The Handbook of the Neuroscience of Multilingualism

Blackwell Handbooks in Linguistics

This outstanding multi-volume series covers all the major subdisciplines within linguistics today and, when complete, will offer a comprehensive survey of linguistics as a whole.

The Handbook of Child Language
Edited by Paul Fletcher & Brian MacWhinney
The Handbook of Phonological Theory, Second Edition
Edited by John A. Goldsmith, Jason Riggle, & Alan C. L. Yu
The Handbook of Sociolinguistics
Edited by Florian Coulmas
The Handbook of Phonetic Sciences, Second Edition
Edited by William J. Hardcastle & John Laver
The Handbook of Morphology
Edited by Andrew Spencer & Arnold Zwicky
The Handbook of Japanese Linguistics
Edited by Natsuko Tsujimura
The Handbook of Contemporary Syntactic Theory
Edited by Mark Baltin & Chris Collins
The Handbook of Language Variation and Change, Second Edition
Edited by J. K. Chambers & Natalie Schilling
The Handbook of Historical Linguistics
Edited by Brian D. Joseph & Richard D. Janda
The Handbook of Language, Gender, and Sexuality, Second Edition
Edited by Susan Ehrlich, Miriam Meyerhoff, & Janet Holmes
The Handbook of Second Language Acquisition
Edited by Catherine J. Doughty & Michael H. Long
The Handbook of Bilingualism and Multilingualism, Second Edition
Edited by Tej K. Bhatia & William C. Ritchie
The Handbook of Pragmatics
Edited by Laurence R. Horn & Gregory Ward
The Handbook of Applied Linguistics
Edited by Alan Davies & Catherine Elder
The Handbook of Speech Perception
Edited by David B. Pisoni & Robert E. Remez
The Handbook of the History of English
Edited by Ans van Kemenade & Bettelou Los
The Handbook of English Linguistics
Edited by Bas Aarts & April McMahon
The Handbook of World Englishes
Edited by Braj B. Kachru, Yamuna Kachru, & Cecil L. Nelson
The Handbook of Educational Linguistics
Edited by Bernard Spolsky & Francis M. Hult
The Handbook of Clinical Linguistics
Edited by Martin J. Ball, Michael R. Perkins, Nicole Müller, & Sara Howard
The Handbook of Pidgin and Creole Studies
Edited by Silvia Kouwenberg & John Victor Singler
The Handbook of Language Teaching
Edited by Michael H. Long & Catherine J. Doughty
The Handbook of Language Contact
Edited by Raymond Hickey
The Handbook of Language and Speech Disorders
Edited by Jack S. Damico, Nicole Müller, & Martin J. Ball
The Handbook of Computational Linguistics and Natural Language Processing
Edited by Alexander Clark, Chris Fox, & Shalom Lappin
The Handbook of Language and Globalization
Edited by Nikolas Coupland
The Handbook of Hispanic Sociolinguistics
Edited by Manuel Díaz-Campos
The Handbook of Language Socialization
Edited by Alessandro Duranti, Elinor Ochs, & Bambi B. Schieffelin

The Handbook of Intercultural Discourse and Communication
Edited by Christina Bratt Paulston, Scott F. Kiesling, & Elizabeth S. Rangel
The Handbook of Historical Sociolinguistics
Edited by Juan Manuel Hernández-Campoy & Juan Camilo Conde-Silvestre
The Handbook of Hispanic Linguistics
Edited by José Ignacio Hualde, Antxon Olarrea, & Erin O'Rourke
The Handbook of Conversation Analysis
Edited by Jack Sidnell & Tanya Stivers
The Handbook of English for Specific Purposes
Edited by Brian Paltridge & Sue Starfield
The Handbook of Spanish Second Language Acquisition
Edited by Kimberly L. Geeslin
The Handbook of Chinese Linguistics
Edited by C.-T. James Huang, Y.-H. Audrey Li, & Andrew Simpson
The Handbook of Language Emergence
Edited by Brian MacWhinney & William O'Grady
The Handbook of Korean Linguistics
Edited by Lucien Brown & Jaehoon Yeon
The Handbook of Speech Production
Edited by Melissa A. Redford
The Handbook of Contemporary Semantic Theory, Second Edition
Edited by Shalom Lappin & Chris Fox
The Handbook of Classroom Discourse and Interaction
Edited by Numa Markee
The Handbook of Narrative Analysis
Edited by Anna De Fina & Alexandra Georgakopoulou
The Handbook of English Pronunciation
Edited by Marnie Reed & John M. Levis
The Handbook of Discourse Analysis, Second Edition
Edited by Deborah Tannen, Heidi E. Hamilton, & Deborah Schiffrin
The Handbook of Bilingual and Multilingual Education
Edited by Wayne E. Wright, Sovicheth Boun, & Ofelia García
The Handbook of Portuguese Linguistics
Edited by W. Leo Wetzels, João Costa, & Sergio Menuzzi
The Handbook of Translation and Cognition
Edited by John W. Schwieter & Aline Ferreira
The Handbook of Linguistics, Second Edition
Edited by Mark Aronoff & Janie Rees-Miller
The Handbook of Technology and Second Language Teaching and Learning
Edited by Carol A. Chapelle & Shannon Sauro
The Handbook of Psycholinguistics
Edited by Eva M. Fernandez & Helen Smith Cairns
The Handbook of Dialectology
Edited by Charles Boberg, John Nerbonne, & Dominic Watt
The Handbook of Advanced Proficiency in Second Language Acquisition
Edited by Paul A. Malovrh & Alessandro G. Benati
The Handbook of the Neuroscience of Multilingualism
Edited by John W. Schwieter

The Handbook of the Neuroscience of Multilingualism

Edited by

John W. Schwieter

With a Special Foreword by

Michel Paradis

WILEY Blackwell

Registered Offices
John Wiley & Sons, Inc., 111 River Street, Hoboken, NJ 07030, USA
John Wiley & Sons Ltd, The Atrium, Southern Gate, Chichester, West Sussex, PO19 8SQ, UK

Editorial Office
The Atrium, Southern Gate, Chichester, West Sussex, PO19 8SQ, UK

For details of our global editorial offices, customer services, and more information about Wiley products visit us at www.wiley.com.

Wiley also publishes its books in a variety of electronic formats and by print-on-demand. Some content that appears in standard print versions of this book may not be available in other formats.

Library of Congress Cataloging-in-Publication Data

Names: Schwieter, John W., 1979– editor.
Title: The handbook of the neuroscience of multilingualism / edited by John
  W. Schwieter.
Description: First edition. | Hoboken, NJ : Wiley-Blackwell, 2019. | Series:
  The handbook of childhood language | Includes bibliographical references
  and index. |
Identifiers: LCCN 2018038791 (print) | LCCN 2018049765 (ebook) | ISBN
  9781119387749 (Adobe PDF) | ISBN 9781119387756 (ePub) | ISBN 9781119387701
  (hardback)
Subjects: LCSH: Multilingualism. | Neurolinguistics. | Cognitive
  neuroscience. | BISAC: LANGUAGE ARTS & DISCIPLINES / Linguistics / General.
Classification: LCC QP411 (ebook) | LCC QP411 .H36 2019 (print) | DDC
  612.8/233–dc23
LC record available at https://lccn.loc.gov/2018038791

Cover Design: Wiley
Cover Image: © Science Photo Library/SuperStock

Set in 10/12 pt Palatino by SPi Global, Pondicherry, India
Printed in Singapore by C.O.S. Printers Pte Ltd

10 9 8 7 6 5 4 3 2 1

This book is dedicated to and in memory of Albert Costa. Albert was an pioneering scholar in the field whose contributions will live on forever. He will be missed dearly.

Contents

List of Figures   xi

List of Tables   xvi

About the Editor   xviii

About the Contributors   xix

Special Foreword   xxxiii
MICHEL PARADIS

Overview of the Handbook   xxxviii
JOHN W. SCHWIETER AND REBECCA MUELLER

Acknowledgements   xlvi

Part I   Theories and Methods   **1**

1   Defining and Assessing Multilingualism   3
KEES DE BOT

2   Cognitive Neuroscience and Multilingualism   19
EDNA ANDREWS

3   What Do Bilingual Models Tell Us About the Neurocognition of Multiple
Languages?   48
ANGELA GRANT, JENNIFER LEGAULT, AND PING LI

4   Psycholinguistic Methods in Multilingual Research   75
ELEONORA ROSSI, KYRA KRASS, AND GERRIT JAN KOOTSTRA

5   Real-Time Measures of the Multilingual Brain   100
NICOLE Y. Y. WICHA, EVA MARÍA MORENO, AND HAYDÉE CARRASCO-ORTÍZ

6   Neuroimaging Studies of Multilingual Speech   121
ANGÉLIQUE M. BLACKBURN

7   In Search of Memory Traces of a Forgotten Language   147
LUDMILA ISURIN

8   Brain Adaptations and Neurological Indices of Processing in Adult Second
Language Acquisition: Challenges for the Critical Period Hypothesis   170
VINCENT DELUCA, DAVID MILLER, CHRISTOS PLIATSIKAS,
AND JASON ROTHMAN

Part II   Neural Representations   **197**

9   Language Organization in the Bilingual and Multilingual Brain   199
NICOLA DEL MASCHIO AND JUBIN ABUTALEBI

10 Bilingual Word Production   214
JANA KLAUS AND HERBERT SCHRIEFERS

11 Multilingualism and Brain Plasticity   230
CHRISTOS PLIATSIKAS

12 Factors Affecting Cortical Representation   252
ANGÉLIQUE M. BLACKBURN

13 The Gift of Language Learning: Individual Differences
in Non-Native Speech Perception   277
BEGOÑA DÍAZ, MIGUEL BURGALETA, AND NURIA SEBASTIAN-GALLES

14 Lexical Organization and Reorganization in the Multilingual Mind   297
GARY LIBBEN AND JOHN W. SCHWIETER

15 Emotion and Emotion Concepts: Processing and Use in Monolingual
and Bilingual Speakers   313
STEPHANIE A. KAZANAS, JARED S. MCLEAN, AND JEANETTE ALTARRIBA

16 Representing, Detecting, and Translating Humour in the Brain   335
JENNIFER HOFMANN AND FRANK A. RODDEN

Part III   Functions and Processes   **355**

17 Multilingualism and Metacognitive Processing   357
PETER BRIGHT, JULIA OUZIA, AND ROBERTO FILIPPI

18 Factors Affecting Multilingual Processing   372
EDALAT SHEKARI AND JOHN W. SCHWIETER

19 Learning and Memory in the Bilingual Mind and Brain   389
ALLISON M. WILCK, JEANETTE ALTARRIBA, ROBERTO R. HEREDIA,
AND JOHN W. SCHWIETER

20 Brain-based Challenges of Second Language Learning in Older Adulthood   408
ZAHRA HEJAZI, JUNGNA KIM, TERESA SIGNORELLI PISANO,
YASMINE OUCHIKH, AVIVA LERMAN, AND LORAINE K. OBLER

21 Language Control and Attention during Conversation: An Exploration   427
    DAVID W. GREEN

22 Cross-Talk Between Language and Executive Control   447
    MARCO CALABRIA, CRISTINA BAUS, AND ALBERT COSTA

23 What Language Experience Tells us about Cognition: Variable Input
    and Interactional Contexts Affect Bilingual Sentence Processing   467
    PAOLA E. DUSSIAS, JORGE R. VALDÉS KROFF, ANNE L. BEATTY-MARTÍNEZ,
    AND MICHAEL A. JOHNS

24 Translation, Interpreting, and the Bilingual Brain: Implications
    for Executive Control and Neuroplasticity   485
    BRUCE J. DIAMOND AND GREGORY M. SHREVE

25 Event-Related Potentials in Monolingual and Bilingual Non-literal
    Language Processing   508
    ANNA SIYANOVA-CHANTURIA, PAOLO CANAL, AND ROBERTO R. HEREDIA

Part IV Impairments and Disorders   531

26 Aphasia in the Multilingual Population   533
    ELISA CARGNELUTTI, BARBARA TOMASINO, AND FRANCO FABBRO

27 Recovery and Rehabilitation Patterns in Bilingual and Multilingual Aphasia 553
    CLAUDIA PEÑALOZA AND SWATHI KIRAN

28 Primary Progressive Aphasia in Bilinguals and Multilinguals   572
    TARYN MALCOLM, AVIVA LERMAN, MARTA KORYTKOWSKA, JET M. J. VONK,
    AND LORAINE K. OBLER

29 Acquired Reading Disorders in Bilingualism   592
    MIRA GORAL

30 Dementia and Multilingualism   608
    MARIANA VEGA-MENDOZA, SUVARNA ALLADI, AND THOMAS H. BAK

31 Schizophrenia and Bilingualism   625
    DARIA SMIRNOVA, SVETA FICHMAN, AND JOEL WALTERS

Part V Cognitive and Neurocognitive Consequences   655

32 Neurocognitive Effects of Multilingualism Throughout the Lifespan:
    A Developmental Perspective   657
    HANNAH L. CLAUSSENIUS-KALMAN AND ARTURO E. HERNANDEZ

33 The Intense Bilingual Experience of Interpreting and Its
    Neurocognitive Consequences   685
    YANPING DONG AND FEI ZHONG

34 The Bilingual Advantage Debate: Quantity and Quality of the Evidence   701
    KENNETH PAAP

35 The Bilingual Advantage Debate: Publication Biases and the Decline Effect   736
    ANGELA DE BRUIN AND SERGIO DELLA SALA

36 Speech-Sign Bilingualism: A Unique Window into the Multilingual Brain   754
    ROBIN L. THOMPSON AND EVA GUTIERREZ-SIGUT

Index   784

List of Figures

Chapter 1

Figure 1 Format of one of the questions asked by Berns et al., 2007.   15

Chapter 2

Figure 1 Dual-stream model of the functional anatomy of language.
Source: Hickok and Poeppel (2007), p. 395.   21

Figure 2 The Jakobsonian speech act model. Source: Adapted from Jakobson
(1957/1987), pp. 66–71.   26

Figure 3 Schematics showing grid placement, function, and resection in 2011 (a)
and 2012 (b). See legend for colour-coded functions.   30

Figure 4 (a) Semantic paraphasias, (b) Performance errors, (c) Phonological
paraphasias, (d) Circumlocutions, (e) Neologisms, (f) No-response
errors. Source: Diagrams from Corina et al. (2010).   32

Chapter 3

Figure 1 The BIA and BIA+ models. The BIA+ model introduces the
task/decision system and distinguishes it from a word identification
system. Bolded boxes include elements that have been added or
modified in the BIA+ model.   50

Figure 2 The inhibitory control model (Green 1998). Note: SAS stands for
supervisory attentional system.   52

Figure 3 The adaptive control model and its neural substrates. Note: ACC/
Pre-SMA = anterior cingulate cortex/pre-supplementary motor area;
IFC = inferior frontal cortex.   64

Chapter 4

Figure 1 Reprinted from 'Incremental interpretation at verbs: Restricting
the domain of subsequent reference'. Source: Altmann and Kamide
(1999, p. 250). Reprinted with permission.   90

Chapter 6

Figure 1   Left lateral aspect of cortical surface, 2016. Source: Hwozdek and
Blackburn, 'Labeled Brain' derivative of 'Brain in Profile'.
Source: Pearish, 2016, openclipart.org, licensed under CCO 1.0.   122

Figure 2   Neural activation during covert word generation. Overlapping
neural activation for all languages in language networks is
displayed in colour for four subjects (S1, S2, S4, S6). Activation,
particularly in the cingulate gyrus and contralateral hemisphere,
increases with decreases in language proficiency from L1 to L4.
Source: Reprinted from Briellmann et al. (2004), Copyright (2004),
with permission from Elsevier.   128

Figure 3   Cognitive control network. (1) Attention: Inferior parietal lobe (IPL)
projects to the prefrontal cortex (PFC) as part of the attentional network
to bias language selection. (2) Conflict detection: Anterior cingulate cortex
(ACC)/pre-SMA signals the PFC and the basal ganglia (BG). (3) Bias:
Fronto-subcortical loop ramps activity from PFC and compares it to other
cortical inputs (e.g. the IPL and pre-SMA). (4) Prediction: The cerebellar
connections to the BG and PFC may play a role in prediction. (5) Output:
Signal spreads to planning and motor cortices (including insula,
pre-motor, and motor). Note that the BG output through the
thalamus (Th). Source: Blackburn, A. M., 2017, 'Language Control
Model 2017', openclipart.org, licensed under CCO 1.0: https://
creativecommons.org/publicdomain/zero/1.0/legalcode.   130

Chapter 8

Figure 1   Diagram of the N400 and P600 components.   177

Figure 2   The neuron and its components. Source: https://commons.wikimedia.
org/wiki/File:Neuron.svg.   181

Figure 3   Examples of grey and white matter within the brain.   182

Figure 4   Select GM regions within the brain.   183

Figure 5   Diagram depicting connectivity of select white matter tracts. Source:
Credit William Hirstein. Diagram by Katie Reinecke. (CC BY 3.0
(http://creativecommons.org/licenses/by/3.0), via Wikimedia
Commons.   184

Chapter 11

Figure 1   The typical parts of a neuron. Source: https://commons.wikimedia.
org/wiki/File:Neuron.svg.   231

Figure 2   A mid-sagittal (a), lateral (b) and mid-axial (c) view of a template brain,
indicating the main grey matter regions that will be discussed in this
chapter. WM, and how it differentiates from cortical and subcortical
GM, is clearly visible in (c).   232

Figure 3   Effects of immersive bilingualism on the shape of subcortical structures. 3a shows the significant surface expansions for bilinguals compared with monolinguals, illustrated in yellow and overlaid on the outline of the bilateral globus pallidus (blue), bilateral putamen (green) and right thalamus (red). 3b shows the portions of the right globus pallidus, where linguistic immersion emerged as a significant predictor of surface expansion. Source: Pliatsikas et al. (2017). Distributed under the terms of the Creative Commons Attribution 4.0 International Licence (http://creativecommons.org/licenses/by/4.0). No changes were made to the original image.   237

Figure 4   Significant bilingual > monolingual differences in FA values (hot colours), expressed in 1-P values (p < 0.05, corrected) and overlaid onto a standard space WM skeleton (green). Source: Pliatsikas et al. (2015).   240

Chapter 13

Figure 1   Brain regions whose activity and/or structure is commonly highlighted by training studies on individual differences in the perception of non-native speech sounds. The list of areas depicted in this figure is not exhaustive. B = bilateral. L = left hemisphere.   281

Figure 2   MMNs obtained for good and poor perceivers of an L2 phoneme contrast in response to a native and a non-native (unknown) phoneme. Good perceivers displayed larger MMN responses than poor perceivers for the two different phonemes. Grey boxes indicate statistical differences between the two groups of bilinguals for an early subcomponent of the MMN (light grey) and a late subcomponent (dark grey). Source: Díaz et al. (2008).   287

Figure 3   (a) Significant negative association between cortical surface area and performance in the lexical decision task, after controlling for performance in prelexical tasks. Bottom figures show significant negative association between cortical thickness and performance in the lexical decision task, before (b) and after (c) controlling for performance in prelexical tasks. All results are corrected for multiple comparisons at the cluster level (familywise error rate < 0.5). Source: Figures adapted from Burgaleta et al. (2014).   291

Chapter 14

Figure 1   The trilingual modified hierarchical model. (Source: Taken from Benati and Schwieter 2017).   305

Chapter 16

Figure 1   Examples of different smiles and laughs.   337

Figure 2 Simplified presentation of the two-stage model after Suls. Source:
          Adapted from Suls (1972).   339
Figure 3 Factors allowing for the categorization of studies on humour and
          neural processing.   343

Chapter 17

Figure 1 Illustration of the conceptual overlap of metacognition and the executive
          system. Source: Adapted from Fernandez-Duque et al. (2000).   359
Figure 2 Two-alternative-forced-choice task employed by Folke et al. (2016).   364

Chapter 19

Figure 1 An example of a simple connectionist model. Conceptual nodes feed into
          larger, more generalized nodes. Thicker lines represent greater
          association strength, which the model indicates as having a higher
          degree of connection between the represented concepts.   393
Figure 2 A conceptual illustration of the revised hierarchical model. Associations
          between the L1 and the shared conceptual store are stronger than those
          between the L2 and the conceptual store. The association from the L2 to
          the L1 is stronger than in the L1 to the L2 direction, indicating the
          assumption that L2 learning occurs by translating words into the
          native language.   394

Chapter 21

Figure 1 The mapping of a speech act.   428
Figure 2 Attentional states at different loci during a speech act.   436

Chapter 34

Figure 1 Boxplots of the mean effect size (bilingual advantage in interference
          scores) when the six extreme outliers from Bialystok et al. (2004) are
          included (left side) compared to when they are deleted (right side).   705
Figure 2 The CSE derived from the Simon task reported in Paap and Greenberg
          (2013), Experiment 3.   719
Figure 3 96% of the population distributions with mean differences of d = 0.1
          overlap.   722

Chapter 35

Figure 1 Number of conference abstracts reporting positive effects of bilingualism
          ('yes'), mixed effects predominantly supporting a bilingual advantage
          ('mixed-yes'), mixed effects predominantly challenging a bilingual advantage
          ('mixed-no'), and abstracts showing no or negative effects of bilingualism
          ('no'). The left side reports abstracts presented until 2012, the right side
          reports abstracts between 2013 and 2015.   745

Figure 2   Percentage of published studies for conference abstracts with positive effects of bilingualism ('yes'), mixed effects predominantly supporting a bilingual advantage ('mixed-yes'), mixed effects predominantly challenging a bilingual advantage ('mixed-no'), and abstracts showing no or negative effects of bilingualism ('no'). The left side shows abstracts presented until 2012, the right side shows abstracts between 2013 and 2015.   746

Chapter 36

Figure 1   Examples of phonological minimal pairs in BSL. Top: *car* and *robot* share location and movement (up and down) parameters, but differ in handshape. Middle: *saxophone* and *computer* share handshape and movement (finger wiggle) features, but differ in location. Bottom: *mouse* and *nose* share handshape and location features, but differ in movement (*mouse*, with a twisting movement and *nose* with a tapping movement).   765

List of Tables

Chapter 3

Table 1 Key regions of interest in studies that provide support to the BIA and IC models. 55

Chapter 6

Table 1 Key multilingual studies regarding cortical overlap of essential language regions and regions involved in control for switching, inhibition, and articulation. 124

Table 2 Key multilingual studies regarding neural substrates of control for switching, inhibition, and articulation. 132

Table 3 Key multilingual studies regarding patient populations. 141

Chapter 7

Table 1 Studies investigating memory traces of a forgotten language. 150

Chapter 12

Table 1 fMRI manipulations of age of acquisition (AoA) and proficiency (Prof) across three or more languages. 259

Chapter 27

Table 1 Patterns of language recovery in bilingual aphasia. 559

Chapter 28

Table 1 Demographic information for 13 published case studies on bilinguals or multilinguals with PPA. 578

Chapter 29

Table 1 Studies of acquired alexia in bilingual individuals. 596

Chapter 31

Table 1   Neurobiological and pathophysiological features associated with schizophrenia as a morbid process and located in brain areas typically involved
in bilingual processing.   627

Table 2   Summary of language and cognitive impairments in schizophrenia
literature.   633

Chapter 34

Table 1   Bilingual advantages in interference control and global RT for
various age groups based on the present meta-analysis.   706

Table 2   Results of tests for bilingual advantages in colour-shape
switching tasks.   710

Table 3   Congruency sequence effects for monolinguals and bilinguals.   721

Chapter 35

Table 1   Overview of the abstracts included in the analysis between 2013
and 2015. The classification 'yes' refers to studies fully supporting
a bilingual advantage. 'Mixed-yes' and 'Mixed-no' respectively refer
to those mainly supporting and mainly challenging a bilingual
advantage. 'No' refers to studies fully challenging a positive effect
of bilingualism on executive control.   743

About the Editor

John W. Schwieter is an Associate Professor of Spanish and Linguistics at Wilfrid Laurier University in Canada where he is also the Director of the Language Acquisition, Multilingualism, and Cognition Laboratory. His research interests include: Psycholinguistic and neurolinguistic approaches to multilingualism and language acquisition; translation and cognition; and second language teaching and learning. He is the Executive Editor of *Bilingual Processing and Acquisition* (Benjamins) and the Co-Editor of *Cambridge Elements in Second Language Acquisition* (Cambridge University Press). Some of his research has appeared in: *Bilingualism: Language and Cognition; The Canadian Journal of Applied Linguistics; Diaspora, Indigenous, and Minority Education; Frontiers in Psychology; Intercultural Education; International Journal of Bilingual Education and Bilingualism; Language Learning; Linguistic Approaches to Bilingualism; The Mental Lexicon; The Spanish Journal of Applied Linguistics; Study Abroad Research in Second Language Acquisition and International Education;* and *Translation, Cognition, & Behavior*. His recent edited books include *The Cambridge Handbook of Language Learning* (2019); *The Handbook of Translation and Cognition* (2017, Wiley Blackwell); *Cognitive Control and Consequences of Multilingualism* (2016); and *The Cambridge Handbook of Bilingual Processing* (2015).

About the Contributors

The CONTRIBUTORS are international experts based at, or affiliated with, institutions and research centres in Australia, Canada, China, England, Germany, Hungary, Italy, Israel, the Netherlands, New Zealand, Russia, Scotland, Spain, Switzerland, and the United States. A short bio of each of the contributors are found below.

Jubin Abutalebi is a Cognitive Neurologist and Professor of Neuropsychology in the Faculty of Psychology at the University San Raffaele and Scientific Institute San Raffaele in Milan, Italy. He is also an Honorary Associate Professor in the Faculty of Education at the University of Hong Kong. Prof. Abutalebi has applied functional and structural neuroimaging methods to the study of language representation, language acquisition, and cognitive functions in populations of bilinguals. The results of his landmark research on bilinguals have been published in the main international neuropsychological, neuroimaging, and neurosciences journals. His research has contributed to enlightening the cerebral basis of language control in bilinguals. He is the Editor-in-Chief of the prestigious international journal *Bilingualism: Language and Cognition* (Cambridge University Press).

Suvarna Alladi is Professor of Neurology at the National Institute of Mental Health and Neurosciences in Bangalore, India, who specializes in cognitive and behavioural neurology. She trained in Neurology in Bangalore, in Cognitive Neurology in Cambridge, UK, and in Cognitive Epidemiology in Edinburgh. Her research interests are Alzheimer's disease, and frontotemporal and vascular dementia, especially in the context of developing countries. Her research group has adapted cognitive tests in Indian languages for dementia diagnosis. Dr. Alladi studies protective impact of lifetime experiences – education and bilingualism on dementia. She co-founded the NGO: Alzheimer's and Related Disorders Society of India, Hyderabad-Deccan, committed to supporting families and persons with dementia.

Jeanette Altarriba is Professor of Psychology and Vice Provost and Dean for Undergraduate Education at the University at Albany, State University of New York (UAlbany), USA, as well as the Director of the Cognition and Language Laboratory at UAlbany. Her research interests include the psychology of language, psycholinguistics, second language acquisition, bilingualism, knowledge representation, eye movements and reading, adaptive memory, and cognition and emotion. She has published her work in numerous scientific journals including *Memory & Cognition*, the *Journal of Memory and Language*, the *International Journal of Bilingualism, Perception and Psychophysics, Cognition and*

Emotion, and *Professional Psychology: Research and Practice*. She is the recipient of an Early Career Award for Teaching and Training from the American Psychological Association and the Collins Fellowship for extraordinary service to the University at Albany.

Edna Andrews is Professor of Linguistics & Cultural Anthropology, Nancy & Jeffrey Marcus Distinguished Professor, Member of the Duke Institute of Brain Sciences and Center for Cognitive Neuroscience, and Chair of the Linguistics Program at Duke University, USA. In 2013, she was awarded the Duke University Scholar/Teacher award. Andrews' most recent book is *Neuroscience and Multilingualism* (2014). Some of her latest articles in cognitive neuroscience and semiotics have been published in the *Journal of Memory and Language, Semiotica*, and *Sign Systems Studies*.

Thomas H. Bak was born and raised in Cracow, Poland. He studied medicine in Germany and Switzerland, obtaining his doctorate with a thesis on acute aphasias from the University of Freiburg in Breisgau, Germany. He worked clinically in psychiatry, neurology, and neurosurgery in Basel, Bern, Berlin, Cambridge, and Edinburgh, with a particular interest in the interaction of movement, language, and cognition in patients with neurodegenerative diseases such as dementia, atypical parkinsonian syndromes, and motor neuron disease. In recent years, Dr. Bak's work has focused increasingly on the impact of language learning and bilingualism/multilingualism on cognitive functions across the lifespan.

Cristina Baus is a Researcher in the Center for Brain and Cognition at the Universitat Pompeu Fabra, Spain. Her main research interests focus on the study of the neurobiological substrates of language production, bilingualism, and sign language. Some of her recent work has appeared in *Acta Psychologica* and *The Cambridge Handbook of Bilingual Processing*.

Anne L. Beatty-Martínez is a PhD student in Spanish and Language Science at the Pennsylvania State University, USA. Her research agenda involves the integration of linguistic, cognitive, and neuroscientific approaches to examine how bilingual experience modulates language processing and cognitive control ability. In her research, she combines experimental approaches, including corpus-elicitation, eye-tracking, and event-related potentials, to study the psycholinguistics of code switching and bilingual language control.

Angélique M. Blackburn is Assistant Professor of Psychology at Texas A&M International University, USA. Her specializations are in cognitive neuroscience and bilingualism. She uses electrophysiology and other neurocognitive methods to investigate the effects of language habits on cognition and how bilinguals manage and switch between two languages with ease. She has recently authored reviews regarding the bilingual brain, neuroimaging techniques for bilingualism research, and the cognitive impact of language habits near cultural/national borders.

Peter Bright is Professor of Psychology and Director of the Brain and Cognition research group at Anglia Ruskin University and a Principal Investigator in the Cambridge Neuroscience Initiative at the University of Cambridge, UK. He was educated at the Universities of Surrey (BSc, 1991), Reading (MSc, 1993) and Cambridge

(PhD, 1999) and has held research positions at the Medical Research Council Cognition and Brain Sciences Unit in Cambridge (1994–1995), King's College in London (1998–2001), and the University of Cambridge (2001–2005). His primary research interests are in memory, intelligence, and executive function and he has published extensively in these fields.

Miguel Burgaleta is a Post-Doctoral Fellow at the Universitat Pompeu Fabra, Spain. He has authored several peer-reviewed articles on bilingualism, brain imaging, and speech perception in journals such as the *Journal of Neuroscience*, *Human Brain Mapping*, and *NeuroImage*.

Marco Calabria is a Researcher in the Center for Brain and Cognition at the Universitat Pompeu Fabra, Spain. His research interests focus on the study of language control and executive control abilities in bilingual speakers with brain damage. Some of his recent work has appeared in the *Journal of Neurolinguistics* and *Neuropsychologia*.

Paolo Canal is a Post-Doctoral Research Fellow in the Laboratorio di Linguistica Nencioni, Scuola Normale Superiore and at the Center for Neurocognition, Epistemology, and Theoretical Syntax in Italy. His research focuses on neurolinguistics, specifically, on the electrophysiological correlates of non-literal language processing, with particular interest in the study of individual differences. He has published in the *Journal of Experimental Psychology: Learning, Memory, and Cognition*, the *Journal of Cognitive Neuroscience*, *Psychophysiology*, and the *Journal of Neurolinguistics*, amongst other publications.

Elisa Cargnelutti is a Researcher in Cognitive Neuroscience at the Scientific Institute IRCCS 'E. Medea', Italy. Her research interests include the functional and anatomical correlates of the cognitive functions, both in physiological and in pathological conditions, with particular reference to language and multilingualism.

Haydée Carrasco-Ortíz is Associate Professor of Psycholinguistics at the Autonomous University of Querétaro, Mexico. She received a PhD in Cognitive Psychology from Aix-Marseille University in France. She was a Postdoctoral Fellow in the NeuroCognition Lab at Tufts University and the McGovern Institute for Brain Research at Massachusetts Institute of Technology. Her research interests include the cognitive and neuronal bases of language comprehension using behavioural and event-related brain potentials (ERPs) techniques. An important goal of her research is to examine the temporal dynamics of the brain while a person is learning and processing a second language.

Hannah L. Claussenius-Kalman is a PhD Student in Cognitive Neuroscience at the University of Houston, USA, where she conducts research in the Laboratory for the Neural Bases of Bilingualism. Her research interests include the neural systems underlying bilingualism and individual differences in foreign language learning success. She plans to use neuroimaging techniques and behavioural studies to improve and make foreign language pedagogy methods more efficient.

Albert Costa is an ICREA Research Professor at the Center for Brain and Cognition at the Universitat Pompeu Fabra, Spain. His research focuses on the cognitive and neural underpinnings of language processing, particularly, on how two languages are

xxii *About the Contributors*

represented and processed by the one brain. Some of his recent work has appeared in *Current Directions Psychological Science* and *Nature Reviews Neuroscience*.

Kees de Bot is Emeritus Professor from the University of Groningen, The Netherlands and Full Professor of Applied Linguistics at the University of Pannonia, Hungary. His research interests include the application of complex dynamic systems theory in second language development and multilingualism, multilingual processing, language attrition, and the history of Applied Linguistics. He is one of the organizers of the 2020 World Congress of the International Association of Applied Linguistics in Groningen.

Angela de Bruin is a Marie Skłodowska-Curie Research Fellow at the Basque Center on Cognition, Brain and Language, Donostia, Spain. She received her PhD from the University of Edinburgh, Scotland, and her research focuses on bilingualism, language switching, executive control, and cognitive ageing.

Nicola Del Maschio is a Post-Doctoral Researcher in the Centre for Neurolinguistics and Psycholinguistics at Vita-Salute San Raffaele University, Italy. His research interests including neurolinguistics, bilingualism, and language and ageing. Some of his work has appeared in *Brain and Language* and *Cerebral Cortex*. He is also an editorial assistant for *Bilingualism: Language and Cognition*.

Sergio Della Sala is Professor of Human Cognitive Neuroscience at the University of Edinburgh, UK. He is the editor of *Cortex*. His research interests include amnesia, visuo-spatial and representational neglect, apraxia, and the cognitive deficits of Alzheimer's disease.

Vincent DeLuca is a postdoctoral researcher in the Department of Psychology at the University of Birmingham in England. He is also affiliated with the Centre for Integrative Neuroscience and Neurodynamics and the Centre for Literacy and Multilingualism at the University of Reading. His research interests include language acquisition/processing, and effects of bi/multilingualism on cognition, neural structure and function.

Bruce J. Diamond is Professor and Founding Director of the Doctoral Program in Clinical Psychology at William Paterson University, USA, where he is also the Director of the Neuropsychology, Cognitive, & Clinical Neuroscience Lab. Diamond is a licensed psychologist specializing in neuropsychology and neurorehabilitation. His research interests include neurologic and neuropsychiatric disorders with an emphasis on information processing, executive function, working memory, and the physiological correlates underlying brain and behaviour relationships. He has published in many prestigious journals and has co-authored a number of chapters examining the cognitive and physiological mechanisms mediating translation and interpretation.

Begoña Díaz is an Assistant Professor at the Universitat Internacional de Catalunya, Spain. She has authored many peer-reviewed articles on bilingualism, speech perception, and syntax in journals such as the *Journal of Neuroscience* and the *Proceedings of the National Academy of Sciences of the United States of America*.

Yanping Dong is Professor of Psycholinguistics, Founding Director of the Chinese Association of Psycholinguistics, and the Founding Director of the Bilingual Cognition and

Education Lab at Guangdong University of Foreign Studies, China. Her research interests include bilingual competence and education across two areas of psycholinguistics: bilingual processing and acquisition, and the complex dynamic systems in students of interpreting. Dong has published widely in prestigious journals such as *Bilingualism: Language and Cognition, Frontiers in Psychology, the Journal of Neurolinguistics,* and *Neuropsychologia.*

Paola E. Dussias is Professor of Spanish, Linguistics, and Psychology at the Pennsylvania State University, USA. Her research examines the conditions under which information from one of the bilingual's languages influences parsing decisions in the other language. Dussias also studies the processing of code-switched language. Her work has been supported by grants from the National Science Foundation (NSF) and the National Institutes of Health. She is the Principle Investigator on a recently awarded grant from NSF to develop an international research programme of training that enables Penn State students to pursue research abroad.

Franco Fabbro is Professor in Clinical Neuroscience at the University of Udine, Italy. He conducts research on the neuropsychology of bilingualism, consciousness, and religion. He has authored numerous articles in international journals and has written several books.

Sveta Fichman is a PhD student who studies clinical features in the narratives of bilingual children with Specific Language Impairment (SLI) at Bar-Ilan University, Israel. Her research focuses primarily on narrative macrostructure (causal relations and referential cohesion). She is also examining fluency markers in L1/Russian-L2/Hebrew bilingual children with and without SLI. Her recent publications have appeared in the *Journal of Communication Disorders* and *Applied Psycholinguistics.*

Roberto Filippi is Associate Professor in the Department of Psychology and Human Development at University College London, Institute of Education, UK, where he is also the Director of the Multilanguage and Cognition Lab (MULTAC), part of the Centre for Language, Literacy & Numeracy. His main research focus is on multilanguage acquisition and its effects on cognitive development from infancy to older age. Some of his recent publications have appeared in *Cognition, Bilingualism: Language and Cognition,* the *Journal of Neuroscience,* and *First Language.*

Mira Goral is Professor of Speech-Language-Hearing Sciences at Lehman College and The Graduate Center of The City University of New York, USA. She has published journal articles and book chapters in the areas of bilingualism, multilingualism, aphasia, language attrition, and language and cognition in ageing, and has co-edited books on bilingual aspects of acquired language disorders and the bilingual mental lexicon. She teaches undergraduate and graduate students and supervises and mentors speech-language-pathology student clinicians.

Angela Grant is a Horizon Postdoctoral Fellow at Concordia University, Canada. She received her PhD in Psychology and Language Science from The Pennsylvania State University in 2017. Her work examines second language processing and its relationship with domain general aspects of cognition such as executive control and memory. Her work has appeared in journals such as *Brain & Language, Cortex,* and *Bilingualism: Language and Cognition*.

David W. Green is Emeritus Professor in the Faculty of Brain Sciences at University College London, UK. His theoretical and neuroimaging research on the cognitive and neural bases of language control in neurologically normal bilingual and multilingual speakers from young adults to the elderly has been combined with applied research into the neural predictors of language recovery in bilingual and multilingual patients following stroke. His recent publications have appeared in *Brain, International Journal of Bilingualism,* and the *Journal of Neuroscience*.

Eva Gutierrez-Sigut is a Researcher at the University of Valencia, Spain. She holds a PhD in Cognitive Neuroscience from the University of La Laguna and has held positions at the University of California, Davis and University College London. Her research investigates the neural signature of language processing in people born deaf, using various research techniques to provide converging evidence. Some of her recent work looks at brain lateralization of sign production and at the role of phonological coding in reading.

Zahra Hejazi is a doctoral student in the Speech-Language-Hearing Sciences department at the City University of New York Graduate Center, USA, and speech and language pathologist. Her research interests include healthy ageing, bilingualism, and aphasia, specifically bilingual aphasia.

Roberto R. Heredia is Regents Professor of Psychology at Texas A&M International University, USA, where he directs the Cognitive Neuroscience Laboratory. He has published in the fields of bilingualism, figurative language processing, social stereotype processing, and evolutionary psychology.

Arturo E. Hernandez is Professor of Psychology at the University of Houston, USA. His research interest is in the neural underpinnings of bilingual language processing and second language acquisition in children and adults. He has used a variety of neuroimaging methods as well as behavioural techniques to investigate these phenomena which have been published in a number of peer-reviewed journal articles. His research has been funded by the National Institutes of Health, the National Science Foundation, and the Alexander von Humboldt Foundation. Hernandez's interest in language learning has also been informed by his own experience as a simultaneous bilingual who learned a third and fourth language in adulthood.

Jennifer Hofmann is a Senior Teaching and Research Fellow in the Department of Personality and Assessment (Institute of Psychology) at the University of Zurich, Switzerland. Her current research interests are in personality and assessment, humour, encoding and decoding of positive emotions, as well as nonverbal behaviour (applying the Facial Action Coding System), with a special interest in laughter.

Ludmila Isurin is Professor in the Department of Slavic and East European Languages and Cultures at The Ohio State University, USA. An interdisciplinary scholar whose research encompasses psycholinguistics and sociolinguistics, social sciences, and humanities, Isurin is the author or co-editor of five books, including two recent books published by Cambridge University Press: *Memory and language: Theoretical and applied approaches to bilingualism* and *Collective remembering: Memory in the world and in the mind*. She also is the author of numerous chapters and journal articles including an award-winning article in *Language Learning*.

Michael A. Johns is a PhD student in Spanish and Language Science at the Pennsylvania State University, USA. His research focuses on the integration of psycholinguistic methodologies, such as eye-tracking, with insights from bilingual corpora to investigate the processing of code-switched speech. A central theme to his research is the role of input and usage in shaping the processing system, and the interaction between external, social factors and internal, cognitive factors.

Stephanie A. Kazanas is Assistant Professor of Psychology at Tennessee Technological University, USA, where she is also the Director of the Cognition Laboratory. Her research interests include emotion word and face processing, adaptive memory, bilingualism/multilingualism, priming, and creativity. Kazanas's work has been published in numerous scientific journals, including the *American Journal of Psychology, Evolutionary Psychology, the Journal of Psycholinguistic Research, Language and Speech*, and *Evolutionary Psychological Science*. She has also received awards for her teaching, including the University at Albany's President's Award for Excellence in Teaching and Tech's EDGE Creative Inquiry Curriculum Grant.

Jungna Kim is doctoral student in the Speech-Language-Hearing Sciences programme in the Graduate Center of the City University of New York, USA. Her research interests include how bilingualism is affected by cognitive abilities, such as interference control, working memory, and executive functions. Her dissertation is about the relationship between interference control and L2 proficiency during L2 auditory comprehension in verbal and non-verbal noise. She obtained her Bachelor's degree in French and English Linguistics at Hankuk University of Foreign Studies in South Korea and completed her Master's degree in Applied Linguistics at Teachers College, Columbia University, focusing on second language acquisition and assessment.

Swathi Kiran is a Professor in the Department of Speech and Hearing Sciences at Boston University, USA, and Assistant in Neurology/Neuroscience at Massachusetts General Hospital. Her research interests focus on lexical-semantic treatment for individuals with aphasia, bilingual aphasia, and neuroimaging of brain plasticity following a stroke. She has over 80 publications across a variety of disciplines, including cognitive neuroscience, neuroimaging, rehabilitation, speech language pathology, and bilingualism. Kiran is a Fellow of the American Speech Language and Hearing Association. Her work has been continually funded by the National Institutes of Health. She is the co-founder and scientific advisor for Constant Therapy (now The Learning Corporation), a software platform for rehabilitation tools after brain injury.

Jana Klaus is a Post-Doctoral Researcher in the Donders Institute for Brain, Cognition, and Behaviour at Radboud University, The Netherlands. Her research focuses on individual differences in monolingual and bilingual language production at the word and sentence level using behavioural and brain stimulation techniques. Some of her recent work has appeared in the *Quarterly Journal of Experimental Psychology, Neuroscience,* and *Brain and Cognition.*

Gerrit Jan Kootstra is a Post-Doctoral Researcher at Radboud University Nijmegen, The Netherlands, and is a Researcher and Lecturer at Windesheim University of Applied Sciences, The Netherlands. His research focuses on the psycholinguistics of bi/multilingualism, specializing in the study of code-switching, structural priming, and interactive alignment in bilingual language production and comprehension. In doing so, he uses both experimental techniques and corpus analyses. At Radboud University, he is currently investigating these themes in bilingual children. At Windesheim University, he is mainly involved with bi/multilingualism in educational settings, translating insights from academic research to classroom practices.

Marta Korytkowska is a doctoral student in the Speech-Language-Hearing Sciences department at the City University of New York Graduate Center, USA. She is a practising Speech-Language Pathologist in the acute care setting with experience in acute rehabilitation, outpatient, and home care settings. Her main areas of research interest include treatment approaches in bilingual populations with language disorders, bilingual aphasia, and the influence of cognition in recovery from aphasia.

Kyra Krass is a doctoral student at the University of Connecticut, USA, working under the direction of Dr. Gerry Altmann. Krass uses eye-tracking, electroencephalography, and functional magnetic resonance imaging techniques to study sentence processing and event representation. Her current research investigates the role that anticipation and affordances play in processing change of state verbs. She is also interested in the individual differences in event representation and the impact of bilingualism on sentence processing.

Jennifer Legault is a neuroscience graduate student at the Pennsylvania State University, USA. Her research interests include examination of behavioural, functional, and structural changes in the brain in response to second language learning. In particular, her research examines the neuroplastic and behavioral effects of second language learning context. Her work has appeared in journals such as *Brain and Cognition, Cortex,* and *Educational Technology Research and Development.*

Aviva Lerman is a doctoral student in the Speech-Language-Hearing Sciences department at the City University of New York Graduate Center, USA. She is a qualified Speech and Language Pathologist and holds a Master's degree specializing in multilingualism and multicultural issues in Speech-Language Pathology. Her research focuses on bilingualism, aphasia, healthy ageing, and dementia.

Ping Li is Professor of Psychology, Linguistics, and Information Sciences & Technology at the Pennsylvania State University, USA, where he also serves as Director of the Center for Brain, Behavior, and Cognition, and Associate Director of the Institute for CyberScience. The goal of his research is to understand the neurocomputational basis of language learning, and its relationship with culture, brain, and technology. Li is Editor-in-Chief of the *Journal of Neurolinguistics* and Associate Editor of *Frontiers in Psychology: Language Sciences.* He previously served as President of *Society for Computers in Psychology* and Program Director of *Cognitive Neuroscience and Perception, Action and Cognition* at the US National Science Foundation. For more information about his research, visit http:// blclab.org.

Gary Libben is Professor of Applied Linguistics and Psychology at Brock University, Canada. His research focuses on the representation and processing of words in the mind, the psycholinguistics of lexical processing across languages, and the development of new methodologies for studying language processing across age groups, language groups, and situational contexts. He is a Fellow of the Royal Society of Canada, has been President of the Canadian Linguistics Association, and was Founding Director of the Centre of Comparative Psycholinguistics at the University of Alberta. He is currently Director of the Words in the World Project.

Taryn Malcolm is a doctoral student in the Speech-Language-Hearing Sciences department at the City University of New York Graduate Center, USA. She has practised as a Speech-Language Pathologist in acute and subacute rehabilitation with a focus on neurogenic disorders. Her main areas of research interest include bilingualism, bilingual aphasia, and neurological processes underlying acquired language disorders. She is currently working on a research project investigating cross-linguistic influence in speakers of Jamaican Creole following immersion in the environment of their second language, English.

Jared S. McLean is a Research Assistant in the Cognition and Language Laboratory at the University at Albany, State University of New York, USA. His research interests include major depressive disorder, substance abuse disorders, multilingualism, and memory of emotion-laden stimuli. He is also a case manager for individuals with substance abuse disorders in New Port Richey, Florida and a research assistant in the Mood and Emotion Laboratory at the University of South Florida.

David Miller is an assistant professor of linguistics in the Department of Hispanic and Italian Studies at the University of Illinois at Chicago in the United States. His research interests include language acquisition, linguistic processing, electroencephalography/ event-related potential methodology, propositional logic, the interface of language, and cognition. Some of his research has appeared in: *Journal of Experimental Psychology: Language, Memory and Cognition* and the *International Journal of Bilingual Education and Bilingualism.*

Eva María Moreno is a Scientist at the Complutense University of Madrid, Spain, where she also received a bachelor's degree in psychology and a PhD in neuroscience. She conducted her dissertation research under the supervision of Dr. Marta Kutas at the University of California, San Diego, where she used event-related potentials to study bilingual sentence comprehension and language switching. Her current research interests include higher order language processes, such as inference making and processing of emotionally charged language and social lies.

Rebecca Mueller is a Research Assistant to the Editor of this Handbook and a President's Gold Scholar award recipient at Wilfrid Laurier University, Canada. During her undergraduate work in Global Studies, she has studied abroad in Israel, Palestine, India, and

Spain. Her interest in language learning stems from her French and Spanish courses and she plans to pursue a career involving both global development and the languages which she is currently studying.

Loraine K. Obler is a Distinguished Professor in Speech-Language-Hearing Sciences and in Linguistics at the City University of New York Graduate Center, USA. Her research interests include bilingualism and the brain, language changes associated with ageing and dementia, cross-language study of aphasia, and the brain bases of special talents like L2 learning. She has written *The Bilingual Brain: Neuropsychological Aspects of Bilingualism* (with Martin Albert), and *Language and the Brain* (with Kris Gjerlow) and recent articles have appeared in *Bilingualism: Language and Cognition* and *Linguistic Approaches to Bilingualism*.

Yasmine Ouchikh is a doctoral student in the Speech-Language-Hearing Sciences programme in the Graduate Center of the City University of New York, USA. Her research interests include understanding how bilingualism affects executive functioning in typical and atypical populations across the lifespan, the relationship between executive dysfunction and language impairment, and second language acquisition in older adulthood.

Julia Ouzia is a Senior Teaching Fellow in the Department of Psychology and Human Development at University College London, Institute of Education, UK. Her research aims to evaluate bilingual cognition through a multidimensional approach, focusing on executive function, selective attention, metacognition, and probabilistic learning. She is also currently involved in various projects evaluating the effect of mindfulness on cognitive control. Julia's recent publications have appeared in the journal *Cognition* and the book *Cognitive control and consequences in the multilingual mind* (2016).

Kenneth Paap is Professor of Psychology at San Francisco State University, USA, and an Emeritus Professor of Psychology at New Mexico State University. His research interests include computational models of letter and word recognition, knowledge elicitation and representation in the design of human-computer interfaces, attention, executive functioning, and bilingual language control. His recent publications on bilingualism have appeared in *Cognitive Psychology, Cortex, Frontiers in Psychology*, and the *Journal of Cognitive Psychology*.

Michel Paradis is Emeritus Professor of Linguistics at McGill University and the Founding Member of the Cognitive Neuroscience Center at the Université du Québec à Montréal, Canada. He is author of the bilingual aphasia test (a double special issue of *Clinical Linguistics & Phonetics* on the uses of the BAT around the world appeared in 2011). His major research interests include the neurolinguistics of bilingualism and the role of implicit and explicit memory in early and late bilinguals. His publications relevant to these topics include *A neurolinguistic theory of bilingualism* (2004) and *Declarative and procedural memory in second languages* (2009).

Claudia Peñaloza is a Post-Doctoral Research Associate in the Aphasia Research Laboratory at Boston University, USA. Her current research focuses on the prediction of rehabilitation outcomes of Spanish/English bilingual speakers with aphasia to determine the optimal language for treatment and the factors that maximize therapy gains and cross-language transfer effects in this population. Peñaloza is also interested in new word learning in aphasia, the cognitive and neural mechanisms that support new learning processes in the adult brain after brain damage, and the potential implications of word learning ability on treatment-induced language recovery.

Christos Pliatsikas is Associate Professor of Psycholinguistics in Bi/Multilinguals in the School of Psychology and Clinical Language Sciences at the University of Reading, UK, where he is also affiliated with the Centre for Literacy and Multilingualism and the Centre for Integrative Neuroscience and Neurodynamics. His research interests include language learning and the brain along with the effects of the bi/multilingual experience on brain structure, function, and cognition. Some of his research has appeared in *Bilingualism: Language and Cognition, Brain Structure and Function, Cerebellum, PLoS ONE,* and the *Proceedings of the National Academy of Sciences.*

Frank A. Rodden is affiliated with the Department of Personality and Assessment in the Institute of Psychology at the University of Zurich, Switzerland. He is currently working as a psychiatrist in a practice in Zurich (Psychcentral). Rodden is a medical doctor, psychiatrist, and senior researcher in cognitive sciences, with a special interest in humour, play, and religion. He worked as a neurosurgeon for eight years.

Eleonora Rossi is an Assistant Professor in the Department of Linguistics at the University of Florida, and a Research Associate at the University of California, Riverside, USA. Her research interests include language processing and bilingualism with the goal of understanding the neurocognitive bases of bilingual language processing and the interactions between language and cognition. In her research, Rossi uses linguistic and behavioural measures of language and cognitive processing, and neuroimaging techniques such as event-related potentials, eye-tracking, and functional and structural measures neuroimaging, including functional magnetic resonance imaging and diffusion tensor imaging.

Jason Rothman is Professor of Psycholinguistics and Bi–/Multilingualism in the School of Psychology and Clinical Language Sciences at the University of Reading, UK, and a Professor II of Linguistics at UiT the Arctic University of Norway. He is the Executive Editor of the journal *Linguistic Approaches to Bilingualism (LAB)* as well as Editor of the book series *Studies in Bilingualism (SiBIL).* Rothman's research focuses on language acquisition and processing in children and adults in addition to the interface between domain general cognition and language. Some of his recent research has appeared in *Bilingualism: Language and Cognition, Second Language Research, Studies in Second Language Acquisition, Language, Cognition and Neuroscience,* and *Frontiers in Psychology.*

Herbert Schriefers is a Professor of Psycholinguistics in the Donders Institute for Brain, Cognition and Behaviour at Radboud University, The Netherlands where he is also Vice Dean of research of the Faculty of Social Sciences. His main research interests concern auditory and visual sentence processing and language production using behavioural and electrophysiological paradigms. Schriefers' recent work has appeared in *Cortex, Journal of Experimental Psychology: Human Perception and Performance, Journal of Cognitive Neuroscience, Journal of Memory and Language,* and *Neuropsychologia.*

John W. Schwieter (see 'About the Editor' above).

Nuria Sebastian-Galles is Professor at the Universitat Pompeu Fabra, Spain. In 2016, she was elected Corresponding Fellow of the British Academy. She was Vice-President of the Scientific Council of the European Research Council until the end of 2016. Sebastian-Galles has authored many peer-reviewed articles on bilingualism, early language development, and speech perception in journals such as *Science, Proceedings of the National Academy of Sciences of the United States of America*, and the *Journal of Neuroscience*.

Edalat Shekari is a PhD Candidate in the Cognitive Science of Language programme at McMaster University, Canada. His research focuses on the L1 and L2 processing and acquisition, complex sentence processing in L1 and L2, the role of cognitive individual differences in L1 and L2 processing, and performance and cognitive consequences of processing input/information in a non-dominant language. Shekari is currently working on processing spoken instructions in L1 and L2 and is examining how language complexity and individual differences in working memory capacity and proficiency affect language processing and real-world task performance in a bilingual's dominant and non-dominant languages.

Gregory M. Shreve is Professor Emeritus of Translation Studies at Kent State University and Professor of Translation at New York University, USA. At Kent State University, he was the founding Director of the Institute for Applied Linguistics and Chair of the Department of Modern and Classical Languages Studies, and was instrumental in establishing one of the first Translation Studies programmes in the United States. Shreve's research interests include text linguistics, cognitive translation studies, empirical approaches to translation studies, and translation informatics. He is the co-author/co-editor of several books including *Translation as Text* (1992), *Cognitive Processes in Translation and Interpreting* (1997), and *Translation and Cognition* (2010).

Teresa Signorelli Pisano is a Visiting Research Scholar in the Speech-Language-Hearing Sciences Program at the City University of New York Graduate Center, USA. She is also a bilingual speech-language pathologist. Her research interests relate to bilingualism across the lifespan in neurotypical and communicatively impaired individuals. Dr. Pisano sits on the Advisory Board for the Clinical Centers at Loyola University and consults in private practice regarding related professional and lay education.

Anna Siyanova-Chanturia is a Senior Lecturer in Applied Linguistics at Victoria University of Wellington, New Zealand. Her interests include: bilingualism; psychological aspects of second language acquisition; usage-based approaches to language acquisition, processing and use; and vocabulary and multiword expressions. Siyanova-Chanturia has used quantitative research methods including corpora, eye movements, and electroencephalography in studies that have appeared in *Language Learning, Studies in Second Language Acquisition, Applied Linguistics*, the *Journal of Experimental Psychology: Learning, Memory, and Cognition, Psychophysiology*, and other venues.

Daria Smirnova is Assistant Professor in the Department of Psychiatry, Narcology, Psychotherapy and Clinical Psychology at Samara State Medical University, Russia, and a Visiting Research Fellow in the Centre for Clinical Research in Neuropsychiatry at the University of Western Australia. She has also served as a consultant in psychiatry and psychotherapy for patients with a variety of psychiatric conditions. Smirnova's primary research interests, informed by her training in general medicine (MD), linguistics, and psycholinguistics, are centred on thought, language and communication disorders, neurocognitive dysfunction, and interpersonal functioning in bilinguals with schizophrenia and their first-degree relatives. Her recent publications have appeared in *Psychiatry Research, Neuropsychologia*, and *Frontiers in Psychiatry*.

Robin L. Thompson is Associate Professor in Psychology at the University of Birmingham, UK. She holds a PhD in cognitive science and linguistics (joint degree) from the University of California, San Diego and has held positions at the Salk Institute, San Diego State University, and University College London. Thompson's research investigates the underlying nature of human language (both signed and spoken) and in particular, how language is related to other aspects of cognition. Some of her recent research published in *Cognition* looks at the role of the production system in sign language comprehension.

Barbara Tomasino is a Researcher in Cognitive Neuroscience at the Scientific Institute IRCCS 'E. Medea', Italy. She works with functional imaging and neuropsychology on healthy participants and neurosurgical patients. She has authored over 40 peer-reviewed publications in international journals in the field of motor action, imagery, language, and perception.

Jorge R. Valdés Kroff is Assistant Professor of Spanish and Linguistics at the University of Florida, USA. He is the Director of the Bilingual Sentence Processing Lab which uses behavioural and eye-tracking methods to investigate how bilinguals adapt their parsing preferences to better anticipate upcoming code switches. Valdés Kroff's recent work focuses on testing whether bilinguals tap into production asymmetries to guide comprehension and recruit greater engagement of cognitive control to rapidly integrate upcoming code switches.

Mariana Vega-Mendoza is a Post-Doctoral Research Associate on the British Arts and Humanities Research Council's Open World Research Initiative 'Multilingualism: Empowering Individuals Transforming Societies (MEITS)' at the University of Edinburgh, working on the impact of foreign language learning on cognitive functions in both healthy ageing and dementia. She holds a PhD in Psychology from the University of Edinburgh, UK, an MA in Hispanic Linguistics from the Ohio State University, a Diploma in Neuropsychology from the REAPRENDE Center for Psychological Rehabilitation at Benemérita Universidad Autónoma de Puebla, and an Honours BA in Psychology from the Universidad Nacional Autónoma de México. With her distinctive background in both neuropsychology and psycholinguistics, she has wide experience on different topics and methodologies of first and second language acquisition, aphasia rehabilitation research, and cognitive assessment of clinical populations such as patients with brain tumours.

Jet M. J. Vonk is a Post-Doctoral Research Scientist at the Taub Institute for Research on Alzheimer's Disease and the Ageing Brain in the Cognitive Neuroscience Division, Department of Neurology at Columbia University Medical Center, USA. She received her PhD in Speech-Language-Hearing Sciences from the Graduate Center of the City University of New York, with a focus on neurolinguistics and cognitive science. Her research interests include language and cognitive changes, and their neurobiological basis, in healthy ageing and dementia (e.g., Alzheimer's disease and primary progressive aphasia).

Joel Walters is Chair of Communication Disorders at Hadassah Academic College, Israel, and Professor Emeritus of Linguistics at Bar-Ilan University. His current research interests focus on a broad range of features of bilingualism and narrative (code switching, fluency, coherence relations, lexis) in a variety of contexts, including bilingual pre-school children (with and without Developmental Language Disorder) and bilingual people with aphasia and schizophrenia. Walters' work has appeared in *Aphasiology*, *Applied Psycholinguistics*, *Bilingualism: Language & Cognition*, *International Journal of Bilingualism*, *Journal of Communication Disorders*, *Linguistic Approaches to Bilingualism*, and *Neuropsychologia* and has been funded by the Israel Science Foundation, the Israel Ministry of Education, the German-Israel Research Foundation (GIF), and the German Ministry of Education (BMBF).

Nicole Y. Y. Wicha is Associate Professor of Neurobiology at the University of Texas at San Antonio, USA. She received a PhD in Cognitive Science from the University of California at San Diego under the direction of Dr. Elizabeth A. Bates and Dr. Marta Kutas. Her dissertation research provided early evidence for prediction during sentence comprehension. She first studied the bilingual brain as a Post-Doctoral Fellow at the Institute of Neural Computation. Her lab continues to investigate language comprehension using ERPs, with an additional focus on how language experience affects other cognitive processes, such as how arithmetic is processed in the developing bilingual brain.

Allison M. Wilck is a PhD Student in Cognitive Psychology at the University at Albany, State University of New York, USA under the mentorship of Dr. Jeanette Altarriba. She has recently published an article on adaptive memory in the *Encyclopaedia of evolutionary psychological science* and has a chapter in the upcoming edition of the *Handbook on language and emotion*. Within the Cognition and Language Laboratory at the University at Albany, State University of New York, she studies various areas of psychology to include adaptive memory, priming, learning judgements and predictions, and emotion word processing.

Fei Zhong is a PhD Student in Linguistics and Applied Linguistics at Guangdong University of Foreign Studies, China. He is currently working on the neurocognitive consequences of interpreting experience under the supervision of Yanping Dong with whom he has a recent paper published in *Neuropsychologia*.

Special Foreword

MICHEL PARADIS

It is no longer necessary, as it might have been 30 years ago, to draw the attention of the research community to the importance of bilingualism, even in countries traditionally considered monolingual. Massive migration worldwide, the increase in travel and the large-scale development of electronic communication media have rendered this phenomenon obvious enough. Speakers of more than one language are no longer an exception in aphasia clinics anywhere. This is reflected in the fact that, in response to the demand, the number of languages of the bilingual aphasia test (available online for free download since 2011 – http://www.mcgill.ca/linguistics/research/bat), has now reached 73 and the validation of several additional versions is in progress around the world. Both clinical and experimental research into multilingualism, including new neuroimaging procedures and new psychological methods, have greatly intensified, as reflected in the present volume. We have seen a considerable surge in research on language acquisition, learning, and use in speakers of more than one language. In parallel, brain research has also increased exponentially over the past two decades. Accordingly, much current research bears on various aspects of the multilingual brain, as evidenced in the contributions to this handbook.

Since the beginning of this century, the apprehension of language has moved away from the Chomskyan view that language is radically different from all other cognitive and motor functions. Rather, language is taken to be grounded in mechanisms of sensory processing and motor control. It is similar to any other cognitive skill in its acquisition and cerebral processing. A number of working hypotheses have emerged. For instance, neurolinguistic studies have argued that declarative metalinguistic and pragmatic knowledge, as well as conceptual representations, are neurofunctionally independent of procedural implicit linguistic competence and susceptible to independent impairment; that motivation is a necessary component of verbal communication; that multiple languages are represented as subsystems of the language neurofunctional system, each subserved by independent microanatomical physiological circuits within the same gross anatomical cerebral areas. Consequently, it has been suggested that aphasia is an impairment of procedural implicit linguistic competence and therefore may not necessarily affect a later-acquired language in the same way as a native language. Different bilingual aphasia recovery patterns thus appear as the result of either impairments in the automatic control over language subsystems that are subject to different threshold level alterations (early bilingualism) and/or of declarative vs. procedural memory dysfunctions (late bilingualism). In addition, whereas the native language is often more impaired in aphasia and Parkinson's disease, later-learned languages are often more impaired in amnesia and Alzheimer's disease.

It has become increasingly apparent that left-hemisphere-based linguistic competence (comprising phonology, morphology, syntax, and semantics) is not sufficient for normal verbal communication. Right-hemisphere-based pragmatic competence (the ability to draw correct inferences from the context and from general knowledge, the interpretation of indirect speech acts, metaphors, puns, affective prosody, and in general of the unspoken component of an utterance) is at least equally necessary. The accrued involvement of the right hemisphere in multilingual speakers is not a question of degrees of lateralization of language competence but of increased use of pragmatics to compensate for a possible lack of competence in one of the languages.

Another widely applicable finding is that results cannot be generalized from single words to *language* in any study of multilingualism, including language lateralization, neuroimaging studies, pre-surgical electrical stimulation, or diagnosis and therapy. Single words are the least likely candidates for investigating *language* representation, given that what makes language most specific as a cognitive function, namely the language system (phonology, morphology, syntax), is supported by procedural memory, whereas isolated words, being explicitly known form-meaning associations, are supported by declarative memory and hence are less focalized in their cortical representation. Neuroimaging studies using single words as stimuli show no difference between monolingual and bilingual individuals, whereas studies that use sentences as stimuli do. Not only can results obtained with single-word stimuli not be generalized to the representation and processing of language (in the way that one normally cannot generalize from a part to the whole), but experiments that use such stimuli address a component that differs radically from the language system.

The radical distinction between conceptual and semantic representations also has multiple implications. Whereas grammatical features are implicitly represented inherently (opaque to introspection), concepts are amenable to reaching consciousness. Word meanings (whose definitions are found in dictionaries, encyclopaedias and textbooks, each corresponding to a word in a given language) must be clearly distinguished from individuals' conceptual representations.

Concepts in monolingual speakers are flexible and dynamic: they constantly evolve with new experience and formal learning. Only (different) portions of their constituent features are activated on each occasion of their use. It has therefore been argued that there are no systematic differences between monolingual and bilingual conceptual functioning, language representation, and language-concept interaction. The contents of representations (i.e. the particular groupings of conceptual features) may – and most likely do – differ amongst individuals, whether monolingual or bilingual, but their nature and modus operandi are the same. The richer the individuals' experience (including the acquisition of other languages), the more differentiated their stock of conceptual representations will be. All other things being equal, bilinguals as a group are likely to have a richer conceptual store, and experiential factors will be modulated by individual cognitive variables. Thus *what* is activated may vary between languages, but the nature of the representations (i.e. what constitutes a conceptual representation) is the same, as are the principles by which they are activated. The variation between the conceptual features that are activated in monolingual native speakers of Swedish when uttering a particular word is of the same kind as that between a Swedish word and its corresponding translation (quasi)equivalent in Japanese. In both cases, the conceptual features they activate are not exactly the same ones, but they are bona fide conceptual features in each case. The brain mechanisms involved in acquiring, representing, and using these concepts are identical. There are thus no neurolinguistic differences in terms of acquisition, organization, and loss between monolingual, bilingual, or multilingual *conceptual* representations, whereas there are semantic and grammatical differences depending on the semantic boundaries and grammatical structures of each language.

Two further working hypotheses have been advantageously used to account for a number of behavioural, clinical, and experimental data: the activation threshold hypothesis and the subset hypothesis. The activation threshold hypothesis proposes that an item is activated when sufficient positive neural impulses have reached its neural substrate. The amount of impulses necessary to activate an item constitutes its activation threshold. Every time an item is activated, its threshold is lowered and fewer impulses are required to reactivate it. Thus, after each activation, the threshold is lowered – but it gradually rises again. If the item is not stimulated, it becomes more and more difficult to activate over time. The threshold is conditioned by recency and frequency of use, and modulated by limbic and neurotransmitter variables. In addition, the selection of a particular item requires that its activation exceed that of any possible alternatives. Production is more vulnerable to attrition than comprehension, as the neurological mechanisms involved require a higher level of activation. Comprehension is therefore easier and will be retained longer than production, in part because the former requires fewer self-generated impulses to reach threshold since, in addition to the internal impulses, external sensory impulses are provided by the verbal input. Several researchers have highlighted the pervasive role of the cerebral systems' activation thresholds, for instance in accounting for differential recovery in multilingual aphasia: Cerebral damage can alter languages' thresholds, which could explain asymmetric impairments. It has proven useful, not only in language pathology, but also in psycholinguistics, childhood bilingualism, heritage speakers, and particularly language attrition studies.

The subset hypothesis states that a bilingual's two languages are subserved by two subsystems of the larger neurofunctional implicit language competence system. As subsystems of language, each (specific) language subsystem has a nature more similar to the other language subsystem(s) than to any other cognitive system and can be independently activated or inhibited. This does not imply that languages are located in different gross neuroanatomical areas; rather, they differ at the microanatomical level, which cannot be detected by current neuroimaging technology but is attested by (preoperative) electrical stimulation of the brain. Neuroimaging studies nevertheless report *largely* overlapping cortical networks, which implies the existence of some non-overlapping areas, often involving executive control and attention, attributable to the extra cognitive/pragmatic effort needed to overcome gaps in second language implicit procedural competence. The subset hypothesis is, moreover, compatible with and has been used to explain instances of dynamic interference, nonce borrowings, and mixing, as well as selective and differential recovery in bilingual speakers with aphasia.

Recently, research has focused particularly on executive control mechanisms. Much discussion has been devoted to the subject and it is raised in 10 of the chapters in this volume. Executive control is central to the declarative/procedural aspects of multilingualism. Every individual without severe mental defects acquires a native language. Some even acquire two or more. However, not everyone who has acquired a first language manages to acquire a second. The numerous causes of inter-individual differences in second language attainment are directly related to several factors intrinsic to declarative memory (e.g. working memory, IQ, focused attention, executive control), to which the normal acquisition of a native language is impervious.

A great deal of discussion is obscured by a lack of distinction between acquisition and learning. Skilled use of a later-learned language often begins as a controlled process which gradually appears to become automatic but, in reality, controlled processing is gradually *replaced* by the use of automatic processing, which is not merely the speeding-up of the controlled process, but the use of a different system which, through practice, develops in parallel. Practice in natural conversational settings engages entities other than those that are controlled. For example, the controlled application of explicit rules is replaced by the automatic use of corresponding implicit computational procedures – explicit rules and implicit procedures being of a different nature, having different contents, and being subserved by different cerebral networks. Executive functions are supported by a broad network of anterior and posterior brain structures including prefrontal grey matter. Neuroimaging studies show anterior cingulate cortex activity during tasks that engage selective attention, working memory, and controlled information processing. It plays a prominent role in the executive control of cognition and, notably, together with the hippocampal system, it is more active during the use of a later-learned language.

Two types of control should be considered: automatic (autonomous) language-specific; and (general, executive, conscious) non-specific control circuits. Executive control involves the attentional system; language-autonomous control does not. As a skill becomes more proficient, processing shifts from the use of one mechanism (controlled, declarative) to another (automatic, procedural). In later language appropriation, there is a shift from reliance on mechanisms that depend on general knowledge (declarative memory) to the autonomous processing of modules (that depend on procedural memory). By eliminating or reducing reliance on higher-level supervisory processes, language performance becomes less subject to monitoring by specialized attentional mechanisms.

A particular question about control in multilingual speakers is how they are able to switch between their languages. In fact, there are two types of switching to be considered: conscious and automatic. The fact that an individual's languages are part of the autonomous implicit neurofunctional language system allows that individual to borrow from or switch between the available subsystems automatically, as a function of the various activation thresholds of the elements involved in the message being elaborated. This is in opposition to a deliberate switch, either in an experimental setting (e.g. name the object in English when the background is red, in Spanish when it is blue) or when consciously perceived circumstances in the environment require it (e.g. because of the arrival of a new person in the conversational group). Thus, switching relies on either executive or autonomous language-specific control.

For the present handbook, John W. Schwieter invited an international array of eminent and promising researchers in applied linguistics, cognitive science, experimental psychology, neuropsychology, and brain imagery to bring their expertise to bear on the key issues that are raised by multilingual phenomena, including theories and methods, neural representations and processes, language impairments, and the cognitive effects of multilingualism. Each author works towards a solution for a problem that contains numerous parameters. Each contribution sheds light from a different perspective and is a welcome step in the direction of a better apprehension of the intricate phenomenon of multilingualism. As a state-of-the art depiction of key issues related to language perception, production, and organization in speakers of multiple languages, this anthology provides an important basis for reflection for students and researchers in any clinical or theoretical aspect of multilingualism.

Overview of the Handbook

JOHN W. SCHWIETER AND REBECCA MUELLER

Human language as a biological window for understanding the brain is perhaps one of the most revealing phenomena available. In fact, our unique ability to acquire and use language(s) should be at the heart of cognitive science, particularly when mapping the organization of the mind. This becomes even more intriguing when considering that the mind is able to handle multiple languages through a complicated control network that is sensitive yet adaptable. Neuroscientific approaches to studying multilingualism continue to gain momentum and uncover valuable insights on how the human brain handles and represents multiple languages. Amongst the world's population, the bilingual/ multilingual brain is far more typical than its monolingual counterpart and, thus, it begs the question as to whether it is more appropriate to study and model the multilingual brain as a default rather than the exception.

Within this multilingual framework, over the last few decades, cognitive psychologists, linguistics, and neurolinguists have explored research questions such as: How does the mind make, store, and lose memories in multiple languages? How do language abilities compare to non-linguistic cognitive abilities? What is the relationship between language and thought? How does multilingualism affect non-linguistic cognition? How does the acquisition of one language from birth differ from acquiring more than one language? How does the mind accommodate language learning later in life? How are words recognized and sentences comprehended? How is speech produced? What are the cognitive mechanisms that underlie the ability for bilinguals to switch back and forth between their languages? As ongoing research is conducted to answer these and many other important research questions, we are getting closer to a comprehensive understanding of the complex relationship between language(s) and the mind.

The Handbook of the Neuroscience of Multilingualism builds on this impetus and reports on topical areas and findings that have formulated and continue to define research trajectories in the field today. In the handbook, the reader will find 36 authoritative, state-of-the-art chapters, which are organized in the following five parts:

Part I: Theories and Methods
Part II: Neural Representations
Part III: Functions and Processes
Part IV: Impairments and Disorders
Part V: Cognitive and Neurocognitive Consequences

In Part I, the handbook opens with a series of chapters dedicated to prominent theories and methods. Chapter 1 by Kees de Bot provides an appropriate starting point for the handbook by offering advice on how multilingualism should be defined and assessed. His view centres on the notion that multilingualism is a dynamic process rather than a state. In line with previous work by Zhao and Li (2010), de Bot argues that the impact of dynamic language competition is a significant factor in multilingual development in which transfer and interaction between languages are dynamic processes, not states. On this backdrop, Edna Andrews, in Chapter 2, reviews prominent theories and methods in the field by focusing on the linguistic and neuroscience contributions that have led to a robust study of brain and language. Her extensive synthesis covers foundational aspects of theory that expose how languages work and their neurological underpinnings (acquisition, maintenance, and loss) along with new methodological applications of electrophysiological and hemodynamic imaging technologies (e.g. cortical stimulation mapping, functional magnetic resonance imaging [fMRI], and longitudinal studies). Andrews concludes her chapter with a commentary on how perspectives have shifted in the field and what future directions should be taken.

Chapter 3, by Angela Grant, Jennifer Legault, and Ping Li, explores what bilingual models add to the conversation on the neurocognition of multiple languages. Inquiries into bilingualism which are addressed in the chapter include: if there is a dual activation of both languages when a bilingual speaks and what the process of language selection entails. The authors also touch on whether a conceptual meaning of an individual word is equivalent across translations or if words have their own separate conceptual meanings. The chapter concludes with a discussion on the mechanisms involved in using neurocognitive methods and offers reviews of bilingual cognitive models and neural evidence that supports that model.

Chapter 4 by Eleonora Rossi, Kyra Krass, and Gerrit Jan Kootstra presents a review of methodologies that have been utilized in psycholinguistics research to address questions pertaining to multilingual processing. Some of these methods include self-paced reading, self-paced listening, eye-tracking for text reading, visual-world eye-tracking, syntactic priming, and syntactic alignment. The chapter exemplifies how these methodologies have been employed to inform multilingual production and comprehension models and comments on the advantages and challenges of utilizing these paradigms in the context of neuroscientific research. In Chapter 5, Nicole Y. Y. Wicha, Eva María Moreno, and Haydée Carrasco-Ortíz offer insight on real-time measures of brain activity that use encephalography to measure the electrical (EEG) and magnetic (MEG) signals of the brain during real-time language comprehension and production. The authors fully discuss these techniques, their advantages and limitations, and the primary brain signatures observed and how to interpret them. Specific focus is given to event-related potential (ERP) studies of language comprehension, which have produced a rich body of work in multilingualism, including single-word recognition, sentence comprehension, language switching, and adult second-language acquisition.

In Chapter 6, Angélique M. Blackburn focuses on neuroimaging techniques such as fMRI and positron emission tomography (PET) that inform our understanding of multilingual speech and its neural underpinnings. The author critically reviews the mapping neural networks involved in lexical selection, phonological retrieval, and articulation.

Collectively, the studies suggest that cortical representations of a multilingual's languages are largely overlapping, and a cortical–subcortical network is engaged to manage language control. Damage to this distributed network hinders control over language switching and frequently engaging this network may lead to neural changes linked to the ability to compensate for loss of cognitive control later in life. Chapter 7 by Ludmila Isurin tracks the development of psycholinguistic and neurolinguistic research on language loss. The author focuses on studies investigating 'the savings effect' in which search for memory traces of a lost language operated on the assumption that a language, once learned but later forgotten, leaves traces in memory that facilitate the relearning of that language later in life. Different methodologies were used to measure the savings effect (e.g. acoustic measurement, phoneme production task, accent perception task, the savings paradigm, fMRI, etc.) in relearning of various domains of the forgotten language.

Vince DeLuca, David Miller, Christos Pliatsikas, and Jason Rothman conclude Part I in their Chapter 8. The authors review EEG/ERP and (f)MRI data to explore the various views regarding the 'critical period' debate and how to best account for the ubiquitously noted differences that align with age of acquisition. Their synthesis shows that the majority of evidence for the critical period in second language (L2) acquisition comes from behavioural experimentation or spontaneous production and from populations of L2 learners who are not exposed to the target language in a way similar to children acquirers. Given the evidence against the notion that the brain remains plastic throughout the lifespan, the neuromaturational basis of the critical period hypothesis is challenged in the chapter.

Part II discusses neural representations in the multilingual brain. The first chapter of the section, Chapter 9 by Nicola Del Maschio and Jubin Abutalebi, reviews results achieved in the field of the functional neuroanatomy of multilingualism. Many of which are yielded PET and fMRI. Multilingualism is discussed as it relates to the functional neuroanatomy of language, specifically the phonological, grammatical, and lexico-semantic processing of multilinguals. The authors review various research theories, including the possibility of languages being represented in separate parts of the brain, amongst others. In Chapter 10, Jana Klaus and Herbert Schriefers dissect bilingual word production, questioning the extent to which a multilingual's languages work separately from one another. Studies are presented with a variety of findings such as the absence of differences that were found between first language (L1) and (L2) production and the increased brain resources required when producing words in L2. Factors such as age of acquisition, proficiency, and immersions are taken into account in the discussion of additional studies. Interestingly, the authors comment on the disadvantages that bilinguals face in certain speech production performances of both their additional and native languages.

Christos Pliatsikas provides insight on brain plasticity in Chapter 11. Particularly, how the brain restructures with the arrival of new linguistic knowledge and how language processes such as grammar, lexicon, and phonology adapt with information from competing languages. The chapter discusses the effects of bilingualism on grey and white matter and the resting state functional connectivity. As mentioned at the start of the chapter, most research is relatively recent; the chapter is thus fittingly concluded with suggestions for additional research. In Chapter 12, Angélique M. Blackburn shifts readers' focus towards factors affecting cortical representation. The overlap in the cortical representation of a multilinguals' languages is of special interest, taking into account the similarity between the languages, the age of acquisition, and the characteristics of the individual such as age, gender, and verbal intelligence. Blackburn also touches on various language acquisition theories as she examines the neural activity needed when using lower proficiency languages versus ones with increased proficiency. Similar to the previous chapter, Blackburn concludes with recommendations for further work in the field.

Chapter 13, by Begoña Díaz, Miguel Burgaleta, and Nuria Sebastian-Galles addresses the individual differences affecting non-native speech perception. The question posed specifically as to why some people appear more natural at language learning is raised as particularly relevant. Preceding a discussion on the controversial critical period hypothesis, age of acquisition, and amount of exposure are presented as exogenous factors affecting L2 input variability. The authors introduce research which compares the brains of monolingual and bilingual brain imaging studies, as well as an in-depth case-study of Spanish-Catalan bilinguals in Catalonia. Concluding the chapter is a discussion on studies involving non-native phoneme contrast.

Gary Libben and John W. Schwieter report on how the multilingual mind is lexically organized and reorganized in Chapter 14. After presenting early work in the field such as an approach entitled *Syntactic Structures* by Noam Chomsky (1957), the authors discuss findings which prove helpful in determining how multilingualism is developed and maintained. The focus then shifts to the metaphors of a multilingual who possesses interacting lexical stores and a multilingual who possessed an entire network of interacting lexical items in a single multilingual lexical store. The complexity necessary for the activation in processing language is exemplified through subword elements. These discoveries are then consequently applied in the context of multilingualism. In Chapter 15, by Stephanie A. Kazanas, Jared S. McLean, and Jeanette Altarriba, processing is alternatively looked at in the scope of emotion and emotion concepts, the form of words and images being one example. The notion that the first language of a bilingual has an emotion processing advantage is supported by a variety of literature. The response evoked by words associated with joyful memories and thoughts or sad memories and thoughts is of significance when contrasting the reaction to words of one's native tongue versus the less prominent reaction with their secondary language. In conjunction with the conclusions drawn in the chapter, thought is given to psychological and clinical treatment for multilinguals.

Jennifer Hofmann and Frank A. Rodden conclude Part II with a comprehensive look at humour in the brain in Chapter 16. By looking at humour production, comprehension, and appreciation, the authors demonstrate the complexity of everyday encounters with humour. The authors then relate these processes specifically to language, touching on the ability or inability to translate something funny from one language to another, and the process that is undergone in doing so. Several case studies provide insight into the processing of humour as a cognitive task and into amusement as the emotional response and behavioural reactions to this humour.

Part III explores the functions and processes of the multilingual brain. Chapter 17 by Peter Bright, Julia Ouzia, and Roberto Filippi begins by exploring the process of metacognition. Much of this chapter provides insight into its overlap with executive control. Acknowledged specifically are conceptual overlap, such as in decision-making, and neural signature overlap, such as decision-making in uncertain situations. The controversial claim as to whether or not multilanguage acquisition benefits executive function is discussed in depth and studies using the alibration curve. Monitoring the difference between confidence and actual performance become particularly releavant to the discussion. In Chapter 18 by Edalat Shekari and John W. Schwieter, the authors discuss the factors which affect multilingual processessing. An in-depth anaylzis of the relationship between working-memory resources and language processing and performance is presented with attention to the benefits and drawbacks of various Span tasks. Alongside this analysis, discussion is included on the age of acquisition – found to correlate with the variability of brain activation – and proficiency level exposure and language use – comparing naturalistic-exposure and classroom exposure. Furthermore, the working memory capacity, processing speed, and language (psycho)typology and language status are discussed at length.

Allison M. Wilck, Jeanette Altarriba, Roberto R. Heredia, and John W. Schwieter, in Chapter 19, examine the function of both learning and memory in the bilingual brain. Theoretical language models are discussed alongside the distinction between compound and coordinate bilingualism. Arguments and various studies are presented which support both the theory that bilinguals obtain an interdependent linguistic store and the independence memory theory. The interlanguage process and organization of different models, including connectionism, hierarchical structures, and language acquisition, are then assessed. In Chapter 20, Zahra Hejazi, Jungna Kim, Teresa Signorelli Pisano, Yasmine Ouchikh, Aviva Lerman, and Loraine K. Obler discuss second language learning in older adulthood and the brain-based challenges associated with it. Cognitive-linguistic changes of this age demographic are presented with respect to their impact on new learning. After discourse as to whether or not older adults have the required potential to learn new languages, second language learning techniques and pedagogies are discussed with respect to the alterations that could be made to enhance efficiency for the changing brains of older adults. Many of these recommendations are formulated on the basis that the declining brain develops compensatory strategies. The methods explored include the use of explicit over implicit feedback, reduced length and speed of instructor speech, and decreased distraction levels.

In Chapter 21, David W. Green explores language control and attention. References to relevant brain processes in conversation include neural synchronization between speaker and listener, through hyperscanning techniques. The relationship between language control in bilinguals and attentional states during a conversation are also discussed, concluding that one complex act can simultaneously encompass distinct attentional acts in the brain. Additionally, conceptual content and language networks are mentioned in the explanation of attentional states, with an analysis of the metastability and network synchrony under the scope of a multilingual. Marco Calabria, Cristina Baus, and Albert Costa utilize Chapter 22 to discuss the interaction that occurs between language and executive control. This relationship with executive control is highlighted especially in comparison with bilingual language control where correlation between the two has been found to range from low to full. Neuroimaging data, as well as cognitive and language deficits that succeed brain damage, are used within several studies that have tested the two controls. These test are reviewed extensively by the authors. Studies are then examined that consider the overlap of reactive and proactive controls, observing how the high demands of bilingualism effect the cooperative dynamics in these controls. Furthermore, bilingual patients with neurodegenerative diseases provide the circumstances necessary for the authors to discuss the relations between linguistic and non-linguistics processes.

Chapter 23, by Paola E. Dussias, Jorge R. Valdés Kroff, Anne L. Beatty-Martínez, and Michael A. Johns, reports on information gathered about cognition from the analysis of the language experience. Specifically, the authors speak about variable input and interactional contexts and how they affect the sentence processing of bilinguals. The discussion on the influence of the L2 on the L1, provides a unique platform to challenge the critical period hypothesis. Code switching is then used to demonstrate the ability of adaptation to different interactional contexts. Studies which use electrophysiological recording methods and those which use behavioural methods of sentence processing are of particular relevance throughout the chapter. In Chapter 24, Bruce J. Diamond and Gregory M. Shreve explore executive control and neuroplasticity in the context of translation, interpreting, and the bilingual brain. First, the different challenges of code switching when translating and interpreting are readily acknowledged. The neuroplasticity perspective looks at the development of bilingualism and the issues that may accompany it, focusing on the working memory and control mechanisms necessary for cross language tasks. The authors examine any alterations or enhancements of information processing that results from the neuroplasticity changes of this development and how it compares to monolinguals who do not undergo this development of bilingualism.

The final topic of the section is presented by Anna Siyanova-Chanturia, Paolo Canal, and Roberto R. Heredia in Chapter 25. The authors explore event-related potentials in the language processing of both monolinguals and bilinguals. Throughout the comparison, several key points include discussion on the way in which ambiguity is handled and also addressed is the way processing figurative speech compares with processing novel/literal phrases. Thereafter, the authors address the question as to which components of event-related potentials are involved in figurative language processing in native and non-native speakers and how the proficiency of a second language affects this processing. Subsequently, there is discussion of results in a comparison of idioms and metaphors, mainly how these types of non-literal language cause different patterns of results.

Part IV looks at language impairments and disorders. The section begins with Chapter 26 in which Elisa Cargnelutti, Barbara Tomasino, and Franco Fabbro explore aphasia in multilinguals. The authors look at the features which differentiate multilinguals and monolinguals with this impairment, as well as the differences between specific languages of a multilingual, not limited to the dominance of a language, the age and manner of aquisition, level of exposure, and emotional ties. An array of clinical patterns of impairment – such as parallel, selective, native, and non-native impairment – help to demonstrate the contributing factors to these profiles. Chapter 27, by Claudia Peñaloza and Swathi Kiran, continues the previous chapter's discussion on multilingual aphasia, focusing on recovery and rehabilitation patterns in such patients. The authors discuss language and cognitive control impairment in bilinguals, looking primarily at the premorbid language-related factors and the lesion factors which affect the degree of impairment. Again examining aphasia in bilinguals specifically, patterns of language recovery and possible neural correlates are identified and treatment efficiency in both of the languages. Neuroimaging evidence of language representation and treatment-induced recovery in these patients is also presented.

Following the theme thus far in Part IV, Chapter 28, by Taryn Malcolm, Aviva Lerman, Marta Korytkowska, Jet M. J. Vonk, and Loraine K. Obler, reports again on aphasia in bilinguals and multilinguals, this time speaking to the results of neurodegeneration and what is called primary progressive aphasia. The authors touch upon three variations of this aphasia: non-fluent, semantic, and logopenic. Centring on the language declines of this aphasia, the factors affecting decline, and the identification of the neural changes occurring in the brain, paint a relevant picture of the language organization in bilingual and multilingual brains. A comparison with Alzheimer's disease – a similar degenerative disease – along with relevant case studies, provide further detail on the contributing factors and ways in which the decline can develop.

Mira Goral, utilizes Chapter 29 to turn the conversation towards the written side of language, exploring acquired reading disorders in bilinguals. Some of the disorders mentioned include phonological, deep, surface, and pure alexia. The author discusses critically whether the degree to which the nature of a reading impairment is determined by orthography, and how the underlying networks associated with reading are implicated by orthography differences. Throughout the chapter, special attention is given to the composition of literature in different languages, comparing the direction that words are read, the size of sound units like phonemes and syllables and their correspondence to graphemes, and the regularity that exists between the written and spoken form. Studies are discussed which present the neuronal networks specialized for reading. In Chapter 30, Mariana Vega-Mendoza, Suvarna Alladi, and Thomas H. Bak discuss dementia and multilingualism. The authors discuss the effects of the degenerative disease on a multilingual and their language abilities and, contrarily, how multilingualism affects the disease, specifically its age of onset and progression. Assuming that multilingualism does delay dementia, the authors look at whether the type of dementia and type of languages have a smaller or greater effect. Various studies are presented which argue for and against the various sides of these controversies and inquiries.

The last topic of the section is Chapter 31, by Daria Smirnova, Sveta Fichman, and Joel Walters, on schizophrenia and bilingualism. The authors review studies on neurobiological underpinnings of schizophrenia and bilingualism, providing a neurological basis for a comparison of the two. A detailed description of linguistics characteristics of both allows the authors to attempt to isolate language phenomena which characterize individuals with the disorder. The potential effects of bilingualism are noted, as well as an approach attempting to integrate linguistic and cognitive elements which constitute a bilingual with schizophrenia.

Part V engages readers with a dialogue on the cognitive and neurocognitive effects of multilingualism. Chapter 32, by Hannah L. Claussenius-Kalman and Arturo E. Hernandez, takes on a developmental perspective, discussing the neurocognitive effects of multilingualism throughout one's lifespan. The chapter starts by looking at the importance of age of acquisition, as well as the role played by individual differences when determining multilingual outcomes. Specifically, the authors look at the genetic basis for cognitive flexibility and code switching and how the success of adult foreign language learners is affected by plasticity. The concept of hyperglots is engaged via age of acquisition and individual differences. As the chapter concludes, executive control, the neuroprotective effects seen in older adults, and the disadvantages and challenges become relevant to the discussion on the constraints of individual differences. In Yanping Dong and Fei Zhong's Chapter 33, the neurocognitive consequences of interpreting are explored. The authors first explore the working memory, where certain advantages are argued to be present beyond those of another bilingual. The magnitude of the span and, more importantly, the efficacy of the functioning are of particular interest. The studies examined are then critiqued, accounting for the unbalanced ages and small sample size in several of the studies. The consequences that interpreting has on inhibitory control are also examined, finding that experience, even though not necessarily enhancing cognitive flexibility, helps enhance executive functioning and has structural and functional neurocognitive consequences.

Kenneth Paap provides insight on the bilingual advantage debate in Chapter 34, through both quantitative and qualitative evidence. As the debate is incredibly common and many publications and studies exist, Paap critiques and dissects the possible biases and inaccuracies that render many unreliable. He attempts to dismiss the typical assumption that bilinguals yield more advantages than monolinguals through analysis of case studies with a positive result, questioning their interpretations, failure to report all findings, and small sample sizes. The claim which is drawn is that, despite popular belief, there are no advantages in executive functioning for bilinguals or, if there are, they only occur very specifically and in undetermined circumstances. In Chapter 35, Angela de Bruin and Sergio Della Sala continue the critique of past studies involved in the bilingual advantage debate. The authors look primarily at publication biases and suggest that researchers interpret findings while keeping in mind that it is more likely that positive findings get published compared to null findings. The decline effect is the second focus of the chapter and there is a discussion on whether this decline of positive findings of the bilingualism advantage relates to publication bias.

In Chapter 36, Robin L. Thompson and Eva Gutierrez-Sigut shift readers' focus towards a different method of communication, exploring speech-sign bilingualism. The authors compare speech-sign bilinguals with spoken language bilinguals, gaining insight into the representation and processing of languages in different sensorimotor modalities in the bilingual's brain, as well as into the relationship between language and general cognitive processes. The chapter compiles research and findings on sign language specifically, mentioning also broader multilingual studies.

Taken together, the five parts in *The Handbook of the Neuroscience of Multilingualism* provide a blueprint for the expansive terrain of this booming research area. The chapters we have presented demonstrate a thriving research field with promising avenues for future work that will only continue to inform our knowledge of the multilingual brain.

REFERENCES

Chomsky, N. (1957). *Syntactic Structures*. The Hague, The Netherlands: de Gruyter.

Zhao, X. and Li, P. (2010). Bilingual lexical interactions in an unsupervised neural network model. *International Journal of Bilingual Education and Bilingualism* 13 (5): 505–524.

Acknowledgements

I am eternally grateful to the invited contributors for their diligence and hard work, without which *The Handbook of the Neuroscience of Multilingualism* would not exist. These scholars have helped to put together a much-needed collection of essential topics that present engaging discussions. A special thank-you goes to Prof. Michel Paradis who graciously accepted my invitation to author the Special Prolegomenon to this *Handbook*. His words of wisdom are indispensable when introducing a handbook of this magnitude.

I would also like to thank the anonymous peer reviewers who were commissioned by Wiley Blackwell to assess my proposal for *The Handbook of the Neuroscience of Multilingualism*. Their suggestions on how to improve the handbook were extremely beneficial to the development of this project. My gratitude also goes to the publisher, John Wiley and Sons, whose support was beyond professional and efficient in the development of this handbook. Tanya McMullin and Manish Luthra deserve special thanks for their excellent assistance and prompt correspondence. Katherine Carr, the copy-editor who meticulously helped to polish up the manuscript, was also an invaluable part of this project. It has been a pleasure to work with John Wiley and Sons on this publication.

Rebecca Mueller was my editorial assistant who put hard work into the preparation of the manuscript. I thankfully acknowledge that financial support to hire her was received from a grant partly funded by Wilfrid Laurier University operating funds and partly by a Social Sciences and Humanities Research Council of Canada Institutional Grant.

A special thank-you goes to Profs. Marc Brysbaert, Martin Pickering, Cathy J. Price, Michael Ullman, and Janet van Hell for their words of endorsement which grace this handbook's back cover. Their assessments are encouraging for both this project and the field. I hope that readers will agree with their reactions to this handbook.

Finally, I am extremely appreciative of the scholars – both internal and external to this handbook – who served as peer reviewers of the individual contributions. It is without a doubt that their knowledge and expertise have strengthened the content of this handbook and its implications for future research. As such, I would like to extend sincere thanks to the following individuals:

Jubin Abutalebi, University San Raffaele, Italy
Edna Andrews, Duke University, USA
Maria Arrendondo, University of British Columbia, Canada
M. Teresa Bajo, University of Granada, Spain

Valentina Bambini, Scuola Normale Superiore di Pisa & IUSS Center for Neurolinguistics and Theoretical Syntax, Italy
Cristina Baus, Universitat Pompeu Fabra, Spain
David Birdsong, University of Texas at Austin, USA
Angélique M. Blackburn, Texas A&M International University, USA
Francesca Martina Branzi, University of Manchester, UK
Peter Bright, Anglia Ruskin University & University of Cambridge, UK
Emanuel Bylund, Stockholm University, Sweden
Marco Calabria, Universitat Pompeu Fabra, Spain
Paolo Canal, Scuola Normale Superiore di Pisa & IUSS Center for Neurolinguistics and Theoretical Syntax, Italy
Elisa Cargnelutti, Scientific Institute, IRCCS E. Medea, Pasian di Prato, Udine, Italy
Gareth Carrol, University of Birmingham, UK
Anna Cieślicka, Texas A&M International University, USA
Brendan Costello, Basque Center on Cognition, Brain and Language, Spain
Kees de Bot, University of Groningen, The Netherlands & University of Pannonia, Hungary
Angela de Bruin, Basque Center on Cognition, Brain and Language, Spain
Jessica De Leon, University of California, San Francisco, USA
Nicola Del Maschio, Vita-Salute San Raffaele University, Italy
Vincent Deluca, University of Reading, UK
Jean-Marc Dewaele, Birkbeck, University of London, UK
Bruce Diamond, William Paterson University, UK
Ton Dijkstra, Radboud University Nijmegen, The Netherlands
Yanping Dong, Guangdong University of Foreign Studies, China
James Dugan, Northern Arizona University, USA
Franco Fabbro, University of Udine, Italy
Aline Ferreira, University of California, Santa Barbara, USA
Julia Festman, Pedagogical University Tyrol, Austria
Roberto Filippi, University College London, UK
Jamile Forcelini, Florida State University, USA
Francesco Foroni, Australian Catholic University, Australia
Marcel Giezen, Basque Center on Cognition, Brain and Language, Spain
Daniel Gile, Université Paris 3 Sorbonne Nouvelle, France
Martin Gitterman, Lehman College & the Graduate Center, City University of New York, USA
Mira Goral, Lehman College, City University of New York, USA & University of Oslo, Norway
Maria Luisa Gorno Tempini, University of California, San Francisco, USA
Sarah Grey, Fordham University, USA
John Grundy, York University, Canada
L. Kirk Hagen, University of Houston–Downtown, USA
Roberto R. Heredia, Texas A&M International University, USA
Ludmila Isurin, Ohio State University, USA
Scott Jarvis, University of Utah, USA

Edith Kaan, University of Florida, USA
Stephanie A. Kazanas, Tennessee Technological University, USA
Merel Keijzer, University of Groningen, The Netherlands
Swathi Kiran, Boston University, USA
Dan Kleinman, University of Illinois at Urbana-Champaign, USA
Iring Koch, RWTH Aachen University, Germany
Barbara Köpke, University of Toulouse II-Le Mirail, France
Gerrit Jan Kootstra, Windesheim University of Applied Sciences & Radboud University
  Nijmegen, The Netherlands
Jennifer Krizman, Northwestern University, USA
Gary Libben, Brock University, Canada
Ping Li, Pennsylvania State University, USA
Fengying Ma, University of Cincinnati, USA
Kara Morgan-Short, University of Illinois at Chicago, USA
Lee Osterhout, University of Washington, USA
Julia Ouzia, Goldsmiths College University of London, UK
Kenneth Paap, San Francisco State University, USA
Daniela Paolieri, University of Granada, Spain
Claudia Peñaloza, Boston University, USA
Christos Pliatsikas, University of Reading, UK
Antoni Rodríguez Fornells, University of Barcelona, Spain
Stefano Rastelli, University of Pavia, Italy
Ingeborg Ribu, University of Oslo, Norway
Eleonora Rossi, University of Florida, USA
Jason Rothman, University of Reading, England & UiT the Arctic University of Norway
Jean Saint-Aubin, University of Moncton, Canada
Mikel Santesteban, University of the Basque Country, Spain
Monika Schmid, University of Essex, UK
Mary Seeman, University of Toronto, Canada
Gregory M. Shreve, Kent State University & New York University, USA
Andrea Stocco, University of Washington, USA
Gretchen Sunderman, Florida State University, USA
Debora Titone, McGill University, Canada
Barbara Tomasino, Scientific Institute, IRCCS E. Medea, Pasian di Prato, Udine, Italy
Barbara Treccani, University of Sassari, Italy
Jorge R. Valdés Kroff, University of Florida, USA
Marilyn Vihman, University of York, UK
Maximiliano Wilson, Laval University, Canada
Brendan Weekes, University of Hong Kong
Janet Werker, University of British Columbia, Canada
Evy Woumans, Ghent University, The Netherlands

Part I   Theories and Methods

1 Defining and Assessing Multilingualism

KEES DE BOT

1. Introduction

In the Western world, monolingualism used to be considered the rule and bilingualism the exception. This belief, which is also reflected in language policy and the treatment of minorities, is not based on the actual situation. There are 30 times more languages than countries, so although there may be a few countries that are monolingual, many are not. Monolingual countries certainly do not exist if we also take dialect differences into account. In addition, 70% of the world's population speak 12% of languages; there are thus only a few 'big' languages: Chinese, Spanish and English score high, but so too do Hindi and Panjabi/Urdu.

When looking at universal scale, there is every reason to assume that, numerically, multilingualism is the rule, and monolingualism is the exception. Nevertheless, for a large part of the Western population, there remains the perception that monolingualism is the 'normal' and desirable situation.

In this handbook, various forms of multilingualism are presented. This chapter focuses on how multilingualism should be defined and how it can be assessed. One of the main points will be that multilingualism should be viewed as a dynamic process rather than a state. Zhao and Li (2010) point to the impact of dynamic language competition as a major force in language development. They view transfer and interaction between languages as dynamic processes, not states. This is a clear break from traditional perspectives on interlanguage (see Bialystok and Sharwood Smith 1985, for a comparison of views).

2. Defining Multilingualism

A distinction should be made between multilingualism at the individual/psycholinguistic level and multilingualism at the group/sociolinguistic level.

Multilingual groups do not necessarily consist of multilingual individuals. A well-known example is Belgium, officially multilingual (Dutch/French/German), yet most

The Handbook of the Neuroscience of Multilingualism, First Edition. Edited by John W. Schwieter.

of its citizens are essentially monolingual with only a rudimentary level of proficiency in the other languages. Given the main theme of this volume, the sociolinguistic perspective is not discussed here any further.

There are many definitions of bi/multilingualism. A simple definition could be: 'use of two or more languages by a language user'. Such a definition faces interpretative problems. An obvious one is: what is one language? Or: what is a language? Is it a set of rules and a list of words, or is it a code in which members of a particular social group communicate with each other, or more fundamentally a symbol of the group to which someone belongs? Actually, it's all of those things and a definition based on just one is insufficient. What exactly is one language? Is a speaker of a dialect who also uses the standard language according to that definition not bilingual? The same holds for different styles and registers in a language or dialect. One solution might be to ask the linguist to draw up a set of criteria that defines two language systems, so they can be named as different languages. Unfortunately, that is not a solution; there are no hard criteria for determining the difference between languages or between languages and dialects (Otheguy et al. 2015). The boundaries that register within a language, between different dialects of a language and even between languages are not clear. In addition, there is a problem with the amount of knowledge one should have of another language system to count as bilingual. One can count the number of strange words that someone knows or the number and difficulty of grammatical rules that one has learned, but that does not tell us very much about language usage and the language user's own estimation. A Dutchman who knows 300 English words and five constructions for simple sentences will probably find himself more bilingual and able to do much more with that knowledge than a Dutchman who knows 300 Moroccan-Arabic words and five sentence constructions, mainly because he can borrow from his first language (L1) for English, but hardly for Arabic.

The solution to the problem should not be sought in formal criteria but in conventions. The Dutch language is not what is found in dictionaries or reference grammar, but what the speakers of that language system think is good. When speakers of a specific Dutch dialect consider themselves able to speak a dialect of Dutch, this is the case, even though the dialect researcher may show that the dialect has as many characteristics of German as Dutch. Here we will be following as a definition: *multilingualism is the daily use of two or more languages*. In the following sections, this will be elaborated by considering why people are of become multilingual, what the role of language contact is, and to what extent multilingualism is a system that can grow or decline depending on the type and amount of use.

3.   Why Is Someone Multilingual?

Though this is not an issue that comes up frequently in neuropsychological research, a relevant question is 'Why is someone bilingual/multilingual?' The answer to this question, the reason for multilingualism, is actually quite simple: 'Because one language is not enough'. Apart from some polyglots or other language lovers, people do not just add a new language to their repertoire. There is always a pragmatic reason, and almost always that motive will be socioeconomic in nature: one can improve oneself or one's children in a socioeconomic sense. In some communities, multilingualism is the norm and children grow up with two or more languages, but even then, there is a motive: with only one language the child cannot participate in daily activities.

The reasons why people become multilingual are also relevant from a neurological perspective: the age at which they learn a new language, the amount of time they invest into learning it, the modality used, the degree to which they lose it (see Bahrick 1984), and the way it is acquired or learned. All these factors have been shown to have an impact on cognitive processing and in the structure of specific parts of the brain. The recent interest in the 'bilingual advantage' suggests that multilingualism has a moderating effect on age-related cognitive decline and leads to a delay of onset of dementia by several years. This may have inspired people worrying about cognitive decline with age, to pick up learning a new language just for the benefits mentioned, but whether learning another language at a later age has the same effects as being bilingual or multilingual from birth, is still a matter of debate.

The need for skills in more than one language may also be temporary, e.g. related to a stay abroad or working conditions. On return, there is no need to use that language anymore, it will not be used at all, and will become lost to some degree. This happens with members of the Latter Day Saints congregation: as part of their education, young men and women are sent to foreign countries to proselytize.They are trained to a very high level of proficiency and sent to a country that may not be their own choice at all. They will live in that country for some time and continue their language learning. Once they come back, they will completely stop using the language they used abroad. Research by Lynne Hansen and her colleagues at University in Hawaii has shown that there is indeed substantial attrition in the years after returning, but at the same time, a lot of supposedly lost knowledge is still accessible (Hansen et al. 2002).

4.   Language Attrition

In addition to the research on attrition mentioned in Section 3, there has been a significant body of research on first and second language attrition (see also Chapter 7 in this volume). When asked about the remaining skills they have of a school-learned foreign language like French in the Netherlands, Germany or the USA, former learners of that language will indicate that 'they lost it all'. However, research on attrition shows that there is much more retention than is assumed. A series of studies by Grendel et al. (1993) on French as a foreign language in the Netherlands and the USA show that it is very difficult to prove that there is attrition: only in situations of no contact at all, will there be some signs of attrition in productive language use, while receptive skills appear to be stable.

There are different types of attrition. The two most relevant ones are the slow decline of well-acquired aspects of a language, which is attested by the work of Bahrick (1984) who showed that even after decades, a significant proportion of the foreign language skills are still available. The other type that has so far not been studied extensively is the immediate forgetting in a learning situation. An example could be a speaker of Danish who is learning a difficult and non-cognate language like Hungarian. They may be in a lesson and may acquire some lexical elements during the lesson, but also during that lesson, elements (words, patterns, pronunciation) that were taught and partly acquired at the beginning of the lesson are gone when tested. It seems as though there is a built-in forgetting mechanism in language learning. Learners need 6–10 repetitions of words before they begin to stick (Nation 2013). Every time it is seen or heard, the level or activation of an element will be elevated and it will be seen as acquired only when it can be produced when tested.

In addition to foreign language attrition, there is also first language attrition (see Chapter 7). This mainly happens in migration settings in which the original language of the home (the heritage language) is taken over by the language spoken in the environment, typically the national language. As with foreign language attrition, research shows that language skills are resilient. Schmid (2010) presented data on German refugees in Britain who emigrated from Nazi Germany in the late 1930s. Some of them gave up using German completely, but when tested decades later, turned out to have kept a considerable part of their German language skills.

In short, a lot of research has been done on first and second language attrition and the data typically shows substantial retention rather than attrition. This is particularly true in settings in which specific languages are not used frequently, but that does not mean that all the skills are completely lost: using a relearning paradigm, it can be shown that some residual knowledge is left which makes relearning easier (Oh et al. 2010; van der Hoeven and de Bot 2012).

5.   The Role of Contact

Multilingualism follows from language contact. Wei (2011) mentions a number of factors that play a role in language contact: politics (conquests, colonization, ethnic cleansing), natural disasters (floods, earthquakes, failed harvests or emergencies), religion (conquests, but also a move to the religious home country, like Israel), culture (the need to know certain languages), economy (migration for economic reasons, ex-pats), education (availability of higher education, language of education other than home language), and technology (ICT, internet and English media).

Though the literature on language attrition clearly shows retention of language skills, the amount and type of contact play a role in the development and maintenance of multilingualism. We simply do not know how much and what type of contact is most effective in language maintenance or, conversely, how little leads to decline. This is an issue in the research on the bilingual advantage mentioned in Section 3. The idea is that multilingualism requires the use of certain executive functions, e.g. for code switching and language selection, and that these domain-specific skills are transferred to domain-independent skills. But what constitutes multilingualism is often far from clear: it can be bilingualism from birth or in early childhood, but also languages learned later in life in a natural or an educational setting. The language contact may stop at some point or be continued over the lifespan. It may be intense or sporadic, intimate or public, rich or poor. So, when it is claimed that early bilingualism has a positive effect on age-related decline, the characteristics of the contact should be established.

6.   Measuring Language Contact

Measuring language contact is notoriously difficult, mainly because (retrospective) data may mispresent the real situation. In the Bialystok et al. (2005) study, a parent questionnaire was used to assess amount of input/use of both languages in the home situation. A number of instruments have been used to assess language contact and often questionnaires on contact and use are administered. Informants or their parents are asked to indicate how often and how much they used what language in a given period (e.g. last week/month). For adolescents and adults, language use diaries have been used frequently (Kim and Starks 2005; Helm 2009). More recently, internet-based methods have been used to assess language use and contact. Zhuravleva et al. (2015) collected data on language use through an internet-based application that required informants to provide information online about languages, settings, and conversational partners used at the moment of reporting. A comparison between post hoc questionnaires, language diaries, and online prompted reports shows that the latter provide richer data, but the informants in the study, all of them university students, raised issues of privacy that prevent the wide application of this type of contact data collection. Two more instruments are used frequently: the language history questionnaire (LHQ, Li et al. 2006) and the language experience and proficiency questionnaire (LEAP-Q, Marian et al. 2007). Although they have been used widely, there is no research to show what type of contact is more effective. Contact can range from intimate conversation to stand-up comedian performances. The learner may also bring specific characteristics, such as the ability to focus and pay attention, working memory capacity, and other executive functions, but also motivation to provide extensive data, privacy control, and experience with an appreciation of social media use to research purposes.

When we go beyond the problems associated with the definition described above and focus on someone who is bilingual, for example, German-English, the level of bilingualism is not easy to determine. In language usage, four skills are usually distinguished: reading, writing, listening, and speaking. Within these skills we can distinguish between subordinate skills: knowledge about sounds/letters, grammatical knowledge, word knowledge, and pragmatic knowledge. Amongst the latter, we understand the whole of conversational conventions, stylistic variation, and the like. In addition, language is used in different situations, in sociolinguistics, usually called 'domains'. These include the work situation, the home situation, but also specific areas such as ecclesiastical activities or special hobbies. Thus, in determining someone's bilingualism, we have three dimensions that play a role: the four skills, the subdivisions within it, and the domains in which the languages are used. To make it even more complicated, we can also distinguish dimensions of skill related to correctness and fluidity. Someone can speak very fluently but make many mistakes, or say little but do so without error. What should then count as the greater language literacy is not so clear.

A relevant question here is whether a 'perfect bilingual' actually exists. In the kinds of research that will be featured in this volume, we look at the relationship of bilingualism with other features, such as intelligence, cognitive functioning, school success, attitude, and the like. Many studies make the assumption of whether or not someone is bilingual and there is a simple bifurcation between the two. Research that is based on this division has been questioned in recent years. It has become increasingly clear that degree of bilingualism is a continuum rather than a dichotomy. As discussed, one must assume a certain lower limit to indicate someone as 'non-bilingual'.

7.   Models of Multilingualism

7.1.   *Language Mode Model*

Grosjean (1982) suggested a model of multilingualism in which languages can be activated to different degrees. Each of the languages can be activated or deactivated depending on characteristics of the language use situation. For a bilingual, the two languages can be activated more or less equally when there is a setting in which both languages can be used, e.g. a conversation with other bilinguals. But someone who is travelling abroad alone with no compatriots to talk to will be in a monolingual mode, with the native language almost completely deactivated and the other language fully activated. As Grosjean put it: 'Bilinguals differ from each other in terms of how much they move along the language mode continuum. Some stay at the monolingual end, while others will move right along the continuum, choosing different points on it depending on the situation, the person they are speaking with, the topic and so on' (Grosjean 2010, p. 42). In Grosjean's model, different languages are seen as separate entities that can be manipulated independent of each other. In the literature on multilingual processing, activation level is often used to describe the state of a multilingual system, but what exactly level of activation is, remains vague. It has to do with accessibility/retrievability and may be related to the amount and type of brain tissue involved or with the degree of effort needed to activate it. In Grosjean's model, level of activation is the core issue, but it is left ill-defined. More recently Grosjean (2016) has developed his 'complementarity principle', according to which, the type and degree of multilingualism will be determined by the individual language user's communicative needs.

If activation level has to do with effort, the question arises whether the cognitive system has a certain amount of resources available for language use and whether this is the same for monolinguals and for multilinguals. The assumption is that managing multiple languages takes more resources than managing one only. If the amount of resource is limited, then activating an additional language will be at the expense of the other languages in the system. There is some research suggesting that having more languages leads to a slowing down of processing (Mägiste 1979), but the effects are small, in the 20–50 ms range.

With respect to the activation of brain tissue, research comparing incipient learners of a second language and more advanced languages suggests that more brain tissue is activated in beginners (see Chapter 12). However, what that means is also far from clear: is the task more demanding in L2 and therefore is more computational power needed? Does more activated brain areas imply more processing power?

7.2. *Multicompetence Model*

In Cook's multicompetence model (2016), the languages do not work independently; use of one has repercussions for the others. In the introduction to the Handbook on Multicompetence, Cook mentions three premises:

- Premise 1: multicompetence concerns the total language system (L1, L2, Ln) in a single mind or community and their interrelationships.
- Premise 2: multicompetence does not depend on the monolingual native speaker.
- Premise 3: multicompetence affects the whole mind, i.e. all language and cognitive systems, rather than language alone.

7.3. *Complex Dynamic Systems Theory (CDST)*

A full description of the application of CDST to multilingualism is beyond the scope of the present chapter (for more detailed accounts see, de Bot 2008; Larsen-Freeman and Cameron 2008; de Bot et al. 2013). There are clear links with Cook's model in that languages are not treated as solitary items, but as part of a larger language system. Language and cognition are embedded and embodied which means that the boundaries between the self and the environment are permeable. CDST looks at development over time and for language and multilingualism, this means that there is no distinction between language use and language learning. Development is dependent on resources and is influenced by initial conditions. Variation is inherent in development and is the motor for change.

Language development is seen as a complex dynamic process which means that many variables play a role in language development, and their interaction may lead to unpredicted and chaotic outcomes. The system is essentially non-modular (Spivey 2007). The claim from a CDST perspective is that it can describe and to a certain extent explain individual patterns of development. CDST also holds that subsystems interact with each other over time. The consequences of a CDST perspective also imply that what applies to the individual mind also applies to the community of users, with the individual embedded in the group.

8. The Multilingual's Brain

A currently prominent question is to what extent multilinguals' brains are different from those of monolinguals or bilinguals. The literature on the impact of multilingualism on executive functions and other cognitive factors has exploded in the last five years. (See Pliatsikas this volume). There are strong indications that the use of multiple languages leads to structural changes in the brain (Li, Legault and Litcofsky 2014; Abutalebi et al. 2011). A basic question in this context is: Do languages have their own neural substrate? Grosjean's model would suggest that different languages can be manipulated independently. Functionally, languages may appear independent of each other and this may reflect different locations for different languages in the brain. The evidence for this is slim. There is data on neuroimaging that are relevant for this discussion. Early studies (such as Kim et al. 1997) suggested that there are different substrates for L1 and L2, but more recent studies have shown that the findings were in fact caused by other factors. Stowe (2006) concludes her review of this literature by stating: 'There is no consistent qualitative difference between the neural architecture supporting processing of (the) two languages' (p. 305).

Various factors have been assumed to lead to different localizations in this particular age of acquisition and level of proficiency, but the argumentation has changed. It is likely that anything acquired early is represented differently compared to what is acquired late, and this applies to language as it does for other aspects of memory and cognition. Differences in proficiency reflect frequency differences that are likely to have an effect on representations. So what leads to differences in processing and localization may be the effect of age of acquisition and frequency and tells us little about differences in neural substrates for different languages. As Paradis (1990) has been arguing for quite some time, differences in proficiency may lead to other strategies being used, that may be reflected in different brain areas showing activation, but again, that is not about the localization of L1 or L2 in itself.

Views on representations and their relation to brain structures have changed considerably over the last decade. Hagoort (2006) summarizes the earlier views as follows: 'Architectural differences in the brain structure are indicative of functional differences and, conversely, that functional differences demand differences in architecture' (p. 93). In other words, differences in processing reflect differences in representation, and because there are differences in processing, there must be differences in representations. Following Hagoort again, the new views on cognition and the brain focus on the plasticity of the brain on the basis of input. 'Functional differences between brain areas are in this perspective mainly due to variability of the input signals in forming functional specializations. Domain specificity of a particular piece of cortex might thus not so much be determined by heterogeneity of brain tissue, but by the way in which its functional characteristics are shaped by the input' (Hagoort 2006, p. 94). This means that use shapes the brain and modularity is not innate but emergent: due to repeated and associated use, certain brain areas will show module-like behaviour. In the same way, it could be argued that different languages in the brain are emergent. Associated use networks will emerge that represent a given language, but these networks are constantly changing and highly individual, because individuals' experiences and contacts with the language will vary.

A number of studies report data based on cortical stimulation. Bello et al. (2006) presented data on multilingual patients and they squarely conclude: 'Sites for each language were distinct and separate' (p. 125), but on the whole, there are mixed findings on localization based on cortical stimulation (Ojemann and Whitaker 1978; Lucas et al. 2004; Cervenka et al. 2011).

So will we ever find evidence for clearly separable networks associated with different languages? It follows from the argument given earlier that this is very unlikely. There is no stable substrate, only instable and constantly varying networks without language labels. Different settings will activate different language forms that have different and constantly changing networks in the brain. It is therefore pointless to continue to try to find the location of different languages. There is an interesting parallel with an earlier discussion in the area of the bilingual brain. For quite some time, it was assumed that in bilinguals the right hemisphere plays a more prominent role in language processing than in monolinguals. Paradis (2004) in a biting commentary has compared this line of research with the search for the Loch Ness Monster. It must be there. We assume that we just have to search harder and in unlikely places, but it is never found. The same holds for languages in the brain. The data available suggests that the same areas are active for different languages, and there may be language specific subnetworks for different languages, but these are yet to be discovered. An interesting finding reported by Xu et al. (2009) is that spoken language and symbolic gestures seem to be processed by a common neural system, but again, the argument could be that at a finer level of granularity they may be different both in localization and in connectivity.

9.   Languages as Separate Entities in our Brain

What evidence is there for stable and language-specific processing and storage? There is a wealth of literature, mainly on the bilingual lexicon in which various experimental techniques have been used to study bilingual processing (for an extensive treatment see de Groot 2011). The discussion has been defined in terms of selective vs. non-selective access (La Heij 2005). The consensus now is that the lexicon is organized in a non-selective way according to Paradis' subset hypothesis (2004, 2009): In the lexicon subsets are formed based on use. Since words of a given language tend to be used together, they form a network. For speakers who often code switch, subsets may develop that consist of words that come from different languages according to an external norm. It should be noticed that for a particular speaker words need not be defined as belonging to one language or another. Paradis' model is clearly usage-based and emergent. What the elements in the lexicon are is not entirely clear: They may be single words, but more likely there will be larger units that are 'sedimented' on the basis of frequency of use. It may well be that 'words' don't have a separate status in the language system at all, since they are hardly ever used in isolation.

The idea of subsets is not limited to the lexicon, the same principles may be at work for syntactic or phonetic patterns. As argued in de Bot (2004) there may be links between elements at different levels that may coactivate each other: a sound that is associated with a specific language may activate elements that 'belong' to that language.

One of the continuing discussions is about whether elements are labelled for language. La Heij (2005) argues that if the conceptual specification is detailed enough, no language labels are needed, while Hartsuiker and Pickering (2007) present a model in which the language tag is an integral part of the conceptual specification. From an emergentist perspective, it is unclear why there should be explicit language tagging, since co-occurrence and associations of linguistic elements with specific settings and interlocutors would suffice to lead to the selection of the right words and thus the right language. This is the general mechanism: language elements are encountered in specific settings and stored as such, and similar settings will lead to the activation of related elements. Elements will thus be associated with language use activities. Elements can be labelled consciously as belonging to a specific language set but language as such does not act as a cue in selection. For monolinguals the associated linguistic elements will come from one language, for a regular code switcher from two or more languages. But again, such labelling is only done post hoc and at a metalinguistic level and it is not necessarily a selection criterion. This means that there may not be separate languages in the brain, but only situation-specific utterances. Such utterances may at a metalinguistic level be labelled as belonging to a specific language, but that does not mean that they are tagged as such in the brain.

The next question then is: Does code switching exist? If there is only one merged system, and the speaker uses those elements that are associated with the setting, there is no switching in the proper sense. The fact that elements from two languages are used does not mean that there are separate languages in the system of a code switcher: a code switcher simply takes the elements that are most appropriate and accessible. To quote Hopper (1998): 'Language is not a general abstract possession that is uniform across the community, but is an emergent fact having its source each individual's experience and life history and in the struggle to accomplish successful communication' (p. 164).

As already mentioned in this chapter, the idea of separate languages in the mind of the second language learner has been generally accepted in the field of applied linguistics. The use of terms like 'transfer' and 'interference' reflects this kind of thinking. Data from very early writers in a second language (L2; Dutch learners of English in the first grade of secondary education, Verspoor et al. 2012) show that at least for this very early stage it is difficult to talk about two language systems. Below are short stories by two early foreign language learners:

Hello dis is my school he staat in apeldoorn. he is very big ai have very veel teachers op my school and ik have er to very veeler zijn to very veel kids op dese school de teachers and de kids walking door de school en have very veel lol de englisch teachers says enlisch

(Hello this is my school it is located in the city of Apeldoorn. it is very big and I have very many teachers at my school and there are very many kids at this school the teachers and the kids walk through the school and have a lot of fun the English teachers speak English).

Hello, i am Arnoud. I sit op the grammar school the Driestar College. I found it well funny. I have nu veel more homework dan first. I hate english and techniek. It are very crazy teachers. We have many leerlingen in the new klas. I have veel friends. I moet heel veel biken to school. It is ongeveer ten tot vijftien km biken.

(Hello, I am Arnoud, I am at the grammar school called Driestar College. I found/find it nice. I now have a lot more homework than before. I hate English and Science & Tehcnology. The teachers are very crazy. We have many pupils in the new class, I have many friends. I have to ride by bike a lot to get to school, it is about 10–15 km to my school)

Data such as these cast at least some doubt on the idea that early learners have separate systems. There can be no doubt that these young writers intend to write in English, but they will be well aware of the fact that what they actually write is a mix. But it is the best they can do.

It has been argued in this contribution that the existence of languages as separate entities can be questioned; rather than a set of distinct systems of words and rules, there may be situation specific sets of utterances that at a metalinguistic level could be labelled as belonging to a given language. This requires a fundamentally different conceptualization of what constitutes a language. In most of the research on multilingualism the existence of languages as separate entities is not questioned and accepting this new perspective on language, which is consistent with a CDST approach to language is so different from the current dominant perspective that it will take time and effort to explore its consequences.

10.   Measuring Multilingual Proficiency

Globally two approaches are used to measure language proficiency: standardized, mostly discrete point tests on the one hand and self-evaluations on the other hand.

In a number of studies, the outcomes of self-evaluation and 'real' proficiency have been compared. Grendel et al. (1993) looked at proficiency in French as a foreign language and used a number of formal test formats (cloze, repetition, lexical decision, translation) and self-evaluations. Her data showed that there are differences in the accuracy of self-evaluations between languages/cultures: Dutch informants tended to overestimate their proficiency, while American students showed less of a gap between tests and self-evaluation. In particular, in studies on language attrition, self-evaluations have been used based on the 'Can-Do' format of the Common European Reference Framework (CEFR). The format used is like the following: 'I can order a simple meal in language X', or 'I can understand an Lx radio news item spoken at a normal speed') Can-Do statements have been related to one of six levels: A1/2, B1/2, and C1/C2. C2 is the native-like level, while A1 reflects very simple language skills. The CEFR allows for a comparison on proficiency which can be very useful for a comparison between studies on the impact of proficiency. Studies comparing self-evaluation and standard tests show contradictory findings. In the studies on language attrition the correlation between the two is fairly low (0.30/0.40), but other studies found higher correlations (Marian et al. 2007). In multilingual neurolinguistic studies, language proficiency is typically measured through very simple self-evaluation tests like 'Rate your speaking proficiency on a scale of 1–10, with 10 as native level, and 1 for very minimal proficiency'. Quite often, language proficiency questionnaires and language use questionnaires are combined in a single instrument, and then statistical procedures are used to find the main contributing factors.

There is a host of instruments and tests to assess proficiency in foreign languages. In addition, there are a number of instruments that look at multilingualism in an integrated way, (i.e. not looking at single languages but looking at the total language system in which, in a traditional approach, the various languages are studied with respect to overlap and difference). A number of instruments have been developed that measure various aspects of languages, but most studies focus on vocabulary. A good example is Lextale (Lemhöfer and Broersma 2012), a five-minute test for English vocabulary knowledge and proficiency. It is based on earlier tests by Meara in which the testees are presented with letter strings that are or are not legal words in the target language. The scores on illegal letter strings provide information on guessing. Huibregste et al. (2002) provide an analytic method to correct for guessing and response style.

The LexTale test is rather widely used and it has been validated by comparing the outcomes of this test with a number of standard tests for English with Dutch and Korean learners of English. They compared the scores on the LexTale test with various other tests including L1–L2 and L2–L1 translation and with self-evaluations, as mentioned an often used format. Correlations between LexTale and translation tasks were fairly high (0.78) for the Dutch participants but much less so for the Korean group (0.50). The authors conclude that LexTALE is a good predictor of English vocabulary knowledge, it correlates high with general measures of proficiency and is clearly superior to self-ratings in predictive power. LexTale is now available for English, Dutch, German, and Korean.

Marian et al. (2007) developed a questionnaire of bilingual language status: LEAP-Q. The goal of the project was to develop a reliable and valid questionnaire for efficient assessment of bilinguals' linguistic profiles, so it combines questions on use and contact with questions on language proficiency. The questionnaire provides information about language experience and proficiency. The authors provide an overview of the use of self-ratings to measure language proficiency and – in contrast to Lemhöfer and Broersma (2012) – conclude that: 'In general, previous research suggests that self-reported language measures are indicative of linguistic ability' (p. 941). At the same time, they conclude that 'ratings of proficiency alone are not sufficient to determine bilingual language status and that bilinguals' language learning and language use experienced play a significant role in shaping their linguistic competence' (p. 942). Proficiency ratings were obtained for speaking, listening, reading, and writing, and rather than being combined into one single aggregate score, the skills were kept separate in the analyses, since individuals may show substantial differences in levels of proficiency for these skills. There were questions on when informants started learning a language, when they started reading, whether they were immersed in a foreign country setting, and how much language exposure of family/friends/reading/TV/Radio/self-instruction was seen as contributing to language learning. The statistical analyses showed that the LEAP-Q has a high validity and internal consistency. It is available for English/Spanish, English/Mandarin, and English/Russian. The questionnaire cannot be used for the assessments of language ability in children with speech disorders, since it has not been tested in these populations.

Another widely used instrument is the LHQ and its internet-based dynamic version (LHQ 2.0). This is an extensive collection of tests aimed at both language proficiency and language uses and contact. 'It allows investigators to dynamically construct individualized LHQs on the fly and allows participant to complete the LHQ online in multiple languages'. (Li et al. 2014, p. 673).

A somewhat older instrument to assess language contact and use in relation with learning is the one by Berns et al. (2007). It gathers fairly detailed information about language use in different modalities and different media, including lyrics from pop-songs. An interesting component is the question asking to what extent a particular source contributed to language proficiency. The question had the format shown in Figure 1.

Indicate how different sources have contributed to your proficiency in language x:

Through school:	.....%
Through media:	.....%
Other sources (explain):	.....%
Total	100%

Figure 1   Format of one of the questions asked by Berns et al., 2007.

11.   Dynamic Assessment

A recent development is the use of dynamic assessment (DA; Lantolf and Poehner 2011). In DA, the focus is on the learning potential of a learner rather than on their (in)abilities. Traditional standardized testing has been criticized for not providing information that is relevant for interventions since it mainly concerns what the learner cannot do. The idea of DA is based on Vygotsky's zone of proximal development (ZPD), which itself is based on what a learner can or cannot do in interaction with a more proficient peer or teacher. The amount and type of information that is provided to the learner reflects their learning potential. Most of the research on DA is done with children, and some studies have included language disorders, but there seems to be little research on DA and bilingual language disorders, though the focus of potential learning is as relevant for healthy people as it is for people with some sort of disorder. The DA approach deviates strongly from traditional forms of testing in that the focus is more on validity than on reliability and more on individual development than on group means. The usability of DA to test bilinguals with language disorders is yet to be established. Not surprisingly, DA shows characteristics of CDST in that it takes into account change over time and the interaction between the individual and the group. Learning potential is not seen as something fixed, but as something that may change in interaction with other factors, such an additional language learning.

To summarize this section: there is still no clear view on the validity of the use of self-evaluations to assess level of proficiency. The correlations between self-assessment and standard tests range from fairly low (0.25) to high (0.75). Several questionnaires have been developed and tested and they provide profiles of different types of learners, which is in line with the tendency in language studies to take individual differences into account. Finally, a new trend is to focus on potential rather than achievement through the use of dynamic assessment.

12.   Conclusion

In this chapter two aspects of multilingualism have been highlighted: its definition and how it can be assessed. Definitions range from a minimal non-balanced level of proficiency to a high-level balanced level. How multilingualism should be defined depends on one's model of what constitutes language. Here we define language as a set of situation-specific utterances that only at the metalinguistic level can be labelled as belonging to a given language. There seems to be no reason to assume the existence of languages as separate entities in the brain that have their own demarcated substrates.

The second aspect concerns the assessment of multilingualism. Again, what can be tested depends on what constitutes language and languages. In neurolinguistic research, self-evaluations have been applied regularly. To what extent self-evaluations are valid and reliable to test language proficiency is a matter of debate: there are contradictory findings on the correlation between self-assessments and other forms of assessments. A promising new development is the use of dynamic assessment that takes learning potential rather than achievement into account.

REFERENCES

Abutalebi, J., Della Rosa, P.A., Green, D.W. et al. (2011). Bilingualism tunes the anterior cingulate cortex for conflict monitoring. *Cerebral Cortex* 22 (9): 2076–2086.

Bahrick, H. (1984). Semantic memory content in permastore: 50 years of memory for Spanish learned in school. *Journal of Experimental Psychology: General* 113: 1–29.

Bello, L., Acerbi, F., Giussani, C. et al. (2006). Intraoperative language localization in multilingual patients with gliomas. *Neurosurgery* 59 (1): 115–125.

Berns, M., de Bot, K., and Hasebrink, U. (2007). *In the Presence of English: Media and European Youth*. New York, NY: Springer.

Bialystok, E., Craik, F.I., and Freedman, M. (2007). Bilingualism as a protection against the onset of symptoms of dementia. *Neuropsychologia* 45 (2): 459–464.

Bialystok, E. and Martin, M.M. (2004). Attention and inhibition in bilingual children: evidence from the dimensional change card sort task. *Developmental Science* 7 (3): 325–339.

Bialystok, E., Martin, M., and Viswanathan, M. (2005). Bilingualism across the lifespan: the rise and fall of inhibitory control. *International Journal of Bilingualism* 9 (1): 103–119.

Bialystok, E. and Sharwood Smith, M. (1985). Interlanguage is not a state of mind: an evaluation of the construct for second-language acquisition. *Applied Linguistics* 6 (2): 101–117.

Bonnet, G. (1998). *L'efficacité de l'enseignement de l'anglais dans l'union européenne*. Paris, France: Ministry of Education.

Cervenka, M., Boatman-Reich, D., Ward, J. et al. (2011). Language mapping in multilingual patients: Electrocorticography and cortical stimulation during naming. *Frontiers in Human Neuroscience* 22 (5): 13.

de Bot, K. (2004). The multilingual lexicon: modeling selection and control. *International Journal of Multilingualism* 1 (1): 17–32.

de Bot, K. (2008). Introduction: second language development as a dynamic process. *Modern Language Journal* 92 (2): 166–178.

de Bot, K. (2016). Multicompetence and complex dynamic systems. In: *The Cambridge Handbook of Linguistic Multi Competence* (ed. V. Cook and L. Wei), 125–141. Cambridge, UK: Cambridge University Press.

de Bot, K., Thorne, S., Lowie, W., and Verspoor, M. (2013). Dynamic systems theory as a comprehensive theory of second language development. In: *Contemporary Approaches to Second Language Acquisition* (ed. M. Mayo, M. Mangado and M. Adrián), 199–202. Amsterdam, The Netherlands: John Benjamins.

de Groot, A.M.B. (2011). *Language and Cognition in Bilinguals and Multilinguals*. New York, NY: Psychology Press.

Grendel, M., Weltens, B., and de Bot, K. (1993). Language attrition: rise and fall of a research topic? *Toegepaste Taalwetenschap in Artikelen* 46/47 (2): 59–68.

Grosjean, F. (1982). *Life with Two Languages: An Introduction to Bilingualism*. Cambridge, MA: Harvard University Press.

Grosjean, F. (2010). *Bilingual Life and Reality*. Cambridge MA: Harvard University Press.

Grosjean, F. (2016). The complementarity principle and its impact on processing, acquisition and dominance. In: *Language Dominance in Bilinguals: Issues of Measurement and Operationalization* (ed. C. Silva-Corvalan and J. Treffers-Daller), 66–84. Cambridge, UK: Cambridge University Press.

Hagoort, P. (2006). What we cannot learn from neuroanatomy about language learnng and language processing: a commentary on uylings. In: *The Cognitive Neuroscience of Second Language Acquisition* (ed. P. Indefrey), 91–97. Malden, MA: Blackwell.

Hansen, L., Umeda, Y., and McKinney, M. (2002). Savings in the relearning of a second language: the effects of time and proficiency. *Language Learning* 52 (2): 653–678.

Hartsuiker, R. and Pickering, M. (2007). Language integration in bilingual sentence production. *Acta Psychologica* 128 (3): 479–489.

Helm, F. (2009). Language and culture in an online context: what can learner diaries tell us about intercultural competence? *Language and Intercultural Communication* 9 (2): 91–104.

Hopper, P. (1998). Emergent grammar. In: *The New Psychology of Language: Cognitive and Functional Approaches to Language Structure* (ed. M. Tomassello), 155–176. Mahwah, NJ: Erlbaum.

Huibregste, I., Admiraal, W., and Meara, P. (2002). Scores on a yes-no vocabulary test: correction for guessing and response style. *Language Testing* 19 (3): 227–245.

Kim, J., Kim, M., Lee, J. et al. (2002). Dissociation of working memory processing associated with native and second languages: PET investigation. *NeuroImage* 15 (4): 879–891.

Kim, K., Relkin, N., Lee, K., and Hirsch, J. (1997). Distinct cortical areas associated with native and second language. *Nature* 388 (9938): 171–174.

Kim, J. and Starks, D. (2005). Language diaries: A case study of language use in the New Zealand Korean community. In: *Languages of New Zealand* (ed. A. Bell, R. Harlow and D. Starks), 343–369. Wellington, New Zealand: Victoria University Press.

La Heij, W. (2005). Selection processes in monolingual and bilingual lexical access. In: *Handbook of Bilingualism* (ed. A. de Groot and J. Kroll), 289–304. Oxford, UK: Oxford University Press.

Lantolf, J.P. and Poehner, M.E. (2011). Dynamic assessment in the classroom: Vygotskian praxis for second language development. *Language Teaching Research* 15 (1): 11–33.

Larsen-Freeman, D. and Cameron, L. (2008). Research methodology on language development from a complex theory perspective. *Modern Language Journal* 92 (2): 200–213.

Lemhöfer, K. and Broersma, M. (2012). Introducing LexTALE: a quick and valid lexical test for advanced learners of English. *Behavior Research Methods* 44 (2): 325–343.

Li, P., Legault, J., and Litcofsky, K.A. (2014). Neuroplasticity as a function of second language learning: anatomical changes in the human brain. *Cortex* 58 (1): 301–324.

Li, P., Sepanski, S., and Zhao, X. (2006). Language history questionnaire: a web-based interface for bilingual research. *Behavior Research Methods* 38 (2): 202–210.

Lucas, T., McKahnn, G., and Ojemann, G. (2004). Functional separation of languages in the bilingual brain: a comparison of electrical stimulation language mapping in 25 bilingual patients and 117 monolingual control patients. *Journal of Neurosurgery* 101 (3): 449–457.

Mägiste, E. (1979). The competing language systems of the multilingual: a developmental study of decoding and encoding processes. *Journal of Verbal Learning and Verbal Behavior* 18: 79–89.

Marian, V., Blumenfeld, H.K., and Kaushanskaya, M. (2007). The language experience and proficiency questionnaire (LEAP-Q): assessing language profiles in bilinguals and multilinguals. *Journal of Speech, Language, and Hearing Research* 50 (4): 940–967.

Melinger, A. (2018). Distinguishing languages from dialects: a litmus test using the picture-word interference task. *Cognition* 172: 73–83.

Nation, I.S.P. (2013). *Teaching & Learning Vocabulary*. Boston, MA: Heinle Cengage Learning.

Oh, J.S., Au, T.K., and Jun, S.-A. (2010). Early childhood language memory in the speech perception of international adoptees. *Journal of Child Language* 37 (5): 1123–1132.

Ojemann, G. and Whitaker, H. (1978). The bilingual brain. *Archives of Neurology* 35 (5): 409–412.

Otheguy, R., García, O., and Reid, W. (2015). Clarifying translanguaging and deconstructing named languages: a perspective from linguistics. *Applied Linguistics Review* 6 (3): 281–307.

Paradis, M. (1990). Language lateralization in bilinguals: Enough already! *Brain and Language* 39: 576–586.

Paradis, M. (2004). *A Neurolinguistic Theory of Bilingualism*. Amsterdam, The Netherlands: John Benjamins.

Paradis, M. (2009). *Declarative and Procedureal Determinants of Second Languages*.

Amsterdam, The Netherlands: John Benjamins.

Schmid, M. (2010). *Language Attrition*. Cambridge, UK: Cambridge University Press.

Spivey, M. (2007). *The Continuity of Mind*. New York, NY: Oxford University Press.

Stowe, L. (2006). When does the neurological basis of first and second language processing differ? Commentary on indefrey. In: *The Cognitive Neuroscience of Second Language Acquisition* (ed. P. Indefrey), 305–311. Malden, MA: Blackwell.

van der Hoeven, N. and de Bot, K. (2012). Relearning in the elderly: age-related effects on the size of savings. *Language Learning* 62 (1): 42–67.

Verspoor, M., Schmid, M.S., and Xu, X. (2012). A dynamic usage based perspective on L2 writing. *Journal of Second Language Writing* 21 (3): 239–263.

Wei, L. (2011). Multilinguality, multimodality, and multicompetence: code-and modeswitching by minority ethnic children in complementary schools. *The Modern Language Journal* 95 (3): 370–384.

Xu, X. (2010). Learning and forgetting of English in Dutch and Chinese students. In: *Unpublished PhD thesis*. The Netherlands: University of Nijmegen.

Zhao, X. and Li, P. (2010). Bilingual lexical interactions in an unsupervised neural network model. *International Journal of Bilingual Education and Bilingualism* 13 (5): 505–524.

Zhuravleva, A., de Bot, K., and Hilton, N.H. (2015). Using social media to measure language use. *Journal of Multilingual and Multicultural Development* 37 (6): 601–614.

2 Cognitive Neuroscience and Multilingualism

EDNA ANDREWS

1. Introduction

Within the first two decades of the twenty-first century, theoretical linguistics, along with one of its newer multidisciplinary subfields, cognitive neurolinguistics, has continued to redefine itself as it becomes one of the central disciplines relevant to the study of human language and the brain. The successful incorporation of imaging technologies into the field has substantially changed the importance of the role of healthy subjects in research. Thus, while neurolinguistics of the twentieth century has predominantly been viewed as a field that studies language-based pathologies, most often forms of aphasia (Ahlsén 2006, pp. 3–5), the current field of cognitive neurolinguistics is actively participating in extending its boundaries beyond the lesion-deficit tradition and becoming an important contributor to cognitive neuroscience. This chapter will present some of the major findings of two types of imaging (hemodynamic/fMRI and electrophysiological/CSM) in the context of the study of multilingualism.

2. Remapping Language in the Human Brain: Moving Away from the *Traditional Model*

One may still find in many contemporary psychology and neuroscience textbooks discussions of brain and language, and these discussions often include or focus exclusively on what Poeppel and Hickok refer to as the *classical model* – the Broca's and Wernicke's areas of the frontal and temporal lobes of the brain respectively (together with the arcuate fasciculus [AF], the band that connects the two regions; cf. Kandel and Schwartz 1991, pp. 7–11; Huttenlocher 2002, p. 49; Dowling 2004, pp. 59–61). These assertions are still made, even though many of the leaders in the neuroscience

The Handbook of the Neuroscience of Multilingualism, First Edition. Edited by John W. Schwieter.
© 2019 John Wiley & Sons Ltd. Published 2019 by John Wiley & Sons Ltd.

community who specifically study language have demonstrated that what Poeppel and Hickok (2004) refer to as the classical model is in fact inadequate in explaining how language works in the brain[1]:

> ... it is now rather uncontroversial that the classical model is (i) empirically wrong in that it cannot reasonably account for the range of aphasic syndromes, (ii) linguistically underspecified to an extent that prohibits contact with theoretical or experimental research on language, and (iii) anatomically underspecified .... there are cortical and subcortical regions that clearly contribute to normal language processing, including the anterior superior temporal lobe, the middle temporal gyrus (MTG), the temporo-parietal junction, the basal ganglia, and many right-hemisphere homologues. Since many areas are relevant in addition to Broca's and Wernicke's areas, it is obvious that the model must be rethought. (p. 5)

Poeppel and Hickok further specify the importance of the non-homogenous anatomical and functional nature of the 'classical speech-related regions'. The above passage underlines the importance of *subcortical* as well as *cortical* regions essential in normal language functioning. The importance of subcortical white matter fibre tracts, in particular, for language(s) is becoming more recognized throughout the neurosurgical and neuroscience communities (cf. Duffau 2008; Duffau et al. 2008; Maldonado et al. 2013; Menjot de Champfleur et al. 2013, and many others).

Poeppel and Hickok (2004) also identify five important trends in the study of language and brain and in models of language processing in the brain that include (i) reanalysis of the Broca's and Wernicke's areas; (ii) an important dorsal-ventral model for language processing that originates in the superior temporal gyrus (STG); (iii) interest in a broader section of cortical regions and subcortical structures that are important in linguistic computation; (iv) interaction of regions responsible for supporting perception/comprehension and production; and (v) the importance of the right hemisphere in models of brain and language (p. 10).[2] This final point is particularly interesting in light of new evidence that clearly demonstrates the importance of both hemispheres in language processing from the smallest levels (phonemic and syllabic) to sentences and discourse (Schirmer et al. 2012, pp. 137–147).

In studies exemplifying point iv above, Poeppel and Hickok (2004) and Hickok and Poeppel (2004) discuss the importance of understanding speech production and comprehension as interrelated phenomena. Their dorsal-ventral stream model of language argues for an essential interface between auditory speech production and motor representations via bilaterally given auditory cortical areas with projections to temporal and parietal regions (2007, p. 395) (Figure 1).

One additional salient point that is made by Poeppel (2008) is the calling out of the epistemological problem of what he calls the 'localization/explanation fallacy' (pp. 19–23). This is manifested in assumptions that brain imaging is a 'privileged type of evidence that forms the basis for explanation of mental life'. Poeppel is very critical of this assumption and insists that functional localization should be seen as an 'intermediate goal ... that requires figuring out *where* things are, before scrutiny

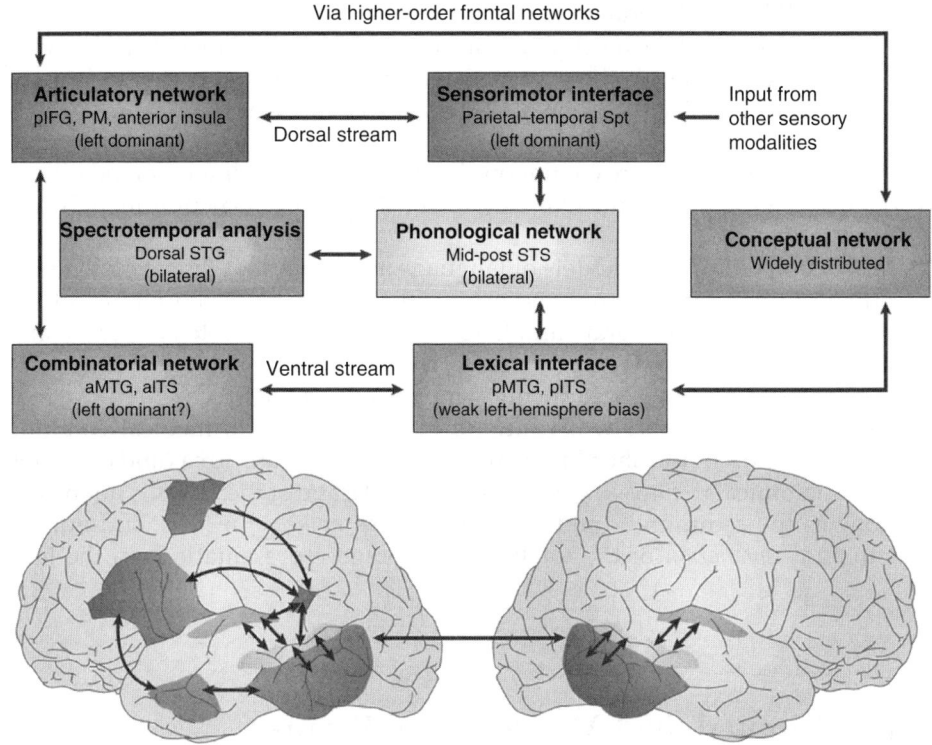

Figure 1   Dual-stream model of the functional anatomy of language. Source: Hickok and Poeppel (2007), p. 395.

turns to the harder and deeper question of *how* things work' (p. 22). Hagoort (2006) also notes that 'the exact nature of these functional specializations is more easily inferred from an analysis of input and connectivity than by looking at the cytoarchitectonic characteristics' (p. 95). Future work must move forward into more nuanced contextualization of localization-based data, and one way this can happen is to reevaluate how *variation* at the individual and group levels is understood and analysed.

Another aspect of the problem of attempting to treat production and comprehension as autonomous processes stems from imagining language processing as a *serial process*. The traditional model indicates that one would expect decoding initially in the temporal lobe, followed by expression in the frontal lobe. The extensive data collected by Ojemann and his colleagues show, using a direct neuronal mapping technique (cortical stimulation mapping [CSM]), that this is not what actually occurs. As Calvin and Ojemann (1994) state:

Our studies didn't find evidence for serial brain wave changes. All sites seemed to be turned on at once, at the beginning of a language event, and they stayed on during the whole event. That's the way many functions in animal cortex seem to be organized, too – parallel activation of dispersed cortical areas (p. 277).

Constructing models of more continuous interactions across different modalities and networks may be a more productive way to construct current neural models of language functioning.

There are compelling new models of language and brain that represent the state of twenty-first-century cognitive neuroscience and that can be tested empirically. The nineteenth-century model of brain and language is not sufficient to accommodate the evidence from pathology and imaging research with healthy subjects. However, this begs the question of why it is so difficult to move beyond the Broca/Wernicke model. I anticipate that these terms will continue to be used in the medical community because they have become a shorthand on a par with Brodmann areas and other abbreviations of anatomical regions in general discourse. Usage of the terms is not problematic as long as the community understands them as *names of regions*, and not as the answer to and *explanation* of the totality of language representations in the human brain.

3.   Multilingual, Not Monolingual Brains

Empirical data gathered from speakers of the world's languages, which number around 5000 at the current time, indicate clearly that most of the world is bilingual or multilingual (de Bot 2009; Crystal 2010). In other words, the monolingual is the exception, not the rule. However, the study of brain and language has often viewed the monolingual brain as the norm. Shifting the focus away from the monolingual brain to the bilingual or multilingual brain is occurring not only in cognitive and neurolinguistics, but also in psycholinguistics and cognitive psychology (cf. Grosjean 1989, 1998, 2001; Cook 2002; Cook et al. 2003). While behavioural studies and linguistic analyses have studied bilingualism and multilingualism for a significant period of time, it is really only in the last two decades that we have seen a shift in perspective with the introduction of important new data on the bilingual and multilingual brain from neurosurgeries, electroencephalography (EEG) and event-related potential (ERP) studies and imaging studies (Paradis 2004; Bhatia and Ritchie 2006). The pioneers in this field are the surgeon and researcher George Ojemann and his colleagues, who began publishing on bilingual brains in the late 1970s.

One of the issues with the study of bilingualism and the brain is the lack of *empirically valid proficiency data* on the subjects included in these studies. The linguistics community has drawn attention to this significant omission, especially Paradis (2004), de Bot (2008, 2009), Andrews et al. (2013), Andrews (2014), and Abutalebi et al. (2013).

Research agendas of brain and language(s) can benefit when taking advantage of fundamental notions central to the field of theoretical linguistics. In fact, the current debates surrounding embodied cognition are embedded in foundational principles of theoretical linguistics and a rethinking of the organization of neurological systems as multimodalities, not modules. Section 4 of this chapter touches on some of the more salient concepts that are relevant to the neuroscience of multilingualism.

4. Foundational Concepts in Linguistic Theory: A Brief Excursus

For an event to become linguistic ... a great many brains must play in unison (Dwight Bolinger 1948, p. 233).

In building a theoretical foundation for understanding human language, there are fundamental properties inherent in all human languages that may be introduced through a working definition of language. I propose the following definition of language and languages as a starting point for this analysis:

> A learned, dynamic, hierarchical, relatively autonomous system of meaning-generating paradigmatic and syntagmatic signs that signify and communicate to oneself and others via *speech communities* and *communities of practice* throughout the life cycle[3]
>
> (Andrews 2014, p. 32).

One of the most important outcomes of this definition is an understanding of language acquisition as a lifelong, dynamic process that is intertwined with maintenance and loss throughout the life span of a speaker. While there may be periods of more intensive acquisition and loss, these three modes of language development are not realized consecutively, but occur simultaneously. This sets the stage for a re-evaluation of how one studies not only first language (L1), but second language (L2) acquisition, processing, and proficiency achievements. Second, this definition places language within the sociocultural context where language is not the product of a single brain, but rather a product of multiple brains in sync with each other and embedded in the cultural context. Once we admit that language is never 'in the one', but rather is an integral part of what it means to be human and a social being, then we are compelled to take the next step and characterize language as a shared phenomenon. In this regard, the field of *cognitive linguistics*, a fundamentally 'usage-based, not rule-based' (Sinha 2007, p. 1270) theory has played a central role in understanding the interactive process-oriented nature of generating and negotiating meanings. Johnson and Lakoff (2002) explain the importance of 'interactional properties' (p. 248) in the following manner: 'Meaning comes, not just from 'internal' structures of the organism (the "subject"), nor solely from "external" inputs (the "objects"), but rather from recurring patterns of engagement between organism and environment'.

Linguistic studies emphasizing the importance of the interaction of language and culture are nothing new (cf. Jakobson 1967/1985). The inevitable interconnectedness of languages and cultures is a powerful prerequisite for any attempt to understand the ontogeny of language development within groups and individuals.[4] Jakobson's (1967/1985) conclusion is that language is 'the fundamental and substantial foundation of culture' (p. 103). What this statement does is to reaffirm the important fact that language is never in the 'one'; it is always a property of a group of speakers. The field of sociolinguistics has contributed significantly to our understanding of how languages are learned and maintained through exposure to groups of speakers in *speech communities* (Hymes 1972) and *communities of practice* (McConnell-Ginet 2003). The fact that speakers are always members of multiple and changing speech communities and communities of practice is explicit in each of these definitions.

The cognitive psychologist, L. Vygotsky (1934/1987, 1934/1999), in his monograph *Thought and Speech*, contributes an important set of experimental data that demonstrates that the trajectory of child development begins in the collective consciousness and individuality occurs in development. This is a very different path of development from the one suggested by Piaget, where the child begins life as an individual and becomes a member of the social/cultural group later. The implication is precisely expressed in the Bolinger quote at the beginning of this section – linguistic events require many brains to 'play in unison'.

4.1. A Quick Glance at Embodied Cognition: Multimodality, not Modularity

Sensory-motor interactive modelling of language and brain systems has become an important part of cognitive neuroscientific discourse over the past 15 years. The debates concerning *embodied cognition* are central to moving forward in understanding the neurological interface of human languages, including fundamental questions of system-level organization of the brain, especially moving towards multimodality modelling over modularity. The analysis by Gallese and Lakoff (2005) emphasizes the importance of multimodal modelling of language and brain, which favours a view of language that takes into account its evolutionary trajectory and characterizes these linguistic structures as becoming part of the sensory-motor system at the neuronal level. Multimodal modelling rejects outright the viability of the modular view of human language. The central arguments presented by Gallese and Lakoff (2005) stress the importance of multimodality, including mirror, premotor, and parietal neurons, and its realization through functional clusters (p. 458). These features are essential in order to move forward with any reasonable theories of brain and language.

However, the kind of sensory-motor alignment that Gallese and Lakoff present is only one type of the significant multimodal aspects of human language and the brain, and the cautionary arguments given in Mahon and Caramazza (2008) are important to keep in mind.[5] The inclusion of *schemas* (instead of *concepts*) by Gallese and Lakoff (2005) ensures the integrity of language as a functionality of brains in cultural space. While their examples provide one important form of the alignment (e.g. English lexeme *grasp*; p. 457), a more pervasive sensory-motor synthesis may be found in (i) the realizations of specific embodied forms of grammatical and lexical meaning as produced/articulated and perceived ([a] *kick* examples – *kick the ball, kick the bucket, kick the habit, you're a kick,* etc., and [b] following Bolinger, /gr/lexemes in English – *grasp, grip, grab, grub, grit, grunt, greed, great, grate, grime, grrh, grizzle, grief,* etc.); (ii) the specific gestures that accompany language-specific lexical categories, i.e. sound-based alternative systems of auditory perception (e.g. lyric and music); and (iii) visual meanings given in written language that are not given in the sound forms (in spellings [e.g. *to/two/too, sea/see/C*] or ideograms).[6]

All types of linguistic meanings are negotiated *in* context and require communities of speakers embedded in *speech communities and communities of practice* to stabilize these meanings. And while there are sensory-motor systems internally determined in the individual organism, there is never language 'in the one'. Language is a consequence of humans interacting in cultural space. We are always multifaceted *users* of language, playing the roles of speakers, hearers and observers (sometimes simultaneously), and we always belong to multiple and variegated dynamically-given speech communities and communities of practice.

4.1.1.   Donald's Intermediate Time Frame and Experimental Design, and Mindsharing   Merlin Donald's (2001) insights into human cognitive evolution illuminate the key moments that led to the development of spoken and written human language, including mimesis, fine motor control, and collective creation of external symbols. There are many things humans have learned to do that are often characterized as automatic or not requiring conscious effort. This type of *automaticity*, which is a phenomenon connected to learned behaviours, should not be confused with innate behaviours:

> Automatization is the end result of a process of repeated sessions of rehearsal and evaluation, which rely heavily on conscious supervision …. Automaticity is not the antithesis of consciousness. It is a necessary complement to it. Moreover, it is one of its by-products
>
> (Donald 2001, p. 57).

One of the ways that Donald (2001) clarifies the problem of defining consciousness is by noting that 'human consciousness cannot be properly isolated and described in the short term' (p. 89). He goes on to explain that while consciousness is 'virtually oblivious of milliseconds' (Donald 2001, p. 89), it may be enacted in frames between 1 and 15 seconds, but it is most interested in the *'intermediate time frame'* that can extend over periods of minutes to hours. Recognizing this important shift away from the ≤15 *seconds* to a more significant period of time (minutes to hours) is essential to take into account when determining the temporal boundaries in ecologically valid experimental design. In particular, Donald differentiates clinical and laboratory methods and the critical role that *time frames* play in research. The return of ecological validity to experimental design and research is essential if cognitive neuroscience research is to move forward (Donald

2001, p. 62). Many experiments of human cognition target only the lower limit of conscious experience, the shorter time frames in which it is impossible to see the full scope of cognitive phenomena like memory and language (Donald 2001, p. 47).

Donald (2001) identifies another crucial component of social intelligence in humans that is more developed than in other species – the ability to perceive and anticipate the intentions of others, to read 'not only our own minds but also those of others' (p. 59). Human language plays a significant role in the ability to 'mindshare', but this type of metacognition is not restricted to a linguistic realization; rather, linguistic utterances may *facilitate* this type of cognition (Donald 2001, p. 60). The key point is to view mindsharing as a 'conscious process not in the representational sense that we explicitly notice and represent every impression but rather in the functional sense that real-time mindreading demands conscious capacity, usually occupying it to the full' (Donald 2001, p. 61). Donald does not idealize human metacognitive ability and 'mindsharing'. In fact, he clearly states that it can be useful in everyday social practice, but it is quite fallible if used as a theoretical method (Donald 2001, 62). It is the backdrop of mindsharing that facilitates a deeper understanding of why human language is *never in the one.*

5.   Approaches to Understanding Linguistic *Meaning* and Speech Acts

The inevitability of translation at all levels of human language is one of the fundamental defining principles of language itself. In fact, defining the role of *translation* in generating meanings and in perception itself are tenets common to many paradigms of theoretical linguistics, sociolinguistics, cognitive linguistics, and neurolinguistics. We have discussed how important ecologically valid modelling and experimental design are in moving the field of cognitive neurolinguistics forward. One way of integrating these perspectives is to present a model of speech acts that can serve as an anchor for understanding and mapping language functions within and across brains. One such heuristic is the Jakobsonian speech act model, consisting of six factors and six functions (Jackobson 1957/1987, pp. 66–71; see Figure 2). Jakobson's model is a dynamic representation of the *minimum* number of factors and functions that are present in each and every speech act; each of these factors and functions are in a hierarchical relationship defined by constant internal renegotiation of dominance within each individual act. In fact, this relative and dynamic hierarchy often results in multiple outcomes within one and the same moment of discourse.[7]

FACTORS/FUNCTIONS
Context/Referential
Message/Poetic

Addresser/Emotive
Addressee/Conative

Contact/Phatic
Code/Metalingual

Figure 2   The Jakobsonian speech act model. Source: Adapted from Jakobson (1957/1987), pp. 66–71.[8]

All individual communication acts are at least *dialogic* and require translation both as an internal mechanism of signification, as well as an external mechanism of signification and communication. However, while such an approach guarantees translation mechanisms, it does not guarantee the achievement of a coherent, meaningful result. Human language in action often leads to *misunderstanding* as well as understanding. Theoretical approaches to language and brain would benefit from incorporating empirical aspects of actual language usage, which includes instability, ambiguity, and redundancy of linguistic meanings, while avoiding notions of idealized speakers and hearers.

6. The Importance of Imaging in Cognitive Neurolinguistic Research

The body of neuroimaging research produced since the mid-1990s is varied, but it contains some very important findings. One of the sticky problems remaining with neuroimaging data is the need to characterize complex cognitive function in terms of a particular morphological region without mapping the larger systems that are essential to the network, a network that is still poorly understood. De Bot (2008) points out this fact by directly addressing the strengths and weaknesses in inductive and deductive models, concluding that as long as we do not have a coherent and comprehension theory of the functioning brain and all of its parts, inductive approaches will be preferred (pp. 113–115). Understanding *variation* at individual and group levels will be essential in moving forward. In the following section, we will look specifically at cortical stimulation mapping (CSM) and functional magnetic resonance imaging (fMRI).

The fact that more than one neural system can subserve what is basically equivalent behaviour is not controversial. The same behaviour may be achieved either by the same underlying neural correlates or by different neural correlates (Huettel et al. 2004, pp. 4; Gullberg and Indefrey 2006, pp. 5–6). We see this again in the broad array of outcomes found in aphasic patients and the variability in recovery across aphasics. When one considers the CSM data from epileptic patients in conjunction with the aphasic data, both sets of results indicate a high variability in language mappings across patients, including fundamentally different localization patterns across and within subjects. I believe, along with many linguists in the community, that this variation is significant and indicates the application of a more complex, multivariate approach to understanding language(s) and the brain. Localization may be a more useful concept if it is understood to be an outcome of network mappings in an individual brain that may be similar and/or different to mappings in other brains. Here again, evidence from CSM in patients who underwent multiple surgeries suggests that while some language-related areas remain stable, others may shift over time within a single individual (cf. Serafini et al. 2013).

6.1.   *Cortical Stimulation Mapping (CSM)*

One of the early and continuing contributions to the study of bilingualism and the brain come from the clinical research done by George Ojemann and his teams of surgeons and neurophysiologists in their work with epileptic patients. Ojemann himself completed over 1100 surgeries, which included the use of CSM, during his career, and many of these patients were bilingual. As early as 1978, Ojemann and Whitaker began publishing their findings using CSM with bilingual patients. Cortical stimulation mapping is an invasive technique developed by Ojemann (following from Penfield's original work of the 1930s) to identify areas related to important functions of production (motor) and comprehension (sensory) in language; it uses an oral object-naming task in order to preserve these functions in surgeries that require removal of tissue (Ojemann 1983, 1991; Haglund et al. 1993, 1994; Serafini et al. 2008, 2013). As Corina et al. (2010) point out, this technique has proven to be quite successful in preserving areas important to motor speech and language comprehension (p. 101).

Beginning with his 1978 publication (Ojemann and Whitaker 1978, pp. 409–412), Ojemann presents data from Dutch/English and English/Spanish bilingual patients. In the initial study using CSM with two bilingual patients, 23 different sites in patient 1 and 22 different sites in patient 2 – which were in the exposed cortical area – were tested multiple times for interference with motor speech. The results showed disturbances in sites for both languages (6 of the 23 sites in patient 1, and 2 of the 22 sites in patient 2), and also disturbances in a single language (7 of patient 1's 23 sites, 7 of patient 2's 22 sites; Ojemann and Whitaker 1978, pp. 410–411). It is important to note that both patients 1 and 2 had a stronger language and a weaker language, that is they were not equally proficient across tasks in both languages.

In over 170 subsequent publications on data from CSM and single-neuron mappings of monolingual and bilingual patients, Ojemann and his colleagues discuss at length the implications of this technique for understanding language representations in the brain. The data sets with bilingual patients involve several languages, including Spanish, Dutch, Chinese, and American Sign Language (ASL). One of the most striking discoveries to come out of data acquired using CSM is the *high degree of variation across subjects in the mapping of motor and sensory aspects of human language*. These studies show the variability in the organization of language centres from brain to brain, including the variable structure of motor naming sites for bilinguals, where they note: (i) the areas of the first and second languages (L1 and L2 respectively) are coterminous; (ii) the areas of L1 and L2 are distinct; (iii) the naming areas vary in size and number and hemispheric placement (Ojemann 1993, p. 220). Furthermore, this unique research demonstrates that stimulation of cortical areas (like Broca's and Wernicke's areas) does not ever cause speech to occur; rather, it is only subcortical electrical stimulation, specifically stimulation of the caudate head and the anterior nuclei of the thalamus, which may induce involuntary speech (Fabbro 1999, p. 83).

This window into the brain using CSM is deeply invasive (and will disappear as alternative robotic surgery techniques are developed), and is only available for patients with medically intractable epilepsy that cannot be controlled by medication. As Corina et al. (2010) notes, some might claim that the epileptic brain is organized in a fundamentally distinct way from the non-epileptic brain, but it is more likely that the evidence of motor speech production areas, which varies somewhat from brain to brain as stated above, remains true for the population at large.

CSM is a powerful and unique source for data of localized neuronal activity for identifying the sensory-motor cortices; but it is also useful in identifying a broader set of regions critical in language representations and function in the brain. These mappings are crucial for pre-surgical data collection in order to eliminate or minimize as much as possible the detrimental effects of the ablation of cortical tissue that is required in epileptic subjects or tumour patients. The data provided by Ojemann and his teams over the years has been a major contributor to what we know about language mapping in monolingual and multilingual brains. Serafini et al. (2013) provides new data resulting from multiple surgeries on the same patient that confirms the dynamic nature of language mappings.

In a 2010 publication, Corina et al. (2010) remind the reader of the potential limitations of this valuable technique, including: (i) intraoperative mappings occur in restricted time frames (from 30 minutes to 3 hours), (ii) sampling of cortical sites may be unequal due to restricted exposure, (iii) patients may be groggy or less responsive since they are coming out of general anaesthesia, (iv) epileptic disorders may cause cortical reorganization that is not indicative of the general population, (v) the degree of spread of the electrical stimulation to neighbouring regions will vary (see also Ojemann 1983, 1991, 1993, 2003; Haglund et al. 1993; Gordon et al. 2001; Roux et al. 2004; Thompson 2005).

In spite of all of these potential issues, it is still the case that CSM has provided a large and unique body of data over several decades on language dysfunction in the brain. This approach yields direct cellular data collected with precise anatomical mappings, while fMRI, for example, measures correlates of blood flow as correlates of neuronal activity in larger parcels of cortical areas. As Corina et al. (2010) state:

> CSM is one of the few techniques that allow direct observation of language dysfunction at an extremely localized neural level … CSM studies have provided evidence that cortex can exhibit functionally specific vulnerabilities for language functions. Direct cortical stimulation has given rise to specific and differentiated errors associated with reading, verbal memory, semantic classes, and differential object naming in bilinguals (pp. 101–102).

The technique of implanting grids of electrodes in an initial surgery, which is later followed by the mappings prior to the resection surgery, includes placing grid sheets onto the cortical surface after the skull is opened and the dura is pulled back, or implantation of longer electrodes into deeper cortical and subcortical areas. The typical temporal grid has electrodes that are 1 cm apart (measured from the centre of each electrode) and 6 cm long by 4 cm wide (length longer than width), while frontal grids are often larger at 8 cm long by 6 cm wide. Figure 3 shows an example of electrode grid placement, function, and resection in a case that required two separate surgeries (2011 [A] and 2012 [B]) (from Serafini et al. 2013).

Critics of the reliability of data obtained using this procedure have noted that resection/ablation of areas where stimulation disrupts language does not always result in aphasias, and that the functional disruption during stimulation is most likely

(a)

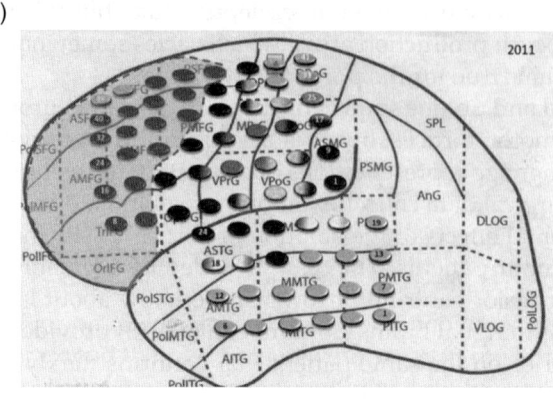

(b)

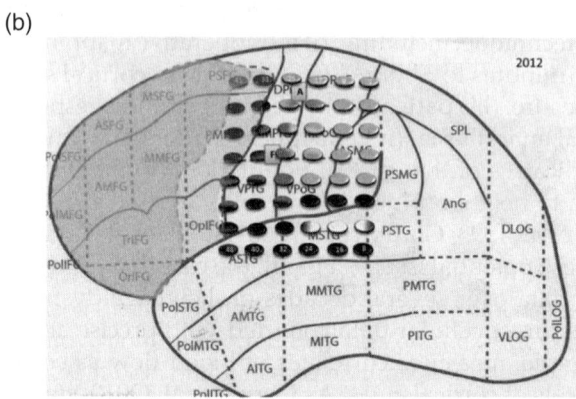

2011		2012		2011 + 2012
Temporal	**Frontal**	**Temporal**	**Frontal**	**Frontal**
○ Auditory (distinct)	○ Face sensory	○ Auditory	⬤ Face motor	⬤ Mouth motor
⬤ Paired trials Visual + Auditory	⬤ Hand sensory	⬤ Auditory Tested	⬤ Counting errors	○ Hand motor
				○ Tongue/mouth sensory
○ Not tested		○ Not tested		○ Not tested
Intraoperative confirmation		Intraoperative confirmation		
		F Face motor		○ Resection
A Hand motor		A Hand motor		

Figure 3   Schematics showing grid placement, function, and resection in 2011 (a) and 2012 (b). See legend for colour-coded functions.

associated with a network of activity and may affect cortical language function that is not near the site of stimulation, and thus the specific neuronal localization is only a small piece of a larger puzzle (e.g. Seeck et al. 2006, pp. 592–594). Also, the most frequent error type, no-response errors, is the least informative about the underlying function that has been disrupted (Corina et al. 2010, p. 103). I would add one additional comment and clarification; there are often cases with epileptic patients with medically refractory epilepsy who undergo a surgical resection of the epileptogenic zone to improve their intractability. It is not an uncommon scenario when the epileptogenic zone overlaps in part with the functional areas for speech or motor/sensory function that prohibit a complete resection required to cure the epilepsy. In such cases, even if the area displays disruption in CSM, ablation may be required. Given the redundancies of motor speech and naming areas in the human brain, there may not be a resulting functional deficit in language function post-surgery. However, with detailed neurocognitive testing deficits in visual or auditory naming or verbal memory are often identified. I would also mention here that what many surgeons refer to as 'basal language centres' are often involved in the anterior subtemporal region and are resected with impunity. In these cases, it is interesting that the recovery rate for motor speech may be quite good after surgery as long as the white matter tracts are preserved. The works of Menjot de Champfleur et al. (2013) and Duffau (2008; Duffau et al. 2008) demonstrate the importance of white matter fibre tracts for language, including the inferior fronto-occipital fasciculus (IFOF), the inferior longitudinal fasciculus (ILF), and the middle longitudinal fasciculus (MdLF). If grey matter is resected, but the subcortical white matter fibre tracts remain intact, the recovery of postoperative dysphasia may be accelerated with fewer persistent problems with word-finding or global aphasia during the recovery process.

Using CSM, Corina et al. (2010) discuss six types of 'naming errors': semantic paraphasias, phonological paraphasias, neologisms, circumlocutions, performance errors, and no-response errors (p. 104; see Figure 4 a–f). The largest number of errors fall under the category of 'no-response' errors at 54%. The second and third largest number of errors were 'performance errors' at 16.4% and semantic paraphasias at 15.1% (Corina et al. 2010, p. 104). These error types are broadly distributed across cortical areas.

In order to appreciate the degree of variation across subjects and the degree to which language-related areas fall well beyond the boundaries of *the traditional model*, consider the following diagrams (Figure 4 a–f) from Corina et al. (2010) that show the spread of different types of linguistic errors (including semantic and phonological paraphasias, performance errors, circumlocutions, neologisms and no-response errors) across cortical sites (pp. 105–108).

The research of Ojemann and his teams supports four very important conclusions: (i) motor speech areas for naming are very variable across subjects, whether they are monolingual or multilingual; (ii) all subjects show some overlap in motor speech naming in multiple languages; (iii) all subjects show distinct motor speech naming centres across multiple languages; and (iv) different types of errors can be evoked by electrical stimulation from different cortical areas (see Serafini et al. 2008, pp. 248–249; Corina et al. 2010, p. 103).

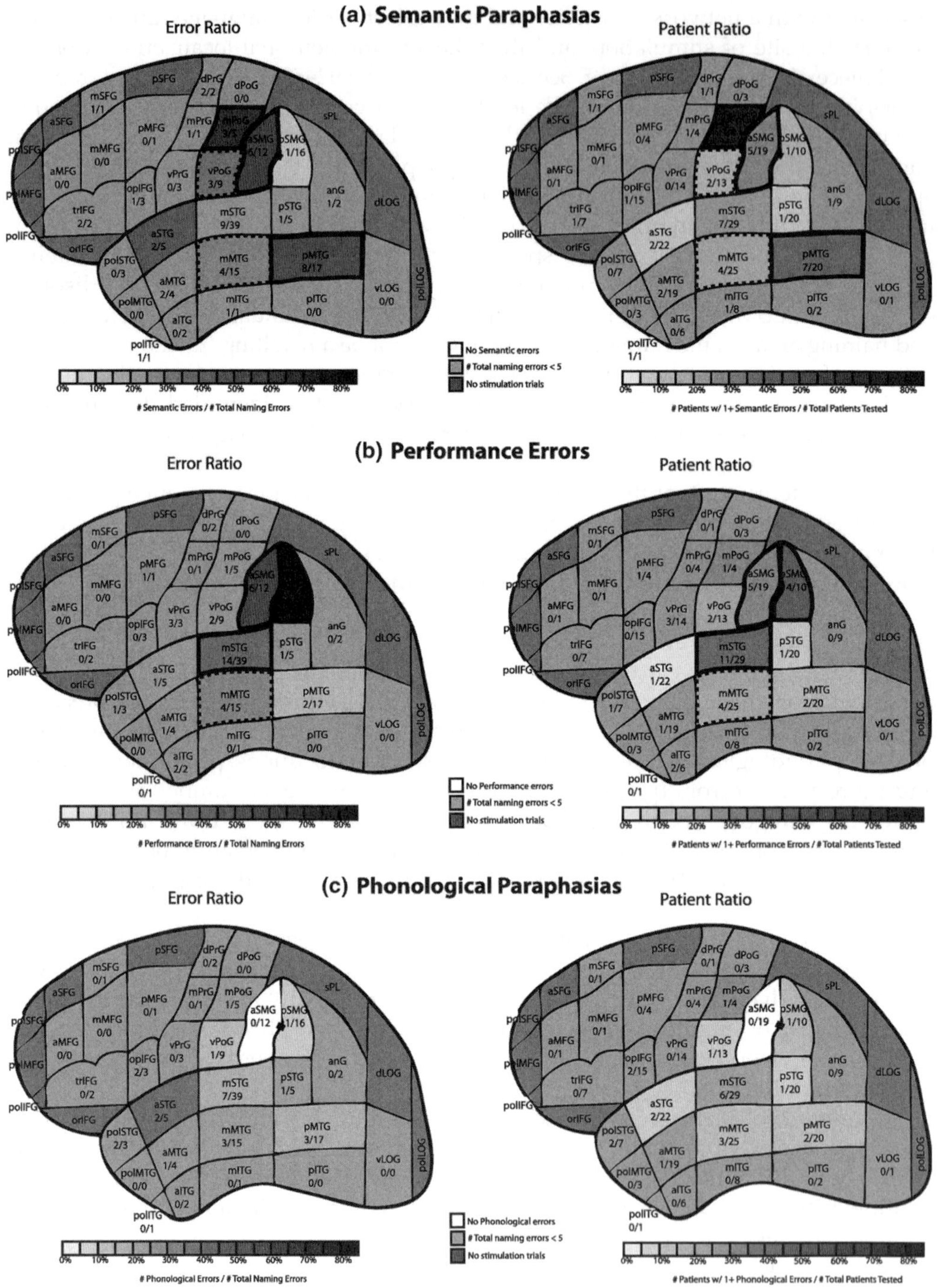

Figure 4   (a) Semantic paraphasias, (b) Performance errors, (c) Phonological paraphasias, (d) Circumlocutions, (e) Neologisms, (f) No-response errors. Source: Diagrams from Corina et al. (2010).

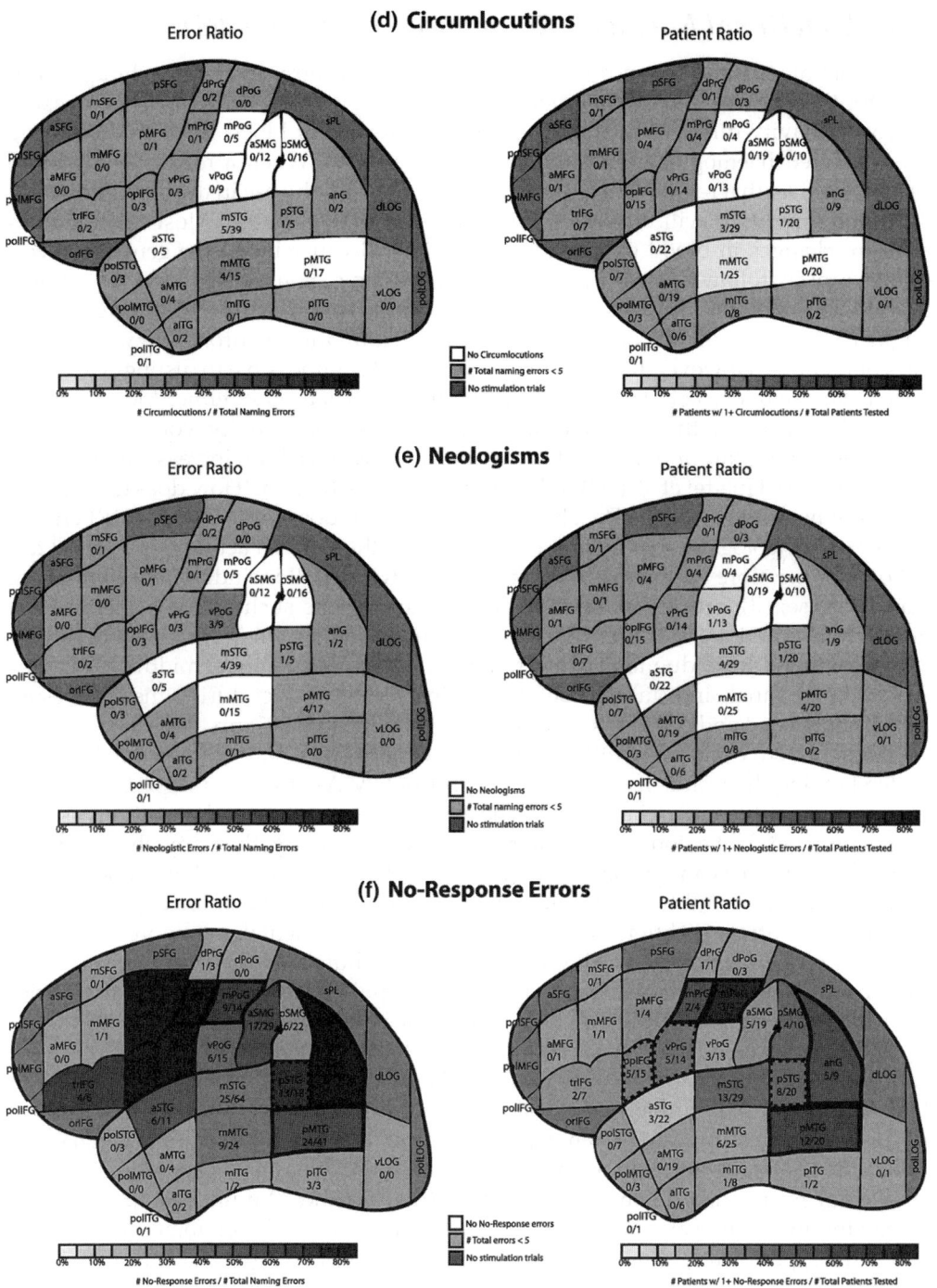

Figure 4 (Continued)

6.2.   *Functional Magnetic Resonance Imaging (fMRI)*

Functional magnetic resonance imaging, is one of the central imaging techniques utilized for the study of human cognition and language(s).[9] While fMRI does not measure neuronal activity directly, but rather through correlates of blood flow by measuring deoxygenated haemoglobin (Huettel et al. 2004, p. 159). When a region of the brain becomes active, that region will require more oxygen and glucose in the blood flow, and the blood flow itself will increase. As Huettel et al. (2004) states: 'Most fMRI studies measure changes in blood oxygenation over time. Because blood oxygenation levels change rapidly following activity of neurons in a brain region, fMRI allows researchers to localize brain activity on a second-by-second basis and within millimeters of its origin' (p. 4). The resulting correlations are not with individual neurons, but with assemblies of neurons. However, Raichle (2001) notes: '… it is impossible to distinguish inhibitory from excitatory cellular activity on the basis of changes in either blood flow or metabolism. Thus, on this view a local increase in inhibitory activity would be as likely to increase blood flow and the fMRI BOLD signal as would a local increase in excitatory activity' (p. 12). Huettel et al. (2004) clearly sum up the situation: 'How does fMRI create images of neuronal activity? The short answer is that it does not! Instead, fMRI creates images of physiological activity that is correlated with neuronal activity' (pp. 127–128).

Some of the more frequently mentioned issues with fMRI include: (i) the significant scanner noise; (ii) 'artifactual signal loss' in brain regions such as the posteromedial orbital frontal and medial anterior temporal regions and the midportion of the ventrolateral temporal lobe, due to proximity to the nasal cavity, sinuses, middle ear cavity, and auditory canal; and (iii) motion of any kind by the subject during the scan, especially whole-head and soft tissue motion (Binder and Price 2001, pp. 195–197).

The subtractive methods utilized in fMRI experiments may lead to confusion in understanding the results if not applied appropriately. As Huettel et al. (2004) state: 'It is important for the researcher to make the experimental and control conditions as similar as possible. If the conditions differ in only one property, then any change in the dependent variable can be confidently attributed to the change in that property. This process is known as subtraction, since one can subtract the value of the dependent variable in the control condition from its value in the experimental condition to quantify the effect of the manipulation. But if the conditions differ in more than one way, then there could be multiple explanations for experimental effects. Any factor that covaries with the independent variable in an experiment is known as a confounding factor' (p. 290). In many cases, the control condition may involve nothing more than subjects lying still in the scanner with their eyes closed; this is often called the 'rest' condition. For language-based experiments, the task condition may involve a broad spectrum of linguistic activities, including listening, speaking, and reading in one or more languages.[10]

Raichle (2001) has argued for rigorous measurement of baseline conditions for fMRI studies for over a decade and more recently (Riachle and Mintun 2006, p. 1249) has turned his attention to an unexpected outcome in positron emission tomography (PET) and fMRI experiments, namely the significant amount of energy (which he calls 'dark energy') 'that the brain normally and continuously expends' that is not connected to the additional energy required for the specific cognitive tasks being studied in the individual imaging experiments.[11]

In order to strengthen the application of fMRI in language-based experiments, it is important to know its limitations. Unless the limitations of the technology are clearly articulated, it becomes impossible to develop more robust experimental design, which will directly impact the validity and broad applicability of the experimental results achieved. One of the most serious issues in using imaging technologies for language study is the design of the experiments and the repeatability of the results. In the following sections, we will address some of the common findings from fMRI studies of language(s) and present suggestions for new language-based imaging studies.

7.   A Glance at fMRI Studies of Language(s)

The question of neural organization of language centres and language-related areas in the brains of bilinguals and multilinguals continues to be a topic of great interest, represented by the significant number of fMRI studies to be found in the literature.[12] Some earlier research suggested that 'early' bilingual or multilingual acquisition is represented differently in the brain than 'late' second- or third-language acquisition. These studies have produced results that are not consistent or that are inconclusive, and more recent studies have shown the importance of proficiency as a more reliable factor than age (Abutalebi et al. 2013).

A number of fMRI studies focus only on monolinguals, or at least involve stimuli from only one language. In those studies that do use bilingual or multilingual subjects, there is little or no empirical evidence that the subjects possessed superior or native proficiency in the languages in which they were supposed to be multilingual, nor was there assurance that parity in multilanguage facility existed throughout the research subjects. What has been missing from most of the studies done heretofore is a more linguistically sophisticated ranking of participants' abilities in multiple languages (beyond self-evaluation) prior to submitting these participants to fMRI procedures. Furthermore, earlier studies have done little to quantify linguistic proficiency. Bilingualism and multilingualism are deeply connected to how speakers of two or more languages live their lives.[13] And proficiency, regardless of the level of attainment, is deeply tied to how and why one uses one's languages.

De Bot (2008) insists that imaging studies of multilingualism must pay attention to this issue not only in *describing* the subject pools, but in *selecting* them as well (pp. 117–119). This means identifying not only the intensity of contact but also the specific terms of the contact. Intensity of contact includes such variables as time frame of language use, educational context,[14] social networks, place where language is used (at home, amongst family, with friends, or at work, with coworkers), level of complexity, specific fields or topics, and so on. Contact also implies that the researcher has information about the backgrounds of the subjects, their language aptitude (as demonstrated by empirically repeatable testing), their level of education, attitudes towards all of their languages (L1, L2, … Ln), all the languages known and how they are used, and the motivation for learning a specific language; the researcher should use this information as criteria for subject selection and experimental design. The field of imaging studies of second language acquisition and bilingualism and multilingualism has the opportunity moving forward to include more information about subjects and a variety of variables that characterize their knowledge of the languages they use.

A summary of Price's meta-analysis of 100 fMRI language studies (2010) provides a general sense of results obtained from fMRI studies of language, as well as insightful comments for future research. For studies of speech comprehension, Price (2010) categorizes activation results into six major categories: prelexical, pseudowords, words, sentence comprehension, semantic/syntactic ambiguity, and word retrieval and articulation (pp. 65–75). Two of the salient points to come from Price's work include noting not only specific activations, but also the overlap in activations within speech production and comprehension (Price 2010, p. 82). In terms of speech production explicitly, she reminds the reader of the difficulties in studying speech production with fMRI because of the artefacts that arise due to mouth and head movements, as well as problems of controlling 'speech production rate, the order of words that are retrieved and the choice of words relating to a semantic theme' (Price 2010, p. 83).

One of the issues that Price identifies at the beginning of her analysis is the usage of different anatomical terms for one and same region across studies and suggests solutions. Price's examples of these terminological difficulties include alternatives for the inferior frontal region (BA 44, Broca's area, and pars opercularis) and for the left temporo-parietal area (supramarginal gyrus or SMG, planum temporal, Sylvian parieto-temporal or Spt, superior temporal gyrus or STG, and the inferior parietal lobe or IPL; Price 2010, p. 63).

Price concludes by noting the importance of further study of bilateral activations, the role of the cerebellum, functional connectivity of language systems using a variety of techniques, including combining fMRI with magnetoencephalography (MEG), event-related potentials (ERP), and transcranial magnetic stimulation (TMS); she also suggest looking more closely at inter-subject variations based on 'behavioral variations, age, multilingualism, lesion studies, or unbiased classification schemes' (Price 2010, p. 83).

7.1. *Language Proficiency Testing, not Self-Reporting: CEFR and MANCOVA*

While the inclusion of proficiency measurements of subjects has long been talked about for neuroimaging studies of language and languages, its inclusion is generally restricted to self-reporting and self-assessment of subjects. The existence of internationally recognized proficiency testing systems like the *Common European Framework* of Reference for Languages (CEFR) – an initiative which began in 1989 and became recognized by EU Council Resolution in November 2001 and one which covers a broader spectrum of world languages than those in the EU – makes it feasible for neuroscience research to treat language proficiency in a more empirically reliable way. CEFR global scales and assessment grids are easily accessible for the six levels (A1, A2, B1, B2, C1, C2) and five sets of tests per level in speaking, reading, audition (also called listening comprehension), grammar/lexicon, and writing. Individuals, universities, and colleges across the globe have access to the tests and to certified testers.

Some of the most important reasons for moving away from self-reporting are its lack of reliability, inconsistencies in the tools used in different groups, problems generalizing results across studies and groups, inherent problems with the questionnaire format, and lack of statistically significant correspondence with more rigorous proficiency measurements. In Andrews et al. (2013), CEFR proficiency testing was conducted multiple times at different levels and close in temporal proximity to fMRI scans conducted over the course of one calendar year.[15]

A multivariate analysis of covariance (MANCOVA), a statistical method within the general linear model with multiple dependent variables and concomitant independent variables, can be a good way to strengthen conclusions in interpreting and understanding activations acquired during neuroimaging. In a longitudinal imaging study of second language acquisition, there is the additional requirement of analysing data collected from a single subject over time as they acquire a new L2. If the first scan is conducted prior to exposure to the L2, each subject may serve as their own control. Different types of proficiency would be tested depending on the protocol and stimuli used in the scan (audition, reading, speaking, etc.). MANCOVA statistical modelling can be used to analyse these data and determine if there is a significant correlation between proficiency and activations obtained during that period of time.

7.2.   *Understanding Activations and Variation: Analysis of fMRI Data*

Significant numbers of fMRI studies of language(s) shows a much broader range of activation across both hemispheres in areas more broadly defined than the traditional Broca/Wernicke targets from the classical model, and these results an keeping with hypotheses and results found in Poeppel and Hickok (2004), Luo and Poeppel (2007), Price (2010), and Andrews et al. (2013). Hagoort (2006) suggests that it is functional anatomy, not structural anatomy, which provides more substantial evidence for understanding language processing and learning (p. 95).

Interpreting the activations recorded from regions of interest (ROIs) in fMRI language studies is strengthened when significance can be found with behavioural data (like proficiency). This is particularly important for bilingual and multilingual fMRI studies where it is common knowledge that a subject may demonstrate higher levels of activation in a condition in a language that they do not know or know poorly than in a language that they know well.

Furthermore, Eklund et al. (2016) reveal some of the potential problems of typical parametric statistical methods used in fMRI analysis, including so-called 'false positives' resulting in studies using the most common software packages for fMRI analysis (AFNI, FSL, and SPM; pp. 7900–7905). Their findings show that results are more reliable for voxel-wise inference and invalid for cluster-based inference (Eklund et al. 2016, p. 7903). Given the fact that activation levels by themselves may not be interpretable (activation levels do not necessarily correlate with knowledge), the importance of including other measurements such as proficiency become critical for strengthening conclusions.

There is also a different type of activation change where specific brain regions may decrease their activity during a task condition. In such an instance, Raichle (2010) and Gusnard and Raichle (2001) offer an explanation using the *default mode network* (DMN). Gusnard and Raichle suggest a way to characterize 'tonically active areas' by calling for a distinction between 'functionally active' and 'activated' (p. 689).

Andrews et al. (2013) took individual variation as a key factor in the analysis by designing an experiment where collect data for individual subjects could be analysed at both the individual subject and group levels. As a departure from many fMRI studies of language, Andrews et al. did not average out individual variations across conditions; rather, individual differences were preserved and a statistical multivariate analysis was used to test for the validity of scanning results with proficiency data across multiple time points.

Variation studies have played a major role in contemporary sociolinguistic theory and practice, but variation has not always been embraced by the general theoretical linguistics community and was often ignored in favour of generalizations and even potential linguistic universals. This was especially true in the fields of morphology and syntax. In imaging studies of language(s), there is a systemic disregard of variation. That is, typical methods of fMRI analysis not only average across runs, but also across groups of subjects (Osterhout et al. [2006] and de Bot [2006] also discuss this problem). As already noted, high brain activation does not mean anything in and of itself. Individual subjects in language studies may have low or high activations in a language in which they are very proficient and low or high activations in a language in which they are not proficient, and activations may change within one and the same subject over time with no active learning going on. Finally, if a subject ardently *tries* to understand a task in an unknown language, they may demonstrate higher activation levels – or they may not engage at all in the task and the activations recorded would not be related at all.

But variation is not only at the level of activations between and across subjects; there are also variations in neural anatomy across subjects (Calvin and Ojemann 1994; Stowe 2006). The question of whether or not bilingual and multilingual users display distinctly different neural anatomy is posed on occasion, but the interpretations are still quite controversial (cf. Maguire et al. 2003; Coggins et al. 2004; Draganski et al. 2004; Mechelli et al. 2004; Indefrey 2006). The general approach is to suggest that acquisition and use of an L2, L3, etc. will yield structural and functional changes to the brain. De Bot (2006) suggests a different position, where it is the structural and functional characteristics of each user's brain that may affect the development of these languages (p. 127).

The mapping of individual activations using Talairach coordinates and various atlases (the Montreal Neurological Institute [MNI] atlas being one of the more popular ones) is also problematic, since even within these systems, there are differences between the brain bank specimens and individual subjects. The complications of spatial normalization of the imaging data of groups of subjects due to differences in normalization paradigms and algorithms can make it almost impossible to compare activations across studies. There are suggestions for best practices and application of specific 'transforms' that can alleviate these issues (cf. Lancaster et al. 2007; Laird et al. 2010). However, it seems that the field of neuroimaging has not fully resolved the issue.

The question of different degrees of variation in brain activations of bilinguals and multilinguals in contrast to monolinguals is fraught with controversy and leads to widely different interpretations. Stowe (2006) notes that the likelihood of variation between L1 and L2 is a product of more complex processing and individual-focused analysis (pp. 305–311). In this vein, Indefrey (2006) look specifically at 30 hemodynamic studies of L1 and L2 processing (pp. 279–304). His general finding is that most of these studies do not find significant differences in the hemodynamic activations of L1 and L2 processing (Indefrey 2006, p. 282). Where there were differences, they seem to be related to three factors: onset (age of acquisition), proficiency, and exposure (Indefrey 2006, p. 299). He notes that it is impossible to obtain any 'insight into the individual variability of activation patterns' since these are reported as group results (Indefrey 2006, p. 289). As noted in the introduction to this chapter, there may be a negative correlation between activation and level of ability, and this pattern may emerge as L2 learners attain higher levels of proficiency.

Michel Paradis (2004) has also written extensively on the problems of interpreting activations in fMRI experiments of language(s) and argues that contradictory results must be addressed:

> If one wishes to claim that very similar experiments designed to isolate the same language processes show activation in non-overlapping cortical areas because these studies use different methodologies, then one must be able to predict which variable will cause which observed activation, and why (p. 157).

By including a multivariate analysis of covariance as part of the fMRI experimental design and analysis, researchers would be able to explain the types of variation that may occur between and across subjects. This is especially important if we recall the type of inter-subject variation found in CSM findings and in light of approaches to brain and language that incorporate a more embodied view of cognition.

8. Towards an Explanation of Bilaterality of Language

One of the central points that has been criticized consistently by the contemporary neurolinguistic community, including those researchers who use fMRI as one of their main imaging techniques for studying language and brain, is the lack of attention to the right hemisphere (esp. Hickok and Poeppel 2000; Bookheimer 2002; Poeppel and Hickok 2004; Stowe et al. 2005; Bozic et al. 2010; Friederici 2012). While there is now more research on language and brain that includes the right hemisphere, there remain unanswered questions about its role and the interactions between the two hemispheres. The data from the Andrews et al. longitudinal fMRI (2013) study consistently show important activations involving both hemispheres with some interesting differences across subjects. Data analysis in the planned follow-up studies will include additional statistical modelling to attempt to provide an explanatory basis for understanding more clearly the role of both hemispheres in language acquisition and maintenance across levels of proficiency.

There are many debates about what fMRI studies of language can and cannot show (see Paradis 2004; de Bot 2008). The Andrews et al. (2013) supports the use of fMRI in understanding second language acquisition and demonstrates that proficiency is a statistically significant effect. It also supports the development of more fMRI longitudinal studies for the study of bilingualism and multilingualism and second language acquisition where proficiency data is included as a key component of the analysis. The drawbacks to fMRI longitudinal studies include high cost and potential subject attrition. The importance of multivariate analysis models including covariance is clear for studies where proficiency measurements and other behavioural empirical data are acquired in conjunction with scanning data.

When combining subject testing and proficiency data with fMRI, it is critical that (i) proficiency testing is the same for all of the subjects in the study, (ii) proficiency tests are used that are recognized internationally (like CEFR) and exist for as many languages of the world as possible, and (iii) it targets multiple linguistic domains, including grammar/

lexicon, reading, listening comprehension, speaking, and writing. The inclusion of reliable proficiency data is crucial to deepening our understanding of results acquired using fMRI technology.

One of the concerns raised by critics of fMRI studies (and PET) is the potential difficulty in comparing the results across studies (see esp. Poeppel 1996; Paradis 2004). The conducting of fMRI studies focusing on bilinguals and/or multilinguals, and second language acquisition at the *discourse level* can strengthen the relevance of results obtained from imaging research. Stowe et al. (2005) discusses the importance of the transition to the sentence (discourse) level away from the word level, how imaging has demonstrated the need for an interactive view of production and comprehension, and the resulting new modelling of brain and language (p. 1006). An additional benefit results in having ecologically valid protocols that will facilitate more reliable results.

Imaging research is an important source of information about the dynamic aspects of the neurological interface of language acquisition, maintenance and loss. As Green et al. (2006), speaking of bilingualism and multilingualism, state: 'Acquisition of another language induces both functional and structural brain changes. Functional neuroimaging methods offer a way to understand individual differences in the process of acquisition and in the manner in which proficiency is expressed both in terms of the nature of the neural representations involved and in their control' (p. 119).

9. Parting Shots: Shifting Perspectives, Conclusions and Future Directions

By moving away from essentialist definitions of language users and articulating non-essentialist variables that are critical to language acquisition (and acquisition of languages) and achievement of the higher levels of proficiency, the experimental baselines for future experiments can be more rigorously defined. Some of these non-essentialist variables include educational background, motivation, aptitude, attitudes towards the specific languages and cultures, individual goals for using these languages and how they are to be used, quality of exposure and instruction, and many more. As I have argued throughout this chapter, these types of variables are critical to improving the interpretability of results achieved in imaging studies of languages.

The past several years have provided important new information on the interactions of proficiency and age. Birdsong (2006) shows that it is proficiency, not age of acquisition or which language comes first, that will be the 'strongest predictor' of degrees of similarity between one's first and second languages (p. 24). And more recently Abutalebi et al. (2013) have shown that proficiency can be a more significant factor than age. Specifically, Abutalebi et al. (2013) show 'for the first time that differences in language proficiency … differentially modulates activity in core regions of the language control network during language switching' (p. 910). More imaging studies that incorporate proficiency, as well as a more nuanced approach to understanding age and ageing are essential for improving experimental design and providing richer conclusions.

Integration of data from the lesion-deficit tradition with data from experiments with healthy subjects can provide additional insights into future research. The importance of ecological validity in the design of studies and experiments and reproducible and reliable proficiency testing data with both of these populations should no longer be an afterthought or add-on to the design itself; rather, it should be a baseline requirement for producing viable research results that will move forward our understanding of language and brain.

The importance of understanding *invariance in variation* has been one of the central concerns of theoretical linguistics of the twentieth and twenty-first centuries. The construction and conducting of imaging studies that include protocols of language that are not only ecologically valid and coupled with behavioural and proficiency data, but also allow for multiple comparisons across and within subjects (including longitudinal), may provide a new perspective on how to answer some of the most challenging issues about brain and language, as well as formulate new questions that can deepen the research paradigms in cognitive neurolinguistics.

NOTES

1   Kandel and Schwartz (1991, p. 845) point out several problems with the traditional model's description of the neurological interface of human language (using the Wernicke-Geschwind version): (i) the lesions of the original patients of Broca and Wernicke were larger and affected more regions than those in modern-day analogues; (ii) the model ignores important subcortical regions (including the left thalamus, left caudate nucleus, and adjacent white matter); (iii) there is a fundamental difference in processing written language that does not involve Wernicke's area and this suggests modality-specific pathways for processing visual and auditory perceptions; and (iv) processing of speech sound and meaning may involve different pathways. (The chapter in Kandel and Schwartz 1991 that critiques the traditional model is by Richard Mayeux and Eric Kandel). Calvin and Ojemann (1994) clearly state the problem: 'The area of cortex related to motor speech functions turns out to be quite wide, involving most of the brain around the sylvian fissure. This is different from what you'd read in most textbooks, where Broca's area is the only place mentioned in conjunction with motor speech' (p. 245). The authors explain not only that the typical definition of Broca's area is incomplete, but also that Broca's patient, Leborgne, displayed a much broader region of damage than what is now referred to as Broca's area. Contemporary data demonstrate that in order for there to be permanent motor language deficits, the entire area around the sylvian fissure must be destroyed, not just the frontal lobe section (1994, p. 245). Finally, electrical stimulation of Broca's area never elicits motor speech.

2   A significant section of Stowe et al. (2005) focuses on the functions of Broca's and Wernicke's areas. In their review of 60 PET and fMRI studies showing activations in these two areas, they make a strong claim that production and comprehension cannot be separated as suggested in the traditional model (2005, p. 1003). This is consistent with the arguments given in Hickok and Poeppel (2004, pp. 1–12; 2007).

3   There are three definitions that are important for understanding our definition of human language: speech communities, communities of practice, signification. Dell Hymes (1972) defines a speech community as 'a community sharing rules for the conduct and interpretation of speech, and rules for the interpretation of at least one linguistic variety' (p. 54). For Hymes, these communities are based on face-to-face interactions. Speakers are members of multiple speech communities and these memberships are dynamic. McConnell-Ginet (2003) defines

communities of practice as follows: 'A community of practice (CofP) is a group of people brought together by some mutual endeavour, some common enterprise in which they are engaged and to which they bring a shared repertoire of resources, including linguistic resources, and for which they are mutually accountable … communities of practice are not free-floating but are linked to one another and to various institutions. They draw on resources with a more general history – languages as well as various kinds of technologies and artefacts' (p. 71–72). Signification, a term used in European structural linguistics and semiotics, can be defined as the prerequisite process of generating meanings that allows humans to have language. Donald (2004) identifies the key to understanding human language as a collective phenomenon when he notes that 'he isolated brain does not come up with external symbols. Human brains collectively invent symbols in a creative and dynamic process' (p. 43). Symbols are invented through executive skills 'that created a nervous system that invented representation out of necessity' (Donald 2004, p. 43.). Using Donald, signification would be the ability to collectively invent innovative and dynamic externalized symbols. Signification is also important to understanding the construction of speech acts. 'There can be no communication act that is a singular event. Rather, all individual communication acts are dialogic in essence and require translation both as an *internal mechanism of signification*, as well as an *external mechanism of signification and communication*' (Andrews 2014, p. 58). The phenomenon of signification does not guarantee a coherent, meaningful result; misunderstanding is as important as understanding (Andrews 2014, p. 58).

4　A simple working definition of culture to parallel the working definition of language may be useful: 'The shared understandings of a collective and the products of those understandings'.

5　Mahon and Caramazza (2008) critique the embodiment hypotheses given by Gallese and Lakoff by specifically focusing on empirical evidence (or lack therein) for the hypothesis. In order to determine which approach (embodied or disembodied) is correct, Mahon and Caramazza argue that it is necessary to understand 'whether the motor system is activated due to "leakage" of (or cascading) activation from an "abstract" conceptual level', or occurs in parallel to (or independently of) activation of the "abstract" conceptual level?' (p. 61). While they suggest that some concepts might include sensory-motor information, they are not convinced that this would be feasible for abstract concepts (Mahon and Caramazza 2008, p. 60). In the end, Mahon and Carammaza reject a disembodied cognition hypothesis as well as the strong version of the embodied cognition hypothesis and call for a new approach – the 'domain-specific sensory motor hypothesis' (Mahon and Caramazza 2008, p. 69).

6　As early as 1948, Dwight Bolinger (1948) is already addressing the question of neurological embodiment: 'To the language learner already familiar with the sound of galloping, the word *galloping* may have seemed appropriate at the very first: but, once learned, *run*, with little or no onomatopoeia, is just as vivid. Whatever its origin, be it as pictorial as an imitative word or as abstract as the numeral *10*, once part of the individual's equipment it can no longer be arbitrary, and cannot "just as well" be something else. "Arbitrary" things are learned in the same way, and with exactly the same systemic results, as "natural" ones. The synapses of the brain are no respecters of any such dichotomy' (p. 233). See also Bolinger (1965, 1975).

7　In brief, a focus on the speaker's intentions or meanings yields a speech event dominated by the *emotive function*; a focus on the hearer commonly found in utterances characterized by commands, imperatives, or other speech acts compelling the addressee to act is called *conative*; a focus on the context results in the *referential function*; a focus on the channel itself – whether it means opening the channel or checking to see if the channel is still viable – is called the *phatic function*; a focus on the code, which is one of the central functions involved in language acquisition across the life cycle, is called *metalingual function*; a focus on the message itself (for its own sake) yields the *poetic function*. It is no coincidence that the term *poetic* is used for this function. This is part of Jakobson's important claim that the basis for language as aesthetic, poetic, or artistic is not peculiar to literature and poetry, but is an ever-present characteristic of all of human language and is embedded in each and every speech act.

8   All of the studies discussed in this section used BOLD fMRI (blood-oxygenation-level dependent contrast functional magnetic resonance imaging).

9   There are numerous outstanding fMRI studies (and meta-analyses) of language(s) that should be mentioned here, including studies by Binder et al. (1995, 1997, 2009), Binder and Price (2001), Price (2000, 2010) and Price et al. (1996a, b, 1999), Diaz and McCarthy (2009, 2014), Abutalebi et al. (2009, 2013), Stowe et al. (2005), Hernandez (2009), Bookheimer (2002) and many others.

10   There are numerous outstanding fMRI studies (and meta-analyses) of language(s) that should be mentioned here, including studies by Binder et al.(1995, 1997, 2001, 2009), Price and Price et al. (1992, 1996a, b, 1999, 2000, 2010), Diaz et al. (2009, 2014), Abutalebi (2008), Abutalebi et al. (2009, 2013), Stowe et al. (2005), Hernandez (2009), Bookheimer (2002) and many others.

11   For a list of important sources of fMRI language studies, including studies of bilingualism and multilingualism, see Andrews (2014, p. 193; Huettel et al. 2004, pp. 196, 277–279;. Huettel et al. 2009.

12   *Languages in Contact* (1953/1968) is the title of Uriel Weinreich's important contribution to the study of bilingualism and multilingualism.

13   Davidson (2006) suggests that the classroom setting may be a good way to 'examine learning on several different timescales' (p. 233). This includes classroom materials, testing, vocabulary, teaching methods, and the order of presentation (Davidson 2006, p. 233).

14   All subjects in Andrews et al. (2013) participated in multiple testing sessions at levels A2 and B1 of the TKRI proficiency exam described above. They were also enrolled in course work and class examinations at both Duke University and St. Petersburg State University. Different types of proficiency (audition, reading, grammar/lexicon) were distinguished and measured and are included in the MANCOVA statistical model to determine if there was a significant relationship between the changes in activations in the ROIs for each subject across the three scans/time points for the Russian-rest condition with changes in proficiency. The result was a p value = 0.01, which supports the research hypothesis that language acquisition is associated with characteristic activations found in the Russian condition (the language being acquired). The lack of significance for the English condition (where p = 0.47) strongly supports the interpretation that non-normal residuals are not distorting the analysis in any important way.

15   Jakobson's model is also compatible with semiotic modelling of communication as given in Sebeok (1991) and Lotman (1990).

REFERENCES

Abutalebi, J. (2008). Neural aspects of second language representation and language control. *Acta Psychologica* 128 (3): 466–478.

Abutalebi, J., Della, R.P.A., Ding, G. et al. (2013). Language proficiency modulates the engagement of cognitive control areas in multilinguals. *Cortex* 49 (3): 905–911.

Abutalebi, J., Tettamanti, M., and Perani, D. (2009). The bilingual brain: linguistic and non-linguistic skills. *Brain and Language* 109 (2–3): 51–54.

Ahlsén, E. (2006). *Introduction to Neurolinguistics*. Amsterdam, The Netherlands: John Benjamins.

Andrews, E. (2014). *Neuroscience and Multilingualism*. Cambridge, UK: Cambridge University Press.

Andrews, E., Frigau, L., Voyvodic-Casabo, C. et al. (2013). Multilingualism and fMRI: longitudinal study of second language acquisition. *Brain Sciences* 3 (2): 849–876.

Bhatia, T.K. and Ritchie, W.C. (2006). *The Handbook of Bilingualism*. Malden, MA: Blackwell.

Binder, J.R., Desai, R.H., Graves, W.W., and Conant, L.L. (2009). Where is the semantic system? A critical review and meta-analysis of 120 functional neuroimaging studies. *Cerebral Cortex* 19 (12): 2767–2796.

Binder, J.R., Frost, J.A., Hammeke, T.A. et al. (1997). Human brain language areas identified by functional magnetic resonance imaging. *The Journal of Neuroscience* 17 (1): 353–362.

Binder, J.R. and Price, C.J. (2001). Functional neuroimaging of language. In: *Handbook of Functional Neuroimaging of Cognition* (ed. R. Cabeza and A. Kingstone), 187–251. Cambridge, MA: MIT Press.

Binder, J.R., Rao, S.M., Hammeke, T.A. et al. (1995). Lateralized human brain language systems demonstrated by task subtraction functional magnetic resonance imaging. *Archives of Neurology* 52 (6): 593–601.

Birdsong, D. (2006). Age and second language acquisition and processing: a selective overview. *Language Learning* 56 (S1): 9–49.

Bolinger, D. (1948). On defining the morpheme. *Word* 4 (1): 18–23.

Bolinger, D. (1965). *Forms of English: Accent, Morpheme, Order*. Cambridge, MA: Harvard University Press.

Bolinger, D. (1975). *Aspects of Language*, 2e. New York, NY: Harcourt Brace Jovanovich.

Bookheimer, S. (2002). Functional MRI of language: new approaches to understanding the cortical organization of semantic processing. *Annual Review of Neuroscience* 25: 151–188.

Bozic, M., Tyler, L.K., Ives, D.T. et al. (2010). Bihemispheric foundations for human speech comprehension. *Proceedings of the National Academy of Sciences of the United States of America* 107 (40): 17439–17444.

Buckner, R.L. and Logan, J. (2001). Functional neuroimaging methods: PET and fMRI. In: *Handbook of Functional Neuroimaging of Cognition* (ed. R. Cabeza and A. Kingstone), 27–48. Cambridge, MA: MIT Press.

Calvin, W.H. and Ojemann, G.A. (1994). *Conversations with Neil's Brain: The Neural Nature of Thought and Language*. Reading, MA: Addison-Wesley.

Coggins, P.E., Kennedy, T.J., and Armstrong, T.A. (2004). Bilingual corpus callosum variability. *Brain and Language* 89 (1): 69–75.

Cook, V. (ed.) (2002). Background to the L2 user. In: *Portraits of the L2 User*, 1–28. Clevedon, UK: Multilingual Matters.

Cook, V., Larossi, E., Stellakis, N., and Tokumaru, Y. (2003). Effects of the L2 on the syntactic processing of the L1. In: *Effects of the Second Language on the First* (ed. V. Cook), 193–213. Clevedon, UK: Multilingual Matters.

Corina, D.P., Loudermilk, B.C., Detwiler, L. et al. (2010). Analysis of naming errors during cortical stimulation mapping: implications for models of language representation. *Brain and Language* 115 (2): 101–112.

Crystal, D. (2010). *The Cambridge Encyclopedia of Language*. Cambridge, UK: Cambridge University Press.

Davidson, D. (2006). Strategies for longitudinal neurophysiology: commentary on Osterhout et al. *Language Learning* 56 (S1): 231–234.

de Bot, K. (2008). Review article: the imaging of what in the multilingual mind? *Second Language Research* 24 (1): 111–133.

de Bot, K. (2009). Multilingualism and aging. In: *The New Handbook of Second Language Acquisition* (ed. T.K. Bhatia and W.C. Ritchie), 425–442. Bingley, UK: Emerald Group Publishing.

Diaz, M.T., Hogstrom, L.J., Zhuang, J. et al. (2014). The influence of written distractor words on brain activity during overt picture naming. *Frontiers in Human Neuroscience* 8: 167.

Diaz, M.T. and McCarthy, G. (2009). A comparison of brain activity evoked by single content and function words: an fMRI investigation of implicit word processing. *Brain Research* 1282: 38–49.

Donald, M. (2001). *A Mind So Rare: The Evolution of Human Consciousness*. New York, NY: Norton.

Donald, M. (2004). The definition of human nature. In: *The New Brain Sciences: Perils and Prospects* (ed. D. Rees and S. Rose), 34–58. Cambridge: Cambridge University Press.

Dowling, J.E. (2004). *The Great Brain Debate: Nature or Nurture?* Washington, DC: Joseph Henry Press.

Draganski, B., Gaser, C., Busch, V. et al. (2004). Neuroplasticity: changes in grey matter induced by training. *Nature* 427 (6972): 311–312.

Duffau, H. (2008). The anatomo-functional connectivity of language revisited. New insights provided by electrostimulation and tractography. *Neuropsychologia* 46 (4): 927–934.

Duffau, H., Peggy, G.S.T., Mandonnet, E. et al. (2008). Intraoperative subcortical stimulation mapping of language pathways in a consecutive series of 115 patients with grade II glioma in the left dominant hemisphere. *Journal of Neurosurgery* 109 (3): 461–471.

Eklund, A., Nichols, T.E., and Knutsson, H. (2016). Cluster failure: why fMRI inferences for spatial extent have inflated false-positive rates. *PNAS* 113 (28): 7900–7905.

Fabbro, F. (1999). *The Neurolinguistics of Bilingualism: An Introduction*. Hove: Psychology Press.

Friederici, A.D. (2012). The cortical language circuit: from auditory perception to sentence comprehension. *Trends in Cognitive Sciences* 16 (5): 262–268.

Gallese, V. and Lakoff, G. (2005). The brain's concepts: the role of the sensory-motor system in conceptual knowledge. *Cognitive Neuropsychology* 22 (3): 455–479.

Gordon, E., Williams, L., Haig, A. et al. (2001). Symptom profile and "gamma" processing in schizophrenia. *Cognitive Neuropsychiatry* 6 (1): 7–19.

Green, D.W., Crinion, J., and Price, C.J. (2006). Convergence, degeneracy and control. *Language Learning* 56 (S1): 99–125.

Grosjean, F. (1989). Neurolinguists, beware! The bilingual is not two monolinguals in one person. *Brain and Language* 36 (1): 3–15.

Grosjean, F. (1998). Studying bilinguals: methodological and conceptual issues. *Bilingualism: Language and Cognition* 1 (2): 131–149.

Grosjean, F. (2001). The bilingual's language modes. In: *One Mind, Two Languages: Bilingual Language Processing* (ed. J.L. Nicol), 284–290. Oxford, UK: Blackwell.

Gullberg, M. and Indefrey, P. (2006). *The Cognitive Neuroscience of Second Language Acquisition*. Malden, MA: Blackwell.

Gusnard, D.A. and Raichle, M.E. (2001). Searching for a baseline: functional imaging and the resting human brain. *Nature Reviews Neuroscience* 2 (10): 685–694.

Haglund, M.M., Berger, M.S., Shamseldin, M. et al. (1994). Cortical localization of temporal lobe language sites in patients with gliomas. *Neurosurgery* 34 (4): 567–576.

Haglund, M.M., Ojemann, G.A., and Blasdel, G.G. (1993). Optimal imaging of bipolar cortical stimulation. *Journal of Neurosurgery* 78 (5): 785–793.

Hagoort, P. (2006). What we cannot learn from neuroanatomy about language learning and language processing: Commentary on Uylings. In: *The Cognitive Neuroscience of Second Language Acquisition* (ed. M. Gullberg and P. Indefrey). Malden, MA: Blackwell.

Hernandez, A.E. (2009). Language switching in the bilingual brain: What's next? *Brain and Language* 109: 133–140.

Hickok, G. and Poeppel, D. (2000). Towards a functional neuroanatomy of speech perception. *Trends in Cognitive Sciences* 4 (4): 131–138.

Hickok, G. and Poeppel, D. (2004). Dorsal and ventral streams: a framework for understanding aspects of the functional anatomy of language. *Cognition* 92: 67–99.

Hickok, G. and Poeppel, D. (2007). The cortical organization of speech processing. *Nature Reviews. Neuroscience* 8 (5): 393–402.

Huettel, S.A., Song, A.W., and McCarthy, G. (2004). *Functional Magnetic Resonance Imaging*. Sunderland, MA: Sinauer Associates.

Huettel, S.A., Song, A.W., and McCarthy, G. (2009). *Functional Magnetic Resonance Imaging*, 2e. Sunderland, MA: Sinauer Associates.

Huttenlocher, P.R. (2002). *Neural Plasticity: The Effects of Environment on the Development of the Cerebral Cortex*. Cambridge, MA: Harvard University Press.

Hymes, D.H. (1972). *Reinventing Anthropology*. New York, NY: Pantheon Books.

Indefrey, P. (2006). A meta-analysis of hemodynamic studies on first and second language processing: which suggested differences can we trust and what do they mean? In: *The Cognitive Neuroscience of Second Language Acquisition* (ed. M. Gullberg and P. Indefrey), 279–304. Malden, MA: Blackwell.

Jakobson, R. (1957/1987). Linguistics and poetics. In: *Language in Literature* (ed. K. Pomorska and S. Rudy), 62–94. Cambridge, MA: Belknap Press of Harvard University Press.

Jakobson, R. (1967/1985). Language and culture. In: *Selected Writings VII* (ed. S. Rudy), 101–112. Berlin, Germany: Mouton.

Jakobson, R. (1985). Communication and Society. In: *Selected Writings VII: Contributions to comparative mythology: Linguistics and Philology 1972–1985* (ed. S. Rudy). Berlin, Germany: Mouton.

Johnson, M. and Lakoff, G. (2002). Why cognitive linguistics requires embodied realism. *Cognitive Linguistics* 13 (3): 245–263.

Kandel, E.R. and Schwartz, J.H. (1991). *Principles of Neural Science*, 3e. Norwalk, CT: Appleton and Lange.

Laird, A.R., Robinson, J.L., McMillan, K.M. et al. (2010). Comparison of the disparity between Talairach and MNI coordinates in functional neuroimaging data: validation of the Lancaster transform. *NeuroImage* 51 (2): 677–683.

Lancaster, J.L., Tordesillas-Gutiérrez, D., Martinez, M. et al. (2007). Bias between MNI and Talairach coordinates analyzed using the ICBM-152 brain template. *Human Brain Mapping* 28 (11): 1194–1205.

Lotman, J.M. (1990). *Universe of the Mind: A Semiotic Theory of Culture. Ann Shukman, (Trs)*. Bloomington: Indiana University Press.

Luo, H. and Poeppel, D. (2007). Phase patterns of neuronal responses reliably discriminate speech in human auditory cortex. *Neuron* 54 (6): 1001–1010.

Maguire, E.A., Spiers, H.J., Good, C.D. et al. (2003). Navigation expertise and the human hippocampus: a structural brain imaging analysis. *Hippocampus* 13 (2): 250–259.

Mahon, B.Z. and Caramazza, A. (2008). A critical look at the embodied cognition hypothesis and a new proposal for grounding conceptual content. *Journal of Physiology, Paris* 102 (1–3): 59–70.

Maldonado, I.L., Menjot de Champfleur, N., Velut, S. et al. (2013). Evidence of a middle longitudinal fasciculus in the human brain from fiber dissection. *Journal of Anatomy* 223 (1): 38–45.

McConnell-Ginet, S. (2003). What's in a name? Social labeling and gender practices. In: *The Handbook of Language and Gender* (ed. J. Holmes and M. Meyerhoff), 69–97. Malden, MA: Blackwell.

Mechelli, A., Crinion, J.T., Noppeney, U. et al. (2004). Neurolinguistics: structural plasticity in the bilingual brain. *Nature* 431 (7010): 757–757.

Menjot de Champfleur, N., Lima, M.I., Moritz-Gasser, S. et al. (2013). Middle longitudinal fasciculus delineation within language pathways: a diffusion tensor imaging study in human. *European Journal of Radiology* 82 (1): 151–157.

Ojemann, G.A. (1983). Brain organization for language from the perspective of electrical stimulation mapping. *Behavioral and Brain Sciences* 6 (2): 189–206.

Ojemann, G.A. (1991). Cortical organization of language. *The Journal of Neuroscience* 11 (8): 2281–2287.

Ojemann, G.A. (1993). Functional mapping of cortical language areas in adults – intraoperative approaches. In: *Electrical and Magnetic Stimulation of the Brain and Spinal Cord* (ed. O. Devinsky, A. Beric and M. Dogali), 155–163. New York, NY: Raven Press.

Ojemann, G.A. (2003). The neurobiology of language and verbal memory: observations from awake neurosurgery. *International Journal of Psychophysiology* 48 (2): 141–146.

Ojemann, G.A. and Whitaker, H.A. (1978). The bilingual brain. *Archives of Neurology* 35 (7): 409–412.

Osterhout, L., MacLaughlin, J., Pitkänen, I. et al. (2006). Novice learners, longitudinal designs and event-related potentials: a means for exploring the neurocognition of second language processing. In: *The Cognitive Neuroscience of Second Language Acquisition* (ed. M. Gullberg and P.

Indefrey), 199–230. Malden, MA: Blackwell Publishers.

Paradis, M. (2004). *A Neurolinguistic Theory of Bilingualism*. Amsterdam, The Netherlands: John Benjamins.

Poeppel, D. (1996). A critical review of PET studies of phonological processing. *Brain and Language* 55 (3): 317–351.

Poeppel, D. (2008). The cartographic imperative: confusing localization and explanation in human brain mapping. In: *Bildwelten des wissens: Ikonographie des gehirns* (ed. H. Bredekamp, M. Bruhn and G. Werner), 1–21. Berlin, Germany: Akademic Verlag.

Poeppel, D. and Hickok, G. (2004). Towards a new functional anatomy of language. *Cognition* 92 (1–2): 1–12.

Price, C.J. (2000). The anatomy of language: contributions from functional neuroimaging. *Journal of Anatomy* 197 (3): 335–359.

Price, C.J. (2010). The anatomy of language: a review of 100 fMRI studies published in 2009. *Annals of the New York Academy of Sciences* 1191 (1): 62–88.

Price, C.J., Green, D.W., and Von, S.R. (1999). A functional imaging study of translation and language switching. *Brain* 1 (22): 2221–2235.

Price, C.J., Wise, R.J., and Frackowiak, R.S. (1996a). Demonstrating the implicit processing of visually presented words and pseudowords. *Cerebral Cortex* 6: 62–70.

Price, C.J., Wise, R., Ramsay, S. et al. (1992). Regional response differences within the human auditory cortex when listening to words. *Neuroscience Letters* 146 (2): 179–182.

Price, C.J., Wise, R.J., Warburton, E.A. et al. (1996b). Hearing and saying. The functional neuro-anatomy of auditory word processing. *Brain: A Journal of Neurology* 119: 919–931.

Raichle, M.E. (2001). Functional neuroimaging: a historical and physiological perspective. In: *Handbook of Functional Neuroimaging of Cognition* (ed. R. Cabeza and A. Kingstone), 3–26. Cambridge, MA: MIT Press.

Raichle, M.E. (2010). Two views of brain function. *Trends in Cognitive Sciences* 14 (4): 180–190.

Raichle, M.E. and Mintun, M.A. (2006). Brain work and brain imaging. *Annual Review of Neuroscience* 29: 449–476.

Roux, F.-E., Lubrano, V., Lauwers-Cances, V. et al. (2004). Intra-operative mapping of cortical areas involved in reading in mono- and bilingual patients. *Brain* 127: 1796–1810.

Schirmer, A., Fox, P.M., and Grandjean, D. (2012). On the spatial organization of sound processing in the human temporal lobe: a meta-analysis. *NeuroImage* 63 (1): 137–147.

Sebeok, T.A. (1991). *A Sign is Just a Sign*. Bloomington: Indiana University Press.

Seeck, M., Pegna, A.J., Ortigue, S. et al. (2006). Speech arrest with stimulation may not reliably predict language deficit after epilepsy surgery. *Neurology* 66 (4): 592–594.

Serafini, S., Friedman, A., Haglund, M., and Gururangan, S. (2008). Identification of distinct and overlapping cortical areas for bilingual naming and reading using cortical stimulation: case report. *Journal of Neurosurgery: Pediatrics* 1 (3): 247–254.

Serafini, S., Grant, G., Haglund, M. et al. (2013). Reorganization and stability for motor and language areas using cortical stimulation. *Brain Sciences* 3 (4): 1597–1614.

Sinha, C. (2007). Cognitive linguistics, psychology, and cognitive science. In: *The Oxford Handbook of Cognitive Linguistics* (ed. D. Geeraerts and H. Cuyckens), 1266–1294. Oxford: Oxford University Press.

Stowe, L.A. (2006). When does the neurological basis of first and second language processing differ? Commentary on Indefrey. *Language Learning* 56: 305–311.

Stowe, L.A., Haverkort, M., and Zwarts, F. (2005). Rethinking the neurological basis of language. *Lingua* 115 (7): 997–1042.

Thompson, P.M. (2005). Abnormal cortical complexity and thickness profiles mapped in Williams syndrome. *Journal of Neuroscience* 25 (16): 4146–4158.

Vygotsky, L.S. (1934/1987). Thinking and speech. In: *The Collected Works of L.S. Vygotsky* (ed. R.W. Rieber and A.S. Carton). New York, NY: Plenum Press.

Vygotsky, L.S. (1934/1999). *Myšlenie i reč*. Moscow, Russia: Labirint.

3 What Do Bilingual Models Tell Us About the Neurocognition of Multiple Languages?

ANGELA GRANT, JENNIFER LEGAULT, AND PING LI

1. Introduction

Although monolingual models of the neurocognition of language continue to dominate the field, in recent years a surge of interest in bilingualism or multilingualism has brought new evidence to our understanding of the neurocognitive mechanisms of language representation and processing. A large number of questions have been asked in the past from a cognitive psychology perspective; for example, when a bilingual speaks, are both languages active? How do bilinguals select between their languages? Are the conceptual meanings associated with individual words shared across translation equivalents, or does each language have a separate conceptual storage space? So far, the answer to each of these, respectively, appears to be 'Yes' (Dijkstra and Van Heuven 2002; Kroll and Stewart 1994; Martin et al. 2009; Midgley et al. 2011; Thierry and Wu 2007); 'It depends' (Costa et al. 1999; Finkbeiner et al. 2006; Green 1998; Kroll et al. 2008); and 'Mostly shared' (Ameel et al. 2005; Pavlenko 2009; Van Hell and De Groot 1998; Zhao and Li 2010). While these questions have been traditionally examined with cognitive and behavioural paradigms, recent studies using neurocognitive methods shed new light on their underlying mechanisms. We provide a review of both the bilingual cognitive models and the neural evidence in support of these models.

2. Activation, Inhibition, and Control

The finding that both of a bilingual's languages are active most of the time leads to the question of how a bilingual is able to successfully select the correct language to use in a particular scenario. While some work suggests that semantic context can constrain the

---

The Handbook of the Neuroscience of Multilingualism, First Edition. Edited by John W. Schwieter.
© 2019 John Wiley & Sons Ltd. Published 2019 by John Wiley & Sons Ltd.

relative activation of each language (Schwartz and Kroll 2006; Titone et al. 2011), a large body of work suggests that the bilingual individual needs to exert a high degree of cognitive control during language processing. An influential model that attempts to account for just this problem is the bilingual interactive activation model (BIA; Dijkstra and Van Heuven 1998).

2.1. The BIA Model

Capitalizing on the mechanisms of the interactive activation (IA) model for monolingual visual word recognition (McClelland and Rumelhart 1981), Dijkstra and van Heuven (1998) proposed the bilingual interactive activation (BIA) model. In the monolingual IA model, there are three levels of nodes, representing features, letters, and words. Between these levels there are two kinds of connections: inhibitory connections between nodes that compete for activation within a level, and across-level connections that cause excitation or inhibition depending on whether features or letters are activated in the recognition process. According to McClelland and Rumelhart (1981), it is these inhibitory and excitatory connections that give rise to the activation of patterns leading to word recognition. The BIA model similarly considered how features, letters, and words interact, but with more complex processes as the interaction occurs in not one, but two languages. Specifically, during reading of a word, feature nodes activate relevant letters, and letter nodes activate words in the relevant language, and words from both languages might interact in the bilingual word recognition processes.

The interactive activation in the BIA model is affected by the reader's proficiency in the language and the current state of language activation. Overall language activation is thought to be affected by recent context, such as previous items in an experimental list, but not by participant expectations. Importantly, because of the interactive nature across languages in the model, activation of features and letters in one language not only spreads to words in that target language, but also to words in the other language. In order to control this cross-language activation, the BIA model proposes a top-down inhibitory control mechanism by using language nodes. First, the language nodes are hypothesized to act as tags that indicate to which language each word belongs. Second, the nodes provide a way to store accumulated activity for each language beyond the word level, and this accumulated activity information is assumed to account for task and situational effects. For example, this function works with the inhibitory control (IC) mechanism (see further discussion on the IC model in Section 2.4) hypothesized to regulate global activity levels for each language, acting as a 'language filter' (Dijkstra and Van Heuven 2002, p. 177).

2.2. The BIA+ Model

The BIA model accounted for orthographic but not semantic or phonological aspects of lexical processing, which limited its ability to account for interactive effects across languages. The BIA+ model (Dijkstra and van Heuven 2002) extended the original BIA model by incorporating semantic and phonological representations and a non-linguistic task/decision system (see Figure 1 for a comparison of the two models). In particular,

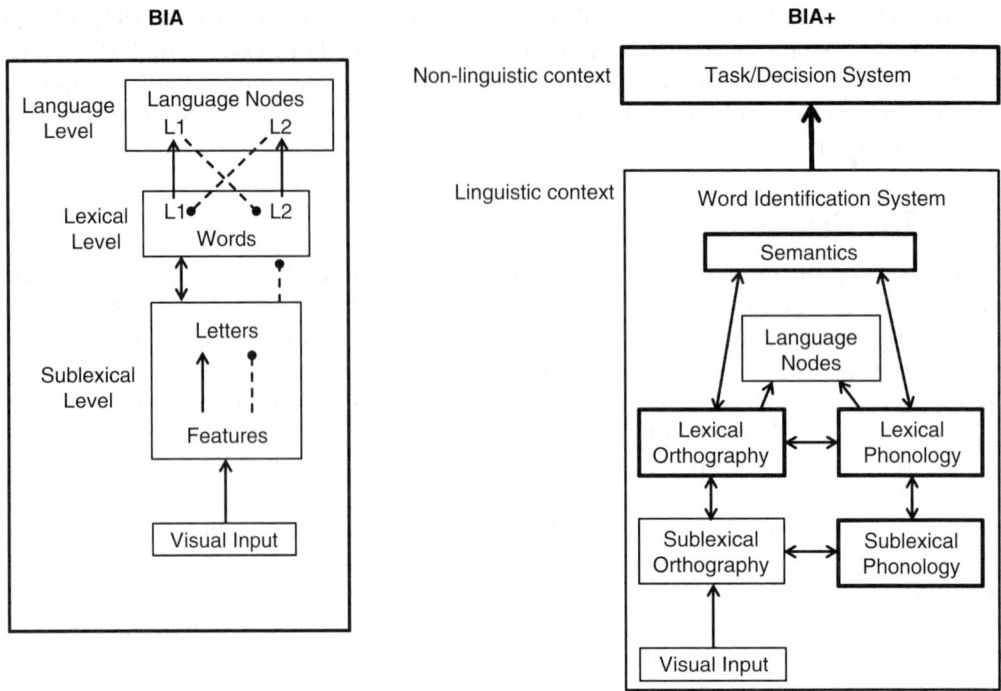

Figure 1   The BIA and BIA+ models. The BIA+ model introduces the task/decision system and distinguishes it from a word identification system. Bolded boxes include elements that have been added or modified in the BIA+ model.

the non-linguistic task/decision system computes processing steps for the current task and determines decision criteria for the task. Unlike in the BIA, non-linguistic expectations by the participants can affect the task system, although the identification system remains theoretically impermeable to these non-linguistic effects. Linguistic context, however, has the ability to affect the identification system (see Dijkstra et al. 2015). The task/decision system receives input from the identification system, which includes its own set of subprocesses. Specifically, when a bilingual reads, the model hypothesizes that the visual input is first processed at the sublexical orthography level, which then connects bidirectionally to the sublexical phonology level and up to the lexical orthography level. From the lexical orthography level, information is passed bidirectionally to the lexical phonology level, and each of those nodes have bidirectional connections to a shared semantic system, as well as bottom-up connections to the language nodes.

The identification system of the BIA+ model retains a similar structure to the system of the BIA model, with the addition of input from phonological and semantic systems. The identification system is joined by a task/decision system, which receives input from the identification system but cannot influence it. Although the BIA+ model represents a significant improvement as compared to BIA, especially with regard to its relevance to neuroimaging evidence, it is still limited in its design as a static model. That is, the model lacks the ability to account for changes in proficiency in one language or another over the lifespan. To capture such changes, Grainger et al. (2010) proposed the developmental variant of the model: the BIA-d model.

Before discussing the BIA-d, however, another developmental simulation of the BIA+ merits attention. Dijkstra et al. (2012) used the BIA+ structure to model lexical processing in simultaneous and late Dutch-English bilinguals. Proficiency and age of acquisition (AoA) were modelled by adjusting the relative frequency of the second language (L2) words (late-learners) and the size of the lexicon (simultaneous). In late learners, the first language (L1) lexicon is considered already established and does not change throughout the simulation (which conflicts with some existing evidence regarding the effect of the L2 on the L1; see Baus et al. 2013; Chang 2012; Linck et al. 2009). In contrast, the L2 lexicon is added gradually after an initial L1-only stage, such that at each following stage L2 words of decreasing frequency are added. When modelling each cohort of words, the model predicts a gradual increase in processing speed in the L2, but these appear to be averaged out in the comparison of the L2 and L1 lexicons overall, as those are depicted with similar processing speeds (which is also in conflict with existing evidence on unbalanced bilinguals, who tend to be slower in L2; e.g. Chauncey et al. 2009; Phillips et al. 2004). In the simulation of simultaneous bilinguals, processing speed is initially faster due to the smaller size of the lexicon, but gradually stabilizes at a rate similar to that predicted for the late-learners (the prediction that simultaneous and late bilinguals engage in lexical processing at similar speeds also conflicts with some existing data; e.g. Sabourin et al. 2014). Thus, while it is possible to adapt the BIA+ to account for aspects of L2 acquisition, the model appears to require more nuanced modification in order to fit existing data. Next, let us examine an alternative developmental form of the BIA, the BIA-d.

2.3. The BIA-d Model

Grainger et al. (2010) proposed a developmental version of the BIA model based on available evidence and models of bilingual lexical access (Dijkstra and Van Heuven 1998; Kroll and Stewart 1994). The BIA-d model's main novel contribution is to describe the development of the inhibitory connections down from the language nodes of the BIA model. Its developmental aspect is based on the predictions of the revised hierarchical model (RHM; Kroll and Stewart 1994). The BIA-d shares the RHM's predictions that lexical processing proceeds through two different routes: L1 to L2 form-based connections; and L2-form to conceptual store connections. The basic assumption is that learners at different proficiency levels utilize these routes to differing degrees. That is, low-proficiency learners are more likely to depend on form-based connections; for example, translation of a word from L2 to L1 in order to understand it shows reliance on a form-based stage. In contrast, more proficient learners, due to their increased exposure to the language, are able to circumvent the L1 and draw directly on the conceptual store. The BIA-d suggests that there is an additional stage beyond the development of these conceptual connections, where form-level inhibitory connections between translation equivalents strengthen pre-existing conceptual connections. The model hypothesizes that these inhibitory connections allow for the improved speed and fluency of L2 use associated with higher levels of L2 proficiency.

It is this final stage of the BIA-d model where it differentiates itself from the RHM – in the development of inhibitory connections between L1 and L2 lexical forms. This time-line is in contrast with what would be predicted by the inhibitory control (IC) model, which predicts more inhibition earlier, rather than later, in learning and will be discussed in Section 2.4 (see also Meade et al. 2018). The consideration of the development that occurs in bilingual representation is a unique feature of the BIA-d model, and is also in line with other computational bilingual models that highlight the importance of learning mechanisms such as the developmental lexicon (DevLex-II) model (Li and Zhao 2013; Zhao and Li 2013), the bilingual single network (BSN) model (Thomas 1997), and the bilingual simple recurrent network (BSRN) model (French 1998; French and Jacquet 2004; see Grosjean and Li 2013).

2.4.   The Inhibitory Control Model

Although the BIA-d was unique in incorporating inhibition into a developmental time-line, it was certainly not the first model to consider the role of inhibition in language production. The IC model, proposed in the late 1990s, explicitly included inhibition in its model name and in the mechanisms that support bilingual processing.

The IC model and the BIA model have some surface level similarities. They both involve a form of language-tagging, assuming that words in individual languages are associated with information about the language to which they belong, and both models utilize task schemas. However, as shown in Figure 2, the way in which these

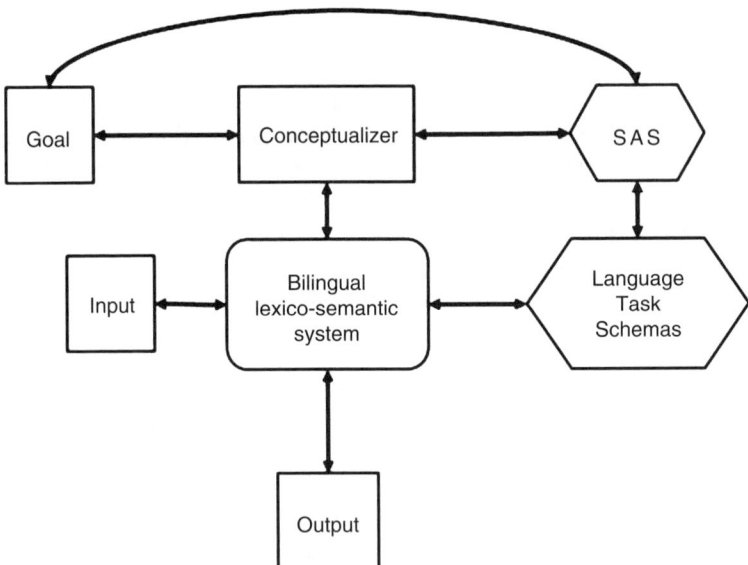

Figure 2   The inhibitory control model (Green 1998). Note: SAS stands for supervisory attentional system.

systems are implemented varies between the two models. Unlike the BIA model, which posited language nodes that could inhibit lexical forms, the IC model tags individual lemmas with language specific information. These tags are typically inhibited or activated by language task schemas, which may compete or cooperate. For example, a lexical decision task has several components, such as seeing the word, reading it, attempting to identify it, identifying it as a word or non-word, and pressing the appropriate button for the selected response. All of these components are wrapped up into its schema. In addition to task schemas, individual lemmas' activation levels may be affected by previous experience or participant intentions. For example, lower levels of proficiency in a language will lead to lower resting activation for words in that language. The model would consequently predict that inhibiting these words would be easier.

In addition to inhibition at the lexical level by the language task schemas, the inhibitory control model also includes non-linguistic control in the form of the supervisory attentional system (SAS; see Norman and Shallice 1986). The language task schemas may be superseded by the SAS, e.g. when performing a new language activity for which we do not have a schema, or when confronted by information that does not fit our preexisting schemas. The SAS can inhibit inappropriate language tags at the lemma level via its connections with the Conceptualizer, and it can also activate appropriate language task schemas, as can be seen in Figure 2.

Although the IC model was proposed two decades ago, its hypotheses continue to be examined in the literature. Liu et al. (2016) extended the IC model to consider how individual differences in inhibition can affect language switching. The authors studied low-proficiency Chinese-English bilinguals that they categorized as either being high or low in inhibitory control abilities based on results from a Simon-switch task. They also asked participants to complete a language-switching task where they had to name pictures while an electroencephalogram (EEG) was recorded. The authors hypothesized that, because L2 switch trials should require more inhibition to suppress the stronger L1, the L2 switch trials should elicit a larger N2 (a negativity occurring around 200 ms) or LPC (a late positive component) component compared to the L1 switch trials. Both components have been associated with inhibition, but because of the difference in timing, they expected that a larger N2 would reflect inhibition at the level of the SAS, while a larger LPC would reflect inhibition at the later lexical response level.

They found that at pre-test, high IC bilinguals showed symmetric behavioural switching costs and while the low IC bilinguals showed asymmetric costs. In the event-related potential (ERP) data, high IC bilinguals showed a larger LPC for L2 switch trials than L1 switch trials, but this effect was absent in the low IC bilinguals. After the pre-test, the low IC bilinguals were given six sessions of training on the Simon-switch task, while the high IC group did not complete any training. At the post-test, both high IC and low IC bilinguals showed symmetric behavioural switching costs. In the ERP data, the LPC did not change for high IC learners, but it did for low IC learners who showed a similar LPC to the high IC bilinguals after training. These data suggested that individual differences in control abilities, as well as linguistic attributes such as proficiency, affect bilingual language processing.

3.   Neural Bases of Cognitive Control in Bilingualism

There has been a wave of research in the last decade that examines the neural basis of bilingual language processing, especially with respect to cognitive control, and the Liu et al. (2016) study discussed above is one of many such examples (see Li et al. 2014, for a review in the context of L2-induced neuroanatomical changes). Most of these studies rely on one of two neuroimaging methods: functional magnetic resonance imaging (fMRI) and ERPs. These two methods complement each other in terms of the evidence they provide. That is, fMRI provides detailed spatial information at the millimetre level about which structures of the brain are involved in a particular task by measuring the blood-oxygenation-level-dependent (BOLD) signal, but measurements of the blood flow in the brain (hemodynamic response) are often slow, and the information about the whole brain (a complete 'volume' of a brain scan) can only be collected approximately once every two seconds. In contrast, ERPs – which are an average of the electrical potential to a particular event (hence, event-related potential or ERP) recorded using electroencephalography – provide highly specific timing information, down to the millisecond, but the spatial information they provide is limited because the information is recorded by electrodes at the scalp. Because of these differences, when referring to fMRI results, we will often talk about activity in a particular brain area (see Table 1 for a summary of all the activity reported in the following sections, organized by brain region), but when referring to ERP results we will often talk about a particular time at which some components, or common ERP responses, occur. More detailed information about these two methods as they apply to research in bilingualism can be found in Grosjean and Li (2013, ch. 10).

The models discussed in Section 2 above, although originally postulated as cognitive models, have been tested in the literature with both fMRI and ERP methods. Below, we review a few key studies that highlight the neural evidence in support of the BIA, BIA+, BIA-d, and IC models. Table 1 provides a summary of the key brain regions and relevant fMRI findings in studies that provide support to the models.

3.1.   *Neural Evidence for the BIA/BIA+ Models*

The two major claims of the BIA models are that first, L1 and L2 lexical networks are integrated, and second, activation of the lexicon is language-independent or language non-selective, which means that lexical items from both languages are initially activated. There appears to be neuroimaging evidence for both of these claims.

3.1.1.   Integrated L1–L2 Lexical Networks   The BIA and BIA+ models hypothesize that bilinguals share a lexical system for their L1 and L2, which has been supported by the neuroimaging literature (see Indefrey 2006; Van Heuven and Dijkstra 2010 for reviews). Isel et al. (2010) examined whether neural networks reflect this shared conceptual lexical system for early versus late French-German adult bilinguals. Their study incorporated a cross-linguistic neural adaptation paradigm to examine repetition enhancement effects for semantic-conceptual representations in response to French and German nouns.

Table 1 Key regions of interest in studies that provide support to the BIA and IC models.

Region of interest	Relevant fMRI findings	Models supported by findings
Anterior Cingulate Cortex (ACC)	• T1 > T2: decreased neural activity (Grant et al. 2015) • Forward switching between L1 and L2 led to activity in the right ACC (Wang et al. 2007) • Inter-language switching > within-language switching in ACC (Abutalebi et al. 2008) • L2>L1 activation during switching in ACC (Abutalebi et al. 2008) • Free>Forced switching led to activation in the ACC (Zhang et al. 2015) • Local inhibition recruits the ACC (Guo et al. 2011)	• IC: Neural activity in control regions decreased over time • IC: Language switching leads to activation in control regions • IC: Inter-language switching recruits cognitive control regions as compared to within-language switching • IC: Task schemas can influence language selection and various tasks lead to differing levels of inhibition • IC: Language-level differences in inhibition exist
Caudate Nucleus (CN)	• Switching between L1 and L2 led to activity in the right CN (Wang et al. 2007) • Inter-language switching > within-language switching in CN (Abutalebi et al. 2008) • L2>L1 activation during switching in ACC (Abutalebi et al. 2008)	• IC: Task switching leads to activation in control regions • IC: Inter-language switching recruits cognitive control regions as compared to within-language switching
Frontal Cortex	• Forward switching between L1 and L2 led to activity in the frontal cortex (Wang et al. 2007) • L2>L1 activation during switching in ACC (Abutalebi et al. 2008)	• IC: Language switching leads to activation in control regions
Inferior Frontal Gyrus (IFG)	• L2–L3 activation during switching in right IFG (de Bruin et al. 2014)	• IC: Processing of L2 and L3 requires less inhibition than L1
Inferior Parietal Lobe (IPL)	• L1>L2 activation during switching in ACC (Abutalebi et al. 2008) • Global inhibition recruits the parietal cortex (Guo et al. 2011)	• IC: L1>L2 switching leads to activation in control regions • IC: Language-level differences in inhibition exist

(Continued)

Table 1 (Continued)

Region of interest	Relevant fMRI findings	Models supported by findings
Insula	• $BI_E > BI_L$: R insula: enhanced repetition effects (Isel et al. 2010) • $BI_L > BI_E$: L insula: enhanced repetition effects (Isel et al. 2010)	• BIA/BIA+: Shared lexical system for early and late bilinguals
Middle Frontal Gyrus (MFG)	• $BI_L > BI_E$: R MFG: enhanced repetition effects (Isel et al. 2010) • T1>T2: decreased neural activity (Grant et al. 2015)	• BIA/BIA+: Shared lexical system for early and late bilinguals • IC: Neural activity in control regions decreased
Prefrontal Cortex (PFC)	• Switching between L1 and L2 led to activity in the bilateral dorsolateral PFC (Wang et al. 2007) • Backward switching led to activity in the lateral PFC (Zhang et al. 2014) • Free>Forced switching led to activation in the dorsolateral and ventrolateral PFC (Zhang et al. 2015) • Global inhibition recruits the dorsolateral PFC (Guo et al. 2011)	• IC: Task switching leads to activation in control regions • IC: task schemas can influence language selection and various tasks lead to differing levels of inhibition • IC: Language-level differences in inhibition exist
Superior Frontal Gyrus (SFG)	• $BI_E > BI_L$: Bilateral SFG: enhanced repetition effects (Isel et al. 2010)	• BIA/BIA+: Shared lexical system for early and late bilinguals
Superior temporal gyrus (STG)	• $BI_E > BI_L$: L STG: enhanced repetition effects (Isel et al. 2010)	• BIA/BIA+: Shared lexical system for early and late bilinguals
Supplementary Motor Area (SMA)	• L2–L3 activation during switching in right pre-SMA (de Bruin et al. 2014) • Free>Forced switching led to activation in the SMA (Zhang et al. 2015) • Local inhibition recruits the SMA (Guo et al. 2011)	• IC: Processing of L2 and L3 requires less inhibition than L1 • IC: Language-level differences in inhibition exist

BIA = bilingual interactive activation; BI_E = early bilinguals; BI_L = late bilinguals; IC = inhibitory control; L1 = native language; L2 = second learned language; L3 = third learned language; T1 = MRI session 1; T2 = MRI session 2.

Repetition enhancement effects have been shown in previous studies in response to repeated stimuli (see James and Gauthier 2005, for a review) and are thought to reflect enhanced or increased neural activity as measured by the BOLD contrast. According to this paradigm, if both early and late bilinguals show repetition enhancement effects in a prefrontal-temporal network including the prefrontal cortex, the anterior insula, and bilateral superior, inferior, and medial temporal gyri, then this is indicative of a shared conceptual representation regardless of the AoA of the L2. On the other hand, if only early bilinguals show repetition enhancement effects in these regions, then L1–L2 shared conceptual representations are likely dependent on AoA (it should be noted that these assumptions are dependent on the spatial resolution of fMRI, which in this study used a smoothing filter of 8 mm). Participants in the study were shown cross-linguistically related or unrelated pairs of words (e.g. on a related trial, participants might see the pair *valise: KOFFER*, both of which mean suitcase), and their task was to make a decision on whether the target word was a natural or man-made item. The results suggested that although there may be some group differences in specific regions, both early and late bilinguals showed repetition enhancement effects in regions comprising the prefrontal-temporal network mentioned above, indicating shared L1–L2 conceptual semantic representations regardless of AoA.

Another study by Leonard et al. (2013) investigated L1 and L2 lexical processing in a unique group of bilinguals: bimodal bilinguals. The authors used a magnetoencephalography (MEG) paradigm to examine neural activation during encoding versus lexico-semantic processing in adults learning American Sign Language (ASL). Encoding of written, spoken, and ASL words have previously shown to occur around 100–200 ms after their presentation, while lexico-semantic processing occurs in a later time window, in the 200–400 ms range (Hickok and Poeppel 2007; Price 2010; Leonard et al. 2010, 2011). During the earlier, encoding time window, participants showed differing networks for English versus ASL words (presented as video clips), with English eliciting activation in the left occipito-temporal and superior temporal cortices, whereas ASL symbols recruited the intraparietal sulcus. During the later time window, indicative of lexico-semantic processing, both English and ASL words showed activation in a left fronto-temporal language network. Therefore, the authors concluded that while neural activation during the encoding stage differed between modalities, lexico-semantic processing at a later stage used a shared frontotemporal network across modalities. The findings from these papers support the hypothesis that L1 and L2 are represented on the same conceptual level, irrespective of AoA and language modality (although possibly distinctly at an earlier encoding stage).

3.1.2. Non-selective Lexical Access   In addition to integrated L1 and L2 networks, the BIA and BIA+ models also propose that lexical access is non-selective. Ng and Wicha (2013) conducted a study that specifically tested this hypothesis. They performed two ERP experiments in Spanish-English balanced bilinguals to examine visual word access: a language-specific lexical decision task (e.g. respond to real words in Spanish) and a language-specific categorical decision task (e.g. respond to Spanish words that refer to a person). They aimed to determine whether (i) language membership inhibits lexical access to non-target (English) words and (ii) whether non-target words could temporarily be treated as targets depending on the semantics of the word. Results from the first experiment showed a larger N400 (a negative-going wave approximately 400 ms post stimulus that is associated with semantic processing) for infrequent words in both the target and non-target languages, which suggests that lexical access to non-target words are not blocked by language membership, in support of the BIA+ model. Importantly, the second experiment in this study was geared towards examining whether the target language used in the task may mediate the timescale of semantic versus language membership processing in balanced bilinguals. Their findings indicated that when Spanish was used as the target language, ERPs first diverged for semantic category at 225 ms, followed by language membership at 350 ms. This is in line with previous studies finding that language membership processing is available either simultaneously with or directly after word retrieval (see Dijkstra and Snoeren 2004, for a review). By contrast, when English was used as the target language, ERPs diverged based on the language used at 150 ms while they diverged based on the word meaning (the semantic category of people versus non-people) at 275 ms, which was interpreted as processing of language membership before semantic information. The authors posited that frequency of language use (English was used more frequently than Spanish for all participants) mediated this relationship, such that when a language is used more frequently, language membership is facilitated and will lead to greater interference when it is not the target language. Interestingly, in another ERP study conducted by Hoversten et al. (2015) that also examined Spanish-English balanced bilinguals, the results based on a Language Go Task (LGT) and a Semantic Go Task (SGT) indicated that across tasks, go trials led to greater positive amplitudes as compared to the no-go trials, with ERP divergences occurring first for the LGT at 300 ms and then for the SGT at 400 ms, indicating that language membership preceded semantics, where N400 frequency effects were found to only partially predict this relationship. The authors propose, based on these data, that language membership may occur early enough in balanced bilinguals to filter word processing, especially when that language is used more frequently, and that semantic processing is ongoing even in the non-target language.

3.2.   *Neural Evidence for the BIA-d Model*

The BIA-d model makes the prediction that with increased proficiency there should be less translation priming between L1 and L2 due to decreasing excitatory connections between the word forms. Further, it proposes that increased inhibition replaces these excitatory connections, and that the inhibition between word forms allows for stronger connections to the semantic store. In the following sections, we review the evidence for these two hypotheses.

3.2.1.   Decreased Excitatory Form-Level Connections   Geyer et al. (2011) investigated the BIA-d's hypothesis that with increased proficiency there should be less translation priming between L1 and L2, due to the development of inhibitory connections between word forms. In their study, they compared within-language repetition effects and between-language translation priming effects on the N400 component, and found symmetrical priming in a sample of highly proficient Russian-English bilinguals. They compared these results to a previous study (Alvarez et al. 2003) investigating less balanced English-Spanish bilinguals, wherein the same paradigm was used but asymmetric priming between languages occurred, with larger priming effects in the L2–L1 direction. Taken together, these findings support the BIA-d hypothesis that increased proficiency results in decreased excitatory connections between lexical forms.

3.2.2. Increased L2 Proficiency Strengthens Connections to the Semantic Store   Another major assumption of the BIA-d is that in adult L2 learners, the L1 has stronger connections to the semantic store, at least at first. In addition, the strength of the L2 connection should be modulated by proficiency. Aparicio et al. (2012) tested this hypothesis by asking French-English-Spanish trilinguals to complete a mixed semantic categorization task while EEG was recorded. They found differences in both latency and amplitude of the N400 component that addressed both of these questions. The latency difference they observed showed that the N400 to L1 words appeared significantly earlier than for L2 or L3 words. Although there was no latency difference between L2 and L3, there was a difference in amplitude, with L3 words showing larger overall amplitude. The authors argued that the earlier latency for the L1 reflects its stronger connection to the semantic store, whereas the differences in amplitude are reflective of the participants' proficiency in their L2 and L3. Consequently, these results suggest that high proficiency does not necessarily always lead to stronger L2-semantic connections, although more research is required to better understand the conditions under which this could occur.

3.2.3. Increased Inhibition Between Word Forms   Perhaps the most important assumption of the BIA-d is that increased proficiency is associated with increased inhibition between word forms. Grant et al. (2015) tested this prediction by asking English-Spanish bilinguals to complete a language decision task during fMRI twice over the course of an academic year. The authors found that, contrary to the predictions of the BIA-d model, activation in areas of the control network (such as the middle frontal gyrus or MFG, and the anterior cingulate cortex or ACC) significantly decreased between testing sessions. In addition, connectivity analyses showed that a typical language processing area, the middle temporal gyrus (MTG), gained connections while the MFG lost connections at a later session. While the data are not entirely clear-cut (e.g. the MFG decreased in activity for homographs but increased for unambiguous Spanish words), the overall pattern offers mixed support for the predictions of the BIA-d. The increase in connectivity with semantic regions supports the BIA-d's prediction that proficiency leads to stronger connections between L2 words and the semantic store, but the decrease in activation and functional connectivity of the control regions conflicts with the BIA-d's proposal that inhibitory connections develop with increased proficiency. The alternative perspective offered by Dijkstra et al. (2012), which predicts lateral inhibition between word forms regardless of proficiency, also does not capture the dynamic pattern of neural recruitment that Grant et al. (2015) observed. In contrast, their results are more in line with the predictions of the IC model (Green, 1998) that bilinguals need less effort of inhibitory control over two languages when proficiency in the L2 increases. We will discuss additional evidence for the IC model in Section 3.3.

3.3. Neural Evidence for the IC Model

The IC model makes several key assumptions that have been tested in the neuroimaging literature. In the following sections, we will discuss evidence for the existence of task schemas, proficiency-modulated lemma activation, and multiple levels of inhibition. We will also discuss a more recent extension of this model in a later section.

3.3.1. Schemas   Christoffels et al. (2013) provided supporting evidence for the concept of task schemas as postulated in the IC (and BIA+) models. In their study, they compared Dutch-English bilinguals' performance on two tasks, a translation task and a naming task, while EEG was recorded. In the translation study, participants saw a word on the screen and were asked to say the translation out loud. The experimenters found that translation direction and homograph status (that is, if the word shared form but not meaning across the two languages) modulated the electrophysiological response to the stimuli. Specifically, they found a larger P2 component (a positive going wave approximately 200 ms post stimulus associated with effort of lexical retrieval) when participants had to translate from L1 to L2. In the opposite direction, from L2 to L1, they found a larger N400. In addition, they also observed a larger N400 when translating homographs compared with unambiguous language stimuli. Interestingly, when the task was changed to reading aloud, the language and homograph effects reduced dramatically. In the naming study there was no behavioural or ERP difference between words named in the L1 versus the L2. In addition, although homographs were named slower overall, there was no accompanying ERP effect. The differing results across the two tasks support the assumption of the IC and BIA+ models that task type influences how and when control is exerted over the language system.

3.3.2. Proficiency-Modulated Lemma Activation   The IC, BIA, and BIA+ models predict that bilinguals have different relative resting activation levels of the lemmas in each of their languages, with less proficient languages having lower activation levels and consequently requiring less effort to inhibit. Support for the idea of proficiency-modulated resting activation has been mixed, with some studies, such as Guo et al. (2013), not finding asymmetric costs between languages of different proficiencies. Guo et al. (2013) studied Uighur-Chinese-English trilinguals when naming digits according to a visually presented cue. The authors examined the n-2 repetition effect – that is, if a participant names in English, then Chinese, then English again, will he benefit from the previous English trial? The authors found a small n-2 repetition effect, but it did not differ between the languages, suggesting that proficiency did not modulate the resting activation of the lemmas. However, this study only required participants to name digits. As we will see below, other studies using more language-like materials have observed the asymmetric costs that the IC model predicts.

Unlike Guo et al. (2013) Wang et al. (2007) did observe asymmetric costs in their fMRI study. They asked Chinese-English bilinguals to perform a switching task where they had to name pictures. They found that switching produced extensive activation in bilateral dorsolateral prefrontal cortex (DLPFC), right cingulate, and caudate (congruent with IC model). Importantly, they also observed different areas of activation depending on the direction of the switch. Forward (L1–L2) but not backward (L2–L1) switching recruited areas typically associated with cognitive control: specifically, the bilateral frontal cortex and ACC. De Bruin et al. (2014) conducted another study of language switching using a picture naming paradigm with Dutch-English-German trilinguals. They also found activation of frontal control areas – specifically the right inferior frontal gyrus (IFG) and pre-supplementary motor area (SMA) – during switches into the participants' less proficient L2 and L3, but not into their L1. Their findings support the idea that the lower resting activation of L2 (and L3) words requires less inhibition than words in the more proficient L1, although the results could also be interpreted as being due to increased excitation necessary to process the L2 and L3.

3.3.3.   Multiple Levels of Inhibition   The IC model predicts that modulation of inhibition based on proficiency is implemented by language task schemas, but the model also predicts that non-linguistic inhibition can occur as implemented by the supervisory attentional system (SAS). This idea of multiple levels of inhibition has been investigated in the neuroimaging literature from different perspectives: linguistically at a local vs. global level, and more broadly comparing language-specific to general executive control.

When we speak about language control at the local and global level, we refer to the concept of reactive, trial-by-trial inhibition compared to sustained inhibition of an entire language. Guo et al. (2011) conducted a study to investigate these phenomena. In their study, they administered a picture-naming task in two orders, L1 first vs. L2 first, both followed by mixed naming. To measure local inhibition, they compared performance on blocked vs. mixed naming across groups. To measure global inhibition, they compared performance in the L1 block vs. the L2 block. They found that local inhibition recruited ACC and SMA, while global inhibition recruited DLPFC and parietal cortex. Their findings support the proposal of different levels of inhibition in the IC model, and additionally provide a way to interpret previous data that had not explicitly considered the difference between these types of control. Another study by Peeters and Dijkstra (2017) also used a picture-naming paradigm to investigate local vs. global language control, with the addition of monolingual virtual interlocutors to cue each language. Across four experiments they found symmetric switch costs in each language, reversed language dominance such that L1 responses were slower than L2 responses, and mixing costs that were limited to the L1. Their EEG data corroborated their behavioural data, showing a late (500–700 ms) centrally distributed negativity to switches regardless of language, as well as an enhanced negativity for the L1-only block compared to both the L2-only block and the L1 non-switch trials in the mixed block. These results suggest that their participants were primarily engaging global, as compared to local, language control – contrary to the predictions of the IC model. The authors suggest that the relatively long response-cue asynchrony in their study could have prevented their observation of more reactive local-level inhibition, and future research is needed to better understand the role of each of these processes in language control.

Other research has concentrated on the distinction between language control and generalized executive control. For example, Zhang et al. (2015) examined the effect of volition (i.e. free vs. forced) on language switching during fMRI scanning. A conjunction analysis of the free and forced switching trials found no spatial overlap between the two trial types, although there was an overall effect of volition that implicated frontoparietal regions including the SMA, ACC, PMC (premotor cortex), DLPFC, ventrolateral PFC and PPC (posterior parietal cortex). These data support the IC model's predictions that task schemas can influence the process of language selection, and also suggest that different tasks may recruit different types or levels of inhibition.

4.   Bilingual Models and the Brain: New Extensions

The neural evidence for or against specific bilingual models as discussed has inspired researchers to further extend their work to new horizons in the last few years. Two new models, the adaptive control model and the conditional routing model have contributed to our understanding on top of the bilingual models and neural evidence discussed above. Additionally, there are several new fruitful directions for exciting research into the study of bilingual language processing and the brain, specifically with regard to brain networks and the connectivity underlying bilingualism, L2-induced structural brain changes, and individual differences in second language learning. In this section, we discuss the two new models, and follow this by looking at the new directions.

4.1.   The Adaptive Control Model

The adaptive control (AC) model (Green and Abutalebi 2013) predicts not just that cognitive control is used during bilingual language comprehension and production, but that the type of cognitive control exerted depends on the context of bilingual language use. Specifically, the AC model outlines three contexts: single-language, dual-language, and dense code switching. Each of these contexts is proposed to have specific effects on the eight different types of cognitive control processes that the authors propose – goal maintenance, interference control, salient cue detection, selective response inhibition, task engagement, task disengagement, and opportunistic planning – and each of these effects is related to particular brain regions.

4.1.1.   Contexts and Processes   In the first context, the single-language context, the use of the two languages is separated entirely by contextual cues. That is, one language may be used exclusively at home, and another exclusively at work. In contrast, dual-language contexts are those where the choice of language is determined primarily by the speaker, rather than the location. The AC model suggests that code switching, or the flexible use of two languages within a conversation, may occur in dual-language contexts, but probably does not occur within single sentences. This contrasts with dense code switching contexts, where both languages are used with multiple speakers in multiple locations, and code switching occurs often and at the intra-sentential level (within single sentences).

These patterns of language use are expected to have particular effects on the eight types of cognitive control outlined in the model. At a general level, bilinguals in single-language contexts will show small changes in goal maintenance and interference control, while those in dual language-contexts will show large changes on the aforementioned aspects of control and small changes on all others except opportunistic planning, which will be primarily affected by dense code-switching environments. First, *goal maintenance* refers to the speakers' ability to set and maintain a task goal, such as speaking in one language but not the other. Maintaining that goal requires *control of interference*. Interference control is composed of two subprocesses, conflict monitoring and interference suppression. The next four types of control are only proposed to be relevant in dual-language contexts, where the cues to use one language or the other are less stable. Consequently, bilinguals in these situations must engage in *salient cue detection* (e.g. noticing when a new speaker enters the room), *selective response inhibition* (to override the current action) and the processes of *task engagement* and *task disengagement*. These processes are considered as separate from *selective response inhibition* due to the global, rather than focal, locus of inhibition and activation that they require. Finally, *opportunistic planning* is defined as 'making use of whatever comes most readily to hand to achieve a goal' (Green and Abutalebi 2013, p. 519). That is, in dense code-switching contexts where all speakers are bilingual, bilinguals are able to use whichever words and grammatical structures that are currently most active to express their meaning.

These contexts and control processes have distinct neural substrates according to the AC model (see Figure 3 for an illustration). Specifically, the parietal cortex has been implicated in the literature on goal maintenance, while the left prefrontal and inferior cortex, the ACC and pre-SMA are related to interference control. These regions are predicted to be more active in single-language contexts. In contrast, bilinguals in dual-language contexts recruit these areas and more, including regions associated with cue detection (right inferior frontal cortex and thalamus), and language switching (pre-SMA, caudate nucleus of the basal ganglia). Finally, dense code switching is predicted to rely on connections between the right cerebellum and the left inferior frontal cortex, which have previously been indicated in the control of morphosyntax and aphasia.

4.1.2. Neural Correlates of Language Control Findings from several recent studies are consistent with the predictions of the AC model (e.g. Blanco-Elorrieta and Pylkkänen 2016; Branzi et al. 2016). For example, Branzi et al. (2016) collected fMRI data while participants named pictures in either their L1 or L2 and found that naming in the L2 after having named in L1 (the L2 local control condition) showed increases in the dorsal ACC and pre-supplementary motor area, which were interpreted as being due to the increased monitoring demands. This interpretation supports the predictions of the AC model that these areas are involved in the monitoring aspect of interference control. In contrast, naming in L1 after having named in L2 (the L1 local control condition) elicited more activation bilaterally in right prefrontal and inferior parietal cortex, which was interpreted as representing response selection, based on findings from behavioural language-switching studies, where naming in L1 becomes more difficult after naming in L2. The differentiation that Branzi et al. make between monitoring systems and response selection systems, however, is not necessarily congruent with the predictions of the AC model, which associates parietal activity with goal maintenance, and left and right inferior frontal activity with interference control and cue detection, respectively. One could make the argument that goal maintenance and interference control are subcomponents of response selection, but future research is needed to reconcile these findings and establish a hierarchy of language control processes and associated neural systems.

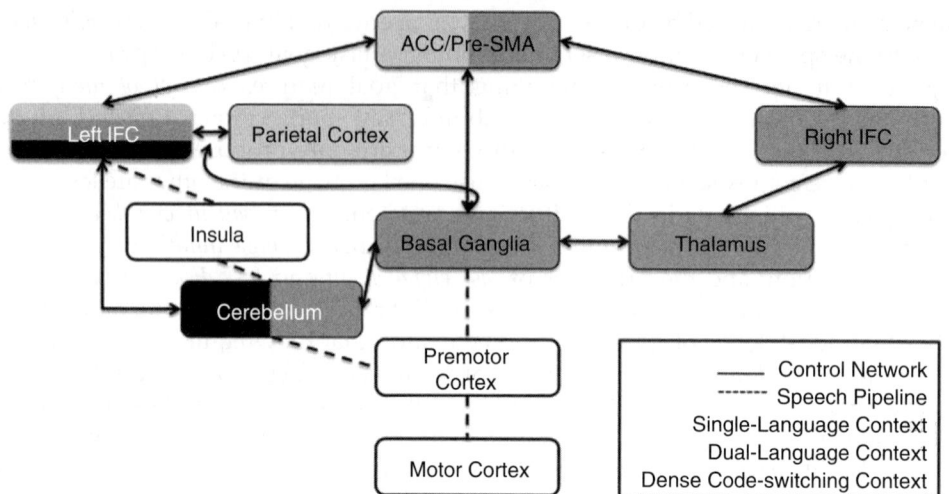

Figure 3   The adaptive control model and its neural substrates. Note: ACC/Pre-SMA = anterior cingulate cortex/pre-supplementary motor area; IFC = inferior frontal cortex.

In another study, Blanco-Elorrieta and Pylkkänen (2016) tested language control in both language comprehension and production, although explanations for any discrepancy between these two modalities are not currently included in the AC model. The authors assessed the neural correlates of these processes using magnetoencephalography (MEG). They found that in production, both language-switching and category-switching elicited activity in the prefrontal cortex, similar to what Branzi et al. (2016) observed in their production study. In comprehension, language-switching relied on the ACC, although category-switching did not. The finding that control regions may be recruited differently during comprehension and production has important implications for the AC model, because bilinguals who could be considered as coming from the same context may have unequal experience in language comprehension compared with production. For example, in situations where languages are differently valued in the community, bilinguals may predominantly understand the heritage language that their family speaks at home, but may not produce that language much themselves and prefer preferring to use the more socially acceptable community language.

4.2.   The Conditional Routing Model

In contrast to the adaptive control model, the conditional routing (CR) model by Stocco et al. (2014), focuses on the deployment of inhibitory control during bilingual language processing and how this may affect generalized executive control skills. The CR model makes predictions about the role of the basal ganglia specifically and the cerebral cortex generally during bilingual language use, and its predictions are based on a computational model, the conditional routing model. The basal ganglia are a set of key subcortical structures that include the caudate, putamen, nucleus accumbens, pallidum, substantia nigra, and subthalamic nuclei, which play significant roles for sequence learning, cognitive control, and categorization (see Braulich and Seger 2013, for review). In the CR model, information flows between cortical regions typically are based on the relative strength of the connections between those regions, which is established via previous practice and reward experience. In their model, the role of the basal ganglia is to increase the strength of the cortical connections that would otherwise not have been selected due to lower resting activation. They note that the striatum (a structure that contains both the caudate and putamen) is particularly well suited to this task due to its internal organization, which mirrors the cortico-cortical network. Furthermore, they have shown that this routing function can be modelled as the execution of conditional rules (i.e. if X, then Y).

Stocco et al. (2014) argued that language switching is a complex task, whose rules often go beyond the type of stimulus–response contingencies encoded within cortico-cortical connections. Consequently, they suggest, based in part on previous evidence (e.g. Abutalebi et al. 2007; Crinion et al. 2006; Wartenburger et al. 2003) that language-switching invokes the basal ganglia due to the necessity of selecting the connection with lower resting activation. Because bilingualism by necessity involves language switching, the authors suggested that bilingualism improves top-down control ability, which includes both language control and general cognitive control. This model is congruent with a number of neuroimaging studies implicating the basal ganglia and specifically the caudate nucleus as being critical for language and cognitive control (e.g. Crinion et al. 2006; Tan et al. 2011; Wang et al. 2013). In short, the conditional routing model suggests that the role of the basal ganglia is to strengthen previously established connections in order to override the currently most active connection, as is necessary during language- or task-switching.

4.2.1. Bilingual Language Use Affects the Basal Ganglia   Recent work by Hervais-Adelman et al. (2015) confirm the CR model's predictions that bilingual language use, and in particular the need to control two languages, draws on and affects the basal ganglia. Hervais-Adelman et al. (2015) conducted a longitudinal study that tested bilinguals at the beginning and the end of simultaneous interpreter training, as well as a control set of proficiency-matched bilinguals, on their abilities to simultaneously interpret and shadow speech. Their univariate analysis found that interpreter training caused a significant decrease in the activity of the right caudate nucleus during interpretation, and an additional supplementary multivariate analysis indicated differences in the thalamus, cerebellum, left IFG, and superior temporal gyrus (STG), sensorimotor and supplementary motor areas, as well as the caudate. Thus, their data suggest that changes to bilingual language use – in this case operationalized as simultaneous interpreter training – actively affects the brain, including the regions of the basal ganglia that the CR models predicts should be affected by bilingualism.

4.2.2. Effects of Bilingualism on Cortical Connections   One way in which the CR model may need to be expanded is in its predictions about the effect of bilingualism on cortical connections. Specifically, two studies that attempted to test the CR model by testing bilingual and monolingual performance on executive control tasks found differences attributed to bilingualism in cortical, in addition to subcortical, networks (Becker et al. 2016; Costumero et al. 2015).

Becker et al. (2016) collected fMRI data while bilingual and monolingual participants performed a rapid instructed learning task. Their dynamic causal modelling analysis (Stephan et al. 2009) tested three network models, each of which included the ACC, caudate, DLPFC, and PPC, as well as the influence of different components of the task, such as encoding and execution. They found that the best model was one where the novel execution aspect of the task modulated the connections between the ACC and DLPFC as well as the ACC and caudate. This result is only partially compatible with the CR model, which predicts that bilinguals use the basal ganglia to affect cortical connections, rather than the ACC. Interestingly, the authors did observe a difference in the connection between the DLPFC and the striatum (composed of the caudate and putamen) between monolinguals and bilinguals, such that while activity in the striatum was positively correlated with activity in the DLPFC in both groups, this relationship was stronger in monolinguals. Becker et al. propose that this may be due to frequent rerouting of information to the DLPFC by the striatum in bilinguals (as predicted by the CR), which could lead to decreased sensitivity of this connection. Whether that is in fact the mechanism is an issue for future research.

In another study testing the effect of bilingualism on executive control, Costumero et al. (2015) examined the BOLD response to a go/no-go task by bilinguals and monolinguals. They hypothesized that the bilinguals would recruit greater activity in areas associated with language control (e.g. the left IFG and the left caudate) compared with monolinguals, and they predicted that the monolinguals would draw more on right IFG and the ACC. Their results were partially consistent with these hypotheses, in that they did observe greater recruitment of left IFG (as well as number of other regions) by bilinguals during task conditions that required more cognitive control, specifically infrequent-go trials and no-go trials. However, the basal ganglia and specifically the caudate were not implicated in these networks, which violates the predictions of the CR model.

5.   New Directions in Understanding the Neural Basis of Multiple Languages

In this final section, we follow up on the above discussion of the bilingual models and point out some new directions in the study of the neurocognitive mechanisms underlying the representation and processing of multiple languages.

5.1.   *Brain Networks Underlying Bilingual Language Processing*

Of the fMRI studies discussed above, only a few (e.g. Becker et al. 2016) moved beyond traditional methods that identify task-associated regions to investigate the underlying functional networks (i.e. relationships between regions). Yet, as demonstrated in the Becker et al. study, examining bilingual brain networks has the potential to inform current and future models of bilingual language processing.

Connectivity studies of bilingual language use have already enriched our knowledge of multiple aspects of bilingualism, including the question of who is likely to become a successful bilingual at all (see Li and Grant 2015 for a review). Veroude et al. (2010) conducted one of the first studies to use this technique. In their study, participants observed weather charts and listened to weather reports given in a foreign language, Mandarin Chinese. Based on participants' performance on a word recognition task after learning, the authors classified the participants into successful learners vs. non-successful learners and compared the functional connectivity of these two groups. The results indicated that the successful learners had greater connectivity between the left and right supramarginal gyrus than the non-successful learners after training. Perhaps more interesting, differences in the participants' connectivity at rest, even before training, was also predictive of their learning success. Participants who would go on to become better learners showed stronger connections between the left SMA and precentral gyrus, as well the insula and rolandic operculum, suggesting that there may be pre-existing differences in the brain connectivity of the participants that predict L2 learning success.

Functional connectivity can also be assessed using EEG. Prat et al. (2016) found that resting state quantitative EEG was able to predict up to 60% of the variance in individuals' second language acquisition success during eight weeks of French training using immersive virtual software. Specifically, they found that power in the beta and low gamma frequencies over right temporo-parietal areas were strongly and positively correlated with second language learning outcomes, whereas behavioural measures of fluid intelligence, working memory, and executive control were not.

Other studies have found that connectivity between particular regions may be indicative of language learning success in specific domains. For example, Xiang et al. (2012) found that structural connectivity in the white matter between the IFG and the posterior temporal lobe is predictive of grammatical success, while the connections between the IFG and parietal lobe are more indicative of vocabulary success. Although studies of structural connectivity (i.e. white matter) are not directly comparable to functional connectivity (which is based on the BOLD signal produced by grey matter), the relationship between these two aspects of the brain is an important area of current and future research. This brings us to the impact of L2 experience on brain structure.

5.2.   Effects of Bilingual Language Use on Brain Structure

A number of recent studies have shown that grey and white matter (neural cell bodies and their connections, respectively) differ between monolinguals and bilinguals, and structural/neuroanatomical as well as functional brain changes result from L2 experience. A recent review of L2-associated structural changes in the brain (Li et al. 2014) outlined various structures that were found to be larger in bilinguals as compared to monolinguals, many of which are implicated in both the language network and the cognitive control network (Abutalebi and Green 2007; see also discussions of the IC and the AC models in Sections 3.3 and 4.1). These findings suggest that many of the same regions that have been shown to differ in terms of neural activation also differ in grey matter structure between monolinguals and bilinguals.

L2 training studies have indicated that (i) the regions that increase in grey matter structure after L2 training (compared to controls) are often also implicated in fMRI studies of language processing, and (ii) some of the regions that showed grey matter changes for L2 training were also found to be greater for those who had undergone non-linguistic training, indicating that experience-dependent neuroplasticity has shared neural substrates for linguistic and non-linguistic tasks (but with some important differences). Importantly, individual differences in L2 proficiency and AoA, along with various cognitive abilities, were associated with many of these L2 experience-related grey matter differences and changes.

In addition to grey matter changes, white matter differences between bilinguals and monolinguals have also been identified in diffusion tensor imaging (DTI) studies, which examine the structural connectivity (white matter) of the brain. Because there have been only a few white matter studies, the results so far are mixed, with some studies showing greater white matter microstructure for bilinguals as compared to monolinguals (Luk et al. 2011), while others the reverse (Cummine and Boliek 2013). García-Pentón et al. (2014) studies showed greater interconnectivity in regions implicated in cognitive control and executive function. In general, these results demonstrate the significant individual variance in white matter microstructure, indicating that L2-related changes or differences are likely dependent on the nature of the task and the age of the learner.

While the observed structural brain changes that occur due to L2 experience are in line with many fMRI studies, there is currently no model for neuroanatomical changes or differences in the brain structure associated with L2 experience. Future investigation into a possible structural model of neural changes, and how these might be affected by variables such as AoA, language proficiency, extent or effort of learning, and nature of the language input, would be beneficial to our understanding of brain, mind, and behavioural relationships in the context of multiple language use and processing (see Li et al., 2014 for discussion).

5.3. *Identifying and Predicting Individual Differences in Bilingualism*

Both the brain networks perspective and the structural brain change studies point to a long-standing question in psychology: Can we identify and predict individual differences in learning? A number of brain imaging studies of L2 learning, inspired by the brain network approach towards individual differences, have been performed (e.g. Sheppard et al. 2012; Xiang et al. 2012; Yang et al. 2015). Multiple authors have espoused the brain network approach towards the understanding of individual differences in recent years (e.g. Bassett et al. 2011; Sporns 2011; Uddin et al. 2011), and new exciting work has shown that data-driven network analysis can serve to fingerprint individual participants' brain functions and structures (e.g. Finn et al. 2015).

One example of this approach in the L2 context comes from Sheppard et al. (2012), who analysed the functional brain networks of participants in a study of tone learning to see if functional brain differences between the successful and less successful learners during auditory discrimination of the acquired tones might characterize the efficiency of the underlying brain networks for learning sound-to-word mappings. In particular, the authors defined the efficiency of the brain networks in terms of the average number of connections (edges) between key brain regions of interest (nodes): the fewer the number of edges needed to go from one node to the other, the more efficient the network is. In their study nodes were based on the Desikan-Killiany atlas, with 998 equally sized nodes per hemisphere. Edges were included in the model when the correlation between any two nodes exceeded a particular threshold (ranging from 0.02 to 0.4, based on the fraction of existing to possible connections). They found that the successful learners and the less successful learners had distinct profiles in their global efficiency as estimated by the small-world network typologies: the former had a more cost-efficient network organization that was positively associated with sound-to-word learning abilities. In addition, the successful learners showed more efficiency in key brain regions that are associated with working memory (e.g. DLPFC and inferior parietal cortex) and speech processing (e.g. middle and inferior temporal cortex).

In another study, Yang et al. (2015) similarly examined second language lexical tone by testing participants in a six-week training session. With a pre-test (T1) and post-test (T2) training and fMRI testing schedule, the participants were scanned at T1 and T2 in response to the same stimuli. A separate group of participants served as a control group who did not go through training but were also scanned at T1 and T2. This procedure allowed the authors to effectively track neural changes underlying both learners' and non-learners' behaviour. A major finding from this study was that the successful learners showed brain network patterns that were significantly different from the patterns of the less successful learners or the non-learners (control participants), as revealed by the effective connectivity analyses using a structural equation modelling (Gates et al. 2011; Gates and Molenaar 2012). Specifically, the successful learners, as compared with both the less successful learners and the non-learners, displayed a network with more connected, better-integrated multi-path nodes at T2 after learning. In addition, the successful learners, as compared with the other two groups, had a better-connected brain network even at T1, that is, even before learning took place. This raised the possibility that we can use brain network analysis to make informed predictions as to who might be the more successful learners in a second language-learning task.

The Yang et al. study further identified a correlation between cognitive ability (IQ), brain activation, and the participants' performance in the L2 learning task. Such a correlation led the authors to hypothesize that there might be relationships underlying individual differences in brain-behaviour correspondences that researchers should examine in future studies. We can better understand individual differences in language learning by identifying variations in cognitive control, working memory, and language aptitude, and these variations can be used as predicting variables for successes or failures in L2 learning, and be related to the underlying neural signatures to clearly reveal the cognition-brain-behaviour relationships. Much more exciting work in the study of brain networks, brain changes, and individual differences awaits researchers interested in multilingualism and second language acquisition.

Acknowledgement

We acknowledge that the writing of this chapter was made possible by grants from the National Science Foundation (BCS-1349110, BCS-1533625) to PL, and from the Research and Graduate Studies Office and the Huck Institutes of the Life Sciences to AG and JL, respectively.

REFERENCES

Abutalebi, J., Annoni, J.M., Zimine, I. et al. (2008). Language control and lexical competition in bilinguals: an event-related fMRI study. *Cerebral Cortex* 18 (7): 1496–1505.

Abutalebi, J., Brambati, S.M., Annoni, J.-M. et al. (2007). The neural cost of the auditory perception of language switches: an event-related functional magnetic resonance imaging study in bilinguals. *The Journal of Neuroscience* 27 (50): 13762–13769. https://doi.org/10.1523/JNEUROSCI.3294-07.2007.

Abutalebi, J. and Green, D. (2007). Bilingual language production: the neurocognition of language representation and control. *Journal of Neurolinguistics* 20 (3): 242–275.

Alvarez, R.P., Holcomb, P.J., and Grainger, J. (2003). Accessing word meaning in two languages: an event-related brain potential study of beginning bilinguals. *Brain and Language* 87 (2): 290–304.

Ameel, E., Storms, G., Malt, B.C., and Sloman, S.A. (2005). How bilinguals solve the naming problem. *Journal of Memory and Language* 53 (1): 60–80.

Aparicio, X., Midgley, K.J., Holcomb, P.J. et al. (2012). Language effects in trilinguals: an ERP study. *Frontiers in Psychology* 3: 402.

Bassett, D.S., Wymbs, N.F., Porter, M.A. et al. (2011). Dynamic reconfiguration of human brain networks during learning. *Proceedings of the National Academy of Sciences* 108 (18): 7641–7646.

Baus, C., Costa, A., and Carreiras, M. (2013). On the effects of second language immersion on first language production. *Acta Psychologica* 142 (3): 402–409. https://doi.org/10.1016/j.actpsy.2013.01.010.

Becker, T.M., Prat, C.S., and Stocco, A. (2016). A network-level analysis of cognitive flexibility reveals a differential influence of the anterior cingulate cortex in bilinguals versus monolinguals. *Neuropsychologia* 85: 62–73.

Blanco-Elorrieta, E. and Pylkkänen, L. (2016). Bilingual language control in perception versus action: MEG reveals comprehension control mechanisms in anterior cingulate cortex and domain-general control of production in dorsolateral prefrontal cortex. *The Journal of Neuroscience* 36 (2): 290–301.

Branzi, F.M., Della Rosa, P.A., Canini, M. et al. (2016). Language control in bilinguals: monitoring and response selection. *Cerebral Cortex* 26 (6): 2367–2380.

Braunlich, K. and Seger, C. (2013). The basal ganglia. *Wiley Interdisciplinary Reviews: Cognitive Science* 4 (April): 135–148. https://doi.org/10.1002/wcs.1217.

Chang, C.B. (2012). Rapid and multifaceted effects of second-language learning on first-language speech production. *Journal of Phonetics* 40 (2): 249–268. https://doi.org/10.1016/j.wocn.2011.10.007.

Chauncey, K., Holcomb, P.J., and Grainger, J. (2009). Primed picture naming within and across languages: an ERP investigation. *Cognitive, Affective, & Behavioral Neuroscience* 9 (3): 286–303. https://doi.org/10.3758/CABN.9.3.286.

Christoffels, I.K., Ganushchak, L., and Koester, D. (2013). Language conflict in translation: an ERP study of translation production. *Journal of Cognitive Psychology* 25 (5): 646–664.

Costa, A., Miozzo, M., and Caramazza, A. (1999). Lexical selection in bilinguals: do words in the bilingual's two lexicons compete for selection? *Journal of Memory and Language* 41 (3): 365–397.

Costumero, V., Rodríguez-Pujadas, A., Fuentes-Claramonte, P., and Ávila, C. (2015). How bilingualism shapes the functional architecture of the brain: a study on executive control in early bilinguals and monolinguals. *Human Brain Mapping* 36 (12): 5101–5112.

Crinion, J., Turner, R., Grogan, A. et al. (2006). Language control in the bilingual brain. *Science* 312: 1537–1540.

Cummine, J. and Boliek, C.A. (2013). Understanding white matter integrity stability for bilinguals on language status and reading performance. *Brain Structure & Function* 218 (2): 595–601.

De Bruin, A., Roelofs, A., Dijkstra, T., and FitzPatrick, I. (2014). Domain-general inhibition areas of the brain are involved in language switching: fMRI evidence from trilingual speakers. *NeuroImage* 90: 348–359. https://doi.org/10.1016/j.neuroimage.2013.12.049.

Dijkstra, T., Haga, F., Bijsterveld, A., and Sprinkhuizen-Kuyper, I. (2012). Lexical competition in localist and distributed connectionist models of L2 acquisition. In: *Memory, Language and Bilingualism: Theoretical and Applied Approaches* (ed. J. Altarriba and L. Isurin), 48–73. Cambridge, UK: Cambridge University Press.

Dijkstra, T. and Snoeren, N. (2004). Appartenance linguistique dans la reconnaissance et la production des mots chez les bilingues. In: *Psycholinguistique Cognitive: Essais en l'honneur de Juan Seguí* (ed. L. Ferrand and J. Grainger), 377–399. Louvain-la-Neuve, Belgique: De Boeck Supérieur doi:10.3917/dbu.ludov.2004.01.0377.

Dijkstra, T., Van Hell, J.G., and Brenders, P. (2015). Sentence context effects in bilingual word recognition: cognate status, sentence language, and semantic constraint. *Bilingualism: Language and Cognition* 18 (4): 597–613. https://doi.org/10.1017/S1366728914000388.

Dijkstra, T. and van Heuven, W.J. (1998). The BIA model and bilingual word recognition. In: *Localist Connectionist Approaches to Human Cognition* (ed. J. Grainger and A.M. Jacobs), 189–225. Maywah, NJ: Lawrence Erlbaum Associates.

Dijkstra, T. and Van Heuven, W.J. (2002). The architecture of the bilingual word recognition system: from identification to decision. *Bilingualism: Language and Cognition* 5 (03): 175–197.

Finkbeiner, M., Gollan, T., and Caramazza, A. (2006). Bilingual lexical access: what is the (hard) problem. *Bilingualism: Language and Cognition* 9 (2): 153–166.

Finn, E.S., Shen, X., Scheinost, D. et al. (2015). Functional connectome fingerprinting: identifying individuals using patterns of brain connectivity. *Nature Neuroscience* 18 (11): 1664–1671.

French, R. M. (1998). A simple recurrent network model of bilingual memory. In *Proceedings of the 20th Annual Conference of the Cognitive Science Society* (pp. 368–373). Mahwah, NJ: Erlbaum.

French, R.M. and Jacquet, M. (2004). Understanding bilingual memory: models and data. *Trends in Cognitive Sciences* 8 (2): 87–93.

García-Pentón, L., Fernández, A.P., Iturria-Medina, Y. et al. (2014). Anatomical connectivity changes in the bilingual brain. *NeuroImage* 84: 495–504.

Gates, K.M. and Molenaar, P. (2012). Group search algorithm recovers effective connectivity maps for individuals in homogeneous and heterogeneous samples. *NeuroImage* 63 (1): 310–319.

Gates, K.M., Molenaar, P., Hillary, F.G., and Slobounov, S. (2011). Extended unified SEM approach for modeling event-related fMRI data. *NeuroImage* 54 (2): 1151–1158.

Geyer, A., Holcomb, P.J., Midgley, K.J., and Grainger, J. (2011). Processing words in two languages: an event-related brain potential study of proficient bilinguals. *Journal of Neurolinguistics* 24 (3): 338–351.

Grainger, J., Midgley, K., and Holcomb, P.J. (2010). Re-thinking the bilingual interactive-activation model from a developmental perspective (BIA-d). In: *Language Acquisition across Linguistic and Cognitive Systems* (ed. M. Kail and M. Hickmann), 267–284. New York, NY: John Benjamins.

Grant, A.M., Fang, S.Y., and Li, P. (2015). Second language lexical development and cognitive control: a longitudinal fMRI study. *Brain and Language* 144: 35–47.

Green, D.W. (1998). Mental control of the bilingual lexico-semantic system. *Bilingualism: Language and Cognition* 1 (02): 67–81.

Green, D.W. and Abutalebi, J. (2013). Language control in bilinguals: the adaptive control hypothesis. *Journal of Cognitive Psychology* 25 (5): 515–530.

Grosjean, F. and Li, P. (2013). *The Psycholinguistics of Bilingualism*. New York, NY: Wiley.

Guo, T., Liu, H., Misra, M., and Kroll, J.F. (2011). Local and global inhibition in bilingual word production: fMRI evidence from Chinese–English bilinguals. *NeuroImage* 56 (4): 2300–2309.

Guo, T., Ma, F., and Liu, F. (2013). An ERP study of inhibition of non-target languages in trilingual word production. *Brain and Language* 127 (1): 12–20.

Hervais-Adelman, A., Moser-Mercer, B., and Golestani, N. (2015). Brain functional plasticity associated with the emergence of expertise in extreme language control. *NeuroImage* 114: 264–274.

Hickok, G. and Poeppel, D. (2007). The cortical organization of speech processing. *Nature Reviews Neuroscience* 8 (5): 393–402.

Hoversten, L.J., Brothers, T., Swaab, T.Y., and Traxler, M.J. (2015). Language membership identification precedes semantic access: suppression during bilingual word recognition. *Journal of Cognitive Neuroscience* 27 (11): 2108–2116.

Indefrey, P. (2006). A meta-analysis of hemodynamic studies on first and second language processing: which suggested differences can we trust and what do they mean? *Language Learning* 56: 279–304. https://doi.org/10.1111/j.1467-9922.2006.00365.x.

Isel, F., Baumgaertner, A., Thrän, J. et al. (2010). Neural circuitry of the bilingual mental lexicon: effect of age of second language acquisition. *Brain and Cognition* 72 (2): 169–180.

James, T.W. and Gauthier, I. (2005). Repetition-induced changes in BOLD response reflect accumulation of neural activity. *Human Brain Mapping* 25: 1–10.

Kroll, J.F., Bobb, S.C., Misra, M., and Guo, T. (2008). Language selection in bilingual speech: evidence for inhibitory processes. *Acta Psychologica* 128 (3): 416–430.

Kroll, J.F. and Stewart, E. (1994). Category interference in translation and picture naming: evidence for asymmetric connections between bilingual memory representations. *Journal of Memory and Language* 33 (2): 149.

Leonard, M.K., Brown, T.T., Travis, K.E. et al. (2010). Spatiotemporal dynamics of bilingual word processing. *NeuroImage* 49 (4): 3286–3294.

Leonard, M.K., Ferjan Ramirez, N., Torres, C. et al. (2013). Neural stages of spoken, written, and signed word processing in beginning second language learners. *Frontiers in Human Neuroscience* 7: 322.

Leonard, M.K., Torres, C., Travis, K.E. et al. (2011). Language proficiency modulates the recruitment of non-classical language areas in bilinguals. *PLoS One* 6 (3): e18240.

Li, P. and Grant, A. (2015). Second language learning success revealed by brain networks. *Bilingualism: Language and Cognition* 19: 657–664.

Li, P., Legault, J., and Litcofsky, K.A. (2014). Neuroplasticity as a function of second language learning: anatomical changes in the human brain. *Cortex* 58: 301–324.

Li, P. and Zhao, X. (2013). Self-organizing map models of language acquisition. *Frontiers in Psychology* 4: 140–153.

Linck, J.A., Kroll, J.F., and Sunderman, G. (2009). Losing access to the native language while immersed in a second language. *Psychological Science* 20 (12): 1507–1515.

Liu, H., Liang, L., Dunlap, S. et al. (2016). The effect of domain-general inhibition-related training on language switching: an ERP study. *Cognition* 146: 264–276.

Luk, G., Bialystok, E., Craik, F.I.M., and Grady, C.L. (2011). Lifelong bilingualism maintains white matter integrity in older adults. *Journal of Neuroscience* 31 (46): 16808–16813.

Martin, C.D., Dering, B., Thomas, E.M., and Thierry, G. (2009). Brain potentials reveal semantic priming in both the 'active' and the 'non-attended' language of early bilinguals. *NeuroImage* 47 (1): 326–333.

McClelland, J.L. and Rumelhart, D.E. (1981). An interactive activation model of context effects in letter perception: I. An account of basic findings. *Psychological Review* 88 (5): 375.

Meade, G., Midgley, K.J., Dijkstra, T., and Holcomb, P.J. (2018). Cross-language neighborhood effects in learners indicative of an integrated lexicon. *Journal of Cognitive Neuroscience* 30: 70–85.

Midgley, K.J., Holcomb, P.J., and Grainger, J. (2011). Effects of cognate status on word comprehension in second language learners: An ERP investigation. *Journal of Cognitive Neuroscience* 23 (7): 1634–1647. https://doi.org/10.1162/jocn.2010.21463.

Ng, S. and Wicha, N.Y. (2013). Meaning first: a case for language-independent access to word meaning in the bilingual brain. *Neuropsychologia* 51 (5): 850–863.

Norman, D.A. and Shallice, T. (1986). Attention to action: willed and automatic control of behaviour. In: *Consciousness & Self-Regulation*, vol. 4 (ed. R.J. Davidson, G.E. Schwartz and D. Shapiro), 1–18. New York, NY: Plenum Press.

Pavlenko, A. (ed.) (2009). *The Bilingual Mental Lexicon: Interdisciplinary Approaches*. Bristol, UK: Multilingual Matters.

Peeters, D. and Dijkstra, T. (2017). *Sustained Inhibition of the Native Language in Bilingual Language Production: A Virtual Reality Approach*. Bilingualism: Language and Cognition doi:10.1017/S1366728917000396.

Phillips, N.A., Segalowitz, N., O'Brien, I., and Yamasaki, N. (2004). Semantic priming in a first and second language: evidence from reaction time variability and event-related brain potentials. *Journal of Neurolinguistics* 17 (2–3): 237–262. https://doi.org/10.1016/S0911-6044(03)00055-1.

Prat, C.S., Yamasaki, B.L., Kluender, R.A., and Stocco, A. (2016). Resting-state qEEG predicts rate of second language learning in adults. *Brain and Language* 157: 44–50.

Price, C.J. (2010). The anatomy of language: a review of 100 fMRI studies published in 2009. *Annals of the New York Academy of Sciences* 1191 (1): 62–88.

Sabourin, L., Brien, C., and Burkholder, M. (2014). The effect of age of L2 acquisition on the organization of the bilingual lexicon: evidence from masked priming. *Bilingualism: Language and Cognition* 17 (3):

542–555. https://doi.org/10.1017/S1366728913000643.

Schwartz, A.I. and Kroll, J.F. (2006). Bilingual lexical activation in sentence context. *Journal of Memory and Language* 55: 197–212. https://doi.org/10.1016/j.jml.2006.03.004.

Sheppard, J.P., Wang, J.P., and Wong, P.C. (2012). Large-scale cortical network properties predict future sound-to-word learning success. *Journal of Cognitive Neuroscience* 24 (5): 1087–1103.

Stephan, K.E., Tittgemeyer, M., Knösche, T.R. et al. (2009). Tractography-based priors for dynamic causal models. *NeuroImage* 47 (4): 1628–1638. doi:10.1016/j.neuroimage.2009.05.096.

Sporns, O. (2011). *Networks of the Brain*. Cambridge, MA: MIT Press.

Stocco, A., Yamasaki, B., Natalenko, R., and Prat, C.S. (2014). Bilingual brain training: a neurobiological framework of how bilingual experience improves executive function. *International Journal of Bilingualism* 18 (1): 67–92.

Tan, L.H., Chen, L., Yip, V. et al. (2011). Activity levels in the left hemisphere caudate–fusiform circuit predict how well a second language will be learned. *Proceedings of the National Academy of Sciences* 108 (6): 2540–2544.

Thierry, G. and Wu, Y.J. (2007). Brain potentials reveal unconscious translation during foreign-language comprehension. *Proceedings of the National Academy of Sciences* 104 (30): 12530–12535.

Thomas, M.S. (1997). Distributed representations and the bilingual lexicon: one store or two? In: *Proceedings of the fourth annual neural computation and psychology workshop* (ed. J. Bullinaria, D. Glasspool and G. Houghton), 240–253. London, England: Springer.

Titone, D., Libben, M., Mercier, J. et al. (2011). Bilingual lexical access during L1 sentence reading: the effects of L2 knowledge, semantic constraint, and L1-L2 intermixing. *Journal of Experimental Psychology. Learning, Memory, and Cognition* 37 (6): 1412–1431. https://doi.org/10.1037/a0024492.

Uddin, L.Q., Supekar, K.S., Ryali, S., and Menon, V. (2011). Dynamic reconfiguration of structural and functional connectivity across core neurocognitive brain networks with development. *The Journal of Neuroscience* 31 (50): 18578–18589.

Van Hell, J.G. and De Groot, A.M.B. (1998). Conceptual representation in bilingual memory: effects of concreteness and cognate status in word association. *Bilingualism: Language and Cognition* 193–211. https://doi.org/10.1017/S1366728998000352.

Van Heuven, W.J. and Dijkstra, T. (2010). Language comprehension in the bilingual brain: fMRI and ERP support for psycholinguistic models. *Brain Research Reviews* 64 (1): 104–122.

Veroude, K., Norris, D.G., Shumskaya, E. et al. (2010). Functional connectivity between brain regions involved in learning words of a new language. *Brain and Language* 113 (1): 21–27.

Wang, X., Wang, Y.Y., Jiang, T. et al. (2013). Direct evidence of the left caudate's role in bilingual control: an intra-operative electrical stimulation study. *Neurocase* 19 (5): 462–469.

Wang, Y., Xue, G., Chen, C. et al. (2007). Neural bases of asymmetric language switching in second-language learners: an ER-fMRI study. *NeuroImage* 35 (2): 862–870.

Wartenburger, I., Heekeren, H.R., Abutalebi, J. et al. (2003). Early setting of grammatical processing in the bilingual brain. *Neuron* 37 (1): 159–170.

Xiang, H., Dediu, D., Roberts, L. et al. (2012). The structural connectivity underpinning language aptitude, working memory, and IQ in the perisylvian language network. *Language Learning* 62 (s2): 110–130.

Yang, J., Gates, K., Molenaar, P., and Li, P. (2015). Neural changes underlying successful second language word learning: an fMRI study. *Journal of Neurolinguistics* 33: 29–49.

Zhang, Y., Huang, P., Song, Z. et al. (2014). In-context language control with production tasks in bilinguals: an fMRI study. *Brain Research* 1585: 131–140.

Zhang, Y., Wang, T., Huang, P. et al. (2015). Free language selection in the bilingual brain: an event-related fMRI study. *Scientific Reports* 5: 11704. https://doi.org/10.1038/srep11704.

Zhao, X. and Li, P. (2010). Bilingual lexical interactions in an unsupervised neural network model. *International Journal of Bilingual Education and Bilingualism* 13: 505–524.

Zhao, X. and Li, P. (2013). Simulating cross-language priming with a dynamic computational model of the lexicon. *Bilingualism: Language and Cognition* 16 (2): 288–303.

4 Psycholinguistic Methods in Multilingual Research

ELEONORA ROSSI, KYRA KRASS, AND GERRIT JAN KOOTSTRA

1. Introduction

The recognition that most of the world's speakers are bilingual (Grosjean and Li 2012) has sparked new areas of psycholinguistic research that examine the way in which bilinguals manage to negotiate the presence of more than one language in the same mind and brain. Despite the difficulty of learning a second language (L2) after a putative critical period for language learning (Johnson and Newport 1991), recent studies have shown that sensitivity to newly learned L2 words can be extremely rapid and efficient even at very early stages of L2 learning and in the absence of a behavioural response (McLaughlin et al. 2004; McLaughlin et al. 2010; Osterhout et al. 2008). At the same time, one of the strongest findings over the last 20 years is that bilingual and multilingual speakers cannot turn off one of their languages at will (Colomé and Miozzo 2010; Costa et al. 2000; Kroll et al. 2006). The phenomenon of language coactivation is incredibly pervasive, suggesting that languages compete for selection even at lower proficiency levels or across modality (Emmorey et al. 2008).

The realization that languages are coactivated in a bilingual's brain has fuelled the question of what neurocognitive mechanisms are in place for monitoring and controlling the relative activations of the two languages. Amongst the various models that have been proposed to account for bilingual language processing, the inhibitory control -IC-model (Green 1998) proposes that bilinguals manage their languages by actively inhibiting their dominant language (L1) to allow fluent production in the weaker language (L2) by engaging a dynamic domain-general neural network involving cortical and subcortical structures to optimally resolve cross-language language competition (Abutalebi and Green 2007). More recently, models have been adapted to include processing and transfer of a third language (Green 2016; Green and Abutalebi 2013), suggesting that the control mechanisms that are in place to control more than two languages are much more variable and malleable than previously thought.

The Handbook of the Neuroscience of Multilingualism, First Edition. Edited by John W. Schwieter.

Over the years, research on the behavioural and cognitive mechanisms of bilingual language acquisition and processing have relied on several methodologies. Even though the relatively recent availability of modern neuroimaging methodologies has allowed researchers to study the neural substrates of bilingual and multilingual language processing with incredible temporal and spatial resolution (see Chapters 5 and 6 of this book), most of the past and current research on bilingualism is based on behavioural psycholinguistic paradigms. However, as will be illustrated throughout this book, most of the behavioural paradigms that will be described in the next sections are used in conjunction with the most recent neural methodologies. The goal of this contribution is therefore to provide an overview of the major behavioural psycholinguistic methods that have been utilized to investigate bilingual/multilingual language processing. In what follows, we will describe those methodologies, and we will exemplify them through the description of seminal studies in the field.

2.   Measuring Lexical Processing

Offline measures of lexical processing, such as accuracy performance during object/picture naming (for production) or object/picture selection (for comprehension), have been foundational to understand the various loci of lexical processing, finally leading to influential models of monolingual language production (e.g. Levelt 1989). Of course, the bi/multilingualism literature has also capitalized on the use of offline lexical measures to understand the architecture of the bilingual lexicon (Costa et al. 1999; Hoshino and Kroll 2008; Kroll and Bogulski 2013; Kroll and Stewart 1994; La Heij 2005). Importantly, even though offline measures of lexical processing are highly valuable, the ability to collect measures of speed (in ms) has offered the opportunity to collect more fine-grained temporal data that allows for a more detailed analysis of bilingual language processing.

2.1.   Lexical Production

As introduced in Section 1, a large body of research has demonstrated that bi/multilingual speakers' languages are constantly activated, even where there is no intention to speak in the L2 or L3. Most of the foundational literature in the field has capitalized on understanding the bases of the bilingual language lexicon and has proposed a number of influential models of bilingual language lexical access, such as the revised hierarchical model (Kroll and Stewart 1994; Kroll et al. 2010) and the BIA models[1] (Dijkstra and Van Heuven 1998; Dijkstra and Van Heuven 2002). Simple paradigms, such as *picture (or word) naming*, have been successfully utilized since the early days of neurolinguistics and experimental cognitive psychology (for a review see Glaser 1992; Snodgrass and Vanderwart 1980). Over the years, these paradigms have also become widely adopted in bilingual research and have allowed researchers to address specific questions about the underlying architecture of the bi/multilingual speech production (Hermans 2012).[2] The main idea behind these tasks is that accuracy and speed of naming reflect the relative level of difficulty in accessing lexical items in the L1, L2, and Lx.

The use of these paradigms has been particularly useful to prove the basic concept of bi/multilingual language coactivation. Seminal studies have revealed that cognate words (i.e. words that share the same form and meaning between two or more languages) are faster to retrieve and to name than control words (Hoshino and Kroll 2008). Bidirectional cognate facilitation effects have also been found in highly proficient bilingual and trilingual children (Poarch and Van Hell 2012) as well as in trilingual adults (Costa et al. 2000). Instead, interlingual homographs share only orthography and phonology while they differ in their meaning (e.g. *pan*, which is a container for cooking in English but a baked food in Spanish meaning bread). Both cognates and interlingual homographs show differential processing patterns compared to control words that have similar lexical properties but little cross-language overlap (e.g. *mesa*, which means table in Spanish). Overall, data from bi/multilinguals showing differential naming performance for non-cognates, cognates, and interlingual homographs has consolidated the idea that bilinguals' lexicons are constantly coactivated and compete for selection, possibly leading to an overall slowing in naming abilities in bilinguals relative to monolinguals as proposed by Ivanova and Costa (2008) and partly supported by Gollan et al. (2005).

Experimental paradigms such as picture and word naming have also been fundamental to the investigation of the structure of the bilingual lexicon and the underlying mechanisms of L2 learning; they have helped in understanding if L2 learning happens by directly accessing the meaning of L2 words rather than going via the L1 translation. While some studies suggested that direct access to meaning was possible for L2 learners at early stages of acquisition (e.g. Duyck and Brysbaert 2004; Potter et al. 1984), other accounts claimed that beginning learners initially rely on an L1–L2 translation route (Kroll and Stewart 1994). Importantly, as proficiency in the L2 increases, reliance on the translation diminishes, and stronger direct access from the L2 word and the conceptual level are established (Sunderman and Kroll 2006). These hypotheses were tested using picture (or word) naming tasks and translation tasks. For example, Kroll and Stewart (1994) had participants name pictures (or printed words) in their L1 or L2. Naming (or translation) accuracies and reaction times (RTs) were recorded, reflecting speed of lexical access. One important finding of those studies is that naming is overall slower in the L2 relative to the L1 and that proficiency in the L2 determines L2 performance, with more proficient L2 speakers naming more accurately and faster (Sunderman and Kroll 2006). This general pattern of performance has been replicated by many studies that have shown that naming in the L1 is faster and more accurate than naming in the L2 (e.g. Hoshino and Kroll 2008; Kroll and Stewart 1994) and that naming in the less proficient L3 is less accurate and slower than naming in the L2 (e.g. Abunuwara 1992; Costa and Santesteban 2004).

A bilingual version of the *picture–picture interference task* has also been used to study bilingual coactivation (Colomé and Miozzo 2010; Morsella and Miozzo 2002). In the monolingual versions of the task, two superimposed pictures are presented simultaneously, and participants were asked to name the picture that they have been pre-trained to name (e.g. 'name the picture that is in the colour green'). Previous research has shown that when the two pictures share phonology, such as wall/wand, naming latencies are faster than for pictures that do not share phonology, such as table/bread (Roelofs 2006).

For bilinguals, the expectation would be to observe the same effect for cognate words if the two languages are coactivated. This is exactly what has been reported by Colomé and Miozzo (2010) who demonstrated that bilinguals show faster RTs when naming picture pairs when they are cognates relative to when the distractor is a non-cognate. Note that related findings of cross-language activation have also been found with pictures combined with words (e.g. Hermans et al. 1998). This shows the versatility of these kinds of tasks.

A large behavioural body of research has capitalized on *language-switching* paradigms, either using item-by-item or blocked-language paradigms. In item-by-item language-switching paradigms, participants switch languages from item to item within a block, while in blocked-language naming paradigms, participants use only one language per experimental block but are required to switch languages across blocks of items. Data from those paradigms have observed that bi/multilinguals' multiple languages are constantly coactivated and competing for selection as well as hypothesized that in order for bilinguals to speak the less dominant of their two languages, they need to inhibit the more dominant of the two languages (e.g. Green 1998; Levy et al. 2007; Linck et al. 2009; Philipp et al. 2007). The idea behind these tasks is that, by having both languages active and engaging participants in switching between their languages, it is possible to reveal the mechanisms underlying bilingual language control.

For example, Meuter and Allport (1999) used the item-by-item language-switching paradigm with bilinguals who were instructed to read numerals aloud as fast as possible. The language that they had to name a given numeral in would be indicated by a colour frame. For example, a blue frame would signify 'name in English', whereas a red frame would mean 'name in French'. The results showed that switching had a cost, shown by longer RTs for switch trials than for non-switch trials. Critically, naming latencies were greater when switching from the L2 to the L1 than when switching from the L1 to the L2. This seemingly counterintuitive result of an asymmetrical switching cost has paved the way to the hypothesis that the strongest language needs to be temporarily inhibited to allow for production in the L2. This proposal has been confirmed by a number of behavioural studies even with trilinguals (Linck et al. 2012); however, there were some mixed results (e.g. Costa and Santesteban 2004), raising the question of whether asymmetrical switching costs are shaped by relative language use and task demands.

Blocked-language switching paradigms instead require naming items in one of the bilingual's two languages in separate blocks of trials. One such example is an event-related potential (ERP) study by Misra et al. (2012), which tested Chinese (L1)-English (L2) bilinguals who named pictures in each of their languages, in different blocks. In that study, to test the inhibitory control hypothesis, the order of naming was counter-balanced across participants, such that some named in L1 first and then in L2, and others named in L2 first and then in L1. Importantly, items were repeated between the blocks. Under normal conditions, repetition of pictures would be expected to produce response facilitation via priming in the subsequent blocks, regardless of which language was to be spoken. However, if inhibition of the strongest language occurs, facilitation effects should be at best eliminated. In line with this last prediction, the behavioural and ERP data revealed that when pictures were named first in the L2 and then were repeated in the L1, naming facilitation was eliminated and an ERP component indexing response conflict (e.g. N200) was observed across the block. Similar behavioural and functional magnetic resonance imaging (fMRI) results were found by Guo et al. (2011) who contrasted item-by-item switching and blocked-language naming performance. Overall, language-switching paradigms have been foundational in revealing the linguistic and cognitive mechanisms at play in bilingual and multilingual language production.

Finally, one language production task that has recently received a lot of attention because of its simplicity and high reliability as a representative measure of proficiency in a given language is the *verbal fluency task*, a short task of verbal ability. Two main variants have been used in the cognitive literature. The first variant is the semantic fluency task (Benton 1968), in which participants are required to name as many items as possible in a given language according to given semantic categories. For example, participants are prompted to name as many 'tools' or as many 'animals' as possible in a given amount of time (typically 30 or 60 seconds). The other variant is the phonological verbal fluency task (Newcombe 1969), which requires participants to name items that start with a given phoneme or letter.

The verbal fluency task has been used in a number of bilingual studies to investigate the mechanisms of bilingual language regulation and to examine the effects that immersion in an L2 environment has on the native language. Given earlier findings that have used the blocked-language naming task and have shown that bilinguals might need to temporarily inhibit the L1 in order to speak in the L2 (e.g. Guo et al. 2011; Misra et al. 2012), Van Assche et al. (2013) used a similar language-blocked phonological verbal fluency task to ask if Dutch-English and Chinese-English bilinguals would show a similar global inhibitory effect on the L1 when accessing words through phonological retrieval. Critically, the task was administered such that a subset of participants performed the letter fluency task in their L1 first and then in the L2, while another subset of participants performed the task in the opposite order. Importantly, participants were instructed to perform the task in both languages for three letters (F/A/S) which was the 'same letter condition', while a subset of other letters were only prompted for Dutch (B/I/L) or English (M/O/N) which was the 'different letter condition'. Performance on the task was compared as a function of the order of the language blocks (L1 or L2 first), the type of bilingual speaker (more proficient Dutch-English or less proficient Chinese-English), and whether the letter cues were the same or different across languages. The results replicated the block order effect reported by Misra et al. (2012) in that letter fluency was reduced for the dominant language when it followed the less dominant language. The groups differed, however, in that only the Chinese-English bilinguals, not the Dutch-English bilinguals, showed these effects globally, regardless of whether the letter cues were repeated or not. The pattern of results suggests that all bilinguals, regardless of their proficiency, show evidence of inhibitory processing, but that proficiency may determine the scope of inhibition. The decrease in fluency in the L1 after an extended time of immersion in the L2 has also confirmed an effect of a general global suppression of the native language (Linck et al. 2009), suggesting that immersion in the L2 environment might play a particularly relevant role for language regulation in L2 learners and bilinguals.

2.2.   *Lexical Comprehension*

Much of the current research in the field has sought to investigate the underlying architecture of bi/multilingual language processing by investigating multiple aspects of language comprehension. At the lexical level, paradigms such as the lexical decision task, the phoneme detection task (Colomé and Miozzo 2010), or the semantic judgement relatedness task have been amongst the major paradigms used to investigate bi/multilingual lexical access and lexical processing.

In a seminal study by Van Hell and Dijkstra (2002), the *lexical decision task* was used to investigate trilingual language coactivation to test the effects of the L2 and the L3 on the native language. During a lexical decision task, participants are simply asked to determine as quickly as possible if the strings of letters they are presented with represent a real word or not. For example, during an English lexical decision task, if 'tuble' is presented, a NO response should be given, while if 'table' is presented, it should trigger a YES response (Menn and Dronkers 2016; Traxler 2011). In Van Hell and Dijkstra (2002), the two groups of Dutch-English-French trilinguals differed in the level of proficiency in French (the L3); one group had higher French proficiency than the other. During the task, participants were presented with words in Dutch (their L1) only. Importantly, they were not aware of the goal of the study; they were recruited from a pool of students who took a final exam in Dutch, English, and French, which identified them as trilingual, but they were asked to participate in a memory study. Experimental items were either cognates with English (the L2), cognates with French (the L3), or non-cognates. Results revealed that both groups of trilinguals processed L1 words that were cognates with the L2 faster than non-cognates. However, only the trilinguals who had high proficiency in French also showed a cognate facilitation effect in the L1 words that were cognates with L3 French. The results from this study are important because they demonstrate that processing words in the L1 coactivates both the L2 and the L3 but that proficiency levels can modulate the observed coactivation effect.

Similar effects have been found in Dutch-English-German trilinguals while they performed a lexical decision task in their L3 German (Lemhöfer et al. 2004). Experimental materials included purely German control words, cognates that overlapped in Dutch and German, and trilingual cognates between Dutch, German, and English. Results showed that RTs for the control words were the slowest. Instead, RTs to trilingual cognates were the fastest, followed by RTs to Dutch-German cognates, thus supporting the language non-selectivity account. A replication of this study tested Polish-English-German trilinguals while they performed a lexical decision task in German, their weakest language (Szubko-Sitarek 2011). Experimental stimuli consisted of Polish-English-German cognates, cognates between Polish and German, and German control words. Results showed a cumulative cognate effect, such that RTs for trilingual cognates were faster than RTs for cognates between Polish and German, which showed faster RTs than control words. In addition to the main results, Szubko-Sitarek (2011) conducted a second experiment in which Polish control words and fillers were used in place of the German control words, therefore boosting the activation of the L1. Results still demonstrated that trilingual cognates were responded to faster than bilingual cognates. However, RTs were overall faster in Experiment 2, suggesting that language coactivation across languages is indeed modulated by experimental or language environment demands.

Dijkstra et al. (1998) used the lexical decision task in three experiments with Dutch-English bilinguals. The goal of the study was to demonstrate that language non-selectivity might be modulated by different language usage requirements, induced through different task manipulations. The experimental material contained control words, cognate words, and interlingual homographs. In the case of interlingual homographs, cross-language activation induced by cross-language word form overlap leads to a coactivation of competing word meanings, whereas in the case of cognates, the cross-language activation induced by word form overlap leads to a coactivation of converging word meanings. In Experiment 1, language 'mode' was induced by having control words that were purely English, while in Experiment 2, Dutch words were also added to the list, factually engaging participants in a bilingual mode and lowering the activation threshold of both languages. Results showed that only for Experiment 2 were interlingual homographs slower than the controls, suggesting that the different experimental demands modulated the magnitude of the language coactivation between the two languages.

Another psycholinguistic paradigm that has been used to investigate bilingual comprehension is the *semantic relatedness paradigm*. In this task, speakers are exposed to a set of pictures or printed words, and they are required to determine as fast as possible whether the two items are semantically related or not. For example, if the word pair CAT DOG is presented, a 'yes' answer should be given, as cat and dog are both animals. On the contrary, the word pair CAT FIG are not semantically related. A number of studies have used this paradigm with elegant cross-linguistic manipulations to unveil mechanisms of bilingual language processing (e.g. Macizo et al. 2010; Martín et al. 2010). For example, Martín et al. (2010) asked Spanish-English bilinguals to perform semantic relatedness judgements when reading English word pairs. Importantly, critical trials contained interlingual homographs which shared form but not meaning across the two languages (i.e. $pan_{English} - pan_{Spanish/bread}$). In the following trial, the word pair included the English translation of the Spanish meaning of the homograph (i.e. bread). Results revealed that bilinguals were slower to judge word pairs that contained a homograph (e.g. pie – toe, given that the Spanish word for toe is 'pie'). Critically, after responding to homographs, bilinguals slowed their responses when its Spanish meaning became relevant in the subsequent trial as compared to a control word pair (e.g. foot – hand). The interference effect found in the first trial was taken as an index of cross-language activation. Given the interference effect stemming from the parallel activation of the two homograph meanings, bilinguals appeared to resolve the interference by suppressing the non-target and competing homograph meaning in order to select the appropriate one.

Overall, there is a great number of behavioural experimental paradigms that have been successfully adapted to testing bi/multilingual language comprehension and have shed light on the bilingual lexical architecture. In Section 3, we will extend our overview to experimental paradigms that have been utilized to tackle bi/multilingual language processing beyond the lexical level.

3.   Measuring Syntactic Processing

Language processing is an extremely complex phenomenon that goes beyond single word level processing. Much of the interest that has fuelled the bilingual and L2 research has revolved around understanding if and to what extent grammatical processing differs in the native and in the second language. Traditionally, offline *end-of-the-sentence grammaticality judgement tasks* have been utilized to collect a speaker's rate and speed of acceptability of a given sentence as a measure of syntactic processing in their various languages (e.g.Johnson and Newport 1989; McDonald 2000). The underlying idea behind this methodology is that higher error rates and longer end-of-the-sentence RTs indicate processing difficulty. However, because language unfolds over time, end-of-the-sentence grammaticality judgements are likely to represent an aggregate of linguistic and cognitive processes that unfold during language comprehension, preventing an accurate determination of the specific point in time at which monolingual and bilingual language processing differ.

As such, more recent psycholinguistic research has relied on experimental paradigms that are sensitive to the time course of syntactic processing as language processing unfolds. For example, *self-paced reading/listening paradigms* (Just et al. 1982) are amongst the major psycholinguistic methods that are used to study syntactic processing such as the comprehension of locally ambiguous sentences, pronominal resolutions, or filler-gap dependencies (e.g. Dallas and Kaan 2008; Felser et al. 2003; Ferreira et al. 1996; Rossi et al. 2017); they are even used to investigate language-switching costs during sentence comprehension (Bultena et al. 2015).

During self-paced reading/listening tasks, participants are instructed to read (or listen) to sentences one word at a time, while they press a button at their own pace to allow words to proceed. In this way, RTs are recorded at each point in the sentence permitting a measure of language processing at each critical point. As such, differently from a typical rapid serial visual presentation (RSVP) paradigm in which words are presented for a specific amount of time (e.g. 300 ms), words appear at the reader's speed (e.g. Gullifer et al. 2013). While for the self-paced listening paradigm there is only one possible variant of the task in which participants press a button to allow for words to advance auditorily, the self-paced reading paradigm can be administered in three variants: (1) cumulative presentation, (2) linear non-cumulative presentation, and (3) centre non-cumulative presentation. The main difference between these variants is whether the words appear on the screen and then disappear at the next button press (as in 2), appear linearly and stay till the end of the sentence (as in 1), or appear in the centre of the screen (as in 3). The most used of the three paradigms is probably the non-cumulative self-paced reading paradigm in which the first word appears at the first space bar press while the remaining words in the sentence are represented by dashes (one dash representing each letter of each word; this task is also called the 'moving window task'). Crucially, the time that elapses between the onset of a word and each subsequent word represents the RT related to each word.

Self-paced reading has been widely used in bilingual research. One recent study that has used this paradigm was conducted by Rossi et al. (2017), who tested how L1 English late L2 Spanish learners process L2-specific pronominal references during sentence comprehension.

In that study, participants read sentences in Spanish that contained Spanish clitic pronouns which were presented either in a correct position (i.e. before the finite verb) or in an incorrect condition (i.e. after the finite verb). The question of interest was whether L2 speakers would be sensitive to clitic pronouns and their position in the sentence. Data from the self-paced reading paradigm revealed that reading times were longer when the clitic pronoun was presented in the incorrect condition, suggesting that L2 Spanish speakers were sensitive to word order violations for that grammatical particle.

So far, we have presented various (but surely not all) psycholinguistic behavioural paradigms that have been and are still utilized to successfully investigate bi/multilingual language production and comprehension from the single word level to the sentence domain. In Section 4, we will introduce a methodological paradigm that has been key to the investigation of language production and comprehension conjointly: structural priming.

4.   Structural Priming

One phenomenon that has received considerable attention over the past couple of decades is *structural priming* (also often called syntactic priming or syntactic persistence). Structural priming refers to the phenomenon that when language users have just heard or produced a sentence with a specific syntactic structure, they tend to reuse that syntactic structure in subsequent utterances and/or their comprehension of subsequent utterances with the same structure is enhanced (see Pickering and Ferreira 2008, for a review; see Dell and Ferreira 2016, for recent insights). One reason why structural priming has received so much attention over the past years is that it appears to have multiple functions that are of interest not only to psycholinguists but also to linguists and sociolinguists. That is, it appears to facilitate fluency of language production (Ferreira and Bock 2006; MacDonald 2013; Schober 2006) and underlie implicit language learning and predictive language processing (Chang et al. 2006; Dell and Chang 2014). It also guides linguistic choices in spontaneous language use between conversation partners in social interaction (e.g. Bresnan et al. 2007; Schenkein 1980; Weiner and Labov 1983), thus enhancing comprehension and mutual intelligibility of each other's utterances (Pickering and Garrod 2004). Priming is a key phenomenon of language use firmly grounded in cognition and social interaction, which appears to link the processes of language comprehension, production, and acquisition (see also Dell and Chang 2014).

Structural priming has not only been investigated as a phenomenon of interest in itself but also most importantly as an experimental tool to measure the representational nature of language production and comprehension. The logic behind this is that, when information is primable, it should represent an existing level of processing (see Branigan and Pickering 2017, for an overview; see Kootstra and Rossi 2017, for a commentary). Based on this logic, Bock (1989) and Bock and Loebell (1990) found that priming of syntactic structures occurs in the absence of thematic, lexical, phonological, and prosodic overlap between the prime and target, thus indicating that syntax is an independent level of representation in language production. Later studies have shown that, despite this independent level of syntactic structure, structural priming effects are still enhanced by lexical overlap between the prime and target (the lexical boost effect; e.g. Cleland and Pickering 2003; Pickering and Branigan 1998; see Mahowald et al. 2016 for a meta-analysis). These findings indicate that lexical and syntactic representations are connected in the minds of language users and have thus critically informed models of language production (cf., Pickering and Branigan 1998).

Structural priming has also been successfully applied as a window into the representational nature of bi/multilingual language use. The underlying idea is that if priming takes place across languages, then the activation of representations in one language influences the activation of representations in the other languages. Cross-language structural priming studies can thus critically inform the development of models on cross-language interactions in bilingual language use beyond the single-word level (see Hartsuiker and Pickering 2008, for more information).

4.1.   *Priming in Language Production*

Most studies on structural priming in bilinguals have focused on the measurement of language production variables. One of the first and most-cited studies on cross-language structural priming is Loebell and Bock (2003). Based on Bock's (1986) seminal work, they used an experimental priming paradigm in which German-English bilinguals were asked to reproduce an auditorily presented sentence with a specific structure (dative alternation, passives vs. actives) in a specific language (either German or English) and then asked to describe a picture in the other language that could be described with the same structure as the just-reproduced sentence. The pictures were thematically unrelated to the priming sentences but could be described by using the structure primed by the just-reproduced sentence or the alternative to the primed structure. Thus, the sentence trials served as prime sentences for subsequent target picture trials, and priming was operationalized as follows: if priming would indeed take place, then this should be evidenced in a significant tendency to use the primed structure over the alternative structure.

Now in a situation such as this, it would be undesirable to have a predictable sequence in which a sentence trial is always followed by a picture trial. This would make the priming manipulation too obvious for the participants and could thus elicit strategic response behaviour. To avoid this, Loebell and Bock (2003) included two more features in their experiment. First, they included a considerable number of filler sentences and pictures which constituted separate sentence trials and picture trials that were randomly ordered in the stimulus lists. Thus, there was no predictable sequence of a picture after each sentence. The second feature that Loebell and Bock included was the use of a cover task: the participants were simply told that they had to reproduce and describe a list of sentences and pictures, some of which would be repeated during the session (which was indeed the case with some of the fillers). The participants were instructed to indicate after each sentence or picture whether they had seen or heard it before in the experimental session. In other words, the participants thought that they were doing a memory task instead of a structural priming task. Using this experimental paradigm, Loebell and Bock indeed found evidence of structural priming across languages.

In addition to this classic memory-task priming paradigm, other techniques have been designed to study priming in (multilingual) language production. One important technique is the *confederate-scripting technique*, developed by Branigan et al. (2000). This technique is similar to Loebell and Bock's (2003) task in the sense that it involves a picture description task, but it differs from Loebell and Bock's paradigm in that it is a dialogue task, involving two participants who take turns in describing pictures to each other. Crucially, one of the participants is a so-called confederate, an actor who is instructed beforehand by the experimenter and whose linguistic behaviour has been scripted, unbeknownst to the real participant. The confederate's scripted picture description functions as the prime sentence for the subsequent picture description by the real participant. Thus, just as with Loebell and Bock's paradigm, the critical question is to what extent the real participants' syntactic choices are influenced by the prime sentence.

The first study to use the confederate-scripting technique in multilingual production is Hartsuiker et al. (2004), who studied priming from Spanish to English of transitive actives, passives, intransitives, and OVS (object-verb-subject) sentences in Spanish-English bilinguals (native speakers of Spanish with moderate or high proficiency in English). The participants took turns with a confederate, who was also a Spanish-English bilingual, to describe cards to each other that depicted simple transitive and intransitive actions. There was a screen between the participant and the confederate, so the participant could not see that the confederate was actually reading aloud a script instead of describing the cards. The confederate always described the cards in Spanish, while the real participants described the cards in English. The question was whether participants' syntactic choices in English would be primed by the structure of a Spanish sentence produced just before by the confederate. Just as in Loebell and Bock's (2003) case, Hartsuiker et al. (2004) included a cover task: in addition to a set of cards to describe (the description set), the participants had a set of 'selection cards', which were used to check whether they corresponded to the dialogue partners' picture descriptions. That is, after either participant finished speaking, the other took the topmost card from their selection box and determined whether it matched their partner's card description. In 50% of the cases, the confederate's picture description did match with the selection card, but this was only the case in filler items. Hartsuiker et al. (2004) indeed found structural priming across languages, a finding that has had a major impact on models of multilingual language production (see Hartsuiker and Pickering 2008).

In addition to the above two picture-description style priming tasks, cross-language structural priming in language production has also been studied by means of sentence completion. Based on Scheepers (2003), Desmet and Declercq (2006) explored whether relative clause attachment can be primed from Dutch to English (e.g. *John met the boss of the employees who* ... where 'who' can refer to 'the boss' but also to 'the employees'). They had Dutch-English bilinguals complete a series of sentences with relative clauses. Prime sentences were Dutch sentences that required either high or low relative clause attachment, based on a gender agreement manipulation on the relative pronoun. Prime sentences were followed by target sentences, which were English sentences that had an ambiguous gender manipulation on the relative pronoun and could therefore be completed either with a high or low attachment. The question of interest was whether choice of relative clause attachment in the English target sentences was influenced by the relative clause attachment of the Dutch prime sentences. This in fact turned out to be the case.

The studies above have prompted many other studies, in which multiple variants of priming tasks have been used to study multiple aspects of structural priming in bilingual language production. For example, Schoonbaert et al. (2007) used the confederate-scripting technique to study boosted effects of cross-linguistic priming when the primes and targets contain translation equivalents (see also Cai et al. 2011); Salamoura and Williams (2006) used verbs with a strong bias towards a specific syntactic structure in Dutch prime sentences to prime syntactic choice in English sentences without biasing verbs; Kantola and van Gompel (2011) used a variant of Desmet and Declercq's (2006) sentence completion task to study within- versus between-language priming in dative sentences and found no differences between the two (though see Travis et al. 2017, for corpus evidence against this conclusion); Kootstra and Doedens (2016) used a variant of Loebell and Bock's priming memory task and found evidence of not only short-term but also long-term cross-language priming. In addition, studies have been done beyond the topic of between-language priming in unilingual sentences, such as within-language priming in the L2 (cf. Flett et al. 2013; Gries and Wulff 2005, 2009; McDonough 2006; McDonough and Trofimovich 2008; Nitschke et al. 2010; Nitschke et al. 2014; Shin and Christianson 2009, 2012) and priming of code switching (i.e. the use of more than one language in the same utterance; Kootstra et al. 2010, 2012). In addition to experimental work, large-scale bilingual corpora of spontaneous conversations have recently become accessible, and statistical techniques to analyse these corpora have become increasingly sophisticated, resulting in the first corpus-based priming results on bilingual language production, thus cross-validating the results from experiments (e.g. Fricke and Kootstra 2016; Torres Cacoullos and Travis 2011, 2017; Travis et al. 2017; see Gries and Kootstra 2017, for a review).

4.2.   *Priming in Language Comprehension*

The studies discussed in Section 4.1 all measured priming of syntactic choice in language production. Importantly, however, priming can also be measured in comprehension, using various measurements and tasks, such as anticipatory eye movements in auditory comprehension of visual-world scenes (e.g. Arai et al. 2007), eye movements and ERP measurements in the reading of garden-path sentences (e.g. Ledoux et al. 2007; Pickering and Traxler 2004; Tooley et al. 2009; Traxler and Tooley 2008), and fMRI repetition suppression and adaptation (Segaert et al. 2012; Weber and Indefrey 2009). Most of these studies have only found structural priming in the case of lexical repetition between prime and target, although there are also studies which have reported structural priming in the absence of lexical repetition between prime and target (see Tooley and Traxler 2010, for a review of structural priming in comprehension).

Weber and Indefrey (2009) were one of the first to study cross-language structural priming in comprehension. In German-English bilinguals, they tested structural priming of passive sentences from German to English and within English, using two methods. The first was a behavioural self-paced reading experiment, based on earlier work by Frazier et al. (1984). Participants read sentences that were presented word by word in a self-paced manner. To study priming, some pairs of sentences constituted prime-target combinations. Target sentences were always passive sentences, whereas prime sentences were either passive sentences or active sentences. If priming would take place, then reading times of passive target sentences should be enhanced after a passive prime sentence compared to after an active prime sentence. To maximize the possibility of finding a priming effect, the verb in the prime sentence was always the same as in the target sentence, because previous studies had shown that verb repetition is an important factor in structural priming in comprehension (e.g. Arai et al. 2007; Ledoux et al. 2007; Tooley et al. 2009). Using this self-paced reading paradigm, Weber and Indefrey found decreased reading times for target sentences preceded by passive prime sentences compared to active prime sentences, both from German to English and within English. The second method Weber and Indefrey used was an fMRI experiment, in which they presented the same stimuli to German-English bilinguals, but then at a fixed presentation time of 350 ms per word. Using this procedure, Weber and Indefrey found a reduced blood-oxygen-level dependent (BOLD) response in specific brain regions after participants had just read a passive prime sentence compared to an active prime sentence, again both within and across languages. This reduced BOLD response as a function of stimulus repetition (i.e. repetition suppression) is a well-known neural measure of priming (Henson 2003). Thus, both behavioural and imaging data provided compelling evidence of cross-language structural priming in bilingual sentence comprehension.

In sum, structural priming in bilinguals can be studied in different ways, with different syntactic structures and languages, and can be measured both on language production and language comprehension variables. Moreover, priming can be studied in both monologue and dialogue settings and can mimic various aspects of language use as they occur in real life. Structural priming is thus a highly versatile technique for the study of language 'as a product' and language 'as an action' (cf., Trueswell and Tanenhaus 2005), combining internal validity (experimental rigour) with ecological validity.

5. Measuring Bilingual Language Processing with Eye-Tracking

In the last part of this chapter, we focus on a methodological technique that has been used frequently in psycholinguistic research on bi/multilingualism: eye-tracking. At its core, this research technique is based on tracking the spontaneous eye movements of individuals who are presented with a variety of linguistic and non-linguistic stimuli. This can be done by presenting full sentences visually, as in reading studies, or by presenting auditory stimuli accompanied by related visual stimuli, as in visual world paradigm studies (e.g. Altmann 2011; Cooper 1974; Rayner 1998). Importantly, eye-tracking reading studies and the visual world paradigm are complementary in that they can address different questions related to language processing. When studying language, reading studies and visual world paradigm studies can add valuable insight into how individuals process written and spoken language. In the sections that follow, we will introduce a number of seminal reading and visual world paradigm studies that exemplify the two methodologies and inform bi/multilingualism literature.

Extensive eye-movement research has been conducted to investigate reading (e.g. Rayner 1998; Rayner et al. 2004). Reading studies that use eye-tracking can record the natural eye movements of an individual in order to capture both the eye movements (saccades) as well as the moments of rest (fixations) that occur during reading. Research shows that information is processed by the reader when the eye is at rest and fixated on one spot (Rayner 1978). Both saccades and fixations can be used when analysing eye-tracking data. When analysing reading data, researchers can look at an individual's saccades during the first reading of a passage (first-pass) or when they reread part of the sentence (second-pass; Rayner 1998). When the content is more challenging for the reader to comprehend, they tend to follow a backward path called a *regression* (Rayner and Pollatsek 2011). Researchers also look at the time individuals spend fixating on different parts of the text. Rayner (1977) found that participants spent longer amounts of time fixating on verbs than other parts of the sentence. It was proposed that longer fixations on the verb suggested that this part of speech is particularly important during sentence processing. The results from this study and others strengthened the proposal that the underlying cognitive processes necessary for reading affect an individual's eye movements. This conclusion is the motivation behind many reading eye-tracking studies both past and present.

Eye-tracking has been an important technique for better understanding of the linguistic and cognitive underpinnings of bi/multilingualism. Research has shown that languages interact with one another in the bi/multilingual's brain. To better understand this proposed phenomenon, Dussias and Sagarra (2007) conducted an eye-tracking reading study to look at the differences between monolingual Spanish speakers, Spanish-English bilinguals with minimal exposure to their L2 (English), and Spanish-English bilinguals who had been immersed in their L2. Generally, when presented with an ambiguous sentence in which one of two nouns is modified by a relative clause, Spanish speakers favour the first noun and English speakers favour the second. This study further investigated this by presenting participants with some sentences that specifically referred to the first noun and other sentences that referred to the second noun. For example, participants heard a sentence like *El policía arrestó a la hermana del criado que estaba enferma desde hacía tiempo* which is translated to 'The police arrested the sister of the servant (male) who had been ill (fem) for a while' (Dussias and Sagarra 2007). Though ambiguous in English, the words *servant* and *ill* in Spanish are coded for grammatical gender which disambiguates the sentence, such that the modified noun in this instance is the sister. The three groups of participants spent varying amounts of time reading the critical adjective (i.e. 'ill') which in the stimuli disambiguated between whether the first or second noun was being modified. Results revealed that the monolinguals and bilinguals with minimal exposure to English showed a trend towards longer reading times in the second noun sentences than the first noun sentences. The bilinguals who had been immersed in an English-speaking environment showed a trend towards longer reading times in the first noun condition than the second. These results suggest that while the monolinguals and individuals with less exposure to their L2 were processing the sentences in a Spanish way (interpreting the first noun as the modified noun), bilinguals exposed to English processed the sentences in a more English way, suggesting that native language processing can change as a function of prolonged immersion in the second language environment.

In addition to reading studies, eye-tracking can also be used in conjunction with the visual world paradigm. The visual world paradigm can be used in language processing research to better understand how individuals process language over time using auditory rather than visually presented language. Tanenhaus et al. (1995) used the visual world paradigm to explore what kind of information is used and when during the processing of sentences containing ambiguous fragments. In this study, participants were shown four pictures on a screen in a quadrant formation. They then heard a sentence like 'Put the apple *on the towel/that's on the towel* in the box' (Tanenhaus et al. 1995). In the four quadrants were objects related to the sentence such as an apple that was on a towel, a box, a towel, and a distractor object. The participants' eye movements were recorded to better understand how individuals interpreted and processed the auditory sentences that were presented. For example, participants looked to the apple, then the towel, then the apple, followed by the box, when hearing 'Put the apple on the towel in the box'. This showed that they had initially interpreted the sentence to be an instruction to place the apple onto the towel rather than the final interpretation of placing the apple that was on the towel into the box. In a condition in which the distractor object had been replaced by an apple (this one was not on a towel), a very different result was observed. When hearing 'on the towel', participants looked only to the apple that was on a towel, showing that they had used the referential ambiguity (i.e. the fact that there were two possible real-world referents for the phrase 'the apple') to disambiguate the sentence. This visual world paradigm eye-tracking technique enables researchers to study the processing of a sentence with excellent time resolution down to the millisecond; prior studies investigating equivalent cases during reading (e.g. Altmann and Steedman 1988) were unable to establish the time-course of these disambiguation effects.

Another seminal study that used the visual world paradigm, this time to investigate *predictive* language processing, was conducted by Altmann and Kamide (1999). Participants were given auditory sentences such as *The boy will move/eat the cake* while looking at a related scene that contained a cake, a boy, and unrelated distractors as shown in Figure 1.

Results showed that when participants heard the verb *eat*, they looked to the cake. Compared to the condition in which they heard *The boy will move the cake*, participants were more likely to look at the cake even *before* the word cake was heard if they had heard the verb *eat*. It was suggested that this result occurred because several objects in the scene were movable but only the cake was edible, thus suggesting the presence of predictive language processing resulting in anticipatory looks to the object in the scene that afforded the action.

While the visual world paradigm was traditionally used to look at sentence processing in monolingual participants, the technique has been adopted to test various hypotheses related to bi/multilingualism. Marian and Spivey (2003) conducted a study with Russian-English bilinguals to investigate bilingual language coactivation. Importantly, this study comprised two experiments: Experiment 1 was run in English, and Experiment 2 was run in Russian to manipulate the language context, which was referred to as 'language mode' (Marian and Spivey 2003; see Grosjean 2001, for more information on the notion of language mode). Crucially, the bilingual nature of the study was not revealed, such that when tested in English, participants were not aware that the stimuli were manipulated to elicit language coactivation between the two languages. Participants were shown several real objects on a table and then were asked to pick up different objects. There

Figure 1   Reprinted from 'Incremental interpretation at verbs: Restricting the domain of subsequent reference'. Source: Altmann and Kamide (1999, p. 250). Reprinted with permission.

were four conditions: no competition, between-language competition, within-language competition, and simultaneous competition. The object that was named (in English or Russian depending on the experiment) would have a lexical competitor in the same language, the second language, both, or neither. For example, in Experiment 1, when asked to pick up the 'plug' there could also be a 'plum' present as an English language competitor and a 'dress' present which is a Russian competitor 'plat'e' (Marian and Spivey 2003). In Experiment 1, participants looked significantly more at the within-language English competitor than the control as well as more to the between-language Russian competitor than a control object suggesting that when processing language, bilingual individuals encounter competition from both known languages. Experiment 2 showed similar results. Individuals looked significantly more to the Russian competitor than the control, and though not significant, there was a trend for participants to look more to the English competitor than the control. Although both languages seem to interfere somewhat when an individual is processing one language, the 'language mode' plays a part in the level of interference of an individual's second language.

Blumenfeld and Marian (2007) used eye-tracking to test coactivation of the English and German languages in English-native bilinguals, German-native bilinguals, and English monolinguals. Participants were asked in English to select an object when four options were presented on a screen. The target object was either an English-German cognate or a non-cognate. Additionally, for half of the stimuli, a German phonological competitor was present as one of the objects (e.g. the target was 'desk' and the competitor was 'Deckel', a lid in English). For both bilingual groups, individuals looked more to the German competitors than the control objects. There was no difference for the monolingual group. When looking at whether the English word was a cognate, German-native bilinguals did not differ. They looked more to the German-competitor than the control regardless of whether the target was a cognate. However, English-native bilinguals only showed more looks to a competitor than the control if the target was a cognate (i.e. an interaction by target-type for bilinguals). These results show that overall the German-native bilinguals coactivated German and English throughout the experiment, while English-native bilinguals activated German only in the presence of cognates.

Similarly, Blumenfeld and Marian (2011) used the visual world paradigm to look at the effects of bilingualism on inhibitory control abilities. In this study, monolingual English-speaking participants and English-Spanish bilinguals were presented with a screen showing four objects, and they were asked to select the object they heard aloud. Phonological competitors were presented with the target picture. For instance, if *plum* were the target item, the picture of a *plug* was presented in the same screen display. Results revealed that for the main task, monolinguals and bilinguals showed an identical pattern of diminished accuracy and longer response times when competitor objects were present as compared to when control items were presented.

Additionally, participants completed a negative priming task designed to determine if they were inhibiting competitors during the main task. During the negative priming task, participants were asked to select a grey asterisk. The location of the asterisk was manipulated so that it was in the same location as the competitor, a control object, or the target object seen in the previous trial. For this negative priming task, there were major differences between the two groups. Monolinguals identified the asterisk fastest when it was in the same position as the target, followed by slower reaction times when it was in the location of the control, and finally followed by slowest reaction times when it was in the same location as the competitor. Bilinguals showed the fastest reaction time when the asterisk was in the same location as the target, and showed slower reactions times in the control and in the competitor positions. When looking at eye movements, both groups launched eye movements quickest when the asterisk was in the same position as the target. The monolingual groups were slower to look to the asterisk when it was in the same position as the competitors than when it was in the same position as the control pictures. The bilingual group showed no difference in timing of looks to the control and competitor conditions. It was suggested that the results indicated that only the monolingual group was able to inhibit the competitors while the bilingual group did not inhibit the language competitor, confirming bilingual language coactivation.

Visual world eye-tracking has been utilized mainly in bilingual populations. However, this methodology could also be used to investigate multilingual populations as various researchers are interested in the impact that a third language has on cognitive processing (e.g. Byers-Heinlein and Werker 2009). Overall, eye-tracking is a useful tool to determine how bi/multilingualism affects linguistic and cognitive processes. Both reading and visual world paradigms can be used to investigate how language processing unfolds over time. Reading studies can help to determine which parts of language may require more cognitive load or can distinguish differences between how monolingual and bi/multilingual individuals interpret written language; visual world paradigm studies can help determine how individuals process language when it is spoken and what lexical items or objects individuals are activating while language unfolds.

6.   Conclusion

In this contribution, we have illustrated the major behavioural methodologies used in psycholinguistic research applied to the investigation of bi-/multilingualism. We have highlighted how such paradigms have been key to understanding the structure of the bilingual lexicon and syntax thanks to measures of accuracy and speed in naming and comprehension of single lexical items and complex sentences. We also discussed how structural priming in bilinguals can be key to linking comprehension and production processes and providing grounds to test various aspects of bilingual language processing in a more naturalistic setting. Finally, we have reviewed how eye-tracking methods permit the study of online predictive processes during bilingual language processing and differences in non-linguistic cognitive abilities that may arise because of speaking two or more languages. Overall, the results from these laboratory designs shed light on the underlying mechanisms that allow for L2 learning and L2 processing and have been foundational to reveal that a bilingual's languages are coactivated and constantly interacting in the bilingual mind and brain.

NOTES

1   The BIA models were principally developed to account for the process of bilingual word recognition rather than word production. Still, the mechanism of bilingual interactive activation specified in the model in combination with the model's notion of a network of lexical and sublexical representations that is shared for both languages has had a major influence on work on bilingual lexical access in general, including word production.
2   Even though naming also involves recognition mechanisms, we have put all the word naming studies under the heading of production for synthesis.

REFERENCES

Abunuwara, E. (1992). The structure of the trilingual lexicon. *European Journal of Cognitive Psychology* 4 (4): 311–322.

Abutalebi, J. and Green, D.W. (2007). Bilingual language production: The neurocognition of language representation and control. *Journal of Neurolinguistics* 20: 242–275.

Altmann, G.T.M. (2011). The mediation of eye movements by spoken language. In: *The Oxford Handbook of Eye Movements* (ed. S.P. Liversedge, I.D. Gilchrist and S. Everling), 979–1003. Oxford, UK: Oxford University Press.

Altmann, G.T.M. and Kamide, Y. (1999). Incremental interpretation at verbs: restricting the domain of subsequent reference. *Cognition* 73 (3): 247–264.

Altmann, G. and Steedman, M. (1988). Interaction with context during human sentence processing. *Cognition* 30 (3): 191–238.

Arai, M., Van Gompel, R.P., and Scheepers, C. (2007). Priming ditransitive structures in comprehension. *Cognitive Psychology* 54 (3): 218–250.

Benton, A.L. (1968). Differential behavioral effects in frontal lobe disease. *Neuropsychologia* 6 (1): 53–60.

Blumenfeld, H.K. and Marian, V. (2007). Constraints on parallel activation in bilingual spoken language processing: examining proficiency and lexical status using eye-tracking. *Language and Cognitive Processes* 22 (5): 633–660.

Blumenfeld, H.K. and Marian, V. (2011). Bilingualism influences inhibitory control in auditory comprehension. *Cognition* 118 (2): 245–257.

Bock, J.K. (1986). Syntactic persistence in language production. *Cognitive Psychology* 18: 355–387.

Bock, J.K. (1989). Closed-class immanence in sentence production. *Cognition* 31: 163–186.

Bock, J.K. and Loebell, H. (1990). Framing sentences. *Cognition* 35: 1–39.

Branigan, H.P. and Pickering, M.J. (2017). An experimental approach to linguistic representation. *Behavioral and Brain Sciences* 40: e282.

Branigan, H.P., Pickering, M.J., and Cleland, A.A. (2000). Syntactic co-ordination in dialogue. *Cognition* 75: B13–B25.

Bresnan, J., Cueni, A., Nikitina, T., and Baayen, R.H. (2007). Predicting the dative alternation. In: *Cognitive Foundations of Interpretation* (ed. G. Bouma, I. Krämer and J. Zwarts), 69–94. Amsterdam, The Netherlands: Royal Netherlands Academy of Science.

Bultena, S., Dijkstra, T., and Van Hell, J.G. (2015). Language switch costs in sentence comprehension depend on language dominance: evidence from self-paced reading. *Bilingualism: Language and Cognition* 18 (3): 453–469.

Byers-Heinlein, K. and Werker, J.F. (2009). Monolingual, bilingual, trilingual: Infants' language experience influences the development of a word-learning heuristic. *Developmental Science* 12 (5): 815–823.

Cai, Z., Pickering, M.J., Yan, H., and Branigan, H.P. (2011). Lexical and syntactic representations between closely related languages: evidence from Cantonese-Mandarin bilinguals. *Journal of Memory and Language* 65: 431–445.

Chang, F., Dell, G.S., and Bock, J.K. (2006). Becoming syntactic. *Psychological Review* 113: 234–272.

Cleland, A.A. and Pickering, M.J. (2003). The use of lexical and syntactic information in language production: evidence from the priming of noun-phrase structure. *Journal of Memory and Language* 49 (2): 214–230.

Colomé, À. and Miozzo, M. (2010). Which words are activated during bilingual word production? *Journal of Experimental Psychology: Learning, Memory, and Cognition* 36 (1): 96.

Cooper, R.M. (1974). The control of eye fixation by the meaning of spoken language: a new methodology for the real-time investigation of speech perception, memory, and language processing. *Cognitive Psychology* 6: 84–107.

Costa, A., Caramazza, A., and Sebastian-Galles, N. (2000). The cognate facilitation effect: implications for models of lexical access. *Journal of Experimental Psychology. Learning, Memory, and Cognition* 26 (5): 1283–1296. doi:10.1037/0278-7393.26.5.1283.

Costa, A., Miozzo, M., and Caramazza, A. (1999). Lexical selection in bilinguals: do words in the bilingual's two lexicons compete for selection? *Journal of Memory and Language* 397: 365–397. doi:10.1006/jmla.1999.2651.

Costa, A. and Santesteban, M. (2004). Lexical access in bilingual speech production: evidence from language switching in highly proficient bilinguals and L2 learners. *Journal of Memory and Language* 50 (4): 491–511.

Dallas, A. and Kaan, E. (2008). Second language processing of filler-gap dependencies by late learners. *Language and Linguistics Compass* 2 (3): 372–388.

Dell, G.S. and Chang, F. (2014). The P-chain: relating sentence production and its disorders to comprehension and acquisition. *Philosophical transactions of the Royal Society of London. Series B, Biological sciences* 369: 20120394.

Dell, G.S. and Ferreira, V.S. (2016). Thirty years of structural priming: an introduction to the special issue. *Journal of Memory and Language* 91: 1–4.

Desmet, T. and Declercq, M. (2006). Cross-linguistic priming of syntactic hierarchical configuration information. *Journal of Memory and Language* 54: 610–632.

Dijkstra, T. and Van Heuven, W.J. (1998). The BIA model and bilingual word recognition. In: *Localist Connectionist Approaches to Human Cognition* (ed. J. Grainger and A.M. Jacobs), 189–225. New York, NY: Psychology Press.

Dijkstra, T. and Van Heuven, W.J. (2002). The architecture of the bilingual word recognition system: from identification to decision. *Bilingualism: Language and Cognition* 5 (3): 175–197.

Dijkstra, T., Van Jaarsveld, H., and Ten Brinke, S. (1998). Interlingual homograph recognition: effects of task demands and language intermixing. *Bilingualism: Language and Cognition* 1 (1): 51–66.

Dussias, P. and Sagarra, N. (2007). The effect of exposure on syntactic parsing in Spanish–English bilinguals. *Bilingualism: Language and Cognition* 10 (1): 101–116.

Duyck, W. and Brysbaert, M. (2004). Forward and backward number translation requires conceptual mediation in both balanced and unbalanced bilinguals. *Journal of Experimental Psychology: Human Perception and Performance* 30 (5): 889.

Emmorey, K., Borinstein, H.B., Thompson, R., and Gollan, T.H. (2008). Bimodal bilingualism. *Bilingualism: Language and Cognition* 11 (1): 43–61.

Felser, C., Marinis, T., and Clahsen, H. (2003). Children's processing of ambiguous sentences: A study of relative clause attachment. *Language Acquisition* 11: 127–163.

Ferreira, F., Anes, M.D., and Horine, M.D. (1996). Exploring the use of prosody during language comprehension using the auditory moving window technique. *Journal of Psycholinguistic Research* 25: 273–290.

Ferreira, V.S. and Bock, J.K. (2006). The functions of structural priming. *Language and Cognitive Processes* 21: 1011–1029.

Flett, S., Branigan, H.P., and Pickering, M.J. (2013). Are non-native structural preferences affected by native language preferences? *Bilingualism: Language and Cognition* 16: 751–760.

Frazier, L., Taft, L., Roeper, T. et al. (1984). Parallel structure: a source of facilitation in sentence comprehension. *Memory & Cognition* 12 (5): 421–430.

Fricke, M. and Kootstra, G.J. (2016). Primed codeswitching in spontaneous bilingual dialogue. *Journal of Memory and Language* 91: 181–201.

Glaser, W.R. (1992). Picture naming. *Cognition* 42 (1): 61–105.

Gollan, T.H., Montoya, R.I., Fennema-Notestine, C., and Morris, S.K. (2005). Bilingualism affects picture naming but not picture classification. *Memory & Cognition* 33 (7): 1220–1234.

Green, D.W. (1998). Mental control of the bilingual lexico- semantic system. *Bilingualism: Language & Cognition* 1 (2): 67–81.

Green, D.W. (2016). Trajectories to third-language proficiency. *International Journal of Bilingualism* doi:10.1177/1367006916637739.

Green, D.W. and Abutalebi, J. (2013). Language control in bilinguals: the adaptive control hypothesis. *Journal of Cognitive Psychology* 25 (5): 515–530.

Gries, S.T. and Kootstra, G.J. (2017). Structural priming within and across languages: a corpus-based perspective. *Bilingualism: Language and Cognition* 20 (2): 235–250.

Gries, S.T. and Wulff, S. (2005). Do foreign language learners also have constructions? Evidence from priming, sorting, and corpora. *Annual Review of Cognitive Linguistics* 3: 182–200.

Gries, S.T. and Wulff, S. (2009). Psycholinguistic and corpus linguistic evidence for L2 constructions. *Annual Review of Cognitive Linguistics* 7: 163–186.

Grosjean, F. (2001). The bilingual's language modes. In: *One Mind, Two Languages: Bilingual Language Processing* (ed. J. Nicol), 1–22. Malden, MA: Blackwell.

Grosjean, F. and Li, P. (2012). *The Psycholinguistics of Bilingualism*. Oxford: Wiley-Blackwell.

Gullifer, J.W., Kroll, J.F., and Dussias, P.E. (2013). When language switching has no apparent cost: lexical access in sentence context. *Frontiers in Psychology* 4: 278.

Guo, T., Liu, H., Misra, M., and Kroll, J.F. (2011). Local and global inhibition in bilingual word production: fMRI evidence from Chinese-English bilinguals. *NeuroImage* 56: 2300–2309.

Hartsuiker, R.J. and Pickering, M.J. (2008). Language integration in bilingual sentence production. *Acta Psychologica* 128: 479–489.

Hartsuiker, R.J., Pickering, M.J., and Veltkamp, E. (2004). Is syntax separate or shared between languages? Cross-linguistic syntactic priming in Spanish-English bilinguals. *Psychological Science* 15: 409–414.

Henson, R. (2003). Neuroimaging studies of priming. *Progress in Neurobiology* 70 (1): 53–81.

Hermans, D. (2012). Formal models of bilingual speech production. In: *The Encyclopedia of Applied Linguistics* (ed. C.A. Chapelle). Oxford, UK: Blackwell doi:10.1002/9781405198431.wbeal0430.

Hermans, D., Bongaerts, T., de Bot, K., and Schreuder, R. (1998). Producing words in a foreign language: can speakers prevent interference from their first language? *Bilingualism: Language and Cognition* 1 (3): 213–229.

Hoshino, N. and Kroll, J.F. (2008). Cognate effects in picture naming: does cross-language activation survive a change of script? *Cognition* 106 (1): 501–511. doi:10.1016/j.cognition.2007.02.001.

Ivanova, I. and Costa, A. (2008). Does bilingualism hamper lexical access in speech production? *Acta Psychologica* 127 (2): 277–288.

Just, M.A., Carpenter, P.A., and Woolley, J.D. (1982). Paradigms and processes in reading comprehension. *Journal of Experimental Psychology: General* 111: 228–238.

Johnson, J.S. and Newport, E.L. (1989). Critical period effects in second language learning: the influence of maturational state on the acquisition of English as a second language. *Cognitive Psychology* 21 (1): 60–99.

Johnson, J.S. and Newport, E.L. (1991). Critical period effects on universal properties of language: the status of subjacency in the acquisition of a second language. *Cognition* 39 (3): 215–258. doi:10.1016/0010-0277(91)90054-8.

Kamide, Y. (2008). Anticipatory processes in sentence processing. *Linguistics and Language Compass* 2 (4): 647–670.

Kantola, L. and van Gompel, R.P.G. (2011). Between- and within-language priming is the same: evidence for shared bilingual representations. *Memory & Cognition* 39: 276–290.

Kootstra, G.J. and Doedens, W.J. (2016). How multiple sources of experience influence bilingual syntactic choice: immediate and cumulative cross-language effects of structural priming, verb bias, and language dominance. *Bilingualism: Language and Cognition* 19 (4): 710–732.

Kootstra, G.J. and Rossi, E. (2017). Moving beyond the priming of single-language sentences: a proposal for a comprehensive model to account for linguistic representation in bilinguals [Peer commentary on "an experimental approach to linguistic representation," by H. P. Branigan & M. J. Pickering]. *Behavioral and Brain Sciences* 40: e297.

Kootstra, G.J., van Hell, J.G., and Dijkstra, T. (2010). Syntactic alignment and shared word order in code-switched sentence production: evidence from bilingual monologue and dialogue. *Journal of Memory and Language* 63: 210–231.

Kootstra, G.J., van Hell, J.G., and Dijkstra, T. (2012). Priming of code-switches in sentences: the role of lexical repetition, cognates, and language proficiency. *Bilingualism: Language and Cognition* 15: 797–819.

Kroll, J.F., Bobb, S.C., and Wodniecka, Z. (2006). Language selectivity is the exception, not the rule: Arguments against a fixed locus of language selection in bilingual speech. *Bilingualism: Language and Cognition* 9: 119–135. doi:10.1017/S1366728906002483.

Kroll, J.F. and Bogulski, C.A. (2013). Cognitive second language acquisition: organization of the second language lexicon. In: *The Encyclopedia of Applied Linguistics* (ed. C.A. Chappelle), 4322–4330. Oxford, UK: Blackwell.

Kroll, J.F. and Stewart, E. (1994). Category interference in translation and picture naming: evidence for asymmetric connections between bilingual memory representations. *Journal of Memory and Language* 33 (2): 149–174.

Kroll, J.F., Van Hell, J.G., Tokowicz, N., and Green, D.W. (2010). The revised hierarchical model: a critical review and assessment. *Bilingualism: Language and Cognition* 13 (3): 373–381.

La Heij, W. (2005). Selection processes in monolingual and bilingual lexical access. In: *Handbook of Bilingualism: Psycholinguistic Approaches* (ed. J.F. Kroll and A.M.B. De Groot), 289–307. New York. NY: Oxford University Press.

Ledoux, K., Traxler, M.J., and Swaab, T.Y. (2007). Syntactic priming in comprehension: evidence from event-related potentials. *Psychological Science* 18 (2): 135–143.

Lemhöfer, K., Dijkstra, T., and Michel, M. (2004). Three languages, one ECHO: cognate effects in trilingual word recognition. *Language and Cognitive Processes* 19 (5): 585–611.

Lemhöfer, K., Schriefers, H., and Indefrey, P. (2014). Idiosyncratic grammars: syntactic processing in second language comprehension uses subjective feature representations. *Journal of Cognitive Neuroscience* 26 (7): 1428–1444.

Levelt, W.J.M. (1989). *Speaking: From Intention to Articulation*. Cambridge, MA: MIT Press.

Levy, B.J., McVeigh, N.D., Marful, A., and Anderson, M.C. (2007). Inhibiting your native language: the role of retrieval-induced forgetting during second language acquisition. *Psychological Science* 18: 29–34.

Linck, J.A., Kroll, J.F., and Sunderman, G. (2009). Losing access to the native language while immersed in a second language: evidence for the role of inhibition in second-language learning. *Psychological Science* 20 (12): 1507–1515.

Linck, J.A., Schwieter, J.W., and Sunderman, G. (2012). Inhibitory control predicts language switching performance in trilingual speech production. *Bilingualism: Language and Cognition* 15 (3): 651–662.

Loebell, H. and Bock, J.K. (2003). Structural priming across languages. *Linguistics* 41: 791–824.

MacDonald, M.C. (2013). How language production shapes language form and comprehension. *Frontiers in Psychology* 4: 226.

Macizo, P., Bajo, T., and Martín, M.C. (2010). Inhibitory processes in bilingual language comprehension: evidence from Spanish–English interlexical homographs. *Journal of Memory and Language* 63 (2): 232–244.

Mahowald, K., James, A., Futrell, R., and Gibson, E. (2016). A meta-analysis of syntactic priming in language production. *Journal of Memory and Language* 91: 5–27.

Marian, V. and Spivey, M. (2003). Competing activation in bilingual language processing: within- and between-language competition. *Bilingualism: Language and Cognition* 6 (2): 97–115.

Martín, M.C., Macizo, P., and Bajo, T. (2010). Time course of inhibitory processes in bilingual language processing. *British Journal of Psychology* 101 (4): 679–693.

McDonald, J.L. (2000). Grammaticality judgments in a second language: influences of age of acquisition and native language. *Applied PsychoLinguistics* 21 (3): 395–423.

McDonough, K. (2006). Interaction and syntactic priming: English L2 speakers' production of dative constructions. *Studies in Second Language Acquisition* 28 (2): 179–207.

McDonough, K. and Trofimovich, P. (2008). *Using Priming Methods in Second Language Research*. Taylor & Francis.

McLaughlin, J., Osterhout, L., and Kim, A. (2004). Neural correlates of second-language word learning: minimal instruction produces rapid change. *Nature Neuroscience* 7: 703. doi:10.1038/nn1264.

McLaughlin, J., Tanner, D., Pitkänen, I. et al. (2010). Brain potentials reveal discrete stages of L2 grammatical learning. *Language Learning* 60: 123–150. doi:10.1111/j.1467-9922.2010.00604.x.

Menn, L. and Dronkers, N.F. (2016). *Psycholinguistics: Introduction and Applications*. Plural Publishing.

Meuter, R.F. and Allport, A. (1999). Bilingual language switching in naming: asymmetrical costs of language selection. *Journal of Memory and Language* 40 (1): 25–40.

Misra, M., Guo, T., Bobb, S.C., and Kroll, J.F. (2012). When bilinguals choose a single word to speak: electrophysiological evidence for inhibition of the native language. *Journal of Memory and Language* 67 (1): 224–237.

Morsella, E. and Miozzo, M. (2002). Evidence for a cascade model of lexical access in speech production. *Journal of Experimental Psychology: Learning, Memory, and Cognition* 28 (3): 555.

Newcombe, F. (1969). *Missile Wounds of the Brain: A Study of Psychological Deficits*. London, UK: Oxford University Press.

Nitschke, S., Kidd, E., and Serratrice, L. (2010). First language transfer and long-term structural priming in comprehension. *Language and Cognitive Processes* 25: 94–114.

Nitschke, S., Serratrice, L., and Kidd, E. (2014). The effect of linguistic nativeness on structural priming in comprehension. *Language, Cognition and Neuroscience* 29: 525–542.

Osterhout, L., Poliakov, A., Inoue, K. et al. (2008). Second-language learning and changes in the brain. *Journal of Neurolinguistics* 21 (6): 509–521.

Philipp, A.M., Gade, M., and Koch, I. (2007). Inhibitory processes in language switching? Evidence from switching language-defined response sets. *European Journal of Cognitive Psychology* 19: 395–416.

Pickering, M.J. and Branigan, H.P. (1998). The representation of verbs: evidence from syntactic priming in language production.

Journal of Memory and Language 39 (4): 633–651.

Pickering, M.J. and Ferreira, V.S. (2008). Structural priming: a critical review. *Psychological Bulletin* 134: 427–459.

Pickering, M.J. and Garrod, S. (2004). Toward a mechanistic psychology of dialogue. *Behavioral and Brain Sciences* 27: 169–190. discussion 190–226.

Pickering, M. J., & Traxler, M. J. (2004). Syntactic priming in comprehension. Paper presented to the CUNY Sentence Conference. College Park, MD.

Poarch, G.J. and van Hell, J.G. (2012). Executive functions and inhibitory control in multilingual children: evidence from second-language learners, bilinguals, and trilinguals. *Journal of Experimental Child Psychology* 113 (4): 535–551. doi:10.1016/j.jecp.2012.06.013.

Potter, M.C., So, K.F., Von Eckardt, B., and Feldman, L.B. (1984). Lexical and conceptual representation in beginning and proficient bilinguals. *Journal of Verbal Learning and Verbal Behavior* 23 (1): 23–38.

Rayner, K. (1977). Visual attention in reading: eye movements reflect cognitive processes. *Memory & Cognition* 5 (4): 443–448.

Rayner, K. (1978). Eye movements in reading and information processing. *Psychological Bulletin* 85 (3): 618–660.

Rayner, K. (1998). Eye movements in reading and information processing: 20 years of research. *Psychological Bulletin* 124 (3): 372–422.

Rayner, K., Ashby, J., Pollatsek, A., and Reichle, E.D. (2004). The effects of requency and predictability on eye fixations in reading: implications for the E-Z reader model. *Journal of Experimental Psychology: Human Perception and Performance* 30 (4): 720–732.

Rayner, K. and Pollatsek, A. (2011). Eye-movement control in reading. In: *Handbook of Psycholinguistics* (ed. M. Traxler and M.A. Gernsbacher), 613–657. Amsterdam, The Netherlands: Academic Press.

Roelofs, A. (2006). Context effects of pictures and words in naming objects, reading words, and generating simple phrases. *The Quarterly Journal of Experimental Psychology* 59 (10): 1764–1784.

Rossi, E., Diaz, M., Kroll, J.F., and Dussias, P.E. (2017). Late bilinguals are sensitive to unique aspects of second language processing: evidence from clitic pronouns word-order. *Frontiers in Psychology* 8 (March): 1–13. doi:10.3389/fpsyg.2017.00342.

Salamoura, A. and Williams, J.N. (2006). Lexical activation of cross-language syntactic priming. *Bilingualism: Language and Cognition* 9: 299–307.

Scheepers, C. (2003). Syntactic priming of relative clause attachments: persistence of structural configuration in sentence production. *Cognition* 89 (3): 179–205.

Schenkein, J. (1980). A taxonomy of repeating action sequences in natural conversation. In: *Language Production*, vol. 1 (ed. B. Butterworth), 21–47. London, UK: Academic Press.

Schober, M.F. (2006). Dialogue and interaction. In: *Encyclopedia of Language and Linguistics* (ed. K. Brown), 564–571. Amsterdam, UK: Elsevier.

Schoonbaert, S., Hartsuiker, R.J., and Pickering, M.J. (2007). The representation of lexical and syntactic information in bilinguals: evidence from syntactic priming. *Journal of Memory and Language* 56: 153–171.

Segaert, K., Menenti, L., Weber, K. et al. (2012). Shared syntax in language production and language comprehension – an fMRI study. *Cerebral Cortex* 22 (7): 1662–1670.

Shin, J.A. and Christianson, K. (2009). Syntactic processing in Korean – English bilingual production: evidence from cross-linguistic structural priming. *Cognition* 112 (1): 175–180.

Shin, J.A. and Christianson, K. (2012). Structural priming and second language learning. *Language Learning* 62 (3): 931–964.

Snodgrass, J.G. and Vanderwart, M. (1980). A standardized set of 260 pictures: norms for name agreement, image agreement, familiarity, and visual complexity. *Journal of Experimental Psychology: Human Learning and Memory* 6 (2): 174.

Sunderman, G. and Kroll, J.F. (2006). First language activation during second language lexical processing: an investigation of lexical form, meaning, and grammatical class. *Studies in Second Language Acquisition* 28 (3): 387–422.

Szubko-Sitarek, W. (2011). Cognate facilitation effects in trilingual word recognition. *Studies in Second Language Learning and Teaching* 1 (2): 189–208.

Tanenhaus, M., Spivey-Knowlton, M., Eberhard, K., and Sedivy, J. (1995). Integration of visual and linguistic information in spoken language comprehension. *Science* 268 (5217): 1632–1634.

Tooley, K.M. and Traxler, M.J. (2010). Syntactic priming effects in comprehension: a critical review. *Language and Linguistics Compass* 4 (10): 925–937.

Tooley, K.M., Traxler, M.J., and Swaab, T.Y. (2009). Electrophysiological and behavioral evidence of syntactic priming in sentence comprehension. *Journal of Experimental Psychology: Learning, Memory, and Cognition* 35 (1): 19.

Torres Cacoullos, R. and Travis, C.E. (2011). Testing convergence via code-switching: priming and the structure of variable subject expression. *International Journal of Bilingualism* 15: 241–267.

Torres Cacoullos, R. and Travis, C.E. (2017). Two languages, one effect: structural priming in spontaneous code-switching. *Bilingualism: Language and Cognition* 19: 733–753.

Travis, C.E., Cacoullos, R.T., and Kidd, E. (2017). Cross-language priming: a view from bilingual speech. *Bilingualism: Language and Cognition* 20 (2): 283–298.

Traxler, M.J. (2011). *Introduction to Psycholinguistics: Understanding Language Science*. Hoboken, NJ: Wiley.

Traxler, M.J. and Tooley, K.M. (2008). Priming in sentence comprehension: strategic or syntactic? *Language and Cognitive Processes* 23 (5): 609–645.

Trueswell, J.C. and Tanenhaus, M.K. (eds.) (2005). *Approaches to Studying World-Situated*

Language Use: Bridging the Language-as-Product and Language-as-Action Traditions. Cambridge, MA: MIT Press.

Van Assche, E., Duyck, W., and Gollan, T.H. (2013). Whole-language and item-specific control in bilingual language production. *Journal of Experimental Psychology: Learning, Memory, and Cognition* 39 (6): 1781.

Van Hell, J.G. and Dijkstra, T. (2002). Foreign language knowledge can influence native language performance in exclusively native contexts. *Psychonomic Bulletin & Review* 9 (4): 780–789. doi:10.3758/BF03196335.

Weber, K. and Indefrey, P. (2009). Syntactic priming in German–English bilinguals during sentence comprehension. *NeuroImage* 46 (4): 1164–1172.

Weiner, E.J. and Labov, W. (1983). Constraints on the agentless passive. *Journal of Linguistics* 19: 29–58.

5 Real-Time Measures of the Multilingual Brain

NICOLE Y. Y. WICHA, EVA MARÍA MORENO, AND HAYDÉE CARRASCO-ORTÍZ

1. Introduction

Language unfolds over time in a dynamic flow of information that the brain must quickly decode at multiple levels of processing, from sound, sight, or touch to meaning. The multilingual brain has the added complexity of accessing the appropriate language(s) in the moment, and maintaining control over which language(s) are used at a given time. Researchers seeking a method that can keep up with this speed and complexity have turned to electroencephalography (EEG), which has served in this role for decades and has become standard practice in the field of language research. Magnetoencephalography (MEG), a complimentary real-time measure of brain activity, is gaining in popularity as it becomes more available to the scientific community. In this chapter, we discuss how these methods have been used to study the multilingual brain. We first introduce the methods, the physiological basis of the data obtained from them, and the advantages and disadvantages of the methods compared to each other and to other neuroimaging techniques. We then briefly present how these techniques have been used to address questions about the multilingual brain, laying a foundation for other chapters in this book that discuss the use of these techniques in specific research areas.

2. Real-Time Measures of the Multilingual Brain

Neurons communicate by causing electromagnetic changes within other neurons (see Luck 2014, for an easy-to-understand explanation of the neural origin of these signals). EEG and MEG measure the product of this communication, the postsynaptic potentials (PSPs) generated by the neurons that are targeted by the communication signal. Because electrical signals decay rapidly with distance, what is measured is not the activity of a single neuron, but the activity from a population of neurons that additively create a

The Handbook of the Neuroscience of Multilingualism, First Edition. Edited by John W. Schwieter.
© 2019 John Wiley & Sons Ltd. Published 2019 by John Wiley & Sons Ltd.

signal large enough to be recorded at a distance. Using amplification methods, these tiny brain signals (on the order of microvolts) can be measured non-invasively from the surface of the scalp (or from the surface of the brain when used intraoperatively, i.e. electrocorticography). Scalp-recorded electromagnetic signals are generated primarily by pyramidal neurons in the neocortex (outermost layer) of the brain, given that pyramidal neurons in a communication network tend to fire synchronously (Hebbian principle, 'fire together wire together'). Hence, EEG and MEG are only partial recordings of brain signals, given that the signals produced by other types of neurons, and by glia (cells that modulate neural signals), cannot be recorded at a distance (e.g. because they are not open source signals, or they do not fire synchronously, or they are too distant). Nevertheless, advantageous for these techniques, pyramidal cells are the predominant neurons in the cortex and they create strong signals (open source dipoles of synchronously firing cells) close to the surface of the brain. Given that any electrical signal has a counter magnetic signal, and vice versa, the same activity from a population of neurons can be measured as a change in either electric currents (EEG) or magnetic fields (MEG). Specifically, EEG and MEG measure activity from a different subset of the same population on cortical neurons (radially or tangentially orientated cells, respectively, relative to the surface of the head). Critically, EEG and MEG are the only non-invasive techniques available for human research that directly measure neural activity.

Encephalographic recordings are complex data sets that can be measured in multiple dimensions. Similar to the way a sound wave is composed of multiple frequencies (i.e. the rates at which air vibrates and hits the eardrum), which together make a complex sound, EEG/MEG signals are also made up of multiple frequency patterns of neural activity. The frequencies can vary from extremely fast signals, such as those emitted by the auditory brain stem structures in response to sounds (e.g. auditory brainstem response – ABR), to the slower cognitive components that we will discuss herein (e.g. N400, P600). In other words, EEG/MEG allows us to track both very rapidly changing and slower changing signals, all on the order of milliseconds, which is the real-time pace of neural activity. We can then look at this neural activity in the time domain, where we can measure *when* changes in brain activity occur, or in the frequency domain, where we can measure *which* frequencies are present in the signal. In this chapter, we will focus primarily on findings in the time domain, which is the dominant method for analysing language-related EEG/MEG data. However, analysis in the frequency domain has also yielded important findings in multilingualism research. For example, neural activity is often more distributed (increased coherence in the frequency domain across recording sites) and more complex for second (L2) language than first (L1) language processes (e.g.Grundy et al. 2017; Reiterer et al. 2011).

Despite measuring related brain signals, there are some discernible differences that set EEG and MEG apart. One of the key benefits of MEG is that it is less susceptible to certain kinds of signal distortion, namely the distortion caused when electrical signals travel through solid structures, such as the skull, making it better than EEG at localizing the neural sources of scalp-recorded signals (see Rommers and Federmeier 2017, for a recent review). That is to say, both techniques only estimate where in the brain the electrical or magnetic signals are coming from, but MEG allows for more reliable localization estimates than EEG. This is important because few non-invasive techniques are capable of measuring brain activity with sufficient precision in both time and space. MEG therefore allows researchers to determine not only when in time neural activity happens, but also what the sources of that signal are. For example, MEG has revealed that the spatiotemporal dynamics of verb generation engages a similar neural trajectory in L1 and L2 from occipital to temporal to inferior frontal cortices, but with a slower time course and additional brain areas (e.g. anterior cingulate) recruited for L2 (Pang and MacDonald 2012). Also, similar to the EEG coherence findings mentioned above, which show a more distributed neural network for L2 than L1, MEG data shows that bilinguals recruit overlapping brain areas in the left hemisphere when reading words in both L1 and L2, but with additional recruitment of homologous regions in the right hemisphere for reading L2 (Leonard et al. 2010).

The large electrical activity caused by movements, such as eye movements and speaking, has limited EEG research primarily to studying language comprehension (rather than production) with the eyes fixed in a single location (e.g. in the centre of a screen). MEG is less susceptible to motor artefacts from blinking or moving the mouth, making it more amenable to language production and natural reading studies (Munding et al. 2016a, b; Pylkkanen et al. 2014). There have also been efforts to overcome these limitations of EEG, for example, by extracting eye movement components using independent components analysis (ICA) or principal components analysis (PCA), or by extracting event-related potentials (ERPs) time-locked to eye movements (fixation related potentials), rather than time locking to the stimulus, in order to measure natural reading (e.g. Ditman et al. 2007; Weiss et al. 2016). Other studies have shown that it is possible to extract language related (ERP) components that are free of (or preceding) articulator artefacts during word production (e.g. Chauncey et al. 2009; Wu and Thierry 2017).

MEG research has been very limited despite its significant advantage as a tool for measuring brain activity with precision in both time and space. The critical reason for this is the accessibility of the technique, which has been improving somewhat in recent years with the availability of more MEG machines at institutions around the world. MEG requires expensive and sophisticated equipment in order to measure the relatively tiny magnetic brain signals without interference from stronger magnetic signals (e.g. magnetic fields of earth; see Baillet 2017 for more detail on MEG technology). As a result, few institutions have MEG machines. In contrast, EEG is relatively inexpensive and user friendly, and has been used much more widely than MEG for all aspects of language research. We therefore focus our review of the literature on the larger contributions from EEG research, citing MEG studies wherever relevant. We will focus on the time domain, describing ERP research starting in Section 4.

3.   Encephalography Compared with Other Methods

The greatest strength of these real-time measures of brain activity is measuring the brain's response to a stimulus as it happens, in real time, with millisecond precision. This is something that behavioural measures and neuroimaging techniques that specialize in localization cannot provide. Chapter 4 discusses how, with the use of clever designs and careful deduction, psycholinguistic methods have provided invaluable behavioural data to develop and refine our understanding of multilingualism. Some methods, such as eye-tracking, have tapped into real-time behaviour that is naturally part of the reading or viewing process during language comprehension. However, psycholinguistic measures are delayed compared to the multiple processes that occur before a behavioural response can be given, and as such are the sum of all the processes that could influence behavior (e.g. sentence parsing, error detection, re-evaluation, etc.) that could influence behaviour. Moreover, most psycholinguistic methods require a behavioural response, such as a forced-choice or offline judgement, which can incur a change in behaviour relative to natural language processes. One advantage of using encephalography is the ability to track changes in brain activity that index these underlying processes with millisecond precision without the need for an overt behavioural response. In this regard, a significant strength of EEG/MEG for multilingual research is the ability to use these non-invasive techniques across the lifespan, including with very young bilingual children (e.g. Conboy et al. 2015; Conboy and Kuhl 2011; Conboy and Mills 2006; Ferjan Ramirez et al. 2014, 2016, 2017; Garcia-Sierra et al. 2011, 2016).

EEG and MEG provide a direct measure of the changes in activity of neurons, with an ability to capture these changes on the order of milliseconds. In contrast, localization techniques rely on a much slower and indirect signal of brain activity that comes from the blood flow that supplies nutrients to neural tissue. This signal functions on the order of seconds not milliseconds, and has a similar summarizing effect as behavioural data, in that the precise millisecond time course of neural responses is collapsed to a single time point. An exception is perhaps transcranial magnetic stimulation (TMS), which is technically also a method for studying the brain in real time, even though it has been used primarily as a localization technique. TMS stimulates the brain using a magnetic field that can lead to excitation or inhibition of neural activity. These stimulations allow researchers to target specific neural tissue with millisecond precision to determine at what point in time that part of the brain becomes critical for a specific behavioural outcome, either modulating normal behaviour or inducing a behaviour (e.g. Holtzheimer et al. 2005). This technique has been underutilized in multilingual research, perhaps for two primary reasons. On the one hand, neural targets specific to being bilingual are hard to isolate, given that there is little evidence for neural tissue that is specific to one language versus another, and we have a limited understanding about what, if any, specific tissue makes a brain uniquely multilingual. For example, no areas of the brain have been identified as critical for comprehending or producing multilingual as opposed to monolingual language (see Chapter 9). On the other hand, localizable areas of the brain that are important for multilingual behaviours, such as the basal ganglia – involved in language control and switching (e.g. Abutalebi et al. 2013; Green and Abutalebi 2013), are also critical for other behaviours, like motor control and planning, and therefore problematic as TMS targets.

Other techniques have been used much more widely to study localization of multilingual processes in the brain, in particular techniques based on magnetic resonance imaging (MRI), as discussed in Chapter 6. Indeed, the most significant limitation of EEG, and to a lesser extent MEG, compared to other neuroimaging methods, like functional MRI (fMRI), is the poor spatial resolution of the measure. EEG and MEG are 'blind' to the neural sources for the scalp recorded EEG/MEG signals. This arises because mapping inversely from the scalp-recorded signal to a neural source creates an ill-posed inverse problem, given that many different combinations of cells (called dipoles) can mathematically add up to the same electrical (or magnetic) signals recorded at the scalp. Importantly, because large enough electrical/magnetic signals can travel great distances instantaneously, they could be generated by neural tissue far from the recording site. Therefore, when interpreting the scalp distribution of EEG data it cannot be assumed that an effect at a particular spot on the scalp necessarily maps onto the brain structures directly beneath that area, or even within that same hemisphere of the brain. With enough recording electrodes (to properly represent the surface of the head), appropriate localization algorithms and converging evidence from other techniques, like fMRI, the sources of an EEG signal can be mathematically estimated (see a review by Jatoi et al. 2014). However, most studies do not attempt to localize EEG sources because of this added burden, and focus instead on the strength of the technique – measuring the timing of brain activity.

Neuroimaging methods, such as fMRI, have helped elucidate some of the neural substrates supporting multilingual processes. However, fMRI is expensive and cumbersome. Functional near infrared spectroscopy (fNIRS) is another non-invasive localization technique that is relatively inexpensive and user friendly, and as such is gaining prominence, especially in very young children, to address the cortical localization of function for language (we recommend the body of work by Ioulia Kovelman and colleagues for a review of this method, e.g. Arredondo et al. 2017; Kovelman 2012; Petitto et al. 2012). fNIRS uses light-emitting diodes and detectors to measure differential rates of light absorption in more versus less active cortical tissue. fNIRS and EEG can be recorded simultaneously with careful arrangement on the scalp of the diodes/light detectors and electrodes, respectively, potentially providing both timing and cortical localization in a relatively inexpensive and user friendly setup. Note that deeper brain tissue cannot be studied since the light emitted by fNIRS diodes does not penetrate far beyond the cortex (in contrast to fMRI). However, the technical challenges (e.g. fMRI-compatible electrodes) and poor signal-to-noise issues from simultaneous recording of EEG and fMRI have limited the usefulness of combining these measures for language research. Future multilingualism research would benefit from combining the findings from both real-time and localization techniques to get a better understanding of both the time course and spatial organization of the multilingual brain. Combining fNIRS and EEG may be a feasible alternative methodology for studying the multilingual brain (compared to MEG or even fMRI).

4.   Interpreting Real-Time Brain Responses in the Multilingual Brain

The most common way of analysing continuously recorded language-related EEG and MEG data is to extract ERPs or event-related fields (ERFs), respectively. ERPs and ERFs can measure the point in time at which electrical signals change in amplitude (magnitude of change), in polarity (direction of change), in latency (time course of the change) and/or in distribution across the scalp. To avoid confusion, we will focus our discussion on ERPs, with the assumption that similar results are observable in ERFs. Segments of EEG data are measured from the onset of an event of interest, either a stimulus or response, and averaged across multiple examples of that event (e.g. grammatical versus ungrammatical words) in order to extract the common brain signature from the background 'neural noise'. The resulting brainwave, the ERP, is made up of a sequence of early sensory brain components, such as the P1-N1-P2 components to a visual stimulus, and later cognitive components, such as the N400 (mN400 in MEG) and P600 (we will discuss these components in greater detail in Section 5).

Naming convention in the field uses N and P for negative-going and positive-going voltage shifts (or peaks), respectively. The numbers following the N or P reflect either the order of the peak (as in the early sensory components, e.g. first positive peak is P1), or the time at which the component was first or is typically observed (e.g. the N400 typically peaks in amplitude at 400 ms after the onset of the stimulus). Some brain components are broad or variable enough that the labels are more descriptive, such as the left anterior negativity (LAN) or the late positive component (LPC). Typically, a change in brain activity earns its place as a component only after its functional role has been operationally defined (e.g. the N400 has been shown in many studies to be a robust response to any meaningful or potentially meaningful stimulus). Importantly, ERP effects are measured as relative amplitudes compared between two conditions (e.g. semantically congruous versus incongruous words), since the absolute amplitude of the component is not, in and of itself, interpretable for cognitive research. In addition to amplitude (magnitude) and polarity (negative versus positive), the timing (latency of the effect onset or peak) and the scalp distribution (which electrodes across the head show the effect) of the components can also be informative (see Otten and Rugg 2005 for more details on the interpretation of these dimensions). To avoid overwhelming the reader, we describe different EEG/MEG components and effects as they become relevant.

The most prominent ERP components used to study multilingualism include ERP components that are especially sensitive to language processes, such as the LAN (and the elusive early LAN, see Steinhauer and Drury 2012), the N400, and the P600 or LPC. Researchers interested in bilingual sentence comprehension, for example, have asked questions about how bilinguals process meaning and grammar compared to native speakers. To address these questions, the N400 – a brain response that is sensitive to the meaning of a word, and the LAN and P600/LPC – brain responses sensitive to grammatical errors, such as word order and morphosyntactic violations in a sentence context, have been widely used. We discuss these brain components in more detail, below, within the domains of adult second language learning and language switching.

Other components not specifically sensitive to language processes, such as the mismatch negativity (MMN), contingent negative variation (CNV), lateralized readiness potential (LRP), P300, and N2, have also been used in clever ways to tap into mechanisms of the bilingual brain. For example, the N2, a measure of attention and inhibition, and the CNV, a measure of anticipatory response preparation, have been used to study language switching, as we discuss in Section 6 (e.g. Jackson et al. 2001; Wu and Thierry 2017). The N2 and P300 (target detection P3b) have been used to measure the availability of one language when attempting to process information selectively in another (e.g. Hoversten et al. 2015, 2017; Ng and Wicha 2013; Rodriguez-Fornells et al. 2005; Wu and Thierry 2012). These studies demonstrate another unique advantage of ERPs. That is, ERPs can measure the brain's response to 'ignored' information and compare that to attended information, in this case addressing the debate over how selective the bilingual brain is when processing language (Kroll et al. 2006; Marian et al. 2003). Similarly, ERPs can measure the brain's response to 'subconscious' processes. For example, despite no apparent effect in behavioural measures, Chinese-English bilinguals showed a repetition effect, the reduction of N400 amplitude to repeated items, for L2 English words that had a concealed link to L1 Chinese character repetition. This occurred during a semantic relatedness task performed exclusively in English, revealing the presence of interference from the presumed ignored L1 (Thierry and Wu 2007).

The use of ERPs to study multilingualism dates back to the seminal work by Weber-Fox and Neville in 1996, which addressed the (still debated) critical period for language learning (Weber-Fox and Neville 1996). Over the subsequent two decades researchers have used encephalography to study many aspects of bilingualism, including how bilinguals differ from monolinguals in phonological category perception (Garcia-Sierra et al. 2016), syntactic processes (Hahne and Friederici 2001; Kotz et al. 2008), lexical access (e.g. Hoversten et al. 2015, 2017; Ng and Wicha 2013; Rodriguez-Fornells et al. 2005), and processes specific to bilinguals, such as second language learning, language switching and cognitive control (e.g. Barac et al. 2016; Carrasco-Ortiz et al. 2017; Moreno et al. 2002; Naylor et al. 2012; Ng et al. 2014). ERPs have even been used to study the effects of being bilingual on other aspects of cognition, such as arithmetic (e.g. Martinez-Lincoln et al. 2015; Salillas and Wicha 2012; Wicha, Dickson and Martinez-Lincoln, 2018). Critically, ERP studies have contributed significantly to our understanding of bilingual speech sound comprehension and word recognition in preverbal multilingual children (e.g. Conboy et al. 2015; Conboy and Kuhl 2011; Conboy and Mills 2006; Garcia-Sierra et al. 2011, 2016).

Many of these studies have provided unique contributions towards our understanding of the multilingual brain, unattainable with other techniques (see relevant chapters in this handbook that address ERP and MEG studies of sentence comprehension in more detail). The rest of this chapter explores two areas of research, adult second language acquisition and language switching (specific areas of expertise for the authors of this chapter) as examples of how encephalographic techniques have been used to study multilingualism.

5.   Real-Time Brain Measures of Adult Second Language Learning

In a neurocognitive framework, the mastery of a second language is thought to involve the ability not only to represent linguistic knowledge, but also to process linguistic input in a native-like manner. Therefore, an important question in bilingualism research addresses whether the neural mechanism used by adult L2 learners to process lexical/ semantic and syntactic knowledge are similar or not to those used in the first language (for neural mechanisms underlying late L1 learning, see Ferjan Ramirez et al. 2016).

Real-time measures of brain activity have provided new insights into these mechanisms and have helped elucidate the nature and time course of the mental representations and processing mechanisms that learners use at different stages of learning for different types of linguistic information, e.g. semantics versus syntax (Bowden et al. 2013; Ojima et al. 2005; Osterhout et al. 2006, 2008; Steinhauer et al. 2009).

The neural mechanisms underlying semantic processing in L2 emerge at the earliest stages of learning (e.g. Osterhout et al. 2006; Weber-Fox and Neville 1996). Lexico-semantic processes appear to engage similar mechanisms in infants and adults for L1 (Travis et al. 2011) and these same mechanisms appear to be in place even in early stages of adult L2 learning (McLaughlin et al. 2004; Osterhout et al. 2006). In fact, after only 14 hours of classroom instruction, adult L2 learners show native-like ERP responses when discriminating between real and pseudo words in their L2 (McLaughlin et al. 2004). This effect is measured on the N400 – a negative-going deflection that was originally observed in response to semantic violations in a sentence context (Kutas and Hillyard 1980), and has since been observed in response to any meaningful or potentially meaningful stimulus across modalities and domains (Kutas and Federmeier 2011). In native speakers, N400 amplitude is larger for pseudowords than real words. After rather minimal exposure, L2 learners show a similar modulation in the L2, even when performance on a lexical decision task was at chance, indicating that the adult brain shows an ability to learn L2 lexical semantics earlier than behavioural findings alone suggest (McLaughlin et al. 2004). The N400 does however show sensitivity to individual differences of L2 factors, such as age of acquisition and proficiency (e.g. Moreno and Kutas 2005; Weber-Fox and Neville 1996), which can independently modulate the timing of the N400 effect. N400 effects starting or peaking later in time are observed in individuals with less proficiency and/or later L2 acquisition, revealing less efficient access to meaning in L2, despite using similar mechanism as in L1.

In contrast, the acquisition of L2 grammatical knowledge is much slower and less consistent across individuals than L2 semantics, and is also accompanied by concomitant changes in a learner's neural systems as a function of L2 proficiency and other factors (e.g. Kasparian et al. 2017; Osterhout et al. 2006; Steinhauer et al. 2009; Tanner et al. 2013). In their seminal study, Weber-Fox and Neville (1996) observed that the brain's response was more affected by later exposure to L2 for syntactic than semantic violations, implicating a critical period for learning grammar in a second language. It was later discovered that L2 learners show a brain response to morphosyntactic anomalies that transitions from a non-native to a native-like brain response with increased proficiency and exposure to L2 (McLaughlin et al. 2010; Osterhout et al. 2006). This transition from an N400 response early in acquisition to a more native-like P600 suggest that L2 learners engage lexical semantic mechanisms in early stages of processing until they are able to implement L2 morphosyntactic rules (see Morgan-Short et al. 2012 on how this difference may also be driven by implicit versus explicit learning). Alternatively, L2 learners may engage in more meaningful processing of the information until detecting grammatical errors becomes more automatic. Importantly, there is significant individual variability across L2 learners, who may transition from the N400 to P600 more quickly or more slowly or not at all. Even more fascinating, this trend appears to reverse with language loss, reverting back to an N400 response (see Kasparian and Steinhauer 2017;

Kasparian et al. 2017 for a discussion on LAN versus N400 effects in attriters). Individual differences in the underlying brain mechanism of an N400 or P600 brain response to morphosyntactic violations are associated with behavioural measures of syntactic proficiency (Tanner et al. 2013), suggesting a qualitative change in the supporting brain mechanisms with increased proficiency in L2 grammar.

In addition to proficiency, exhibiting an N400 or a P600 response to morphosyntactic violations is partially explained by other factors like L1–L2 similarity (McLaughlin et al. 2010), and sociological factors, such as the learner's motivation to learn and age of arrival in the L2 environment (Tanner et al. 2014). Indeed, studies have revealed several factors to be regulators of the acquisition of L2 grammar (see Caffarra et al. 2015, Morgan-Short 2014, and van Hell and Abdollahi 2017 for recent reviews), including age of acquisition (AoA; Weber-Fox and Neville 1996, 2001), language proficiency (Dowens et al. 2010; Hahne 2001; Hahne and Friederici 2001; Ojima et al. 2005; Rossi et al. 2006), and the degree of similarity between L1 and L2 (Carrasco-Ortiz et al. 2017; Foucart and Frenck-Mestre 2011; McLaughlin et al. 2010; Tokowicz and MacWhinney 2005). Amongst these, AoA has been one of the most complicated and controversial effects.

A standard assumption in L2 research is that the capacity to fully master a new language diminishes with age. This is most evident in learning the speech sounds of a new language, given that the phonetic categories we perceive as adults are established early in life (e.g. Ferjan Ramirez et al. 2017). Similarly, the persistent difficulty amongst adult L2 learners in fully mastering some aspects of language, namely grammar, had been explained by 'critical period' effects, or biological constraints, such as brain-maturation processes (Johnson and Newport 1989; Pakulak and Neville 2011; Weber-Fox and Neville 1996). These studies suggested that when a language is acquired after the so-called critical period, the brain responses to processing grammatical structure are not native-like. Even after many years of immersion and practice in L2, learners may still fail to show evidence of native-like processing for certain syntactic structures (Foucart and Frenck-Mestre 2011, 2012; Hahne et al. 2006; Kubota et al. 2003, 2004; Kubota et al. 2005; Meulman et al. 2014). However, the data obtained for AoA effects on L2 learning are far from consistent and the idea of a critical period has since been softened to a sensitive, yet flexible, period (for a review, see Pallier 2007).

Early on, Weber-Fox and Neville (1996) measured the native English response to sentences with word-order violations (e.g. 'The scientist criticized Max's of proof the theorem'.), and observed an early left anterior negativity (ELAN, N125), followed by a later left anterior negativity (LAN, N300–500), and a subsequent P600. Note that the interpretation of ELAN/LAN effects is controversial due to inconsistency across studies in observing LANs and the possibility that the LAN is actually a distorted N400 (see Tanner 2015; Molinaro et al. 2015; Steinhauer and Drury 2012; Guajardo and Wicha, 2014). Regardless of the debate, L2 speakers showed a different ERP pattern as a function of their AoA. The anterior negativity had a bilateral distribution for individuals who learned the L2 when they were 11 years old or older. The P600 was comparable to that of native speakers only in bilinguals who learned L2 by 10 years of age, and otherwise was delayed (AoA 11–13 years) or altogether absent (AoA 16+ years). The authors argued that these differences in the ERP response to syntactic violations were due to maturational effects (critical period around age 10).

Since this early seminal study, ERP studies have demonstrated that this sensitive period is malleable, and other factors such as proficiency level can modulate the brain response to syntax independently of AoA (Diaz et al. 2016; Hahne 2001; Hahne and Friederici 2001; Rossi et al. 2006). Proficiency has even been implicated in whether or not non-classical languages areas in the brain are engaged in L2 processing (Leonard et al. 2011). Here we introduce just a few of the studies, classic and recent, that have shown effects of proficiency on the brain response to syntactic processes in sentence comprehension. Hahne and Friederici 2001 showed that word order violations in German elicited a delayed P600 effect, but no ELAN in high proficiency learners, and a complete absence of the native like ELAN and P600 in less proficient late learners. Similarly, Ojima et al. (2005) demonstrated that proficiency can modulate the ERP response to subject-verb agreement violations in L2 English. Here again neither a LAN nor P600 effect was observed in less proficient speakers, while a LAN effect with no subsequent P600 was observed in highly proficient L2 speakers, even though AoA was controlled across groups (see also Chen et al. 2007; Meulman et al. 2014).

These two studies suggest that proficiency changes the brain response to L2 syntax, although they demonstrated no native-like attainment. In contrast, Rossi et al. (2006) showed that German sentences containing syntactic-category anomalies and agreement violations elicited comparable ERP signatures in native speakers and high proficiency L2 learners, but not in low proficiency L2 learners, who showed a delayed ERP pattern for syntactic-category violations, and only a P600 effect with no native-like LAN for agreement violations. Subsequently, Rossi et al. (2014) revealed that highly proficient late L2 learners can show mastery of features that are encoded on a grammatical morpheme (gender and number) even when these are absent in the native language (e.g. Spanish clitic pronouns that are absent in L1 English). Similarly, Dowens et al. (2010) showed that late English learners of Spanish who had been exposed to their L2 for at least 12 years also demonstrated native-like processing (early negativity and P600) in response to gender agreement violations. Finally, Bowden et al. (2013) showed that with sufficient proficiency late L2 learners can attain native-like syntactic processing (LAN/P600) even when the language is learned as late as university-level instruction. These studies show a strong association between native-like brain patterns and syntactic proficiency, especially for morphosyntax, and provide compelling evidence against a strong critical period hypothesis.

Another strong predictor of native-like brain activity is the degree of linguistic similarity between L2 and L1 (see Clahsen and Felser 2006, for a review). Tokowicz and MacWhinney (2005) investigated the effects of English-L1 on comprehending Spanish-L2 using three different types of syntactic violations: tense marking, which is comparable between L1 and L2; number agreement, which differed in application between L1 and L2; and gender agreement, which only occurred in the L2. L2 learners showed a native-like P600 effect for syntactic anomalies that were either similar between L1 and L2 (tense marking) or only present in L2 (gender agreement), but not for violations involving features that differed between languages (number agreement). The findings were interpreted under the competition model (MacWhinney 2004; MacWhinney and Bates 1989), according to which overlapping syntactic constructions in L1 and L2 allow for facilitation, while cross-language mismatches hinder L2 processing due to competition. Similarly, Carrasco-Ortiz et al. (2017) examined the effect of similarity in individuals with low proficiency where dependence on L1 grammar might be expected when processing the weaker L2. Whereas, native speakers of French showed a typical P600 for gender agreement violations, native speakers of Spanish who were low proficiency French learners exhibited a negativity – reminiscent of the N400 effects observed by Osterhout and colleagues (2006), but only for nouns that had the same lexical gender across languages. The L2 learners showed no effect in response to gender violations on nouns with conflicting gender across languages. These findings suggest that L2 learners used gender information from L1 at the lexical level to process agreement in L2, but engaged non-native mechanisms (N400 rather than a P600) even when agreement operates similarly in both languages.

Indeed, L2 grammar appears to be learned faster when features are shared between L1 and L2 than when the L2 features are new (McLaughlin et al. 2010; Osterhout et al. 2006). A longitudinal study conducted by Osterhout and colleagues (2006) followed English-speaking learners of French at one month, four months, and eight months of instruction. Participants read sentences in French containing verb agreement errors (*Tu adores/adorez* le français.* – 'You love/loves* French'.), or determiner-noun agreement errors (*Tu manges des hamburgers/hamburger* pour diner.* – 'You are having hamburgers/ hamburger* for dinner'.). Native speakers showed a P600 to both types of morphosyntactic violations. Results for L2 learners in the first month of instruction revealed an N400 effect to verb agreement violations, which operates similarly in French and English. Later in learning, this N400 was replaced by a P600 effect with amplitude increasing proportionally with the amount of instruction. In contrast, determiner-noun agreement violations, a grammatical feature unique to L2, did not elicit an effect and did not change significantly over the one year of instruction (see also Steinhauer et al. 2009; White et al. 2012, for effects of proficiency and language similarity). These results suggest that language similarity influences the rate at which L2 grammar features are mastered, and interacts with proficiency to elicit native-like brain responses.

In summary, ERP studies (and a handful of MEG studies, e.g. Bastarrika and Davidson 2017; Leonard et al. 2011) have been critical for understanding if and when an adult second language learner will exhibit native-like brain responses when comprehending a second language. ERPs have been especially helpful in revealing different processing stages in the acquisition of grammatical structures in L2, with a qualitative shift from semantic-like N400s to more native-like P600s in response to syntactic violations. The rate at which this transition occurs is driven by individual differences in age of acquisition and proficiency, as well as linguistic similarity between L1 and L2.

6. Real-Time Brain Measures of Language Switching

Another area of bilingual research that has benefited from real-time brain measures is in the exploration of language switching. ERPs can provide insight into the cognitive processes that take place before a language switch occurs in production (e.g. naming digits or pictures in alternating languages), as well as from the moment a language switch occurs during comprehension. In this section we briefly present a sample of studies that have measured the brain signatures for language switching, first in production then during written sentence comprehension, in bilinguals and professional simultaneous interpreters. We conclude with a recent MEG study that examined the brain network for language switching in an attempt to address the controversial bilingual advantage hypothesis (e.g. the notion of better attentional control in bilinguals than monolinguals), and a discussion of ecological validity in studying code switching.

Most studies examining the cost of switching between languages during production have aimed to test whether it is more difficult to switch in one direction than the other, for example, from L1 into L2 than vice versa. In studies measuring response times, paradoxically longer naming times are observed when naming in the stronger L1 after naming in L2 than vice versa (Christoffels et al. 2007; Costa and Santesteban 2004; Jackson et al. 2001; Kroll et al. 2006). This switching asymmetry has been explained as either the need to inhibit L1 more strongly in order to use L2 (than vice versa) or a more general difficulty in accessing words in L2. The first ERP study to look at this paradoxical effect used a number-naming task and showed electrophysiological evidence for this asymmetrical switch cost (Jackson et al. 2001). A negative-going amplitude deflection occurred at frontocentral electrodes around 310 ms after a language switch, but only when switching from L1 to L2, and not from L2 to L1. This negativity resembled an N2, which has been related to response-inhibition and is typically observed in go/no-go tasks where a response must be suppressed on certain trials. This finding suggested that in order to switch into L2, L1 had to be inhibited, but not the other way around.

Recently, Wu and Thierry (2017) showed results consistent with this observation using the contingent negative variation, or CNV, which occurs in preparation for a response and is sustained from the moment a cue to respond is given until the response itself is given (Walter et al. 1964). The CNV was used to explore a bilingual's preparation for naming a picture in each of their languages. Naming pictures in both L1 and L2 elicited a CNV around 500 ms after a language cue was provided compared to when subjects received a 'remain-silent' cue. The CNV was larger, however, in response to the cue to name-in-L2 compared to name-in-L1. The authors interpreted this finding as evidence that stronger proactive inhibition is needed to inhibit L1 in order to name in L2, than vice versa (Wu and Thierry 2017).

However, ERP studies of producing a code switch have not been entirely consistent with this conclusion, at times showing an opposite switch asymmetry or modulations at later ERP components, such as the N400 (Christoffels et al. 2007; Verhoef et al. 2010). In one study, a larger frontocentral negativity was observed for non-switch than switch trials, perhaps reflecting the need to inhibit on any switch trial. Then subsequently, between 350 and 500 ms post-cue onset, an asymmetrical switch cost emerged, with larger N400 amplitude when switching from L1 to L2, but not vice versa (Chang et al. 2016). This finding implies that the locus of the asymmetrical switch cost may be in lexical-semantic retrieval when naming in L2 after naming in L1 – hence the N400, rather than inhibition of L1, per se. Note however that this study, similar to Jackson et al. (2001), used numbers, which may be less like other words given their highly overlearned nature, which may drive some of the difference across languages. Another ERP study using a picture-naming task showed a similar modulation of an N400-like posterior negativity in response to a language cue that indicated which language to subsequently name in and appeared 750 ms before the picture to be named (Verhoef et al. 2010). Again, the effect was observed for switches into L2, but not switches into L1, which may signal difficulty of disengaging the non-target native L1 in order to access words in L2.

In brief, naming in a language-switching context creates a cost, which is often observed more strongly in one direction of switching, namely switching into the L2. ERP components such as the N2 and CNV indicate that global and proactive inhibition of L1 is needed to facilitate naming in L2. However, the N400 is also modulated under certain circumstances, revealing a cost in accessing lexical-semantic information in L2. Importantly, the brain response to producing language switches appears to depend on critical factors such as language use, and particularly whether bilinguals are typically exposed to language switches in their daily life (Christoffels et al. 2007). Further studies are needed to systematically manipulate the predictability of the switch (percentage of switch vs. non-switch trials), the immediacy of the response (if one is required), and the nature of the stimuli to fully understand the consequences of switching languages during language production.

As in language production, the N400 has been a useful tool for understanding the impact of language switching during sentence comprehension. One question in this domain is how the bilingual lexicon(s) is organized. For example, are words that have the same meaning across languages (translations, e.g. friend – *amigo*) treated the same as words with similar meanings within a language (synonyms, e.g. friend – buddy)? Moreno et al. (2002) tested this in Spanish-English bilinguals using sentences with highly predictable endings and idioms. They observed that unexpected within-language synonyms elicited a typical N400 response in bilinguals, with larger amplitude for a synonym than the expected word. In contrast, language switches elicited a frontocentral negativity followed by a large posterior late positivity, or LPC (450–850 ms). Thus, unexpected language switches were not processed in the same way as unexpected within-language synonyms, even if the word was highly predictable within the sentence context, such as in idioms. Interestingly, the amplitude and peak latency of this LPC effect was modulated by the participants' proficiency in L2. Individuals with higher proficiency in L2 showed earlier peak latency and smaller LPC amplitude than individuals with lower proficiency. A later study showed that similar LPCs are observed for language switches on both nouns and verbs in a bilingual story context, regardless of where in the story the switch occurred (early or later; Ng et al. 2014). This suggests that the LPC effect has more to do with sentence-level processing than discourse level contextually driven integration.

An important consideration when studying bilinguals is that not all bilinguals share the same experience with how they use their languages. For example, simultaneous interpreters regularly comprehend in two languages and rapidly translate or switch from one language into another (Proverbio et al. 2004). Considering that some environmental contexts prompt more switching behaviour that others, a recent study by Beatty-Martinez and Dussias (2017) compared two types of bilinguals. One group was immersed in a dual-language context with early and continued exposure to language switches in speech, and the other group was immersed in a single language environment with little-to-no exposure to language switches. Their study addressed the brain's sensitivity to a violation of grammatical gender in the switched language. Language switches were of the sort found in naturalistic corpora (e.g. 'Su mamá le pidió que colocara el/la <u>fork</u> next to every dish', 'Her mother asked her to put the MASC/FEM fork next to every dish'). In bilinguals who frequently switched, the N400 component was modulated for switched English nouns that violated the grammatical gender of the Spanish translations. In contrast, non-language-switchers showed a P2 modulation, an ERP typically associated with processing orthographic level information, to any switches regardless of gender agreement (gender match/mismatch). Therefore, language experience, in particular whether switching is a daily or infrequent phenomenon in a bilingual's environment, shapes the specific brain response to switches in language comprehension. This observation that bilinguals process switches differently based on how much experience they have with switching languages is consistent with findings from an unpublished data set from the lead author's lab (Blackburn 2013). The frequency of language switching differentially benefited bilinguals on different tasks. Namely, bilinguals who frequently switched were more sensitive to reading language switches in a sentence context, whereas bilinguals who rarely switched, and therefore continuously inhibit one language while using the other, showed stronger effects of inhibition on non-linguistic switching tasks.

In this regard, it has been argued that switching between languages engages similar neural mechanism as the ability to switch between tasks more generally (e.g. Abutalebi et al. 2013). In turn, some have argued that switching languages may be one of the factors modulating performance on non-language tasks where bilinguals have shown an advantage over monolinguals (see de Bruin et al. 2015, for a recent review on the bilingual advantage debate). A recent MEG study addressed this debate by comparing bilinguals who heard, versus produced, switches (Blanco-Elorrieta and Pylkkanen 2016). Participants had to either name or match an auditory input to visually presented playing cards. Language switching in production and a non-language category-switching task both recruited bilateral (left and right hemisphere) dorsolateral prefrontal cortex (dlPFC), a brain area associated with cognitive control. In contrast, language switching in comprehension recruited the left anterior cingulate cortex (ACC), a brain area associated with attention that was not critical for general category switching. Thus, in addition to considering an individual's use of language switches, it is important to consider that production and comprehension of switches may have different constraints and underlying neural mechanisms. While switching in production seems to share cognitive resources with switching tasks in other domains, switching in comprehension may involve brain activity that is specific for switches in the language domain.

Another consideration in language-switching studies is the language modality. Although it is not uncommon to read language switches in written text, such as in novels by authors like Sandra Cisneros (2002) or in everyday texts and emails, the above mentioned studies may suffer from poor ecological validity since language switching is more common in natural conversation or when interpreting between individuals (with the exception of bimodal bilinguals, who can switch between signed and spoken languages or use both languages simultaneously; for a recent example of the differences in language processing between unimodal and bimodal bilinguals; see Meade et al. 2017). However, because of the limitations and challenges of time locking continuous brain activity to continuous language, there are no studies of which we are aware in the spoken or signed modality. This is an important direction for future research in comprehending mixed language passages in real-world situations (including unimodal and bimodal conversations).

In summary, ERP and MEG studies suggest that using an L2 requires the effortful active inhibition of the native language (Chang et al. 2016; Christoffels et al. 2007; Jackson et al. 2001). These studies show that the comprehension system is altered by a language switch in a qualitatively different way than a within-language lexical switch, and the response to a language switch changes with language proficiency in L2 (Moreno et al. 2002). Moreover, the mechanisms for language switching in production and task switching, more generally seem to share neural networks, whereas language switching in comprehension relies on different cortical structures (Blanco-Elorrieta and Pylkkanen 2016). It remains to be determined how variables such as the predictability of the switch and the sensory modality (spoken/written/signed) contribute to the modulation of brain responses during language switching.

7. Conclusion

To date, real-time measures of brain activity have been used in clever ways to uncover the underlying timing and structure of the multilingual brain. For example, they have allowed us to study the subconscious presence of an unused language, beyond what behavioural measures can tell us (Wu and Thierry 2012), and to measure an infant's response to native sounds and words in their two languages (Ferjan Ramirez et al. 2017). We discussed in this chapter how by measuring the latency and amplitude of N400, LAN, and P600 responses in L2 speakers, the idea of a critical period to learn a second language has been softened to a sensitive, yet flexible, period. Also, by monitoring these ERP effects longitudinally we have learned that as proficiency in L2 increases adult L2-learners show a qualitative shift in the strategy for processing L2 grammar (Osterhout et al. 2006, 2008), and that this process is modulated by factors such as cross-language similarity (Carrasco-Ortiz et al. 2017; McLaughlin et al. 2010; Steinhauer et al. 2009; Tokowicz and MacWhinney 2005). ERP and MEG measures of language switching have revealed different neural mechanisms and consequences of switching during production (Chang et al. 2016; Christoffels et al. 2007; Jackson et al. 2001; Verhoef et al. 2010; Wu and Thierry 2017) versus comprehension (Moreno and Kutas 2005; Ng et al. 2014; Proverbio et al. 2004), and these brain responses are sensitive to the everyday environment within which a bilingual lives (Beatty-Martinez and Dussias 2017).

EEG remains the predominant measure of real-time brain activity for multilingualism research, and language processing more generally. MEG research is becoming more available and is a highly useful tool for studying both the timing and localization of function for language in the bilingual brain. As newer electrode technologies develop, researchers might begin to record EEG in less constraining environments (i.e. outside the lab) and perhaps study bilingualism in harder to reach populations, such as children in lower socioeconomic neighbourhoods far from a laboratory setting (e.g. Garcia-Sierra et al. 2011). In brief, EEG and MEG are still the best (if not the only) measures of real-time brain activity and will continue to flourish as tools for studying the multilingual brain.

REFERENCES

Abutalebi, J., Della Rosa, P.A., Ding, G. et al. (2013). Language proficiency modulates the engagement of cognitive control areas in multilinguals. *Cortex* 49 (3): 905–911. doi:10.1016/j.cortex.2012.08.018.

Arredondo, M.M., Hu, X.S., Satterfield, T., and Kovelman, I. (2017). Bilingualism alters children's frontal lobe functioning for attentional control. *Dev. Sci.* 20 (3): doi:10.1111/desc.12377.

Baillet, S. (2017). Magnetoencephalography for brain electrophysiology and imaging. *Nat. Neurosci.* 20 (3): 327–339. doi:10.1038/nn.4504.

Barac, R., Moreno, S., and Bialystok, E. (2016). Behavioral and electrophysiological differences in executive control between monolingual and bilingual children. *Child Dev.* 87 (4): 1277–1290. doi:10.1111/cdev.12538.

Bastarrika, A. and Davidson, D.J. (2017). An event related field study of rapid grammatical plasticity in adult second-language learners. *Front. Hum. Neurosci.* 11: 12. doi:10.3389/fnhum.2017.00012.

Beatty-Martinez, A.L. and Dussias, P.E. (2017). Bilingual experience shapes language processing: evidence from codeswitching. *J. Mem. Lang.* 95: 173–189. doi:10.1016/j.jml.2017.04.002.

Blackburn, A. M. (2013). *A study of the relationship between code switching and the bilingual advantage: Evidence that language use modulates neural indices of language processing and cognitive control* (Doctoral dissertation). Retrieved from The University of Texas at San Antonio. (Accession No. 978-1-3036-5119-9).

Blanco-Elorrieta, E. and Pylkkanen, L. (2016). Bilingual language control in perception versus action: MEG reveals comprehension control mechanisms in anterior cingulate cortex and domain-general control of production in dorsolateral prefrontal cortex. *J. Neurosci.* 36 (2): 290–301. doi:10.1523/JNEUROSCI.2597-15.2016.

Bowden, H.W., Steinhauer, K., Sanz, C., and Ullman, M.T. (2013). Native-like brain processing of syntax can be attained by university foreign language learners. *Neuropsychologia* 51 (13): 2492–2511. doi:10.1016/j.neuropsychologia.2013.09.004.

de Bruin, A., Treccani, B., and Della Sala, S. (2015). Cognitive advantage in bilingualism: an example of publication bias? *Psychol. Sci.* 26 (1): 99–107. doi:10.1177/0956797614557866.

Caffarra, S., Molinaro, N., Davidson, D., and Carreiras, M. (2015). Second language syntactic processing revealed through event-related potentials: an empirical review. *Neurosci. Biobehav. Rev.* 51: 31–47.

Carrasco-Ortiz, H., Herrera, A.V., Jackson-Maldonado, D. et al. (2017). The role of language similarity in processing second language morphosyntax: evidence from ERPs. *Int. J. Psychophysiol.* 117: 91–110. doi:10.1016/j.ijpsycho.2017.04.008.

Chang, S., Xie, J., Li, L. et al. (2016). Switch costs occur at lemma stage when bilinguals name digits: evidence from language-switching and event-related potentials. *Front. Psychol.* 7: 1249. doi:10.3389/fpsyg.2016.01249.

Chauncey, K., Holcomb, P.J., and Grainger, J. (2009). Primed picture naming within and across languages: an ERP investigation. *Cogn. Affect. Behav. Neurosci.* 9 (3): 286–303. doi:10.3758/CABN.9.3.286.

Chen, L., Shu, H., Liu, Y.Y. et al. (2007). ERP signatures of subject-verb agreement in L2 learning. *Biling. Lang. Congn.* 10 (2): 161–174. doi:10.1017/S136672890700291x.

Christoffels, I.K., Firk, C., and Schiller, N.O. (2007). Bilingual language control: an event-related brain potential study. *Brain Res.* 1147: 192–208. doi:10.1016/j.brainres.2007.01.137.

Cisneros, S. (2002). *Caramelo*. New York, NY: Alfred A. Knopf.

Clahsen, H. and Felser, C. (2006). How native-like is non-native language processing? *Trends Cogn. Sci.* 10 (12): 564–570. doi:10.1016/j.tics.2006.10.002.

Conboy, B.T., Brooks, R., Meltzoff, A.N., and Kuhl, P.K. (2015). Social interaction in infants' learning of second-language phonetics: an exploration of brain-behavior relations. *Dev. Neuropsychol.* 40 (4): 216–229. doi:10.1080/87565641.2015.1014487.

Conboy, B.T. and Kuhl, P.K. (2011). Impact of second-language experience in infancy: brain measures of first- and second-language speech perception. *Dev. Sci.* 14 (2): 242–248. doi:10.1111/j.1467-7687.2010.00973.x.

Conboy, B.T. and Mills, D.L. (2006). Two languages, one developing brain: event-related potentials to words in bilingual toddlers. *Dev. Sci.* 9 (1): F1–F12. doi:10.1111/j.1467-7687.2005.00453.x.

Costa, A. and Santesteban, M. (2004). Bilingual word perception and production: two sides of the same coin? *Trends Cogn. Sci.* 8 (6): 253; author reply 254. doi:10.1016/j.tics.2004.04.005.

Diaz, B., Erdocia, K., de Menezes, R.F. et al. (2016). Electrophysiological correlates of second-language syntactic processes are related to native and second language distance regardless of age of acquisition. *Front. Psychol.* 7: 133. doi:10.3389/fpsyg.2016.00133.

Ditman, T., Holcomb, P.J., and Kuperberg, G.R. (2007). An investigation of concurrent ERP and self-paced reading methodologies. *Psychophysiology* 44 (6): 927–935. doi:10.1111/j.1469-8986.2007.00593.x.

Dowens, M.G., Vergara, M., Barber, H.A., and Carreiras, M. (2010). Morphosyntactic processing in late second-language learners. *J. Cogn. Neurosci.* 22 (8): 1870–1887.

Ferjan Ramirez, N., Leonard, M.K., Davenport, T.S. et al. (2016). Neural language processing in adolescent first-language learners: longitudinal case studies in American sign language. *Cereb. Cortex* 26 (3): 1015–1026. doi:10.1093/cercor/bhu273.

Ferjan Ramirez, N., Leonard, M.K., Torres, C. et al. (2014). Neural language processing in adolescent first-language learners. *Cereb. Cortex* 24 (10): 2772–2783. doi:10.1093/cercor/bht137.

Ferjan Ramirez, N., Ramirez, R.R., Clarke, M. et al. (2017). Speech discrimination in 11-month-old bilingual and monolingual infants: a magnetoencephalography study. *Dev. Sci.* 20 (1): doi:10.1111/desc.12427.

Foucart, A. and Frenck-Mestre, C. (2011). Grammatical gender processing in L2: electrophysiological evidence of the effect of L1-L2 syntactic similarity. *Biling. Lang. Congn.* 14 (3): 379–399. doi:10.1017/S136672891000012x.

Foucart, A. and Frenck-Mestre, C. (2012). Can late l2 learners acquire new grammatical features? Evidence from ERPS and eye-tracking: Corrigendum. *Journal of Memory and Language* 67 (1): 238. http://dx.doi.org/10.1016/j.jml.2012.02.009.

Garcia-Sierra, A., Ramirez-Esparza, N., and Kuhl, P.K. (2016). Relationships between quantity of language input and brain responses in bilingual and monolingual infants. *Int. J. Psychophysiol.* 110: 1–17. doi:10.1016/j.ijpsycho.2016.10.004.

Garcia-Sierra, A., Rivera-Gaxiola, M., Percaccio, C.R. et al. (2011). Bilingual language learning: an ERP study relating early brain responses to speech, language input, and later word production. *J. Phon.* 39 (4): 546–557. doi:10.1016/j.wocn.2011.07.002.

Green, D.W. and Abutalebi, J. (2013). Language control in bilinguals: the adaptive control hypothesis. *J. Cogn. Psychol. (Hove)* 25 (5): 515–530. doi:10.1080/20445911.2013.796377.

Grundy, J.G., Anderson, J.A.E., and Bialystok, E. (2017). Bilinguals have more complex EEG brain signals in occipital regions than monolinguals. *NeuroImage* 159: 280–288. doi:10.1016/j.neuroimage.2017.07.063.

Guajardo, L.F. and Wicha, N.Y. (2014). Morphosyntax can modulate the N400 component: event related potentials to gender-marked post-nominal adjectives. *NeuroImage* 91: 262–72.

Hahne, A. (2001). What's different in second-language processing? Evidence from event-related brain potentials. *J. Psycholinguist. Res.* 30 (3): 251–266. doi:10.1023/A:1010490917575.

Hahne, A. and Friederici, A.D. (2001). Processing a second language: late learners' comprehension mechanisms as revealed by event-related brain potentials. *Biling. Lang. Congn.* 4 (02): 123–141.

Hahne, A., Mueller, J.L., and Clahsen, H. (2006). Morphological processing in a second language: behavioral and event-related brain potential evidence for storage and decomposition. *J. Cogn. Neurosci.* 18 (1): 121–134. doi:10.1162/089892906775250067.

van Hell, J.G. and Abdollahi, F. (2017). Individual variation in syntactic processing in the second language: electrophysiological approaches. In: *Developmental Perspectives in Written Language and Literacy* (ed. E. Segers and P. van den Broek), 257–273. Amsterdam, The Netherlands: John Benjamins.

Holtzheimer, P., Fawaz, W., Wilson, C., and Avery, D. (2005). Repetitive transcranial magnetic stimulation may induce language switching in bilingual patients. *Brain Lang.* 94 (3): 274–277. doi:10.1016/j.bandl.2005.01.003.

Hoversten, L.J., Brothers, T., Swaab, T.Y., and Traxler, M.J. (2015). Language membership identification precedes semantic access: suppression during bilingual word recognition. *J. Cogn. Neurosci.* 27 (11): 2108–2116. doi:10.1162/jocn_a_00844.

Hoversten, L.J., Brothers, T., Swaab, T.Y., and Traxler, M.J. (2017). Early processing of orthographic language membership information in bilingual visual word recognition: evidence from ERPs. *Neuropsychologia* 103: 183–190. doi:10.1016/j.neuropsychologia.2017.07.026.

Jackson, G., Swainson, R., Cunnington, R., and Jackson, S. (2001). ERP correlates of executive control in language-switching. *NeuroImage* 13 (6): S322–S322.

Jatoi, M.A., Kamel, N., Malik, A.S., and Faye, I. (2014). EEG based brain source localization comparison of sLORETA and eLORETA.

Australas. Phys. Eng. Sci. Med. 37 (4): 713–721. doi:10.1007/s13246-014-0308-3.

Johnson, J.S. and Newport, E.L. (1989). Critical period effects in 2nd language-learning: the influence of maturational state on the acquisition of English as a 2nd language. *Cogn. Psychol.* 21 (1): 60–99. doi:10.1016/0010-0285(89)90003-0.

Kasparian, K. and Steinhauer, K. (2017). When the second language takes the lead: neurocognitive processing changes in the first language of adult attriters. *Front. Psychol.* 8: 389. doi:10.3389/fpsyg.2017.00389.

Kasparian, K., Vespignani, F., and Steinhauer, K. (2017). First language attrition induces changes in online morphosyntactic processing and re-analysis: an ERP study of number agreement in complex Italian sentences. *Cogn. Sci.* 41 (7): 1760–1803. doi:10.1111/cogs.12450.

Kotz, S.A., Holcomb, P.J., and Osterhout, L. (2008). ERPs reveal comparable syntactic sentence processing in native and non-native readers of English. *Acta Psychol.* 128 (3): 514–527. doi:10.1016/j.actpsy.2007.10.003.

Kovelman, I. (2012). Neuroimaging methods. In: *Research Methods in Child Language: A Practical Guide* (ed. E. Hoff), 43–59. Wiley-Blackwell.

Kroll, J.F., Bobb, S.C., and Wodniecka, Z. (2006). Language selectivity is the exception, not the rule: arguments against a fixed locus of language selection in bilingual speech. *Biling. Lang. Congn.* 9 (2): 119–135. https://doi.org/10.1017/S1366728906002483.

Kubota, M., Ferrari, P., and Roberts, T.P. (2003). Magnetoencephalography detection of early syntactic processing in humans: comparison between L1 speakers and L2 learners of English. *Neurosci. Lett.* 353 (2): 107–110.

Kubota, M., Ferrari, P., and Roberts, T.P. (2004). Human neuronal encoding of English syntactic violations as revealed by both L1 and L2 speakers. *Neurosci. Lett.* 368 (2): 235–240. doi:10.1016/j.neulet.2004.07.027.

Kubota, M., Inouchi, M., Ferrari, P., and Roberts, T.P. (2005). Human magnetoencephalographic evidence of early syntactic responses to c-selection violations of English infinitives and gerunds by L1 and L2 speakers. *Neurosci. Lett.* 384 (3): 300–304. doi:10.1016/j.neulet.2005.04.095.

Kutas, M. and Federmeier, K.D. (2011). Thirty years and counting: finding meaning in the N400 component of the event-related brain potential (ERP). *Annu. Rev. Psychol.* 62: 621–647. doi:10.1146/annurev.psych.093008.131123.

Kutas, M. and Hillyard, S.A. (1980). Reading senseless sentences: brain potentials reflect semantic incongruity. *Science* 207 (4427): 203–205.

Leonard, M.K., Brown, T.T., Travis, K.E. et al. (2010). Spatiotemporal dynamics of bilingual word processing. *NeuroImage* 49 (4): 3286–3294. doi:10.1016/j.neuroimage.2009.12.009.

Leonard, M.K., Torres, C., Travis, K.E. et al. (2011). Language proficiency modulates the recruitment of non-classical language areas in bilinguals. *PLoS One* 6 (3): e18240. doi:10.1371/journal.pone.0018240.

Luck, S.J. (2014). *An Introduction to the Event-Related Potential Technique*, 2e. Cambridge, MA: The MIT Press.

MacWhinney, B. (2004). A multiple process solution to the logical problem of language acquisition. *Journal of Child Language* 31 (4): 883–914.

MacWhinney, B. and Bates, E.A. (1989). *The Crosslinguistic Study of Sentence Processing*. Cambridge, UK: Cambridge University Press.

Marian, V., Spivey, M., and Hirsch, J. (2003). Shared and separate systems in bilingual language processing: converging evidence from eyetracking and brain imaging. *Brain Lang.* 86 (1): 70–82.

Martinez-Lincoln, A., Cortinas, C., and Wicha, N.Y.Y. (2015). Arithmetic memory networks established in childhood are changed by experience in adulthood. *Neurosci. Lett.* 584: 325–330. doi:10.1016/j.neulet.2014.11.010.

McLaughlin, J., Osterhout, L., and Kim, A. (2004). Neural correlates of second-language word learning: minimal instruction produces rapid change. *Nat. Neurosci.* 7 (7): 703–704. doi:10.1038/nn1264.

McLaughlin, J., Tanner, D., Pitkanen, I. et al. (2010). Brain potentials reveal discrete stages of L2 grammatical learning. *Lang. Learn.* 60: 123–150. doi:10.1111/j.1467-9922.2010.00604.x.

Meade, G., Midgley, K.J., Sevcikova Sehyr, Z. et al. (2017). Implicit co-activation of American sign language in deaf readers: an ERP study. *Brain Lang.* 170: 50–61. doi:10.1016/j.bandl.2017.03.004.

Meulman, N., Stowe, L.A., Sprenger, S.A. et al. (2014). An ERP study on L2 syntax processing: when do learners fail? *Front. Psychol.* 5: 1072. doi:10.3389/fpsyg.2014.01072.

Molinaro, N., Barber, H.A., Caffarra, S., and Carreiras, M. (2015). On the left anterior negativity (LAN): the case of morphosyntactic agreement. *Cortex* 66: 156–159. doi:10.1016/j.cortex.2014.06.009.

Moreno, E.M., Federmeier, K.D., and Kutas, M. (2002). Switching languages, switching palabras (words): an electrophysiological study of code switching. *Brain Lang.* 80 (2): 188–207. doi:10.1006/brln.2001.2588.

Moreno, E.M. and Kutas, M. (2005). Processing semantic anomalies in two languages: an electrophysiological exploration in both languages of Spanish-English bilinguals. *Brain Res. Cogn. Brain Res.* 22 (2): 205–220. doi:10.1016/j.cogbrainres.2004.08.010.

Morgan-Short, K. (2014). Electrophysiological approaches to understanding second language acquisition: a field reaching its potential. *Annu. Rev. Appl. Linguist.* 34: 15–36.

Morgan-Short, K., Steinhauer, K., Sanz, C., and Ullman, M.T. (2012). Explicit and implicit second language training differentially affect the achievement of native-like brain activation patterns. *J. Cogn. Neurosci.* 24 (4): 933–947. doi:10.1162/jocn_a_00119.

Munding, D., Dubarry, A.S., and Alario, F.X. (2016a). MEG studies of word production:

what next? *Lang. Cogn. Neurosci.* 31 (4): 480–483. doi:10.1080/23273798.2016.1153117.

Munding, D., Dubarry, A.S., and Alario, F.X. (2016b). On the cortical dynamics of word production: a review of the MEG evidence. *Lang. Cogn. Neurosci.* 31 (4): 441–462. doi:10.1080/23273798.2015.1071857.

Naylor, L.J., Stanley, E.M., and Wicha, N.Y. (2012). Cognitive and electrophysiological correlates of the bilingual Stroop effect. *Front. Psychol.* 3: 81. doi:10.3389/fpsyg.2012.00081.

Ng, S., Gonzalez, C., and Wicha, N.Y. (2014). The fox and the Cabra: an ERP analysis of reading code switched nouns and verbs in bilingual short stories. *Brain Res.* 1557: 127–140. doi:10.1016/j.brainres.2014.02.009.

Ng, S. and Wicha, N.Y. (2013). Meaning first: a case for language-independent access to word meaning in the bilingual brain. *Neuropsychologia* 51 (5): 850–863. doi:10.1016/j.neuropsychologia.2013.01.017.

Ojima, S., Nakata, H., and Kakigi, R. (2005). An ERP study of second language learning after childhood: effects of proficiency. *J. Cogn. Neurosci.* 17 (8): 1212–1228. doi:10.1162/0898929055002436.

Osterhout, L., McLaughlin, J., Pitkanen, I. et al. (2006). Novice learners, longitudinal designs, and event-related potentials: a means for exploring the neurocognition of second language processing. *Lang. Learn.* 56: 199–230. doi:10.1111/j.1467-9922.2006.00361.x.

Osterhout, L., Poliakov, A., Inoue, K. et al. (2008). Second-language learning and changes in the brain. *J. Neurolinguistics* 21 (6): 509–521. doi:10.1016/j.jneuroling.2008.01.001.

Otten, L.J. and Rugg, M.D. (2005). Interpreting event-related brain potentials. In: *Event-Related Potentials: A Methods Handbook* (ed. T.C. Handy), 3–16. Cambridge, MA: The MIT Press.

Pakulak, E. and Neville, H.J. (2011). Maturational constraints on the recruitment of early processes for syntactic processing. *J. Cogn. Neurosci.* 23 (10): 2752–2765. doi:10.1162/jocn.2010.21586.

Pallier, A. (2007). Critical periods in language acquisition and language attrition. In: *Studies in Bilingualism*, vol. 33 (ed. M.S. Köpke, M. Schmid, M. Keijzer and S. Dostert), 155–168. Amsterdam, The Netherlands: John Benjamins.

Pang, E.W. and MacDonald, M.J. (2012). An MEG study of the spatiotemporal dynamics of bilingual verb generation. *Brain Res.* 1467: 56–66. doi:10.1016/j.brainres.2012.05.054.

Petitto, L.A., Berens, M.S., Kovelman, I. et al. (2012). The "perceptual wedge hypothesis" as the basis for bilingual babies' phonetic processing advantage: new insights from fNIRS brain imaging. *Brain Lang.* 121 (2): 130–143. doi:10.1016/j.bandl.2011.05.003.

Proverbio, A.M., Leoni, G., and Zani, A. (2004). Language switching mechanisms in simultaneous interpreters: an ERP study. *Neuropsychologia* 42 (12): 1636–1656. doi:10.1016/j.neuropsychologia.2004.04.013.

Pylkkanen, L., Bemis, D.K., and Elorrieta, E.B. (2014). Building phrases in language production: an MEG study of simple composition. *Cognition* 133 (2): 371–384. doi:10.1016/j.cognition.2014.07.001.

Reiterer, S., Pereda, E., and Bhattacharya, J. (2011). On a possible relationship between linguistic expertise and EEG gamma band phase synchrony. *Front. Psychol.* 2: 334. doi:ARTN 33410.3389/fpsyg.2011.00334.

Rodriguez-Fornells, A., van der Lugt, A., Rotte, M. et al. (2005). Second language interferes with word production in fluent bilinguals: brain potential and functional imaging evidence. *J. Cogn. Neurosci.* 17 (3): 422–433. doi:10.1162/0898929053279559.

Rommers, J. and Federmeier, K.D. (2017). Electrophysiological methods. In: *Research Methods in Psycholinguistics and the Neurobiology of Language* (ed. A.M.B. de Groot and P. Hagoort). Hoboken, NJ: Wiley Blackwell.

Rossi, S., Gugler, M.F., Friederici, A.D., and Hahne, A. (2006). The impact of proficiency on syntactic second-language processing of German and Italian: evidence from event-related potentials. *J. Cogn. Neurosci.* 18 (12): 2030–2048. doi:10.1162/jocn.2006.18.12.2030.

Rossi, E., Kroll, J.F., and Dussias, P.E. (2014). Clitic pronouns reveal the time course of processing gender and number in a second language. *Neuropsychologia* 62: 11–25. doi:10.1016/j.neuropsychologia.2014.07.002.

Salillas, E. and Wicha, N.Y. (2012). Early learning shapes the memory networks for arithmetic: evidence from brain potentials in bilinguals. *Psychol. Sci.* 23 (7): 745–755. doi:10.1177/0956797612446347.

Steinhauer, K. and Drury, J.E. (2012). On the early left-anterior negativity (ELAN) in syntax studies. *Brain Lang.* 120 (2): 135–162. doi:10.1016/j.bandl.2011.07.001.

Steinhauer, K., White, E.J., and Drury, J.E. (2009). Temporal dynamics of late second language acquisition: evidence from event-related brain potentials. *Second. Lang. Res.* 25 (1): 13–41. doi:10.1177/0267658308098995.

Tanner, D. (2015). On the left anterior negativity (LAN) in electrophysiological studies of morphosyntactic agreement: a commentary on "grammatical agreement processing in reading: ERP findings and future directions" by Molinaro et al., 2014. *Cortex* 66: 1–7. doi:10.1016/j.cortex.2014.04.007.

Tanner, D., Inoue, K., and Osterhout, L. (2014). Brain-based individual differences in online L2 grammatical comprehension. *Biling. Lang. Congn.* 17 (2): 277–293. doi:10.1017/S1366728913000370.

Tanner, D., McLaughlin, J., Herschensohn, J., and Osterhout, L. (2013). Individual differences reveal stages of L2 grammatical acquisition: ERP evidence. *Biling. Lang. Congn.* 16 (2): 367–382. doi:10.1017/S1366728912000302.

Thierry, G. and Wu, Y.J. (2007). Brain potentials reveal unconscious translation during foreign-language comprehension. *Proc. Natl. Acad. Sci. U. S. A.* 104 (30): 12530–12535. doi:10.1073/pnas.0609927104.

Tokowicz, N. and MacWhinney, B. (2005). Implicit and explicit measures of sensitivity to violations in second language grammar: an event-related potential investigation. *Stud. Second. Lang. Acquis.* 27 (2): 173–204. doi:10.1017/S0272263105050102.

Travis, K.E., Leonard, M.K., Brown, T.T. et al. (2011). Spatiotemporal neural dynamics of word understanding in 12- to 18-month-old-infants. *Cereb. Cortex* 21 (8): 1832–1839. doi:10.1093/cercor/bhq259.

Verhoef, K.M., Roelofs, A., and Chwilla, D.J. (2010). Electrophysiological evidence for endogenous control of attention in switching between languages in overt picture naming. *J. Cogn. Neurosci.* 22 (8): 1832–1843. doi:10.1162/jocn.2009.21291.

Walter, W.G., Cooper, R., Aldridge, V.J. et al. (1964). Contingent negative variation: an electric sign of sensorimotor association and expectancy in the human brain. *Nature* 203: 380–384.

Weber-Fox, C.M. and Neville, H.J. (1996). Maturational constraints on functional specializations for language processing: ERP and behavioral evidence in bilingual speakers. *J. Cogn. Neurosci.* 8 (3): 231–256. doi:10.1162/jocn.1996.8.3.231.

Weber-Fox, C.M. and Neville, H.J. (2001). Sensitive periods differentiate processing of open- and closed-class words: an ERP study of bilinguals. *J. Speech Lang. Hear. Res.* 44 (6): 1338–1353.

Weiss, B., Knakker, B., and Vidnyanszky, Z. (2016). Visual processing during natural reading. *Sci. Rep.* 6: 26902. doi:10.1038/srep26902.

White, E.J., Genesee, F., and Steinhauer, K. (2012). Brain responses before and after intensive second language learning: proficiency based changes and first language background effects in adult learners. *PLoS One* 7 (12): e52318. doi:10.1371/journal.pone.0052318.

Wicha, N.Y., Dickson, D., and Martinez-Lincoln, A. (2018). Arithmetic in the bilingual brain. In D. Berch, D. Geary & K. Mann Koepke (Eds.), Language and Culture in Mathematical Cognition, Mathematical Cognition and Learning Series, Vol. 4, Academic Press: San Diego, CA.

Wu, Y.J. and Thierry, G. (2012). Unconscious translation during incidental foreign language processing. *NeuroImage* 59 (4): 3468–3473. doi:10.1016/j.neuroimage.2011.11.049.

Wu, Y.J. and Thierry, G. (2017). Brain potentials predict language selection before speech onset in bilinguals. *Brain Lang.* 171: 23–30. doi:10.1016/j.bandl.2017.04.002.

6 Neuroimaging Studies of Multilingual Speech

ANGÉLIQUE M. BLACKBURN

1. Introduction

Neuroimaging techniques such as functional magnetic resonance imaging (fMRI) have clarified our understanding of multilingual speech and its neural underpinnings. Functional MRI allows us to detect neural activity during one task relative to another (for a review of neuroimaging techniques to study bilingualism, see Blackburn, forthcoming). In addition to mapping neural networks involved in lexical selection and articulation, these studies have predominantly focused on the following: the degree of overlap in the cortical representation of each language; how multilinguals are able to select, control, and switch between languages; whether this need for language control protects against age-related cognitive decline; and models of multilingualism and recovery treatments based on neuroimaging case studies of multilingual patients. Together, results from these studies suggest that cortical representations of a multilingual's languages are overlapping, but not identical, and a cortical–subcortical network is engaged to manage language control. Damage to this distributed network hinders control over language selection and switching. Although the effects of using the language control network are still under investigation, frequently engaging this network may be responsible for neural changes linked to the ability to compensate for loss of cognitive control later in life.

2. Bilingual Speech Networks

Much of what we know about the multilingual language system has been garnered from bilingual neuroimaging studies. In these studies, bilinguals and/or monolinguals are asked to read, listen to, or generate single words (Briellmann et al. 2004), sentences (Chee et al. 1999b; Hasegawa et al. 2002), or stories (Bloch et al. 2009; Kim et al. 1997); make semantic or syntactic judgements (Luke et al. 2002); translate between languages (Price et al. 1999); or perform other language tasks (Rodriguez-Fornells et al. 2002).

The Handbook of the Neuroscience of Multilingualism, First Edition. Edited by John W. Schwieter.
© 2019 John Wiley & Sons Ltd. Published 2019 by John Wiley & Sons Ltd.

Often during speech tasks, participants are asked to silently generate words or narrate stories, as any movement from speaking may obscure the data (Rodriguez-Fornells et al. 2005). These studies have helped us map bilingual language networks and revealed how the brain manages more than one language.

In brief, bilingual studies have identified a left-lateralized frontotemporal language network that includes the middle and inferior frontal gyri (MFG/IFG), posterior temporal region, and motor areas in the precentral gyrus, as well as associated language control areas including subcortical structures and the anterior cingulate cortex (ACC) (see Figure 1 for a diagram of cortical gyri). Depending on the specific task during speech production, visual processing regions (i.e. the occipital lobe, inferior temporal gyrus, fusiform) may also be engaged during stimulus perception and processing (e.g. Videsott et al. 2010). Activation in the temporal region is related to lexical-semantic retrieval (Indefrey and Levelt 2000). The prefrontal cortex (PFC), ACC, and subcortical structures including the basal ganglia, aid in controlled language processes (Abutalebi 2008; Abutalebi and Green 2007, 2008). The MFG and IFG are engaged during lexical selection and planning (Thompson-Schill et al. 1997, 1999). The insula is involved in monitoring and speech planning (Bamiou et al. 2003), and the supplementary motor area (SMA), motor areas in the precentral gyrus, and cerebellum are associated with articulation (Crinion et al. 2006). Depending on the task and conditions being contrasted, different aspects of this network show different degrees of activation.

When contrasting monolinguals and bilinguals, no specific regions appear to be differentially activated, which has been taken as evidence of similar, but not necessarily identical, language networks for monolinguals and bilinguals (for reviews, see Blackburn 2016, 2018). Although a few studies have found distinct regions for each language (Dehaene et al. 1997; Kim et al. 1997), most have reported largely overlapping

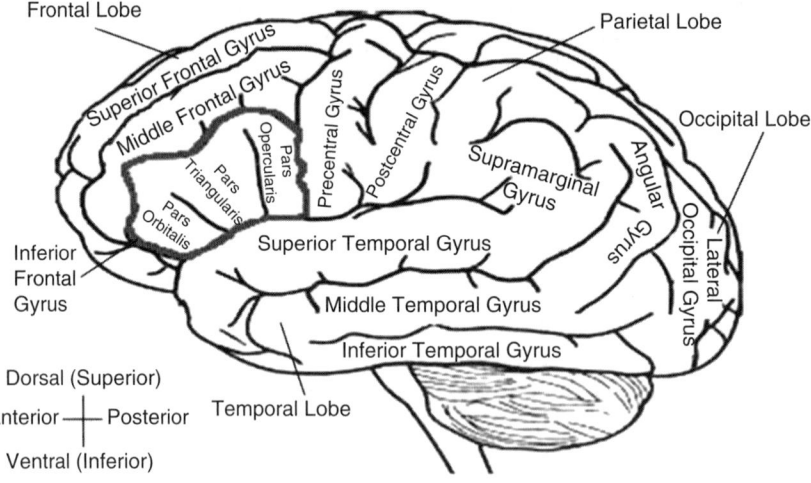

Figure 1   Left lateral aspect of cortical surface, 2016. Source: Hwozdek and Blackburn, 'Labeled Brain' derivative of 'Brain in Profile'. Source: Pearish, 2016, openclipart.org, licensed under CCO 1.0.

representation for each language (e.g. Chee et al. 1999a, b; Illes et al. 1999; Perani et al. 1998). It should be noted that many of these studies may lack the spatial resolution necessary to distinguish language-specific regions (see F. E. Roux et al. 2003 for a comparison of fMRI and direct cortical stimulation techniques with greater spatial resolution), and the inability to reject the null hypothesis does not warrant the conclusion that these networks are necessarily the same (Rodriguez-Fornells et al. 2006).

When differential representation of a bilingual's languages is observed with fMRI, it often can be explained either by morphosyntactic, visual, or phonological differences between languages (e.g. Tan et al. 2001, 2003) or by more extensive activation for bilinguals in brain regions associated with controlling two languages (e.g. Kovelman et al. 2008). For instance, the IFG is an area involved in word selection, as evidenced by greater activity in this region when monolinguals must select between competing responses such as 'couch' and 'sofa' (Thompson-Schill et al. 1997, 1999). A Spanish-English bilingual might also activate the translations of couch and sofa, 'el sofá' and 'el diván'. Even when operating only in one language, additional activation is often observed in bilinguals in the IFG, presumably because bilinguals must select from more competing responses (Kovelman et al. 2008). To manage interference from these competitors, more activation is also observed in the language control network, including the ACC, basal ganglia, and PFC (see Section 3.2.1) of bilinguals than monolinguals. Finally, articulation may be more effortful and require more monitoring for bilinguals, resulting in greater activation in areas associated with articulation and post-articulatory feedback, including the precentral gyrus, planum temporale, and superior temporal gyrus (STG; Parker Jones et al. 2012).

3. Multilingual Speech Networks

Multilingual studies provide insight about how language representation differs when managing languages of different strengths or that were acquired at different times and in different ways (see Table 1). In one of the earliest fMRI studies of multilinguals, two languages that were spoken currently and for at least five years were compared to a third language that had been studied for two to four years but not regularly used (Yetkin et al. 1996). Five males were asked to silently generate words beginning with a given letter in their first (L1), second (L2), and third (L3) languages. In every subject, greater frontal and parietal activity, including the IFG, MFG, precentral gyrus, and SMA, was observed for the less fluent, later acquired, and less regularly used L3 compared to L1 and L2. A similar trilingual study of verbal fluency also showed activation in frontotemporal language areas and regions related to articulation, as well as the ACC, for all three languages. The patterns were not explicitly discussed, but different patterns of activation within the IFG (BA 44/45) were found for each language (Wattendorf et al. 2001). Although these studies were not designed to independently test intricate aspects of language networks or the factors that contribute to differences in them, the use of multilinguals allowed for a within-subject comparison of languages. Rather than simply comparing bilinguals and monolinguals or the first and second language, researchers studying multilinguals were able to conclude that differences in experience with each

Table 1 Key multilingual studies regarding cortical overlap of essential language regions and regions involved in control for switching, inhibition, and articulation.

	Research question	Task	Contributing factors tested	Main findings	Significance
Early Multilingual Studies					
Yetkin et al. (1996)	Cortical overlap of languages	Covert Word Generation	Prof, AOA, exposure (conflated)	Greater frontal and parietal activity for less known language	Demonstrated benefit of using trilinguals for within-subject comparison; illustrated importance of factors
Wattendorf et al. (2001)	Cortical overlap of languages	Covert Verbal Fluency		Similar activation in frontotemporal regions, different pattern in IFG	Demonstrated benefit of using trilinguals for within-subject comparison; showed cortical representation is not identical across languages
Cortical Overlap Evidence from fMRI studies					
Vingerhoets et al. (2003)	Overlap of non-native languages	Covert Word Fluency/Picture Naming; Reading	Prof, exposure, and AOA	Common language areas for all languages; greater activation and recruitment of additional areas for non-native languages; differences across tasks	Demonstrated that differences in overlap may be proficiency- and task-related

Study		Task		Findings	
Bloch et al. (2009)	Overlap in simultaneous, early, and late bilinguals with later-acquired L3	Covert Narration	AOA	Early L2 exposure linked to greater overlap of the later-acquired L3 with L1	Showed that early life bilingualism impacts subsequent acquisition of additional languages (develops a bilingual network onto which subsequently acquired languages register)
Briellmann et al. (2004)	Overlap in quadralinguals with varying proficiency	Covert Noun-Verb Generation	Prof	Additional activity recruited for lower proficiency languages	Used quadrilinguals to investigate graded differences in proficiency and showed a shared language network across languages
Videsott et al. (2010)	Overlap in quadralinguals with varying proficiency	Overt Picture Naming	Prof (not dissociated from AOA)	Increased activity in left IFG and cerebellum for lower proficiency; increased right PFC activity for higher proficiency languages	Use of quadrilinguals revealed differences based on proficiency in two languages acquired after the early developmental years

AOA = age of acquisition; Prof = proficiency; IFG = inferior frontal gyrus; PFC = prefrontal cortex.

language result in different neural activity, with more extensive activity and different patterns of activity within language regions for lesser known languages.

3.1. *Overlap in Cortical Representation during Speech Production*

A number of studies have shown a large degree of cortical overlap in the frontotemporal language networks in each of a bilingual's languages. The degree of overlap is impacted by a number of factors, including but not limited to age of acquisition (AOA), relative proficiency, exposure to each language, number of languages learned, and processes specific to the language or task (see Chapter 12, this volume). Many of these studies have used a word fluency task similar to that used by Yetkin and colleagues (1996) or a covert narration task, in which participants silently narrate the events of the previous day. Unlike bilingual studies, where comparison of non-native languages with different properties (e.g. proficiency, AOA) necessarily requires a between-group design, comparing languages of multilinguals allows the participants to serve as their own controls. Within-group comparisons are advantaged because cortical activation patterns tend to vary between subjects (Dehaene et al. 1997; Seghier et al. 2004).

Using a within-subjects design, Vingerhoets et al. (2003) compared three languages within a group of multilinguals while they performed three tasks: reading comprehension, and two silent production tasks – picture naming and a similar word fluency task to that employed in Yetkin and colleagues' multilingual study. This design enabled comparison of cortical overlap between non-native languages in both production and processing, and allowed the researchers to probe the effects of proficiency, language exposure, and AOA on the degree of cortical overlap. They found different patterns of activation across tasks, but within each task, common language areas were engaged for all three languages, with a greater degree of activation and recruitment of additional areas for the non-native languages compared to the L1.

The additional areas recruited were dependent on the task. During the production tasks, widespread enhancement of frontal activity, including the inferior frontal cortex, was found for the non-native languages, especially in the left hemisphere. In particular, picture naming in the non-native languages resulted in additional left-lateralized activation compared to the native language, despite equivalent performance on the task. This observation led the authors to propose that additional neural activity in the non-native languages enabled the participants to perform at a comparable level to the higher proficiency L1. The authors attributed the widespread enhancement of left frontal activation in non-native languages to less automatic processes that might rely on subvocalization, phonological awareness, and greater lexical retrieval effort.

Studying multilinguals also provides the unique opportunity to determine how early-life bilingualism impacts subsequent acquisition of additional languages. In order to assess how the age of bilingual language development contributes to cortical representation of subsequent languages, Bloch et al. (2009) compared cortical activity during a silent narration task in simultaneous bilinguals who were either merely exposed to or experienced direct interaction in their L2 from birth, early sequential bilinguals who acquired their L2 between the ages of one to five years, and late bilinguals who acquired

L2 later in life, all of whom had all acquired fluency in a third language later in life. As expected, early acquisition of the L2 resulted in greater overlap of L1 and L2, with gradually more variability in neural activation in language regions (PFC, ACC, and STG) being observed with increases in the age of L2 acquisition. Interestingly, compared to late L2 acquisition, early L2 exposure was also associated with greater overlap of the later-acquired L3, even if early exposure was passive rather than direct interaction. This indicates that exposure to a second language early in life develops a bilingual language network onto which subsequently acquired languages register. If developed early, this system is able to manage the demands of additional languages in a way that a language system developed in a monolingual environment cannot (Bloch et al. 2009). Developing this overlapping bilingual network may partially account for easier acquisition of subsequent languages after the L2.

In a rare fMRI study of quadrilinguals, Briellmann et al. (2004) also found substantial overlap between four languages. Generating verbs (e.g. swim) associated with provided nouns (e.g. fish) activated the language network typically observed when accessing words from memory (the MFG), producing words (the IFG), and performing speech tasks (STG, left angular gyrus, and ACC). Consistent with bilingual studies, proficiency modulated the degree of activation within this shared language network, with additional activity recruited for lower proficiency languages (Figure 2). In addition, greater deactivation of the posterior cingulate cortex (PCC) was observed as language proficiency decreased. The authors suggested that deactivation of the PCC reflects allocation of resources to more anterior systems to accommodate the higher cognitive demands of operating in a less proficient language. Patterns of activation were not modulated by AOA in this study, but this variable was not directly manipulated and the contrast (before or after two years of age) was smaller and earlier than in most studies. The use of quadrilinguals provided the unique opportunity to investigate graded differences in proficiency and showed that a shared language network can accommodate at least four of a multilingual's languages.

Videsott et al. (2010) also compared a homogenous group of quadrilinguals during a picture-naming task. Like earlier studies, they found that all three languages activated the frontotemporal language network and associated control regions, as well as networks specific to the task. They also found an effect of proficiency: the later-acquired, lower-proficiency language exhibited more left IFG activity than the native language and more cerebellar activity than both higher proficiency languages. The authors postulated that enhanced cerebellar activity reflects increased motor planning demands in the less fluent language, and activity in the IFG reflects the greater need to resolve competition from the L1. In contrast, both native and non-native high proficiency languages engaged more right prefrontal activity, and the signal in this region positively correlated with naming accuracy in the non-native languages. The researchers concluded that demonstrating proficiency during production relies on the right PFC, which may play a role in monitoring and resolving competition between lexical items. It is important to note that proficiency and AOA could not be dissociated in this study, as the lower proficiency language was recruited much later (13–14 years) than the higher proficiency non-native language (4–5 years), but the multilingual sample revealed differences based on proficiency in two languages acquired after the early developmental years when compared with the native language.

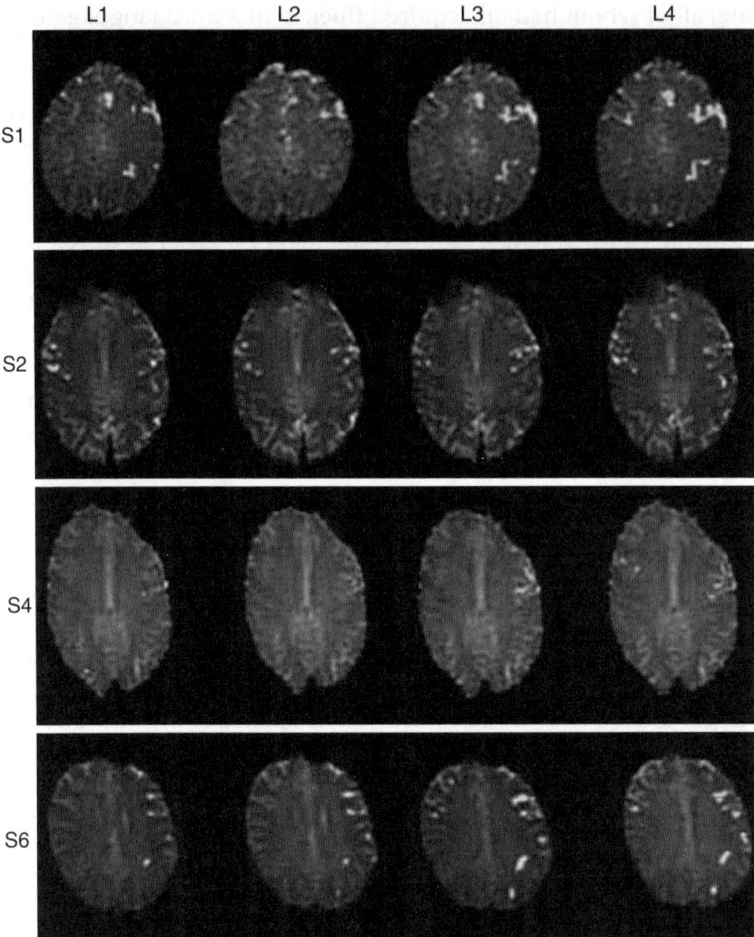

Figure 2   Neural activation during covert word generation. Overlapping neural activation for all languages in language networks is displayed in colour for four subjects (S1, S2, S4, S6). Activation, particularly in the cingulate gyrus and contralateral hemisphere, increases with decreases in language proficiency from L1 to L4. Source: Reprinted from Briellmann et al. (2004), Copyright (2004), with permission from Elsevier.

Together these studies have found that production in each of a multilingual's languages relies on a similar frontotemporal system, but that the exact networks engaged are task-dependent. A partially overlapping language system appears to subserve up to four, and likely all, of a multilingual's languages. It is crucial to note that although a general frontotemporal network appears to be used for each language, it is likely that these networks are overlapping, but not identical. Functional MRI studies may lack the fine-grained spatial resolution to distinguish spatially distinct representations within specific regions of the language network (Rodriguez-Fornells et al. 2006). While the general networks appear to be similar, neurosurgery studies allow for greater spatial resolution and point to partial evidence of language-specificity of neural substrates (Bello et al. 2006; Roux and Trémoulet 2002) with some degree of overlap (Fernandez-Coello et al. 2017, as will be discussed in Section 3.3). Although beyond the scope of this chapter, the reader is referred to critiques of the validity and reliability of neuroimaging studies and convergence with other methods (de Bot 2008; Paradis 2004).

Studying multilinguals has allowed for within-subject comparisons of two or more non-native languages, as well as manipulations of AOA and proficiency. In most cases, the less proficient language recruited additional resources, most notably in the left IFG, and possibly allocation of resources to more anterior systems to accommodate the higher cognitive demands of operating in a less proficient language. AOA also impacted cortical overlap, with later exposure to multilingualism leading to more variability in the language networks of both the L2 and L3. This suggests that early exposure to multilingualism impacts development of language networks and representation of subsequent languages.

3.2. *Multilingual Language Control*

3.2.1. *Language-Switching Networks*

The above studies illustrate a substantial degree of cortical overlap between languages; however, the degree of overlap appears to depend on the relative strength, exposure, and AOA of each language. It has been proposed that extended activation in the weaker languages reflects increased effort and reliance on control mechanisms to manage interference from the stronger language and less automatic processing in the weaker one (Abutalebi 2008). Language switching, which requires control, provides a means to unravel control mechanisms engaged for languages of differing strengths. We know from neuroimaging studies of bilingualism that switching between languages involves a frontoparietal-subcortical cognitive control network (Abutalebi and Green 2008). In these studies, bilinguals typically name pictures or digits in the language indicated by a cue. There is usually a response time cost when the required language switches from the previous trial (switch trials) compared to staying the same (non-switch trials; Meuter and Allport 1999).

Language switching is associated with enhanced activity in a cognitive control network that includes the left PFC, ACC, pre-SMA, inferior parietal lobe (IPL), and left caudate nucleus and putamen of the basal ganglia (Figure 3; for reviews, see Abutalebi and Green 2008, 2016). The ACC is routinely activated in both language and non-language tasks that involve monitoring and detecting conflict, such as the conflict a multilingual faces when choosing between translation equivalents in different languages (Abutalebi et al. 2011; van Veen and Carter 2002). When conflict is detected, the ACC/pre-SMA signals the PFC. The PFC, most notably the dorsolateral prefrontal cortex (DLPFC), is involved in attention, decision-making, response/language selection, and inhibition and has consistently been identified as a key player during language switching (Hernandez 2009; Hernandez et al. 2000; Ma et al. 2014). The PFC and other cortical structures send information regarding the task to the caudate nucleus, which biases responses to override the previous language and allow switching into the new one (Stocco and Prat 2014; Stocco et al. 2014). The basal ganglia in turn project back to the cortical structures (via the thalamus) to shift the focus of attention when required.

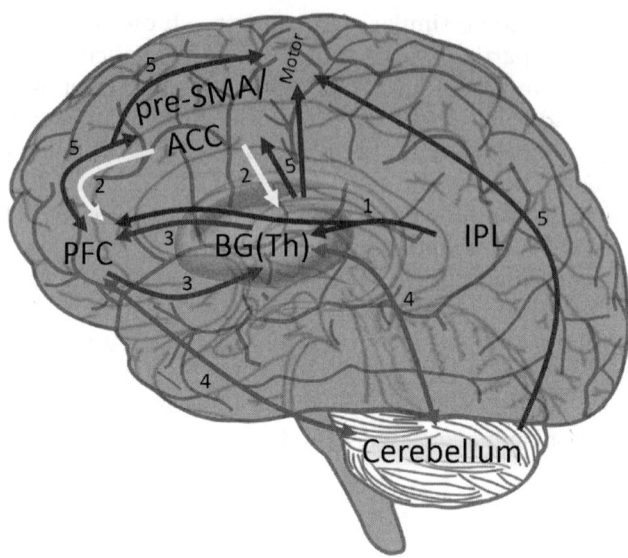

Figure 3 Cognitive control network. (1) Attention: Inferior parietal lobe (IPL) projects to the prefrontal cortex (PFC) as part of the attentional network to bias language selection. (2) Conflict detection: Anterior cingulate cortex (ACC)/pre-SMA signals the PFC and the basal ganglia (BG). (3) Bias: Fronto-subcortical loop ramps activity from PFC and compares it to other cortical inputs (e.g. the IPL and pre-SMA). (4) Prediction: The cerebellar connections to the BG and PFC may play a role in prediction. (5) Output: Signal spreads to planning and motor cortices (including insula, pre-motor, and motor). Note that the BG output through the thalamus (Th). Source: Blackburn, A. M., 2017, 'Language Control Model 2017', openclipart.org, licensed under CCO 1.0: https://creativecommons.org/publicdomain/zero/1.0/legalcode.

In the prefrontal region, the MFG and IFG are often engaged during switching and likely play a role in resolving competition between potential responses during word selection (Abutalebi et al. 2008; Guo et al. 2011; Luk et al. 2012; Wang et al. 2007; Zhang et al. 2015). Stimulating the posterior MFG and regions in the pars triangularis of the IFG impacts language switching independently of single language naming, although disrupting activity in the MFG elicits opposing effects (involuntary vs. delayed switching) in single language and language-switching contexts (Sierpowska et al. 2013). This suggests that the MFG may be a critical area in top-down regulation of appropriate schemas related to the task at hand and therefore a key region involved in language switching (Sierpowska et al. 2013, 2018). Disrupting the connection between semantic retrieval areas in the temporal lobe and the IFG also elicits involuntary language switching (i.e. the superior longitudinal fasciculus; Moritz-Gasser and Duffau 2009). The left and right IFG may serve the opposing functions of selecting the desired response and inhibiting the undesired one (Aron et al. 2007). It has been suggested that the DLPFC and left IFG may work together to select new stimulus–response mappings under conditions of moderate semantic interference (Canini et al. 2016). Once a response is selected, a signal spreads to motor planning areas (insula and SMA) to prepare for articulation. Activity in other areas is sometimes identified during language switching. The IPL, including the supramarginal gyrus (SMG) and angular gyrus, is active when attention is required to monitor the context. The SMG, which has been implicated in language switching during both fMRI and electrical stimulation mapping studies (Sierpowska et al. 2013), is associated with attention and phonological processing; it may be involved in inhibiting the previously used language in order to switch into the other (Toro et al. 2008; Van Heuven et al. 2008). A fronto-cerebellar circuit may play a role in prediction based on context (Abutalebi and Green 2016). Finally, activity in regions associated with semantic retrieval (i.e. the middle temporal gyrus), visual processing (i.e. the occipital region and inferior temporal lobe, including the fusiform gyrus), and articulation (i.e. the pre-SMA, SMA, and precentral gyrus) is observed during switching (Hernandez 2009; Hernandez et al. 2000; Luk et al. 2012). The exact network engaged depends on phonological and orthographic similarity of the languages, individual differences in language experience, and task demands, such as whether the switching is voluntary or indicated by a cue (for a review, see Blackburn 2018; Ma et al. 2014; Zhang et al. 2015).

3.2.2. Language-Switching Studies in Multilinguals   A deficit in the bilingual literature is that it is difficult to dissociate effects of language acquisition order (L1 vs. L2) and proficiency. To independently test proficiency effects in bilinguals, it is often necessary to compare at least two groups of bilinguals with different proficiencies in their L2. To eliminate between-group confounds, Abutalebi et al. (2013a) took advantage of varying proficiencies in languages that multilinguals acquired around the same stage in life. They compared switching out of the stronger L1 into either a high-proficiency L2 acquired around six years of age or a medium-proficiency L3 acquired around the age of eight. As an additional comparison, monolinguals were asked to switch between two language tasks in their L1. The researchers posited that switching effects that were independent of proficiency and obtained for both within- and between-language switching reflect task monitoring, as when multilinguals monitor the language context. In contrast, switching effects that were modulated by proficiency were thought to reflect different levels of control needed to inhibit languages of different strengths (see Table 2 for key language control studies).

The prefrontal region did not manifest effects of switching, which the authors proposed was due to the role of this region in maintaining task rules in order to operate in one language. They found that the pre-SMA/ACC were engaged for switching into all three languages, regardless of the proficiency level, implicating these regions in monitoring. In contrast, the left caudate was engaged when monolinguals performed a within-language switching task, and was progressively more engaged when multilinguals switched into the L1, L2, and L3. That is, the greatest caudate activity was observed when switching out of the strongest language into the weakest language, demonstrating specificity of the caudate in resolving conflict, especially regarding response selection under conditions of high interference from another language (see also Abutalebi et al. 2013b). The impact of these findings was twofold. First, they showed that the language control networks were not specific to multilinguals, but that multilinguals and monolinguals use similar control networks to monitor tasks and resolve conflict as a result of interference.

Table 2 Key multilingual studies regarding neural substrates of control for switching, inhibition, and articulation.

	Research question	Task	Factors tested	Main findings	Significance
Language Control					
Abutalebi et al. (2013)	Language switching network	Overt Language Switching (Picture Naming)	Prof	Pre-SMA/ACC for switching in all languages; caudate involved for all switching (including monolingual) and highest level of activation when switching into the weakest language	1. Showed language control networks are not specific to multilinguals 2. Showed dissociable effects of proficiency on areas of the language control networks that are responsible for different aspects of cognitive control
de Bruin et al. (2014)	Role of inhibition in language switching	Overt Language Switching	Prof; AOA	1. Switching out of the stronger language involves the right IFG and pre-SMA; linked to behavioural inhibition effects 2. Selective inhibition of L1; little inhibition is needed to suppress the weaker languages when using the first language, even in a mixed-language context	1. Demonstrated that inhibition is similarly engaged to switch out of the first language into subsequently acquired languages, regardless of L2/L3 proficiency and AOA 2. Showed inhibition via the right IFG/pre-SMA is specifically engaged to switch out of the stronger first language

Articulatory Control

Study		Task		Results	Implications
Wattendorf et al. (2014)	Overlap of articulatory control based on AOA	Covert Sentence Production	AOA	Same language network regardless of AOA; language control networks related to articulation for all three languages differed based on L2 AOA	Indicated that late multilinguals may not develop frontal-subcortical sensorimotor loops that enable switching between articulatory systems in the same way as early multilinguals; early developed systems are used for later-acquired languages
Abutalebi et al. (2013)	Overlap of articulatory control based on proficiency	Overt Language Switching	Prof (conflated with AOA)	Extended control activation for L2 and L3; putamen selectively activated for less proficient L3	Implicated left putamen and frontostriatal network in managing the articulatory demands of a non-nativelike language
Waldron and Hernandez (2013)	Overlap of sensorimotor/ articulatory control based on AOA	Covert Past Tense Verb Generation	AOA	Early bilinguals showed more activation than late bilinguals in motor and articulatory regions (including the putamen)	Suggested sensorimotor network is developed as early bilinguals acquire two languages through sensorimotor means; later languages rely on control and memory networks

AOA = age of acquisition; Prof = proficiency; IFG = inferior frontal gyrus; pre-SMA = pre-supplementary motor area; ACC = anterior cingulate cortex.

Second, they demonstrated dissociable effects of proficiency on areas of the language control networks that are responsible for different aspects of cognitive control.

The fact that more caudate activity was generated to switch out of the stronger language into the weaker languages, and that the degree of activity progressed with larger changes in relative proficiency between languages, is consistent with the inhibitory control (IC) hypothesis. According to this hypothesis, words in each language compete for selection; stronger languages cause more interference when producing words in a weaker language, and this interference must be inhibited so that words in the weaker language can be selected (Green 1998). The IC hypothesis has received support from behavioural and ERP studies (e.g. Blackburn 2013; cf. Costa and Santesteban 2004; Kroll et al. 2008; Linck et al. 2012).

In an effort to specifically test the role of inhibition during overt language switching, de Bruin et al. (2014) compared activation in two regions associated with inhibition, the right IFG (rIFG) and pre-SMA. In accordance with the IC model, they predicted that more inhibition would be needed to suppress the stronger L1 than the L2 and L3, resulting in greater activation of these areas when switching from L1 into the weaker languages. Consistent with this prediction, switching out of L1 increased activation in the rIFG and pre-SMA. In contrast, non-switch and switch trials into L1 revealed no difference in inhibition areas, substantiating the IC model claim that inhibition would be specifically needed to switch out of the stronger language.

The reported activations were associated with behavioural effects linked to inhibition. The authors reported a weak link between activation in these regions for L1 inhibition and IC ability as measured on a non-language task (the Simon task). In addition, stronger IC ability was associated with larger switch costs into the L1 but smaller switch costs into the weaker language, suggesting that more inhibition is exerted in individuals with enhanced IC ability specifically to suppress the stronger language when switching into the weaker languages. A correlation in this direction corroborates the proposal that language switching relies on and strengthens a general cognitive inhibition network (Abutalebi and Green 2008).

In addition to inhibition-related activation, switching out of the first language into a weaker language increased activation in other areas related to cognitive control: the left precuneus, the right cuneus, and the right anterior and posterior cingulate cortices. Importantly, no differences were found between L2 and L3, suggesting that the inhibition and control mechanisms are similarly engaged to switch out of the first language into subsequently acquired languages, even if they are acquired at a different point in time or a different level of proficiency has been attained.

This is consistent with the finding by Abutalebi et al. (2013a) that monitoring when switching out of the L1 into a less proficient language is independent of proficiency in the weaker language; however, their discovery of L2/L3 differences in the caudate would suggest that proficiency influences the degree of conflict. Because inhibition-related activity does not differ between L2 and L3, this conflict may arise from relative accessibility of the non-native languages, rather than inhibiting the L1 to different degrees. In other words, inhibition of the L1 may be consistent for production in all weaker languages, but lower availability of the L3 than the L2 may drive the prefrontal-subcortical loop through the striatum harder to ramp activation of the desired language response.

To test the effects of context, de Bruin and colleagues (2014) also compared mixed blocks, in which more than one language was used, with single-language blocks. Similar results were found, with context not impacting inhibition-related engagement during L1 naming, but greater activation in the rIFG and marginally greater activation in the pre-SMA for switches out of L1 into the L2 and L3 compared to L2/L3 naming in a single-language context. This further substantiated their claim that inhibition via the rIFG/pre-SMA is specifically engaged to switch out of the stronger first language, but inhibition is not necessarily required to switch out of weaker languages.

However, this contrast does not allow an independent comparison of mixed vs. single-language context, as the researchers reported the effects of the switch trials in the mixed block compared to the non-switch trials in the single-language block. Typically, the non-switch trials in the mixed and single-language blocks are directly compared to isolate the effects of context in the absence of a switching confound. Because this comparison was not reported, it is difficult to assess whether L1 was globally inhibited during the mixed context or inhibited only when switching out of this language. Despite this, the lack of difference in these regions for switching into the L1 in either context indicates that no or relatively little inhibition is needed to suppress the weaker languages when using the first language in a mixed-language context. This conclusion was supported by behavioural data indicating greater response time delays in L1 naming in a mixed-language context relative to delays in L2 and L3. Further substantiation comes from a multilingual behavioural study demonstrating a link between general IC ability on the Simon task and reduced switch costs related to the L1 only (Linck et al. 2012). Thus, in line with the IC model, the first language appears to be selectively inhibited during language switching.

Finally, consistent with the language production studies reviewed above, naming pictures in the weaker languages activated a more extensive brain network than naming in L1. Greater L2 activation was found in areas related specifically to inhibition (the left IFG and left pre-SMA), as well as regions involved in control and switching (the bilateral putamen, right caudate nucleus, and cerebellum), sensory perception, articulation, and cognition. These findings implicate a more complex network for L1 than L2 interference suppression which involves inhibition, attention during perception, articulation, and other aspects of cognitive control.

It is noteworthy that the pre-SMA was involved in both switching studies. Activation in this region was independent of proficiency in the study by Abutalebi et al. (2013a), but enhanced for inhibiting the stronger language in the investigation by de Bruin et al. (2014), leading the researchers to assume its role in monitoring and inhibition, respectively. It should be noted that while both studies generated regions of interest (ROIs) within the average range for the pre-SMA (Mayka et al. 2006), the ROIs were defined differently. In the former study, the selected ROI encompassed the left pre-SMA, while the latter study included the right pre-SMA. In addition, a monitoring role may have been observed in the former analysis because the pre-SMA was clustered with the ACC, a region known for its role in monitoring. Neuronal studies in macaques have shown that the pre-SMA is involved in switching from an automatic action to a controlled one by suppressing interference from the automatic action and subsequently signalling the subthalamic nucleus (STN) of the basal ganglia (Isoda and Hikosaka 2007). A single-cell experiment showed that the pre-SMA contains neurons that inhibit the unwanted automatic response and/or boost the desired controlled response, implicating this area in both inhibition of automatic responses and facilitation of controlled processes (Isoda and Hikosaka 2008). In turn, the pre-SMA projects to the STN, which contains a high proportion of neurons that function to inhibit undesired actions during switching.

Together, these studies suggest a role for the pre-SMA in resolving conflict, but may reflect conflict incurred by disengaging from one language and shifting to the other, even when interference is low. It is possible that the ACC monitors and detects conflict, the pre-SMA is involved in resolving conflict that occurs regardless of relative proficiency when disengaging one language to switch into another, and the rIFG (which projects to the STN; Jahfari et al. 2011) and STN are involved in inhibiting any additional interference from the stronger language. Further research is needed regarding the specific role of the pre-SMA in language switching, and lateralization of activity in this region. Since the pre-SMA implements the resolved course of action through the STN, which also contains inhibition-specific neurons, inclusion of the STN as a ROI would be beneficial in future studies regarding inhibition during language switching.

To summarize, neuroimaging studies of bilinguals have revealed a cortical–subcortical network involved in language switching which includes the left PFC, ACC, caudate nucleus, IPL, and the pre-SMA/SMA. Multilingual studies have exploited proficiency differences between languages to test the degree of inhibition required within this network when switching out of the L1 into an equally- or less-proficient language. These manipulations have revealed dissociable areas of the language control networks that are responsible for different aspects of cognitive control and are modulated differently by proficiency. By comparing effects of proficiency on activity across regions during language switching, researchers have concluded that the ACC appears to be involved in task monitoring, the caudate is involved in selection of the less proficient language, and the rIFG is involved in inhibition specifically of the stronger L1 when switching into the weaker languages. Further research is necessary to determine the role of the pre-SMA and STN, but it is likely that the pre-SMA resolves conflict by both inhibiting the prior task and biasing responses in the STN towards the desired task. The STN also likely plays a role in inhibition during language switching. Finally, comparisons of multilinguals and monolinguals have revealed that language control mechanisms for multilinguals rely on the same conflict resolution networks as monolingual language usage.

3.2.3. Controlled Articulation and Lexical Selection in Multilinguals   It should be noted that while many fMRI studies of speech production use a covert speech task due to movement artefact during articulation, fMRI and positron emission tomography (PET; another imaging method) techniques for reducing artefact during speech exist (Gracco et al. 2005). Overt speech production, which may be ideal when speech processes are under investigation, necessitates specific acquisition techniques, participant training to reduce movement, and complex prepossessing of the data to correct for motion-relation artefact (e.g. as performed in the study by de Bruin et al. 2014, see Section 3.2.2; for a comprehensive discussion and motion-reduction techniques, the reader is directed to Xu et al. 2014). Some studies have shown that covert and overt production reveal similar effects (e.g. Shuster and Lemieux 2005); however, direct comparisons of overt and covert speech have led researchers to conclude that the neural substrates of covert speech are not simply those of overt speech excluding areas specific to motor execution (Huang et al. 2002).

In particular, covert speech production may not fully address non-native activity that results from mismatch between auditory feedback and internal representations, monitoring, and feedback control of the speech motor-control system (Simmonds et al. 2011). Researchers have found enhanced activity for the L2 vs. L1 in the basal ganglia (e.g. Klein et al. 1994) and motor areas (e.g. Waldron and Hernandez 2013), and for bilinguals compared to monolinguals during articulatory monitoring (Parker Jones et al. 2012). These studies suggest that non-native-like pronunciation may stem from reliance on existing L1 systems or underdeveloped sensorimotor feedback systems for a late learned L2, and that pronunciation of unfamiliar phonemes may require greater engagement of these systems (Simmonds et al. 2011; see Table 2, Articulatory Control, for key studies in multilinguals). Multilinguals provide a ripe resource to study potential shifts in these systems with reductions in accent or even with increased L2 practice without demonstrating accent improvement. In this case, two non-native languages with different degrees of accent or active exposure could be directly compared during overt production.

In line with the sensorimotor developmental hypothesis, Wattendorf et al. (2014) compared network activity in multilinguals with early or late exposure to a second language. This comparison allowed them to determine if the language and control networks developed differently as a result of acquiring the second language in parallel or subsequent to the first language. They identified the same essential language network for each language, regardless of AOA; however, language control networks for all three languages differed based on L2 AOA. Early multilinguals showed more activation than late multilinguals in areas associated with language selection and articulation, including the left IFG, SMA/motor cortex, ACC, and the striatum. In contrast, late multilinguals preferentially activated the posterior STG, which is involved in controlling phonological representations. Differences in control networks related to articulation led the researchers to conclude that late multilinguals may not develop frontal-subcortical sensorimotor loops that enable switching between articulatory systems in the same way as early multilinguals who learn at least two languages simultaneously (Wattendorf et al. 2014). Furthermore, similar activation patterns for the L3 and earlier learned languages revealed that developmental effects impact the management of subsequently learned languages. Thus, learning two languages early in life affects the development of control and articulatory paths used for all languages, including those learned later in life.

Further support for the importance of early multilingual exposure on control network development was found in an MRI study of multilingual children (Della Rosa et al. 2013). Greater multilingual competence was associated with better conflict management during an attention task and structural changes in the IPL, a region involved in attention. This suggests a link between development of attentional control networks and multilingual competence: the ability to proficiently manage multiple languages may rely on and/or strengthen attentional control networks.

In a clever dissociation of cortical overlap related to articulation and cognitive control, Abutalebi et al. (2013b) used an overt language-switching paradigm with multilinguals who achieved native-like proficiency in their L2 and moderate proficiency in their L3. It should be noted that because AOA was much earlier for the L2 (five to six years) than the L3 (10 years), proficiency and AOA were not able to be fully dissociated. When only comparing non-switch trials, naming activated the same frontotemporal language network in all three languages, and mimicked activations found when monolinguals performed the task. Of interest, the high-proficiency L2 recruited additional activation in the ACC and pars opercularis of the IFG. The L3 also recruited and further extended activation in these regions, and additionally activated the left putamen. Neural activity during L3 naming was correlated with grey matter volume in the left putamen, which was denser in the multilinguals than in the monolinguals. The authors proposed a role for the left putamen in managing the articulatory demands of using a non-native-like language, and suggested experience-driven structural changes in this region as a result of mastering a multilingual articulatory repertoire. They also noted that this pattern of activation is consistent with increased functional connectivity of the putamen and pars opercularis for a less-proficient language compared to the L1 (Dodel et al. 2005), implicating this frontal-striatal network in managing the articulatory and phonological demands of operating in a moderately proficient language. Alternatively, the authors suggested a role of the putamen in controlling articulation in a less automatic language.

In contrast, switching out of the strongest language into the weakest language did not engage the putamen. According to the IC hypothesis, suppressing the strongest language in order to switch from L1 to L3 should require the greatest level of cognitive control. In line with this hypothesis, switching from L1 to L3 engaged the caudate nucleus, a region implicated in language control and consistently activated during switching tasks (Abutalebi et al. 2000; Crinion et al. 2006). Thus switching involved the caudate, but not the putamen, while naming in the weakest language involved the putamen and to a lesser degree, the caudate. The authors concluded that naming in the weaker language engages the putamen to manage the articulatory demands and the caudate to control interference from the stronger languages.

At first glance, these findings are somewhat difficult to reconcile with a bilingual study of past tense generation published the same year. In this study, early bilinguals showed more activation than late bilinguals in motor and articulatory regions of the left hemisphere, including the insula, putamen, and SMA (Waldron and Hernandez 2013). They also showed more activity in the left STG, which the authors attributed to a phonological lexical retrieval strategy. Since proficiency was controlled, the researchers argued that this pattern reflects reliance on a sensorimotor network that is developed as early bilinguals acquire two languages through sensorimotor means. In contrast, second languages acquired later in life are not thought to be acquired via the same sensorimotor means, but rather through cognitive control and memory circuits. Also, because late bilinguals acquire their L2 after the L1 is entrenched, the L2 maps onto the L1 network, resulting in more interference of L1 and a need for cognitive control to use L2. This was supported by enhanced activation for late bilinguals in areas related to memory, cognitive control, and reading-based strategies: the hippocampus, superior/middle frontal gyrus, and angular gyrus, respectively.

These somewhat opposing results regarding putamen activity for early vs. late multilinguals might cause us to question whether activation in the putamen for early bilinguals reflects sensorimotor-driven acquisition and lexical access or if the putamen is engaged during production in the weaker language to manage articulatory demands during naming. While the tasks used in both of these studies involved lexical selection, the task requirements were quite different. Waldron and Hernandez's 2013 study, in which past tense forms of visually presented verbs were generated, tapped into direct vs. rule-based verb formation, whereas the picture-naming paradigm used by Abutalebi and colleagues required lexical selection of noun forms in the face of interference (by virtue of operating in a mixed language context). Thus, activation in Waldron and Hernandez's study reflects processing routes for memory and rule-based retrieval of irregular and regular verbs, respectively; while activity in the latter study reflects lexical selection and related control processes. Importantly, in the former study, more left putamen activity was found for early bilinguals than late bilinguals, but only for the regular verbs. Late bilinguals, in contrast, showed activation in regions related to memory for regular verbs. Regular verb conjugation is thought to rely on application of rules, which is known to involve the basal ganglia (cf. Sach et al. 2004; Stocco and Prat 2014; Ullman et al. 1997). Thus, the greater putamen activity for early bilinguals in this study may have been driven by engaging a rule-application mechanism for regular verbs rather than retrieving regular verbs from memory.

Additionally, the impact of AOA and proficiency differ across aspects of language, including morphological processing (sensitive to AOA) in Waldron and Hernandez's study and lexical-semantic retrieval (sensitive to proficiency) in the investigation by Abutalebi et al. (2013a; see Chapter 12, this volume, for additional discussion). Abutalebi et al. (2013b) reviewed production and phonological studies that showed enhanced putamen activity in the L2 vs. L1 for various levels of L2 proficiency and AOA. Activity in the putamen consistently differs between L1 and L2 on tasks that require articulation, but further investigation is needed regarding the impact of AOA and proficiency across tasks and whether putamen activity reflects sensorimotor development of languages learned in parallel or articulatory effort. Despite somewhat different findings, these studies both illustrate the engagement of different control networks for L1 and L2 as a result of AOA and/or proficiency. In both cases, the L2 relied on cognitive control mechanisms not necessarily engaged for the L1.

In summary, lexical selection and articulation investigations have again shown similar language networks in each of a multilingual's languages, with additional resources for controlled production in the weaker or later learned languages. By manipulating AOA, researchers have corroborated the proposal that learning two languages early in life affects the development of control and articulatory networks. By manipulating proficiency, multilingual studies have also verified a role for the caudate in switching and implied a role for the putamen in controlling articulatory demands in a weaker language.

3.2.4. Protection against Age-Related Cognitive Decline   There is evidence that years of exerting language control builds cognitive reserve, which protects against age-related or pathological neurodegeneration (Schweizer et al. 2012). A comparison of multilingual and bilingual patients with dementia using single-photon emission computed tomography (SPECT), a neuroimaging technique, revealed slower degeneration and functional inactivity in the multilingual (Liu et al. 2012). Slower progression of dementia in the multilingual corroborates findings from a number of bilingual studies and implies that recruiting additional cortical activity to control multiple languages has long-term benefits to cognitive reserve (Perani and Abutalebi 2015). It should be briefly noted, however, that while some meta-analyses and reviews of the literature have found support for a bilingual advantage in cognitive control (Adesope et al. 2010), other meta-analyses have led a number of researchers to conclude that the observed effects are due to publication bias or methodological/statistical artefacts (de Bruin et al. 2015; Paap 2017).

From investigations mostly of bilingualism, researchers have proposed that neuroprotective effects of multilingualism may occur because: (i) controlling multiple languages strengthens the areas which later are subject to neurodegeneration, making them more efficient and therefore more resilient to the effects of neurodegeneration, (ii) additional networks recruited to manage multiple languages may compensate for those that are degenerating, or (iii) multilingualism delays the posterior-to-anterior shift that occurs during normal ageing (Calabria et al. 2017). One multilingual study has revealed that the bilingual benefit to cognitive reserve increases (before eventually plateauing) with additional languages (Perquin et al. 2013). Thus, differences in cortical activity between native and non-native languages probably reflect controlled processing, which alters the networks over time and enhances their resilience to the symptoms of ageing and pathology.

3.3.   *Evidence from Patient Populations*

Case studies of patients have substantiated experimental findings of an overlapping, but not entirely identical, neural substrate for both languages, with a cognitive control network to manage controlled language processing (Table 3). In line with this conclusion, languages recover in parallel in most aphasia incidents, but unequal recovery in about a third of cases may be explained by damage to extended areas needed for the L2 or subcortical lesions affecting control (Briellmann et al. 2004).

Likewise, one PET study of a multilingual patient showed overlapping, but slightly different, activation during production tasks in three languages, especially in the IFG (Klein et al. 2002). Although the typical pattern of enhanced activation specifically for L2 was not necessarily observed, differences were found in the inferior temporal gyrus for the two first languages compared with a later learned language. Inconsistencies amongst languages were also observed in the angular gyrus and middle temporal gyrus. Patient data, especially of this patient whose language was represented in the right hemisphere, must be interpreted cautiously, but these findings support the conclusion of substantial, but not identical, overlap between languages.

Despite overwhelming overlap, the neuroimaging studies described above have shown slight differences in functional connectivity or patterns of activation within a region. This finding is confirmed with cortical stimulation mapping (CSM), a justifiable technique in populations undergoing surgery. CSM has revealed that although areas are largely overlapping, the precise sites for language production are both shared and distinct. CSM in a multilingual revealed shared representation within the IFG, with additional sites that were specific to the later-acquired, but highly proficient L3 (Lubrano et al. 2012), confirming neuroimaging findings of extended activation for languages acquired after L1 (e.g. Vingerhoets et al. 2003). However, subcortical substrates were shared.

Shared subcortical representation implies that damage to these regions, should affect language control, but not necessarily the languages themselves. To test whether aphasia recovery following a subcortical lesion involves control, Abutalebi et al. (2009) trained one such patient only in his L2. This patient was experiencing unintended switching and equal anomia in both languages. Crucially, the control issues remained but reversed

Table 3 Key multilingual studies regarding patient populations.

	Research question	Task	Factors tested	Main findings	Significance
Klein et al. (2002)	Overlap for native vs. early and late non-native languages	PET: Overt Word Repetition and Synonym Generation	Prof	Overlapping, but different activation in the IFG, angular gyrus, and MTG	Found shared and distinct activation across languages
Lubrano et al. (2012)	Overlap for L1 and later-acquired L3	Cortical Stimulation Mapping: Picture-Naming	AOA	Shared representation within the IFG and subcortical structures with additional IFG sites distinct to the later-acquired language	Confirmed some language distinct regions with high spatial resolution
Abutalebi et al. (2009)	Whether recovery following subcortical lesion involves control	fMRI Across Treatment: Overt Picture Naming	Prof	Improvement in trained language accompanied a shift in control region activation for that language	Demonstrated role of subcortical structures in control, especially for L2

AOA = age of acquisition; Prof = proficiency; IFG = inferior frontal gyrus; MTG = middle temporal gyrus.

with L2 training. Before training, the patient switched mostly into L1, but after training, the patient was more likely to switch into L2. As L2 improved with training, access to L1 worsened. Improved L2 access was accompanied by extension of the classic language areas, a functional shift in control region activation (the caudate and ACC) from the L1 to the L2, and increased connectedness of the control and language networks.

Together, these investigations support the proposal that much of the enhanced activation for the L2 reported in normal multilingual populations reflects control processes. These studies also substantiate the claim that cortical representation of languages is largely overlapping, but not identical. Some activation differences are due to control, but later-acquired or less-proficient languages register to both shared and extended language regions.

4. Conclusion

To conclude, multilingual neuroimaging studies provide the unique opportunity to compare multiple non-native languages to a native language, eliminating between-group confounds found in some bilingualism studies. These investigations have provided insight about how language representation and control differs when managing languages of different strengths or that were acquired at different times during development.

There is substantial evidence that production in each of a multilingual's languages relies on a shared frontotemporal system, with recruitment of additional resources for weaker languages and more variability when multilingual exposure occurs later in development. Additional resources involve a cortical–subcortical control network which includes the left PFC, ACC, left caudate nucleus and putamen, IPL, and the pre-SMA/SMA. Areas of language control networks that are responsible for different aspects of cognitive control are modulated differently by proficiency. In particular, speaking or switching into a weaker language activates regions involved in suppressing interference from the stronger language. Age of multilingual exposure affects the development of control and articulatory networks. Differences in cortical activity across languages mostly reflect enhanced language control, which alters the networks over time and boosts their resilience to the symptoms of ageing and pathology. Findings from patient studies have corroborated the hypotheses of both shared and distinct representation, and that differences in fMRI activation are likely due to representation of non-native languages in extended language areas and engagement of control networks. More research is needed regarding the role of individual aspects of the control network, especially of the pathways in the basal ganglia that mediate inhibition of interference.

REFERENCES

Abutalebi, J. (2008). Neural aspects of second language representation and language control. *Acta Psychologica* 128 (3): 466–478.

Abutalebi, J., Annoni, J.M., Zimine, I. et al. (2008). Language control and lexical competition in bilinguals: an event-related fMRI study. *Cerebral Cortex* 18: 1496–1505.

Abutalebi, J., Della Rosa, P.A., Ding, G. et al. (2013a). Language proficiency modulates the engagement of cognitive control areas in multilinguals. *Cortex* 49 (3): 905–911. doi: 10.1016/j.cortex.2012.08.018.

Abutalebi, J., Della Rosa, P.A., Gonzaga, A.K.C. et al. (2013b). The role of the left putamen in multilingual language production. *Brain and Language* 125: 307–315.

Abutalebi, J., Della Rosa, P.A., Green, D.W. et al. (2011). Bilingualism tunes the anterior cingulate cortex for conflict monitoring. *Cerebral Cortex* 22: 2076–2086. doi: 10.1093/cercor/bhr287.

Abutalebi, J. and Green, D.W. (2007). Bilingual language production: the neurocognition of language representation and control. *Journal of Neurolinguistics* 20: 242–275.

Abutalebi, J. and Green, D.W. (2008). Control mechanisms in bilingual language production: neural evidence from language switching studies. *Language & Cognitive Processes* 23 (4): 557–582.

Abutalebi, J. and Green, D.W. (2016). Neuroimaging of language control in bilinguals: neural adaptation and reserve. *Bilingualism: Language and Cognition* 19 (4): 689–698. doi:10.1017/S1366728916000225.

Abutalebi, J., Miozzo, A., and Cappa, S.F. (2000). Do subcortical structures control 'language selection' in polyglots? Evidence from pathological language mixing. *Neurocase: The Neural Basis of Cognition* 6 (1): 51–56. doi:10.1080/13554790008402757.

Abutalebi, J., Rosa, P.A., Tettamanti, M. et al. (2009). Bilingual aphasia and language control: a follow-up fMRI and intrinsic connectivity study. *Brain and Language* 109: 141–156.

Adesope, O.O., Lavin, T., Thompson, T., and Ungerleider, C. (2010). A systematic review and meta-analysis of the cognitive correlates of bilingualism. *Review of Educational Research* 82 (2): 207–245.

Aron, A.R., Behrens, T.E., Smith, S. et al. (2007). Triangulating a cognitive control network using diffusion-weighted magnetic resonance imaging (MRI) and functional MRI. *The Journal of Neuroscience* 27 (14): 3743–3752. doi:10.1523/jneurosci.0519-07.2007.

Bamiou, D.E., Musiek, F.E., and Luxon, L.M. (2003). The insula (Island of Reil) and its role in auditory processing. *Brain Research Reviews* 42 (2): 143–154.

Bello, L., Acerbi, F., Giussani, C. et al. (2006). Intraoperative language localization in multilingual patients with gliomas. *Neurosurgery* 59 (1): 115–125. discussion 115-125.

Blackburn, A. M. (2013). *A study of the relationship between code switching and the bilingual advantage: Evidence that language use modulates neural indices of language processing and cognitive control.* Doctoral dissertation, University of Texas at San Antonio, San Antonio.

Blackburn, A.M. (2016). MRI methods in bilingual reading comprehension. In: *Methods in Bilingual Reading Comprehension Research* (ed. R.R. Heredia, J. Altarriba and A.B. Cieślicka), 313–352. New York, NY: Springer.

Blackburn, A.M. (2018). The bilingual brain. In: *An Introduction to Bilingualism: Principles and Processes*, 2e (ed. J. Altarriba and R.R. Heredia), 107–138. London, UK: Psychology Press.

Blackburn, A.M. (forthcoming). The bilingual brain: mechanical tools. In: *The Bilingual Brain Unwrapped* (ed. R.R. Heredia and A.B. Cieślicka). London, UK: Psychology Press.

Bloch, C., Kaiser, A., Kuenzli, E. et al. (2009). The age of second language acquisition determines the variability in activation elicited by narration in three languages in Broca's and Wernicke's area. *Neuropsychologia* 47 (3): 625–633.

de Bot, K. (2008). The imaging of what in the multilingual mind? [The cognitive neuroscience of second language acquisition, M. Gullberg, P. Indefrey]. *Second Language Research* 24 (1): 111–133.

Briellmann, R.S., Saling, M.M., Connell, A.B. et al. (2004). A high-field functional MRI study of quadri-lingual subjects. *Brain and Language* 89 (3): 531–542.

de Bruin, A., Roelofs, A., Dijkstra, T., and FitzPatrick, I. (2014). Domain-general inhibition areas of the brain are involved in language switching: FMRI evidence from trilingual speakers. *NeuroImage* 90: 348–359.

de Bruin, A., Treccani, B., and Sala, S.D. (2015). Cognitive advantage in bilingualism: an example of publication bias? *Psychological Science* 26 (1): 99–107.

Calabria, M., Cattaneo, G., and Costa, A. (2017). It is time to project into the future: 'bilingualism in healthy and pathological aging'. *Journal of Neurolinguistics* 43 (Part A): 1–3.

Canini, M., Della Rosa, P.A., Catricalà, E. et al. (2016). Semantic interference and its control: a functional neuroimaging and connectivity study: semantic interference and its control. *Human Brain Mapping* 37 (11): 4179–4196.

Chee, M.W.L., Caplan, D., Soon, C.S. et al. (1999a). Processing of visually presented sentences in Mandarin and English studied with fMRI. *Neuron* 23 (1): 127–137.

Chee, M.W.L., Tan, E.W.L., and Thiel, T. (1999b). Mandarin and English single word processing studied with functional magnetic resonance imaging. *Journal of Neuroscience* 19 (8): 3050–3056.

Costa, A. and Santesteban, M. (2004). Lexical access in bilingual speech production: evidence from language switching in highly proficient bilinguals and L2 learners. *Journal of Memory and Language* 50: 491–511.

Crinion, J., Turner, R., Grogan, A. et al. (2006). Language control in the bilingual brain. *Science* 312: 1537–1540.

Dehaene, S., Dupoux, E., Mehler, J. et al. (1997). Anatomical variability in the cortical representation of first and second language. *NeuroReport* 8 (17): 3809–3815.

Della Rosa, P.A., Videsott, G., Borsa, V.M. et al. (2013). A neural interactive location for multilingual talent. *Cortex* 49 (2): 605–608.

Dodel, S., Golestani, N., Palllier, C. et al. (2005). Condition-dependent functional connectivity: syntax networks in bilinguals. *Philosophical Transactions of the Royal Society of London* 360 (1457): 921–935.

Fernandez-Coello, A., Havas, V., Juncadella, M. et al. (2017). Age of language acquisition and cortical language organization in multilingual patients undergoing awake brain mapping. *Journal of Neurosurgery* 126 (6): 1912–1923.

Gracco, V.L., Tremblay, P., and Pike, B. (2005). Imaging speech production using fMRI. *NeuroImage* 26 (1): 294–301.

Green, D.W. (1998). Mental control of the bilingual lexico-semantic system. *Bilingualism: Language and Cognition* 1: 67–81.

Guo, T., Misra, M., and Kroll, J.F. (2011). Local and global inhibition in bilingual word production: fMRI evidence from Chinese-English bilinguals. *NeuroImage* 56 (4): 2300–2309.

Hasegawa, M., Carpenter, P.A., and Just, M.A. (2002). An fMRI study of bilingual sentence comprehension and workload. *NeuroImage* 15 (3): 647–660.

Hernandez, A. (2009). Language switching in the bilingual brain: What's next? *Brain and Language* 109: 133–140.

Hernandez, A., Martinez, A., and Kohnert, K. (2000). In search of the language switch: an fMRI study of picture naming in Spanish-English bilinguals. *Brain and Language* 73: 421–431.

Huang, J., Carr, T.H., and Cao, Y. (2002). Comparing cortical activations for silent and overt speech using event-related fMRI. *Human Brain Mapping* 15 (1): 39–53.

Illes, J., Francis, W.S., Desmond, J.E. et al. (1999). Convergent cortical representation of semantic processing in bilinguals. *Brain and Language* 70 (3): 347–363.

Indefrey, P. and Levelt, W.J.M. (2000). The neural correlates of language production. In: *The New Cognitive Neurosciences*, 2nde (ed. M.S. Gazzaniga), 845–865. Cambridge, MA: MIT Press.

Isoda, M. and Hikosaka, O. (2007). Switching from automatic to controlled action by monkey medial frontal cortex. *Nature Neuroscience* 10 (2): 240–248.

Isoda, M. and Hikosaka, O. (2008). Role for subthalamic nucleus neurons in switching from automatic to controlled eye movement. *The Journal of Neuroscience* 28 (28): 7209–7218.

Jahfari, S., Waldorp, L., van den Wildenberg, W.P. et al. (2011). Effective connectivity reveals important roles for both the hyperdirect (fronto-subthalamic) and the indirect (fronto-striatal-pallidal) fronto-basal ganglia pathways during response inhibition. *The Journal of Neuroscience* 31 (18): 6891–6899.

Kim, K.H.S., Relkin, N.R., Lee, K.M., and Hirsch, J. (1997). Distinct cortical areas associated with native and second languages. *Nature* 388 (6638): 171–174.

Klein, D., Milner, B., Zatorre, R.J. et al. (2002). Cerebral organization in a right-handed trilingual patient with right-hemisphere speech: a positron emission tomography study. *Neurocase* 8 (5): 369–375.

Klein, D., Zatorre, R.J., Milner, B. et al. (1994). Left putaminal activation when speaking a second language: evidence from PET. *Neuroreport* 5 (17): 2295–2297.

Kovelman, I., Baker, S.A., and Petitto, L.-A. (2008). Bilingual and monlingual brains compared: a functional magnetic resonance imaging investigation of syntactic processing and a possible 'neural signature' of bilingualism. *Journal of Cognitive Neuroscience* 20 (1): 153–169.

Kroll, J.F., Bobb, S.C., Misra, M., and Guo, T. (2008). Language selection in bilingual speech: evidence for inhibitory processes. *Acta Psychologica* 128 (3): 416–430.

Linck, J.A., Schwieter, J.W., and Sunderman, G. (2012). Inhibitory control predicts language switching performance in trilingual speech production. *Bilingualism: Language and Cognition* 15 (3): 651–662.

Liu, Y.C., Yip, P.K., Fan, Y.M., and Meguro, K. (2012). A potential protective effect in multilingual patients with semantic dementia: two case reports of patients speaking Taiwanese and Japanese. *Acta Neurologica Taiwanica* 21 (1): 25–30.

Lubrano, V., Prod'homme, K., Démonet, J.-F., and Köpke, B. (2012). Language monitoring in multilingual patients undergoing awake craniotomy: a case study of a German–English–French trilingual patient with a WHO grade II glioma. *Journal of Neurolinguistics* 25 (6): 567–578.

Luk, G., Green, D.W., Abutalebi, J., and Grady, C. (2012). Cognitive control for language switching in bilinguals: a quantitative meta-analysis of functional neuroimaging studies. *Language & Cognitive Processes* 27 (10): 1479–1488.

Luke, K.-K., Liu, H.-L., Wai, Y.-Y. et al. (2002). Functional anatomy of syntactic and semantic processing in language comprehension. *Human Brain Mapping* 16: 133–145.

Ma, H., Hu, J., Xi, J. et al. (2014). Bilingual cognitive control in language switching: an fMRI study of English-Chinese late bilinguals. *PLoS One* 9 (9): e106468.

Mayka, M.A., Corcos, D.M., Leurgans, S.E., and Vaillancourt, D.E. (2006). Three-dimensional locations and boundaries of motor and premotor cortices as defined by functional brain imaging: a meta-analysis. *NeuroImage* 31 (4): 1453–1474.

Meuter, R.F.I. and Allport, A. (1999). Bilingual language switching in naming: asymmetrical costs of language selection. *Journal of Memory and Language* 40: 25–40.

Moritz-Gasser, S. and Duffau, H. (2009). Evidence of a large-scale network underlying language switching: a brain stimulation study. *Journal of Neurosurgery* 111 (4): 729–732.

Paap, K. (2017). Bilingualism and executive functioning. In: *An Introduction to Bilingualism: Principles and Processes* (ed. J. Altarriba and R. Heredia), 190–224. London, UK: Psychology Press.

Paradis, M. (2004). Neuroimaging studies of the bilingual brain. In: *A Neurolinguistic Theory of Bilingualism*, 153–186. Amsterdam, The Netherlands: John Benjamins.

Parker Jones, O., Green, D.W., Grogan, A. et al. (2012). Where, when and why brain activation differs for bilinguals and monolinguals during picture naming and reading aloud. *Cerebral Cortex* 22 (4): 892–902.

Perani, D. and Abutalebi, J. (2015). Bilingualism, dementia, cognitive and neural reserve. *Current Opinion in Neurology* 28 (6): 618–625.

Perani, D., Paulesu, E., Galles, N.S. et al. (1998). The bilingual brain. Proficiency and age of acquisition of the second language. *Brain* 121 (10): 1841–1852.

Perquin, M., Vaillant, M., Schuller, A.-M. et al. (2013). Lifelong exposure to multilingualism: new evidence to support cognitive reserve hypothesis. *PLoS One* 8 (4): e62030.

Price, C.J., Green, D.W., and Studnitz, R.V. (1999). A functional imaging study of translation and language switching. *Brain* 122: 2221–2235.

Rodriguez-Fornells, A., De Diego Balaguer, R., and Münte, T.F. (2006). Executive control in bilingual language processing. *Language Learning* 56: 133–190.

Rodriguez-Fornells, A., Rotte, M., Heinze, H.J. et al. (2002). Brain potential and functional MRI evidence for how to handle two languages with one brain. *Nature* 415: 1026–1029.

Rodriguez-Fornells, A., van der Lugt, A., Rotte, M. et al. (2005). Second language interferes with word production in fluent bilinguals: brain potential and functional imaging evidence. *Journal of Cognitive Neuroscience* 17: 422–433.

Roux, F.E., Boulanouar, K., Lotterie, J.A. et al. (2003). Language functional magnetic resonance imaging in preoperative assessment of language areas: correlation with direct cortical stimulation. *Neurosurgery* 52 (6): 1335–1345. discussion 1345–1337.

Roux, F.-E. and Trémoulet, M. (2002). Organization of language areas in bilingual patients: a cortical stimulation study. *Journal of Neurosurgery* 97 (4): 857–864.

Sach, M., Seitz, R.J., and Indefrey, P. (2004). Unified inflectional processing of regular and irregular verbs: PET study. *NeuroReport* 15 (3): 533–537.

Schweizer, T.A., Ware, J., Fischer, C.E. et al. (2012). Bilingualism as a contributor to cognitive reserve: evidence from brain atrophy in Alzheimer's disease. *Cortex* 48 (8): 991–996.

Seghier, M.L., Lazeyras, F., Pegna, A.J. et al. (2004). Variability of fMRI activation during a phonological and semantic language task in healthy subjects. *Human Brain Mapping* 23 (3): 140–155.

Shuster, L.I. and Lemieux, S.K. (2005). An fMRI investigation of covertly and overtly produced mono- and multisyllabic words. *Brain and Language* 93 (1): 20–31.

Sierpowska, J., Fernandez-Coello, A., Gomez-Andres, A. et al. (2018). Involvement of the middle frontal gyrus in language switching as revealed by electrical stimulation mapping and functional magnetic resonance imaging in bilingual brain tumor patients. *Cortex* 99 (Supplement C): 78–92.

Sierpowska, J., Gabarrós, A., Ripollés, P. et al. (2013). Intraoperative electrical stimulation of language switching in two bilingual patients. *Neuropsychologia* 51 (13): 2882–2892.

Simmonds, A., Wise, R., and Leech, R. (2011). Two tongues, one brain: imaging bilingual speech production. *Frontiers in Psychology* 2 (166): doi:10.3389/fpsyg.2011.00166.

Stocco, A. and Prat, C.S. (2014). Bilingualism trains specific brain circuits involved in flexible rule selection and application. *Brain and Language* 137: 50–61.

Stocco, A., Yamasaki, B., Natalenko, R., and Prat, C.S. (2014). Bilingual brain training: a neurobiological framework of how bilingual experience improves executive function. *International Journal of Bilingualism* 18 (1): 67–92.

Tan, L.H., Liu, H.-L., Perfetti, C.A. et al. (2001). The neural system underlying Chinese logograph reading. *NeuroImage* 13 (5): 836–846.

Tan, L.H., Spinks, J.A., Feng, C.M. et al. (2003). Neural systems of second language reading are shaped by native language. *Human Brain Mapping* 18 (3): 158–166.

Thompson-Schill, S.L., d'Esposito, M., Aguirre, G.K., and Farah, M.J. (1997). Role of the left inferior prefrontal cortex in retrieval of semantic knowledge: a reevaluation. *Proceedings of the National Academy of Sciences* 94: 14792–14797.

Thompson-Schill, S.L., d'Esposito, M., and Kan, I.P. (1999). Effects of repetition and competition on activity in left prefrontal cortex during word generation. *Neuron* 23: 513–522.

Toro, R., Fox, P.T., and Paus, T. (2008). Functional coactivation map of the human brain. *Cerebral Cortex* 18 (11): 2553–2559.

Ullman, M.T., Corkin, S., Coppola, M. et al. (1997). A neural dissociation within language: evidence that the mental dictionary is part of declarative memory,

and that grammatical rules are processed by the procedural system. *Journal of Cognitive Neuroscience* 9 (2): 266–276.

Van Heuven, W.J.B., Schriefers, H., Dijkstra, T., and Hagoort, P. (2008). Language conflict in the bilingual brain. *Cerebral Cortex* 18: 2706–2716.

van Veen, V. and Carter, C. (2002). The anterior cingulate as a conflict monitor: fMRI and ERP studies. *Physiology & Behavior* 77 (477–482).

Videsott, G., Herrnberger, B., Hoenig, K. et al. (2010). Speaking in multiple languages: neural correlates of language proficiency in multilingual word production. *Brain and Language* 113 (3): 103–112.

Vingerhoets, G., Van Borsel, J., Tesink, C. et al. (2003). Multilingualism: an fMRI study. *NeuroImage* 20 (4): 2181–2196.

Waldron, E.J. and Hernandez, A.E. (2013). The role of age of acquisition on past tense generation in Spanish–English bilinguals: an fMRI study. *Brain and Language* 125 (1): 28–37.

Wang, Y., Xue, G., Chen, C. et al. (2007). Neural basis of asymmetric language switching in second-language learners: an ER-fMRI study. *NeuroImage* 35: 862–870.

Wattendorf, E., Festman, J., Westermann, B. et al. (2014). Early bilingualism influences early and subsequently later acquired languages in cortical regions representing control functions. *International Journal of Bilingualism* 18 (1): 48–66.

Wattendorf, E., Westermann, B., Zappatore, D. et al. (2001). Different languages activate different subfields in Broca's area. *NeuroImage* 13: 624.

Xu, Y., Tong, Y., Liu, S. et al. (2014). Denoising the speaking brain: toward a robust technique for correcting artifact-contaminated fMRI data under severe motion. *NeuroImage* 103: 33–47.

Yetkin, O., Zerrin Yetkin, F., Haughton, V.M., and Cox, R.W. (1996). Use of functional MR to map language in multilingual volunteers. *American Journal of Neuroradiology* 17 (3): 473–477.

Zhang, Y., Wang, T., Huang, P. et al. (2015). Free language selection in the bilingual brain: an event-related fMRI study. *Scientific Reports* 5: 11704.

7   In Search of Memory Traces of a Forgotten Language

LUDMILA ISURIN

1.   Introduction

A language that an individual once spoke or to which they were exposed is as susceptible to being forgotten as any other information stored in long-term memory. The phenomenon of language forgetting, which often is referred to as language attrition or language loss, has been studied extensively in the last few decades. While the loss of the knowledge of a foreign/second language (L2) primarily concerns the pedagogical aspects of language maintenance over the time of disuse (e.g. summer break for students), first language (L1) forgetting in the context of a second language (L2) environment represents a bigger challenge for researchers (see Köpke et al. 2007; Schmid et al. 2004, for more details regarding studies on L1 attrition). Because the main focus on L1 forgetting is in adults, the field of L1 attrition seemingly lacks sufficient evidence on how the process operates in international adoptees, whose L1 input often is disrupted or completely terminated when a child is removed from the native country and placed in a new linguistic context. What remains even more fascinating is the attempt to trace memory of a lost childhood language in adults who were adopted as infants or small children or who were exposed to a language in their childhood and later never were exposed to or used that language. The remnants of such memory are believed to facilitate the relearning of the forgotten language in adulthood or at least benefit the better discrimination of certain linguistic items in the lost language. This line of thinking has motivated numerous studies discussed here.

In this chapter, we will be looking at recent psycholinguistic and neurolinguistic research that attempted to uncover a lost or suppressed childhood language both in adult and young adoptees as well as in those who were exposed to the language in childhood or learned a foreign language and later claimed to have forgotten it. In particular, this chapter focuses on those studies where the search for memory traces of a lost language operates on the assumption that a language, once learned but later forgotten, leaves imprints in the person's brain that later facilitate relearning or identification of that language. Different methodologies were used in order to measure this effect: age-regression

The Handbook of the Neuroscience of Multilingualism, First Edition. Edited by John W. Schwieter.
© 2019 John Wiley & Sons Ltd. Published 2019 by John Wiley & Sons Ltd.

hypnosis; functional magnetic resonance imaging (fMRI); and behavioural tasks, such as phoneme production task, accent perception task, grammaticality judgement test, and the savings paradigm, in uncovering various aspects of the forgotten language (i.e. phonological contrast, vocabulary, syntax, etc.). Moreover, researchers looked into different populations, such as adult adoptees (those who were adopted as children but were tested as adults), child adoptees (those who were adopted as young children and tested a few years later), childhood overhearers (those who were exposed to another language in their childhood – not necessarily speaking it – and later had limited or no exposure to the language), and second language learners (those who once learned a foreign language in a formal or informal setting, but later did not use it or had very limited exposure to their forgotten L2). The majority of studies provided evidence supporting the existence of memory traces of a forgotten language, especially in phonology. However, a few studies did not find any evidence for the existence of such memory remnants, which leaves the present research area open for further investigation.

The structure of the chapter aims to introduce the reader to different approaches used in studies tapping into memory traces of a lost language (i.e. hypnosis, fMRI, and behavioural tasks, including the savings paradigm). Where appropriate, each section devoted to a particular approach will look into different populations (e.g. childhood overhearers, adult/child adoptees, or L2 learners). In order to understand better the process of language forgetting, especially in young children, we first will turn to a few case studies, as scant as such reports are, where the linguistic performance of adoptees was recorded as soon as they joined their new families.

2.   Language Forgetting in Adoptees

The age factor in language acquisition, both first and second, often is related to the so-called critical age hypothesis (see Birdsong 2006, for an overview). According to this hypothesis, there is a time window within which the ultimate acquisition of the language should occur (i.e. from birth to puberty). Different accounts explain this phenomenon, including the notion of brain plasticity, which postulates that in the process of brain maturation some brain plasticity necessary for language acquisition/retention changes (Neville and Bavelier 2002). This makes young children more susceptible to losing their language due to the lack of exposure to it. Although an in-depth discussion of the hypothesis is outside the scope of this chapter, it should be noted that the relatively fast language forgetting in young children can be viewed through the prism of this hypothesis. The language that was not fully acquired in young children tends to deteriorate rather quickly and this becomes especially evident in cases of international adoptees. Longitudinal studies on language loss in adoptees are rather rare, so despite the methodological flaws, as acknowledged by the authors of the studies discussed here, and the insufficient evidence such studies provide, they offer a unique insight into the real process of language loss outside a well-controlled laboratory setting.

Isurin (2000) investigated the longitudinal case of a nine-year-old Russian girl adopted by an American family. After the girl was brought to the US, any exposure to Russian abruptly stopped. The girl did not know any English prior to her arrival in the

US; neither of her adoptive parents spoke any Russian. The author, herself a Russian-English bilingual, conducted regular sessions over a period of 13 months, looking into both L1 attrition and L2 acquisition as well as serving as an intermediary communicator between the child and her new parents. The main focus of the study was on the fast process of lexical attrition in L1 correlated with the acquisition of translation equivalents in L2: the girl showed forgetting of those Russian words for which she had learned English equivalents.[1] Amongst a few lexical categories that became the focus of Isurin's (2000) study, nouns and verbs were compared both in terms of L1 forgetting and L2 acquisition. Verbs showed a slower rate of L2 acquisition and L1 loss compared with nouns. It should be noted that L1 comprehension – albeit not specifically investigated in that particular adoptee – also suffered, and, after three years in the US, was no longer intact.

Nicoladis and Grabois (2002) reported a case of a much younger child, a 17-month-old Chinese girl adopted by an English-speaking Canadian mother. They primarily focused on the switch to a new language (English) in such a young child. The researchers conducted a series of observational sessions in Cantonese and English, respectively, and videotaped the interaction with the child for the independent analysis. They examined the child's language production and comprehension, focusing on words that she used or understood without contextual support. Also, special note was taken as far as the child's use of symbolic play, gestures, and eye contact used to communicate. The study showed a remarkably fast pace of English acquisition and Cantonese loss. By the fourth session – a month after the study began – the child no longer showed any signs of understanding decontextualized Cantonese. The authors concluded that the ease of the switch to English experienced by the child indicates a high degree of plasticity at least until that young age. However, they also acknowledged the limitation of the study: the data on initial language knowledge was obtained four weeks after the child was brought to the US, which makes it problematic to assess the actual rate of L1 loss in such a young adoptee.

The above finding agrees with what was reported by psychologists working with adoptees. For example, Gindis (2005) gives an account, based mostly on the accumulated cases in psychological practice, of the dramatic language loss in adoptees of three to four years of age. According to him, abrupt immersion in an English-speaking environment leads to the reduction of the L1 linguistic skills to a practically non-functional level: Expressive language skills will deteriorate greatly in three months for a six-year-old adoptee, whereas receptive language may stay intact for longer. However, within six months to a year, all functional use of the native language will disappear. Wickes and Slate (1996) explored psychological issues related to transracial adoptees' acculturation in a new country on a sample of 175 Korean adoptees[2] ranging in age from 17 to 39 years at the time of the study and recommended that ideally children should be adopted internationally before 18 months of age (i.e. before the developmental milestone of two-word sentences in the child's native language). Besides the functional side of the L2 development in children upon their adoption or immigration, scholars emphasized the emotional impact of such a switch to a new language.

In the rest of this chapter we will be looking into different methodological approaches to the study of memory remnants of a lost language, both in adoptees and non-adoptees. Table 1 shows an annotated summary of all studies discussed in the next three sections.

Table 1 Studies investigating memory traces of a forgotten language.

Study	L1 or L2	Forgotten language	Linguistic context	Method	n	Findings
As (1962)	L1	Swedish	English	Age regression hypnosis	1	When regressed to 5 years of age, significantly more language was remembered in the hypnotic stage than in the normal condition.
Au and Romo (1997)	L2	Korean	English	Comprehension test; grammaticality judgement	18	Relearners outperformed first time learners.
	L2	Spanish	English	Production test; grammaticality judgement	31	Relearners outperformed first time learners.
Au et al. (2002)	L2	Spanish	English	Acoustic measurements; phonological assessment; morphosyntax production	200	Significant advantage in phonology but not morphosyntax for childhood overhearers (n = 11) over late L2 learners.
Au et al. (2008)	L1	Spanish	English	Sentence and narrative accent rating; morphosyntax assessment; grammaticality judgement	200	Childhood speakers (n = 10) outperformed childhood overhearers and late L2 learners in phonology and grammaticality (both production and comprehension, including sentence perception in noise).
Bowers et al. (2009)	L2	Hindi Zulu	English	Relearning of phoneme contrasts	7	No preserved knowledge on initial testing but after practice (15–20 sessions) a subset (under the age of 40) regained sensitivity to a phoneme contrast from their childhood language.
Broersma et al. (2016)	L1	Chinese (Mandarin and Cantonese)	Dutch	Perception and production of Mandarin or Cantonese Chinese affricate and tone contrasts	97	22 Cantonese adoptees and 23 Dutch controls; 26 Mandarin adoptees and 26 Dutch controls. At the pre-test, the adopted children did not outperform the Dutch control children. After re-exposure, however, adoptees did outperform Dutch controls both in perception and production.

Study	L1/L2	Original language	Testing language	Task	n	Findings
Choi et al. (2017)	L1	Korean	Dutch	Phoneme perception and production; identification and rating tasks	58	Adult adoptees (n = 29) outperformed controls both in perception and production, regardless of the age of adoption (prelinguistic infants or toddlers/ older children).
de Bot and Stoessel (2000)	L2	Dutch	English	Savings paradigm	2	Advantage in the rate of relearning 'old' words over 'new' ones.
de Bot et al. (2004)	L2 L2 L2	German French French	English Dutch Dutch	Savings paradigm	21 30 12	Support for the savings effect. The savings paradigm can be very useful for testing long-term forgetting and retention.
Fromm (1970)	L1	Japanese	English	Age regression hypnosis	1	When regressed to 3 years of age the participant lapsed into rapid Japanese that as a little child he spoke but did not remember any of later in his life.
Footnick (2007)	L2	Mina	French	Age regression hypnosis	1	By the sixth session the participant regained more knowledge of Mina than at the beginning of the experiment despite being instructed, while in the hypnotic state, to forget everything that he said and remembered.
Hansen et al. (2002)	L2	Korean Japanese	English	Savings paradigm	302	The results confirmed the savings effect for the L2 vocabulary items that once had been learned but had not been used for a long period of time.
Hyltenstam et al. (2009)	L1	Korean	Swedish	Phonemic discrimination task	32	Adoptees (n = 23) relearning Korean outperformed native Swedish learners of Korean as L2 in phoneme discrimination but not in grammaticality judgement.
	L1	Spanish	Swedish		195	Adoptees (4) tested on L2 (Swedish) knowledge via a broad range of instruments. L2 was found not entirely native-like when compared to native Swedish speakers.

(Continued)

Table 1 (Continued)

Study	L1 or L2	Forgotten language	Linguistic context	Method	n	Findings
Isurin and Seidel (2015)	L1	Unknown	English	Savings paradigm	1	Based on the results of post-tests, the memory of the relearned 'old' words was better than memory of 'new' words. Controls did not show that 'old' words inherently were easier to learn. Russian or Ukrainian suggested as the lost language.
Knightly et al. (2003)	L2	Spanish	English	Phonetic analyses; accent ratings; grammaticality judgement; narrative and verb-phrase production	45	Pronunciation advantage for the childhood overhearers (n = 15); no benefit in morphosyntax.
Montrul (2011)	L1	Spanish	English	Oral production and written tasks aimed at testing morphosyntactic knowledge		Adoptee demonstrated native-like knowledge of English and significant attrition in Spanish.
Oh et al. (2010)	L1	Korean	English	Phoneme perception	25	Adult adoptees (n = 12, 11 adopted at the mean age of 5 months, one at the age of 3 years) reliably outperformed novice learners in identifying some Korean phonemes.
Oh et al. (2003)	L1	Korean	English	Phoneme perception and production	31	Childhood speakers (n = 15) were as good as native speakers at hearing the phonemic contrasts and outperformed novice learners and childhood hearers (n = 6) in phoneme production.
Oh, Au, Jun, & Lee, (forthcoming)	L1	Korean	English	Phoneme identification and production	38	Adult adoptees (adopted before age 1 year) comprised learner adoptees (n = 19) and adoptees who did not take Korean classes (n = 19). Advantage in phoneme perception and production for adoptees after 2-week re-exposure to Korean.
Pallier et al. (2003)	L1	Korean	French	Language identification; word recognition; fMRI	8	No advantage for adoptees. The fMRI data revealed no differences in brain activation when adoptees listened to Korean vs. to an unknown language.

Study	L1/L2	Language	Task		Findings
Singh et al. (2011)	L1	Hindi	Phoneme discrimination task	27	Adoptees (n = 8) performed better than controls after minimal training.
Park (2015)	L1	Korean	Perception test	35	Adoptees (n = 21) outperformed controls only in perception of Korean obstruents. Instrumental motivation of controls offered as a possible explanation of weak effects.
Pierce et al. (2016)	L1	Chinese	Tone discrimination task; fMRI	44	Similar brain activation to Chinese linguistic elements in adoptees (n = 21) and Chinese L1 speakers (n = 12), both differed from monolingual French children (n = 11).
Tees and Werker (1984)	L1/ L2	Hindi	Perception discrimination task	33	Limited early exposure to Hindi in 9 (out of 10) participants contributed to better performance on the task.
Van der Hoeven and de Bot (2012)	L2	French	Savings paradigm	45	Older participants (mean age 76) showed greater advantage in relearning old words than younger learners (mean age 22.4).
Ventureyra et al. (2004)	L1	Korean	Phoneme discrimination task	42	Adoptees (n = 18) showed no advantage of early experience with language for its availability later in life. Only small advantage for later re-exposure was found.

3.   Age Regression Hypnosis in Uncovering Suppressed Language

Although hypnosis often is not recognized as a valid scientific method and studies that have focused on suppressed language using age regression hypnosis as the main approach are extremely rare – with only three reported cases – the findings are intriguing and deserve a brief discussion. The age regression technique is used in hypnosis in order to bring mental images to the mind of an individual and ask them to describe those images, aiming at the individual's speech production in the suppressed language. A participant for such a study first is tested for 'hypnotic responsiveness' and ideally should be characterized as highly hypnotizable.

The earliest study on age regression hypnosis with the aim to uncover a suppressed childhood language by As (1962), involved an 18-year-old male student (S.) who was born in Finland to Swedish-speaking parents and spoke Swedish at home until the age of five. Due to his parents' divorce he was brought to the US by his mother, where his exposure to Swedish partly continued in the family until S. was eight years old. Then Swedish was replaced by English as his second stepfather spoke only English. At the time of the study, S. maintained almost no memories prior to the age of 10 years old and claimed that he did not remember any Swedish, except for a few words. Prior to the first hypnosis session, a list of 56 simple questions in Swedish that a child of five years of age is expected to understand was pre-tested on the participant with no feedback on correctness of responses provided. During the first four hypnotic sessions no mention of the target language was made. However, during the last session the same set of questions used in the pre-test was introduced and S. showed a significant improvement in understanding Swedish. To illustrate, when asked to count to 10 in Swedish before hypnosis he could not recall a single number, whereas under hypnosis he correctly named 6 out of 10 numbers. The author was cautious enough not to extend the findings of the experiment beyond the study but recommended 'that the method of attempted recovery of forgotten language be employed in further research in hypnotic age regression' (As 1962, p. 28).

In another study published a few years later, the researcher (Fromm, 1970) came across her participant rather incidentally while observing a hypnosis session conducted by her assistant. The participant (Don) was a 26-year-old student of Japanese descent who was born and raised in the US.; his parents were second-generation Japanese immigrants who were born in the US. Don claimed to have no knowledge of Japanese, yet when regressed to three years of age, he broke into rapid Japanese in a high-pitched child's voice and spoke like this for 15–20 minutes. When progressed forward to age 7, he reverted to English. This finding puzzled the researcher who did not know the participant's background, but assumed that based on her participant's age, he was likely to have spent his early childhood in an internment camp for Japanese Americans following the Japanese attack on Pearl Harbor. Later her assumption was corroborated by the participant's testimony. During the following therapy sessions Don regained progressively more knowledge of the forgotten language. There was another intriguing finding in the study: after the researcher could not induce Japanese in Don without clearly suggesting it, she chose to use a word in Japanese (*hai,* which means 'yes') that phonologically over-laps with the English 'hi'. After Don heard the word he repeated it three times and then lapsed into excited Japanese. Although Fromm did not emphasize this particular part of her experiment, we may look into recent evidence from an experimental study on code switching where 'false friends' along with cognates produced a significant effect in a lan-guage switch by a Russian-English habitual code switcher (Broersma et al. 2009). The authors suggested that such overlap between bilinguals' two languages at the semantic and/or phonological levels does activate both languages of a bilingual and a switch to another language is more likely to take place (see Clyne 2003, for the original idea behind the triggering hypothesis).

A third and more recent study involving age regression hypnosis in uncovering the suppressed language (Footnick 2007) was conducted on a 21-year-old male student (CK) who was born and raised in Paris apart from spending a few years in early childhood (from 2 years and 6 months, to six years and no months [hereafter pre-sented in the form 2; 6 to 6; 0]) in Togo where he spoke Mina, a language he did not speak after he returned to Paris. During six sessions of age regression hypnosis CK showed inconsistent linguistic behaviour, prompting the researcher to suggest that he was actively blocking the suppressed language. However, by the sixth session he regained more knowledge of Mina than he had at the beginning of the experiment. This finding is intriguing indeed, as at the end of each session and while still in the hypnotic state, CK directly was instructed to forget everything that he had remem-bered during the session and information was not shared with him until later in the study. The reported study started with a follow-up fMRI investigation in mind. However, due to CK's recovery of comprehension of Mina when he was out of hyp-nosis it was unlikely that any difference in his brain activation before, during, and after hypnosis would be detected. Yet Footnick called for the incorporation of fMRI studies into future research involving age regression hypnosis. We may argue, how-ever, that given their own problems, such as the use of inter-subject averaging (without looking into individual variations), the lack of knowledge of the physiological basis of cerebral blood flow changes, and the multiple unintended secondary processes, to name a few (see Paradis 2004, pp. 158–166, for more discussion) such incorporation of the fMRI technique may lend the hypnosis approach more credibility in the scientific world but not necessarily shed more light on the uncovering of forgotten languages under age regression hypnosis.

Studies on hypnosis aimed at uncovering the suppressed/forgotten language pro-vide an interesting insight into the human brain and its ability to retrieve information that supposedly was not accessible outside the hypnotic state. Such inaccessibility of the language can be qualified as language suppression or repression. As Ecke (2004) points out, the difference between suppression and repression 'lies in the possibility to con-sciously retrieve the target information, which is presumed possible in the first case, whereas it is expected [to be] impossible in the second' (p. 324). Since age regression hypnosis operates on the assumption that an individual has no conscious awareness of the procedure, we may suggest that the age regression hypnosis taps into the repressed knowledge of the lost language or the knowledge that was *intentionally* suppressed, which represents the common opinion amongst cognitive psychologists when it concerns the semantic difference between suppression and repression (Ecke 2004, p. 324). As fascinating and intriguing as the above three studies are, there has been more focus on finding remnants of a forgotten language using more traditional (behavioural) or more advanced neurological (fMRI) approaches.

4.   fMRI Studies in Uncovering Memory Remnants of a Lost Language

The aim of the fMRI technique in studies on language loss is to identify any difference in brain activation as a result of exposure to linguistic stimuli. However, Paradis (2004) cautioned about the potential overestimation of the neuroimagining findings. In his words, 'neuroimagining is new, exciting, and colourful; it is also very expensive, and hence prestigious. As a result, it runs the risk of being overrated and used for purposes beyond its true scope' (p.153).

Although there are many studies looking into the difference between early and late bilinguals through the use of the fMRI technique (see Birdsong 2006, for an overview) there were only two such studies looking into memory traces of a forgotten language and both involved adoptees whose first language supposedly was forgotten. The first one, testing adult adoptees, did not find any effect (Pallier et al. 2003), whereas another, looking into much younger adoptees, did (Pierce et al. 2016).

4.1.   *Adult Adoptees*

The first study (Pallier et al. 2003) has attracted much attention in the field, mostly due to the lack of evidence that other studies using behavioural techniques seem to provide, and this has led to extensive debate amongst scholars working on memory traces of a lost language.

Pallier et al. (2003) studied a group of adult adoptees (i.e. Korean children adopted between the ages of 3 and 8) to French-speaking families. In addition to two behavioural tasks (language and word recognition), they used the fMRI technique to detect any difference in brain activation when the participants were discriminating between the languages (Korean was placed in a group of a few other languages, both related and unrelated to Korean) or words coming from different languages. The fMRI results found no difference in brain activation between adoptees and the control group of native French speakers, indicating no residual memory of the childhood language. The authors discussed their findings through the prism of the crystallization hypothesis that, first, stipulates that the later a second language is learned, the more the cortical representations of the second and the first languages will differ. Second, the hypothesis predicts that exposure to the first language should leave long-lasting traces in the neural circuits subserving language processing. Since the study did not find any support for the crystallization hypothesis, the authors concluded that 'when a second language is learned early on, this acquisition does not necessarily involve different brain systems than those involved in learning the native language' (Pallier et al. 2003, p. 158).

Having found no evidence of the remnants of the childhood language preserved in the speakers' memory, the authors left open the possibility that implicit traces of linguistic knowledge were preserved, but not accessible, through the tasks employed in their study. They acknowledged that a different instrument – a relearning task – might provide different results.

4.2. *Child Adoptees*

Since Pallier et al.'s (2003) study was the first – and for many years has remained the only – study where brain imaging (fMRI) was used and it found no evidence of traces of memory for the lost language in adoptees, a recent study involving Chinese adoptees in French-speaking Canada deserves attention (Pierce et al. 2016). The study tested whether early established neural representations for language persist despite discontinuation of that language. In their study, much younger adoptees were investigated (i.e. ages 9–17, adopted at 12; 8 months of age, on average) and their performance was compared with that of two other groups: a group of age-matched Chinese L1 speakers who immigrated with their parents to French-speaking Canada and spoke Chinese as their L1 before acquiring French as their L2, and a group of age-matched French monolinguals who never were exposed to Chinese before. A tonal discrimination task showed similar brain activation in adoptees and Chinese L1 speakers, whereas both groups differed from a group of control French monolinguals. The authors concluded that 'the similarity between adoptees and Chinese speakers clearly illustrates that early-acquired information is maintained in the brain and that early experiences unconsciously influence neural processing for years, if not indefinitely' (Pierce et al. 2016, p. 17314) and that 'the brain exhibits tremendous plasticity and a pronounced ability to adapt to its environment' (p. 17318).

The question remains why Pallier et al. (2003) did not find any indication of brain activation in their adoptees while using the same fMRI technique as Pierce et al. (2016) did. One possible explanation may come from the age difference between the participants in the two studies: Pallier et al.'s (2003) adoptees were older at the time of the adoption and could have been more distanced from their experience with the lost language. However, because they were adopted at an older age than Pierce et al.'s (2016) adoptees, they arguably could retain more traces of memory for their birth language.

5. Behavioural Tasks in Uncovering Memory Remnants of a Lost Language

The use of the fMRI technique remains less prevalent in the field of language loss and the majority of studies explored the issue of memory traces by using behavioural tasks, such as re-exposing the participants to the supposedly lost language and looking for any possible relearning advantage over control groups that never knew the language in question. Here the studies can be broken down into those that were conducted on childhood overhearers and on adoptees.

5.1.   Childhood Overhearers

One of the earliest studies conducted on perception discrimination of sounds amongst those who were learning the language as L2 (Hindi) and those who had prior exposure to Hindi in early childhood suggested the presence of memory remnants for the forgotten language (Tees and Werker 1984). However, it was not until a few contemporary scholars started looking into this issue in more depth that we acquired a better picture of what is happening when an individual is re-exposed to a reportedly forgotten childhood language. Amongst those, Terry Au, Janet Oh, and their colleagues have been contributing to this line of research for the last 20 years. In the earliest publication (Au and Romo 1997), two studies conducted on college language learners of Korean and Spanish, respectively, were reported. In both studies, the researchers looked at possible advantages for better language learning for those students who were exposed to the target language in their childhood: overhearers (who were exposed to the language but never spoke it), addressees (who were spoken to only), and limited speakers (who spoke for several years during early childhood), versus first-time learners. A clear advantage in production, comprehension, and grammaticality judgement tasks was reported for the participants who had prior exposure to the target language in their childhood. The results found in these experiments encouraged the authors to continue their pursuit of memory remnants of a lost language in the reacquisition of that language. In the following two decades, there were other publications by Au (2012) and her group of researchers (Au and Oh 2009; Au et al. 2002, 2008; Knightly et al. 2003; Oh et al. 2010; Oh, Au, Jun, & Lee, forthcoming; Oh et al. 2003). The reported studies compared the performance of childhood language overhearers with typical late L2 learners (Au et al. 2002; Knightly et al. 2003), childhood speakers, with childhood overhearers and late L2 learners (Au et al. 2008; Oh et al. 2003) on a variety of experimental tasks, such as phonological assessment, phoneme perception/production, morphosyntax production, accent rating, grammaticality judgement, and so forth.

Evidence for preserved implicit knowledge of a forgotten childhood language also was reported by Bowers, Mattys, and Cage (2009). The seven adult participants of their study were individuals who at some point in their childhood knew either Hindi or Zulu due to their parents' work abroad and never used the language in their everyday life past their childhoods. They were tested on phoneme discrimination in the respective childhood languages. Initially the participants did not show any preserved knowledge of their childhood languages. However, after intensive practice was provided (15–20 sessions), they showed a relearning effect. Also, the younger participants (under the age of 40) outperformed the older participants (over the age of 40) and the control group (i.e. native speakers of English with no prior exposure to those two languages) in relearning the contrasting phonemes. The authors acknowledged the small size of their sample and concluded that preserved implicit knowledge of the once lost language, now practised or relearned, could not easily be detected by less robust or less intrusive behavioural measures, such as extensive re-exposure to the lost language. It remains unclear why most of the studies reported by Au and colleagues did show the relearning advantage despite not having such repetitive training trials for their participants.

The above studies provided evidence of a long-lasting advantage of early childhood exposure to the target language for the later relearning of that language, with the phonological effect remaining strong, whereas morphosyntactic performance did not benefit significantly from such exposure.

5.2. *Adoptees*

Later there were two additional studies that involved now adult adoptees. Oh et al. (2010) investigated whether phoneme perception differs between a group of adult adoptees from Korea and novice learners of Korean as L2. Importantly, the participants (n = 12) had been adopted before the age of one year (i.e. before the stage when actual speech production happens) with the exception of one adoptee who was adopted at the age of three years. The results of the study provided evidence of a significant advantage of a very early exposure to the language – albeit with no speech production yet – for the later ability to be better attuned to the target language. The most recent study coming from the same group of researchers (Oh et al. forthcoming) reconfirmed the prior findings. This time, the participants comprised adult adoptees from Korea who were taking Korean classes in college and a group of adult adoptees from Korea who had never taken any classes in Korean and who were not enrolled in them at the time of the study. All participants were adopted before the age of one year. The study showed a clear advantage in phoneme perception and production for adoptees after two weeks of re-exposure to Korean compared with those who had no such exposure. However, the authors were cautious of making big claims and acknowledged the absence of baseline data for adoptee relearners. In the absence of that baseline, they added a group of adoptees who did not take any classes in Korean and matched them on all demographic variables with learner-adoptees. Yet, as they rightly pointed out, the learner adoptees might have been more motivated to learn Korean and motivation and interest in Korean culture may play a critical role in these group differences.

After Pallier et al. (2003) did not find any evidence of memory traces in their study using the fMRI approach, Pallier and his colleagues (Ventureyra et al. 2004) conducted another study that adopted a behavioural approach and tested phoneme discrimination in Korean by a different group of Korean adoptees raised by French-speaking families in France, Switzerland, and Belgium. Their age at the time of adoption ranged between 3 and 9 years old. In this study, half of the adoptees had no re-exposure to Korean since childhood and the other half had been re-exposed to Korean during short trips to Korea that ranged from 10 days to 6 months. In contrast to other studies using the same behavioural tasks, the results of this study were not different from those in Pallier et al.'s (2003) study: no difference was found between the linguistic performance of adoptees (regardless of re-exposure) and native speakers of French. The authors acknowledged that formal extensive exposure, rather than just short touristic visits, might be the essential element required for evidence of residual memory of a lost L1 to surface.

By the time the above study was published, Au and her colleagues had found evidence for the traces of memory of a lost language in two of their earlier studies (Au et al. 2002; Au and Romo 1997). Thus, in their recent articles they have acknowledged the null findings in Pallier et al. (2003) and Ventureyra et al. (2004) by offering their explanation of differing results. According to the authors, the disparity may stem from the difference between storage strength and retrieval strength of childhood memories.[3] Storage strength depends on how well something was learned originally, whereas retrieval strength depends on current usage, making the retrieval by participants in Pallier et al. (2003) rather weak (Au and Oh 2009, p. 273). By the same token, the absence of the relearning experience in Pallier et al.'s (2003) sample contributes to the weak strength of retrieval and makes the results different from those in Oh et al.'s (2010) sample (pp. 1129–1130).

The null findings in the studies by Pallier et al. (2003) and Ventureyra et al. (2004) were further challenged by Hyltenstam et al. (2009). Their study consisted of two parts. First, Korean adoptees in Sweden (adopted at the age of 3 months and 10 and a half years), unexposed to Korean since their adoption for an average of 22 years, but formally studying or having studied Korean at the time of the research, were found to have more significant results on the voice onset time (VOT) phonemic discrimination task than the group of native Swedish speakers who formally learned Korean as a foreign language as adults. However, adoptees underperformed compared to native Swedish speakers on the grammaticality judgement task, possibly due to less advantageous learning conditions for adoptees who spent less time on formally learning Korean as adults than their native Swedish counterparts. This concurs with the earlier findings by Au et al. (2002) and as Hyltenstam et al. (2009) suggested, the remnants of the adoptees' L1 seem to consist primarily of basic features of the childhood language phonology and phonetics rather than of more complex grammatical features. Second, a small sample of Latino Spanish adoptees in Sweden underperformed compared to native Swedish speakers in the 'nativeness' of their Swedish. This suggests that a severely terminated exposure to native Spanish did not lead to any advantage for the acquisition of Swedish in those adoptees. Based on the results of the study (the first component, in particular), Hyltenstam et al. (2009) argued that the search for L1 memory traces in adoptees 'requires a methodological approach different from that pursued by Pallier et al., and Ventureyra et al. If there are remnants of a seemingly lost L1, these are most likely not easily retrievable for the individual. It is reasonable to believe that a re-exposure to this language is necessary to boost accessibility' (p. 132).

In other words, the authors argued that the evidence in Pallier et al. (2003) and Ventureyra et al. (2004) should be interpreted as support of severe L1 attrition rather than the lack of residual memory for the lost L1, for no repetitive re-exposure to the lost language was used in those studies. They further suggest that had a re-exposure to Korean taken place during a longer period of time (in the case of Ventureyra's adoptees), the evidence for the remnants of memory would have been clearer. Montrul (2011) agrees with Hyltenstam et al. (2009) that age effect and the effects of re-exposure and relearning should be considered in studies on language attrition in adoptees. Her case study involved an adult adopted from Guatemala at the age of nine by an American family who had no exposure to Spanish during her childhood years. The adoptee was re-exposed to the L1 from age 14 and showed significant attrition of morphosyntactic knowledge of Spanish but, as the author argues, not to the degree demonstrated by Korean adoptees in Pallier et al. (2003) and Ventureyra et al. (2004).

The study by Hyltenstam et al. (2009) was further expanded by Park (2015) using the same pool of adoptees. Additional statistical analyses provided conflicting evidence on the adoptees' advantage in the relearning of their birth language. Only one part of the test – perception of Korean obstruents – showed that adoptees had better results than the best-performing Swedes. Assuming that Korean obstruents represent some of the most difficult sounds for Swedish learners and Swedes had a higher motivation for studying Korean and better learning conditions than the adoptees, the author considered the advantage shown by the adoptees in that test as an indication of residual memory for the lost language in adoptees.

Contrary to the majority of studies conducted on adult adoptees, Singh et al. (2011) reported the phonological advantage in much younger adoptees. The participants were adopted from India by American families on average at the age of two years. Mean age at the time of testing for adoptees was 12; 1. No significant difference between the adoptee group and the non-adopted group was found during the initial testing; the adoptees, however, significantly improved in perceptual discrimination over the control group after minimal training. This further emphasizes the role of re-exposure – as minimal or as extensive as it may be – in uncovering the remnants of memory of a severely lost childhood language.

Support for the role of re-exposure in finding the phonological advantage in adoptees recently has been provided by another study on adult Korean adoptees; this time the study came from the Netherlands (Choi et al. 2017). The participants comprised 29 adult adoptees from Korea and 29 native Dutch speakers. Moreover, the group of adoptees was split into two subgroups depending on whether they were adopted as prelinguistic infants (n = 15) or as toddlers and young children ranging in age between 1; 5 and 5; 10 at the time of adoption (n = 15). Extensive training (13 sessions over a period of 10–12 days) aimed at exposing the participants to phonemic contrast; post-tests, both in perception and production, concluded each session. The results of the study showed that adoptees' production scores improved significantly more across the training period than control participants' scores. Moreover, there was no significant difference between the two groups of adoptees, suggesting that even those who were adopted at the prelinguistic stage retained enough of the initial exposure to Korean phonology to facilitate a later relearning of that language. Another intriguing finding concerned a possible transfer that exists between perception knowledge and production skills: only for adoptees, production success correlated significantly with the rate of learning in perception. Similar findings came from another study on much younger adoptees, this time Cantonese and Mandarin adoptees in the Netherlands (Broersma et al. 2016). For the Cantonese group (n = 22), children were adopted at the age of 2; 2, on average, and were tested at the age of 7; 5, on average, and the Dutch control group (n = 23) was age matched. Similarly, for the Mandarin group (n = 26), children were adopted at the age of 2; 4, on average, and were at the age of 7; 4 at the time of testing. The Dutch control group (n = 26) was also age matched. Participants were tested for the perception and production of phonological contrast (affricate contrast and tone contrast). At the pre-test, the adopted children did not outperform the Dutch control children. After re-exposure, however, adoptees did outperform Dutch controls both in perception and production.

As the above studies suggest, behavioural techniques tapping into the remnants of a lost childhood language proved successful in providing evidence of advantage in relearning the lost language. However, the biggest advantage was reported for phonology, with other linguistic areas not showing consistent findings across studies. Moreover, the advantage mainly was found through extensive re-exposure to the language and it was evident both in adult adoptees and child adoptees. The clear evidence of the phonological advantage is not surprising given the young age at which participants were removed from their early linguistic environment. As Au and Oh (2009) noted, 'given the massive brain cell death and pruning of synapses in early brain development…, it is possible that childhood language memory might not survive for so many years with little or no further exposure to the language. Even if it did, it might not be readily accessible' (p. 273). The need for extensive re-exposure to the lost language in order to detect the relearning advantage, acknowledged by numerous scholars, further suggests that the traces of memory for the lost childhood language might be so minimal that it cannot be discovered instantly through the use of behavioural techniques. Also, it remains unclear what role the temporal distance separating adoptees from the time of their adoption may play in the accessibility of the native language memory. Although recent findings on adoptees who were much younger at the time of the study suggest that such memory traces are available either without any re-exposure (Pierce et al. 2016) or after some minimal training (Broersma et al. 2016; Choi et al. 2017; Singh et al. 2011), the same can be said about the majority of other studies conducted on adult adoptees. In other words, behavioural techniques used in the discussed studies did find support for the remnants of the lost language in the individuals' memory; however, the strongest evidence was reported for the phonological memory.

6.   The Savings Paradigm

The above studies on the remnants of memory for a lost childhood language did not necessarily include the relearning technique. However, the major assumption on which the savings paradigm operates is that the residual memory for the learned information could produce the 'savings' effect during the subsequent relearning of that information.

The idea of memory traces that benefit the relearning the old information goes back to Ebbinghaus (1885), the founding father of experimental psychology who provided the first documented scientific evidence of memory retention, repetition effect, forgetting, and the savings effect. As in other cases of early studies in experimental psychology, Ebbinghaus used himself as the only subject of experimentation and found that increased repetition during a period of study provided savings in relearning that information at a later time. Almost a century later, Nelson (1978) continued that line of thought and used the relearning task to see whether there is a relearning advantage of old items over new items. Although the task used word-number pairs and was disassociated from any meaningful learning that happens in real life, it laid the foundation for the new approach that assumed that the residual memory for the learned information could produce the 'savings' effect during the subsequent relearning of that information. Nelson's reconceptualization of Ebbinghaus's savings idea, known as the savings paradigm, later was applied in a series of studies on L2 loss, starting with a ground-breaking study by de Bot and Stoessel (2000).

The savings paradigm approach is not fundamentally different from a few notions that have remained influential in the field of L2 attrition. The most well-known hypothesis in L2 attrition research is the regression hypothesis (e.g. Cohen 1975; Olshtain 1989). It predicts that the path of attrition is the reverse of the path of acquisition (the first things learned remain longest in memory, whereas the last things learned are the first things forgotten). Also, an amount of the lexical knowledge in L2 that was not forgotten shortly after the learning phase supposedly stays intact in an individual's memory, forming what Bahrick (1984) called the 'permastore.' These two fundamental notions agree with the principle on which the savings paradigm is postulated: the linguistic knowledge acquired first or earlier will leave much stronger traces in memory and can be more easily reactivated through re-exposure to that knowledge later in life.

6.1.   Child L2 Learners

When first applied to the study of the residual memory of the forgotten language, de Bot and Stoessel (2000) expanded the paradigm by suggesting that if an individual knew certain linguistic items at one point, there is a high likelihood that other items in that language were not known to them during the original stage of learning. Thus the contrast between 'old' and 'new' knowledge is drawn along that line. The rate of relearning of 'old' items over 'new' items is considered the major control factor in studies employing the paradigm. All studies conducted within the savings paradigm framework used lexical items as the main experimental stimuli, whereas the studies reviewed above mostly employed a phonetic discrimination task. Moreover, all but one (Isurin and Seidel 2015) of the studies within the savings paradigm framework looked into a lost L2, whereas the above studies on the savings effect primarily looked into adoptees' lost birth language.

In their original study (de Bot and Stoessel 2000), the participants were two German adults (siblings) who had learned Dutch as an L2 in their childhood while living in the Netherlands and had not used it since then. They were tested for their remaining L2 skills in a series of relearning sessions. 'Old' words were those that they were assumed to know as children and 'new' words were those that they were unlikely to know as children, excluding any words from the stimulus pool that were recognized by participants during the initial pre-testing. The authors also hypothesized that a lost language may 'reactivate' itself if performance – on both recall and recognition – improves over time. The results of the study provided support for the savings hypothesis and showed an obvious advantage of relearning 'old' words over 'new' ones. Although this first study within the savings paradigm framework used a control group, the authors wondered whether it shed more light on their findings. While there was a noticeable increase of remembered words for both participants in the study, the control group showed much variability in its performance, which could be attributed to the participants' different learning strategies rather than to a prior exposure to the language. Subsequent studies that adopted this line of thought did not use a control group in their design (except for Isurin and Seidel 2015, as discussed in Section 6.3). Further supporting evidence for the savings effect came from a methodologically similar follow-up study using foreign language learners of German in the US and French in the Netherlands (de Bot et al. 2004). This study provided implications for language teaching and showed that indeed 'the savings paradigm can be very useful for testing long-term forgetting and retention on the basis of global estimates of preattrition knowledge' (de Bot et al. 2004, p. 381).

6.2. *Adult L2 Learners*

The savings paradigm approach was embraced by Lynne Hansen, a leading scholar in L2 attrition research. In a large-scale study involving 302 missionaries who lived either in Korea or Japan but then for years had no exposure to the respective languages, the savings paradigm was used to tap into the residual memory for those languages (Hansen et al. 2002). 'Old' words were contrasted to 'new' pseudowords. The results confirmed the savings effect for the L2 vocabulary items that once had been learned but had not been used for a long period of time. Moreover, the authors concluded that the effect found was the most robust reported to date.[4]

The latest study using the savings paradigm to investigate L2 forgetting (Van der Hoeven and de Bot 2012) added an additional variable (i.e. age) and looked at three groups of participants who had learned French as L2 in school. The oldest group (mean age 76) showed the highest savings effect: older participants showed greater advantage in relearning old words than younger learners (mean age 22.4). The authors hypothesized that the older learners could have a larger vocabulary to start with due to the higher prestige of French in Dutch society at the time when they learned it and that they could make more use of French in their lifetime than the younger participants. The age-related decline in cognitive abilities might have affected the learning of new words rather than the relearning of old words.

6.3. *Adult Adoptee*

An intriguing case of language recovery in an adoptee recently has been reported by Isurin and Seidel (2015). Due to a closed case adoption, their 33-year-old participant did not know her linguistic or ethnic background prior to her adoption at the age of three years old. While going through psychotherapy, she recovered some childhood memories and bits and pieces of a lost childhood language. In order to determine what her lost language was and whether she still retained remnants of it, the researchers had to act quickly to bring relevant methods into their study. They chose to use the savings paradigm technique, which by then had provided strong evidence in uncovering traces of a lost language. Having assumed that the paradigm is a relevant method, they expanded and reconceptualized it when applying it in their study. Also, they added a control group, which traditionally is deemed unnecessary in experimental designs within the savings paradigm framework. The control group comprised 12 female native English-speaking undergraduate students who had no prior exposure to any Slavic languages. The results of the study suggested a high probability that the lost childhood language in their adoptee was either Russian or Ukrainian. The typological closeness of the two languages and the limited vocabulary that a three-year-old child knows did not allow the researchers to move beyond this conclusion.

Compared with numerous studies on adoptees and overhearers reported in the Section 5, the studies employing the savings paradigm operate on the same assumption, that the previously learned language leaves imprints in the individual's brain and such imprints can be detected through the re-exposure to that language later in life. However, the technique implies a more rigorous control over the rate of relearning, which constitutes the savings effect, and it involves only one linguistic area, lexicon. Also, the use of the savings paradigm is not limited to the study of adoptees and childhood learners; primarily, it was used in studies on adult L2 learners. Therefore, discussing the 'savings paradigm' studies separately from other studies that looked into the memory traces for forgotten languages served only one purpose: to illustrate different behavioural approaches to the study of memory traces for a forgotten language.

7. Conclusion

The last two decades have seen a few exciting trends in studies on multilinguals. The emerging line of thought, in which scholars tap into remnants of memory of a lost childhood language, is one of those. Regardless of some inconsistencies in findings and possible methodological flaws, this new direction promises to broaden our knowledge about the human brain and the elusive memories of a language that a child was exposed to even before conscious language learning took place. What do we learn about human memory and the human brain through the studies discussed in this chapter? If we assume that the information once learned and later forgotten indeed leaves imprints in the individual's brain, as postulated by Ebbinghaus (1885), we may see evidence of such remnants of memory in those who were exposed to the language early in life and later had such exposure terminated. A few decades of research on lost childhood language have shown that language deterioration in children happens rather fast as a result of the terminated linguistic input. Longitudinal case studies on adoptees are rather infrequent in literature. Thus scholars turned to an intriguing question: How much of the earlier learned language – or traces thereof – were still preserved in those learners who knew a language in their childhood or young adulthood but had not used it since? Here the research followed a few trends.

First, a few studies with the use of an age regression hypothesis produced fascinating results, albeit ones not always accepted as valid in the scientific community. When individuals were regressed to the age at which they spoke a supposedly forgotten language, the language re-emerged and sometimes was connected closely to the individual's sense of self at the time when the language was in use.

Second, there were numerous studies on adult adoptees who had not spoken the birth language since their adoption. The majority of those studies used behavioural tasks, such as phoneme perception/discrimination, production, accent rating, and so forth. The participants either were re-exposed to or retrained in the target language or the task was applied without any preliminary training. All those studies, regardless of re-exposure, found the evidence of the remnants of memory for a lost childhood language; such evidence was particularly strong and rather consistent across studies in one linguistic area, phonology. However, the importance of re-exposure to the language in order to find traces thereof was emphasized in a few studies. What is more intriguing is that such memory traces were detected in those who were adopted as prelinguistic infants. The same was confirmed for non-adoptees (i.e. those who happened to be exposed to the language in their childhood while speaking a different native language). However, there were two studies – both co-authored by Pallier – that did not find the memory traces in adoptees: one used the fMRI technique in addition to a few behavioural tasks and another used a standard behavioural task that was employed widely in other studies where the effect was found. Surprisingly, a recent study on adoptees with the use of the same fMRI technique did find a difference in brain activation, something that Pallier and his colleagues did not. Unfortunately, given that this line of research involving adoptees has produced such overwhelming evidence supporting the presence of memory for early childhood language and that the only two studies that did not are widely acknowledged in the literature, Pallier and colleagues did not proceed with conducting another experiment, which either would have reinforced their previous claims or refuted them. An engaging intellectual debate based on scientific evidence always contributes to our better understanding of how the human mind/brain works.

Third, a traditional approach in cognitive psychology, known as the savings paradigm, that involves the relearning of forgotten knowledge was adopted by de Bot and Stoessel (2000) and later applied in a few other studies. All of these studies supported the idea of better relearning/retention of those items that had been known to an individual versus those items that represented new knowledge. If studies on memory traces outside the savings paradigm approach involved both L1 and L2 forgotten by the participants, the methodology, known as the 'savings paradigm', focused exclusively on L2. However, a recent study by Isurin and Seidel (2015) has reconceptualized and expanded the framework by applying it to an unusual case of an adult adoptee who did not know her linguistic background prior to adoption.

The majority of techniques tapping into memory traces of a forgotten language are behavioural tasks, with the only two studies that used the fMRI technique providing conflicting evidence. Why are behavioural, and not only neurological, techniques relevant for the field of neuroscience? As a relatively young field, the neuroscience of multilingualism faces its own challenges in terms of study participants (e.g. difficulties in finding participants for studies on bilingual aphasia) and the general reliability and high cost of fMRI studies (Paradis 2004). Therefore, any emerging evidence related to human memory and the human mind provides a direction in which a more advanced, yet not necessarily more ground-breaking or technologically reliable, research should go. After all, the concept of mind and memory, as elusive as they may seem, can physically be located only in one human organ, the brain.

NOTES

1   This finding triggered an experimental study that tested the role of conceptual overlap in L1 forgetting (see Isurin and McDonald 2001).
2   According to the authors, the National Committee for Adoption (1988) reported that half of the transracial adoptions in the United States comprised predominantly Korean children adopted by white Americans. This may explain why Koreans represented the major adoptee population (both in the US and in Europe) in studies discussed in this chapter.
3   For a more detailed explanation of these phenomena, see Bjork and Bjork (1992).
4   Hansen et al. 2002, refer to a few additional studies that reported the savings effect. However, those studies were presented at a symposium and no subsequent publications could be found.

REFERENCES

As, A. (1962). The recovery of forgotten language knowledge through hypnotic age regression: a case report. *American Journal of Clinical Hypnosis* 5: 24–29.

Au, T.K. (2012). Access to childhood language memory: implications for cognitive development. In: *Access to Language and Cognitive Development* (ed. M. Siegal and L. Surian), 176–191. New York, NY: Oxford University Press.

Au, T.K. and Oh, J.S. (2009). Korean as a heritage language. In P. Li (General Ed.). In: *Handbook of East Asian Psycholinguistics, Part III: Korean Psycholinguistics* (ed. C. Lee, G.B. Simpson and Y. Kim), 269–275. London, UK: Cambridge University Press.

Au, T.K., Oh, J.S., Knightly, L. et al. (2008). Salvaging a childhood language. *Journal of Memory and Language* 58 (4): 998–1011.

Au, T.K. and Romo, L.F. (1997). Does childhood language experience help adult learners? In: *The Cognitive Processing of Chinese and Related Asian Languages* (ed. H.-C. Chen), 417–441. Hong Kong, China: Chinese University Press.

Au, T.K., Romo, L.F., Knightly, L. et al. (2002). Overhearing a language during childhood. *Psychological Science* 13: 238–243.

Bahrick, H.P. (1984). Fifty years of second language attrition: implications for programmatic research. *Modern Language Journal* 68: 105–118.

Birdsong, D. (2006). Age and second language acquisition and processing: a selective overview. *Language Learning* 56 (1): 9–49.

Bjork, R. and Bjork, E. (1992). A new theory of disuse and an old theory of stimulus fluctuation. In: *From Learning Processes to Cognitive Processes: Essays in Honor of William K. Estes*, vol. 2 (ed. A. Healy, S. Kosslyn and R. Shiffren), 35–67. Hillsdale, NJ: Erlbaum.

de Bot, K., Martens, V., and Stoessel, S. (2004). Finding residual lexical knowledge: the "savings" approach to testing vocabulary. *International Journal of Bilingualism* 8 (3): 373–382.

de Bot, K. and Stoessel, S. (2000). In search of yesterday's words: reactivating a long-forgotten language. *Applied Linguistics* 21 (3): 333–353.

Bowers, J., Mattys, S., and Cage, S. (2009). Preserved implicit knowledge of a forgotten childhood language. *Psychological Science* 20 (9): 1064–1069.

Broersma, M., Isurin, L., de Bot, K., and Butlena, S. (2009). Triggered code-switching: evidence from Dutch-English and Russian-English data. In: *Multidisciplinary Approaches to Code Switching* (ed. L. Isurin, D. Winford and K. de Bot), 103–129. Amsterdam, The Netherlands: John Benjamins.

Broersma, M., Zhou, W., & Choi, J. (2016). *New sounds or old sounds? International adoptees' relearning of birth language phonology.*

Presented at the *8th International Symposium on the Acquisition of Second-Language Speech* (New Sounds 2016), Aarhus, Denmark.

Choi, J., Cutler, A., and Broersma, M. (2017). Early development of abstract language knowledge: evidence from perception-production transfer of birth-language memory. *The Royal Society Open Science* 4: 160660.

Clyne, M. (2003). *Dynamics of Language Contact*. Cambridge, UK: Cambridge University Press.

Cohen, A.D. (1975). Forgetting a second language. *Language Learning* 24: 55–68.

Ebbinghaus, H. (1885). *Memory: A Contribution to Experimental Psychology*. New York, NY: Columbia University Press.

Ecke, P. (2004). Language attrition and theories of forgetting: a cross-disciplinary review. *International Journal of Bilingualism* 8 (3): 321–354.

Footnick, R. (2007). A hidden language. Recovery of a 'lost' language is triggered by hypnosis. In: *Language Attrition: Theoretical Perspectives* (ed. B. Köpke, M. Schmid, M. Keijzer and S. Dostert), 169–189. Amsterdam, The Netherlands: John Benjamins.

Fromm, E. (1970). Age regression with unexpected reappearance of a repressed childhood language. *International Journal of Clinical and Experimental Hypnosis* 18: 79–88.

Gindis, B. (2005). Cognitive, language, and educational issues of children adopted from overseas orphanages. *Journal of Cognitive Education and Psychology* 4 (3): 291–315.

Hansen, L., Umeda, Y., and McKinney, M. (2002). Savings in the relearning of second language vocabulary: the effect of time and proficiency. *Language Learning* 52 (4): 653–678.

Hyltenstam, K., Bylund, E., Abrahamsson, N., and Park, H.-S. (2009). Dominant-language replacement: the case of international adoptees. *Bilingualism: Language and Cognition* 12 (2): 121–140.

Isurin, L. (2000). 'Deserted island' or a child's first language forgetting. *Bilingualism: Language and Cognition* 3 (2): 151–166.

Isurin, L. and McDonald, J. (2001). Retroactive interference from translation equivalents: implications for first language forgetting. *Memory & Cognition* 29: 312–319.

Isurin, L. and Seidel, C. (2015). Traces of memory for a lost childhood language: the savings paradigm expanded. *Language Learning Journal* 65 (4): 761–790.

Knightly, L., Jun, S.-A., Oh, J.S., and Au, T.K. (2003). Production benefits of childhood overhearing. *Journal of the Acoustical Society of America* 114: 465–474.

Köpke, B., Schmid, M.S., Keijzer, M., and Dostert, S. (eds.) (2007). *Language Attrition: Theoretical Perspectives*. Amsterdam, The Netherlands: John Benjamins.

Montrul, S. (2011). First language retention and attrition in an adult Guatemalan adoptee. *Language, Interaction and Acquisition* 2 (2): 276–311.

National Committee for Adoption, Inc. (1988). *Adoption Factbook* (DHHS Publication No.9). Washington, DC: U.S. Government Printing Office.

Nelson, T. (1978). Detecting small amounts of information in memory: savings for non-recognized items. *Journal of Experimental Psychology: Human Learning and Memory* 4 (5): 453–468.

Neville, H. and Bavelier, D. (2002). Human brain plasticity: evidence from sensory deprivation and altered language experience. In: *Progress in Brain Research* (ed. M.A. Hofman, G.J. Boer, A.J.G.D. Holtmaat, et al.), 177–188. Amsterdam, The Netherlands: Elsevier Science BV.

Nicoladis, E. and Grabois, H. (2002). Learning English and losing Chinese: a case study of a child adopted from China. *International Journal of Bilingualism* 6: 441–454.

Oh, J.S., Au, T.K., and Jun, S.-A. (2010). Early childhood language memory in the speech perception of international adoptees. *Journal of Child Language* 37: 1123–1132.

Oh, J.S., Jun, S.-A., Knightly, L.M., and Au, T.K. (2003). Holding on to childhood language memory. *Cognition* 86: B5–B64.

Olshtain, E. (1989). Is second language attrition the reversal of second language acquisition? *Studies in Second Language Acquisition* 11: 151–165.

Pallier, C., Dehaene, S., Poline, J. et al. (2003). Brain imaging of language plasticity in adopted adults: can a second language replace the first? *Cerebral Cortex* 13: 155–161.

Paradis, M. (2004). *A Neurolinguistic Theory of Bilingualism*. Amsterdam, The Netherlands: John Benjamins.

Park, H.-S. (2015). Korean adoptees in Sweden: Have they lost their first language completely? *Applied PsychoLinguistics* 36: 773–797.

Pierce, L.J., Klein, D., Chen, J.-K. et al. (2016). Mapping the unconscious maintenance of a lost first language. *Proceedings of the National Academy of Sciences of the United States of America* 111: 17314–17319.

Schmid, M., Köpke, B., Keijzer, M., and Weilemar, L. (eds.) (2004). *First Language Attrition: Interdisciplinary Perspectives on Methodological Issues*. Amsterdam, The Netherlands: John Benjamins.

Singh, L., Liederman, J., Mierzejewski, R., and Barners, J. (2011). Rapid reacquisition of native phoneme contrasts after disuse: you do not always lose what you do not use. *Developmental Science* 14 (5): 949–959.

Tees, R. and Werker, J. (1984). Perceptual flexibility: maintenance or recovery of the ability to discriminate non-native speech sounds. *Canadian Journal of Psychology* 38: 579–590.

Van der Hoeven, N. and de Bot, K. (2012). Relearning in the elderly: age-related effects on the size of savings. *Language Learning* 62 (1): 42–67.

Ventureyra, V., Pallier, C., and Yoo, H.-Y. (2004). The loss of first language phonetic perception in adopted Koreans. *Journal of Neurolinguistics* 17: 79–91.

Wickes, K. and Slate, J. (1996). Transracial adoption of Koreans: a preliminary study of adjustment. *International Journal for the Advancement of Counseling* 19: 187–195.

8 Brain Adaptations and Neurological Indices of Processing in Adult Second Language Acquisition
Challenges for the Critical Period Hypothesis

VINCENT DELUCA, DAVID MILLER,
CHRISTOS PLIATSIKAS, AND
JASON ROTHMAN

1. Introduction

Stemming from the seminal work of Penfield and Roberts (1959) and Lenneberg (1967), a major question in adult language learning studies – indeed one that transcends all paradigms – has involved the extent to which adult language acquisition and processing is destined to be fundamentally different in adulthood compared to childhood. The basis of the original claims of the critical period hypothesis (CPH) (Lenneberg 1967) regards neurological maturation after puberty; brain plasticity is said to be lost or greatly reduced, rendering the mechanisms that underlie language learning necessarily distinct and thus disadvantaging adults. No one denies that child and adult developmental paths differ; however, the evidence that is used to support critical/sensitive period effects are decisively not clear (see Abrahamsson and Hyltenstam 2009; DeKeyser 2000; Long 2005, 2013, as compared to Bialystok and Hakuta 1994; Birdsong and Molis 2001; Birdsong and Vanhove 2016; Birdsong 2014; Rothman 2008, for review and opposing views). With few exceptions, the vast majority of 'relevant evidence' on the matter comes from behavioural experimentation or spontaneous production, most often from second language (L2) populations not exposed to the target language in a way similar to child L1 acquirers (e.g. adults tend to be classroom learners and children tend to be

The Handbook of the Neuroscience of Multilingualism, First Edition. Edited by John W. Schwieter.
© 2019 John Wiley & Sons Ltd. Published 2019 by John Wiley & Sons Ltd.

naturalistic learners). In the past two decades, technologies have progressed that permit us to have a renewed look at the critical period debate. That the healthy brain remains plastic throughout the lifespan is no longer controversial within neurocognitive psychology (see Fuchs and Flügge 2014, for review). And so, the neuromaturational basis of the critical period hypothesis advocated originally in Lenneberg (1967) and assumed by many ever since is necessarily challenged. In this chapter, we focus on how neurolinguistic evidence – electroencephalography/event-related potential (EEG/ERP) and (functional) magnetic resonance imaging ((f)MRI) data – can help us adjudicate between various views regarding the critical period debate and how to best account for the ubiquitously noted differences that align with age of acquisition effects in language acquisition/processing.

2. Reframing Questions and the Evidence Base for the Critical Period Hypothesis

There is no question that a typical adult is able to learn a second language (L2), at least to various degrees of grammatical and communicative competences. It is also equally clear that age of onset (AoO) for adult non-native acquisition negatively correlates with success, whenever success is measured against typical native, monolingual outcomes. Despite the fact that we all probably know someone who is so successful at adult L2 acquisition that we can hardly believe they are not a native speaker of language X, one cannot ignore the fact that coming across such individuals is a remarkable occurrence. Indeed, most adult L2 learners, even those who have very high communicative and grammatical competences, show various degrees of differences to the average native monolingual speaker, especially in phonology but also in other domains of grammar such as morphosyntax and lexis. In actuality, however, the semblance of rarity might be (inadvertently) misleading. After all, to determine how remarkable finding such a diamond in the rough truly is one would need to assume that equipotentiality for success is held constant across all L2 learners. If true, then finding 1–5% – an estimate accepted in the literature, see Long 2005, 2013 – of learners who achieve indistinguishable performance abilities compared to natives would make that select group especially talented indeed; a true rarity. If, however, it were the case that only a small subset of all L2 learners turn out to have been under conditions that could have resulted in competencies indistinguishable from native speakers and that the vast majority of the so-called exceptional L2 learners fit squarely into this subset group, then the exceptionality of the few becomes ever less impressive or special. It is simply a reflection of opportunity. While there is no question that some individuals seem to show a talent for language learning in adulthood, that outcome variability characterizes adult L2 acquisition/processing, that motivation matters and/or that measurable linguistic/language aptitude plays a predictive role in at least classroom L2 acquisition success (e.g. Carroll 1973, 1990; Carroll and Sapon 1959; Dörnyei 2001, 2005; Dörnyei and Skehan 2003; Harley and Hart 1997; Robinson 1997, 2005); showing this, however distinct from typical child L1 acquisition overall, does not necessarily mean that child L1 versus adult L2 language acquisition is fundamentally different. To start, individual differences, albeit to a different degree, also pertain to native monolingual outcomes, especially when one considers various proxies related to accessing qualities and quantities of input, such as education/literacy and other indices of socioeconomic status (SES; e.g. Dąbrowska 1997, 2012). Pertaining to the underlying mental mechanisms implicated, no one would claim that acquiring language is fundamentally different for socioeconomically privileged as compared to disadvantaged native, monolinguals a priori. Rather, we would hypothesize that extraneous variables that coincide with SES conspire to explain the surface variance and we would seek to tease them apart. As is the case of L1 acquisition outcomes when competence/performance/processing is compared against a far-reaching standardized norm, differences in typical L2 acquisition versus typical L1 acquisition might just as likely reflect opportunity for an individual to have had any chance to converge on the comparative norm competence than be indicative of any fundamental difference itself. By happenstance, then, there is perhaps more conformity in child monolingual outcomes overall because there is less opportunity for variation given the naturalistic context of a native environment and the impossibility that another grammar, which by definition they do not have, imposes influence. A possible exception would be the case of balanced, early bi/multilingualism outcomes when two languages are acquired at the same time from the time of birth (or very early) and typically when the community itself is a bi/multilingual one (a proxy for many things related to opportunities for acquisition, use, and maintenance over time). Even in such environments, and despite the fact that children maintain a difference between the two (or more) grammars from very early on, the two languages exercise some influence on each other.

Is it really the case that native-like linguistic convergence after puberty is impossible due to some neurological maturation cutting off the mechanisms by which language is acquired/processed in childhood? Or, is it more likely that child L1 versus adult L2 outcome differences reflect a series of co-conspiring variables that have little or nothing to do with changes to the brain that would preclude native-like acquisition and processing past a specific age of exposure? If we accept that most adults learning an L2 simply do not experience anything close to the conditions under which typical child L1 acquisition occurs, then expecting in the first place that most could have had any chance to emerge with so-called native-like competence seems inherently unreasonable. As pointed out by Rothman and Guijarro-Fuentes (2010) and Ortega (2013), the focus of adult L2 acquisition/processing outcome research needs to shift from a default position of assumed impossibility and exceptionality to one that accepts adult additive bilingualism as normal and weighs fairly the potential role that differences in context bring to bear. Only then can we seek to better understand what underlies the gamut of L2 outcome variability, both manifested in differences from monolinguals but also differences across bilingual groups and individuals. If we were to do so, we would note a shift in how the fundamental questions are framed. In equal measure, we would be preoccupied with, amongst others, the following two questions: (i) What underlies 'opportunity for success' in the context of adult L2 acquisition?, and (ii) Is the gold standard benchmark of the educated native speaker norm a fair comparison at all in the first place?

The above questions relate non-trivially to the long-standing debates surrounding the CPH application to adult L2 acquisition (see Bialystok and Hakuta 1994; Birdsong and Molis 2001; Long 2005, 2013; Rothman 2008, for summaries and contrasting views) as well as the 'comparative fallacy' observation in bilingualism studies more generally (e.g. Bley-Vroman 1983; Hopp and Schmid 2013; Ortega 2013; Rothman and Guijarro-Fuentes 2010). Do differences that typify child L1 versus adult L2 development and ultimate attainment stem from a biologically based maturational critical period[1] for language learning after which adults are unable to acquire and process an L2 in qualitatively the same way as L1 native speakers? Is there a biologically induced age effect – in whole or in part – for accessing/using domain-general cognitive and/or domain-specific linguistic mechanisms that guide language acquisition and processing in children? After all, we should have no disagreements that any answer to these immediately presented questions is credible only to the extent that evidence used to support an affirmative or negative answer is predicated on sound and fair comparisons. To this end, we might ask: Was the critical period hypothesis ever intended to be debated from the view of typical L2 acquisition in adulthood? This is a fair question to ask on at least two fronts: (i) in consideration of all the disparities inherent to L1–L2 comparison that could muddy the comparative waters in the first place and (ii) the original proposals for a linguistic critical period itself are based exclusively on monolingual data and make only the most tangential reference to adult L2 learning by the original authors. We must bear in mind that when Lenneberg (1967) originally coined the CPH he was not directly talking about a critical period for learning an additional language for individuals who had already experienced normal L1 acquisition in early childhood. It is also worth recalling that the evidence that led him to offer the CPH was based exclusively on language recovery differences between children and adults who suffered from aphasia – or language loss after neurological injury. Observing that children were substantially more successful prior to puberty in language recovery as compared to post-pubescent adults with similar injuries paved the road to hypothesizing that there is something fundamentally different about the brain's ability to deal with language depending on age. From there, case studies of linguistic isolates in childhood such as Genie (Curtiss 1977) and Chelsea (Curtiss 1988) and deaf studies where exposure to a first language can be significantly delayed (Mayberry 1993, 1994) give strong support to Lenneberg's claims. However, all such studies deal with the acquisition/recovery of a primary, first language. And so, it seems pretty clear that if no language is acquired prior to puberty or if a monolingual loses language after puberty, there are serious consequences related to the brain's ability to recover a complete computational system that shares the universal characteristic of natural human grammars.

Does it follow from the above that an adult who has successfully established and utilized their language networks of the brain and has fully acquired a previous language (minimally an L1) would also be confronted with the same underlying obstacles for L2 acquisition as an individual somehow deprived of L1 acquisition does when exposed to an L1 as an adult? A quick comparison of what the language of late L1 acquirers looks like as compared to even relatively nascent L2 learners with accordingly low proficiency shows that they are qualitatively very different. Genie, the linguistic isolate discovered just after puberty, for example, was indeed able to acquire a considerably large lexicon and string several words together. However, her language never progressed past a telegraphic stage, essentially lacking any functional properties of what we would call natural human syntax. A quick glance in Curtiss (1977) at Genie's production shows how difficult it would be even for a native speaker of English to understand what she produces at all. This is true after countless hours of specific and purposeful interventions by world-renowned linguists and psychologists. An average adult L2 speaker, on the other hand, even after a few semesters of classes, is able to hold meaningful conversations – however limited in topic – and although their production usually contains various degrees of L2 grammatical errors and reflects transfer from their L1 and more, the structure of their language is clearly complex and accords with the universal constraints of natural human grammars (see discussion in White 2003, 2008, Rothman and Slabakova 2017). Over time, unlike the case of Genie, proficiency, and fluency improves dramatically. Our point is not to suggest that L2 acquisition is an easy, non-trivial task nor that all researchers studying L2 acquisition agree on what can be concluded from the evidence in the literature, but rather that there are sharp differences in the production and comprehension of linguistic isolates like Genie even after years of exposure with specific interventions and the average, moderately successful L2 learner.

When considering the many interrelated questions above, it is important to keep in mind what extraneous factors could lead to the observable differences between typical L1 and adult L2 acquisition if indeed the underlying mechanisms for both are one and the same. Virtually all monolingual children (i) grow up in an environment that surrounds them with significant quantities of high-quality input from native speakers, (ii) do not have to deal with cross-linguistic influence/transfer from previously acquired languages affecting the path of development, like learners with previous linguistic experience do, and (iii) have an inherent need to acquire at least one language through which they will be able to encode the world around them and use it to communicate their thoughts, needs, and desires. Conversely, many adults acquiring an L2 (i) have limited access to native target input, (ii) receive and must filter through significant amounts of non-native input (e.g. from classmates, other immigrants), (iii) have to deal with influences from their previous linguistic knowledge (i.e. cross-linguistic influence/transfer) that can hinder as much as it helps, and (iv) do not need the L2 to encode the world in which they express themselves with conceptual structures already mapped onto their L1.

Of course it is possible that there is a simple explanation to child L1 versus adult L2 differences; the latter group simply no longer has the same abilities for language acquisition and processing (e.g. Abrahamsson and Hyltenstam 2008, 2009; Bley-Vroman 1989, 2009; Bylund et al. 2012, 2013; Clahsen and Felser 2006; Clahsen and Muysken 1989; DeKeyser 2000; Granena and Long 2013; Hawkins and Chan 1997; Johnson and Newport 1989; Long 2005; Meisel 2011; Tsimpli and Dimitrakopoulou 2007). Relative successes in adult L2 performances are not ignored under such a position; but they are understood as by-products of adults' generally high ability to learn patterns, the mapping of the L2 lexicon onto the structure of their L1 and/or their metalinguistic knowledge about the L2. However, such a position does not seem to herald the relative weight the variables we have discussed throughout might contribute. Many have suggested that indeed such variables and others conspire, in various constellations, to explain the gamut of observable differences that others liken to a critical period effect. Such a perspective circumvents the need to claim that child versus adult acquisition processes are fundamentally different, while still acknowledging the problem of explanation. In Bialystok and

Hakuta's words, morphosyntax 'remains accessible throughout life, even though the circumstances of our lives may muddy that access (1994, pp. 86)'.

The above claim is supported by at least four distinct types of evidence, the first corresponding to the ageing brain in general and the others specifically to language acquisition/processing evidence from adults. Recall that the whole notion of a critical period was originally predicated on the proposal that the modular mind was deeply affected by neurological maturation. It was hypothesized that when the brain becomes fully lateralized, corresponding roughly to puberty as claimed by Lenneberg (1967), brain plasticity – non-pathological, morphological changes to the structure of the adult brain affecting its ability to reorganize or redistribute function as needed – would decline and with it our ability to acquire language, at least an L1. We now know, however, that the brain remains much more malleable throughout the lifespan than previously claimed, meaning there is no sharp decline in neurological plasticity[2] culminating around puberty in general (see Fuchs and Flügge 2014) and certainly not as related to language (see Chapter 11). This alone already questions the tenability of the original argument, at least the neurological claims upon which it was based. On balance, however, whether or not the brain remains plastic in general does not necessarily mean that there is no critical period for language itself or a neurologically based explanation for the increased difficulty in language learning as a function of age, for example, gradual fibre tract maturation may impact how language acquisition happens in childhood and in adulthood. Better evidence against (a strong version of) a critical period affecting sequential adult L2 acquisition comes from three types of linguistic research: (i) that showing very successful older learner exceptions to the general L2 acquisition outcome, (ii) that showing acquisition of discrete properties of grammar such as very complex syntax that could not have been transferred from the L1, is not explicitly taught in a classroom setting, and which is not easily deduced from the learner input alone, and (iii) significant neurolinguistic/processing data that fail to show qualitative differences in the acquisition outcomes and/or real-time processing by adults for particular domains for which measurable critical period effects are predicted. The remainder of this chapter will introduce the reader in much greater detail to type (iii) evidence, which to date has factored much less than type (i) and (ii) evidence into argumentation debated in the linguistic literature (see Rothman and Slabakova 2017, for review of [i] and [ii]) on L2 acquisition despite compelling reasons to the contrary.

Questioning the notion of a critical period for language acquisition is indeed supported by a large body of psycholinguistic and neurolinguistic research that has focused on whether or not L2 learners make use of the same linguistic processing mechanisms, routines, and strategies in the L2 as native speakers of a given language and in what domains of language (dis)similarities arise (e.g. Alemán Bañón et al. 2014, 2017; Friederici et al. 2002; Hahne 2001; Hahne and Friederici 2001; McDonald 2006; Morgan-Short et al. 2012; Osterhout et al. 2006; Pliatsikas et al. 2017; Rossi et al. 2006; Tokowicz and MacWhinney 2005; Weber-Fox and Neville 1996). Although this research follows the tradition of native vs. non-native comparisons, which we have questioned above as potentially fostering unfair comparative expectations as related to offline behavioural performance, the fact that L2 learners overall display qualitative similarities in how they process L2 grammar is thus even more impressive. Within this research, as we will see in greater detail in Section 3, the use of event-related potentials (ERPs) has proven a fruitful methodology to differentiate between purely behavioural measures and those more closely associated with implicit and automatic neural processes, a level at which we might expect extraneous variables as those discussed above would have less of an effect on performance. A general assumption in the above line of work has been that if late L2 learners (after any potential critical period) show similar processing procedures/strategies in the L2 as compared to native speakers, then there must not be crucial fundamental differences in the neural substrates of L2 processing, thus challenging the predictive validity of the CPH. Although much smaller in quantity of studies, and with a shorter temporal tradition, neuroimaging studies using (f)MRI of adult L2 learners, as we will review in much greater detail, show no evidence to suggest that there is loss of language-related neural plasticity and/or that language areas of the brain recruited for particular linguistic functions are any different between monolinguals and adult L2 learners. Taken together, we will argue that the evidence from neurolinguistic methods provides a particularly strong basis to argue against the CPH's application to adult L2 acquisition and rather show just how similar language learning is between children and adults, even when the cards are seemingly stacked against the adult learner by comparison.

3.   A Brief Description of ERPs and their Use in Language Processing Research

ERPs provide a non-invasive method to investigate electrophysiological correlates of mental processes. ERPs emerge as a result of small voltages (measured in microvolts) that are generated in the brain when large groups of neurons fire in synchrony due to the onset of specific cognitive, sensory, or motor events.

ERP data over the last several decades have offered great insight into language processing. One of the more noteworthy discoveries from these data is that of qualitatively different brain signatures resulting from different types of linguistic stimuli. The fact that the brain responds uniquely to different aspects of language processing, giving rise to reliably distinct ERP signatures, enables researchers to tease apart various types of linguistic processing (e.g. grammatical repair versus failed expectation). For example, the brain responds differently to a morphosyntactic violation as instantiated in a grammatical gender or number violation in Spanish, Portuguese, Dutch, and Arabic than it does to a semantic incongruency or a failed expectation of upcoming information. A qualitatively similar distinction would be made for overt case marking violations in German, Icelandic, Korean, and Turkish, also compared to failed expectations of upcoming information or semantic incongruences. While they are not useful for pinpointing brain locations implicated in specific types of processing – MRI and magneto-encephalography (MEG), for example, would be much better for such questions – ERPs allow for a better examination of a participant's sensitivity to a given stimulus at its precise onset and computation by relying on high temporal resolution in the measure of milliseconds. Therefore, if L2 and native control groups show qualitatively different brain responses to the same stimuli, this can be taken as a reflection of differences at a so-called level of linguistic representation that ultimately leads to the use of distinct

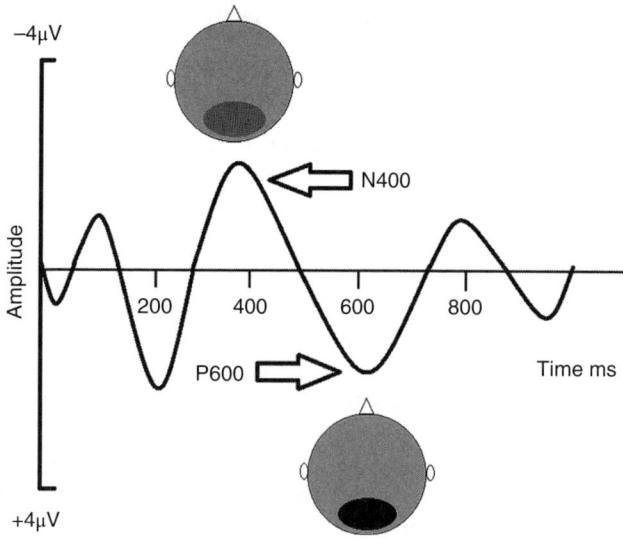

Figure 1   Diagram of the N400 and P600 components.

processing mechanisms (e.g. see Alemán Bañón et al. 2014; 2017; Clahsen and Felser 2006; Phillips and Ehrenhofer 2015). It is worth noting, however, that while specific ERP components associated with language processing of one kind or another arguably may not reflect linguistic representation per se (Sassenhagen et al. 2014; Tanner et al. 2017), they do emerge reliably in monolingual and advanced bilingual datasets examining any given linguistic property.

The two most common ERP components associated with, though not specific to, linguistic processing are the N400 and the P600 (see Figure 1), which will be the primary components discussed in the cited research herein. The N400 is said to reflect lexico-semantic processes, strength of lexical associations, and implausibility (failed expectation), emerging as a negative going wave roughly between 250 and 500 ms post-stimulus (e.g. Kutas and Hillyard 1980; see also Lau et al. 2008 for review). In contrast, morphosyntactic violations amongst native speakers and indeed some L2ers elicit a P600, which is a positive-going waveform that emerges roughly between 500 and 900 ms post-stimulus in central-parietal electrodes of the EEG cap (e.g. Hagoort et al. 1993). This effect has been argued to arise due to various aspects of morphosyntactic processing such as reanalysis (e.g. Osterhout and Holcomb 1992), repair (see Molinaro et al. 2011, for review) and integration (e.g. Kaan et al. 2000).

3.1.   *Do L2 Learners Process Language in a Native-like Way? What ERP Research Implies about the Critical Period*

As noted in Section 2, L2 learners often find themselves at various stages of non-native-likeness concerning language abilities in the L2. This L2 variability has been attributed to individual differences, from variation in sources of input (i.e. classroom instruction as compared to naturalistic acquisition) to differences in intelligence and specific linguistic aptitude. Additionally, general issues such as the so-called critical period for language learning, claimed to be maturationally conditioned by age, have been argued to constrain L2 ultimate attainment. Importantly, adult L2 learners have also been shown to vary with respect to their native-likeness depending on the type of linguistic property under investigation. That is, while they often converge on native-like patterns of N400 emergence in studies examining semantic anomalies (e.g. Hahne and Friederici 2001; Isel 2007; Ojima et al. 2005; Weber-Fox and Neville 1996), they also often differ from native-like morphosyntactic processing in studies examining P600 effects, especially in cases where the learners' L1 and L2 are typologically or structurally dissimilar (e.g. Foucart and Frenck-Mestre 2011; Sabourin and Haverkort 2003; Sabourin and Stowe 2008). For example, Ojima and colleagues tested Japanese learners of English at two levels of proficiency with respect to their ERP responses to both syntactic and semantic violations. Their conclusion was that the cortical processing of an L2 is similar to that of an L1, particularly as proficiency increases in the L2, stating 'we obtained little evidence for an absolute critical period effect and discontinuity between L1 and L2 learning' (Ojima et al. 2005, p. 1223). Moreover, Gabriele et al. (2013) investigated English-speaking learners of Spanish at three distinct levels of proficiency in the domain of gender and number agreement. The authors showed that at low levels of proficiency, learners revealed slightly emerging P600 effects for gender and number violations. Intermediate learners, on the other hand, showed an overall advantage for number over gender given that the L1 has number but not gender, but as a whole these learners' ERPs did not differ qualitatively from those of the native speakers. The advanced learners showed no preference for number or gender and their ERPs paralleled those of the native speakers. While more robust P600 effects emerged as a consequence of increased L2 proficiency, the underlying processing mechanism of gender and number in the learner groups was found to be qualitatively similar to that of the native groups. In this vein, an increasing number of recent studies reveal a continuity between native and non-native systems of processing. This is true in cases where the L1 and L2 are similar with respect to the feature being tested (e.g. Tokowicz and MacWhinney 2005), where a feature, such as gender, is instantiated differently in two languages (e.g. Frenck-Mestre et al. 2008; Gillon Dowens et al. 2011; Rossi et al. 2006) for syntactic ambiguity and syntactic anomalies (Kotz et al. 2008), and even in artificial language learning paradigms (Morgan-Short et al. 2010). It is important to note that while some of the aforementioned research has led to idiosyncratic conclusions, particularly with respect to specific variables that contribute to native-like processing in L2 learners – such as the impact of phonological realization, age of acquisition, proficiency and L1 transfer, linguistic structure, and type of training on processing – overall it does show that under specifically controlled conditions L2 learners can process morphosyntactic information in a qualitatively similar way to native speakers (see Kotz 2009 for review of ERP research on L2 processing of morphosyntax).

Needless to say, the results across studies and domains of language being tested have been somewhat mixed with respect to the reported status of syntactic processes amongst L2 learners. However, as highlighted by Tanner et al. (2013), the studies that have failed to find traditional P600 effects amongst learners in cases of morphosyntactic processing used grand average analyses of ERP data. The grand averaging procedure is a method by which one groups all learners together and takes average amplitude measurements of all trials across all conditions, in spite of the well-documented individual linguistic variability amongst L2 learners, causing the subtle differences between individuals to be lost. Osterhout et al. (2006) and McLaughlin et al. (2010) also highlight that for the reasons mentioned above, interpreting null results in L2 studies using ERPs can be problematic, precisely because of the averaging procedure. For example, as McLaughlin et al. (2010) and Tanner et al. (2013) note, electrophysiological effects present in cases of either (i) only a few trials but for most subjects or (ii) a few subjects but most trials, can be obscured by the averaging procedure, particularly due to extraneous noise in the raw EEG. Additionally, any variability in the timing of the effect across trials and individual subjects can further diminish the size of the effect when doing ERP grand averages (see also Luck 2005). Therefore, Tanner et al. (2013) propose that when examining L2 learners – particularly given the inherent individual linguistic variability amongst learners more generally – one must take care to consider the individual differences amongst subjects by using appropriate statistical regressions to observe within-groups differences that are camouflaged by grand averaging. However, findings discovered on the backbone of a grand averaging analysis are not invalid. Rather, researchers suggest that longitudinal designs adopted by Osterhout et al. (2006) or appropriate statistical measures to tease apart individual differences can be ecologically valid alternatives.

Of particular relevance to the question of whether or not there is a critical period for language acquisition are the findings in ERP research showing qualitative (and quantitative) shifts in ERP signatures associated with increased proficiency in the L2. This means that such ERP data can be used a proxy to show 'learning' over time, or minimally a change in state over the course of L2 learning in which processing is shifting qualitatively. Studies showing increased native-like processing over time thus reveal that processing is related to acquisition of grammar itself, and because the change in state is ever more native-like, then processing is more plastic than the CPH leads one to believe. For example, Tanner et al. (2013) report a systematic ERP difference across individual learners. Subject-verb agreement violations produced N400 effects amongst some of their learners while producing P600 effects in others. Because of the inherent differences amongst L2 learners' working memory, as well as size of vocabulary, for example, interpretation of their results was challenging. One of the possibilities put forward by the authors for such response differences was that they were merely a reflection of more durable (cognitive) traits, in which case these differences would be expected to persist over time irrespective of gradient L2 proficiency. However, the more compelling argument made was that of a progressive shift in processing stages, putting some learners at one stage and others at another, an argument which would ultimately require longitudinal ERP data for its support at the individual level. Indeed, such longitudinal data exist. Reporting the ERP results of first-year French learners, Osterhout et al. (2012) tested French subject-verb agreement violations amongst first-year learners and showed that after only one month of instruction, morphosyntactic violations, which are relevant to the P600, produced N400 effects in most learners. After a slightly longer period of seven months of instruction most learners then showed a P600 effect. Very interestingly, at the middle stage of testing, which was at four months of instruction, the grand average ERPs showed a biphasic (i.e. positive and negative) N400-P600 effect. In other words, as the learners increased their proficiency and grammatical competency, the initial N400 gradually shifted to a P600 across the instructional period. It is worth noting, however, that Osterhout and colleagues revealed that an individual analysis of subjects provided evidence that some learners showed an N400 and others a P600 to the same set of agreement violations.

In sum, while results may very well be varied across tasks, the evidence is clear that in specifically controlled conditions L2 learners can process linguistic information similarly to native speakers. Furthermore, collective evidence from studies examining individual differences points in the direction of progressive stages through which learners pass during language acquisition. Taken together, these data suggest that while L2 learners clearly exhibit variability in their individual language capacities, they are also capable of converging on native-like processing strategies as measured via ERPs. Recall that the foundation of the original claims of a critical period for language acquisition relies on the notion of neurological maturation after puberty, affecting the very ability to acquire and process language in a native-like manner. However, a careful examination of contemporary neurolinguistic research in L2 acquisition suggests that, irrespective of any potential maturational effects that may take place in the stages moving from childhood into adulthood, L2 learners – under the right circumstances and when tested with appropriate methodologies – can show tendencies of native-like language processing. This evidence contradicts the notion that the brain is incapable of learning a second language well into adulthood and calls for a more careful examination of theories claiming that maturational effects constrain specific domains of language processing.

4. Brain Plasticity in Adulthood: Evidence from (f)MRI

As discussed, the CPH is predicated on a proposed general decline of neuroplasticity; however, recent work has shown neuroplasticity to extend to L2 acquisition/learning in adulthood (see for review Bialystok 2016a, b; García-Pentón et al. 2016) and moreover occur via the same neural substrates as for those who learn the L2 in childhood, suggesting that biological maturation does not affect the brain's capacity to deal with/adapt to the task of novel language learning in adulthood. What evidence of this type means for the CPH will be the focus of this section.

4.1. *Magnetic Resonance Imaging (MRI)*

MRI is a non-invasive neuroimaging technique which uses strong magnetic fields and radiofrequency pulses to produce detailed images of structures and processes inside the body. While a wide range of imaging techniques may be employed, here we discuss two such protocols relevant to brain plasticity and processing: static/structural scans detailing aspects of specific structures and pathways within the brain, and functional MRI (fMRI) scans which can document neural processes both at rest and in relation to stimuli.

In neuroimaging research, MRI can be used to assess differences in brain structure and function between sample populations or between individuals within a given population, with respect to specific external experiences or experimental stimuli. Structural differences can be examined via grey matter (GM), including GM volume (e.g. Ashburner and Friston 2000), cortical thickness (CT; e.g. Ad-Dab'bagh et al. 2005), and changes in surface area (Patenaude et al. 2011). Structural connectivity in white matter (WM) can also be measured in terms of fractional anisotropy (FA) and mean diffusivity (MD) values, amongst others (e.g. Smith et al. 2006) which provide indices of the degree of water diffusivity in the white matter tracts of the brain (for details see following section). Functional differences are measured in terms of connectivity between various regions (e.g. Beckmann and Smith 2004) at rest or during tasks, or functional activation of specific regions during a task/stimulus presentation (e.g. Smith et al. 2004).

5. Brain Structure and Regions of Interest

To more effectively discuss the nature of changes within the brain, we first lay out the basic architecture of the brain and local regions of interest with respect to language processing and control.

The brain is comprised of neurons, which serve as both centres of computation and communication between regions (Figure 2). The neuron is formed of two main sections: the body (soma) in which electrical signals are both collected and produced, and the axon, in which information is conveyed between regions. The axon is covered in a pale-coloured lipid layer called myelin, which is used for both insulation and to increase efficiency of information transfer. Due to their pale colour, these axon bodies form what is termed the 'white matter' within the brain. Bundles of axons form white matter tracts which transfer information between both neighbouring and remote regions of the brain. The neuron bodies form the 'grey matter' of the brain in which computations take place (Figure 3). Increased exposure to specific experiences is known to incur neuroplastic changes – namely both increased

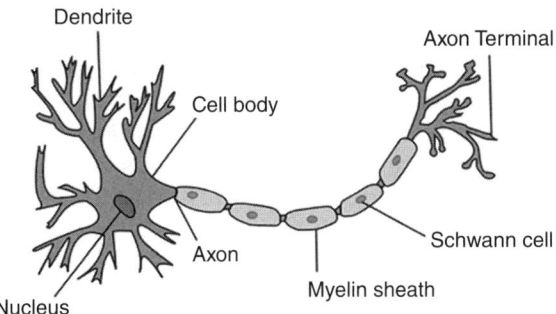

Figure 2   The neuron and its components. Source: https://commons.wikimedia.org/wiki/File:Neuron.svg.

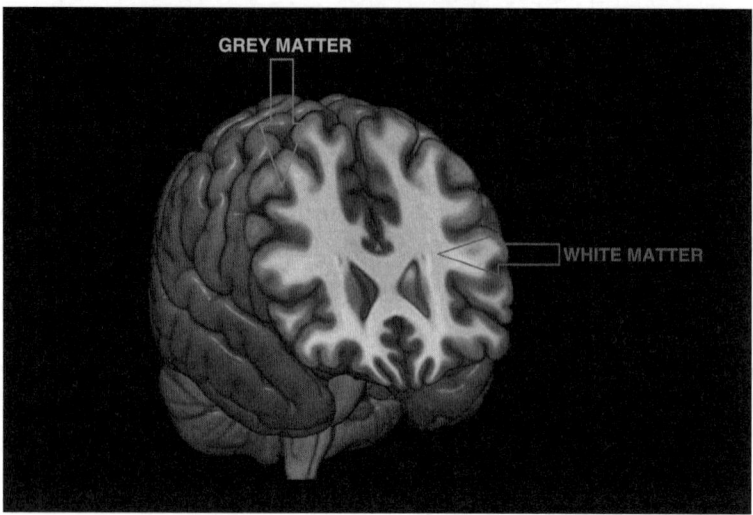

Figure 3   Examples of grey and white matter within the brain.

GM in specific regions (increasing computational capacity commensurate to increased processing load), and in related tracts (reflecting increased efficiency of communication between relevant regions).

Various areas of the brain have been associated with different computational processes, with information transfer between them being associated with different tracts or pathways. Several regions and pathways/tracts of the brain have been implicated in both processes related to language processing and control. Furthermore, these regions are known to operate in conjunction with one another, forming networks of language processing and control (for further discussion see Friederici and Gierhan 2013; Green and Abutalebi 2013). Several key regions and pathways are discussed below to facilitate the unpacking of the (f)MRI research done in the following section.

Several grey matter regions are implicated in language processing and control functions. Frontal and cortical regions, including the dorsolateral prefrontal cortex (DLPFC) and anterior cingulate cortex (ACC), and supramarginal gyrus (SMG) have been implicated in several higher-order cognitive functions, including language control in processing and production (Abutalebi and Green 2016; Luk et al. 2011). Other regions including the left inferior frontal gyrus (IFG), inferior parietal lobule (IPL;including the supramarginal gyrus [SMG]), superior temporal gyrus (STG), middle frontal gyrus (MFG), and middle temporal gyrus (MTG; Figure 4) have been implicated in syntactic and lexico-semantic processing (Frenck-Mestre et al. 2005; Hickok and Poeppel 2007; Hofstetter et al. 2016; Petersson et al. 2012; Stein et al. 2012; Veroude et al. 2010). Several subcortical structures including the caudate nucleus and putamen have been implicated in phonological processing and control (Abutalebi and Green 2016). The right hippocampus (RHC) and anterior temporal lobe (ATL) are involved in vocabulary acquisition processes (Pliatsikas et al. 2014b). Finally, the cerebellum, which has extensive

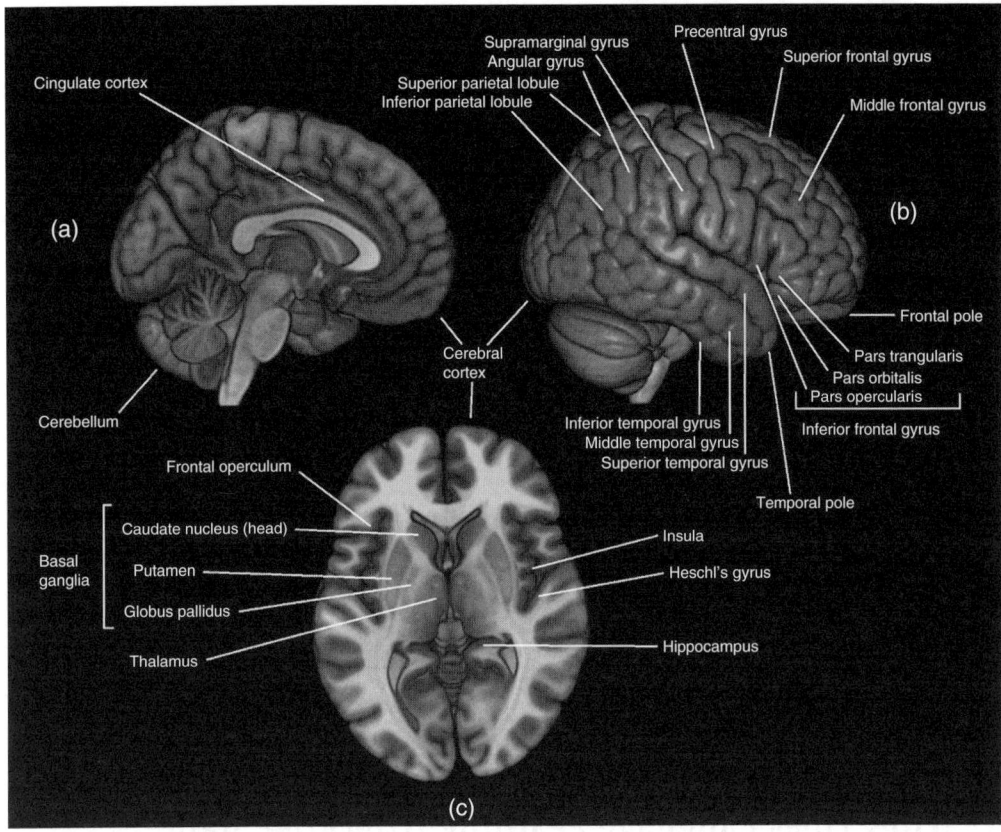

Figure 4 Select GM regions within the brain.

connections across the brain, is thought to be involved in several processes related to language, including facilitating language production and automating language processing and production (Booth et al. 2007).

With respect to white matter pathways, several have been implicated in language-related processes connecting corresponding regions to form language control and processing/production networks (Friederici 2009). The corpus callosum (CC) connects both hemispheres and has been implicated in language control processes, specifically interhemispheric communication in executive functioning and lateralization of brain functions (Luk et al. 2011; Schlegel et al. 2012). The inferior fronto-occipital fasciculus (IFOF; Figure 5) connects frontal and occipital regions for both hemispheres, and has been implicated in semantic processing (Leclercq et al. 2010). Finally, the superior longitudinal fasciculus (SLF; Figure 5) is a ventral pathway, connecting the left IFG to temporal areas such as the STG and MTG, and is implicated in several language functions including semantic, syntactic, and phonological processing (Friederici 2009; Pliatsikas et al. 2015).

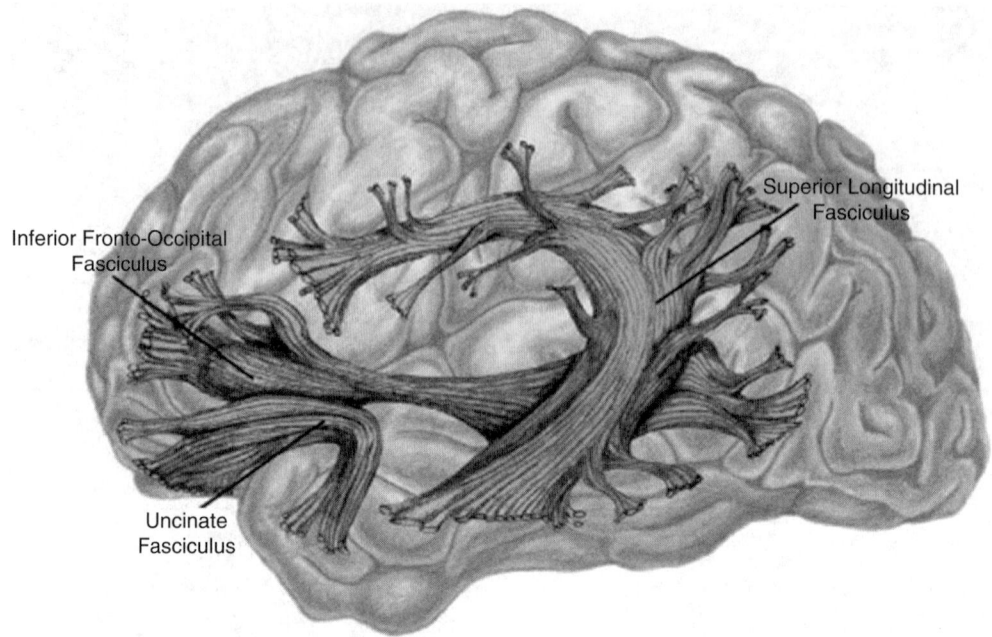

Figure 5   Diagram depicting connectivity of select white matter tracts. Source: Credit William Hirstein. Diagram by Katie Reinecke. (CC BY 3.0 (http://creativecommons.org/licenses/by/3.0), via Wikimedia Commons.

6.   How Does Language Learning Affect the Brain? Structural and Functional Evidence for Bilingualism-Induced Neuroplasticity

A number of studies, both longitudinal and cross-sectional, have found brain adaptations to language learning in at a variety of stages of acquisition, from hours (Hofstetter et al. 2016), to weeks (Mamiya et al. 2016), to months (e.g. Hosoda et al. 2013; Mårtensson et al. 2012; Stein et al. 2012). Some variability exists between studies with respect to the specific area of the brain affected (García-Pentón et al. 2016). However, when the evidence is considered as a whole, results are fairly consistent with respect to adaptations both in terms of region affected and what effects occur. That is, GM and WM in brain regions and pathways implicated in language control are found to adapt commensurately with increases in use of the additional language.

Most of the evidence for neuroplasticity in adult L2 acquisition stems from longitudinal and training studies. While some variation exists between study designs, the general format follows: a scan prior to a language training program and then scans during and/or after the program along with behavioural tests. This allows for the study to examine plastic changes in the brain commensurate to the period of learning. Several such studies report grey matter adaptations in language-related regions. For example,

Mårtensson et al. (2012) examined neural effects of L2 acquisition in young adults in the Swedish military training to be interpreters, which involves a 10-month training process. GM volume increases were found in the STG, MFG, and RHC for the interpreters over a control group (psychology and cognitive science students at a local university). Within the trainee interpreters, there was a significant correlation found between GM volume and proficiency (as established by their performance in the course) for all areas found to significantly change (MFG, STG, and RHC). Plastic adaptations have also been found, both in isolation and in relation to language proficiency, in regions including the left SMG (Osterhout et al. 2008), left IFG and ATL (Stein et al. 2012). Longitudinal studies have also found several WM pathways to increase in integrity following L2 acquisition in adulthood. Mamiya and colleagues (2016) examined the effects of L2 immersion on WM integrity by testing newly arrived Chinese students to the United States completing an intensive English language course. Regarding effects of immersion, increases in FA values in the right SLF were positively correlated with both time spent in the language course and proficiency measures. Other studies find WM adaptations in relation to language learning in the CC and bilateral SLF (Schlegel et al. 2012), IFG-to-caudate pathway and right SLF (Hosoda et al. 2013), and WM beneath the IFG, MFG, and IPL (Hofstetter et al. 2016).

Taken together, the available evidence pertaining to both grey and white matter growth in the context of longitudinal and training studies in adult language learning overwhelmingly points in the direction of continued, general brain plasticity, already challenging the predicating tenet of the CPH – that lateralization correlates with decline of plasticity – first offered by Lenneberg (1967). It is important to keep in mind how this conclusion was made in 1967; that is in the absence of modern technologies whose application to this domain in recent years seems to point in the opposite direction. As discussed, Lenneberg based his arguments on observations of language recovery pattern differences in aphasic children versus adults. MRI affords us the opportunity to literally see first hand if the 1967 predictions hold. Evidence from the above studies clearly suggest they do not. Moreover, the relative growth in grey and white matter supports not only continued generalized plasticity, but indeed that there is something specific to language learning itself. This is true because the areas of the brain that are affected in L2 acquisition are precisely those known to be implicated in grammatical representations and processing itself within monolingual acquisition and evoked in real-time language processing of specific functions in adult monolinguals.

A handful of cross-sectional studies have also found evidence for brain plasticity in adulthood in response to language acquisition or immersion (Kuhl et al. 2016; Pliatsikas et al. 2015; Rossi et al. 2017). Pliatsikas et al. (2015) examined specifically the effects of L2 immersion in late-acquired L2 learners of English in comparison to monolingual controls. They report increased integrity in several WM tracts including bilaterally the CC, IFOF, and SLF. Similarly, the study by Rossi et al. (2017) found increases in the IFOF, inferior longitudinal fasciculus (ILF), anterior thalamic radiation (ATR), and ucinate fasciculus (UF) in late-acquired L2 Spanish native English speakers over monolingual controls. Crucially, both studies found patterns of WM increase in late-acquired L2 bilinguals in a similar manner to child L2 bilinguals, whether tested as adults (Luk et al. 2011; Olsen et al. 2015) or in childhood (Mohades et al. 2015), suggesting that highly similar plastic processes are available in L2 learning in adulthood. Of significance in the context of relating these findings to what they might imply for the CPH is the fact the neural adaptations discussed here are similar to those adaptations seen in L2 acquisition in children, an age at which exceedingly few would deny that the brain is still plastic and that cognitive and linguistic mechanisms which underlie first language acquisition are available.

Functional adaptations have also been found with respect to L2 acquisition and use for adult learners, although fMRI studies on non-native processing remain limited. These adaptations have been found in both natural language acquisition, and in artificial grammar learning (AGL) experimental training paradigms, the latter of which is especially interesting for the CPH precisely because it isolates the acquisition of syntax in the absence of other linguistic properties. Regarding natural language acquisition, a study by Veroude et al. (2010) found increased functional connectivity in several regions including the bilateral IFG, STG, and MTG in native Dutch speakers following initial exposure to Chinese. With respect to later stages of acquisition, Frenck-Mestre et al. (2005) examined neural activation patterns during articulation in the L1 and L2 for early- and late-acquired English-French bilinguals and found no significant differences in terms of location or strength of activation between groups in either language. Of particular interest for this chapter is evidence related to whether adult L2 learners of a language process symbolic aspects of the newly acquired language in a native-like fashion, and whether this is expressed in markers of brain activity that are indistinguishable between native and non-native speakers (Roberts et al. 2018). Unsurprisingly, the limited available literature has focused on aspects of language acquisition that have been considered unattainable by adult learners, particularly abstract grammatical processing in L2, which according to models such as the shallow structure hypothesis (SSH; Clahsen and Felser 2006), is subject to critical periods. However, the available evidence does not consistently support the SSH (for review, see Abutalebi 2008; Roncaglia-Denissen and Kotz 2016). For example, in the domain of morphology, Pliatsikas et al. (2014a) found no difference in the brain regions activated in native and non-native speakers of English for the processing of past tense inflection. However, the same authors showed that non-native processing of inflection correlated with volumetric changes in the cerebellum, suggesting dynamic restructuring of the brain for the acquisition of a grammatical rule (see Section 5; Pliatsikas et al. 2014b). Similar patterns for inflectional processing were reported by Prehn et al. (2017), but without the volumetric effects, whereas De Grauwe and colleagues (2014) also reported native-like L2 processing of Dutch derivation. In the domain of syntax the evidence remains extremely scarce. However, in a recent study Pliatsikas et al. (2017) reported native-like patterns of brain activation for the processing of abstract syntactic elements (intermediate traces of wh-movement) by late L2 learners with extensive immersion to an L2 speaking environment, as opposed to learners of equal proficiency but with limited immersion. This finding suggests a shift in the areas involved in syntactic processing as an effect of long-term usage of an additional language, which can be interpreted as an expression of plasticity at the functional level. An obvious implication of this type of findings is that any models on L2 grammatical processing should take into account other factors apart from AoA, especially those related to frequency and amount of L2 usage.

Finally, with respect to AGL paradigms, recruitment of language-related regions has been found. A study by Petersson et al. (2012) examined neural substrates of artificial grammar learning in young adults. After a five-week training period, artificial grammar strings learning activated sections of the left IFG, and this area was activated to a greater extent when syntactically anomalous strings were processed. The response of the left IFG to syntactically anomalous strings has been corroborated by others, along with implications of the caudate being recruited in processing of grammatical strings (Forkstam et al. 2006). Considered together, the functional evidence suggests that highly similar brain regions and networks are recruited in L2 processing/production, regardless of AoA/AoO, further challenging the assumptions of the CPH.

As is the case with virtually all available behavioural studies, it should be noted that there are some differences in brain adaptation amongst later L2 learners. However, these are less likely to do with differences in AoA than they are to differences in language experience, specifically quantities or quality of input used or available to the L2 learner, as has been argued for L1–L2 superficial differences with behavioural experimentation (see Rothman and Guijarro-Fuentes 2010). In some cases, this may be due to overall time spent actively learning or using the L2. Pliatsikas et al. (2017) found converging evidence in immersed, late-acquired L2 speakers of English, with respect to plastic adaptations in the subcortical structures. A highly immersed bilingual population (average of eight years living in the UK) showed expansions in several structures including the bilateral thalamus, globus pallidus, and putamen, as compared to a monolingual control group. A low immersed group (less than four years in the UK) was found to have both expansions and contractions in the right caudate nucleus, with contractions in the left putamen, caudate, and thalamus compared to the monolingual controls. Crucially for our discussion, this pattern of effects in the highly immersed bilingual speakers replicated those found in simultaneously acquired bilinguals in an earlier study by Burgaleta et al. (2016), suggesting that quantity of input received may be telling of individual differences in outcomes of brain adaptations in the L2, and that age of acquisition à la CPH is not deterministic. The difference in overall time spent learning or using the novel language being the largest predictor of neural change is corroborated in other studies, for example in L2 vocabulary acquisition by adults (Bellander et al. 2016). Individual differences of proficiency have also been noted to correlate to differences in the extent of neural plasticity, although not the location. This is true of both functional connectivity changes (Veroude et al. 2010), and for structural plasticity (recall that both Mårtensson et al. 2012 and Mamiya et al. 2016 found correlations between extent of neuroplasticity and measured L2 proficiency levels). Crucially, however, the location of adaptation did not change significantly between learners, suggesting that at least the same neural substrates were serving this adaptation. Moreover, it would fair to conclude that those with less proficiency and, thus, relatively less extent of plastic adaptations would, with the passing of time, match the more proficient learners. Learning does not happen at the same rate for each individual, yet learning of grammar itself seems to be what in these cases drives the plastic effects. This alone further challenges the CPH specifically for language.

All in all, the current evidence from an array of neuroimaging techniques and foci suggest that the same neural substrates are available to both children and adults for L2 acquisition and processing, and in a highly similar capacity, which is not in line with the tenets of the CPH.

Future research needs to examine in further detail specific experience-based factors which co-occur with language acquisition and use, such as L2 immersion, daily use of both languages, and contexts of use (e.g. single language, dual language, dense code switching), amongst others (for further discussion see Abutalebi and Green 2016; Bialystok 2016a, b). However, to date relatively few studies have examined these factors. Future experimental designs should move away from categorical distinction within these factors and instead focus on them as continuous regressors and how they facilitate or moderate the process of language acquisition and, by extension, neural plasticity. By better understanding the potentially deterministic variables in neuroplasticity and language acquisition, we may better understand the trajectory of the L2 learner through the process of acquisition and use. Longitudinal designs are another useful method by which to account for individual differences in L2 acquisition and use. While some have found aspects of brain adaptations in training paradigms, exceedingly few have examined the process of language acquisition naturalistically. Within-subjects designs such as these allow for us to control potentially conflating inter-subject factors and isolate common neural adaptations which are unique to the L2 experience.

7. Conclusion

While true that L2 learners exhibit significant variability regarding their end-state linguistic competence, this chapter has attempted to weigh in on how best to interpret this general trend as it relates to the CPH in light of neurolinguistic data. Such data are important to consider for two non-intersecting reasons: (i) they tend to be overlooked by L2 acquisition researchers who do not actively work with neurolinguistic methodologies despite providing crucial insights and (ii) they are perhaps a privileged type of data precisely because the very notion of the CPH was built on proposals of brain maturation that at the time were not directly testable, but now are. In doing so, we outlined a wide range of studies from both EEG/ERP and (f)MRI research that provide convincing evidence challenging the central tenet of the CPH, namely, that biological neural maturation would result in the adult brain being incapable of acquiring and processing a subsequent language as happens when a primary language is acquired in childhood. Taken together, the evidence indicates that the neural substrates and processes underlying language acquisition and production in the L2 are maximally comparable to those in L1 across the lifespan. Any maturational constraints that might apply are not specific to language learning, especially to the extent that they create critical periods, but are generic constraints brought about by healthy ageing and they apply to other aspects of cognition (e.g. memory). While showing so does nothing to negate the very observable differences in path and outcome between typical L1 and adult L2 acquisition, it does suggest that other variables conspire to account for these differences, that is, there is no true fundamental difference in how language is acquired and processed, irrespective of age.

NOTES

1   We use the term critical period in a catch-all way for ease of exposition, ever mindful that it is not a monolithic, simplistic construct. That is, we use the term as a proxy for either a singular absolute critical period for all domains of grammar, multiple critical periods applying at different times to distinct domains of grammar (e.g. an earlier one for phonology as compared to syntax), or even sensitive periods that apply gradually over time as opposed to a sharp critical period effect. For our immediate purposes explaining the differences and the literature that debates them is peripheral to the points of focus in the present discussion.

2   In this chapter, the term 'brain plasticity' refers to non-pathological changes in brain structure and function as a result of certain experiences. With respect to structure, based on the available methods, these changes can normally be observed at the macroscopic level, i.e. regional increases/decreases in grey/white matter volume and/or density, whereas changes at the microscopic level (i.e. changes at the size of single neurons, dendritic loss, synaptic pruning) can only be inferred, but not directly tested, as the underlying cause of volumetric increases/decreases. At the functional level, we refer to changes in patterns of activation of, or connectivity between, brain areas, which either (i) shift from L2-specific to native-like patterns as a result of increased L2 usage and general experience or (ii) represent unique L2 patterns reflecting the increased needs that are brought about by the need to juggle two languages. In all cases, we interpret these changes as evidence for a dynamic, plastic system which constantly changes as a response to increased needs for the acquisition, processing, and control of an additional language

REFERENCES

Abrahamsson, N. and Hyltenstam, K. (2008). The robustness of aptitude effects in near-native second language acquisition. *Studies in Second Language Acquisition* 30 (04): 481–509.

Abrahamsson, N. and Hyltenstam, K. (2009). Age of onset and native-likeness in a second language: listener perception versus linguistic scrutiny. *Language Learning* 59 (2): 249–306.

Abutalebi, J. (2008). Neural aspects of second language representation and language control. *Acta Psychologica* 128 (3): 466–478. doi:10.1016/j.actpsy.2008.03.014.

Abutalebi, J. and Green, D.W. (2016). Neuroimaging of language control in bilinguals: neural adaptation and reserve. *Bilingualism: Language and Cognition* 1–10. doi:10.1017/S1366728916000225.

Ad-Dab'bagh, Y., Singh, V., Robbins, S., Lerch, J., Lyttelton, O., Fombonne, E., & Evans, A. (2005). Native space cortical thickness measurement and the absence of correlation to cerebral volume. In K. Zilles (Ed.), Proceedings of the 11th Annual Meeting of the Organization for Human Brain Mapping. Toronto: Elsevier.

Alemán Bañón, J., Fiorentino, R., and Gabriele, A. (2014). Morphosyntactic processing in advanced second language (L2) learners: an event-related potential investigation of the effects of L1–L2 similarity and structural distance. *Second Language Research* 30 (3): 275–306.

Alemán Bañón, J., Miller, D., and Rothman, J. (2017). Morphological variability in second language learners: an examination of electrophysiological and production data. *Journal of Experimental Psychology. Learning,*

Memory, and Cognition doi:10.1037/
xlm0000394.

Ashburner, J. and Friston, K.J. (2000). Voxel-based morphometry – the methods. *NeuroImage* 11 (6): 805–821. doi:10.1006/nimg.2000.0582.

Beckmann, C.F. and Smith, S.M. (2004). Probabilistic independent component analysis for functional magnetic resonance imaging. *IEEE Transactions on Medical Imaging* 23 (2): 137–152. doi:10.1109/TMI.2003.822821.

Bellander, M., Berggren, R., Mårtensson, J. et al. (2016). Behavioral correlates of changes in hippocampal gray matter structure during acquisition of foreign vocabulary. *NeuroImage* 131: 205–213. doi:10.1016/j.neuroimage.2015.10.020.

Bialystok, E. (2016a). The bilingual adaptation: how minds accommodate experience. *Psychological Bulletin* 143 (3): 233–262. doi:10.1037/bul0000099.

Bialystok, E. (2016b). The signal and the noise: finding the pattern in human behavior. *Linguistic Approaches to Bilingualism* 6 (5): 517–534. doi:10.1075/lab.15040.bia.

Bialystok, E. and Hakuta, K. (1994). *In Other Words: The Psychology and Science of Second Language Acquisition*. New York, NY: Basic Books.

Birdsong, D. (2014). The critical period hypothesis for second language acquisition: tailoring the coat of many colors. In: *Essential Topics in Applied Linguistics and Multilingualism* (ed. M. Pawlak and D. Singleton), 43–50. New York, NY: Springer.

Birdsong, D. and Molis, M. (2001). On the evidence for maturational constraints in second language acquisition. *Journal of Memory and Language* 44: 235–249.

Birdsong, D. and Vanhove, J. (2016). Age of second language acquisition: critical periods and social concerns. In: *Language and the Human Lifespan Series. Bilingualism across the Lifespan: Factors Moderating Language Proficiency* (ed. E. Nicoladis and S. Montanari), 163–181. Washington, DC: American Psychological Association.

Bley-Vroman, R. (1983). The comparative fallacy in interlanguage studies: the case of systematicity. *Language Learning* 33 (1): 1–17.

Bley-Vroman, R. (1989). What is the logical problem of foreign language learning? In: *Linguistic Perspectives on Second Language Acquisition* (ed. S.M. Gass and J. Schachter), 1–68. Cambridge, UK: Cambridge University Press.

Bley-Vroman, R. (2009). The evolving context of the fundamental difference hypothesis. *Studies in Second Language Acquisition* 31 (02): 175–198.

Booth, J.R., Wood, L., Lu, D. et al. (2007). The role of the basal ganglia and cerebellum in language processing. *Brain Research* 1133: 136–144. doi:10.1016/j.brainres.2006.11.074.

Burgaleta, M., Sanjuán, A., Ventura-Campos, N. et al. (2016). Bilingualism at the core of the brain. Structural differences between bilinguals and monolinguals revealed by subcortical shape analysis. *NeuroImage* 125: 437–445. doi:10.1016/j.neuroimage.2015.09.073.

Bylund, E., Abrahamsson, N., and Hyltenstam, K. (2012). Does first language maintenance hamper nativelikeness in a second language? *Studies in Second Language Acquisition* 34 (02): 215–241.

Bylund, E., Hyltenstam, K., and Abrahamsson, N. (2013). Age of acquisition effects or effects of bilingualism in second language ultimate attainment. In: *Sensitive Periods, Language Aptitude, and Ultimate L2 Attainment* (ed. G. Granena and M. Long), 69–101. Amsterdam, The Netherlands: John Benjamins.

Carroll, J.B. (1973). Implications of aptitude test research and psycholinguistic theory for foreign-language teaching. *Linguistics* 11 (112): 5–14.

Carroll, J.B. (1990). Cognitive abilities in foreign language aptitude: then and now. In: *Language Aptitude Reconsidered* (ed. T.S. Parry and C.W. Stansfield), 11–27. Englewood Cliffs, NJ: Prentice Hall.

Carroll, J.B. and Sapon, S.M. (1959). *Modern Language Aptitude Test*. San Antonio, TX: Psychological Corporation.

Clahsen, H. and Felser, C. (2006). Grammatical processing in language learners. *Applied PsychoLinguistics* 27 (1): 3–42.

Clahsen, H. and Muysken, P. (1989). The UG paradox in L2 acquisition. *Interlanguage Studies Bulletin (Utrecht)* 5 (1): 1–29.

Curtiss, S. (1977). *Genie: A Psycholinguistic Study of a Modern Day 'Wild Child'*. New York, NY: Academic.

Curtiss, S. (1988). Abnormal language acquisition and grammar: evidence for the modularity of language. In: *Linguistics: The Cambridge Survey: Volume 2, Linguistic Theory: Extensions and Implications* (ed. F.J. Newmeyer), 96–116. New York, NY: Routledge.

Dąbrowska, E. (1997). The LAD goes to school: a cautionary tale for nativists. *Linguistics* 35: 735–766.

Dąbrowska, E. (2012). Different speakers, different grammars: individual differences in native language attainment. *Linguistic Approaches to Bilingualism* 2 (3): 219–253.

De Grauwe, S., Lemhöfer, K., Willems, R.M., and Schriefers, H. (2014). L2 speakers decompose morphologically complex verbs: fMRI evidence from priming of transparent derived verbs. *Frontiers in Human Neuroscience* 8 (October): 1–12. doi:10.3389/fnhum.2014.00802.

DeKeyser, R.M. (2000). The robustness of critical period effects in second language acquisition. *Studies in Second Language Acquisition* 22 (04): 499–533.

Dörnyei, Z. (2001). *Motivational Strategies in the Language Classroom*. Cambridge, UK: Cambridge University Press.

Dörnyei, Z. (2005). *The Psychology of the Language Learner*. Mahwah, NJ: Erlbaum.

Dörnyei, Z. and Skehan, P. (2003). Individual differences in second language learning. In: *The Handbook of Second Language Acquisition* (ed. C.J. Doughty and M.H. Long), 589–630. Oxford, UK: Blackwell.

Forkstam, C., Hagoort, P., Fernandez, G. et al. (2006). Neural correlates of artificial syntactic structure classification. *NeuroImage* 32 (2): 956–967. doi:10.1016/j.neuroimage.2006.03.057.

Foucart, A. and Frenck-Mestre, C. (2011). Grammatical gender processing in L2: electrophysiological evidence of the effect of L1–L2 syntactic similarity. *Bilingualism: Language and Cognition* 14 (3): 379–399.

Frenck-Mestre, C., Anton, J.L., Roth, M. et al. (2005). Articulation in early and late bilinguals' two languages: evidence from functional magnetic resonance imaging. *NeuroReport* 16 (7): 761–765. doi:10.1097/00001756-200505120-00021.

Frenck-Mestre, C., Osterhout, L., McLaughlin, J., and Foucart, A. (2008). The effect of phonological realization of inflectional morphology on verbal agreement in French: evidence from ERPs. *Acta Psychologica* 128 (3): 528–536.

Friederici, A.D. (2009). Pathways to language: Fiber tracts in the human brain. *Trends in Cognitive Sciences* 13 (4): 175–181. doi:10.1016/j.tics.2009.01.001.

Friederici, A.D. and Gierhan, S.M.E. (2013). The language network. *Current Opinion in Neurobiology* 23 (2): 250–254. doi:10.1016/j.conb.2012.10.002.

Friederici, A.D., Steinhauer, K., and Pfeifer, E. (2002). Brain signatures of artificial language processing: evidence challenging the critical period hypothesis. *Proceedings of the National Academy of Sciences* 99 (1): 529–534.

Fuchs, E. and Flügge, G. (2014). Adult neuroplasticity: more than 40 years of research. *Neural Plasticity* doi:10.1155/2014/541870.

Gabriele, A., Fiorentino, R., and Bañón, J.A. (2013). Examining second language development using event-related potentials: a cross-sectional study on the processing of gender and number agreement. *Linguistic Approaches to Bilingualism* 3 (2): 213–232.

García-Pentón, L., Fernández García, Y., Costello, B. et al. (2016). The neuroanatomy of bilingualism: how to turn a hazy view into the full picture. *Language, Cognition and Neuroscience* 3798 (September): 1–25. doi:10.1080/23273798.2015.1068944.

Gillon Dowens, M., Guo, T., Guo, J. et al. (2011). Gender and number processing in

Chinese learners of Spanish–evidence from event related potentials. *Neuropsychologia* 49 (7): 1651–1659.

Granena, G. and Long, M.H. (2013). Age of onset, length of residence, language aptitude, and ultimate L2 attainment in three linguistic domains. *Second Language Research* 29 (3): 311–343.

Green, D.W. and Abutalebi, J. (2013). Language control in bilinguals: the adaptive control hypothesis. *Journal of Cognitive Psychology* 25: 1–16. doi:10.1080/20445911.2013.796377.

Hagoort, P., Brown, C., and Groothusen, J. (1993). The syntactic positive shift (SPS) as an ERP measure of syntactic processing. *Language and Cognitive Processes* 8 (4): 439–483.

Hahne, A. (2001). What's different in second-language processing? Evidence from event-related brain potentials. *Journal of Psycholinguistic Research* 30 (3): 251–266.

Hahne, A. and Friederici, A.D. (2001). Processing a second language: late learners' comprehension mechanisms as revealed by event-related brain potentials. *Bilingualism: Language and Cognition* 4 (2): 123–141.

Harley, B. and Hart, D. (1997). Language aptitude and second language proficiency in classroom learners of different starting ages. *Studies in Second Language Acquisition* 19 (3): 379–400.

Hawkins, R. and Chan, C.Y.H. (1997). The partial availability of universal grammar in second language acquisition: the 'failed functional features hypothesis'. *Second Language Research* 13 (3): 187–226.

Hickok, G. and Poeppel, D. (2007). The cortical organization of speech processing. *Nature Reviews. Neuroscience* 8 (5): 393–402. doi:10.1038/nrn2113.

Hofstetter, S., Friedmann, N., and Assaf, Y. (2016). Rapid language-related plasticity: microstructural changes in the cortex after a short session of new word learning. *Brain Structure and Function* doi:10.1007/s00429-016-1273-2.

Hopp, H. and Schmid, M.S. (2013). Perceived foreign accent in L1 attrition and L2 acquisition: the impact of age of acquisition and bilingualism. *Applied Psycholinguistics* doi: 10.1017/S0142716411000737.

Hosoda, C., Tanaka, K., Nariai, T. et al. (2013). Dynamic neural network reorganization associated with second language vocabulary acquisition: a multimodal imaging study. *The Journal of Neuroscience* 33 (34): 13663–13672. doi:10.1523/JNEUROSCI.0410-13.2013.

Isel, F. (2007). Syntactic and referential processes in second-language learners: event-related brain potential evidence. *Neuroreport* 18 (18): 1885–1889.

Johnson, J.S. and Newport, E.L. (1989). Critical period effects in second language learning: the influence of maturational state on the acquisition of English as a second language. *Cognitive Psychology* 21 (1): 60–99.

Kaan, E., Harris, A., Gibson, E., and Holcomb, P. (2000). The P600 as an index of syntactic integration difficulty. *Language and Cognitive Processes* 15 (2): 159–201.

Kotz, S.A. (2009). A critical review of ERP and fMRI evidence on L2 syntactic processing. *Brain and Language* 109 (2–3): 68–74.

Kotz, S.A., Holcomb, P.J., and Osterhout, L. (2008). ERPs reveal comparable syntactic sentence processing in native and non-native readers of English. *Acta Psychologica* 128 (3): 514–527.

Kuhl, P.K., Stevenson, J., Corrigan, N.M. et al. (2016). Neuroimaging of the bilingual brain: structural brain correlates of listening and speaking in a second language. *Brain and Language* 162: 1–9. doi:10.1016/j.bandl.2016.07.004.

Kutas, M. and Hillyard, S.A. (1980). Event-related brain potentials to semantically inappropriate and surprisingly large words. *Biological Psychology* 11 (2): 99–116.

Lau, E.F., Phillips, C., and Poeppel, D. (2008). A cortical network for semantics: (De) constructing the N400. *Nature Reviews: Neuroscience* 9 (12): 920.

Leclercq, D., Duffau, H., Delmaire, C. et al. (2010). Comparison of diffusion tensor imaging tractography of language tracts and intraoperative subcortical stimulations.

Journal of Neurosurgery 112 (3): 503–511. doi:1 0.3171/2009.8.JNS09558.

Lenneberg, E.H. (1967). The biological foundations of language. *Hospital Practice* 2 (12): 59–67.

Long, M.H. (2005). *Second Language Needs Analysis*. Cambridge, UK: Cambridge University Press.

Long, M.H. (2013). Maturational constraints on child and adult SLA. In: *Sensitive Periods, Language Aptitude, and Ultimate L2 Attainment* (ed. G. Granena and M. Long), 3–42. Amsterdam, UK: John Benjamins.

Luck, S.J. (2005). *Event-Related Potentials: A Methods Handbook*. Cambridge, MA: MIT Press.

Luk, G., Bialystok, E., Craik, F.I.M., and Grady, C.L. (2011). Lifelong bilingualism maintains white matter integrity in older adults. *Journal of Neuroscience* 31 (46): 16808–16813. doi:10.1523/JNEUROSCI.4563-11.2011.

Luk, G., Green, D.W., Abutalebi, J., and Grady, C. (2011). Cognitive control for language switching in bilinguals: a quantitative meta-analysis of functional neuroimaging studies. *Language and Cognitive Processes* 27 (10): 1479–1488. doi:10.1080/01690965.2011.6 13209.

Mamiya, P.C., Richards, T.L., Coe, B.P. et al. (2016). Brain white matter structure and COMT gene are linked to second-language learning in adults. *Proceedings of the National Academy of Sciences* 1–6. doi:10.1073/pnas.1606602113.

Mårtensson, J., Eriksson, J., Bodammer, N.C. et al. (2012). Growth of language-related brain areas after foreign language learning. *NeuroImage* 63 (1): 240–244. doi:10.1016/j.neuroimage.2012.06.043.

Mayberry, R.I. (1993). First-language acquisition after childhood differs from second-language acquisition: the case of American sign language. *Journal of Speech, Language, and Hearing Research* 36 (6): 1258–1270.

Mayberry, R. (1994). The importance of childhood to language acquisition: evidence from American Sign Language. In: *The Development of Speech Perception* (ed. J.

Goodman and H. Nusbaum), 57–90. Cambridge, MA: MIT Press.

McDonald, J.L. (2006). Beyond the critical period: processing-based explanations for poor grammaticality judgment performance by late second language learners. *Journal of Memory and Language* 55 (3): 381–401.

McLaughlin, J., Tanner, D., Pitkänen, I. et al. (2010). Brain potentials reveal discrete stages of L2 grammatical learning. *Language Learning* 60 (s2): 123–150.

Meisel, J.M. (2011). *First and Second Language Acquisition: Parallels and Differences*. Cambridge, UK: Cambridge University Press.

Mohades, S.G., Van Schuerbeek, P., Rosseel, Y. et al. (2015). White-matter development is different in bilingual and monolingual children: a longitudinal DTI study. *PLoS One* 10 (2): 1–16. doi:10.1371/journal.pone.0117968.

Molinaro, N., Barber, H.A., and Carreiras, M. (2011). Grammatical agreement processing in reading: ERP findings and future directions. *Cortex* 47 (8): 908–930.

Morgan-Short, K., Sanz, C., Steinhauer, K., and Ullman, M.T. (2010). Second language acquisition of gender agreement in explicit and implicit training conditions: An event-related potential study. *Language Learning* 60 (1): 154–193. doi:10.1111/j.1467-9922.2009.00554.x.

Morgan-Short, K., Steinhauer, K., Sanz, C., and Ullman, M.T. (2012). Explicit and implicit second language training differentially affect the achievement of native-like brain activation patterns. *Journal of Cognitive Neuroscience* 24 (4): 933–947.

Ojima, S., Nakata, H., and Kakigi, R. (2005). An ERP study of second language learning after childhood: effects of proficiency. *Journal of Cognitive Neuroscience* 17 (8): 1212–1228.

Olsen, R.K., Pangelinan, M.M., Bogulski, C.A. et al. (2015). The effect of lifelong bilingualism on regional grey and white matter volume. *Brain Research* 1612: 128–139. doi:10.1016/j.brainres.2015.02.034.

Ortega, L. (2013). SLA for the 21st century: disciplinary progress, transdisciplinary relevance, and the bi/multilingual turn. *Language Learning* 63 (s1): 1–24.

Osterhout, L. and Holcomb, P.J. (1992). Event-related brain potentials elicited by syntactic anomaly. *Journal of Memory and Language* 31 (6): 785–806.

Osterhout, L., Kim, A., and Kuperberg, G.R. (2012). The neurobiology of sentence comprehension. In: *The Cambridge Handbook of Psycholinguistics* (ed. M. Spivey, K. McRae and M. Joannisse), 365–389. Cambridge: Cambridge University Press.

Osterhout, L., McLaughlin, J., Pitkänen, I. et al. (2006). Novice learners, longitudinal designs, and event-related potentials: a means for exploring the neurocognition of second language processing. *Language Learning* 56 (s1): 199–230.

Osterhout, L., Poliakov, A., Inoue, K. et al. (2008). Second-language learning and changes in the brain. *Journal of Neurolinguistics* 21 (6): 509–521. doi:10.1016/j.jneuroling.2008.01.001.

Patenaude, B., Smith, S.M., Kennedy, D.N., and Jenkinson, M. (2011). A Bayesian model of shape and appearance for subcortical brain segmentation. *NeuroImage* 56 (3): 907–922. doi:10.1016/j.neuroimage.2011.02.046.

Penfield, W. and Roberts, L. (1959). *Speech and Brain Mechanisms*. Princeton, NJ: Princeton University Press.

Petersson, K.M., Folia, V., and Hagoort, P. (2012). What artificial grammar learning reveals about the neurobiology of syntax. *Brain and Language* 120 (2): 83–95. doi:10.1016/j.bandl.2010.08.003.

Phillips, C. and Ehrenhofer, L. (2015). The role of language processing in language acquisition. *Linguistic Approaches to Bilingualism* 5 (4): 409–453.

Pliatsikas, C., DeLuca, V., Moschopoulou, E., and Saddy, J.D. (2017). Immersive bilingualism reshapes the core of the brain. *Brain Structure and Function* 222 (4): 1785–1795. doi:10.1007/s00429-016-1307-9.

Pliatsikas, C., Johnstone, T., and Marinis, T. (2014a). fMRI evidence for the involvement of the procedural memory system in morphological processing of a second language. *PLoS One* 9 (5): e97298. doi:10.1371/journal.pone.0097298.

Pliatsikas, C., Johnstone, T., and Marinis, T. (2014b). Grey matter volume in the cerebellum is related to the processing of grammatical rules in a second language: a structural voxel-based morphometry study. *Cerebellum* 13 (1): 55–63. doi:10.1007/s12311-013-0515-6.

Pliatsikas, C., Johnstone, T., and Marinis, T. (2017). An fMRI study on the processing of long-distance wh-movement in a second language. *Glossa* 2 (1): 1–22. doi:10.5334/gjgl.95.

Pliatsikas, C., Moschopoulou, E., and Saddy, J.D. (2015). The effects of bilingualism on the white matter structure of the brain. *Proceedings of the National Academy of Sciences* 112 (5): 1334–1337. doi:10.1073/pnas.1414183112.

Prehn, K., Taud, B., Reifegerste, J. et al. (2017). Neural correlates of grammatical inflection in older native and second-language speakers. *Bilingualism* 21 (1): 1–12. doi:10.1017/S1366728916001206.

Roberts, L., Gonzalez Alonso, J., Pliatsikas, C., and Rothman, J. (2018). Evidence from neurolinguistic methodologies: can it actually inform linguistic/language acquisition theories and translate to evidence-based applications? *Second Language Research* 34 (1): 125–143. doi:10.1177/0267658316644010.

Robinson, P. (1997). Generalizability and automaticity of second language learning under implicit, incidental, enhanced, and instructed conditions. *Studies in Second Language Acquisition* 19 (2): 223–247.

Robinson, P. (2005). Cognitive abilities, chunk-strength, and frequency effects in implicit artificial grammar and incidental L2 learning: replications of Reber, Walkenfeld, and Hernstadt (1991) and Knowlton and squire (1996) and their relevance for SLA. *Studies in Second Language Acquisition* 27 (2): 235–268.

Roncaglia-Denissen, M.P. and Kotz, S.A. (2016). What does neuroimaging tell us about morphosyntactic processing in the brain of second language learners? *Bilingualism* 19 (4): 665–673. doi:10.1017/S1366728915000413.

Rossi, E., Cheng, H., Kroll, J.F. et al. (2017). Changes in white-matter connectivity in late second language learners: evidence from diffusion tensor imaging. *Frontiers in Psychology* 8: 1–15. doi:10.3389/fpsyg.2017.02040.

Rossi, S., Gugler, M.F., Friederici, A.D., and Hahne, A. (2006). The impact of proficiency on syntactic second-language processing of German and Italian: evidence from event-related potentials. *Journal of Cognitive Neuroscience* 18 (12): 2030–2048.

Rothman, J. (2008). Why all counter-evidence to the critical period hypothesis in second language acquisition is not equal or problematic. *Language and Linguistics Compass* 2 (6): 1063–1088.

Rothman, J. and Guijarro-Fuentes, P. (2010). Input quality matters: some comments on input type and age-effects in adult SLA. *Applied Linguistics* 31 (2): 301–306.

Rothman, J. and Slabakova, R. (2017). The generative approach SLA and its place in ModernSecond language studies. *Studies in Second Language Acquisition* 1–26. doi:10.1017/S0272263117000134.

Sabourin, L. and Haverkort, M. (2003). Neural substrates of representation and processing of a second language. *Language Acquisition and Language Disorders* 30: 175–196.

Sabourin, L. and Stowe, L.A. (2008). Second language processing: when are first and second languages processed similarly? *Second Language Research* 24 (3): 397–430.

Sassenhagen, J., Schlesewsky, M., and Bornkessel-Schlesewsky, I. (2014). The P600-as-P3 hypothesis revisited: single-trial analyses reveal that the late EEG positivity following linguistically deviant material is reaction time aligned. *Brain and Language* 137: 29–39.

Schlegel, A.A., Rudelson, J.J., and Tse, P.U. (2012). White matter structure changes as adults learn a second language. *Journal of Cognitive Neuroscience* 24 (8): 1664–1670. doi:10.1162/jocn_a_00240.

Smith, S.M., Jenkinson, M., Johansen-Berg, H. et al. (2006). Tract-based spatial statistics: voxelwise analysis of multi-subject diffusion data. *NeuroImage* 31 (4): 1487–1505. doi:10.1016/j.neuroimage.2006.02.024.

Smith, S.M., Jenkinson, M., Woolrich, M.W. et al. (2004). Advances in functional and structural MR image analysis and implementation as FSL. *NeuroImage* 23 (Suppl. 1): doi:10.1016/j.neuroimage.2004.07.051.

Stein, M., Federspiel, A., Koenig, T. et al. (2012). Structural plasticity in the language system related to increased second language proficiency. *Cortex* 48 (4): 458–465. doi:10.1016/j.cortex.2010.10.007.

Tanner, D., Grey, S., and van Hell, J.G. (2017). Dissociating retrieval interference and reanalysis in the P600 during sentence comprehension. *Psychophysiology* 54 (2): 248–259.

Tanner, D., McLaughlin, J., Herschensohn, J., and Osterhout, L. (2013). Individual differences reveal stages of L2 grammatical acquisition: ERP evidence. *Bilingualism: Language and Cognition* 16 (2): 367–382.

Tokowicz, N. and MacWhinney, B. (2005). Implicit and explicit measures of sensitivity to violations in second language grammar: an event-related potential investigation. *Studies in Second Language Acquisition* 27 (2): 173–204.

Tsimpli, I.M. and Dimitrakopoulou, M. (2007). The interpretability hypothesis: evidence from wh-interrogatives in second language acquisition. *Second Language Research* 23 (2): 215–242.

Veroude, K., Norris, D.G., Shumskaya, E. et al. (2010). Functional connectivity between brain regions involved in learning words of a new language. *Brain and Language* 113 (1): 21–27. doi:10.1016/j.bandl.2009.12.005.

Weber-Fox, C.M. and Neville, H.J. (1996). Maturational constraints on functional specializations for language processing: ERP and behavioral evidence in bilingual speakers. *Journal of Cognitive Neuroscience* 8 (3): 231–256.

White, L. (2003). *Second Language Acquisition and Universal Grammar*. Cambridge, UK: Cambridge University Press.

White, L. (2008). Different? Yes. Fundamentally? No. Definiteness effects in the L2 English of Mandarin speakers. In Proceedings of the 9th generative approaches to second language acquisition conference (GASLA 2007) (pp. 251–261). Somerville, MA: Cascadilla Proceedings Project.

Part II   Neural Representations

9 Language Organization in the Bilingual and Multilingual Brain

NICOLA DEL MASCHIO AND JUBIN ABUTALEBI

1. Introduction

Language is often taken to be the trait that most prominently distinguishes humans from other species (Berwick et al. 2013). When mapping language function in the brain, of particular interest is the unique human capacity to acquire, store, and use more than one language efficiently. Compensating for the acknowledged limitations of the anatomoclinical method (see Démonet et al. 2005), the application of neuroimaging technologies to the functional anatomy of cognition has provided remarkable insights into the representation and processing of multiple languages in the living, intact brain (Abutalebi et al. 2005). In this chapter, we offer a narrative review of the most relevant results so far achieved in the field of the cerebral basis of multilingualism using positron emission tomography (PET) and functional magnetic resonance imaging (fMRI). The impact of multilingual experience on the functional neuroanatomy of language will be discussed with special reference to the critical components of spoken language processing: sound, grammar, and meaning. Within the context of a volume focusing on the cognitive (neuro)science of multilingualism, it is worth clarifying that unless otherwise specified we will use the term 'multilingualism' to indicate the regular use of more than one language and the term 'second language (L2)' to indicate any language other than the native (L1).

Few people in modern globalized societies are strictly monolingual in the sense of having no knowledge or exposure to a second language (Grosjean and Li 2013). Multilingualism, however, is not an all-or-nothing phenomenon. Multilingual experience is increasingly recognized as a complex construct sensitive to a number of distinct but interacting variables, including the age at which L2 is acquired (AoA), the amount and quality of L2 input (exposure), and the level of attained L2 knowledge (proficiency).

The Handbook of the Neuroscience of Multilingualism, First Edition. Edited by John W. Schwieter.
© 2019 John Wiley & Sons Ltd. Published 2019 by John Wiley & Sons Ltd.

These factors not only yield heterogeneous profiles of multilingual users, but also affect the neurobiology of multilingualism (Perani et al. 1998, 2003; Abutalebi et al. 2013; Luk and Bialystok 2013; Liu and Cao 2016). Two major approaches were adopted to probe the neural substrates of multilingual competence: the neuropsychological observation of impaired language function in multilingual aphasics, and the functional neuroimaging investigation of normal language in healthy multilinguals. The aphasiological literature has not been successful in defining the neural localization of multiple languages, nor in illuminating the mechanisms underlying their simultaneous management. Rather, selective language impairment and unequal recovery patterns for different languages led many researchers to believe that different languages were represented in distinct brain structures or even different hemispheres (Scoresby-Jackson 1867; Albert and Obler 1978). More recently, substantial neuroimaging evidence has established that all languages learned are supported by a common neural mechanism (for reviews, see Higby et al. 2013; Mouthon et al. 2013; Costa and Sebastián-Gallés 2014), L2 representation converging with that of an already-specified L1 network (Green 2003; Abutalebi and Green 2007). Noteworthy, this convergence is modulated by experience-related factors inherent to the studied populations, such as the time of L2 onset and the level of L2 proficiency (see Liu and Cao 2016). Based on the 'critical period hypothesis' (CPH; Penfield and Roberts 1959; Lenneberg 1967), according to which the capacity to acquire a language is tied to age-dependent loss of cortical plasticity with maturation, a fundamental difference has been posited between the acquisition of L1 and L2 in late L2 learners, due to maturational decay of L2 capability (e.g. Bley-Vroman 1988; Johnson and Newport 1989; Newport 1990). Although much greater plasticity than previously conjectured has been reported for late multilinguals (Abutalebi et al. 2014, 2015; Steinhauer 2014; Pliatsikas et al. 2017), the individual and cumulative effects of AoA, proficiency, and exposure on L2 learning are still a matter of intense debate (Hernandez and Li 2007; Birdsong and Vanhove 2016; Berken et al. 2017). Relevant to this chapter, language processing components seem to be differentially sensitive to AoA and proficiency effects, AoA having greater impact on phonological and grammatical processes, proficiency having greater impact on lexico-semantic and control processes (Johnson and Newport 1989; Werker and Tees 2005; Hernandez and Li 2007; Saito 2015; Sugiura et al. 2015; Berken et al. 2017).

In the remainder of this chapter, we will first examine the neural underpinnings of phonological, grammatical, and lexico-semantic processing in multilinguals, and then conclude by illustrating how the brain controls more than one language.

2.   Brain Basis of L2 Phonology

Phonological competence is the ability to recognize and produce the distinctive sound patterns of a language. In monolingual speakers, phonological processing is subserved by specialized networks in the left hemisphere. Within 'dual stream' models of language processing (Hickok and Poeppel 2004, 2007; Saur et al. 2008; see also Friederici 2015), a dorsal pathway projecting from the posterior superior temporal plane to the premotor cortex links the incoming speech signals with speech motor programs for articulation, thereby supporting critical aspects of sensorimotor integration for speech production based on previous auditory input. Whilst early cortical stages of acoustic-phonological analysis occur bilaterally adjacent both anteriorly and posteriorly to Heschl's gyrus (Binder et al. 2000; Hickok and Poeppel 2007), speech processing becomes progressively more left-lateralized to temporal, parietal, and frontal cortices as signals become more 'speech-like' (Hickok and Poeppel 2007). A significant exception to this leftward asymmetry is represented by the neural computation of suprasegmental features and emotional prosody (Belyk and Brown 2014; Sammler et al. 2015).

In line with neuroimaging literature on multilingual language processing more generally, PET and fMRI studies point in the direction of a shared neural circuitry housing L1 and L2 phonological processing (Golestani 2015). Differences in the extent and intensity of activation within this circuitry are particularly prominent during initial stages of L2 learning and when L2 is processed with low or moderate proficiency (e.g. Golestani and Zatorre 2004; Marian et al. 2017). It continues to be debated, however, whether L1 and L2 activation patterns are more divergent for late vs. early multilinguals irrespective of attained level of L2 knowledge (Frenck-Mestre et al. 2005; Berken et al. 2015; Marian et al. 2017).

Despite proficient knowledge of L2 grammar and vocabulary, mastering non-native sounds may be challenging. Although early vs. late learning is generally associated with higher ultimate proficiency in L2 speech (e.g. Oyama 1976; Flege 1988; Flege et al. 1999; Moyer 1999), evidence has been provided that an early start as such does not automatically lead to native-like mastery (Thompson 1991; Flege et al. 1995; Pallier et al. 1997; Flege et al. 2006). The predictive value of several factors other than L2 AoA has been documented at both behavioural and neural levels, including the amount of continued L1 use and the characteristics of L2 input (see Piske et al. 2001; Frenck-Mestre et al. 2005; Flege and MacKay 2011). As shown by ample experimental work, previous language experience acts as a filter through which foreign speech is perceived and produced (e.g. Miyawaki et al. 1975; Bohn and Flege 1990). It has been suggested that the neural commitment to the acoustic properties of L1 may interfere with the perception of new sounds at an auditory or early-phonetic level, as L2 learners tend to rely on acoustic cues that are perceptually salient in L1 but not reliable for sound categorization in L2 (Kuhl 2000; Iverson et al. 2003; Zhang et al. 2005). The influence of prior linguistic experience (Best 1995; Kuhl 2000; Flege 2002), the effects of perceptual narrowing during development (see Werker and Tees 2005), the amount and quality of L2 input (see Lecumberri et al. 2010), as well as the age-dependent loss of neuromuscular plasticity for speech motor control (Simmonds et al. 2011) have been identified as potential sources of the persistent foreign accent frequently exhibited by late L2 learners.

Experimental studies on phonetic learning provided useful insights into the neuroplastic mechanisms underlying the acquisition of non-native speech patterns (e.g. Callan et al. 2003; Golestani and Zatorre 2004; Wang et al. 2007; Moser et al. 2009). During initial stages of L2 training, non-native vs. familiar contrasts were found to be associated with less-efficient processing in frontotemporal areas for speech computation and greater recruitment of cortico-subcortical networks for executive control. On the other hand, post-training activation patterns for non-native contrasts crucially converged onto those observed during the identification of familiar speech, with less demand on the executive control system (e.g. Callan et al. 2003, 2004; Golestani and Zatorre 2004; Wang et al. 2007). These longitudinal data alluded to progressive cortical changes as a function of increasing proficiency, with a more automated and bottom-up processing succeeding to the initial cost of processing unfamiliar sounds. More generally, these findings suggest that neural representations for language processing may be continuously shaped with learning across the life span.

It has also been proposed that multilingualism per se or, rather, the advantage of being multilingual, would come at the expense of increased demands on word retrieval, articulation, and post-articulatory monitoring in production contexts. According to this view, although higher levels of expertise and use may reduce between-language phonological competition and facilitate production, multilinguals would experience an additional processing load with respect to monolinguals due to the constant management of a composite articulatory repertoire. Parker-Jones et al. (2012), for instance, used fMRI to contrast the neural signatures of monolingual vs. multilingual speakers engaged in overt picture-naming, reading aloud and semantic decisions in only their first language. Higher activations for multilinguals were found in the left dorsal precentral gyrus, Broca's area, the superior temporal gyrus, and the temporal plane for naming and reading aloud. Interestingly, monolinguals showed greater activity in the same areas when task demands were increased. The authors interpreted these findings as suggesting that multilingual language production exploits a system that is also used in monolinguals (Abutalebi and Green 2007), with additional processing demands arising from the need to control for cross-linguistic interference during word retrieval, articulatory planning, articulation, and auditory-motor feedback.

Overall, although a limited number of functional neuroimaging studies have examined the brain basis of L2 phonology, the literature consistently provided evidence for a shared networked system of brain areas for L1 and L2 speech. The reported L1–L2 activation differences appear to be modulated by how well a second language is spoken and – possibly – by the time of L2 onset. In production, additional processing demands may be imposed on multilingual speakers due to competing representations extending over the entire speech pipeline, from articulatory planning to post-articulatory monitoring.

3.   Brain Basis of L2 Grammar

Grammatical competence is the ability to recognize and produce the distinctive grammatical structures of a language. Contemporary linguistics generally partitions grammatical competence into two subcomponents: morphological and syntactic competence. The former allows for the generation and processing of morphologically complex words (i.e. inflected, derived, and compound words; Aronoff 1976); the latter allows for the generation and processing of an unbounded array of hierarchically and recursively constructed sentences (Chomsky 1957). Inflectional processes, which produce grammatical variants of the same lexeme within given syntactic slots, are considered to straddle the morphology-syntax interface.

According to dual-route models of morphological processing (e.g. Pinker and Prince 1988; Pinker and Ullman 2002), whilst irregular forms are stored and retrieved as wholes from declarative memory, the combinatorial structure of regular complex words is processed online via rule-based decomposing strategies. The computation of regular word forms in monolingual speakers is subserved by a left frontotemporal/basal ganglia circuit (Vannest et al. 2005; Marangolo et al. 2006; Meinzer et al. 2009; Bozic and Marslen-Wilson 2010; Pliatsikas et al. 2014a). The processing of irregular word forms has been associated with the recruitment of regions implicated in the retrieval and processing of lexical meaning such as the bilateral superior and middle temporal gyri (Binder et al. 2009; Bozic and Marslen-Wilson 2010) and with a decreased engagement of the left inferior frontal gyrus (e.g. Tyler et al. 2005), the main locus of rule-based morphological parsing. It is however unclear whether producing grammatical variants of the same lexeme (inflexion) and forming new lexemes from existing ones (derivation) recruit overlapping systems, or whether inflectional and derivational processes may involve partially different neural mechanisms (see Bozic and Marslen-Wilson 2010).

Syntactic processing in monolinguals, on the other hand, draws on a cortico-subcortical network that comprises Broca's area, the posterior superior temporal gyrus, the basal ganglia and possibly the cerebellum (Cappa 2012; Friederici and Gierhan 2013). The pathway connecting Broca's area and the posterior superior temporal gyrus (i.e., the arcuate fasciculus) has been claimed to support the processing of syntactically complex structures (Friederici and Gierhan 2013).

It is reasonable to argue that while vocabulary development uses associative learning processes that are adaptable to late L2 learners, the explicit learning of L2 grammar in adulthood may exploit mechanisms that are qualitatively different from those governing the acquisition of first-language grammar (see DeKeyser 2005, 2012; Clahsen and Felser 2006a). Ullman's declarative/procedural model (Ullman 2001, 2004, 2016) provided a rationale for this argument. The model proposes that L1 processing relies on two memory systems underpinned by distinct neural structures: a declarative system for the acquisition and use of lexico-semantic knowledge (rooted in left temporal circuits), and a procedural system for the acquisition and use of grammatical rules (rooted in Broca's area and the basal ganglia). The model predicts that when an L2 is learned later in life, the speaker's procedural resources are impoverished or no longer available. As a result, the processing of L2 grammar would rely heavily on the declarative system and much less on procedural mechanisms. Although an admittedly meagre amount of functional neuroimaging work has been conducted on grammatical processing in L2 speakers, the literature has so far contradicted the maturational constraints proposed by Ullman's model: data collected from heterogeneous profiles of L2 users and typologically different languages revealed that the neural architecture of grammatical competence in monolinguals and multilinguals is substantially comparable. In contrast with Ullman's predictions, the network which early and late multilinguals recruit when processing L2 grammar comprises the left inferior frontal gyrus and the dorsal striatum (for reviews, see Abutalebi 2008; Kotz 2009). Noteworthy, in late and low proficiency multilinguals these regions are driven more extensively, supposedly reflecting less automaticity for L2 grammatical processing (e.g. Abutalebi 2008; Prehn et al. 2017).

With reference to L2 morphological parsing, a left frontotemporal/basal ganglia circuit has been consistently associated with the computation of predictable word structure, whether inflectionally or derivationally complex words were used as experimental stimuli (Sakai et al. 2004; Tatsuno and Sakai 2005; Lehtonen et al. 2009; Bick et al. 2011; Pliatsikas et al. 2014b). In a cross-sectional fMRI study on L2 inflexion, Pliatsikas et al. (2014b) reported that monolinguals and late proficient multilinguals equally engaged frontotemporal areas, the caudate nuclei and the right cerebellum to process regularly inflected items. These findings were interpreted as indicating a common computational strategy for both groups, irrespective of the age at which L2 was acquired by multilingual speakers. Along similar lines, training studies exploring the acquisition of L2 inflectional morphology in late multilinguals (e.g. Sakai et al. 2004; Tatsuno and Sakai 2005) reported a cortical mechanism underlying the processing of L2 morphosyntax identical to that of L1. Of note, a more efficient processing in the left inferior frontal gyrus positively correlated with participants' learning improvements (Sakai et al. 2004), pointing towards the convergent neural representation of L2 grammar within an already-specified L1 network (Green 2003; Abutalebi and Green 2007).

Neuroimaging investigations of L2 syntax showed a common cortico-subcortical system underpinning syntactic processing in L1 and L2, with activation patterns being modulated by L2 proficiency and syntactic distance or complexity (Wartenburger et al. 2003; Golestani et al. 2006; Indefrey 2006; Kotz 2009; Sebastian et al. 2011; Consonni et al. 2013). Stronger activations for low-proficiency or late-learned L2s in Broca's area, prefrontal cortices, the basal ganglia, and the cerebellum have been associated with the need to suppress interference from syntactic constructions of non-target languages (Abutalebi and Green 2007). A syntactic distance effect was detected by Jeong et al. (2007), who compared the activation patterns of native Korean speakers engaged in sentence comprehension in Korean (L1) and Japanese and English (L2s). A stronger activation in the left Broca's area and the right cerebellum was found when participants performed the comprehension task in English, while activation in these regions did not differ significantly between Korean and Japanese. The authors interpreted these results as reflecting a syntactic distance effect between English and the other two languages, supposedly similar to each other in terms of core syntax. Nonetheless, an open question remains as to whether complex syntactic structures such as non-local dependencies are processed in a native-like manner by late L2 learners (Weber et al. 2016), or whether a late-learned L2 implies different processes and representations for complex vs simple syntactic structures (see Clahsen and Felser 2006b; Suh et al. 2007).

Taken together, these functional neuroimaging findings show a common cortico-subcortical network underpinning grammar processing in L1 and L2, with activation patterns being modulated by L2 proficiency, distance and/or complexity of grammatical structures and possibly AoA.

4.   Brain Basis of L2 Lexico-Semantics

Semantic competence is the ability to extract meaning from linguistic structure. In monolingual speakers, the representation and control of semantic knowledge reflect the joint activation of a widely distributed neural system (Cappa 2012; Jefferies 2013). Within dual-stream models of language processing (Hickok and Poeppel 2004, 2007; Saur et al. 2008; see also Friederici 2015), a ventral pathway projecting bilaterally from the posterior superior temporal plane to the middle and inferior frontotemporal cortices supports sound-to-meaning mapping and language comprehension. At the cortical level, the neuroimaging literature has implicated a number of regions as being involved in lexico-semantic tasks, including the left posterior middle temporal gyrus, the ventral occipitotemporal cortex, the anterior temporal lobes, and the left middle and inferior frontal gyri (Binder et al. 2009). Subcortical engagement has been associated with word meaning extraction in the context of competing alternatives (Mestres-Missé et al. 2008) as well as with reward mechanisms during successful word learning (Ripollés et al. 2014).

In both L1 and L2 as aforementioned, multilinguals tend to perform worse than monolingual speakers on lexical tasks, as indexed by lower fluency rates (e.g. Rosselli et al. 2000) and slower picture-naming (e.g. Ivanova and Costa 2008). It has been proposed that competition from the non-target language could delay or impoverish lexical access in the language selected (Green 1998), whilst higher levels of language proficiency and use may reduce competition and facilitate retrieval (Michael and Gollan 2005; de Bruin et al. 2016).

With respect to phonology and grammar, the lexico-semantic domain has been relatively well studied by means of functional neuroimaging. Experimental work involving single-word tasks widely attested the contribution of L2 proficiency in modulating neural activation for lexical processing (Illes et al. 1999; Chee et al. 2001; Abutalebi 2008). It has been consistently reported that when the degree of L2 proficiency is comparable to that of L1, shared neural networks in the left frontal and temporo-parietal regions are recruited. On the other hand, disparities in activation patterns in frontal and subcortical structures exist when semantic competence is unbalanced for L1 and L2 (see Indefrey 2006). Consonni et al. (2013), for instance, used fMRI to evaluate word generation and sentence comprehension in two groups of highly proficient multilinguals only differing in AoA. Whereas one group learned Italian and Friulian from birth, the second group learned Italian in kindergarten or primary school. All participants were highly proficient in both languages, but more exposed to Italian than Friulian. The results indicated a complete overlap of neural activations for L1 and L2 during both production and comprehension tasks. However, additional activation for the less-exposed language was detected in the left thalamic region, known to be involved in language monitoring processes (Mestres-Missé et al. 2008; Wahl et al. 2008). This last finding was interpreted as confirming psycholinguistic evidence that decreased exposure to a given language enhances controlled processing for that language. Other studies documented additional brain activity in the left inferior frontal gyrus and other prefrontal regions for multilinguals with low L2 proficiency (e.g. Perani et al. 2003; Rüschemeyer et al. 2005; Marian et al. 2007). Abutalebi et al. (2007) showed that L1 naming in a multilingual context (as compared with monolingual contexts) was associated with increased activation in the left caudate and the anterior cingulate cortex, with greater involvement of these areas when participants were using a less proficient L2. One interpretation is that the processes required to produce language become more automatic, requiring less domain-general executive control as the language becomes more familiar.

Overall, lexico-semantic processing in multilinguals is associated with similar brain regions as in monolinguals, with greater recruitment of the prefrontal cortex when the level of L2 proficiency and/or exposure is low or moderate. The processing of word-meaning in a late-learned L2 deploys neural resources that do not diverge substantially from those used in L1.

5.   Brain Basis of Language Control

Language control refers to the set of cognitive abilities that enable multilinguals to use a target language while monitoring for potential interference from language(s) not in use but constantly active in the multilingual mind (Green 1986, 1998). This complex control task is orchestrated by a cortico-subcortical network largely overlapping with the neural infrastructure for domain-general executive control functions (Abutalebi and Green 2007, 2016). Executive control may be characterized as a multicomponential construct comprising a range of mechanisms that support flexible, goal-directed behaviour by representing task-relevant information in order to guide action (Yeung 2013). An intervention of the executive control system in multilingual language processing has been attributed to the need of selectively attending to one language, monitoring speech from other languages' intrusions and switching from a language to another (Green 1998; Abutalebi and Green 2007; Kroll et al. 2008). Functional neuroimaging evidence has shown that multilinguals activate neural circuits that lie outside the classical perisylvian language network, such as the dorsolateral prefrontal cortex, the supplementary motor area, the anterior cingulate cortex, the bilateral caudate, and the cerebellum (Hervais-Adelman et al. 2011; Luk et al. 2012; Abutalebi and Green 2016; Pliatsikas and Luk 2016). This pattern has been consistently detected across varying language pairs such as Chinese-English (e.g. Wang et al. 2007; Guo et al. 2011), Spanish-Catalan (e.g. Garbin et al. 2011), and German-French (Abutalebi et al. 2008). The anterior cingulate cortex, in particular, stands out as a critical component mediating the monitoring of conflicting information, whether in verbal or in non-verbal domains (Carter et al. 1999; Crinion et al. 2006; Hernandez 2009; Abutalebi et al. 2012; Branzi et al. 2016). When comparing the conflict resolution abilities of multilingual and monolingual speakers on executive control tasks, a lower activation in the anterior cingulate cortex of multilinguals was significantly correlated with greater local grey matter volume, suggesting a special tuning of this region for the simultaneous management of multiple languages (Abutalebi et al. 2012). Not surprisingly, the processing demands in multilingual speakers were shown to be particularly taxing in low-proficiency subjects, who seem to heavily rely on the active suppression of the native language when speaking an L2. In contrast, highly proficient multilinguals would select and maintain their language output with minimal interference from the unintended language(s) (Abutalebi and Green 2007; Costa et al. 2016).

Overall, these findings suggest that the control of more than one language is accomplished through a combination of interwoven activities in a neural network that supports not only language processing but also executive attention. Most importantly, these findings imply that multilingual experience has consequences beyond language processing. Whether these consequences are beneficial for multilingual individuals as compared to monolinguals both at the cognitive and neural level is currently intensely debated (Paap and Greenberg 2013; Valian 2015; Bialystok et al. 2016; Del Maschio et al. 2018; Maschio 2018; Fedeli 2018; Abutalebi 2018).

6. Conclusion

In this chapter, we offered a narrative review of the most relevant results so far achieved in the field of the functional neuroanatomy of multilingualism. Functional neuroimaging data contrasting L1 and L2, both within and between groups, provided evidence for a shared networked system of brain areas underpinning the representation of linguistic knowledge, regardless of the modality of language input and the typological features of individual languages. The principles governing the architecture of phonology, grammar, and lexico-semantics in L1 and L2 appear to be analogous, with differences in associated activation patterns resulting from a more effortful L2 processing rather than from differences in the actual representation of language systems. A less-proficient language is generally linked with a more widely distributed cluster of activations within and in proximity of the classical language regions, arguably reflecting a compensatory mechanism necessary to perform a difficult task such as speaking an L2. Moreover, low levels of proficiency are typically correlated with greater recruitment of frontal and subcortical circuitries that support executive control functions, arguably indicating a low level of automatism for L2 processing compared to L1. Whereas the impact of L2 proficiency and exposure on the cerebral basis of multilingualism is fairly well established, the role of AoA is still controversial. If certain linguistic subdomains seem to be more sensitive than others to the age at which an L2 is acquired, it remains unclear whether the diminished computational efficiency displayed by some late L2 learners is the result of hard maturational constraints or other factors.

To conclude, there is ample agreement that multilingualism represents a privileged window into the invariant and experience-dependent aspects of human language. Advancing our knowledge of how multiple language processing shapes the brain has far-reaching consequences that exceed the domain of neurolinguistics, opening up new opportunities for the study of learning mechanisms, neural specialization and brain plasticity. There is of course still much we do not know about the effects of multilingualism on the mind/brain and the experience-related factors that lead to them. It is equally undeniable, however, that an increasingly multilingual world requires rapid advancements in the study of the multilingual brain to shape the future agenda of educational and intervention policies.

REFERENCES

Abutalebi, J. (2008). Neural aspects of second language representation and language control. *Acta Psychologica* 128 (3): 466–478.

Abutalebi, J., Annoni, J.M., Zimine, I. et al. (2007). Language control and lexical competition in bilinguals: an event-related fMRI study. *Cerebral Cortex* 18 (7): 1496–1505.

Abutalebi, J., Annoni, J.M., Zimine, I. et al. (2008). Language control and lexical competition in bilinguals: an event-related fMRI study. *Cerebral Cortex* 18 (7): 1496–1505.

Abutalebi, J., Canini, M., Della Rosa, P.A. et al. (2015). The neuroprotective effects of bilingualism upon the inferior parietal lobule: a structural neuroimaging study in aging Chinese bilinguals. *Journal of Neurolinguistics* 33: 3–13.

Abutalebi, J., Canini, M., Della Rosa, P.A. et al. (2014). Bilingualism protects anterior temporal lobe integrity in aging. *Neurobiology of Aging* 35 (9): 2126–2133.

Abutalebi, J., Cappa, S.F., and Perani, D. (2005). What can functional neuroimaging tell us about the bilingual brain. In: *Handbook of Bilingualism: Psycholinguistic Approaches* (ed. J.F. Kroll and A.M.B. De Groot), 497–515. Oxford, UK: Oxford University Press.

Abutalebi, J., Della Rosa, P.A., Ding, G. et al. (2013). Language proficiency modulates the engagement of cognitive control areas in multilinguals. *Cortex* 49 (3): 905–911.

Abutalebi, J., Della Rosa, P.A., Green, D.W. et al. (2012). Bilingualism tunes the anterior cingulate cortex for conflict monitoring. *Cerebral Cortex* 22 (9): 2076–2086.

Abutalebi, J. and Green, D.W. (2007). Bilingual language production: the neurocognition of language representation and control. *Journal of Neurolinguistics* 20 (3): 242–275.

Abutalebi, J. and Green, D.W. (2016). Neuroimaging of language control in bilinguals: neural adaptation and reserve. *Bilingualism: Language and cognition* 19 (4): 1–10.

Albert, M.L. and Obler, L.K. (1978). *The Bilingual Brain: Neuropsychological and Neurolinguistic Aspects of Bilingualism*. New York, NY: Academic Press.

Aronoff, M. (1976). *Word Formation in Generative Grammar*. Cambridge, MA: MIT Press.

Belyk, M. and Brown, S. (2014). Perception of affective and linguistic prosody: an ALE meta-analysis of neuroimaging studies. *Social Cognitive and Affective Neuroscience* 9 (9): 1395–1403.

Berken, J.A., Gracco, V.L., Chen, J.K. et al. (2015). Neural activation in speech production and reading aloud in native and non-native languages. *NeuroImage* 112: 208–217.

Berken, J.A., Gracco, V.L., and Klein, D. (2017). Early bilingualism, language attainment, and brain development. *Neuropsychologia* 98: 220–227.

Berwick, R.C., Friederici, A.D., Chomsky, N., and Bolhuis, J.J. (2013). Evolution, brain, and the nature of language. *Trends in cognitive sciences* 17 (2): 89–98.

Best, C.T. (1995). A direct realist view of cross-language speech perception. In: *Speech Perception and Linguistic Experience: Theoretical and Methodological Issues in Cross-Language Speech Research* (ed. W. Strange), 167–200. Timonium, MD: York Press.

Bialystok, E., Abutalebi, J., Bak, T.H. et al. (2016). Aging in two languages: implications for public health. *Ageing Research Reviews* 27: 56–60.

Bick, A.S., Goelman, G., and Frost, R. (2011). Hebrew brain vs. English brain: language modulates the way it is processed. *Journal of Cognitive Neuroscience* 23 (9): 2280–2290.

Binder, J.R., Desai, R.H., Graves, W.W., and Conant, L.L. (2009). Where is the semantic system? A critical review and meta-analysis of 120 functional neuroimaging studies. *Cerebral Cortex* 19: 2767–2796.

Binder, J.R., Frost, J.A., Hammeke, T.A. et al. (2000). Human temporal lobe activation by speech and nonspeech sounds. *Cerebral Cortex* 10 (5): 512–528.

Birdsong, D. and Vanhove, J. (2016). Age of second language acquisition: critical periods and social concerns. In: *Bilingualism Across the Lifespan: Factors Moderating Language Proficiency* (ed. E. Nicoladis and S. Montanari), 163–182. Berlin, Germany: De Gruyter Mouton/American Psychological Association.

Bley-Vroman, R. (1988). The fundamental character of foreign language learning. In: *Grammar and Second Language Teaching: A Book of Readings* (ed. W. Rutherford and M. Sharwood Smith), 19–30. Rowley, MA: Newbury House.

Bohn, O.S. and Flege, J.E. (1990). Interlingual identification and the role of foreign language experience in L2 vowel perception. *Applied PsychoLinguistics* 11 (3): 303–328.

Bozic, M. and Marslen-Wilson, W. (2010). Neurocognitive contexts for morphological complexity: dissociating inflection and derivation. *Lang & Ling Compass* 4 (11): 1063–1073.

Branzi, F.M., Della Rosa, P.A., Canini, M. et al. (2016). Language control in bilinguals: monitoring and response selection. *Cerebral Cortex* 26 (6): 2367–2380.

Callan, D.E., Jones, J.A., Callan, A.M., and Akahane-Yamada, R. (2004). Phonetic perceptual identification by native-and second-language speakers differentially activates brain regions involved with acoustic phonetic processing and those involved with articulatory–auditory/orosensory internal models. *NeuroImage* 22 (3): 1182–1194.

Callan, D.E., Tajima, K., Callan, A.M. et al. (2003). Learning-induced neural plasticity associated with improved identification performance after training of a difficult second-language phonetic contrast. *NeuroImage* 19 (1): 113–124.

Cappa, S.F. (2012). Imaging semantics and syntax. *NeuroImage* 61 (2): 427–431.

Carter, C.S., Botvinick, M.M., and Cohen, J.D. (1999). The contribution of the anterior cingulate cortex to executive processes in cognition. *Reviews in the Neurosciences* 10 (1): 49–58.

Chee, M.W., Hon, N., Lee, H.L., and Soon, C.S. (2001). Relative language proficiency modulates BOLD signal change when bilinguals perform semantic judgments. *NeuroImage* 13 (6): 1155–1163.

Chomsky, N. (1957). *Syntactic Structures*. The Hague, The Netherlands: Mouton.

Clahsen, H. and Felser, C. (2006a). Grammatical processing in language learners. *Applied PsychoLinguistics* 27 (1): 3–42.

Clahsen, H. and Felser, C. (2006b). How native-like is non-native language processing? *Trends in Cognitive Sciences* 10 (12): 564–570.

Consonni, M., Cafiero, R., Marin, D. et al. (2013). Neural convergence for language comprehension and grammatical class production in highly proficient bilinguals is independent of age of acquisition. *Cortex* 49 (5): 1252–1258.

Costa, A., Branzi, F.M., and Avila, C. (2016). Bilingualism: switching. In: *Neurobiology of Language* (ed. G. Hickok and S. Small), 419–430. Cambridge, MA: Academic Press.

Costa, A. and Sebastián-Gallés, N. (2014). How does the bilingual experience sculpt the brain? *Nature Reviews Neuroscience* 15 (5): 336.

Crinion, J., Turner, R., Grogan, A. et al. (2006). Language control in the bilingual brain. *Science* 312 (5779): 1537–1540.

de Bruin, A., Della Sala, S., and Bak, T.H. (2016). The effects of language use on lexical processing in bilinguals. *Language, Cognition and Neuroscience* 31 (8): 967–974.

DeKeyser, R.M. (2005). What makes learning second-language grammar difficult? A review of issues. *Language Learning* 55 (S1): 1–25.

DeKeyser, R.M. (2012). Age effects in second language learning. In: *Handbook of Second Language Acquisition* (ed. S. Gass and A. Mackey), 442–460. London, UK: Routledge.

Del Maschio, N., Fedeli, D., and Abutalebi, J. (2018). Bilingualism and Aging: Why Research Should Continue, *Linguistic Approaches to Bilingualism* (online print).

Démonet, J.F., Thierry, G., and Cardebat, D. (2005). Renewal of the neurophysiology of language: functional neuroimaging. *Physiological Reviews* 85 (1): 49–95.

Flege, J.E. (1988). Factors affecting degree of perceived foreign accent in English sentences. *The Journal of the Acoustical Society of America* 84 (1): 70–79.

Flege, J.E. (2002). Interactions between the native and second-language phonetic systems. In: *An Integrated View of Language Development: Papers in Honor of Henning Wode* (ed. P. Burmeister, T. Piske and A. Rohde), 217–244. Trier, Germany: Wissenschaftlicher Verlag.

Flege, J.E., Birdsong, D., Bialystok, E. et al. (2006). Degree of foreign accent in English sentences produced by Korean children and adults. *Journal of Phonetics* 34 (2): 153–175.

Flege, J.E. and MacKay, I. (2011). What accounts for 'age' effects on overall degree of foreign accent? In: *Achievements and Perspectives in the Acquisition of Second Language Speech: New Sounds*, vol. 2 (ed. M. Wrembel, M. Kul and K. Dziubalska-Kołaczyk), 65–82. Bern, Switzerland: Peter Lang.

Flege, J.E., Munro, M.J., and MacKay, I.R. (1995). Factors affecting strength of perceived foreign accent in a second language. *The Journal of the Acoustical Society of America* 97 (5): 3125–3134.

Flege, J.E., Yeni-Komshian, G.H., and Liu, S. (1999). Age constraints on second-language acquisition. *Journal of Memory and Language* 41 (1): 78–104.

Frenck-Mestre, C., Anton, J.L., Roth, M. et al. (2005). Articulation in early and late bilinguals' two languages: evidence from functional magnetic resonance imaging. *NeuroReport* 16 (7): 761–765.

Friederici, A.D. (2015). White matter pathways for speech and language processing. In: *The Human Auditory System: Fundamental Organization and Clinical Disorders*, vol. 129 (ed. G.G. Celesia and G. Hickok), 177–186. New York, NY: Elsevier.

Friederici, A.D. and Gierhan, S.M. (2013). The language network. *Current Opinion in Neurobiology* 23 (2): 250–254.

Garbin, G., Costa, A., Sanjuan, A. et al. (2011). Neural bases of language switching in high and early proficient bilinguals. *Brain and Language* 119 (3): 129–135.

Golestani, N. (2015). Neuroimaging of phonetic perception in bilinguals. *Bilingualism: Language and Cognition* 19 (4): 1–9.

Golestani, N., Alario, F.X., Meriaux, S. et al. (2006). Syntax production in bilinguals. *Neuropsychologia* 44 (7): 1029–1040.

Golestani, N. and Zatorre, R.J. (2004). Learning new sounds of speech: reallocation of neural substrates. *NeuroImage* 21 (2): 494–506.

Green, D.W. (1986). Control, activation, and resource: a framework and a model for the control of speech in bilinguals. *Brain and Language* 27 (2): 210–223.

Green, D.W. (1998). Mental control of the bilingual lexico-semantic system.

Bilingualism: Language and Cognition 1 (2): 67–81.

Green, D.W. (2003). The neural basis of the lexicon and the grammar in L2 acquisition. In: *The Interface Between Syntax and the Lexicon in Second Language Acquisition* (ed. R. van Hout, A. Hulk, F. Kuiken and R. Towell), 197–218. Amsterdam, The Netherlands: John Benjamins.

Grosjean, F. and Li, P. (2013). Bilingualism: a short introduction. In: *The Psycholinguistics of Biblingualism* (ed. F. Grosjean and P. Li), 5–25. Malden, MA: Wiley-Blackwell.

Guo, T., Liu, H., Misra, M., and Kroll, J.F. (2011). Local and global inhibition in bilingual word production: fMRI evidence from Chinese–English bilinguals. *NeuroImage* 56 (4): 2300–2309.

Hernandez, A.E. (2009). Language switching in the bilingual brain: What's next? *Brain and Language* 109 (2): 133–140.

Hernandez, A.E. and Li, P. (2007). Age of acquisition: its neural and computational mechanisms. *Psychological Bulletin* 133 (4): 638–650.

Hervais-Adelman, A.G., Moser-Mercer, B., and Golestani, N. (2011). Executive control of language in the bilingual brain: integrating the evidence from neuroimaging to neuropsychology. *Frontiers in Psychology* 2: 234.

Hickok, G. and Poeppel, D. (2004). Dorsal and ventral streams: a framework for understanding aspects of the functional anatomy of language. *Cognition* 92 (1): 67–99.

Hickok, G. and Poeppel, D. (2007). The cortical organization of speech processing. *Nature Reviews Neuroscience* 8 (5): 393–402.

Higby, E., Kim, J., and Obler, L.K. (2013). Multilingualism and the brain. *Annual Review of Applied Linguistics* 33: 68–101.

Illes, J., Francis, W.S., Desmond, J.E. et al. (1999). Convergent cortical representation of semantic processing in bilinguals. *Brain and Language* 70 (3): 347–363.

Indefrey, P. (2006). A meta-analysis of hemodynamic studies on first and second language processing: which suggested differences can we trust and what do they mean? *Language Learning* 56 (s1): 279–304.

Ivanova, I. and Costa, A. (2008). Does bilingualism hamper lexical access in speech production? *Acta Psychologica* 127 (2): 277–288.

Iverson, P., Kuhl, P.K., Akahane-Yamada, R. et al. (2003). A perceptual interference account of acquisition difficulties for non-native phonemes. *Cognition* 87 (1): 47–57.

Jefferies, E. (2013). The neural basis of semantic cognition: converging evidence from neuropsychology, neuroimaging and TMS. *Cortex* 49 (3): 611–625.

Jeong, H., Sugiura, M., Sassa, Y. et al. (2007). Effect of syntactic similarity on cortical activation during second language processing: a comparison of English and Japanese among native Korean trilinguals. *Human Brain Mapping* 28 (3): 194–204.

Johnson, J.S. and Newport, E.L. (1989). Critical period effects in second language learning: the influence of maturational state on the acquisition of English as a second language. *Cognitive Psychology* 21 (1): 60–99.

Kotz, S.A. (2009). A critical review of ERP and fMRI evidence on L2 syntactic processing. *Brain and Language* 109 (2): 68–74.

Kroll, J.F., Bobb, S.C., Misra, M., and Guo, T. (2008). Language selection in bilingual speech: evidence for inhibitory processes. *Acta Psychologica* 128 (3): 416–430.

Kuhl, P.K. (2000). A new view of language acquisition. *Proceedings of the National Academy of Sciences* 97 (22): 11850–11857.

Lecumberri, M.L.G., Cooke, M., and Cutler, A. (2010). Non-native speech perception in adverse conditions: a review. *Speech Communication* 52 (11): 864–886.

Lehtonen, M., Vorobyev, V., Soveri, A. et al. (2009). Language-specific activations in the brain: evidence from inflectional processing in bilinguals. *Journal of Neurolinguistics* 22 (5): 495–513.

Lenneberg, E.H. (1967). *Biological Foundations of Language*. New York, NY: Wiley.

Liu, H. and Cao, F. (2016). L1 and L2 processing in the bilingual brain: a meta-analysis of neuroimaging studies. *Brain and Language* 159: 60–73.

Luk, G. and Bialystok, E. (2013). Bilingualism is not a categorical variable: interaction between language proficiency and usage. *Journal of Cognitive Psychology* 25 (5): 605–621.

Luk, G., Green, D.W., Abutalebi, J., and Grady, C. (2012). Cognitive control for language switching in bilinguals: a quantitative meta-analysis of functional neuroimaging studies. *Language & Cognitive Processes* 27 (10): 1479–1488.

Marangolo, P., Piras, F., Galati, G., and Burani, C. (2006). Functional anatomy of derivational morphology. *Cortex* 42 (8): 1093–1106.

Marian, V., Bartolotti, J., Rochanavibhata, S. et al. (2017). Bilingual cortical control of between- and within-language competition. *Scientific Reports* 7 (1): 11763.

Marian, V., Shildkrot, Y., Blumenfeld, H.K. et al. (2007). Cortical activation during word processing in late bilinguals: similarities and differences as revealed by functional magnetic resonance imaging. *Journal of Clinical and Experimental Neuropsychology* 29 (3): 247–265.

Meinzer, M., Lahiri, A., Flaisch, T. et al. (2009). Opaque for the reader but transparent for the brain: neural signatures of morphological complexity. *Neuropsychologia* 47 (8): 1964–1971.

Mestres-Missé, A., Camara, E., Rodriguez-Fornells, A. et al. (2008). Functional neuroanatomy of meaning acquisition from context. *Journal of Cognitive Neuroscience* 20 (12): 2153–2166.

Michael, E.B. and Gollan, T.H. (2005). Being and becoming bilingual. In: *Handbook of Bilingualism: Psycholinguistic Approaches* (ed. J.F. Kroll and A.M.B. de Groot), 389–407. New York, NY: Oxford University Press.

Miyawaki, K., Jenkins, J.J., Strange, W. et al. (1975). An effect of linguistic experience: the discrimination of [r] and [l] by native speakers of Japanese and English. *Perception & Psychophysics* 18 (5): 331–340.

Moser, D., Fridriksson, J., Bonilha, L. et al. (2009). Neural recruitment for the production of native and novel speech sounds. *NeuroImage* 46 (2): 549–557.

Mouthon, M., Annoni, J.M., and Khatebc, A. (2013). The bilingual brain. *Swiss Archives of Neurology and Psychiatry* 64 (8): 266–273.

Moyer, A. (1999). Ultimate attainment in L2 phonology. *Studies in Second Language Acquisition* 21 (1): 81–108.

Newport, E.L. (1990). Maturational constraints on language learning. *Cognitive Science* 14 (1): 11–28.

Oyama, S. (1976). A sensitive period for the acquisition of a nonnative phonological system. *Journal of Psycholinguistic Research* 5 (3): 261–283.

Paap, K.R. and Greenberg, Z.I. (2013). There is no coherent evidence for a bilingual advantage in executive processing. *Cognitive Psychology* 66 (2): 232–258.

Pallier, C., Bosch, L., and Sebastián-Gallés, N. (1997). A limit on behavioral plasticity in speech perception. *Cognition* 64 (3): 9–17.

Parker-Jones, ō., Green, D.W., Grogan, A. et al. (2012). Where, when and why brain activation differs for bilinguals and monolinguals during picture naming and reading aloud. *Cerebral Cortex* 22 (4): 892–902.

Penfield, W. and Roberts, L. (1959). *Speech and Brain Mechanisms*. Princeton, NJ: Princeton University Press.

Perani, D., Abutalebi, J., Paulesu, E. et al. (2003). The role of age of acquisition and language usage in early, high-proficient bilinguals: an fMRI study during verbal fluency. *Human Brain Mapping* 19 (3): 170–182.

Perani, D., Paulesu, E., Galles, N.S. et al. (1998). The bilingual brain. Proficiency and age of acquisition of the second language. *Brain* 121 (10): 1841–1852.

Pinker, S. and Prince, A. (1988). On language and connectionism: analysis of a parallel distributed processing model of language acquisition. *Cognition* 28 (1): 73–193.

Pinker, S. and Ullman, M.T. (2002). The past and future of the past tense. *Trends in Cognitive Sciences* 6 (11): 456–463.

Piske, T., MacKay, I.R., and Flege, J.E. (2001). Factors affecting degree of foreign accent in an L2: a review. *Journal of Phonetics* 29 (2): 191–215.

Pliatsikas, C., DeLuca, V., Moschopoulou, E., and Saddy, J.D. (2017). Immersive bilingualism reshapes the core of the brain. *Brain Structure and Function* 222 (4): 1785–1795.

Pliatsikas, C., Johnstone, T., and Marinis, T. (2014a). Grey matter volume in the cerebellum is related to the processing of grammatical rules in a second language: a structural voxel-based morphometry study. *The Cerebellum* 13 (1): 55–63.

Pliatsikas, C., Johnstone, T., and Marinis, T. (2014b). fMRI evidence for the involvement of the procedural memory system in morphological processing of a second language. *PLoS One* 9 (5): e97298.

Pliatsikas, C. and Luk, G. (2016). Executive control in bilinguals: a concise review on fMRI studies. *Bilingualism: Language and Cognition* 19 (4): 699–705.

Prehn, K., Taud, B., Reifegerste, J. et al. (2017). Neural correlates of grammatical inflection in older native and second-language speakers. *Bilingualism: Language and Cognition* 21 (1): 1–12.

Ripollés, P., Marco-Pallarés, J., Hielscher, U. et al. (2014). The role of reward in word learning and its implications for language acquisition. *Current Biology* 24 (21): 2606–2611.

Rosselli, M., Ardila, A., Araujo, K. et al. (2000). Verbal fluency and repetition skills in healthy older Spanish-English bilinguals. *Applied Neuropsychology* 7 (1): 17–24.

Rüschemeyer, S.A., Fiebach, C.J., Kempe, V., and Friederici, A.D. (2005). Processing lexical semantic and syntactic information in first and second language: fMRI evidence from German and Russian. *Human Brain Mapping* 25 (2): 266–286.

Saito, K. (2015). The role of age of acquisition in late second language oral proficiency attainment. *Studies in Second Language Acquisition* 37 (4): 713–743.

Sakai, K.L., Miura, K., Narafu, N., and Muraishi, Y. (2004). Correlated functional changes of the prefrontal cortex in twins induced by classroom education of second language. *Cerebral Cortex* 14 (11): 1233–1239.

Sammler, D., Grosbras, M.H., Anwander, A. et al. (2015). Dorsal and ventral pathways for prosody. *Current Biology* 25 (23): 3079–3085.

Saur, D., Kreher, B.W., Schnell, S. et al. (2008). Ventral and dorsal pathways for language. *Proceedings of the National Academy of Sciences* 105 (46): 18035–18040.

Scoresby-Jackson, R.E. (1867). Case of aphasia with right hemiplegia. *Edinburgh Medical Journal* 12 (8): 696–706.

Sebastian, R., Laird, A.R., and Kiran, S. (2011). Meta-analysis of the neural representation of first language and second language. *Applied PsychoLinguistics* 32 (4): 799–819.

Simmonds, A.J., Wise, R.J., and Leech, R. (2011). Two tongues, one brain: imaging bilingual speech production. *Frontiers in Psychology* 2: 166.

Steinhauer, K. (2014). Event-related potentials (ERPs) in second language research: a brief introduction to the technique, a selected review, and an invitation to reconsider critical periods in L2. *Applied Linguistics* 35 (4): 393–417.

Sugiura, L., Ojima, S., Matsuba-Kurita, H. et al. (2015). Effects of sex and proficiency in second language processing as revealed by a large-scale fNIRS study of school-aged children. *Human Brain Mapping* 36 (10): 3890–3911.

Suh, S., Yoon, H.W., Lee, S. et al. (2007). Effects of syntactic complexity in L1 and L2: an fMRI study of Korean–English bilinguals. *Brain Research* 1136: 178–189.

Tatsuno, Y. and Sakai, K.L. (2005). Language-related activations in the left prefrontal regions are differentially modulated by age, proficiency, and task demands. *The Journal of Neuroscience* 25 (7): 1637–1644.

Thompson, I. (1991). Foreign accents revisited: the English pronunciation of Russian immigrants. *Language Learning* 41 (2): 177–204.

Tyler, L.K., Stamatakis, E.A., Post, B. et al. (2005). Temporal and frontal systems in speech comprehension: an fMRI study of past tense processing. *Neuropsychologia* 43 (13): 1963–1974.

Ullman, M.T. (2001). A neurocognitive perspective on language: the declarative/procedural model. *Nature Reviews Neuroscience* 2 (10): 717–726.

Ullman, M.T. (2004). Contributions of memory circuits to language: the declarative/procedural model. *Cognition* 92 (1): 231–270.

Ullman, M.T. (2016). The declarative/procedural model: a neurobiological model of language learning, knowledge, and use. In: *Neurobiology of Language* (ed. G. Hickok and S.L. Small), 953–968. San Diego, CA: Elsevier.

Valian, V. (2015). Bilingualism and cognition. *Bilingualism: Language and Cognition* 18 (01): 3–24.

Vannest, J., Polk, T.A., and Lewis, R.L. (2005). Dual-route processing of complex words: new fMRI evidence from derivational suffixation. *Cognitive, Affective, & Behavioral Neuroscience* 5 (1): 67–76.

Wahl, M., Marzinzik, F., Friederici, A.D. et al. (2008). The human thalamus processes syntactic and semantic language violations. *Neuron* 59 (5): 695–707.

Wang, Y., Xue, G., Chen, C. et al. (2007). Neural bases of asymmetric language switching in second-language learners: an ER-fMRI study. *NeuroImage* 35 (2): 862–870.

Wartenburger, I., Heekeren, H.R., Abutalebi, J. et al. (2003). Early setting of grammatical processing in the bilingual brain. *Neuron* 37 (1): 159–170.

Weber, K., Luther, L., Indefrey, P., and Hagoort, P. (2016). Overlap and differences in brain networks underlying the processing of complex sentence structures in second language users compared with native speakers. *Brain Connectivity* 6 (4): 345–355.

Werker, J.F. and Tees, R.C. (2005). Speech perception as a window for understanding plasticity and commitment in language systems of the brain. *Developmental Psychobiology* 46 (3): 233–251.

Yeung, N. (2013). Conflict monitoring and cognitive control. In: *The Oxford handbook of cognitive neuroscience*, vol. 2 (ed. K.N. Ochsner and S. Kosslyn), 275–299). The Cutting Edges. Oxford, UK/New York, NY: Oxford University Press.

Zhang, Y., Kuhl, P.K., Imada, T. et al. (2005). Effects of language experience: neural commitment to language-specific auditory patterns. *NeuroImage* 26 (3): 703–720.

10   Bilingual Word Production

JANA KLAUS AND HERBERT SCHRIEFERS

1.   Introduction

Language production is a complex cognitive process which requires the selection of an appropriate lexical entry and its phonological properties in order to articulate a to-be-expressed concept (e.g. Levelt et al. 1999; Roelofs 1992). Despite this enormous computational effort, humans produce words, ideally conjoined to conceptually, syntactically, grammatically, and phonologically correct sentences, in a fairly automatic way, at a high speed, and without unreasonable amounts of errors. On top of this, about half of the world is bilingual (Bialystok et al. 2012; Grosjean 2010), meaning that next to their native language, they use one (or more) languages on a more or less regular basis. Intuitively, this increases the cognitive demands imposed during speaking exponentially. However, bilinguals and multilinguals master this task remarkably well: language intrusions happen rarely (Poulisse 2000; Poulisse and Bongaerts 1994), and bilinguals and multilinguals are able to switch between languages without much effort. Nevertheless, how two languages work together on the behavioural, neurophysiological, and hemodynamic level has not been fully understood.

Before turning to the neuroscientific aspect of how two languages are represented in a speaker's brain, we should point out that even on a behavioural level, it is not clear to what extent a speaker's two languages operate separately from each other (or not). While it is assumed that the conceptual system is shared by both languages (e.g. Costa 2004; de Bot 1992), there is still debate about whether lexical and phonological features work in a distinct or combined fashion. In other words, the question of whether lexical selection and subsequent processes are target language-specific (i.e. both languages are activated, but the non-target language does not compete for selection) or target language non-specific (i.e. both languages compete for selection) in bilinguals has not been satisfactorily settled yet. The majority of behavioural studies has provided evidence for the hypothesis that lexical entries from both languages compete for selection, a problem solved by active inhibition of the language which is not to be used in the present context (Green 1998; Hermans et al. 1998; Jacobs et al. 2016; Kroll et al. 2008; Misra et al. 2012;

The Handbook of the Neuroscience of Multilingualism, First Edition. Edited by John W. Schwieter.
© 2019 John Wiley & Sons Ltd. Published 2019 by John Wiley & Sons Ltd.

Spalek et al. 2014). However, other studies also identified situations in which no selection for competition occurred, arguing for target language-specific lexical selection (Colomé 2001; Costa et al. 1999; Costa and Caramazza 1999). More recently, lexical selection has been discussed as a dynamic process which can act both target language-specific and non-specific (e.g. Boukadi et al. 2015; Costa et al. 2003; Hermans et al. 2011; Kroll et al. 2006). The constant improvement of methodologies to investigate the neural substrates underlying successful bilingual speech production has helped to provide additional insights into its mechanisms. In this chapter, we will review studies that investigated the functional and neuroanatomical representations of first and second languages during single-word production in healthy bilingual speakers. We will emphasize three related aspects: (i) Are the languages of bilinguals underpinned by common or distinct brain regions during production? (ii) What are the neurophysiological signatures of timing aspects of bilingual word production? and (iii) To what extent are potential dissociations modulated by moderating factors such as age of acquisition, proficiency, and immersion of the L2?

2. Bilingual Word Production: Common or Distinct Neural Signatures?

In the last two decades, a substantial number of studies investigated to what extent a speaker's first and second languages are represented by the same neural substrates. The majority of these studies have provided evidence for the single-network hypothesis (Abutalebi and Green 2007), which has been continuously updated in recent years to account for new findings (Abutalebi and Green 2016; Green and Abutalebi 2013). At its core, this framework assumes largely shared neural representations of the first language (L1) and second language (L2). Specifically, it purports that both cortical and evolutionarily older subcortical structures are involved in language control and lexical selection. Further, speaking in any one language creates a competition process at both the cortical and the subcortical levels which is resolved by inhibition processes. Critically, in the case of bilinguals, managing separate linguistic systems (i.e. with respect to syntax, phonology, and prosody) requires an adaptation process, which results in similar, but nevertheless distinct processing of L1 and L2. In other words, the theory suggests that bilingual speakers (i) process their L1 differently from their L2, and (ii) also process their L1 differently compared with purely monolingual speakers. In this section, we will provide an overview of studies that look at neural activations during bilingual word production. This has been addressed both in single-language and mixed-language contexts, which we will present in the two following subsections. We will mainly focus on within-speaker comparisons which allow us to evaluate directly to what extent native production differs from non-native production.

2.1. *Production in a Single-Language Context*

One of the first studies that investigated hemodynamic differences between L1 and L2 word production was conducted by Klein et al. (1995). In their positron emission tomography (PET) study, four English-French bilinguals were asked to generate a rhyme word or a synonym in response to an auditorily presented word, either in their L1 or their L2. Behaviourally, participants were slower and less accurate during L2 synonym generation, while there were no differences in the rhyme word generation task. On the hemodynamic level, higher activation was observed in left inferior frontal cortex (Brodmann areas [BAs] 45 and 47) and dorsolateral prefrontal cortex (BAs 8, 9, and 46) compared to a baseline task (word repetition). However, no differences were found between L1 and L2 production, suggesting that word generation is subserved by identical neural substrates in L1 and L2. In a similar study, Klein et al. (1999) asked seven Mandarin-English bilinguals to generate nouns and verbs in response to an auditory cue, either in their L1 or L2. On the behavioural level, generating words in L2 took longer and resulted in more naming errors. Again, however, this processing deficit was not paralleled in the hemodynamic response: both L1 and L2 naming caused higher activity in the left inferior cortex compared to a baseline task, but there were no significant differences between L1 and L2 naming. Thus, although participants were late learners of L2, there was no evidence for distinct neuronal signatures, in line with the single-network hypothesis.

Chee et al. (1999) compared 15 early and 9 late Chinese-English bilinguals in a functional magnetic resonance imaging (fMRI) study using a covert word completion task. Participants were visually presented with either the beginning or the end of a word and instructed to produce the full word (e.g. 'cou' to generate a word like 'couple' or 'ter' to generate a word like 'water'), or they were shown a single Mandarin character and instructed to generate a compound. Compared to fixation as the control task, word generation increased activity in prefrontal, temporal, and parietal regions as well as the supplementary motor area. However, no significant differences were found between L1 and L2 word generation, or between early and late bilinguals, again suggesting that L1 and L2 word retrieval recruit the same neural regions.

De Bleser et al. (2003), in a PET study, tested Flemish-French bilinguals in a covert picture-naming task investigating the production of cognates. In bilingual speakers, cognates (i.e. words which have a similar form in the two languages) are typically named faster than non-cognates (Costa et al. 2000, 2005). Behaviourally (in an overt production task prior to the scanning session), this effect was indeed obtained: naming in L2 was overall slower compared to L1, but naming non-cognates in L2 additionally slowed naming latencies compared with cognates. With respect to the hemodynamic response, activation was comparable between L1 cognates, L1 non-cognates, and non-cognates of the much later acquired L2. Only the presumably most difficult condition (i.e. L2 non-cognates) elicited higher activation in left inferior frontal and temporoparietal regions (BAs 44, 47, and 20), again suggesting a role of these region in effortful lexical retrieval during L2 production as reported by Hernandez et al. (2000, 2001).

Perani et al. (2003) tested 11 highly proficient Spanish-Catalan bilinguals in a phonemic verbal fluency task. In the experiment, participants were asked to covertly generate as many words as possible beginning with a given letter in one of the two languages. Note that all had acquired their L2 (either Catalan or Spanish) at the age of three and showed no differences in proficiency. The fMRI results, however, did show a dissociation between the L1 and the L2 which was acquired in early childhood: Generating words in a speaker's L2 resulted in an increased neural response compared to L1. Interestingly, this pattern differed depending on whether speakers were

Catalan-Spanish or Spanish-Catalan speakers. While both groups showed higher activation in the left inferior and middle frontal gyrus and in the insula, Catalan-born speakers recruited additional resources in the left premotor cortex, left inferior parietal lobule, left caudate nucleus, and right inferior frontal gyrus. Importantly, the Catalan-born group was exposed less to their L2, so increases in activation compared to the Spanish-born group were interpreted as reflecting more effortful lexical processing. Overall, this study provides evidence that even with an early age of acquisition, producing words in L2 requires more resources, which is additionally modulated by exposure to the L2.

Extending the investigations to trilingual speakers, Vingerhoets et al. (2003) tested 12 native Dutch speakers with varying degrees of proficiency in their L2 and L3 (French and English) in a covert picture naming task and a phonemic verbal fluency task. Behavioural performance prior to the fMRI session indicated that fluency scores differed between all languages, and picture naming performance (measured as percent correct) was best for the L1, but comparable between the L2 and the L3. Imaging during the fluency task showed activation of left frontal and medial frontal/cingulate areas as well as of the left superior parietal lobule and a small right (anterior) temporal-(inferior) frontal region for all languages. When the task was carried out in the L2 and L3, respectively, an additional activation of left posterior temporal regions was found (BA 21). Note that Perani et al. (2003) had not obtained increased posterior temporal activation in a comparable task. However, their participants were highly proficient and immersed in both their L1 and L2, potentially resulting in a more automated (i.e. less effortful) use of the non-native language. In the picture naming task, all languages recruited medial/superior frontal and occipital (BAs 18 and 19) regions bilaterally. Covert naming in L2 and L3 additionally showed activation in left frontal superior parietal and temporal-occipital areas. When compared across languages, the right cuneate area (BA 19) was significantly more activated during L1 naming, whereas L2 and L3 showed additional predominantly left hemispheric medial frontal and inferior lateral frontal activation. Vingerhoets et al. (2003) concluded that speech production in a foreign language relies on largely overlapping areas, but that a proficiency deficit necessitates the recruitment of additional neural resources, predominantly in left frontal and posterior temporal regions. These findings, again, converge with those reported in previous studies attributing a supporting role of frontal and temporal areas to more effortful word production.

Liu et al. (2010) investigated neural differences during blocked L1 and L2 picture-naming in 24 Chinese-English speakers. Compared with L1 naming, L2 naming resulted in higher error rates and elicited higher activation in left inferior frontal, precentral, and lingual gyri, the left cuneus, and supplementary motor areas, putamen, globus pallidus, caudate nucleus and cerebellum bilaterally. In line with previous findings, this increased activation across widespread areas was attributed to the recruitment of additional neural resources during the less-automatic L2 production process, specifically with respect to lexical retrieval, articulatory processing, and cognitive control.

Another fMRI study on multilingual speakers was conducted by Videsott et al. (2010). Twenty native speakers of Ladin, a language spoken by a small community in South Tyrol, who were also proficient in Italian (L2), German (L3), and English (L4), were tested in an overt picture-naming task that required the production of Ladin, Italian, and English nouns in separate blocks. Pre-experimental tests revealed that English was spoken with the lowest proficiency, which was confirmed by the highest error rates in this language compared to Ladin and Italian. Compared with L1 production, English picture-naming resulted in higher activation in the left inferior frontal gyrus (BAs 6 and 44) and the cerebellum; compared with L2 production, only the cerebellum showed a stronger signal during English naming. Furthermore, composite proficiency scores for English and Italian were correlated with the neural response in the right dorsolateral prefrontal cortex (BA 45), such that higher proficiency was associated with higher activation in this region. This is at odds with other findings reporting lower cortical activity with increasing proficiency (Abutalebi and Green 2007). However, in line with the results reported by Vingerhoets et al. (2003) on trilingual speakers, this study found an important role of the cerebellum in low-proficiency word production. Recall that Vingerhoets et al. (2003) only found increased activity in frontal and temporal regions during non-native word generation in trilingual speakers. Videsott et al. (2010) thus show that, at relatively low proficiency and in the presence of three competitor languages, the cerebellum may play a coordinating role for successful production.

Parker Jones et al. (2012) investigated speech production in 31 L2 speakers of English using a variety of production tasks. Depending on the visual display, participants, who had different first languages (Greek or European languages with a Latin-based script), were required to name objects, read out words, or respond '1, 2, 3' to a string of non-objects or Greek symbols, either in their L2 (English), or for the Greek participants, also in their L1. Behaviourally, the bilinguals performed equally well in both languages and did not differ from a group of 36 matched monolingual English speakers. The hemodynamic response, however, did show significant differences between the monolingual and bilingual group. During picture naming and word reading, bilinguals showed higher activation than monolinguals in the left central sulcus, the planum temporale, superior temporal gyrus, inferior frontal gyrus and anterior insula. Interestingly, this increase was found even when bilingual participants responded in their L1. Furthermore, when the bilinguals were divided into two groups depending on how many languages they spoke overall (i.e. two vs. at least three), it was found that those who spoke three or more languages showed higher activation in the planum temporale, pars triangularis, and insula. The authors concluded that areas related to more effortful monolingual production underlie bilingual word production. For instance, effects of lexical frequency, which affects production performance in monolinguals, have been localized in the pars triangularis (Graves et al. 2007). Speaking several languages, similarly, is considered to make lexical selection more difficult, recruiting resources from the same region.

2.2.   *Production in a Mixed-Language Context*

Hernandez et al. (2000) conducted an fMRI study in which they tested six early highly proficient Spanish-English bilinguals in a cued switching task. Participants were asked to name pictures in response to a printed naming instruction ('say' or 'diga' on each trial). Both L1 and L2 naming showed comparable activity in the dorsolateral prefrontal cortex (BA 9 and 46), the supramarginal gyrus (BA 40), inferior frontal gyrus (BAs 44 and 45), and superior temporal gyrus (BA 22). However, when comparing activity between blocks that required naming in only one language to blocks in which participants had to switch constantly between the two languages, the dorsolateral prefrontal cortex was activated more in the latter. Overall, these findings provided evidence for the involvement of the left dorsolateral prefrontal cortex in executive functioning. In a similar study, Hernandez et al. (2001) tested six early Spanish-English bilinguals who were more dominant in their L2 (English) than in their L1. The results replicated those from Hernandez et al. (2000), such that activation patterns in left frontal regions were comparable between languages in the blocked naming condition, and the dorsolateral prefrontal cortex showed increased activity in the mixed naming condition. This again supports the notion that producing words in one's L1 and L2 recruits similar neural regions (in single-language contexts, at least), while the dorsolateral prefrontal cortex serves as a control structure in situations where rapid switches between languages are required.

Rodriguez-Fornells et al. (2005) employed a different approach to investigate word production in bilinguals. In a tacit picture-naming task to measure phonological competition in Spanish-German bilinguals, participants were asked to give a speeded button response to a picture. Specifically, a button press was required if the name of a given object (either in L1 or L2, depending on block) started with a consonant, but no response was required if it started with a vowel. To investigate cross-language activation, the objects were selected such that for half of the trials, both the L1 and the L2 name would require the same response (e.g. pressing a button in response to the picture of a syringe, which is 'jeringuilla' in Spanish and 'Spritze' in German, as opposed to pliers, which translates to 'alicates' in Spanish and 'Zange' in German). Eleven early Spanish-German bilinguals who at the time of testing reported to be more fluent in their L2 carried out this task in an fMRI session. Compared with a German monolingual control group, bilinguals were slower both when naming in their L1 and L2. Furthermore, reaction times were faster when both the L1 target word and the L2 translation required the same response, compared with a condition in which the target word began with a vowel, but the translation with a consonant, or vice versa. On the hemodynamic level, this difference was manifested in higher activity when the onset of the target word and the translation were incongruent (i.e. the target word started with a vowel but the translation with a consonant, or vice versa) in left frontal regions (BAs 9 and 46) and the supplementary motor area (BA 6), as well as the anterior cingulate cortex (BAs 24 and 32). These regions were thus interpreted as playing a crucial role in language selection. Note that the finding of higher activity in frontal regions coincides with increased activity in dorsolateral prefrontal cortex in language switching (Hernandez et al. 2000, 2001). This provides evidence that greater involvement of the dorsolateral prefrontal cortex when language selection is difficult can be demonstrated with different language-switching tasks.

Continuing investigations on the hemodynamics of language switching, Abutalebi et al. (2008) conducted an fMRI study in which they contrasted naming in L1 and L2 in both single-language and mixed-language contexts. Twelve German-French bilinguals completed three tasks, amongst which there was an object naming task that required switching between L1 and L2. In this condition, no latency differences were found between L1 and L2 naming, but error rates were higher for L2 naming. Comparing the hemodynamic response between L1 and L2 naming in this mixed-language context revealed higher activation during L2 naming predominantly in the left cingulate cortex, but also left inferior frontal gyrus (BAs 44, 45, and 47), middle frontal gyrus (BAs 10 and 46), precentral gyrus, right dorsal frontal gyrus (BA 9), right anterior cingulate cortex and putamen, and the caudate nucleus bilaterally. This increased activity was interpreted as reflecting higher processing demands during lexical selection in the non-dominant language and additionally provided further evidence for the involvement of frontal, but also subcortical regions during L2 production.

Addressing inhibition mechanisms in bilingual production, Guo et al. (2011) examined inhibitory processes during L1 and L2 production in 24 Chinese-English bilinguals. Specifically, the authors investigated how global inhibition (i.e. complete suppression of the non-target language) and local inhibition (i.e. restricted suppression of a specific set of lexical representations) are manifested in bilinguals. Participants first were asked to name pictures solely in their L1 or L2, and afterwards in a mixed block which required continuous switching between languages. In a purely behavioural session following the fMRI session the authors found that globally (i.e. when L1 and L2 naming occurred in separate blocks), participants were slower and less accurate when they named pictures in their L2 compared with their L1. However, whether participants had started with their L1 or L2 did not affect naming performance. As for the local inhibition effects, which were operationalized by comparing performance between blocked and mixed naming, L1 mixed naming was slower and elicited more errors than L1 blocked naming, while L2 mixed naming was faster than L2 blocked naming. In the fMRI study, an increased activity during L1 naming following L2 naming was found in left dorsolateral prefrontal cortex, left temporal and parietal regions, and right postcentral gyrus, which were interpreted in terms of interference suppression and enhanced articulatory and visual control. By contrast, L2 naming following L1 naming only increased activity in the right cuneus and precuneus, which was ascribed to participants' awareness of picture presentation, given that these regions are linked to visual processing. Relative to blocked naming, mixed naming activated frontal regions including the dorsal anterior cingulate gyri bilaterally, supplementary motor area, precuneus, and pre- and postcentral gyri. Importantly, no differences were found between L1 and L2 naming in the mixed compared to the blocked naming condition. Especially the dorsal anterior cingulate cortex, precuneus, and supplementary motor area were interpreted as exerting control, inhibition, and selection functions during continuous language switching, which ascribes an important role of frontal and parietal regions in bilingual language control.

Finally, Abutalebi et al. (2013) reported evidence for the involvement of subcortical structures in multilingual word production. Fourteen native speakers of German who had acquired their L2 (Italian) at kindergarten age and their L3 (English) at school were tested in a mixed naming task. The authors found similar activation for L1, L2, and L3 naming, with increasingly higher activation of the pars opercularis and anterior cingulate cortex when naming in the later-acquired language. Additionally, L3 naming increased activation in the left putamen. Subsequent voxel-based morphometry analysis showed that compared with a matched group of monolinguals, the trilingual speakers displayed increased grey matter density in the left putamen. This study thus provided striking evidence for the role of the left putamen in multilinguals, which has been interpreted as a control region for articulation in a less proficient language. In accordance with this finding, Burgaleta et al. (2016) recently demonstrated expanded subcortical structures, specifically the bilateral putamen and thalamus, left globus pallidus, and right caudate nucleus, in bilingual speakers (see also Pliatsikas et al. 2017, for complementary findings). This finding supports the notion that especially subcortical areas are susceptible to anatomical changes in response to bilingualism (but see Mechelli et al. 2004, for evidence for increased grey matter density in the left inferior parietal cortex in bilinguals).

In summary, findings from PET and fMRI studies have provided ample evidence that word production in L1 and L2 is largely subserved by the same neural structures, namely the well-established frontotemporal language network with contributions from superior parietal regions and the supplementary motor area, both in single- and mixed-language contexts. Moreover, subcortical structures have been related to production beyond the native language, which, next to control regions like the dorsolateral prefrontal cortex and the anterior cingulate cortex, may play a crucial role in language selection in multilinguals in situations of language switching. Critically, comparable activation for L1 and L2 naming, as well as higher activation during L2 naming has been reported. This dissociation can partly be explained by a difference in L2 proficiency and immersion levels of the tested speakers. Typically, higher proficiency and immersion result in more native-like cortical signatures (see Section 4), so discrepancies between studies may have been caused by examining different study populations (i.e. early vs. late bilinguals). A most interesting endeavour for future research would be to directly compare otherwise 'matched' individuals from different proficiency and immersion spectra to get a more detailed picture of how these factors contribute to different cortical responses during production.

Critically, with the current state of affairs, most studies differ on too many aspects to allow for solid direct comparisons, thus hindering further theoretical advances which would allow to account for discrepancies between studies. These aspects concern, amongst others, sample size and statistical power, types of populations investigated, and proficiency measures used. It would be very useful to have at least some 'standardization' of these aspects in future research.

3. The Neurophysiology of Timing Aspects of Bilingual Word Production

Bilingualism often comes at a cost in terms of speech production performance. That is, bilinguals usually name pictures more slowly in their L2 than in their L1 (for an overview, see Hanulová et al. 2011), but on top of this, they also often name pictures more slowly in their L1 (Ivanova and Costa 2008; Sadat et al. 2012), experience more tip-of-the-tongue states (Gollan and Acenas 2004), and score lower on verbal fluency tasks compared with monolingual speakers (Gollan et al. 2002; Portocarrero et al. 2007). While this may in part be explained by a greater cognitive control demand or linguistic intrusions from the L2 on the L1 (Costa and Sebastián-Gallés 2014), the weaker links hypothesis (Gollan et al. 2005, 2008) has addressed this phenomenon in terms of relative frequency. Contrary to monolingual speakers, bilinguals can refer to a to-be-expressed concept with two words instead of one, decreasing the frequency of the individual words. Put differently, the links between semantics and phonology in L1 and L2 are weaker, rendering this 'bilingual disadvantage' ultimately the result of a functional frequency effect (see also Poulisse and Bongaerts 1994).

One way of testing this hypothesis experimentally is by comparing lexical frequency effects in monolingual and bilingual speakers. In L1 production, high-frequency words are produced faster than low-frequency words (Oldfield and Wingfield 1965; Wingfield 1968). In a behavioural experiment, Gollan et al. (2008) investigated whether this L1 finding translates into L2 production and whether bilinguals differ from monolinguals. Fifty-seven Spanish-English bilinguals who were more dominant in their L2 (English) produced high- and low-frequency words in response to pictures either in their L1 or their L2, or in the language that first came to mind. Compared to matched English-speaking monolinguals, bilinguals named pictures more slowly in their L2, but also showed a larger frequency effect. Additionally, comparing bilinguals' naming latencies in L1 and L2 showed that the frequency effect was larger for the L1, which was the non-dominant language. The authors concluded that a decrease in use (i.e. the non-dominance of the L1) weakens the activation of the lexical entries of that language, which is especially pronounced for low-frequency words. In a similar vein, Ivanova and Costa (2008) showed that, compared with Spanish monolinguals, Spanish-Catalan speakers who dominantly spoke Spanish showed a larger frequency effect, while the size of this effect did not differ between monolinguals and Catalan-Spanish bilinguals whose dominant language was Catalan.

Building on this rationale, Strijkers et al. (2010) conducted an event-related potential (ERP) study in which highly proficient Spanish-Catalan ($N = 16$) and Catalan-Spanish ($N = 16$) speakers named pictures manipulated for lexical frequency in Spanish (i.e. either the L1 or the L2). Behaviourally, a similarly sized frequency effect was found for both groups, implying that high proficiency in L2 abolishes frequency effect differences observed as a function of language dominance (Gollan et al. 2008; Ivanova and Costa 2008). ERP amplitudes including the P2, P3, and N3 component, were larger for low-frequency words starting around 180 ms after picture onset for both groups of speakers, suggesting that bilinguals rapidly access lexical properties of a target word, regardless of whether it is named in their first or second language. The items in this study additionally were chosen such that cognate status could be investigated as well. As with word frequency, non-cognates elicited larger ERP amplitudes (P2, P3, and N3) starting at around 190 ms after picture onset, with no differences between the two speaker groups. However, in L1 speakers, the frequency effect preceded the cognate effect, whereas they co-occurred in L2 speakers. Furthermore, overall P2 amplitudes were larger in L2 naming. It should be noted, however, that these two differences were small and statistically not robust, which may at least partly be caused by the fact that the authors employed a between-speaker design. To account for this caveat, Strijkers et al. (2013) contrasted the temporal signatures of word frequency in L1 and L2 naming *within* 40 early Spanish-Catalan bilinguals. Unlike previous findings with bilinguals who are highly proficient in both languages, the behavioural frequency effect was larger for blocked naming in L2 compared to L1. ERP modulations were found as a function of word frequency (low vs. high) and response language (L1 vs. L2) from 140 ms after picture onset onwards, with low-frequency and L2 words eliciting a stronger response than high-frequency and L1 words. The latter effect was restricted to the participant group that started naming in L1. According to the authors, participants who started speaking in L2 had a stronger need to suppress L1 in this block, subsequently making L1 less accessible in the second block. Overall, the results of this study were taken as evidence for cortical differences between L1 and L2 naming already at the onset of lexical access.

Christoffels et al. (2007) investigated the cognate facilitation effect in a group of 24 unbalanced German-Dutch bilinguals. Participants named cognate and non-cognate words either in a single-language (L1 or L2) or a mixed-language context which required switching between L1 and L2. In the single-language context, a larger behavioural cognate facilitation effect was observed for L2 compared to L1 naming, accompanied by larger negative amplitudes during cognate naming starting as early as 275 ms after picture onset. Surprisingly, in the mixed-language condition, cognates were named faster than non-cognates in L1 compared to L2 naming. Given that the cognate facilitation effect indexes to what extent the non-target language is activated, this finding was interpreted as a more effortful suppression of the more dominant non-target language (L1). With respect to switching between L1 and L2, non-switch trials caused shorter naming latencies and larger negative amplitudes than switch trials, with the ERP effect being present for L1 naming in the early time window and for both languages in the later time window. Overall, the authors concluded that in mixed language conditions (i.e. when switching between L1 and L2), language control is exerted primarily by actively inhibiting the more proficient and more dominant language rather than by modulating activation levels of the weaker L2.

In order to assess both spatial and temporal signatures of bilingual word production, Pang and MacDonald (2012) conducted a magnetoencephalography (MEG) study. Twelve bilingual participants with varying first and second languages were asked to produce action names in response to pictures, either in their L1 or their L2. Those who performed the task in their native language showed activation of the left inferior frontal gyrus (BA 47) up to 400 ms after picture onset, as well as activation in the left frontal cortex (BAs 9, 13, and 47). By contrast, L2 production was characterized by sustained right insula (BA 13) activation and an early involvement (50–200 ms) of the right anterior cingulate cortex (BA 32). Based on previous findings from semantic judgement tasks, the authors related the insular desynchrony to L2 proficiency, and activation of the right anterior cingulate cortex to conflict and error monitoring.

In summary, ERP studies have provided behavioural support for the weaker links hypothesis, such that languages which are spoken less frequently or with lower proficiency elicit larger word frequency and cognate effects (cf. Strijkers et al. 2013). On the ERP (and MEG) level, however, diverging results have been reported. Importantly, the experimental procedure of the reported studies varied substantially (e.g. with respect to between/within-participant comparisons, mixed vs. blocked naming, L1 vs. L2 naming). Future research should therefore attempt to further clarify which factors influence the emergence of different brain potentials in bilinguals. A comparatively simple way to achieve this is by replicating existing studies to see whether previously obtained results are robust (Button et al. 2013). Moreover, it seems reasonable to focus future research on mixed-language contexts as this is a scenario more common to bilingual speakers and a better candidate to uncover differences in the electrophysiological response.

4.   Factors Moderating Neural Representations of Bilingual Word Production

In the previous sections we purposefully interspersed details about the language background of speakers examined in the respective studies, because intuitively it makes a lot of sense that differences in L2 usage and proficiency may shape the representation and word production of bilinguals differentially. This intuition has received much empirical support. In the following, we will provide an overview of how age of acquisition, proficiency, and immersion may modulate bilingual word production in behavioural, electrophysiological, and hemodynamic measures.

Whether an early versus late acquisition of a second language affects the degree to which it is mastered is still a matter of ongoing debate. While it has originally been argued that there is a critical period of L2 acquisition, by now a bulk of research has found opposing evidence (Singleton 2005; Vanhove 2013). However, with respect to neural differences, it has been shown that in the domain of syntax, differences do exist, with higher connectivity between relevant language regions observed for highly proficient speakers compared with less-proficient speakers during L2 sentence production (Abutalebi 2008; Dodel et al. 2005). In the lexico-semantic domain, by contrast, no robust neural differences have been found (Indefrey 2006; Perani and Abutalebi 2005). A recent meta-analysis by Hengshuang Liu and Cao (2016), however, reports a crucial role of age of acquisition in mediating neural differences. That is, compared with L1 processing, L2 processing in late bilinguals was found to activate the left superior frontal gyrus (BAs 8 and 9) to a greater degree than in early bilinguals, arguing for a greater planning demand in late bilinguals. Additionally, the left fusiform gyrus (BA 37) of early bilinguals was activated more during L1 processing, which was interpreted as a parallel activation of the two orthographies. Note, however, that this meta-analysis did not focus exclusively on word production studies, but also included semantic and phonological judgement, comprehension, and repetition tasks. Thus, the direct influence of age of acquisition on neural differences in bilingual production cannot be derived from these results.

A less ambiguous factor modulating neural differences in bilingual word production is the proficiency level at which bilinguals master their second language. Notably, although there is no clear-cut standard as to how to quantify proficiency (scores used as regressors are often composites of highly variable and unstandardized measures), which may obscure between- and within-language comparisons, the evidence on proficiency effects on neural representations in bilinguals is fairly clear. The strongest finding is that less-proficient bilinguals activate left prefrontal regions to a greater extent than highly proficient bilinguals. This finding has been related to increased cognitive control demands (Abutalebi 2008). In line with the convergence hypothesis (Green 2003), these differences diminish with increasing L2 proficiency. That is, as L2 production becomes more native-like, the need to exert cognitive control in juggling the two languages appears to decrease, and a speaker's two languages activate identical areas (Perani and Abutalebi 2005). Abutalebi and Green (2007) argued for three different possibilities determining less prefrontal activity with higher L2 proficiency. First, high proficiency likely results in stronger neural connections between a concept and its lexico-semantic and phonological properties, which in turn facilitates lexical retrieval. Second, high L2 proficiency may decrease the need to inhibit the L1 during L2 production. The more proficient speakers are in their L2, the more automatic L2 processing becomes, reducing interference from L1. Third, high proficiency invariably results in less cognitive effort as the L2 will have become more practised and retrieval thus more automatic. As a result, except for language-switching situations, conflict resolution between L1 and L2 concepts may be less demanding, thus reducing the involvement of prefrontal regions. Note that cognitive control is inherent to all three possibilities. In sum, it can be assumed that high proficiency reduces the need for conscious control processes.

Directly related to the concept of proficiency is the degree to which bilinguals are exposed to their second language. Although constant practice undoubtedly has a beneficial effect on mastering a second language, there is evidence that high immersion in an L2 environment influences neural representations on top of proficiency. For instance, Perani et al. (2003) reported that the exposure to a speaker's L2 differentially affects neural activations in picture naming. Despite comparable degrees of proficiency, less-immersed speakers showed stronger activations in parietal and prefrontal regions including the left caudate nucleus. Analogous to experience and practice effects in monolingual naming (Thompson-Schill et al. 1999), Perani and Abutalebi (2005) thus argued for immersion as an additional factor modulating the neurobiological underpinnings of bilingual word production. More direct evidence for this claim comes from a recent study by Pliatsikas et al. (2017) who compared structural MRI scans of bilingual speakers currently living in an L2 environment to bilinguals without daily exposure to the L2. Compared with monolinguals, the highly immersed speakers showed a bilateral expansion of the putamen and globus pallidus, and right thalamus, while the bilateral thalamus and putamen were contracted in the less immersed speakers. Additionally, high immersion, quantified as the time living in the L2 environment, predicted the expansion of the right globus pallidus. These findings were taken as support for an exposure-related theory in which a bilingual's brain dynamically exhibits remarkable plasticity as a function of exposure to the second language.

5.   Conclusion

In this chapter, we have reviewed cognitive neuroscience studies investigating bilingual word production. While many studies reported comparable neurophysiological and hemodynamic signals for both L1 and L2 processing, there is also ample evidence that more effortful processing in L2 results in higher activation of left frontal and temporal areas, and that a number of areas (e.g. the dorsolateral prefrontal cortex, the anterior cingulate cortex, and the supplementary motor areas) appear to be specialized for the coordination of a speaker's two languages within a control network. Furthermore, speaker-specific factors such as L2 proficiency and exposure have been shown to influence neural representations. Many methodological advances have provided a clearer picture of the mechanisms underlying bilingual speech production, although they have not been immune to criticism (García-Pentón et al. 2017). Finally, one should keep in mind that the vast majority of the studies have investigated bilingual production at the word-level, although, as we mentioned in the introduction, this is a simplification of natural language production which usually occurs at the sentence and discourse level.

Similar to the investigation of monolingual language production, it will therefore remain a conceptual and methodological challenge to further illuminate the neurobiological processes of bilingual language production at the sentence and discourse level.

REFERENCES

Abutalebi, J. (2008). Neural aspects of second language representation and language control. *Acta Psychologica* 128 (3): 466–478. doi:10.1016/j.actpsy.2008.03.014.

Abutalebi, J., Annoni, J.-M., Zimine, I. et al. (2008). Language control and lexical competition in bilinguals: an event-related fMRI study. *Cerebral Cortex* 18: 1496–1505. doi:10.1093/cercor/bhm182.

Abutalebi, J. and Green, D.W. (2007). Bilingual language production: the neurocognition of language representation and control. *Journal of Neurolinguistics* 20 (3): 242–275. doi:10.1016/j.jneuroling.2006.10.003.

Abutalebi, J. and Green, D.W. (2016). Neuroimaging of language control in bilinguals: neural adaptation and reserve. *Bilingualism: Language and Cognition* 19 (4): 689–698. doi:10.1017/S1366728916000225.

Abutalebi, J., Rosa, P., Della, A. et al. (2013). The role of the left putamen in multilingual language production. *Brain and Language* 125 (3): 307–315. doi:10.1016/j.bandl.2012.03.009.

Bialystok, E., Craik, F.I.M., and Luk, G. (2012). Bilingualism: consequences for mind and brain. *Trends in Cognitive Sciences* 16 (4): 240–250. doi:10.1016/j.tics.2012.03.001.

Boukadi, M., Davies, R., and Wilson, M.A. (2015). Bilingual lexical selection as a dynamic process: evidence from Arabic-French bilinguals. *Canadian Journal of Experimental Psychology* 69 (4): 297–313. doi:10.1037/cep0000063.

Burgaleta, M., Sanjuán, A., Ventura-Campos, N. et al. (2016). Bilingualism at the core of the brain. Structural differences between bilinguals and monolinguals revealed by subcortical shape analysis. *NeuroImage* 125: 437–445. doi:10.1016/j.neuroimage.2015.09.073.

Button, K.S., Ioannidis, J.P.A., Mokrysz, C. et al. (2013). Power failure: why small sample size undermines the reliability of neuroscience. *Nature Reviews Neuroscience* 14 (5): 365–376. doi:10.1038/nrn3475.

Chee, M.W.L., Tan, E.W.L., and Thiel, T. (1999). Mandarin and English single word processing studied with functional magnetic resonance imaging. *Journal of Neuroscience* 19: 3050–3056.

Christoffels, I.K., Firk, C., and Schiller, N.O. (2007). Bilingual language control: an event-related brain potential study. *Brain Research* 1147: 192–208. doi:10.1016/j.brainres.2007.01.137.

Colomé, À. (2001). Lexical activation in bilinguals' speech production: language-specific or language-independent? *Journal of Memory and Language* 45: 721–736. doi:10.1006/jmla.2001.2793.

Costa, A. (2004). Speech production in bilinguals. In: *The Handbook of Bilingualism* (ed. T.K. Bhatia and W.C. Ritchie), 201–223. Oxford, UK: Blackwell doi:10.1002/9780470756997.ch8.

Costa, A. and Caramazza, A. (1999). Is lexical selection in bilingual speech production language-specific? Further evidence from Spanish–English and English–Spanish bilinguals. *Bilingualism: Language and Cognition* 2 (3): 231–244.

Costa, A., Caramazza, A., and Sebastian-Galles, N. (2000). The cognate facilitation effect: implications for models of lexical access. *Journal of Experimental Psychology: Learning, Memory, and Cognition* 26 (5): 1283–1296. doi:10.1037/0278-7393.26.5.1283.

Costa, A., Colomé, À., Gómez, O., and Sebastián-Gallés, N. (2003). Another look at cross-language competition in bilingual speech production: lexical and phonological factors. *Bilingualism: Language and Cognition* 6 (3): 167–179. doi:10.1017/S1366728903001111.

Costa, A., Miozzo, M., and Caramazza, A. (1999). Lexical selection in bilinguals: do words in the bilingual's two lexicons compete for selection? *Journal of Memory and Language* 41 (3): 365–397. doi:10.1006/jmla.1999.2651.

Costa, A., Santesteban, M., and Caño, A. (2005). On the facilitatory effects of cognate words in bilingual speech production. *Brain and Language* 94 (1): 94–103. doi:10.1016/j.bandl.2004.12.002.

Costa, A. and Sebastián-Gallés, N. (2014). How does the bilingual experience sculpt the brain? *Nature Reviews Neuroscience* 15: 336–345. doi:10.1038/nrn3709.

De Bleser, R., Dupont, P., Postler, J. et al. (2003). The organisation of the bilingual lexicon: a PET study. *Journal of Neurolinguistics* 16: 439–456.

de Bot, K. (1992). A bilingual production model: Levelt's 'speaking' model adapted. *Applied Linguistics* 13: 1–24.

Dodel, S., Golestani, N., Pallier, C. et al. (2005). Condition-dependent functional connectivity: syntax networks in bilinguals. *Philosophical Transactions of the Royal Society B: Biological Sciences* 360 (1457): 921–935. doi:10.1098/rstb.2005.1653.

García-Pentón, L., Fernández García, Y., Costello, B. et al. (2017). The neuroanatomy of bilingualism: how to turn a hazy view into the full picture. *Language, Cognition and Neuroscience* 31 (3): 303–327. doi:10.1080/23273798.2015.1068944.

Gollan, T.H. and Acenas, L.-A.R. (2004). What is a TOT? Cognate and translation effects on tip-of-the-tongue states in Spanish-English and Tagalog-English bilinguals. *Journal of Experimental Psychology: Learning, Memory, and Cognition* 30 (1): 246–269. doi:10.1037/0278-7393.30.1.246.

Gollan, T.H., Montoya, R.I., Cera, C., and Sandoval, T.C. (2008). More use almost always a means a smaller frequency effect: aging, bilingualism, and the weaker links hypothesis. *Journal of Memory and Language* 58 (3): 787–814. doi:10.1016/j.jml.2007.07.001.

Gollan, T.H., Montoya, R.I., Fennema-Notestine, C., and Morris, S.K. (2005). Bilingualism affects picture naming but not picture classification. *Memory & Cognition* 33 (7): 1220–1234.

Gollan, T.H., Montoya, R.I., and Werner, G.A. (2002). Semantic and letter fluency in Spanish-English bilinguals. *Neuropsychology* 16 (4): 562–576. doi:10.1037/0894-4105.16.4.562.

Graves, W.W., Grabowski, T.J., Mehta, S., and Gordon, J.K. (2007). A neural signature of phonological access: distinguishing the effects of word frequency from familiarity and length in overt picture naming. *Journal of Cognitive Neuroscience* 19 (4): 617–631. doi:10.1162/jocn.2007.19.4.617.

Green, D.W. (1998). Mental control of the bilingual lexico-semantic system. *Bilingualism: Language and Cognition* 1: 67–81. doi:10.1017/S1366728998000133.

Green, D.W. (2003). Neural basis of lexicon and grammar in L2 acquisition: the convergence hypothesis. In: *The Lexicon-Syntax Interface in Second Language Acquisition* (ed. R. van Hout, A. Hulk, F. Kuiken and R. Towell), 197–218. Amsterdam, The Netherlands: John Benjamins.

Green, D.W. and Abutalebi, J. (2013). Language control in bilinguals: the adaptive control hypothesis. *Journal of Cognitive Psychology* 25 (5): 515–530. doi:10.1080/20445911.2013.796377.

Grosjean, F. (2010). *Bilingual: Life and Reality*. Cambridge, MA: Harvard University Press.

Guo, T., Liu, H., Misra, M., and Kroll, J.F. (2011). Local and global inhibition in bilingual word production: fMRI evidence from Chinese-English bilinguals. *NeuroImage* 56 (4): 2300–2309. doi:10.1016/j.neuroimage.2011.03.049.

Hanulová, J., Davidson, D.J., and Indefrey, P. (2011). Where does the delay in L2 picture naming come from? Psycholinguistic and neurocognitive evidence on second language word production. *Language and Cognitive*

Processes 26 (7): 902–934. doi:10.1080/01690965.2010.509946.

Hermans, D., Bongaerts, T., de Bot, K., and Schreuder, R. (1998). Producing words in a foreign language: can speakers prevent interference from their first language? *Bilingualism: Language and Cognition* 1 (3): 213–229. doi:10.1017/S1366728998000364.

Hermans, D., Ormel, E., van Besselaar, R., and van Hell, J. (2011). Lexical activation in bilinguals' speech production is dynamic: how language ambiguous words can affect cross-language activation. *Language and Cognitive Processes* 26 (10): 1687–1709. doi:10.1080/01690965.2010.530411.

Hernandez, A.E., Dapretto, M., Mazziotta, J., and Bookheimer, S. (2001). Language switching and language representation in Spanish–English bilinguals: an fMRI study. *NeuroImage* 14 (2): 510–520. doi:10.1006/nimg.2001.0810.

Hernandez, A.E., Martinez, A., and Kohnert, K. (2000). In search of the language switch: an fMRI study of picture naming in Spanish–English bilinguals. *Brain and Language* 73 (3): 421–431. doi:10.1006/brln.1999.2278.

Indefrey, P. (2006). A meta-analysis of hemodynamic studies on first and second language processing: which suggested differences can we trust and what do they mean? *Language Learning* 56 (s1): 279–304. doi:10.1111/j.1467-9922.2006.00365.x.

Ivanova, I. and Costa, A. (2008). Does bilingualism hamper lexical access in speech production? *Acta Psychologica* 127 (2): 277–288. doi:10.1016/j.actpsy.2007.06.003.

Jacobs, A., Fricke, M., and Kroll, J.F. (2016). Cross-language activation begins during speech planning and extends into second language speech. *Language Learning* 66 (2): 324–353. doi:10.1111/lang.12148.

Klein, D., Milner, B., Zatorre, R.J. et al. (1995). The neural substrates underlying word generation: a bilingual functional-imaging study. *Proceedings of the National Academy of Sciences of the United States of America* 92 (7): 2899–2903. doi:10.1073/PNAS.92.7.2899.

Klein, D., Milner, B., Zatorre, R.J. et al. (1999). Cerebral organization in bilinguals: a PET study of Chinese-English verb generation. *Neuroreport* 10: 2841–2846.

Kroll, J.F., Bobb, S.C., Misra, M., and Guo, T. (2008). Language selection in bilingual speech: evidence for inhibitory processes. *Acta Psychologica* 128 (3): 416–430. doi:10.1016/j.actpsy.2008.02.001.

Kroll, J.F., Bobb, S.C., and Wodniecka, Z. (2006). Language selectivity is the exception, not the rule: arguments against a fixed locus of language selection in bilingual speech. *Bilingualism: Language and Cognition* 9 (2): 119–135. doi:10.1017/S1366728906002483.

Levelt, W.J., Roelofs, A., and Meyer, A.S. (1999). A theory of lexical access in speech production. *Behavioral and Brain Sciences* 22 (1): 1-38-1-75. doi:10.1017/S0140525X99001776.

Liu, H. and Cao, F. (2016). L1 and L2 processing in the bilingual brain: a meta-analysis of neuroimaging studies. *Brain and Language* 159: 60–73. doi:10.1016/j.bandl.2016.05.013.

Liu, H., Hu, Z., Guo, T., and Peng, D. (2010). Speaking words in two languages with one brain: neural overlap and dissociation. *Brain Research* 1316: 75–82. doi:10.1016/j.brainres.2009.12.030.

Mechelli, A., Crinion, J.T., Noppeney, U. et al. (2004). Neurolinguistics: structural plasticity in the bilingual brain. *Nature* 431 (7010): 757–757. doi:10.1038/431757a.

Misra, M., Guo, T., Bobb, S.C., and Kroll, J.F. (2012). When bilinguals choose a single word to speak: electrophysiological evidence for inhibition of the native language. *Journal of Memory and Language* 67 (1): doi:10.1016/j.jml.2012.05.001.

Oldfield, R.C. and Wingfield, A. (1965). Response latencies in naming objects. *The Quarterly Journal of Experimental Psychology* 17 (4): 273–281.

Pang, E.W. and MacDonald, M.J. (2012). An MEG study of the spatiotemporal dynamics of bilingual verb generation. *Brain Research* 1467: 56–66. doi:10.1016/j.brainres.2012.05.054.

Parker Jones, O., Green, D.W., Grogan, A. et al. (2012). Where, when and why brain activation differs for bilinguals and monolinguals during picture naming and reading aloud. *Cerebral Cortex* 22 (4): 892–902. doi:10.1093/cercor/bhr161.

Perani, D. and Abutalebi, J. (2005). The neural basis of first and second language processing. *Current Opinion in Neurobiology* 15 (2): 202–206. doi:10.1016/j.conb.2005.03.007.

Perani, D., Abutalebi, J., Paulesu, E. et al. (2003). The role of age of acquisition and language usage in early, high-proficient bilinguals: an fMRI study during verbal fluency. *Human Brain Mapping* 19 (3): 170–182. doi:10.1002/hbm.10110.

Pliatsikas, C., DeLuca, V., Moschopoulou, E., and Saddy, J.D. (2017). Immersive bilingualism reshapes the core of the brain. *Brain Structure and Function* 222 (4): 1785–1795. doi:10.1007/s00429-016-1307-9.

Portocarrero, J., Burright, R., and Donovick, P. (2007). Vocabulary and verbal fluency of bilingual and monolingual college students. *Archives of Clinical Neuropsychology* 22 (3): 415–422. doi:10.1016/j.acn.2007.01.015.

Poulisse, N. (2000). Slips of the tongue in first and second language production. *Studia Linguistica* 54 (2): 136–149. doi:10.1111/1467-9582.00055.

Poulisse, N. and Bongaerts, T. (1994). First language use in second language production. *Applied Linguistics* 15 (1): 36–57. doi:10.1093/applin/15.1.36.

Rodriguez-Fornells, A., van der Lugt, A., Rotte, M. et al. (2005). Second language interferes with word production in fluent bilinguals: brain potential and functional imaging evidence. *Journal of Cognitive Neuroscience* 17 (3): 422–433. doi:10.1162/0898929053279559.

Roelofs, A. (1992). A spreading-activation theory of lemma retrieval in speaking. *Cognition* 42 (1–3): 107–142.

Sadat, J., Martin, C.D., Alario, F.X., and Costa, A. (2012). Characterizing the bilingual disadvantage in noun phrase production.

Journal of Psycholinguistic Research 41: 159–179. doi:10.1007/s10936-011-9183-1.

Singleton, D. (2005). The critical period hypothesis: a coat of many colours. *International Review of Applied Linguistics in Language Teaching* 43 (4): 269–285. doi:10.1515/iral.2005.43.4.269.

Spalek, K., Hoshino, N., Wu, Y.J. et al. (2014). Speaking two languages at once: unconscious native word form access in second language production. *Cognition* 133 (1): 226–231. doi:10.1016/j.cognition.2014.06.016.

Strijkers, K., Baus, C., Runnqvist, E. et al. (2013). The temporal dynamics of first versus second language production. *Brain and Language* 127 (1): 6–11. doi:10.1016/j.bandl.2013.07.008.

Strijkers, K., Costa, A., and Thierry, G. (2010). Tracking lexical access in speech production: electrophysiological correlates of word frequency and cognate effects. *Cerebral Cortex* 20 (4): 912–928. doi:10.1093/cercor/bhp153.

Thompson-Schill, S.L., D'Esposito, M., and Kan, I.P. (1999). Effects of repetition and competition on activity in left prefrontal cortex during word generation. *Neuron* 23: 513–522.

Vanhove, J. (2013). The critical period hypothesis in second language acquisition: a statistical critique and a reanalysis. *PLoS One* 8 (7): e69172. doi:10.1371/journal.pone.0069172.

Videsott, G., Herrnberger, B., Hoenig, K. et al. (2010). Speaking in multiple languages: neural correlates of language proficiency in multilingual word production. *Brain and Language* 113: 103–112. doi:10.1016/j.bandl.2010.01.006.

Vingerhoets, G., Van Borsel, J., Tesink, C. et al. (2003). Multilingualism: an fMRI study. *NeuroImage* 20 (4): 2181–2196. doi:10.1016/j.neuroimage.2003.07.029.

Wingfield, A. (1968). Effects of frequency on identification and naming of objects. *The American Journal of Psychology* 81 (2): 226–234.

11 Multilingualism and Brain Plasticity

CHRISTOS PLIATSIKAS

1. Introduction

The literature on how additional languages are acquired and processed has been comprehensive, and now spans several decades, as other chapters in this book illustrate. However, until recently the brain structure correlates of the acquisition and use of additional languages were significantly underresearched. In other words, how does language learning 'force' the brain to restructure in order to (i) accommodate all the new incoming linguistic knowledge and (ii) become efficient in handling competing information from two or more languages at the various levels of processing (grammar, lexicon, phonology)? Interest in these research questions was kindled around the early 2000s, when advances in neuroimaging methods such as magnetic resonance imaging (MRI) allowed cognitive neuroscientists to measure the structure of the brain and correlate it to the acquisition of new knowledge and/or skills. For example, Maguire et al. (2000) showed significantly increased volume in the hippocampi of London taxi drivers, a brain region that is crucial for navigation. This finding, along with subsequent findings regarding brain restructuring as result of the acquisition of new knowledge or skills (e.g. Draganski et al. 2006; Park et al. 2009) highlighted the brain's capacity to restructure, also known as neuroplasticity, in order to provide more efficient task-specific functionality and connectivity. Such findings led researchers to inquire whether the cognitively demanding task of handling two languages requires restructuring of brain regions involved in linguistic processing and executive control, in order to manage both the acquisition of multiple languages and the skills necessary to control and choose amongst them.

This chapter provides a contemporary snapshot of the literature on multilingualism-induced changes in the brain, including theoretical suggestions about the origin and the nature of these changes. The structure of this chapter will be as follows: After a brief overview of the anatomy of the neuron and the brain, the chapter will turn to grey matter (Section 3), and specifically to the available effects on the cortical, subcortical, and cerebellar grey matter. This will be followed by a review of the effects on white

The Handbook of the Neuroscience of Multilingualism, First Edition. Edited by John W. Schwieter.
© 2019 John Wiley & Sons Ltd. Published 2019 by John Wiley & Sons Ltd.

matter (Section 4), and of the much smaller literature on resting state functional connectivity (Section 5). Following that, Section 6 will examine separately the findings in older bilinguals, and the chapter will conclude with a summary of the available evidence and suggestions for further research. Evidence from both unimodal and bimodal bilinguals as well as from multilinguals will be examined. For the purposes of this chapter, 'bilingualism' and 'multilingualism' will not be examined separately; this is because evidence from multilinguals remains extremely scarce, and the reported findings so far have not revealed a different pattern of effects from that found in bilinguals.

2.   The Building Blocks: Grey and White Matter in the Brain

Before reviewing the effects of multilingualism on the structure of the brain, it is useful to describe the building blocks of the nervous system that collectively undergo these changes, the brain cells, or *neurons*. A typical neuron in the brain has three main parts: the *cell body* is responsible for collecting and synthesizing electrical signals that arrive from other neurons through the *dendrites*; along with the dendrites, the cell body is responsible for producing new signals to be propagated to neighbouring neurons. This is carried out by the *axon*, the main 'avenue' by which information from a neuron is communicated to neighbouring ones. The axons are covered by a lipid layer, the myelin, which gives them a pale colour and acts as an insulation providing efficient communication between brain areas. See Figure 1, for an illustration of a typical neuron.

In the brain, the cell bodies are concentrated mainly on the cortical and the cerebellar surface, with the exception of some subcortical clusters, such as the basal ganglia and the thalamus (see Section 3.2). Such high concentrations of cell bodies are referred to as grey matter (GM), in contrast to white matter (WM), which refers to high concentrations of myelinated axons, just below the cortical or cerebellar surface. Figure 2 illustrates a typical high-definition MRI scan showing the contrast between GM and WM and identifying the main GM regions that will be discussed in the remainder of this chapter.

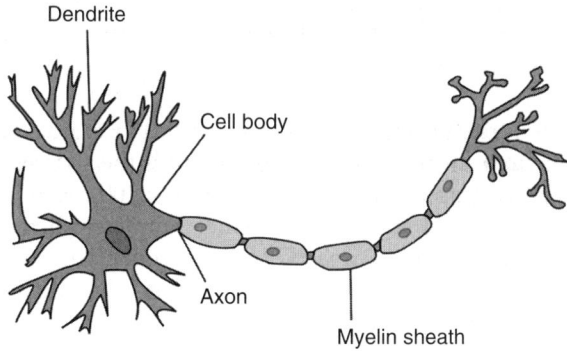

Figure 1   The typical parts of a neuron. Source: https://commons.wikimedia.org/wiki/File:Neuron.svg.

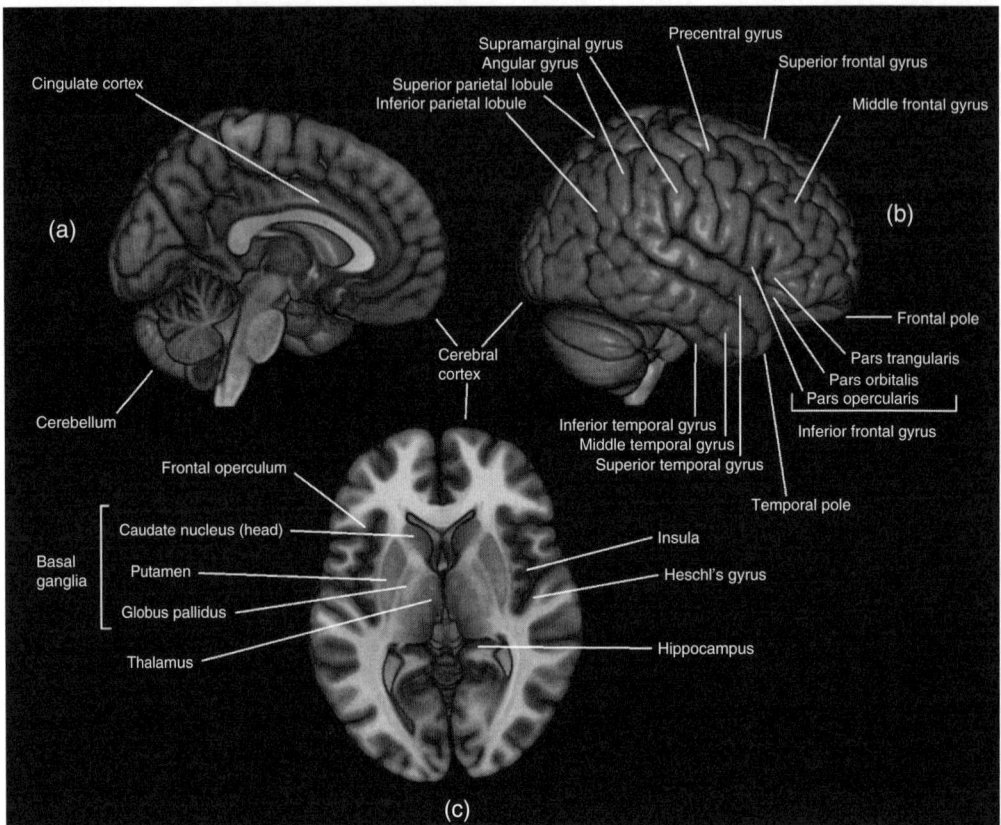

Figure 2   A mid-sagittal (a), lateral (b) and mid-axial (c) view of a template brain, indicating the main grey matter regions that will be discussed in this chapter. WM, and how it differentiates from cortical and subcortical GM, is clearly visible in (c).

3.   The Effects of Bi–/Multilingualism on the Grey Matter of the Brain

As already mentioned, structural GM changes are thought to underlie internal restructuring of the affected area, in order for it to cope with the increased demands of the acquisition and use of a complex skill (Maguire et al. 2000). Researchers have used a variety of methods to study GM, including measuring indices such as cortical thickness (CT) and extent of cortical surface area (CSA). However, the most commonly used method in the field is voxel-based morphometry (VBM; Mechelli et al. 2005), which measures GM density or volume in a given region. It is important to note that, no matter which index is used, the available analytical methods cannot describe the microstructural changes that take place in the GM; for example, it is not clear whether GM increases are due to increase in the size of the cell bodies, the increase in the number of dendrites, or of the size of neuropil (the brain tissue surrounding the neurons that includes astrocytes and other glial cells) or other reasons.

3.1.   Cerebral Cortex

The effects of bi–/multilingualism on the cortical GM structure were the first to be studied and reported. The study that kick-started the field was by Mechelli et al. (2004), who used VBM and revealed increased GM density for bilinguals vs. monolinguals in a region roughly corresponding to the left posterior supramarginal gyrus (SMG), an area related to verbal fluency. Importantly, GM density in this region was significantly correlated to both the age of acquisition (AoA) of the bilinguals' second language (L2), as well as their L2 proficiency. This finding was the first to suggest that the bilingual experience might 'sculpt' the brain, and was followed by a significant number of subsequent studies, which produced interesting, yet diverse, results regarding the effects of bilingualism on brain structure. For example, Ressel et al. (2012) showed increased volume for bilinguals vs. monolinguals in bilateral Heschl's gyrus (HG), which is suggested to be the main part of the primary auditory cortex (Wong et al. 2008). Moreover, Grogan et al. (2012) compared bilinguals to multilinguals (three to six languages), and reported increased GM density for the multilingual group in the posterior SMG and its right hemisphere homologue. Furthermore, they reported a significant correlation between GM density in the left IFG pars opercularis (IFGop) and the participants' performance in a letter fluency task in the second language (L2) for the bilingual group. Effects in the left SMG were also reported by Elmer et al. (2014), along with effects in regions such as the left anterior cingulate cortex (ACC) and IFG pars triangularis (IFGtr), and bilateral IFGop and insula (INS). This study compared simultaneous interpreters to multilingual controls, and interestingly revealed *reduced* GM volume in all these regions for the interpreters, as well as negative correlations between these volumes and the number of hours of interpreting that the participants reported; however, in comparing similar groups, Becker et al. (2016) reported increase in the volume of the left frontal pole for the interpreters. Nevertheless, and similar to Elmer et al. (2014), Kaiser et al. (2015) reported reduced GM volume for multilinguals who learned their native language (L1) and L2 simultaneously compared to multilinguals who learned their L2 later in life, in bilateral IFG and middle frontal gyrus (MFG), the right middle temporal gyrus (MTG), the left inferior temporal gyrus, and the right IPL. More recently, Olulade et al. (2016) reported increased GM volume in a widespread network of cortical regions for bilinguals versus monolinguals. In the left hemisphere, these included regions within the dorsolateral prefrontal cortex (DLPFC), including the MFG and the precentral gyrus (PCG), and also the IFG, inferior middle and superior occipital gyri, cuneus and posterior MTG. In the right hemisphere, they included the IFG, MFG, superior frontal gyrus (SFG), frontal operculum, inferior parietal lobule (IPL), MTG, and the superior temporal gyrus (STG). At the same time, reduced volume for bilinguals was reported primarily in occipital and parahippocampal regions in both hemispheres. Finally, Felton et al. (2017) reported greater thickness in the right ACC for bilinguals vs. monolinguals, and the opposite pattern for the left ACC, which they interpreted as evidence for bilingualism-induced maturity in the left ACC, and plasticity in the right ACC. The ACC has been strongly linked to executive control, and as such it is a highly important region for bilinguals who constantly have to select amongst language alternatives; indeed, Abutalebi et al. (2012) showed that GM density in the ACC positively correlated with the bilinguals' performance in a conflict monitoring task (flanker).

Several studies focused on L2 AoA as a predictor of structural changes in the cortex. For example, Klein et al. (2014) compared cortical thickness in simultaneous bilinguals (L2 AoA: 0–3 years), early (4–7 years) and late (8–13 years) sequential bilinguals, and monolinguals. They revealed greater thickness in the left IFGop and IFGtr for both the sequential bilingual groups compared to monolinguals; additionally, the late sequential bilingual group revealed reduced cortical thickness in the right IFG pars orbitalis (IFGorb), compared with all other groups, and a similar effect was reported for the early sequential bilingual group compared with the monolinguals only. Notably, L2 AoA was significantly correlated with these changes, in that the later the AoA, the thicker the left IFG and superior parietal lobule (SPL), and the thinner the right IFG (RIFG), across all bilingual subjects. In a similar vein, Wei et al. (2015) showed L2 AoA to negatively correlate with GM volume in the right angular gyrus (AG) and SPL. Finally, Berken and colleagues (2016b) compared simultaneous vs. sequential (L2 AoA: 5+ years) bilinguals and revealed increased GM density for the former group in the left posterior INS, right DLPFC and bilateral occipital areas. Conversely, they only reported higher GM density in the bilateral premotor cortex for the sequential group, who also revealed positive correlations between how native-like their L2 accent was and GM density in the several regions, including the bilateral IPL, the left IFG, and the right HG.

More evidence about multilingualism-induced structural changes has been provided by longitudinal training studies. These typically included cohorts of participants enrolled into an intensive language training program, usually on L2 vocabulary only, who were scanned before and after their training. In an early longitudinal study, Osterhout et al. (2008) reported a significant volumetric increase in the left SMG in a small group of participants enrolled in an intensive nine-week language training course, further confirming the role of this region in L2 learning (see also Della Rosa et al. 2013, for similar effects in children in a partly overlapping region). More recently, Mårtensson and colleagues (2012) tested interpreters enrolled in an intensive training program, and revealed volumetric increases in bilateral hippocampus and the left MFG, IFG and STG, compared to a control group (see also Bellander et al. 2016, for similar hippocampal increases for L2 vocabulary training). Stein et al. (2012) also observed significant volume increases in the left MFG, IFGtr, IFGorb and anterior temporal lobe (ATL) of English students learning German in a naturalistic environment for five months, and these changes were predicted by the participants' success in a proficiency test administered at both test points. Similarly, in an L2 vocabulary training study, Hosoda et al. (2013) showed that the volume of the left IFGop, STG/SMG and ACC positively correlated to the size of the vocabulary that their participants had acquired; moreover, in a longitudinal study, Hosoda et al. showed that vocabulary learning-induced volumetric increases in the right IFG disappeared after a period of no L2 training. Finally, in a recent longitudinal study Hervais-Adelman et al. (2017) compared trainee simultaneous interpreters enrolled in a 14-month-long course with multilingual control participants tested over the same period of time. At the end of the training period, the interpreters showed increases in the cortical thickness of the left posterior STG, SMG and planum temporale (PT), as well as the right SPL, AG, intraparietal sulcus (IPS) and SFG. This is a more widespread pattern than the ones reported in previous training studies – however, this might be related to the fact that interpreter training is a more global and structured task than the vocabulary training employed in the previous studies, and also to the fact that the trainee interpreters were compared with an already multilingual population.

3.1.1. Effects on Cortical Grey Matter: What Do they Tell us?   The available literature presents a rather complicated picture of the effects of multilingualism on cortical structure. However, a few regions are very often reported to be affected by the multilingual experience. Notably, this includes a cluster of regions in the parietal cortex, mostly on the left hemisphere but sometimes also bilaterally, comprising the adjacent SPL and IPL (the latter including the SMG and AG), as well as the IPS which separates them. These regions are known to underlie lexicosemantic processing, and more specifically to link the semantics and phonology of newly acquired words (Richardson et al. 2010). A role in vocabulary acquisition and processing is attributed to the left ATL (i.e. the temporal pole and anterior parts of the STG, MTG and inferior temporal gyrus [ITG]) and hippocampus (L. Li et al. 2017), which are also affected by the multilingual experience. Therefore, restructuring of these regions possibly signifies their increased recruitment for the purposes of vocabulary acquisition in a non-native language and/or for controlling the selection of various naming alternatives. Furthermore, bilingualism appears to restructure other temporal regions which are mainly implicated in low-level phonological processing such as the *STG* and the *HG*, a region whose volume is also related to the ability to learn and perceive non-native sounds (Golestani 2014). Another cluster of regions that are affected by the multilingual experience are located in the prefrontal cortex, particularly in the ventrolateral prefrontal cortex (VLPFC; including all the subregions of the IFG) and the dorsolateral prefrontal cortex (DLPFC; including the MFG and PCG). Along with the also commonly affected ACC, this cluster of regions is central to domain-general executive control, and has an important role in a widespread language control network which is heavily involved in language selection and control in bilinguals (Abutalebi and Green 2016). More specifically, in this model, the prefrontal regions have the task of selecting the appropriate language amongst several alternatives, whereas the ACC is proposed to monitor correct responses when several languages compete, especially in demanding language-switching conditions. Summing up, structural evidence suggests that the multilingual experience restructures cortical regions that are central to three major aspects of speaking more than one languages: phonological acquisition and processing, lexicosemantic acquisition and processing, and language switching and control.

3.2. Subcortical

The evidence relating to the effects of multilingualism on subcortical structures, including the basal ganglia and the thalamus, is significantly more limited than the evidence for the cerebral cortex, but also more consistent. However, it is worth examining them separately from the cortex, because regions such as the caudate nucleus, the putamen, and the thalamus are proposed to have special roles in acquiring and controlling more than one language, along with several cortical regions (see Section 3.1) and the cerebellum (see Section 3.3; Abutalebi and Green 2016). The first evidence for structural reorganization of subcortical nuclei was provided by Grogan et al. (2009), who, by using VBM, revealed that the volume of the head of the left caudate nucleus (LCN) correlated positively with bilinguals' L2 phonemic fluency. The same structure was found to have greater GM volume in bimodal bilinguals of spoken and sign Chinese, compared to monolingual Chinese speakers (Zou et al. 2012). This was interpreted as indicative of the central role that the LCN has in switching between languages (Abutalebi et al. 2008; Crinion et al. 2006), and crucially, irrespective of the modality in which each language is processed. In an L2 vocabulary training study (Hosoda et al. 2013), the volume of bilateral caudate was found to increase with L2 vocabulary training, and to positively correlate with the level of L2 vocabulary that was acquired. Another VBM study showed volumetric increases in the left putamen of female multilinguals compared with monolinguals (Abutalebi et al. 2013b). Importantly, the volume of the left putamen in this group was also correlated to the activation of this region for a picture-naming task only in their L3, which was acquired later in life than their L1 and L2. This suggests that the left putamen might be crucial for the acquisition and processing of additional languages later in life, and the increases in size might reflect the need for it to reorganize to accommodate the increased articulatory demands of a later-acquired language.

More recently, Burgaleta et al. (2016) compared simultaneous bilinguals to monolinguals with FIRST (Patenaude et al. 2011), a Bayesian analytical approach that is optimized for detecting shape changes in subcortical structures. They reported expansion of the bilateral putamen and thalamus, the right caudate nucleus, and the left globus pallidus for bilinguals (see also Berken et al. 2016b, for similar effects in the left putamen for simultaneous, but not sequential, bilinguals). Interestingly, a similar pattern of effects emerged in a study from my lab (Pliatsikas et al. 2017) for highly immersed sequential bilinguals versus monolinguals. More specifically, our results showed expansion of the bilateral putamen and globus pallidus, as well as the right thalamus, while the expansion of the globus pallidus directly correlated with the amount of time the bilinguals had spent in the L2-speaking country (see Figure 3). However, when we examined a group of sequential bilinguals with equal proficiency but a limited amount of bilingual immersion, they showed only minor restructuring of the bilateral caudate nucleus compared with monolinguals, and no other effects.

3.2.1.   Effects on Subcortical Grey Matter: What Do they Tell us?   In all available studies, the effects on the putamen were attributed to its central role in language production, and especially to its suggested role of *controlling articulatory processes* (Abutalebi and Green 2016). Since both the immersed bilinguals in Pliatsikas et al. and those in Burgaleta et al. have spent considerable amounts of time in an immersive environment, it is to be expected that they face increased switching needs at the level of production, which are reflected as restructuring of the putamen. This suggestion might also apply to the putaminal volumetric increases observed for simultaneous vs. sequential bilinguals in

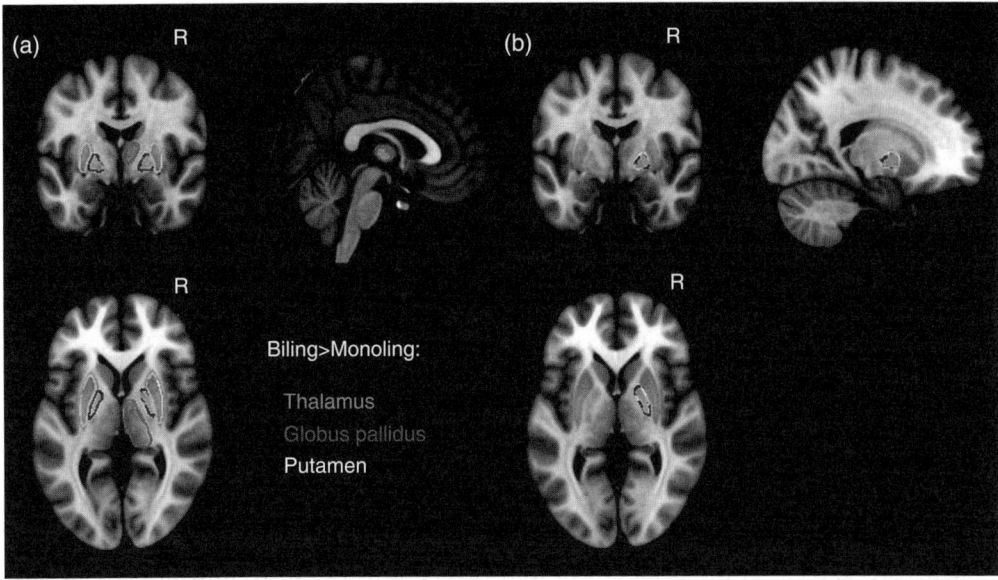

Figure 3 Effects of immersive bilingualism on the shape of subcortical structures. 3a shows the significant surface expansions for bilinguals compared with monolingual overlaid on the outline of the bilateral globus pallidus, bilateral putamen and right thalamus. 3b shows the portions of the right globus pallidus, where linguistic immersion emerged as a significant predictor of surface expansion. Source: Pliatsikas et al. (2017). Distributed under the terms of the Creative Commons Attribution 4.0 International Licence (http://creativecommons.org/licenses/by/4.0). No changes were made to the original image.

Berken et al. 2016b, as the former group should have had more experience in switching between languages. Less is known about the role in bilingual processing of the globus pallidus, which has been shown to activate in L2 *production* tasks (Liu et al. 2010; Stein et al. 2009). The significant restructuring of the globus pallidus in both studies, combined with the effects on its neighbouring putamen, potentially further highlight the role of this structure in L2 production, which seems to increase as a function of immersion, as the significant correlation in Pliatsikas et al. (2017) suggests. With respect to the thalamus, its role in bilingual language production has been highlighted with special reference to its connections between the basal ganglia (putamen, caudate nucleus) and the cerebellum, and it is thought to control the selection of lexical and semantic representations during language production (Abutalebi and Green 2016). As with the effects in the basal ganglia, the reported reshaping of the thalamus potentially reflects increased involvement of this nucleus in language control during production and/or speech monitoring control. Finally, with respect to the caudate nucleus, it is worth noting that significant reshaping in the LCN is usually observed in bilinguals with limited immersion or in bimodal bilinguals. The LCN has been suggested to have a central role in switching between languages in a variety of tasks, and it is especially activated when language proficiency is low (Abutalebi et al. 2013a; Abutalebi and Green 2016). Notably, Elmer et al. (2014) reported *reduced* volume of the bilateral caudate nucleus for simultaneous multilingual interpreters compared to multilingual controls, suggesting that LCN volumetric increases do not apply to highly experienced language switchers, like interpreters. This explanation might also apply to the presence of LCN restructuring in groups with limited bilingual experience.

3.3. The Cerebellum

Similar to the subcortical structures, the cerebellum does not appear very often in the relevant literature. Originally thought to be primarily involved in motor control, the cerebellum is now widely recognized to have significant cognitive functions (Koziol et al. 2014). In the bilingual literature, it has been suggested to have a prominent role in language control, which is further highlighted by its extensive connections with parts of the language control network such as the basal ganglia, the thalamus, and the bilateral IFG (Abutalebi and Green 2016). The limited available evidence points to structural effects in the cerebellum that can be attributed to multilingual experience. For example, Filippi et al. (2011) identified a region in the right posterior cerebellum (VIIIA) where GM volume correlated positively with how efficiently bilinguals suppressed interference from their L1 while performing a comprehension task in their L2. Similarly, research from my lab identified three cerebellar clusters (in bilateral Crus I/II and right V) which were activated in an L2 grammatical task (Pliatsikas et al. 2014a), and whose GM volume was higher for sequential bilinguals versus monolinguals (Pliatsikas et al. 2014b). Crucially, the volume of the affected regions positively correlated with how fast they processed morphologically complex verbs in their L2; however, these effects were not replicated in a recent study by Prehn et al. (2017). Volumetric increases in bilateral parts of the cerebellum (in left VIIIB and right VIIIa/IX) were also reported in Burgaleta et al. (2016) for simultaneous bilinguals vs. monolinguals. Finally, Berken et al. (2016b) showed that GM density in the left cerebellar vermis correlated positively with how native-like the accent of a group of sequential bilinguals was. It is possible that different regions of the cerebellum are sensitive to different aspects of language processing, and this might explain the topographic variety in the results. The existing evidence is too limited for appropriate interpretations to be attempted, but the findings of these studies point to several well-known roles of the cerebellum, including language control (Abutalebi and Green 2016), as well as speech production and comprehension and grammatical acquisition and processing (De Smet et al. 2013). The relative scarcity of cerebellar, compared to cerebral, findings could be due to various reasons, including the type of the multilingual experience of the tested groups; indeed, the available evidence all comes from individuals that were immersed in bilingual environments and active users of both their languages. Therefore, it might be that cerebellar changes only occur after a sufficient amount of multilingual experience; however, more research is needed to confirm this suggestion.

4. The Effects of Bi–/Multilingualism on the White Matter of the Brain

The reported changes in local GM volume and/or shape are thought to accommodate the additional linguistic information that is being acquired, as well as to facilitate efficient language switching and control. However, language processing also entails communication between brain regions that are not necessarily located next to each other. This is provided by several major WM tracts, or bundles of axons, which connect the cerebral cortex with the basal ganglia, the thalamus, and the cerebellum. Consequently, researchers on multilingualism have also focused on whether bilingualism can affect WM structure in order to provide more efficient structural connectivity. Typically, and besides VBM-style volumetric approaches, structural connectivity across the WM is measured by means of how water-diffusive the WM tracts are, i.e. how permeable the myelin is to water molecules. Several measures have been used: Axial diffusivity (AD) measures water diffusion parallel to the WM tract; Radial Diffusivity (RD) measures water diffusion perpendicular to the tract; Mean Diffusivity (MD) is the average diffusivity across all directions at a given tract; Fractional anisotropy (FA) is the most commonly used diffusivity measure, and measures the directional asymmetry of water diffusion. In brief, high FA and AD, and low RD and MD, are usually treated as indication for low diffusivity caused by higher amounts of myelin, which can be due to increased axonal density or myelination within a tract.

Coggins et al. (2004) were the first to report bilingualism-induced WM changes, by comparing scans of long-term bilinguals vs. monolinguals and showing larger volume in the anterior midbody of the corpus callosum (CC) for the bilingual group. This finding was followed up by several studies which used more modern automated techniques, such as tract-based spatial statistics (TBSS; Smith et al. 2006). Luk et al. (2011) compared elderly lifelong bilinguals and monolinguals and revealed increased FA for the former group in a number of WM tracts. The affected tracts included the CC, the bilateral superior longitudinal fasciculus (SLF), the right inferior fronto-occipital fasciculus (IFOF) and the right uncinate fasciculus (UF). Crucially, the same tracts were reported in the majority of the follow-up studies: For example, Mohades et al. (2012) reported increased FA in the left IFOF for simultaneous bilingual children compared with both sequential bilingual and monolingual children, but also reduced FA compared with monolingual children only in a tract extending from the CC to the orbitofrontal lobe. Interestingly, when the same groups were tested again after two years (Mohades et al. 2015), while the FA values in the left IFOF increased for all groups, the increase was higher for the sequential bilingual group, with the authors suggesting that myelination of this tract is 'directly related with the years of being bilingual' (p. 11). In a subsequent study from my lab Pliatsikas et al. 2015, we compared sequential bilinguals that were highly immersed in a bilingual environment and found increased FA in very similar tracts to those reported in Luk et al. (2011), namely the CC and the IFOF, UF, and SLF, bilaterally (Figure 4; see also Rahmani et al. 2017, for further analysis of these data confirming that the FA increases correlated with the amount of immersion in a bilingual environment). A similar pattern was also recently reported by Rossi et al. (2017) even for

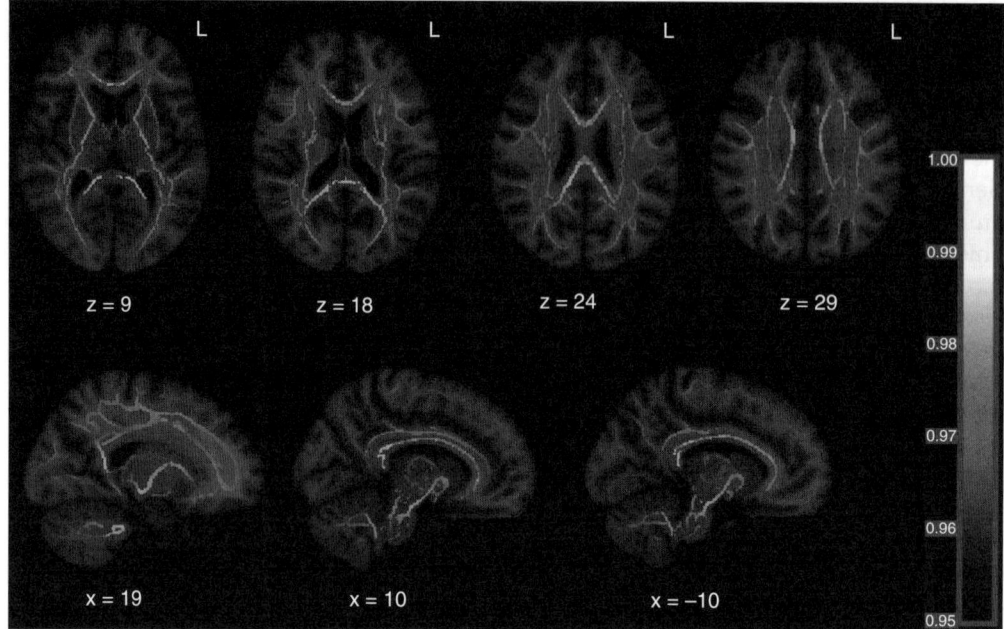

Figure 4   Significant bilingual > monolingual differences in Fractional Anisotropy projected on a standard space skeleton and expressed in 1-P values (p < 0.05, corrected). Source: Pliatsikas et al. (2015).

bilinguals with limited immersion, but the effects significantly correlated with their L2 AoA, further suggesting that these effects cannot be viewed independently of factors pertaining to the amount of L2 experience that bilinguals have. Further evidence for the link between FA and bilingual experience has been provided by Nichols and Joanisse (2016), who reported positive correlations between L2 AOA and FA values in the left ILF, arcuate fasciculus (AF), and the CC, and between L2 proficiency and FA in the right ILF, AF, and the forceps minor (FM), a frontal extension of the CC. Similarly, Singh et al. (2018) reported a significant correlation between L2 proficiency and RD in the right SLF for bilinguals, along with increases in mean MD, RD, and AD for bilinguals compared with monolinguals in the right SLF and FM. Increased volume of the mid-anterior CC for bilinguals was also recently reported by Felton et al. (2017), replicating the earliest findings by Coggins et al. (2004). Moreover, Hämäläinen et al. (2017) reported higher FA in the left AF, lower MD in the right AF and higher MD in the bilateral IFOF for early simultaneous bilinguals vs. late sequential bilinguals. Finally, García-Pentón et al. (2014) used a network-based approach to reveal increased connectivity for early bilinguals vs. monolinguals in a network connecting the left IFG, STG, SFG, SMG, and INS, and a network connecting the left superior occipital gyrus, right SFG, left superior parietal gyrus, left superior temporal pole and left AG.

Similar to GM, important evidence on how WM is affected by multilingual experience has also been provided by several language training studies. For example, Schlegel et al. (2012) collected monthly scans from a group of participants enrolled in a nine-month intensive L2 training course, and compared them to a control group. They reported a parametric increase in the FA of several WM tracts, including the CC, and particularly in tracts that connect regions that are crucial for bilingual processing, such as the bilateral IFG and caudate nucleus, and the left anterior and posterior STG. In another training study, Hosoda et al. (2013) demonstrated increases in the myelination of a tract connecting the right IFG to the head of the right caudate nucleus, after a 16-week training program. Importantly, the same participants were tested again a year after the program had finished, during which time they reported no use of their newly acquired language. At that testing point all the additional myelination had effectively disappeared, suggesting that any bilingualism-related effects in the WM are dynamic in nature and depend on continuous bilingual usage. Similarly, Xiang et al. (2015) reported increases in the FA of the right AF at the beginning of an L2 immersion course, which were reduced, however, as a function of increased proficiency. Moreover, Mamiya et al. (2016) showed that the amount of time that L2 learners spent in a language immersion programme correlated positively with FA and negatively with RD in bilateral SLF; crucially, and reminiscent of the Hosoda et al. results, these effects started to disappear after the immersion programme had ended. The sensitivity of the WM in language learning was recently demonstrated even more dramatically by Hofstetter et al. (2017), who reported changes in regional FA in the left parietal cortex after only one hour of vocabulary training in L2. Moreover, in the same study, the degree of myelination in the left SLF correlated significantly with the participants' rate of vocabulary learning.

Despite the apparent congruence of the available findings, in that bilingualism appears to enhance the intergity of several language-related WM tracts, some contradictory evidence has also been reported. For example, Cummine and Boliek (2013) failed to replicate previously reported FA increases for bilinguals, but reported FA increases (and concurrent MD decreases) for monolinguals instead, in the right IFOF and bilateral anterior thalamic radiation (ATR; see also Singh et al. 2018); however, they also reported lower MD for bilinguals in the left IFOF and FM. Cummine and Boliek attributed this pattern of effects to the fact that their bilingual group were late learners with limited L2 experience. Similarly, Kuhl et al. (2016) reported higher FA and lower RD and MD for monolinguals vs. bilinguals in 21 different cortical WM tracts and in the cerebellum, which they also attributed to their participants' limited immersion in a bilingual environment. Notably, Kuhl and colleagues also reported that the bilinguals' amount of experience in speaking and listening to their L2 correlated positively with FA and/or negatively with RD and MD in tracts such as the left IFOF, SLF, UF, ATR and inferior longitudinal fasciculus (ILF), and the CC, further suggesting that the myelination of these tracts is actively modulated by the bilingual experience. Moreover, Elmer et al. (2011) reported significant *reductions* in FA values in several cortical and subcortical regions across the brain, notably including the CC, for simultaneous interpreters versus controls (who were not specified, however, as monolinguals or bi–/multilinguals). Elmer and colleagues interpreted this finding as evidence for increased efficiency in their highly trained interpreter group. It is worth noting here that, similar to GM effects, interpreters presented idiosyncratic patterns that are not readily comparable to the effects observed in the rest of the bilinguals and/or monolinguals.

4.1.   *Effects on White Matter: What Do they Tell us?*

The increasing evidence on the effects of bilingualism on WM allows for certain patterns to be identified. The affected tracts will be discussed in this section, based on the model proposed by Friederici and Gierhan (2013). One of them is the IFOF, which is defined as one of the ventral pathways connecting the frontal cortex to posterior parts of the brain, such as the posterior temporal cortex and the occipital and parietal cortices. More specifically, the IFOF connects regions that are well-documented to underlie semantic processing, such as the IFG, MTG, AG and posterior STG. A similar role in semantic processing has also been proposed for the ILF, which is also suggested to be part of the same ventral pathway (Mandonnet et al. 2007). The other ventral pathway connecting frontal and temporal regions is the UF, also frequently shown to be affected by the multilingual experience. Specifically, the UF connects the IFG to anterior regions of the temporal cortex, and has been implicated in syntactic processing. Other tracts that have been repeatedly reported in the bilingual literature are the SLF and AF, which form two dorsal pathways connecting frontal and temporal areas. More specifically, the AF connects the IFGop to the middle and posterior STG, and the SLF is a more complex tract, primarily connecting the MTG and the STG to the premotor cortex via the parietal cortex, as well as frontal regions to the AG and SMG. Both pathways are thought to be crucial for speech repetition and for processing of complex syntactic structures. The remaining tracts are less frequently reported in the neurolinguistic literature. Nevertheless, the CC is crucial for interhemispheric communication, and it is proposed to underlie executive control (Just et al. 2007) with its frontal extension, the FM, providing connectivity between the two frontal lobes; a related tract in the region is the ATR, which connects anterior and medial portions of the thalamus to the frontal cortex. Summing up, the available evidence points to bilingualism affecting the myelination of tracts which are fundamental for several aspects of linguistic processing, such as semantics, syntax and phonology, as well as for executive control, which is crucial for bilinguals who constantly have to choose amongst several language alternatives. It is possible that the increased linguistic and language control demands that bilinguals face require efficient communication between brain regions, which is expressed as increased myelination of the connecting tracts.

5.   What about Function?

Along with the emerging literature on the structural changes in the brain, several researchers have also turned their attention to whether the observed alterations in local GM volume and/or WM integrity are also related to altered function of the brain. Although this chapter is primarily concerned with changes in brain structure, it is also worth reviewing the small but informative literature on the effects of multilingualism on the resting state connectivity of the brain, i.e. changes in the default functional connectivity expressed when no task is present, as an additional index of multilingualism-induced brain plasticity, which, similar to structural connectivity, is task- and context-independent.

The literature on the effects of bilingualism on resting state connectivity remains limited, with the majority of the available studies on brain function in bilinguals using cognitive or linguistic tasks in fMRI designs (see Pliatsikas and Luk 2016; Roberts et al. 2018, for reviews). For example, Li et al. (2015) compared Chinese bimodal bilinguals to monolinguals and showed *decreased* connectivity for the former group between the ACC, a region linked to language control, and temporal regions related to spoken language processing, such as the left STG. They attributed this finding to the fact that the bimodal bilinguals used their spoken language overall less often than the monolinguals. Moreover, Becker et al. (2016) reported increased connectivity between the left frontal pole and the left IFG and MTG for professional interpreters compared to multilingual controls, which they attributed to the increased demands brought about by simultaneous interpreting. More recently, a few studies have directly tested the effects of L2 AoA on resting state connectivity, by comparing simultaneous to sequential bilinguals. For example, Berken and colleagues (2016a) used a seed-based approach and showed increased functional connectivity for simultaneous bilinguals between the left and right IFG, and between these regions and regions related to language control, such as the right DLPFC, bilateral IPL and bilateral posterior cerebellum, resembling the patterns reported in Luk et al. (2011). Crucially, in sequential bilinguals, the strength of the functional connectivity between the bilateral IFG and the right IPL correlated with the AoA of the L2: The earlier the acquisition, the stronger the connections. This study was followed up by Kousaie et al. (2017), who showed that activity in a seed in the ventro-medial prefrontal cortex (VMPFC) correlated positively with activity within the Default Mode Network (DMN; posterior cingulate cortex, VMPFC, AG and parahippocampal gyri), which is shown to reduce activity during cognitive tasks, while greater reduction in its activity is related to better performance in tasks requiring executive control; moreover, the same seed revealed negative correlations with activity in regions of the task-positive attention network, including bilateral IFG, DLPFC, and SPL, and the left IPL. Kousaie and colleagues also reported significant effects of L2 AoA, in that the anticorrelations between their seed and two regions from the attention network (namely bilateral DLPFC) were stronger for simultaneous vs. sequential bilinguals, indicating better cognitive control for the former group. More effects of L2 AoA were also reported by Liu and colleagues (X. Liu et al. 2017), who showed that, compared with late bilinguals, early bilinguals had higher functional connectivity between a 'phonological' network (comprising left ITG, IFGtr, IPL, cuneus and right ITG, IFGtr, SPL and MFG) and (i) a 'semantic' network (right IFGop, IFGorb, MTG, MFG, SMG and left AG) and (ii) a 'syntactic' network (left MFG, SFG and right cerebellum).

5.1.   Effects on Resting State Functional Connectivity: What Do they Tell us?

Although the literature on the effects of bilingualism on resting state connectivity remains limited, the available evidence mainly points to changes in the connectivity between language and executive control regions that have already been identified to show volumetric and/or shape increases in multilinguals (see Section 3.1), and are connected by the white matter tracts that are also affected by multilingualism (see Section 4).

Importantly, these effects appear to depend on the L2 AoA, in that the earlier the L2 is acquired the more efficient language processing and control is, a pattern perhaps related to the structural changes found in WM and subcortical GM for simultaneous and/or early bilinguals. In all, the limited available evidence suggests that functional and structural connectivity are inextricably related and are similarly affected by multilingual experience, and as such they should be studied and used together in order to understand the general effects of multilingualism on cognition and the brain.

6.   Bilingualism and the Ageing Brain

It is worth pointing out that the vast majority of the available evidence on the effects of bilingualism on the brain comes from young and healthy populations. Given recent debates regarding the extent to which bi–/multilingualism might provide a benefit in older age, also referred to as a cognitive reserve (Bialystok 2009), and suggestions that it might even delay the onset of dementia (Alladi et al. 2013), it is interesting to examine separately evidence from older bilinguals. This will help determine whether the proposed cognitive reserve has its neurological correlates, i.e. whether the reported 'reinforcement' of GM and WM regions and functional networks which are related to language processing and control, results in a 'neural reserve', expressed as better preservation and/or slower decline of these regions, and/or better connectivity between them, which in turn give rise to the reported cognitive benefits in older age (Perani and Abutalebi 2015).

Despite the importance of the matter, and the vivid discussions that surround it, evidence from elderly populations remains scarce. For example, Abutalebi et al. (2014) revealed greater GM volume in the left ATL for elderly bilingual versus monolingual participants, which they attributed to faster age-related GM decline for the monolingual group, arguing for neuroprotective effects of bilingualism in older age (see also Olsen et al. 2015). Crucially, GM volume in that region correlated positively with the bilinguals' performance in an L2 naming task, highlighting the importance of this region for L2 vocabulary acquisition and retrieval. This finding suggests that the increased lexico-semantic demands that the bilinguals face throughout their lives lead to structural reorganization of this region, which in turn delays age-related decline. Similar effects have also been reported for bimodal bilinguals, who also showed better-preserved GM in regions such as the left INS and hippocampus (L. Li et al. 2017). In another study Abutalebi and colleagues (2015a) also reported greater GM volume in the bilateral SMG for elderly bilinguals compared with monolinguals. Notably, the GM volume in the left SMG correlated positively with the bilinguals' performance in an L2 naming task, whereas the GM volume in the right SMG correlated with their amount of L2 immersion. Finally, in a separate study, Abutalebi and colleagues (2015b) also reported greater GM volume in the ACC for older bilinguals versus monolinguals, further suggesting that the increased usage of this area for the purposes of language switching in bilinguals led to its structural 'reinforcement'.

With respect to WM, the literature remains even more limited. Since the seminal study by Luk et al. (2011; see Section 4) only a handful of studies have looked at elderly bilinguals. Of them, Olsen et al. (2015) used a VBM approach and reported increased WM volume across the frontal lobe for elderly bilinguals vs. monolinguals, which also positively correlated to their performance in a Stroop task, linking WM volume to efficient executive control. More recently, Anderson et al. (2018) reported increased AD in the left SLF for older bilinguals compared to monolinguals.

In terms of functional connectivity, only two studies have looked at older bilinguals: the first resting state evidence was provided by Luk et al. (2011), who reported increased functional connectivity for elderly bilinguals vs. monolinguals between the bilateral IFG and a widespread network including bilateral temporal, parietal and occipital regions, and the LCN. Crucially, this finding was paired with enhanced structural connectivity for the same bilingual group compared to monolinguals (see Section 4), further highlighting that brain plasticity in bilinguals can be concurrently expressed in both structural and functional changes. Grady et al. (2015) looked at the effects of bilingualism on predefined resting state networks that underlie executive control, a cognitive skill in which bilinguals are suggested to outperform monolinguals (for a review, see Valian 2015). Grady et al. reported stronger intrinsic functional connectivity for older bilinguals vs. monolinguals in two major networks: The frontoparietal control network (DLPFC, IFG, IPL), thought to control the involvement of other networks in cognitive tasks, and the DMN.

Of particular mention are three studies which reported *worse* preserved brain in bilinguals compared to monolinguals: Schweizer et al. (2012) studied CT scans of patients with Alzheimer's disease (AD) and found more widespread atrophy for bilinguals versus monolinguals. Similarly, Gold et al. (2013) reported decreased FA and increased RD in the bilateral IFOF and left ILF and fornix in a group of elderly bilinguals compared with monolinguals, where the bilingual group had higher incidence of preclinical AD. More recently, Perani et al. (2017) reported significantly more severe cerebral hypometabolism in a bilingual group diagnosed with AD compared with a monolingual group with AD. Notably, in all three studies bilinguals matched or even outperformed monolinguals in several cognitive tasks, despite their more pronounced brain pathology.

In all, the evidence from older bilinguals seems to form two main patterns, which are related to each other: on the one hand, healthy bilinguals show better-preserved GM and WM in several key regions related to language processing and executive control, sometimes accompanied by more efficient functional connectivity and better performance in tasks related to executive control. Still, it is not clear whether the better preserved structures are a result of 'more' tissue being in place in bilinguals, or of faster decline of these regions for monolinguals, or both. Nevertheless, the reported cognitive reserve appears to be indeed related to better preserved brain structure. On the other hand, bilinguals diagnosed with AD seem to have at least equivalent performance in cognitive tests to monolinguals with less severe neurodegeneration. This pattern suggests efficient *compensatory mechanisms* in bilinguals with AD, e.g. more efficient usage of the spared brain tissue, which are still not very well understood, but nevertheless constitute a different expression of neural reserve in older age. In other words, bilingualism appears to 'optimise' brain architecture throughout the life, making it more efficient in the face of tissue loss in older age, and this potentially is a result of the extensive experience of using multiple languages and switching between them.

7. Conclusion and Further Directions

The above review of the available evidence of the effects of bi–/multilingualism on brain structure and connectivity highlights a few interesting points: first of all, it can now safely be claimed that the experience of learning and using more than one language induces plasticity in the brain, even in late language learners. The changes are not random, but affect brain regions and networks that are central to language acquisition and processing, especially controlling and switching between more than one languages. It also seems that changes in structural connectivity are not independent from changes in functional connectivity; it is therefore worth testing and viewing the two sources of information in a combined manner. Finally, it appears that the well-known and documented effects of multilingualism on cognition (see other chapters in this book) are very likely related to changes in the structure and connectivity of the multilingual brain. This is still a new field, with several issues to be addressed and clarified. Future studies should aim to carefully control experience-based factors, such as the amount and type of immersion in multilingual environments, as well as to carefully measure other experiences that can lead to neuroplasticity (e.g. music, sports, and video games), although we still don't fully understand how neuroplasticity caused by these experiences compares with that caused by multilingualism. Additionally, future research should devise longitudinal designs in order to study the progression of these changes, take into account individual differences in brain structure and function that might be related to the degree of neuroplasticity (for reviews see Golestani 2014; Li and Grant 2016), and critically, combine behavioural, functional, and structural brain data, in order to get a thorough understanding of multilingualism-induced brain plasticity.

REFERENCES

Abutalebi, J., Annoni, J.-M., Zimine, I. et al. (2008). Language control and lexical competition in bilinguals: an event-related FMRI study. *Cerebral Cortex* 18 (7): 1496–1505. doi:10.1093/cercor/bhm182.

Abutalebi, J., Canini, M., Della Rosa, P.A. et al. (2015a). The neuroprotective effects of bilingualism upon the inferior parietal lobule : a structural neuroimaging study in aging Chinese bilinguals. *Journal of Neurolinguistics* 33: 3–13. doi:10.1016/j.jneuroling.2014.09.008.

Abutalebi, J., Canini, M., Della Rosa, P.A. et al. (2014). Bilingualism protects anterior temporal lobe integrity in aging. *Neurobiology of Aging* 35 (9): 2126–2133. doi:10.1016/j.neurobiolaging.2014.03.010.

Abutalebi, J., Della Rosa, P.A., Ding, G. et al. (2013a). Language proficiency modulates the engagement of cognitive control areas in multilinguals. *Cortex* 49 (3): 905–911. doi:10.1016/j.cortex.2012.08.018.

Abutalebi, J., Della Rosa, P.A., Gonzaga, A.K.C. et al. (2013b). The role of the left putamen in multilingual language production. *Brain and Language* 125 (3): 307–315. doi:10.1016/j.bandl.2012.03.009.

Abutalebi, J., Della Rosa, P.A., Green, D.W. et al. (2012). Bilingualism tunes the anterior cingulate cortex for conflict monitoring. *Cerebral Cortex* 22 (9): 2076–2086. doi:10.1093/cercor/bhr287.

Abutalebi, J. and Green, D.W. (2016). Neuroimaging of language control in bilinguals: neural adaptation and reserve. *Bilingualism: Language and Cognition* 19 (4): 689–698. doi:10.1017/S1366728916000225.

Abutalebi, J., Guidi, L., Borsa, V. et al. (2015b). Bilingualism provides a neural reserve for aging populations. *Neuropsychologia* 69: 201–210. doi:10.1016/j.neuropsychologia. 2015.01.040.

Alladi, S., Bak, T.H., Duggirala, V. et al. (2013). Bilingualism delays age at onset of dementia, independent of education and immigration status. *Neurology* 81 (22): 1938–1944. doi:10.1212/01. wnl.0000436620.33155.a4.

Anderson, J.A.E., Grundy, J.G., De Frutos, J. et al. (2018). Effects of bilingualism on white matter integrity in older adults. *NeuroImage* 167: 143–150. doi:10.1016/j.neuroimage. 2017.11.038.

Becker, M., Schubert, T., Strobach, T. et al. (2016). Simultaneous interpreters vs. professional multilingual controls: group differences in cognitive control as well as brain structure and function. *NeuroImage* doi:10.1016/j.neuroimage.2016.03.079.

Bellander, M., Berggren, R., Mårtensson, J. et al. (2016). Behavioral correlates of changes in hippocampal gray matter structure during acquisition of foreign vocabulary. *NeuroImage* 131: 205–213. doi:10.1016/j.neuroimage.2015.10.020.

Berken, J.A., Chai, X.J., Chen, J.-K. et al. (2016a). Effects of early and late bilingualism on resting-state functional connectivity. *Journal of Neuroscience* 36 (4): 1165–1172. doi:10.1523/JNEUROSCI. 1960-15.2016.

Berken, J.A., Gracco, V.L., Chen, J.-K., and Klein, D. (2016b). The timing of language learning shapes brain structure associated with articulation. *Brain Structure and Function* 221 (7): 3591–3600. doi:10.1007/ s00429-015-1121-9.

Bialystok, E. (2009). Bilingualism: the good, the bad, and the indifferent. *Bilingualism: Language and Cognition* 12 (1): 3. doi:10.1017/ S1366728908003477.

Burgaleta, M., Sanjuán, A., Ventura-Campos, N. et al. (2016). Bilingualism at the core of

the brain. Structural differences between bilinguals and monolinguals revealed by subcortical shape analysis. *NeuroImage* 125: 437–445. doi:10.1016/j.neuroimage. 2015.09.073.

Coggins, P.E., Kennedy, T.J., and Armstrong, T.a. (2004). Bilingual corpus callosum variability. *Brain and Language* 89 (1): 69–75. doi:10.1016/S0093-934X(03)00299-2.

Crinion, J.T., Turner, R., Grogan, A. et al. (2006). Language control in the bilingual brain. *Science* 312 (5779): 1537–1540. doi:10.1126/science.1127761.

Cummine, J. and Boliek, C.A. (2013). Understanding white matter integrity stability for bilinguals on language status and reading performance. *Brain Structure & Function* 218 (2): 595–601. doi:10.1007/ s00429-012-0466-6.

De Smet, H.J., Paquier, P.F., Verhoeven, J., and Mariën, P. (2013). The cerebellum: its role in language and related cognitive and affective functions. *Brain and Language* 127 (3): 334–342. doi:10.1016/j.bandl.2012. 11.001.

Della Rosa, P.A., Videsott, G., Borsa, V.M. et al. (2013). A neural interactive location for multilingual talent. *Cortex* 49 (2): 605–608. doi:10.1016/j.cortex.2012.12.001.

Draganski, B., Gaser, C., Kempermann, G. et al. (2006). Temporal and spatial dynamics of brain structure changes during extensive learning. *Journal of Neuroscience* 26 (23): 6314–6317. doi:10.1523/JNEUROSCI. 4628-05.2006.

Elmer, S., Hänggi, J., and Jäncke, L. (2014). Processing demands upon cognitive, linguistic, and articulatory functions promote grey matter plasticity in the adult multilingual brain: insights from simultaneous interpreters. *Cortex* 54: 179–189. doi:10.1016/j.cortex.2014.02.014.

Elmer, S., Hänggi, J., Meyer, M., and Jäncke, L. (2011). Differential language expertise related to white matter architecture in regions subserving sensory-motor coupling, articulation, and interhemispheric transfer. *Human Brain Mapping* 32 (12): 2064–2074. doi:10.1002/hbm.21169.

Felton, A., Vazquez, D., Ramos-Nunez, A.I. et al. (2017). Bilingualism influences structural indices of interhemispheric organization. *Journal of Neurolinguistics* 42: 1–11. doi:10.1016/j.jneuroling.2016.10.004.

Filippi, R., Richardson, F.M., Dick, F. et al. (2011). The right posterior paravermis and the control of language interference. *Journal of Neuroscience* 31 (29): 10732–10740. doi:10.1523/JNEUROSCI.1783-11.2011.

Friederici, A.D. and Gierhan, S.M.E. (2013). The language network. *Current Opinion in Neurobiology* 23 (2): 250–254. doi:10.1016/j.conb.2012.10.002.

García-Pentón, L., Fernández, A.P., Iturria-Medina, Y. et al. (2014). Anatomical connectivity changes in the bilingual brain. *NeuroImage* 84: 495–504. doi:10.1016/j.neuroimage.2013.08.064.

Gold, B.T., Johnson, N.F., and Powell, D.K. (2013). Lifelong bilingualism contributes to cognitive reserve against white matter integrity declines in aging. *Neuropsychologia* 51 (13): 2841–2846. doi:10.1016/j.neuropsychologia.2013.09.037.

Golestani, N. (2014). Brain structural correlates of individual differences at low-to high-levels of the language processing hierarchy: a review of new approaches to imaging research. *International Journal of Bilingualism* 18 (1): 6–34. doi:10.1177/1367006912456585.

Grady, C.L., Luk, G., Craik, F.I.M., and Bialystok, E. (2015). Brain network activity in monolingual and bilingual older adults. *Neuropsychologia* 66: 170–181. doi:10.1016/j.neuropsychologia.2014.10.042.

Grogan, A., Green, D.W., Ali, N. et al. (2009). Structural correlates of semantic and phonemic fluency ability in first and second languages. *Cerebral Cortex* 19 (11): 2690–2698. doi:10.1093/cercor/bhp023.

Grogan, A., Parker Jones, O., Ali, N. et al. (2012). Structural correlates for lexical efficiency and number of languages in non-native speakers of English. *Neuropsychologia* 50 (7): 1347–1352. doi:10.1016/j.neuropsychologia.2012.02.019.

Hämäläinen, S., Sairanen, V., Leminen, A., and Lehtonen, M. (2017). Bilingualism modulates the white matter structure of language-related pathways. *NeuroImage* 152: 249–257. doi:10.1016/j.neuroimage.2017.02.081.

Hervais-Adelman, A., Moser-Mercer, B., Murray, M.M., and Golestani, N. (2017). Cortical thickness increases after simultaneous interpretation training. *Neuropsychologia* 98: 212–219. doi:10.1016/j.neuropsychologia.2017.01.008.

Hofstetter, S., Friedmann, N., and Assaf, Y. (2017). Rapid language-related plasticity: microstructural changes in the cortex after a short session of new word learning. *Brain Structure and Function* 222 (3): 1231–1241. doi:10.1007/s00429-016-1273-2.

Hosoda, C., Tanaka, K., Nariai, T. et al. (2013). Dynamic neural network reorganization associated with second language vocabulary acquisition: a multimodal imaging study. *The Journal of Neuroscience* 33 (34): 13663–13672. doi:10.1523/JNEUROSCI.0410-13.2013.

Just, M.A., Cherkassky, V.L., Keller, T.A. et al. (2007). Functional and anatomical cortical underconnectivity in autism: evidence from an FMRI study of an executive function task and corpus callosum morphometry. *Cerebral Cortex* 17 (4): 951–961. doi:10.1093/cercor/bhl006.

Kaiser, A., Eppenberger, L.S., Smieskova, R. et al. (2015). Age of second language acquisition in multilinguals has an impact on gray matter volume in language-associated brain areas. *Frontiers in Psychology* 6: 1–9. https://doi.org/10.3389/fpsyg.2015.00638.

Klein, D., Mok, K., Chen, J.-K., and Watkins, K.E. (2014). Age of language learning shapes brain structure: a cortical thickness study of bilingual and monolingual individuals. *Brain and Language* 131: 20–24. doi:10.1016/j.bandl.2013.05.014.

Kousaie, S., Chai, X.J., Sander, K.M., and Klein, D. (2017). Simultaneous learning of two languages from birth positively impacts intrinsic functional connectivity and cognitive control. *Brain and Cognition* 117: 49–56. doi:10.1016/j.bandc.2017.06.003.

Koziol, L.F., Budding, D., Andreasen, N. et al. (2014). Consensus paper: the cerebellum's role in movement and cognition. *The Cerebellum* 13 (1): 151–177. doi:10.1007/s12311-013-0511-x.

Kuhl, P.K., Stevenson, J., Corrigan, N.M. et al. (2016). Neuroimaging of the bilingual brain: structural brain correlates of listening and speaking in a second language. *Brain and Language* 162: 1–9. doi:10.1016/j.bandl.2016.07.004.

Li, L., Abutalebi, J., Emmorey, K. et al. (2017). How bilingualism protects the brain from aging: insights from bimodal bilinguals. *Human Brain Mapping* 38 (8): 4109–4124. doi:10.1002/hbm.23652.

Li, L., Abutalebi, J., Zou, L. et al. (2015). Bilingualism alters brain functional connectivity between "control" regions and 'language' regions: evidence from bimodal bilinguals. *Neuropsychologia* 71: 236–247. doi:10.1016/j.neuropsychologia.2015.04.007.

Li, P. and Grant, A.M. (2016). Second language learning success revealed by brain networks. *Bilingualism: Language and Cognition* 19 (4): 657–664. doi:10.1017/S1366728915000280.

Liu, H., Hu, Z., Guo, T., and Peng, D. (2010). Speaking words in two languages with one brain: neural overlap and dissociation. *Brain Research* 1316: 75–82. doi:10.1016/j.brainres.2009.12.030.

Liu, X., Tu, L., Wang, J. et al. (2017). Onset age of L2 acquisition influences language network in early and late Cantonese-Mandarin bilinguals. *Brain and Language* 174: 16–28. doi:10.1016/j.bandl.2017.07.003.

Luk, G., Bialystok, E., Craik, F.I.M., and Grady, C.L. (2011). Lifelong bilingualism maintains white matter integrity in older adults. *The Journal of Neuroscience* 31 (46): 16808–16813. doi:10.1523/JNEUROSCI.4563-11.2011.

Maguire, E., Gadian, D.G., Johnsrude, I.S. et al. (2000). Navigation-related structural change in the hippocampi of taxi drivers. *Proceedings of the National Academy of Sciences of the United States of America* 97 (8): 4398–4403. doi:10.1073/pnas.070039597.

Mamiya, P.C., Richards, T.L., Coe, B.P. et al. (2016). Brain white matter structure and COMT gene are linked to second-language learning in adults. *Proceedings of the National Academy of Sciences* 113 (26): 7249–7254. doi:10.1073/pnas.1606602113.

Mandonnet, E., Nouet, A., Gatignol, P. et al. (2007). Does the left inferior longitudinal fasciculus play a role in language? A brain stimulation study. *Brain* 130 (3): 623–629. doi:10.1093/brain/awl361.

Mårtensson, J., Eriksson, J., Bodammer, N.C. et al. (2012). Growth of language-related brain areas after foreign language learning. *NeuroImage* 63 (1): 240–244. doi:10.1016/j.neuroimage.2012.06.043.

Mechelli, A., Crinion, J.T., Noppeney, U. et al. (2004). Neurolinguistics: structural plasticity in the bilingual brain. *Nature* 431 (7010): 757–757. doi:10.1038/431757a.

Mechelli, A., Price, C.J., Friston, K.J., and Ashburner, J. (2005). Voxel-based morphometry of the human brain: methods and applications. *Current Medical Imaging Reviews* 1 (2): 105–113. doi:10.2174/1573405054038726.

Mohades, S.G., Struys, E., Van Schuerbeek, P. et al. (2012). DTI reveals structural differences in white matter tracts between bilingual and monolingual children. *Brain Research* 1435: 72–80. doi:10.1016/j.brainres.2011.12.005.

Mohades, S.G., Van Schuerbeek, P., Rosseel, Y. et al. (2015). White-matter development is different in bilingual and monolingual children: a longitudinal DTI study. *PLoS One* 10: e0117968. doi:10.1371/journal.pone.0117968.

Nichols, E.S. and Joanisse, M.F. (2016). Functional activity and white matter microstructure reveal the independent effects of age of acquisition and proficiency on second-language learning. *NeuroImage* 143: 15–25. doi:10.1016/j.neuroimage.2016.08.053.

Olsen, R.K., Pangelinan, M.M., Bogulski, C. et al. (2015). The effect of lifelong bilingualism on regional grey and white matter volume. *Brain Research* 1612: 128–139. doi:10.1016/j.brainres.2015.02.034.

Olulade, O.A., Jamal, N.I., Koo, D.S. et al. (2016). Neuroanatomical evidence in support of the bilingual advantage theory. *Cerebral Cortex* 26 (7): 3196–3204. doi:10.1093/cercor/bhv152.

Osterhout, L., Poliakov, A., Inoue, K. et al. (2008). Second-language learning and changes in the brain. *Journal of Neurolinguistics* 21 (6): 509–521. doi:10.1016/j.jneuroling.2008.01.001.

Park, I.S., Lee, K.J., Han, J.W. et al. (2009). Experience-dependent plasticity of cerebellar vermis in basketball players. *The Cerebellum* 8 (3): 334–339. doi:10.1007/s12311-009-0100-1.

Patenaude, B., Smith, S.M., Kennedy, D.N., and Jenkinson, M. (2011). A Bayesian model of shape and appearance for subcortical brain segmentation. *NeuroImage* 56 (3): 907–922. doi:10.1016/j.neuroimage.2011.02.046.

Perani, D. and Abutalebi, J. (2015). Bilingualism, dementia, cognitive and neural reserve. *Current Opinion in Neurology* 28 (6): 618–625. doi:10.1097/WCO.0000000000000267.

Perani, D., Farsad, M., Ballarini, T. et al. (2017). The impact of bilingualism on brain reserve and metabolic connectivity in Alzheimer's dementia. *Proceedings of the National Academy of Sciences* 114 (7): 1690–1695. doi:10.1073/pnas.1610909114.

Pliatsikas, C., DeLuca, V., Moschopoulou, E., and Saddy, J.D. (2017). Immersive bilingualism reshapes the core of the brain. *Brain Structure and Function* 222 (4): 1785–1795. doi:10.1007/s00429-016-1307-9.

Pliatsikas, C., Johnstone, T., and Marinis, T. (2014a). fMRI evidence for the involvement of the procedural memory system in morphological processing of a second language. *PLoS One* 9 (5): e97298. doi:10.1371/journal.pone.0097298.

Pliatsikas, C., Johnstone, T., and Marinis, T. (2014b). Grey matter volume in the cerebellum is related to the processing of grammatical rules in a second language: a structural voxel-based morphometry study. *The Cerebellum* 13 (1): 55–63. doi:10.1007/s12311-013-0515-6.

Pliatsikas, C. and Luk, G. (2016). Executive control in bilinguals: a concise review on fMRI studies. *Bilingualism: Language and Cognition* 53 (9): 1689–1699. doi:10.1017/CBO9781107415324.004.

Pliatsikas, C., Moschopoulou, E., and Saddy, J.D. (2015). The effects of bilingualism on the white matter structure of the brain. *Proceedings of the National Academy of Sciences* 112 (5): 1334–1337. doi:10.1073/pnas.1414183112.

Prehn, K., Taud, B., Reifegerste, J. et al. (2017). Neural correlates of grammatical inflection in older native and second-language speakers. *Bilingualism: Language and Cognition* 21 (1): 1–12. doi:10.1017/S1366728916001206.

Rahmani, F., Sobhani, S., and Aarabi, M.H. (2017). Sequential language learning and language immersion in bilingualism: diffusion MRI connectometry reveals microstructural evidence. *Experimental Brain Research* 235 (10): 2935–2945. doi:10.1007/s00221-017-5029-x.

Ressel, V., Pallier, C., Ventura-Campos, N. et al. (2012). An effect of bilingualism on the auditory cortex. *The Journal of Neuroscience* 32 (47): 16597–16601. doi:10.1523/JNEUROSCI.1996-12.2012.

Richardson, F.M., Thomas, M.S.C., Filippi, R. et al. (2010). Contrasting effects of vocabulary knowledge on temporal and parietal brain structure across lifespan. *Journal of Cognitive Neuroscience* 22 (5): 943–954. doi:10.1162/jocn.2009.21238.

Roberts, L., Gonzalez Alonso, J., Pliatsikas, C., and Rothman, J. (2018). Evidence from neurolinguistic methodologies: can it actually inform linguistic/language acquisition theories and translate to evidence-based applications? *Second Language Research* 34 (1): 125–143. doi:10.1177/0267658316644010.

Rossi, E., Cheng, H., Kroll, J.F. et al. (2017). Changes in white-matter connectivity in late second language learners: evidence from diffusion tensor imaging. *Frontiers in Psychology* 8: 1–15. doi:10.3389/fpsyg.2017.02040.

Schlegel, A.A., Rudelson, J.J., and Tse, P.U. (2012). White matter structure changes as adults learn a second language. *Journal of Cognitive Neuroscience* 24 (8): 1664–1670. doi:10.1162/jocn_a_00240.

Schweizer, T.A., Ware, J., Fischer, C.E. et al. (2012). Bilingualism as a contributor to cognitive reserve: evidence from brain atrophy in Alzheimer's disease. *Cortex* 48 (8): 991–996. doi:10.1016/j.cortex. 2011.04.009.

Singh, N.C., Rajan, A., Malagi, A. et al. (2018). Microstructural anatomical differences between bilinguals and monolinguals. *Bilingualism: Language and Cognition* 21 (5): 995–1008. doi:10.1017/S1366728917000438.

Smith, S.M., Jenkinson, M., Johansen-Berg, H. et al. (2006). Tract-based spatial statistics: Voxelwise analysis of multi-subject diffusion data. *NeuroImage* 31 (4): 1487–1505. doi:10.1016/j.neuroimage.2006.02.024.

Stein, M., Federspiel, A., Koenig, T. et al. (2009). Reduced frontal activation with increasing 2nd language proficiency. *Neuropsychologia* 47 (13): 2712–2720. doi:10.1016/j.neuropsychologia.2009.05.023.

Stein, M., Federspiel, A., Koenig, T. et al. (2012). Structural plasticity in the language system related to increased second language proficiency. *Cortex* 48 (4): 458–465. doi:10.1016/j.cortex.2010.10.007.

Valian, V. (2015). Bilingualism and cognition. *Bilingualism: Language and Cognition* 18: 3–24. doi:10.1017/S1366728914000522.

Wei, M., Joshi, A.A., Zhang, M. et al. (2015). How age of acquisition influences brain architecture in bilinguals. *Journal of Neurolinguistics* 36: 35–55. doi:10.1016/j.jneuroling.2015.05.001.

Wong, P.C.M., Warrier, C.M., Penhune, V.B. et al. (2008). Volume of left Heschl's gyrus and linguistic pitch learning. *Cerebral Cortex* 18 (4): 828–836. doi:10.1093/cercor/bhm115.

Xiang, H., van Leeuwen, T.M., Dediu, D. et al. (2015). L2-proficiency-dependent laterality shift in structural connectivity of brain language pathways. *Brain Connectivity* 5 (6): 349–361.

Zou, L., Ding, G., Abutalebi, J. et al. (2012). Structural plasticity of the left caudate in bimodal bilinguals. *Cortex* 48 (9): 1197–1206. doi:10.1016/j.cortex.2011.05.022.

12 Factors Affecting Cortical Representation

ANGÉLIQUE M. BLACKBURN

1. Introduction

Neuroimaging studies of the multilingual brain have shown largely overlapping cortical representation for each language, managed by a cortical-subcortical control network. Language use relies on a left-lateralized frontotemporal network which includes the middle and inferior frontal gyri (MFG/IFG), posterior temporal region, and associated motor planning, visual, and auditory perception areas. When a multilingual must choose between responses from different languages (e.g. *amour* [love] vs. love), potential responses, especially those used more recently or frequently, are thought to compete and interfere with selection. Networks involved in cognitive control are thought to interact with other elements of language networks to monitor the context and check for errors, inhibit interference, switch between languages, select the correct grammatical rules and lexical items, and perform additional controlled processes necessary for managing the languages (Abutalebi and Green 2007, 2008). The control network involves the anterior cingulate cortex (ACC) and a loop that ramps activity from the prefrontal cortex (PFC), in particular the left IFG, through the basal ganglia, back to the cortex (for a detailed explanation, see Chapter 6 in this volume).

The degree of overlap across languages in this control network and language-specific networks is modulated by a number of factors. The task, similarity between languages, and an individual's age, gender, and verbal intelligence all affect cortical representation of languages. The largest contributors are proficiency and age of acquisition (AoA) of each language. In brief, proficiency has a greater effect on lexical-semantic and control processes, while AoA appears to profoundly affect phonological and grammatical processes. Other factors of interest are the method of second language acquisition, language dominance, and more recently, specific aspects of language experience. In this chapter, I will discuss the impact of each of these factors on the structure and function of language and control networks in light of theories regarding multiple language acquisition.

The Handbook of the Neuroscience of Multilingualism, First Edition. Edited by John W. Schwieter.
© 2019 John Wiley & Sons Ltd. Published 2019 by John Wiley & Sons Ltd.

2.   Language Properties

2.1.   *Language- and Task-Specific Attributes*

One of the most obvious factors that might contribute to differences in cortical representation is the language being used; however, an overwhelming number of studies have shown a remarkably similar left frontotemporal network supporting a wide range of languages (e.g. Briellmann et al. 2004; Videsott et al. 2010; Vingerhoets et al. 2003). Despite much overlap, some cortical differences are incurred by specific attributes of the language or language features related to the experimental task. For example, the visual–spatial complexity of Chinese characters requires recruitment of visual cortex not necessarily involved in processing English words, particularly in the right hemisphere (Tan et al. 2001, 2003, 2005). Some differences in neural activity manifest as a result of morphosyntactic differences between languages (Kovelman et al. 2008; Suh et al. 2007). Additional neural resources are also recruited for a language learned later in life when the task requires attention to prosodic elements of the language (Gandour et al. 2007). In fact, not only do different tasks recruit different aspects of language and cognitive control networks, but the degree of overlap between languages may differ across tasks depending on the interactions of other factors and the task demands (Vingerhoets et al. 2003). Thus, although a wide range of languages have been shown to activate the same basic language network (Bloch et al. 2009; Briellmann et al. 2004; Wattendorf et al. 2014), language- and task-specific attributes affect the precise neural pathways engaged.

2.2.   *Language Similarity*

Bilingual studies have shown similar patterns of activation for different languages, even when the languages are typologically distant, such as English and Mandarin (Klein et al. 1999). Multilinguals afford the opportunity to contrast cortical overlap between two similar languages and two dissimilar languages. To test the import of prosodic and syntactic similarity between languages, Jeong et al. (2007) compared neural activity during auditory sentence comprehension in the native Korean language to the similar Japanese and dissimilar English languages. As in other studies, similar activation in the superior temporal cortex (STS/STG) was observed for all languages, with additional activation in the pars triangularis of the left IFG for the non-native languages. Auditory comprehension in English enhanced activation in the right cerebellum and pars opercularis of the left IFG and activity in the right superior temporal cortex, which the researchers attributed to the syntactic and prosodic dissimilarity, respectively. Despite equivalent proficiency in English and Japanese, the latter did not differ from Korean in these regions, indicating that differences were due to language similarity rather than proficiency. Another trilingual study tested whether language similarity influenced patterns of assimilation (that second language (L2) maps onto existing first language (L1) networks) or accommodation (that L2 recruits additional networks) (Perfetti and Liu 2005). Functional MRI activation in Korean trilinguals during a visual rhyming judgement task in one of their L2's (English) patterned like that of native Korean speakers when the orthographic transparency of L2 was similar to Korean, but like native speakers of their other L2 (Chinese) when the L2 was more distant from Korean (Kim et al. 2016). These results suggest that the L2 maps onto existing L1 networks when it is similar to L1, but additional networks are needed to accommodate the L2 when it is more orthographically opaque than L1. Together, these studies showed comparable cortical activation across languages, and that the degree of overlap in cortical representation depends in part on language similarity.

2.3.   *Language Modality*

The effects of language modality on language representation have also been investigated. Comparison of networks involved during picture-naming in signed and spoken languages has revealed similar lexical-semantic representation, but modality-dependent differences in other aspects of language (Emmorey et al. 2002). In addition to the classic left-lateralized language networks, there is evidence that the use of signed languages requires additional resources in the right hemisphere, especially of the posterior parietal region, and within regions of the left hemisphere associated with somatosensory and visual-motor integration (i.e. left inferior parietal lobe [IPL], including the supramarginal gyrus, and posterior left temporal areas; for a review, see Corina et al. 2012). Corina et al. (2012) proposed that modality-driven differences in cortical overlap may be due to processing that is specific to the visual–spatial characteristics of operating in a signed modality or the unique syntactic properties of the signed language under investigation.

2.4.   *Summary*

Despite small differences in supplementary areas related to specific aspects of visual processing, articulation, or linguistic elements of a specific language, patterns of activation across languages are mostly consistent (Bloch et al. 2009; Briellmann et al. 2004; Perani et al. 2003). The pattern of L1 and L2 activation is considerably overlapping during both comprehension (Abutalebi et al. 2001) and production, regardless of whether the languages are closely or distantly related (Bloch et al. 2009) or in the same modality. Thus, most researchers have concluded that different languages activate a shared language system (e.g. Briellmann et al. 2004; Perani and Abutalebi 2005).

3.   Individual Differences

3.1.   *Verbal Intelligence*

Although not many neuroimaging studies of multilinguals have directly measured the significance of gender, verbal intelligence, and age on the degree of cortical overlap between languages, cortical stimulation mapping (CSM) studies have suggested that these factors play a role in language organization. It is important to keep in mind that these recordings were conducted in patient populations undergoing surgery, so observed effects may not generalize to the population at large. One such study showed that individuals with larger representative language areas exhibited lower verbal intelligence (Ojemann et al. 1989). In addition, different levels of verbal intelligence were associated with different patterns of localization in the temporal lobe (Ojemann 1989, in Ojemann et al. 1989), indicating that verbal intelligence is linked to the pattern and extent of representation.

3.2. Gender

A consistent link between gender, language abilities, and neural organization has not yet been identified. There is some evidence from studies in patient populations that language is represented differently in males and females, with parietal substrates (in addition to frontal and/or temporal substrates) being more likely in males, while the same functions are likely to be represented in frontal sites of females (Ojemann et al. 1989). Certain language-related developmental disorders (e.g. stuttering, autism, and dyslexia) are also more prevalent in males than females, but it remains unclear whether these deficits stem from gender-related differences in the cortical organization of language (Wallentin 2009). In normal populations, there is some evidence of female advantages in some language abilities, especially in vocabulary acquisition during early development; however, most of these effects disappear during childhood or are linked to differences in task-related strategies (Wallentin 2009).

While structural differences do exist across genders (Chen et al. 2007; Good et al. 2001), a consistent structural difference related to language has not been identified in normal populations. A number of studies have reported more left lateralization of language in males than in females (for a review, see Wallentin 2009) or different patterns of lateralization (Kaiser et al. 2007). However, multiple meta-analyses of gender-related differences in language lateralization have led to the conclusion that either no effect exists (Sommer et al. 2004, 2008) or slight increases in laterality effects observed in males could be attributed to different task-related strategies used by males and females or publication biases rather than organizational differences in the brain (Medland et al. 2002).

To conclude, gender differences in development and laterality of language networks may exist, but authors who have extensively reviewed this topic have cautioned that the link between gender and language organization is unresolved due to methodological issues and publication bias in the field (Kaiser et al. 2009; Wallentin 2009).

3.3. Age

Of course, developmental changes occur with age, but one question is whether age is predictive of language organization. As the brain develops and language performance improves during early childhood, language becomes lateralized to the left hemisphere (by around three to five years of age), activation of the semantic networks increases, and activity related to the default mode network decreases during language tasks, which has been attributed to increases in task-relevant regions and/or reduced top-down control as language skills are acquired (Weiss-Croft and Baldeweg 2015). Weiss-Croft and Baldeweg (2015) have proposed that decreases in activation of frontal-parietal regions coupled with increased activation of lower-level sensorimotor regions during language tasks reflect a shift along an anterior–posterior gradient as language processing becomes more automatic. They suggest that with the maturation of dorsal tracts in the language network connecting frontal language areas to more posterior motor and sensory processing regions, processing can be relegated to lower-level posterior regions to automatize language. Of interest, during normal ageing, a reversal of this shift – from activation in sensory processing regions to more frontal and parietal regions involved in top-down control – during performance of various cognitive tasks is thought to reflect compensation for age-related deficits in posterior networks (Davis et al. 2008).

Multilingual studies have indicated that while similar language organization has been observed in both young and older bilinguals (Ojemann et al. 1989), multilinguals do not exhibit the typical age-related posterior–anterior shift during tasks that require cognitive control (Ansaldo et al. 2015). Multilingualism also appears to impact cortical efficiency of the cognitive control networks in normally ageing adults, with fewer and smaller clusters of neural activation than monolinguals (Berroir et al. 2017). This is reminiscent of the effects of other individual factors, with more cortical efficiency in cases of higher verbal intelligence, higher proficiency, earlier acquisition, and more practised language control (see Section 3.4). While age may not directly affect cortical overlap of languages, multilingualism has different effects across the lifespan regarding regions of growth and degeneration in language control networks (Schweizer et al. 2012), and will be discussed further.

3.4. Genetics

Even our genetics may influence cortical representation of language and efficiency of language control. Genetic factors have been shown to shape the structure of language areas (Thompson et al. 2001). Genetic differences may also predispose language and cognitive ability (e.g. Lai et al. 2000; Vargha-Khadem et al. 2005), perhaps by affecting the cognitive control networks necessary to manage two languages.

In particular, genetic differences related to the neurotransmitter, dopamine, may impact the development of multilingual control systems. It has been proposed that dopamine in the striatum plays a role in modulating the control network and improving control processes with practice (Blackburn 2013; Stocco et al. 2010). The role of dopamine in language control is supported by reduced language control in patients with Parkinson's symptoms compared to healthy controls (Cattaneo et al. 2015). Since Parkinson's symptoms occur due to degeneration of dopaminergic networks in the basal ganglia, this finding implicates striatal dopamine in language control.

Bilinguals who achieve higher education in their second language are more likely to carry a dopamine allele that is linked to individual differences in cognitive control, suggesting that this allele benefits young bilinguals who attend school in their second language (Hernandez et al. 2015; Vaughn et al. 2016). Individuals with greater striatal dopamine receptor availability also demonstrate enhanced cognitive control (Ghahremani et al. 2012), and bilingualism appears to compensate for loss of this control resulting from neurodegeneration (Bialystok et al. 2007). Although more research is needed to understand the interaction of genetics and experience, these connections suggest that a dopaminergic network that aids bilinguals early in life may be strengthened by bilingual language use and compensate for the symptoms of age-related neural degeneration later in life. It will not be long before researchers measure transient and long-term dopaminergic receptor density in the striatum of bilinguals to test how bilingual language usage alters this network and whether transient neurochemical changes during language learning transfer to other cognitive systems (Blackburn, forthcoming). While this type of research is in its infancy, researchers are beginning to understand the genetic factors that impact multilingual language representation, acquisition, and control.

4. Language Acquisition and Ability

4.1. Age of Acquisition

There is substantial research investigating whether acquiring a second language either simultaneously with the first language, or at least early during development impacts the formation of language and/or control networks (e.g. K. H. S. Kim et al. 1997; Waldron and Hernandez 2013; Wartenburger et al. 2003). Much of our knowledge regarding the impact of AoA on cortical representation was discovered by comparing the overlap of L1 and L2 in bilinguals who either acquired their L2 early or later in life. The distinction between early and late varies considerably, in part because different aspects of language acquisition (e.g. phonemic categorization, grammar, vocabulary, etc.) have different developmental time courses. Most researchers define the cut-off for a later- acquired language between school age (~6 years) and puberty.

Typically, the earlier the AoA in bilinguals, the more overlap in cortical representation of L1 and L2 (K. H. S. Kim et al. 1997), with later-acquired languages generally eliciting more activation in areas involved in language selection and control, especially in the PFC and basal ganglia, than those acquired early in life (Kovelman et al. 2008; Perani et al. 2003; Wartenburger et al. 2003). Although less common, a few studies have reported greater activation within the language network for early bilinguals compared with later bilinguals, which may be attributed to enhanced use of sensorimotor processing resources within the language networks rather than reliance on executive function (e.g. Mahendra et al. 2003; Waldron and Hernandez 2013) or to greater coactivation of stimulus features (e.g. orthography) in languages acquired together early in life (Liu and Cao 2016). A recent meta-analysis confirmed increased activations in frontal areas for the L2 in late learners, but increased activation in areas related to orthographic processing for the L1 in early learners, suggesting an impact of AoA in both the connectivity and cross-language activation of sensorimotor networks needed for processing of L1 and in the additional networks recruited for controlled processing of L2 in late learners (Liu and Cao 2016).

Importantly, different aspects of language are differentially impacted by AoA. While AoA has shown little impact on cortical representation of the lexical-semantic systems (Abutalebi 2008; Indefrey 2006), it has been shown to affect cortical activity during grammatical tasks (Wartenburger et al. 2003). Both Ullman (2001) and Paradis (1994,

2013) have argued that this difference lies in how word properties and grammatical rules are represented in the brain. Declarative memory is required for the lexico-semantic (e.g. word meanings) aspects of language and involves the left temporal lobe, regardless of when or how many languages are learned. In contrast, both Ullman (2001) and Paradis (2013) assert that because grammar is implicitly acquired for the L1, L1 grammar is governed by rule-based applications that involve a frontal-striatal network, while grammar acquired explicitly at a later AoA depends on declarative memory. Support for this model has come from dissociations in neural activity related to rule-based vs. direct memory retrieval of words and differences in grammatical processing in patients with conditions that affect the basal ganglia (Ullman 2001; Ullman et al. 1997). In addition, increased activation in the basal ganglia as proficiency in L2 increases can been taken as support for a shift from declarative to procedural processing (Golestani et al. 2006). However, Abutalebi (2008) has pointed out that this increase may instead reflect increases in automaticity and cognitive control.

Rather than separate systems subserving grammar in the L1 and L2, Perani and Abutalebi (2005) concluded that the same neural system subserves grammar in both of a bilingual's languages, but the later-acquired language recruits additional resources within this system. During production, late bilinguals tend to recruit a more extensive cognitive control network than early bilinguals, including the dorsolateral prefrontal cortex (DLPFC) and IPL (Waldron and Hernandez 2013). However, early bilinguals also show some neural differences between L1 and L2 production. For instance, more sensorimotor activity has been observed in early bilinguals when generating verbs in L2 than in L1 (Waldron and Hernandez 2013). Similarly to production, common areas are responsible for comprehension of both languages in early bilinguals, with differences between languages manifesting in late bilinguals and modulated by proficiency (greater differences with lower proficiency; for a review, see Blackburn 2016; e.g. Price et al. 1999).

Some of these differences in early and late bilinguals, especially those in sensorimotor regions, may be linked to the method of acquisition. Later-acquired languages are often explicitly learned via visual means, while earlier in life, languages are acquired implicitly in the sensorimotor domain. It has been suggested that not only the AoA, but also the method and modality of acquisition will result in different cortical representation of each language (Diéguez-Vide et al. 2012).

In many of the bilingualism studies, AoA and proficiency were conflated. Multilingual investigations have allowed us to dissociate the effects of AoA and proficiency by comparing non-native languages of similar proficiencies that were acquired at different times (see Table 1 for multilingual studies manipulating these factors). These studies have also enabled us to determine how acquiring two languages impacts the development of language and supporting networks and the acquisition of subsequent languages. Multilingualism findings converge with the conclusion from bilingualism research: the age of second language acquisition is a major determinant in the development of the language network. Multilinguals who are exposed to two languages simultaneously from birth develop a homogenous language network that accommodates each of their languages (Cherodath and Singh 2015), even when the third language is acquired later in life (Bloch et al. 2009). In contrast, multilinguals who acquire their second language

Table 1 fMRI manipulations of age of acquisition (AoA) and proficiency (Prof) across three or more languages.

Authors	Factor	AoA/Prof	Task	Group Comparisons	Language Overlap	Findings
Briellmann et al. 2004	Prof AoA	Quadrilinguals, variable parameters	Noun verb generation	Within-group Good vs. poor prof Early vs. late	Yes: in language areas: MFG, IFG, STG, left IPL(Pa), and contralateral areas	1. Low vs. High Prof: Greater BOLD response in all language areas, more deactivation of PCC 2. AoA: No effect (but not manipulated)
Yetkin et al. 1996	Prof	L2: Fluent (> 5 years) L3: Non fluent (AoA = 2–4 years, not regular conversing)	Covert verbal fluency	Within-group	Yes: Precentral, lateral prefrontal gyri: IFG, MFG	1. Low (L3) vs. High (L2) Prof: Greater activation 2. High Prof (L2) vs. L1: No difference
Abutalebi et al. 2013a	Prof	L2: High-prof (AoA ~ 6 years) L3: Moderate-prof (AoA ~ 8 years)	Language switching; Overt picture naming	Within-group	Yes: Pre-SMA/ACC	1. Prof does not impact pre-SMA/ACC 2. Switching from L1 --> Moderate Prof (L3): Increases left caudate
De Bruin et al. 2014	Prof	L2: High-prof (AoA = 10 years) L3: Moderate-prof (AoA = 12.6 years)	Language switching; Overt picture-naming	Within-group	N/A (L2 and L3 switch and mix effects: No difference)	1. Switching from L1-->High or Moderate Prof (L2/L3) vs. non-switch: Increases rIFG and pre-SMA (and left precuneus, right PCC, right cuneus, right ACC) 2. Switching into L1 vs. Non-Switch L1: No effects 3. Naming High/Moderate Prof (L2/L3) vs. L1: Left IFG, left pre-SMA, right SMA, left pre–/postcentral gyrus, right Heschl's gyrus, right postcentral gyrus, right insula, cingulate cortex, left and right occipital, cerebellum, putamen, right caudate 4. Naming L1 vs. L2/L3: No effects

(Continued)

Table 1 (Continued)

Authors	Factor	AoA/Prof	Task	Group Comparisons	Language Overlap	Findings
Videsott et al. 2010	Prof	L2: High-prof (AoOA ~5 years) L3: High-prof (AoA ~7 years) L4: Lower-prof (AoA ~14 years)	Overt picture naming	Within-group	Yes: PFC including IFG, insula, ACC, occipital/inferior temporal, HCF, precentral gyrus, SMA, cerebellum	1. High Prof (L1 and L2) vs. Low Prof (L4): Right PFC 2. Low Prof (L4) vs. L1: Left IFG, cerebellum 3. Low Prof (L4) vs. High Prof (L2): Cerebellum
Vingerhoets et al. 2003	Prof	L2: AoA = 10.3 L3: AoA = 13.5, Variable prof, good on average	Word fluency, Picture-naming, Reading comprehension	Within-group	Yes: task-dependent areas overlap for all languages, with additional activation for non-native	1. Non-native (L2 and L3) vs. L1: More extensive activation within native language networks and additional activation (exact areas depend on the task), especially left IFG 2. Effects of exposure observed during comprehension
Abutalebi et al. 2013b	Prof	L2: High-prof (AoA ~ 5-6 years) L3: Low-prof (AoA>10 years)	Overt picture-naming (Switching paradigm)	Within-group	Yes: (for all three languages and compared to monolinguals): Occipital/left inferior temporal/fusiform, premotor, left IFG, left MFG, ACC	1. High Prof (L2) vs. L1: IFG (pars opercularis) and ACC 2. Low Prof (L3) vs. L1: More extended IFG (pars opercularis) and ACC, and left putamen
Della Rosa et al. 2013*	Talent	L2/L3: Intermediate competence and exposure L4: Lower competence and exposure	Structural MRI scans/Attentional Network Task	Talent vs. GMV increases over 1 year	N/A	Higher Multilingual Talent: Greater GMV increases in left IPL

Study	AoA	Proficiency	Method	Exposure/Timing		Findings
Kaiser et al. 2015*	AoA	L2: Proficient, simultaneous or sequential L3: Proficient, AoA>9 years	Structural MRI scans	Simultaneous (AoA = birth) Sequential (AoA>2 years)	N/A	1. Simultaneous vs. Sequential: Lower GMV in medial frontal gyrus, bilateral IFG, right medial temporal gyrus, right posterior IPL, left inferior temporal gyrus 2. Sequential vs. Simultaneous: No effects
Bloch et al. 2009	AoA	L2: Medium-High Prof (simultaneous or sequential) L3: Medium-High Prof (AoA>9 years)	Covert narration	Simultaneous Active/Passive Exposure, Sequential (1–5 years), Late (AoA>9 years)	Yes: for all languages	1. Early L2 Groups: Low variability all three languages 2. Late L2 Group: High variability in language areas for all three languages
Wattendorf et al. 2014	AoA	L2: Prof (AoA early/late) L3: Prof (but lower prof ratings than L2; AoA>9 years)	Covert narration	Early: L2 AoA<3 years. Late: L2 AoA>9 years	Yes: for all languages: Left prefrontal (IFG), STS, IPL, SMA, PCC, dorsolateral premotor/SMA, visual, cerebellar	1. Early L2 vs. Late L2 Group: Left frontostriatal for all languages (IFG [BA 44/45], SMA, left ACC, left striatum) 2. Late L2 vs. Early L2 Group: Left posterior STG 3. All Conditions Except L1 for Late Group: Striatum and IFG 4. Language differences – Early vs. Late: left DLPFC, left fusiform

*Structural MRI, not fMRI.

Anterior cingulate cortex (ACC), Blood-oxygen-level dependent (BOLD), Dorsolateral prefrontal cortex (DLPFC), Grey Matter Volume (GMV), Hippocampal formation (HCF), Inferior frontal gyrus (IFG), Inferior parietal lobe (IPL), Middle frontal gyrus (MFG), Pars angularis (Pa), Posterior cingulate cortex (PCC), Prefrontal cortex (PFC), Superior temporal gyrus/sulcus (STG/STS), Supplementary motor area (SMA), Talent = (Multilingual Competence x Attentional Skills).

later in life generally show a higher degree of activation for the L2 and L3 than the L1 (Bloch et al. 2009; Vingerhoets et al. 2003). This indicates that development of the language system and the control systems with which it interacts is moulded by the environment.

One hypothesis is that if two languages are learned simultaneously, representation will be shared, resulting in cortical overlap. A subsequently learned language will register to adjacent areas. In accordance with this hypothesis, one CSM investigation identified shared sites within the left IFG for all of a patient's languages, with extended representation in this region for a later-acquired, but highly proficient language (Lubrano et al. 2012).

Another hypothesis is that early life bilingualism provides an environment in which a bilingual language system develops to manage two languages. General cognitive control systems that aid in language control develop concurrently with both language systems in early bilinguals. Concurrent development may result in greater overlap of language and more general control systems, as evidenced by the use of language systems to perform non-language tasks (Garbin et al. 2010). In contrast, if a second language is learned after development of cognitive control networks, it can converge onto the existing language and control systems; the exact timing of acquisition will determine the neurostructural changes necessary to accommodate the new language (for reviews, see Berken et al. 2015; Blackburn 2018a). Thus, for multilinguals, the age of second language acquisition should be a major determinant in the interaction of language and control systems, even for subsequently learned languages.

Evidence that early multilingualism impacts the interaction of language and cognitive control was found in a study comparing early multilinguals who acquired a second language before the age of three years with late multilinguals who acquired their L2 after nine years (Wattendorf et al. 2014). In both cases, the multilinguals later acquired a third language, attaining high proficiency and regularly using all three languages. Controlling for proficiency and exposure allowed the researchers to independently assess the effect of L2 AoA on systems engaged when using a subsequently acquired language. During silent sentence production, some differences were observed between languages acquired at different times, even within early multilinguals. Compared with late-learned languages, those learned early engaged regions involved in retrieval of contextual information associated with verbal stimuli (that is, integrating stimuli into a context): the left fusiform gyrus and left MFG. However, representations were mostly shared. All three languages activated a common left-lateralized language system for all multilinguals, including the premotor and supplementary motor areas (SMA; Brodmann area [BA] 6), IFG (BA 44/45), STS (BA 21/22), IPL, bilateral posterior cingulate gyrus, visual cortex, and right cerebellum. Sentence production in each language also involved a supporting control system including the left PFC, bilateral ACC, and the left posterior STG.

However, the early and late multilinguals in this study exhibited differences in activation of control networks (Wattendorf et al. 2014). Despite using only one language at a time, early multilinguals showed greater activity than late multilinguals for all languages in a control network implicated in language selection and articulation, including the left frontal (the IFG, SMA/motor cortex, ACC) and subcortical (the striatum) regions.

Thus, the language control networks developed as a result of early multilingualism differ from those developed in a monolingual context and can be recruited for subsequently learned languages later in life. In contrast, late multilinguals showed more activity in the left posterior STG, which the authors suggested reflects control of phonological representations when multilingualism occurs later in life. The authors proposed that late multilinguals cannot rely on frontal-subcortical sensorimotor loops that develop when languages are learned in parallel, so they must instead recruit other task-specific regions. Additionally, the striatum and IFG (BA 47) were engaged for both groups in all conditions except for L1 in late multilinguals, the unique condition in which multilinguals were using a language that was acquired independently of other languages or the need for cross-linguistic selection and control. This may indicate less interference and need for control solely when operating in a high proficiency language that was acquired independently of other languages. The researchers interpreted the results within the emergentist theory – that languages learned in parallel are consolidated and require the development of selection mechanisms that are recruited for control of all languages. Importantly, in accord with previous studies (Bloch et al. 2009) and the emergentist theory, the L2 AoA impacted a subsequently learned language.

This theory is in accord with the finding that multilingual competency during childhood is associated with neurostructural changes in cognitive control areas (Della Rosa et al. 2013). In addition, Kaiser et al. (2015) reported that structural effects of learning two languages simultaneously or successively persist into adulthood. Although they did not find differences in the classic language areas, simultaneous bilinguals who later became fluent in a third language exhibited less grey matter volume in extended language areas than successive fluent trilinguals. Differences were found in areas related to lexical-semantic representation, text comprehension, and vocabulary acquisition. This is in line with functional magnetic resonance imaging (fMRI) studies showing overlap in language areas, but more variable activity for late multilinguals, regardless of similar L3 acquisition (Bloch et al. 2009). The fact that different neurostructural patterns were observed despite L3 acquisition in both cases substantiates the claim that early bilingual exposure gives rise to an efficient bilingual network that can accommodate additional languages.

In summary, AoA profoundly affects cortical representation of languages and language control networks. Compared to early AoA, a later AoA results in less overlap of language networks, with more variable activity within them and additional recruitment of distinct resources, reflecting potentially different mechanisms of phonological and grammatical processing. Although some differences are observed in lexico-semantic regions, the effect of AoA on this aspect of language processing is less pronounced. Acquiring multiple languages early in life develops sensorimotor and language control networks which differ from those of late multilinguals and which are used for subsequently acquired languages.

4.2. *Proficiency*

Proficiency is one of the most studied determinants of cortical overlap between languages, and its effects have been dissociated from the effect of AoA and linguistic factors (for a review, see Abutalebi et al. 2001; Briellmann et al. 2004). In general, each of a multilingual's languages activates a similar frontotemporal network (for a review, see Abutalebi 2008), with the weaker language incurring greater activation in language areas (Briellmann et al. 2004; Hasegawa et al. 2002; Wartenburger et al. 2003; Yetkin et al. 1996) and recruiting additional brain regions (Abutalebi et al. 2013b; Leonard et al. 2011). When two languages are of similar proficiency, a greater degree of overlap is observed (Abutalebi et al. 2001).

In particular, studies using a wide range of language tasks have linked lower proficiency to greater prefrontal control, especially increased activation in the left IFG (BA 47) and the MFG (BA 46; e.g. Hernandez and Meschyan 2006; Videsott et al. 2010; Vingerhoets et al. 2003; Wartenburger et al. 2003). The left IFG is a critical component identified both in language and in controlled processes outside of the linguistic domain. Furthermore, activity in the left IFG is influenced not only by proficiency, but also AoA (Hernandez et al. 2007). Differential activity in this region is even detected within the native language for words acquired at different times (Fiebach et al. 2003). Thus, enhanced activity of the left IFG may be linked to controlled selection that suffers from interference due to a prepotent response from an earlier-acquired word or effortful retrieval of less available items.

In addition to enhanced prefrontal activity, the less proficient language engages other supporting areas. These include other elements of the control network, including the cerebellum (Videsott et al. 2010) and left caudate (Abutalebi et al. 2013a). The weaker language also elicits more delays in activation and there is some evidence for bilateral representation in areas homologous to the left-lateralized language network (cf. Indefrey 2006; Leonard et al. 2010). For instance, while covert verb generation in the first language has been shown to recruit the left DLPFC and IFG, this same task in L2 recruits the homologous right DLPFC and a delayed response in the right IFG (Pang 2012). The IFG is also coactivated with the IPL to a greater degree in lower proficiency bilinguals during complex sentence processing than in native speakers, implying greater attentional demands of operating in the less automatic language (Weber et al. 2016). Activation in the motor areas is also delayed and additional resources in the ACC and insula are recruited. Activation of these additional areas may reflect conflict-monitoring and controlled processing of the more difficult L2 (Pang 2012). Many of these effects, including enhanced activation of the left IFG, decrease as proficiency increases (e.g. Golestani et al. 2006; Leonard et al. 2010).

Like AoA, proficiency differentially impacts cortical representation of different aspects of language. In contrast to AoA, proficiency has less of an impact on grammatical processing, but greatly impacts lexical-semantic systems. It should be noted, however, that even when similar areas are activated, proficiency appears to modulate functional connectivity within grammatical systems (Dodel et al. 2005). Lexical and semantic retrieval tasks in lower proficiency languages generally recruit additional brain regions, most notably the PFC as stated above, whereas attaining native-like proficiency diminishes differences between languages during lexical-semantic access (Abutalebi 2008). Thus, using a lower proficiency language does not only impact activation within the language network, but also recruits additional regions to manage the demands of operating in a less proficient language. These findings support Green's (2003) convergence hypothesis that the second language is learned within the context of an already developed first language and L2 representations converge onto this system; as proficiency in the second language increases, differences in cortical activation of the languages diminish.

One possible explanation for the increase in neural activity for lower-proficiency languages is the additional cognitive demand of operating in the less-proficient language. Increasing the task difficulty in the less-proficient, but not the more-proficient language, increases neural activation within the same network, suggesting an increase in activity to accommodate the greater cognitive demand in the less-proficient language (Hasegawa et al. 2002). The increase in activity observed for a less-proficient language may reflect greater activity of the same neurons or an increase in the number of neurons needed to handle the greater cognitive load of operating in the weaker language. As multilinguals become more experienced with a language, neural activity within the language network may become more efficient for that language (Indefrey 2006). This hypothesis is supported by CSM investigations showing larger essential language areas involved in naming in the less-proficient language than the more-proficient one (Ojemann and Whitaker, as cited in Ojemann et al. 1989).

Another idea is that as familiarity and frequency of words in the L2 increase, a shift away from reliance on interference suppression of the L1 to a more language selective mechanism may decrease activity in the left IFG and eliminate apparent differences between languages (Schwieter and Sunderman 2011). This proposal is partially supported by fMRI and behavioural evidence showing that the L1 is specifically inhibited during switching (for a review, see Chapter 6 in this volume), but subsequently acquired languages with similar proficiency and AoA do not exhibit differences in inhibition as measured by switch costs (response delays during switching) and the degree of activation in inhibition-related brain regions, i.e. the IFG and pre-SMA (De Bruin et al. 2014). In contrast, larger proficiency differences between non-native languages enhance switch cost asymmetries, indicating greater inhibition of the stronger languages (Schwieter and Sunderman 2011).

Another complementary explanation is that as proficiency is attained, a shift is observed from more controlled processing at the cortical level to more automatic processing via a cortical-subcortical circuit (Abutalebi 2008). Controlled processing refers to the conscious effort to retrieve lexical terms, articulate sounds, and follow the rules according to the task goals. In line with this proposal, increased L2 proficiency is associated with a shift from more prefrontal activation to an increase in basal ganglia engagement (Golestani et al. 2006). A shift from prefrontal to subcortical processing via the basal ganglia has been observed with gains in automaticity of other acquired skills (e.g. soccer) as a result of practice (Bishop et al. 2013; Knowlton et al. 1996). According to the conditional routing hypothesis, the basal ganglia receive competing cortical inputs and prioritize those relevant to the goal. Practice increases the ability of the basal ganglia to bias cortical activity and flexibly modify behaviour (Stocco et al. 2014). Thus, proficiency effects may reflect a shift to automatic processing via a subcortical network with L2 practice.

Finally, increased proficiency is associated with an increase in the grey matter volume of both the temporal lobes (Abutalebi et al. 2014) and IPL (Della Rosa et al. 2013; Mechelli et al. 2004). As noted by Abutalebi and Green (2016), these regions are amongst the first impacted by ageing and mild cognitive impairment, suggesting that structural changes related to multilingual proficiency may be a source of multilingualism's protective effect during ageing and pathology.

In summary, lower-proficiency languages are typically subserved by the same frontotemporal network as higher-proficiency languages, but the additional effort and control needed to operate in a weaker language drives the language areas more and recruits additional resources. As proficiency increases, non-native languages may converge onto the existing networks for the native language, become more accessible with increased familiarity and frequency, experience less interference from the L1, require less activity for efficient processing, and shift to more automatic processing via a subcortical network. These changes are associated with long-term neurostructural modifications that may serve a protective function during neurodegeneration.

4.3.   *Language Dominance*

Proficiency and AoA are often confounded. Researchers have attempted to dissociate these factors by observing bilinguals who have become dominant in their second language. In one such study of visual and auditory lexical processing, similar activation was found in the frontotemporal language network for both languages, but more activity was observed in bilateral posterior visual areas for the less dominant native language during semantic retrieval. This suggests that additional resources are recruited to manage semantic access in the less proficient language, either by extension of an existing mechanism or due to reliance on a perceptual semantic system rather than the abstract system represented in the frontotemporal network (Leonard et al. 2011). The results implicate proficiency, not AoA, in the recruitment of additional resources; however, these factors interact in some aspects of language representation.

4.4.   *Interaction of AoA and Proficiency*

Importantly, proficiency and AoA are often linked, and there is evidence that these factors interact in the development of neural networks. An interaction of these factors has been observed during comprehension in bilinguals, such that a shared neural network represents both languages when they are acquired early, but proficiency modulates the degree of overlap in late bilinguals. That is, early bilinguals and late high-proficiency bilinguals demonstrate overlapping representations for each language, but late low-proficiency bilinguals have different patterns of activation (Abutalebi et al. 2001; see also Liu and Cao 2016). This implies that learning two languages simultaneously yields overlap in the systems, but that later-learned languages converge onto the existing system only when enough fluency is obtained.

Although changes in proficiency have been shown to alter activation patterns in adulthood, relative proficiency of each language early in life also likely affects the course of development. Proficient management of multiple languages during childhood is linked to performance on attentional tasks and structural changes in the attentional control networks (specifically the pars angularis of the left IPL; Della Rosa et al. 2013). Thus, multilingual competency may arise due to interactions with other cognitive systems during development. Researchers are still investigating the impact of relative proficiencies and other factors (such as linguistic environment) on the development of language and control systems.

5.   Language Experience

5.1.   *Exposure*

Like proficiency, more exposure to a second language is associated with diminished differences between L1 and L2 activation, especially in regions associated with controlled language use. Catalan native speakers with less exposure to their L2 (Spanish) showed greater left lateral prefrontal and inferior parietal activation during a verbal fluency task than Spanish native speakers living in a region with high exposure to their L2 (Catalan; Perani et al. 2003). Importantly, even though these two groups demonstrated similar proficiency and acquired their second language early (around kindergarten), more extensive activation for the later-acquired language was modulated by exposure, with more exposure related to a decrease in the extent of activation. Similarly, activity in the left lateral PFC decreases even as monolinguals gain experience with a language task (Thompson-Schill et al. 1999). Thus, activity in the left lateral frontal cortex during L2 production may reflect more controlled processing for languages with less exposure. This suggests that some of the differences in L1 and L2 activation stem from difficulty or unfamiliarity with using the L2.

Other studies have also found an effect of exposure on language control. More activity has been observed in the ACC and left caudate during auditory comprehension when switching into a language with less exposure (Abutalebi et al. 2007). Even after only 30 days of differential exposure to two early, high-proficiency languages, bilinguals showed increased activity in the ACC for silent narration in the less-exposed language, as well as marginal negative correlations between exposure and activity in the pars opercularis of the left IFG, the left MFG, and the left caudate (Tu et al. 2015). Since this effect occurred so rapidly, the researchers suggested that lack of exposure to a language may decrease lexical availability, driving both lexical access and cognitive control during retrieval.

The effects of exposure on neural activation also depend on the task. Although one study revealed only a minor effect of exposure during picture-naming, reading comprehension in the same participants showed increased activation in the left inferior frontal cortex for a non-native language with low exposure compared to a non-native language with high exposure (Vingerhoets et al. 2003). Additional bilateral inferior frontal activation was also observed for the low-exposed language compared to the native language. The researchers suggested that this difference in inferior frontal activation may reflect a different mechanism of visual word form recognition as a consequence of exposure. A word fluency task showed a different pattern, with greater activity in frontal and parietal regions for the more-exposed language. In this case, performance was enhanced in the more-exposed language, implicating a possible interaction of performance and exposure that is yet to be explored (Vingerhoets et al. 2003). Together, these studies indicate that prefrontal activity decreases with exposure, but that this effect is modulated by the task and performance.

5.2.   *Language Environment and Use*

Even when different multilinguals have the same language exposure, they may not use their languages in the same way. As yet, no known neuroimaging studies of cortical representation based on language habits have been conducted. However, behavioural and electrophysiological studies have provided evidence that language habits impact both language and general cognitive abilities and underlying neural activity (Blackburn 2018b). In particular, individuals living in bilingual communities may experience a high degree of language interference as they must be prepared to switch readily between languages with changes in the conversation or context. Managing language interference and switching between languages frequently throughout the day in a dual-language context incurs benefits and enhanced neural activity related to language switching, task switching, and interference suppression (Blackburn 2013; Hartanto and Yang 2016; cf. Johnson et al. 2015; Verreyt et al. 2016). Some bilinguals reside in dense code-switching environments, in which it is common to alternate effortlessly between languages within a conversation (Green & Abutalebi 2013). In this context, language may be used creatively and a high level of monitoring is necessary to process unpredictable language switches, conferring benefits in creativity, cognitive flexibility, and monitoring (Hofweber et al. 2016; Kharkhurin and Wei 2015). Research has shown that language context has short-term effects on activation of control structures (i.e. the caudate Abutalebi et al. 2008); these effects may be linked to long-term neurostructural changes (Zou et al. 2012). As research regarding language habits and environment expands into the neuroimaging domain, it will be possible to test predictions regarding structural and functional connectivity changes as a result of time spent in different language contexts. For instance, compared with multilinguals in a dense code-switching environment and those who generally use a single language at a time, multilinguals who reside in a dual-language context may exhibit more efficient language control networks and possibly less deterioration of these networks during ageing (Green and Wei 2014).

6.   Number of Languages and Neuroprotection

As mentioned in Section 4.2, acquiring multiple languages appears to have a protective effect against age-related brain atrophy and neurodegeneration. Speaking at least two languages has been associated with protection against the symptoms of Alzheimer's disease and other forms of dementia (Bialystok et al. 2007; Craik et al. 2010; Schweizer et al. 2012), either by increasing the efficiency and resilience of language and control networks or by developing functionally connected networks that compensate for those that are lost with age or pathology (Perani and Abutalebi 2015). Bilingualism has been associated with preserving white matter integrity during ageing (Luk et al. 2011) and structural and functional connectivity changes in the language and control networks (e.g. Li et al. 2015; Perani et al. 2017; Zou et al. 2012). In fact, simply learning a second language or halting language training can rapidly alter white matter integrity in the right hemisphere (Hosoda et al. 2013) and in language areas (Schlegel et al. 2012).

Of interest is what factors impact these protective alterations in the multilingual brain. Both AoA and proficiency have been correlated with structural modifications of bilingualism (Mechelli et al. 2004). In addition, the number of languages acquired correlates with protection against cognitive impairment and enhanced cognitive performance in older populations, even when controlling for other factors affecting cognitive ageing such as education, age, and leisure activities (Kavé et al. 2008; Perquin et al. 2013). In one such study of multilinguals, researchers assessed the language, leisure, and neuropsychological background of 232 participants to model how each of these features impacts the probability of exhibiting cognitive impairment without dementia (Perquin et al. 2013). The results indicated a benefit of multilingualism that peaks at three languages learned early in life, with seven times more protection for trilinguals than bilinguals and 13 times more protection when two of the languages were acquired simultaneously and early in life. Thus, using two or more languages appears to protect against cognitive ageing, with the greatest benefits found for learning at least three languages earlier in life, but the benefits plateau as the number of acquired languages increases beyond three. This may be related to the functional and structural changes associated with managing two or more languages.

7. Conclusion

In conclusion, there is overwhelming evidence that languages share overlapping cortical representation, although differences arise due to the task, language attributes, individual differences, and experience. Additional regions are often engaged to handle aspects of processing that are specifically related to the task and language, including language modality. Low proficiency, later AoA, and lower verbal intelligence are linked to more extensive and variable activation in regions surrounding and supporting the language networks. Acquiring multiple languages early in life appears to develop a language control and articulatory network which differs from that of late multilinguals and is used for subsequently acquired languages. Using lower-proficiency languages requires greater neural activity, especially within the control network, but as proficiency increases, language networks may become more efficient, the L2 may converge with the L1, and a shift to subcortical automatic processing may occur. Similarly, activity in control regions, most notably the left IFG, decreases with exposure, but this effect is modulated by the task and performance.

It should be briefly noted that the additional areas recruited for specialized language functions or more difficult processing often involve the right hemisphere. For instance, languages that require special attention to visuospatial processing (e.g. Mandarin and signed language) involve greater right hemisphere activation in the visual cortex. Learning a second language results in changes to white matter tracks in the right hemisphere and compared with L1, operating in the less-proficient L2 recruits additional cognitive control regions in the right hemisphere. Thus, the right hemisphere may serve in part to provide additional resources for expansion of the left-lateralized language networks during learning or when the system is taxed.

More research is needed regarding individual differences in genetics and gender, which likely play a role in organization. Although in its infancy, researchers are also starting to recognize the importance of language environment, both currently and during development, on cortical representation. Because researchers recognize the importance of these factors, future investigations are likely to take individual differences into account. Some effects of these individual differences, such as enhancement of bilingualism's neuroprotection with early multilingual exposure, demonstrate that individual variability affects language and control networks in a way that significantly impacts cognition.

REFERENCES

Abutalebi, J. (2008). Neural aspects of second language representation and language control. *Acta Psychologica* 128 (3): 466–478. https://doi.org/10.1016/j.actpsy.2008.03.014.

Abutalebi, J., Annoni, J.-M., Zimine, I. et al. (2008). Language control and lexical competition in bilinguals: an event-related fMRI study. *Cerebral Cortex* 18: 1496–1505.

Abutalebi, J., Brambati, S., M., Annoni, J.-M. et al. (2007). The neural cost of the auditory perception of language switches: an event-related functional magnetic resonance imaging study in bilinguals. *The Journal of Neuroscience* 27 (50): 13762–13769.

Abutalebi, J., Canini, M., Della Rosa, P.A. et al. (2014). Bilingualism protects anterior temporal lobe integrity in aging. *Neurobiology of Aging* 35 (9): 2126–2133. https://doi.org/10.1016/j.neurobiolaging.2014.03.010.

Abutalebi, J., Cappa, S.F., and Perani, D. (2001). The bilingual brain as revealed by functional neuroimaging. *Bilingualism: Language and Cognition* 4 (2): 179–190. https://doi.org/10.1017/S136672890100027X.

Abutalebi, J., Della Rosa, P.A., Ding, G. et al. (2013a). Language proficiency modulates the engagement of cognitive control areas in multilinguals. *Cortex* 49 (3): 905–911. https://doi.org/10.1016/j.cortex.2012.08.018.

Abutalebi, J., Della Rosa, P.A., Gonzaga, A.K.C. et al. (2013b). The role of the left putamen in multilingual language production. *Brain and Language* 125: 307–315.

Abutalebi, J. and Green, D.W. (2007). Bilingual language production: the neurocognition of language representation and control. *Journal of Neurolinguistics* 20: 242–275.

Abutalebi, J. and Green, D.W. (2008). Control mechanisms in bilingual language production: neural evidence from language switching studies. *Language & Cognitive Processes* 23 (4): 557–582.

Abutalebi, J. and Green, D.W. (2016). Neuroimaging of language control in bilinguals: neural adaptation and reserve. *Bilingualism: Language and Cognition* 19 (4): 689–698. https://doi.org/10.1017/S1366728916000225.

Ansaldo, A.I., Ghazi-Saidi, L., and Adrover-Roig, D. (2015). Interference control in elderly bilinguals: appearances can be misleading. *Journal of Clinical and Experimental Neuropsychology* 37 (5): 455–470. https://doi.org/10.1080/13803395.2014.990359.

Berken, J.A., Gracco, V.L., Chen, J.-K., and Klein, D. (2015). The timing of language learning shapes brain structure associated with articulation. *Brain Structure and Function* 1–10. https://doi.org/10.1007/s00429-015-1121-9.

Berroir, P., Ghazi-Saidi, L., Dash, T. et al. (2017). Interference control at the response level: functional networks reveal higher efficiency in the bilingual brain. *Journal of Neurolinguistics* 43 (Part A): 4–16. https://doi.org/10.1016/j.jneuroling.2016.09.007.

Bialystok, E., Craik, F.I., and Freedman, M. (2007). Bilingualism as a protection against the onset of symptoms of dementia. *Neuropsychologia* 45: 459–464.

Bishop, D.T., Wright, M.J., Jackson, R.C., and Abernethy, B. (2013). Neural bases for anticipation skill in soccer: an fMRI study. *Journal of Sport and Exercise Psychology* 35 (1): 98–109. https://doi.org/10.1123/jsep.35.1.98.

Blackburn, A. M. (2013). *A study of the relationship between code switching and the bilingual advantage: evidence that language use modulates neural indices of language processing and cognitive control*. PhD Neurobiology, University of Texas at San Antonio, San Antonio.

Blackburn, A.M. (2016). MRI methods in bilingual reading comprehension. In: *Methods in Bilingual Reading Comprehension Research* (ed. R.R. Heredia, J. Altarriba and A.B. Cieślicka), 313–352. New York, NY: Springer New York.

Blackburn, A.M. (2018a). The bilingual brain. In: *An Introduction to Bilingualism: Principles and Processes*, 2nde (ed. J. Altarriba and R.R. Heredia), 107–138. London, UK: Psychology Press.

Blackburn, A.M. (2018b). Cognitive impact of bilingualism and language habits at the borders of cultures and nations. In: *Inquiries into Literacy Learning and Intercultural Competency in a World of Border Tensions* (ed. T. Huber and P.S. Roberson), 141–166. Charlotte, NC: Information Age Publishing.

Blackburn, A.M. (forthcoming). The bilingual brain: mechanical tools. In: *The Bilingual Brain Unwrapped* (ed. R.R. Heredia and A.B. Cieślicka). London, UK: Psychology Press.

Bloch, C., Kaiser, A., Kuenzli, E. et al. (2009). The age of second language acquisition determines the variability in activation elicited by narration in three languages in Broca's and Wernicke's area. *Neuropsychologia* 47 (3): 625–633. https://doi.org/10.1016/j.neuropsychologia.2008.11.009.

Briellmann, R.S., Saling, M.M., Connell, A.B. et al. (2004). A high-field functional MRI study of quadri-lingual subjects. *Brain and Language* 89 (3): 531–542. https://doi.org/10.1016/j.bandl.2004.01.008.

Cattaneo, G., Calabria, M., Marne, P. et al. (2015). The role of executive control in bilingual language production: a study with Parkinson's disease individuals. *Neuropsychologia* 66: 99–110. https://doi.org/10.1016/j.neuropsychologia.2014.11.006.

Chen, X., Sachdev, P.S., Wen, W., and Anstey, K.J. (2007). Sex differences in regional gray matter in healthy individuals aged 44–48 years: a voxel-based morphometric study. *NeuroImage* 36 (3): 691–699. https://doi.org/10.1016/j.neuroimage.2007.03.063.

Cherodath, S. and Singh, N.C. (2015). The influence of orthographic depth on reading networks in simultaneous biliterate children. *Brain and Language* 143 (Supplement C): 42–51. https://doi.org/10.1016/j.bandl.2015.02.001.

Corina, D.P., Lawyer, L.A., and Cates, D. (2012). Cross-linguistic differences in the neural representation of human language: evidence from users of signed languages. *Frontiers in Psychology* 3: 587. https://doi.org/10.3389/fpsyg.2012.00587.

Craik, F.I., Bialystok, E., and Freedman, M. (2010). Delaying the onset of Alzheimer disease: bilingualism as a form of cognitive reserve. *Neurology* 75: 1726–1729.

Davis, S.W., Dennis, N.A., Daselaar, S.M. et al. (2008). Qué PASA? The posterior-anterior shift in aging. *Cerebral Cortex* (New York, N.Y.: 1991) 18 (5): 1201–1209. https://doi.org/10.1093/cercor/bhm155.

De Bruin, A., Roelofs, A., Dijkstra, T., and FitzPatrick, I. (2014). Domain-general inhibition areas of the brain are involved in language switching: FMRI evidence from trilingual speakers. *NeuroImage* 90: 348–359.

Della Rosa, P.A., Videsott, G., Borsa, V.M. et al. (2013). A neural interactive location for multilingual talent. *Cortex* 49 (2): 605–608. https://doi.org/10.1016/j.cortex.2012.12.001.

Diéguez-Vide, F., Gich-Fullà, J., Puig-Alcántara, J. et al. (2012). Chinese–Spanish–Catalan trilingual aphasia: a case study. *Journal of Neurolinguistics* 25 (6): 630–641. https://doi.org/10.1016/j.jneuroling.2012.01.002.

Dodel, S., Golestani, N., Palllier, C. et al. (2005). Condition-dependent functional connectivity: syntax networks in bilinguals. *Philosophical Transactions of the Royal Society of London* 360 (1457): 921–935.

Emmorey, K., Damasio, H., McCullough, S. et al. (2002). Neural systems underlying spatial language in American sign language. *NeuroImage* 17 (2): 812–824.

Fiebach, C.J., Friederici, A.D., Muller, K. et al. (2003). Distinct brain representations for early and late learned words. *NeuroImage* 19 (4): 1627–1637.

Gandour, J., Tong, Y., Talavage, T. et al. (2007). Neural basis of first and second language processing of sentence-level linguistic prosody. *Human Brain Mapping* 28 (2): 94–108. https://doi.org/10.1002/hbm.20255.

Garbin, G., Sanjuan, A., Forn, C. et al. (2010). Bridging language and attention: brain basis of the impact of bilingualism on cognitive control. *NeuroImage* 53 (4): 1272–1278. https://doi.org/10.1016/j.neuroimage.2010.05.078.

Ghahremani, D.G., Lee, B., Robertson, C.L. et al. (2012). Striatal dopamine D(2)/D(3) receptors mediate response inhibition and related activity in frontostriatal neural circuitry in humans. *The Journal of neuroscience: The Official Journal of the Society for Neuroscience* 32 (21): 7316–7324. https://doi.org/10.1523/JNEUROSCI.4284-11.2012.

Golestani, N., Alario, F.X., Meriaux, S. et al. (2006). Syntax production in bilinguals. *Neuropsychologia* 44 (7): 1029–1040. https://doi.org/10.1016/j.neuropsychologia.2005.11.009.

Good, C.D., Johnsrude, I., Ashburner, J. et al. (2001). Cerebral asymmetry and the effects of sex and handedness on brain structure: a voxel-ased morphometric analysis of 465 normal adult human brains. *NeuroImage* 14 (3): 685–700. https://doi.org/10.1006/nimg.2001.0857.

Green, D.W. (2003). Neural basis of lexicon and grammar in L2 acquisition: the convergence hypothesis. In: *The Lexicon-Syntax Interface in Second Language Acquisition* (ed. R. van Hout, A. Hulk, F. Kuiken and R. Towell), 197–218. Amsterdam, UK: John Benjamins.

Green, D.W. and Abutalebi, J. (2013). Language control in bilinguals: The adaptive control hypothesis. *Journal of Cognitive Psychology* 25 (5): 515–530.

Green, D.W. and Wei, L. (2014). A control process model of code-switching. *Language, Cognition and Neuroscience* 29 (4): 499–511. doi: 10.1080/23273798.2014.882515.

Hartanto, A. and Yang, H. (2016). Disparate bilingual experiences modulate task-switching advantages: a diffusion-model analysis of the effects of interactional context on switch costs. *Cognition* 150: 10–19. https://doi.org/10.1016/j.cognition.2016.01.016.

Hasegawa, M., Carpenter, P.A., and Just, M.A. (2002). An fMRI study of bilingual sentence comprehension and workload. *NeuroImage* 15 (3): 647–660. https://doi.org/10.1006/nimg.2001.1001.

Hernandez, A., Greene, M.R., Vaughn, K.A. et al. (2015). Beyond the bilingual advantage: the potential role of genes and environment on the development of cognitive control. *Journal of Neurolinguistics* 35: 109–119. https://doi.org/10.1016/j.jneuroling.2015.04.002.

Hernandez, A., Hofmann, J., and Kotz, S.A. (2007). Age of acquisition modulates neural activity for both regular and irregular syntactic functions. *NeuroImage* 36 (3): 912–923. https://doi.org/10.1016/j.neuroimage.2007.02.055.

Hernandez, A. and Meschyan, G. (2006). Executive function is necessary to enhance lexical processing in a less proficient L2: evidence from fMRI during picture naming. *Bilingualism: Language and Cognition* 9 (2): 177–188.

Hofweber, J., Marinis, T., and Treffers-Daller, J. (2016). Effects of dense code-switching on executive control. *Linguistic Approaches to Bilingualism* 6 (5): 648–668. https://doi.org/10.1075/lab.15052.hof.

Hosoda, C., Tanaka, K., Nariai, T. et al. (2013). Dynamic neural network reorganization associated with second language vocabulary acquisition: a multimodal imaging study. *The Journal of Neuroscience* 33 (34): 13663–13672. https://doi.org/10.1523/jneurosci.0410-13.2013.

Indefrey, P. (2006). A meta-analysis of hemodynamic studies on first and second language processing: which suggested differences can we trust and what do they mean? *Language Learning* 56: 279–304.

Jeong, H., Sugiura, M., Sassa, Y. et al. (2007). Effect of syntactic similarity on cortical activation during second language processing: a comparison of English and Japanese among native Korean trilinguals. *Human Brain Mapping* 28 (3): 194–204. https://doi.org/10.1002/hbm.20269.

Johnson, H. A., Sawi, O., & Paap, K. R. (2015). *Language switching frequency in bilinguals is inconsistently linked to executive functioning.* Paper presented at the Cognitive Neuroscience Society, San Francisco, CA.

Kaiser, A., Eppenberger, L.S., Smieskova, R. et al. (2015). Age of second language acquisition in multilinguals has an impact on gray matter volume in language-associated brain areas. *Frontiers in Psychology* 6 (638): https://doi.org/10.3389/fpsyg.2015.00638.

Kaiser, A., Haller, S., Schmitz, S., and Nitsch, C. (2009). On sex/gender related similarities and differences in fMRI language research. *Brain Research Reviews* 61 (2): 49–59. https://doi.org/10.1016/j.brainresrev.2009.03.005.

Kaiser, A., Kuenzli, E., Zappatore, D., and Nitsch, C. (2007). On females' lateral and males' bilateral activation during language production: a fMRI study. *International Journal of Psychophysiology* 63 (2): 192–198. https://doi.org/10.1016/j.ijpsycho.2006.03.008.

Kavé, G., Eyal, N., Shorek, A., and Cohen-Mansfield, J. (2008). Multilingualism and cognitive state in the oldest old. *Psychology and Aging* 23 (1): 70–78. https://doi.org/10.1037/0882-7974.23.1.70.

Kharkhurin, A.V. and Wei, L. (2015). The role of code-switching in bilingual creativity. *International Journal of Bilingual Education and Bilingualism* 18 (2): 153–169. https://doi.org/10.1080/13670050.2014.884211.

Kim, K.H.S., Relkin, N.R., Lee, K.M., and Hirsch, J. (1997). Distinct cortical areas associated with native and second languages. *Nature* 388 (6638): 171–174. https://doi.org/10.1038/40623.

Kim, S.Y., Qi, T., Feng, X. et al. (2016). How does language distance between L1 and L2 affect the L2 brain network? An fMRI study of Korean–Chinese–English trilinguals. *NeuroImage* 129 (Supplement C): 25–39. https://doi.org/10.1016/j.neuroimage.2015.11.068.

Klein, D., Milner, B., Zatorre, R.J. et al. (1999). Cerebral organization in bilinguals: a PET study of Chinese-English verb generation. *NeuroReport* 10 (13): 2841–2846.

Knowlton, B.J., Mangels, J.A., and Squire, L.R. (1996). A neostriatal habit learning system in humans. *Science* 273: 1399–1402.

Kovelman, I., Baker, S.A., and Petitto, L.-A. (2008). Bilingual and monlingual brains compared: a functional magnetic resonance imaging investigation of syntactic processing and a possible 'neural signature' of bilingualism. *Journal of Cognitive Neuroscience* 20 (1): 153–169.

Lai, C.S.L., Fisher, S.E., Hurst, J.A. et al. (2000). The SPCH1 region on human 7q31: genomic characterization of the critical interval and localization of translocations associated with speech and language disorder. *The American Journal of Human Genetics* 67 (2): 357–368. https://doi.org/10.1086/303011.

Leonard, M.K., Brown, T.T., Travis, K.E. et al. (2010). Spatiotemporal dynamics of bilingual word processing. *NeuroImage* 49 (4): 3286–3294. https://doi.org/10.1016/j.neuroimage.2009.12.009.

Leonard, M.K., Torres, C., Travis, K.E. et al. (2011). Language proficiency modulates the recruitment of non-classical language areas in bilinguals. *PLoS One* 6 (3): e18240. https://doi.org/10.1371/journal.pone.0018240.

Li, L., Abutalebi, J., Zou, L. et al. (2015). Bilingualism alters brain functional connectivity between "control" regions and 'language' regions: evidence from bimodal bilinguals. *Neuropsychologia* 71: 236–247. https://doi.org/10.1016/j.neuropsychologia.2015.04.007.

Liu, H. and Cao, F. (2016). L1 and L2 processing in the bilingual brain: a meta-analysis of neuroimaging studies. *Brain and Language* 159 (Supplement C): 60–73. https://doi.org/10.1016/j.bandl.2016.05.013.

Lubrano, V., Prod'homme, K., Démonet, J.-F., and Köpke, B. (2012). Language monitoring in multilingual patients undergoing awake craniotomy: a case study of a German–English–French trilingual patient with a WHO grade II glioma. *Journal of Neurolinguistics* 25 (6): 567–578. https://doi.org/10.1016/j.jneuroling.2011.08.002.

Luk, G., Bialystok, E., Craik, F.I., and Grady, C. (2011). Lifelong bilingualism maintains white matter integrity in older adults. *The Journal of Neuroscience* 31 (46): 16808–16813.

Mahendra, N., Plante, E., Magloire, J. et al. (2003). fMRI variability and the localization of languages in the bilingual brain. *NeuroReport* 14 (9): 1225–1228. https://doi.org/10.1097/01.wnr.0000081877.45938.43.

Mechelli, A., Crinion, J.T., Noppeney, U. et al. (2004). Neurolinguistics: structural plasticity in the bilingual brain. *Nature* 431 (7010): 757–757.

Medland, S.E., Geffen, G., and McFarland, K. (2002). Lateralization of speech production using verbal/manual dual tasks: meta-analysis of sex differences and practice effects. *Neuropsychologia* 40 (8): 1233–1239.

Ojemann, G. (1989). Some brain mechanisms for reading. In: *Brain and Reading* (ed. C.V. Euler), 47–59. New York, NY: MacMillan.

Ojemann, G., Ojemann, J., Lettich, E., and Berger, M. (1989). Cortical language localization in left, dominant hemisphere. An electrical stimulation mapping investigation in 117 patients. *Journal of*

Neurosurgery 71 (3): 316–326. https://doi.org/10.3171/jns.1989.71.3.0316.

Pang, E.W. (2012). Neuroimaging studies of bilingual expressive language representation in the brain: potential applications for magnetoencephalography (MEG). *Neuroscience Bulletin* 28 (6): 759–764. https://doi.org/10.1007/s12264-012-1278-7.

Paradis, M. (1994). Neurolinguistic aspects of implicit and explicit memory: implications for bilingualism. In: *Implicit and Explicit Learning of Second Languages* (ed. N. Ellis), 393–419. London, UK: Academic Press.

Paradis, M. (2013). Late-L2 increased reliance on L1 neurocognitive substrates: a comment on Babcock, Stowe, Maloof, Brovetto & Ullman (2012). *Bilingualism: Language and Cognition* 16 (3): 704–707. https://doi.org/10.1017/S1366728913000011.

Perani, D. and Abutalebi, J. (2005). The neural basis of first and second language processing. *Current Opinion in Neurobiology* 15 (2): 202–206. https://doi.org/10.1016/j.conb.2005.03.007.

Perani, D. and Abutalebi, J. (2015). Bilingualism, dementia, cognitive and neural reserve. *Current Opinion in Neurology* 28 (6): 618–625. https://doi.org/10.1097/wco.0000000000000267.

Perani, D., Abutalebi, J., Paulesu, E. et al. (2003). The role of age of acquisition and language usage in early, high-proficient bilinguals: an fMRI study during verbal fluency. *Human Brain Mapping* 19 (3): 170–182. https://doi.org/10.1002/hbm.10110.

Perani, D., Farsad, M., Ballarini, T. et al. (2017). The impact of bilingualism on brain reserve and metabolic connectivity in Alzheimer's dementia. *Proceedings of the National Academy of Sciences* 114 (7): 1690–1695. https://doi.org/10.1073/pnas.1610909114.

Perfetti, C.A. and Liu, Y. (2005). Orthography to phonology and meaning: comparisons across and within writing systems. *Reading and Writing* 18 (3): 193–210. https://doi.org/10.1007/s11145-004-2344-y.

Perquin, M., Vaillant, M., Schuller, A.-M. et al. (2013). Lifelong exposure to multilingualism: new evidence to support cognitive reserve hypothesis. *PLoS One* 8 (4): e62030. https://doi.org/10.1371/journal. pone.0062030.

Price, C.J., Green, D.W., and Studnitz, R.v. (1999). A functional imaging study of translation and language switching. *Brain* 122: 2221–2235.

Schlegel, A.A., Rudelson, J.J., and Tse, P.U. (2012). White matter structure changes as adults learn a second language. *Journal of Cognitive Neuroscience* 24 (8): 1664–1670. https://doi.org/10.1162/jocn_a_00240.

Schweizer, T.A., Ware, J., Fischer, C.E. et al. (2012). Bilingualism as a contributor to cognitive reserve: evidence from brain atrophy in Alzheimer's disease. *Cortex* 48 (8): 991–996.

Schwieter, J.W. and Sunderman, G. (2011). Inhibitory control processes and lexical access in trilingual speech production. *Linguistic Approaches to Bilingualism* 1 (4): 391–412.

Sommer, I.E., Aleman, A., Bouma, A., and Kahn, R.S. (2004). Do women really have more bilateral language representation than men? A meta-analysis of functional imaging studies. *Brain* 127 (Pt 8): 1845–1852. https://doi.org/10.1093/brain/awh207.

Sommer, I.E., Aleman, A., Somers, M. et al. (2008). Sex differences in handedness, asymmetry of the planum temporale and functional language lateralization. *Brain Research* 1206: 76–88. https://doi. org/10.1016/j.brainres.2008.01.003.

Stocco, A., Lebiere, C., and Anderson, J.R. (2010). Conditional routing of information to the cortex: a model of the basal ganglia's role in cognitive coordination. *Psychological Review* 117 (2): 541–574. https://doi. org/10.1037/a0019077.

Stocco, A., Yamasaki, B., Natalenko, R., and Prat, C.S. (2014). Bilingual brain training: a neurobiological framework of how bilingual experience improves executive function. *International Journal of Bilingualism* 18 (1): 67–92. https://doi.org/10.1177/1367006912456617.

Suh, S., Yoon, H.W., Lee, S. et al. (2007). Effects of syntactic complexity in L1 and L2; an fMRI study of Korean–English bilinguals. *Brain Research* 1136: 178–189. https://doi. org/10.1016/j.brainres.2006.12.043.

Tan, L.H., Liu, H.-L., Perfetti, C.A. et al. (2001). The neural system underlying Chinese logograph reading. *NeuroImage* 13 (5): 836–846.

Tan, L.H., Spinks, J.A., Eden, G.F. et al. (2005). Reading depends on writing, in Chinese. *Proceedings of the National Academy of Sciences* 102 (24): 8781–8785.

Tan, L.H., Spinks, J.A., Feng, C.M. et al. (2003). Neural systems of second language reading are shaped by native language. *Human Brain Mapping* 18 (3): 158–166.

Thompson-Schill, S.L., d'Esposito, M., and Kan, I.P. (1999). Effects of repetition and competition on activity in left prefrontal cortex during word generation. *Neuron* 23: 513–522.

Thompson, P.M., Cannon, T.D., Narr, K.L. et al. (2001). Genetic influences on brain structure. *Nature Neuroscience* 4 (12): 1253–1258. https://doi.org/10.1038/nn758.

Tu, L., Wang, J., Abutalebi, J. et al. (2015). Language exposure induced neuroplasticity in the bilingual brain: a follow-up fMRI study. *Cortex* 64: 8–19. https://doi. org/10.1016/j.cortex.2014.09.019.

Ullman, M.T. (2001). The neural basis of lexicon and grammar in first and second language: the declarative/procedural model. *Bilingualism: Language and Cognition* 4 (2): 105–122. https://doi.org/10.1017/S1366728901000220.

Ullman, M.T., Corkin, S., Coppola, M. et al. (1997). A neural dissociation within language: evidence that the mental dictionary is part of declarative memory, and that grammatical rules are processed by the procedural system. *Journal of Cognitive Neuroscience* 9 (2): 266–276. https://doi.org/10.1162/jocn.1997.9.2.266.

Vargha-Khadem, F., Gadian, D.G., Copp, A., and Mishkin, M. (2005). FOXP2 and the neuroanatomy of speech and language.

Nature Reviews Neuroscience 6: 131. https://doi.org/10.1038/nrn1605.

Vaughn, K.A., Ramos Nuñez, A.I., Greene, M.R. et al. (2016). Individual differences in the bilingual brain: the role of language background and DRD2 genotype in verbal and non-verbal cognitive control. *Journal of Neurolinguistics* 40: 112–127. https://doi.org/10.1016/j.jneuroling.2016.06.008.

Verreyt, N., Woumans, E., Vandelanotte, D. et al. (2016). The influence of language-switching experience on the bilingual executive control advantage. *Bilingualism: Language and Cognition* 19 (1): 181–190. https://doi.org/10.1017/S1366728914000352.

Videsott, G., Herrnberger, B., Hoenig, K. et al. (2010). Speaking in multiple languages: neural correlates of language proficiency in multilingual word production. *Brain and Language* 113 (3): 103–112. https://doi.org/10.1016/j.bandl.2010.01.006.

Vingerhoets, G., Van Borsel, J., Tesink, C. et al. (2003). Multilingualism: an fMRI study. *NeuroImage* 20 (4): 2181–2196.

Waldron, E.J. and Hernandez, A.E. (2013). The role of age of acquisition on past tense generation in Spanish–English bilinguals: an fMRI study. *Brain and Language* 125 (1): 28–37. https://doi.org/10.1016/j.bandl.2013.01.002.

Wallentin, M. (2009). Putative sex differences in verbal abilities and language cortex: a critical review. *Brain and Language* 108 (3): 175–183. https://doi.org/10.1016/j.bandl.2008.07.001.

Wartenburger, I., Heekeren, H.R., Abutalebi, J. et al. (2003). Early setting of grammatical processing in the bilingual brain. *Neuron* 37 (1): 159–170. https://doi.org/10.1016/S0896-6273(02)01150-9.

Wattendorf, E., Festman, J., Westermann, B. et al. (2014). Early bilingualism influences early and subsequently later acquired languages in cortical regions representing control functions. *International Journal of Bilingualism* 18 (1): 48–66. https://doi.org/10.1177/1367006912456590.

Weber, K., Luther, L., Indefrey, P., and Hagoort, P. (2016). Overlap and differences in brain networks underlying the processing of complex sentence structures in second language users compared with native speakers. *Brain Connectivity* 6 (4): 345–355. https://doi.org/10.1089/brain.2015.0383.

Weiss-Croft, L.J. and Baldeweg, T. (2015). Maturation of language networks in children: a systematic review of 22 years of functional MRI. *NeuroImage* 123 (Supplement C): 269–281. https://doi.org/10.1016/j.neuroimage.2015.07.046.

Yetkin, O., Zerrin Yetkin, F., Haughton, V.M., and Cox, R.W. (1996). Use of functional MR to map language in multilingual volunteers. *American Journal of Neuroradiology* 17 (3): 473–477.

Zou, L., Ding, G., Abutalebi, J. et al. (2012). Structural plasticity of the left caudate in bimodal bilinguals. *Cortex* 48: 1197–1206. https://doi.org/10.1016/j.cortex.2011.05.022.

13 The Gift of Language Learning
Individual Differences in Non-Native Speech Perception

BEGOÑA DÍAZ, MIGUEL BURGALETA, AND NURIA SEBASTIAN-GALLES

1. Introduction

The most distinctive feature of non-native language learning is the large variability between individuals' capacities to perceive and produce the sounds of the target language. Indeed, while variation in native language (L1) is quite limited, and attributed to either differences in socioeconomic factors or to language learning pathologies, performance in a second language (L2) varies remarkably. In the present chapter, we will review the evidence accounting for individual differences in second language processing.

In Section 2, we will present a general overview of how certain factors relating to L2 input variability affect individual differences. We have named these 'exogenous factors'. Because factors such as age of acquisition and amount of exposure to a second language affect language learning overall, this section will take a general language learning perspective. In this section, we will also discuss current knowledge of the critical period hypothesis, a core debate in explaining individual differences in non-native language processing. The notion of L1–L2 language distance is also presented, a topic sometimes neglected in studies on individual variability in non-native speech perception. In Section 3, we will present an overview of brain imaging studies where monolinguals and bilinguals have been compared. This section provides a general framework to better integrate the results described in the following section, highlighting the differences in the neural substrate that the learning of a second phonological system induces in the brain.

Section 4 constitutes the core of this chapter. It reviews variability induced by endogenous factors, that is, what is commonly known as aptitude in the acquired language. This section is divided into two subsections. In the first we will present studies where a non-native phoneme contrast has been learned through laboratory training, usually through short and intense learning regimes. On the positive side, such studies provide precise control over the amount of exposure individuals receive; but on the negative

---

The Handbook of the Neuroscience of Multilingualism, First Edition. Edited by John W. Schwieter.
© 2019 John Wiley & Sons Ltd. Published 2019 by John Wiley & Sons Ltd.

side, they have low ecological value. A significant share of the research examined in this subsection has investigated the individual differences in learning the Hindi dental retroflex in natives of English. The following subsection presents studies investigating individual differences resulting from learning in natural contexts. The research strategy of these studies is to compare individuals who have been exposed to a new language during equally protracted periods of time, but who differ in a significant way in their non-native speech perceptual abilities. Unlike in laboratory training, these studies do not provide precise information about the exposure individuals have had, but they represent the result of learning a new language in more similar ways to the first language. The chapter ends with a conclusion summarizing the main findings and pointing to potential new lines of research.

2.   Exogenous Factors that Influence Language Learning

Bilinguals learn their second language in a wide range of personal circumstances. For example, some bilinguals learn their second language early in life, while others do it later. They can also differ in the way they learn the new language, some learning at school, others when changing country of residence. One significant group of exogenous sources of individual variation in language exposure relates to the speaker's personal history; the two most investigated being the age at which a language was learned (age of acquisition) and the amount of exposure.

In general, the earlier a language is learned the better the speaker is at mastering it (Flege and MacKay 2004; Flege et al. 1999; Mayo et al. 1997). The beneficial effects of early acquisition are at the centre of one of the main debates in the field of bilingual research: whether there is a critical or optimal period for second language acquisition (Epstein et al. 1996; Juffs 2011; Li 2009; Werker and Tees 2005). The popular versions of this hypothesis assume that after a certain age (often puberty), it is virtually impossible to learn a second language like a native. Such statements neglect current knowledge regarding the biology of critical periods and the complex structure of the language system.

Research with animal models has shown that the opening and closing of critical periods depend on complex molecular interactions, and some evidence exists that such models may also apply to human language learning (for a review see Werker and Hensch 2015). Additionally, language learning entails the acquisition of several types of linguistic knowledge (phonological rules, morphosyntactic rules, vocabulary, etc.), each recruiting different brain structures and networks (Hickok and Poeppel 2007). It has been well-established that brain structures mature at different rates and that different networks become functional at different moments in development. For instance, auditory areas mature within the first months of life, while prefrontal structures have more protracted maturational periods (Huttenlocher 1999; Huttenlocher and Dabholkar 1997; Pujol et al. 2006). As a consequence, early influence of the environment on language learning will be maximal for those aspects of language that heavily recruit auditory areas, such as phonological aspects, but will be less significant for other language domains (such as syntax or vocabulary). It is therefore not surprising that several studies show that the optimal period for learning the phonological aspects of a language is within the first two years of life. Studies on bilingual adult populations have shown that the perception of speech sounds that are unique to the non-native language can be compromised even in relatively early acquisition (at four years of age: Pallier et al. 1997; Sebastian-Galles and Soto-Faraco 1999, or seven years: Caramazza et al. 1973).

The other main exogenous factor for non-native language learning is the amount of experience the listener has with the non-native language, both in terms of use and exposure (Flege et al. 1997). Although there is a strong correlation between age of acquisition and amount of exposure, different studies suggest these factors affect language learning in specific ways (Wartenburger et al. 2003). One group of particular interest in the study of the relative contributions of age of acquisition versus amount of exposure/use, is that of individuals who have learned both languages from birth (simultaneous bilinguals). There are just a handful of studies investigating speech perception in simultaneous bilinguals. These studies converge in showing that language dominance in the first years of life plays a critical role in bilinguals' speech processing abilities (Cutler et al. 1992; Dupoux et al. 2010).

Finally, the similarities and differences between the learner's native language and the learned language are also important in determining individual differences. Although it can be said that a particular phoneme or language is more or less difficult to acquire, the truth is that difficulty depends largely on the relationship between the speakers' native language and the non-native one. For instance, Japanese and Chinese native speakers experience great difficulties in pronouncing the English phoneme /r/, as in *rabbit*, but Spanish or Greek natives do not experience such difficulties. Although none of the four languages contain this sound in their inventories, Spanish and Greek can easily map their native /r/ sound onto the English one. This is something that Japanese or Chinese speakers cannot do because, unlike Spanish and Greek, Japanese and Chinese lack rhotic phonemes.

In summary, learning a second language involves a series of endogenous factors, resulting in important variability of the properties of the second language input to which a learner is exposed. Such variability plays a critical role in second language attainment.

3. Brain Differences Between Monolinguals and Bilinguals

Language experience shapes the structure and function of the brain. Functional magnetic resonance imaging (fMRI) studies have revealed that bilinguals show increased brain activity compared with monolinguals in regions related to word retrieval and articulatory processes (Parker Jones et al. 2012) as well as to cognitive control areas involved in language switching (Abutalebi 2008; Abutalebi and Green 2007; Indefrey 2006). At the structural level, increased grey matter volume associated with bilingualism is observed in temporo-parietal areas related to vocabulary acquisition, and in primary auditory cortices (Abutalebi et al. 2015; Mechelli et al. 2004; Ressel et al. 2012), as well as other cortical and subcortical grey matter regions (Abutalebi et al. 2012; Burgaleta et al. 2016;

Pliatsikas et al. 2014, 2017). Moreover, structural connectivity – a brain feature that is also essential for supporting cognitive processes – has been shown to differ between bilinguals and monolinguals, for instance in the white matter integrity of commissural and association tracts (Luk et al. 2011; Mohades et al. 2012; Gold et al. 2013; Pliatsikas et al. 2014), as well as in left-lateralized language networks (García-Pentón et al. 2014). Interestingly, exogenous variables such as the age at which a second language is acquired modulates bilinguals' brain morphology (although in complex ways; for a review see Li et al. 2014).

However, brain differences are not only present between monolinguals and bilinguals, but also amongst bilinguals. Even if exogenous factors fundamentally shape non-native language proficiency, there is a significant amount of variability in non-native performance that cannot be explained by these factors alone: some bilinguals excel at performing in their non-native language and are indistinguishable from natives, while others show very poor accuracy even for an early-acquired language (Díaz et al. 2012; Sebastian-Galles and Baus 2005). So, what makes a person 'gifted' at learning a non-native language?

4.   Endogenous Factors that Influence Learning and Brain

Individuals differ greatly in their perception of non-native languages despite having similar learning conditions. No matter the nature of the learning (in a laboratory or natural learning situations), some people manage to reach high levels of proficiency in a non-native language, while others remain stuck at very low levels, even in the most favourable conditions, such as early language acquisition and ample exposure to the language (Díaz et al. 2012; Sebastian-Galles and Baus 2005). The question as to why some individuals excel while others struggle with perceiving non-native speech sounds (i.e. phonemes) is a topic that has received relatively little attention from neuroscientists. However, in recent years the study of individual variability in non-native language learning has become an emerging field since mastering languages is becoming an increasingly necessary skill in our global world. Furthermore, determining the cognitive and brain areas that correlate with non-native perception proficiency has the potential to provide new insights into the brain mechanisms involved in language function. In the following section we review studies that have investigated the basis of individual variability in non-native language learning that cannot be attributed to exogenous factors.

4.1.   *Training Studies*

Over the past three decades a growing body of evidence has revealed the substantial variability in performance that individuals display when learning non-native speech sounds. Some of this work exploits the now popular Hindi dental–retroflex contrast amongst stop consonants, which is hard for English speakers to detect, even after training (Golestani and Zatorre 2009). A prolific line of research has since been built on this evidence, seeking to understand the neural basis of such individual differences. To this end, researchers have relied mostly on magnetic resonance imaging. Figure 1 depicts

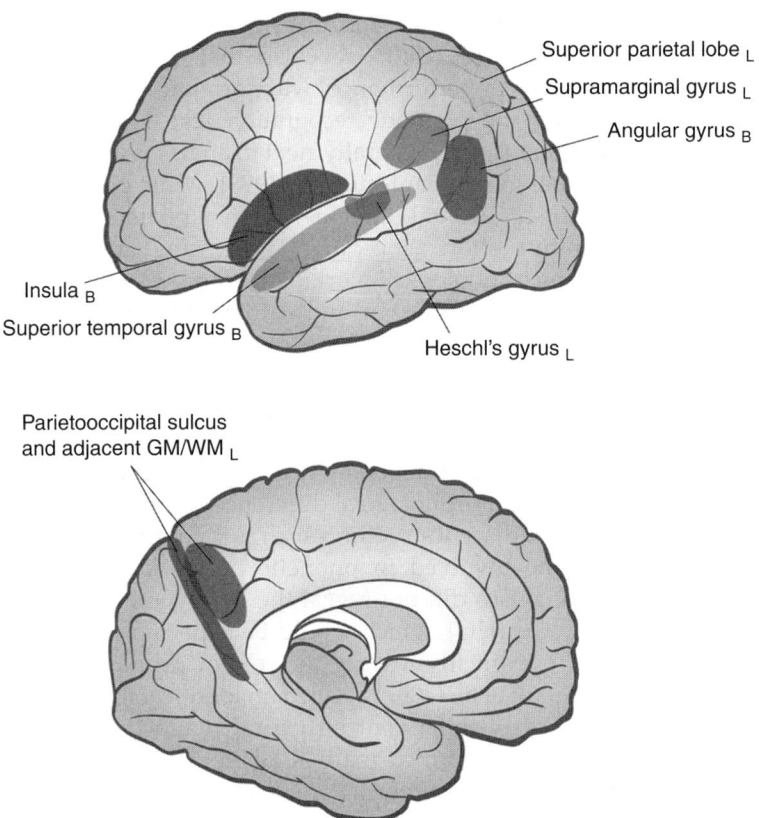

Figure 1   Brain regions whose activity and/or structure is commonly highlighted by training studies on individual differences in the perception of non-native speech sounds. The list of areas depicted in this figure is not exhaustive. B = bilateral. L = left hemisphere.

some of the brain regions most commonly identified in this literature. A pioneering functional study on this topic was carried out by Golestani and Zatorre (2004), who investigated brain activity using fMRI in a group of English-speaking participants before and after two weeks' training to discriminate the dental–retroflex contrast. The authors synthesized a continuum of seven stimuli that ranged from pure retroflex to pure dental. During the training sessions, at each trial participants were first presented with one of the two stimuli at the ends of the continuum (sounds 1 and 7) and were asked to categorize it as 'sound A' (dental) or 'sound B' (retroflex), receiving feedback right after their response. Once an individual achieved a high performance in the discrimination of those two sounds, the experiment jumped to the next pair of sounds (2 and 6), thus increasing task difficulty. During the pre- and post-training fMRI acquisitions, participants were tested on their ability to distinguish between dental and retroflex prototype sounds, and in-scanner task performance was evaluated. At the behavioural level, the expected individual differences were observed, with some participants presenting a steeper progression during training, while others learned more slowly. Furthermore, imaging results revealed that behavioural improvement after training (pre-post changes in performance) was correlated with the post-training fMRI signal captured during the phonetic recognition test. Good learners showed greater activation in the angular gyrus bilaterally, next to areas involved in phonological processing (i.e. supramarginal gyrus; Paulesu et al. 1993), while poor learners showed increased activation in the insula-frontal-opercular regions bilaterally, which might be the result of greater cognitive effort ('top-down' processing) and/or the usage of rehearsal strategies relying on phonological working memory components.

Further analyses of the dataset in Golestani and Zatorre (2004) focused on brain morphology, aimed at identifying structural predictors of individual differences in training performance. Such analyses were reported by Golestani et al. (2002) who observed that learning rates were predicted by left parietal morphology, including greater white matter density and a more posteriorly located parieto-occipital sulcus in fast learners; these results were replicated in an independent dataset (Golestani et al. 2007). The authors hypothesized that these morphological differences may arise from the indirect influence of the size or shape of adjacent structures such as the angular and supramarginal gyri, which are known to be involved in phonetic processing, as just mentioned. Interestingly, whole-brain analyses did not reveal the involvement of primary speech regions, such as Heschl's gyrus (HG), which would be expected to contribute to non-native speech perception. To explicitly test for the role of primary auditory areas in learning performance, Golestani et al. (2007) applied an identical training protocol to an independent sample which also underwent structural magnetic resonance imaging (MRI) acquisition. The authors performed manual labelling of the left and right HG, observing larger left HG, as well as greater leftward asymmetry, in fast learners compared with slow learners – an observation that was replicated when reanalysing Golestani et al. (2002)'s dataset. Fast learners were also more likely to present duplication or splitting of the HG, a morphological pattern that is also observed in expert phoneticians (Golestani et al. 2011). The implication of HG in accounting for individual differences in learning rates was interpreted in light of the role of this structure in processing rapidly changing auditory information. Furthermore, the right insula appeared to be superiorly displaced in slower learners, underscoring the role of insular regions initially observed at the functional level (Golestani and Zatorre 2004).

An additional piece of evidence highlighting the relevance of parietal and fronto-opercular/insular regions when learning to distinguish the dental-retroflex contrast was provided by Ventura-Campos et al. (2013), who focused on the resting-state functional connectivity (FC) between these regions as a predictor of individual differences in phonetic learning. Resting-state FC, as measured by fMRI, captures the temporal correlation of low-frequency fluctuations in brain activity across brain regions at rest. In two independent samples, Ventura-Campos et al. (2013) showed that the strength of pre-training FC between the left superior parietal lobe and the left fronto-opercular/insular region predict individual differences in performance after a training procedure similar to those implemented by Golestani and colleagues in a sample of Spanish-speaking participants (who also experience difficulties with the dental-retroflex contrast).

A second line of training-based research that has generated compelling evidence regarding the neural basis of individual differences in non-native speech perception has focused on the variability displayed by individuals when learning to identify words based on their pitch pattern. In contrast to the studies reviewed above, where participants are trained in pure phonetic discrimination, this complementary perspective contextualizes the ability to perceive non-native speech sounds within the boundaries of sound-to-word mapping processes. A representative selection of the brain areas highlighted by these studies can be found in Figure 1. One of the first neuroimaging studies that considered the contribution of non-native speech sounds in word learning was conducted by Wong et al. (2007). The authors generated a set of auditory stimuli comprising English pseudowords with pitch patterns that resembled a subset of those found in Mandarin tones (level, rising, and falling). As such, each pseudoword had three variants, one per tone. Native English-speaking participants without previous exposure to tone languages were trained to associate these sounds with pictures of objects during an average of eight sessions (around two weeks). At the end of each training session, participants were presented with the 18 trained words, and were asked to match them with their corresponding pictures. Before and after training, participants underwent fMRI acquisition while asked to discriminate the pitch patterns of the pseudowords, showing that successful learners had greater activation in the left superior temporal gyrus following training, whereas poor learners showed increased activity in the right superior temporal and inferior frontal gyri (involved in non-linguistic pitch perception), as well as in the left insula and in left posterior parietal regions – two areas mentioned above with regard to their role in the perception of the dental-retroflex contrast.

Interestingly, in a structural study using the same sample, Wong et al. (2008) reported a greater volume of the left Heschl's gyrus in successful learners. In other words, the size of the left HG was a significant predictor of both accuracy and speed of learning during training. As the authors mention, this result complements those of Golestani et al. (2007) by showing that left HG volume is not only associated with rapid temporal processing and non-lexical phonetic learning, but also with the learning of lexically relevant acoustic cues. Providing further structural evidence, Wong et al. (2011) employed the same training protocol in a new sample and focused on the predictive power of white matter integrity, as measured by diffusion tensor imaging. Fractional anisotropy, an index of white matter integrity, was found to predict task performance in the left parieto-temporal area. This region was identified as part of a ventral sound-to-meaning pathway, according to the dual-stream model (Hickok and Poeppel 2007). This finding, along with the implication of HG in non-native speech perception underscored by Wong et al. (2008) and Golestani et al. (2007), highlights the contribution of low level acoustic mechanisms in the emergence of individual differences in phonemic learning. This notion was recently expanded on by Deng et al. (2016), who acquired resting-state fMRI from a sample of participants that underwent the same training protocol as devised by Wong and colleagues. Instead of focusing on functional connectivity, Deng and colleagues investigated the amplitude of low-frequency fluctuations (ALFF), which characterizes regional brain activity at rest. They observed that ALFF values in the left superior temporal gyrus were significant predictors of the amount of learning after training. This is consistent with observations by Wong and Perrachione (2007), who reported increased activity in this region after training, as well as with those of Wong et al. (2011), which suggest an important role of the white matter pathways running along the left superior temporal gyrus, serving as a backbone to the ventral pathway involved in sound-to-word mapping.

In summary, research on the training of perceptual skills of non-native speech sounds emphasizes the role of primary acoustic mechanisms underlying individual differences in phonemic learning, as illustrated by the involvement of the structure and function of Heschl's gyrus. In addition, temporo-parietal areas and ventral pathway elements of language processing also contribute to this variability and suggest that individual differences in sound-to-word mapping mechanisms are of relevance independently of whether training focuses on purely phonetic contrasts or on the perception of speech sounds in a lexical context.

4.2.   Natural Language Learning Studies

Another important line of research investigates individual variability in L2 speech perception in bilinguals who have acquired their second language in natural environments. The study of individual differences in this population provides information on the factors that modulate final speech perception attainment rather than just the initial learning stages. Although natural learning entails a reduction of control of language input, it mirrors the complexities of native language learning, enabling the investigation of the organization of the speech perception system. Most models of (native) speech perception assume the existence of a hierarchy of interacting phonological processes before the lexical and morphosyntactic representations are accessed (Hickok and Poeppel 2000; Klatt 1979; McClelland and Elman 1986; Norris 1994; Poeppel et al. 2008). These models propose that initial processes analyse acoustic-phonetic information in order to identify the phonemes embedded in the speech signal. The output of these initial computations provides the input for the following phonolexical processes, which involves mapping the identified phonemes onto the appropriate lexical entries. As a result, if difficulties in phonological processes are present, deficient processing at higher levels of the system is expected. For instance, the difficulties of Japanese listeners at the segmental level in discriminating the English contrast /r/–/l/ may lead to difficulties at the lexical level when discriminating the English words /rock/–/lock/ (Strange and Dittman 1984).

The pioneer study by Sebastian-Galles and Baus (2005) investigated the patterns of individual variability in bilinguals' speech perception across phonological domains. This study took advantage of the well-known difficulties of Spanish(L1)-Catalan(L2) bilinguals in discriminating some Catalan-specific contrasts. The bilinguals under study had acquired Spanish in the first years of their lives but were not continuously exposed to Catalan until the age of three to four years. Catalan and Spanish are official languages in Catalonia. This means that both social interaction and mandatory schooling ensure that bilinguals are highly skilled in both languages and homogenous in socioeconomic level. Previous research had established that these bilinguals encountered difficulties in discriminating the two mid-front Catalan vowels /e/–/ɛ/, with both vowels being perceived as the Spanish mid-front vowel /e/, which possess phonetic traits intermediate to the two mid-front Catalan vowels (Pallier et al. 1997; Sebastian-Galles et al. 2005,

2006; Sebastian-Galles and Soto-Faraco 1999). Interestingly, Sebastian-Galles and Baus (2005) found that the percentage of bilinguals behaving as monolinguals depended on the nature of the stimuli and of the tasks employed, and hypothesized that such variability might relate to the specific phonological representations required by each experimental task.

These authors tested 80 Spanish-dominant Spanish-Catalan bilinguals in three behavioural tasks. A categorization task consisting of a seven-step continuum of synthesized isolated vowels ranging from /e/ to /ɛ/ was used to measure bilinguals' ability to categorize the Catalan vowels (Pallier et al. 1997). This task assessed the processing of acoustic-phonemic information. The second task was a modified gating task (adapted from Sebastian-Galles and Soto-Faraco 1999). The stimuli were naturally produced minimal pairs (i.e. words that differ in one speech sound only, such as /rock/ and /lock/) that differed in the critical vowels /e/ and /ɛ/, such as 'Pere' (/perə/, 'Peter') and 'pera' (/pɛrə/, 'pear'). Participants heard incremental segments of a word ('gates') until the whole word had been presented. This task measured whether participants could use coarticulation cues to correctly identify the Catalan vowels, making phoneme identification more complex than in the categorization task on isolated vowels. The third task was an auditory lexical decision task in which pseudowords were made by exchanging two vowels, the critical stimuli involving swapping /e/ and /ɛ/ (Sebastian-Galles et al. 2005). This task required participants not only to accurately perceive the vowel contrast but also to match the stimuli with the representations in the lexicon, thus assessing phonolexical processing. The comparison of bilinguals' performance across the three tasks showed that a higher percentage of bilinguals performed within the Catalan natives' performance range in the categorization task (68.3%) as compared to the gating task (46.6%); performance decreased further for the lexical decision task (18.3%). At the individual level, the results of 90% of the bilinguals followed a hierarchical structure of phonological processes: good performance in the acoustic-phonetic tasks (i.e. identification and gating tasks) was necessary, though not sufficient, for accurate performance in the phonolexical task (i.e. lexical decision task).

Sebastian-Galles and Baus (2005) studied highly competent bilinguals who had learned the non-dominant language in natural settings and at a very early age. As a result, these bilinguals had been significantly exposed to the non-dominant language in the first years of life. Díaz and coworkers (Díaz et al. 2012) investigated whether graded performance across tasks would also be present for bilinguals who were both less skilled and had been less exposed to their non-dominant language. They tested 55 Dutch-dominant Dutch-English bilinguals who had learned English at the age of 10–12 in the course of mandatory schooling. These bilinguals usually struggle to discriminate the two English mid-front unrounded vowels /æ/ and /ɛ/, which are perceptually assimilated to the only available mid-front unrounded Dutch vowel /ɛ/ (Broersma and Cutler 2011; Cutler et al. 2004; Weber and Cutler 2004). The late Dutch-English bilinguals were tested in three behavioural tasks involving the critical English /æ/–/ɛ/ contrast: a categorization task, a word identification task, and a lexical decision task. The categorization and lexical decision tasks were analogous to those in the study of Sebastian-Galles and Baus (2005), but adapted to English stimuli. In the word identification task participants were presented with English minimal pairs that differed in the critical English vowels /æ/

and /ɛ/ and had to select the corresponding picture from two alternatives. This task assessed the accuracy of phonological representations for lexical access. The results showed that the percentage of bilinguals who scored within the performance range of English natives decreased from the categorization task (43.63%) to the lexical decision task (12.72%) and the word identification task (9.09%). The individual performance pattern of 86% of the bilinguals followed a hierarchical structure of speech perception processes: good proficiency in the acoustic-phonetic task (i.e. the identification task) was a prerequisite for achieving good proficiency in the phonolexical tasks (i.e. the lexical decision and word identification tasks), but it did not ensure accuracy in the phonolexical tasks. The findings on early (Sebastian-Galles and Baus 2005) and late bilinguals (Díaz et al. 2012) both show great individual variability in L2 speech perception amongst bilinguals with homogenous L2 experience, and a graded performance across phonological processes.

An important characteristic of the populations studied by Sebastian-Galles and Baus (2005) and Díaz et al. (2012) was their homogeneity in terms of age of acquisition, type of learning, use of their languages, and, most likely, motivation to learn the non-dominant language. Thus, the individual variability observed is unlikely to originate from such exogenous factors. Díaz and collegues (2008) investigated whether individual variability in speech perception originates from differences in auditory skills or, rather, in speech-specific abilities. With this aim, they selected two groups of bilinguals from the same sample studied by Sebastian-Galles and Baus (2005), representing the two extremes of the bilingual perception ability distribution: one group of bilinguals was consistently comparable to Catalan natives in all the L2 tasks (good perceivers, GPs) and the other group performed more poorly than Catalan natives in all three tasks (poor perceivers, PP). The two groups were tested for their capacity to perceive native and unknown speech sounds as well as pure tones by means of the mismatch negativity (MMN) response. The MMN is an event-related potential (ERP) that appears in the electroencephalographic recording when the auditory system detects an acoustic change (Näätänen et al. 2007). The typical experimental procedure to measure the MMN involves continuous repetition of a sound (either a tone or a speech sound), considered the standard stimuli, with random interspersed presentation of another sound, called deviant. In response to the deviant sounds, the auditory system shows a frontal negativity, with a reversed polarity at temporal sites that peaks 100 ms after the onset of the deviant. The MMN is generated by two sets of neural generators: a superior temporal generator that is functionally involved in comparing the incoming auditory input with a memory trace and a frontal generator that participates in the orienting of attention towards a detected change in the auditory input (Escera et al. 1998; Giard et al. 1990; Yago et al. 2001). The activity of the MMN generators can be inferred from the amplitude and latency of the MMN at frontal and mastoid electrodes, respectively (note, however, that ERPs do not directly measure the activity of the neural sources). As such, the MMN can be used to investigate the contribution of each MMN source to potential differences between GPs and PPs. A relevant advantage of using the MMN response is that it can be assessed during passive listening while participants are reading or watching a silent movie. The MMN during passive listening is thus not dependent on cognitive processes related to task demands, strategies, or motivation to perform a task. A crucial characteristic of the MMN for the issue of individual variability is that its amplitude directly relates to the magnitude of the perceived change: the bigger the change, the bigger the amplitude of the MMN. Consequently, the MMN captures perceptual capacities for linguistic and non-linguistic stimuli (Alho et al. 1993; Amenedo and Escera 2000; Näätänen et al. 1997; Nenonen et al. 2005; Winkler et al. 1999).

In Díaz and collegues' (2008), the MMN was measured for tones of different frequency (standard: 1000 Hz; deviants: 1030, 1060, and 1090 Hz), duration (standard: 200 ms; deviants: 120, 80, and 40 ms), and order pattern (standard: alternating tones such as ABABAB; deviants: tone repetitions such as ABABAA). In addition, the MMN was measured for the vowel contrast /e/–/o/ from the participants' native language, Spanish, and a vowel contrast unknown to the bilinguals, the Estonian /ö/–/o/. GPs and PPs showed equivalent responses for non-linguistic conditions involving the discrimination of tones, suggesting that they had similar non-linguistic perceptual capacities. However, differences between the groups emerged for phoneme perception: GPs showed larger MMNs for native and unknown vowels as compared to PPs (see Figure 2). These findings suggest the existence of a common ability for the perception of speech sounds regardless of language familiarity (i.e. native, L2, or unknown) that does not depend on general auditory perception. In other words, differences in the learning of speech-sounds stems from variability in a speech-specific perception capability. Interestingly, the differences between GPs and PPs were present at frontal electrodes, but similar MMN responses were measured at mastoid electrodes. As mentioned, mastoid electrodes measure the MMN temporal generator engaged in the comparison of sensory information with memory representations, whereas the frontal electrodes measure the frontal generator, which is associated with the triggering of involuntary attention when an auditory change is detected. According to this functional distinction

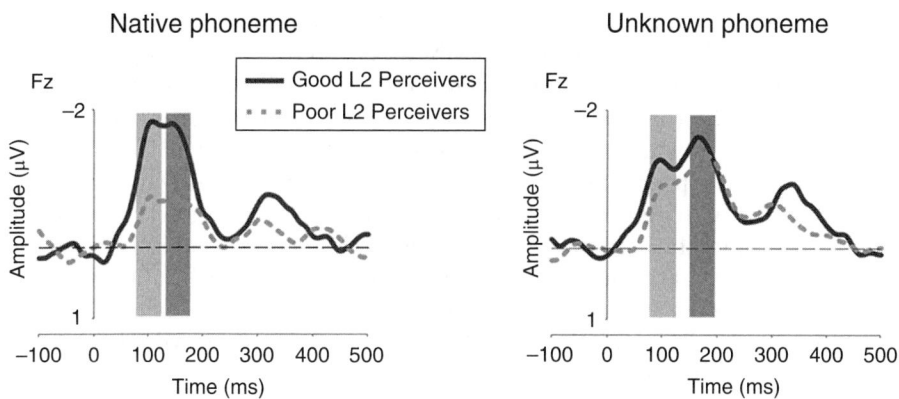

Figure 2 MMNs obtained for good and poor perceivers of an L2 phoneme contrast in response to a native and a non-native (unknown) phoneme. Good perceivers displayed larger MMN responses than poor perceivers for the two different phonemes. Grey boxes indicate statistical differences between the two groups of bilinguals for an early subcomponent of the MMN (light grey) and a late subcomponent (dark grey). Source: Díaz et al. (2008).

of the MMN, the lack of differences between GPs and PPs at temporal electrodes suggests that both groups are similar in their ability to represent the phonetic auditory sensory information and to integrate this information into memory representations. Following this rationale, the differences at frontal sites suggest that the two groups may differ in the cognitive mechanism that allows them to reallocate attentional resources to novel speech sounds.

These conclusions are supported by converging evidence from studies on late and less-skilled bilinguals and different language combinations (Díaz et al. 2016; Jakoby et al. 2011). For instance, Díaz et al. (2016) used a very similar experimental paradigm to Díaz et al. (2008) to study the MMN responses of Dutch(L1)-English(L2) bilinguals. From the same population tested in Díaz et al. (2012), they categorized the Dutch-English bilinguals as GPs and PPs based on their behavioural discrimination of an English vowel contrast. The bilinguals were tested in their discrimination sensitivity to the same non-linguistic acoustic stimuli as in Díaz et al. (2008; i.e. changes in tone frequency, duration, and order pattern) but the linguistic conditions were adapted to the bilinguals' languages. The participants in Díaz et al. (2008) were Spanish-Catalan bilinguals. Both of the bilinguals' languages used only spectral cues to differ between phonemes (e.g. /e/–/o/). However, in some languages such as Dutch, Finnish, or Japanese, phonemes can differ not only in spectral but also duration cues. For instance, the length of the vowel is the only difference between the Dutch words 'maan' ('moon') and 'man' ('man'). Díaz et al. (2012) took advantage of the rich phonological properties of Dutch and tested the Dutch-English bilinguals in their perception of the two phonological cues: duration, with the vowel contrast /ɔ:/–/ɔ/, and spectral, with the vowel contrast /ɑ/–/ɔ/. In addition, they presented participants with an unknown vowel contrast that differed in nasalization, the French /ɔ̃/–/ɔ/, and the English contrast used for participant selection, /ɛ/ and /æ/. The results paralleled those of Díaz et al. (2008). The MMN for the non-linguistic stimuli was similar for the two groups of bilinguals but GPs showed larger MMNs for all kinds of speech stimuli at frontal electrodes only (not at the mastoids). In early bilinguals the larger MMN was present in GPs compared to PPs for all types of speech sounds, but not for tones (Díaz et al. 2008) and late bilinguals (Díaz et al. 2016), suggesting the existence of a single speech perception capability for all the bilinguals' languages regardless of the age at which the language is learned or of language proficiency. The proposal of a shared speech perception ability across bilinguals' languages is in line with neuroimaging findings that show a common brain network for the lexical and grammatical processing of native and second languages (for reviews, see Perani and Abutalebi 2005; Indefrey 2006). Moreover, the similar location of the MMN differences between GPs and PPs at frontal electrodes for early and late bilinguals suggests that phoneme abilities are tightly linked to the activity of the MMN frontal generator, which is engaged in triggering attention towards auditory changes, regardless of the age at which a language is initially learned.

A potential caveat of Díaz et al. (2008, 2016) is that they used ERPs, which do not fully capture the underlying neural oscillatory patterns. ERPs rely on averaging across trials. As the result of averaging, the responses that are induced by the stimuli but not stimuli phase-locked are lost as they are cancelled out when averaging across trials. Thus, the lack of differences in the MMN amplitude between GPs and PPs for tone discrimination and at temporal electrodes for speech changes could potentially hide differences in the underlying neural oscillations. To address this potential issue, Jin and coworkers (2014) used time-frequency analysis to investigate the oscillatory neural patterns associated with success in phoneme learning. They analysed the oscillatory rhythms underlying auditory discrimination of GPs and PPs to tone and phoneme changes measured by Díaz et al. (2008). The spectral analysis revealed similar oscillatory patterns for GPs and PPs when processing tone changes. However, differences emerged between the groups for native speech discrimination. GPs showed an increase in the theta band power (4–8 Hz) for the native deviant phonemes compared to PPs at frontocentral electrodes only, but the two groups were similar in their neural activity for the unknown phoneme. The theta band has consistently been associated with the auditory discrimination processes reflected in the MMN response (Bishop and Hardiman 2010; Fuentemilla et al. 2008; Hsiao et al. 2009; Ko et al. 2012). Overall, findings by Jin et al. (2014) resemble those from Díaz et al. (2008, 2016), apart from the lack of difference between the groups for the unknown phoneme. The group differences for the native deviant phoneme alone suggest that GPs and PPs differ maximally in the processing of familiar speech sounds. The authors put forward the hypothesis that lifelong experience with native contrasts may result in better neural representations for GPs than for PPs, while the lack of previous experience with unknown sounds could diminish (or even abolish) the differences between GPs and PPs in detecting unknown contrasts. The study of the cause of the different outcomes regarding unfamiliar phoneme processing between the ERP and time-frequency analysis will require future work.

Little is yet known about the brain underpinnings of individual variability in speech perception in bilingual populations. Two studies using structural MRI looked to shed light on the brain characteristics that relate to speech perception abilities (Burgaleta et al. 2014; Sebastian-Galles et al. 2012). The two MRI studies compared GPs and PPs (selected from the same population tested by Sebastian-Galles and Baus (2005), following the same criteria as in Díaz et al. (2008). These studies can determine the brain areas that are preferentially engaged in phonological processing because this is presumably the only variable that differs between the two groups of bilinguals. Sebastian-Galles et al. (2012) compared the brain morphology of GPs and PPs. Specifically, they used voxel-based morphometry (VBM) to investigate whether GPs and PPs differed in brain grey and/or white matter volume across the entire brain. The analyses revealed that PPs had larger white matter volume in the right insulo/fronto-opercular region compared to GPs. The authors further examined whether this difference in white matter did actually relate with participants' phoneme discrimination abilities as indexed by the MMN to native phoneme discrimination assessed by Díaz et al. (2008). They found that white matter volume correlated negatively with the MMN amplitude: the more white matter volume, the smaller the MMN. Interestingly, the right insulo/fronto-opercular region has been put forward as part of the brain network involved in the generation of the MMN, and has been functionally linked to the detection of auditory changes that are difficult to perceive (Opitz et al. 2002). In light of this functional property, the larger white matter volume of the right insulo/fronto-opercular region in PPs was interpreted by Sebastian-Galles and collaborators (2012) as being a compensatory mechanism for achieving accurate phonological processing. This interpretation fits well with the results by Golestani and Zatorre (2004; reviewed in the Section 4.1) who found in a training study that poor learners increasingly activated the insula-frontal-opercular regions bilaterally. The authors argued that such an area might be recruited by cognitive effort and/or the use of rehearsal strategies relying on phonological working memory components.

Sebastian-Galles et al. (2012) also compared the volume of GPs and PPs' Heschl's gyrus as training studies suggest that auditory processing skills may play a role in individual differences in non-native phonemic learning. However, the two groups were comparable in this regard. The contrasting findings in terms of the involvement of auditory areas in the variability of non-native speech perception might indicate that auditory skills are relevant at initial stages of learning (as in training studies), but that given sufficient exposure to the non-native sounds (as in the natural learning studies) such low-level auditory skills may no longer play a crucial role in learning.

Burgaleta and collaborators (2014) studied the relation between cerebral cortical morphology and phonological skills in PPs and GPs. Overall, PPs and GPs did not differ in their cortical measurements. Yet, the assessment of the association between L2 speech perception tasks (categorization task, gating task, and lexical decision task) from Sebastian-Galles and Baus (2005) and cortical morphology revealed that poor performance in the lexical decision task was associated with increased cortical thickness in the left middle and inferior temporal gyrus (see Figure 3), regions that support the mapping from phonology to meaning (Price 2012), and are preferentially engaged in the processing of difficult associations between speech sounds and lexical representations (Heim et al. 2009). The thicker cortex in these regions for poor performance in the lexical decision task was interpreted as reflecting long-term experience with challenging situations in sound-to-meaning mapping situations. Overall, the two MRI studies on individual variability showed enlarged brain morphology for poor speech perception, possibly caused by an attempt by the language system to optimize speech perception in difficult situations. However, the evidence is not sufficient to determine whether these brain morphological correlates of speech perception abilities are related to a compensatory mechanism or rather are present at birth, leading to the variability in phonological skills.

In summary, the studies reviewed here demonstrate the large individual variability that is present in the learning of new languages. Systematic analysis of the proficiency attained in a second language has provided evidence that supports a hierarchical organization of speech perception processes. Furthermore, electrophysiological studies show that individual differences in the perception of a second language relate positively to the perception of native and unknown speech sounds, suggesting the existence of a general phonological ability that is expressed in a similar fashion across the languages to which the listener is exposed. This phonological ability is therefore independent of the listeners' familiarity with the given language. Such a finding implies that the degree of learning of new speech sounds might be predicted by the listener's capabilities with the already acquired native language. The current working hypothesis is that talent for learning new speech sounds relies on attention mechanisms that allocate computational resources to the processing of new speech sounds. These individual differences in language perception are also characterized by individual differences in brain morphology in right frontal and left temporal brain regions, which are relevant to auditory and speech processing.

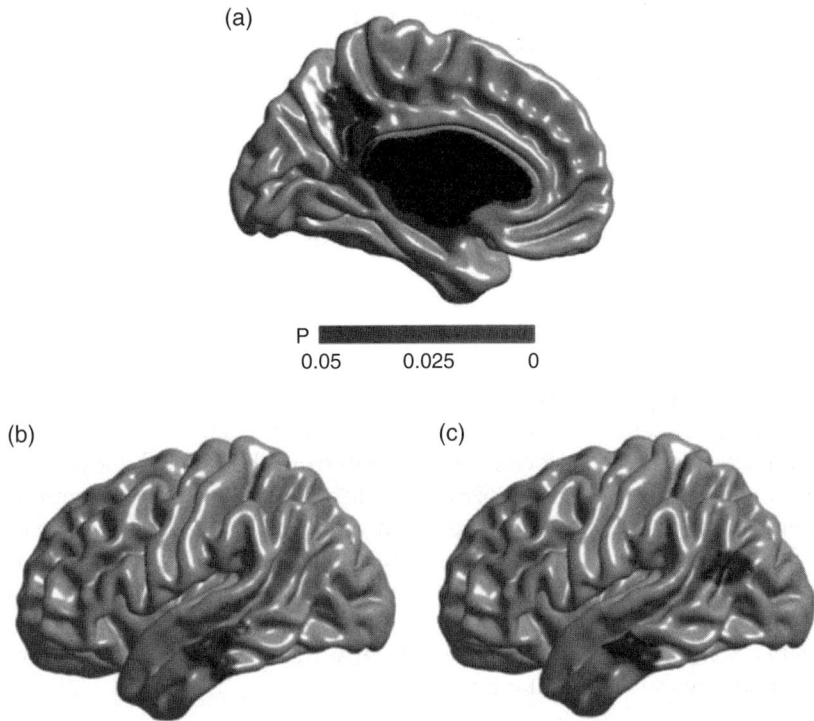

Figure 3   (a) Significant negative association between cortical surface area and performance in the lexical decision task, after controlling for performance in prelexical tasks. Bottom figures show significant negative association between cortical thickness and performance in the lexical decision task, before (b) and after (c) controlling for performance in prelexical tasks. All results are corrected for multiple comparisons at the cluster level (familywise error rate < 0.5). Source: Figures adapted from Burgaleta et al. (2014).

5.   Conclusion

How proficient an individual will be in a non-native language is the result of a complex equation where both exogenous and endogenous factors play important roles. In the present chapter we have focused on studies showing that endogenous factors, in particular those related with what is commonly understood to be *aptitude*, critically shape final attainment. In this review, we have not assessed the importance of other significant endogenous factors, such as motivation, or social status of the language. In doing so we do not deny the importance of such factors, but knowledge of the neural mechanisms underlying such factors is still lacking at present.

Our review reveals that individual differences in giftedness for languages are tied in with neural networks relating to speech processing mechanisms. Although the existing data does not allow conclusions to be drawn regarding the extent to which these neural underpinnings are the cause or the consequence of ease of language learning, the way

Spanish-Catalan bilinguals learned their second language together with the relationship between native and non-native speech processing favours the existence of some sort of genetic origin. To our knowledge, there are no studies linking genetics and individual differences in non-native speech perception. However, a recent study linking dyslexia (a language processing pathology associated to phonological processing deficits) to specific genetic variants and to variation in the late component of the MMN (Müller et al. 2017) shows promising future avenues of how to link the neural substrates of individual differences in non-native speech processing to its genetic basis.

Acknowledgements

Díaz received funding from the People Programme (Marie Curie Actions) of the European Union's Seventh Framework Programme (FP7/2007–2013) under REA grant agreement n 32867 and a postdoctoral fellowship from the Spanish Government (Juan de la Cierva fellowship JCI-2012–12678). Burgaleta received funding from the Spanish Government (Juan de la Cierva Incorporación grant IJCI-2015–25056). Sebastian-Galles received funding from the European Commission Seventh Framework Programme (FP7/2007–2013): ERG grant agreement number 323961 (UNDER CONTROL); the Spanish Ministerio de Economía y Competitividad (PSI201566918-P), the Catalan Government (SGR 2014–1210), and the 'ICREA Acadèmia' prize for excellence in research, funded by the Generalitat de Catalunya.

REFERENCES

Abutalebi, J. (2008). Neural aspects of second language representation and language control. *Bilingualism: Functional and Neural Perspectives* 128: 466–478.

Abutalebi, J., Canini, M., Della Rosa, P.A. et al. (2015). The neuroprotective effects of bilingualism upon the inferior parietal lobule: a structural neuroimaging study in aging Chinese bilinguals. *Journal of Neurolinguistics* 33: 3–13.

Abutalebi, J., Della Rosa, P.A., Green, D.W. et al. (2012). Bilingualism tunes the anterior cingulate cortex for conflict monitoring. *Cerebral Cortex* 22: 2076–2086.

Abutalebi, J. and Green, D. (2007). Bilingual language production: the neurocognition of language representation and control. *Journal of Neurolinguistics* 20: 242–275.

Alho, K., Huotilainen, M., Tiitinen, H. et al. (1993). Memory-related processing of complex sound patterns in human auditory cortex: a MEG study. *NeuroReport* 4: 391–394.

Amenedo, E. and Escera, C. (2000). The accuracy of sound duration representation in the human brain determines the accuracy of behavioural perception. *European Journal of Neuroscience* 12: 2570–2574.

Bishop, D.V.M. and Hardiman, M.J. (2010). Measurement of mismatch negativity in individuals: a study using single-trial analysis. *Psychophysiology* 47: 697–705.

Broersma, M. and Cutler, A. (2011). Competition dynamics of second-language listening. *Quarterly Journal of Experimental Psychology* 64: 74–95.

Burgaleta, M., Baus, C., Díaz, B., and Sebastian-Galles, N. (2014). Brain structure is related to speech perception abilities in bilinguals. *Brain Structure and Function* 219: 1405–1416.

Burgaleta, M., Sanjuán, A., Ventura-Campos, N. et al. (2016). Bilingualism at the core of the brain. Structural differences between bilinguals and monolinguals revealed by subcortical shape analysis. *NeuroImage* 125: 437–445.

Caramazza, A., Yeni-Komshian, G., Zurif, E., and Carbone, E. (1973). The acquisition of a new phonological contrast: the case of stop consonants in French-English bilinguals. *Journal of the Acoustical Society of America* 54: 421–428.

Cutler, A., Mehler, J., Norris, D.G., and Segui, J. (1992). The monolingual nature of speech segmentation by bilinguals. *Cognitive Psychology* 24: 381–410.

Cutler, A., Weber, A., Smits, R., and Cooper, N. (2004). Patterns of English phoneme confusions by native and non-native listeners. *Journal of the Acoustical Society of America* 116: 3668–3678.

Deng, Z., Chandrasekaran, B., Wang, S., and Wong, P.C.M. (2016). Resting-state low-frequency fluctuations reflect individual differences in spoken language learning. *Cortex* 76: 63–78.

Díaz, B., Baus, C., Escera, C. et al. (2008). Brain potentials to native phoneme discrimination reveal the origin of individual differences in learning the sounds of a second language. *Proceedings of the National Academy of Sciences of the United States of America* 105: 16083–16088.

Díaz, B., Mitterer, H., Broersma, M. et al. (2016). Variability in L2 phonemic learning originates from speech-specific capabilities: an MMN study on late bilinguals. *Bilingualism: Language and Cognition* 19: 955–970.

Díaz, B., Mitterer, H., Broersma, M., and Sebastian-Galles, N. (2012). Individual differences in late bilinguals' L2 phonological processes: from acoustic-phonetic analysis to lexical access. *Learning and Individual Differences* 22: 680–689.

Dupoux, E., Peperkamp, S., and Sebastian-Galles, N. (2010). Limits on bilingualism revisited: stress "deafness" in simultaneous French-Spanish bilinguals. *Cognition* 114: 266–275.

Epstein, S.D., Flynn, S., and Martohardjono, G. (1996). Second language acquisition: theoretical and experimental issues in contemporary research. *Behavioral and Brain Sciences* 19: 677–714.

Escera, C., Alho, K., Winkler, I., and Näätänen, R. (1998). Neural mechanisms of involuntary attention to acoustic novelty and change. *Journal of Cognitive Neuroscience* 10: 590–604.

Flege, J.E., Bohn, O., and Jang, S. (1997). Effects of experience on non-native speakers' production and perception of English vowels. *Journal of Phonetics* 25: 437–470.

Flege, J.E. and MacKay, I.R.A. (2004). Perceiving vowels in a second language. *Studies in Second Language Acquisition* 26: 1–34.

Flege, J.E., MacKay, I.R., and Meador, D. (1999). Native Italian speakers' perception and production of English vowels. *The Journal of the Acoustical Society of America* 106: 2973–2987.

Fuentemilla, L., Marco-Pallarés, J., Münte, T.F., and Grau, C. (2008). Theta EEG oscillatory activity and auditory change detection. *Brain Research* 1220: 93–101.

García-Pentón, L., Pérez Fernández, A., Iturria-Medina, Y. et al. (2014). Anatomical connectivity changes in the bilingual brain. *NeuroImage* 84: 495–504.

Giard, M.H., Perrin, F., Pernier, J., and Bouchet, P. (1990). Brain generators implicated in the processing of auditory stimulus deviance: a topographic event-related potential study. *Psychophysiology* 27: 627–640.

Gold, B.T., Johnson, N.F., and Powell, D.K. (2013). Lifelong bilingualism contributes to cognitive reserve against white matter integrity declines in aging. *Neuropsychologia* 51: 2841–2846.

Golestani, N., Molko, N., Dehaene, S. et al. (2007). Brain structure predicts the learning of foreign speech sounds. *Cerebral Cortex* 17: 575–582.

Golestani, N., Paus, T., and Zatorre, R. (2002). Anatomical correlates of learning novel speech sounds. *Neuron* 35: 997–1010.

Golestani, N., Price, C.J., and Scott, S.K. (2011). Born with an ear for dialects? Structural plasticity in the expert phonetician brain. *Journal of Neuroscience* 31: 4213–4220.

Golestani, N. and Zatorre, R. (2004). Learning new sounds of speech: reallocation of neural substrates. *NeuroImage* 21: 494–506.

Golestani, N. and Zatorre, R. (2009). Individual differences in the acquisition of second language phonology. *Brain and Language* 109: 55–67.

Heim, S., Eickhoff, S.B., Ischebeck, A.K. et al. (2009). Effective connectivity of the left BA 44, BA 45, and inferior temporal gyrus during lexical and phonological decisions identified with DCM. *Human Brain Mapping* 30: 392–402.

Hickok, G. and Poeppel, D. (2000). Towards a functional neuroanatomy of speech perception. *Trends in Cognitive Sciences* 4: 131–138.

Hickok, G. and Poeppel, D. (2007). The cortical organization of speech processing. *Nature Reviews Neuroscience* 8: 393–402. doi:10.1038/nrn2113.

Hsiao, F.J., Wu, Z.A., Ho, L.T., and Lin, Y.Y. (2009). Theta oscillation during auditory change detection: an MEG study. *Biological Psychology* 81: 58–66.

Huttenlocher, P.R. (1999). Dendritic and synaptic development in human cerebral cortex: time course and critical periods. *Journal of Developmental Neuropsychology* 16: 347–349.

Huttenlocher, P.R. and Dabholkar, A.S. (1997). Regional differences in synaptogenesis in human cerebral cortex. *Journal of Comparative Neurology* 387: 167–178.

Indefrey, P. (2006). A meta-analysis of hemodynamic studies on first and second language processing: which suggested differences can we trust and what do they mean? *Language Learning* 56: 279–304.

Jakoby, H., Goldstein, A., and Faust, M. (2011). Electrophysiological correlates of speech perception mechanisms and individual differences in second language attainment. *Psychophysiology* 48: 1517–1531.

Jin, Y., Díaz, B., Colomer, M., and Sebastian-Galles, N. (2014). Oscillation encoding of individual differences in speech perception. *PLoS One* 9: e100901.

Juffs, A. (2011). Second language acquisition. *Wiley Interdisciplinary Reviews: Cognitive Science* 2: 277–286.

Klatt, D.H. (1979). Speech perception: A model of acoustic-phonetic analysis and lexical access. *Journal of Phonetics* 7: 279–312.

Ko, D., Kwon, S., Lee, G.-T. et al. (2012). Theta oscillation related to the auditory discrimination process in mismatch negativity: oddball versus control paradigm. *Journal of Clinical Neurology* 8: 35–42.

Li, P. (2009). Lexical organization and competition in first and second languages: computational and neural mechanisms. *Cognitive Science* 33: 629–664.

Li, P., Legault, J., and Litcofsky, K.A. (2014). Neuroplasticity as a function of second language learning: anatomical changes in the human brain. *Cortex* 58: 301–324.

Luk, G., Bialystok, E., Craik, F.I., and Grady, C.L. (2011). Lifelong bilingualism maintains white matter integrity in older adults. *Journal of Neuroscience* 31: 16808–160813.

Mayo, L.H., Florentine, M., and Buus, S. (1997). Age of second-language acquisition and perception of speech in noise. *Journal of Speech, Language, and Hearing Research* 40: 686–693.

McClelland, J.L. and Elman, J.L. (1986). The TRACE models of speech perception. *Cognitive Psychology* 18: 1–86.

Mechelli, A., Crinion, J.T., Noppeney, U. et al. (2004). Structural plasticity in the bilingual brain. *Nature* 431: 757.

Mohades, S.G., Struys, E., Van Schuerbeek, P. et al. (2012). DTI reveals structural differences in white matter tracts between bilingual and monolingual children. *Brain Research* 1435: 72–80.

Müller, B., Schaadt, G., Boltze, J. et al. (2017). ATP2C2 and DYX1C1 are putative modulators of dyslexia-related MMR. *Brain and Behavior: A Cognitive Neuroscience Perspective* 7: e00851. doi:10.1002/brb3.851.

Näätänen, R., Lehtokoski, A., Lennes, M. et al. (1997). Language-specific phoneme representations revealed by electric and magnetic brain responses. *Nature* 385: 432–434.

Näätänen, R., Paavilainen, P., Rinne, T., and Alho, K. (2007). The mismatch negativity (MMN) in basic research of central auditory processing: a review. *Clinical Neurophysiology* 118: 2544–2590.

Nenonen, S., Shestakova, A., Huotilainen, M., and Näätänen, R. (2005). Speech-sound duration processing in a second language is specific to phonetic categories. *Brain and Language* 92: 26–32.

Norris, D. (1994). Shortlist: a connectionist model of continuous speech recognition. *Cognition* 52: 189–234.

Opitz, B., Rinne, T., Mecklinger, A. et al. (2002). Differential contribution of frontal and temporal cortices to auditory change detection: fMRI and ERP results. *NeuroImage* 15: 167–174.

Pallier, C., Bosch, L., and Sebastian-Galles, N. (1997). A limit on behavioral plasticity in speech perception. *Cognition* 64: B9–B17.

Parker Jones, O., Green, D.W., Grogan, A. et al. (2012). Where, when and why brain activation differs for bilinguals and monolinguals during picture naming and reading aloud. *Cerebral Cortex* 22: 892–902.

Paulesu, E., Frith, C.D., and Frackowiak, R.S.J. (1993). The neural correlates of the verbal component of working memory. *Nature* 362: 342–345.

Perani, D. and Abutalebi, J. (2005). The neural basis of first and second language processing. *Current Opinion in Neurobiology* 15: 202–206.

Pliatsikas, C., DeLuca, V., Moschopoulou, E., and Saddy, J.D. (2017). Immersive bilingualism reshapes the core of the brain. *Brain Structure and Function* 222: 1785–1795.

Pliatsikas, C., Johnstone, T., and Marinis, T. (2014). Grey matter volume in the cerebellum is related to the processing of grammatical rules in a second language: a structural voxel-based morphometry study. *Cerebellum* 13: 55–63.

Poeppel, D., Idsardi, W.J., and van Wassenhove, V. (2008). Speech perception at the interface of neurobiology and linguistics. *Philosophical Transactions of the Royal Society, B: Biological Sciences* 363: 1071–1086.

Price, C.J. (2012). A review and synthesis of the first 20 years of PET and fMRI studies of heard speech, spoken language and reading. *NeuroImage* 62: 816–847.

Pujol, J., Soriano-Mas, C., Ortiz, H. et al. (2006). Myelination of language-related areas in the developing brain. *Neurology* 66: 339–343.

Ressel, V., Pallier, C., Ventura-Campos, N. et al. (2012). An effect of bilingualism on the auditory cortex. *Journal of Neuroscience* 32: 16597–16601.

Sebastian-Galles, N. and Baus, C. (2005). On the relationship between perception and production in L2 categories. In: *Twenty-First Century Psycholinguistics: Four Cornerstones* (ed. A. Cutler), 279–292. New York, NY: Erlbaum.

Sebastian-Galles, N., Echeverria, S., and Bosch, L. (2005). The influence of initial exposure on lexical representation: comparing early and simultaneous bilinguals. *Journal of Memory and Language* 52: 240–255.

Sebastian-Galles, N., Rodriguez-Fornells, A., de Diego-Balaguer, R., and Díaz, B. (2006). First- and second-language phonological representations in the mental lexicon. *Journal of Cognitive Neuroscience* 18: 1277–1291.

Sebastian-Galles, N., Soriano-Mas, C., Baus, C. et al. (2012). Neuroanatomical markers of individual differences in native and non-native vowel perception. *Journal of Neurolinguistics* 25: 150–162.

Sebastian-Galles, N. and Soto-Faraco, S. (1999). Online processing of native and non-native phonemic contrasts in early bilinguals. *Cognition* 72: 111–123.

Strange, W. and Dittman, S. (1984). Effects of discrimination training on the perception of /r-l/ by Japanese adults learning English. *Perception and Psychophysics* 36: 131–145.

Ventura-Campos, N., Sanjuán, A., González, J. et al. (2013). Spontaneous brain activity predicts learning ability of foreign sounds. *Journal of Neuroscience* 33: 9295–9305.

Wartenburger, I., Heekeren, H.R., Abutalebi, J. et al. (2003). Early setting of grammatical processing in the bilingual brain. *Neuron* 37: 159–170.

Weber, A. and Cutler, A. (2004). Lexical competition in non-native spoken-word recognition. *Journal of Memory and Language* 50: 1–25.

Werker, J.F. and Hensch, T.K. (2015). Critical periods in speech perception: new directions. *Annual Review of Psychology* 66: 173–196.

Werker, J.F. and Tees, R.C. (2005). Speech perception as a window for understanding plasticity and commitment in language systems of the brain. *Developmental Psychobiology* 46: 233–251.

Winkler, I., Kujala, T., Tiitinen, H. et al. (1999). Brain responses reveal the learning of foreign language phonemes. *Psychophysiology* 36: 638–642.

Wong, F., Chandrasekaran, B., Garibaldi, K., and Wong, P. (2011). White matter anisotropy in the ventral language pathway predicts sound-to-word learning success. *Journal of Neuroscience* 31: 8780–8785.

Wong, P.C. and Perrachione, T.K. (2007). Learning pitch patterns in lexical identification by native English-speaking adults. *Applied PsychoLinguistics* 28: 565–585.

Wong, P., Perrachione, T., and Parrish, T. (2007). Neural characteristics of successful and less successful speech and word learning in adults. *Human Brain Mapping* 28: 995–1006.

Wong, P., Warrier, C., Penhune, V. et al. (2008). Volume of left Heschl's Gyrus and linguistic pitch learning. *Cerebral Cortex* 18: 828–836.

Yago, E., Escera, C., Alho, K., and Giard, M.H. (2001). Cerebral mechanisms underlying orienting of attention towards auditory frequency changes. *NeuroReport* 12: 2583–2587.

14 Lexical Organization and Reorganization in the Multilingual Mind

GARY LIBBEN AND JOHN W. SCHWIETER

1. Introduction

Anyone who speaks and understands two or more languages will have immediate and personal experience of the ways in which the lexicon of a language differs from the lexicon of a person. Lexicons of separate languages can be compiled as separate books or databases. Such separation, however, is not possible for the lexicon of a person, which is an integrated knowledge system in a single mind/brain. How, then, can an integrated lexical system acquire, maintain, couple, and decouple lexical elements of two or more languages? This is the fundamental question in the understanding of the multilingual mental lexicon and the topic of this chapter.

The notion of a mental lexicon may have first emerged in Treisman's (1961) dissertation as being the storehouse, or listing, of words in the mind. However, over a half a century later, developments in psycholinguistic research suggest that the mental lexicon may be better explained from a dynamic and integrated perspective (Libben and Goral 2015). Indeed, for speakers of two or more languages, their language systems are continuously interactively evolving and adapting to the needs of the communicative demands of the environment. Libben et al. (2017a) argue that 'adequate modeling of the (bilingual) mental lexicon requires an understanding not only of dynamicity and integration as individual constructs but also of the manner in which they interact with each other and with key phenomena in bilingual lexical processing' (p. 2). Under these assumptions, researchers are now entertaining the idea that the mental lexicon of the multilingual mind may be the default rather than the exception to a monolingual mental lexicon (Vaid and Meuter 2017).

In this chapter, we discuss the manner in which recent developments in mental lexicon research have created new implications for the understanding of how multilingualism develops and how it is maintained across the lifespan. We consider multilinguals to be persons who are able to understand and speak two or more languages.

The Handbook of the Neuroscience of Multilingualism, First Edition. Edited by John W. Schwieter.
© 2019 John Wiley & Sons Ltd. Published 2019 by John Wiley & Sons Ltd.

Under this view, multilingualism includes bilingualism, trilingualism, etc. In Section 2, we discuss the notion of a mental lexicon within the context of its historical roots in generative linguistics and psycholinguistics. This is followed by an examination of two dominant metaphors in the literature: one in which the multilingual person is characterized as possessing interacting lexical stores and the other in which the multilingual person is characterized as possessing a network of interacting lexical items in a single multilingual lexical store. Throughout the chapter, we explore the special role that structurally-complex words may play in the organization of words in the mind and how the specific nature of a multilingual's lexical system is shaped by the linguistic – and specifically, morphological – properties of the languages.

2.   The Notion of a Mental Lexicon

The fundamental challenge in understanding the nature of linguistic knowledge in the mind and brain is that, whereas the external manifestations of language are open to observation, the mental representations and operations that enable language activity are not. This may be an inherent challenge. On the other hand, it may simply be a temporary one that is awaiting resolution through a yet-to-be-discovered research technology. But, whatever the eventual outcome in the study of language representation and processing will be, our present situation is one in which language researchers have no direct observational access to putative linguistic structures in the mind or brain. For this reason, they are reliant on constructs that generate predictions that can be related to observable language activity. The mental lexicon is exactly such a construct.

The mental lexicon may constitute the key to our understanding of the nature of language organization among multilingual persons. The reason for this is that it is the theoretical space in which the fundamental tension inherent in multilingual language ability is most clear. The inherent tension is simply this: multilingualism seems to require that words of different languages both be separated and be related. Thus, the multilingual mental lexicon must be a cognitive system whose organization creates both connection and isolation. Moreover, it must be able to do so under conditions of constant change. More than any other aspect of language knowledge, the knowledge of words seems to be in a state of flux over the lifespan. A language user will be acquiring (and perhaps losing) words and modifying connections among them over time. This dynamicity, while present for all language users, is heightened in the case of multilingualism. Current evidence suggests that multilingualism requires both the online integration and differentiation of language-specific lexical forms. All other things being equal, multilinguals will have a larger lexical store than monolinguals and their lexical systems will undergo more change across the lifespan. Thus, the study of the multilingual mental lexicon may offer language researchers the greatest access presently available to an understanding of the fundamental features of linguistic knowledge in action.

In recent years, substantial progress has been made in the understanding of multilingual lexical representation and processing through the lens of the evolving characterization of the mental lexicon. In the next sections, we discuss these developments by first tracing the roots of the construct in both the linguistic and psycholinguistic literature.

2.1. Roots in Generative Linguistics

The roots of the notion of a lexicon as part of (and indeed the backbone of) a language date back to antiquity. In order, however, to present the backdrop to more recent developments in the conceptualization of the multilingual mental lexicon, it may suffice to begin by focusing on a particular body of grammatical scholarship that emerged with the publication of Chomsky's (1957) *Syntactic Structures*. This approach, first known under the term 'transformational generative grammar' will serve to highlight important contrasts in the ways in which lexical knowledge was seen from a purely grammatical vs. a processing perspective in the second half of the twentieth century. As we will see, those contrasts have been in some ways transcended as researchers have moved from early formulations to models that take into consideration the structural complexities of words both within and across languages.

From the outset, the notion of a lexicon that was distinct theoretically from the syntactic component of a language system was a core feature of generative grammar. It was explicit in Chomsky's (1970) paper entitled 'remarks on nominalization' and became known within the framework as *lexicalism*. In the *lexicalist* framework, the syntactic component of a native speaker's grammar is supplied with words that are part of a separate component, the lexicon. The manner in which this lexicon is structured and the manner in which new words are created within it were the subject of a number of key subsequent publications in the 1970s and 1980s. In the framework of Halle (1973), the fundamental unit of the lexicon was the morpheme. In the seminal work of Aronoff (1976), it was claimed that words, rather than morphemes, were the fundamental units of representation and word formation. This work was followed by major contributions of William (1981) and Di Sciullo and Williams (1987), which tackled the seemingly simple, but in fact quite thorny, issue of what constitutes a word in the grammar of a language and in the grammar of an individual.

A key feature of generative approaches to the lexicon was the view that the lexicon was a list of exceptions, i.e. those aspects of the grammar that could not be derived by rule. This seems intuitively appealing if one considers that a grammar is a system of rules, constraints, and/or regularities, but a simple word, almost by definition, is an arbitrary association of form and meaning. Thus, the lexicon, in the generative framework was essentially a listing of idiosyncratic forms. This view was expressed perhaps most cleverly by Di Sciullo and Williams (1987): 'The lexicon is like a prison – it contains only the lawless, and the only thing its inmates have in common is lawlessness' (p. 3).

It should be noted that the simple (and likely false) dichotomy between rules and idiosyncratic words was recognized and addressed by several influential approaches to theoretical morphology beginning with the work of Jackendoff (1975), who captured the relationship among complex words sharing elements through 'redundancy rules' and Booj's (2010) *Construction Morphology*. Anderson's *A-Morphous Morphology* (Anderson 1992), contains a nuanced treatment of simple, affixed, and compound words. The core of his approach is the rejection of the view that morphologically complex words can be characterized as containing morphemes. Also noteworthy in Anderson's landmark book is the extremely poignant epigraph with which it begins: 'Linguistics will become a science when linguists begin standing on one another's shoulders instead of on one another's toes' (p. viii).

2.2. Roots in Psycholinguistics

The term 'mental lexicon', in its psycholinguistic sense, gained common usage in the psycholinguistic literature at roughly the same time that the notions of the lexicon and lexical operations were being elaborated in the generative literature. The psycholinguistic perspective was, however, quite different. The source of that difference can be tied to methodological matters. From the 1970s onward, the lexical processing literature was dominated by a single methodological paradigm – visual lexical decision. In its most basic form, the visual lexical decision task is one in which a language user is presented with a letter string on the screen of a computer and is asked to decide whether that letter string is or is not a word of his/her language by pressing a key labelled 'yes' or a key labelled 'no' as quickly as possible. Psycholinguistic experiments using this paradigm typically measured a participant's response accuracy (% 'yes' responses for existing words; % 'no' responses for nonwords) as well as response latency in milliseconds. The lexical decision paradigm proved itself to be sensitive to differences among word types in both a robust and reliable manner. With it, lexical processing researchers were able to document processing speed differences associated with a variety of lexical characteristics, including frequency, length, concreteness, and part of speech. The data yielded by these experiments were used to develop and test models of the functional architecture of the mental lexicon.

It is important to note that the conceptualization of the mental lexicon that was developed and tested with this methodological approach was one that was dominated by considerations of lexical access. This is in stark contrast to the lexicon in the generative linguistic framework, which had as its focus word formation and structure. In the theoretical linguistic literature, little attention was paid to matters of speed or ease of access. However, in the psycholinguistic literature, these were exactly the considerations that were used to create models of the mental lexicon. In the very influential work of Forster (1976), for example, differences in lexical decision latencies to higher frequency words vs. lower frequency words were used to claim that the mental lexicon could be seen as a frequency ordered list. It was claimed that during lexical access, this list was searched from the top downward, so that lower frequency words (the ones lower down on the list) took longer to process because to get at them, the mental search process had to go past the lexical listings that were higher in the list.

The metaphor of the mental lexicon as a list received challenge from a number of competing approaches in which frequency effects, for example, were captured by rather different sorts of metaphors. In Morton's (1969) logogen model, differences in recognition speed between high-frequency and low-frequency words were captured by the postulation that words essentially were in a random-access store (modelled after the approach of Selfridge 1959) but that each lexical representation in that store had an activation threshold that was dynamically adjusted on the basis of experience. Thus, higher frequency words, because they had been activated more often, came to be activated more easily (i.e. had reduced activation thresholds). This approach to the functional architecture of the mental lexicon was incorporated into models of word reading such as that proposed by Coltheart et al. (1977). Their approach, in turn, was challenged by connectionist approaches to the organization of the mental lexicon, which employed distributed representations for words and, thus, claimed to be better able to capture the spread of association from one recognized word to others in a lexical network (e.g. Seidenberg and McClelland 1989).

3.   Structurally Complex Words as the Meeting Ground

In many ways, our discussion of the linguistic and psycholinguistic roots of research on the human lexicon might appear to be a narrative of two solitudes. Historically, one approach was concerned with how lexical structures meet grammatical structures and how words are formed. The other approach was concerned with how words are accessed.

Indeed, as long as the fundamental units considered in lexical modelling are structurally simple ones, that narrative could very well have remained one of two solitudes. But it has not, and the reason for this is that a consideration of structurally complex words has created the meeting ground between the two traditions. This was a development that was necessary to meet the basic requirements of observational adequacy in the study of lexical representation and processing. Although it might seem that 'normal' words are structurally simple ones (e.g. *cat, dog*), the fact is that most words of a language, even a language as morphologically simple as English, are prefixed, suffixed, or compounded. This fact has great consequences for the architecture of the multilingual lexicon and for the relation of morphology to psycholinguistic models of the mental lexicon. The reason for this is that words that contain other words (e.g. *handy, handstand, walker, catwalk*) have a dual character. On the one hand, they are clearly linked formally to the simple words *hand, stand, walk*, and *cat* from which they were formed. Yet, they also maintain an idiosyncratic character. Even if a speaker of English already knows the meanings of these simple words, the meanings and usage of the derived and compound words must also be learned. It is because of their dual nature that derived and compound words create the key bridge between the linguistic notion of a lexicon and the psycholinguistic notion of a mental lexicon.

In a seminal study of the processing of prefixed words, Taft and Forster (1975) claimed that words such as *refill* and *uncover* are stripped of their prefixes in visual word recognition. This processing claim was associated with the representational claim that such prefixed forms do not have their own representations in the mental lexicon, but rather are understood through links between separately stored prefixes (e.g. *re-, un-*) and stems (e.g. *fill, cover*). In a paper published the following year, Taft and Forster (1976) made a similar proposal for the representation and processing of compound words. Compounds were claimed to be represented in the mental lexicon in a decomposed, morpheme-based form and to be decomposed morphologically during online visual processing.

In the four decades since the initial work of Taft and Forster (1975, 1976), a very rich psycholinguistic literature has developed on how derived and compound words are represented and processed. Alternatives to full decomposition models such as that proposed by Taft and Forster included so-called horse-race models (e.g. Bertram et al. 2000; Schreuder and Baayen 1995), in which visual lexical processing is characterized as a competition between whole word access and morphological decomposition, as well as models such as that proposed by Giraudo and Grainger (2001), in which it is claimed that access to morphological constituents is achieved through prior activation of the whole word. Several more recent publications have questioned the assumption that the notion of a morpheme, as a construct inherited from the theoretical linguistic literature, is appropriate to the characterization of mental lexical representations (e.g. Baayen 2014; Libben 2017).

In addition to the overarching questions concerning the representation and processing of derived and compound words as entire classes, many psycholinguistic studies have investigated whether subclasses of derived and compound words may be represented and processed differently. One prominent example of this is the treatment of so-called semantically-opaque words (Bell and Schäfer 2016). These words often have been considered an exotic subclass. However, as can be seen in the examples above, many (perhaps the majority) of derived and compound words can be considered to be semantically opaque. It would be almost impossible, for example, to deduce the meaning of *handy* in English from the meanings of the stem *hand* and the suffix -*y*. Similarly, it would be difficult to deduce that in the dominant meanings of *catwalk* ('a narrow bridge' or 'a platform used by fashion models'), it is people who are walking, not cats. More extreme examples include compound words such as *cakewalk*, for which the etymological relation to *cake* has been lost in its current meaning and use.

It turns out, that matters of semantic opacity have profound consequences for models of the mental lexicon as an integrated knowledge store. They also have important implications for multilingualism. If it is the case that lexical processing involves the activation of the lexical elements of all words, including those that are semantically opaque (Marelli et al. 2017), then the constituent *cat* will be activated in the processing of *catwalk* and *cake* will be activated during the processing of *cakewalk*. This will result in a routine state of lexical interference (Smolka and Libben 2017). Under this view, a core feature of the cognitive system that we call the mental lexicon is the capacity to manage such interference. Libben (2014) has claimed that in a lexical system that has evolved to maximize the opportunity for meaning creation, interference is a routine feature of lexical activity. In addition, if it is the case that the multilingual lexicon also shows massive interconnectivity, then the processing of *cakewalk* may not only activate *cake* in English, but will do so in other languages as well.

A masked visual priming study with Chinese-English bilinguals, reported by Zhang et al. (2011) offers an example of this interconnectivity. Their study was built upon the fact that Chinese has many compounds that are semantically opaque. For example, the Chinese word for *thing*, is an exocentric compound composed of the elements *east* and *west*. In their study, Chinese-English bilinguals participated in a lexical decision task with masked priming. A prime word was shown on the computer screen for 59 milliseconds immediately preceding the target stimulus for which a lexical decision was required. The key masked primes were constituents of Chinese compounds that were translation equivalents of the target English word. Thus, the English word *thing* was preceded by the English target *east* (a constituent of *east–west*, the Chinese word for *thing*). The authors found significant facilitation for first constituents such as these. They also found the reverse effect, namely that for bilingual participants, the English word *thing* primed the English target *east*. The authors conclude from this that participants rapidly and automatically translated English words into Chinese and then decomposed the translated compounds into their constituents. Irrespective of whether this actually corresponds to the sequence of cognitive events, the data demonstrate how between-language associations that involve subword elements play a role in online lexical processing.

The effects reported by Zhang et al. (2011) are made more dramatic by the fact that, visually, Chinese and English words are fully distinct. Therefore, the associations must be at a form-independent, lexical level.

In a study that also investigated the processing of compounds among bilinguals whose languages have very different writing systems (English and Hebrew), Libben et al. (2017b) found that subword priming (e.g. presentation of the prime *gold* followed by the target *goldfish)* were evidenced for both languages of Hebrew-English bilinguals. Moreover, these priming effects were comparable for both within-language and between-language priming. Thus seeing *gold* facilitated the processing of goldfish. But so did seeing the Hebrew translation of gold (i.e. זהב). Similarly, seeing English constituents facilitated processing of compounds in Hebrew, the native language of all participants.

The findings of Libben et al. (2017b) reinforce the conclusion that connections in the multilingual lexicon do not simply involve whole words. In addition, the fact that subword primes in the second language (L2) facilitated compound recognition in the native language points to how acquiring lexical knowledge in a new language may force a reorganization of the lexical system as a whole.

As a first example of potential dynamic multilingual reorganization of lexical structures, consider the English word *turkey*. It is represented in French as the word *dinde*. In Hebrew, it is represented as the compound תַרְנְגוֹל הוֹדוּ (literally 'rooster Indian'). Through the explicit compound representation, it is likely that the native speaker of French will be able to reanalyse the opaque form *dinde* (which was originally *coq d'inde* in French) as the French phrase *of India* (d'*Inde)*, with just the apostrophe dropped.

As a second example, consider the word *dandelion* in English, which came into English from the French *dent de lion* (literally: 'tooth of lion'). In many languages, the word for *dandelion* is a compound composed of the constituents *tooth* and *lion* (e.g. Spanish, Italian, Portuguese, German, Norwegian, Hebrew). One might imagine that the interaction among these lexical representations would enable the multilingual speaking English and one or more of these languages to have a structured representation for the English word *dandelion* (though recognition that it is the French *dent-de-lion)* that a monolingual speaker of English would be very unlikely to have.

And, finally, consider the compound system of a multilingual as a whole: in English, all compound words have their modifiers first and their main element last (so that a *horserace* must be a type of *race* and a *racehorse* must be a type of *horse*). In many languages, it is exactly the opposite. And, in languages such as French, Italian, and Farsi, both orders are attested. The consequence of this, if indeed the multilingual mental lexicon is characterized by massive lexical connectivity, is that there is a drive towards the development of a unified system in which compound ordering is less fixed overall, so that *racehorse* and *horserace* might require some ambiguity resolution for the trilingual in the online lexical processing of English.

The discussion above highlights the ways in which morphological phenomena within and across languages create a need for dynamic reorganization within the multilingual lexicon. The reason for this is that, as has been shown across many psycholinguistic investigations, the mental lexicon is characterized by great connectivity among both word and subword units. In Section 4, we examine the consequences of this connectivity for modelling the multilingual lexicon.

4.   Modelling Multilingual Connections and the Functional Architecture of the Mental Lexicon

Research on the bilingual and multilingual lexicon is best described as coming out of the psycholinguistic tradition described in the Section 2.2. Its primary focus has been on issues of lexical access and the implications of lexical processing data for hypotheses concerning the functional architecture of the mental lexicon. But, as we will see below, by examining whether knowing two or more languages involves having two or more lexicons, the study of the multilingual lexicon has linked lexical processing research to the most fundamental questions regarding the relation between linguistic and conceptual structures.

Two enduring questions in research on the bilingual lexicon have concerned whether bilinguals' languages are integrated and whether lexical access is a selective or non-selective procedure (see recent reviews by Kroll 2017; Kroll and Ma 2017; Kroll et al. 2013). Overwhelming support for the observation that bilinguals activate both their languages in parallel has come from a wealth of studies looking at both word recognition (Dijkstra 2005; Dijkstra and Van Heuven 2002; Shook and Marian 2013; Van Heuven et al. 1998) and word production (Costa et al. 1999; De Groot and Starreveld 2015; Kroll and Gollan 2014; Poarch and van Hell 2012; Starreveld et al. 2014).

Perhaps short of some neurological intervention or in extreme cases of language attrition (Schmid 2010), it is highly improbable that one of the bilingual's languages can be 'turned off'. Consequently, the presence of activated words in both languages requires lexical access to be a competitive procedure which takes into account activated alternatives (in both languages) and resolves such competition at higher levels. These non-selective, dynamic accounts to lexical access can be seen in models of bilingual word recognition (Dijkstra and Van Heuven 2002; Shook and Marian 2013) and production (Costa 2005; Costa et al. 1999; Schwieter and Sunderman 2008) in addition to models of the bilingual memory (Kroll and Stewart 1994; Pavlenko 2009).

One explanation of the bilingual memory which demonstrates the consequences of persistent activation and competition between languages is the revised hierarchical model (RHM; Kroll and Stewart 1994). This developmental account identifies L2 proficiency as a modulating factor of lexical processing. The model argues that at beginning stages of adult L2 acquisition, learners rely on existing links between first language (L1) words and their meanings to access a shared conceptual system. As L2 proficiency increases, so does the ability to directly access meaning without the need to rely on L1 lexical links. While much work has supported the RHM (Sholl et al. 1995; Schwieter and Sunderman 2009; Sunderman and Kroll 2006; Talamas et al. 1999), there are some inconsistent findings to still be clarified (see Brysbaert and Duyck 2010; Duyck and Brysbaert 2004).

Researchers have also shown that conceptual restructuring occurs when new words are learned to accommodate for word-to-concept mapping (Athanasopoulos 2009, 2011; Athanasopoulos and Kasai 2008; Cook et al. 2006). Building on this and the hypotheses in the RHM, Pavlenko (2009) put forth a multimodal representation of the conceptual system which consists of revised categories she argued are fully shared, partially overlapping, or entirely language-specific. Pavlenko's modified hierarchical model (MHM) presents a dynamic account of conceptual and lexical processing that incorporates conceptual and semantic transfer (Jarvis and Pavlenko 2008). The MHM, like the RHM, maintains the developmental progression from lexical to conceptual mediation as L2 proficiency increases.

Keeping with the notion that concepts can restructure to become fully shared, partially shared, or language-specific during L2 acquisition, Benati and Schwieter (2017) speculated as to how the MHM could be extended to learning a third language. In their proposed trilingual modified hierarchical model (TMHM; see Figure 1), the

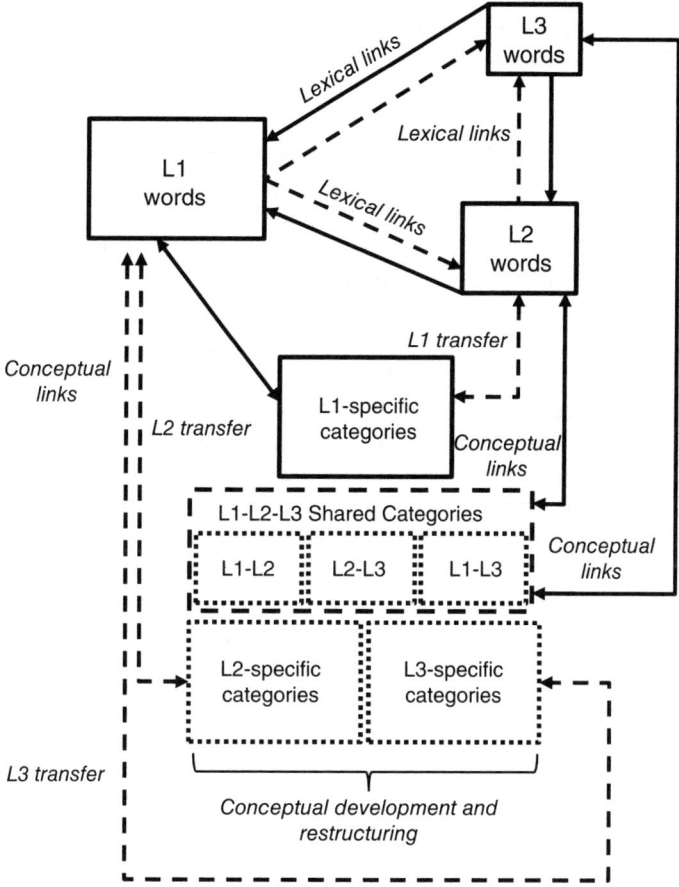

Figure 1 The trilingual modified hierarchical model. (Source: Taken from Benati and Schwieter 2017).

idea of conceptual restructuring and target-like development of linguistic categories couple with the argument that both L2 and L3 word learning can trigger conceptual reorganizing. However, empirical tests of the TMHM are needed as noted by the authors:

> The addition of an L3 implies that lexical mediation from the L3 to the L2 can occur (although empirical support would be needed to tease apart whether the preferred path of lexical mediation for the L3 would be via L1 or L2 words and whether these things are modulated by other factors). For instance, when an English (L1), Spanish (L2), Italian (L3) language learner is asked to name an L3 word (e.g., *gatto*), he/she may have to access its meaning by first associating it with the L2 word (e.g., *gato*) rather than with the L1 word *cat*. L3-to-L2 word association may be sensitive to factors such as cognate status, language typologies, lexical robustness (i.e., an element of proficiency in which automaticity of word retrieval is due to the familiarity with and frequency of its access; Schwieter and Sunderman 2008, 2009), and overall proficiency level. Future studies should test the modulating nature of these variables while also keeping in mind that lexical transfer may also trigger syntactic transfer (Benati and Schwieter, p. 267).

The predictions of the TMHM align with many of the findings from L3 studies and models which have attempted to address the complex issue of syntactic transfer (Alonso and Rothman 2016; Bardel and Falk 2007, 2012; de Bot and Jaensch 2015; Falk and Bardel 2011; Hammarberg 2009, 2010; Jaensch 2013; Mykhaylyk et al. 2015; Rothman 2011, 2013, 2015; Slabakova 2016; William and Hammarberg 1998).

In addition to syntactic transfer and the lexical-conceptual restructuring posited in the TMHM, it is important to consider the effect of parallel language activation on how bilinguals process their languages. At the lexical level, several studies suggest that languages converge (Ameel et al. 2005; Benati and Schwieter 2017; Malt et al. 2015). Consequently, bilinguals must adapt to these dynamic changes as they occur and be able to apply them in situations in which they are not only merited but also contextually appropriate (Green and Abutalebi 2013). Under this assumption, bilingual experience alone could shape the way bilinguals process their languages and adapt to such processes over time. Some of the most recent research that is being hotly debated is the possibility that these adaptive changes are exemplary at showcasing bilingualism as a model of neural plasticity (Baum and Titone 2014; Kroll 2017; Li et al. 2014). For instance, fresh characterizations view the bilingual as a 'mental juggler who negotiates and resolves cross-language competition with the consequence that he or she gains juggling expertise that spills over into the domain of general cognition functions' (Kroll 2017, pp. 38–39). Recent research has shown some support for this metaphor, with a few caveats that identify critical and modulating factors such as how supportive their speech community is of the two languages (Lauchlan et al. 2013), language immersion (Baus et al. 2013; Linck et al. 2009) and whether they often code switch in daily lives (Green and Wei 2014; Schwieter and Ferreira 2016).

The research summarized above has demonstrated that understanding of the functional architecture of the human lexical processing system can be significantly deepened through a consideration of bilingual and multilingual processing. Moreover, the TMHM – while currently based on empirical work that informed its bilingual counterpart, the MHM, demonstrates the manner in which the cognitive dynamics of bilingual processing can generalized to trilingual (and, in principle, n-lingual) cognitive architectures. If indeed, as we have noted, it is highly improbable that one of the multilingual's languages can be 'turned off', this suggests a system of extraordinary complexity and dynamic balance. Although cases of simultaneous early bilingualism are common, the acquisition of subsequent languages typically develops over an individual's life history. The consequence of this, as hypothesized in the TMH, is that the lexical system of the multilingual may always be in a dynamic state of readjustment, in which lexical items may be both recoupled, and decoupled.

5. Concluding Remarks

In this chapter, we have discussed the mental lexicon as the cognitive system that constitutes the capacity for conscious and unconscious lexical activity (Jarema and Libben 2007). We traced the roots of the notion of a lexicon in generative linguistics as well as its roots in the psycholinguistics of visual lexical processing. We noted how models of the bilingual lexicon and multilingual lexicon create an opportunity to understand more deeply how lexical and conceptual knowledge may be intertwined in the mind and how a consideration of structurally complex words may require that we see the mental lexicon as a self-organizing system whose chief property may be plasticity. This perspective underlines the fundamental difference between the *lexicon of a language* and *the lexicon of a person*. In essence, both are models. But they are models of very different things. The lexicon of a language is a model of the external lexical manifestations of the language activity of a speech community at a specific time or over time. The lexicon of a person is a model of the cognitive system that both creates and is created by their language activity.

REFERENCES

Ameel, E., Storms, G., Malt, B., and Sloman, S. (2005). How bilinguals solve the naming problem. *Journal of Memory and Language* 53: 60–80.

Anderson, S. (1992). *A-Morphous Morphology*. Cambridge, UK: Cambridge University Press.

Aronoff, M. (1976). *Word Formation in Generative Grammar*. Cambridge, MA: MIT Press.

Athanasopoulos, P. (2009). Cognitive representation of color in bilinguals: the case of Greek blues. *Bilingualism: Language and Cognition* 12 (1): 83–95.

Athanasopoulos, P. (2011). Cognitive restructuring in bilingualism. In: *Thinking and Speaking in Two Languages* (ed. A. Pavlenko), 29–65. Bristol, UK: Multilingual Matters.

Athanasopoulos, P. and Kasai, C. (2008). Language and thought in bilinguals: the case of grammatical number and nonverbal classification preferences. *Applied PsychoLinguistics* 29 (1): 105–121.

Baayen, R. (2014). Experimental and psycholinguistic approaches to studying derivation. In: *The Handbook of Derivational Morphology* (ed. R. Lieber and P. Stekauer), 95–117. Oxford, UK: Oxford University Press.

Bardel, C. and Falk, Y. (2007). The role of the second language in third language acquisition: The case of Germanic syntax. *Second Language Research* 23 (4): 459–484.

Bardel, C. and Falk, Y. (2012). The L2 status factor and the declarative/procedural distinction. In: *Third language acquisition in adulthood (pp. 61–78). Philadelphia, PA/ Amsterdam* (ed. J. Cabrelli Amaro, S. Flynn and J. Rothman). The Netherlands: John Benjamins.

Baum, S. and Titone, D. (2014). Moving toward a neuroplasticity view of bilingualism, executive control and aging. *Applied PsychoLinguistics* 5: 857–894.

Baus, C., Costa, A., and Carreiras, M. (2013). On the effects of second language immersion on first language production. *Acta Psychologica* 142 (3): 402–409.

Bell, M. and Schäfer, M. (2016). Modelling semantic transparency. *Morphology* 26: 157–199.

Benati, A. and Schwieter, J.W. (2017). Input processing and processing instruction: pedagogical and cognitive considerations for L3 acquisition. In: *L3 Syntactic Transfer: Models, New Developments, and Implications* (ed. T. Angelovska and A. Hahn), 253–275. Amsterdam, The Netherlands: Benjamins.

Bertram, R., Schreuder, R., and Baayen, R. (2000). The balance of storage and computation in morphological processing: the role of word formation type, affixal homonymy, and productivity. *Journal of Experimental Psychology: Learning, Memory, and Cognition* 26: 419–511.

Booj, G. (2010). *Construction Morphology*. Oxford, UK: Oxford University Press.

Brysbaert, M. and Duyck, W. (2010). Is it time to leave behind the revised hierarchical model of bilingual language processing after fifteen years of service? *Bilingualism: Language and Cognition* 13: 359–371.

Chomsky, N. (1957). *Syntactic Structures*. The Hague, The Netherlands: de Gruyter.

Chomsky, N. (1970). Remarks on nominalization. In: *Readings in English Transformational Grammar* (ed. R. Jacobs and P. Rosenbaum), 184–221. Waltham, MA: Ginn.

Coltheart, M., Davelaar, E., Jonasson, J., and Besner, D. (1977). Access to the internal lexicon. In: *Attention and Performance* (ed. S. Dornic), 535–556. London, UK: Academic Press.

Cook, V., Bassetti, B., Kasai, C. et al. (2006). Do bilinguals have different concepts? The case of shape and material in Japanese L2 users of English. *International Journal of Bilingualism* 10 (2): 137–152.

Costa, A. (2005). Lexical access in bilingual production. In: *The Handbook of Bilingualism: Psycholinguistic Approaches* (ed. J. Kroll and A. de Groot), 308–325. New York, NY: Oxford University Press.

Costa, A., Miozzo, M., and Caramazza, A. (1999). Lexical selection in bilinguals: do words in the bilingual's two lexicons compete for selection? *Journal of Memory and Language* 41: 365–397.

De Bot, K. and Jaensch, C. (2015). What is special about L3 processing? *Bilingualism: Language and Cognition* 18 (2): 15.

De Groot, A. and Starreveld, P. (2015). Parallel language activation in bilinguals' word production and its modulating factors: a review and computer simulations. In: *The Cambridge Handbook of Bilingual Processing* (ed. J.W. Schwieter), 389–415. Cambridge, UK: Cambridge University Press.

Di Sciullo, A.-M. and Williams, E. (1987). *On the Definition of Word*. Cambridge MA: MIT Press.

Dijkstra, T. (2005). Bilingual word recognition and lexical access. In: *The Handbook of Bilingualism: Psycholinguistic Approaches* (ed. J. Kroll and A. de Groot), 179–201. New York, NY: Oxford University Press.

Dijkstra, T. and Van Heuven, W. (2002). The architecture of the bilingual word recognition system: from identification to decision. *Bilingualism: Language and Cognition* 5: 175–197.

Duyck, W. and Brysbaert, M. (2004). Forward and backward number translation requires conceptual mediation in both balanced and unbalanced bilinguals. *Journal of Experimental Psychology: Human Perception and Performance* 30 (5): 889–906.

Falk, Y. and Bardel, C. (2011). Object pronouns in German L3 syntax: Evidence for the L2 status factor. *Second Language Research* 27 (1): 59–82.

Forster, K. (1976). Accessing the mental lexicon. In: *New Approaches to Language Mechanisms* (ed. R. Wales and E. Walker), 257–287. Amsterdam, The Netherlands: North-Holland.

Giraudo, H. and Grainger, J. (2001). Priming complex words: evidence for supralexical representation of morphology. *Psychonomic Bulletin and Review* 8 (1): 127–131.

Gonzalez Alonso, J. and Rothman, J. (2017). Coming of age in L3 initial stages transfer models: deriving developmental predictions and looking towards the future. *International Journal of Bilingualism* 21 (6): 683–697.

Green, D. and Abutalebi, J. (2013). Language control in bilinguals: the adaptive control hypothesis. *Journal of Cognitive Psychology* 25 (5): 515–530.

Green, D. and Wei, L. (2014). A control process model of code-switching. *Language, Cognition and Neuroscience* 29: 499–511.

Halle, M. (1973). Prolegomena to a theory of word formation. *Linguistic Inquiry* 4: 3–16.

Hammarberg, B. (2009). *Processes in Third Language Acquisition*. Edinburgh, Scotland: University of Edinburgh Press.

Hammarberg, B. (2010). The languages of the multilingual: Some conceptual and terminological issues. *International Review of Applied Linguistics in Language Teaching* 48 (2–3): 91–104.

Jaensch, C. (2013). Third language acquisition: Where are we now? *Linguistic Approaches to Bilingualism* 3 (1): 73–93.

Jackendoff, R. (1975). Morphological and semantic regularities in the lexicon. *Language* 51 (3): 639–671.

Jarema, G. and Libben, G. (2007). Matters of definitions. In: *Core Perspectives on the Mental Lexicon* (ed. G. Jarema and G. Libben), 1–12. Oxford, UK: Elsevier.

Jarvis, S. and Pavlenko, A. (eds.) (2008). *Crosslinguistic Influence in Language and Cognition*. New York, NY: Routledge.

Kroll, J. (2017). The bilingual lexicon: a window into language dynamics and cognition. In: *Bilingualism: A Framework for Understanding the Mental Lexicon* (ed. M. Libben, M. Goral and G. Libben), 27–48. Amsterdam, The Netherlands/Philadelphia, PA: Benjamins.

Kroll, J. and Gollan, T. (2014). Speech planning in two languages: what bilinguals tell us about language production. In: *The Oxford Handbook of Language Production* (ed. V. Ferreira, M. Goldrick and M. Miozzo), 165–181. Oxford, UK: Oxford University Press.

Kroll, J., Gullifer, J., and Rossi, E. (2013). The multilingual lexicon: the cognitive and neural basis of lexical comprehension and production in two languages. *Annual Review of Applied Linguistics* 33: 102–127.

Kroll, J. and Ma, F. (2017). The bilingual lexicon. In: *The Handbook of Psycholinguistics* (ed. H. Cairns and E. Fernandez), 294–319. Malden, MA/Oxford, UK: Wiley-Blackwell.

Kroll, J. and Stewart, E. (1994). Category interference in translation and picture naming: evidence for asymmetric connections between bilingual memory representations. *Journal of Memory and Language* 33: 149–174.

Lauchlan, F., Parisi, M., and Fadda, R. (2013). Bilingualism in Sardinia and Scotland: exploring the cognitive benefits of speaking a 'minority' language. *International Journal of Bilingualism* 17: 43–56.

Li, P., Legault, J., and Litcofsky, K. (2014). Neuroplasticity as a function of second language learning: anatomical changes in the human brain. *Cortex* 58: 301–324.

Libben, G. (2014). The nature of compounds: a psychocentric perspective. *Cognitive Neuropsychology* 31: 8–25.

Libben, G. (2017). The quantum metaphor and the organization of words in the mind. *Cultural Cognitive Science* 1: 49–55.

Libben, G. and Goral, M. (2015). How bilingualism shapes the mental lexicon. In: *The Cambridge Handbook of Bilingual Processing* (ed. J.W. Schwieter), 631–644. Cambridge, UK: Cambridge University Press.

Libben, M., Goral, M., and Libben, G. (2017a). The dynamic lexicon: complex words in bilingual minds. In: *Bilingualism: A Framework for Understanding the Mental Lexicon* (ed. M. Libben, M. Goral and G. Libben), 1–7. Amsterdam, The Netherlands/ Philadelphia, PA: Benjamins.

Libben, G., Goral, M., and Baayen, R. (2017b). Dynamicity and compound processing in bilinguals. In: *Bilingualism: A Framework for Understanding the Mental Lexicon* (ed. M. Libben, M. Goral and G. Libben), 199–218. Amsterdam, The Netherlands/ Philadelphia, PA: Benjamins.

Linck, J., Kroll, J., and Sunderman, G. (2009). Losing access to the native language while immersed in a second language: evidence for the role of inhibition in second language learning. *Psychological Science* 20: 1507–1515.

Malt, B., Li, P., Pavlenko, A. et al. (2015). Bidirectional lexical interaction in late immersed Mandarin-English bilinguals.

Journal of Memory and Language 82: 86–104.

Marelli, M., Gagné, C., and Spalding, T. (2017). Compounding as abstract operation in semantic space: investigating relational effects through a large-scale, data-driven computational model. *Cognition* 166: 207–224.

Morton, J. (1969). Interaction of information in word recognition. *Psychological Review* 76: 165–178.

Mykhaylyk, R., Mitrofanova, N., Rodina, Y., and Westergaard, M. (2015). The linguistic proximity model: The case of verb-second revisited. In: *Proceedings of the 39th Annual Boston University Conference on Language Development* (ed. E. Grillo and K. Jepson), 337–349. Somerville, MA: Cascadilla.

Pavlenko, A. (2009). Conceptual representation in the bilingual lexicon and second language vocabulary learning. In: *The Bilingual Mental Lexicon: Interdisciplinary Approaches* (ed. A. Pavlenko), 125–160. Bristol, UK: Multilingual Matters.

Poarch, G. and van Hell, J. (2012). Cross-language activation in children's speech production: evidence from second language learners, bilinguals, and trilinguals. *Journal of Experimental Child Psychology* 111: 419–438.

Rothman, J. (2011). L3 syntactic transfer selectivity and typological determinacy: the typological primacy model. *Second Language Research* 27 (1): 107–217.

Rothman, J. (2013). Cognitive economy, non-redundancy and typological primacy in L3 acquisition: evidence from initial stages of L3 romance. In: *Romance Languages and Linguistic Theory*, vol. 2011 (ed. S. Baauw, F. Dirjkoningen and M. Pinto), 217–248. Philadelphia, PA/Amsterdam, The Netherlands: John Benjamins.

Rothman, J. (2015). Linguistic and cognitive motivations for the typological primacy model (TPM) of third language (L3) transfer: Timing of acquisition and proficiency considered.

Bilingualism: Language and Cognition 18 (2): 179–190.

Schmid, M. (2010). Languages at play: the relevance of L1 attrition to the study of bilingualism. *Bilingualism: Language and Cognition* 13: 1–7.

Schreuder, R. and Baayen, H. (1995). Modeling morphological processing. In: *Morphological Aspects of Language Processing* (ed. L. Feldman), 131–154. Hillsdale, NJ: Erlbaum.

Schwieter, J.W. and Ferreira, A. (2016). Effects of cognitive control, lexical robustness, and frequency of codeswitching on language switching. In: *Cognitive Control and Consequences of Multilingualism* (ed. J.W. Schwieter), 193–216. Amsterdam, The Netherlands/ Philadelphia, PA: Benjamins.

Schwieter, J.W. and Sunderman, G. (2008). Language switching in bilingual speech production: in search of the language-specific selection mechanism. *The Mental Lexicon* 3 (2): 214–238.

Schwieter, J.W. and Sunderman, G. (2009). Concept selection and developmental effects in bilingual speech production. *Language Learning* 59 (4): 897–927.

Seidenberg, M. and McClelland, J. (1989). A distributed, developmental model of visual word recognition. *Psychological Review* 96: 523–568.

Selfridge, O. (1959). Pandemonium: a paradigm for learning. In: *Proceedings of the Symposium on Mechanisation of Thought Processes* (ed. D. Blake and A. Uttley), 511–529. Richmond, UK: H.M. Stationery Office.

Sholl, A., Sankaranarayanan, A., and Kroll, J. (1995). Transfer between picture naming and translation: a test of asymmetries in bilingual memory. *Psychological Science* 6 (1): 45–49.

Shook, A. and Marian, V. (2013). The bilingual language interaction network for comprehension of speech. *Bilingualism: Language and Cognition* 16: 304–324.

Slabakova, R. (2016). The scalpel model of third language acquisition. *International Journal of Bilingualism* 21 (6): 651–665.

Smolka, E. and Libben, G. (2017). Semantic transparency and compounding. *Language, Cognition and Neuroscience* 32 (4): 514–531.

Starreveld, P., de Groot, A., Rossmark, B., and van Hell, J. (2014). Parallel language activation during word processing in bilinguals: evidence from word production in sentence context. *Bilingualism: Language and Cognition* 17: 258–276.

Sunderman, G. and Kroll, J. (2006). First language activation during second language lexical processing: an investigation of lexical form meaning and grammatical class. *Studies in Second Language Acquisition* 28: 387–422.

Taft, M. and Forster, K. (1975). Lexical storage and the retrieval of prefixed words. *Journal of Verbal Learning and Verbal Behavior* 14: 630–647.

Taft, M. and Forster, K. (1976). Lexical storage and retrieval of polymorphemic and polysyllabic words. *Journal of Verbal Learning and Verbal Behavior* 15: 607–620.

Talamas, A., Kroll, J., and Dufour, R. (1999). From form to meaning: stages in the acquisition of second-language vocabulary. *Bilingualism: Language and Cognition* 2: 45–58.

Treisman, A. (1961). *Attention and speech.* Unpublished doctoral dissertation. Oxford, England: University of Oxford.

Vaid, J. and Meuter, R. (2017). Languages without borders: reframing the study of the bilingual mental lexicon. In: *Bilingualism: A Framework for Understanding the Mental Lexicon* (ed. M. Libben, M. Goral and G. Libben), 8–39. Amsterdam, The Netherlands/ Philadelphia, PA: Benjamins.

Van Heuven, W., Dijkstra, T., and Grainger, J. (1998). Orthographic neighborhood effects in bilingual word recognition. *Journal of Memory and Language* 39: 458–483.

William, E. (1981). On the notions 'lexically related' and 'head of a word'. *Linguistic Inquiry* 12: 245–274.

William, S. and Hammarberg, B. (1998). Language switches in L3 production: implications for a polyglot speaking model. *Applied Linguistics* 19: 295–333.

Zhang, T., Van Heuven, W., and Conklin, K. (2011). Fast automatic translation and morphological decomposition in Chinese-English bilinguals. *Psychological Science* 22 (10): 1237–1242.

15 Emotion and Emotion Concepts

Processing and Use in Monolingual and Bilingual Speakers

STEPHANIE A. KAZANAS, JARED S. MCLEAN, AND JEANETTE ALTARRIBA

1. Introduction

Recent work with monolingual and bilingual speakers has focused on the role of emotion in the encoding, storage, and retrieval of information and experiences. The current chapter explores the ways in which emotion processing – in the form of words, images, and other stimuli – differs across a bilingual's two languages. Findings from the behavioural, physiological, neuroimaging, and clinical literatures support the notion of a bilingual's first language (L1) garnering emotion processing advantages and preferences. As a set, these works are discussed with regards to language proficiency and experience, particularly the domains of language dominance and learning environments.

First, work with behavioural tasks has revealed the strength and durability of emotion concepts in the native language with regards to the activation of corresponding emotional words in memory, as compared to words in a second language (L2), and this effect is mitigated by word type: emotion word (e.g. *love, joy*) processing in L1 is facilitated to a greater extent than emotion-laden word (e.g. *cancer, butterfly*) processing. The behavioural section describes how these types of tasks can inform our understanding of emotional language and its representation, across a bilingual's L1 and L2, with the relevant work indicating that emotional memories are tied to and influenced by the language of that experience. These connections are observed as bilingual participants reflect on their own memories, as well as when they respond to more implicit, experimental stimuli.

Physiological work and related findings from electrophysiological measures and neuroimaging have also shown similar L1 advantages, with faster, more dynamic responses and activity. Recent work has shown stronger physiological responses to

The Handbook of the Neuroscience of Multilingualism, First Edition. Edited by John W. Schwieter.
© 2019 John Wiley & Sons Ltd. Published 2019 by John Wiley & Sons Ltd.

emotional expressions, words, and prose in a bilingual's L1, showing the persistence of these effects across a wide range of stimuli. Neural data show similar patterns of greater, more widespread activity in L1, relative to L2. The more applied fields of clinical and counselling psychology have utilized findings from these domains to provide more complete treatment plans for their patients: offering translation services and flexible bilingual interviews, as well as managing a patient's religious and cultural needs. The importance of this line of work cannot be overstated, given the growing bilingual population and the need for these specialized mental health services. As a set, these basic and applied approaches highlight the role of linguistic and cultural considerations in cognitive, biological, and clinical psychology.

2.   Behavioural Work

Data from behavioural work on emotion processing typically stem from the fields of cognitive science and cognitive psychology with particular emphasis on the types of tasks and approaches that uncover language representation and processing. In this section, work that focuses on emotion word processing in L1 and L2 will be discussed as a function of the types of tasks and methodological approaches that have been readily applied, in this area of research (for additional discussions on word processing across languages, see Chapters 4, 18, and 19 in this volume). Work that investigates bilingual memory, attention, and emotion word processing, emotional Stroop tasks and bilingualism, and emotion's influence on reading, word ratings, and lexical decisions will be reviewed. How do these methods and approaches help to inform what we know about emotional language, its mental representation and processing in L1 and L2? To begin with, emotional interactions and contexts help to form the way in which mental representations of emotional language develop in young children, as interactions between parents and children drive the development of this type of language and conceptual learning from a very early age (Chen et al. 2012). In their work, Chen et al. identified the ways in which the language chosen by parents to convey emotional expressions influences children's emotional development. Parents tend to shift to L2 either to match the cultural expectations in the child's surroundings, or to maintain emotional distance, possibly allowing for discussions without the arousal component that might come with discussing emotional events in the L1. By shifting language use at appropriate times during discourse that involves emotional topics, emotional understanding and emotion regulation can become refined and lead to better outcomes for children in terms of their social competence and their behavioural adjustment. By examining language shifts during emotional encounters, these authors were able to add to the literature regarding emotional adjustment and regulation for bilingual children. This is merely one example of how examining the representation and use of emotional language can help to enhance communication and promote overall well-being. Others include the deliberate use of L1 versus L2 in real-world decision-making, psychotherapy, marketing, and forensics (Altarriba and Kazanas 2017; Caldwell-Harris 2015; Costa and Dewaele 2012). In fact, the use of the L1 may provide distinct advantages over the L2, in cases where the arousal component might elicit more and richer facts related to a given situation, such as when one is an eyewitness to a traumatic event (but see Pavlenko 2012). More will be said about these applied notions in Section 4.

The following section, Section 2, is divided into two main areas: (i) a review of theory and data regarding the encoding, storage, and retrieval of emotional words – basic information on emotion word representation; and (ii) a review of literature concerning word processing and comprehension. The first part includes a basic overview on how we distinguish, or otherwise characterize, emotional words and how they are coded in memory, as measured by time-sensitive presentation paradigms such as the rapid serial visual presentation (RSVP) technique, and the Stroop task. Both approaches are described in Section 2. Knowing a bit about how these words are coded or otherwise represented in memory, in both a first and a second language, the second part of this section examines how higher order processing occurs in terms of reviewing work focused on the processing, reading, and comprehension of emotional stimuli. Thus, the following sections move from issues of basic encoding and memory representation to the higher order cognitive processes involved in reading and word comprehension.

2.1.   *Emotion Word Acquisition, Storage, and Retrieval*

It is said that language itself forms the glue by which individuals develop and use categories of knowledge including emotion categories in either language. Some argue that it is that very emotional vocabulary or emotional language that allows one to understand, perceive, and actually construct meaning when speaking with others or observing others using emotional language. This form of constructionism allows individuals to not only make sense of what they currently perceive in an interaction but to better predict the outcome of that interaction, particularly if it is emotional in nature (Lindquist et al. 2015). Thus, it is important to know exactly how emotion words and concepts are acquired, stored, and retrieved – information that is typically gathered via an examination of cognitive/behavioural data.

Work in the area of bilingual memory and attention has underscored the notion that memories are 'tagged' with language, such that part of the conceptual representations that are retained within a memory are typically encoded with the language in which it was experienced. In their seminal review, Holland and Kensinger (2010) underscore the notion that autobiographical memories contain information about specific, personal events, and that emotions are part of those memories influencing not only how they are encoded but also how they are retrieved. In fact, the emotional mode or context at the time of retrieval can influence the way in which memories are accessed and recalled. This notion can be expanded to the idea that those memories that are recalled are further influenced by the language in which they were both experienced and retrieved (Isurin 2017). It is quite clear from work on personal narratives, language discourse via cues or prompts, and the recording of mixed-language information that the very language in which emotional events were experienced influences the recollection of those memories and indeed, may even exert an influence on reconstructing memories from an earlier period in one's life. Isurin notes that individuals who have undergone immigrations that were unplanned have particular remembrances from certain periods in their lives that are either richer due to using the L1 which was most active before immigration, or poorer when L2 may be used, a newly acquired language that was not active when the memories were first encoded. It is quite likely the case that arousal and accompanying neural mechanisms also play a role in cementing memories that are activated from past, emotional events.

In terms of empirical, laboratory evidence, researchers have applied cognitive techniques in uncovering the ways in which L1 and L2 may differ in terms of emotional intensity. Ferré et al. (2010) tested Spanish-Catalan bilinguals' memories for positive, negative, and neutral words. Participants were asked to assess the pleasantness of these words which appeared in either Spanish or Catalan. They then participated in a free recall task. Participants revealed better memory for the emotional words, as compared to the neutral words, in both of their languages. This was true both for this sample and for a sample of Spanish-English bilinguals who were exposed to the words in both languages though they had learned their L1 earlier in their lives than their L2. All in all, these groups of participants were highly proficient in both languages, and the authors argued that it was this proficiency that revealed no differences in their abilities to recall words in both languages. In other demonstrations in the literature, differences are detected, however, when indeed bilinguals are less than highly proficient in both languages, and/or when they have lived in an environment that is more biased, linguistically towards one or the other language (see e.g. Altarriba and Bauer 2004).

Using an RSVP technique, Colbeck and Bowers (2012) presented monolingual English, native speakers and bilingual, English-Chinese speakers with taboo words embedded within sets of neutral words. The participants' task was to view the stream of words presented at a rate of one word every 100 milliliseconds (ms) and then to report the colour word at the conclusion of each stream. Each stream contained taboo words, but participants were asked to ignore any emotion words and focus on the words that appeared in colour. The inclusion of the taboo words slowed processing of the colour words and hampered the ability to identify those words. Most interesting was the fact that for the English-Chinese bilinguals, taboo words in Chinese were less problematic than taboo words that appeared in L1 – English. Thus, there was an L2 advantage in the ability to recollect emotion words, highlighting the notion that the first language may store emotion words more strongly than the second language. That is, emotion words in L1 tend to capture attention more readily than emotion words in the L2.

Paradigms, such as the one above that capitalizes on an interference effect to determine how attention is directed by emotional stimuli, provide evidence to support the notion that emotion captures attention (see e.g. Altarriba and Basnight-Brown 2010, for work involving the affective Simon task). Another paradigm that also reveals this finding is the emotional Stroop task. In the standard Stroop task (Stroop 1935), a word is presented in a colour, and an individual is asked to name that colour as quickly and as accurately as possible, disregarding the word itself. For example, the word GREEN might appear in blue, thus, the response would be 'blue'. Colour naming is disrupted in this case, the incongruent case, as compared to the situation in which the word and the colour are the same (e.g. the word GREEN appears in the colour green). In the case of emotion words, words such as happy or sad appear in coloured font, and the task is again, to name the colour of the word. Demonstrations of the emotional Stroop effect often include words in a neutral category (e.g. boat parts) that have been controlled in terms of frequency and length, as a comparison condition. Typically, emotion words that appear in colour are responded to more slowly than emotionally neutral words. The emotional component of the words tends to capture attention and interfere with the participant's ability to name its colour. Sutton et al. (2007) presented proficient Spanish-English bilinguals with emotion and neutral words in English and in Spanish and asked them to name the colour in which the words appeared. Interference effects were found in both languages for these participants, though the effects were numerically stronger in L2, where neutral words were responded to much more quickly than neutral items in L1. Thus, while these participants were highly proficient in both languages and showed a slowing in response times to emotional words in both languages, colour naming was indeed quicker for these participants for neutral words in L2 than in L1. This result likely stems from the fact that these participants were more practised readers of English, given that they had been in English-speaking schools for the greater part of their lives. Similar results have also been reported with late Finnish-English bilinguals (Eilola et al. 2007; however, see Winskel 2013 for a report of language differences for late Thai-English bilinguals as a function of language proficiency).

Researchers interested in how emotion affects memory processes have investigated what has been termed the emotional enhancement of memory (EEM) effect (see Hamann 2001, for a review). Studies examining the neurophysiology of emotion processing have underscored the important role of arousal and in particular, the amygdala, in playing a key role in driving explicit memory for positive and negative emotional stimuli. Plainly stated, emotional arousal can enhance memory in many situations, and can also impair memory particularly in cases where there are high levels of stress and cortisol release occurs to a certain extent. On occasion, it appears that this effect is stronger in the L1 – that is, memory for emotion words has been enhanced for bilinguals' first language in unexpected tests of free recall for word lists and assorted memory tasks, as compared to the second language (see e.g. Anooshian and Hertel 1994; Baumeister et al. 2017). However, on occasion, the data suggest that L2 might display stronger EEM effects but only in situations where participants are asked to deeply process the emotional connotation of words or phrases in the L2 (see e.g. Ayçiçeği and Harris 2004). More will be said regarding the psychophysiological correlates of emotion processing, in Section 3.1.

2.2.   *Emotion Word Processing and Comprehension*

Interestingly, while emotion words tend to lengthen response times for naming the colour in which they appear, recent reading research indicates that emotion words are read more quickly via the typical course of reading than are neutral words (Knickerbocker et al. 2015). English-speaking monolinguals were asked to read sentences that contained an emotion word, positive or negative, or a neutral word. The sentences were identical except for the inclusion of the emotional word or neutral word (e.g. Nora found her *chair/passion* about a year ago). Eye movements were measured using an Eyelink 1000 eye-tracking device. Readers processed the negative and positive words more quickly than the neutral words as evidenced by faster reading rates, first fixations, and total reading times. Thus, emotion words as processed in these monolingual participants actually sped up reading of typical sentences rather than posing interference. Thus, the combination of stimuli, language dominance, proficiency, and word type moderates eye movements in reading. This work should be extended to include bilingual populations and multilingual readers in order to examine the ways in which reading in the two languages influences the record of eye movements, in these situations.

As mentioned in Section 2.1, having participants rate words for their attributes is another way that researchers have distinguished the representation of emotion words as compared to neutral words. Altarriba (2003) asked Spanish-English bilinguals to rate concrete (e.g. *perro* 'dog'), abstract (e.g. *mente* 'mind'), and emotion (e.g. *feliz* 'happy') Spanish words on one of three dimensions: concreteness, imageability, or context-availability. The concreteness scale included concrete and abstract anchors, and asked participants to rate words on this seven-point scale. Concrete words label an object that is tangible or perceptible. Words were also rated in terms of how easily a participant could think of an image representing the word – the imageability scale. Finally, the context-availability scale asks about the ease or difficulty of thinking of a context in which a word might be included (e.g. the title of a song or play, the title of a book, a commonly-used object). Emotion words were rated as less concrete but more easily pictured than abstract words. Interestingly, emotion words and abstract words in Spanish received equal ratings for context-availability. This finding was in direct contrast to earlier work in which emotion words in English were not rated as highly in terms of their context availability in English-speaking monolinguals (Altarriba et al. 1999). Altarriba concluded that emotion words are learned quite early in an L1 linguistic context that provides a complex learning environment for those words. Those emotion words are encoded more richly and deeply in terms of their semantic components, as compared to concrete words, and thus, context plays a large role in terms of the representation of L1 emotion words as compared to their L2 counterparts.

Finally, a task that has been applied to the investigation of emotion word representation in L1 and L2 for monolingual and bilingual speakers is the lexical decision task. In its simple form, this task asks participants to decide whether a word is a real word in a given language (e.g. *box*) or a nonword that is typically pronounceable in a given language (e.g. *blit*). Participants are asked to respond as quickly and as accurately as possible. Unbeknownst to the participant, there can be occasions where two successive words are related in some manner either semantically (e.g. *cat-dog*) or antonymically (e.g. *day-night*) or perhaps phonologically (e.g. *lamp-damp*). The first word or prime often facilitates responses to the second word or target indicating that there is a relationship between the two words in the mental lexicon. Primes and targets can be words, pictures, objects or take other forms. Lindquist et al. (2006) found that presenting emotion words as primes (e.g. *anger*) and setting up a situation in which the emotion word was satiated produced a slowing down of responses to faces depicting that emotion. That is, once an emotion has been activated and primed to a given extent, it then makes it more difficult to identify that emotion in the faces of others. These kinds of demonstrations are important in the understanding of emotion perception particularly when it involves a human face. In cases that do not involve the satiation of emotion, it has been shown, however, that response times are faster when facial posture matches the valence of a subsequent sentence than in the case in which they mismatch (Havas et al. 2007). Thus, emotion comprehension can affect both the perception of faces, as well as, the comprehension of language in the form of sentence reading.

Altarriba and Bauer (2004) were the first to discuss the ways in which emotion words prime each other, but often fail to prime other classes of words, namely, abstract words. When emotion words appear as primes and targets and are semantically related to one another, they tend to show facilitation in lexical decision times as compared to cases in which two emotion words are not semantically related – a semantic priming effect. Abstract words also tend to prime related emotion words; however, the reverse is not the case. The authors discuss these findings in terms of the 'fan effect' in which emotion words have a larger number of related or associated items making it difficult for any single (abstract) item to receive the level of activation needed to show a priming effect. In this way, emotion words were shown to be readily distinguishable from abstract words. Kazanas and Altarriba (2016) demonstrated that emotion words elicited faster reaction times in a lexical decision task as compared to emotion-laden words (e.g. words like *cancer* or *death* that are emotional but do not name an emotion state). This effect occurred only in English, however, for Spanish-English bilinguals, indicating that emotion words were more deeply coded in the L2 for these bilinguals, at first appearing to contradict earlier reports of stronger emotionality in L1 versus L2. In fact, in this study, even though the bilinguals learned English later in life, L2 became the more dominant language and the language that was practised more readily by these participants in both spoken and written form. Degner et al. (2012) also reported significant affective priming for participants in their dominant language (in this case, their L1, German) and reported similar findings in L2, French, but only where there were high levels of immersion and the frequency of the words in that language was high, as well. Thus, it is the case that dominance is not always equated with 'first language learned' for bilingual populations, particularly in the United States. Context seems to serve a moderating role beyond linguistic proficiency, in these types of paradigms. These findings – reflecting the differences between early and late bilingualism – replicate across behavioural, psychophysiological, and neuroimaging work, with additional implications for clinical settings.

In summary, the current section introduced notions regarding the benefits that can accrue by switching languages between L1 and L2 when processing emotional stimuli. The typical findings indicate that while L2 might be used to distance oneself from the arousal or intensity that co-occurs with the processing of emotional language, this is only the case when L2 is the subordinate or later-learned language. Knowing the interplay between languages and emotion in bilingual speakers can help inform a variety of real-life situations in applied settings, some of which will be explored towards the end of the current work. Additionally, the present section reviewed the ways in which emotion words are coded or characterized in our mental representations in terms of imageability, concreteness, and the like, noting that tests that capitalize on interference effects (e.g. RSVP paradigms; Stroop tasks) help to uncover situations in which L1 or L2 is the language in which emotions are deeply coded for a bilingual speaker. Most important, emotions are tagged in the language in which they are situated such that L1 might be rendered the most 'emotional language' if indeed emotions were learned, reinforced, and coded when L1 was the active or current language, in the bilingual's learning experience. If L2 words are newly coded and not deeply situated in memory, they may in fact show less interference in Stroop tasks or related tasks as they have yet to garner all of the intensity and arousal components of the more proficient L1.

3.   Psychophysiological and Neuroimaging Work

Recently, researchers have begun to pair behavioural tasks with physiological and neuroimaging methods, using various equipment to examine differences in emotional experiences across a bilingual's L1 and L2 (for related discussions on bilingualism using these technologies and equipment, see Chapters 2, 9, and 14 in this volume). For example, the behavioural tasks discussed previously – reading, Stroop, lexical decision, rating, and so on – have been paired with equipment to measure bilingual's facial expressivity, skin conductance, electrophysiology, and neural activity. This section discusses these collaborative efforts, as well as more unique endeavours, again highlighting the ways in which emotion processing and expression in a bilingual's L1 compares with their L2. As was the case with behavioural data, differences in emotion processing are often a function of language experience.

3.1.   *Psychophysiological Work*

One common finding across physiological works is greater expression and activity when bilinguals activate and process emotional information in their L1, relative to their L2. Common measures in these lines of investigation include facial electromyography (EMG) and skin conductance responses (SCRs), distinguished by their ability to discriminate the nature of emotional experiences and stimuli: In many ways, EMG is better suited for measuring differences in valence, while SCRs are better suited for measuring levels of arousal (e.g. Bradley and Lang 2000; Lang et al. 1993, 1998). In one recent example, Foroni (2015) assessed facial muscle activity when Dutch-English bilinguals read sentences that contained verbal descriptions of emotional expressions (e.g. *I am smiling; I am not grinning*). In part, these kinds of investigations allow researchers to also examine whether L1 processing engages the motor cortex to a greater extent than a bilingual's L2. In an interesting finding, both sentence form and language affected muscle simulation (L1 Dutch results described by Foroni and Semin 2013). With affirmative sentences, participants displayed similar reactions in their L1 and L2; reading sentences such as, *I am smiling* led to participants activating the zygomatic major muscle. However, with negative sentences, similar reactions were not observed across L1 and L2. When presented with *I am not grinning* in a bilingual's L1, Foroni and Semin (2013) observed relaxation and inhibition (i.e. relaxed zygomatic muscles); these effects were not observed in their L2 (Foroni 2015). Overall, smaller reactions in L2 were likened to partial, or weaker simulations: Emotional language processing in L1 likely relies on simulations of *meaning*, as described in the emotional expressions. The somatic correlates of these expressions are weaker in a bilingual's L2, the result of weaker semantic connections (Foroni 2015; Foroni and Semin 2013).

Researchers have also paired facial EMG with other behavioural tasks. Recently, Baumeister et al. (2017) examined facial muscle activity when Spanish-English and English-Spanish bilinguals performed categorization and recognition tasks. In the categorization task, participants categorized words according to whether they were associated or not associated with emotion, with words including those related to happiness and anger. Replicating patterns of behavioural data discussed in Section 2, participants categorized more effectively in their L1, which Baumeister et al. indicated was not a reflection of their word fluency. These behavioural data were supported by increased facial responsiveness in their L1, in both the zygomatic and corrugator muscles. Moreover, SCRs, a measure of autonomic arousal, were stronger for emotion words in L1, with no differences between emotion and neutral word processing in L2. These patterns were also replicated with recognition data, collected 24 hours later. Together, these findings indicate reduced activity and general differences from an embodiment perspective, suggesting that emotion processing in a bilingual's L1 is grounded in embodied simulations: how emotions are experienced and learned during childhood will differ from the L2 learning environment.

Caldwell-Harris and colleagues (Caldwell-Harris and Ayçiçeği-Dinn 2009; Harris et al. 2003, 2006) have adopted a similar hypothesis, arguing that the emotional context of L1 learning is met with an earlier age of acquisition and generally greater proficiency, the consequence of interpersonal and motivating learning environments with family members and friends. Their SCR data largely support an L1 advantage, with higher SCRs for emotional information presented in a bilingual's L1, relative to their L2. In many of their early investigations, bilinguals rated a variety of emotional words and phrases: insults, reprimands, taboo words, endearments, and so on. SCRs were often correlated with ratings, with more negative phrases (e.g. reprimands) prompting higher SCR amplitudes and unpleasantness ratings (Harris et al. 2003). Some participants also remarked that the auditory presentation led them to remember hearing a family member speaking those reprimands (p. 573). Similar findings were observed with late Spanish-English bilinguals displaying heightened sensitivity to reprimands presented in Spanish (Harris 2004). This pattern of data has also been observed with other samples of late Turkish-English bilinguals who had learned English in intensive educational settings and self-reported their English proficiency as 'fair' or 'good' (Caldwell-Harris and Ayçiçeği-Dinn 2009). Lending further support for the emotional contexts of learning hypothesis, this difference in sensitivity across languages is not often observed with early bilinguals, such as those participants whose L1 and L2 learning environments were well-matched. Moreover, Harris (2004) reported comparable SCRs for L1 and L2 taboo words amongst these early bilinguals. Thus, observed differences in emotional reactivity with these measures is often a function of the language learning experience and environment.

As a result, these physiological investigations often depict L2 emotion processing as less extreme, with bilinguals experiencing fewer or reduced physiological responses, relative to L1 emotion processing (Eilola and Havelka 2010). One recent exception to this pattern compared SCRs for words rated for their emotional intensity. Sampling Chinese-English bilinguals, Caldwell-Harris et al. (2010) identified cultural constraints that affect emotion expression. Many of their late learners preferred English for expressing anger and intimacy, challenging the findings discussed previously with other bilingual samples. Moreover, increases in SCR amplitudes for English endearments were observed with bilinguals who reported high Chinese usage. For these bilinguals, whose language experiences resemble those sampled in other studies, the role of culture adds a new layer of complexity. In many ways, the English language permits them to be more emotionally expressive than their L1 Chinese, with this freedom observed in their preference ratings and SCR data. Again, these multimethod investigations are particularly useful for clarifying the specific nature of L1 and L2 differences.

3.2. *Electrophysiological Work*

Other measures of sensitivity include those that can be gleaned from event-related potentials (ERPs) using electroencephalogram (EEG) recordings. These data provide unique insights across the timecourse of cognitive processes, including the automatic, early access of emotional information in a bilingual's L1 and the more delayed access to their L2. With these ERP investigations, common findings include an early component – the early posterior negativity (EPN) – detected at left temporo-occipital electrode sites, believed to indicate the spontaneous activation of a word's emotional connotation. With late bilinguals, this ERP component is delayed when emotional stimuli are presented in their L2. Conrad et al. (2011) detected this delayed EPN with late Spanish-German and German-Spanish bilinguals, who performed a lexical decision task (LDT) with positive, negative, and neutral words. The EPN was delayed 50–100 ms during L2 processing, for both groups of bilingual participants. Interestingly, overall ERP effects were stronger for negative words than for positive words in German (in both L1 and L2), yet stronger for positive words than for negative words in Spanish (also in both L1 and L2), highlighting the important consideration of language-specific findings in these paradigms. Of equal importance, additional investigations have shown that the durability of these differences in emotion activation do not appear to be confounded by proficiency, frequency of use, or other relevant multilingual factors (Opitz and Degner 2012).

  A bit later in the timecourse of emotion word processing, another ERP component can distinguish L1 from L2 processing. A negative wave peaking approximately 400 ms poststimulus onset (N400) can be detected across centroparietal electrode sites. The N400 is thought to be modulated by several linguistic functions. One of these, semantic integration, can be observed in tasks that ask participants to process competing information, as is the case with variants of the Stroop (1935) task. In one of these, Fan et al. (2016) presented late Chinese-English bilinguals with emotion words superimposed on faces, creating a set of congruent (*happy* presented with a happy face) and incongruent (*happy* presented with an angry face) trials. This conflict-related N400, activated by competing emotional information, was met with congruency effects only in a bilingual's L1. Thus, the interference is more readily apparent in L1, as more attention is given to emotional information in conflict. Another function of the N400 appears to be related to affective valence. For example, Jończyk et al. (2016) presented a number of emotional sentences with congruent and incongruent endings to a sample of late Polish-English bilinguals. The N400 component was enhanced by Polish sentences as compared to English sentences – replicating the L1 advantage for processing emotional information – and this was particularly the case for negative sentences (e.g. *Gloria accidentally poured boiling water over herself and was burnt*). These data suggest that late bilinguals can experience their L2 in an incomplete, shallow manner, with especially limited access to the complex connotations of negative words. These effects are visible with methodology that tap the early timecourse of word processing (ERPs) as well as those that permit slower, more effortful emotion processing (SCRs).

3.3.   *Neuroimaging and Related Work*

Data displaying neural activity – the structures and coordination in emotion processing – are not quite as cohesive. While some studies do imply an L1 advantage, with increased activity in brain regions when processing emotional information in L1 (e.g. Hernandez 2009; Hsu et al. 2015), others show similar patterns of activation when processing emotional information in L1 and L2 (e.g. Yang et al. 2017), or different patterns of activity altogether (e.g. Chen et al. 2015). These mixed findings are early in terms of their recent publication and rapid advances in technology, though they highlight the need for further research in this area: sampling new populations of bilinguals with a wide array of emotional materials.

Neuroimaging studies examining emotion processing often depict activity in the amygdala, regardless of positive or negative valence (Garavan et al. 2001; Hamann and Mao 2002; Hamann et al. 2002), as well as generally greater interhemispheric communication when processing emotional information (even in a bilingual's L2; Jończyk 2015). Interestingly, data collected by Hernandez (2009) using functional magnetic resonance imaging (fMRI) has shown increased activity in a number of brain regions – including the amygdala – even when participants process neutral information. In his study, early Spanish-English bilinguals performed a picture-naming task, with language-naming instructions mixed or blocked. Importantly, words included fruit and furniture exemplars, which score in the neutral range on a number of emotion dimensions (e.g. arousal, valence). Thus, amygdala activity, heightened during Spanish trials, suggests that a bilingual's L1 may benefit from more widespread neural activity. Moreover, these data lend support to the notion that a bilingual's L1 may be more generally emotional (at least, in a visual form), relative to their L2. This seems to be the case even when bilinguals have a great deal of experience with each language, as was the case with Hernandez's (2009) early bilinguals, who reported an average L2 age of acquisition of five years old.

General L1 advantages appear in other brain regions, as well. Using excerpts from J. K. Rowling's Harry Potter novels, Hsu et al. (2015) had late German-English bilinguals provide emotion ratings on valence, arousal, fearfulness, and happiness dimensions to positive, negative, and neutral passages. Ratings were consistent with fMRI data, with differences in valence, fear, and happiness ratings across L1 and L2, along with greater L1 activity in the bilateral visual cortices (a possible explanation for the data reported by Hernandez 2009), left precentral gyrus, and amygdala. In many cases, these patterns of increased L1 activity were observed across all passages, in other cases, increased activity was restricted to the emotional passages.

Other fMRI data refute some of these general increases in neural activity during L1 processing, suggesting *qualitative* differences in L1 and L2 emotion processing. In one recent example, Chen et al. (2015) had late Chinese-English bilinguals perform a variety of lexical and executive function tasks (the LDT, operation span (OSPAN), and Simon tasks) with positive, negative, and neutral words while simultaneously collecting ERP and fMRI data. Regions activated during emotion word processing included the left superior frontal gyrus, middle occipital gyrus, and left cerebellum, while the superior parietal lobe had greater activation for neutral word processing, relative to positive and negative word processing. Of these regions, several patterns of activation differed across

L1 and L2 processing. In the middle occipital gyrus, negative and neutral words in the bilingual's L1 produced greater activation than positive words, with no response detected for emotion words in their L2. Additional differences were observed in the left cerebellum, with opposite patterns detected across L1 and L2: positive words produced weaker activation than neutral words in their L1 and greater activation than neutral words in their L2. Again, these data suggest some general differences in emotion processing across L1 and L2. However, some recent work with computational modelling has suggested that neural activity collected from 38 brain regions when reading in one language – including sentences pertaining to people, places, actions, and feelings – can also predict neural activity for sentence-reading in another language. Yang et al. (2017) found that neural activity collected during English reading was largely similar to reading in Portuguese amongst Portuguese monolinguals and Portuguese-English bilinguals. Findings from these predictive models are important, though tentative given the need for simple, concrete sentences that are well-matched across sentence types (e.g. *The family was happy*; *The street was dark*).

Findings from psychophysiological and neuroimaging work – with data measuring facial muscle activity, skin conductance, event-related potentials, and neural activity – largely support an L1 advantage in emotion processing. The advantage appears in many forms: greater physiological reactivity, earlier electrophysiological activity in the brain, and so on. Many of these findings, however, rely on data collected with late bilinguals: sampling participants whose language-learning experience greatly differs across their two languages (i.e. differences in terms of age of acquisition; Caldwell-Harris and Ayçiçeği-Dinn 2009; Harris et al. 2003, 2006; differences in terms of culture; Caldwell-Harris et al. 2010). Despite these limitations, the L1 advantage does persist across this wide variety of measures and experimental stimuli, including words (Baumeister et al. 2017; Chen et al. 2015; Conrad et al. 2011; Harris 2004), pictures (Fan et al. 2016; Hernandez 2009), sentences (Foroni 2015; Foroni and Semin 2013; Jończyk et al. 2016), and prose passages (Hsu et al. 2015). Real-world applications of these L1 and L2 comparisons follow in Section 4, with an emphasis on the preferred language in emotional settings.

4.   Applied Work in Clinical and Counselling Settings

Laboratory and applied research findings derived from behavioural, psychophysiological, and neuroimaging studies have been utilized in clinical and counselling settings to improve mental health services for bilingual individuals (see also Chapter 31 in this volume). This section elaborates on the intricacies involved when working with bilingual clients, and differences in cognition and expression of emotion between L1 and L2 usage; the impact interpreters can have on healthcare outcomes; and culture-specific treatment strategies.

4.1.   Research Findings and Implications for Practice

Research shows that language is a primary means through which emotions are labelled and expressed (Altarriba et al. 1999), and a client's native language is often the one that is considered more emotional (Altarriba 2003; Santiago-Rivera and Altarriba 2002).

Since bilingual speakers periodically use more than one language to identify and convey their emotions, providing bilingual therapy poses a unique and intricate challenge (Bager-Charleson et al. 2017; Rolland et al. 2017).

De Zulueta (2006) acknowledged that language has an intrinsic link to our sense of identity, and using different languages is associated with experiencing changes in self-image (Pavlenko 2006). The research establishes that individuals tend to represent emotion words differently in their two languages and typically associate these words with a broader range of emotion in their L1 (Altarriba and Santiago-Rivera 1994). Various experimental studies assert that autobiographical recall differs depending on whether the language of encoding is congruent with the one of retrieval (Altarriba 2002, 2006; Altarriba and Canary 2004; Marian and Neisser 2000; Schrauf 2003; Schrauf and Durazo-Arvizu 2006). Since recalling memories in the encoding language is shown to increase detail and emotional intensity, clinicians are challenged to obtain the most accurate information possible from their bilingual clients (Byford 2015; Harris et al. 2006; Marian and Neisser 2000).

Bilingual speakers can employ a technique known as code switching, which occurs when a speaker substitutes a word or phrase in a single language with a counterpart in another (Bhatia and Ritchie 1996; Heredia and Altarriba 2001; MacSwan 2013). Fortunately, code switching appears to offer a plausible strategy for bilingual therapists and their clients to use during therapy (Dewaele and Costa 2013). Potential explanations for code switching by bilinguals include wanting to express themselves more accurately and to be better understood (Altarriba 2003; Grosjean 2010), non-equivalence between language concepts (Wierzbicka 1997), and an occasional lack of word-to-word translation across languages (Altarriba 2003; Basnight-Brown and Altarriba 2016).

Evidence suggests that bilinguals can use a less dominant language to serve as a distancing function for discussing troubling events (Altarriba 2008; Pérez Foster 1998; Pitta et al. 1978), which Marcos (1976) named the 'detachment effect' (see also Pavlenko 2012). Ideally, a skilled therapist would be able to assess the situation and lead the patient to switch languages in a way that best allows for memories and emotions to be accessed (Santiago-Rivera and Altarriba 2002). Therapists have demonstrated shifting languages as a strategy to build the therapeutic alliance by bonding with their clients, intentionally managing resistance and engagement in the therapeutic process, facilitating disclosure and expression of emotions, and improving communication and understanding (Sprowls 2002). Although code switching presents a potentially valuable therapeutic technique, many bilingual therapists have had to informally train themselves due to a lack of formal training specifically for providing bilingual therapy (Verdinelli and Biever 2009; a recent review of the neurorehabilitation literature strongly recommends additional training for bilingual clients, Altarriba and Kazanas 2017).

Processing emotion language in L1 and L2 can have significant implications in a range of domains, such as confrontation and decision-making. Caldwell-Harris and Ayçiçeği-Dinn (2009) demonstrated that participants report more affective discomfort in L1 than L2 when lying, which implies that a lack of emotionality in L2 can promote suspects to lie and make false confessions when being interrogated in that language. In contrast, Keysar et al. (2012) have identified that fewer decision-making biases are an advantage provided by lower emotional expression in L2 than L1 (see also Costa et al. 2014).

Since bilingual speakers pose a challenge to therapists, sufficient knowledge and understanding of bilingual cognition and emotional expression is imperative for providing effective treatment. Improving access to formal training for clinicians interested in serving bilingual speakers is essential in locations with increasing bilingual populations.

4.2.   Use of Interpreters in Clinical Settings

Without interpreters, effective communication between some clinicians and their patients is a difficult obstacle to overcome. When a clinician and their patient do not share a language, using an interpreter is often the most convenient solution to this problem. However, this strategy comes with a multitude of potential benefits and pitfalls.

Many providers expect interpreters to serve in a neutral conduit role, in which information is transferred from one language to another in a word-for-word, machine-like fashion (Brämberg and Sandman 2013; Fatahi et al. 2008; Rosenberg et al. 2007). By serving in this role, it is standard for the interpreter to emulate the affective state of the patient when relaying information to the clinician, rather than their own (Hsieh 2009). Having an interpreter communicate the emotional expressions and affective content of the client can help ensure favourable provider–patient interactions (Avery 2001; Farini 2013).

Not only can interpreters bridge language gaps, but they may also ease the therapeutic process by providing insight regarding the patient's culture and values to the clinician. Moreover, positive side interactions with the interpreter may allow clients to feel more comfortable about revealing sensitive information to their provider (Penn and Watermeyer 2012). Interpreters can also increase comfort in therapy by reaching out to the patient and other community members with the intent to break cultural barriers. Research investigating the impact and role of interpreters in diagnostic interviews describes clinicians reporting high confidence in their assessments due to interpreters providing unbiased, accurate information (Zayas et al. 2007).

Despite the potentially positive aspects of using an interpreter, there are some issues regarding their influence on adverse healthcare outcomes. First, there is concern that a patient's beliefs, experiences, and emotions may be distorted or lost during interpretation (Singh 2016). Second, without the adequate clinical knowledge and cross-cultural training, an interpreter may inadvertently heighten, minimize, or overlook a patient's or a provider's emotions and emotion work (i.e. emotional management; Hsieh and Nicodemus 2015). Third, the use of an interpreter can often interfere with the therapeutic engagement, not only in the areas of gender, age, religion, cultural, and hierarchical values but also in the discussion of sensitive issues (Nijad 2003). Fourth, Vasquez and Javier (1991) pointed out that interpreters have been found to potentially jeopardize the treatment process by gaining a sense of power in their position, attempting to take on the role of the therapist, and interjecting their own opinions about diagnoses and treatment. Finally, since formally trained mental health interpreters are scarce and patients have a right to an interpreter of their choice (i.e. refusing the one provided) clinicians may face the ethical tension between respect for patient autonomy and their commitment to non-maleficence and beneficence (Searight and Searight 2009). Furthermore, interpreters from collectivist cultures that de-emphasize autonomy may possess a worldview emphasizing family or collectively held information, which poses a confidentiality risk (Searight and Gafford 2005; Sue and Sue 1987). Ultimately, it is the clinician's responsibility to ensure that the interpreter demonstrates competence to provide services while also protecting patient confidentiality and avoiding dual relationships (APA 2017).

Researchers have noted that there is a growing demand for interpreters with formal training to assist clinicians providing therapy, but such interpreters are in short supply. Musser-Granski and Carrillo (1997) have suggested that areas of focus for training and educating interpreters in the United States should include the following: (i) English language and American culture; (ii) mental health terminology, concepts, and interventions; (iii) interpretation of words and affect; (iv) crisis intervention; (v) interviewing techniques; and (vi) beginning counselling skills. Paone and Malott (2008) recommended that before conducting a therapy session, counsellors and interpreters ought to have a discussion to agree on specific practices, goals of the appointment, and potentially challenging topics; ideally, they should also rehearse before the session begins. Although the use of interpreters in therapy can be advantageous, further research and practice must orient towards improving therapeutic engagement and communication with bilingual and bicultural patients.

4.3.   *Cultural Issues and Culture-Specific Treatment Strategies*

It is necessary to understand the impact that cultural background has on a person's emotional expression and sense of identity. To illustrate, research on cultural differences in emotional expression has found that individualist and collectivist cultures differ significantly on the acceptance of emotional expression, with individualist cultures having higher expressivity norms (Matsumoto et al. 2008). Consideration of cultural factors in therapy with bilingual and bicultural populations is crucial to increasing the quality of treatment and decreasing dropout rates (Flaskerud 1986).

Unfortunately, minority populations have been found to underutilize mental health services and have a higher rate of termination of treatment than white Americans (Nadeem et al. 2007; Sue et al. 2009). Negative attitudes and stereotypes concerning mental illness are prevalent amongst ethnic-minority populations, and in family-centred cultures, psychological issues are typically not discussed outside the family (Gary 2005). When these individuals have difficulty, they are expected to turn to clergy, family members, elders, family doctors, or religion/spirituality (Martinovic and Altarriba 2013). Consequently, members of family-centred cultures tend to only seek help outside the family as a last resort (Willerton et al. 2008).

Discrimination, language barriers, acculturation, and poverty are some of the common impediments that contribute to higher rates of mental illness than in other clients (Anderson 1983; Maduro 1983; Muecke 1983; Sue and Morishima 1982). As compared with people born in the United States, individuals with low acculturation and limited English proficiency were only half as likely to seek mental health care (Snowden et al. 2007). The disparity between these groups emphasizes how language and culture are barriers that continue to deter minorities from utilizing mental health services.

To improve treatment for minority groups, some researchers have directed their focus towards refining education and training for multicultural counsellors. Sue et al. (1992) suggested that therapists interested in becoming culturally skilled ought to receive training in traditional assessment techniques and attain awareness of their stereotypes and those of other cultural, racial, and ethnic groups. Recommendations also include acquiring the latest research knowledge and skills related to the following areas: (i) ethnic and cultural groups; (ii) religious/spiritual beliefs and family structure of the groups under consideration; and (iii) sociopolitical structures and institutions surrounding a given client (Sue et al. 1992). Additionally, language match between a therapist and their client has been associated with a lower dropout rate and an increased length of treatment (Willerton et al. 2008). Thus, therapists are encouraged to assess and match languages with their patients whenever possible (Andrés-Hyman et al. 2006; Sue et al. 1992).

Intriguingly, researchers have also found that patients often resist points made directly (Barker 1985). Littmann (1985) suggested metaphors can be used to reach an emotional part of an individual that may be too adamantly defended to be otherwise accessible. Moreover, using culturally preferred terms to discuss psychological issues can help increase rapport with the client by reflecting an understanding of their distress, while avoiding the stigma sometimes associated with mental illness (Snowden et al. 2007; Willerton et al. 2008).

It is evident that obstacles such as discrimination, language barriers, cultural differences, socioeconomic factors, and stigmas associated with mental illness can negatively influence healthcare outcomes for people belonging to various cultural, racial, or ethnic groups. To counter such hindrances, training clinicians to become culturally skilled is vital for increasing the quality and utilization of mental health services amongst bilingual and bicultural individuals.

5.   Conclusions and Recommendations for Future Research

Emotion work conducted with bilingual individuals has offered valuable theoretical and applied insights. Recent work has shown that late bilinguals do prefer the language they had acquired early in life; during emotional situations they rely on that language in a range of everyday and clinical settings. These preferences are supported by behavioural and physiological differences in emotion processing across a bilingual's two languages: faster, more accurate emotion activation, more durable emotional memories, and more dynamic reactivity and neural activation, most often in their L1. L2 responses are often slower and more effortful during behavioural tasks, with weaker physiological responses and patterns of electrophysiological and neural activity. While these methods are varied in their focus and purpose, they draw similar conclusions in L1 dominance for emotion processing. The exceptions to these observations are few, though important. For one, matching proficiency across a bilingual's languages can minimize or even eliminate word processing differences (Ferré et al. 2010). These balanced bilinguals – and also those bilinguals whose L2 has become their more dominant language – are not as likely to show L1 advantages.

Future work, primarily in the applied literature, would greatly benefit from understanding how behavioural and physiological differences translate into differences in a bilingual's emotional experiences and expressions. The implications for bilingual therapy and its training, particularly a flexible, bilingual mode of therapy are of the utmost importance in these investigations. Permitting this bilingual mode of therapy is particularly important in preserving the accuracy of a bilingual speaker's emotional expressions, minimizing translation and interpretation difficulty, and promoting cultural understanding in these settings.

Finally, we recommend future research adopt a multimethod approach to investigate these differences in emotion processing: our understanding of current findings is overwhelmingly (with few exceptions) limited to single-method approaches with a single bilingual sample. Future research would largely benefit from more broad examinations of emotion effects in laboratory and applied settings, adding a range of stimuli, equipment, tasks, and language experience.

REFERENCES

Altarriba, J. (2002). Bilingualism: language, memory and applied issues. *Online Readings in Psychology and Culture* 4 (2): 1–10.

Altarriba, J. (2003). Does cariño equal "liking"? A theoretical approach to conceptual nonequivalence between languages. *International Journal of Bilingualism* 7 (3): 305–322.

Altarriba, J. (2006). Cognitive approaches to the study of emotion-laden and emotion words in monolingual and bilingual memory. *Bilingual Education and Bilingualism* 56: 232–256.

Altarriba, J. (2008). Expression of emotion as mediated by context. *Bilingualism: Language and Cognition* 11 (2): 165–167.

Altarriba, J. and Basnight-Brown, D.M. (2010). The representation of emotion vs. emotion-laden words in English and Spanish in the affective Simon task. *International Journal of Bilingualism* 15: 310–328.

Altarriba, J. and Bauer, L.M. (2004). The distinctiveness of emotion concepts: a comparison between emotion, abstract, and concrete words. *American Journal of Psychology* 117: 389–410.

Altarriba, J., Bauer, L.M., and Benvenuto, C. (1999). Concreteness, context availability, and imageability ratings and word associations for abstract, concrete, and emotion words. *Behavior Research Methods* 31 (4): 578–602.

Altarriba, J. and Canary, T.M. (2004). The influence of emotional arousal on affective priming in monolingual and bilingual speakers. *Journal of Multilingual and Multicultural Development* 25 (2–3): 248–265.

Altarriba, J. and Kazanas, S.A. (2017). Neurorehabilitation with Hispanic/Latino populations: clinical perspectives on interprofessional communication. *SIG 2 Perspectives on Neurophysiology and Neurogenic Speech and Language Disorders* 2 (3): 132–141.

Altarriba, J. and Santiago-Rivera, A.L. (1994). Current perspectives on using linguistic and cultural factors in counseling the Hispanic client. *Professional Psychology: Research and Practice* 25 (4): 388–397.

American Psychological Association (2017). *Ethical Principles of Psychologists and Code of Conduct*. Washington, DC: American Psychological Association.

Anderson, J.N. (1983). Health and illness in Pilipino immigrants. *Western Journal of Medicine* 139 (6): 811–819.

Andrés-Hyman, R.C., Ortiz, J., Añez, L.M. et al. (2006). Culture and clinical practice:

recommendations for working with Puerto Ricans and other Latinas (os) in the United States. *Professional Psychology: Research and Practice* 37 (6): 694–701.

Anooshian, L.J. and Hertel, P.T. (1994). Emotionality in free recall: language specificity in bilingual memory. *Cognition and Emotion* 8: 503–514.

Avery, M. P. B. (2001). The role of the health care interpreter: An evolving dialogue. *National Council on Interpreting in Health Care.*

Ayçiçeği, A. and Harris, C.L. (2004). Bilinguals' recall and recognition of emotion words. *Cognition and Emotion* 18: 977–987.

Bager-Charleson, S., Dewaele, J.-M., Costa, B., and Kasap, Z. (2017). A multilingual outlook: can awareness-raising about multilingualism affect therapists' practice? A mixed-method evaluation. *Language and Psychoanalysis* 6 (2): 1–21.

Barker, P. (1985). *Using Metaphors in Psychotherapy*. New York, NY: Brunner/Mazel.

Basnight-Brown, D.M. and Altarriba, J. (2016). Multiple translations in bilingual memory: processing differences across concrete, abstract, and emotion words. *Journal of Psycholinguistic Research* 45: 1219–1245.

Baumeister, J.C., Foroni, F., Conrad, M. et al. (2017). Embodiment and emotional memory in first v. Second language. *Frontiers in Psychology* 8: 394.

Bhatia, T.K. and Ritchie, W.C. (1996). Bilingual language mixing, universal grammar, and second language acquisition. In: *Handbook of Second Language Acquisition* (ed. W.C. Ritchie and T.K. Bhatia), 627–688. San Diego, CA: Academic Press.

Bradley, M.M. and Lang, P.J. (2000). Affective reactions to acoustic stimuli. *Psychophysiology* 37 (2): 204–215.

Brämberg, E.B. and Sandman, L. (2013). Communication through in-person interpreters: a qualitative study of home care providers' and social workers' views. *Journal of Clinical Nursing* 22 (1–2): 159–167.

Byford, A. (2015). Lost and gained in translation: the impact of bilingual clients'

choice of language in psychotherapy. *British Journal of Psychotherapy* 31 (3): 333–347.

Caldwell-Harris, C.L. (2015). Emotionality differences between a native and foreign language: implications for everyday life. *Current Directions in Psychological Science* 24 (3): 214–219.

Caldwell-Harris, C.L. and Ayçiçeği-Dinn, A. (2009). Emotion and lying in a non-native language. *International Journal of Psychophysiology* 71 (3): 193–204.

Caldwell-Harris, C.L., Tong, J., Lung, W., and Poo, S. (2010). Physiological reactivity to emotional phrases in mandarin-English bilinguals. *International Journal of Bilingualism* 15 (3): 329–352.

Chen, S.H., Kennedy, M., and Zhou, Q. (2012). Parents' expression and discussion of emotion in the multilingual family: does language matter? *Perspectives on Psychological Science* 7 (4): 365–383.

Chen, P., Lin, J., Chen, B. et al. (2015). Processing emotional words in two languages with one brain: ERP and fMRI evidence from Chinese–English bilinguals. *Cortex* 71: 34–48.

Colbeck, K.L. and Bowers, J.S. (2012). Blinded by taboo words in L1 but not L2. *Emotion* 12 (2): 217–222.

Conrad, M., Recio, G., and Jacobs, A.M. (2011). The time course of emotion effects in first and second language processing: a cross-cultural ERP study with German–Spanish bilinguals. *Frontiers in Psychology* 2: 351.

Costa, B. and Dewaele, J.-M. (2012). Psychotherapy across languages: beliefs, attitudes and practices of monolingual and multilingual therapists with their multilingual patients. *Language and Psychoanalysis* 1 (1): 19–41.

Costa, A., Foucart, A., Arnon, I. et al. (2014). 'Piensa' twice: on the foreign language effect in decision making. *Cognition* 130 (2): 236–254.

De Zulueta, F. (2006). *From Pain to Violence: The Traumatic Roots of Destructiveness*. London, UK: Wiley.

Degner, J., Doycheva, C., and Wentura, D. (2012). It matters how much you talk: on the automaticity of affective connotations of first and second language words. *Bilingualism: Language and Cognition* 15: 181–189.

Dewaele, J.-M. and Costa, B. (2013). Multilingual clients experience of psychotherapy. *Language and Psychoanalysis* 2 (2): 31–50.

Eilola, T.M. and Havelka, J. (2010). Behavioural and physiological responses to the emotional and taboo Stroop tasks in native and non-native speakers of English. *International Journal of Bilingualism* 15 (3): 353–369.

Eilola, T.M., Havelka, J., and Sharma, D. (2007). Emotional activation in the first and second language. *Cognition and Emotion* 21 (5): 1064–1076.

Fan, L., Xu, Q., Wang, X. et al. (2016). Neural correlates of task-irrelevant first and second language emotion words: evidence from the emotional face–word Stroop task. *Frontiers in Psychology* 7: 1672.

Farini, F. (2013). The pragmatics of emotions in interlinguistic healthcare settings. *Research in Language* 11 (2): 163–187.

Fatahi, N., Hellström, M., Skott, C., and Mattsson, B. (2008). General practitioners' views on consultations with interpreters: a triad situation with complex issues. *Scandinavian Journal of Primary Health Care* 26 (1): 40–45.

Ferré, P., García, T., Fraga, I. et al. (2010). Memory for emotional words in bilinguals: do words have the same emotional intensity in the first and in the second language? *Cognition and Emotion* 24 (5): 760–785.

Flaskerud, J.H. (1986). The effects of culture-compatible intervention on the utilization of mental health services by minority clients. *Community Mental Health Journal* 22 (2): 127–141.

Foroni, F. (2015). Do we embody second language? Evidence for 'partial' simulation during processing of a second language. *Brain and Cognition* 99: 8–16.

Foroni, F. and Semin, G.R. (2013). Comprehension of action negation involves inhibitory simulation. *Frontiers in Human Neuroscience* 7: 209.

Garavan, H., Pendergrass, J.C., Ross, T.J. et al. (2001). Amygdala response to both positively and negatively valenced stimuli. *NeuroReport* 12: 2779–2783.

Gary, F.A. (2005). Stigma: barrier to mental health care among ethnic minorities. *Issues in Mental Health Nursing* 26 (10): 979–999.

Grosjean, F. (2010). *Bilingual: Life and Reality*. Cambridge: MA: Harvard University Press.

Hamann, S. (2001). Cognitive and neural mechanisms of emotional memory. *Trends in Cognitive Sciences* 5: 394–400.

Hamann, S.B., Ely, T.D., Hoffman, J.M., and Kilts, C.D. (2002). Ecstasy and agony: activation of the human amygdala in positive and negative emotion. *Psychological Science* 13: 135–141.

Hamann, S. and Mao, H. (2002). Positive and negative emotional verbal stimuli elicit activity in the left amygdala. *NeuroReport* 13: 15–19.

Harris, C.L. (2004). Bilingual speakers in the lab: psychophysiological measures of emotional reactivity. *Journal of Multilingual and Multicultural Development* 25 (2/3): 223–247.

Harris, C.L., Ayçiçeği, A., and Gleason, J.B. (2003). Taboo words and reprimands elicit greater autonomic reactivity in a first language than in a second language. *Applied Psycholinguistics* 24: 561–579.

Harris, C.L., Gleason, J.B., and Ayçiçeği, A. (2006). When is a first language more emotional? Psychophysiological evidence from bilingual speakers. In: *Bilingual Minds: Emotional Experience, Expression, and Representation* (ed. A. Pavlenko), 257–283. Clevedon, UK: Multilingual Matters.

Havas, D.A., Glenberg, A.M., and Rinck, M. (2007). Emotion simulation during language comprehension. *Psychonomic Bulletin & Review* 14 (3): 436–441.

Heredia, R.R. and Altarriba, J. (2001). Bilingual language mixing: why do bilinguals code-switch? *Current Directions in Psychological Science* 10: 164–168.

Hernandez, A.E. (2009). Language switching in the bilingual brain: What's next? *Brain and Language* 109 (2): 133–140.

Holland, A.C. and Kensinger, E.A. (2010). Emotion and autobiographical memory. *Physics of Life Reviews* 7 (1): 88–131.

Hsieh, E. (2009). Bilingual health communication: medical interpreters' construction of a mediator role. In: *Communicating to Manage Health and Illness* (ed. D. Brashers and D. Goldsmith), 135–160. New York, NY: Routledge.

Hsieh, E. and Nicodemus, B. (2015). Conceptualizing emotion in healthcare interpreting: a normative approach to interpreters' emotion work. *Patient Education and Counseling* 98 (12): 1474–1481.

Hsu, C.-T., Jacobs, A.M., and Conrad, M. (2015). Can Harry Potter still put a spell on us in a second language? An fMRI study on reading emotion-laden literature in late bilinguals. *Cortex* 63: 282–295.

Isurin, L. (2017). *Collective Remembering: Memory in the World and in the Mind*. Cambridge, UK: Cambridge University Press.

Jończyk, R. (2015). Hemispheric asymmetry of emotion words in a non-native mind: a divided visual field study. *Laterality* 20 (3): 326–347.

Jończyk, R., Boutonnet, B., Musial, K. et al. (2016). The bilingual brain turns a blind eye to negative statements in the second language. *Cognitive, Affective, & Behavioral Neuroscience* 16: 527–540.

Kazanas, S.A. and Altarriba, J. (2016). Emotion word processing: effects of word type and valence in Spanish–English bilinguals. *Journal of Psycholinguistic Research* 45 (2): 395–406.

Keysar, B., Hayakawa, S.L., and An, S.G. (2012). The foreign-language effect: thinking in a foreign tongue reduces decision biases. *Psychological Science* 23 (6): 661–668.

Knickerbocker, H., Johnson, R.L., and Altarriba, J. (2015). Emotion effects during reading: influence of an emotion target word on eye movements and processing. *Cognition and Emotion* 29: 784–806.

Lang, P.J., Bradley, M.M., and Cuthbert, B.N. (1998). Emotion, motivation, and anxiety: brain mechanisms and psychophysiology. *Biological Psychiatry* 44 (12): 1248–1263.

Lang, P.J., Greenwald, M.K., Bradley, M.M., and Hamm, A.O. (1993). Looking at pictures: affective, facial, visceral, and behavior reactions. *Psychophysiology* 30: 261–273.

Lindquist, K.A., Barrett, L.F., Bliss-Moreau, E., and Russell, J.A. (2006). Language and the perception of emotion. *Emotion* 6 (1): 125–138.

Lindquist, K.A., MacCormack, J.K., and Shablack, H. (2015). The role of language in emotion: predictions from psychological constructionism. *Frontiers in Psychology* 6: 444.

Littmann, S.K. (1985). Foreword. In: *Using Metaphors in Psychotherapy* (ed. P. Barker), vii–viii. New York, NY: Brunner/Mazel.

MacSwan, J. (2013). Code-switching and grammatical theory. In: *The Handbook of Bilingualism and Multilingualism*, 2nd ed. (ed. T.K. Bhatia and W.C. Ritchie), 323–350. London, UK: Routledge.

Maduro, R. (1983). Curanderismo and Latino views of disease and curing. *Western Journal of Medicine* 139 (6): 868–874.

Marcos, L.R. (1976). Linguistic dimensions in the bilingual patient. *American Journal of Psychoanalysis* 36 (4): 347–354.

Marian, V. and Neisser, U. (2000). Language-dependent recall of autobiographical memories. *Journal of Experimental Psychology: General* 129 (3): 361–368.

Martinovic, I. and Altarriba, J. (2013). Bilingualism and emotion: implications for mental health. In: *The Handbook of Bilingualism and Multilingualism* (ed. T.K. Bhatia and W.C. Ritchie), 292–320. London, UK: Routledge.

Matsumoto, D., Yoo, S.H., and Fontaine, J. (2008). Mapping expressive differences around the world: the relationship between emotional display rules and individualism versus collectivism. *Journal of Cross-Cultural Psychology* 39 (1): 55–74.

Muecke, M.A. (1983). In search of healers: southeast Asian refugees in the American health care system. *Western Journal of Medicine* 139 (6): 835–840.

Musser-Granski, J. and Carrillo, D.F. (1997). The use of bilingual, bicultural paraprofessionals in mental health services: issues for hiring, training, and supervision. *Community Mental Health Journal* 33 (1): 51–60.

Nadeem, E., Lange, J.M., Edge, D. et al. (2007). Does stigma keep poor young immigrant and US-born black and Latina women from seeking mental health care? *Psychiatric Services* 58 (12): 1547–1554.

Nijad, F. (2003). A day in the life of an interpreter in adult mental health. In: *Understanding Mental Health Work Using Interpreters* (ed. R. Tribe and H. Raval). London, UK: Routledge.

Opitz, B. and Degner, J. (2012). Emotionality in a second language: It's a matter of time. *Neuropsychologia* 50 (8): 1961–1967.

Paone, T.R. and Malott, K.M. (2008). Using interpreters in mental health counseling: a literature review and recommendations. *Journal of Multicultural Counseling and Development* 36 (3): 130–142.

Pavlenko, A. (2006). Bilingual selves. In: *Bilingual Minds: Emotional Experience, Expression and Representation* (ed. A. Pavlenko), 1–33. Clevedon, OH: Multilingual Matters.

Pavlenko, A. (2012). Affective processing in bilingual speakers: disembodied cognition? *International Journal of Psychology* 47: 405–428.

Penn, C. and Watermeyer, J. (2012). When asides become central: small talk and big talk in interpreted health interactions. *Patient Education and Counseling* 88 (3): 391–398.

Pérez Foster, R.M. (1998). *The Power of Language in the Clinical Process: Assessing and Treating the Bilingual Person*. Northvale, NJ: Jason Aronson.

Pitta, P., Marcos, L.R., and Alpert, M. (1978). Language switching as a treatment strategy with bilingual patients. *The American Journal of Psychoanalysis* 38: 255–258.

Rolland, L., Dewaele, J.-M., and Costa, B. (2017). Multilingualism and psychotherapy: exploring multilingual clients' experiences of language practices in psychotherapy. *International Journal of Multilingualism* 14 (1): 69–85.

Rosenberg, E., Leanza, Y., and Seller, R. (2007). Doctor–patient communication in primary care with an interpreter: physician perceptions of professional and family interpreters. *Patient Education and Counseling* 67 (3): 286–292.

Santiago-Rivera, A.L. and Altarriba, J. (2002). The role of language in therapy with the Spanish-English bilingual client. *Professional Psychology: Research and Practice* 33 (1): 30–38.

Schrauf, R.W. (2003). A protocol analysis of retrieval in bilingual autobiographical memory. *International Journal of Bilingualism* 7 (3): 235–256.

Schrauf, R.W. and Durazo-Arvizu, R. (2006). Bilingual autobiographical memory and emotion: theory and methods. In: *Bilingual Minds: Emotional Experience, Expression and Representation* (ed. A. Pavlenko), 284–311. Clevedon, OH: Multilingual Matters.

Searight, H.R. and Gafford, J. (2005). Cultural diversity at the end of life: issues and guidelines for family physicians. *American Family Physician* 71 (3): 515–522.

Searight, H.R. and Searight, B.K. (2009). Working with foreign language interpreters: recommendations for psychological practice. *Professional Psychology: Research and Practice* 40 (5): 444–451.

Singh, S. (2016). Cognitive behaviour therapy in a second language. *Mental Health Practice* 20 (3): 23–29.

Snowden, L.R., Masland, M., and Guerrero, R. (2007). Federal civil rights policy and mental health treatment access for persons with limited English proficiency. *American Psychologist* 62 (2): 109–117.

Sprowls, C. (2002). Bilingual therapists' perspectives of their language related self-experience during therapy. *Dissertation Abstracts International*, 63(04), 2076B. (UMI No. 3052139).

Stroop, J.R. (1935). Studies of interference in serial verbal reactions. *Journal of Experimental Psychology* 18 (6): 643–662.

Sue, D.W., Arredondo, P., and McDavis, R.J. (1992). Multicultural counseling competencies and standards: a call to the profession. *Journal of Counseling & Development* 70 (4): 477–486.

Sue, S. and Morishima, J.K. (1982). *The Mental Health of Asian Americans: Contemporary Issues in Identifying and Treating Mental Problems*. San Francisco, CA: Jossey-Bass.

Sue, D. and Sue, S. (1987). Cultural factors in the clinical assessment of Asian-Americans. *Journal of Consulting and Clinical Psychology* 55: 479–487.

Sue, S., Zane, N., Nagayama Hall, G.C., and Berger, L.K. (2009). The case for cultural competency in psychotherapeutic interventions. *Annual Review of Psychology* 60: 525–548.

Sutton, T.M., Altarriba, J., Gianico, J.L., and Basnight-Brown, D.M. (2007). The automatic access of emotion: emotional Stroop effects in Spanish–English bilingual speakers. *Cognition and Emotion* 21 (5): 1077–1090.

Vasquez, C. and Javier, R.A. (1991). The problem with interpreters: communicating with Spanish-speaking patients. *Psychiatric Services* 42 (2): 163–165.

Verdinelli, S. and Biever, J.L. (2009). Spanish–English bilingual psychotherapists: personal and professional language development and use. *Cultural Diversity and Ethnic Minority Psychology* 15 (3): 230–242.

Wierzbicka, A. (1997). *Understanding Cultures through their Key Words*. New York, NY: Oxford University Press.

Willerton, E., Dankoski, M.E., and Martir, J.F.S. (2008). Medical family therapy: a model for addressing mental health disparities among Latinos. *Families, Systems, & Health* 26 (2): 196–206.

Winskel, H. (2013). The emotional Stroop task and emotionality rating of negative and neutral words in late Thai–English bilinguals. *International Journal of Psychology* 48 (6): 1090–1098.

Yang, Y., Wang, J., Bailer, C. et al. (2017). Commonality of neural representations of sentences across languages: predicting brain activation during Portuguese sentence comprehension using an English-based model of brain function. *NeuroImage* 146: 658–666.

Zayas, L.H., Cabassa, L.J., Perez, M.C., and Cavazos-Rehg, P.A. (2007). Using interpreters in diagnostic research and practice: pilot results and recommendations. *The Journal of Clinical Psychiatry* 68 (6): 924–928.

16 Representing, Detecting, and Translating Humour in the Brain

JENNIFER HOFMANN AND FRANK A. RODDEN

1. Introduction

1. Some things are funny. A considerable part of those funny things are transported or created by language.
2. Some funny things can be translated into other languages and they remain funny.
3. Some funny things can*not* be translated into another language without losing their humour.
4. Some non-funny things are funny because of attempts to translate them.

Sentences (1)–(4) show how closely humour is linked to language and how difficult the translation of humour may be. Humour, language, and translation is an important topic to linguists and experts of translation studies and has received growing attention in the past three decades (see for example, Attardo 2017; Maitland 2017). Yet, fewer studies have looked at *individuals* (as opposed to humorous material) and how they deal with humour and its translation, as well as the neural processes relating to this (see also Vaid 2000; Vaid et al. 2003). Moreover, no studies have addressed the relationship between humour, translation, and neural processes in individuals with a bilingual or multilingual background.

We believe that the knowledge from psychology *on individuals* and – in the case of language dependent humor- the knowledge from linguistics and translation studies on *humorous materials* can inform the cognitive scientist. This knowledge will help to enrich study designs, the operationalization of humour, and the interpretation of results in studies on the represenation, detection and translation of humor in the brain. Thus, we aim at providing an overview of fundamental issues concerning humour and a review of the state of the art literature from an interdisciplinary perspective. In the first part of

The Handbook of the Neuroscience of Multilingualism, First Edition. Edited by John W. Schwieter.
© 2019 John Wiley & Sons Ltd. Published 2019 by John Wiley & Sons Ltd.

the chapter, we will focus on issues of the humour definitions, humour and language, as well as the translation of humour from one language to another. In the second part of the chapter, we will elaborate on the processing of humour in the brain, present a review on the currently existing studies and briefly elaborate on humour and language learning. We differentiate between humour processing as a cognitive task, amusement as the emotional response to humour, and the motor/behavioural reactions (smiling or laughter). In the third part of the chapter, we will present a conclusion on the reviewed studies and offer hypotheses on humour and the multilingual brain. Thus, the current chapter aims at bringing together pieces of the puzzle that inform about the neural processing of humour in the bilingual or multilingual brain; but at this point in time, it can only give directions, no final answers.

2.   What Is Humour?

In order to investigate humour, we first need to establish a shared vocabulary on humour and define which aspects of humour are of interest. While we all have an idea of what humour is, the question of the definition of humour is not as straightforward as one might expect, especially when adapting a multidisciplinary point of view. Different (conflicting) terminological systems exist across disciplines and no agreed definition of either term – humour or sense of humour – exists (cf. Ruch 2004, 2007).

   While the concept of humour is nowadays most often used as an umbrella term for *all* the phenomena in the field of the laughable and funny (see Roeckelein 2002), humour may also be seen as a worldview of smiling at the adversities and imperfections of life (cf. Ruch 2007). In the latter sense, humour may be seen as a cognitive-affective style of dealing with situations and life in general. This style allows for the development of a positive or light side in unfortunate and serious situations. Thus, humour allows one to at least find such situations or mishaps marginally amusing or to being able to see a funny side (see Ruch 2001, 2004). In this notion, humour is in opposition to concepts such as wit or sarcasm, which may all be seen as different comic styles in the field of 'the comic' (see Schmidt-Hidding 1963).

   The psychology of humour refers to the study of humour and people, not humorous materials only (e.g. Martin 2007; Ruch 2007). Psychological humour studies aim at describing, explaining, predicting, and controlling humorous behaviour. By this understanding, humour exists in several aspects, including humour production, humour comprehension and appreciation, emotional responses to humorous stimuli, behavioural styles expressing humour, and cognitive and motivational aspects.

   Humour production entails the active generation of humour: for example, in response to conversation partners, or even professionally (e.g. comedians). *Humour comprehension* denotes the capability of understanding humour (i.e. the joke), of being able to explain what makes the joke funny, or to be able to give an explanation of the mechanism of a punch line. *Humour appreciation* is our personal liking (or disliking) of the humour. Usually, two nearly orthogonal components of positive and negative responses can be separated to assess humour appreciation (e.g. Ruch and Rath 1993).

Figure 1   Examples of different smiles and laughs.

Humour appreciation is linked to comprehension, but the two are distinct processes. Based on comprehension and appreciation, we also experience emotional responses to humour: *amusement*. This amusement may be correlated with the behavioural markers of *smiling* and *laughter* (see Figure 1 for examples of smiles and laughs).

Concerning cognitive and motivational processes and importantly for the link of humour and language, there is agreement that for humour to occur, individuals need to be in a relatively relaxed, relatively stress-free frame of mind and motivational state, or need to be willing to switch into such a state of mind.[1] Individuals process humour in a playful rather than serious frame of mind (see McGhee 1979), or need to be in a paratelic (i.e. activity-oriented, playful) motivational state as opposed to a telic (i.e. serious) motivational state (Apter 2001). Humour was claimed to involve a non-bona fide rather than bona fide mode of communication (see Raskin 1985). Humour is thus different from most other forms of communications we encounter, which are based on serious, goal-oriented, rationale thinking and speaking. Also, humour has been claimed as being a form of play, a play with ideas (McGhee 1979). Consequently, humour also plays with language (words, grammar, syntax), norms, cultural stereotypes, and knowledge.

Lastly, an important distinction is to be drawn between humour and laughter (for an overview see Hofmann and Ruch 2017; Martin 2007; Ruch and Hofmann 2013). While early theoretical accounts and empirical studies often mix the terms or use humour and laughter as synonyms, the two phenomena need to be kept apart. Laughter has many functions and elicitors beyond humour. Thus, while smiling and laughter (see Figure 1 for some examples) are behavioural markers of amusement elicited by humour, they also occur without amusement. Also, there is amusement experienced in the absence of smiling and laughter.

3.   Humour and Language

The uniqueness of humour poses a variety of challenges for its study in neuroscience. Some basic emotions can be studied in other animals (i.e. when things are not going how we want them to go, we get angry, so do dogs. We are afraid of some things, so are apes). For a brain scientist, animal models of behaviour are valuable tools. Unfortunately, such models are simply not available for the study of humour because no other animals experience humour in the way that we do. For example Panksepp, Burgdorf, and their colleagues could show that rats experience positive affect and this is behaviourally shown in respiration patterns and vocalizations that are very similar to our laughter. 50Hz ultrasonic vocalizations in rats are typically elevated by hedonic stimuli, elicited by tickling, and suppressed by averse stimuli (e.g. Burgdorf et al. 2011; Panksepp 1998; Panksepp and Burgdorf 2000, 2003). Thus, we can conclude that rats (and many other animals) experience joy. Yet, the dissection of joy into such facets as *amusement*, relief, gratitude, and schadenfreude (amongst others), has not been made for animals as it has been proposed for humans.

Moreover, while there is a fair share of research on play and playfulness in primates (which may be seen as forms of humour), all of these studies are restricted to certain forms of play or humour which do not include one of the main thrusts of this book: *language*. Thus, while we acknowledge the existence of non-language-related humour and playfulness, apparent in infants (Rothbart 1973; Scheiner et al. 2002; Sroufe and Waters 1976) and primates (e.g. Darwin 1872; Davila-Ross et al. 2009; Van Hooff 1972; Vettin and Todt 2005), non-verbal humour it is not the primary subject of this chapter.

4.   Theories of Verbal Humour

Several theories deal with the processing of humour, (psychological) mechanisms in the generation and response to humour and the functions of humour (for an overview, see Chapman and Foot 1992; Keith-Spiegel 1972). Narrowing the focus from humorous material in general (which also includes visual puns, cartoons, and slapstick humour which may not rely on language altogether) to verbal humour, we present two lines of research that are important to the study of the neuroscience of humour, translation, and bilingualism.

So called 'cognitive theories' (Ruch 2008) typically deal with the structural properties of funny stimuli or the ways in which such stimuli are processed by individuals. Suls (1972) put forward a two-stage model for the appreciation of jokes and cartoons. He presented the idea that a fair share of humour is based on (i) the experience of an incongruity between two objects, elements of an object or events, and accompanying expectations, and (ii) its resolution (see Figure 2).

In the first stage, the listener detects the incongruity in the punch line (i.e. the ending of the joke is inconsistent with the expectation). The resolution of the problematical incongruity is stage two. It possibly leads to laughter or puzzlement, if the resolution is not found (see Figure 2). There is general agreement that these two stages exist in the process of perceiving and understanding humour (see for example McGhee et al. 1990). While incongruity is a necessary but not sufficient condition for humour, the resolving of the incongruity may not always lead to the perception of something being funny. The lack of a resolution may also be a reason for something being perceived as funny: so called 'nonsense jokes' based on no or only partial resolution (see Ruch 1992). Importantly, Suls's (1972) account was criticized for only explaining humour comprehension, but not appreciation (cf. McGhee and Goldstein 1972). It was argued that for the experience of humour, a *third stage* is needed that concludes on the resolution

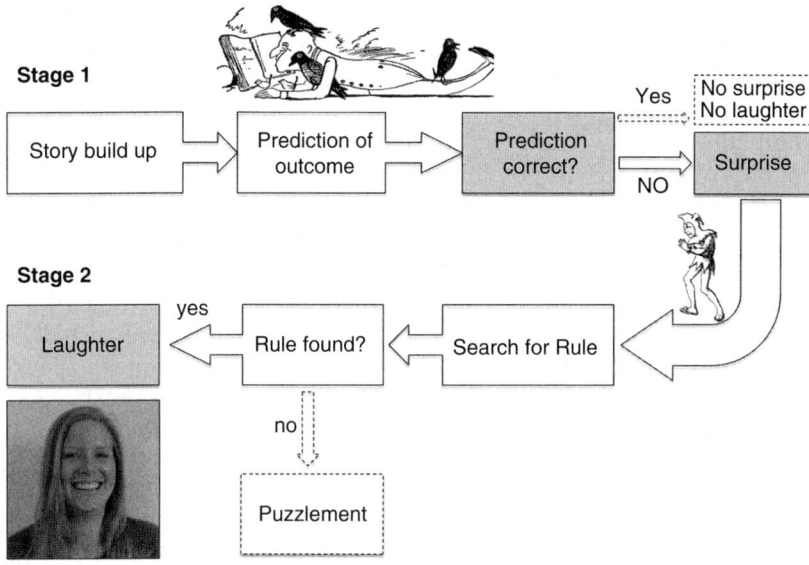

Figure 2 Simplified presentation of the two-stage model after Suls. Source: Adapted from Suls (1972).

actually being *nonsensical*. According to Ruch (2008), the third stage allows one to distinguish humour from a problem-solving process.

Supporting the significance of incongruity and resolution in the processing of humorous stimuli, Ruch (1981, 1992) studied the appreciation of verbal jokes and cartoons from a personality psychology point of view. He identified a bimodal taxonomy of verbal humour, covering two structure factors (incongruity resolution and nonsense) and one content factor (sexual humour, no other content factor occurred). The model and its accompanying test were labelled the 3WD (in German, *Drei Witz Dimensionen*: three joke dimensions). In incongruity-resolution humour, the initial resolution can be solved, as suggested in the model of Suls (1972). In nonsense jokes, the initial resolution cannot, or only partially be resolved (example: *What is the difference between a sparrow? None, whatsoever. Both legs are of similar length, especially the left one*). Within the two structure factors, the contents of the jokes are of various themes (except sex), but they are similar in the cognitive processes involved (i.e. solving the incongruity or not). In the third factor (sexual humour), the joke or cartoon may be based on one of the two structure factors, but the content is always related to sexual themes. The three factors 'are considered to provide an exhaustive taxonomy in classifying jokes and cartoons at a general level. They consistently explain approximately 40% of the total variance' (Ruch 1992, p. 30). Moreover, the three factors have proven to be cross-nationally stable and many studies have shown that individuals do differ in their appreciation of incongruity-resolution, nonsense, and sexual humour. These differences also relate to other individual differences variables, such as sensation seeking, conservatism/liberalism, as well as art and music preferences (for an overview, see Ruch 1992).

The second line of research to be presented stems from linguistics. The semantic theory of humour (Raskin 1985) adds knowledge to the understanding of verbal humour, or more specifically, to jokes. Raskin defines the conditions and factors that make a text funny. A text is funny when two necessary and sufficient conditions are met: the piece must be compatible with two different scripts and the two scripts must be opposite (in the sense of oppositions such as possible/impossible, real/unreal, etc.; Raskin 1985). To exemplify, individuals associate manifold information with single words. For example, hearing the sentence, '*it's a lovely table*' (see Raskin 2008, p. 11) may lead the listener to think about *furniture*. Only the second sentence ('*I love the sixth row data*') *disambiguates* the word to the intended meaning of a table also being a *chart*. Following Raskin, humour often includes such 'intended ambiguity' while 'normal language' usually seeks to resolving ambiguity. The theoretical account by Raskin has been claimed to be an account that follows the logic of incongruity-resolution theory (see Attardo 1997). Extending the account by Raskin (1985), Attardo and Raskin (1991) presented the general theory of verbal humour (GTVH). This theory postulates six hierarchically structured 'knowledge resources': script opposition; logical mechanism (somewhat equivalent to the third stage of incongruity-resolution theories: the understanding of the resolution being nonsensical, funny); the situation (additional information that comes with a script which is not funny, but necessary to understand a joke); target (what is known about the target of the joke); narrative strategy (e.g. joke, riddle); and language (e.g. syntactic, lexical choices).

Ruch et al. (1993) found empirical support for most of the predictions of the theory, but not the hierarchical structure of the knowledge resources as initially postulated. Hempelmann and Ruch (2005) continued the work on the GTVH with an interdisciplinary approach and analysed the jokes of the 3WD with the GTVH. They found that jokes of the type incongruity-resolution were medium in degree of incongruity and degree of residual incongruity, very simple to complex in terms of degree of resolution, and contained diverse script oppositions and logical mechanisms. The narrative strategies used involve text and cartoons with one panel, and targets were frequently involved. Nonsense jokes and cartoons were characterized by a high degree of incongruity and a high degree of residual incongruity, and the degree of resolution ranged from very simple to very complex. There were fewer cartoons with an actual/not actual script opposition while possible/impossible script oppositions occurred more often. Targets were rarely involved and diverse logical mechanisms were used. Also, a higher number of panels was typical for cartoons (Hempelmann and Ruch 2005).

To conclude, the GTVH allows for an analysis of humorous texts, which might be helpful in the process of offline translations of humour in a second language. Furthermore, the factors found by Ruch (3WD) may be fruitful in studying different neural responses to the different types of humour in bilingual or multilingual individuals.

4.1. The Translation of Humour: Translatability, Equivalence, and Compromises

Functioning humour (we explicitly leave out cases of failed humour, which are easily achieved by bad translations, unbridgeable gaps in knowledge between agents of different cultures/language groups, bad timing, or inadequate contexts; see Bell 2015) depends on contextual, environmental, social, and personal factors. 'Translation of humour' as the phrase is used in this chapter is based on shared knowledge about the world, a shared social background (cf. Raskin 1985), and a shared language (see Chiaro 2008).

Studies on humour translation are typically found in the fields of 'translation studies' and linguistics. Researchers have mostly focused on looking at the translation of humour in *written literature* (cf. Laurian and Nilsen 1989), and only few researchers have dedicated their attention to oral communication and/or multimedia texts (see Chiaro 2008; Pavlicek and Pöchhacker 2002; Vandaele 2002). For both types of materials and communication forms, researchers have developed different strategies to deal with the translation of humour. These strategies range from, as Attardo (2008) puts it, 'pragmatic translation (i.e., respecting the perlocutionary goal of humor, but abandoning the sense of the original text)', to simply 'ignoring the humor and perhaps replacing it with another joke, even elsewhere in the text' (pp. 126–127).

While 'translatability' determines whether humorous material is translatable at all or not, 'equivalence' refers to the degree of closeness of the original humorous instance to the translation, with different forms of equivalence being possible (for a discussion see Chiaro 2008). Reaching equivalence means that the goal of the humour (i.e. wanting to amuse the perceiver) should be kept, while the text or spoken humour may be changed to a significant extent in order to reach this goal. In the final analysis, this means that spectators of, say dubbed films in two cultures, may both judge a film as having been funny – although they laughed neither at the same places, nor at the same punch lines (see Chiaro 2003).

Some kinds of humour are deemed to be 'notoriously untranslatable' (Chiaro 2008, p. 571), meaning that they lack translatability altogether. This kind of humour can involve puns, as the chances of being able to do a pun on the same word in two different languages is extremely small. Even more, Chiaro (2008) points out that even the chances of finding the same type of pun (i.e. a homonym or a homophone) are even smaller. Humour based on wordplay, irregular word order, different sounds of words or unusual collocations, may only very rarely be directly and equivalently translated into another language. Therefore, translations of humour based on play with language often ends in a 'linguistic compromise' (Chiaro 2008) where the formal equivalence is sacrificed in order to reach dynamic equivalence. Humour based on play with ideas or concepts may be translated more easily, but will create difficulties when the ideas or concepts inherent in the funny core are specific to a cultural group (and may not be known in another cultural group). In such cases, radical changes may have to be made to accommodate the knowledge of the target culture into which the joke is translated, leading to a 'cultural compromise' (Chiaro 2008). The latter may even involve changing the target of a joke (i.e. the person which is the target of a joke), changing the context, etc. Sometimes, in order to reach the ultimate goal (i.e. eliciting amusement), even cultural and linguistic compromises are needed when translating verbal humour (Chiaro 2008).

Yet, as Davies (2005) argued with respect to jokes, many jokes are translatable into different languages without having to change the content. In these jokes there is either (i) shared knowledge across cultures (i.e. laughing at the cowardly Italians: see Davies 1998) or (ii) the target groups of jokes can easily be replaced by regional target groups (i.e. the British laughing at the Irish, the Americans laughing at the Poles). Problems do arise when scripts or ideas are unique to a certain group or culture. With respect to *jokes*, Davies (2005) categorized three types of jokes. First, transposable jokes with shared scripts across cultures (in these, nothing much needs to be changed for the joke to be understood with a fairly literal translation; see also unrestricted jokes, Zabalbeascoa 2005). For example (Low 2011):

Nancy: Winston, if I were your wife, I would put poison in your coffee.

Winston: Nancy, if I were your husband, I would drink it.

Second, Davies describes switchable jokes (jokes which exist in one culture but have a more or less equivalent in another culture, jokes which target a different locally known group). Third are problematic jokes (jokes in which scripts are unique and would not be understood in another cultural context).

Although mostly relating to the translation of written material, one might use the dimensions of *equivalence* and *compromise* to judge the quality of translations of humour of bilingual individuals in studies. Moreover, the categorization of jokes (i.e. by Davies 2005) may be used to categorize the initial stimuli and vary their difficulty in studies on individuals' ability to translate jokes from one language to another[2]. For example, a study could test the translation abilities of bilinguals with varying anchor stimuli (differing in translatability and joke type), judge the quality by obtaining ratings of funniness and aversiveness (by peers or experts) and by rating the degree of equivalence and compromise.

Beyond these general remarks, other opportunities and difficulties will arise from the person of the translator and will depend upon their inclination to humour, humour abilities (humour understanding, humour production), and humour preferences. Humorous instances may be detected or not, and if detected, the 'translator' may be able to come up with an equivalently funny translation. Unfortunately, very few articles exist that have empirically studied the effects of translation on humour understanding and appreciation of the audience (for a discussion and exception see Antonini 2005; Chiaro 2007; Denton and Ciampi 2012). To the knowledge of the authors, no empirical studies have investigated the relationships between the translators' personality and sense of humour, and the relationship to the features and quality of translations.

4.2.   *Humour Processing and Appreciation: Neural Processes*

Similarly, to the knowledge of the authors, there are no studies that have investigated humour processing in the bilingual or multilingual brain. Thus, we have to approach the issue from the knowledge on the processes involved: the translation process (see Chapter 24 in this volume), the processing of non-literal and figurative language (see Chapter 25, this volume), meaning activation, and humour processing in general.

The areas of the brain that extract meaning from words have been partially known for over a hundred years but have become much more precise since the beginning of this century (Pulvermüller 2013). Humour or funniness has no 'meaning', but rather comes into existence when the meaning of a situation (or, in the case of translation, of a sentence) can/must be seen in a totally different framework (cf. Eysenck 1942). Inasmuch as two separate meanings are always present when humour occurs, the areas of the

Categorization		Differentiations	
Aspect of humour	Cognitive processing	Detection	
		Comprehension	
		Production	
		Impairment	
	Affective process	Appreciation (funniness/aversiveness)	of types or individual differences
		Amusement/mirth	
		Impairment	
	Differentiation	Cognitive vs. affective	
		Comprehension vs. elaboration	
Method	Non-invasive	EEG	
		MEG	
		fMRI	
	Invasive	PET	
		Surgery/Stimulation	
Conditions	Humorous vs. not humorous		
	Humorous vs. not humorous vs. garden path		
	Incongruity resolution vs. nonsense vs. not humorous		
	"Bright" vs. "dark" types		
	exaggeration vs. ambiguity vs. "bridging-inference" types		
Type of stimulus	Verbal	e.g. puns, semantic jokes, jokes requiring mentalizing	
	Visual	e.g. cartoons	
	Multimedia	e.g. videos, TV clips	
Type of participants	Clinical cases		
	Individuals with lesions		
	Healthy Individuals		

Figure 3   Factors allowing for the categorization of studies on humour and neural processing.

brain involved in deriving meaning from words are necessary and will be active when humour is perceived. Consequently, those parts of the brain dedicated to the derivation of meaning from words will be active when humour is being translated into a second language.

Next, we will focus on studies that have specifically utilized funny materials and considered the neural processes and responses in the brain. These studies were conducted in one language context, with most studies naming the language the study was conducted in and probably including native speakers of this given language (with some studies not providing any language related details at all). The existing studies may be categorized according to methodological decisions, dependent variables, or the target population. Figure 3 gives an overview on the different factors which may allow categorizing the existing studies.

4.2.1.   Studies Utilizing EEG and ERPs   Beginning with the simpler techniques, studies using electroencephalography (EEG) have shown changes in the patterns of brain waves upon the presentation of humour to the subject (e.g. Papousek et al. 2013; Ramaraju et al. 2015) along with differences in bright types of humour (laughing with) and dark types of humour (laughing at; see Papousek et al. 2017). By studying event-related potentials' (ERPs – a refinement of the EEG technique in which brain waves related to events can be measured) – changes were detected when the subject was presented with jokes as opposed to non-funny stories (Mayerhofer and Schacht 2015). It was further possible to detect significant interhemispheric differences in joke processing between left-handers and right-handers (Coulson and Lovett 2004) and between good and poor joke comprehenders (Coulson and Kutas 2001). These differences were dependent on the hemisphere to which the punchlines of jokes were presented, with the semantic activation of the right hemisphere facilitating joke comprehension (Coulson and Williams 2005). Moreover, joke enjoyment (humour appreciation) has also been studied using ERPs (Du et al. 2013; Mensen et al. 2014). In contrast to the results of Coulson and Kutas (2001), Du and colleagues (2013) found support for the three stage model of humour processing (with the first stage denoting humour detection, followed by the resolution of an incongruity, and the last stage being the appreciation of the humour). Funny stimuli (as compared to unfunny stimuli) initially elicited a more negative ERP deflection across the frontocentral scalp regions (the left temporal gyrus and the left medial frontal gyrus were localized as the generators in dipole analysis, possibly involved in the detection of an incongruent element). Then, funny stimuli elicited a more negative deflection over the frontocentral scalp regions and a more positive ERP deflection over posterior scalp regions (with the anterior cingulate cortex being located as the generator in dipole analysis, possibly involved in the forming of novel/alternative associations). Lastly, funny items elicited a more positive ERP deflection over anterior and posterior scalp regions (middle frontal gyrus and gyrus fusiformis as generators, possibly related to the enjoyment).

4.2.2. Studies Utilizing fMRI, PET, SPECT and MEG   Neuroimaging techniques, functional magnetic resonance imaging (fMRI), positron emission tomography (PET), single photon emission computed tomography (SPECT), and magnetoencephalography (MEG) have made it possible to determine which areas of the brain are active during the processing of humour and laughter. Consequently, studies about the assignment of brain areas involved in the detection, conception, and enjoyment of humour have increased tremendously. A deeper discussion of the areas of the brain found to be active in these studies would make this a much longer chapter (for an extensive overview, see Rodden 2018I, II) and a thorough summary of all fMRI studies (and one PET study) up to the year 2013 can be found in a publication by Vrticka et al. (2013).

Using PET, Iwase et al. (2001) discovered that during humour-induced smiling or laughter (elicited by funny films), a selective increase in regional blood flow was present bilaterally in the subjects' supplementary motor areas, left putamena, visual association areas, left anterior temporal cortex (ATC), left uncus (close to the hippocampus), and the orbitofrontal and medial prefrontal cortices. Additionally, it was discovered that the experience of humour engages elements of an important 'reward system', a network of subcortical regions including the nucleus accumbens (a key component of the mesolimbic dopaminergic reward system; Berns 2004; Mobbs et al. 2003). These findings were confirmed by Osaka and Osaka (2005) and expanded to include more extended areas of the reward system.

Comparing funny stimuli with non-funny counterparts, Wild et al. (2006) had subjects viewing funny nonverbal cartoons vs. nearly-identical but non-funny cartoons.

The cortical regions selective for humour perception (left temporo-parietal junction: TPJ, left prefrontal cortex (PFC)), humour-induced smiling (bilateral activity in the basal temporal lobes), and voluntary grinning (bilateral facial regions of the motor cortex) were reported. In a similar investigation, Bartolo et al. (2006) presented nonverbal cartoons that were funny vs. non-funny. They found a somewhat different distribution of areas of activity, namely, the right inferior frontal gyrus (RIFG), the left superior temporal gyrus (STG), the left middle temporal gyrus (MTG) and the left cerebellum. Moreover, a few studies looked into gender differences in neural processing of funny vs. unfunny materials. Azim and colleagues (2005) showed that although both men and women share an extensive cerebral humour-response strategy, there are differences in brain activation in the reward centres elicited by humour. Females showed more activity in the left PFC in response to humour than males did, and also more activity in the mesolimbic reward system, including the nucleus accumbens. Kohn and colleagues (2011) also used funny vs. non-funny cartoons as stimuli in an fMRI approach. They replicated some of the findings by Azim et al. (2005) but not others: it was found that in women responding to funny cartoons, activation was found primarily in the ventral system, including the amygdala, insula, and anterior cingulate cortex, whereas men showed activation in both the ventral (emotional processing) and dorsolateral prefrontal cortex. A resolution of the differences will have to await further investigations.

Using fMRI, Amir and colleagues (2013) and coworkers measured the differences between the brain's processing of humour and non-humorous insight. They found that the brain activity associated with non-humorous insight was a subset of the activity associated with humorous insight and that the humorous condition was accompanied uniquely and bilaterally by activations in the temporal poles: the temporo-occipital junctions extending to the temporo-parietal junction and the media prefrontal cortex. The importance of this network in the processing of humour was further supported by the correlation between the degree of activation and the 'funniness'. Marinkovic et al. (2010) aimed at determining the temporal sequence of humour-specific event locations in the brain using the MEG technique (which has greater temporal precision than fMRI). While lying in the MEG apparatus, subjects viewed jokes with punchlines that were either funny, non-funny (but semantically congruent), or incongruent while their MEGs were being recorded. The earliest response to all these stimuli (funny, non-funny, incongruent) was, as expected, in the visual cortex. From there, the activity spread towards the front of the brain via the ventral visual stream and was left-lateralized in the antero-ventral occipital area. Activation encompassed the anterior left temporal area and then, by 400 ms, moved on to the left inferior prefrontal regions. From 700 to 1150 ms the main effect was seen in the right dorsolateral prefrontal cortex, indicating a unique sensitivity in this region for funny punchlines.

Moreover, several studies have compared different types of humorous stimuli. Goel and Dolan (2001) segregated the cognitive and affective components of humour by using fMRI as subjects listened to puns and semantic jokes. The two types of humour were associated with patterns of cerebral activity easily distinguished from one another. Also, enjoying cartoons involving incongruity-resolution produced more activity in the temporo-parietal junction, inferior frontal gyrus, and ventromedial prefrontal cortex than simpler cartoons did (Samson et al. 2008). In a later study of cerebral activation during incongruity-resolution humour vs. nonsense humour, the TPJ was active along with the anterior medial frontal cortex and the superior frontal gyri, bilaterally (Samson et al. 2009). Different types of jokes (exaggeration, ambiguity, bridging-inference) gave rise to characteristic cerebral activity patterns but in all jokes the left dorsolateral prefrontal cortex and ventral anterior cingular cortex were active (Chan and Lavallee 2015). Another recent investigation of neural correlates of sex differences in joke processing considered three types of verbal jokes (Chan 2016). Women exhibited greater cerebral activity than men while processing the jokes in the temporo-parietal-mesiocortical-motor cortex and also while processing 'exaggeration jokes' in the frontomesolimbic network. 'Ambiguity jokes' elicited greater cerebral activity in men in the frontal paralimbic network. All joke types elicited greater activation in the anterior prefrontal gyrus of women than in those of men, whereas men showed greater activation than women in the dorsal prefrontal cortex.

Thus, different types of humorous materials relate to different neural responses. Furthermore, the different process involved in humour can be separated too. According to a study by Chan et al. (2012), humour comprehension is associated with activity bilaterally in the frontal gyri and the left frontal superior gyrus. Humour elaboration (appreciation, enjoyment) is associated with activity in the left ventroledial prefrontal cortex, and bilaterally in the amygdalae and the parahippocampal gyri. According to an fMRI study by Akimoto and colleagues (2014) in which first-person-view stories involving irony were examined, the right anterior superior temporal gyrus seemed to be responsible for representing conceptual knowledge of irony: the medial prefrontal cortex and the right anterior inferior temporal gyrus appeared to underlie the understanding of the context in which the irony is expressed. The degree of irony varied with the intensity of the cerebral activity in the right amygdala, hippocampus, parahippocampal gyrus, and the right dorsolateral prefrontal cortex.

In an fMRI investigation using closely related sentences as stimuli, Shibata et al. (2014) showed that 'the perception of funniness' elicited activity in the cognitive networks (language and semantic networks: inferior frontal gyrus, middle temporal gyrus, superior temporal gyrus, superior frontal gyrus, and inferior parietal lobule), as well as in the affective networks in the mesolimbic reward regions (regions around the base of the brain that are involved in the feeling of pleasure). It should be noted, however, that the separation of emotional experience and expression has recently been questioned (Caruana 2017).

In a study of humour appreciation by Campbell and colleagues (2015), the superior frontal gyrus also was active in association with humor appreciation and the TPJ with humor comprehension. Moreover, Campbell et al. (2015) were able to tease apart the activity of the brain when it detects attempts at humour and when it enjoys it. Humour comprehension was found to be correlated with cerebral activity in the left inferior frontal gyrus, bilaterally in the temporal poles and in the temporoparietal junctions, supplementary motor area-cingulate cortex, the post-central gyrus, bilateral posterior ventral regions including the fusiform gyrus and the cerebellum. The enjoyment/appreciation of humour was associated with regions of activation in the bilateral substantia nigra, bilateral amygdala, and the left frontal superior gyrus (see also Caruana 2017, however).

4.2.3. Studies Utilizing Invasive Techniques   With respect to invasive research techniques, humour and laughter have been studied using intraoperative (open) brain stimulation since van Buren's experiments in 1961. These have been studied by a number of neurosurgeons since then (Arroyo et al. 1993; Fish et al. 1993; Fried et al. 1998; Schmitt et al. 2006; Sperli et al. 2006) and areas of the brain involved in humour and laughter have been catalogued.

4.3.   Summary: Translating Humour in the Brain

To sum up the reported findings: activity related to humour and mirth has been consistently reported in the temporal lobes near the junctions of the parietal or occipital lobes, and at the temporal poles, the prefrontal cortex and the classical reward systems of the brain. When the ideal, successful translation of a text occurs, the text will at best be as funny in the language into which it has been translated as it is in the native language. It seems thus reasonable to believe that those parts of the brain involved in the detection and enjoyment of humour will also be implicated after the work is translated. Therefore, we assume that when enjoying humour in a second language, the same parts of the brain should be involved as for the processing of humour in the mother-tongue. Yet, it might be expected that the brain areas involved in the translation, the finding of meaning of words and the humour in the second language will lead to further neural involvement. If the text is not translated by a machine, it will be translated by a bilingual person and the literature on bilingual people is rather large (for example, García-Pentón et al. 2016; Grundy et al. 2017; Pliatsikas et al. 2017). Yet, the neural processes when processing humour in a second language in real time has not been studied so far. To the knowledge of the authors, no study on the online translation of humour and its accompanying neural processes has been conducted.

5.   Humour and Language Learning

Humour has been deemed a special language competency, or more extremely, humour has been seen as a form of mastery over a given language, as well as the culture, norms, and themes associated with the people speaking this language (see for example, Nilsen 1989). For example, in order to understand and produce incongruity-resolution humour, one needs to know about words (lexical components, semantic and conceptual components; cf. Pavlenko 2000) and about themes or scripts that could have more than one (opposing) meaning. Thus, to produce humour, one must have mastered the rules of a language and a culture's norms and desirable behaviour, in order to play with these elements (see also 'humor as a play with ideas', McGhee 1979; or Vaid 2000 who deems humour as a special form of figurative language). Kersten (2009) utilized a mixed-method approach to investigate the humour in narrations in the second language (L2) acquisition in elementary school children. She concludes that humour was being used by the children in order to cope with the linguistic inadequacies of the L2 skills. With a different spin, Pomerantz and Bell (2007) argue that playing with words and language (while learning an L2) can elicit amusement, but more importantly, it contributes to the expansion of a learner's communicative repertoires and deepens their knowledge of the correct and more creative use of language. Investigating the humour use of couples with a bilingual, cross-cultural background (long-term relationships), Chiaro (2009) finds, in a mixed-method approach, that couples often report having made special efforts to teach their own humour to their partners in order to learn and appreciate their partner's humour and the humour's cultural specifics. In similar vein, the work of Bell (e.g. Bell 2005, 2007) shows that in interactions between L2 learners and native speakers, humour is more carefully used and placed, but seldom causes problems (for a discussion of failed humour, see Bell 2015).

6. Conclusion

The interplay of humour and languages is a very difficult and tedious – but it is a rewarding area to look at more closely. As Vaid (2006) summarized:

> Yet, the research on humor use in multiple language users would greatly enrich our understanding of bilingualism, as well as our understanding of humor. For students of bilingualism, the study of humor would broaden the study of language from decontextualized, representational aspects of language to contextualized, performativity aspects. For students of humor, the study of humor use among multiple language users would deepen awareness of the ways in which humor comprehension depends on shared, tacit linguistic and cultural knowledge (p. 152).

Humour can be a very sharp tool in a society and understanding the utility of that tool well enough to make a funny statement funny in another language shows a high degree of proficiency not only in the languages involved but also in the two cultures. Humour can also *arise* from multilingualism. Some idiomatic expressions in one language translate poorly or not at all into another language thus giving rise to the failed expectations that are the substrate of humour. In German the very common expression *'Jetzt haben wir den Salat'* is a phrase that expresses frustration at preparations that have been made but to no avail. *'Now we have the salad'* is its linguistically perfect translation into English – but the meaning of the phrase is lost totally. That total lack of coherence is what makes it funny. Such humoristic material may be voluntarily produced by speakers of two languages (cf. code switching; see also Davies 2003; Leeds 1992). Thus, the mastery of two languages allows those individuals to play with language, as well as playing with common mistakes beginners would make (for a variety of examples, see Vaid 2006). Moreover, the switching between two languages and explicit use of two language and culture backgrounds has been claimed to be an indicator for giftedness (Hughes et al. 2006). Thus, the study of humour in multilingualism does not only target attempts to translate humour or produce adequate humour in the second language, but also play with the 'misuse' of language to amuse.

As we said at the start, an understanding of the interrelationships amongst humour and the multilingual brain is still in its infancy, but growing fast. Experiments that need to be done include testing to see how individuals of bilingual or multilingual backgrounds differ in *humour appreciation* and *humour production* in their native and second language. At best, passive appreciation and active production (in both languages) may be tested. Importantly, humour-related traits need to be considered – and maybe controlled for when humour is studied, as individuals habitually differ in how easily amusement is elicited, how likely or unlikely they are to engage in humour and understand humour, and which type of humour they prefer (see Ruch and Hofmann 2012). Moreover, there are individuals who systematically misperceive humour (i.e. individuals with a fear of being laughed at (gelotophobia); see Ruch et al. 2014, for a review) and these individuals may hugely distort the results when undetected. Thus, humour-related traits that may override effects of bilingualism or multilingualism should be controlled for (or studied in their own right). Similar influences were shown for humour-related moods that may impact on the elicitation of amusement.

Moreover, studying humour in all its natural forms will not be possible (e.g. spontaneously occurring humour in interactions will be difficult to study) – but this is a problem of most disciplines studying humour (see also López and Vaid 2017, for thoughts on the psycholinguistic study of humour). Also, the interaction of laughter and humour should be studied more closely. It is clear that laughter should not be used as a single indicator for humour comprehension and/or appreciation, as laughter may stem from other elicitors than amusement. Future studies may investigate more closely what emotions humorous stimuli elicit, whether it is pure amusement, or maybe emotion blends (i.e. amusement and disgust in toilet humour, or amusement and contempt in ridicule; or amusement and relief), or other emotions altogether, including schadenfreude, as it was shown that these emotions or emotion blends may also go along with laughter (see Hofmann et al. 2017), yet they may go along with different neural responses. Concerning the *sense of humour*, studies are needed to help determine whether there is a basic humour of the person or whether the humour of a bilingual or multilingual person varies with his or her spoken language. How the representation, detection, and translation of humour with a human brain is accomplished still remains largely mysterious, but – as this chapter shows – a beginning has been made.

Acknowledgements

The authors would like to thank the editor for his guidance and the foundation Humour Hilft Heilen for their ongoing support of studies on humour. We are thankful to Richard Bruntsch and the two anonymous reviewers for their comments on a prior version of this manuscript.

NOTES

1 The willingness/ability to switch into a playful mode, the liking of humorous interactions, and the threshold for amusement to be elicited, is subject to individual differences in the sense of humour and the temperamental basis of the sense of humour, as well as being dependent on mood (e.g. state cheerfulness, seriousness, and being in a bad mood; for an overview, see Ruch and Hofmann 2012).

2 Several researchers have formulated guidelines for the translation of humour (e.g. Attardo 2002; Zabalbeascoa 2005), yet those rules may be more of interest to offline translations and unlikely to be applied in 'normal human encounters'.

REFERENCES

Akimoto, Y., Sugiura, M., Yomogida, Y. et al. (2014). Irony comprehension: social conceptual knowledge and emotional response. *Human Brain Mapping* 35 (4): 1167–1178.

Amir, O., Biederman, I., Wang, Z., and Xu, X. (2013). Ha ha! Versus aha! A direct comparison of humor to non-humorous insight for determining the neural correlates of mirth. *Cerebral Cortex* 25 (5): 1405–1413.

Antonini, R. (2005). The perception of subtitled humor in Italy. *Humor: International Journal of Humor Research* 18 (2): 209–225.

Apter, M.J. (ed.) (2001). *Motivational Styles in Everyday Life: A Guide to Reversal Theory.* Washington, DC: American Psychological Association.

Arroyo, S., Lesser, R.P., Gordon, B. et al. (1993). Mirth, laughter and gelastic seizures. *Brain* 116: 575–780.

Attardo, S. (1997). The semantic foundations of cognitive theories of humor. *Humor: International Journal of Humor Research* 10 (4): 395–420.

Attardo, S. (2002). Translation and humour: An approach based on the general theory of verbal humour (GTVH). *The Translator* 8 (2): 173–194.

Attardo, S. (2008). A primer for the linguistics of humor. In: *The Primer in Humor Research* (ed. V. Raskin), 101–156. Berlin, Germany: Mouton de Gruyter.

Attardo, S. (ed.) (2017). *The Routledge Handbook of Language and Humor.* London, UK: Taylor & Francis.

Attardo, S. and Raskin, V. (1991). Script theory revis(it)ed: joke similarity and joke representation model. *Humor: International Journal of Humor Research* 4: 293–347.

Azim, E., Mobbs, D., Jo, B. et al. (2005). Sex differences in brain activation elicited by humor. *PNAS* 102: 16496–16501.

Bartolo, A., Benuzzi, F., Nocetti, L. et al. (2006). Humor comprehension and appreciation: an fMRI study. *Journal of Cognitive Science* 18: 1789–1798.

Bell, N.D. (2005). Exploring L2 language play as an aid to SLL: a case study of humor in NS–NNS interaction. *Applied Linguistics* 26 (2): 192–218.

Bell, N.D. (2007). How native and non-native English speakers adapt to humor in intercultural interaction. *Humor: International Journal of Humor Research* 20 (1): 27–48.

Bell, N.D. (2015). *We Are Not Amused: Failed Humor in Interaction.* Berlin, Germany: Mouton de Gruyter.

Berns, G.S. (2004). Something funny happened to reward. *Trends in Cognitive Science* 8 (5): 193–194.

Burgdorf, J., Panksepp, J., and Moskal, J.R. (2011). Frequency–modulated 50kHz ultrasonic vocalizations: a tool for uncovering the molecular substrates of positive affect. *Neuroscience & Biobehavioral Reviews* 35: 1831–1836.

Campbell, D.W., Wallace, M.G., Modirrousta, M. et al. (2015). The neural basis of humour comprehension and humour appreciation: the roles of the temporoparietal junction and superior frontal gyrus. *Neuropsychologia* 79 (A): 10–20.

Caruana, F. (2017). The integration of emotional expression and experience: a pragmatist review of recent evidence from brain stimulation. *Emotion Review* 2017: 1–12.

Chan, Y.-C. (2016). Neural correlates of sex/gender differences in humor processing for different joke types. *Frontiers in Psychology* 7: 536.

Chan, Y.-C., Chou, T.-L., Chen, H.-C., and Liang, K.-C. (2012). Segregating the comprehension and elaboration processing of verbal jokes: an fMRI study. *NeuroImage* 61: 899–906.

Chan, Y.-C. and Lavallee, J. (2015). Temporo parietal and frontal-parietal lobe contributions to theory of mind and executive control: an fMRI study of verbal jokes. *Frontiers in Psychology* 6: 1285.

Chapman, A.J. and Foot, H.C. (eds.) (1992). *Humor and Laughter: Theory, Research, and Applications*, 2nde. New York, NY: Transaction Publishers.

Chiaro, D. (2003). The implications of the quality of translated verbally expressed humour and the success of big screen comedy. *Antares* VI: 14–20.

Chiaro, D. (2007). The effect of translation on humour response. In: *Doubts and Directions in Translation Studies* (ed. Y. Gambier, M. Shlesinger and R. Stolze), 137–152. London, UK: John Benjamins.

Chiaro, D. (2008). Verbally expressed humor and translation. In: *The Primer in Humor Research* (ed. V. Raskin), 569–608. Berlin, Germany: Mouton de Gruyter.

Chiaro, D. (2009). Cultural divide or unifying factor? In: *Humor in Interaction* (ed. N.R. Norrick and D. Chiaro), 211–232. London, UK: John Benjamins.

Coulson, S. and Kutas, M. (2001). Getting it: human event-related brain response to jokes in good and poor comprehenders. *Neuroscience Letters* 316: 71–74.

Coulson, S. and Lovett, C. (2004). Handedness, hemispheric asymmetries and joke comprehension. *Cognitive Brain Research* 19: 275–288.

Coulson, S. and Williams, R. (2005). Hemispheric asymmetries and joke comprehension. *Neuropsychologia* 43: 128–141.

Davies, C. (2005). European ethnic scripts and the translation and switching of jokes. *Humor: International Journal of Humor Research* 18: 147–160.

Davies, C. (1998). *Jokes and their Relation to Society*. Berlin, Germany: Mouton de Gruyter.

Davies, C.E. (2003). How English-learners joke with native speakers: an interactional sociolinguistic perspective on humor as collaborative discourse across cultures. *Journal of Pragmatics* 35 (9): 1361–1385.

Davila-Ross, M., Owren, M.J., and Zimmermann, E. (2009). Reconstructing the evolution of laughter in great apes and humans. *Current Biology* 19: 1106–1111.

Darwin, C. (1872). *The Expression of the Emotions in Man and Animals*. London, UK: John Murray.

Denton, J. and Ciampi, D. (2012). A new development in audiovisual translation studies: focus on target audience perception. *LEA-Lingue e letterature d'Oriente e d'Occidente* 1: 399–422.

Du, X., Qin, Y., Tu, S. et al. (2013). Differentiation of stages in joke comprehension: evidence from an ERP study. *International Journal of Psychology* 48: 149–157.

Eysenck, H.-J. (1942). The appreciation of humor: an experimental and theoretical study. *British Journal of Psychology* 32: 295–309.

Fish, D., Gloor, P., Quesney, F., and Olivier, A. (1993). Clinical responses to electrical brain stimulation of the temporal and frontal lobes in patients with epilepsy. Pathophysiological implications. *Brain* 116: 394–414.

Fried, I., Wilson, C.L., MacDonald, K.A., and Behnke, E.J. (1998). Electric current stimulated laughter. *Nature* 391: 650–650.

García-Pentón, L., Fernández Garcia, Y., Costello, B. et al. (2016). The neuroanatomy of bilingualism: how to turn a hazy view into the full picture. *Language, Cognition and Neuroscience* 31: 303–327.

Goel, V. and Dolan, R.J. (2001). The functional anatomy of humor: segregating cognitive and affective components. *Nature Neuroscience* 4: 237–238.

Grundy, J., Anderson, J., and Bialystok, E. (2017). Neural correlates of cognitive processing in monolinguals and bilinguals. *Annals of the New York Academy of Sciences* 1396: 183–201.

Hempelmann, C.F. and Ruch, W. (2005). 3 WD meets GTVH: breaking the ground for interdisciplinary humor research. *Humor: International Journal of Humor Research* 18 (4): 353–387.

Hofmann, J., Platt, T., and Ruch, W. (2017). Laughter and smiling in 16 positive emotions. *IEEE Transactions on Affective Computing*, Special Issue on Laughter 8: doi:10.1109/TAFFC.2017.2737000.

Hofmann, J. and Ruch, W. (2017). Laughter. In: *Oxford Bibliographies Online* (ed. D.S. Dunn). New York, NY: Oxford University Press.

Hughes, C.E., Shaunessy, E.S., Brice, A.R. et al. (2006). Code switching among bilingual and limited English proficient students: possible indicators of giftedness. *Journal for the Education of the Gifted* 30 (1): 7–28.

Iwase, M., Ouchi, Y., Okada, H. et al. (2001). Neural substrates of human facial expression of pleasant emotion induced by comic films: a pet study. *NeuroImage* 17: 758–768.

Keith-Spiegel, P. (1972). Early conceptions of humor: varieties and issues. In: *The Psychology of Humor* (ed. J.H. Goldstein and P.E. McGhee), 4–42. New York, NY: Academic Press.

Kersten, K. (2009). Humor and interlanguage in a bilingual elementary school setting. In: *Humor in Interaction* (ed. N.R. Norrick and D. Chiaro), 187–210. London, UK: John Benjamins.

Kohn, N., Kellermann, T., Gur, R.C. et al. (2011). Gender differences in the neural correlates of humor processing: implications for different processing modes. *Neuropsychologia* 49: 888–897.

Laurian, A.M. and Nilsen, D.L.F. (1989). Humor and translation. Special issue of. *META: Journal des Traducteurs* 34 (1).

Leeds, C. (1992). Bilingual Anglo-French humor: an analysis of the potential for humor based on the interlocking of the two languages. *Humor: International Journal of Humor Research* 5: 129–148.

López, B.G. and Vaid, J. (2017). Psycholinguistic approaches to humor. In: *Routledge Handbook of Language and Humor* (ed. S. Attardo), 267–281. London, UK: Taylor & Francis.

Low, P.A. (2011). Translating jokes and puns. *Perspectives* 19: 59–70. doi:10.1080/0907676X.2010.493219.

Maitland, S. (ed.) (2017). *What Is Cultural Translation?* London, UK: Bloomsbury Academic.

Marinkovic, K., Baldwin, S., Courtney, M.G. et al. (2010). Right hemisphere has the last laugh: neural dynamics of joke appreciation. *Cognitive, Affective & Behavioral Neuroscience* 11: 113–130.

Martin, R.A. (2007). *The Psychology of Humor*. New York, NY: Academic Press.

Mayerhofer, B. and Schacht, A. (2015). From incoherence to mirth: neuro-cognitive processing of garden-path jokes. *Frontiers in Psychology* 6: 550.

McGhee, P.E. (1979). *Humor: Its Origin and Development*. San Francisco, CA: W. H. Freeman and Company.

McGhee, P.E. and Goldstein, J. (1972). *The Psychology of Humor*. New York, NY: Academic Press.

McGhee, P.E., Ruch, W., and Hehl, F.J. (1990). A personality-based model of humor development during adulthood. *Humor: International Journal of Humor Research* 3: 119–146.

Mensen, A., Poryazova, R., Schwartz, S., and Khatami, R. (2014). Humor as reward mechanism: event-related potentials in the healthy and diseased brain. *PLoS One* 9: e85978.

Mobbs, D., Greicius, M.D., Abdel-Azim, E. et al. (2003). Humor modulates the mesolimbic reward centers. *Neuron* 40: 1041–1048.

Nilsen, D. (1989). Better than the original: humorous translations that succeed. *Meta* 34: 112–124.

Osaka, N. and Osaka, M. (2005). Striatal reward areas activated by implicit laughter induced by mimic words in humans: a functional magnetic resonance imaging study. *NeuroReport* 16: 1621–1624.

Panksepp, J. (1998). *Affective Neuroscience: The Foundations of Human and Animal Emotions*. Oxford, UK: Oxford University Press.

Panksepp, J. and Burgdorf, J. (2000). 50-kHz chirping (laughter?) in response to conditioned and unconditioned tickle-induced reward in rats: effects of social housing and genetic variables. *Behavioural Brain Research* 115: 25–38.

Panksepp, J. and Burgdorf, J. (2003). 'Laughing' rats and the evolutionary antecedents of human joy? *Physiology and Behavior* 79: 533–547.

Papousek, I., Ruch, W., Rominger, C. et al. (2017). The use of bright and dark types of humor is rooted in the brain. *Scientific Reports* 7: 42967.

Papousek, I., Schulter, G., Rominger, C. et al. (2013). The fear of other person's laughter: poor neuronal protection against social signals of anger and aggression. *Psychiatry Research* 235: 61–68.

Pavlenko, A. (2000). New approaches to concepts in bilingual memory. *Bilingualism: Language and Cognition* 2: 209–230.

Pavlicek, M. and Pöchhacker, F. (2002). Humour in simultaneous conference interpreting. *The Translator* 8: 385–400.

Pliatsikas, C., DeLuca, V., Moschopoulou, E., and Saddy, J. (2017). Immersive bilingualism reshapes the core of the brain. *Brain Structure and Function* 222: 1785–1795.

Pomerantz, A. and Bell, N.D. (2007). Learning to play, playing to learn: FL learners as multicompetent language users. *Applied Linguistics* 28: 556–578.

Pulvermüller, F. (2013). How neurons make meaning: brain mechanisms for embodied and abstract-symbolic semantics. *Trends in Cognitive Sciences* 17: 458–470.

Ramaraju, S., Izzidien, A., & Roula, M. (2015). The detection and classification of the mental state elicited by humor from EEG patterns. *Conference Proceedings: 37th Annual International Conference of the IEEE Engineering in Medicine and Biology Society*, 1472–1475.

Raskin, V. (1985). *Semantic Mechanisms of Humor*. Dordrecht, The Netherlands: D. Reidel.

Raskin, V. (ed.) (2008). *The Primer of Humor Research*, vol. 8. Berlin, Germany: Walter de Gruyter.

Rodden, F. A. (2018). The neurology and psychiatry of humor, smiling and laughter: A tribute to Paul McGhee. Part I. Introduction and clinical studies. *Humor*, 31(2), 339–371.

Rodden, F. A. (2018). The neurology and psychiatry of humor, smiling, and laughter: a tribute to Paul McGhee Part II. neurological studies and brain imaging. *Humor*, 31(2), 373–399.

Roeckelein, J.E. (2002). *The Psychology of Humor: A Reference Guide and Annotated Bibliography*. Westport, UK: Greenwood Press.

Rothbart, M. (1973). Laughter in young children. *Psychological Bulletin* 80: 247–256.

Ruch, W. (1981). Humor and personality: a three-modal analysis. *Zeitschrift für Differentielle und Diagnostische Psychologie* 2: 253–273.

Ruch, W. (1992). Assessment of appreciation of humor: studies with the 3 WD humor test. In: *Advances in Personality Assessment*, vol. 9 (ed. J.N. Butcher and C.D. Spielberger), 27–75. Hillsdale, NJ: Erlbaum.

Ruch, W. (2001). The perception of humor. In: *Emotion, Qualia, and Consciousness* (ed. A.W. Kaszniak), 410–425. Tokyo, Japan: Word Scientific Publisher.

Ruch, W. (2004). Humor. In: *Character Strengths and Virtues: A Handbook and Classification* (ed. C.P. Peterson and M.E.P. Seligman), 583–598. Washington, DC: American Psychological Association.

Ruch, W. (2007). Foreword and overview– sense of of humor: a new look at an old concept. In: *The Sense of Humor: Explorations of a Personality Characteristic* (ed. W. Ruch), 3–14. New York, NY: Mouton de Gruyter.

Ruch, W. (2008). The psychology of humor. In: *A Primer of Humor* (ed. V. Raskin), 17–100. Berlin, Germany: Mouton de Gruyter.

Ruch, W., Attardo, S., and Raskin, V. (1993). Toward an empirical verification of the general theory of verbal humor. *Humor: International Journal of Humor Research* 6 (2): 123–136.

Ruch, W. and Hofmann, J. (2012). A temperament approach to humor. In: *Humor and Health Promotion* (ed. P. Gremigni), 79—113. Hauppauge, NY: Nova Science Publishers.

Ruch, W. and Hofmann, J. (2013). Humor. In: *Oxford Bibliographies Online* (ed. D.S. Dunn). New York, NY: Oxford University Press.

Ruch, W., Hofmann, J., Platt, T., and Proyer, R.T. (2014). The state-of-the art in gelotophobia research: a review and some theoretical extensions. *Humor: International Journal of Humor Research* 27: 23–45. doi:10.1515/humor-2013-0046.

Ruch, W. and Rath, S. (1993). The nature of humor appreciation: toward an integration of perception of stimulus properties and affective experience. *Humor: International Journal of Humor Research* 6: 363–384.

Samson, A., Hempelmann, C., Huber, O., and Zysset, S. (2009). Neural substrates of incongruity-resolution and nonsense humor. *Neuropsychologia* 47: 1023–1033.

Samson, A., Zysset, S., and Huber, O. (2008). Cognitive humor processing: different logical mechanisms in nonverbal cartoons: an fMRI study. *Social Neuroscience* 3: 125–140.

Scheiner, E., Hammerschmidt, K., Jürgens, U., and Zwirner, P. (2002). Acoustic analyses of developmental changes and emotional expression in the preverbal vocalizations of infants. *Journal of Voice* 16: 509–529.

Schmidt-Hidding, W. (1963). *Europäische Schlüsselwörter. Band I. Humor und Witz* [European keywords Vol. I. Humor and jokes]. Munich, Germany: Huber.

Schmitt, J., Janszky, J., Woermann, F. et al. (2006). Laughter and the mesial and lateral premotor cortex. *Epilepsy and Behavior* 8: 773–775.

Shibata, M., Terasawa, Y., and Umeda, S. (2014). Integration of cognitive and affective networks in humor comprehension. *Neuropsychologia* 65: 137–145.

Sperli, F., Spinelli, L., Pollo, C., and Seeck, M. (2006). Contralateral smile and laughter, but no mirth, induced by electrical stimulation of the cingulate cortex. *Epilepsia* 47: 440–443.

Sroufe, L.A. and Waters, E. (1976). The ontogenesis of smiling and laughter: a perspective on the organization of development in infancy. *Psychological Review* 83: 173–189.

Suls, J.M. (1972). A two-stage model for the appreciation of jokes and cartoons: an information-processing analysis. In: *The Psychology of Humor: Theoretical Perspectives and Empirical Issues* (ed. J.H. Goldstein and P.E. McGhee), 81–100. New York, NY: Academic Press.

Vaid, J. (2000). New approaches to conceptual representations in bilingual memory: the case for studying humor interpretation. *Bilingualism: Language and Cognition* 3: 28–30.

Vaid, J., Hull, R., Heredia, R. et al. (2003). Getting a joke: the time course of meaning activation in verbal humor. *Journal of Pragmatics* 35: 1432–1449.

Vaid, J. (2006). Joking across languages: perspectives on humor, emotion and bilingualism. In: *Bilingual Minds: Emotional Experience, Expression and Representation* (ed. A. Pavlenko), 152–182. Clevedon, UK: Multilingual Matters.

van Buren, T. (1961). Sensory, motor and autonomic effects of mesial temporal stimulation in man. *Journal of Neurosurgery* 18: 273–288.

Van Hooff, J.A.R.A.M. (1972). A comparative approach to the phylogeny of laughter and smiling. In: *Non-verbal Communication* (ed. R.A. Hinde), 209–240. Cambridge, UK: Cambridge University Press.

Vandaele, J. (Ed.). (2002). Translating humor (Special issue). *The Translator*, 8.

Vettin, J. and Todt, D. (2005). Human laughter, social play, and play vocalizations of non-human primates: an evolutionary approach. *Behavior* 142: 217–240.

Vrticka, P., Neely, M., Walter, E. et al. (2013). Sex differences during humor appreciation in child sibling-pairs. *Social Neuroscience* 8: 291–304.

Wild, B., Rodden, F.A., Rapp, A. et al. (2006). Humor and smiling: cortical regions selective for cognitive, affective and volitional components. *Neurology* 66: 887–893.

Zabalbeascoa, P. (2005). Humor and translation – an interdiscipline. *Humor: International Journal of Humor Research* 18: 186–207.

Part III   Functions
and Processes

17 Multilingualism and Metacognitive Processing

PETER BRIGHT, JULIA OUZIA, AND ROBERTO FILIPPI

1. Introduction

Modern understanding of the term 'metacognition' encompasses two levels of processing: a lower level *awareness* or *knowledge* of one's own thoughts and a higher level *regulation* or *control* of our thinking (Paris and Winograd 1990; Fernandez-Duque et al. 2000; McCormick 2003; Fleming et al. 2014). For example, we may be aware that our thinking about someone or something is unfair or biased, but this awareness does not necessarily result in an attempt to regulate and correct that thinking. Cognition and metacognition are, therefore, mutually dependent functions that serve our ability to understand and interact with our environment in an adaptive, goal-directed manner. Without effective metacognition, we would not be able to adjust our cognitive strategies towards goal-achievement because we would lack insight into ongoing levels of performance (Gollwitzer and Schaal 1998). This notion of metacognition both as a comparatively passive (knowledge/awareness) function and an active (regulatory/control) function is problematic because it renders the term rather inseparable from the well-established concept of executive function: both are concerned with top-down monitoring and control of cognition in the service of ongoing goal-directed behaviour. In order to progress theory on metacognitive processing, therefore, it is crucial to determine the conceptual relationship between the two, not least because advances in theoretical knowledge are unlikely to be realized by replacing one (arguably) poorly defined concept with another.

The claim that multilanguage acquisition drives advantages in executive function is currently an issue of vigorous debate in the literature. To the extent that the claim is true, we might predict a multilingual benefit in metacognitive ability commensurate with the level of overlap between the two concepts. Until recently, however, the literature has been largely silent on this issue and the only study to date that has directly and empirically compared metacognitive performance in multilingual and monolingual participants indicates a multilingual disadvantag*e* (Folke et al. 2016).

The Handbook of the Neuroscience of Multilingualism, First Edition. Edited by John W. Schwieter.
© 2019 John Wiley & Sons Ltd. Published 2019 by John Wiley & Sons Ltd.

In this chapter, we critically review evidence for overlap and divergence in the neural and psychological basis of metacognition and executive function, and consider the implications for current debate on the proposed cognitive advantages associated with the acquisition and regular use of two or more languages.

2. Metacognitive Regulation and Executive Function: Conceptual Overlap

Executive function refers to higher-order cognitive processes that together allow us to function effectively in complex environments (Baddeley and Hitch 1974; Norman and Shallice 1986; Baddeley 2017). Terms such as attentional control, inhibition, planning, sustained/selective attention, task switching, and error monitoring can all be grouped under the conceptual umbrella of executive function. The widely accepted fundamental assumptions of this executive or attentional system are (i) limited capacity (our resources are limited in the sense that we can only process a portion of the information available to us at one time; Broadbent 1958; Desimone and Duncan 1995), and (ii) selectivity (optimally, selection of information into the system is biased towards that information currently relevant to ongoing goals; Norman and Shallice 1986). Of course, an environment can be complex not only in terms of physical characteristics and visual 'noise' with different objects competing for our attention. It can also exert complexity across other input modalities, in which, for example, auditory information from multiple sources can compete for our attention. One crucial issue is whether the limited capacity and goal-directed selectivity of our executive system can somehow be enhanced or otherwise benefit from the continuous, intense competition associated with multilingual environments. Although this issue has received attention in the literature, those cognitive mechanisms most influenced by the enhanced competition associated with multilingual contexts remains unresolved. Here, we focus on the relationship between executive function and metacognitive abilities and consider whether and how multilingualism might impact upon them.

The concept of metacognition originated in the early 1970s with the work of John Flavell and others (e.g. Flavell 1971; Butterfield et al. 1973; Brown 1975). The early focus was on metamemory, which Flavell described as the knowledge and monitoring of memory storage and retrieval. When used effectively, metamemory skills ensure optimized memory performance via the regulatory process of calibrating subjective estimates of performance against actual performance, with the latter modified accordingly (Roebers 2017). Thus, the notions of active control as well as more passive monitoring were incorporated, with the broader concept of metacognition formally introduced by Flavell (1979) to encompass the monitoring and control of all declarative cognitive activity. If we accept that executive function and metacognitive regulation serve the coordination of domain-general cognitive activity in the service of goal-relevant behaviour, it is reasonable to challenge the assumption that they are dissociable functions.

Figure 1 Illustration of the conceptual overlap of metacognition and the executive system. Source: Adapted from Fernandez-Duque et al. (2000).

On a theoretical level, it has been argued that metacognition operates on two interacting levels – the object level (bottom-up cognitive monitoring) and the meta-level (top-down control; Nelson and Narens 1990, 1994). Fernandez-Duque et al. (2000) raised similarities in this conceptualization with Norman and Shallice's (1986) model of executive function, in which a higher-level supervisory attentional mechanism monitors and manipulates automatic processes (action schemas), thereby exhibiting control over them. According to this view, the meta-level and executive systems operate comparably in the way that they modulate information via top-down control (see Figure 1).

Intuitively, therefore, if metacognition is closely associated with mechanisms of cognitive control (i.e. selective attention, response inhibition, task switching, etc.), we would expect to observe metacognitive advantages alongside benefits in executive function. Empirical evidence has supported this argument of a positive correlation between measures of metacognitive and executive function, demonstrating that inhibitory control correlates with the ability to accurately apply rules in decision-making tasks (Souchay and Isingrini 2004; Del Missier et al. 2010). It has also been claimed that attentional shifting between task constraints supports the ability to provide consistent/accurate performance judgements (Del Missier et al. 2010) as well as prospective confidence judgements (feeling-of-knowing) on a metamemory task involving memorizing cue-target word combinations (Boduroglu et al. 2014).

There are clearly important similarities between modern conceptualizations of metacognition and executive function, both referring to systems that serve our ability to think and behave in a purposive, goal-directed manner when confronted with complex situations in which multiple responses are available to us at any one time (i.e. in our typical daily lives). Orchestration of our activities relies not only on our ability to overturn strong goal-irrelevant response tendencies (e.g. overturning the urge to go back to sleep after the early morning alarm has sounded) or to sustain our attention on a difficult task through to completion, but also to understand the relationship between our actions and objective performance towards our goals. Without accurate monitoring of our ongoing learning and performance (i.e. in situations in which our subjective judgement of our cognitive performance is poorly calibrated with actual performance), we are unable to optimally regulate our knowledge or strategies in the service of goal attainment.

3.   Metacognitive Regulation and Executive Function: Neuroanatomical Considerations

Aside from evaluating the theoretical functional overlap between metacognitive regulation and executive function, Fernandez-Duque et al. (2000) provided initial pointers with regards to the discussion of the neuroanatomical overlap in the two systems. The fundamental tenet of their argument is that mechanisms associated with high-level cognitive control, such as conflict resolution, monitoring, and emotional regulation, are a necessary element of successful metacognition. To a far greater extent, executive function has attracted a concerted effort by neuropsychologists and cognitive neuroscientists to identify and tease apart the underlying neural mechanisms that together serve our ability to produce complex goal-directed behaviour. This literature identifies widely distributed networks serving high-level cognitive control, with fundamental importance attributed to regions of the frontal lobes. Broadly speaking, both metacognitive and executive control serve the optimization of performance and decision-making in novel and uncertain situations (e.g. Woolgar et al. 2010; Fedorenko et al. 2013), and it therefore seems intuitive to predict overlap in their neural signatures. In interpreting this literature, however, caution must be applied due to the challenge of disentangling activity associated with lower-order processing (i.e. task-specific perceptual information, memory content, etc.) from the higher-order or 'meta' processes that are the target of investigation (i.e. the active monitoring and regulation of performance; Roebers 2017). Thus, we need to distinguish between activity associated with passive *awareness* of our level of performance on a given task and that associated with *regulation* and *modulation* of our behaviour in the service of improving our performance.

A broad network of frontal areas, including the anterior cingulate cortex and supplementary motor area, the orbitofrontal cortex, the dorsolateral prefrontal cortex, as well as non-frontal cortical and subcortical structures are implicated in high-level executive control (Fernandez-Duque et al. 2000). The role of frontoparietal connectivity in the service of executive attentional control and psychometric intelligence is also an important theme in the literature.

In comparison with executive function, our knowledge of the neuroanatomical basis of metacognition is limited, and while earlier studies provide broad consistency with neuropsychological studies of executive function (i.e. a sensitivity to frontal lesions), they lack anatomical specificity. Janowsky et al. (1989) reported metamemory impairments in patients with frontal lesions (but intact metamemory in temporal lobe amnesic patients). They also identified metamemory impairment in patients with Korsakoff syndrome (in which frontal involvement is typically implicated in addition to diencephalic disturbance), consistent with an important role of the frontal lobes in metamemory judgements (see also Parkin et al. 1988; Modirrousta and Fellows 2008). A review of neuropsychological studies provides confirmatory evidence that the neural correlates of metamemory are distinct from fundamental primary memory encoding and retrieval processes, and are served, in large part, by the frontal lobes (Pannu and Kaszniak 2005). Consistent with this proposed dissociation in the networks serving meta- and primary memory functions a recent transcranial direct current stimulation (tDCS) study, in which the dorsolateral prefrontal cortex was positively stimulated, indicated reduced confidence ratings in a visual short-term memory task (in comparison to a sham condition) despite intact trial accuracy (Bona and Silvanto 2014).

Recent developments in structural imaging technology have provided the opportunity for more accurate lesion delineation and quantification, and a more precise characterization of frontal involvement in metamemory is emerging. Our ability to monitor and estimate our performance on memory tasks can be separated into prospective and retrospective judgements. The former is characterized as 'feeling of knowing' how well we will perform on some future task, while the latter refers to judgement of how well we have performed on a completed task or trial. In a structural magnetic resonance imaging (MRI) study of abstinent alcoholics and neurologically healthy controls, Le Berre et al. (2016) found evidence for a structure–function double dissociation in which volumetric measurements of the insular cortex selectively covaried with feeling-of-knowing judgements and frontolimbic volumes selectively covaried with retrospective confidence judgements (consistent with the literature on metamemory impairment in Korsakoff syndrome, as outlined above). Other studies indicate that prospective judgements may be supported by medial prefrontal cortex structures, whilst retrospective judgements depend on lateral prefrontal cortex (Fleming and Dolan 2012). For example, although lesions in the ventromedial prefrontal cortex are associated with decreased feeling-of-knowing accuracy, the accuracy of confidence judgements is preserved (Schnyer et al. 2004). Conversely, retrospective confidence judgements may be impaired following rostrolateral prefrontal lesions while actual task execution performance is unaffected (Fleming and Dolan 2012). The anterior cingulate cortex has also been identified as an important part of a distributed metacognition network, with functional neuroimaging and electrophysiological evidence for a key role in prediction and monitoring of task performance, and detection of novelty or conflict (e.g. Metcalfe et al. 2012; Do Lam et al. 2012; for reviews see Roebers 2017; Schwartz and Metcalfe 2017).

Together, these findings provide a potential neurocognitive link between metacognition, executive function and the cognitive advantages reported in bilinguals, particularly in light of the previously suggested involvement of the prefrontal and anterior cingulate cortices in bilingual language control (Abutalebi and Green 2007). Nevertheless, research evaluating the relationship between attentional set shifting (on the trail making test; Reitan 1958), which is considered to be an important executive control mechanism, and metacognitive efficiency did not detect a relationship between the two functions (Palmer et al. 2014). Given the argument that the multilingual advantage may derive in large part from the demands associated with regular switching between two or more languages (e.g. Bialystok et al. 2012; Wiseheart et al. 2016), such findings raise the possibility that advantages may well be observed in aspects of executive function, but leave metacognitive abilities unaffected, or even disadvantaged (as has been reported by Folke et al. 2016, discussed in Section 5). Other authors have, however, reported links between metacognitive control over task performance and other components of executive function, such as response inhibition (Souchay and Isingrini 2004; Pansky et al. 2009). Problems in definition and separability amongst concepts/labels such as task/set shifting, response inhibition, sustained attention, updating etc., continue to obfuscate the ability to clearly and selectively identify *specific* mechanisms of executive function, and the relationship between each of these mechanisms and metacognitive functions therefore remains uncertain. Overall, whilst the considerations outlined above certainly support the notion of a conceptual and neuroanatomical overlap of metacognitive regulation and executive function, future research systematically addressing this issue is required in order to clarify the degree of dissociability amongst these systems. There is likely to be unity and diversity within and between executive and metacognitive operations and the current lack of clarity represents a significant obstacle to progress.

4. Description and Critique of Methods Used for Measuring Metacognition

Metacognitive awareness is often quantified via confidence judgements in relation to a specific measure of cognitive task performance, such as accuracy or error rate (e.g. De Martino et al. 2013; Schwartz and Díaz 2014; Yeung and Summerfield 2014). This degree of fit between an individual's estimate of performance and actual performance is commonly referred to as *calibration* (Keren 1991; Nelson 1996; Bol and Hacker 2012), and allows identification of overconfidence and underconfidence in actual performance. It is considered a fundamental requirement for the successful regulation of ongoing purposive behaviour, because it is only through accurate calibration of actual against self-estimated performance that optimal efficiency in performance can be achieved. Consistent with this claim, for example, a large body of evidence indicates that actual achievement in educational settings is highly sensitive to calibration accuracy (for a review, see Bol and Hacker 2012).

Historically, then, the relationship between confidence and actual performance has been evaluated via a calibration curve (Hart 1967), in which the objectivity or precision of an individual's monitoring of task performance is plotted against actual performance (Nelson 1984; Kornell et al. 2007; Roebers 2017). However, the limitations of this approach have been challenged on the basis of failure to distinguish between an individual's metacognitive sensitivity (or accuracy) and their bias towards over- or underconfidence; the former tends to be task specific but the latter is typically more of a stable or enduring tendency (Fleming and Lau 2014; Fleming et al. 2016), although it has been shown to interact in some cases with straightforwardness of the task (Gigerenzer et al. 1991; Fleming et al. 2016). Cortical stimulation studies have provided confirmatory evidence that confidence judgements and objective accuracy can be interrupted independently of each other and are therefore served by (at least partially) independent networks (Fleming et al. 2015; Rahnev et al. 2016).

Signal detection theory can be applied to isolate metacognitive sensitivity from confidence bias because it provides separate measures for each of these components. However, studies have shown that the sensitivity index (or d') remains confounded by metacognitive bias, due to violation of distribution assumptions (e.g. Evans and Azzopardi 2007; Fleming and Lau 2014). In response to this problem, Maniscalco and Lau (2012, 2014) developed meta-d' which offers a more robust measure of metacognitive accuracy (e.g. Baird et al. 2013; Barrett et al. 2013) with metacognitive efficiency

(MRatio) computed as the fraction between meta-d′ and d′ (Fleming and Lau 2014) such that an MRatio of 1 would denote confidence ratings that perfectly reflect first order accuracy. The advantages of this approach have been recognized in the literature and meta-d′ has already been exploited in a range of studies (e.g. Charles et al. 2013; Lee et al. 2013; McCurdy et al. 2013; Folke et al. 2016).

The literature has not, to date, provided consistent evidence for a stable metacognitive ability within participants and across tasks, possibly due to the considerable empirical difficulty of quantifying performance-confidence relationships, which is inherently more subjective and challenging than quantification of task performance itself (Fleming and Dolan 2012). Authors typically, therefore, recommend very large numbers of trials to elicit reliable and consistent estimation of metacognitive performance (see also Kelemen et al. 2000). Nevertheless, individual variability in metacognitive sensitivity across trials and between tasks may be of interest in its own right, and we do not currently know whether stability vs. lability covaries with other variables of theoretical interest, such as psychometric intelligence or mechanisms associated with multilingualism.

5. Metacognition and Multilingualism

Despite the large body of literature focused on the impact of multilanguage learning on executive function, and the suggestions concerning a conceptual and neural overlap between cognitive control and metacognition, very few studies have explicitly addressed the possibility that multilingualism may impact metacognitive processing. Research on bilingualism indicates that bilingual university students have better insight into their reading comprehension abilities compared with their monolingual peers (Ransdell et al. 2006), that children who learned a second language in a formal context display an increased awareness and use of communicational strategies (Le Pichon Vorstman et al. 2009; Le Pichon et al. 2010), and that proficient multilingualism is associated with the flexible use of grammatical (Kemp 2009) as well as reading strategies (García et al. 1998).

However, to date, there is only one report in the published literature evaluating general metacognitive abilities in multilingual individuals that are not related to their linguistic performance. Folke et al. (2016) administered a two-alternative-forced-choice task across two experiments. First, participants had to determine which one of two circles contained the most number of dots (first order task). Following on from this, participants had to state their confidence in their choice (second order task; see Figure 2 for an illustration). In one experiment, in which the first order task was not time-constrained, bilinguals were found to respond faster than monolinguals but were significantly less metacognitively efficient, with efficiency mathematically determined by the difference between expected and observed performance (as detailed in the Section 4). The findings suggested that in comparison with monolinguals, bilinguals tended to feel less confident in trials they completed correctly and more confident in trials where their performance was incorrect. In a second experiment in which the response time window for the first order task was experimentally constrained,

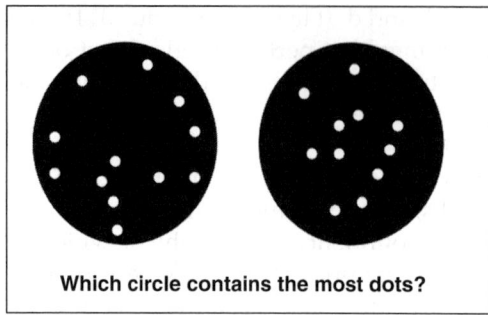

Which circle contains the most dots?

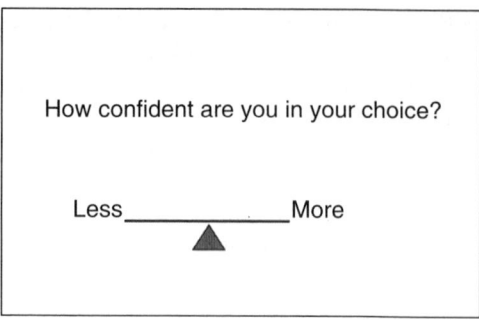

How confident are you in your choice?

Less_____More

Figure 2   Two-alternative-forced-choice task employed by Folke et al. (2016).

the bilingual metacognitive disadvantage was replicated despite statistically equal response times in the two groups. Therefore, the metacognitive disadvantage in the bilingual group appeared robust, and unrelated to group differences in visual discrimination speed and/or reaction times.

This finding of a metacognitive disadvantage is seemingly at odds with the literature. For example, in their systematic review and meta-analysis of 63 studies of the cognitive correlates of bilingualism, Adesope et al. (2010) identified a reliable association between bilingualism and meta*linguistic* awareness. To resolve this apparent discrepancy, it is instructive to consider the relationship between metacognitive and metalinguistic processing. Although, intuitively, 'meta' abilities may be considered a family of interrelated functions, metacognitive, and metalinguistic awareness may be served – at least in part – by distinct cognitive mechanisms. Thus, while metalinguistic skills have traditionally been understood as a subset of metacognition abilities, evidence that they share precisely the same underpinning mechanisms is an assumption arguably lacking in a solid evidence base (for discussion of this theme, see Van Kleeck 1982). This argument mirrors the uncertain relationship between metacognition and executive function. The relationship between executive function and psychometric intelligence is also fiercely debated in the literature (e.g. Deary 2001; Kane and Engle 2002; Duncan et al. 2008; Carroll and Bright 2016) and the relationship of the 'bilingual advantage' to psychometric intelligence is similarly complicated (e.g. Peal and Lambert 1962; Bialystok and Martin 2004; for a review see Barac et al. 2014). At a conceptual level, these labels given to mechanisms of high-level cognition are very difficult to tease apart, to the extent that we cannot confidently argue that they either refer to dissociable cognitive systems or otherwise identify the extent to which component processes are shared across these 'systems'.

Despite these issues, evidence that there may be metacognitive disadvantages associated with multilingualism and that these coexist with advantages in executive function and metalinguistic ability indicates some level of dissociability amongst the proposed systems – and that we might also observe disparity in the underlying neural signatures. In a recent review, Roebers (2017) sought to bring together the literature on metacognition and executive function and build a unifying framework to promote theoretical understanding of cognitive self-regulation. The extent to which the process of becoming multilingual may facilitate or interfere with such domain general self-regulatory skills is an important question yet the literature to-date focuses on executive function and neglects metacognition, possibly because the two research fields are rooted in quite different research traditions. Consolidating executive function and metacognition research and applying this to specific contexts such as multilingual cognition, therefore, constitutes an important avenue for future inquiry.

6. Executive Function, Metacognition and Multilingualism

In Abutalebi and Green's (2007) model of language processing in bilinguals, both languages are served by a common distributed network, but multilanguage contexts place additional demands on left prefrontal cortex, anterior cingulate cortex, parietal cortex and left caudate nucleus, all regions associated with inhibitory control (e.g. Bunge et al. 2002; Durston et al. 2002; Wiecki and Frank 2013) and metacognition (e.g. Chua et al. 2006; Molenberghs et al. 2016). In the Molenberghs et al. functional MRI study, increased confidence in performance on a social and cognitive reading test was associated with increased caudate activity but *lower* metacognitive accuracy. Evidence that the left and/or right caudate nucleus (along with other subcortical structures including the thalamus and putamen) is significantly larger in bilinguals than monolinguals (Zou et al. 2012; Burgaleta et al. 2016) is consistent with a striatal gating system that controls the neocortical recruitment serving language processing and control (e.g. Stocco et al. 2014). It also raises the possibility, though speculative, that emotion regulation via the striatum may differentially affect the relationship between metacognitive judgement of task performance and actual performance in multilinguals and monolinguals. Whatever the nature of the cortical and subcortical developmental effects of multilanguage acquisition, converging evidence is emerging that multilingualism impacts on a broad, distributed network of brain regions, including both primary language and domain general/nonverbal processing sites involved in emotional regulation and higher-level cognitive control. Within this system, structures associated with executive attention and the resolution of response competition (particularly the frontoparietal network and anterior cingulate cortex) are most likely to be the primary hub driving structural change in the rest of the system in the service of operating more effectively in complex multilingual environments.

7. Conclusion

Over the past decade, the bilingual advantage has broadened from a relatively narrow focus on inhibitory control to incorporate theory of mind (Rubio-Fernández and Glucksberg 2012), rule-based learning (Stocco and Prat 2014), reactive and proactive control (Morales et al. 2013), visuo-spatial memory (Kerrigan et al. 2017) and controlling verbal interference in speech comprehension (Filippi et al. 2012; Filippi et al. 2015). The claim that the process of becoming bilingual may impact on metacognitive abilities adds to this broadening focus, but may also benefit the resolution of ongoing debate about the selectivity of cognitive changes associated with multilingualism. One obstacle to progress in this regard is the tendency in the literature to treat executive function as a unitary frontoparietal system recruited in response to all manner of cognitive demand, yet performance across so-called executive function tasks is highly variable and inter-correlations are sometimes low (Miyake et al. 2000). In their large-scale recent review, Friedman and Miyake (2017) break executive function down into three intermediate components: inhibition, updating in working memory, and task-set shifting. This characterization is not meant to imply three unitary and dissociable constructs serving broader executive control, but it does provide a framework for a finer-grained analysis of the 'family resemblance' of impairment typically observed in patients with dysexecutive syndrome following frontal lobe damage, and the types of error produced by neurologically healthy participants on complex tasks. In our view, frameworks such as that proposed by Friedman and Miyake (2017) provide a sensible basis for identifying fractionation of processes associated with executive control.

In conclusion, in the only laboratory study of metacognitive effects associated with multilingualism published to date, a metacognitive disadvantage was observed (Folke et al. 2016), and this raises a theoretically compelling argument for future research not only to replicate and further characterize this effect, but potentially to exploit it in order to better characterize unity and diversity in the relationships amongst components of executive function and metacognition. Further work is needed to confirm the strength and direction of any changes in metacognitive abilities associated with multilanguage acquisition. Possible avenues for future research include exploration of early vs. late language acquisition, the language in which tasks were conducted (e.g. native/primary vs. secondary language) and the particular characteristics of individuals' bilingual experience, all of which are potentially important moderating factors in this relationship.

Acknowledgement

This work was supported by the Leverhulme Trust UK (RPG-2015-024) and the British Academy (SG162171).

REFERENCES

Abutalebi, J. and Green, D. (2007). Bilingual language production: the neurocognition of language representation and control. *Journal of Neurolinguistics* 20 (3): 242–275.

Adesope, O.O., Lavin, T., Thompson, T., and Ungerleider, C. (2010). A systematic review and meta-analysis of the cognitive correlates of bilingualism. *Review of Educational Research* 80 (2): 207–245.

Baddeley, A.D. (2017). Modularity, working memory and language acquisition. *Second Language Research* 33: 299–311.

Baddeley, A.D. and Hitch, G. (1974). Working memory. *Psychology of Learning and Motivation* 8: 47–89.

Baird, B., Smallwood, J., Gorgolewski, K.J., and Margulies, D.S. (2013). Medial and lateral networks in anterior prefrontal cortex support metacognitive ability for memory and perception. *Journal of Neuroscience* 33 (42): 16657–16665.

Barac, R., Bialystok, E., Castro, D.C., and Sanchez, M. (2014). The cognitive development of young dual language learners: a critical review. *Early Childhood Research Quarterly* 29 (4): 699–714.

Barrett, A.B., Dienes, Z., and Seth, A.K. (2013). Measures of metacognition on signal-detection theoretic models. *Psychological Methods* 18 (4): 535.

Bialystok, E., Craik, F.I., and Luk, G. (2012). Bilingualism: consequences for mind and brain. *Trends in Cognitive Sciences* 16 (4): 240–250.

Bialystok, E. and Martin, M.M. (2004). Attention and inhibition in bilingual children: evidence from the dimensional change card sort task. *Developmental Science* 7 (3): 325–339.

Boduroglu, A., Tekcan, A.İ., and Kapucu, A. (2014). The relationship between executive functions, episodic feeling-of-knowing and confidence judgements. *Journal of Cognitive Psychology* 26 (3): 333–345.

Bol, L. and Hacker, D.J. (2012). Calibration research: where do we go from here? *Frontiers in Psychology* 3: 1–6.

Bona, S. and Silvanto, J. (2014). Accuracy and confidence of visual short-term memory do not go hand-in-hand: behavioral and neural dissociations. *PLoS One* 9 (3): e90808.

Broadbent, D. (1958). *Perception and Communication*. London, UK: Pergamon Press.

Brown, A.L. (1975). The development of memory: knowing about knowing, and knowing how to know. In: *Advances in Child Development and Behavior*, vol. 10 (ed. H.W. Reese), 103–152. New York, NY: Academic Press.

Bunge, S.A., Dudukovic, N.M., Thomason, M.E. et al. (2002). Immature frontal lobe contributions to cognitive control in children: evidence from fMRI. *Neuron* 33 (2): 301–311.

Burgaleta, M., Sanjuán, A., Ventura-Campos, N. et al. (2016). Bilingualism at the core of the brain. Structural differences between bilinguals and monolinguals revealed by subcortical shape analysis. *NeuroImage* 125: 437–445.

Butterfield, E.C., Wambold, C., and Belmont, J.M. (1973). On the theory and practice of improving short-term memory. *American Journal of Mental Deficiency* 77: 654–669.

Carroll, E.L. and Bright, P. (2016). Involvement of Spearman's g in conceptualisation versus execution of complex tasks. *Acta Psychologica* 170: 112–126.

Charles, L., Van Opstal, F., Marti, S., and Dehaene, S. (2013). Distinct brain mechanisms for conscious versus subliminal error detection. *NeuroImage* 73: 80–94.

Chua, E.F., Schacter, D.L., Rand-Giovannetti, E., and Sperling, R.A. (2006). Understanding metamemory: neural correlates of the cognitive process and subjective level of confidence in recognition memory. *NeuroImage* 29 (4): 1150–1160.

Deary, I.J. (2001). Human intelligence differences: towards a combined experimental-differential approach. *Trends in Cognitive Sciences* 5 (4): 164–170.

De Martino, B., Fleming, S.M., Garrett, N., and Dolan, R.J. (2013). Confidence in value-based choice. *Nature Neuroscience* 16 (1): 105–110.

Del Missier, F., Mäntylä, T., and Bruine de Bruin, W. (2010). Executive functions in decision making: an individual differences approach. *Thinking and Reasoning* 16 (2): 69–97.

Desimone, R. and Duncan, J. (1995). Neural mechanisms of selective visual attention. *Annual Review of Neuroscience* 18 (1): 193–222.

Do Lam, A.T., Axmacher, N., Fell, J. et al. (2012). Monitoring the mind: the neurocognitive correlates of metamemory. *PLoS One* 7 (1): e30009.

Duncan, J., Parr, A., Woolgar, A. et al. (2008). Goal neglect and Spearman's g: competing parts of a complex task. *Journal of Experimental Psychology: General* 137 (1): 131.

Durston, S., Thomas, K.M., Yang, Y. et al. (2002). A neural basis for the development of inhibitory control. *Developmental Science* 5 (4): F9–F16.

Evans, S. and Azzopardi, P. (2007). Evaluation of a 'bias-free' measure of awareness. *Spatial Vision* 20 (1): 61–77.

Fedorenko, E., Duncan, J., and Kanwisher, N. (2013). Broad domain generality in focal regions of frontal and parietal cortex. *Proceedings of the National Academy of Sciences* 110 (41): 16616–16621.

Fernandez-Duque, D., Baird, J.A., and Posner, M.I. (2000). Executive attention and metacognitive regulation. *Consciousness and Cognition* 9 (2): 288–307.

Filippi, R., Leech, R., Thomas, M.S. et al. (2012). A bilingual advantage in controlling language interference during sentence comprehension. *Bilingualism: Language and Cognition* 15 (4): 858–872.

Filippi, R., Morris, J., Richardson, F.M. et al. (2015). Bilingual children show an advantage in controlling verbal interference during spoken language comprehension. *Bilingualism: Language and Cognition* 18 (3): 490–501.

Flavell, J.H. (1971). First discussant's comments: what is memory development the development of? *Human Development* 14: 272.

Flavell, J.H. (1979). Metacognition and cognitive monitoring: a new area of cognitive–developmental inquiry. *American Psychologist* 34 (10): 906.

Fleming, S.M. and Dolan, R.J. (2012). The neural basis of metacognitive ability. *Philosophical Transactions of the Royal Society of London, B Biological Sciences* 367: 1338–1349.

Fleming, S.M. and Lau, H.C. (2014). How to measure metacognition. *Frontiers in Human Neuroscience* 8: 443.

Fleming, S.M., Maniscalco, B., Ko, Y. et al. (2015). Action-specific disruption of perceptual confidence. *Psychological Science* 26 (1): 89–98.

Fleming, S.M., Massoni, S., Gajdos, T., and Vergnaud, J.C. (2016). Metacognition about the past and future: quantifying common and distinct influences on prospective and retrospective judgments of self-performance. *Neuroscience of Consciousness* 2016 (1): niw018.

Fleming, S.M., Ryu, J., Golfinos, J.G., and Blackmon, K.E. (2014). Domain-specific impairment in metacognitive accuracy following anterior prefrontal lesions. *Brain* 137 (10): 2811–2822.

Folke, T., Ouzia, J., Bright, P. et al. (2016). A bilingual disadvantage in metacognitive processing. *Cognition* 150: 119–132.

Friedman, N.P. and Miyake, A. (2017). Unity and diversity of executive functions: individual differences as a window on cognitive structure. *Cortex* 86: 186–204.

García, G.E., Jiménez, R.T., and Pearson, P.D. (1998). Metacognition, childhood bilingualism, and reading. In: *Metacognition in Educational Theory and Practice* (ed. D.J. Hacker, J. Dunlosky and A.C. Graesser), 193–219. Mahwah, NJ: Erlbaum.

Gigerenzer, G., Hoffrage, U., and Kleinbölting, H. (1991). Probabilistic mental models: a brunswikian theory of confidence. *Psychological Review* 98 (4): 506.

Gollwitzer, P.M. and Schaal, B. (1998). Metacognition in action: the importance of implementation intentions. *Personality and Social Psychology Review* 2 (2): 124–136.

Hart, J.T. (1967). Memory and the memory-monitoring process. *Journal of Verbal Learning and Verbal Behavior* 6: 685–691.

Janowsky, J.S., Shimamura, A.P., and Squire, L.R. (1989). Memory and metamemory: comparisons between patients with frontal lobe lesions and amnesic patients. *Psychobiology* 17 (1): 3–11.

Kane, M.J. and Engle, R.W. (2002). The role of prefrontal cortex in working-memory capacity, executive attention, and general fluid intelligence: an individual-differences perspective. *Psychonomic Bulletin & Review* 9 (4): 637–671.

Kelemen, W.L., Frost, P.J., and Weaver, C.A. (2000). Individual differences in metacognition: evidence against a general metacognitive ability. *Memory & Cognition* 28 (1): 92–107.

Kemp, C. (2009). Defining multilingualism. In: *The Exploration of Multilingualism: Development of Research on L3, Multilingualism and Multiple Language Acquisition*, vol. 6 (ed. L. Aronin and B. Hufeisen), 11–27. Amsterdam: John Benjamins.

Keren, G. (1991). Calibration and probability judgements: Conceptual and methodological issues. *Acta Psychologica* 77 (3): 217–273.

Kerrigan, L., Thomas, M.S., Bright, P., and Filippi, R. (2017). Evidence of an advantage in visuo-spatial memory for bilingual compared to monolingual speakers. *Bilingualism: Language and Cognition* 20 (3): 602–612.

Kornell, N., Son, L.K., and Terrace, H.S. (2007). Transfer of metacognitive skills and hint seeking in monkeys. *Psychological Science* 18 (1): 64–71.

Lee, T.G., Blumenfeld, R.S., and D'Esposito, M. (2013). Disruption of dorsolateral but not ventrolateral prefrontal cortex improves unconscious perceptual memories. *Journal of Neuroscience* 33: 13233–13237.

Le Berre, A.P., Müller-Oehring, E.M., Kwon, D. et al. (2016). Differential compromise of prospective and retrospective metamemory monitoring and their dissociable structural brain correlates. *Cortex* 81: 192–202.

Le Pichon, E., de Swart, H., Vorstman, J., and van den Bergh, H. (2010). Influence of the context of learning a language on the strategic competence of children. *International Journal of Bilingualism* 14 (4): 447–465.

Le Pichon Vorstman, E., de Swart, H., Ceginskas, V., and van den Bergh, H. (2009). Language learning experience in school context and metacognitive awareness of multilingual children. *International Journal of Multilingualism* 6 (3): 258–280.

Maniscalco, B. and Lau, H. (2012). A signal detection theoretic approach for estimating metacognitive sensitivity from confidence ratings. *Consciousness and Cognition* 21 (1): 422–430.

Maniscalco, B. and Lau, H. (2014). Signal detection theory analysis of type 1 and type 2 data: Meta-d′, response-specific meta-d′, and the unequal variance SDT model. In: *The Cognitive Neuroscience of Metacognition*, 25–66. Heidelberg, Germany: Springer Berlin Heidelberg.

McCormick, C.B. (2003). Metacognition and learning. In: *Handbook of Psychology*, vol. 7 (ed. W.M. Reynolds and G.E. Miller), 79–102. Hoboken, NJ: Wiley.

McCurdy, L.Y., Maniscalco, B., Metcalfe, J. et al. (2013). Anatomical coupling between distinct metacognitive systems for memory and visual perception. *Journal of Neuroscience* 33: 1897–1906.

Metcalfe, J., Butterfield, B., Habeck, C., and Stern, Y. (2012). Neural correlates of people's hypercorrection of their false beliefs. *Journal of Cognitive Neuroscience* 24 (7): 1571–1583.

Miyake, A., Friedman, N.P., Emerson, M.J. et al. (2000). The unity and diversity of executive functions and their contributions to complex "frontal lobe" tasks: a latent variable analysis. *Cognitive Psychology* 41 (1): 49–100.

Modirrousta, M. and Fellows, L.K. (2008). Medial prefrontal cortex plays a critical and selective role in 'feeling of knowing'metamemory judgments. *Neuropsychologia* 46 (12): 2958–2965.

Molenberghs, P., Trautwein, F.M., Böckler, A. et al. (2016). Neural correlates of metacognitive ability and of feeling confident: a large-scale fMRI study. *Social Cognitive and Affective Neuroscience* 11 (12): 1942–1951.

Morales, J., Gómez-Ariza, C.J., and Bajo, M.T. (2013). Dual mechanisms of cognitive control in bilinguals and monolinguals. *Journal of Cognitive Psychology* 25 (5): 531–546.

Nelson, T.O. (1984). A comparison of current measures of the accuracy of feeling-of-knowing predictions. *Psychological Bulletin* 95: 109–133.

Nelson, T.O. (1996). Consciousness and metacognition. *American Psychologist* 51 (2): 102.

Nelson, T.O. and Narens, L. (1990). Metamemory: a theoretical framework and new findings. *Psychology of Learning and Motivation* 26: 125–173.

Nelson, T.O. and Narens, L. (1994). Why investigate metacognition? In: *Metacognition: Knowing about Knowing* (ed. J. Metcalfe and A. Shimamura), 1–25. Cambridge, MA: Bradford Books.

Norman, D.A. and Shallice, T. (1986). Attention to action. In: *Consciousness and Self-Regulation*, 1–18. New York, NY: Springer US.

Palmer, E.C., David, A.S., and Fleming, S.M. (2014). Effects of age on metacognitive efficiency. *Consciousness and Cognition* 28: 151–160.

Pannu, J.K. and Kaszniak, A.W. (2005). Metamemory experiments in neurological populations: a review. *Neuropsychology Review* 15 (3): 105–130.

Pansky, A., Goldsmith, M., Koriat, A., and Pearlman-Avnion, S. (2009). Memory accuracy in old age: cognitive, metacognitive, and neurocognitive determinants. *European Journal of Cognitive Psychology* 21 (2–3): 303–329.

Parkin, A.J., Bell, W.P., and Leng, N.R. (1988). A study of metamemory in amnesic and normal adults. *Cortex* 24 (1): 143–148.

Paris, S.G. and Winograd, P. (1990). How metacognition can promote academic learning and instruction. In: *Dimensions of Thinking and Cognitive Instruction*, vol. 1 (ed. B.F. Jones and L. Idol), 15–51. Hillsdale, NJ: Erlbaum.

Peal, E. and Lambert, W.E. (1962). The relation of bilingualism to intelligence. *Psychological Monographs: General and Applied* 76 (27): 1–23.

Rahnev, D., Nee, D.E., Riddle, J. et al. (2016). Causal evidence for frontal cortex organization for perceptual decision making. *Proceedings of the National Academy of Sciences* 113 (21): 6059–6064.

Ransdell, S., Barbier, M.L., and Niit, T. (2006). Metacognitions about language skill and working memory among monolingual and bilingual college students: when does multilingualism matter? *International Journal of Bilingual Education and Bilingualism* 9 (6): 728–741.

Reitan, R.M. (1958). Validity of the trail making test as an indicator of organic brain damage. *Perceptual and Motor Skills* 8 (3): 271–276.

Roebers, C.M. (2017). Executive function and metacognition: towards a unifying framework of cognitive self-regulation. *Developmental Review* 45: 31–51.

Rubio-Fernández, P. and Glucksberg, S. (2012). Reasoning about other people's beliefs: bilinguals have an advantage. *Journal of Experimental Psychology: Learning, Memory, and Cognition* 38 (1): 211.

Schnyer, D.M., Verfaellie, M., Alexander, M.P. et al. (2004). A role for right medial prefrontal cortex in accurate feeling-of-knowing judgments: evidence from patients with lesions to frontal cortex. *Neuropsychologia* 42 (7): 957–966.

Schwartz, B.L. and Díaz, F. (2014). Quantifying human metacognition for the neurosciences. In: *The Cognitive Neuroscience of Metacognition*, 9–23. Heidelburg, Germany: Springer Berlin Heidelberg.

Schwartz, B.L. and Metcalfe, J. (2017). Metamemory: An update of critical findings. In: *Reference Module in Neuroscience and Biobehavioral Psychology*. Amsterdam, Netherlands: Elsevier Press.

Souchay, C. and Isingrini, M. (2004). Age related differences in metacognitive control: role of executive functioning. *Brain and Cognition* 56 (1): 89–99.

Stocco, A. and Prat, C.S. (2014). Bilingualism trains specific brain circuits involved in flexible rule selection and application. *Brain and Language* 137: 50–61.

Stocco, A., Yamasaki, B., Natalenko, R., and Prat, C.S. (2014). Bilingual brain training: a neurobiological framework of how bilingual experience improves executive function. *International Journal of Bilingualism* 18 (1): 67–92.

Van Kleeck, A. (1982). The emergence of linguistic awareness: a cognitive framework. *Merrill-Palmer Quarterly* 28 (2): 237–265.

Wiecki, T.V. and Frank, M.J. (2013). A computational model of inhibitory control in frontal cortex and basal ganglia. *Psychological Review* 120 (2): 329.

Wiseheart, M., Viswanathan, M., and Bialystok, E. (2016). Flexibility in task switching by monolinguals and bilinguals. *Bilingualism: Language and Cognition* 19 (1): 141–146.

Woolgar, A., Parr, A., Cusack, R. et al. (2010). Fluid intelligence loss linked to restricted regions of damage within frontal and parietal cortex. *Proceedings of the National Academy of Sciences* 107 (33): 14899–14902.

Yeung, N. and Summerfield, C. (2014). Shared mechanisms for confidence judgements and error detection in human decision making. In: *The Cognitive Neuroscience of Metacognition*, 147–167. Heidelburg, Germany: Springer Berlin Heidelberg.

Zou, L., Ding, G., Abutalebi, J. et al. (2012). Structural plasticity of the left caudate in bimodal bilinguals. *Cortex* 48 (9): 1197–1206.

18 Factors Affecting Multilingual Processing

EDALAT SHEKARI AND JOHN W. SCHWIETER

1. Introduction

Although generally the same areas of the brain are activated during language use in skilled multilinguals (de Bot and Jaensch 2015) and late bi/multilinguals are able to demonstrate native-like performance, language processing can be affected by a number of individual and interacting factors. Individual differences in working memory (WM) capacity (WMC), proficiency level, the age of acquisition (AoA), exposure and language use, processing speed, language (psycho)typology, and language status are among the most influential factors that affect processing in multilinguals (Caffarra et al. 2015; Roberts 2012; Roncaglia-Denissen and Kotz 2016; Sagarra 2017; van den Noort et al. 2014; see also Chapter 23 in this volume). Some of these factors may not have a role in processing the first language (L1), but they critically influence language processing and representations in the second/third language (L2/L3). In most cases, processing depends on the interaction between factors (Pliatsikas and Marinis 2013) and one factor may attenuate or modulate the influence of other factors.

In this chapter, we review the relationship between WM resources, language processing, and performance along with other identified factors that affect multilingual processing: language proficiency, L2 age of acquisition, exposure and language use, processing speed, and language typology and language status. We also provide a discussion of implications for future work.

2. Working Memory Capacity

WM is a multicomponent, limited capacity system that is responsible for the temporary maintenance and simultaneous processing of the information (Baddeley 2003, 2007, 2012; Baddeley and Hitch 1974). WM can store limited amounts of information – three to five chunks (Cowan 2001; Unsworth and Engle 2007) – for immediate and accurate recall

The Handbook of the Neuroscience of Multilingualism, First Edition. Edited by John W. Schwieter.
© 2019 John Wiley & Sons Ltd. Published 2019 by John Wiley & Sons Ltd.

during a limited amount of time (i.e. less than a minute). Thus, due to these limitations, individual differences in WMC (i.e. the extent to which normal adults vary in their WMC; Linck et al. 2014) is considered a variant of the cognitive individual differences that are associated with performing various cognitive and linguistic tasks. WM has been demonstrated to have a role in L1 and L2 vocabulary learning, reading and listening comprehension, oral and written proficiency, learning L2 sounds, and L2 sentence processing (Daneman and Hannon 2007; Engle 2001; Felser and Roberts 2007; Gathercole and Baddeley 1993; Juffs and Harrington 2011; Martin and Ellis 2012; O'brien et al. 2006; Service 1992, 2012; Williams 2012; also see Linck et al. 2014 for a meta-analysis).

2.1. *Measuring Working Memory Capacity*

WMC is measured by both simple and complex span tasks. Simple span tasks such as word span, letter span, nonword span, and forward digit span mainly measure the storage function of WM, whereas complex span tasks simultaneously tap both the processing (executive control) and storage (short-term memory) functions of WM. A commonly-used complex span task is the reading span task (RST; Daneman and Carpenter 1980) or its spoken variant, the listening span task (Mackey et al. 2010). Participants are required to either read or listen to sequences of sentences, two to six in length (Juffs and Harrington 2011), and memorize the last word of each sentence for later recall. A grammaticality judgement task or semantic plausibility task is followed by each sentence to check the speed and accuracy. The latter task acts as a distractor and taxes both processing and storage functions of WM, causing the whole procedure to be more demanding on the cognitive system. The automated or computerized versions of the RST (Unsworth et al. 2009) are now widely used in place of the original paper- or card-based version.

The operation span task (OSpan; Turner and Engle 1989) is another technique that measures complex memory span. In the OSpan task, participants are asked to read aloud sets of mathematical operations while computing the outcome at the same time. They then verify whether the answer is correct or incorrect and memorize the letter or word displayed which they are asked to recall later. The sets vary from two or three to six or seven in length and the unrelated sets of letters or words must be recalled (verbally or non-verbally) in the original serial order. Following Unsworth et al. (2005) and Unsworth et al. (2009), some researchers have used the computerized version of the OSpan task, called the automated operation span. In this task, participants read aloud and solve simple math problems one at a time by pressing the 'Yes' button if the solution is correct or the 'No' button if it is incorrect. After each problem, participants read aloud a word. At the end of each set, they recall the words in the order in which they were presented. A three-item set (taken from Unsworth et al., 2005) would look like:

$$\text{is } (8/2) - 1 = 1? \text{ Bear}$$

$$\text{is } (6*1) + 2 = 8? \text{ Drill}$$

$$\text{is } (10 * 2) - 5 = 15? \text{ Job}$$

$$???$$

(p. 499)

The experimental math equations are simplistic and the items to be recalled are checked for frequency, number of characters, phonemes, syllables, imaginability, familiarity, and concreteness.

Like the RST, the OSpan task measures the simultaneous processing and storage of information. Although operations replaced the sentences in the RST, the task demands were largely unchanged (Conway et al. 2005). One advantage of the OSpan task over the RST is that it does not require the knowledge of language and, thus, lessens the demand on comprehension (Juffs and Harrington 2011). The OSpan may avoid confounding the relationship between the RST and language proficiency (Lu 2015). Conway et al. (2005) suggest that replacing the words to be recalled with letters can further reduce the dependence on language. In addition to the OSpan task, the backward digit span (Kormos and Sáfár 2008), in which participants are required to recall presented sets of digits in reverse order, can decrease the effect of language. Unlike simple measures of WM, complex span tasks such as the RST and OSpan task push WM storage to the limit in the face of processing demands to engage executive attention processes (Conway et al. 2005), thus making the task more demanding on the cognitive system. Reading sentences aloud in the RST or solving mathematical operations and recalling words in the OSpan task can further burden the WM resources, make the tasks more demanding, and prevent rehearsal. Both tasks are reliable and valid measures of individual differences in WMC and are highly correlated with other linguistically-demanding tasks such as reading comprehension. Furthermore, automated versions of complex span tasks allow the experimenters to collect the data related to the accuracy and speed of processing.

2.2.   *Language Effects in Multilinguals*

So far, theoretical accounts have not considered separate WM components for the additional language(s) a bilingual has acquired. Some studies suggest that there are no differences in WMC in L1 and L2, which means that WMC is language independent (Harrington and Sawyer 1992; Osaka and Osaka 1992; Osaka et al. 1993). However, other studies (Coughlin and Tremblay 2013; Service et al. 2002; Shekari and Service 2017a; van den Noort et al. 2006) found that bi/multilinguals exhibit larger WMC in their dominant language and that their L2/L3 WMC is affected by L2/L3 proficiency level. For example, the findings of the study by Service et al. (2002) revealed that lower proficiency in L2 consumes the L2 learners' internal resources, resulting in lower reading span scores in less-skilled bilinguals. Van den Noort et al. (2006) tested a group of L1 Dutch, L2 German, and L3 Norwegian multilinguals using simple and complex memory span tasks. The results of the study revealed differences in performance in all three languages. Participants had larger functional WMC in the L1, followed by the L2, then L3. Thus, WM resources in less-skilled bilinguals can be affected by presenting the input in a non-dominant language. In other words, the cognitive internal resources interact with L2/L3 language proficiency. Because language learning, development, and processing are dynamic processes (de Bot 2012; de Bot et al. 2007; Lowie and de Bot et al. 2015) and can be improved by experience with the target language over time, WMC in L2/L3 may reach the level of L1 as the result of mastery in L2/L3 proficiency.

2.3. Effects on Language Processing

Individual differences in WMC influence language processing and performance in L1, L2, and L3. A number of studies have found that there is a relationship between WMC and language processing, with an advantage exhibited by individuals with a higher WMC in terms of: sentence comprehension; resolving syntactic ambiguity; integrating pragmatic, lexical-semantic, and syntactic information for efficient processing; and being sensitive to (morpho)syntactic violations (Dai 2015; Dussias and Piñar 2010; Farmer et al. 2017; Havik et al. 2009; Hopp 2014; Just et al. 1996; Kim and Christianson 2017; Mackey et al. 2010; Medina et al. 2017; Sagarra and Herschensohn 2010; Shekari and Service 2017a; Williams 2006).

There is still debate on the relationship between WMC and L2 syntactic processing. Some studies (Dussias and Piñar 2010; Havik et al. 2009; McDonald 2006, 2008; Reichle et al. 2016; Sagarra and Herschensohn 2010) suggest that individuals with a higher WMC perform better than those with a lower WMC regarding syntactic processing. In contrast, other studies found no significant relationship between individual differences in WMC and (online) syntactic processing (Caplan and Waters 2005; Coughlin and Tremblay 2013; Felser and Roberts 2007; Waters and Caplan 2002). The debates led to two different approaches to memory for syntactic processing. The separate sentence interpretation resource (SSIR) hypothesis (Caplan and Waters 1999) considers a distinct specialized verbal working memory system for syntactic processing, whereas the single resources (SR) model (Just and Carpenter 1992) considers unitary WM resources for performing all verbal tasks. Caplan and Waters (1999) presented evidence from various sources on the relationship between individual differences in WM and efficiency of syntactic processing, memory load, and syntactic processing among three groups including: patients with poor short-term memory and WM, patients with aphasia and various brain lesions, and healthy participants. Their study supported the notion that there is a specialization in the verbal WM system for syntactic processing which is neither affected by WMC nor the external load and does not differ between participants with a higher or lower WMC.

Coughlin and Tremblay (2013) examined the role of proficiency and WMC in processing short- and long-distance number agreement dependencies between object clitics and their antecedents in French by moderately and highly proficient English-French bilinguals. The results revealed that although both groups showed sensitivity to agreement violations in the offline acceptability judgement task, only highly-proficient bilinguals showed more sensitivity to number agreement violations in the online self-paced reading task. Highly proficient bilinguals had lower WM scores in L2 than in L1 and there was a weak relationship between L2 performance and L2 WMC. The researchers argued that proficiency and WMC modulate sensitivity to agreement morphology in sentence processing.

In two self-paced reading experiments, Kim and Christianson (2017) investigated the effects of WMC on processing globally ambiguous relative clauses among proficient Korean-English bilinguals. They examined whether the effects of WMC on processing strategies patterned differently across the L1 and L2. The target sentences contained a complex noun phrase (NP1 – of – NP2) and a modifying relative clause (RC). In English, the RC follows the complex noun phrase, NP1 – of – NP2 – RC, and English native speakers generally have a preference for attaching the RC low to the NP2. In contrast, in Korean, a head-final language, the RC precedes the complex noun phrase, RC – NP1 – uy – NP2,[1] and native Korean speakers resolve the ambiguity by attaching the RC high to the NP1. Kim and Christianson assessed participants' WMC using the RST in the L1. The results revealed that participants employed appropriate processing strategies to disambiguate the target sentences in L1 and L2. WMC was found to be a factor that affected ambiguity resolution in L1 and L2. However, only skilled bilinguals with a larger WMC were sensitive to the potential RC ambiguity and could retain both interpretations in WM to resolve the ambiguity. This was consistent with the predictions of the capacity constrained parsing model (MacDonald et al. 1992), namely that an increase in WMC led to longer reading times in the critical region.

In another study, Dussias and Piñar (2010) investigated the processing of long-distance *wh*-extraction (e.g. Who$_i$ did the police know t_i killed the pedestrian?) in a grammaticality judgement task. They tested a group of proficient late Chinese-English bilinguals whose L1 did not have an overt *wh*-movement. They used Waters and Caplan's (1996) version of the RST to measure subjects' WMC and examined if there was a correlation with L2 sentence processing. The results revealed that the reading patterns of the bilinguals with a higher WMC were similar to those of native speakers of English (especially those with a greater WMC). This suggested that these bilinguals had access to the same plausibility information and employed it the same as English monolinguals. On the other hand, the lower-WMC L2 group failed to attend to and employ the lexical-semantic information during L2 sentence comprehension the same as the higher-WMC L2 group and English monolinguals. Overall, their results revealed that L2 sentence processing requires adequate internal resources to access and integrate different sources of information.

Contrary to capacity-based approaches to L2 processing, Cunnings (2017) states that the difference in L1 and L2 processing can be related to the quality of representations in memory which includes memory encoding, storage, and retrieval operations. He argues that cue-based approaches to individual differences to L2 processing emphasize the quality of representation in memory while individual differences in WMC measures have a role in capacity-based approaches to L2 processing.

3.   Proficiency

The degree of proficiency in a non-native language can affect language processing and performance in bi/multilinguals. Roberts (2012) notes that processing input in the L2 can put a strain on the processing system, particularly in less-proficient L2 learners. Unlike L1 processing that is an automatic process, processing input in a non-dominant language for less-proficient late L2 learners is indeed more demanding for the cognitive system and relies on more cognitive resources as shown in several studies (Green 1998; Linck et al. 2014; Meschyan and Hernandez 2006; Perani and Abutalebi 2005). While having greater WM resources may result in more efficient processing, the extra load imposed by a non-dominant language or language complexity may cause processing deficiency, inaccurate language representation, and poor task performance among less-proficient L2 learners.

The degree of proficiency interacts with other variables such as WM resources and influences processing and task performance in L2/L3 (Coughlin and Tremblay 2013; Hummel 2009). An increase in proficiency can attenuate the burden imposed by a once-weaker language. In multilingual studies using neuroimaging techniques, L2/L3 learners with low proficiency levels showed additional brain activity, mostly in pre-frontal areas, in languages in which they were not fluent and activated fewer neural substrates for sentence and discourse level processing in the left temporal lobe (Briellmann et al. 2004; De Bleser et al. 2003; de Bot and Jaensch 2015; Perani and Abutalebi 2005; Perani et al. 1998). On the other hand, proficient L2/L3 learners are more efficient in processing, have more accurate representations and responses, and can demonstrate native-like processing (Bel et al. 2016; Keating 2017; Rossi et al. 2017; Shekari and Service 2016; Tanner et al. 2014; van Hell and Tokowicz 2010). The results from event-related potential (ERP) studies testing phonological, morphological, syntactic, and morphosyntactic processing have revealed that proficient bilinguals are able to display similar native-like ERP signatures in response to syntactic or morphosyntactic violations (Liang and Chen 2014; McLaughlin et al. 2010; White et al. 2017; also see van den Noort et al. 2014; van Hell and Tokowicz 2010, for analyses of some neuroimaging studies). Linck et al. (2015) state that the degree of proficiency in the L3 changes the amount of cross-language interactions between the three languages. For instance, L2 influences phonological processing in less-proficient L3 learners; however, the L2 effects are attenuated by the increase in L3 proficiency.

In a priming paradigm study, Liang and Chen (2014) compared the morphological processing mechanisms of highly-proficient and less-proficient Chinese-English bilinguals. The ERPs showed that proficient L2 learners exhibited priming effects in morphological conditions at 350–400 ms, 400–450 ms, and 500–550 ms while no such effects were observed for less-proficient L2 learners for any of these time conditions. They observed a stronger correlation between proficiency and the magnitude of ERP priming effect in morphological conditions than semantic and form conditions. They suggested that the decomposition of regular inflected primes (e.g. *walked* to *walk+ed*) left a trace in the episodic memory which facilitated the access of the target, '*walk*', hence leading to an attenuated N400 component. In contrast, less-proficient L2 learners showed no priming effect within the N400 range, suggesting no decomposition of the prime and no facilitation to access the target word. Their results are consistent with Ullman's (2004, 2005) declarative/procedural memory model, suggesting that the proficiency level of L2 learners is a dynamic process that can result in a change in L2 learners' word processing as they become more proficient.

4.   Age of Acquisition

The effect of L2/L3 age of acquisition (e.g. early vs. late bi/multilinguals) on language learning and processing has been widely studied (Archila-Suerte et al. 2015; Bloch et al. 2009; DeKeyser 2013, 2017; van den Noort et al. 2014; Roncaglia-Denissen and

Kotz 2016; Wattendorf and Festman 2008; Wattendorf et al. 2014). In most cases, L2 learners are divided into early and late groups and their performance on various language processing tasks is compared. Although proficiency and extensive experience with the target language are good predictors of language processing in multilinguals, morphosyntactic processing is affected by AoA when proficiency is matched (Sakai et al. 2009). AoA can also affect the cerebral representation of language. In an fMRI study, Bloch et al. (2009) investigated the effect of AoA on cerebral activation during language production in proficient multilinguals. The results of the study revealed that the age of L2 acquisition correlated with and modulated the variability of brain activation in all three languages, with low variability in early multilinguals and higher variability in late multilinguals. There was an increase in the individual variation of local cerebral activation in Broca's and Wernicke's areas in the later-acquired languages (regardless of typological differences between the acquired languages). In another fMRI study, Wattendorf et al. (2014) investigated the impact of early bilingualism on the organization of the cortical language network during sentence production in early multilinguals, who acquired the L2 before the age of three, and late multilinguals, who acquired L2 and L3 after the age of nine, respectively. Their findings revealed that brain areas commonly involved in sentence processing and bilingual language control were activated in both early and late multilinguals during the performance of the narrative task. However, the AoA influenced the subsequently learned languages irrespective of whether they had been acquired early or late. Their results showed regional differences in neural activity in both groups. While early multilinguals exhibited higher neural activity in prefrontal (and subcortical) areas that involve language and cognitive controls, higher neural activity was registered in the posterior superior temporal gyrus (pSTG) in late multilinguals. They propose that 'early learning of two languages has a pervasive effect on a neural network that is presumed to regulate language control in bilinguals at different processing levels, which include even subcortical structures' (p. 14).

There is a strong relationship between the onset of AoA and L2/L3 phonological processing. In an fMRI study using the pre-attentive listening paradigm, Archila-Suerte et al. (2015) investigated the effect of L2 AoA, socioeducational status (SES), and L2 proficiency on L2 phonological processing among a group of Spanish-English bilinguals. The results showed that although early and late bilinguals with similar SES had similar performance in speech production, AoA was the main factor that affected the neural processing of L2 speech sounds in brain areas involving speech perception and executive processes. Bilinguals (both early and late) with lower SES showed increased activity in the inferior parietal lobule compared to bilinguals with higher SES suggesting that 'bilingualism can serve to counteract the negative effects of low socioeducational environments on cognition' (p. 46). When compared with monolingual English speakers, the results suggested that early L1 acquisition recruits expected temporal regions in speech perception processing, whereas early acquisition of two languages increases the engagement of prefrontal regions that are involved in WM to process L2 speech sounds. The study suggests that AoA has an important role in L2 phonological processing and interacts with other individual variables such as L2 proficiency and SES.

5.   Exposure and Language Use

Experience with L2/L3 input and frequency of its use can alter processing mechanisms, reduce L1 transfer effects, and ultimately result in native-like processing (Frenck-Mestre 2002; Kroll et al. 2015; Pliatsikas and Marinis 2013; Shekari and Service 2017b). In a self-paced reading study, Pliatsikas and Marinis investigated the ways in which L2 learners process regular and irregular English past tense inflexion at the sentence level by using real forms (regular/irregular) and forms that included violations (regularized/irregularized). They further examined whether the type of exposure in L2, namely naturalistic vs. classroom, would affect morphological processing in bilinguals. They recruited two groups of highly proficient Greek-English bilinguals: an L2 group with the naturalistic-exposure tested in the UK and another L2 group with the classroom-exposure tested in Greece. The distinction was made to investigate the possible effect of naturalistic L2 exposure on processing. The inflected and pseudo-inflected forms were embedded in one sentence each. The results revealed that L2 learners showed the same effects as native speakers of English in applying the rule-based decomposition mechanism by processing regularly inflected forms slower than irregular verbs. The type of L2 exposure did not affect the morphological decomposition and both groups showed similar effects, with small variations in processing regularized verbs. These results supported the notion that dual-system processing for inflectional morphology is accessible to both native speakers of English and L2 learners and that the morphological processing was largely affected by the overall amount of exposure to L2 input. The researchers argue that the effect of L2 exposure on morphological decomposition was not modulated by proficiency since they controlled for the proficiency level and AoA for both L2 groups. Their findings are consistent with the predictions of Ullman's (2004, 2005) declarative/procedural memory model that L2 grammar processing relies more on the declarative memory system in less-proficient L2 learners and may come to rely on the procedural memory system as L2 learners become more proficient. However, in some other studies (Muñoz 2008; Silva and Clahsen 2008), the effect of L2 exposure on L2 processing was modulated by other individual differences such as proficiency, AoA, cognitive resources, or a combination of them.

   Frequency- and usage-based approaches to language learning and processing can show the role of L2/L3 intensive experience on processing. According to probabilistic or exposure-based processing models of sentence processing, such as the tuning hypothesis (Mitchell et al. 1995), the accumulated exposure to L2 can account for the shift in processing strategies for L2 input. For example, during ambiguity resolution, the parser is assumed to tune its parsing preferences based on the overall distribution of forced disambiguation preferences it has encountered and resolved in the past. This may also make bilinguals abandon their L1 parsing mechanisms in favour of L2. Thus, the tuning hypothesis predicts that parsing preferences will change if the reader or listener has been exposed to an unusual preponderance of one ambiguity resolution type compared to another during some period prior to testing (Dussias and Sagarra 2007). The statistical and artificial grammar learning and the effects of training in which subjects are exposed to a specific structure before or between experiments (Morgan-Short et al. 2010; Wells et al. 2009) can further support the effects of language experience and use on multilingual processing (Kroll et al. 2015).

Babcock et al. (2012) examined the morphological processing of English past tense inflected forms among native English speakers and L1 Chinese or Spanish speakers learning L2 English. The researchers were interested in how storage/decomposition distinctions might be influenced by factors such as L2 proficiency, AoA, and length of residence/exposure to an L2. Their results revealed that processing inflected forms in the L2 did not always depend on the same mechanisms as in the L1. The critical factors of proficiency, length of residence/exposure, and AoA yielded less dependence on storage and more on composition while the native language of L2 learners had no effects on L2 morphological processing. Babcock et al. suggested that the computational mechanism underlying at least some aspects of language (e.g. rule-governed aspects of inflectional morphology) continue to be affected by the factors mentioned above. This confirms Ullman (2012) and Clahsen and Felser's (2006) predictions that increasing exposure or proficiency can lead to the native-like morphological decomposition, even in late L2 acquisition.

Further support for the role of exposure and experience with the target language come from statistical learning, priming effects, and training subjects on infrequent structures, for example, the increased exposure to more object relative clauses facilitates interpretation and processing speed (Brandt et al. 2017; Christiansen and Chater 2016; Deng et al. 2017; Hopp 2016; Morgan-Short et al. 2012; Wells et al. 2009). In Deng et al.'s study, participants who received short-/long-term training showed more sensitivity to the subject-verb agreement violations than a control group. In addition, the attrition of an L1 in an L2 environment (see Schmid 2016, for a review; see also Chapter 7 in this volume) and backward processing transfer in which L2 parsing strategies are applied to process L1 input (Dussias and Sagarra 2007) also show that exposure to the target language and the frequency of its use can alter the processing strategies in favour of the dominant language.

6.   Processing Speed

Another factor to consider in our discussion is processing speed. The effect of speed is more robust in studies where online (real-time) and speeded techniques are employed to test processing efficiency. Bilinguals usually exhibit longer reading/response times while processing input in L2/L3 or doing a task in their non-dominant language, especially in experiments that use online, time-locked, speeded, or time-stressed paradigms (Frenck-Mestre 2002; Hopp 2010). However, proficient L2 learners are able to demonstrate a native-like processing (Hopp 2010). Roberts (2012) believes that processing speed could relate to efficiency in several different processes undertaken during language comprehension including orthography/sound decoding, lexical access, integration of syntactic and other information, and the prediction or anticipation of up-and-coming input. Since a bilingual's languages are activated in parallel and are accessible simultaneously during production and comprehension (Kroll and Ma 2017; Kroll et al. 2006, 2012), bilinguals are usually slower than monolinguals when it comes to processing.

In a battery of four experiments, Hopp (2010) investigated the processing of case and subject-verb agreement in German under time pressure in speeded grammaticality judgements. Advanced and near-native learners of L2 German were tested who had either English, Russian, or Dutch as an L1. The participants viewed the stimuli at five speeds ranging from 250 ms (speed 1) to 71 ms per word (speed 5). The results showed that the subject-verb agreement was less affected by speed and was processed robustly by all L2 groups under increased processing load, with a significant decrease in accuracy in speed 5. However, only L1 Russian bilinguals performed at the level of German native speakers in processing the German case and advanced L2 groups, irrespective of L1, were not sensitive to case in speeded processing. Hopp argued that this could be caused either by L1 effects or greater computational strains of L2 processing, especially in less-proficient bilinguals. Furthermore, he suggests that for L2 learners, case marking under speeded conditions is subject to an earlier breakdown than for native speakers. Overall, the results of the study suggest that late L2 learners can reach the level of native-like processing in the domain of L2 inflexion. However, L1 and task demands can cause non-native-like processing, resulting in reduced processing efficiency and non-native-like L2 inflexion.

7. Language Typology and Language Status

The linguistic relatedness between a multilingual's languages can affect language processing and can manifest in lexicon organization, phonology, morphology, syntax, morphosyntax, and parsing mechanisms. Typologically-different or-similar language families, e.g. Korean/Chinese, Chinese/Japanese, and English, are often studied to investigate the effects of language distance on processing (Carrasco-Ortíz et al. 2017; Dai 2015; D'Anselmo et al. 2013; Jeong et al. 2007; Kim et al. 2016; Liu et al. 2017; Park-Johnson 2017; Tolentino and Tokowicz 2011). Liu et al'.s ERP study on the L2 production of inflected words in Korean L1 and Chinese L1 bilinguals revealed that morphosyntactic similarities between Korean and English modulated processing. While Korean bilinguals and native speakers of English followed the same processing mechanisms, Chinese bilinguals did not, indicating that morphosyntactic similarities had a modulatory effect on producing regular and irregular past tense verbs in English.

L3 processing can be positively or negatively influenced by L1 and L2 cross-linguistic similarities or differences. Llama, Cardoso, and Collins (2010) investigated whether language distance or L2 status phonologically influence L3 production. The researchers defined L2 status as 'any languages the speaker knows in addition to the L1' (p. 40). They tested two groups of trilingual learners: English-French-Spanish and French-English-Spanish. These participants produced Spanish words containing voiceless stops onset in stressed position. While these three languages share the same phonemes /p, t, k/, they differ in voice onset time (VOT). The voiceless stops are aspirated in the stressed onset position in English and have long lags but they lack aspiration in French and Spanish and have short lags. The results revealed that L2 status was the determining factor in selecting the source language for the aspiration feature of

L3 words. For the English-French-Spanish group, the suppression of aspiration in L2 resulted in L3 Spanish VOT values that were closer to those of L2. However, in the French-English-Spanish group, the production of L3 stops was influenced by L2 English and had longer VOT values than required in L3 Spanish.

The role of psychotypology in trilingual processing of cognates can further explain how different languages interact during multilingual processing. Szubko-Sitarek (2015) investigated the influence of psychotypology and L2 status on the representation of cognates in the multilingual lexicon. Using a lexical decision task, the researcher tested a group of Polish-English-German trilinguals. The stimuli included Polish-German cognates (e.g. *DACH*, meaning *roof* in Polish and German), English-German cognates that overlapped in orthography and meaning but were different in Polish (e.g. *FINGER*; Polish: *palec*), and German control words that were different from both their English and Polish translations (e.g. *GELD*; English: *money*; Polish: *pienia̜dze*). The lexical decision task was conducted in the weakest language and mean reaction times were calculated for the cognates with English, Polish, and the non-cognates. The results revealed that Polish-German (L1–L3) cognates and control words were processed faster than L2–L3 cognates. Szubko-Sitarek explained that trilinguals' extensive experience with German, more than English, modulated the effect of language psychotypology. The results are contrary to hypotheses which predict that psychotypology and the L2 status have a robust effect on transfer (Foote 2009).

8. Conclusion

Overall, language processing in proficient multilinguals seems to be qualitatively similar to that of native speakers. However, it is quantitatively affected by several individual variables or a combination of them. Individual differences in WMC, proficiency, AoA, exposure, processing speed, and language typology and status are the most studied factors in most psycholinguistic and neurolinguistic studies looking at multilingual processing. The factors that influence such processing interact with each other and the role of one factor may undergo significant changes as the result of the development/ shift in other variables. Future multilingual studies not only should consider and control for these factors, but also should contemplate how they might modulate the effects of each other. Since it is not always easy to recruit or match the participants according to the desired criteria or control for interfering variables, using mixed-effects regression models for data analyses are more appropriate. As proficiency and language processing are dynamic processes, longitudinal studies can best reveal any changes in processing mechanisms as the result of the shift in the individual differences that affect language processing in multilinguals.

NOTE

1   -uy is a genitive case marker in Korean.

REFERENCES

Archila-Suerte, P., Zevin, J., and Hernandez, A. (2015). The effect of age of acquisition, socioeducational status, and proficiency on the neural processing of second language speech sounds. *Brain and Language* 141: 35–49.

Babcock, L., Stowe, J., Maloof, C. et al. (2012). The storage and composition of inflected forms in adult-learned second language: a study of the influence of length of residence, age of arrival, sex and other factors. *Bilingualism: Language and Cognition* 15 (4): 820–840.

Baddeley, A. (2003). Working memory and language: an overview. *Journal of Communication Disorders* 36 (3): 189–208.

Baddeley, A. (2007). *Working Memory, Thought, and Action*. Oxford, UK: Oxford University Press.

Baddeley, A. (2012). Working memory: theories, models, and controversies. *Annual Review of Psychology* 63: 1–29.

Baddeley, A. and Hitch, G. (1974). Working memory. In: *The Psychology of Learning and Motivation* (ed. G. Bower), 47–89. New York, NY: Academic Press.

Bel, A., Sagarra, N., Comínguez, J., and García-Alcaraz, E. (2016). Transfer and proficiency effects in L2 processing of subject anaphora. *Lingua* 184: 134–159.

Bloch, C., Kaiser, A., Kuenzli, E. et al. (2009). The age of second language acquisition determines the variability in activation elicited by narration in three languages in Broca's and Wernicke's area. *Neuropsychologia* 47 (3): 625–633.

Brandt, S., Nitschke, S., and Kidd, E. (2017). Priming the comprehension of German object relative clauses. *Language Learning and Development* 13 (3): 241–261.

Briellmann, R., Saling, M., Connell, A. et al. (2004). A high-field functional MRI study of quadri-lingual subjects. *Brain and Language* 89 (3): 531–542.

Caffarra, S., Molinaro, N., Davidson, D., and Carreiras, M. (2015). Second language syntactic processing revealed through event-related potentials: an empirical review. *Neuroscience & Biobehavioral Reviews* 51: 31–47.

Caplan, D. and Waters, G.S. (1999). Verbal working memory and sentence comprehension. *Behavioral and Brain Sciences* 22 (1): 77–94.

Caplan, D. and Waters, G. (2005). The relationship between age, processing speed, working memory capacity, and language comprehension. *Memory* 13 (3–4): 403–413.

Carrasco-Ortíz, H., Herrera, A., Jackson-Maldonado, D. et al. (2017). The role of language similarity in processing second language morphosyntax: evidence from ERPs. *International Journal of Psychophysiology* 117: 91–110.

Christiansen, M. and Chater, N. (2016). *Creating Language: Integrating Evolution, Acquisition, and Processing*, 169–196. Cambridge, MA: MIT Press.

Clahsen, H. and Felser, C. (2006). Grammatical processing in language learners. *Applied PsychoLinguistics* 27 (1): 3–42.

Conway, A., Kane, M., Bunting, M. et al. (2005). Working memory span tasks: a methodological review and user's guide. *Psychonomic Bulletin & Review* 12 (5): 769–786.

Coughlin, C. and Tremblay, A. (2013). Proficiency and working memory based explanations for nonnative speakers' sensitivity to agreement in sentence processing. *Applied PsychoLinguistics* 34 (3): 615–646.

Cowan, N. (2001). The magical number 4 in short-term memory: a reconsideration of mental storage capacity. *Behavioral and Brain Sciences* 24: 87–185.

Cunnings, I. (2017). Parsing and working memory in bilingual sentence processing. *Bilingualism: Language and Cognition* 20 (4): 659–678.

Dai, Y. (2015). Working memory in L2 sentence processing: the case with relative clause attachment. In: *Working Memory in Second Language Acquisition and Processing* (ed. Z. Wen, M. Mota and A. McNeil), 105–124. Bristol, UK: Multilingual Matters.

Daneman, M. and Carpenter, P. (1980). Individual differences in working memory and reading. *Journal of Verbal Learning and Verbal Behavior* 19 (4): 450–466.

Daneman, M. and Hannon, B. (2007). What do working memory span tasks like reading span really measure? In: *The Cognitive Neuroscience of Working Memory* (ed. N. Osaka, R. Logie and M. D'Esposito), 21–42. Oxford, UK: Oxford University Press.

D'Anselmo, A., Reiterer, S., Zuccarini, F. et al. (2013). Hemispheric asymmetries in bilinguals: tongue similarity affects lateralization of second language. *Neuropsychologia* 51 (7): 1187–1194.

De Bleser, R., Dupont, P., Postler, J. et al. (2003). The organisation of the bilingual lexicon: a PET study. *Journal of Neurolinguistics* 16 (4): 439–456.

de Bot, K. (2012). Rethinking multilingual processing: from a static to a dynamic approach. In: *Third Language Acquisition in Adulthood* (ed. S. Flynn, J. Rothman and J. Cabrelli Amara), 79–93. Amsterdam, The Netherlands/Philadelphia, PA: Benjamins.

de Bot, K. and Jaensch, C. (2015). What is special about L3 processing? *Bilingualism: Language and Cognition* 18 (2): 130–144.

de Bot, K., Lowie, W., and Verspoor, M. (2007). A dynamic systems theory approach to second language acquisition. *Bilingualism: Language and Cognition* 10 (1): 7–21.

DeKeyser, R. (2013). Age effects in second language learning: stepping stones toward better understanding. *Language Learning* 63: 52–67.

DeKeyser, R. (2017). Age in learning and teaching grammar. In: *The TESOL Encyclopedia of English Language Teaching* (ed. J.I. Liontas), 1–6. Wiley-Blackwell.

Deng, T., Dunlap, S., and Chen, B. (2017). Effects of input training on second language syntactic representation entrenchment. *International Journal of Bilingualism* 21 (1): 3–20.

Dussias, P. and Piñar, P. (2010). Effects of reading span and plausibility in the reanalysis of wh-gaps by Chinese-English second language speakers. *Second Language Research* 26 (4): 443–472.

Dussias, P. and Sagarra, N. (2007). The effect of exposure on syntactic parsing in Spanish-English bilinguals. *Bilingualism: Language and Cognition* 10 (1): 101–116.

Engle, R. (2001). What is working memory capacity? In: *The Nature of Remembering: Essays in Honor of Robert G. Crowder* (ed. H. Roediger, J. Nairne, I. Neath and A. Suprenant), 297–314. Washington, DC: American Psychological Association.

Farmer, T., Fine, A., Misyak, J., and Christiansen, M. (2017). Reading span task performance, linguistic experience, and the processing of unexpected syntactic events. *The Quarterly Journal of Experimental Psychology* 70 (3): 413–433.

Felser, C. and Roberts, L. (2007). Processing wh-dependencies in a second language: a cross-modal priming study. *Second Language Research* 23 (1): 9–36.

Foote, R. (2009). Transfer in L3 acquisition: the role of typology. In: *Third Language Acquisition and Universal Grammar* (ed. Y. Leung), 89–114. Bristol, UK: Multilingual Matters.

Frenck-Mestre, C. (2002). An on-line look at sentence processing in the second language. *Advances in Psychology* 134: 217–236.

Gathercole, S. and Baddeley, A. (1993). Phonological working memory: a critical building block for reading development and vocabulary acquisition? *European Journal of Psychology of Education* 8 (3): 259–272.

Green, D. (1998). Mental control of the bilingual lexico-semantic system. *Bilingualism: Language and Cognition* 1 (2): 67–81.

Harrington, M. and Sawyer, M. (1992). L2 working memory capacity and L2 reading skill. *Studies in Second Language Acquisition* 14 (1): 25–38.

Havik, E., Roberts, L., Van Hout, R. et al. (2009). Processing subject-object ambiguities in the L2: a self-paced reading study with

German L2 learners of Dutch. *Language Learning* 59 (1): 73–112.

Hopp, H. (2010). Ultimate attainment in L2 inflection: performance similarities between non-native and native speakers. *Lingua* 120 (4): 901–931.

Hopp, H. (2014). Working memory effects in the L2 processing of ambiguous relative clauses. *Language Acquisition* 21: 250–278.

Hopp, H. (2016). Learning (not) to predict: grammatical gender processing in second language acquisition. *Second Language Research* 32 (2): 277–307.

Hummel, K. (2009). Aptitude, phonological memory, and second language proficiency in nonnovice adult learners. *Applied PsychoLinguistics* 30 (2): 225–249.

Jeong, H., Sugiura, M., Sassa, Y. et al. (2007). Effect of syntactic similarity on cortical activation during second language processing: a comparison of English and Japanese among native Korean trilinguals. *Human Brain Mapping* 28 (3): 194–204.

Juffs, A. and Harrington, M. (2011). Aspects of working memory in L2 learning. *Language Teaching* 44 (2): 137–166.

Just, M. and Carpenter, P. (1992). A capacity theory of comprehension: individual differences in working memory. *Psychological Review* 99 (1): 122–149.

Just, M., Carpenter, P., and Keller, A. (1996). The capacity theory of comprehension: new frontiers of evidence and arguments. *Psychological Review* 103 (4): 773–780.

Keating, G. (2017). L2 proficiency matters in comparative L1/L2 processing research. *Bilingualism: Language and Cognition* 20 (4): 700–701.

Kim, J. and Christianson, K. (2017). Working memory effects on L1 and L2 processing of ambiguous relative clauses by Korean L2 learners of English. *Second Language Research* 33 (3): 365–388.

Kim, S., Qi, T., Feng, X. et al. (2016). How does language distance between L1 and L2 affect the L2 brain network? An fMRI study of Korean-Chinese-English trilinguals. *NeuroImage* 129: 25–39.

Kormos, J. and Sáfár, A. (2008). Phonological short-term memory, working memory and foreign language performance in intensive language learning. *Bilingualism: Language and Cognition* 11 (2): 261–271.

Kroll, J., Bobb, S., and Wodniecka, Z. (2006). Language selectivity is the exception, not the rule: arguments against a fixed locus of language selection in bilingual speech. *Bilingualism: Language and Cognition* 9 (2): 119–135.

Kroll, J., Dussias, P., Bice, K., and Perrotti, L. (2015). Bilingualism, mind, and brain. *Annual Review of Linguistics* 1 (1): 377–394.

Kroll, J., Dussias, P., Bogulski, C., and Valdes Kroff, J. (2012). Juggling two languages in one mind: what bilinguals tell us about language processing and its consequences for cognition. In: *The Psychology of Learning and Motivation* (ed. B. Ross), 229–262. San Diego, CA: Academic Press.

Kroll, J.F. and Ma, F. (2017). The bilingual lexicon. In: *The Handbook of Psycholinguistics* (ed. E.M. Fernández and H.S. Cairns), 294–319. Hoboken, NJ: Wiley.

Liang, L. and Chen, B. (2014). Processing morphologically complex words in second-language learners: the effect of proficiency. *Acta Psychologica* 150: 69–79.

Linck, J., Michael, E., Golonka, E. et al. (2015). Moving beyond two languages: the effects of multilingualism on language processing and language learning. In: *The Cambridge Handbook of Bilingual Processing* (ed. J.W. Schwieter), 665–694. Cambridge, UK: Cambridge University Press.

Linck, J., Osthus, P., Koeth, J., and Bunting, M. (2014). Working memory and second language comprehension and production: a meta-analysis. *Psychonomic Bulletin & Review* 21 (4): 861–883.

Liu, H., Dunlap, S., Tang, Y. et al. (2017). The modulatory role of L1 and L2 morphosyntactic similarity during production of L2 inflected words: an ERP study. *Journal of Neurolinguistics* 42: 109–123.

Llama, R., Cardoso, W., and Collins, L. (2010). The influence of language distance and language status on the acquisition of L3 phonology. *International Journal of Multilingualism* 7 (1): 39–57.

Lowie, W. and de Bot, K. (2015). Variability in bilingual processing. In: *The Cambridge Handbook of Bilingual Processing* (ed. J.W. Schwieter), 234–254. Cambridge, UK: Cambridge University Press.

Lu, Y. (2015). Working memory, cognitive resources and L2 writing performance. In: *Working Memory in Second Language Acquisition and Processing* (ed. Z. Wen, M. Mota and A. McNeil), 175–188. Bristol, UK: Multilingual Matters.

MacDonald, M., Just, M., and Carpenter, P. (1992). Working memory constraints on the processing of syntactic ambiguity. *Cognitive Psychology* 24 (1): 56–98.

Mackey, A., Adams, R., Stafford, C., and Winke, P. (2010). Exploring the relationship between modified output and working memory capacity. *Language Learning* 60 (3): 501–533.

Martin, K. and Ellis, N. (2012). The roles of phonological STM and working memory in L2 grammar and vocabulary learning. *Studies in Second Language Acquisition* 34 (3): 379–413.

McDonald, J. (2006). Beyond the critical period: processing-based explanations for poor grammaticality judgment performance by late second language learners. *Journal of Memory and Language* 55 (3): 381–401.

McDonald, J. (2008). Differences in the cognitive demands of word order, plural, and subject-verb agreement constructions. *Psychonomic Bulletin & Review* 15 (5): 980–984.

McLaughlin, J., Tanner, D., Pitkänen, I. et al. (2010). Brain potentials reveal discrete stages of L2 grammatical learning. *Language Learning* 60 (2): 123–150.

Medina, A., Callender, A., Brantmeier, C., and Schultz, L. (2017). Inserted adjuncts, working memory capacity, and L2 reading. *System* 66: 69–86.

Meschyan, G. and Hernandez, A. (2006). Impact of language proficiency and orthographic transparency on bilingual word reading: an fMRI investigation. *NeuroImage* 29 (4): 1135–1140.

Mitchell, D., Cuetos, F., Corley, M., and Brysbaert, M. (1995). Exposure-based models of human parsing: evidence for the use of coarse-grained (nonlexical) statistical records. *Journal of Psycholinguistic Research* 24 (6): 469–488.

Morgan-Short, K., Finger, I., Grey, S., and Ullman, M. (2012). Second language processing shows increased native-like neural responses after months of no exposure. *PLoS One* 7 (3): e32974.

Morgan-Short, K., Sanz, C., Steinhauer, K., and Ullman, M. (2010). Second language acquisition of gender agreement in explicit and implicit training conditions: an event-related potential study. *Language Learning* 60 (1): 154–193.

Muñoz, C. (2008). Symmetries and asymmetries of age effects in naturalistic and instructed L2 learning. *Applied Linguistics* 29 (4): 578–596.

O'brien, I., Segalowitz, N., Collentine, J., and Freed, B. (2006). Phonological memory and lexical, narrative, and grammatical skills in second language oral production by adult learners. *Applied PsychoLinguistics* 27 (3): 377–402.

Osaka, M. and Osaka, N. (1992). Language-independent working memory as measured by Japanese and English reading span tests. *Bulletin of the Psychonomic Society* 30 (4): 287–289.

Osaka, M., Osaka, N., and Groner, R. (1993). Language-independent working memory: evidence from German and French reading span tests. *Bulletin of the Psychonomic Society* 31 (2): 117–118.

Park-Johnson, S. (2017). Crosslinguistic influence of wh-in-situ questions by Korean-English bilingual children. *International Journal of Bilingualism* 21 (4): 419–432.

Perani, D. and Abutalebi, J. (2005). The neural basis of first and second language processing. *Current Opinion in Neurobiology* 15 (2): 202–206.

Perani, D., Paulesu, E., Santesteban Galles, N. et al. (1998). The bilingual brain: proficiency and age of acquisition of the second language. *Brain* 121 (10): 1841–1852.

Pliatsikas, C. and Marinis, T. (2013). Processing of regular and irregular past tense morphology in highly proficient second language learners of English: a self-paced reading study. *Applied PsychoLinguistics* 34 (5): 943–970.

Reichle, R., Tremblay, A., and Coughlin, C. (2016). Working memory capacity in L2 processing. *Probus* 28 (1): 29–55.

Roberts, L. (2012). Individual differences in second language sentence processing. *Language Learning* 62: 172–188.

Roncaglia-Denissen, M. and Kotz, S. (2016). What does neuroimaging tell us about morphosyntactic processing in the brain of second language learners? *Bilingualism: Language and Cognition* 19 (4): 665–673.

Rossi, E., Diaz, M., Kroll, J., and Dussias, P. (2017). Late bilinguals are sensitive to unique aspects of second language processing: evidence from clitic pronouns word-order. *Frontiers in Psychology* 8: 342.

Sagarra, N. (2017). Longitudinal effects of working memory on L2 grammar and reading abilities. *Second Language Research* 33 (30): 341–363.

Sagarra, N. and Herschensohn, J. (2010). The role of proficiency and working memory in gender and number agreement processing in L1 and L2 Spanish. *Lingua* 120 (8): 2022–2039.

Sakai, K., Nauchi, A., Tatsuno, Y. et al. (2009). Distinct roles of left inferior frontal regions that explain individual differences in second language acquisition. *Human Brain Mapping* 30 (8): 2440–2452.

Schmid, M. (2016). First language attrition. *Language Teaching* 49 (2): 186–212.

Service, E. (1992). Phonology, working memory, and foreign-language learning. *The Quarterly Journal of Experimental Psychology* 45 (1): 21–50.

Service, E. (2012). Working memory in second language acquisition: phonological short-term. In: *The Encyclopedia of Applied Linguistics* (ed. C. Chappelle). Wiley-Blackwell.

Service, E., Simola, M., Metsaenheimo, O., and Maury, S. (2002). Bilingual working memory span is affected by language skill. *European Journal of Cognitive Psychology* 14: 383–407.

Shekari, E. and Service, E. (2016). *Native-like L2 processing, a possibility in proficient late bilinguals*. Paper presented at the Psycholinguistics Shorts (PsychoShorts) conference. University of Ottawa, Ottawa, Canada.

Shekari, E. and Service, E. (2017a). *Working memory capacity as the predictor of L2 processing and task performance in bilinguals*. Paper presented at the 2017 Linguistic Association of Canada and the United States (LACUS) conference. McMaster University, Hamilton, Canada.

Shekari, E. and Service, E. (2017b). *Processing Syntactically Complex Sentences in Skilled Late Adult Bilinguals*. Poster presented at the TESL Canada conference 2017, Niagara Falls, Canada.

Silva, R. and Clahsen, H. (2008). Morphologically complex words in L1 and L2 processing: evidence from masked priming experiments in English. *Bilingualism: Language and Cognition* 11 (2): 245–260.

Szubko-Sitarek, W. (2015). *Multilingual Lexical Recognition in the Mental Lexicon of Third Language Users*. New York, NY: Springer.

Tanner, D., Inoue, K., and Osterhout, L. (2014). Brain-based individual differences in online L2 grammatical comprehension. *Bilingualism: Language and Cognition* 17 (2): 277–293.

Tolentino, L. and Tokowicz, N. (2011). Across languages, space, and time: a review of the role of cross-language similarity in L2 (Morpho) syntactic processing as revealed by fMRI and ERP methods. *Studies in Second Language Acquisition* 33 (1): 91–125.

Turner, M. and Engle, R. (1989). Is working memory capacity task dependent? *Journal of Memory and Language* 28 (2): 127–154.

Ullman, M. (2004). Contributions of memory circuits to language: the declarative/procedural model. *Cognition* 92: 231–270.

Ullman, M. (2005). A cognitive neuroscience perspective on second language acquisition: the declarative/procedural model. In:

Processing Approaches to Adult SLA: Theory and Practice (ed. C. Sanz), 141–178. Washington, DC: Georgetown University Press.

Ullman, M. (2012). The declarative/ procedural model. In: *Routledge Encyclopedia of Second Language Acquisition* (ed. P. Robinson), 135–158. New York, NY: Routledge.

Unsworth, N. and Engle, R. (2007). The nature of individual differences in working memory capacity: active maintenance in primary memory and controlled search from secondary memory. *Psychological Review* 114: 104–132.

Unsworth, N., Heitz, R., Schrock, J., and Engle, R. (2005). An automated version of the operation span task. *Behavior Research Methods* 37 (3): 498–505.

Unsworth, N., Redick, T., Heitz, R. et al. (2009). Complex working memory span tasks and higher-order cognition: a latent-variable analysis of the relationship between processing and storage. *Memory* 17 (6): 635–654.

van den Noort, M., Bosch, P., and Hugdahl, K. (2006). Foreign language proficiency and working memory capacity. *European Psychologist* 11 (4): 289–296.

van den Noort, M., Struys, E., Kim, K. et al. (2014). Multilingual processing in the brain. *International Journal of Multilingualism* 11 (2): 182–201.

van Hell, J. and Tokowicz, N. (2010). Event-related brain potentials and second language learning: syntactic processing in late L2 learners at different L2 proficiency levels. *Second Language Research* 26 (1): 43–74.

Waters, G. and Caplan, D. (1996). The measurement of verbal working memory capacity and its relation to reading comprehension. *Quarterly Journal of Experimental Psychology* 59 (1): 51–75.

Waters, G. and Caplan, D. (2002). Working memory and online syntactic processing in Alzheimer's disease: studies with auditory moving window presentation. *The Journals of Gerontology Series B: Psychological Sciences and Social Sciences* 57 (4): 298–311.

Wattendorf, E. and Festman, J. (2008). Images of the multilingual brain: the effect of age of second language acquisition. *Annual Review of Applied Linguistics* 28: 3–24.

Wattendorf, E., Festman, J., Westermann, B. et al. (2014). Early bilingualism influences early and subsequently later acquired languages in cortical regions representing control functions. *International Journal of Bilingualism* 18 (1): 48–66.

Wells, J., Christiansen, M., Race, D. et al. (2009). Experience and sentence processing: statistical learning and relative clause comprehension. *Cognitive Psychology* 58 (2): 250–271.

White, E., Titone, D., Genesee, F., and Steinhauer, K. (2017). Phonological processing in late second language learners: the effects of proficiency and task. *Bilingualism: Language and Cognition* 20 (1): 162–183.

Williams, J. (2006). Incremental interpretation in second language sentence processing. *Bilingualism: Language and Cognition* 9 (1): 71–88.

Williams, J. (2012). Working memory and SLA. In: *Handbook of Second Language Acquisition* (ed. S. Gass and A. Mackey), 427–441. New York, NY: Routledge.

19 Learning and Memory in the Bilingual Mind and Brain

ALLISON M. WILCK, JEANETTE
ALTARRIBA, ROBERTO R. HEREDIA,
AND JOHN W. SCHWIETER

1. Introduction

Bilingual speakers operate independently in their first (L1) or second language (L2), or interdependently in which both languages interact simultaneously as in language mixing or code switching. How do bilingual (or multilingual) speakers organize their linguistic systems in the brain? Are the languages organized in the same or separate brain regions? This chapter explores various aspects and assumptions of models of bilingual language processing and organization. A brief overview of theoretical language models is provided to include a discussion of the distinction between compound and coordinate bilingualism, as well as models of connectionism, hierarchical structures, and a recently proposed model of language acquisition. The underlying assumptions of these theories and models will be assessed with a focus on interlanguage processing and organization.

One purpose of this chapter is to underscore the importance of bilingual research to aid in the refinement of existing theoretical constructs that distinguish between conceptual meaning and lexical representations, for example, and to provide further evidence for structural assumptions of language processing models (Altarriba and Soltano 1996). Bilingual research, in addition to helping us understand an individual with knowledge of two or more languages, provides yet another opportunity to assess, correct, and expand existing models and theories of language processing. Bilingualism provides a unique perspective for understanding how words and sentences are learned, encoded, stored, and retrieved from memory.

Additionally, how meaning is derived from language, both within and between languages, must be considered from several perspectives to include the nature of the words, how and when the language has been acquired by the individual, and the consistency of processing across languages in a given context. Overall, the bilingual and L2 literature

The Handbook of the Neuroscience of Multilingualism, First Edition. Edited by John W. Schwieter.
© 2019 John Wiley & Sons Ltd. Published 2019 by John Wiley & Sons Ltd.

supports the view that there are various layers of information extracted from words (e.g. physical features, conceptual meaning) that become interlinked with the acquisition of new languages (e.g. Velan and Frost 2007, 2011; Wong et al. 2011). Within the bilingual mind, the research largely supports models that incorporate a mixed linguistic representation: some aspects of language share a common store while others are separate with language specificity. By studying language processing in bilinguals and multilinguals, a better understanding of how information is generally integrated into human memory can be obtained.

2.   Overview of Theories and Models of Bilingual/ Multilingual Memory

Human memory is a rich and complex system that has been researched in a variety of capacities for decades from working memory (e.g. Baddeley 2003; Baddeley and Hitch 1974) to long-term memory (Lynch 2004). However, there is not an undisputed understanding of how information is processed, stored, and retrieved in memory (see Baddeley et al. 2015), and there have been numerous models proposed on how language is processed in memory (see French and Jacquet 2004; Kroll and Tokowicz 2005). Research findings from bilinguals and multilinguals have led to the development of models that attempt to account for how individuals with knowledge of more than one language store and extract information within and across languages. In this section, we provide a brief overview of a number of models addressing bilingual and multilingual language processing, beginning with the fundamental debate between memory store organizations and concluding with more recent and well-defined models (for additional discussions on models of bilingual language processing, see Heredia and Cieślicka 2018).

2.1.   *Language Memory Stores*

The seminal research into the uniqueness of bilingual language processing and representation comes from Ervin and Osgood (1954). The distinction between compound and coordinate bilingualism provides the basis for today's models. Compound bilinguals are those who became proficient in an L2 by relating and matching the to-be-learned concepts back to those in their L1. Connecting the new language concepts to those already in memory, it was proposed that there would be an overlap of representations such that all linguistic information would be stored in one location within the brain. On the other hand, coordinate bilinguals are those who acquired a new language in a context that is distinct from any previous language knowledge. For example, if an individual learned English in the home through immersion, but was explicitly taught French in a classroom, then these two languages would come to have separate representations. Under these conditions, English words and their French translations would not be interpreted as having identical meanings and associations. Therefore, word translations would not be processed and stored equivalently, and words from each language would have their own cognitive store.

An important underlying distinction between these types of bilinguals is the implication that the individual must encode information in a context-specific manner. In other words, for each word bilinguals encounter, they must make note of the learning conditions, so as to later be able to retrieve the meaning of the word in accordance with its appropriate language. Although acquisition may be affected by learning context (Segalowitz and Freed 2004), this theory does not allow for the possibility of alterations as a product of experience with the languages after the initial learning or from the nature of the linguistic codes themselves (see Kopeliovich 2006; cross-linguistic word features will be discussed further in Section 4 below).

In the present-day literature, it is a rarity to encounter the compound versus coordinate bilingualism distinction. Although Ervin and Osgood (1954) generated their understanding based on how language was acquired, the current debate tends to focus on how linguistic information is stored and processed in memory. Updating and expanding their seminal proposal, the more recent psycholinguistic literature investigates if linguistic information in individuals with knowledge of more than one language is stored within a single mental lexicon, or among multiple, separate stores. If multiple stores indeed exist, the degree of interaction and interconnectivity between them remains a topic of discussion.

Theorists supporting a single, interdependent linguistic store largely argue that the concepts represented by words are stored as language-free abstract meanings (see Heredia and Cieślicka 2018, for a review of the literature supporting the shared memory hypothesis). These concepts are then 'tagged' with labels corresponding to the word or phrase associated with each known language. For example, the conceptual representation for the place one lives will be tagged in an English-Spanish bilingual with both *house* and *casa*. Therefore, when this concept becomes activated, both labels would be accessible for use, and the bilingual can attend to the tag that is most applicable for the current conversation. This shared memory hypothesis predicts that the underlying concepts of information learned in one language (e.g. $3 + 4 = 7$, or *seven* in English) will be able to be retrieved in one's L2 (*siete* in Spanish) without the need to relearn the notion in each tongue. Tasks that emphasize a conceptual focus and accentuate attention towards *the meaning* of words, such as recall and recognition tests of semantic meaning and relational processing, often garner support for an interdependence model of bilingual and multilingual language processing (see Heredia and Cieślicka 2018).

In contrast to a single memory store is the separate or independence memory hypothesis (Kolers 1963). This stance posits that linguistic information is processed, stored, and retrieved unimodally, with each learned language having its own distinct memory store. The separation of lexicons is proposed to emphasize the quantitative differences of words and concepts learned between languages. These differences can be derived by comparing linguistic aspects such as word morphology, phonology, orthography, or learnability. Furthermore, interactions between stores only occur through translation processes, and therefore, information obtained in one language store is often not available to another. Support for this hypothesis comes from experiments that utilize tasks that are sensitive to data-driven or perceptually-based factors (e.g. lexical decision tasks). Additional evidence for this hypothesis comes from tasks involving code switching (i.e. alternating between a bilingual's two languages within a single sentence). For example, intermixed

English-Spanish sentences (e.g. *dame una hamburguesa sin LETTUCE por favor*) take English-Spanish bilinguals longer to process than do the monolingual equivalents (*give me a hamburger without LETTUCE please*; Heredia and Altarriba 2001). When assessed using the separate language stores hypothesis, these results can be explained with one language store being fully searched for each word's meaning before searching another, with search typically beginning in the speaker's primary language or the language that is currently more activated (e.g. Dijkstra and Van Heuven 2002; Soares and Grosjean 1984).

To combine the concepts of both the interdependent and independent memory store hypotheses, models with separate but interconnected bilingual memory stores have been proposed. One of the more well-known models, the bilingual dual-coding theory (Paivio and Desrochers 1980), predicts that each language of a bilingual speaker has a separate store for its verbal code that can function independently. Within each verbal code, there is information pertaining to the specific language's word labels and syntax. Although stored separately, these verbal systems are linked through translation equivalents. The stronger the labels are between languages for a given concept map onto each other, the stronger and more accessible the links are. For example, the translation equivalents of *cheese* in English and *fromage* in French produce a stronger association, as compared to the related concepts of *cheese* and *pain* (bread in French).

Importantly, the bilingual dual-coding theory can also account for many language type effects with the inclusion of a third, language-free image store that is linked to the verbal stores. Language type effects refer to differences in attention, reaction time, or other responses because of manipulations in word type (e.g. abstract, concrete, emotion [words describing an affective state, such as *joyful*], or emotion-laden [words that evoke emotion, such as *funeral*]), or language presentation. There is ample evidence for a bilingual concreteness effect in which tangible objects (e.g. *chair, tiger, bottle*) are better recalled from memory than abstract words (e.g. *dream, love, death*; Altarriba and Bauer 2004; de Groot 1992; Farley et al. 2012). It is important to note that tangible objects or nouns score high in imagery accessibility and often have a single translation between languages, while abstract words are lower in imageability and often map onto multiple translations (see Altarriba 2003). Therefore, concrete nouns can activate meaning from all three stores (L1, L2, and imagery) of the bilingual dual-code model, while abstract and other word types are often limited to only the verbal encodings.

The search for a structural and functional understanding of how language is processed in memory continues to be a predominant area of research in the fields of neuroscience and psycholinguistics. Whether there exists a single mental lexicon that encompasses all linguistic information, separate stores for each language, or some combination of these is an ongoing discussion. However, many models have been proposed that incorporate the acquisition and recall of various lexical properties that can be organized according to their underlying theoretical assumptions.

2.2. Connectionist Models

Connectionist models of linguistic acquisition come from the field of cognitive psychology. These models function to bridge linguistic knowledge and organization with the mechanisms that operate them. In general, connectionism has been used to describe

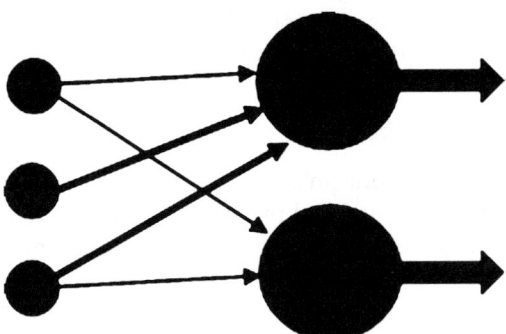

Figure 1   An example of a simple connectionist model. Conceptual nodes feed into larger, more generalized nodes. Thicker lines represent greater association strength, which the model indicates as having a higher degree of connection between the represented concepts.

behaviours that can be attributed to neuronal connections or other basic units. When describing language acquisition, it is common to refer to these basic conceptual units as *nodes* that interact through weighted connections (see Figure 1). Connections are formed when associations between nodes are created, and their connective strength is increased as learning occurs. This learning can arise from interactions with the environment that allow for broad categories and rules to develop to link concepts together. For example, when learning the meaning of an unfamiliar word, the features of the individual letters must first be interpreted and then connected to form a meaningful word unit. Once the unit has been established as a word, meaning can be applied to it and this meaning can be grouped together with concepts already established in memory.

One of the most cited connectionist word recognition models is the bilingual interactive activation model (BIA; Dijkstra and Van Heuven 2002), currently modified to the BIA+ model (Chauncey et al. 2008; Grainger et al. 2010). This network model posits that information about the physical appearance of word features initiates the activation of letter recognition, followed by word recognition and semantic comprehension. These various lexical levels interact to identify a meaning for the presented words, with the underlying assumption that activation is not language specific. Information across all of an individual's known languages is integrated in a single lexicon, with a given word being recognized as belonging to a specific language. When presented within a language task, the information from both languages will become activated simultaneously until enough evidence is gathered to determine the language most appropriate to continue using for processing. For example, if the letters PAN are presented to an English-Spanish bilingual, the possible conceptual meanings for this word will be activated across both languages so that the English definition of a cooking utensil and the Spanish definition of bread will be generated. The definitional meaning most relevant or contextually appropriate wins the competition for activation. As connections between an L1 and L2 become strengthened through proficiency, translation equivalency, or semantic links, the representations from both languages become integrated to form a lateral inhibitory network. With strong connections, information regarding the more dominant and proficient language can be more easily inhibited and suppressed during L2 processing to allow for more efficient communication.

2.3.   *Hierarchical Models*

While connectionist models provide an account for how multiple languages can become connected within the mind, hierarchical models offer an alternative account to explain this process using interdependent memory. These models propose the existence of a single store for each language as well as a common store. In addition to processing information of a word from its individual features, combined letter form, and conceptual meaning, hierarchical models also assign a relative weight and location of the L1 and L2 connections between these parts of information.

The revised hierarchical model (Kroll and Stewart 1994) is one of the most cited models in the bilingual language literature. As common to hierarchical models, it is proposed that the shared concepts for words with equivalent meanings are stored in a common conceptual system, but the individual words are divided at the lexical level by language. Importantly, this model suggests that L1 words are directly linked to their meaning in the conceptual store while subsequent languages must route through the L1 to reach the conceptual store.

To explain lexical development and processing in L2 acquisition, the revised hierarchical model predicts that learners initially link the L2 words onto their L1 translations, which are already connected to the conceptual store (see Figure 2). As proficiency develops in the L2, a link directly from its language's lexical store to the conceptual store is made. Hence a second connection to conceptual meaning is made. However, this L2–conceptual link is weaker than the L1–conceptual link. This unbalanced connection creates asymmetrical mappings between words and concepts in bilingual

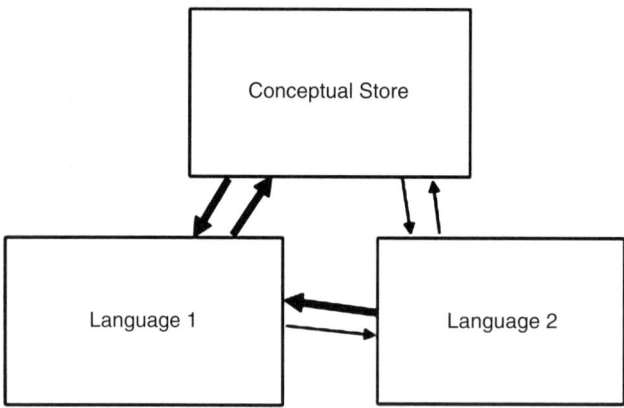

Figure 2   A conceptual illustration of the revised hierarchical model. Associations between the L1 and the shared conceptual store are stronger than those between the L2 and the conceptual store. The association from the L2 to the L1 is stronger than in the L1 to the L2 direction, indicating the assumption that L2 learning occurs by translating words into the native language.

memory. Support for the asymmetrical mapping assumption has been provided by research on L1 and L2 translational speeds that indicates bilinguals tend to be faster at translating words from an L2 to the L1 (e.g. Tokowicz and Kroll 2007), as the model would assert the L2–L1 direction can occur via a direct lexical access route as opposed to an indirect, conceptually-mediated route.

Although the revised hierarchical model has been widely accepted, it also has its critics. In particular, the concept of asymmetrical mapping has been called into question. Both novice and expert bilinguals have been shown to demonstrate conceptual interference effects within and between languages during a Stroop task, which requires participants to ignore the conceptual meaning of words while only attending to lexical features (Altarriba and Mathis 1997; but see Kroll and Tokowicz 2005, for a counter-argument to this finding). In addition, proficient bilinguals demonstrate priming effects of semantic categorization in the L2–L1 direction, indicating a conceptual link between the languages (Finkbeiner et al. 2004; Wang and Forster 2010). The revised hierarchical model stipulates that newly acquired languages gain meaning by relying on lexical representations. However, these results indicate that bilinguals of all skill levels can form both conceptual and lexical links for L2 words. While this model has been used to guide research on language acquisition, it is important to continue to adapt and generate bilingual and multilingual language frameworks that can encompass the empirical findings in the literature (Brysbaert and Duyck 2010; Brysbaert et al. 2010).

2.4.   *Model of L3/LN Acquisition*

While the underlying assumptions that make up the models discussed above could be expanded to incorporate third language (L3) acquisition and processing, research on multilinguals has indicated that these populations can be unique. Recently, a new model of language acquisition has been proposed that specifically encompasses multilingual (fluency in more than two languages) language processing. This model has been used to emphasize the uniqueness of language acquisition as stemming from a variety of lexical representations becoming interconnected.

The scalpel model (Slabakova 2016) provides a new set of ideas on how existing knowledge of languages can facilitate (or selectively hinder) the learning of a new language. Language processing does not occur in isolation. The concepts of integrating grammars across languages is a primary basis for this model. The model proposes that transference of information between languages occurs with 'scalpel-like' precision to extract the relevant grammars that aid in making meaning or translating the present words. This metaphor is used to encompass the notion that the learning of a new language occurs at the level of syntactic and word features by selectively drawing on the properties of languages already in memory. Aspects of a newly acquired language are broken down and compared to already stored languages, and thus can be influenced by linguistic features. Furthermore, this model stipulates that the transfer of knowledge from one language to another does not necessarily occur during the initial acquisition phase. Rather, concepts acquired in any language can influence the encoding and retrieval of other languages, previously stored or to-be-learned.

The scalpel model emphasizes cognitive, experiential, and linguistic influences on new language acquisition such that languages already in memory can both facilitate and inter-fere with new language acquisition. In this vein, frequency effects become a consideration for language learning. Learning a new language that appears to be similar to an already proficient language in memory can benefit the individual in quickly picking up aspects that are consistent across both. For example, cognates (i.e. words sharing meaning and form across languages; English: *composition* and Spanish: *composición*) tend to be identified in fluent bilinguals faster than they are identified by individuals not fluent in both languages. However, in the case of circumstances when there is a false similarity between languages, interference from stored linguistic information can hinder learning. For example, Bulgarian adolescents learning English as an L2 have been shown to overgeneralize the rules of morphology of their L1 onto their L2 (Harakchiyska 2011). When translating sentences, Bulgarian speakers often extend the rules of pluralization to uncountable nouns that do not have a pluralized form in English as they would in their native tongue. Thus, the sen-tence 'I do my *homework* at home' may be incorrectly written as 'I do my *homeworks* [sic] at home'. Overall, the scalpel model attempts to incorporate the idea of foundational information transfer between languages as a tool for L3 (or more) acquisition. However, the model acknowledges that there are practical limitations to this transference that can cause issues depending on the specifics of the language combinations.

3.   Methodological Considerations for L2 Studies

The brief overview of various models of bilingual and multilingual language processing provided in Section 2 generates an understanding for how the focus of these theoretical models can vary. A main underlying dispute involves the structure of mental lexicons, namely if there exists a single, interdependent store or multiple, independent language stores. At issue is whether the conceptual properties of words are extracted and stored together, independent of language, or are superimposed with specific lexical features. The use of bilingual research has become a valuable tool for assessing and updating assumptions of language processing, in general. Bilinguals are able to represent the meaning of words with multiple lexical codes (e.g. a pet that meows can be labelled as *cat* or *gato* for an English-Spanish bilingual), while monolinguals cannot. By varying the degree of similarity of lexical codes and overlap of processing within an individual, each model's explanations and predictions will necessarily differ for linguistic aspects such as language acquisition, production, comprehension, memory, and translation abilities.

Advances in technology have allowed these models and their underlying assump-tions to be evaluated with greater acuity and precision (see van Heuven and Dijkstra 2010). Section 3 reviews the existing empirical data for the models described above and how these models are able to account for these findings.

3.1.   *fMRI and ERP*

The models of language processing that have gained the most popularity are limited in their predictions of a theoretical structure for *how* processing occurs. Most do not pro-vide explicit predictions for *where* in the brain the processing occurs (but see Indefrey and Levelt 2004, for an attempt to link functional components to theory). However, technologies do allow for language processing to be localized and compared between the processing of an L1, L2, or LN (languages acquired beyond the L2).

Functional magnetic resonance imaging (fMRI) detects changes in blood flow as a proxy to measure brain activity. As blood flow to an area increases, it is taken as an indication that neuronal activity in that area is occurring above the typical resting rate. Although fMRI provides high-quality images that detail where activation is localized, it produces low temporal resolution. Thus, information provided with fMRI is useful for identifying where in the brain neuronal activity is occurring, but not for creating a time-line of activation. Identifying the specific brain structures involved in tasks of reading and listening can allow for a comparison of the processing between languages, ultimately providing support for a single language store or multiple stores.

Event-related potentials (ERPs) are an alternative measure of brain activity in response to a sensory or cognitive stimulus as recorded by changes in voltage. Substantial changes indicate greater neuronal activation. In contrast to fMRI, measures from ERP provide low image resolution but high temporal resolution allowing for the study of rapidly occurring linguistic processing with precise timing of the activation at various stages (Morgan-Short 2014; Morgan-Short and Tanner 2014; Swaab et al. 2012). For models that provide sequential stages or differentiation of lexical properties, and therefore involve a time course of processing, ERPs can be used to evaluate these assumptions. By comparing the results of location activation information from fMRI with the precise timing of neuronal changes from ERP, researchers can generate a detailed understanding for the physical processing of language.

Looking at patterns of brain activity has allowed for the testing of assumptions corresponding to the theoretical considerations presented in Section 2. For example, what happens at a neurological level when translating words between languages? Palmer et al. (2010) addressed this question with fully proficient Spanish-English and English-Spanish bilinguals. Participants were presented with Spanish and English concrete and abstract word pairs with the task of indicating if both words shared a common meaning or not. ERP recordings were taken during the task to examine lexical-semantic activation during word translation. The results showed a larger peak of the N400 (a common marker of semantic activation; see Kutas and Federmeier 2011; see Lau et al. 2008, for a discussion of lexical and semantic aspects of the N400) when translating in the L2–L1 direction, regardless of word type, than in the L1–L2 direction. The authors explained this finding in terms of an asymmetrical link between the L1–conceptual store and L2–conceptual store as proposed by the revised hierarchical model of language processing. The greater L2–L1 activation of the N400, the authors argued, demonstrated the additional semantic activation that needed to occur during a conceptual judgement due to the less direct, and therefore weaker, connections between the L2 and the conceptual store. When the L1 is presented first, there is a more direct and fast link to its translation equivalent in the L2. The path to make a conceptual judgement is primed, thereby reducing the amplitude and effort required of the neurological response. These results are indeed accounted for by the revised hierarchical model that proposes a direct link from the L1 to the conceptual store.

Although much information can be garnered from studying the neurological components of language processing with fMRI and ERP technologies, these methodologies present several limitations that merit acknowledgment for assessing theoretical assumptions. First, there are practical constraints for the types of tasks that can be performed while participants are connected to the brain-scanning equipment. This physical limitation reduces the number of naturalistic behavioural measures that can be recorded, as these machines often require the participant to minimize motion. Consequently, comparing data obtained about brain activity to behavioural data must be done with caution as natural reading behaviours typically involve more freedom of bodily movement. Second, although information about where and when in the brain linguistic information is processed when performing a particular task can be obtained from these techniques, neither the underlying causes for brain activation patterns nor an evaluation of the process can be observed. Data obtained from fMRI and ERP technologies are used to imply correlations between task performance and neurological activation. Therefore, neurological data alone cannot be used for evaluating causality, as indicated by many of the word identification models. To create a fuller understanding of the data obtained from fMRI and ERP studies, a combination of results with behavioural data from experimental paradigms should be considered (but see Grey et al. 2017; McLaughlin et al. 2004).

Moreover, when interpreting fMRI and ERP data, results indicating an overlap or separation of brain activation do not necessarily imply the absence of an alternative explanation (Hernandez et al. 2005). By considering where language is processed, an understanding of its function and physical structure can be obtained. However, the possibility remains that there is a neural separation of linguistic representations. A localized brain region can account for the processing of an L2 to a differing degree than an L1, or at differing time courses. In other words, while the physical processing of two languages (e.g. letter analysis) may occur in given brain regions with varying degrees of activation, a higher-order representation (e.g. semantic meaning) can overlap between all languages. This disambiguation cannot be clarified using these methods alone.

3.2.   Behavioural Methodologies

There are many experimental designs that allow for the analysis of behavioural data. Various experimental results obtained using tasks that provide insight into the processing of language through behavioural responses will be discussed in this section, in relation to learning and memory.

Lexical priming, in which the recent experience of a given language input or previously presented word influences the processing of a subsequently presented language or word, has been used to study implicit learning. This learning can occur not only at the level of individual words (e.g. associating the meaning of a presented word with a concept or related words), but also with syntactic structure (Hartsuiker and Bernolet 2017). Languages that are learned in an informal or immersive setting, such as by children at home, often incorporate an implicit understanding for proper syntax by mimicking the sentence structure produced by others. When attempting to learn an L2, information about the syntax of an L1 is often applied to the L2. This can occur even when the proper syntax between languages does not match precisely. Furthermore, bilinguals tend to process phrases across languages faster if the translation is literal or familiar and the sentence structures of both languages match, as opposed to unfamiliar or figurative meanings (Carrol and Conklin 2015, 2017). The formulaic structure from one language can carry over into another language and can facilitate processing if the structures are equated, but disrupt processing speed if different. Furthermore, the learned structure of an L2 can become formulaic and, when the formula is not followed, language comprehension will require more time and effort. These studies in figurative language, for example, indicate that priming can occur at the multiword level across languages and that familiar phrases can be stored in the mental lexicon as both individual words and as a whole meaningful unit.

A recent study assessing audiovisual speech cues demonstrated how language familiarity and proficiency can moderate speakers' strategies for processing speech. Barenholtz et al. (2016) had English monolinguals and English-Spanish bilinguals watch videos of balanced (equally proficient in both languages) bilingual speakers in conversation. Participants watched and listened to clips with speakers in either a language in which they were proficient (English) or an unfamiliar language (Spanish or Icelandic) while an infrared-based eye-tracking system recorded their eye movements. An analysis of eye movements indicated that when asked to monitor the conversation, the individual spent the most time looking at the mouth of a speaker if she used an unfamiliar language, but not if the language was familiar. However, when attention was not explicitly directed towards the conversation, eye movements were focused on the mouth as often as they were to the eyes of the speaker, regardless of whether or not the language was familiar. The authors concluded that language familiarity acts as a mediator for attention to enhance perceptual comprehension. This attentional strategy is particularly important when learning to integrate physical speech production (mouth movements) with acoustic information, such as when acquiring a new language (see Lewkowicz and Hansen-Tift 2012, for a similar study on infants with congruent results).

Understanding the role of factors that influence language learning and comprehension, such as familiarity and visual focal points, helps to distinguish the kind of information most relevant to language learning and comprehension at various stages of proficiency. Because the behavioural responses between an L2 learner and proficient speaker differ, consideration for context and degree of experience with a particular language should be considered when evaluating how it is being processed.

4. Distinguishing the Memory Models

Although the extant literature presents multiple models to explain language learning and memory, the underlying assumptions have also been evaluated with scientific research. At this point, it is still unclear exactly how the mental lexicon is structured and where information pertaining to known languages is stored and processed. However, the evidence from cognitive psychology and neuroscience points towards models that combine both integrated conceptual stores as well as language-specific feature stores. Furthermore, how lexical information is engaged within memory is influenced by the specific properties of the language representations. This section explores findings related to how languages are processed in terms of their lexical units and the underlying nature of these representations.

4.1. Findings Related to Levels of Language Representation

Much of the information discussed thus far has primarily focused on language processing at the word level. However, in the real world, language is primarily conveyed by combining words into phrases or sentences. When assessing sentence processing, as compared to word processing, it is important to consider models for their ability to incorporate the enhanced complexity of syntax and grammar, as well as the increased burden placed on working memory to hold more pieces of information simultaneously (Hamrick and Ullman 2016). Data from ERPs have indicated that sentence processing presented between an individual's languages can vary based on the manner of acquisition for the given language (see Morgan-Short et al. 2012 for a study of adults learning an artificial language). The L1 is typically learned as a child in immersive informal environments, such as the home, where sentence structure and phrasings are spoken by the parents. However, L2 is often acquired through formal schooling where proper syntax and grammar are explicitly emphasised and taught. Regardless of the context in which one learns, there tend to be similar behavioural patterns that demonstrate proficiency. Yet, differing patterns of brain activity between processing languages learned under formal (i.e. explicit), and informal (i.e. implicit) learning conditions indicate language processing differences.

Once a language has been acquired, the frequency with which specific words or phrases are encountered within a language can play a role in linguistic processing or accessibility. That is, words that are commonly encountered tend to be read faster than uncommon words. This general effect is referred to as the word frequency effect. This robust finding has been found in isolated word identification tasks and also word processing tasks involving words in combination (e.g. Monsell et al. 1989; Segui et al. 1982). This effect has largely been studied in monolingual populations, with frequency referring to the commonality of a given word's occurrence within a language. However, for a fully proficient bilingual, word frequency might depend heavily on the bilingual's dominant language. Does the word frequency effect occur within and between the bilingual's languages?

To address this question, Cop et al. (2015) analysed the eye movements of English monolingual and Dutch-English bilinguals while reading a novel. Monolinguals read a text in English while the bilingual group read half of the novel in the L1 and half in the L2. Levels of proficiency were also assessed for each language within the bilingual group. The results indicated that monolinguals and unbalanced bilinguals (having unequal levels of proficiency between an L1 and L2) showed similar sized word frequency effects when reading in their respective L1. However, balanced bilinguals (equally proficient in both languages) showed an even larger effect in both languages.

Cop et al. (2015) also found that bilinguals tended to make more fixations while reading in their L2 as compared to their L1. The increased rate of fixations resulted in a reduction of reading speed and overall longer reading times. Surprisingly, the ability to process high-frequency words quickly decreased in both L1 and L2 as the level of L1 proficiency increased. However, this effect was not influenced by L2 proficiency. The authors argued that this finding could be explained in terms of a weaker association between word form and meaning in an L2 than an L1, which can be affected by proficiency level. That is, the more proficient an individual is in each language, the larger the size of the mental lexicon for that language. Because the size of the frequency effect was identical between monolinguals and the unbalanced bilinguals, both of which were only highly proficient in one language, the authors concluded that the same underlying lexical processing mechanisms were operating for both groups. Comparable results have been found using computer connectionist models that support language proficiency resulting from an increased lexicon size as effectively reducing frequency effects for that language (Monaghan et al. 2017). Overall, these results support an interdependent conceptual store in the bilingual lexicon, with size of the mental lexicon as a main factor for enhancing lexical access and thereby the frequency effect. Furthermore, individual differences in lexical processing can arise as a factor of multilanguage processing with respect to language exposure.

4.2. Findings Related to the Nature of Language Representations

Although the structure of language can impact its processing across languages, the inherent properties of the representations play a key role, as well. It has been well-established that word type is an important consideration for understanding language processing in monolinguals to include where attention is directed, processing speed, and ability to recall (for a recent overview of monolingual versus bilingual emotion word processing see Wilck & Altarriba, in press). Similar effects have been found in L2 processing. For example, Sutton et al. (2007) demonstrated that emotion words (e.g. English: *sad*, Spanish: *triste*), as compared to neutral words (e.g. English: *table*, Spanish: *mesa*), capture attention across languages in highly proficient Spanish-English bilinguals.

Although word type has been shown to influence processing across languages, and emotion words increase selective attention over neutral words, it is not necessarily the case that the degree of emotionality translates well across languages. Altarriba (2003) collected ratings of concreteness (i.e. tangibility of a word), imageability (i.e. how easy it is to picture the word), and context availability (i.e. how easy it is to generate examples of the word) for Spanish concrete (e.g. *perro* [dog], *tijeras* [scissors]), abstract (*consejo* [advice], *verdad* [truth]), and emotion (e.g., *encantado* [delighted], *miedo* [fear]) words from Spanish-English bilinguals. Emotion words produced the lowest ratings of concreteness, but the highest ratings of imageability and context availability. However, when Spanish emotion words were compared to their English translations (e.g. Altarriba et al. 1999), Spanish words had a higher average context availability rating. In other words, Spanish emotion words generated more meanings than their English counterparts. Altarriba argued that words in one language, especially emotion words, may not precisely and singularly translate into another language. If a bilingual's understanding of concepts in the L1 and L2 differs, then the perceptual representations between an L1 and L2 must also differ.

To investigate the differences in conceptual versus perceptual representations of information across languages, Altarriba and colleagues employed a variety of experimental paradigms using bilingual populations. To examine if bilingual language information is processed according to its higher-level conceptual information or at its lower-level (i.e.

lexical level), a series of eye-tracking studies was performed (Altarriba et al. 1996). Fluent Spanish–English bilinguals read mixed-language sentences while their eye movements were recorded. When the eye focused on a word in the sentence that had a language switched, it tended to produce a longer fixation than if the word was in Spanish (the bilinguals' L1) and was highly expected based on the contextual cues. For example, it took longer for participants to process the word *dinero* in the sentence 'He wanted to deposit all of his *dinero* at the credit union' than if the translated word was the expected English equivalent, *money*, or if there were no contextual cues for the target word. The authors concluded that sentence context and word expectations were influenced by both the conceptual information provided by the context (prediction ability) and the lexical information (word in English or Spanish). The increased processing time required to comprehend sentences that switched from an L2 into the L1, as compared to a purely monolingual presentation, indicated that presentation mode was a crucial factor in reading comprehension. Retrieval of semantic information is dependent on the language in which information is encoded. These findings suggest support for language processing models with assumptions of separate stores for conceptual and lexical information.

In another attempt to provide evidence for a semantic or lexical overlap across languages, Altarriba and Soltano (1996) examined the repetition blindness effect in bilingual memory. Briefly, the repetition blindness effect refers to an individual's inability to recall the presentation of a repeated word, often explored using a rapid serial visual presentation task, in which words are presented one at a time. Most studies of this effect have been conducted within a single language, although the few experiments using bilingual populations have indicated meaningful differences (see Martin and Altarriba 2016 for a discussion). Altarriba and Soltano were interested in understanding if the conceptual overlap (word meaning) between equivalent translations would be enough to produce the repetition blindness effect, or if lexical overlap (similarity of word form) of the physical features was required. For example, the English word *book* and the French word *livre* both refer to a compilation of words on pages, although the letters that make up the words are not similar. Spanish-English bilinguals were presented with sentences (Experiment 1B) or word lists (Experiment 2) consisting of intermixed Spanish and English words. On half of the trials, a word was repeated in either the same (e.g. *sour–sour*) or the alternative language via its translation (*sour-agrio*), and the remaining trials had no repeated words. Therefore, on trials where the repeated word was in the same language, there would be repetition of both the semantic and lexical code. However, if the repeated word was presented in the alternative language, then the lexical code would differ while the conceptual meaning would remain the same.

The results indicated that a repetition blindness effect occurred when a word was repeated within the same language, but not if the second presentation was a translation equivalent. Regardless of whether the words were presented in the context of a sentence or as seemingly unconnected words in a list, participants were able to recall the occurrence of both word presentations with the same conceptual meaning if the lexical features were distinct. However, in the absence of grammar and syntactical structure, the repetition of a non-cognate word (i.e. translations that share a meaning but not form) across languages aided in the recall of the repeated word. Altarriba and Soltano (1996) argued that words presented in list form were being processed at a conceptual level, with semantic overlap facilitating translational recall. When assessing words across languages, it appears that overlap of physical features plays a vital role in merging the concepts together as one and producing repetition blindness. In the case of non-cognate translations, both items are easily processed as separate entities, thus enabling recallability for both words even though they share a conceptual meaning. Comparable results indicating that semantic similarity does not aid in generating useful information when reading to any greater extent than does orthographic similarity have been found in Spanish-English bilinguals in eye movements (see for example, Altarriba et al. 2001). Across multiple experiments, Altarriba and colleagues concluded that language processing does not occur solely at the conceptual level and that the physical features of individual words are considered when encoding and retrieving information from the mental lexicon.

5.   Conclusions and Suggestions for Future Directions

Language learning and memory has been a popular topic across many domains, including psychology and neuroscience. The research reviewed in this chapter has integrated the findings of language processing with respect to various models of acquisition, storage, and retrieval. Although there are aspects from each model that can be supported, the overall evidence has largely supported those with a single, interdependent language memory store (see French and Jacquet 2004, for further discussion). Data from various tasks, such as code switching (Heredia and Altarriba 2001) and reading (Altarriba et al. 1996; Cop et al. 2015), seem to support assumptions of hierarchical level processing, with the physical features of words being encoded and retrieved separately from the conceptual meanings.

Bilingual speakers have been identified as a useful resource for studying various levels of language representation. This population has the unique ability to garner the same conceptual information from words with orthographically and phonologically distinct features. The research reviewed throughout this chapter indicates that bilinguals can store and utilize two sets of symbols that represent one concept (e.g. Heredia and Altarriba 2001). Capitalizing on this population's unique mental representations can allow for the disambiguation of semantic meaning versus lexical features. In a monolingual population, these features are inherently overlapping. However, bilinguals are able to map multiple lexical labels onto a single conceptual meaning, thus allowing the possibility to determine the degree of influence on processing from each. Importantly, these can be studied within the same individual and thus within the same language processing system. Engaging bilinguals and multilinguals in research can effectively influence theory on general language processing. The continued use of this population as a research tool in linguistic research is encouraged to aid in the understanding of how language is represented across all individuals and is not limited to benefiting only those with knowledge of more than one language.

Future investigations of language, memory, and learning should continue to explore and obtain support for the various underlying assumptions of the proposed models. Furthermore, the present models should be assessed for reliability and precision with multilingual populations. Are all consecutively learned languages stored and represented in the mind in the same way as an L1 or L2? Future research should be aimed at providing answers to this and related questions.

REFERENCES

Altarriba, J. (2003). Does cariño equal 'liking'? A theoretical approach to conceptual nonequivalence between languages. *The International Journal of Bilingualism* 7 (3): 305–322.

Altarriba, J. and Bauer, L.M. (2004). The distinctiveness of emotion concepts: a comparison between emotion, abstract, and concrete words. *The American Journal of Psychology* 117 (3): 389–410.

Altarriba, J., Bauer, L.M., and Benvenuto, C. (1999). Concreteness, context availability, and imageability ratings and word associations for abstract, concrete, and emotion words. *Behavior Research Methods, Instruments, & Computers* 31 (4): 578–602.

Altarriba, J., Kambe, G., Pollatsek, A., and Rayner, K. (2001). Semantic codes are not used in integrating information across eye fixations in reading: evidence from fluent Spanish-English bilinguals. *Perception & Psychophysics* 63 (5): 875–890.

Altarriba, J., Kroll, J.F., Sholl, A., and Rayner, K. (1996). The influence of lexical and conceptual constraints on reading mixed-language sentences: evidence from eye fixations and naming times. *Memory & Cognition* 24 (4): 477–492.

Altarriba, J. and Mathis, K.M. (1997). Conceptual and lexical development in second language acquisition. *Journal of Memory and Language* 36: 550–568.

Altarriba, J. and Soltano, E.G. (1996). Repetition blindness and bilingual memory: token individuation for translation equivalents. *Memory & Cognition* 24 (6): 700–711.

Baddeley, A. (2003). Working memory: looking back and looking forward. *Nature Reviews Neuroscience* 4 (10): 829–839.

Baddeley, A., Eysenck, M.W., and Anderson, M.C. (2015). *Memory*, 2nd. New York, NY: Psychology Press.

Baddeley, A.D. and Hitch, G. (1974). Working memory. In: *Recent Advances in Learning and Motivation*, vol. 8 (ed. G. Bower), 47–89. New York, NY: Academic Press.

Barenholtz, E., Mavica, L., and Lewkowicz, D.J. (2016). Language familiarity modulates relative attention to the eyes and mouth of a talker. *Cognition* 147: 100–105.

Brysbaert, M. and Duyck, W. (2010). Is it time to leave behind the revised hierarchical model of bilingual language processing after fifteen years of service? *Bilingualism: Language and Cognition* 13 (3): 359–371.

Brysbaert, M., Verreyt, N., and Duyck, W. (2010). Models as hypothesis generators and models as roadmaps. *Bilingualism: Language and Cognition* 13 (3): 1–2.

Carrol, G. and Conklin, K. (2015). Eye-tracking multi-word units: some methodological questions. *Journal of Eye Movement Research* 7 (5): 1–11.

Carrol, G. and Conklin, K. (2017). Cross language lexical priming extends to formulaic units: evidence from eye-tracking suggests that this idea 'has legs'. *Bilingualism: Language and Cognition* 20 (2): 299–317.

Chauncey, K., Grainger, J., and Holcomb, P.J. (2008). Code-switching effects in bilingual word recognition: a masked priming study with event-related potentials. *Brain and Language* 105 (3): 161–174.

Cop, U., Keuleers, E., Drieghe, D., and Duyck, W. (2015). Frequency effects in monolingual and bilingual natural reading. *Psychonomic Bulletin & Review* 22 (5): 1216–1234.

de Groot, A.M.B. (1992). Determinants of word translation. *Journal of Experimental Psychology: Learning, Memory, and Cognition* 18 (5): 1001–1018.

Dijkstra, T. and Van Heuven, W.J. (2002). The architecture of the bilingual word recognition system: from identification to decision. *Bilingualism: Language and Cognition* 5 (3): 175–197.

Ervin, S.M. and Osgood, C.E. (1954). Second language learning and bilingualism. *Journal of Personality and Social Psychology* 58: 139–145.

Farley, A.P., Ramonda, K., and Liu, X. (2012). The concreteness effect and the bilingual lexicon: the impact of visual stimuli attachment on meaning recall of abstract L2 words. *Language Teaching Research* 16 (4): 449–466.

Finkbeiner, M.S., Forster, K., Nicol, J., and Nakamura, K. (2004). The role of polysemy in masked semantic and translation priming. *Journal of Memory and Language* 51 (1): 1–22.

French, R.M. and Jacquet, M. (2004). Understanding bilingual memory: models and data. *Trends in Cognitive Sciences* 8 (2): 87–93.

Grainger, J., Midgley, K., and Holcomb, P.J. (2010). Re-thinking the bilingual interactive-activation model from a developmental perspective (BIA-d). In: *Language Acquisition across Linguistic and Cognitive Systems* (ed. M. Kail and M. Hickman), 267–283. Philadelphia, PA: John Benjamins.

Grey, S., Tanner, D., and van Hell, J.G. (2017). How right is left? Handedness modulates neural responses during morphosyntactic processing. *Brain Research* 1669: 27–43.

Hamrick, P. and Ullman, M.T. (2016). A neurocognitive perspective on retrieval interference in L2 sentence processing. *Bilingualism: Language and Cognition* 20 (4): 687–688.

Harakchiyska, T. (2011). Overgeneralization as a strategy for the acquisition of L1 and L2 noun, morphology (the category of number). *Научни Трудове На Русенския Университет* 63 (50): 115–123.

Hartsuiker, R.J. and Bernolet, S. (2017). The development of shared syntax in second language learning. *Bilingualism: Language and Cognition* 20 (2): 219–234.

Heredia, R.R. and Altarriba, J. (2001). Bilingual language mixing: why do bilinguals code-switch? *Current Directions in Psychological Science* 10 (5): 164–168.

Heredia, R.R. and Cieślicka, A.B. (2018). Bilingual mental models. In: *An Introduction to Bilingualism: Principles and Processes*, 2nd (ed. J. Altarriba and R.R. Heredia), 37–67. New York, NY: Routledge.

Hernandez, A., Li, P., and MacWhinney, B. (2005). The emergence of competing modules in bilingualism. *Trends in Cognitive Sciences* 9 (5): 220–225.

Indefrey, P. and Levelt, W.J. (2004). The spatial and temporal signatures of word production components. *Cognition* 92 (1–2): 101–144.

Kolers, P.A. (1963). Interlingual word associations. *Journal of Verbal Learning and Verbal Behavior* 2 (4): 291–300.

Kopeliovich, S. (2006). *Reversing language shift in the immigrant family: A case-study of a Russian-speaking community in Israel* (Doctoral dissertation, Bar-Ilan University).

Kroll, J.F. and Stewart, E. (1994). Category interference in translation and picture naming: evidence for asymmetric connections between bilingual memory representations. *Journal of Memory and Language* 33: 149–174.

Kroll, J.F. and Tokowicz, N. (2005). Models of bilingual representation and processing: looking back and to the future. In: *Handbook of Bilingualism: Psycholinguistic Approaches* (ed. J.F. Kroll and A.M.B. DeGroot), 531–553. New York, NY: Oxford University Press.

Kutas, M. and Federmeier, K.D. (2011). Thirty years and counting: finding meaning in the N400 component of the event-related brain potential (ERP). *Annual Review of Psychology* 62: 621–647.

Lau, E.F., Phillips, C., and Poeppel, D. (2008). A cortical network for semantics: (De) constructing the N400. *Nature Reviews Neuroscience* 9: 920–933.

Lewkowicz, D.J. and Hansen-Tift, A.M. (2012). Infants deploy selective attention to the mouth of a talking face when learning speech. *Proceedings of the National Academy of Sciences* 109 (5): 1431–1436.

Lynch, M.A. (2004). Long-term potentiation and memory. *Physiological Reviews* 84 (1): 87–136.

Martin, J.M. and Altarriba, J. (2016). Rapid serial visual presentation: bilingual lexical and attentional processing. In: *Methods in Bilingual Reading Comprehension Research* (ed. R. Heredia, J. Altarriba and A. Cieślicka), 61–98. New York, NY: Springer.

McLaughlin, J., Osterhout, L., and Kim, A. (2004). Neural correlates of second-language word learning: minimal instruction produces rapid change. *Nature Neurosciene 7* (7): 703–704.

Monaghan, P., Chang, Y., Welbourne, S., and Brysbaert, M. (2017). Exploring the relations between word frequency, language exposure, and bilingualism in a computational model of reading. *Journal of Memory and Language* 93: 1–21.

Morgan-Short, K. (2014). Electrophysiological approaches to understanding second language acquisition: a field reaching its potential. *Annual Review of Applied Linguistics* 34: 15–36.

Morgan-Short, K., Steinhauer, K., Sanz, C., and Ullman, M.T. (2012). Explicit and implicit second language training differentially affect the achievement of native-like brain activation patterns. *Journal of Cognitive Neuroscience* 24: 933–947.

Morgan-Short, K. and Tanner, D. (2014). Event-related potentials (ERPs). In: *Research Methods in Second Language Psycholinguistics* (ed. J. Jegerski and B. VanPatten), 127–152. New York, NY: Routledge.

Monsell, S., Doyle, M.C., and Haggard, P.N. (1989). Effects of frequency on visual word recognition tasks: where are they? *Journal of Experimental Psychology: General* 118: 43–71.

Paivio, A. and Desrochers, A. (1980). A dual-coding approach to bilingual memory. *Canadian Journal of Psychology/Revue Canadienne de Psychologie* 34 (4): 388–399.

Palmer, S.D., van Hooff, J.C., and Havelka, J. (2010). Language representation and processing in fluent bilinguals: electrophysiological evidence for asymmetric mapping in bilingual memory. *Neuropsychologia* 48 (5): 1426–1437.

Segalowitz, N. and Freed, B.F. (2004). Context, contact, and cognition in oral fluency acquisition: learning Spanish in at home and study abroad contexts. *Studies in Second Language Acquisition* 26 (2): 173–199.

Segui, J., Mehler, J., Frauenfelder, U., and Morton, J. (1982). The word frequency effect and lexical access. *Neuropsychologia* 20 (6): 615–627.

Slabakova, R. (2016). The scalpel model of third language acquisition. *International Journal of Bilingualism* 21 (6): 651–665.

Soares, C. and Grosjean, F. (1984). Bilinguals in a monolingual and a bilingual speech mode: the effect on lexical access. *Memory & Cognition* 12 (4): 380–386.

Sutton, T.M., Altarriba, J., Gianico, J.L., and Basnight-Brown, D.M. (2007). The automatic access of emotion: emotional Stroop effects in Spanish–English bilingual speakers. *Cognition and Emotion* 21 (5): 1077–1090.

Swaab, T.Y., Ledoux, K., Camblin, C.C., and Boudewyn, M.A. (2012). Language-related ERP components. In: *Oxford Handbook of Event-Related Potential Components* (ed. S.J. Luck and E.S. Kappenman), 397–440. New York, NY: Oxford University Press.

Tokowicz, N. and Kroll, J.F. (2007). Number of meanings and concreteness: consequences of ambiguity within and across languages. *Language and Cognitive Processes* 22 (5): 727–779.

van Heuven, W.J. and Dijkstra, T. (2010). Language comprehension in the bilingual brain: fMRI and ERP support for psycholinguistic models. *Brain Research Reviews* 64 (1): 104–122.

Velan, H. and Frost, R. (2007). Cambridge University versus Hebrew University: the impact of letter transposition on reading English and Hebrew. *Psychonomic Bulletin & Review* 14 (5): 913–918.

Velan, H. and Frost, R. (2011). Words with and without internal structure: what determines the nature of orthographic and morphological processing? *Cognition* 118 (2): 141–156.

Wang, X. and Forster, K.I. (2010). Masked translation priming with semantic categorization: testing the sense model. *Bilingualism: Language and Cognition* 13 (3): 327–340.

Wilck, A.M. and Altarriba, J. (in press). Emotion words in monolingual and bilingual cognitive psycholinguistic research. In: *Handbook on Language and Emotion* (ed. G. Schiewer, J. Altarriba and N.B. Chin). de Gruyter: Berlin, Germany.

Wong, A.C.N., Qu, Z., McGugin, R.W., and Gauthier, I. (2011). Interference in character processing reflects common perceptual expertise across writing systems. *Journal of Vision* 11 (1): 1–13.

20 Brain-based Challenges of Second Language Learning in Older Adulthood

ZAHRA HEJAZI, JUNGNA KIM, TERESA SIGNORELLI PISANO, YASMINE OUCHIKH, AVIVA LERMAN, AND LORAINE K. OBLER

1. Introduction

Our brains change as a part of normal ageing. This often presents cognitive challenges for older adults (OAs), ages 60–65 years and older, also known as 'third agers'. Older adults, relative to when they were younger, may demonstrate difficulty remembering names and learning new skills, for example. In this chapter, we review the brain-based, cognitive-linguistic changes that come in the third age of life and how they may impact new learning, with a particular focus on learning a foreign language. We review what is known about foreign or second-language acquisition (SLA) and how second language (L2) teaching pedagogies may be designed to enhance learning in OAs in response to their changing brains.

Learning an L2 has become increasingly important in a world whose cultural and linguistic diversity is expanding and interacting. Despite decades of investigation on age-influenced SLA, little empirical research has addressed OA learners. Given that the National Institute on Aging in the United States estimates dramatic increases for this already sizeable population worldwide, the need to secure social–emotional, physical, and intellectual well-being for them is increasingly relevant (e.g. He et al. 2016). When one also considers the declines in these modalities associated with ageing, the need becomes even greater.

The idea of OAs learning an L2 is appealing for many reasons. For older immigrants coming to a new country and a new language, learning an L2 is often crucial for daily life (see Pot et al. 2017). The social benefits of L2 acquisition in less urgent circumstances are fairly well known, such as effective communication with family members who speak that L2 as their primary language and enriched tourism experiences/or leisure activities

The Handbook of the Neuroscience of Multilingualism, First Edition. Edited by John W. Schwieter.
© 2019 John Wiley & Sons Ltd. Published 2019 by John Wiley & Sons Ltd.

amongst others. Second language acquisition is also gaining attention because of possible cognitive benefits. For example, bilingualism has been suggested to delay the onset of dementia by three to five years in a number of studies, most notably in works by Ellen Bialystok and colleagues (e.g. Bialystok et al. 2007). This cognitive benefit is presumed to be associated with the processes involved in using two or more languages; thus, the process of SLA itself may be beneficial. For example, Bak et al. (2014) revealed positive effects of bilingualism on cognition in their longitudinal study. The researchers compared just over 850 monolingual and bilingual speakers' performance at age 11 and then at ages 71–74 years on a series of cognitive measures. Results indicated that bilingual speakers performed significantly better than expected, relative to that predicted by their baseline testing. Having controlled for other demographics, the authors believed bilingualism had a protective impact on cognition. Both early and late bilinguals evidenced benefits, though differentially, relative to their childhood intelligence scores. Similarly, Antoniou and colleagues have described cognitive training as a way to buffer against cognitive decline in OAs and explain that L2 learning is one type of cognitive training that may be effective in this way (e.g. Antoniou et al. 2013; Antoniou and Wright 2017). However, Calvo et al. (2016) point out that not all studies indicate an L2 advantage or benefit. They note the data are inconsistent and offer suggestions to improve research paradigms (see Lehtonen et al.'s 2018 meta-analysis of the literature).

With the appeal, if not need, for OAs to learn an L2, why is there so little primary research on this topic? It may be partly due to anecdotally driven, common negative perceptions amongst OAs–and their instructors – regarding L2 learning in older age. Indeed, legitimate age-related constraints may contribute to difficulties in language learning. It is widely accepted that adults generally have more difficulty learning a second language relative to children. There is substantial evidence that learning an L2 in childhood results in higher eventual proficiency than learning as an adult (e.g. Krashen 1982; Krashen et al. 1979). However, this does not mean that adults cannot successfully learn new languages even later in life. The question, we believe, is not *if* OAs can learn an L2, but to what level of proficiency across the different language domains can they do so, and which pedagogical approaches are most effective.

2. Brain-based Cognitive-Linguistic Changes in Healthy Ageing

The literature defines healthy OAs as those individuals over a certain age (typically 60–65 years or older) who are free of disease and disability despite a decline in various skills. For example, normal ageing processes include diminishing hearing (e.g. Baltes and Lindenberger 1997) and vision (e.g. Owsley 2011), both peripheral processes that are important to language functioning and learning and, in part, brain-based. The brain-based changes governing language and cognition, however, are the most significant in terms of communication and so we address those here in detail.

Language is one of the most complex cognitive skills and it involves manipulating a symbol system to communicate wants and ideas between and amongst individuals. It is interconnected and modulated by other cognitive processes, such as memory and attention, thereby making language and cognition difficult to dissociate (Anderson 2013; Kohnert 2004; Luria 1966). Since a comprehensive review is beyond the scope of this chapter, we will review changes in the primary neuroanatomical structures and language behaviours. See Burke and Shafto (2008), Abrams et al. (2010), and Shafto and Tyler (2014) for more detailed reviews on brain and language changes in ageing.

2.1. Brain Anatomical Changes

Language is typically lateralized to the left cerebral hemisphere. Classic regions associated with language production and comprehension include Broca's area, located in the inferior frontal lobe and Wernicke's area in the superior posterior temporal lobe. Additional structures related to language include gyri in the inferior regions of the parietal lobe, the anterior temporal lobe, and connecting fibres (white matter tracts). Two main streams have been identified within the language network: the dorsal (upper) stream, closely associated with language production, and the ventral (lower) stream, closely associated with language comprehension (e.g. Hickok and Poeppel 2007). These streams involve predominantly cortical language regions as well as white matter pathways, with the dorsal stream mapping sound to articulation and the ventral stream mapping sound to meaning (Hickok and Poeppel 2007; Saur et al. 2008).

Additional areas that are implicated in language processing include the prefrontal cortex and distributed networks across other cortical and subcortical regions. For example, the hippocampus is a subcortical structure crucial for memory and the hippocampus and surrounding cortices are involved in encoding novel information, consolidating and integrating memories, as well as language processing (see Duff and Brown-Schmidt 2012; Horner and Doeller 2017; Strange et al. 1999). Additionally, cognitive control depends on substantial prefrontal regions in a network with subcortical regions, inferior parietal cortex, and anterior cingulate cortex. Part of this cognitive control network is directly involved in language monitoring and inhibition in monolinguals and bilinguals, as well as switching between languages in bilinguals (Abutalebi and Green 2007; Cohen 2017).

Neuroimaging research shows changes in these brain areas in healthy ageing. For example, Broca's and Wernicke's areas show a decrease in activation levels in OAs relative to younger adults (YAs; e.g. Rotte 2005). Age-related decline begins in middle adulthood in some brain regions. For instance, throughout the brain, cortical grey matter decreases in volume, starting around age 30 years with an increased rate of decline starting around age 80 years (Allen et al. 2005). White matter volume also decreases with age (Michielse et al. 2010).

There is variability across individuals regarding the degree and types of neuronal change but total brain volume decreases atrophy in healthy ageing (Fjell and Walhovd 2010; Raz et al. 2005). This atrophy is most likely due to a reduction in synapses that connect between neurons rather than actual neuronal loss (Fjell and Walhovd 2010), although myelinated (well-insulated) axons are notably reduced by almost 50% between ages 20 and 80 years (Marner et al. 2003). In healthy OAs, some regions show faster volume loss than others, such as the prefrontal cortex and parts of the temporal lobe where semantic processing and auditory comprehension are subserved (e.g. Raz et al. 2005). Additionally, some of the greatest atrophy in healthy ageing has been found in the hippocampus (Raz et al. 2005), responsible for many aspects of memory.

Although neurological decline in ageing has been well-documented, there are also other anatomical changes in the brain that may result in compensatory strategies in OAs. For example, decreased activation for encoding verbal information has been found in the left inferior frontal lobe; this is more likely to accompany increased activation in the right hemisphere homologue in OAs, more so than in YAs (e.g. Buckner 2003; Grady and Craik 2000; Park et al. 2001). Interestingly, these right hemisphere compensatory patterns were more common in OAs than in YAs (Buckner 2004). For example, Cabeza et al. (2002) found that higher-functioning OAs recruited prefrontal cortical areas bilaterally in word-memory tasks. This may suggest that compensatory strategies in OAs may, in part, be due to the contribution of the right hemisphere as argued in Obler et al. 2010, with respect to naming in OA.

2.2. Cognitive Changes

Behavioural changes occur along with the neurological changes in ageing. Here we address the typical changes one sees in cognitive functioning in OAs. Cognition mediates all types of learning across the lifespan, including a set of mental actions or mechanisms that contribute to language processes, such as memory, problem-solving, reasoning, planning, and inhibition (Anderson 2013; Kohnert 2004; Luria 1966). Cognitive functions increase through childhood then decline in adults with advancing age, though, as with neurological changes, not all in the same way or at the same rate within and across individuals. This variation may explain some of the L2 learning differences seen amongst children, YAs, and OAs that we address below. In part, these cognitive differences reflect the ways in which brain networks are strengthened with maturation and learning and may diminish with disuse and age-related neuronal loss. The cognitive changes that have particular influence in language functioning throughout life are cognitive slowing and changes in episodic memory, working memory, cognitive control, and attention.

Cognitive functions gradually slowdown in OAs; this is often termed *cognitive slowing*. Cognitive slowing refers to an age-related decline in speed of processing or functional processing in various cognitive activities (e.g. Zanto and Gazzaley 2017), and are generally considered to be more susceptible to decline than language functions (Shafto and Tyler 2014).

2.2.1. Changes in Episodic and Working Memory   Episodic memory is a type of memory characterized by the ability to remember information that has undergone consolidation into long-term, more permanent memory. It plays a role in word finding (Craik and Tulving 1975; Tulving and Thomson 1973) and sentence and action memory (Burke and MacKay 1997). Episodic memory is also susceptible to change in older adulthood – even for words known for many years – in that word retrieval becomes less efficient relative to younger adulthood (Meinzer et al. 2014; Seidenberg et al. 2013). Seidenberg et al. (2013), for example, investigated the relationship between episodic memory decline and proper noun retrieval in two groups of (presumably monolingual) OAs ages 65–90 years. The participants were placed into a declining or stable group based on their scores on a series of cognitive measures. Participants viewed printed proper names and made judgements indicating whether or not the name was of a famous person. Behavioural outcomes indicated that the declining group was less accurate in identifying contemporary famous names (from 1995 to 2005) compared to the stable group. The two groups, however, were equally accurate regarding famous names from an earlier era (from 1950 to 1965). Data from MRI testing indicated that group episodic memory performance scores correlated with hippocampal volumes.

Working memory (WM), in contrast to episodic memory, is a cognitive function that temporarily stores and processes information required for complex tasks such as language comprehension and learning. Looking at the components of Baddeley's model (2010), one can see how closely WM and language are connected: Baddeley's oft-cited paradigm comprises a central executive component that serves as an attentional control system to short-term storage systems for visual and phonological information called the visuo-spatial scratch pad and the phonological loop respectively. There is also a system for storing chunks of multidimensional sensory information called the episodic buffer.

Studies exploring age-related changes in WM show a reduced capacity of WM between younger and older adults (e.g. Hasher and Zacks 1988). Such studies have shown that WM is positively correlated with sentence comprehension (e.g. Goral et al. 2011; Salis 2011). Salis (2011) found, for example, that OAs experience more difficulty in comprehending syntactically complex discourse than YAs. This age-related difference, however, diminished with syntactically simple sentences. Moreover, Salis found that greater WM span (e.g. the ability to repeat back a list of words) correlated significantly with complex sentence comprehension for both their younger and older groups. This suggests that WM span is important for complex sentence processing across adulthood and that age-related processing difference can be attributed, at least in part, to limitations in WM resources.

2.2.2.   Changes in Cognitive Control   Cognitive control governs goal-directed activities in the face of competition (e.g. Cohen 2017). Inhibition, the ability to suppress irrelevant information, is a type of cognitive control. Research shows that OAs are slower than YAs in non-verbal inhibitory control tasks, such as the Simon task (Simon and Rudell 1967). In the Simon task, participants respond selectively to certain stimuli but not to others (Sommers and Danielson 1999; West and Alain 2000), inhibiting the tendency to respond to interference. While the Simon task does not capture the process completely (Kroll and Bialystok 2013), Simon-task studies indicate an age-related decline to resisting interference. Other support comes from the electrophysiology literature. For example, OAs were found to inhibit task-irrelevant information less efficiently than YAs (Alain and Woods 1999) and evidenced smaller mismatch negativity (MMN) on irrelevant auditory distractors during a visual discrimination task. This indicated that the OAs had reduced inhibitory control of sensory stimuli relative to YAs. Alain and Woods note that this decreased inhibitory control of sensory stimuli in the prefrontal cortex, where inhibition was measured, may account for the age-related declines in visual discrimination tasks with auditory interference.

2.2.3. Changes in Attention Related to cognitive control and inhibition is the function of attention. This cognitive mechanism comprises subtypes such as sustained, selective, divided, and attention switching. Sustained attention facilitates focus on a given target, selective attention permits focus on one target over another, divided attention addresses focus on concurrent multiple targets, and attention switching facilitates focusing back and forth between two different target stimuli (see Gilsky 2007 for more information). All subtypes of attention are important to learning and language functioning.

Similar to other cognitive functions, the attentional system also declines with age. OAs tend to have slower and less accurate performance than YAs when asked to detect visual (e.g. Hommel et al. 2004) and/or auditory (e.g. Singh et al. 2008) stimuli in the presence of interference, indicating an age-related slowing in the selective attentional system. However, the impact of ageing on attention appears to be task-dependent. Older adults tend to show ageing-related decline on sustained attention tasks, but relatively better preserved selective attention (Gilsky 2007). Dividing or switching attention amongst multiple inputs or tasks, as well as attention tasks involving a visual search, are also more challenging for OAs than YAs (Commodari and Guarnera 2008; West 2004). Moreover, declines in auditory selective and sustained attention are pivotal to spoken language functioning, and comprehending speech in noisy situations is particularly difficult for OAs compared with YAs (Gosselin and Gagné 2011), independent of peripheral hearing problems.

2.3. Linguistic Changes

It is generally accepted that linguistic competence remains relatively preserved across the lifespan (see Shafto and Tyler 2014). Most OAs are able to communicate as effectively as YAs. There are, nonetheless, functional language declines associated with healthy ageing in different domains and to varying degrees across individuals. For example, cognitive slowing, which we discussed in Section 2.2 with respect to general cognitive functions, may influence linguistic performance in OAs. Indeed, studies have shown that OAs are slower than YAs in language control tasks (Calabria et al. 2015; Ivanova et al. 2016). For example, older bilingual adults responded more slowly than younger ones in naming pictures of objects, and they were less efficient in switching languages when they were cued to do so (Calabria et al. 2015; Ivanova et al. 2016). Also, OAs were slower in verbal fluency tasks than YAs (i.e. listing items from a given category in a given time frame; Gollan et al. 2002). Since the literature on the relationship between cognitive and linguistic slowing in ageing is highly limited, this will be an area for developing research in the future.

Similarly, functional language declines may be affected by factors that affect cognitive reserve. The term *cognitive reserve* refers to the resilience or resistance to cognitive decline in normal ageing or in the presence of a degenerative disease such as Alzheimer's disease and other forms of dementia (e.g. Alladi et al. 2013; Stern 2002). There is evidence that this functional decline can be slowed by certain activities or conditions throughout the lifespan. For example, cognitive reserve may be affected by education and experience, language background and bilingualism, usage patterns, and occupation (e.g. LaBarge et al. 1986; Le Carret et al. 2003; Scarmeas and Stern 2004; Tun and

Wingfield 1997). Neurophysiological research indicates that people with good cognitive reserve perform better on intellectual tasks than their degree of brain deterioration might predict (e.g. Buckner 2004). This in turn affects their linguistic abilities.

Arguably, the most well-known language challenge for OAs is the 'tip-of-the-tongue' phenomenon linked to problems with word retrieval, also known as *lexical access* (e.g. Burke et al. 1991). Healthy adults can often overcome word retrieval difficulties given a phonemic cue which prompts recall of a given word, showing that the words are not lost, but rather they are harder to retrieve (e.g. James and Burke 2000; Nicholas et al. 1985). Juncos-Rabadán and Iglesias (1994) found that advancing age is accompanied by problems with comprehension, repetition, judgement, writing and reading. Indeed, Obler et al. (1991) reported that advancing age was associated with increased reaction time and errors in comprehending syntactically more complex structures relative to simple ones. There is also evidence that in OAs language difficulty manifests with more complex linguistic components (such as comprehension) relative to less complex ones (such as naming skills; e.g. Obler and Albert 1981).

3.   Second Language Acquisition (SLA)

Individuals who master an L2 after achieving communicative competence in their first language (L1) as a child, are considered sequential bilinguals. Those who study an L2 formally are often referred to as second language learners (SLLs) and may also be considered sequential bilinguals. While there is a long history of research looking at SLA, most research investigates L2 development in children or college-aged young adults; as mentioned in the Introduction to this chapter, comparatively little empirical research has addressed OAs. In this section, we address this small body of research on older learners, using the general SLA literature when necessary to provide context.

3.1.   Age and Language Development

The importance of age to language development was emphasized by Lenneberg (1967) who developed Penfield and Roberts' (1959) notion of a critical period for language learning and proposed puberty as a boundary for the brain's ability to acquire a new language. Johnson and Newport (1989) tested this hypothesis with respect to SLA. They compared English grammar proficiency in Korean- and Chinese-L1 speakers immersed in an L2 English environment to their age of immigration. Their results evidenced a negative relationship such that grammatical knowledge decreased as a function of age of arrival to a new country/language environment. The results highlighted a particular importance of age to L2 morphosyntax and support the sensitive period hypothesis. This hypothesis argues that individuals show varied abilities while learning different L2 domains and that age-related decline in the ability to learn a language is gradual rather than abrupt (Long 1990).

Studies of critical and sensitive periods in childhood burgeoned in the late twentieth century. Age-related differences across adulthood, however, were virtually not considered. It was generally understood, from the earlier critical period research and cultural perceptions, that the neural plasticity (i.e. the brain's ability to change) that permitted language learning ended before adulthood. Recent neurophysiology studies, however, have transformed views on adult language-learning. Current research suggests that the brain retains some degree of plasticity throughout adulthood (see Li et al. 2014; Merzenich et al. 2014). Moreover, we see that considerable changes may occur in the cortical areas of the brain that largely mediate language even in late life (e.g. Fratiglioni et al. 2004; Guglielman 2012). This, along with the fact that many YAs and OAs succeed in learning an L2 to greater or lesser extent (Ramírez Gómez 2016), indicates that language learning is definitely still possible after puberty.

Age may also be important to SLA because the underlying cognitive mechanisms involved in language learning are purportedly different in children and in adults. Bley-Vroman (1988) and Paradis (2009), for example, propose that children rely on implicit knowledge when learning an L2 whereas adults rely on explicit knowledge. Ellis (1994) explains that implicit learning is a process that occurs naturally and does not require conscious effort. Explicit learning, in contrast, is a selective operation and requires conscious functions and attention. There are dissenting views in the L2 literature, however. DeKeyser (1997), for example, suggests that YAs require explicit learning for general grammatical components when learning an L2. In contrast, Ellis (1994) claims that acquiring the phonetic and phonological features of a new word involves implicit learning in general, but that the semantic features require explicit learning. It is important to note that these claims are largely theoretical; thus more empirical research is needed to test these assertions.

While the pool is small, a number of studies assess L2 learning in OAs and provide some insight into how OAs learn an L2. Lenet and her colleagues, for example, taught Latin word order to younger and older English-speaking adults ages 18–21 and 66–81 years, respectively (Lenet et al. 2011). Half of each age group received explicit feedback and correction when they made an error. Participants were told whether their answers were right or wrong and were given the correct form. The other half received less explicit feedback whereby they were simply told whether their response was correct or not. The OAs benefited more from the less-explicit feedback condition, whereas the YAs benefited more from the more-explicit feedback condition. Additionally, older adults commented that the more explicit feedback was presented too quickly. The authors postulated that additional explicit feedback may have interfered with the OAs' ability to learn the rules since they may have tried to memorize the feedback that explained their error.

In a similar study, Cox and Sanz (2015) taught Latin vocabulary and word order to younger and older English-Spanish bilinguals ages 19–27 and 60–82 years, respectively. Some older participants had studied Latin in school, but not for more than three years and not for, at least, the past 20 years. Also, while OAs had significantly more education than the YAs, participants had no experience learning other languages with case marking, as Latin has. The study sought to determine the influence of explicit instruction with practice versus explicit instruction only. Explicit instruction involved reviewing thematic roles in English and how these are marked by case in Latin. Practice, then, involved several tasks: reading or listening to sentences in Latin and then translating them to English and/or pointing to a photo from two options that depicted the sentence. Following explicit instruction only, OAs performed less optimally and less successfully than did the YAs. However, when both groups were tested two weeks later, after receiving explicit instruction with practice, their performance did not significantly differ.

As described above, WM is important to general language learning and SLA. Mackey and Sachs (2012) investigated the relationship between WM and interaction-driven learning in older L2 learners. Native Spanish-speakers ages 65–89 years engaged in a number of working memory tasks and held conversations in English with native speakers. The language learners were guided in conversation with various prompts (e.g. picture sequences) and given feedback (e.g. recasts and clarification). The results indicated that OAs with better WM showed improvement in an immediate post-test and sustained skills in a delayed post-test period compared with those with a weaker WM.

3.2.   *Cognitive-linguistic Aptitude and L2 Acquisition*

Linguistic aptitude is an important variable in learning an L2 (e.g. Dörnyei 2014), but it has not, to our knowledge, been studied in OAs. Ramírez Gómez (2016) describes linguistic aptitude as an innate ability to learn a new language. She notes that it includes inherent memory and attention abilities. Supporting this notion is work by Rodriguez-Fornells et al. (2006) and Mackey and Sachs (2012), for example, who show that better WM and attention skills are in general associated with better linguistic aptitude in SLA. Researchers in the field of bilingualism suggest that non-linguistic, cognitive factors are central components of L2 aptitude, accounting for individual differences at any age (e.g. Bialystok and Hakuta 1999; Skehan 1986).

Working memory is an important component of language aptitude and is a strong predictor of written and auditory L2 sentence processing as well as discourse comprehension (e.g. Linck et al. 2014). One of the earliest studies on WM and L2 development examined the L1 and L2 WM capacity relationship and L2 reading skills in Japanese advanced learners of English aged 25–30 years (Harrington and Sawyer 1992). Results revealed a significant link between performance on an L2 reading skills task and WM measured in L2, suggesting that better WM supported better reading performance and L2 performance. Many positive correlations have been observed between WM and L2, including L2 vocabulary learning (Gathercole et al. 1999; Verhagen and Leseman 2016), oral proficiency (Payne and Whitney 2002), grammatical form (Leeser 2007), speech production and performance (Ahmadian 2012; Gass and Lee 2011; Kormos and Trebits 2011), and L2 listening and reading comprehension (Alptekin and Erçetin 2010; Osaka et al. 1993). However, this robust relationship has been found primarily in studies of young adults and children in the literature. Future research will determine whether this relationship occurs in OAs as well.

4.   The Neurobiology of First and Second Languages

Neuroimaging research on healthy adults shows that first and second languages largely use the same neural processing systems despite some differences in neural representation. The neural bases for first and second languages are not stable, but rather change as L2 develops, and age of acquisition (AoA), proficiency, and L2 exposure all impact L2 neural organization (Perani and Abutalebi 2005; Perani et al. 2003). Looking at AoA, Wartenburger et al. (2003) found that adults who had acquired their L2 before age six showed no difference in L1 and L2 activation during grammar tasks. Those who acquired their L2 after that age showed more activation for L2 than for L1. This suggests that the later bilinguals needed additional neural resources for L2 to achieve comparable performance in grammatical tasks in the two languages even though the same brain regions were recruited.

Not all findings indicate an AoA-related impact, however. Second language differences for lexical retrieval have been noted to be related to proficiency, rather than to AoA. While the same left-hemisphere regions around the Sylvian fissure were activated in both L1 and L2, less-proficient speakers recruited additional neural resources relative to more-proficient speakers, such as from prefrontal regions usually associated with cognitive control (De Bleser et al. 2003; Perani and Abutalebi 2005). However, the findings regarding proficiency are not always consistent either. While also showing differences in neural substrate involvement between high- and low-proficiency speakers, Perani et al. (1998) found an opposing pattern with a different processing task. Looking at sentence and discourse comprehension, Perani and colleagues found that low-proficiency speakers evidenced less neural substrate involvement in the temporal lobes and temporo-parietal regions compared with high-proficiency L2 speakers. Furthermore, later research by Perani and colleagues in 2003 found that experience and practice may affect cerebral representation more than proficiency; participants with varying amounts of L2 exposure, but comparable proficiency, presented different left dorsolateral frontal lobe profiles (Perani et al. 2003). How the neuroanatomy of an L2 in OAs will compare with what we know to date, based on younger individuals, remains to be seen and merits further investigation.

5. Designing L2 Experiences to Enhance Older Adults' L2 Learning

The process of developing L2 learning programs for OAs must largely be extrapolated from the general ageing and L2 literature until more empirical research is done. Ramírez Gómez's (2016) book, *Language Teaching and the Older Adult: The Significance of Experience* and Danuta Gabryś-Barker's edited (2017) book *Third Age Learners of Foreign Language* are the most comprehensive resources regarding older L2 learners. They review characteristics of older learners and their instructors, the influence of experience, and pedagogical considerations. We recommend a number of their suggestions here that are particularly pertinent to the brain and cognitive issues we have discussed and consider outcomes of the other studies we have reported on (e.g. Cox and Sanz 2015). We highlight additional suggestions in light of our review of the brain-based cognitive changes seen in normal ageing.

5.1. *Normal Ageing and Pedagogical Approaches*

Regarding general ageing considerations, in Section 2 we reviewed cognitive changes OAs experience in healthy ageing including potential memory, attention, cognitive, and linguistic processing limitations. We have also discussed physiological changes in hearing and vision that can impact these processes. In response to such potential changes, Ramírez Gómez (2016) makes a number of suggestions that limit cognitive load and facilitate focus. For example, she recommends that instruction sessions be shorter rather than longer and that lessons focus on one linguistic component rather than on several at a time. Additionally, she suggests that instructors reduce their rate of speech as necessary, using relatively simple sentences rather than complex ones. She proposes mitigating auditory and visual noise in the instruction area and using larger fonts for printed materials. Moreover, Gabry-Barker's (2017) contributors (e.g. Green 2017; Singleton 2017), report on several qualitative studies regarding pedagogical approaches to facilitate L2 teaching in OAs. Recommendations include resources to strengthen the memorization process following OAs' reported need and to provide feedback (e.g. performance evaluation) so older learners know what to expect during instruction.

With respect to the use of feedback and explicit instruction, it may be wise to consider VanPatten's processing instruction theory (e.g. Culman et al. 2009). This suggests that explicit instruction is not sufficient for learning and that, in addition to explicit statements, teaching materials should be presented systematically so that learners can automatize rules. The small body of literature available on explicit feedback for OAs suggests that a limited degree of feedback can be helpful (e.g. Cox and Sanz 2015), while too much appears to interfere with learning (e.g. Lenet et al. 2011). This accords with Ramírez Gómez's (2016) recommendation of clearly describing activity goals, essentially a form of limited explicit instruction. Similarly, Doughty (2008) recommends encouraging adults to attend to aspects of the L2 that are different from those of the L1 and pointing out crucial elements for processing the L2, an approach that would seem ideal for older learners.

Recall that Cox and Sanz (2015), found practice to be helpful for OAs. They observed that OAs, given the opportunity to practice and to consolidate information over two weeks, caught up with YA learners. Yet, in their performance immediately after the learning session, YAs outperformed OAs. Methods like these, which involve providing incremental information with systematic support like scaffolding, may facilitate learning an L2 as reported by Chen (personal communication 2017) from experiences teaching English to older Chinese immigrants who arrived in the US aged 50–60 years.

5.2.   *SLA and Pedagogical Approaches*

Regarding SLA in general and how it may interact with potential ageing deficits, attention and attentional control are salient factors. It is largely believed that, although access to both languages is available to bilinguals at any time, they suppress one language when speaking another (e.g. Meuter and Allport 1999). Work by Rodriguez-Fornells et al. (2006) suggests that a dominant language requires greater attentional control to suppress it than does a non-dominant language. For OAs learning an L2 for the first time, in light of their life-long experience of using one language, their attentional limitations may result in more intrusion errors during L2 learning than for YAs.

In order to compensate for this potential attention decline in OAs during L2 learning, L2 learners must notice or be aware of L2 linguistic forms and structures in order for the input to be internalized and accessible (Bergsleithner 2011; Doughty 2008; Schmidt 1990). The concept of *awareness*, rather than attention, has been more commonly addressed in SLA research. Awareness involves conscious cognizance during L2 acquisition, whereas attention can be effectively engaged without the learner being aware. Researchers argue that conscious awareness of learning is involved in explicit learning (e.g. Reber 1993) and supports input enhancement (e.g. Sharwood-Smith 1981). For example, Doughty, and Williams (1998) emphasize a 'focus on form' pedagogy, in which learners are trained to consciously pay attention to the grammatical forms of the language so that they can acquire it better. Older adults may rely on explicit relative to implicit processing to learn an L2, due to their declining attentional control, but, as mentioned, too much explicit instruction may be detrimental and therefore must be carefully monitored.

6. Conclusion

While age-related decline in neural reserve and cognitive functioning would appear to bode ill for L2 learning in OAs, their brains have also been reported to develop compensatory brain mechanisms to deal with problems with lexical retrieval and with challenging comprehension. These compensatory strategies that develop over time in OAs can be harnessed by addressing and perhaps enhancing them in the classroom.

Two debates can be extracted from the minimal literature on L2 learning in older adulthood: (i) whether or not OAs really do have a harder time than YAs learning a new language, and (ii) whether more-explicit teaching helps OAs more than less-explicit teaching. The first debate has two sides: many L2 teachers and older students compare themselves to their younger counterparts (or to themselves at earlier ages) and report that learning an L2 later in life is harder than it was previously. This they attribute to difficulty with hearing, attention, and memory if not to additional brain-related physiological changes. The other side of this debate, which Ramírez Gómez and others espouse, argues optimistically that OAs can learn an L2; they just need to be taught in the ways that best address their cognitive strengths. We note that these positions are not mutually exclusive. That is, while OAs may have more difficulty learning a second language than in their youth, teaching them in ways that address their cognitive strengths will offer them tools to compensate for their age-related decline in neural reserve and cognitive functioning. Whether this compensation will permit them to achieve the same ultimate proficiency as YAs remains to be tested.

Amongst the approaches that researchers have prescribed to facilitate L2 learning in OAs are those that address learning-based abilities that decline in many OAs. Ensuring scaffolding to assure success and providing written materials in visible font to complement auditory stimuli that may be hard to distinguish, should increase the success of learning an L2. Additionally, extra time for drills, breaks to permit consolidation of learned materials, encouraging learners to reflect on what learning style works best for them (e.g. Kotik-Friedgut 2008) and to take responsibility for employing this knowledge in their free time are all recommended, though not yet based on definitive experiments. Avoiding multitasking and other potential distractions during language learning is obviously important for focusing attention to materials that will be learned. While sufficient high-quality sleep and exercise have been shown to enhance the brain's ability to learn generally in younger and older adults (Borota et al. 2014; Mazzoni et al. 1999; Winter et al. 2007), their cumulative benefit should be examined in relation to L2 learning in OAs because these factors may also enhance their attention and learning abilities.

In sum, we conclude that teaching OAs an L2 is possible, but (i) instruction should fit their learning needs and cognitive abilities, and (ii) it is not known whether there is any limit on the proficiency they will achieve. One pedagogical tool that directs the second debate in the field is the use of explicit teaching materials, especially for syntax and morphosyntax, but also for lexical semantics. However, those researchers who have experimented with explicit methodologies for OAs have seen mixed results, and explicit instruction is likely most beneficial when paired with practice (e.g. Cox and Sanz 2015). We conclude that more work remains to be done to determine whether certain types of explicit feedback may succeed where others do not, either for OAs learning an L2 as a group, or for individuals amongst them. Perhaps, for example, those with more successful prior experience learning another L2 via explicit teaching methods are those who may most benefit from explicit teaching and/or feedback in older adulthood, consistent with Ramírez Gómez's findings on how 'experience' with L2 learning can predict better learning of yet a new language in older adulthood.

While there are changes in older adults' brains, which may be offset by compensatory processes allowing for OAs to successfully learn a second language under the right learning conditions, we should also take into account that learning an L2 will bring about further changes in the brain, possibly resulting in better cognitive reserve, therefore we recommend that OAs do not shy away from learning a second language, and that teachers do not shy away from teaching them in ways that best permit successful L2 learning.

Acknowledgements

Thanks to Zhilong Xie and Stanley Chen for discussions on L2 learning in older adults; to Taryn Malcolm for comments on an early draft of the chapter and for suggesting additional papers we have referred to; to Tatiana Talavera for her participation in the early stages of the current chapter and designing a related research study on second language learning in older adults; to Merel Keijzer and an anonymous reviewer for their helpful comments on a previous draft; and to Bella Kotik-Friedgut for a discussion on individual differences in L2 learning style.

REFERENCES

Abrams, L., Farrell, M.T., and Margolin, S.J. (2010). Older adults' detection of misspellings during reading. *The Journals of Gerontology Series B: Psychological Sciences and Social Sciences* 65 (6): 680–683.

Abutalebi, J. and Green, D. (2007). Bilingual language production: the neurocognition of language representation and control. *Journal of Neurolinguistics* 20 (3): 242–275.

Ahmadian, M.J. (2012). The relationship between working memory capacity and L2 oral performance under task-based careful online planning condition. *TESOL Quarterly* 46 (1): 165–175.

Alain, C. and Woods, D.L. (1999). Age-related changes in processing auditory stimuli during visual attention: evidence for deficits in inhibitory control and sensory memory. *Psychology and Aging* 14 (3): 507.

Alladi, S., Bak, T.H., Duggirala, V. et al. (2013). Bilingualism delays age at onset of dementia, independent of education and immigration status. *Neurology* 81 (22): 1938–1944.

Allen, J.S., Bruss, J., Brown, C.K., and Damasio, H. (2005). Normal neuroanatomical variation due to age: the major lobes and a parcellation of the temporal region. *Neurobiology of Aging* 26 (9): 1245–1260.

Alptekin, C. and Erçetin, G. (2010). The role of L1 and L2 working memory in literal and inferential comprehension in L2 reading. *Journal of Research in Reading* 33 (2): 206–219.

Anderson, J.R. (2013). *The Architecture of Cognition*. New York, NY: Psychology Press.

Antoniou, M., Gunasekera, G.M., and Wong, P.C. (2013). Foreign language training as cognitive therapy for age-related cognitive decline: a hypothesis for future research. *Neuroscience & Biobehavioral Reviews* 37 (10): 2689–2698.

Antoniou, M. and Wright, S.M. (2017). Uncovering the mechanisms responsible for why language learning may promote healthy cognitive aging. *Frontiers in Psychology* 8: 2217.

Baddeley, A. (2010). Working memory. *Current Biology* 20 (4): R136–R140.

Bak, T.H., Nissan, J.J., Allerhand, M.M., and Deary, I.J. (2014). Does bilingualism influence cognitive aging? *Annals of Neurology* 75 (6): 959–963.

Baltes, P.B. and Lindenberger, U. (1997). Emergence of a powerful connection between sensory and cognitive functions across the adult life span: a new window to the study of cognitive aging? *Psychology and Aging* 12 (1): 12.

Bergsleithner, J.M. (2011). The role of noticing and working memory capacity in L2 oral performance. *Organon* 26 (51): 217–243.

Bialystok, E., Craik, F.I., and Freedman, M. (2007). Bilingualism as a protection against the onset of symptoms of dementia. *Neuropsychologia* 45 (2): 459–464.

Bialystok, E. and Hakuta, K. (1999). Confounded age: linguistic and cognitive factors in age differences for second language acquisition. In: *Second Language Acquisition and the Critical Period Hypothesis* (ed. D. Birdsong), 161–181). Mahwah, NJ: Erlbaum.

Bley-Vroman, R. (1988). The fundamental character of foreign language learning. In: *Grammar and Second Language Teaching: A Book of Readings* (ed. W. Rutherford and M. Sharwood Smith), 19–30. Rowley, MA: Newbury House.

Borota, D., Murray, E., Keceli, G. et al. (2014). Post-study caffeine administration enhances memory consolidation in humans. *Nature Neuroscience* 17 (2): 201–203.

Buckner, R.L. (2003). Functional-anatomic correlates of control processes in memory. *Journal of Neuroscience* 23 (10): 3999–4004.

Buckner, R.L. (2004). Memory and executive function in aging and AD: multiple factors that cause decline and reserve factors that compensate. *Neuron* 44 (1): 195–208.

Burke, D.M. and MacKay, D.G. (1997). Memory, language, and ageing. *Philosophical Transactions of the Royal Society of London B: Biological Sciences* 352 (1363): 1845–1856.

Burke, D.M., MacKay, D.G., Worthley, J.S., and Wade, E. (1991). On the tip of the tongue: what causes word finding failures in young and older adults? *Journal of Memory and Language* 30 (5): 542–579.

Burke, D.M. and Shafto, M.A. (2008). Language and aging. In: *The Handbook of Aging and Cognition*, vol. 3 (ed. F.I.M. Craik and T.A. Salthouse), 373–443. Mahwah, NJ: Erlbaum.

Cabeza, R., Anderson, N.D., Locantore, J.K., and McIntosh, A.R. (2002). Aging gracefully:

compensatory brain activity in high-performing older adults. *NeuroImage* 17 (3): 1394–1402.

Calabria, M., Branzi, F.M., Marne, P. et al. (2015). Age-related effects over bilingual language control and executive control. *Bilingualism: Language and Cognition* 18 (1): 65–78.

Calvo, N., García, A.M., Manoiloff, L., and Ibáñez, A. (2016). Bilingualism and cognitive reserve: a critical overview and a plea for methodological innovations. *Frontiers in Aging Neuroscience* 7: 249.

Cohen, J.D. (2017). Cognitive control: core constructs and current considerations. In: *The Wiley Handbook of Cognitive Control* (ed. T. Egner), 3–28. New York, NY: Wiley.

Commodari, E. and Guarnera, M. (2008). Attention and aging. *Aging Clinical and Experimental Research* 20 (6): 578–584.

Cox, J.G. and Sanz, C. (2015). Deconstructing PI for the ages: explicit instruction vs. practice in young and older adult bilinguals. *International Review of Applied Linguistics in Language Teaching* 53 (2): 225–248.

Craik, F.I. and Tulving, E. (1975). Depth of processing and the retention of words in episodic memory. *Journal of Experimental Psychology: General* 104 (3): 268–294.

Culman, H., Henry, N., and VanPatten, B. (2009). The role of explicit information in instructed SLA: an on-line study with processing instruction and German accusative case inflections. *Die Unterrichtspraxis/Teaching German* 42 (1): 19–31.

De Bleser, R., Dupont, P., Postler, J. et al. (2003). The organisation of the bilingual lexicon: a PET study. *Journal of Neurolinguistics* 16 (4): 439–456.

DeKeyser, R.M. (1997). Beyond explicit rule learning. *Studies in Second Language Acquisition* 19 (2): 195–221.

Dörnyei, Z. (2014). *The Psychology of the Language Learner: Individual Differences in Second Language Acquisition*. Abingon, UK: Routledge.

Doughty, C.J. (2008). Instructed SLA: constraints, compensation, and enhancement. In: *The Handbook of Second Language Acquisition* (ed. C. Doughty and M.H. Long), 256–310. Malden, MA: Blackwell.

Doughty, C. and Williams, J. (1998). Pedagogical choices in focus on form. In: *Focus on Form in Classroom Second Language Acquisition* (ed. C. Doughty and J. Williams), 197–261. New York, NY: Cambridge University Press.

Duff, M.C. and Brown-Schmidt, S. (2012). The hippocampus and the flexible use and processing of language. *Frontiers in Human Neuroscience* 6: 69.

Ellis, R. (1994). *The Study of Second Language Acquisition*. Oxford, UK: Oxford University.

Fjell, A.M. and Walhovd, K.B. (2010). Structural brain changes in aging: courses, causes and cognitive consequences. *Reviews in the Neurosciences* 21 (3): 187–222.

Fratiglioni, L., Paillard-Borg, S., and Winblad, B. (2004). An active and socially integrated lifestyle in late life might protect against dementia. *Lancet Neurology* 3 (6): 343–353.

Gabryś-Barker, D. (ed.) (2017). *Third Age Learners of Foreign Languages*. Bristol, UK: Multilingual matters.

Gass, S. and Lee, I. (2011). Working memory capacity, inhibitory control, and proficiency in a second language. In: *Modeling Bilingualism: From Structure to Chaos*, vol. 43 (ed. M.S. Schmid and W. Lowie), 59–84. Amsterdam, The Netherlands: John Benjamins.

Gathercole, S.E., Service, E., Hitch, G.J. et al. (1999). Phonological short-term memory and vocabulary development: further evidence on the nature of the relationship. *Applied Cognitive Psychology* 13 (1): 65–77.

Gilsky, E.L. (2007). Changes in cognitive function in human aging. In: *Brain Aging: Models, Methods, and Mechanisms* (ed. D.R. Riddle), 3–20. Boca Raton, FL: CRC Press.

Gollan, T.H., Montoya, R.I., and Werner, G.A. (2002). Semantic and letter fluency in Spanish English bilinguals. *Neuropsychology* 16 (4): 562.

Goral, M., Clark-Cotton, M., Spiro, A. III et al. (2011). The contribution of set switching and working memory to sentence processing in older adults. *Experimental Aging Research* 37 (5): 516–538.

Gosselin, P.A. and Gagné, J.P. (2011). Older adults expend more listening effort than young adults recognizing speech in noise. *Journal of Speech, Language, and Hearing Research* 54 (3): 944–958.

Grady, C.L. and Craik, F.I.M. (2000). Changes in memory processing with age. *Current Opinion in Neurobiology* 10: 224–231.

Green, D. (2017). The interactional challenge: L2 learning and use in the Third Age. In: *Third Age Learners of Foreign Languages* (ed. D. Gabryś-Barker), 31–47. Bristol, UK: Multilingual Matters.

Guglielman, E. (2012). The ageing brain: neuroplasticity and lifelong learning. *eLearning Papers* 29: 1–7.

Harrington, M. and Sawyer, M. (1992). L2 working memory capacity and L2 reading skill. *Studies in Second Language Acquisition* 14 (1): 25–38.

Hasher, L. and Zacks, R.T. (1988). Working memory, comprehension, and aging: a review and a new view. *Psychology of Learning and Motivation* 22: 193–225.

He, W., Goodkind, D., and Kowal, P.R. (2016). *An Aging World: 2015*. Washington, DC: United States Census Bureau.

Hickok, G. and Poeppel, D. (2007). The cortical organization of speech processing. *Nature Reviews Neuroscience* 8 (5): 393.

Hommel, B., Li, K.Z., and Li, S.C. (2004). Visual search across the life span. *Developmental Psychology* 40 (4): 545–558.

Horner, A.J. and Doeller, C.F. (2017). Plasticity of hippocampal memories in humans. *Current Opinion in Neurobiology* 43: 102–109.

Ivanova, I., Murillo, M., Montoya, R.I., and Gollan, T.H. (2016). Does bilingual language control decline in older age? *Linguistic Approaches to Bilingualism* 6 (1): 86–118.

James, L.E. and Burke, D.M. (2000). Phonological priming effects on word retrieval and tip-of-the-tongue experiences in young and older adults. *Journal of Experiment: Learning, Memory, and Cognition* 26 (6): 1378–1391.

Johnson, J.S. and Newport, E.L. (1989). Critical period effects in second language learning: the influence of maturational state on the acquisition of English as a second language. *Cognitive Psychology* 21 (1): 60–99.

Juncos-Rabadán, O. and Iglesias, F.J. (1994). Decline in the elderly's language: evidence from cross-linguistic data. *Journal of Neurolinguistics* 8 (3): 183–190.

Kohnert, K. (2004). Cognitive and cognate-based treatments for bilingual aphasia: a case study. *Brain and Language* 91 (3): 294–302.

Kormos, J. and Trebits, A. (2011). Working memory capacity and narrative task performance. In: *Second Language Task Complexity: Researching the Cognition Hypothesis of Language Learning and Performance* (ed. P. Robinson), 267–286. Amsterdam, The Netherlands: John Benjamins.

Kotik-Friedgut, B. (2008). *Enhancement of autonomy in language learners*. In: *Studies in Language and Language Education* (ed. A. Stavans and I. Kupferberg), 243–260. Jerusalem, Israel: The Hebrew University Magnes Press.

Krashen, S.D. (ed.) (1982). *Child-Adult Differences in Second Language Acquisition*. Rowley, MA: Newbury House Publishers.

Krashen, S.D., Long, M.A., and Scarcella, R.C. (1979). Age, rate and eventual attainment in second language acquisition. *TESOL Quarterly* 13 (4): 573–582.

Kroll, J.F. and Bialystok, E. (2013). Understanding the consequences of bilingualism for language processing and cognition. *Journal of Cognitive Psychology* 25 (5): 497–514.

LaBarge, E., Edwards, D., and Knesevich, J.W. (1986). Performance of normal elderly on the Boston Naming Test. *Brain and Language* 27 (2): 380–384.

Le Carret, N., Lafont, S., Letenneur, L. et al. (2003). The effect of education on cognitive performances and its implication for the constitution of the cognitive reserve. *Developmental Neuropsychology* 23 (3): 317–337.

Leeser, M.J. (2007). Learner-based factors in L2 reading comprehension and processing grammatical form: topic familiarity and working memory. *Language Learning* 57 (2): 229–270.

Lehtonen, M., Soveri, A., Laine, A. et al. (2018). Is bilingualism associated with enhanced executive functioning in adults? A meta-analytic review. *Psychological Bulletin* 144 (4): 394–425.

Lenet, A.E., Sanz, C., Lado, B. et al. (2011). Aging, pedagogical conditions, and differential success in SLA: an empirical study. In: *Implicit and Explicit Language Learning: Conditions, Processes, and Knowledge. SLA and Bilingualism* (ed. C. Sanz and R.P. Leow), 73–84. Washington, DC: Georgetown University Press.

Lenneberg, E.H. (1967). The biological foundations of language. *Hospital Practice* 2 (12): 59–67.

Li, P., Legault, J., and Litcofsky, K.A. (2014). Neuroplasticity as a function of second language learning: anatomical changes in the human brain. *Cortex* 58: 301–324.

Linck, J.A., Osthus, P., Koeth, J.T., and Bunting, M.F. (2014). Working memory and second language comprehension and production: a meta-analysis. *Psychonomic Bulletin & Review* 21 (4): 861–883.

Long, M.H. (1990). Maturational constraints on language development. *Studies in Second Language Acquisition* 12 (3): 251–285.

Luria, A.R. (1966). *Higher Cortical Functions in Man*. New York, NY: Basic Books.

Mackey, A. and Sachs, R. (2012). Older learners in SLA research: a first look at working memory, feedback, and L2 development. *Language Learning* 62: 704–740.

Marner, L., Nyengaard, J.R., Tang, Y., and Pakkenberg, B. (2003). Marked loss of myelinated nerve fibers in the human brain with age. *Journal of Comparative Neurology* 462 (2): 144–152.

Mazzoni, G., Gori, S., Formicola, G. et al. (1999). Word recall correlates with sleep cycles in elderly subjects. *Journal of Sleep Research* 8 (3): 185–188.

Meinzer, M., Lindenberg, R., Sieg, M.M. et al. (2014). Transcranial direct current stimulation of the primary motor cortex improves word-retrieval in older adults. *Frontiers in Aging Neuroscience* 6: 1–9.

Merzenich, M.M., Van Vleet, T.M., and Nahum, M. (2014). Brain plasticity-based therapeutics. *Frontiers in Human Neuroscience* 8: 385.

Meuter, R.F. and Allport, A. (1999). Bilingual language switching in naming: asymmetrical costs of language selection. *Journal of Memory and Language* 40 (1): 25–40.

Michielse, S., Coupland, N., Camicioli, R. et al. (2010). Selective effects of aging on brain white matter microstructure: a diffusion tensor imaging tractography study. *NeuroImage* 52 (4): 1190–1201.

Nicholas, M., Obler, L., Albert, M., and Goodglass, H. (1985). Lexical retrieval in healthy aging. *Cortex* 21 (4): 595–606.

Obler, L.K. and Albert, M.L. (1981). Language and aging: a neurobehavioral analysis. In: *Aging: Communication Processes and Disorders* (ed. D. Beasley and G.A. Davis), 107–121. New York, NY: Grune & Stratton.

Obler, L.K., Fein, D., Nicholas, M., and Albert, M.L. (1991). Auditory comprehension and aging: decline in syntactic processing. *Applied PsychoLinguistics* 12 (4): 433–452.

Obler, L.K., Rykhlevskaia, E., Schnyer, D. et al. (2010). Bilateral brain regions associated with naming in older adults. *Brain and Language* 113: 113–123.

Osaka, M., Osaka, N., and Groner, R. (1993). Language-independent working memory: evidence from German and French reading span tests. *Bulletin of the Psychonomic Society* 31 (2): 117–118.

Owsley, C. (2011). Aging and vision. *Vision Research* 51 (13): 1610–1622.

Paradis, M. (2009). *Declarative and Procedural Determinants of Second Languages*, vol. 40. Amsterdam, The Netherlands: John Benjamins.

Park, D.C., Polk, T.A., Mikels, J.A. et al. (2001). Cerebral aging: integration of brain and behavioral models of cognitive function. *Dialogues in Clinical Neuroscience* 3: 151–165.

Payne, J.S. and Whitney, P.J. (2002). Developing L2 oral proficiency through synchronous CMC: output, working memory, and interlanguage development. *CALICO Journal* 20 (1): 7–32.

Penfield, W. and Roberts, L. (1959). *Speech and Brain Mechanisms*. Princeton, NJ: Princeton University Press.

Perani, D. and Abutalebi, J. (2005). The neural basis of first and second language processing. *Current Opinion in Neurobiology* 15 (2): 202–206.

Perani, D., Abutalebi, J., Paulesu, E. et al. (2003). The role of age of acquisition and language usage in early, high-proficient bilinguals: an fMRI study during verbal fluency. *Human Brain Mapping* 19 (3): 170–182.

Perani, D., Paulesu, E., Galles, N.S. et al. (1998). The bilingual brain. Proficiency and age of acquisition of the second language. *Brain: A Journal of Neurology* 121 (10): 1841–1852.

Pot, A., Keijzer, M., and de Bot, K. (2017). Enhancing language awareness in migrants' third age to promote well-being. In: *Third Age Learners of Foreign Languages* (ed. D. Gabryś-Barker), 176–200. Bristol, UK: Multilingual Matters.

Ramírez Gómez, D. (2016). *Language Teaching and the Older Adult: the Significance of Experience*, vol. 103. Bristol, UK: Multilingual Matters.

Raz, N., Lindenberger, U., Rodrigue, K.M. et al. (2005). Regional brain changes in aging healthy adults: general trends, individual differences and modifiers. *Cerebral Cortex* 15 (11): 1676–1689.

Reber, A.S. (1993). *Implicit Learning and Tacit Knowledge: An Essay on the Cognitive Unconscious*. Oxford, UK: Oxford University Press.

Rodriguez-Fornells, A., De Diego Balaguer, R., and Münte, T.F. (2006). Executive control in bilingual language processing. *Language Learning* 56 (s1): 133–190.

Rotte, M. (2005). Age-related differences in the areas of Broca and Wernicke using functional magnetic resonance imaging. *Age and Ageing* 34 (6): 609–613.

Salis, C. (2011). Understanding of auditory discourse in older adults: the effects of syntax and working memory. *Aphasiology* 25 (4): 529–539.

Saur, D., Kreher, B.W., Schnell, S. et al. (2008). Ventral and dorsal pathways for language. *Proceedings of the National Academy of Sciences* 105 (46): 18035–18040.

Scarmeas, N. and Stern, Y. (2004). Cognitive reserve: implications for diagnosis and prevention of Alzheimer's disease. *Current Neurology and Neuroscience Reports* 4 (5): 374–380.

Schmidt, R. (1990). The role of consciousness in second language learning. *Applied Linguistics* 11: 129–158.

Seidenberg, M., Kay, C.D., Woodard, J.L. et al. (2013). Recognition of famous names predicts cognitive decline in healthy elders. *Neuropsychology* 27 (3): 333.

Shafto, M.A. and Tyler, L.K. (2014). Language in the aging brain: the network dynamics of cognitive decline and preservation. *Science* 346 (6209): 583–587.

Sharwood-Smith, M. (1981). Consciousness-raising and the second language learner. *Applied Linguistics* 2: 159–168.

Simon, J.R. and Rudell, A.P. (1967). Auditory SR compatibility: the effect of an irrelevant cue on information processing. *Journal of Applied Psychology* 51 (3): 300–304.

Singh, G., Pichora-Fuller, M.K., and Schneider, B.A. (2008). The effect of age on auditory spatial attention in conditions of real and simulated spatial separation. *The Journal of the Acoustical Society of America* 124 (2): 1294–1305.

Singleton, D. (2017). Really late learners: some research contexts and some practical hints. In: *Third Age Learners of Foreign Languages* (ed. D. Gabryś-Barker), 19–30. Bristol, UK: Multilingual Matters.

Skehan, P. (1986). The role of foreign language aptitude in a model of school learning. *Language Testing* 3 (2): 188–221.

Sommers, M.S. and Danielson, S.M. (1999). Inhibitory processes and spoken word recognition in young and older adults: the interaction of lexical competition and semantic context. *Psychology and Aging* 14 (3): 458.

Stern, Y. (2002). What is cognitive reserve? Theory and research application of the reserve concept. *Journal of the International Neuropsychological Society* 8 (3): 448–460.

Strange, B.A., Fletcher, P.C., Henson, R.N.A. et al. (1999). Segregating the functions of human hippocampus. *Proceedings of the National Academy of Sciences* 96 (7): 4034–4039.

Tulving, E. and Thomson, D.M. (1973). Encoding specificity and retrieval processes in episodic memory. *Psychological Review* 80 (5): 352.

Tun, P.A. and Wingfield, A. (1997). Language and communication: fundamentals of speech communication and language processing in old age. In: *Handbook of Human Factors and the Older adult* (ed. A.D. Fisk and W.A. Rogers), 125–149. San Diego, CA: Academic Press.

Verhagen, J. and Leseman, P. (2016). How do verbal short-term memory and working memory relate to the acquisition of vocabulary and grammar? A comparison between first and second language learners. *Journal of Experimental Child Psychology* 141: 65–82.

Wartenburger, I., Heekeren, H.R., Abutalebi, J. et al. (2003). Early setting of grammatical processing in the bilingual brain. *Neuron* 37 (1): 159–170.

West, R. (2004). The effects of aging on controlled attention and conflict processing in the Stroop task. *Journal of Cognitive Neuroscience* 16 (1): 103–113.

West, R. and Alain, C. (2000). Age-related decline in inhibitory control contributes to the increased Stroop effect observed in older adults. *Psychophysiology* 37 (2): 179–189.

Winter, B., Breitenstein, C., Mooren, F.C. et al. (2007). High impact running improves learning. *Neurobiology of Learning and Memory* 87 (4): 597–609.

Zanto, T.P. and Gazzaley, A. (2017). Cognitive control and the ageing brain. In: *The Wiley Handbook of Cognitive Control* (ed. T. Egner), 476–490. New York, NY: Wiley.

21 Language Control and Attention during Conversation
An Exploration

DAVID W. GREEN

1. Introduction

Experimental and neuroimaging research on language control has mostly required participants to name depicted objects or describe simple scenes in response to imperative cues as to the language of use (e.g. Costa and Santesteban 2004; Linck et al. 2012). Suitable designs dissociate regions involved in the intention to use a given language from the actual processes of execution (e.g. Reverberi et al. 2015); identify the neural regions and networks involved in switching between languages in the performance of simple tasks (e.g. Luk et al. 2012, for a meta-analysis); and identify, behaviourally at least, the consequences of a free choice of language of use (Gollan and Ferreira 2009). Such trial by trial explorations are complemented by studies that explore the carry-over effects of naming in one language in a block of trials on naming in a second language in a second block of trials (see Kroll and Gollan 2014, for review). Both event-related potential (ERP) (Branzi et al. 2014) and functional magnetic resonance imaging (fMRI) data (Branzi et al. 2015; Guo et al. 2011) indicate a cost to naming in the dominant language after a block of trials naming in the less dominant language. From a theoretical point of view, such research strongly suggests that language control involves multiple levels. We can, for example, distinguish control at the level of the whole language (the global level or the schema level) from control at the item or local level (Green 1998). Yet our ambition must be to develop both theory and procedures to look at the dynamics of language use and its neural bases in speakers of more than one language in a key site of language use in our everyday lives: conversation. Research examining language switching within a sentence (e.g. Declerck and Philipp 2015), and more particularly dialogue (e.g. Liu et al. 2017; Pivneva et al. 2012), is closer to the concerns here. The present aim is to explore some high-level aspects of these dynamics in terms of processes of language control and attentional fields or states.

The Handbook of the Neuroscience of Multilingualism, First Edition. Edited by John W. Schwieter.

Conversation allows us to coordinate action with others. It exemplifies the cycles of perception and action that infuse our lives. In turn-taking, participants express and reply to speech acts. Conversation is also typically multimodal. As participants speak, they gesture, monitor their own speech and assess the facial and gestural communicative signals of their addressee and so adjust their turn. We take the talking and understanding involved as a point of departure in our exploration of the neural bases of language control in speakers of more than one language (referred to as bilingual speakers from now on in this chapter). We distinguish between the language networks, whose representations and connections make utterances possible, and the control processes that act on these networks, or on their outputs, to achieve a communicative goal.

Figure 1 (after Green 2018) provides a schematic for the production and comprehension of speech acts during conversation (see the key for a fuller description). The figure depicts a control hierarchy with the speech act intention at the top level and processes of language control at a lower level. In mapping the intention into speech, activated conceptual representations are distinguished from the language networks (Paradis 2004) with output from the language networks into a speech plan gated according to the processes of language control (e.g. Green and Abutalebi 2013). We elaborate on this aspect of the proposal in Section 2. The figure also indicates that covert speech contributes to understanding and predicting the speech of the other party as in analysis by synthesis type models (Halle and Stevens 1962; Skipper et al. 2017). Comprehension processes are involved too as a speaker monitors their own output.

A more elaborate version would display a comparable sketch depicting the other participant and their mutual embedding in the multimodal context of face-to-face conversation. The figure omits any depiction of the ongoing representation such as any

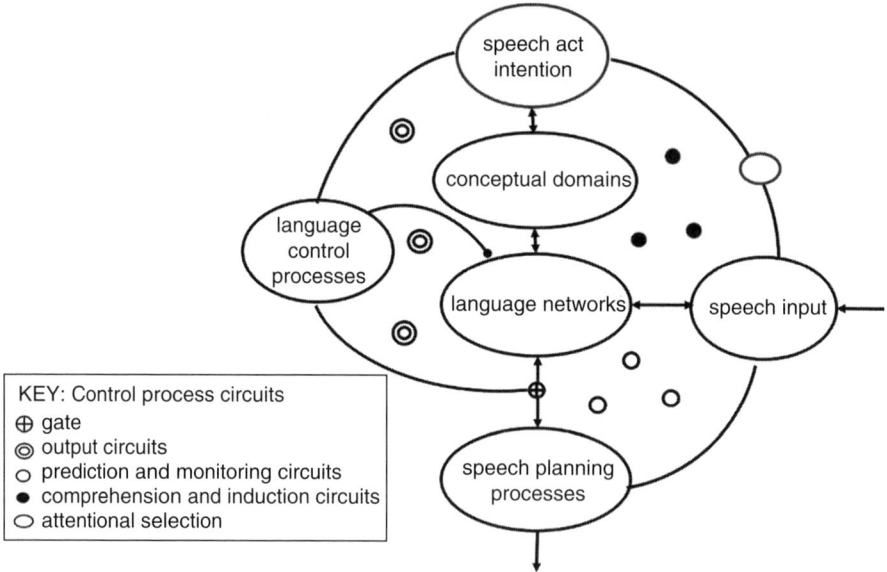

KEY: Control process circuits
⊕ gate
◎ output circuits
○ prediction and monitoring circuits
● comprehension and induction circuits
○ attentional selection

Figure 1   The mapping of a speech act.

temporary representation of the other's speech or a representation of the discourse model to date but does depict the intimate relation between speech production processes and the comprehension of another's speech and own speech (see also Pickering and Garrod 2013). In both cases, heard words or phrases can prime items and constructions in the language network. Where a word or phrase is unknown, induction processes infer reference, and meaning from the context of the utterance. The intention to speak about a particular topic, recruits knowledge represented in a conceptual domain and drives activation of lexical concepts and constructions in the language networks. These networks are functionally separable but intertwined (e.g. Hartsuiker et al. 2004) and are likely interspersed in the same neural regions (Paradis 2004) that are widely distributed (see Price 2012). Outputs from the networks are gated for entry into the planning process (see section 2 for discussion). Speaking is guided by a plan that precedes its execution (Lashley 1951). Multiple reciprocal connections between frontal and subcortical structures may serve to construct the plan (Kriete et al. 2013) but we still know little of the neuroanatomical details involved. There is no need for a full specification of the utterance plan before starting to speak. Rather execution of part of it, such as producing a noun phrase, can be interleaved with the incremental construction of the plan for the remainder of a clause before its execution in turn. An important point is that items in the plan are active in parallel. How are items serialized for production? A competitive queuing (CQ) network provides an answer that is neuroanatomically plausible (Bohland et al. 2009; Grossberg 1978; Houghton 1990). A CQ network consists of a planning layer and a linked competitive choice layer. Items with the highest level of activation as the utterance unfolds enter the planning layer. Selection is achieved by a competitive process in which the item with the highest activation at that moment in time suppresses all other items in the choice layer and so allows the most active item in the planning layer to be released. Once the item is released its activation in the planning layer is suppressed allowing the next most active item to be readied for selection via the choice layer and the cycle repeats. Many such CQ networks are required as a communicative goal is progressively mapped through a hierarchy of production levels into overt speech.

Each conversational turn entails an intricate mesh of processes. We draw out the control demands in a little more detail to set the background for our exploration of speech acts and attention. Language control processes are bidirectional. They are triggered bottom-up (e.g. via the speech of the other person) and top-down (via the speaker's intentions) to realize the production and comprehension of speech acts. During comprehension, possible meanings of words and sentences may be momentarily considered and discarded (e.g. Dahan and Gaskell 2007) with control processes dynamically evoked to overcome misinterpretations (Hsu and Novick 2016). During production, alternative ways of referring to an object or expressing a speech act compete for selection with overt speech occasionally explicitly halted for pragmatic or affective reasons. We sometimes do need to 'bite our tongues'.

Given that the modal interval between turns in a conversation can be quite short (Levinson 2016) listeners may go further than incrementally updating their discourse model. They may predict the ending of the current speaker's turn. They may do more based on the shared model. They may envisage its unfolding content and incipiently shape their response to it. In the right circumstances they may even formulate a precise response as they listen. Experimental data support this possibility (see Bögels and Levinson 2017, for a review). Bögels et al. (2015) used a quiz format and recorded ERP responses as participants understood and replied to questions that either permitted an answer to be retrieved before the question end (e.g. 'Which character, also called 007, appears in the famous movies?') or that did not (e.g. Which character from the famous movies is also called 007?'). The large ERP positivity, localized to regions involved in language production, indicate that participants start to formulate their answer as soon as the question allows them to do so (i.e. in the example question, at '007'). In everyday conversation, such early formulation, together with the stance the listener takes to the issue at hand, can help a listener's readiness to respond. Characterized in this way conversational fluency presumes skilled management of the control demands involved. Does the use of more than language increase these demands relative to the demands faced by monolingual speakers? Plausibly yes.

In contrast to the perceptual experience of monolingual speakers, a multilingual auditory and visual environment affords potentially meaningful, competing communicative signals in more than one language. In consequence, bilingual speakers become adept at tracking the fundamental frequency differences between different language in order to select and sustain attention to a current conversation (Krizman et al. 2012). Even speaking or listening in one language may evoke additional competing linguistic representation from another language (e.g. Parker-Jones et al. 2012). Relative to monolingual speakers, language processing in bilingual speakers may also be less automatic and so more demanding of control (e.g. Abutalebi and Green 2007). The mapping between meaning and spoken form, for instance, may be slower than in picture-naming (e.g. Gollan et al. 2008) and articulating these forms less well practised. On the comprehension side, word recognition processes can be slower (e.g. Shook et al. 2015), inducing delays in the incremental updating of the discourse model and predictions of upcoming content.

We follow MacDonald (2013) in supposing that speakers can minimize problems of speech planning and produce easier over more difficult utterance forms. As members of a speech community, such forms are also ones that speakers encounter as listeners. They can be used to predict upcoming speech and so, arguably, facilitate response and the fluency of turn-taking. Here the reduced community experience of bilingual speakers in each language might impose a constraint on conversational fluency as their repertoire of spoken collocations and formulaic phrases may be less extensive. On the other hand, any reduced experience may be compensated by a bottom-up process of control: reusing the wording and phrases in a prior turn. Indeed, reuse (see MacDonald 2013) may be optimal where words or phrases label referents in a shared discourse model. It can prompt alignment across linguistic levels (e.g. Pickering and Garrod 2013) though differences in linguistic expertise between native and non-native speakers may constrain such alignment (e.g. Costa et al. 2008). Fluency in responding is also aided by the fact that there are different ways to convey meaning. But there is a cost to such flexibility. Non-selected alternatives must be rapidly suppressed to ensure that the selected words are correctly articulated (MacDonald 2013).

Given this background to control demands, how might we relate language control during a speech act to attentional states? We can set the present exploration in a wider context. There is general agreement that in order for a person to meet their current goals, attentional processes are needed to select amongst diverse competing stimuli and thoughts and ensure their effective processing and response, i.e. their modulation (Chun et al. 2011). The targets for selection and modulation are set by cognitive control processes (e.g. Botvinick and Braver 2015; Chun et al. 2011). In the context of a speech act, these are metacontrol processes (Green and Abutalebi 2013) that set the parameters for the processes of language control (e.g. to speak in one language rather than another or to code switch) and the goals of the speech act (e.g. to describe a view or to reminisce). They set the nature of attention in different linguistic, perceptual, memorial, and motor domains and so induce particular attentional states. The present proposal concerns the nature of these states during a speech act in speakers of more than one language.

We know from personal experience that distinct attentional states can coexist. We can walk or drive almost on autopilot whilst holding a conversation. But are such dissociable states possible within a single complex act such as holding a conversation? Let's grant that our ability to coordinate with others requires the integration of activity in functionally separable neural networks. Let's grant too that activity within a network or networks is shaped by attentional processes (Harris and Thiele 2011) that can be directed externally or internally (see Chun et al. 2011; Lavie et al. 2014) and can be focused more or less broadly (e.g. Eriksen and Yeh 1985; Leech and Sharp 2014; Wachtel 1967). We contend then that a complex activity (such as holding a conversation) involves the coordination of networks in potentially separate attentional states. More specifically, nested within a sustained state of attention to the ongoing conversation, a speech act is a coupling of the processes of language control with ones associated with the processing information about a given conceptual domain or topic. This coupling can invoke a number of dissociable attentional states: ones associated with the speech act intention and with the form of language use (e.g. use of just one language in a given context) and ones induced through the topic of conversation (e.g. remembering a dream). Conversation is a joint enterprise (Clark 1996) and so the corollary of this line of argument is that similar, dissociable attentional states are induced in the listener as they build representations or mental simulations tracking those evoked by the speech of their conversational partner. Such a possibility is consistent with evidence that brain activity is synchronized between speaker and listener (Stephens et al. 2010).

We start by considering the levels of language control identified in Figure 1 and the nature of the attentional field or state induced (Section 2). We then consider states associated with the processing of different types of topic (Section 3). An integrative section (Section 4) considers the multiple states induced through the coupling of language control processes and the conversational topic. A final section (Section 5) reviews the exploration and considers prospects for theoretical and experimental advance.

2.   Language Control and Attentional States

Our everyday lives indicate that our attention can be narrowly focused on a specific feature or mental object or can be more broadly focused. This dimension of an attentional state is pertinent to language control. At the top-level of the control hierarchy, speakers intend to achieve a communicative goal with a specific speech act. Ensuring that the goal is met requires a narrow focus of attention to avoid the distraction of alternative competing communicative goals. However, exactly how that intention is realized depends on the contexts of language use. Is it possible that language use can induce an attentional state different from that associated with the top-level of the control hierarchy? To explore this possibility, we consider the control demands of the different contexts of language use.

We contrast three contexts of language use: single language, dual language, and code-switching contexts (Green 2011; Green and Abutalebi 2013). We use the single language context to describe a selection mechanism. In a single language context successive conversational turns are in just one language. An example of such a context is the one faced by a migrant worker whose native language is not spoken in the work place. Switching to the native language would fail to circumvent a communication problem: only the non-native language must be selected. On the face of it, the solution is easy: completely inhibit the language not in use. Indeed, some theorists adopt this proposal (e.g. Muysken 2000). Mechanistically if there are reciprocal inhibitory connections between the two languages at a global level, the intentional activation of one language will lead to the automatic and active suppression of the other. However, experimental evidence rather counts against the sufficiency of the global inhibition proposal as the non-selected language appears active and capable of interfering with production (e.g. Bergman et al. 2015; Liu et al. 2014; see, Kroll et al. 2015, for a review). Such activation includes syntactic constructions (Liu et al. 2017). Activation, it seems, can reach to the level of word form, even in a language that is not produced (e.g. Blumenfeld and Marian 2013; Christoffels et al. 2007; Costa et al. 2000; Hoshino and Thierry 2011). Constructing an utterance plan may then require selecting a relevant structure in the intended language and selecting amongst competing items that may be from both languages (see also Stocco et al. 2014, for a related view). How is this achieved? We do not know for certain but can sketch a solution.

We need a solution that tolerates the parallel activation of items in both languages even in single language contexts. The mechanism required may be identical to that which rapidly suppresses alternative, non-selected items, in the speech plans of monolingual speakers. It inhibits such items only once they become active ('reactive inhibition', Green 1998). We also need a solution that covers the range of language use. The solution adopted here (see Figure 1) is that speakers gate the output of the language system into the speech plan (Green 1986, 1998). The context of use can then determine the precise form of the gating (Green and Abutalebi 2013; Green and Wei 2014). In a single language context, the control process gates entry of the non-target language into the speech plan. There is competitive control with the selection of one language at the expense of the other. The same applies in the dual language context. Here both languages are in use but with different addressees (e.g. Catalan-Spanish speakers in Barcelona: Rodriguez-Fornells et al. 2012). Indeed, which language is used may be contingent on the one the parties initially used together. If so, deviation from habitual use by one party might be felt as a rupture in the tone of the relationship and require explanation.[1]

Both the single language context and the dual language context require the competitive control of the two languages with the control demand arguably heightened in the dual language context because both languages are in play. The narrow attentional state induced in these two language contexts aligns with that required at the intentional level of control. By contrast, in our third context of language use, the attentional states at these two levels of the control hierarchy can dissociate. In code switching, bilingual speakers switch between their languages to the same addresses and within the same utterance. Code switching allows the cooperative control of the two language so that items and constructions from either language can enter the speech plan subject to their appropriateness (Green and Wei 2014).[2] In such a case, attention can be broadened to cover both language networks though the extent of such broadening hinges on the nature of code switching.

The nature of code switching is community-dependent (Muysken 2000). In fact, one type, 'alternation', arguably also recruits competitive control as stretches of one language alternate between utterances within a conversational turn. Two other types more obviously require cooperative control. In 'insertion', words or whole constituents from one language are inserted into the utterance of another that provides the matrix language (e.g. Myers-Scotton and Jake 2000). Inserted items might be adapted to the local syntactic context to create a novel form: For example, adding a German particle (–*ieren*) to a French verb such as *choisir* to create *choisieren* (Edwards and Gardner-Chloros 2007, p. 82; see also Gardner-Chloros 2009). For insertion, suppression of items from the non-matrix language, can be lifted, contingently within a clause. In a third type, congruent lexicalization, a common language structure is realized with words/morphemes from each language, permitting contributions from each language that would count as non-constituents in each language as in this example: 'wan heri *gedeelte* de ondro *beheer* fu *gewapende machten* [one whole part is under control of the armed forces]' (Sranan/Dutch; Bolle, 1994, p. 75; cited in Muysken 2000, p. 139). Some language pairs permit particularly dense code switching (dense CS). In Mandarin-English, code switching items from different lexical categories in the two languages can be combined to yield a well-formed sentence without any overt morphological adjustment. In the following example (Li Wei personal communication), English prepositions, adjectives, and nouns are switched, but in positions that grammatically require verbs and other lexical categories: '你 (*ni*) up stairs, 走到底 (*zoudaodi*) end,向 (*xiang*) left,最 (*zui*) front那张(*nazhang*). [You go upstairs, walk to the very end, turn left, the one at the forefront.]').

In the case of congruent lexicalization, or instances of dense CS, speakers can form utterances opportunistically with items from either language based on their relative accessibility. There is no necessary gating of one language and items can be foraged from either language network consistent with broad attention (Green and Wei 2016). However, such a control state may also increase the need to suppress alternatives that would otherwise be gated from entry into the speech plan under competitive control. Such suppression as noted earlier in this section is also required in the speech production of monolingual speakers.

2.1.   Signatures of Attentional State During Language Control

We can look for signatures of the attentional state in measures of different types. Where control is heightened, as in the dual language context compared to a single language context, there should be greater resistance to non-verbal interference. An ingenious experiment by Wu and Thierry (2013) found supportive evidence. Bilingual Welsh-English participants responded to a non-verbal flanker task in which they pressed a button to indicate the direction of a central target arrow presented on a computer screen. On congruent trials, flanking arrows point in the same direction as the target arrow whereas on incongruent trials they point in the opposite direction inducing interference. In their novel design, Welsh-English bilingual speakers showed reduced interference when words from both languages (a dual language context) were interposed between flanker trials compared with when words from only one language (a single language context) were interposed (see also Hommel et al. 2011 for evidence of the benefits of dual language use on a convergent thinking task).

As a further signature we can draw on research that establishes a link between pupil dilation and the trade-off between exploiting a given resource and exploring an alternative resource. Selective language control *exploits* the resources of just one language. By contrast, cooperative language control, and especially, open control elicited for dense CS, threads together words and phrases from each language in order to convey intended meaning. This type of control *explores* the resources of each language. Research implicates neuroadrenergic signals from the locus coeruleus (LC) in the exploitation/exploration trade-off (Aston-Jones and Cohen 2005) and remarkably, pupil diameter provides a non-invasive index of its activity (De Gree et al. 2014; Jepma and Nieuwenhuis 2011). Pupil dilation responds to different classes of LC signals: tonic and phasic, and these two classes are inversely related (Gilzenrat et al. 2010; Smallwood et al. 2011). Increased tonic activity yields higher baseline pupil diameter. Research shows that baseline pupil diameter increases with shifts to exploration and individual differences in pupil diameter are predictive of the extent of exploratory choices in decision-making tasks (Jepma and Nieuwenhuis 2011; see also Franklin et al. 2013 for converging evidence from a study of 'mind-wandering' in reading.) An intriguing possibility then is that pupil diameter could also be an index of language control. If dense CS induces a broad attentional state (i.e. exploring functionally distinct language networks), baseline pupil diameter should increase during periods of dense CS. A counter-prediction can be tested. Prior research indicates a link between increased cognitive effort and event-related (i.e. phasic) pupil diameter: event-related pupil diameter increases with cognitive effort (Kahneman 1973; Kahneman and Beatty 1996). If, contrary to the present hypothesis, dense CS demands a narrow attentional state because of repeated demands to switch between languages, event-related pupil diameter should increase during dense CS. It should also dramatically amplify activation in the network typically recruited during language switching (e.g. anterior cingulate cortex/pre-SMA, caudate; Luk et al. 2012). We discuss further indices of language control states in Section 4.

3.   Attentional States and Topics With Their Neural Signatures

Conversations cover different topics. Participants may talk about what they see in front of them (an external orientation) or may discuss some aspects of their internal worlds (an internal orientation) such as their pasts or possible futures. The required focus of attention may also be narrow ('How many petals does it have?') or broad ('What's good about it?'). Though the nature of the topic, with its specific orientation and focus, may not constrain the nature of language control (e.g. single language use or code switching) it will affect the networks supporting speech production. Objects and events that are the current topic of conversation, and active in the current speech act, must have their representations in the conceptual domain bound to representations and constructions in the language network. Current neuroimaging data suggest that different attentional networks and regions will support this binding.

Neuroimaging data only weakly constrain our inferences about the networks that support binding because the bulk of research to data has concerned experimental tasks (e.g. name this object) that demand a narrow external focus and have not, to our knowledge, explored attentional networks in a conversational context. However, we can envisage some possibilities. Leech and Sharp (2014) on the basis of an insightful analysis of extensive experimental and clinical data make the case that the posterior cingulate cortex is a crucial structure in tuning the focus of attention. The posterior cingulate cortex is part of the default mode network that includes, as core regions, the posterior cingulate cortex, anterior prefrontal cortex, and medial temporal lobe. The term default mode or task-negative network turns out to be a misnomer as core regions, for example the posterior cingulate cortex (Andrews-Hanna et al. 2010), are actively recruited in task performance involving shifts between dissimilar tasks (e.g. Crittenden et al. 2015) in accord with the proposals of Leech and Sharp (2014).

The posterior cingulate cortex is strongly connected to different networks involved in attentional control and to other parts of the default mode network typically activated during the resting state. Here we consider just two networks involved in attentional control: the dorsal attentional network and the frontoparietal control network. The former comprises the frontal eye fields and the intraparietal sulci (Corbetta and Shulman 2002) whereas the latter comprises a number of regions of the prefrontal cortex that coactivate with the anterior cingulate, anterior inferior parietal lobule, and anterior insular cortex (Vincent et al. 2008).

In line with Leech and Sharp (2014), we consider the four attentional states formed by the pairing of attentional orientation (external/internal) and breadth (narrow/broad) and outline some expected neural correlates. A conversational topic that involves describing a visual scene or an event unfolding in real time (e.g. a race or a game) would seem to require an external narrow attentional state. At a minimum, we should expect engagement of regions in the dorsal attentional network and in the frontoparietal control network to meet the attentional demand. If the proposals of Leech and Sharp (2014) generalize to conversational topics of this type, activity in these networks should be anti-correlated with activity in a dorsal region of the posterior cingulate cortex. A broad external attentional state corresponds to one in which we are attentive to any changes in the state of the world. Talking about changes in the patterns of light or cloud or the sudden appearance of a meteor shower at twilight, may reflect such a state. Leech and Sharp (2014) suppose that such a state will also implicate the frontoparietal control network. However, unlike the previous narrow attentional state, network properties will be moderated by increased functional connectivity with the dorsal posterior cingulate so that attention can be captured by salient external events.

What about attentional states associated with an internal orientation? A conversation about a specific autobiographical event would seem to require a narrow internal focus. Neuroimaging data suggest coactivation of a ventral region of the posterior cingulate cortex, and another region of the default mode network, the retrosplenial cortex, together with parts of the frontoparietal control network (Vann et al. 2009). Expert meditators perhaps exemplify a sustained state of internally focused attention and functional connectivity analysis shows increased connectivity between ventral posterior cingulate cortex and the frontoparietal control network (Brewer et al. 2011). Leech and Sharp (2014) propose that sustaining such a state would also involve increased anti-correlation with the dorsal attentional network. Lastly, what might be expected of topics that require an internal broad attentional state such as daydreaming out loud or musing about the future? To the extent this attentional state is more freewheeling, and exploratory, we can look to resting-state functional imaging data. These reveal relatively high levels of posterior cingulate activity along with other parts of the default mode network and anti-correlated activity between ventral posterior cingulate cortex and the dorsal attentional network (Fox et al. 2005).

4.   Attentional States and Their Dynamics in a Speech Act

We have identified possible neural signatures of attentional states associated with the processing of different topics. These states drive the binding of the conceptual and language networks and can dissociate from the attentional states associated with language control (see Figure 2 for an illustration).

Figure 2 selects components from Figure 1 to indicate that attentional states can be linked to different levels in the speech production hierarchy (speech act intention and

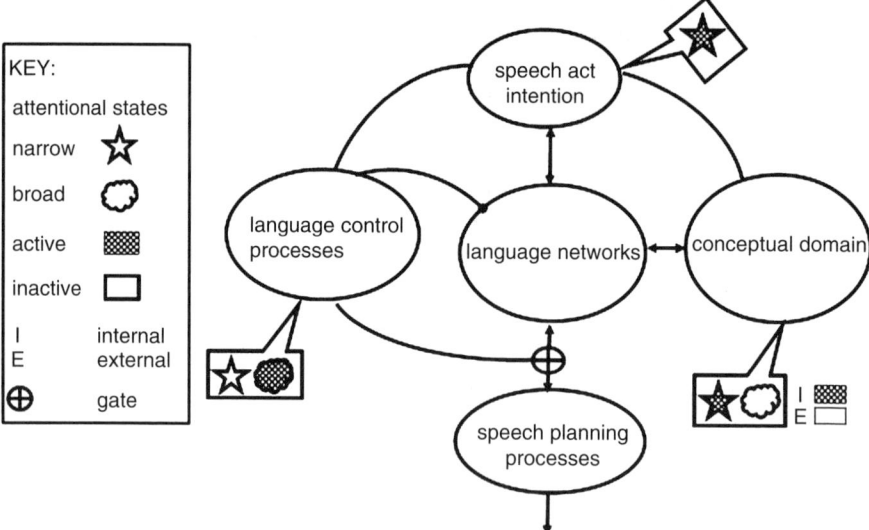

Figure 2   Attentional states at different loci during a speech act.

language control processes) and linked with respect to activation in the conceptual domain for a specific topic. Illustrated is a case where a narrow attentional state associated with the topic co-occurs with a broad attentional state associated with language control (i.e. during the production of dense code switching). An attentional state associated with language control may also differ, as here, from the narrow attentional state associated with the communicative intention.

So, for example, a topic demanding a narrow focus of attention would allow dense code switching (if that is the practice of participants) that is hypothesized to require a broader attentional state. If, on the other hand, a multiplicity of attentional states is precluded because the brain tolerates only one attentional state for a given duration then the behavioural outcome is clear: a topic demanding a narrow focus of attention precludes dialogue involving dense code switching. Likewise, selective language use would preclude discussion of a topic, or reporting on a topic, a daydream perhaps, that requires a broad attentional focus. How likely are these outcomes? Well it is an empirical matter but if a multiplicity of states is possible then these states should be discernible in the patterns of neural activity.[3] For instance, the pattern of activity associated with dense code switching when discussing a topic requiring a broad focus of attention should also be evident when the topic involves a narrow focus of attention. Multivariate pattern analysis may prove a fruitful tool to explore these questions.

A further question related to attentional states is the neural mechanisms that allow us to move between them. Participants may talk about topics requiring a narrow external focus and shift to talking about ones involving a broad internal focus. It follows that the brain must be able to transition between these states both during speech production and speech comprehension. How language is used can also change and this is apparent in corpus-based analyses. In Section 2.1, we referred to cooperative language control in a code-switching context. In fact, code-switched utterances can constitute a small proportion of utterances. Fricke and Kootstra (2016) in their rich analyses of the Bangor-Miami corpus (Deuchar et al. 2014) report just 5.8%. As they argue, opportunities for code switching, triggered bottom-up by priming from the previous discourse in their data, or, in other data, more specifically by cognates (Broersma 2009; Broersma and De Bot 2006; Clyne 2003), are not invariably taken up. We can say that code switching involves top-down control processes that 'allow' such priming to capture speech output. For present purposes, it follows that conversations in such contexts require transitions between a broad attentional state induced during code switching and a narrow attentional states induced during the use of a single language. The precise nature of a code switch is relevant. Beatty-Martínez and Dussias (2017) suggest that code switches that conform to community norms may induce a preparatory shift from a narrow to a broad attentional state.

How do speakers and listeners move between different attentional states? Brains may be specially adapted to maintain stable states and also to move to other states. The world, after all, is not unvaryingly stable (cf. Chialvo 2010). Two measures of the activity are useful for characterizing what is involved in transitioning between different states: network synchrony and network metastability (Shanahan 2010). Network synchrony refers to the extent to which regional and network activity coheres. Network metastability refers how such synchrony (coherence) changes over time. Narrow-focus attentional states require high synchrony and low metastability so that coactivation amongst the participating networks can be maintained over time to perform the task. Such a state resists interference from competing possibilities. By contrast, a broad-focus attentional state requires low synchrony and high metastability and does permit capture by other possibilities. Our earlier contrast also applies: high synchrony and low meta-stability permits exploitation of a given resource whereas high metastability and low synchrony allows a more exploratory mode. If these identities are accepted, we can associate measures of neural dynamics not only to the processing of topic information but also to the process of language control itself. For example, selective language use would require low metastability to avoid interference whereas dense code switching permits capture by competing possibilities. If so, differences in language control will be reflected in a measure of metastability with dense code switching associated with higher metastability. If, by contrast, dense code switching involves a hyper-competitive state, then there would be no association with higher metastability during periods of dense code switching.

Whatever is the empirical case, tuning the degree of metastability may be a means to transition between attentional states that vary in their focus. Leech and Sharp (2014) adopt this possibility and propose that dorsal posterior cingulate cortex tunes the metastability of the brain as a whole, especially when attention is externally oriented. (Ventral posterior cingulate cortex, they suggest, may fulfil the same function for inter-nally oriented attention). We diverge from their claim because if it were the case that metastability is tuned for the brain as a whole it would preclude the conjecture that there can be a multiplicity of co-occurring attentional states. We propose instead that if dorsal posterior cingulate is a mechanism for tuning metastability then it must achieve concurrent states that differentially tune topic and language related networks.

5.   Review and Conclusion

Our exploration of the relationship between language control in bilinguals and atten-tional states during a conversation leads to the conjecture that the mind/brain can be in simultaneously distinct attentional states within a single complex act. Given evidence of neural synchronization between speaker and listener dissociability of attentional states in the current speaker will also entrain such states in the listener. The possibility of mul-tiple attentional states arises because any speech act is a coupling of attentional states associated with the processing of a given topic content and ones associated with lan-guage control.

Topics may refer to events or objects in the external or internal world and may require a narrow or a broad focus of attention. For instance, retrieving a specific autobiograph-ical memory demands a narrow internally directed attentional state whereas associating evening clouds to the shapes of different animals requires a broad, externally directed attentional state. Neuroimaging research, admittedly using much more prosaic tasks, indicates that different neural networks mediate these different states. From the point of view of utterance production, topic-associated attentional states drive the coupling of conceptual content and the language networks. A speech act then can evoke distinct, and simultaneously active attentional states in neural regions and networks supporting that coupling. Viewed in the context of conversation evoked attentional states are identical to the configuration of the control processes needed to map topic content into speech under different demands of language control.

Attentional states associated with language control are locatable at different levels of the production hierarchy. Maintaining the high-level goal of holding a conversation means that both parties need to avoid being unnecessarily distracted by other ongoing events. There is a need for sustained attention. It is likely this involves the coordinated response of numerous cortical, subcortical, and cerebellar regions (e.g. Rosenberg et al. 2016). Indeed, in terms of attentional networks, a plausible argument could be made that conversation recruits the cingulo-opercular network to sustain attention, a fronto-parietal control network and dorsal attention network to avoid distraction and interference, and the default mode network to detect salient events such as a change in the context of interaction to vary the language of use. However, the contention here is that the precise nature of such coordination will depend on the content and context of the conversation. At the level of a given speech act speakers need to focus their attention so that their utterance is appropriate to the ongoing conversation. Precisely how they communicate their intended meaning, though, depends on the conversational context. Bilingual speakers may need to use just one of their languages. Such usage requires competitive control in which words and constructions of the non-selected language are not part of the speech plan. Competitive control requires a narrow focus of attention in which speakers exploit the resources of just one of their languages. By contrast, the conversational context may permit other bilingual speakers to explore the resources of both their languages – the utterance plan weaves items and constructions from either language network. Language control is cooperative (see Section 2 for further detail) and, especially in dense code switching, the attentional state is broad rather than narrow.

On this formulation, during a speech act, the attentional properties of co-occurring attentional states associated with topic processing and language control may not cohere. A broad state of attention associated with topic processing may co-occur with a narrow state of attention associated with language control as in selective language use.[4] Conversely, broad attentional control associated with dense code switching could be coupled with a narrow attentional state associated with topic processing (Figure 2 provides an illustration). A necessary prediction from this formulation is that attentional signals within language-sensitive regions and networks should be dissociable from those associated with topic processing. Such signals might be reflected in the patterns of coactivation of different networks and directly in measures of neural dynamics. Such measures are also useful for determining how the brain transitions between different attentional states associated with a change in topic or a change in language use.

Key dynamical measures (Shanahan 2010) are synchrony (the extent of synchrony in the pattern of coactivation of different networks) and metastability (the extent to which such synchrony changes over time). We followed Leech and Sharp (2014) and identified low metastability (high synchrony) with narrow focus attentional states and high metastability (low synchrony) with broad focus attentional states. The conjecture that there are co-existing different attentional states is therefore equivalent to the claim about differences in the metastability of different networks. In an extension of Leech and Sharp

(2014), we suppose that the dorsal posterior cingulate cortex can tune the degree of metastability both respect to the processing of topic information and language control and so mediate transitions between attentional states.[5]

How plausible is our conjecture about language control and attentional states during conversation in bilingual speakers? It relies on a set of identifications and assumptions. We identified differences in attentional state with the degree of metastability. This is theoretically interesting and plausible, but it is important to have converging evidence about attentional states. A broad attentional state should increase distractibility. Given the goal is to explore language control and attentional states during conversation we need to be able to track the impact of experimental interventions on ongoing behaviour. We need subtle, sensitive, and replicable interventions that differentiate topic and language control states. Given the claim that attentional states are entrained in speaker and listener studies we also need further research using techniques that examine neural response during conversation. Studies using functional near-infrared spectroscopy (fNIRS; e.g. Jiang et al. 2012) establish the viability of hyperscanning and further developments with optimally pumped magnetometers (see Knappe et al. 2014) offer a further exciting prospect for studies of synchrony.

We also envisaged that dorsal posterior cingulate cortex would initiate transitions between attentional states for both topics and language control. However, the implementation is likely to be different in these two cases because language control involves mechanisms that reflect recurrent control demands in the use of one language or another (Green and Abutalebi 2013). However, whatever the details of the mechanism, the prediction according to our conjecture is that dense code switching increases metastability in the networks mediating language control (e.g. a left frontal-right cerebellar circuit).

We do not know if there are multiple, potentially dissociable attentional states during a speech act because we have not looked. If there are, these must be integrated to form the neural substrate of our conscious experience during a conversation. The binding of representations across the production hierarchy points to the nature of this integration. Tononi et al. (2016) speak of conscious perception as integrated neural information patterns. Research on the perception of simple signals using electrocorticography (Haun et al. 2017) support this theoretical position. With further development, we can dare to imagine a future in which we establish an isomorphism between the phenomenological structure of experience and neural patterns.

In conclusion, we explored the relationship between language control and attentional states as bilinguals talk to one another about different topics and control their use of language in different ways. Hyperscanning techniques provide a way to explore the synchrony between speaker and listener as different attentional states are entrained. Our exploration leads to the conjecture of concurrent dissociable attentional states during a speech act. To refute the conjecture requires exploration of the neural dynamics during speech production and comprehension. Measures of network synchrony and metastability offer suitable indices and when combined with measures of the integration of neural patterns across production levels during a speech act may allow us to chart the neural substrate of our subjective experience of holding a conversation.

Acknowledgement

I am grateful to the reviewers for constructive comments and suggestions.

NOTES

1   The use of one language in a dual language context may also be topic-dependent. In a research laboratory, for instance, technical discussion may be in one language, English perhaps, where technical concepts are lexicalized and shared with other members of the group with a switch to a mutually shared native language (e.g. Italian, German) for other topics (see Grosjean 1982 for discussion of language-specific vocabulary knowledge).

2   Green (2018) makes a specific proposal about utterance planning in code switching by extending the work of Kriete et al. (2013, see description for Figure 1) that provides a neuroanatomically plausible way to generate a sentence plan.

3   The exploratory/exploitative trade-offs of different attentional states may exert joint effects on a measure such as pupil dilation. If so, sensitivity will be maximized by contrasting coherent narrow attentional states (selective language use and narrow focus topics) with coherent broad attentional states (dense code switching and broad attentional topics). A better prospect for testing multiple concurrent attentional states is to examine changes in neural data under different conversational contexts.

4   The precise language target of competitive control depends on the contexts of use. In a single language or dual language context, the target of suppression, can be items in language A in one context but language B in another. From a conceptual point of view, contexts of use recruit different higher-order or metacontrol states. Shifting between contexts of use requires a transition between these high-order states that configure a pre-established set of control processes (Green and Abutalebi 2013). Inducing cooperative language control (a broad attentional state) might then involve allowing this alternative state to dominate in which gating into the utterance plan is not language selective.

5   Our 2-D characterization of attentional states is not intended to be exhaustive. Other attentional states are accessible to us. For instance, a certain state of immersion (a partial suspension of the inner/outer dichotomy perhaps) might better capture the attentional and phenomenological state that issued in Bashō's (1684/1965) haiku as he watches the sea at dusk from the shoreline, and expressed in different form in this translation by Nobuyuki Yuasa:

Over the darkened sea,
Only the voice of a flying duck
Is visible –
In soft white.

REFERENCES

Abutalebi, J. and Green, D.W. (2007). Bilingual language production: the neurocognition of language representation and control. *Journal of Neurolinguistics* 20: 242–275.

Andrews-Hanna, J.R., Reidler, J.S., Sepulcre, J. et al. (2010). Functional-anatomic fractionation of the brain's default network. *Neuron* 65: 550–562.

Aston-Jones, G. and Cohen, J.D. (2005). An integrative theory of locus coeruleus-norepinephrine function: adaptive gain and optimal performance. *Annual Review of Neuroscience* 28: 403–450.

Bashō, M. (1684/1965). *The Narrow Road to the Deep North and Other Travel Sketches*. N. Yuasa (Trs.). London, UK: Penguin Classics.

Beatty-Martínez, A.L. and Dussias, P.E. (2017). Bilingual experience shapes language processing: evidence from code-switching. *Journal of Memory and Language* 95: 173–189.

Bergman, C., Sprenger, S.A., and Schmid, M.S. (2015). The impact of language co-activation on L1 and L2 speech fluency. *Acta Psychologica* 161: 25–35.

Blumenfeld, H.K. and Marian, V. (2013). Parallel activation and cognitive control during spoken word recognition in bilinguals. *Journal of Cognitive Psychology* 25: 547–567.

Bögels, S. and Levinson, S.C. (2017). The brain behind the response: insights into turn-taking in conversation from neuroimaging. *Research on Language and Social Interaction* 50: 71–89.

Bögels, S., Magyari, L., and Levinson, S.C. (2015). Neural signatures of response planning occur midway through an incoming question in conversation. *Scientific Reports* 5: 12881.

Bohland, J.W., Bullock, D., and Guenther, F.H. (2009). Neural representations and mechanisms for the performance of simple speech sequences. *Journal of Cognitive Neuroscience* 22: 1504–1529.

Botvinick, M. and Braver, T. (2015). Motivation and cognitive control: from behavior to neural mechanism. *Annual Review of Psychology* 66: 83–113.

Branzi, F.M., Della Rosa, P.A., Canini, M. et al. (2015). Language control in bilinguals: monitoring and response selection. *Cerebral Cortex* 26: 2367–2380.

Branzi, F.M., Martin, C.D., Abutalebi, J., and Costa, A. (2014). The after-effects of bilingual language production. *Neuropsychologia* 52: 102–116.

Brewer, J.A., Worhunsky, P.D., Gray, J.R. et al. (2011). Meditation experience is associated with differences in default mode network activity and connectivity. *Proceedings of the National Academy of Sciences United States of America* 108: 20254–20259.

Broersma, M. (2009). Triggered codeswitching between cognate languages. *Bilingualism: Language and Cognition* 12: 447–462.

Broersma, M. and De Bot, K. (2006). Triggered codeswitching: a corpus-based evaluation of the original triggering hypothesis and a new alternative. *Bilingualism: Language and Cognition* 9: 1–13.

Chialvo, D.R. (2010). Emergent complex neural dynamics. *Nature Physics* 6: 744–750.

Christoffels, I.K., Firk, C., and Schiller, N.O. (2007). Bilingual language control: an event-related brain potential study. *Brain Research* 1147: 192–208.

Chun, M.M., Golomb, J.D., and Turk-Browne, N.B. (2011). A taxonomy of external and internal attention. *Annual Review of Psychology* 62: 73–101.

Clark, H.H. (1996). *Using Language*. Cambridge, UK: Cambridge University Press.

Clyne, M. (2003). *Dynamics of Language Contact*. Cambridge, UK: Cambridge University Press.

Corbetta, M. and Shulman, G.L. (2002). Control of goal-directed and stimulus-driven attention in the brain. *Nature Reviews Neuroscience* 3: 201–215.

Costa, A., Caramazza, A., and Sebastián-Gallés, N. (2000). The cognate facilitation effect: implications for models of lexical access. *Journal of Experimental Psychology: Learning, Memory and Cognition* 26: 1283–1296.

Costa, A., Pickering, M.J., and Sorace, A. (2008). Alignment in second language dialogue. *Language and Cognitive Processes* 23: 528–556.

Costa, A. and Santesteban, M. (2004). Lexical access in bilingual speech production: evidence from language switching in highly proficient bilinguals and L2 learners. *Journal of Memory and Language* 50: 491–511.

Crittenden, B.M., Mitchell, D.J., and Duncan, J. (2015). Recruitment of the default mode network during a demanding act of executive control. *eLife* 4: e06481.

Dahan, D. and Gaskell, M.G. (2007). Temporal dynamics of ambiguity resolution: evidence from spoken word recognition. *Journal of Memory and Language* 57: 483–501.

De Gree, J.W., Knapen, T., and Donner, T.H. (2014). Decision-related pupil dilation reflects upcoming choice and individual bias. *Proceedings of the National Academy of Sciences* 111: E618–E625.

Declerck, M. and Philipp, A.M. (2015). A sentence to remember: instructed language switching in sentence production. *Cognition* 137: 166–173.

Deuchar, M., Davies, P., Herring, J. et al. (2014). Building bilingual corpora. In: *Advances in the Study of Bilingualism* (ed. E.M. Thomas and I. Mennen), 93–110. Bristol, UK: Multilingual Matters.

Edwards, M. and Gardner-Chloros, P. (2007). Compound verbs in code switching: bilinguals making do? *International Journal of Bilingualism* 11: 73–91.

Eriksen, C.W. and Yeh, Y.Y. (1985). Allocation of attention in the visual field. *Journal of Experimental Psychology: Human Perception and Performance* 11: 583–597.

Fox, M.D., Snyder, A.Z., Vincent, J.L. et al. (2005). The human brain is intrinsically organized into dynamic, anticorrelated functional networks. *Proceedings of the National Academy of Sciences Unites States America* 102 (27): 9673–9678.

Franklin, M.S., Broadway, J.M., Mrazek, M.D. et al. (2013). Window to the wandering mind: pupillometry of spontaneous thought while reading. *The Quarterly Journal of Experimental Psychology* 66: 2289–2294.

Fricke, M. and Kootstra, G.J. (2016). Primed codeswitching in spontaneous bilingual dialogue. *Journal of Memory and Language* 91: 181–201.

Gardner-Chloros, P. (2009). *Code-Switching*. Cambridge, UK: Cambridge University Press.

Gilzenrat, M.S., Nieuwenhuis, S., Jepma, M., and Cohen, J.D. (2010). Pupil diameter tracks changes in control state predicted by the adaptive gain theory of locus coeruleus function. *Cognitive, Affective, & Behavioral Neuroscience* 10: 252–269.

Gollan, T.H. and Ferreira, V.S. (2009). Should I stay or should I switch? A cost benefit analysis of voluntary language switching in young and aging bilinguals. *Journal of Experimental Psychology: Learning, Memory and Cognition* 35: 640–665.

Gollan, T.H., Montoya, R.I., Cera, C., and Sandoval, T.C. (2008). More use almost always means a smaller frequency effect: aging, bilingualism and the weaker links hypothesis. *Journal of Memory and Language* 58: 787–784.

Green, D.W. (1986). Control, activation and resource: a framework and a model for the control of speech in bilinguals. *Brain and Language* 27: 210–223.

Green, D.W. (1998). Mental control of the bilingual lexico-semantic system. *Bilingualism: Language and Cognition* 1: 67–81.

Green, D.W. (2011). Language control in different contexts: the behavioural ecology of bilingual speakers. *Frontiers in Psychology* 2: 103.

Green, D.W. (2018). Language control and code-switching. *Languages* 3: 8.

Green, D.W. and Abutalebi, J. (2013). Language control in bilinguals: the adaptive control hypothesis. *Journal of Cognitive Psychology* 25: 515–530.

Green, D.W. and Wei, L. (2014). A control process model of code-switching. *Language, Cognition and Neuroscience* 29: 499–511.

Green, D.W. and Wei, L. (2016). Code-switching and language control. *Bilingualism: Language and Cognition* 19: 883–884.

Grosjean, F. (1982). *Life with Two Languages: An Introduction to Bilingualism*. Cambridge, MA: Harvard University Press.

Grossberg, S. (1978). A theory of human memory: self-organization and performance of sensory-motor codes, maps, and plans.

In: *Progress in Theoretical Biology* (ed. R. Rosen and F. Snell), 233–374. New York, NY: Academic Press.

Guo, T., Liu, H., Misra, M., and Kroll, J.F. (2011). Local and global inhibition in bilingual word production: fMRI evidence from Chinese–English bilinguals. *NeuroImage* 56: 2300–2309.

Halle, M. and Stevens, K. (1962). Speech recognition: a model and a program for research. *IRE Transactions on Information Theory* 8: 155–159.

Harris, K. and Thiele, A. (2011). Cortical state and attention. *Nature Reviews Neuroscience* 12: 507–512.

Hartsuiker, R.J., Pickering, M.J., and Veltkamp, E. (2004). Is syntax separate or shared between languages? *Psychological Science* 15: 409–414.

Haun, A.M., Oizumi, M., Kovach, C.K. et al. (2017). Conscious perception as integrated information patterns in human electrocorticography. *eNeuro* https://doi.org/10.1523/ENEURO.0085-17.2017.

Hommel, B., Colzato, L.S., Fischer, R., and Christoffels, I.K. (2011). Bilingualism and creativity: benefits in convergent thinking come with loses in divergent thinking. *Frontiers in Psychology* 2: 273.

Hoshino, N. and Thierry, G. (2011). Language selection in bilingual word production: electrophysiological evidence for cross-language competition. *Brain Research* 1371: 100–109.

Houghton, G. (1990). The problem of serial order: a neural network model of sequence learning and recall. In: *Current Research in Natural Language Generation* (ed. R. Dale, C. Mellish and M. Zock), 287–319. London, UK: Academic Press.

Hsu, N.S. and Novick, J.M. (2016). Dynamic engagement of cognitive control modulates recovery time from misinterpretation during real-time language processing. *Psychological Science* 27: 572–582.

Jepma, M. and Nieuwenhuis, S. (2011). Pupil diameter predicts changes in the exploration–exploitation trade-off: evidence for the adaptive gain theory. *Journal of Cognitive Neuroscience* 23: 1587–1596.

Jiang, J., Dai, B., Peng, D. et al. (2012). Neural synchronisation during face-to-face communication. *Journal of Neuroscience* 32: 16064–16069.

Kahneman, D. (1973). *Attention and Effort*. Englewood Cliffs, NJ: Prentice-Hall.

Kahneman, D. and Beatty, J. (1996). Pupil diameter and load on memory. *Science* 154: 1583–1585.

Knappe, S., Sander, T., and Trahms, L. (2014). Optically-pumped magnetometers for MEG. In: *Magnetoencephalography* (ed. S. Supek and C.J. Aine), 993–999. Heidelberg, Germany: Springer Verlag.

Kriete, T., Noelle, D.C., Cohen, J.D., and O'Reilly, R.C. (2013). Indirection and symbol-like processing in the prefrontal cortex and basal ganglia. *Proceedings of the National Academy of Sciences United States of America* 110: 16390–16395.

Krizman, J., Marian, V., Shook, A. et al. (2012). Subcortical encoding of sound is enhanced in bilinguals and relates to executive function advantages. *Proceedings of the National Academy of Sciences* 109: 7877–7881.

Kroll, J.F., Dussias, P.E., Bice, K., and Perrotti, L. (2015). Bilingualism, mind, and brain. In: *Annual Review of Linguistics*, vol. 1 (ed. M. Liberman and B.H. Partee), 377–394.

Kroll, J.F. and Gollan, T.H. (2014). Speech planning in two languages: what bilinguals tell us about language production. In: *The Oxford Handbook of Language Production* (ed. V. Ferreira, M. Goldrick and M. Miozzo), 165–181. Oxford, UK: Oxford University Press.

Lashley, K.S. (1951). The problem of serial order in behavior. In: *Cerebral Mechanisms in Behavior: The Hixon Symposium* (ed. L.A. Jeffress), 112–136. New York, NY: Wiley.

Lavie, N., Beck, D.M., and Konstantinou, N. (2014). Blinded by the load: attention, awareness and the role of perceptual load. *Philosophical Transactions of the Royal Society B* 369: 20130205.

Leech, R. and Sharp, D.J. (2014). The role of the posterior cingulate cortex in cognition and disease. *Brain* 137: 12–32.

Levinson, S.C. (2016). Turn-taking in human communication-origins and implications for language processing. *Trends in Cognitive Sciences* 20: 6–14.

Linck, J.A., Schwieter, J.W., and Sunderman, G. (2012). Inhibitory control predicts language switching performance in trilingual speech production. *Bilingualism: Language and Cognition* 15: 651–662.

Liu, H., Dunlap, S., Wu, M.S. et al. (2017). Inhibitory control predicts quasi language switching performance: evidence from face-to-face dialogue. *Language, Cognition and Neuroscience* 32: 695–708.

Liu, H., Rossi, S., Zhou, H., and Chen, B. (2014). Electrophysiological evidence for domain-general inhibitory control during bilingual language switching. *PLoS One* 9: e110887.

Luk, G., Green, D.W., Abutalebi, J., and Grady, C. (2012). Cognitive control for language switching in bilinguals: a quantitative meta-analysis on functional neuroimaging studies. *Language and Cognitive Processes* 27: 1479–1488.

MacDonald, M.C. (2013). How language production shapes language form and comprehension. *Frontiers in Psychology* 4: 226.

Muysken, P. (2000). *Bilingual Speech: A Typology of Code-mixing*. Cambridge, UK: Cambridge University Press.

Myers-Scotton, C. and Jake, J.L. (2000). Testing the 4-M model. *International Journal of Bilingualism* 4: 1–8.

Paradis, M. (2004). *A Neurolinguistic Theory of Bilingualism*. Amsterdam, The Netherlands: John Benjamins.

Parker-Jones, O., Green, D.W., Grogan, A. et al. (2012). Where, when and why brain activation differs for bilinguals and monolinguals during picture naming and reading aloud. *Cerebral Cortex* 22: 892–902.

Pickering, M.J. and Garrod, S. (2013). An integrated theory of language production and comprehension. *Behavioral and Brain Sciences* 36: 329–347.

Pivneva, I., Palmer, C., and Titone, D. (2012). Inhibitory control and L2 proficiency modulate bilingual language production: evidence from spontaneous monologue and dialogue speech. *Frontiers in Psychology* 3 (57): 1–15.

Price, C.J. (2012). A review and synthesis of the first 20 years of PET and fMRI studies of heard speech, spoken language and reading. *NeuroImage* 62: 816–847.

Reverberi, C., Kuhlen, A., Abutalebi, J. et al. (2015). Language control in bilinguals: intention to speak vs. execution of speech. *Brain and Language* 144: 1–9.

Rodriguez-Fornells, A., Krämer, U.M., Lorenzo-Sava, U. et al. (2012). Self-assessment of individual differences in language switching. *Frontiers in Psychology* 2: 388.

Rosenberg, M.D., Finn, E.S., Scheinost, D. et al. (2016). A neuromarker of sustained attention from whole-brain functional connectivity. *Nature Neuroscience* 19: 165–179.

Shanahan, M. (2010). Metastable chimera states in community-structured oscillator networks. *Chaos* 20: 013108.

Shook, A., Goldrick, M., Engstler, C., and Marian, V. (2015). Bilinguals show weaker lexical access during spoken sentence comprehension. *Journal of Psycholinguistic Research* 44: 789–802.

Skipper, J.I., Devlin, J.T., and Lametti, D.R. (2017). The hearing ear is always found close to the speaking tongue. *Brain and Language* 164: 77–105.

Smallwood, J., Brown, K.S., Tipper, C. et al. (2011). Pupillometric evidence for the decoupling of attention from perceptual input during offline thought. *PLoS One* 6: e18298.

Stephens, G.J., Silbert, L.J., and Hasson, U. (2010). Speaker-listener neural coupling underlies successful communication. *Proceedings of the National Academy of Sciences United States of America* 107: 14425–14430.

Stocco, A., Yamasaki, B., Natalenko, R., and Prat, C.S. (2014). Bilingual brain training: a neurobiological framework of how bilingual experience improves executive function. *International Journal of Bilingualism* 18: 67–92.

Tononi, G., Boly, M., Massimini, M., and Koch, C. (2016). Integrated information theory: from consciousness to its physical substrate. *Nature Reviews Neuroscience* 17: 450–461.

Vann, S.D., Aggleton, J.P., and Maguire, E.A. (2009). What does the retrosplenial cortex do? *Nature Reviews Neuroscience* 10: 792–802.

Vincent, J.L., Kahn, I., Snyder, A.Z. et al. (2008). Evidence for a frontoparietal control system revealed by intrinsic functional connectivity. *Journal of Neurophysiology* 100: 3328–3342.

Wachtel, P.L. (1967). Conceptions of broad and narrow attention. *Psychological Bulletin* 68: 417–429.

Wu, Y.J. and Thierry, G. (2013). Fast modulation of executive function by language context in bilinguals. *Journal of Neuroscience* 33: 13533–13537.

22 Cross-Talk Between Language and Executive Control

MARCO CALABRIA, CRISTINA BAUS, AND ALBERT COSTA

1. Introduction

Language production is the set of processes that are involved in translating thoughts into speech, including the selection of a concept to express, the retrieval of the corresponding words and their morphological properties, and the planning and monitoring of the articulatory aspects of the speech output. The orchestration of these processes is supervised by control mechanisms that some scholars have argued are related to the executive control (EC) system (e.g. Piai et al. 2013; Roelofs and Piai 2011; Shao et al. 2012, 2015). The interaction between control and linguistic processes is especially apparent in the context of bilingualism because of bilingual language control (BLC), where bilingual speakers must not only select the language in which they want to conduct verbalization (according to the communicative setting) but also avoid potential interferences from the irrelevant language. In this chapter, we review current knowledge about the relationship between language control and EC mechanisms in bilingual speakers.

Some psycholinguistic and cognitive models of bilingual language production have proposed a clear link between these two domains of control (e.g. Green 1986), whereas others have not addressed this issue (Baus et al. 2015; Costa et al. 1999; Finkbeiner et al. 2006; La Heij 2005). Recent research on this issue has proposed a more specific framework that details the relation between the linguistic and non-linguistic components, such as the adaptive control hypothesis (Green and Abutalebi 2013). Moreover, this proposal explains the extent to which each cognitive control process may adapt to language context demands (from a single- to a dual-language situation to code switching). Besides describing the cognitive processes that underlie the BLC system, the same authors have also proposed a neural account of the brain areas that are related to such processes (Abutalebi and Green 2016).

The most common strategy to assess the relationship between the two domains of control is to compare people's performance on control tasks that involve linguistic and

The Handbook of the Neuroscience of Multilingualism, First Edition. Edited by John W. Schwieter.
© 2019 John Wiley & Sons Ltd. Published 2019 by John Wiley & Sons Ltd.

non-linguistic processes. The argument is that if BLC and EC share at least some of their mechanisms, there should be a correlation between performances on these two tasks. However, research on healthy individuals has not always supported this straightforward prediction. Some studies have indicated poor correlations between individuals' performance on BLC tasks, such as language switching, and on EC tasks (Branzi et al. 2016; Calabria et al. 2012, 2015; Klecha, 2013; Prior and Gollan 2013; Weissberger et al. 2012; for a review see Declerck and Philipp 2015); others have reported a certain degree of correlation (Gross and Kaushanskaya 2016; Festman and Münte 2012; Festman et al. 2010) or complete correlation (Declerck et al. 2017).

In order to complement these findings, researchers have begun to explore new perspectives and methodologies, such as neuroimaging and neuropsychology. Assessing the commonalities and similarities between the underlying brain networks of BLC and EC is a way to investigate the domain-general versus domain-specific nature of such mechanisms. Similarly, studying the relationship between deficits of linguistic and non-linguistic control can contribute to an understanding of similar or different cognitive mechanisms of control across domains.

In this chapter, we review studies that have tested BLC and EC in the same population of bilingual speakers by focusing on neuroimaging data and cognitive and language deficits following brain damage.

2.   Theoretical Perspectives

One critical point in studying the cross-talk between language and EC in bilinguals is the complexity of the concept of control in these two domains. Particularly, language control has been labelled differently according to each of the existing psycholinguistic models. Similarly, EC is an umbrella term that includes several subsystems; some are characterized by a certain degree of specificity, and others are less specific. The possibility of having few or many subsystems has therefore led to a large number of models, which range from more 'monolithic' architectures to more 'compartmentalized' ones (for reviews, see Diamond 2013; Jurado and Rosselli 2007; Munakata et al. 2011).

One common problem amongst all proposals for both language and EC is that it is becoming more and more difficult to measure each subsystem through experimental tasks. Given the disagreement about the general architecture of the systems, it is slightly problematic to interpret the experimental results in terms of cognitive processes and their reliability (e.g. Paap and Sawi 2016). Consequently, understanding the relationship between the control mechanisms that are common to both domains remains a challenging task that requires converging evidence from several fields ranging from cognition to neuroimaging to neuropsychology.

An exhaustive review of both language and non-linguistic control models is beyond the scope of this chapter. However, given that not all psycholinguistic models are in agreement regarding the involvement of EC in BLC, we briefly explain their assumptions. Similarly, we describe the main EC models for investigating the cross-talk between language and non-linguistic control in the context of bilingualism.

Two prominent groups of models have been proposed for lexical retrieval in bilinguals: those that claim the involvement of language-specific mechanisms and those that support the engagement of non-language specific mechanisms. According to the first group, lexical access is not a competitive process between languages but is rather implemented by selection mechanisms similarly to lexical selection in monolinguals (Baus et al. 2015; Costa et al. 1999; Finkbeiner et al. 2006; Hartsuiker et al. 2008; La Heij 2005). Thereby, speaking in one language would activate the selection process (at the lexical or conceptual level) in the intended language without considering potential competitors in the other language. These models do not explicitly relate the control processes to more domain-general EC ones; therefore, according to this view, word retrieval entails linguistic processes only.

Conversely, language non-specific models assume that words in both languages compete during lexical selection (e.g. Green 1986; Poulisse and Bongaerts 1994). The most widely known version is likely the inhibitory control model (ICM) by Green (1986). The main assumption of this model is that inhibition allows bilinguals to resolve competition between languages: once the goal to speak in one language is established, a 'supervisory attentional system' (Norman and Shallice 1986) activates the 'task schema' for one language and inhibits lexical items in the other.

One assumption of Green's ICM model is that inhibition is reactive in the sense that it is applied only after the activation of lexical representations of the non-intended language. A further assumption is that the activation of previously inhibited representations requires time; therefore, a stronger inhibition takes longer to overcome. It follows that the recovery from dominant language (L1) inhibition would require more time and cognitive resources than recovery from non-dominant (L2) inhibition, as its amount is proportional to the relative strength of the languages in terms of proficiency and dominance. Typically, switching from L1 to L2 should be less costly than switching in reverse (Costa and Santesteban 2004; Costa et al. 2006; Declerck and Philipp 2015; Macizo et al. 2012; Peeters et al. 2014; Philipp et al. 2007; for a review on asymmetry in language switching, see Bobb and Wodniecka 2013).

As noted earlier in this section, several models describe the architecture of the EC system and adopt different views of its mechanisms. However, inhibitory control is one process that most of these EC models include. Indeed, in the Miyake et al. model (2000), inhibitory control, updating, and shifting constitute the three distinctive components. Updating monitors the information during the task, shifting refers to the process that underlies the ability to switch between tasks, and inhibition suppresses prepotent non-target responses. Despite recent revision of this framework, its general architecture has not changed dramatically. In the most recent version of the model (Miyake and Friedman 2012), inhibition remains a crucial component of the EC system; however, it is now described as a more general factor that shares importance with updating and shifting. Inhibition also plays a central role in other, more monolithic versions of the EC system. For instance, Munakata et al. (2011) have proposed a unified account that includes two types of inhibition, namely directed global inhibition and indirect competitive inhibition. The former maintains abstract information that is relevant to the functions, whereas the latter amplifies the most active representations and suppresses competitors in order to achieve a goal. These two types of inhibition are not exclusive, and the prefrontal cortex implements them via connections with cortical and subcortical areas.

As noted, there are several other potential accounts to describe the functioning of the EC system (Botvinick et al. 2001, 2004; Diamond 2013; Jurado and Rosselli 2007; Norman and Shallice 1986; Stuss and Alexander 2000; Verhaeghen and Cerella 2002). However, the dual mechanisms of control model (DCM) by Braver (2012) has recently raised interest in the context of bilingualism and control.

The DCM distinguishes between two main processes of control, namely proactive and reactive. Proactive control is defined as a sustained type of control that actively maintains a goal, promotes cognitive flexibility, and facilitates the processing of possible upcoming conflicts. Reactive control, in contrast, is a more transient type of control that resolves interference when it is detected (e.g. trial by trial). A similar framework for language control in bilinguals has recently been introduced and especially explains the nature of language-switching mechanisms (e.g. Abutalebi and Green 2007; Christoffels et al. 2007; Grosjean 2013; Ma et al. 2016). According to this framework, proactive control would manage the activation levels of the two languages prior to the activation of specific lexical items. Reactive control is instead responsible for resolving transient interference between languages, for instance in the case of switching languages. This distinction has become relevant in the context of bilingualism because both types of mechanisms (and their behavioural indexes) have been studied in order to investigate their overlap across various domains of control that are both linguistic and non-linguistic. Moreover, there is some evidence that non-linguistic reactive and proactive control can cooperate more dynamically in bilingual speakers as a result of the high demands of a dual-language context. Indeed, bilinguals outperform monolinguals in situations that require a more flexible adjustment to the involvement of proactive and reactive control (Morales et al. 2013; for the modulation of the frontoparietal network in the interplay of these types of control, see Morales et al. 2015).

Finally, the adaptive control hypothesis that Green and Abutalebi (2013) have recently proposed is of interest for the flexibility of EC processes with respect to the demand of the language context. The authors have argued that the control process adapts to the interactional context that confronts bilingual speakers. Green and Abutalebi (2013) have defined three types of interactional contexts: the single-language context, in which the two languages are used in distinct environments; the dual-language context, in which bilingual speakers switch between languages with different speakers; and the dense code-switching context, in which bilingual speakers mix languages in the course of a single utterance. They have additionally defined the following eight cognitive control processes: goal maintenance, conflict monitoring, interference suppression, salient cue detection, selective response inhibition, task engagement, task disengagement, and opportunistic planning. These control processes would occur flexibly according to the interactional context. For instance, the dual-language context would be the most demanding because it requires bilingual speakers to use most of these EC processes. Moreover, given the high frequency of switching in comparison to the single-language context, speakers have to monitor the language conflict and suppress interference from the language that is not in use (goal maintenance, conflict monitoring, and interference suppression).

In Section 3, we aim to determine how the cross-talk between EC and BLC has been studied by focusing on inhibitory control, the dichotomy of proactive and reactive control, and the flexibility of these processes. We first describe studies that have investigated the overlap between the brain areas in charge of linguistic and non-linguistic control in bilinguals. Then, we discuss studies of bilingual speakers with brain diseases, such as aphasia and neurodegenerative disorders.

3. Neural Basis of BLC and EC

This section deals with this research question: How are the networks responsible for domain-general EC and BLC related? This question has been mostly addressed by examining the brain activity that is elicited by language-related and non-linguistic tasks (for reviews on neuroimaging of BLC, see Luk et al. 2011; for non-linguistic control in bilinguals, see Pliatsikas and Luk 2016).

The most exhaustive model that describes the brain areas associated with BLC is likely the model that Abutalebi and Green (2007, 2008) have proposed and recently updated under the adaptive control hypothesis (Abutalebi and Green 2016; Green and Abutalebi 2013). It is relevant to discuss this model because it offers insight into the link between the brain areas associated with BLC and those related to the EC system.

This model considers the prefrontal cortex to be the main neural hub and conceptualizes it as a top-down control device that processes task-relevant representations. The prefrontal cortex is connected with posterior areas (parietal cortex), which creates a circuit that manages selection amongst competing responses. Specifically, the parietal cortex is involved in the maintenance of task representation and updates it through a working memory process. Two more areas connected with the prefrontal cortex are crucial for efficient cognitive control. The first is the anterior cingulate cortex, which has the prominent role of detecting the presence of the conflict and then sending information to the prefrontal cortex to implement the response selection. The second set of areas connected to the prefrontal cortex is the basal ganglia, which are mainly related to motor control but also to sequence planning and task-switching abilities (Graybiel et al. 1994; Hikosaka and Isoda 2010). Abutalebi and Green (2007) have proposed this general framework of cognitive control and accordingly adapted it to BLC. They have examined a series of studies that have mainly investigated the neural network of language switching, word translation, or both – two tasks which supposedly require control of the two languages for their high cognitive demand.

The prefrontal cortex is involved in response selection and inhibition, and its activation has been found to increase when bilinguals name pictures and switch languages compared to in a non-switching condition (e.g. Branzi et al. 2016; Garbin et al. 2011; Geranmayeh et al. 2014; Hernandez et al. 2001; Luk et al. 2011). The parietal cortices (left and right parietal lobules) maintain language and task representation (Jackson et al. 2001), and similarly to the EC, the anterior cingulate cortex detects and modulates the language conflict (cross-language interference and switching). According to Abutalebi and Green (2007), the basal ganglia play a more specific role in language control, including the selection and control of the language in use in terms of its activation, inhibition, or both. Indeed, some studies have highlighted that the activation of the prefrontal cortex and basal ganglia is modulated by the linguistic context in which bilinguals are situated. For instance, Abutalebi et al. (2008) have demonstrated that the left caudate is activated only when a language switch is required (dual-language context) and not when participants must switch intralingually (single-language context). Similarly, Crinion et al. (2006) have indicated that the activation of the left caudate occurs only in cross-language conditions of priming. In their study, bilingual participants were presented with sequential word pairs and instructed to judge their semantic relatedness. Crucially, the target word was in either the same or a different language. The results revealed heightened activation of the left head of the caudate when word pairs were in different languages (dual-language context) but not when they were in the same language. Moreover, lesion and brain stimulation studies have revealed the vital role of this area in language control through the finding that electrical stimulation (Wang et al. 2012) and brain damage over the left caudate consequently generate pathological language switching and mixing (see 'Brain damage and deficits of EC and BLC').

Recently, in the context of the adaptive control hypothesis, it has been proposed that language context may influence the activation of the frontal and subcortical structures (Green and Abutalebi 2013). For the dual-language context, where bilinguals need to switch back and forth between languages, this hypothesis predicts changes in the subcortical structures for the activation and inhibition of the two languages. Moreover, frontal lobes, in connection with basal ganglia, would be more strongly activated in their involvement in monitoring conflict and suppressing cross-language interference. Conversely, in the single-language context, as the suppression of the non-target language extends over time, there would not be involvement of basal ganglia.

The idea that two control systems might depend on the very similar neural network has suggested the hypothesis of brain difference between bilinguals and monolinguals. The EC brain network has been of special interest because it is supposed to benefit from the overlap with BLC (for a review, see Pliatsikas and Luk 2016). Along this line of studies, research has illustrated that bilinguals and monolinguals either use different brain areas or use certain areas with different degrees of efficiency while performing EC tasks. For instance, Garbin et al. (2010) have found that monolinguals use a more extended brain network, including the right inferior gyrus, anterior cingulate cortex, and left inferior parietal lobe, for non-linguistic abilities of switching. Bilinguals instead rely more heavily on the left inferior frontal lobe, which is a brain area also belonging to BLC network. In a further study, Rodríguez-Pujadas et al. (2013) have reported that bilinguals use more numerous language control areas (left caudate, left inferior, and middle frontal gyri) than monolinguals in task switching. Recently, researchers have also demonstrated that bilinguals use the left inferior gyrus and the anterior cingulate cortex more efficiently (reduced activation) than monolinguals during task switching (Gold et al. 2013).

These differences between monolinguals and bilinguals suggest a potential role of BLC in modulating the brain activity of the non-linguistic EC network. Specifically, these findings suggest that such overlap between the two control systems relies on the most anterior part of the network, including the inferior frontal lobule and the anterior cingulate cortex. Interestingly, Abutalebi and Green (2007) have proposed the connection between these two areas to be a common locus for language control and resolution of non-linguistic conflict in their BLC model. Moreover, it has recently been found that the more efficient brain activity of the anterior cingulate cortex in bilinguals correlates positively with its grey matter volume, which supports a further link with the BLC network (Abutalebi et al. 2012).

To find more direct evidence of the cross-talk between BLC and EC, some authors have compared brain activation in the same populations of bilinguals in linguistic and non-linguistic control tasks (Coderre et al. 2015; De Baene et al. 2015; Weissberger et al. 2015). To test whether inhibitory control involves similar areas for the two domains of control, Coderre et al. (2015) have compared the brain activation of bilinguals performing a linguistic and a non-linguistic version of a flanker task (conflict resolution task). The conjunction analysis has revealed a straightforward result: monolinguals do not exhibit any evidence of using common brain areas in performing the two tasks, whereas bilinguals presented an overlap in the left inferior frontal gyrus. In line with the suggestion of indirect evidence of an overlap, the authors have concluded that this area is fundamental for both language processing and cognitive control in bilingualism.

However, for switching abilities, the results are less clear. Weissberger et al. (2015) have compared brain activation for language switching and task switching in bilinguals, and the results have revealed a more complex scenario. In an overall analysis, Weissberger et al. (2015) have reported a similar activation for the tasks for an extensive neural network that includes cortical and subcortical areas. However, when they considered the type of trial (switch or non-switch) in the conjunctional analysis, they found certain differences between task activations. In particular, for switch trials, language switching activated the bilateral thalamus, posterior cingulate, right caudate, and cingulate gyrus more than task switching did. For non-switch trials, there was greater activation of frontal, parietal, temporal, occipital, cingulate, insular, and subcortical areas for task switching than for language switching. Besides the explanation of all of these differences in brain activation, the conclusion from this study is that the overlap between BLC and EC is only partial.

In partial contradiction with the results of Weissberger et al. (2015), De Baene et al. (2015) have found evidence of a more clear overlap of brain circuitries. De Baene et al. (2015) have compared a language-switching task in Spanish, Basque, and English and a task-switching activity with colour, motion, and gender as sorting criteria. In their analysis of the brain activations, they determined that the prefrontal cortex (lateral and medial) and the parietal lobule (inferior and superior) were both active in the two tasks. In addition to the commonalties between the two neural networks, some differences were also found. For language switching, there was activation of the areas related to phonological processing due to the verbal nature of the task. For task switching, there was activation of the dorsal premotor cortex because it is an area related to action preparation.

In sum, the current evidence of a common neural network of the BLC and the EC system does not seem to support a complete overlap between these two domains but only a partial overlap for frontal and posterior parietal areas. The inferior and superior frontal gyri are the most likely to be common brain areas for the domain-general control of inhibition and conflict resolution, whereas the posterior parietal areas are likely for working memory and maintenance of task representations (Abutalebi and Green 2007).

4.   Brain Damage and Deficits of EC and BLC

Language-control deficits and their relationship with deficits of the non-linguistic domain have been studied in bilingual patients with aphasia, pathological language switching, and neurodegenerative diseases. There are at least two reasons for the research interest in studying this relationship in pathological populations.

First, this context allows researchers to investigate whether control mechanisms in both domains are similarly affected by brain disease under the hypothesis of their domain-general nature (association of deficits) or if they are domain-specific in that the mechanisms that can be affected for language control cannot be affected for non-linguistic control, or vice versa (dissociation of deficits). In the specific context of neuro-degenerative diseases, this relationship can be explored in pathologies that affect the EC system and the brain areas involved in BLC, namely those that damage the basal ganglia, such as Parkinson's disease (PD) and Huntington's disease. These types of pathologies are well characterized for their deficits over the EC system and therefore quite useful for comparison with current knowledge about language control in bilinguals (Calabria et al. 2017; Lorenzen and Murray 2008; Murray 2017; Paradis 2008).

Second, some researchers have suggested explaining differential or selective language impairments (one language more affected than the other) as a consequence of deficits of control processes. Indeed, according to the 'dynamic view', selective language recovery reflects an imbalance between activation and inhibition of the two languages as deficits of language selection. That is, a selective loss of one language would be due to increased inhibition following brain damage. Therefore, this overinhibition would raise the activation threshold, which would in turn make selection more difficult for the more impaired language than for the spared one (Abutalebi and Green 2007; Green 2008; Green et al. 2010; Paradis 1999, 2008). Thus, lexical representations per se are not affected by brain damage but rather by the control processes behind language activation and inhibition (as part of the BLC system). The hypothesis of affected control processes in bilingual aphasia have implied that also non-linguistic EC might contribute to language deficits. Therefore, the study of control mechanisms in patients with bilingual aphasia would offer insight into the language recovery pattern and implementation approaches for speech therapy that take into account the role of non-linguistic control processes.

4.1.   *Pathological Language Switching and Mixing*

Problems in BLC may lead to rather striking linguistic behaviour, such as pathological language mixing and pathological language switching (Abutalebi et al. 2000; Aglioti et al. 1996; Aglioti and Fabbro 1993; Ansaldo et al. 2010; Calabria et al. 2014; Fabbro et al. 2000; Garcia-Caballero et al. 2007; Kong et al. 2014; Leemann et al. 2007; Mariën et al. 2005). The former refers to the uncontrolled mixing of elements of two languages within a single utterance, and the latter entails involuntarily alternating languages across different utterances (Ansaldo and Marcotte 2007). These pathological behaviours are due to damage within the BLC network, specifically over the subcortical (basal ganglia and subthalamic regions), the frontal areas and their connections with striatal structures, or both these subcortical and frontal areas. For example, Abutalebi et al. (2000) have reported the case of a trilingual (Armenian–English–Italian) female (A.H.) who developed a non-fluent aphasia characterized by pathological language switching between these languages in speech production after a subcortical white matter infarction adjacent to the left caudate nucleus. Similarly, Aglioti et al. (1996) have recounted a bilingual patient (E.M.) who, after a stroke in the left capsular-putaminal region, suffered cross-language intrusions during spontaneous speech. In a further study, Fabbro et al. (2000) have described a patient who produced his dominant language (Friulian) half of the time when requested to speak in his non-dominant language (Italian), and vice versa, and who had a lesion over the left anterior cingulate and the frontal lobe. Finally, a study by Mariën et al. (2005) is relevant for detailing the crucial areas related to BLC and their damage. After a subcortical lesion, the patient, an English-Dutch bilingual, produced mixed words composed of the first part of a word in Dutch with a suffix in English (pathological language mixing). However, when perfusion in the left frontal lobe and left caudate returned to normal levels, these problems disappeared.

Although these studies indicate that specific lesions can dramatically affect language control in bilinguals, it is not clear whether this is due to concomitant deficits of EC. Indeed, a few studies have investigated the performance of these patients in EC, and some have only used general neuropsychological tests, though not in a systematic way. For instance, in Fabbro et al.'s (2000) study, their patient did not exhibit impaired performance on attention assessment tests. However, Leemann et al. (2007) have described a patient who had deficits in EC tasks (perseverations), and Mariën et al. (2005) have reported one who had 'a decrease in general cognitive abilities', especially for the performance subscale of the intelligence quotient (IQ) test. Recently, Kong et al. (2014) have specifically tested the role of EC deficits in a Cantonese-English-Mandarin trilingual speaker named Dr T., who engaged in involuntary language switching when speaking in Cantonese. The patient was tested in two EC tasks that involve inhibition and interference (Stroop colour-word test) and shifting abilities (Wisconsin card-sorting test). For both tasks, the patient was impaired, which led the authors to conclude that linguistic and non-linguistic control processes are closely linked. Moreover, considering that the patient had a lesion over his left frontal lobe, the researchers concluded that this was an area common to both BLC and EC. Similar results were found for a Catalan-Spanish bilingual patient (R.M.) who Calabria et al. (2014) have noted for the overlapping of deficits between domain-general EC and BLC. Besides the neuropsychological and linguistic assessments of spontaneous speech, these authors have also evaluated switching abilities with a language-switching task and non-linguistic task switching. In the language-switching task, R.M. made several intrusions when required to switch into her dominant language (as she did in spontaneous speech), and her accuracy in task switching was significantly impaired compared with age-matched healthy controls. Moreover, her EC abilities were tested for inhibition in a conflict task (flanker); in this case, R.M. scored poorly compared with healthy controls. These studies, which specifically tested EC in bilingual patients with language-control deficits, have revealed a certain degree of overlap between these two domains, at least for inhibitory control in conflict resolution and switching abilities. However, given the limited amount of evidence from these patients and the behavioural evidence from healthy bilinguals that indicates a limited overlap between EC and BLC, the consistency of this pattern is uncertain. In the next section, we examine the contributions of studies that have investigated EC deficits in bilingual speakers with aphasia.

4.2.   *Bilingual Aphasia and EC*

In addition to the interest in studying BLC and EC in patients who possess specific language control deficits, research in the past 10 years has extended to bilingual speakers with aphasia. These patients have classical language impairments, but they do not necessarily engage in pathological switching or mixing. However, it is still relevant to acknowledge the role of EC in bilingual aphasia since the deficits in some cases of differential language impairment (one more affected than the other) may rely on control, for instance due to exaggerated inhibition or activation (see 'dynamic view' in Green 2008). Indeed, although similar impairment in both languages is more frequent (about 60% of cases), estimates claim that approximately 20–30% of bilingual speakers with aphasia exhibit differential recovery (Ansaldo and Marcotte 2007; Fabbro 2001; Paradis 2001). Research on the role of non-linguistic EC deficits in patients with bilingual aphasia is limited to a small number of studies; however, their crucial role on language impairment is apparent in their (negative) impact on language outcomes in monolingual speakers with aphasia (Kuzmina and Weekes 2017; Murray 2012; Murray 2017).

The involvement of brain areas related to control in language improvement after speech therapy offer some indication of such overlap between EC and BLC. Abutalebi et al. (2009) have longitudinally examined the effect of neural plasticity due to speech therapy in a Spanish-Italian bilingual patient with aphasia. After therapy, in addition to the increased activation of the language network, including prefrontal and temporal areas, they also observed persistent activation of the control network (left caudate and anterior cingulate cortex), but only for the language that was trained, namely Italian. Given that the anterior cingulate cortex is one of the brain areas responsible for response resolution and selection in conflict conditions (e.g. Botvinick et al. 2001), the authors have concluded that this is indirect evidence of the involvement of EC in BLC. Similarly, a recent study by Radman et al. (2016) has identified the anterior cingulate cortex as an essential area for selective language recovery in patients with bilingual aphasia. Specifically, it found that the coupling of the anterior cingulate cortex and one of the areas of the language network (left inferior frontal gyrus) became stronger for the recovered language over time. Taken together, these results suggest a broad connection between EC and BLC; however, as non-linguistic abilities were not measured, this remains indirect evidence.

In recent years, the issue of EC deficits amongst bilingual patients with aphasia has attracted interest, especially amongst speech pathology researchers. Most of the available studies to date have examined the contribution of EC in language comprehension using lexical decision or semantic priming tasks (Dash and Kar 2014; Gray and Kiran 2015; Green et al. 2010; Verreyt et al. 2013) and have assessed only a few cases for word production (Faroqi-Shah et al. 2016). Moreover, almost all studies have compared linguistic performance to non-linguistic inhibition using a flanker task (Dash and Kar 2014; Gray and Kiran 2015; Green et al. 2010; Verreyt et al. 2013) or inhibition for verbal material (Faroqi-Shah and Waked 2010).

The two patients that Green et al. (2010) have described are the first examples of the dissociation between language and non-linguistic control. Their study featured two patients with different brain lesions: Pt1 over subcortical areas (putamen and globus pallidus) and Pt2 in the left frontal and temporal areas (territory of the left-middle cerebral artery) and occipital regions. Pt1 was pathological in the linguistic control task (Stroop) but less pathological than healthy controls in the non-linguistic one (flanker). Pt2 demonstrated less affected linguistic control and more impaired non-linguistic control. After considering the lesion and behavioural data from these two patients together, Green et al. (2010) have suggested that the different neural network affected by brain damage explains the dissociation regarding the domain of the control abilities. So, a lesion in the putamen and globus pallidus (Pt1) was consistent with damage of the language control device, whereas a lesion over the parietal cortex (Pt2) was more damaging for the interplay between linguistic and non-linguistic control mechanisms. Following this initial evidence of a certain degree of dissociation between the two domains, other group studies with patients with bilingual aphasia have explored this question. In summary, most of these studies have found a partial overlap between EC and BLC.

Dash and Kar (2014) have investigated the possible overlap of inhibitory control in language and non-linguistic control amongst four aphasic patients with English as L2 and Telugu, Hindi, or Urdu as L1 (in two versions of a flanker task). In the linguistic version, flankers were letters from L1 to L2, whereas for the non-linguistic version, they used congruent and incongruent arrows. They identified no correlation for the performance between the two tasks and therefore concluded in favour of dissociation, as Green et al. (2010) have proposed. However, it is difficult to understand how patients performed in terms of impairment for BLC and EC given that they were not compared to a healthy group of participants.

Results from Gray and Kiran (2015) also support an incomplete overlap. These researchers have employed the flanker task to measure EC deficits and semantic priming to further measure language impairment in Spanish-English patients with aphasia (n = 10). In the semantic priming task, patients generally did not reflect the expected semantic facilitation found in healthy controls, which suggests deficits in the language domain. However, in the flanker task, patients scored the same as controls on both accuracy and speed. These results imply no contribution of EC deficits to the language impairment of bilinguals.

A further study by Faroqi-Shah et al. (2016) has assessed the relation between control deficits and speech production in picture naming and verbal fluency in English-Tamil bilingual speakers with aphasia. It used a cognitive control task with verbal material (Stroop task) rather than a non-linguistic control task; nevertheless, as previous studies have indicated, the performance of the two tasks was uncorrelated.

Most of the studies described thus far (excluding Green et al. 2010) have tested patients with parallel recovery and noted an inconsistent relationship between non-linguistic control deficits (when found) and language performance. Therefore, one possibility is that the role of EC deficits might be less crucial when the two languages are similarly affected. Indeed, according to the dynamic view of language recovery, the BLC and EC would be more strongly impacted in patients who exhibit differential language impairment. Following this idea, Verreyt et al. (2013) have tested language deficits with lexical decisions and EC with a flanker task in a French-Dutch bilingual speaker with aphasia (H.D.M.) who experienced a greater effect in Dutch than in French. Specifically, the language performance of H.D.M. was less accurate in Dutch than in French when the two languages were mixed in the lexical decision task, and his performance on the flanker task was also less accurate, especially for incongruent trials, in comparison to healthy controls. Hence, this result suggests that the presence of similar deficits of control in both domains is more reliable in cases of differential language impairment.

In sum, aphasia studies that have explored the cross-talk between BLC and EC have yielded mixed findings, with some indications favouring an incomplete overlap between the two systems. However, this preliminary conclusion is seemingly restricted to inhibitory control and to patients with parallel language impairment. Further studies should explore other EC components, such as working memory and switching abilities, to determine whether these non-linguistic control mechanisms are more closely related to language control deficits in bilingual speakers.

4.3. Bilingual Language Control and EC in Neurodegenerative Diseases

A recent line of research on the cross-talk between BLC and EC has studied bilingual patients with neurodegenerative diseases. Similar to studies on bilingual aphasia, this research has explored impacts on language control in patients who have EC deficits due to the disease. In the context of bilingualism, few studies have investigated the relationship between these two domains in PD patients. An extensive body of literature has demonstrated that in addition to the movement disorders that characterize this pathology, EC is compromised in the early stages of the disease. The EC processes that PD mainly affects include set-shifting, planning, inhibitory control, conflict resolution, decision-making, and working memory (see the review by Dirnberger and Jahanshahi 2013; Kudlicka et al. 2011), according to studies that have used neuropsychological measures and experimental tasks (e.g. flanker task, Wylie et al. 2009; Simon task, Praamstra and Plat 2001; task switching, Cools et al. 2001; Hayes et al. 1998). These deficits have been related to dysfunctions of the basal ganglia and their striatal connections to the frontal cortex (Narayanan et al. 2013), which are brain areas in the neural network of BLC, as described earlier (Abutalebi and Green 2008, 2016; Luk et al. 2011). Therefore, the hypothesis is that there could be some overlap in deficits for both BLC and EC in bilingual patients with PD.

To date, only a few studies have investigated the impact of PD on language processing in bilinguals. Therefore, it is difficult to conclude its effects on language control. Two studies (Zanini et al. 2004, 2010) have evidenced that PD leads to difficulty with sentence and syntactic comprehension as well as to spontaneous speech production. In the first study (Zanini et al. 2004), the authors tested both Friulian-Italian bilinguals with PD and healthy controls in a sentence comprehension task, syntactic judgement tasks, and an EC task (Wisconsin card-sorting test). The main result was that PD patients were impaired in syntactic processing, and particularly in their dominant language (Friulian). Moreover, in line with findings for monolinguals, performance on EC tasks correlated with that on the sentence comprehension task, which suggests a link between grammatical processing and EC. Johari et al. (2013) have recently replicated similar results in Azari-Farsi bilinguals.

Finally, Zanini et al. (2010) have found that bilingual individuals with PD produced more morphological, phonological, and syntactic errors compared to controls, and particularly in L1 speech production. The authors have interpreted their results according to the declarative procedural model, which explains different linguistic impairments in terms of the dissociation between procedural and declarative memories that underlie more or less explicit processing (Ullman 2001; Ullman et al. 1997). Bilinguals would more implicitly learn the dominant and early-acquired language and would depend more on procedural memory in doing so, whereas they would explicitly learn the late-acquired second language (e.g. at school) through declarative memory. The fact that the frontobasal ganglia network processes procedural memories accounts for the greater deficits of bilingual PD patients in their dominant language.

However, Zanini et al. (2004) have also reported a positive correlation between performance in linguistic and non-linguistic tasks, which permits the possibility that EC deficits may contribute to language impairments in their bilingual PD patients (see Adrover-Roig et al. 2011, for a differential impairment of L1 and L2 due to EC deficits).

Recently, in order to explore the cross-talk between EC and BLC, Cattaneo et al. (2015) have specifically examined the performance of bilingual PD patients in linguistic and non-linguistic tasks. Under the hypothesis of a shared neural network between the two systems and the known control deficits of PD patients, they predicted similar deficits in the linguistic and the non-linguistic domain. The authors used a language-switching task and non-linguistic task switching in which participants were required to name pictures (in Catalan or Spanish) or to match images according to specific criteria (shape or colour). The critical point was that the naming language or sorting criterion changed in some trials (switch trials). The difference in reaction times between switch trials and non-switch trials (in two consecutive trials with the same naming language or same sorting criterion) was calculated as switch cost. The results reveal that patients have higher switch costs than healthy controls do for the language-switching task but not for non-linguistic task switching. In addition to this index of control, Cattaneo et al. (2015) have successfully measured mixing cost as the difference of reaction times between non-switch and single trials, where single trials were those named in the non-mixed conditions, such as only one naming language to use or only one sorting criterion. For this second measure of control, patients with greater impairment in EC exhibited similar impairment in both language and non-linguistic task switching. Thus, bilingual PD patients reflected similarities across tasks for mixing costs but not for switch costs.

Despite the complexity of these results, the interpretation can be framed in the context of the DCM by Braver (2012), which postulates two types of control, namely proactive and reactive. The measures of these two types of control would be the mixing cost and the switch cost, respectively. According to this dual-process account, Cattaneo et al. (2015) have explained the results as follows. Reactive control (indexed by switch cost) is not a mechanism shared between BLC and EC (domain-specific), as it was differentially affected across domains in PD patients. Moreover, this result replicates the findings of previous studies that note no correlation between linguistic and non-linguistic costs (Branzi et al. 2016; Calabria et al. 2012, 2015; Declerck and Philipp 2015). However, proactive control (indexed by mixing cost) appears to be a shared mechanism between these two systems (domain-general) because it was similarly affected across domains in bilingual PD patients. Proactive control is seemingly dependent on other EC subcomponents, but its nature is still under debate. For example, it may be related to working memory mechanisms, such as the demand to maintain task goals that are available in a dual-task situation (e.g. Braver et al. 2003). Indeed, beyond their function as crucial processes of the non-linguistic EC system, working memory and updating also play a role in speech production for word planning, maintaining, and updating lexical selection processes (dual-task interference condition, Piai et al. 2013; Roelofs and Piai 2011). Therefore, the interpretation of proactive control in terms of working memory and updating subcomponents would offer a new perspective of the nature of the cross-talk between BLC and EC.

5.   Conclusion

In this chapter, we have reviewed the available evidence on the cross-talk between BLC and EC with a focus on findings from neuropsychology and neuroimaging. Given the complexity of this issue at both the methodological and the theoretical level, behavioural data from healthy bilinguals need to be complemented by other approaches. Therefore, examining bilingual speakers following brain damage and the underlying neural network of control might be two ways to gather new data on this issue.

As we noted in the Introduction to this chapter, the complexity of the architecture of language control – and even more so for EC – drastically complicates the study of their relationship. Indeed, there are several models for BLC that postulate various degrees of association with non-linguistic models. Moreover, since researchers disagree about the general frame of non-linguistic control processes, it is challenging to determine which subcomponents to investigate amongst several potential candidates. In fact, these difficulties have led most studies to explore specific subcomponents (e.g. inhibitory control) in both language and non-linguistic tasks, and other EC components (e.g. working memory) have received little attention. Future research should complement the scenario by including tasks that engage other EC processes and should attempt to determine the utility of more recent frameworks (proactive vs. reactive control proposals).

The general conclusion from data that are currently available from neuropsychology and neuroimaging is that the overlap of mechanisms between BLC and EC is partial. From dissociations of deficits in patients with bilingual aphasias for these two domains of control to partially different brain networks, the data seem to suggest a certain degree of domain specificity of BLC over EC. However, especially in the case of patients, it is important to note that the evidence is not exhaustive, as it is limited to inhibitory control or conflict resolution. Indeed, as reviewed, most studies have evaluated inhibitory control and have primarily employed the same task (flanker). Moreover, few researchers have investigated the language production system and have limited their investigations to the receptive/comprehension system. Since these two language systems rely on relatively different control processes, we need to determine their specific relation with the non-linguistic ones.

One potential population with which to expand this research is bilingual patients with neurodegenerative diseases, as it would offer the possibility to test large samples of individuals with well-described deficits of EC (Calabria et al. 2017). In this case, studying the consequence of EC deficits on language control may reveal the point at which the two systems are linked and on which subprocesses this occurs (working memory, conflict monitoring, shifting, or inhibition).

A similar conclusion is possible regarding the partial overlap between the two domains of control for neuroimaging data. The number of available papers in this field is notably limited, and most evidence derives from studies that have not explored the neural basis of EC and language control within the same bilinguals. Therefore, it would be premature to develop firm conclusions. Hopefully, with the intensifying interest in this issue and improvements in the techniques, research can amass an increasing amount of high-quality data, which can allow for integration with data from brain-damaged individuals and from age-related disorders.

Acknowledgements

This work was supported by grants from the Agencia Estatal de Investigación (AEI, National Research Agency) and Fondo Europeo de Desarrollo Regional (FEDER, European Regional Development Fund) (Projects: PSI2017-84539-P, PSI2014-52181-P, PSI2017-87784-R), the Catalan Government (2017 SGR 268), and the European Union's Seventh Framework Programme for research, technological development and demonstration under grant agreement no. 613465 - AThEME. Marco Calabria was supported by the Ramón y Cajal F Programme (RYC-2013-14013)

REFERENCES

Abutalebi, J., Annoni, J.M., Zimine, I. et al. (2008). Language control and lexical competition in bilinguals: an event-related fMRI study. *Cerebral Cortex* 18 (7): 1496–1505.

Abutalebi, J., Della Rosa, P.A., Green, D.W. et al. (2012). Bilingualism tunes the anterior cingulate cortex for conflict monitoring. *Cerebral Cortex* 22 (9): 2076–2086.

Abutalebi, J., Della Rosa, P.A., Tettamanti, M. et al. (2009). Bilingual aphasia and language control: a follow-up fMRI and intrinsic connectivity study. *Brain and Language* 109 (2–3): 141–156.

Abutalebi, J. and Green, D.W. (2007). Bilingual language production: the neurocognition of language representation and control. *Journal of Neurolinguistics* 20: 242–275.

Abutalebi, J. and Green, D.W. (2008). Control mechanisms in bilingual language production: neural evidence from language switching studies. *Language & Cognitive Processes* 23 (4): 557–582.

Abutalebi, J. and Green, D.W. (2016). Neuroimaging of language control in bilinguals: neural adaptation and reserve. *Bilingualism: Language and Cognition* 19 (April): 1–10.

Abutalebi, J., Miozzo, M., and Cappa, S.F. (2000). Do subcortical structures control 'language selection' in polyglots? Evidence from pathological language mixing. *Neurocase* 6: 51–56.

Adrover-Roig, D., Galparsoro-Izagirre, N., Marcotte, K. et al. (2011). Impaired L1 and executive control after left basal ganglia damage in a bilingual Basque-Spanish person with aphasia. *Clinical Linguistics & Phonetics* 25: 480–498.

Aglioti, S., Beltramello, A., Girardi, F., and Fabbro, F. (1996). Neurolinguistic and follow-up study of an unusual pattern of recovery from bilingual subcortical aphasia. *Brain: A Journal of Neurology* 119 (Pt 5): 1551–1564.

Aglioti, S. and Fabbro, F. (1993). Paradoxical selective recovery in a bilingual aphasic following subcortical lesions. *NeuroReport* 4 (12): 1359–1362.

Ansaldo, A.I. and Marcotte, K. (2007). Language switching and mixing in the context of bilingual aphasia. In: *Studying Communication Disorders in Spanish Speakers: Theoretical, Research, and Clinical Aspects* (ed. J.G. Centeno, L.K. Obler and R.T. Anderson). Cleveland, UK: Multilingual Matters.

Ansaldo, A.I., Saidi, L.G., and Ruiz, A. (2010). Model-driven intervention in bilingual aphasia: evidence from a case of pathological language mixing. *Aphasiology* 24 (2): 309–324.

Baus, C., Branzi, F.M., and Costa, A. (2015). On the mechanism and scope of language control in bilingual speech production. In: *The Cambridge Handbook of Bilingual processing* (ed. J.W. Schwieter). Cambridge: Cambridge University Press.

Bobb, S.C. and Wodniecka, Z. (2013). Language switching in picture naming: what asymmetric switch costs (do not) tell us about inhibition in bilingual speech planning. *Journal of Cognitive Psychology* 25 (5): 568–585.

Botvinick, M.M., Braver, T.S., Barch, D.M. et al. (2001). Conflict monitoring and cognitive control. *Psychological Review* 108 (3): 624–652.

Botvinick, M.M., Cohen, J.D., and Carter, C.S. (2004). Conflict monitoring and anterior cingulate cortex: an update. *Trends in Cognitive Sciences* 8 (12): 539–546.

Branzi, F.M., Calabria, M., Boscarino, M.L., and Costa, A. (2016). On the overlap between bilingual language control and domain-general executive control. *Acta Psychologica* 166: 21–30.

Branzi, F.M., Della Rosa, P.A., Canini, M. et al. (2016). Language control in bilinguals: monitoring and response selection. *Cerebral Cortex* 26 (6): 2367–2380.

Braver, T.S. (2012). The variable nature of cognitive control: a dual-mechanisms framework. *Trends in Cognitive Sciences* 16 (2): 106–113.

Braver, T.S., Reynolds, J.R., and Donaldson, D.I. (2003). Neural mechanisms of transient and sustained cognitive control during task switching. *Neuron* 39 (4): 713–726.

Calabria, M., Branzi, F.M., Marne, P. et al. (2015). Age-related effects over bilingual language control and executive control. *Bilingualism* 18 (1): 65–78.

Calabria, M., Cattaneo, G., and Costa, A. (2017). It is time to project into the future: 'bilingualism in healthy and pathological aging'. *Journal of Neurolinguistics* 43: 1–3.

Calabria, M., Hernández, M., Branzi, F.M., and Costa, A. (2012). Qualitative differences between bilingual language control and executive control: evidence from task-switching. *Frontiers in Psychology* 3 (2): 399.

Calabria, M., Marne, P., Romero-Pinel, L. et al. (2014). Losing control of your languages: a case study. *Cognitive Neuropsychology* 31 (3): 266–286.

Cattaneo, G., Calabria, M., Marne, P. et al. (2015). The role of executive control in bilingual language production: a study with Parkinson's disease individuals. *Neuropsychologia* 66: 99–110.

Christoffels, I.K., Firk, C., and Schiller, N.O. (2007). Bilingual language control: an event-related brain potential study. *Brain Research* 1147 (1): 192–208.

Coderre, E., Smith, L., Jason, F. et al. (2015). The functional overlap of executive control and language processing in bilinguals. *Bilingualism* 19 (3): 417–488.

Cools, R., Barker, R.A., Sahakian, B.J., and Robbins, T.W. (2001). Mechanisms of cognitive set flexibility in Parkinson's disease. *Brain: A Journal of Neurology* 124 (Pt 12): 2503–2512.

Costa, A., Miozzo, M., and Caramazza, A. (1999). Lexical selection in bilinguals: do words in the bilingual's two lexicons compete for selection? *Journal of Memory and Language* 41: 365–397.

Costa, A. and Santesteban, M. (2004). Lexical access in bilingual speech production: evidence from language switching in highly proficient bilinguals and L2 learners. *Journal of Memory and Language* 50: 491–511.

Costa, A., Santesteban, M., and Ivanova, I. (2006). How do highly proficient bilinguals control their lexicalization process? Inhibitory and language-specific selection mechanisms are both functional. *Journal of Experimental Psychology: Learning, Memory, and Cognition* 32 (5): 1057–1074.

Crinion, J., Turner, R., Grogan, A. et al. (2006). Language control in the bilingual brain. *Science* 312 (5779): 1537–1540.

Dash, T. and Kar, B.R. (2014). Bilingual language control and general purpose cognitive control among individuals with bilingual aphasia: evidence based on negative priming and flanker tasks. *Behavioural Neurology* 2014: 679706.

De Baene, W., Duyck, W., Brass, M., and Carreiras, M. (2015). Brain circuit for cognitive control is shared by task and language switching. *Journal of Cognitive Neuroscience* 27 (9): 1752–1765.

Declerck, M., Grainger, J., Koch, I., and Philipp, A.M. (2017). Is language control just a form of executive control? Evidence for overlapping processes in language switching and task switching. *Journal of Memory and Language* 95: 138–145.

Declerck, M. and Philipp, A.M. (2015). A review of control processes and their locus in language switching. *Psychonomic Bulletin and Review* 22 (6): 1630–1645.

Diamond, A. (2013). Executive functions. *Annual Review of Pshycology* 64 (9): 135–168.

Dirnberger, G. and Jahanshahi, M. (2013). Executive dysfunction in Parkinson's disease: a review. *Journal of Neuropsychology* 7 (2): 193–224.

Fabbro, F. (2001). The bilingual brain: bilingual aphasia. *Brain and Language* 79: 201–210.

Fabbro, F., Skrap, M., and Aglioti, S. (2000). Pathological switching between languages after frontal lesions in a bilingual patient. *Journal of Neurology, Neurosurgery, and Psychiatry* 68 (5): 650–652.

Faroqi-Shah, Y., Sampson, M., Pranger, M., and Baughman, S. (2016). Cognitive control, word retrieval and bilingual aphasia: is there a relationship? *Journal of Neurolinguistics* 1–15.

Faroqi-Shah, Y. and Waked, A.N. (2010). Grammatical category dissociation in multilingual aphasia. *Cognitive Neuropsychology* 27 (2): 181–203.

Festman, J. and Münte, T.F. (2012). Cognitive control in Russian-German bilinguals. *Frontiers in Psychology* 3: 115.

Festman, J., Rodriguez-Fornells, A., and Münte, T.F. (2010). Individual differences in control of language interference in late bilinguals are mainly related to general executive abilities. *Behavioral and Brain Functions* 13 (6): 5.

Finkbeiner, M., Gollan, T.H., and Caramazza, A. (2006). Lexical access in bilingual speakers: what's the (hard) problem? *Bilingualism: Language and Cognition* 9 (2): 153–166.

Garbin, G., Costa, A., Sanjuan, A. et al. (2011). Neural bases of language switching in high and early proficient bilinguals. *Brain and Language* 119 (3): 129–135.

Garbin, G., Sanjuan, A., Forn, C. et al. (2010). Bridging language and attention: brain basis of the impact of bilingualism on cognitive control. *NeuroImage* 53 (4): 1272–1278.

Garcia-Caballero, A., Garcia-Lado, I., Gonzalez-Hermida, J. et al. (2007). Paradoxical recovery in a bilingual patient with aphasia after right capsuloputaminal infarction. *Journal of Neurology, Neurosurgery, and Psychiatry* 78 (1): 89–91.

Geranmayeh, F., Wise, R.J.S., Mehta, A., and Leech, R. (2014). Overlapping networks engaged during spoken language production and its cognitive control. *Journal of Neuroscience* 34 (26): 8728–8740.

Gold, B.T., Kim, C., Johnson, N.F. et al. (2013). Lifelong bilingualism maintains neural efficiency for cognitive control in aging. *The Journal of Neuroscience* 33 (2): 387–396.

Gray, T. and Kiran, S. (2015). The relationship between language control and cognitive control in bilingual aphasia. *Bilingualism: Language and Cognition* 19: 1–20.

Graybiel, A.M., Aosaki, T., Flaherty, A.W., and Kimura, M. (1994). The basal ganglia and adaptive motor control. *Science* 265 (5180): 1826–1831.

Green, D.W. (1986). Control, activation, and resource: a framework and a model for the control of speech in bilinguals. *Brain and Language* 27 (2): 210–223.

Green, D.W. (2008). Bilingual aphasia: adapted language networks and their control. *Annual Review of Applied Linguistics* 28 (1): 25–48.

Green, D.W. and Abutalebi, J. (2013). Language control in bilinguals: the adaptive control hypothesis. *Journal of Cognitive Psychology* 25 (5): 515–530.

Green, D.W., Grogan, A., Crinion, J. et al. (2010). Language control and parallel recovery of language in individuals with aphasia. *Aphasiology* 24 (2): 188–209.

Grosjean, F. (2013). Bilingual and monolingual language modes. In: *The Encyclopedia of Applied Linguistics* (ed. C. Chapelle), 489–493. Hoboken, NJ: Blackwell.

Gross, M. and Kaushanskaya, M. (2016). Contributions of nonlinguistic task-shifting to language control in bilingual children. *Bilingualism* 21 (1): 1–14.

Hartsuiker, R.J., Costa, A., and Finkbeiner, M. (2008). Bilingualism: functional and neural perspectives. *Acta Psychologica* 128 (3): 413–415.

Hayes, A.E., Davidson, M.C., Keele, S.W., and Rafal, R.D. (1998). Toward a functional analysis of the basal ganglia. *Journal of Cognitive Neuroscience* 10 (2): 178–198.

Hernandez, A.E., Dapretto, M., Mazziotta, J., and Bookheimer, S. (2001). Language switching and language representation in Spanish-English bilinguals: an fMRI study. *NeuroImage* 14 (2): 510–520.

Hikosaka, O. and Isoda, M. (2010). Switching from automatic to controlled behavior: cortico-basal ganglia mechanisms. *Trends in Cognitive Sciences* 14 (4): 154–161.

Jackson, G.M., Swainson, R., Cunnington, R., and Jackson, S.R. (2001). ERP correlates of executive control during repeated language switching. *Bilingualism: Language and Cognition* 4 (2): 169–178.

Johari, K., Ashrafi, F., Zali, A. et al. (2013). Grammatical deficits in bilingual Azari: Farsi patients with Parkinson's disease. *Journal of Neurolinguistics* 26 (1): 22–30.

Jurado, M.B. and Rosselli, M. (2007). The elusive nature of executive functions: a review of our current understanding. *Neuropsychology Review* 17 (3): 213–233.

Klecha, A. (2013). Language and task switching in Polish-English bilinguals. *Psychology of Language and Communication* 17 (1): 17–36.

Kong, A.P.H., Abutalebi, J., Lam, K.S.Y., and Weekes, B. (2014). Executive and language control in the multilingual brain. *Behavioural Neurology* 527951.

Kudlicka, A., Clare, L., and Hindle, J.V. (2011). Executive functions in Parkinson's disease: systematic review and meta-analysis. *Movement Disorders* 26 (13): 2305–2315.

Kuzmina, E. and Weekes, B.S. (2017). Role of cognitive control in language deficits in different types of aphasia. *Aphasiology* 31 (7): 765–792.

La Heij, W. (2005). Selection processes in monolingual and bilingual lexical access. In: *Handbook of Bilingualism: Psycholinguistic Approaches* (ed. J.F. Kroll and A.M.B. de Groot), 289–307. New York, NY: Oxford University Press.

Leemann, B., Laganaro, M., Schwitter, V., and Schnider, A. (2007). Paradoxical switching to a barely-mastered second language by an aphasic patient. *Neurocase* 13 (3): 209–213.

Lorenzen, B. and Murray, L.L. (2008). Bilingual aphasia: a theoretical and clinical review. *American Journal of Speech-Language Pathology* 17: 299–317.

Luk, G., Green, D.W., Abutalebi, J., and Grady, C. (2011). Cognitive control for language switching in bilinguals: a quantitative meta-analysis of functional neuroimaging studies. *Language and Cognitive Processes* 27 (10): 1479–1488.

Ma, F., Li, S., and Guo, T. (2016). Reactive and proactive control in bilingual word production: an investigation of influential factors. *Journal of Memory and Language* 86: 35–59.

Macizo, P., Bajo, T., and Paolieri, D. (2012). Language switching and language competition. *Second Language Research* 28 (2): 131–149.

Mariën, P., Abutalebi, J., Engelborghs, S., and De Deyn, P.P. (2005). Pathophysiology of language switching and mixing in an early bilingual child with subcortical aphasia. *Neurocase: Case Studies in Neuropsychology, Neuropsychiatry, and Behavioural Neurology* 11 (6): 385–398.

Miyake, A. and Friedman, N.P. (2012). The nature and organization of individual differences in executive functions: four general conclusions. *Current Directions in Psychological Science* 21 (1): 8–14.

Miyake, A., Friedman, N.P., Emerson, M.J. et al. (2000). The unity and diversity of executive functions and their contributions to complex 'frontal lobe' tasks: a latent variable analysis. *Cognitive Psychology* 41: 49–100.

Morales, J., Gómez-Ariza, C.J., and Bajo, M.T. (2013). Dual mechanisms of cognitive control in bilinguals and monolinguals. *Journal of Cognitive Psychology* 25 (5): 531–546.

Morales, J., Yudes, C., Gómez-Ariza, C.J., and Bajo, M.T. (2015). Bilingualism modulates dual mechanisms of cognitive control: evidence from ERPs. *Neuropsychologia* 66: 157–169.

Munakata, Y., Herd, S., Chatham, C. et al. (2011). A unified framework for inhibitory control. *Trends in Cognitive Sciences* 15 (10): 453–459.

Murray, L.L. (2012). Attention and other cognitive deficits in aphasia: presence and relation to language and communication measures. *American Journal of Speech-Language Pathology* 21 (2): S51–S64.

Murray, L. (2017). Focusing attention on executive functioning in aphasia. *Aphasiology* 31 (7): 721–724.

Narayanan, N.S., Rodnitzky, R.L., and Uc, E.Y. (2013). Prefrontal dopamine signaling and cognitive symptoms of Parkinson's disease. *Reviews in the Neurosciences* 24 (3): 267–278.

Norman, D. and Shallice, T. (1986). Attention to action. In: *Consciousness and Self-Regulation: Advances in Research and Theory* (ed. R.J. Davidson, G.E. Schwartz and D. Shapiro), 1–18. New York, NY: Plenum Press.

Paap, K.R. and Sawi, O. (2016). The role of test-retest reliability in measuring individual and group differences in executive functioning. *Journal of Neuroscience Methods* 274: 81–93.

Paradis, M. (1999). Acquired aphasia in bilingual speakers. In: *Acquired Aphasia*, 3rde (ed. M. Taylor Sarno), 531–549. London, UK: Academic Press.

Paradis, M. (2001). Bilingual and polyglot aphasia. In: *Handbook of Neuropsychology* (ed. R.S. Berndt), 69–91. Amsterdam, The Netherlands: Elsevier Science.

Paradis, M. (2008). Bilingualism and neuropsychiatric disorders. *Journal of Neurolinguistics* 21: 199–230.

Peeters, D., Runnqvist, E., Bertrand, D., and Grainger, J. (2014). Asymmetrical switch costs in bilingual language production induced by reading words. *Journal of Experimental Psychology. Learning, Memory, and Cognition* 40 (1): 284–292.

Philipp, A.M., Gade, M., and Koch, I. (2007). Inhibitory processes in language switching: evidence from switching language-defined response sets. *European Journal of Cognitive Psychology* 19 (3): 395–416.

Piai, V., Roelofs, A., Acheson, D.J., and Takashima, A. (2013). Attention for speaking:

domain-general control from the anterior cingulate cortex in spoken word production. *Frontiers in Human Neuroscience* 7: 832.

Pliatsikas, C. and Luk, G. (2016). Executive control in bilinguals: a concise review on fMRI studies. *Bilingualism: Language and Cognition* 53 (9): 1689–1699.

Poulisse, N. and Bongaerts, T. (1994). First language in second language production. *Applied Linguistics* 15: 36–57.

Praamstra, P. and Plat, F.M. (2001). Failed suppression of direct visuomotor activation in Parkinson's disease. *Journal of Cognitive Neuroscience* 13 (1): 31–43.

Prior, A. and Gollan, T.H. (2013). The elusive link between language control and executive control: a case of limited transfer. *Journal of Cognitive Psychology* 25 (5): 622–645.

Radman, N., Mouthon, M., Di Pietro, M. et al. (2016). The role of the cognitive control system in recovery from bilingual aphasia: a multiple single-case fMRI study. *Neural Plasticity* 2016: 8797086.

Rodríguez-Pujadas, A., Sanjuán, A., Ventura-Campos, N. et al. (2013). Bilinguals use language-control brain areas more than monolinguals to perform non-linguistic switching tasks. *PLoS One* 8 (9): e73028.

Roelofs, A. and Piai, V. (2011). Attention demands of spoken word planning: a review. *Frontiers in Psychology* 2: 307.

Shao, Z., Roelofs, A., Martin, R.C., and Meyer, A.S. (2015). Selective inhibition and naming performance in semantic blocking, picture-word interference, and color-word Stroop tasks. *Journal of Experimental Psychology: Learning, Memory, and Cognition* 41 (6): 1806–1820.

Shao, Z., Roelofs, A., and Meyer, A.S. (2012). Sources of individual differences in the speed of naming objects and actions: the contribution of executive control. *The Quarterly Journal of Experimental Psychology* 65 (10): 1927–1944.

Stuss, D.T. and Alexander, M.P. (2000). Executive functions and the frontal lobes: a conceptual view. *Psychological Research* 63 (3–4): 289–298.

Ullman, M.T. (2001). The neural basis of lexicon and grammar in first and second language: the declarative/procedural model. *Bilingualism: Language and Cognition* 4: 105–122.

Ullman, M.T., Corkin, S., Coppola, M. et al. (1997). A neural dissociation within language: evidence that the mental dictionary is part of declarative memory, and that grammatical rules are processed by the procedural system. *Journal of Cognitive Neuroscience* 9 (2): 266–276.

Verhaeghen, P. and Cerella, J. (2002). Aging, executive control, and attention: a review of meta-analyses. *Neuroscience and Biobehavioral Reviews* 26 (7): 849–857.

Verreyt, N., De Letter, M., Hemelsoet, D. et al. (2013). Cognate effects and executive control in a patient with differential bilingual aphasia. *Applied Neuropsychology* 20 (3): 221–230.

Wang, X., Wang, Y.Y., Jiang, T. et al. (2012). Direct evidence of the left caudate's role in bilingual control: an intra-operative electrical stimulation study. *Neurocase* 19 (5): 462–469.

Weissberger, G.H., Gollan, T.H., Bondi, M.W. et al. (2015). Language and task switching in the bilingual brain: bilinguals are staying, not switching, experts. *Neuropsychologia* 66: 193–203.

Wylie, S.A., van den Wildenberg, W.P.M., Ridderinkhof, K.R. et al. (2009). The effect of Parkinson's disease on interference control during action selection. *Neuropsychologia* 47 (1): 145–157.

Zanini, S., Tavano, A., and Fabbro, F. (2010). Spontaneous language production in bilingual Parkinson's disease patients: evidence of greater phonological, morphological and syntactic impairments in native language. *Brain and Language* 113 (2): 84–89.

Zanini, S., Tavano, A., Vorano, L. et al. (2004). Greater syntactic impairments in native language in bilingual Parkinsonian patients. *Journal of Neurology, Neurosurgery, and Psychiatry* 75 (12): 1678–1681.

23 What Language Experience Tells us about Cognition

Variable Input and Interactional Contexts Affect Bilingual Sentence Processing

PAOLA E. DUSSIAS, JORGE R. VALDÉS KROFF, ANNE L. BEATTY-MARTÍNEZ, AND MICHAEL A. JOHNS

1. Introduction

Adult learners often find it difficult to acquire a high level of proficiency in a second language (L2). L2 learners are purportedly unable to learn subtle nuances of the L2 grammar (e.g. Johnson and Newport 1989), they often speak the L2 with an accent (Piske et al. 2001), and they process the L2 differently from first language and/or monolingual (L1) speakers, particularly in the domain of complex syntax (Clahsen and Felser 2006). These general observations are reported even when high levels of L2 proficiency have been attained, and despite many years of study and exposure to the second language. Consequently, a question that has dominated the adult L2 sentence processing literature is why there are apparent constraints on the level of proficiency that adult learners typically reach in their ability to process words and sentences in their second language. Results demonstrating failure to acquire the L2 natively have been widespread (e.g. Clahsen and Muysken 1986, 1989) and have fuelled proposals on the existence of hard constraints on late L2 learning (Bley-Vroman 1990) and L2 processing (Clahsen and Felser 2006). The traditional account has been that individuals who learn a second language past early childhood are unable to fully acquire the L2 syntax (e.g. Clahsen and Muysken 1986) or to process the L2 in an L1-like fashion (e.g. Clahsen and Felser 2006). To explain what L2 learners can do with the L2, the proposal has been that they use compensatory strategies to speak and to process the L2 that are based on semantic and pragmatic information, but that they are not sensitive to complex syntactic operations (e.g. filler-gap dependencies).

The Handbook of the Neuroscience of Multilingualism, First Edition. Edited by John W. Schwieter.

In the past 15 years, a premier method that has been used to examine whether L2 language processing is fundamentally similar to or different from native language processing is electroencephalography (EEG). Time-averaged event-related potentials (ERPs) derived from EEG have served as the benchmark measure to characterize differences and similarities in L2 learners by revealing which processing components approximate the neural signatures of native speakers. The vast majority of neurocognitive studies focusing on the presence or absence of ERP effects in L2 learners have yielded somewhat mixed results. Early electrophysiological studies suggest that L2 speakers are less sensitive than native speakers when processing syntactic violations relative to semantic ones (Hahne 2001; Hahne and Friederici 2001; Weber-Fox and Neville 1996). Recent studies, on the other hand, have shown that some learners manage to successfully achieve L1-like performance in the L2 within the domain of syntactic processing; the evidence has demonstrated that late L2 learners who have become proficient in the L2 show many of the same brain signatures in the L2 that are seen in L1 speakers (e.g. Morgan-Short et al. 2012; Steinhauer et al. 2009). To illustrate, a study by Caffarra et al. (2015) examined the role of L2 factors on three ERP components associated with syntactic processing: early left anterior negativity (eLAN), left anterior negativity (LAN), and P600 (for a discussion of the different ERP components, see Chapter 5, this volume). They report that eLAN effects,[1] which are typically found when L1 speakers process phrase structure violations (e.g. Friederici 1995; Friederici and Weissenborn 2007) are also found in highly proficient L2 speakers. Likewise, LAN effects for morphosyntactic violations have been observed in ERP studies where L2 speakers have had more than five years of immersion in the L2 environment; and P600 effects are observed in relation to the processing of morphosyntactic features, such as grammatical gender and number, in spite of significant syntactic differences between the L1 and L2 grammars (e.g. Dowens et al. 2011).

Despite the documented similarities, an important caveat of the ERP research on L2 sentence processing is that the interpretation of the effects rests on the assumption of homogeneity across individuals, and this is true even when monolingual speakers are the target of study. Notwithstanding, recent evidence suggests that ERP responses are sensitive to individual differences both in the L1 (Pakulak and Neville 2010) and in the L2 (Tanner et al. 2013); it has also been argued that under certain conditions, the modulation and/or absence of an ERP effect may be an artefact of individual processing strategies (e.g. Nieuwland and Van Berkum 2008; Tanner et al. 2014). In other words, it is becoming increasingly clear that individuals display considerable variability in their responses to natural language input (Qi et al. 2017). Given this, an important aspect to consider in the comparison between native and L2 processing is the role of the speakers' linguistic experience and of variation in the input to which they are exposed (see discussion in Boland et al. 2016). The assumption underlying most L2 processing research, and which we would argue should be revised, has been that of an ideal and uniform native language processor. Most research on L2 processing has compared the performance of first and second language speakers, with little consideration of the inherent variability that characterizes speakers' linguistic experience and the input to which speakers are exposed. For example, work investigating the role of individual differences in L1 reading proficiency has shown a tight correlation between letter name and sound knowledge in the L1 and resulting early literacy skills in the L2 (Cárdenas-Hagan et al. 2007). Likewise, L2 proficiency and L1 reading ability interact to predict L2 reading ability (Lee and Schallert 1997). While little, if any, work has been conducted on the variability underlying specific parsing strategies, the finding that the L2 can affect the L1 (Kroll and Dussias 2016) in much the same way that the L1 affects the L2 suggests that variability in the L1 may affect subsequent learning and processing in the L2.

The assumption of a uniform and highly efficient L1 processor has long been challenged and acknowledged in the L1 processing literature, with evidence for individual variation in L1 speakers (e.g. Caplan and Waters 1999; Farmer et al. 2012; Just and Carpenter 1992; Pakulak and Neville 2010; Tanner and Van Hell 2014), and with strategies in L1 language processing that are sometimes 'good enough' (e.g. Ferreira and Patson 2007). While speakers of the same variety tend to converge on the cues and strategies that they employ, there nonetheless exists great heterogeneity and variation in how comprehenders approach sentence processing in their native language (Farmer et al. 2012). Yet, many L2 processing studies that have observed mismatches between L1 and L2 processing routines have not considered the inherent variability that exists in native speaker processing. The aim of this chapter is to discuss recent findings that demonstrate how variability in the linguistic experiences of bilingual speakers and in the ability of bilingual speakers to learn from these experiences, might impact bilingual language processing. The goal is to show that linguistic experience – the input that comprehenders receive – and the interactional contexts in which bilinguals find themselves serve an influential role in L2 speaker language processing. We do this first by briefly discussing several illustrative studies that demonstrate how the first language system of speakers adapts to L2 input. We have chosen to discuss the influence of the L2 on the L1 because it provides a dramatic illustration of the permeability of the language system that challenges the traditional interpretation of critical periods for language learning and language comprehension. We then follow with a discussion of a particular case of bilingual speech – code switching – to illustrate how adaptation to different interactional contexts modulates the processing of codeswitched language. As much as possible, we will present studies that have employed electrophysiological recording methods. We will additionally discuss studies that have used behavioural methods of sentence processing (i.e. reaction time and eye-tracking), especially when neuroscience evidence is not available to illustrate a particular point.

2. The Role of Variable Input in Monolingual Language Processing

It is of little debate in the monolingual sentence processing literature that individual differences affect language processing. The early work examined individual variability in syntactic processing through the lens of verbal working memory, demonstrating that individuals who scored higher on tests of working memory tended to more easily parse difficult syntactic structures compared with those who scored lower (e.g. King and Just 1991). For instance, some studies have found that individuals with higher working memory exhibited faster reading times on object relatives (e.g. 'The reporter that the senator attacked admitted the error') – a difficult English structure to parse – compared with individuals with lower working memory (Just and Carpenter 1992). Recent work suggests, however, that the story does not end here: linguistic experience and the patterns and strategies that speakers use vis-à-vis the input also affect language processing. To take an example from the monolingual processing literature, Wells et al. (2009) directly manipulated input-driven experience in a self-paced reading study of object and subject relatives. They examined two groups of monolingual comprehenders. One group participated in three training sessions in which they were exposed to various complex English structures, but not subject or object relatives. A second group also completed three training sessions, but they saw an equal number of subject and object relatives. Upon testing, the authors found that participants exposed to relative clauses had significantly faster reading times compared with those who were not exposed, suggesting less difficult processing for the exposure group. Importantly, because the two groups were matched on working memory, the results suggest that the individuals' linguistic experience with the particular structure affected processing beyond effects of working memory. Further evidence on the key role of input and experience in monolingual processing comes from studies that incorporate sociolinguistic variation. In a self-paced reading experiment, Squires (2014), for instance, examined participants' processing of different agreement conditions in English: the standard (singular + doesn't) and (plural + don't), the non-standard (singular + don't), attested in African American English Vernacular (Weldon 1994), and an unattested structure (plural + doesn't). Participants varied across various social traits, in particular sex, socioeconomic status, and race. The results showed that while all participants experienced increased processing difficulty when reading the unattested (plural + doesn't) structure, only White participants were disrupted by the non-standard (singular + don't) structure; African American participants, presumably with greater experience to this structure, showed little to no processing costs compared to their processing of the standard structure. The results of this study highlight the key role of linguistic experience in shaping individuals' language processing abilities.

Monolingual speakers' sensitivity to experience is also reported to emerge rapidly. Kim and Gilley (2013) used both ERPs and magnetoencephalography (MEG) to examine how exposure to different patterns of syntactic anomalies affects predictive processing in native speakers. One group was exposed to a consistent anomaly: a doubled preposition where the second preposition was always 'for' (e.g. The thief was caught by for police). A second group saw the same type of anomaly, but the doubled preposition varied between at, of, on, for, from, over, or with. In response to the syntactic anomaly, both groups showed an N170 component, as well as the classic P600 effect. The group which was exposed to the consistent 'for' anomaly, however, also showed an enhanced P1 component; the variable group did not. Because it has been suggested that the P1 is implicated in both attention (Hillyard et al. 1998) and arousal (Vogel and Luck 2000), the authors argued that it reflects participants' sensitivity to the anomaly during the course of the experimental session; that is, its continuing appearance heightened participants' expectation for the same upcoming anomaly.

All three of the studies described above and many others (Fine and Jaeger 2016; Fraundorf and Jaeger 2016; Kleinschmidt and Jaeger 2015) demonstrate the key role of linguistic experience in shaping native language processing. This modulation may be short-term and adaptive in nature (Kim and Gilley 2013) or it may be the result of long-term, community-based norms (Squires 2014). Short-term adaptation may be driven by changes in an individual's expectations or predictions about upcoming input, in turn affecting how participants react to deviations from norms in the moment. Hopp (2016), for example, found that German native speakers stopped using grammatical gender information predictively when gender assignment and agreement errors were present in filler materials (we discuss this in greater detail in Section 3). Long-term exposure-based changes, however, reflect at least some shift in the underlying representations, such that the new or unfamiliar structure becomes entrenched in the individual's linguistic system. This process is similar to 'syntactic satiation' (Snyder 2000; Do and Kaiser 2017), in which the frequent exposure to ungrammatical structures leads to individuals accepting these structures more and processing them more easily. One view, proposed by Pajak et al. (2016) regards the linguistic system 'as a set of language models (or mini-grammars) that encode the hierarchical structure of the listener's linguistic environment and that are continuously being adapted to incoming input' (p. 913). The highest mini-grammar in this system takes precedence, such that small fluctuations in the subsumed mini-grammars (capturing dialectal or environmental variation) need not influence the speaker's own speech. Under a usage-based approach, however, such mini-grammars need not be posited, as this approach connects the linguistic structure to external, social factors, and this system is susceptible to executive processes (attention, suppression, interference resolution, etc.; see Tamminga 2016; see also Hay and Foulkes 2016 for a review and empirical evidence for this approach).

Variability in L1 language processing should thus be considered the norm, rather than the exception. Indeed, the study of individual differences has formed a key component in psycholinguistic work on monolingual sentence processing (King and Just 1991; Tanner and Van Hell 2014). Nonetheless, psycholinguistic work examining the processing of bilingual speech has often upheld the monolingual monolithic comparison, treating bilingualism – in whatever form it takes – as some deviation from this norm (e.g. Montrul 2006). Despite its ubiquity in monolingual sentence processing studies, however, variability in individuals who speak two or more languages has only recently begun to be explored. Rather, most of the literature focusing on L2 processing has sought to compare L1 and L2 processing dichotomously, determining what is similar and what is different. We argue here that an approach that connects L2 language processing with language experience and basic cognitive principles is more compatible with our current knowledge of the architectural underpinnings of the systems responsible for language acquisition and language processing, and a more fruitful approach in future studies of L2 sentence processing.

3.   The Role of Variable Input in Bilingual Language Processing

Models of late L2 learning have largely assumed stability of the L1. Yet, recent research on bilingual language processing shows that the L1 changes dynamically in different contexts, for even highly proficient bilinguals. One of the key discoveries is that bilinguals experience coactivation between their two languages in production and comprehension, in both visual and spoken language modalities, and even when the situational context strongly points towards staying in one language alone. This foundational principle is known as non-selectivity (e.g. Dijkstra 2005; Kroll et al. 2006, 2012) and has led to an overwhelming focus on how bilinguals are able to comprehend and produce in one language alone. Because of the overwhelming evidence in favour of non-selectivity, researchers have hypothesized that bilinguals recruit domain-general cognitive mechanisms such as inhibition, increased attentional control, and/or conflict monitoring in order to successfully process in one language (e.g. Green 1998; Hilchey and Klein 2011; Meuter and Allport 1999). The parallel activation of the bilingual's two languages has several consequences, including cross-language activation at all levels of language processing. The availability of both languages affects not only the activation of the two languages and the resulting mechanisms of cognitive control (Kroll and Bialystok 2013) but also the way in which each of the two languages is processed, suggesting a language system that is highly adaptive. Being bilingual is not only about acquiring and using the L2 but also about the ways that the native or dominant L1 changes in response to the L2. These changes have been observed at every level of language use, from the lexicon to the syntax and phonology and often are quite subtle. They are unlike the native language transfer phenomena discussed in the context of L2 'interlanguage competence' that began in the 1950s (e.g. Lado 1957) and continues to date (for example, the 2013 workshop in Geneva organized by Julia Herschensohn and Martha Young-Scholten), which often result in obvious deviations of the L2 target that are easily discernible in learners' linguistic productions (see, for example, Choi and Lardiere 2006; Hopp 2010; White 2003) and that have given adult L2 learning its notoriety.

Word recognition studies were the first to have revealed robust effects of the L1 on the L2 (e.g. Dijkstra 2005; Schwartz et al. 2007) and also effects of the L2 on the L1 for proficient bilinguals (e.g. Van Assche et al. 2009; Van Hell and Dijkstra 2002). We now know that effects of L2 on L1 are not restricted to the lexicon. At the morphosyntactic level, Hopp (2016), for example, examined the predictive use of grammatical gender in an intermediate group of English learners of German. Results of an eye-tracking experiment indicated that L2 learners who behaved non-L1-like with respect to L2 gender assignment in an offline task not only made erroneous predictions based on gender in an online comprehension task but also abandoned gender as a predictive cue altogether. While it may seem that this merely points to the key role of proficiency and its relation to predictive processing in the L2, a second experiment suggested that the story is more nuanced. German L1 speakers completed a similar comprehension task as the L2 learners but with one additional modulation: half of the speakers received target-like input, where gender features always agreed. The other half, however, was exposed to non-target-like input (through the filler items), where gender features were non-agreeing. Hopp found that the L1 speakers in this treatment group also abandoned gender as a predictive cue, just like the L2 learners in the previous experiment. In this case, it was the L1 speakers who came to exhibit L2-like behaviours.

Equally fast changes to the L1 processing system have been reported when proficient bilinguals are exposed to auditory sentences spoken with L2 accented speech. In one

ERP study, Romero-Rivas et al. (2016) presented Spanish-Catalan bilingual speakers with sentences that ended in three types of words. Highly semantically constrained words, (e.g. underlined in *Lo tenía en la punta de la lengua, pero no conseguía recordar aquella palabra* [He had it on the tip of his tongue, but was unable to remember that <u>word</u>]), words that were semantically related to the target, and semantically unrelated words. Participants heard the sentences in two conditions: in one condition, the sentences were spoken by an L1 speaker of Spanish; in the other, the sentences were spoken by French and Italian speakers with an L2 accent in Spanish. Sentences with the L1 accent produced the expected attenuation of the N400 amplitude for highly semantically constrained words compared to semantically related words; there was also an attenuated N400 amplitude for semantically related words compared with semantically unrelated words. For *word* in the example above, the semantically related condition given the sentence context was *expression* and the unrelated condition was *date*, because it bears no semantic relationship to the most expected item, though it is still a plausible continuation given the sentence context. However, listening to L2 accented speech eliminated the difference previously observed in integrating semantically related and unrelated words.

Changes to the L1 have been found under conditions of immersion in the L2. Recent work on L2 syntactic processing using ERPs has shown that amount of exposure to L2 naturalistic input has been linked to brain signatures that reflect high levels of automaticity in L2 parsing processes and to neural correlates implicated in the early detection of syntactic mismatch in grammatical features (e.g. Caffarra et al. 2015; Friederici 2002; Mueller 2005). Exposure to the variability present in the input as well as the diverse interactional contexts are presumed to confer high levels of automaticity during syntactic processing in the L2 (Caffarra et al. 2015). If prolonged naturalistic exposure can have profound effects on how a second language is processed by reversing processing strategies that result from transfer of L1 information (Frenck-Mestre 2002) and by causing shifts in L2 processing routines from lexically driven to structurally driven (Pliatsikas and Marinis 2013), an important aspect of the comparison between L2 and L1 speaker performance is to consider how immersion experience might affect L1 processing. One might expect, for example, that experience in a second-language environment should also produce changes in syntactic processing in the native language. Dussias and Sagarra (2007; Fernández, 2003) investigated this hypothesis by examining the effect of intense contact with English on the resolution of syntactically ambiguous relative clauses in Spanish. Native Spanish and native English speakers differ in how they interpret temporarily ambiguous relative clauses like *Alguien disparó al hijo de la actriz que estaba en el balcón* [Someone shot the son of the actress who was on the balcony]. When asked *Quién estaba en el balcón?* [Who was on the balcony?], monolingual Spanish speakers typically respond 'the son' (i.e. high attachment preference), whereas monolingual English speakers respond 'the actress' (low attachment preference) (Carreiras and Clifton 1999). Using eye-tracking methodology while reading, Dussias and Sagarra (2007) found that Spanish-English bilinguals immersed in a Spanish-speaking environment processed the ambiguity using a high attachment strategy. This was an expected finding. The interesting result was that bilinguals living in an English-speaking (i.e. L2) environment strongly favoured the low attachment strategy when reading in Spanish, their first language. That is, for these speakers, exposure to a preponderance of English constructions resolved in favour of low attachment rendered this interpretation more available, resulting in a low attachment preference when reading in their first language. These results highlight how the seemingly stable L1 system is open to influence from the L2 once individuals become proficient in the L2 (e.g. Gollan et al. 2008).

The influence of the L2 on the L1 has also been reported in conditions of L1 immersion. Oliveira et al. (2017) examined whether adult Brazilian Portuguese-English bilinguals differed from monolingual Brazilian Portuguese speakers in their processing of depictive constructions (e.g. *Ele comeu o salmão cru* [He eats the salmon raw], which are shared between the two languages, and of resultative constructions (e.g. He wiped the table clean/*Ele esfregou a mesa limpia*), which are grammatical only in English. Although the surface syntactic word order of resultatives also exists in Brazilian Portuguese, its only licit interpretation is that of a depictive meaning (e.g. He wiped the clean table). The authors found that the two groups of speakers provided similar ratings in an acceptability judgement task; however, the bilingual group showed shorter reaction times in an online sentence processing task for the resultative construction relative to monolinguals, a finding that the authors interpreted as resulting from the influence of the L2 on the L1.

Changes to the L1 have also been observed within a short timescale in the laboratory. These dynamic changes are sensitive to recency of re-exposure to input, and may be partly reversed by it. Above we discussed work by Dussias and colleagues (Dussias and Sagarra 2007) that examined the resolution of structural conflicts when bilinguals read sentences containing syntactically ambiguous relative clauses. A study in progress extends this finding to examine whether changes in the L1 can be triggered in a laboratory setting by exposing bilinguals to particular syntactic structures. In other words, can extensive exposure to particular structures trigger changes 'back' to L1-like parsing preferences as well as movement 'forward' to L2-like parsing preferences, even for bilinguals who have not previously demonstrated L2-like processing preferences? Past findings from the child sentence processing literature suggest that exposure experience can affect children's sentence processing routines (e.g. Cuetos et al. 1996). Similar findings have been reported with adult monolingual speakers, demonstrating powerful implicit learning properties that characterize the human language system. As stated earlier, the notorious difficulties that L1 English speakers experience when processing object-extracted relative clauses such as 'The reporter that the senator attacked admitted the error' relative to subject-extracted relative clauses such as 'The reporter that attacked the senator admitted the error' (e.g. Traxler et al. 2002) disappear with increased exposure to object-relatives (Wells et al. 2009). If the parser's configuration is related to language exposure (e.g. Gennari and MacDonald 2009; MacDonald and Seidenberg 2006) and language contact, then bilinguals' processing routines are expected to change as a function of the frequency with which the relevant structure appears in an experimental session. Ongoing experiments on intervention in language exposure provide support for the dynamic nature of parsing. In one study (Carlson et al. in prep), L1 Spanish-L2 English bilinguals identified as being either high attachers or low attachers (via an eye-tracking study) participated in a five-day intervention, during which they read short paragraphs containing relative clauses in which a syntactically ambiguous relative clause was resolved in favour of the opposite attachment site from the one that the bilinguals had previously demonstrated. That is, participants who favoured high attachment received a low attachment treatment, and those who favoured low attachment received a high attachment treatment. In addition, half the participants received the intervention in Spanish and the other half in English. Participants returned to the lab after the intervention to participate in two subsequent eye-tracking studies, one that assessed the immediate effect of the intervention and one that assessed the effect of the intervention a week after it was completed. Ongoing analyses show that those participants who originally preferred high attachment switched to a low attachment preference and participants who originally showed a low attachment strategy switched to a high attachment preference. Like the results on bilingual word recognition alluded to earlier in this section (Dijkstra 2005; Schwartz et al. 2007), these findings suggest that not only does the L1 affect the L2 but that the L2 can come to influence the L1 (for a similar 'reversal effect' in anaphoric processing, see Chamorro et al. 2016). The literature reviewed above suggests that changes in the L1 as a result of L2 experience are driven by both short- and long-term modulations to statistical properties of the input. The finding that experience in one language can affect the other through shared or related structures or strategies suggests that the L1 or native language holds no de facto special status, but merely enjoys greater entrenchment than the L2 – a characteristic readily modulated by both internal (cognitive control, e.g. Segalowitz and Hulstijn 2005) and external (exposure and environment, e.g. Schmid and Köpke 2007) factors.

4. Variability in Bilingual Language Use and its Implications for Language Processing

In our view, the heterogeneity in linguistic exposure that is experienced by bilingual speakers has important implications for language processing. Elsewhere we have discussed that when bilinguals read, listen to speech, or plan utterances in one language, information is also activated in the other language (see Kroll et al. 2012, for a review). One consequence of the parallel activation of the bilinguals' two languages is the ability of highly proficient bilinguals to code switch. Code switching is a structured and creative linguistic behaviour broadly defined as the fluid alternation between languages in discourse (Poplack 1980). The ubiquity with which certain bilingual communities engage in code-switching challenges the strong unilingual perspective prevalent in psycholinguistics research. Instead, it points towards the necessity to maintain heightened coactivation between multiple languages and an ability to flexibly move between the two languages, which requires the seamless and successful integration of two grammars at multiple linguistic levels, i.e. phonology, morphology, syntax, and discourse. Consequently, how bilinguals systematically engage and disengage their languages in real time becomes a new and important avenue of inquiry for understanding bilingual sentence processing and language control (Green and Abutalebi 2013; Kroll et al. 2015).

In the nascent literature on neurolinguistic and psycholinguistic approaches to code switching, two main threads of inquiry have emerged: whether integrating code-switched speech is costlier than unilingual sentence processing and how bilinguals adapt their parsing strategies to better anticipate upcoming code switches. The first approach pairs code-switched stimuli with unilingual stimuli and tests whether integrating code-switched text or speech is costly relative to non-switched or unilingual speech/text. The underlying logic behind this approach is that it is unusual for humans to engage in behaviour that is more costly or less efficient; therefore, because many bilinguals engage in code-switched speech, processing costs should be minimal, at least under certain linguistic contexts and amongst certain bilingual speakers. Nevertheless, analogous to the switch costs observed in the cued language-switching literature (e.g. Meuter and Allport 1999), code-switched stimuli are often read more slowly (Altarriba et al. 1996), recruit greater neural activity in prefrontal and anterior cingulate brain areas – all areas related to cognitive control (Abutalebi and Green 2008; Abutalebi et al. 2007), and often elicit differential patterns of electrical activity (Kutas et al. 2009) relative to unilingual stimuli. Overall, this literature poses an interesting paradox as to why bilinguals customarily engage in code switching given that it incurs additional processing costs relative to unilingual language. A noteworthy point is that switch costs can be modulated by a number of factors, and this is part of an ongoing discussion as to why behavioural data and ERP measures of switch costs are not always consistent across studies.

Amongst language-related ERP components, the N400 and the late positive complex (LPC) have been associated with processing code switches (see Van Hell et al. 2015, for a review). The LPC has been observed both in meaningful code-switched sentences (Moreno et al. 2002) and in code-switched discourse contexts (Ng et al. 2014). This ERP component is typically sensitive to the processing of an improbable event (Kutas and Hillyard 1980) and is commonly associated to sentence-level integration and reanalysis. The N400 component on the other hand, has been found to be a sensitive measure of the critical word's expectancy (Kutas and Federmeier 2011). Code-switching studies that have observed this component have interpreted it as a processing cost related to lexico-semantic integration (Proverbio et al. 2004).

Emerging experimental evidence indicates that switch costs are modulated by the direction of the code switch (i.e. from the dominant to the weaker language or vice versa) both in behavioural and ERP data. For example, a recent study by Litcofsky and van Hell (2017) tested the influence of language dominance on the processing of intra-sentential code switching, using behavioural (self-paced reading) and ERP techniques. In the behavioural study, reading times were significantly slower for code-switched sentences relative to unilingual sentences. In the ERP study, an LPC was observed at the site where the code switch took place but only when switching from the dominant into the weaker language. Consistent with the latter observation, Bultena et al. (2015) found that switching to the weaker language was more costly than switching to the dominant language using a shadowing task. However, they also found that switch costs decreased with increasing L2 proficiency, suggesting that switch costs may be driven by experience with the L2. Other behavioural studies have found that switch costs appear to be reduced depending on the grammatical structure (Tarlowski et al. 2013) or may be absent altogether in inter-sentential switches (Gullifer et al. 2013).

Only recently have studies begun to uncover switch cost modulations, but their relative contributions and the degree to which they interact remain unclear. Critically, the extant literature lacks reference to the various contexts of language experience to which bilinguals are exposed and the recurrent forms of conversational exchanges in which they engage when communicating in a natural setting. An emerging trend in psycholinguistic research seeks to build a more nuanced view of variation in language processing. For bilinguals, the shift in emphasis towards the everyday conversational use of language is captured by the adaptive control hypothesis (Green and Abutalebi 2013), which postulates that different interactional contexts impose different communicative demands on speakers' language control processes. Indeed, there is growing evidence that individuals learn and attend to distributional variation in the input. However, while such adaptation is a fundamental process of individuals of all language backgrounds, many questions remain concerning the role of experience in guiding online sentence processing. Moreover, understanding the interactional demands of different contexts calls for a systematic assessment of the relationship amongst language processing, language use, and the contexts in which these take place. In this respect, the study of code switching provides a unique lens to examine such interactions underlying processing adaptation and variation. Because code switching emerges in some bilingual communities but not in others, it provides a venue to examine the consequences of exposure and adaptation to variation in code-switched speech and text.

Adamou and Shen (2017) carried out a study examining the processing of code-switched sentences as a function of the frequency of use of specific code-switching patterns. Using a bimodal picture-sentence matching task, they tested whether switching costs were modulated by exposure to specific code-switching patterns from a well-established code-switching community. Stimuli included ecologically valid and ecologically non-valid code switches that were created based on an analysis of code-switching preferences in natural conversations from the community under study. Although participants responded the fastest to unilingual sentences overall, a more fine-grained analysis, based on the statistical frequencies of the switches in natural speech, revealed that switched trials that were based on frequently occurring examples in the corpus were just as fast as unilingual trials. Thus, these findings illustrate the importance of taking the switching preferences of the community into consideration and support an experience-based approach to the study of code switching.

This study also highlights the link to a second approach emerging in the neurolinguistic and psycholinguistic study of code switching, namely, how bilinguals adapt to rapidly integrating code-switched speech. This approach is novel in that it starts from the premise that code switching is ubiquitous and regardless of whether it results in switch costs, bilinguals engage in it. Therefore, bilingual code switchers must adapt their parsing strategies in order to accommodate to this linguistic behaviour. Crucially, this approach builds upon two observations that are well-known from the sociolinguistic study of code switching: not all bilinguals frequently code switch (e.g. Poplack 1988) and different patterns of code-switching structure emerge in different bilingual communities (e.g. insertional, alternational, congruent lexicalization; see Muysken 2000, for detailed explanation).

These two observations have important psycholinguistic implications for language processing: bilinguals who code switch are more sensitive to code-switching structures that are consistent with attested distributional patterns and should therefore demonstrate facilitated processing as compared to unattested code switches. Conversely, bilinguals who do not frequently code switch should not show differential processing to attested vs. unattested code switches, as these code switches are virtually all unattested to bilingual non-code switchers. Indeed, recent research has shown that distributional regularities involving attested code-switching patterns act as cues heightening the probability of upcoming switches (Fricke et al. 2016; Guzzardo Tamargo et al. 2016; Valdés Kroff et al. 2017). Moreover, these observations also predict variability amongst speakers who engage and do not engage in code switching (e.g. Beatty-Martínez and Dussias 2017; Valdés Kroff et al. 2018). To illustrate this approach, Beatty-Martínez and Dussias (2017) conducted a study using two groups of bilinguals who differed in code-switching experience. The goal of the study was to examine the consequences of adaptation to language processing across different communities of speakers. The first experiment analysed ERPs to compare the processing of code switches that were either rarely attested or commonly attested in bilingual corpora from a habitual code-switching community. For code switchers, rarely attested code switches evoked an N400 effect in comparison to common code switches, suggesting greater difficulty with lexical integration. Non-code switchers, on the other hand, processed these two types of code switches similarly. Furthermore, non-code switchers showed greater frontal EEG activity to switching, regardless of switch type, most likely reflecting detection of a language change during early monitoring stages of language processing. The participants additionally completed a map task that elicited naturaly produced speech to assess their code-switching tendencies and behaviours. Code switchers switched more often than non-code switchers, and their code-switching preferences robustly reflected the conditions that were more easily processed in the ERP experiment. Together, the findings underscore how the processing of code-switched language largely depends on bilinguals' language experience, namely on the type of code-switching strategies available in their discourse environment.

5.   Conclusion

Language experience is complex and variable, and it is in this view that understanding the sources of variation in language processing can reveal fundamental dynamics of the language system (Boland et al. 2016). In this chapter, we have reviewed the empirical evidence on how comprehenders adapt to and change their processing strategies by tuning into the input they receive, a mechanism that applies to both L1 and L2 processing. The emerging evidence suggests that learning and using two languages changes the language system: the two languages begin to converge, becoming more similar and less monolingual-like (e.g. Ameel et al. 2005). To understand the factors that underlie processing variability, researchers have called for an ecological approach that considers the natural speech of the interactional context in which speakers typically use their language(s) (e.g. Abutalebi and Green 2016; Baum and Titone 2014; MacDonald 2013; Valdés Kroff et al. 2018). In this light, instead of asking if L2 learners process sentences similarly to L1 speakers, we may examine the ways in which L2 learners are sensitive to variability as is the case for L1 speakers.

The fact that L1 speakers and L2 learners may both converge and diverge in terms of language processing is not at all surprising when we take into consideration the inherent variability of language processing itself, and the influential role of linguistic experience. Kaan (2014) argues that the mechanisms that underlie L1 and L2 sentence processing are fundamentally the same. What differs – or rather, what yields differences – are 'several interdependent sets of factors, all of which are subject to individual differences' (p. 261). This includes input-driven factors such as frequency and context (i.e. immersion vs. classroom learning), language-specific factors like competition, and variation in cognitive abilities and resources. The linkage between language experience and processing has several implications for the way psycholinguists design experiments and draw conclusions with respect to issues of language and domain general cognition. We propose here a shift in the way bilingual language processing research moves forward that considers variability in language experience not as a source of noise but rather as a source of evidence.

NOTE

1 We note that the interpretation of the functional significance for the eLAN is unclear; in fact, Steinhauer and Drury (2012) have questioned the reliability and validity of eLAN effects by noting the presence of artefacts.

REFERENCES

Abutalebi, J., Brambati, S.M., Annoni, J.-M. et al. (2007). The neural cost of the auditory perception of language switches: an event-related functional magnetic resonance imaging study in bilinguals. *The Journal of Neuroscience* 27: 13762–13769.

Abutalebi, J. and Green, D.W. (2008). Control mechanisms in bilingual language production: neural evidence from language switching studies. *Language and Cognitive Processes* 23: 557–582.

Abutalebi, J. and Green, D.W. (2016). Neuroimaging of language control in bilinguals: neural adaptation and reserve. *Bilingualism: Language and Cognition* 19: 689–698.

Adamou, E. and Shen, X.R. (2017). There are no language switching costs when codeswitching is frequent. *International Journal of Bilingualism* https://doi.org/10.1177/1367006917709094.

Altarriba, J., Kroll, J.F., Sholl, A., and Rayner, K. (1996). The influence of lexical and conceptual constraints on reading mixed-language sentences: evidence from eye fixations and naming times. *Memory and Cognition* 24: 477–492.

Ameel, E., Sotrms, G., Malt, B.C., and Sloman, S.A. (2005). How bilinguals solve the naming problem. *Journal of Memory and Language* 53: 60–80.

Baum, S. and Titone, D. (2014). Moving toward a neuroplasticity view of bilingualism, executive control, and aging. *Applied PsychoLinguistics* 35: 857–894.

Beatty-Martínez, A.L. and Dussias, P.E. (2017). Bilingual experience shapes language processing: evidence from codeswitching. *Journal of Memory and Language* 95: 173–189.

Bley-Vroman, R. (1990). The logical problem of foreign language learning. *Linguistic Analysis* 20: 3–49.

Boland, J.E., Kaan, E., Valdés Kroff, J.R., and Wulff, S. (2016). Psycholinguistics and variation in language processing. *Linguistic Vanguard* 2 (s1).

Bultena, S., Dijkstra, T., and Van Hell, J.G. (2015). Switch cost modulations in bilingual sentence processing: evidence from shadowing. *Language, Cognition, and NeuroScience* 30: 586–605.

Caffarra, S., Molinaro, N., Davidson, D., and Carreiras, M. (2015). Second language syntactic processing revealed through event-related potentials: an empirical review. *Neuroscience and Biobehavioral Reviews* 51: 31–47.

Caplan, D. and Waters, G.S. (1999). Verbal working memory and sentence comprehension. *Behavioral and Brain Science* 22: 77–126.

Cárdenas-Hagan, E., Carlson, C.D., and Pollard-Durdola, S.D. (2007). The cross-linguistic transfer of early literacy skills: the role of initial L1 and L2 skills and language of instruction. *Language, Speech and Hearing Services in Schools* 38: 249–259.

Carlson, M., Halberstadt, L., & Dussias, P. E. (in prep). Re-learning to parse a first language: The role of experience in sentence comprehension.

Carreiras, M. and Clifton, C. (1999). Another word on parsing relative clauses: Eyetracking evidence from Spanish and English. *Memory and Cognition* 27: 826–833.

Chamorro, G., Sorace, A., and Sturt, P. (2016). What is the source of L1 attrition? The effect of recent L1 re-exposure on Spanish speakers under L1 attrition. *Bilingualism: Language and Cognition* 19: 520–532.

Choi, M.H. and Lardiere, D. (2006). The interpretation of wh-in-situ in Korean second language acquisition. In: *Language Acquisition and Development: Proceedings of GALA 2005* (ed. A. Belletti, E. Bennati, C. Chesi, et al.), 125–135. Cambridge, UK: Cambridge Scholars Press.

Clahsen, H. and Felser, C. (2006). Grammatical processing in language learners. *Applied PsychoLinguistics* 27: 3–42.

Clahsen, H. and Muysken, P. (1986). The availability of universal grammar to adult and child learners – a study of the acquisition of German word order. *Second Language Research* 2: 93–119.

Clahsen, H. and Muysken, P. (1989). The UG paradox in L2 acquisition. *Second Language Research* 5: 1–29.

Cuetos, F., Mitchell, D.C., and Corley, M. (1996). Parsing in different languages. In: *Language Processing in Spanish* (ed. M. Carreiras, J.E. García-Albea and N. Sebastián-Gallés), 147–190. Mahwah, NJ: Erlbaum.

Dijkstra, T. (2005). Bilingual word recognition and lexical access. In: *Handbook of Bilingualism: Psycholinguistic Approaches* (ed. J.F. Kroll and A.M.B. De Groot), 179–201. New York, NY: Oxford University Press.

Do, M. and Kaiser, E. (2017). The relationship between syntactic satiation and syntactic priming: A first look. *Frontiers in Psychology* 25: doi: 10.3389/fpsyg.2017.01851.

Dowens, M.G., Guo, T., Guo, J. et al. (2011). Gender and number processing in Chinese learners of Spanish-evidence from event related potentials. *Neuropsychologia* 49: 1651–1659.

Dussias, P.E. and Sagarra, N. (2007). The effect of exposure on syntactic parsing in Spanish-English bilinguals. *Bilingualism, Language & Cognition* 10: 101–116.

Farmer, T.A., Misyak, J.B., and Christiansen, M.H. (2012). Individual differences in sentence processing. In: *Cambridge Handbook of Psycholinguistics* (ed. M.J. Spivey, M.F. Joannisse and K. McRae), 353–364. Cambridge, UK: Cambridge University Press.

Fernández, E.M. (2003). *Bilingual Sentence Processing: Relative Clause Attachment in English and Spanish*. Amsterdam, The Netherlands: Benjamins.

Ferreira, F. and Patson, N.D. (2007). The 'good enough' approach to language comprehension. *Language and Linguistics Compass* 1: 71–83.

Fine, A.B. and Jaeger, T.F. (2016). The role of verb repetition in cumulative syntactic priming in comprehension. *Journal of Experimental Psychology: Learning, Memory, and Cognition* 42: 1362–1376.

Fraundorf, S. and Jaeger, T.F. (2016). Readers generalize adaptation to newly-encountered dialectal structures to other unfamiliar structures. *Journal of Memory and Language* 91: 28–58.

Frenck-Mestre, C. (2002). An on-line look at sentence processing in a second language. In: *Bilingual Sentence Processing* (ed. R.R. Heredia and J. Altarriba), 217–236. Amsterdam, The Netherlands: Elsevier.

Fricke, M., Kroll, J.F., and Dussias, P.E. (2016). Phonetic variation in bilingual speech: a lens for studying the production-comprehension link. *Journal of Memory and Language* 89: 110–137.

Friederici, A.D. (1995). The time course of syntactic activation during language processing: a model based on neurophysiological and neurophysiological data. *Brain and Language* 50: 259–281.

Friederici, A.D. (2002). Towards a neural basis of auditory sentence processing. *Trends in Cognitive Science* 6: 78–84.

Friederici, A.D. and Weissenborn, J. (2007). Mapping sentence form onto meaning: the syntax-semantic interface. *Brain Research* 1146: 50–58.

Gennari, S.P. and MacDonald, M.C. (2009). Linking production and comprehension processes: the case of relative clauses. *Cognition* 111: 1–23.

Gollan, T.H., Montoya, R.I., Cera, C.M., and Sandoval, T.C. (2008). More use almost always means a smaller frequency effect: aging, bilingualism, and the weaker links hypothesis. *Journal of Memory and Language* 58: 787–814.

Green, D.W. (1998). Mental control of the bilingual lexico-semantic system. *Bilingualism: Language and Cognition* 1: 67–81.

Green, D.W. and Abutalebi, J. (2013). Language control in bilinguals: the adaptive control hypothesis. *Journal of Cognitive Psychology* 25: 515–530.

Gullifer, J.W., Kroll, J.F., and Dussias, P.E. (2013). When language switching has no apparent cost: lexical access in sentence context. *Frontiers in Psychology* 4: 1–13.

Guzzardo Tamargo, R.E., Valdés Kroff, J.R., and Dussias, P.E. (2016). Using codeswitching as a tool to study the link between production and comprehension. *Journal of Memory and Language* 89: 138–161.

Hahne, A. (2001). What's different in second-language processing? evidence from event-related brain potentials. *Journal of Psycholinguistic Research* 30: 251–266.

Hahne, A. and Friederici, A.D. (2001). Processing a second language: late learners' comprehension mechanisms as revealed by event-related brain potential. *Bilingualism: Language and Cognition* 4: 123–141.

Hay, J. and Foulkes, P. (2016). The evolution of medial /t/ over real and remembered time. *Language* 92: 298–330.

Hilchey, M.D. and Klein, R.M. (2011). Are there bilingual advantages on nonlinguistic interference tasks? Implications for the plasticity of executive control processes. *Psychonomic Bulletin Review* 18: 625–658.

Hillyard, S.A., Vogel, E.K., and Luck, S.J. (1998). Sensory gain control (amplification) as a mechanism of selective attention: electrophysiological and neuroimaging evidence. *Philosophical Transactions of the Royal Society: Biological Sciences* 353: 1257–1270.

Hopp, H. (2010). Ultimate attainment in L2 inflection: performance similarities between non-native and native speakers. *Lingua* 120: 901–931.

Hopp, H. (2016). Learning (not) to predict: grammatical gender processing in second language acquisition. *Second Language Research* 32: 277–307.

Johnson, J.S. and Newport, E.L. (1989). Critical period effects in second language learning: the influence of maturational state on the acquisition of English as a second language. *Cognitive Psychology* 21: 60–99.

Just, M.A. and Carpenter, P.A. (1992). A capacity theory of comprehension: individual differences in working memory. *Psychological Review* 99: 122–149.

Kaan, E. (2014). Predictive sentence processing in L2 and L1: what is different? *Linguistic Approaches to Bilingualism* 4: 257–282.

Kim, A.E. and Gilley, P.M. (2013). Neural mechanisms of rapid sensitivity to syntactic anomaly. *Frontiers in Psychology* 4 (45).

King, J. and Just, M.A. (1991). Individual differences in syntactic processing: the role of working memory. *Journal of Memory and Language* 30: 580–602.

Kleinschmidt, D. and Jaeger, T.F. (2015). Robust speech perception: recognizing the familiar, generalizing to the similar, and adapting to the novel. *Psychological Review* 122: 148–203.

Kroll, J.F. and Bialystok, E. (2013). Understanding the consequences of bilingualism for language processing and cognition. *Journal of Cognitive Psychology* 25 (5): 497–514.

Kroll, J.F., Bobb, S., and Wodniecka, Z. (2006). Language selectivity is the exception, not the rule: arguments against a fixed locus of language selection in bilingual speech. *Bilingualism: Language and Cognition* 9: 119–135.

Kroll, J.F., Bogulski, C.A., and McClain, R. (2012). Psycholinguistic perspectives on second language learning and bilingualism: the course and consequence of cross–language competition. *Linguistic Approaches to Bilingualism* 2 (1): 1–24.

Kroll, J. F., & Dussias, P. E. (2016). Language and productivity for all Americans. *American Academy of Arts and Sciences*. Commission on Language Learning.

Kroll, J.F., Dussias, P.E., Bice, K., and Perrotti, L. (2015). Bilingualism, mind, and brain. *Annual Review of Linguistics* 1: 377–394.

Kroll, J.F., Dussias, P.E., Bogulski, C.A., and Valdés Kroff, J.R. (2012). Juggling two languages in one mind: what bilinguals tell us about language processing and its consequences for cognition. In: *The Psychology of Learning and Motivation*, vol. 56 (ed. B. Ross), 229–262. San Diego, CA: Academic Press.

Kutas, M. and Federmeier, K.D. (2011). Thirty years and counting: finding meaning in the N400 component of the event-related brain potential (ERP). *Annual Review of Psychology* 62: 621–647.

Kutas, M. and Hillyard, S.A. (1980). Reading senseless sentences: brain potentials reflect semantic incongruity. *Science* 207: 203–205.

Kutas, M., Moreno, E., and Wicha, N. (2009). Codeswitching and the brain. In: *The Cambridge Handbook of Linguistic Codeswitching* (ed. B.E. Bullock and A.J. Toribio), 289–306. Cambridge, UK: Cambridge University Press.

Lado, R. (1957). *Linguistics across Cultures*. Ann Arbor, MI: Michigan University Press.

Lee, J.W. and Schallert, D.L. (1997). The relative contribution of L2 language proficiency and L1 reading ability to L2 reading performance: a test of the threshold hypothesis in an EFL context. *TESOL Quarterly* 31 (4): 713–739.

Litcofsky, K.A. and Van Hell, J.G. (2017). Neural correlates of intra-sentential codeswitching: switching direction affects switching costs. *Neuropsychologia* 97: 112–139.

MacDonald, M.C. (2013). How language production shapes language form and comprehension. *Frontiers in Psychology* 4: 1–16.

MacDonald, M.C. and Seidenberg, M.S. (2006). Constraint satisfaction accounts of lexical and sentence comprehension. In: *Handbook of Psycholinguistics*, 2nde (ed. M.J. Traxler and M.A. Gernsbacher), 581–611. London, UK: Elsevier.

Meuter, R.F. and Allport, A. (1999). Bilingual language switching in naming: asymmetrical costs of language selection. *Journal of Memory and Language* 40: 25–40.

Montrul, S. (2006). On the bilingual competence of Spanish heritage speakers: syntax, lexical-semantics and processing. *International Journal of Bilingualism* 10: 37–69.

Moreno, E.M., Federmeier, K.D., and Kutas, M. (2002). Switching languages, switching palabras (words): an electrophysiological study of code switching. *Brain and Language* 80: 188–207.

Morgan-Short, K., Steinhauer, K., Sanz, C., and Ullman, M.T. (2012). Explicit and implicit second language training differentially affect the achievement of native-like brain activation patterns. *Journal of Cognitive Neuroscience* 24: 933–947.

Mueller, J.L. (2005). Electrophysiological correlates of second language processing. *Second Language Research* 21: 152–174.

Muysken, P. (2000). *Bilingual Speech: A Typology of Code-Mixing*. Cambridge, UK: Cambridge University Press.

Ng, S., Gonzalez, C., and Wicha, N.Y.Y. (2014). The fox and the Cabra: an ERP analysis of reading code switched nouns and verbs in bilingual short stories. *Brain Research* 1557: 127–140.

Nieuwland, M.S. and Van Berkum, J.J.A. (2008). The interplay between semantic and referential aspects of anaphor noun phrase resolution: evidence from ERPs. *Brain and Language* 106: 119–131.

Oliveira, C.S.F., Souza, R.A., and Oliveira, F.L.P. (2017). Bilingualism effects on L1 representation and processing of argument structure. *Journal of the European Second Language Association* 1: 23–37.

Pajak, B., Fine, A.B., Kleinschmidt, D.F., and Jaeger, F. (2016). Learning Additional Languages as Hierarchical Probabilistic Inference: Insights From First Language Processing. *Language Learning* 66: 900–944.

Pakulak, E. and Neville, H.J. (2010). Proficiency differences in syntactic processing of monolingual native speakers indexed by event-related potentials. *Journal of Cognitive Neuroscience* 22: 2728–2744.

Piske, T., MacKay, I.R.A., and Flege, J.E. (2001). Factors affecting the degree of foreign accent in an L2: a review. *Journal of Phonetics* 29: 191–215.

Pliatsikas, C. and Marinis, T. (2013). Processing empty categories in a second language: when naturalistic exposure fills the (intermediate) gap. *Bilingualism: Language and Cognition* 16: 167–182.

Poplack, S. (1980). Sometimes I'll start a sentence in Spanish y termino en español:

towards a typology of codeswitching. *Linguistics* 18: 581–618.

Poplack, S. (1988). Contrasting patterns of codeswitching in two communities. In: *Codeswitching: Anthropological and Sociolinguistic Perspectives* (ed. M. Heller), 215–244. The Hague, The Netherlands: Mouton de Gruyter.

Proverbio, A.M., Leoni, G., and Zani, A. (2004). Language switching mechanisms in simultaneous interpreters: an ERP study. *Neuropsychologia* 42: 1636–1656.

Qi, Z., Beach, S.D., Finn, A.S. et al. (2017). Native-language N400 and P600 predict dissociable language-learning abilities in adults. *Neuropsychologia* 98: 177–191.

Romero-Rivas, C., Martin, C.D., and Costa, A. (2016). Foreign-accented speech modulates linguistic anticipatory processes. *Neuropsychologia* 85: 245–255.

Schmid, M.S. and Köpke, B. (2007). Bilingualism and attrition. In: *Language Attrition: Theoretical Perspectives* (ed. B. Köpke, M.S. Schmid, M. Keijzer and S. Dostert), 1–7. Amsterdam, The Netherlands: John Benjamins.

Schwartz, A.I., Kroll, J.F., and Diaz, M. (2007). Reading words in Spanish and English: mapping orthography to phonology in two languages. *Language & Cognitive Processes* 22: 106–129.

Segalowitz, N. and Hulstijn, J. (2005). Automaticity in bilingualism and second language learning. In: *Handbook of Bilingualism: Psycholinguistic Approaches* (ed. J.F. Kroll and A.M.B. de Groot), 371–388. New York, NY: Oxford University Press.

Snyder, W. (2000). An experimental investigation of syntactic satiation effects. *Linguistic Inquiry* 31: 575–582.

Squires, L. (2014). Social differences in the processing of grammatical variation. *University of Pennsylvania Working Papers in Linguistics* 20 (2): 178–188.

Steinhauer, K. and Drury, J.E. (2012). On the early left-anterior negativity (ELAN) in syntax studies. *Brain and Language* 120: 135–162.

Steinhauer, K., White, E.J., and Drury, J.E. (2009). Temporal dynamics of late second language acquisition: evidence from event-related brain potentials. *Second Language Research* 25: 13–41.

Tamminga, M. (2016). Persistence in phonological and morphological variation. *Language Variation and Change* 28 (3): 335–356.

Tanner, D., Inoue, K., and Osterhout, L. (2014). Brain-based individual differences in on-line L2 grammatical comprehension. *Bilingualism: Language and Cognition* 17: 277–293.

Tanner, D., McLaughlin, J., Herschensohn, J., and Osterhout, L. (2013). Individual differences reveal stages of L2 grammatical acquisition: ERP evidence. *Bilingualism: Language and Cognition* 16: 367–382.

Tanner, D. and Van Hell, J.G. (2014). ERPs reveal individual differences in morphosyntactic processing. *Neuropsychologia* 56: 281–301.

Tarlowski, A., Wodniecka, Z., and Marzecová, A. (2013). Language switching in the production of phrases. *Journal of Psycholinguistic Research* 42: 103–118.

Traxler, M.J., Morris, R.K., and Seely, R.E. (2002). Processing subject and object relative clauses: evidence from eye movements. *Journal of Memory and Language* 47: 69–90.

Valdés Kroff, J.R., Dussias, P.E., Gerfen, C. et al. (2017). Experience with codeswitching modulates the use of grammatical gender during sentence processing. *Linguistic Approaches to Bilingualism* 7: 163–198.

Valdés Kroff, J.R., Guzzardo Tamargo, R.E., and Dussias, P.E. (2018). Experimental contributions of eye-tracking to the understanding of comprehension processes while hearing and reading code-switches.

Linguistic Approaches to Bilingualism 8: 98–133.

Van Assche, E., Duyck, W., Hartsuiker, R.J., and Diependaele, K. (2009). Does bilingualism change native-language reading? Cognate effects in a sentence context. *Psychological Science* 20: 923–927.

Van Hell, J.G. and Dijkstra, T. (2002). Foreign language knowledge can influence native language performance in exclusively native contexts. *Psychonomic Bulletin & Review* 9: 780–789.

Van Hell, J.G., Litcofsky, K.A., and Ting, C.Y. (2015). Sentential codeswitching: cognitive and neural approaches. In: *The Cambridge Handbook of Bilingual Processing* (ed. J.W. Schweiter), 459–482. Cambridge, UK: Cambridge University Press.

Vogel, E.K. and Luck, S.J. (2000). The visual N1 component as an index of a discrimination process. *Psychophysiology* 37: 190–203.

Weber-Fox, C. and Neville, H.J. (1996). Maturational constraints on functional specializations for language processing: ERP and behavioral evidence in bilingual speakers. *Journal of Cognitive Neuroscience* 8: 231–256.

Weldon, T. (1994). Variability in negation in African American vernacular English. *Language Variation and Change* 6: 359–397.

Wells, J.B., Christiansen, M.H., Race, D.S. et al. (2009). Experience and sentence processing: statistical learning and relative clause comprehension. *Cognitive Psychology* 58: 250–271.

White, L. (2003). Fossilization in steady state L2 grammars: persistent problems with inflectional morphology. *Bilingualism: Language and Cognition* 6: 129–141.

24 Translation, Interpreting, and the Bilingual Brain
Implications for Executive Control and Neuroplasticity

BRUCE J. DIAMOND AND
GREGORY M. SHREVE

1. Introduction

This chapter examines some of the ways in which acquisition and continued use of two languages in communicative situations over a sustained period can influence the development of the 'bilingual brain'. There is credible evidence that the structure and function of the brain can be altered over time (Bialystok et al. 2016; Green and Abutalebi 2013), perhaps as an adaptive response to the particular constraints of bilingual communication and, in particular, to the unique changes associated with the experience, training and operations performed by interpreters and translators (Diamond and Shreve 2010). One of the unique conditions of bilingual communication is 'language switching', when two languages are activated during the performance of a cross-language activity such as translation or interpreting (Abutalebi and Green 2007, 2016).

Such switching involves costs, including the possibility of the two languages interfering with one another, or effects such as increased processing time on certain tasks. However, over time, the bilingual brain appears to alter to mitigate these costs. One example is the improved attentional and executive control that some studies have reported. Some of the neurophysiological changes precipitated by bilingual performance may confer cognitive advantages beyond the task-specific language domain, to non-linguistic domains as well.

Research into bilingualism has employed an increasingly sophisticated variety of models and technologies to examine the cognitive and neurophysiological mechanisms engaged during the performance of 'cross-language' tasks by bilinguals. This research also provides useful insight into the structural and functional neuroplastic changes in

The Handbook of the Neuroscience of Multilingualism, First Edition. Edited by John W. Schwieter.
© 2019 John Wiley & Sons Ltd. Published 2019 by John Wiley & Sons Ltd.

the brain that can occur as bilingual facility develops under the influence of long-term bilingual communication (Pliatsikas et al. 2015, 2017).

Neuroplastic changes involve, as one would expect, language specific areas, but also appear to include changes to, for example, general executive processing systems. As a result of these changes there may be both cognitive advantages and disadvantages for the bilingual individual. Some of the advantageous changes (such as improved executive control) may not only enhance performance in the particular cross-language task domain (e.g. interpreting or translating) but could also confer, as a side effect, an advantage in other non-language task areas (Bialystok et al. 2016). Bilinguals appear to possess two separate lexical systems reflecting brain regions and the connections between them and mediated by a common conceptual system (Diamond et al. 2015). According to Wong et al. (2016), the lexical systems comprising the neural substrates identified with phonology, morphology, syntax, and semantics, show the largest degree of divergence in structure, function, and connectivity between bilinguals and monolinguals. The observed development of the affected brain regions closely parallels language development, with the developmental sequence thought to be phonological development, followed by semantic development, and finally syntactic development (Wong et al. 2016). The lexical and conceptual systems come online during cross-language tasks and both languages appear to be accessible even when one language is being used (Bialystok 2009; Dijkstra et al. 1999; Kroll et al. 2006).

Because research shows that both lexical systems are activated during such tasks, some sort of executive control mechanism is posited to explain how bilinguals can select the appropriate 'active' language during task performance (Diamond et al. 2015). Bilinguals must speak, read, write, translate, or interpret in the language that is contextually relevant during the course of a cross-language task; there must be a mechanism that enables switching between the relevant lexical systems when needed (Colome 2001; Costa and Caramazza 1999; Kroll and Peck 1998; Lee and Williams 2001). An increasing body of research supports the idea that executive and attentional control mechanisms, as well as working memory, are crucial elements mediating the language-switching process (Elmer 2012).

Cross-language task research indicates that task-related language switching incurs cognitive processing costs with respect to speed and efficiency (Diamond et al. 2015). These processing costs appear to be asymmetric, with the direction of switching influencing the costs incurred. For example, reactivation time for a dominant language may be longer, based on the idea that the dominant language production schema requires greater inhibition and a greater allocation of resources in order to reactivate it (e.g. Meuter and Allport 1999). The long-term activation of the executive control mechanisms associated with switching may also confer both language-specific and general cognitive processing advantages – and possibly some disadvantages as well (Bogulski et al. 2015; Scaltritti et al. 2017).

Potential advantages and disadvantages conferred by the development of bilingualism are influenced and modified by cultural and developmental contexts, as well as the by the timing of language acquisition, and, as we propose, by the long-term practice of professional bilingual tasks. This chapter explores the issues surrounding the development of bilingualism from a neuroplasticity perspective, focusing particularly on working memory and control mechanisms invoked during cross-language tasks and how any ensuing neuroplastic changes related to those mechanisms may alter or enhance information processing relative to monolinguals.

2. Bilingualism and the Control of Switching and Interference

While only one language may be in use during a bilingual task, a significant body of work suggests that both language systems are active and accessible in bilinguals (Bialystok 2009; Dijkstra et al. 1999; Kroll et al. 2006). Given that, how do proficient bilinguals consistently generate 'correct' language forms in highly demanding language task contexts (e.g. simultaneous interpreting; and it should be emphasized that interpreting is a very specific task/skill, so any findings from interpreting may not readily be applicable to all bilinguals).

Interpreting would require, for instance, that the listening language be suppressed while the speaking language is promoted to emerge into speech production. This inhibition–activation cycle, what we are calling language switching, is thought to be mediated by executive control processes that serve as regulatory mechanisms to modulate attentional focus, all in order to achieve a smooth transfer from language to another efficiently (Diamond et al. 2015). In fact, there is general agreement that brain areas involved in the executive control of switching tasks unrelated to language are the same areas involved in switching between languages (Pliatsikas and Luk 2016).

However, the repeated transitions from one language to another during a cross-language task may not always be a smooth process. The dual activation of the two languages potentially produces interference, a cognitive cost that could be expressed in longer and less efficient inhibition–activation cycles and language transfer times (compared to a monolingual context; Diamond et al. 2015). In addition, there may be an undesirable influence of one language on the comprehension or production of the other. For example, second language (L2) reading and L2 lexical decision tasks in the comprehension stage of translation, to first language (L1) writing in the production stage involve alternately activating, inhibiting, and then reactivating competing L1 and L2 language action schemas, along the lines of the inhibitory control (IC) model (Green 1998). This *switching between schemas* imposes *costs* at both the production level (Meuter and Allport 1999) and at the input level (von Studnitz and Green 1997).

The extent and severity of cross-linguistic interference may be modified by the nature and extent of bilingual experience; that is, how well established the underlying lexical networks are, or how well the experience-derived content of the lexical and conceptual networks fits with task demands. The task context may also promote interference. Thus, while cross-linguistic interference is more likely to be seen during the early acquisition of the second language (i.e. less proficient bilinguals), it may also be observed in more proficient bilinguals, who may be performing under highly stressful task conditions such as interpreting (Kroll and Sunderman 2003). Cross-linguistic interference is more likely when the nature of the utterances or texts involved requires knowledge of concepts, lexical items or syntactic patterns that might not have been previously experienced (when translating specialized technical materials, for instance).

Interference may also arise if, during the transition from one language to the other, bilinguals fail to sufficiently inhibit the irrelevant lexicon. Yet another interference situation occurs when the bilingual is operating in monolingual mode and the second language is not needed in the task at all. While some work suggests that the dual lexica in bilinguals are independent, other research suggests that even in monolingual contexts the supposedly 'irrelevant' language is activated partially and in parallel and then deactivated or suppressed.

This may suggest that in bilingual individuals language comprehension and production are distributed along a language-mixing continuum between the two languages (Spivey and Marian 1999).

If this view is correct, then one should find evidence of switching costs, such as declines in processing speed, as well as the progressive development of control systems to address those costs. For instance, in a recent study, processing speed on a bilingual switch task involving alternating Spanish-English words was found to be significantly slower than processing on a non-linguistic switch task. In other words, while there was no difference between bilinguals and monolinguals on a non-linguistic switching task involving working memory (WM) and executive control, the addition of a linguistic switching component significantly slowed processing speed. It appears that linguistic switching results in a cycle of activation and inhibition, with inhibition of the more salient L1 activation requiring greater executive control resources. L1 inhibition also appeared to carry over to subsequent L1 trials, resulting in less efficient processing overall (Diamond et al. 2015).

Over time, one can expect greater efficiency in language control to arise due to the bilingual's need to control interference from the non-target language during cross-language tasks, or even when simply speaking in single- or mixed-language contexts (Weissberger et al. 2015). If inhibition of the non-target language becomes semi-automatic, fewer executive resources would be needed to inhibit L1 activation, which would help enhance overall bilingual language processing performance. This is in line with the idea that the sustained practice of bilingual communication can, under the right conditions, induce 'adaptive' cognitive changes with a concomitant neuroplastic expression as expressed, for example, in the adaptive control hypothesis (Green and Abutalebi 2013).

The capability to control which language is active at a point in a given task and to switch between two languages may be mediated by neurocognitive mechanisms that are shared with non-linguistic task-switching processes. In other words, the control mechanism may not be specific to the language system. To investigate whether switching control mechanisms are unique to language or invoke more general control processes, a recent functional magnetic resonance imaging (fMRI) study employed a hybrid (event-related and blocked) design using a colour-shape switching and language-switching paradigm involving 19 Spanish-English bilingual university students. The results confirmed previous work suggesting shared mechanisms of switching across language and non-language domains, i.e. involving prefrontal and parietal areas that are implicated in tasks involving cognitive and executive-attentional control mechanisms, and represent general rather than language-specific executive control (Brass et al. 2005; D'Esposito et al. 1995; Nebel et al. 2005; Shallice 1994; Swainson et al. 2003), but also greater efficiency for sustaining the inhibition of the non-target language compared with the non-target task (Weissberger et al. 2015).

It is thought that the control of multiple languages may require domain-general executive control in bilinguals, thus suggesting that executive control and language systems become intertwined, with evidence suggesting how and where executive control and language processes overlap in the bilingual brain. Thus, using fMRI data from a flanker task with linguistic and non-linguistic distractors and a semantic categorization task, functional overlap was demonstrated in the left inferior frontal gyrus (LIFG) in bilinguals. No overlap occurred in monolinguals. The flanker task involves congruent, incongruent, and neutral stimuli that require executive processes in order to control response inhibition in appropriate contexts. These findings provide support for the concurrent recruitment of executive control mechanisms during bilingual language processing and the engagement of domain-general and non-linguistic control mechanisms suggesting functional overlap of language and executive control in the bilingual brain (Coderre et al. 2016).

Additional evidence showing functional and structural overlap in linguistic and non-linguistic switching tasks was reported in a study using fMRI in 36 healthy, right-handed, early, and highly proficient Spanish (L1)-Basque (L2) bilingual college students who had a good knowledge of English (L3). The L2 was acquired, on average, before the age of three years. Overlap in brain activation between switch-specific activity in a linguistic switching task and a closely matched non-linguistic switching task was demonstrated, providing more direct evidence that, in these bilinguals, highly similar brain circuits are involved in language control and domain-general cognitive control (De Baene et al. 2015).

There is, however, some evidence suggesting that *early* bilinguals and monolinguals use different brain areas when performing non-linguistic executive control tasks. In examining brain activity in early bilinguals and monolinguals during a manual stop-signal paradigm, Rodríguez-Pujadas et al. (2014) reported that bilinguals and monolinguals did not show significant differences in the task. However, despite no differences in task performance, monolinguals activated the anterior cingulate cortex more often than bilinguals when performing the stop-signal task, and bilinguals used the anterior cingulate more efficiently than monolinguals to monitor nonlinguistic cognitive conflicts. This may suggest that early bilingualism may exert a differential effect on the development and invocation of neural circuitry mediating executive control (Rodríguez-Pujadas et al. 2014).

Grant et al. (2015) conducted a longitudinal fMRI study examining cognitive control in second language (L2) acquisition over the course of one academic year. While in the scanner, participants judged the language membership of unambiguous first and second language words, as well as interlingual homographs. Based on ROI and connectivity analyses, increased exposure to the L2 is associated with decreased activation in control areas such as the anterior cingulate cortex and increased connectivity with semantic processing regions such as the middle temporal gyrus. The authors interpreted these results as suggesting that cognitive control plays a greater initial role in L2 acquisition and that the findings have significant implications for understanding developmental and neurocognitive models of second language lexical processing.

In a study examining whether early bilinguals use more language-related networks than monolinguals while performing a go/no-go task that includes infrequent no-go and go trials, RTs and accuracy did not differ between the groups. However, an independent component analysis (ICA) showed that bilinguals used the left frontoparietal network and the salience network more than monolinguals while processing 'go infrequent cues' and 'no-go cues', respectively (Costumero et al. 2015). The results were also interpreted as suggesting that the executive control networks that comprise the left inferior frontal gyrus during cognitive control tasks operate differently in bilinguals versus monolinguals. This implies that the practice of bilingual communication does, in fact, induce neuroplastic changes.

Similarly, young adult bilinguals and monolinguals demonstrate similar response times on incongruent (interference suppression) and no-go trials (response inhibition). In fact, discrete regions of activation have been identified using fMRI, showing that bilinguals and monolinguals show similar regions of activation for no-go trials. In contrast, a different set of brain regions was activated for congruent and incongruent trials. Monolinguals activated the left temporal pole and left superior parietal regions during the incongruent trials whereas bilinguals showed activation in bilateral frontal, temporal, and subcortical regions. These findings provide some evidence that there may be a bilingual-specific control network for interference suppression involving executive and attentional control processes. However, it also appears as if bilinguals and monolinguals may share common pathways during response suppression (Luk et al. 2010). This suggests shared executive and attentional control processes in bilinguals and monolinguals, but there is also evidence for a more elaborated bilingual-specific control network for interference suppression.

Clearly, the successful completion of cross-language tasks, especially those performed at a professional level, such as translation or interpreting, would require some executive control mechanism to mitigate the effects of interference. From the previous studies, it seems as if control systems are engaged early to mitigate the negative effects of having two active language systems. While the development of switching control and interference suppression mechanisms in monolinguals and bilinguals share common pathways, changes in the brain appear to be more elaborated in the bilingual brain and parallel the development of proficiency.

3.   Implications for Translating and Interpreting

The ability of an interpreter listening to an L2 interlocutor to respond effectively in the L1 and not the L2 and, similarly, that of a translator to read a source text segment in the L2 and write a target text segment in the L1 would thus seem to rest on the efficacy of control mechanisms activated to minimize cross-linguistic interference. Although the task constraints of translation and interpreting are quite different, particularly with respect to the time allotted for the task, there is little reason to assume that there are major structural and functional differences in the bilingual cognitive system that supports both activities.

The control of switching and the suppression of interference via executive control mechanisms incur cognitive costs including slower processing speed, lower accuracy, a decreased ability to process multiple streams of information, and an overall degradation in processing efficiency. Tasks like interpreting or translating necessarily involve a significant amount of switching and increased opportunities for cross-language interference (an example being the processing of cognate words that point to different concepts).

Translation and interpreting, although they are different tasks, involve a characteristic alternation – switching – of language segment comprehension and production. In translating and simultaneous interpreting, input source segments must be understood, and once their sense has been constructed, must be recast as output target segments. In consecutive interpreting, L2 and L1 alternate; L2 listening and L1 speaking alternate with L1 listening and L2 speaking during turn taking. The interpretation of a long dialogue or a translation of a complex text are not identical processes – differences in task factors such as time constraints and differences in language modality (speaking/listening versus reading/writing) certainly differentiate them cognitively. But both most likely engage the same bilingual memory and control systems; there is little reason to assume otherwise. Such cross-language activities involve processing particular linguistic input using the source lexical store, developing a sense of its meaning via access to the common conceptual store, and then accessing the target store to produce the necessary output.

The source side of this equation is an L2 comprehension schema that alternates with an L2 production schema on the target side. There is a sustained cyclic activation, inhibition, and reactivation of competing L1 and L2 language action schemas along the lines of the inhibitory control model (Green 1998). During cross-language task performance, it is to be expected that cognitive resources will be expended for language processing, but, further, control resources must be allocated to successfully negotiate the language switches inherent in the alternation of these schemas. While translation and interpreting are not, as we have indicated, identical processes, they share many features and incur similar kinds of costs due to language schema alternation. Executive costs are incurred at both the production (speaking, writing) and input stages (listening, reading) when switching between language schemas. In translation, certain issues may also be exacerbated due to the continuous presence of the source text, such as 'the involuntary persistence of the previous language set' which is referred to by Meuter and Allport (1999). In interpreting, control mechanisms may be under additional strain due to the faster alternation of the production and comprehension schemas relative to translation. Studies of the costs of language switching in naming and lexical decision tasks (Meuter and Allport 1999; von Studnitz and Green 1997) indirectly support the idea of switching costs being incurred in both translation and interpreting and point to some of the underlying mechanisms that both processes would share.

Given the finite nature of processing resources, there would clearly be a diminished set of resources available to be allocated in response to any other task demands. This pressure on cognitive resources likely precipitates the effects mentioned earlier in this section, including lower accuracy, increased processing time, and degradation of processing. The effects would be greater, of course, in schema configurations such as interpreting where the course of language switching is much faster than in translating. There would be no language-switching costs at all in pure monolinguals enacting similar schemas (listening, for instance, followed by paraphrasing).

3.1.   *The Case of Simultaneous Interpreting*

Further insight into the nature of the costs incurred by language switching is provided by recent findings by Diamond et al. (2015) who report that Spanish-English bilinguals are significantly slower in processing L2 English input words than English mono-linguals are in processing L1 English input words. Moreover, processing speed on a computer-based, 2-back, bilingual switch task, in which the participants were presented with a variable alternating schedule of Spanish or English words, was significantly slower than processing speed on either the Spanish or English processing conditions alone. This suggests that switching between languages, even when it involves only single words, incurs processing costs that reduce processing speed within both the L1 and L2. One can only imagine the costs involved in more complex bilingual tasks.

It is well established in the literature that consecutive and (especially) simultaneous interpreting are complex bilingual language activities, with much of the current theoret-ical work suggesting that memory and attention play major mediating roles in the inter-preting process (Cowan 2000; Frauenfelder and Schriefers 1997; Gile 2009; Moser-Mercer 2000; Pöchhacker 2004). That makes interpreting an interesting case in support of our general thesis; that the successful accomplishment of bilingual tasks incurs costs that need to be managed and involves the significant involvement of executive control mechanisms.

Specifically, simultaneous interpreting requires active listening to the input language while simultaneously maintaining virtually any extracted source information in short-term memory, and planning and producing an articulation in the target language. The whole complex process involves not just listening and speaking, but also demands on working memory during complex language switching. The interpreter must exercise executive control of the output language under conditions of divided attention and inhibit the articulatory codes of the input language (Elmer 2012).

Insight into the complexity and difficulty of simultaneous interpreting is provided by a study of 24 advanced student interpreters (with 12–60 months of practice in simulta-neous interpreting). The interpreters performed a digit span task under four different conditions: after listening, after shadowing, after articulatory suppression, and after simultaneous interpreting. Digit span performance was significantly poorer following simultaneous interpreting compared to any of the other conditions. This was interpreted as suggesting that simultaneous interpretation is the most complex task of the four con-ditions with performance decrements likely due to phonological interference and greater processing burdens imposed by performing a concurrent working memory task (Darò and Fabbro 1994).

It is thought that when switching between any two languages L1 and L2 during task performance, the dominant (L1) schema requires greater inhibition to effectively pro-cess the L2 language schema. Overall processing speed is consequently slower because reactivation time for the L1 is longer and requires more extensive implementation of executive resources (e.g. Meuter and Allport 1999). Stroop and Stroop-like tasks that are thought to reflect inhibitory control have been used to examine language-switching functions and costs (Schwieter and Ferreira 2013, 2016). Stroop tasks are used as models for examining language-switching costs based on the premise that these tasks share, at least some cognitive computational similarities with language-switching tasks. Both operations require the inhibition of dominant response schemas. Executive burden is measured as the difference in reaction times with and without interference. In the case of the Stroop, a no-interference condition would involve a trial in which the word Green is written in green, whereas in an interference trial, Green would be written in the colour red. The participants in an experiment would normally be faster in processing trials (i.e. determining a match or mismatch) in which both word and colour are congruent.

Switching costs can also be incurred when switching operations involve words and objects in classification tasks. In one study, one of the costs was expressed as a selective decline in memory encoding for task-relevant. Degradation of task-relevant encoding may suggest that information stored about the task itself is less salient, less available for retrieval, and may, in fact, be more vulnerable to loss due to switching interference information (Richter and Yeung 2012). The implication here is that switching costs may include not only well-documented declines in accuracy and efficiency, but also degradation of the saliency of stored information about the task – this may adversely impact the efficacy of interpreting and translation, with the effects more pronounced in interpreting due to the transitory nature of the spoken source input. In translation there may be a similar loss, but it might be mitigated by strategies such as rereading and rewriting. In the case of interpreting, switching may also add to an already fraught cognitive processing situation due to the demands of parallel processing, which is often seen in interpreting, but rarely in translation (Gile 2009).

In examining the neurophysiological substrates of simultaneous interpreting, five professional simultaneous interpreters were monitored using fMRI while the participants overtly interpreted or simply repeated sentences with a simple subject-verb-object structure. The findings indicate that the pars triangularis was commonly activated across participants during interpretation from the L2 to the L1. The other brain regions of what is characterized as a 'control network' showed a strong inter-individual variability during both L2–L1 and L1–L2 tasks. It was proposed that *the* pars triangularis plays a crucial role within the language-control network in supporting simultaneous language processing (Elmer 2016). Moreover, the pars triangularis showed directional effects. That is, the findings suggest that it plays a role in supporting interpretation from L2 to L1, while other putative control networks appeared to be more variable with respect to directional effects. Taken together, these findings and interpretations are consistent with the idea that language-switching tasks necessarily involve effective control systems in order to succeed and that some of these systems appear to exhibit directional effects as well.

4.   Neuroplasticity and Cross-Language Task Performance

We have claimed that the performance of cross-language tasks like translation and interpreting involve the activation of L1 and L2 language systems and switching between them. Bilingual performance necessitates repeated cycles of the inhibition and activation of these systems and must integrate working memory and a variety of control mechanisms to allow such tasks to complete successfully.

The extent of exposure to cross-language tasks has an effect not just on the strength of the lexical networks involved but most likely also on those control and memory mechanisms that arise to mitigate any interference effects. It seems clear that as cross-language task experience is accumulated, we would find neurophysiological evidence that brain structure and function is modified. We have already cited some evidence that this occurs. From an expertise acquisition perspective, language networks and control systems should be adapting, under appropriate conditions, to improve switching performance and mitigate the costs of switching. Thus, there are indications of practice-induced language network plasticity as well as evidence of changes in control systems.

Using diffusion-weighted MRI (DW-MRI) tractography techniques and a network-based statistic (NBS) procedure, a recent study found that two structural subnetworks exhibited greater white matter (WM) tract connectivity in bilinguals versus monolinguals. This finding may suggest that there is greater white matter brain plasticity in bilinguals. These subnetworks included the left frontal and parietal/temporal regions, the left occipital and parietal/temporal regions, and the right superior frontal gyrus. All these regions have been implicated in both language processing and monitoring and may suggest that in order to deal with two languages, bilinguals develop specialized language subnetworks. Taken together, it appears as though bilingualism does modify the axonal structural organization of brain networks, conferring greater connectivity and more efficient subnetworks in mostly language regions and some frontal regions than is observed in monolinguals (García-Pentón et al. 2014).

Along the same lines, an interesting longitudinal study used magnetic resonance imaging (MRI) to measure cortical thickness in conference (simultaneous) interpreting trainees before and after completing a Master's programme in the profession. The study reported finding cortical thickening in multiple regions after completion of training. Cortical thickening occurred in regions serving lower level, phonetic processing, i.e. the left posterior superior temporal gyrus, the anterior supramarginal gyrus, and the planum temporale (Hervais-Adelman et al. 2017). There was also thickening of the right angular gyrus (thought to mediate higher-level formulation of propositional speech) and the right dorsal premotor cortex, which is putatively involved in the conversion of items from working memory into a sequence and in domain-general executive control and attention (right parietal lobule). The findings also imply that interpreter training may confer some protection against normal, age-related cortical thinning – implying that other regimens with similar processing demands may also induce cortical thickening.

5.   Bilingualism: Advantages and Disadvantages

We have proposed that the long-term practice of bilingual tasks may induce some intriguing changes in the structure and function of the brain involving not only language networks, but also memory and control (see Brito et al. 2014; MacNamara and Conway 2014; Zhou and Krott 2016, amongst others). These changes are quite possibly adaptive, meaning that they serve to improve task performance. The particular character of cross-language tasks places demands on control and memory that are different from the demands of monolingual tasks. Switching, interference control, and the cyclic mediation of the L2 lexical representation to the L1 representation via the conceptual store (so-called 'transfer' in the translation studies literature), place the language mediator (translator or interpreter) at a processing disadvantage. With practice, we assume, some of this disadvantage can be compensated for. Indeed, the notion of 'adaptive compensation' via repeated practice is at the heart of expertise studies in psychology.

From the notion of the language mediator's disadvantage we can turn to some possible advantages of bilingualism and the changes it induces. Given the ubiquitous nature of language and its intense usage, it is argued that bilingualism is a prime catalyst for modifying cognitive and brain systems beyond just language centres and processing (Bialystok 2017). We seem to have evidence that changes induced by the repetition of bilingual tasks may improve bilingual task performance, in the domain, or should, if expertise studies are correct. For instance, as mentioned in Section 4, the Hervais-Adelman et al. (2017) study reported increases in cortical thickness in brain regions linked to specific task requirements in simultaneous interpreting, thus potentially counteracting normal age-related cortical thinning. But a recent meta-analysis has reported that bilingualism is also positively associated with a range of other more general cognitive benefits, including being able to outperform monolinguals on combined measures of metalinguistic and metacognitive awareness, on measures of abstract and symbolic representation, attentional control, and problem solving. In other words, some neuroplastic reorganization improves performance on the specific bilingual task set, and exerts more general effects. It should, however, be noted that there was significant variability in the effect sizes reported in these studies, suggesting that more replication and extension studies are needed. In addition, the evidence suggests that earlier, rather than later, acquisition of a second language has a higher probability of being associated with greater metalinguistic and metacognitive awareness (Adesope et al. 2010).

5.1. *Advantages in Metalinguistics and Judging Grammaticality*

Some early research suggesting that bilingualism was associated with cognitive advantages was based on work with monolingual and bilingual children performing metalinguistic tasks. For instance, Cummins's 1978 study of Irish-English bilingual children seemed to demonstrate that bilingualism was associated with the ability to recognize the essentially arbitrary nature of linguistic reference. Based on study results, Cummins concluded that bilingual experience brought about an enhanced capacity to recognize and analyse language structure – metalinguistic awareness. These studies had their theoretical roots in the work of Vygotsky (1962). He proposed that the ability to separate words and their meanings and view their interrelationship as arbitrary is an essential foundation for higher cognitive thought. This insight is also crucial to professional translating and interpreting.

There is evidence supporting the idea that the separation of word and meaning is more advanced in bilingual children (Bialystok 2001). Bilingual children also appear to have greater proficiency compared with monolinguals in judging the grammaticality of anomalous sentences, which requires sustained and effortful attention, as well as the efficient filtering out of distractions (Bialystok 1986; Cromdal 1999). Bilingual children may also demonstrate greater proficiency at set shifting and, do so, at earlier stages in development than monolingual children (Bialystok 1999; Bialystok and Martin 2004).

In a similar manner, bilingual adults have exhibited smaller P600 event-related potentials (ERPs) in grammatical but silly sentences (Moreno et al. 2010). The sentences were grammatically correct, and so smaller P600s are consistent with the idea that greater violations of grammaticality lead to enhanced P600 amplitudes (Friederici et al. 1993). In essence, the P600 provided an index of the separation of grammaticality from meaning in bilinguals. That is, greater violations of grammaticality produce enhanced P600 amplitudes, while grammatically correct yet meaningless sentences produce smaller P600s. Taken together, these findings are consistent with the thesis that executive and attentional control processes are enhanced in bilinguals.

5.2. Component Language Structures, Cognitive and L1 Linguistic Attentional Control

A review article evaluating the effects of bilingualism on phonological, lexical-semantic, and syntactic aspects of language processing reported that bilinguals generally showed increased volume in component language structures serving phonological, lexical-semantic, and syntactic processing, as well as connective tracts between these brain regions compared with monolinguals. The authors concluded that the reviewed studies indicated that stronger cognitive control in bilinguals is accompanied by increased grey and white matter volume and regional activation in the frontoparietal network and basal ganglia (Wong et al. 2016). Overall, these studies suggest that greater cognitive control is supported by increased white matter or myelinated fibres which allow for more rapid transmission and efficient connectivity between regions rich in grey matter or neuronal cell bodies and glia.

Some intriguing recent evidence suggests that proficiency in a second language has a positive impact on linguistic attentional control in one's L1. This conclusion is supported by a study in which 22 monolinguals (18–30 years) and 19 bilinguals (18–30 years) completed two conditions of an alternating-runs task-switching paradigm in their first language. There was a relational condition which involved processing spatial prepositions and a non-relational condition which involved processing concrete nouns and adjectives. Monolinguals exhibited significantly greater attention control burden in the relational condition than the non-relational condition. Bilinguals performed similarly in both conditions (Duncan et al. 2016). In other words, bilinguals showed enhanced attentional and executive control in their L1 compared with monolinguals, who experienced a greater attentional control burden than bilinguals. This may suggest that bilingualism confers a processing advantage with respect to the L1.

While much of the literature suggests that bilingual individuals have better executive control than monolinguals, outperforming monolinguals on a variety of tasks that measure non-linguistic executive functioning, the neural bases of this capability remain largely unknown. In a study comparing bilinguals and monolinguals on a rapid instructed task learning (RITL) paradigm (Cole et al. 2013), it was reported that bilinguals were faster than monolinguals in applying novel rules, with the authors concluding that bilinguals show greater adaptive modulation of striatal activity than monolinguals (Stocco and Prat 2014). It was hypothesized that this change in executive functioning arises from the need to flexibly select and apply rules when speaking multiple languages and that this flexible behaviour may strengthen the functioning of the frontostriatal loops that direct signals to the prefrontal cortex.

5.3. *Cognition*

Ljungberg et al. (2013), in a longitudinal study of bilinguals and monolinguals, examined episodic memory recall and both verbal letter and category fluency. Monolingual and bilingual participants (n = 178) between 35 and 70 years at baseline showed that bilinguals outperformed monolinguals at the first testing session and across time, both in episodic memory recall and in letter fluency. The rate of change across ages was similar for bilinguals and monolinguals, with no bilingual advantages found in the category fluency task. These findings suggest that bilinguals had a cognitive advantage in processing episodic memory and in letter fluency, which is consistent with a bilingual executive control advantage that may have been associated with enhance encoding and retrieval processes, particularly for the types of memory that require executive control (e.g. episodic and verbal recall; Grant et al. 2014).

An underlying putative mechanism accounting for these results may be based on advantages in frontal lobe function and in making connections between the prefrontal cortex (PFC) and posterior areas of the cortex, which are thought to be critical for successful recollection (Dobbins and Davachi 2006). In other words, the strengthening of both frontal and temporal cortical pathways may be a result of bilingualism as well as enhanced levels of cognitive reserve (Grant et al. 2014), which may lead to more efficient episodic and verbal recall and a greater capacity for the executive control of memory processing.

Executive processing advantages also appear to extend to children as well. For example, findings from an ERP study using an executive control task suggest that when monolingual and bilingual children are engaged in a task involving a complex set of cognitive processing demands, e.g. monitoring, response selection, and response inhibition, bilingual children appear to show more efficient neural processing (Barac 2012).

Cognitive advantages also appear to extend to vocabulary as suggested in a cross-sectional study, where it was reported that bilateral frontal-subcortical-parietotemporal areas, predominantly in the right hemisphere, may underlie superior L2 vocabulary ability in late L2 learners. It was reported that grey matter volume in the inferior frontal gyrus pars opercularis (IFGop), as well as connectivity of the IFGop with the caudate nucleus and the superior temporal gyrus/supramarginal gyrus (STG/SMG), predominantly in the right hemisphere, were positively correlated with development of L2 vocabulary competence (Hosoda et al. 2013).

These authors then implemented a cohort study involving 16 weeks of L2 training in university students. It was reported that the training intervention increased both IFGop volume and the reorganization of white matter, including the IFGop-caudate and IFGop-STG/SMG pathways in the right hemisphere, with 'positive' plastic changes correlating with gains in L2 ability in the trained group versus controls. The authors proposed that the right hemispheric network exhibits plasticity and can be reorganized

into language-related areas that reflect reorganization of the neural substrates responding to linguistic experiences (Hosoda et al. 2013). These findings support the notion of
adaptive compensation with neuroplastic expression, introduced in Section 2.

6.   Neuroprotective Effects of Bilingualism in Normal Ageing and in Neurodegenerative Disease

Older adult bilinguals have shown better perceptual switching performance than
their monolingual peers. For instance, Gold et al. (2013), examined younger and older
adult monolinguals and bilinguals, using fMRI while they performed a perceptual
switching test. Like younger adults, bilingual older adults outperformed their monolingual peers while displaying decreased activation in left lateral frontal cortex and
cingulate cortex. Lower blood oxygenation level-dependent response in frontal
regions accounted for 82% of the variance in the bilingual task-switching reaction time
advantage, with decreased activation directly correlated with better task-switching
performance.

   These results may suggest that lifelong bilingualism can offset or, at least, mitigate
age-related declines in the neural efficiency of cognitive control processes. The results
also support our general contention that long-term bilingualism, because of the need to
deal with language switching, induces adaptive change; here, one might argue, improvements in language switching have positively impacted task switching – possibly due to
overall improvement in cognitive control. This is supported by the decreased activation
or lower blood oxygenation level-dependent response within frontal regions which suggests greater levels of processing efficiency.

   In a study that investigated whether a greater opportunity for language switching
contributes to a bilingual advantage, Italian-Venetian dialect bilinguals (lower switching frequency) were compared to Italian monolinguals in the flanker task. No advantages were reported. This is in contrast with Catalan-Spanish bilinguals who experience
frequent opportunities of language switching and who do show bilingual advantages.
The findings were interpreted as suggesting that language switching, particularly the
frequency with which it occurs, plays a role in mediating a bilingual advantage (Scaltritti
et al. 2017). This result is also consonant with our thesis that the nature and extent of
bilingual experience are critical factors in whether the bilingual brain reorganizes to
promote improved performance.

   As we can see, there is some intriguing evidence that structural and functional
changes due to the practice of bilingualism can confer some cognitive advantages. Can
such advantages have more profound effects? Could, for instance, lifelong bilingual
experience any neuroprotective effects in neurodegenerative disease? In essence, can
bilingualism slow the progression of neurodegenerative disease? There is, in fact, some
evidence across multinational studies suggesting that speaking two or more languages
may delay the onset of dementia, including both frontotemporal dementia and vascular
dementia. Putative mechanisms may involve cognitive reserve which is manifested as a
reorganization and strengthening of neural networks that enhance executive control
(Freedman et al. 2014).

In support of the idea that bilingualism may exert neuroprotective effects, a retrospective study examined patients in a memory clinic who had been diagnosed with dementia. Following exclusion of patients who could not be confidently classified, 184 remaining patients (91 monolingual, 93 bilingual) remained, with two-thirds meeting criteria for probable Alzheimer's disease (AD) and one-third suffering from other dementias. In evaluating the age at which the formal consensual diagnosis of dementia was made by the medical team, the mean age was 75.4 years for monolinguals and 78.6 years for bilinguals (Bialystok et al. 2007). A number of studies that have examined patient records (Craik et al. 2010) or tested patients from the same clinic used in the original study (Bialystok et al. 2014) have supported this finding. Furthermore, the findings have been replicated by other researchers in a number of studies (e.g. Wilson et al. 2015; Woumans et al. 2015), including a study conducted in India (which included a sample with diverse educational and economic backgrounds) that replicated the four and a half year delay in time of dementia diagnosis (Alladi et al. 2013).

While some research suggests that multilingualism may increase the level of protection against dementia (Perquin et al. 2013), it also appears as if socioeconomic and demographic factors may act as intervening variables in modifying the neuroprotective effects of certain groups (Chertkow et al. 2010). In addition, there are interactions with education, bilingual proficiency, and age of onset of AD (Gollan et al. 2011).

The incidence of Alzheimer's disease was evaluated in 93 countries that were rated in terms of the mean number of languages spoken by the population. Interestingly, they report a significant decline in the incidence of AD with increasing multilingualism, a relationship that became stronger when an estimate of life expectancy was included in the model. The authors controlled for the effects of wealth and literacy and interpreted the results as being consistent with an overall protective effect of bilingualism (Klein et al. 2016).

6.1. *Neuroprotective Effects and Incidence Studies*

In order to investigate whether multilanguage experience exerts neuroprotective effects against dementia, incidence studies have been used in which cohorts of healthy adults with various backgrounds or experiences are followed over time to determine the rate of dementia onset. The relatively small number of incidence studies that have investigated whether bilingualism plays a role in decreasing the likelihood of dementia has generally reported no significant effects (Crane et al. 2009, 2010; Hack et al. 2012; Ljungberg et al. 2016; Sanders et al. 2012; Zahodne et al. 2014), although there are exceptions (e.g. Wilson et al. 2015).

While the Zahodne et al. (2014) study suggested that greater bilingualism was associated with a lower incidence of dementia and later onset of symptoms, it is posited that, overall, the design and statistical structure of these studies may preclude or highly restrict their ability to definitively answer the question of whether bilingualism exerts neuroprotective effects with respect to dementia. Clearly, there may be multiple factors that differentiate population samples, and that impact the incidence of dementia; bilingualism is one such factor.

7.   Disadvantages or Neutrality

There is some evidence that bilinguals may be at a disadvantage or exhibit no greater advantage in performing some tasks (Adesope et al. 2010). For example, some work suggests that lexical access in bilinguals may be less efficient (Diamond et al. 2015) due to the activation of two competing language systems (Bialystok 2009). This between-language interference may also explain a bilingual fluency disadvantage that has also been reported (Sandoval et al. 2010). A review found that a number of studies reporting better performance amongst bilinguals versus monolinguals on tasks involving executive switching and inhibition have not been replicated (Gasquoine 2016). Studies that have suggested that the age of onset of Alzheimer's disease occurred about four years later for bilinguals have also not been confirmed in more rigorously controlled work. In addition, neuroimaging studies examining regional grey and white matter volume in bilinguals versus monolinguals have shown inconsistent results with respect to what regions differed and the nature of those differences (Gasquoine 2016).

Inconsistencies in the literature may be attributable to publication bias, statistical flaws, and failures to match groups on potentially confounding variables. For example, in a study involving 52 bilingual and 53 monolingual speakers that used simple and complex WM) span tasks, no bilingual advantage in WM capacity was reported (Ratiu and Azuma 2015). Some of the discrepancies in the literature may be based on differential task demand characteristics and the idea that cognitive advantages are not necessarily a function of the bilingualism itself, but instead are derived from the active use of those languages in various communicative tasks (Diamond and Shreve 2017). This is consonant with the idea that it is language 'tasks' (such as translating or interpreting) that confer the advantage – and that failure to account for the 'nature' of how bilingualism is practised, for how long, and with what kind of frequency, can be a problem in study design.

Diamond et al. (2015) reported that there were no significant differences between bilinguals (aggregated across all subtypes) and monolinguals on the 2-back executive non-linguistic switch task. However, the findings were more nuanced. That is, when the bilinguals were divided into 'late sequential' and 'simultaneous' learners, there were some cognitive advantages for simultaneous versus late sequential bilingual learners, perhaps suggesting that the timing of language learning may be a mediating factor in influencing the degree of cognitive advantage across linguistic and non-linguistic cognitive domains.

8.   Conclusion

Bilinguals raised in environments where both languages are actively used in communication appear to develop a more enhanced processing control facility than is observed in environments that involve more passive kinds of language acquisition. This type of bilingual language immersion or active use during later developmental stages, even into adulthood, may also help foster the development of more efficient executive control processes overall. Taken together, the literature supports the idea that positive effects are derived not just from early bilingual exposure but also (and perhaps critically) from sustained active use of the two languages in communication. The finding that bilinguals who revert to monolingualism performed at an intermediary level relative to monolinguals and bilinguals (Bogulski et al. 2015) also supports this interpretation. Such findings also support the idea that prolonged and continued practice of bilingual tasks (as with language professionals) may confer cognitive advantages – for both early and late acquirers.

Age of acquisition (e.g. Dehaene et al. 1997; Kim et al. 1997) and proficiency levels (Perani et al. 1998) seem to modify the location, interconnections, and intensity of activation in the bilingual brain. Generally, the earlier a language is learned and the higher proficiency is attained in L2, the more grey matter intensity and white matter integrity are observed. However, we might argue that it is actually the length, continuity, and intensity of exposure (as opposed to absolute age of acquisition) that causes these changes. In many practising bilinguals, these three conditions are often correlated.

Processing advantages may also be attributable to exposure to tasks that require extensive executive set shifting or language shifting (Scaltritti et al. 2017). Such skills are integral to the processes mediating translation and interpreting that involve shifting between comprehension tasks (reading, listening) in one language and production tasks (speaking, writing) in another. Moreover, executive set shifting would be a requisite skill if both languages are activated during comprehension and production tasks. That is, bilinguals would need to invoke executive control mechanisms in order to manage appropriate language selection.

Functioning within a bilingual setting may provide multiple contexts that foster enhancement of executive control processes. For example, some communication may involve comprehension and production tasks that cross languages. Therefore, hearing one parent in the L1 and then speaking to the other parent in the L2 during conversation promotes engagement in active language control switching behaviours (Shreve and Diamond 1997) in children. And, of course, professional cross-language tasks, sustained over the course of a career may induce similar control system enhancement.

There seems to be a potential association between bilingualism, neuroplastic changes, and cognitive advantages. For example, there is evidence showing cortical thickening in interpreter trainees over the course of training. There is also a growing body of work suggesting that bilingualism is associated with a range of benefits across multiple cognitive domains, including outperforming monolinguals on a number of measures from attentional control to problem-solving and episodic memory recall.

Research exploring the impact of the bilingual experience on health and well-being was also considered as some of this work suggests that the bilingual experience may confer protective effects on the brain that slow various pathologic processes. Specifically, some research suggests that bilingualism may slow the progression of neurodegenerative disease. A word of caution is needed here as there are a variety of potential confounds that can help explain or, at least, contribute to observed advantages.

Overall, some available evidence seems to indicate that the unique conditions of sustained bilingual communication – the language switching involved in moving between production and comprehension schemas – precipitates detectable neuroplastic changes. Not only do language-specific areas of the brain alter in structure and function, but control mechanisms also appear to change in an apparently adaptive way. Further, the necessary engagement of executive control and even memory mechanisms to mitigate and accommodate to the costs of bilingualism seem to have detectable and sustained effects on other processing domains that can be interpreted as a durable cognitive advantage.

Acknowledgements

The authors would like to thank Daniel Mattei for his editorial support in preparing this manuscript as well as Katherine Makarec for her contributions.

REFERENCES

Abutalebi, J. and Green, D.W. (2007). Bilingual language production: the neurocognition of language representation and control. *Journal of Neurolinguistics* 20 (3): 242–275.

Abutalebi, J. and Green, D.W. (2016). Neuroimaging of language control in bilinguals: neural adaptation and reserve. *Bilingualism: Language and Cognition* 19 (4): 689–698.

Adesope, O.O., Lavin, T., Thompson, T., and Ungerleider, C. (2010). A systematic review and meta-analysis of the cognitive correlates of bilingualism. *Review of Educational Research* 80: 207–245. doi:10.3102/0034654310368803.

Alladi, S., Bak, T.H., Duggirala, V. et al. (2013). Bilingualism delays age at onset of dementia, independent of education and immigration status. *Neurology* 81: 1938–1944. doi:10.1212/01.wnl.0000436620.33155.a4.

Barac, R. (2012). *Neuroplasticity in young bilingual children: Evidence from ERPs in an executive control task* (Doctoral dissertation, York University, Toronto, Canada).

Bialystok, E. (1986). Factors in the growth of linguistic awareness. *Child Development* 57: 498–510. doi:10.1111/j.1467-8624.1986.tb00048.x.

Bialystok, E. (1999). Cognitive complexity and attentional control in the bilingual mind. *Child Development* 70: 636–644. doi:10.1111/1467-8624.00046.

Bialystok, E. (2001). *Bilingualism in Development: Language, Literacy, & Cognition*. Cambridge, UK: Cambridge University Press.

Bialystok, E. (2009). Bilingualism: the good, the bad, and the indifferent. *Bilingualism: Language and Cognition* 12: 3–11. doi:10.1017/S1366728908003477.

Bialystok, E. (2017). The bilingual adaptation: how minds accommodate experience. *Psychological Bulletin* 143: 233–262. doi:10.1037/bul0000099.

Bialystok, E., Abutalebi, J., Bak, T.H. et al. (2016). Aging in two languages: implications for public health. *Ageing Research Reviews* 27: 56–6.

Bialystok, E., Craik, F.I., Binns, M.A. et al. (2014). Effects of bilingualism on the age of onset and progression of MCI and AD: evidence from executive function tests. *Neuropsychology* 28: 290–304. doi:10.1037/neu0000023.

Bialystok, E., Craik, F.I., and Freedman, M. (2007). Bilingualism as a protection against the onset of symptoms of dementia. *Neuropsychologia* 45: 459–464. doi:10.1016/j.neuropsychologia.2006.10.009.

Bialystok, E. and Martin, M.M. (2004). Attention and inhibition in bilingual children: evidence from the developmental change card sort task. *Developmental Science* 7: 325–339.

Bogulski, C.A., Rakoczy, M., Goodman, M., and Bialystok, E. (2015). Executive control in fluent and lapsed bilinguals. *Bilingualism: Language and Cognition* 18: 561–567. doi:10.1017/S1366728914000856.

Brass, M., Ullsperger, M., Knoesche, T.R. et al. (2005). Who comes first? The role of the prefrontal and parietal cortex in cognitive control. *Journal of Cognitive Neuroscience* 17: 1367–1375.

Brito, N.H., Grenell, A., and Barr, R. (2014). Specificity of the bilingual advantage for memory: examining cued recall, generalization, and working memory in monolingual, bilingual, and trilingual toddlers. *Frontiers in Psychology* 5: 1369. doi:10.3389/fpsyg.2014.01369.

Chertkow, H., Whitehead, V., Philips, N. et al. (2010). Multilingualism (but not always bilingualism) delays the onset of Alzheimer disease: evidence from a bilingual community. *Alzheimer's Disease & Associated Disorders* 24: 118–125. doi:10.1097/WAD.0b013e3181ca1221.

Coderre, E.L., Smith, J.F., van Heuven, W.J.B., and Horwitz, B. (2016). The functional overlap of executive control and language processing in bilinguals. *Bilingualism: Language and Cognition* 19: 471–488. doi:10.1017/S1366728915000188.

Cole, M.W., Laurent, P., and Stocco, A. (2013). Rapid instructed task learning: a new window into the human brain's unique capacity for flexible cognitive control. *Cognitive, Affective, & Behavioral Neuroscience* 13 (1): 1–22.

Colome, A. (2001). Lexical activation in Bilinguals' speech production: language-specific or language-independent. *Journal of Memory and Language* 45 (4): 721–736.

Costa, A. and Caramazza, A. (1999). Is lexical selection in bilingual speech production language-specific? Further evidence from Spanish-English and English-Spanish bilinguals. *Bilingualism: Language and Cognition* 2: 231–244.

Costumero, V., Rodríguez-Pujadas, A., Fuentes-Claramonte, P., and Ávila, C. (2015). How bilingualism shapes the functional architecture of the brain: a study on executive control in early bilinguals and monolinguals. *Human Brain Mapping* 36: 5101–5112. doi:10.1002/hbm.22996.

Cowan, N. (2000). Processing limits of selective attention and working memory: potential implications for interpreting. *Interpreting* 5: 117–146. doi:10.1075/intp.5.2.05cow.

Craik, F.I., Bialystok, E., and Freedman, M. (2010). Delaying the onset of Alzheimer disease: bilingualism as a form of cognitive reserve. *Neurology* 75: 1726–1729. doi:10.1212/WNL.0b013e3181fc2a1c.

Crane, P.K., Gibbons, L.E., Arani, K. et al. (2009). Midlife use of written Japanese and protection from late life dementia. *Epidemiology* 20: 766–774. doi:10.1097/EDE.0b013e3181b09332.

Crane, P.K., Gruhl, J.C., Erosheva, E.A. et al. (2010). Use of spoken and written Japanese did not protect Japanese-American men from cognitive decline in late life. *The Journals of Gerontology Series B: Psychological Sciences and Social Sciences* 65B: 654–666. doi:10.1093/geronb/gbq046.

Cromdal, J. (1999). Childhood bilingualism and metalinguistic skills: analysis and control in young Swedish-English bilinguals. *Applied PsychoLinguistics* 20: 1–20.

Cummins, J. (1978). Metalinguistic development of children in bilingual education programs: data from Irish & Canadian Ukrainian-English programs. In: *The Fourth Locus Forum 1977* (ed. M. Paradis), 29–40. Columbia, SC: Hornbeam Press.

Darò, V. and Fabbro, F. (1994). Verbal memory during simultaneous interpretation: effects of phonological interference. *Applied Linguistics* 15: 365–381. doi:10.1093/applin/15.4.365.

De Baene, W., Duyck, W., Brass, M., and Carreiras, M. (2015). Brain circuit for cognitive control is shared by task and language switching. *Journal of Cognitive Neuroscience* 9: 1752–1765. doi:10.1162/jocn_a_00817.

Dehaene, S., Dupoux, E., Mehler, J. et al. (1997). Anatomical variability in the cortical representation of first and second language. *NeuroReport* 8: 3809–3815.

D'Esposito, M., Detre, J.A., Alsop, D.C. et al. (1995). The neural basis of the central executive system of working memory. *Nature* 378: 279–281.

Diamond, B.J. and Shreve, G.M. (2010). Neural and physiological correlates of translation and interpreting in the bilingual brain; recent perspectives. In: *Translation and Cognition* (ed. G. Shreve and E. Angelone), 289–321. Philadelphia, PA: Johns Benjamin.

Diamond, B.J. and Shreve, G.M. (2017). Neurocognitive factors, bilingualism, deliberate practice and the optimization of translation expertise. In: *The Handbook of Translation and Cognition* (ed. J.W. Schwieter and A. Ferreira), 476–495. Malden, MA/ Oxford, UK: Wiley-Blackwell.

Diamond, B.J., Shreve, G.M., Golden, A., and Durán-Narucki, V. (2015). Processing speed, switching and cognitive control in the bilingual brain. In: *The Development of Translation Competence: Theories and Methodologies from Psycholinguistics and Cognitive Science* (ed. J.W. Schwieter and A. Ferreira), 200–238. Newcastle upon Tyne, UK: Cambridge Scholars Publishing.

Dijkstra, T., Grainger, J., and van Heuven, W.J.B. (1999). Recognition of cognates and interlingual homographs: the neglected role of phonology. *Journal of Memory and Language* 41: 496–518. doi:10.1006/jmla.1999.2654.

Dobbins, I.G. and Davachi, L. (2006). Functional neuroimaging of episodic memory. In: *Handbook of Functional Neuroimaging of Cognition*, 2nde (ed. R. Cabeza and A. Kingstone), 229–268. Cambridge, MA: MIT Press.

Duncan, H.D., Segalowitz, N., and Phillips, N.A. (2016). Differences in L1 linguistic attention control between monolinguals and bilinguals. *Bilingualism: Language and Cognition* 19: 106–121. doi:10.1017/S136672891400025X.

Elmer, S. (2012). The investigation of simultaneous interpreters as an alternative approach to address the signature of multilingual speech processing. *Zeitschrift für Neuropsychologie* 23: 105–116. doi:10.1024/1016-264X/a000068.

Elmer, S. (2016). Broca pars triangularis constitutes a 'hub' of the language-control network during simultaneous language translation. *Frontiers in Human Neuroscience* 10: 491. doi:10.3389/fnhum.2016.00491.

Frauenfelder, U.H. and Schriefers, H. (1997). A psycholinguistic perspective on simultaneous interpretation. *Interpreting* 2: 55–89. doi:10.1075/intp.2.1-2.03fra.

Freedman, M., Alladi, S., Chertkow, H. et al. (2014). Delaying onset of dementia: are two languages enough? *Behavioural Neurology* 2014 (808137): 1–8. doi:10.1155/2014/808137.

Friederici, A.D., Pfeifer, E., and Hahne, A. (1993). Event-related brain potentials during natural speech processing: effects of semantic, morphological and syntactic violations. *Cognitive Brain Research* 1: 183–192. doi:10.1016/0926-6410(93)90026-2.

García-Pentón, L., Fernández, A.P., Iturria-Medina, Y. et al. (2014). Anatomical connectivity changes in the bilingual brain. *NeuroImage* 84: 495–504. doi:10.1016/j.neuroimage.2013.08.064.

Gasquoine, P.G. (2016). Effects of bilingualism on vocabulary, executive functions, age of dementia onset, and regional brain structure. *Neuropsychology* 30: 988–997. doi:10.1037/neu0000294.

Gile, D. (2009). *Basic Concepts and Models for Interpreter and Translator Training*. Amsterdam, The Netherlands: John Benjamins.

Gold, B.T., Kim, C., Johnson, N.F. et al. (2013). Lifelong bilingualism maintains neural efficiency for cognitive control in aging. *Journal of Neuroscience: The Official Journal of the Society for Neuroscience* 33: 387–396. doi:10.1523/JNEUROSCI.3837-12.2013.

Gollan, T.H., Salmon, D.P., Montoya, R.I., and Galasko, D.R. (2011). Degree of bilingualism predicts age of diagnosis of Alzheimer's disease in low-education but not in highly educated Hispanics. *Neuropsychologia* 49: 3826–3830. doi:10.1016/j. neuropsychologia.2011.09.041.

Grant, A., Dennis, N.A., and Li, P. (2014). Cognitive control, cognitive reserve, and memory in the aging bilingual brain. *Frontiers in Psychology* 5 (1401): 1–10. doi:10.3389/fpsyg.2014.01401.

Grant, A.M., Fang, S.Y., and Li, P. (2015). Second language lexical development and cognitive control: a longitudinal fMRI study. *Brain and Language* 144: 35–47. doi:10.1016/j. bandl.2015.03.010.

Green, D. (1998). Mental control of the bilingual lexico-semantic system. *Bilingualism: Language and Cognition* 1: 67–81. doi:10.1017/S1366728998000133.

Green, D.W. and Abutalebi, J. (2013). Language control in bilinguals: the adaptive control hypothesis. *Journal of Cognitive Psychology* 25 (5): 515–530.

Hack, E., Tyas, S., Dubin, J. et al. (2012). Does multilingualism reduce the risk or delay the onset of dementia?: findings from the Nun study. *Alzheimer's & Dementia* 8: 3–149. doi:0.1016/j.jalz.2012.05.1368.

Hervais-Adelman, A., Moser-Mercer, B., Murray, M.M., and Golestani, N. (2017). Cortical thickness increases after simultaneous interpretation training. *Neuropsychologia* 98: 212–219. doi:10.1016/j. neuropsychologia.2017.01.008.

Hosoda, C., Tanaka, K., Nariai, T. et al. (2013). Dynamic neural network reorganization associated with second language vocabulary acquisition: a multimodal imaging study. *Journal of Neuroscience* 33: 13663–13672. doi:10.1523/JNEUROSCI.0410-13.2013.

Kim, K., Relkin, N., Lee, K., and Hirsch, J. (1997). Distinct cortical areas associated with native and second languages. *Nature* 388: 171–174. doi:10.1038/40623.

Klein, R., Christie, J., and Parkvall, M. (2016). Does multilingualism affect the incidence of Alzheimer's disease?: a worldwide analysis by country. *SSM – Population Health* 2: 463–467. doi:10.1016/j.ssmph.2016.06.002.

Kroll, J., Bobb, S., and Wodniecka, Z. (2006). Language selectivity is the exception not the rule: arguments against a fixed locus of language selection in bilingual speech. *Bilingualism: Language and Cognition* 9: 119–135.

Kroll, J. F., and Peck. A. (1998). Competing activation across a bilingual's two languages: Evidence from picture naming. Paper presented at the 43rd Annual Meeting of the International Linguistic Association, New York, NY.

Kroll, J. and Sunderman, G. (2003). Cognitive processes in second language learners and bilinguals: the development of lexical and conceptual representations. In: *The Handbook of Second Language Acquisition* (ed. C.J. Doughty and M.H. Long), 104–129. Malden, MA: Blackwell Publishing.

Lee, M.W. and Williams, J.N. (2001). Lexical access in spoken word production by bilinguals: evidence from the semantic competitor priming paradigm. *Bilingualism: Language and Cognition* 4 (3): 233–248.

Ljungberg, J.K., Hansson, P., Adolfsson, R., and Nilsson, L.-G. (2016). The effect of language skills on dementia in a Swedish longitudinal cohort. *Linguistic Approaches to Bilingualism* 6: 190–204. doi:10.1075/lab.14031.lju.

Ljungberg, J.K., Hansson, P., Andrés, P. et al. (2013). A longitudinal study of memory advantages in bilinguals. *PLoS One* 8: 1–8. doi:10.1371/journal.pone.0073029.

Luk, G., Anderson, J., Craik, A.E. et al. (2010). Distinct neural correlates for two types of inhibition in bilinguals: response inhibition versus interference suppression. *Brain and Cognition* 74: 347–357. doi:10.1016/j.bandc. 2010.09.004.

MacNamara, B.N. and Conway, A.R.A. (2014). Novel evidence in support of the bilingual advantage: influences of task demands and experience on cognitive control and working memory. *Psychonomic Bulletin & Review* 21 (2): 520–525. doi:10.3758/ s13423-013-0524-y.

Meuter, R. and Allport, A. (1999). Bilingual language switching in naming: asymmetrical costs of language selection. *Journal of Memory and Language* 40: 25–40. doi:10.1006/jmla.1998.2602.

Moreno, S., Bialystok, E., Wodniecka, Z., and Alain, C. (2010). Conflict resolution in sentence processing by bilinguals. *Journal of Neurolinguistics* 27: 50–74. doi:10.1016/j.jneuroling.2013.09.002.

Moser-Mercer, B. (2000). Simultaneous interpreting: cognitive potential and limitations. *Interpreting* 5: 83–94. doi:10.1075/intp.5.2.03mos.

Nebel, K., Wiese, H., Stude, P. et al. (2005). On the neural basis of focused and divided attention. *Cognitive Brain Research* 25: 760–776.

Perani, D., Paulesu, E., Galles, N.S. et al. (1998). The bilingual brain: proficiency and age of acquisition of the second language. *Brain: A Journal of Neurology* 121 (10): 1841–1852.

Perquin, M., Vaillant, M., Schuller, A.M. et al. (2013). Lifelong exposure to multilingualism: new evidence to support cognitive reserve hypothesis. *PLoS One* 8: 1–7. doi:10.1371/journal.pone.0062030.

Pliatsikas, C., DeLuca, V., Moschopoulou, E., and Saddy, J.D. (2017). Immersive bilingualism reshapes the core of the brain. *Brain Structure and Function* 222 (4): 1785–1795.

Pliatsikas, C. and Luk, G. (2016). Executive control in bilingual: a concise review on fMRI studies. *Bilingualism: Language and Cognition* 19 (4): 699–705.

Pliatsikas, C., Moschopoulou, E., and Saddy, J.D. (2015). The effects of bilingualism on the white matter structure of the brain. *PNAS* 112 (5): 1334–1337. doi:10.1073/pnas.1414183112.

Pöchhacker, F. (2004). *Introducing Interpreting Studies*. London, UK: Routledge.

Ratiu, I. and Azuma, T. (2015). Working memory capacity: is there a bilingual advantage? *Journal of Cognitive Psychology,* 27: 1–11. doi:10.1080/20445911.2014.976226.

Richter, F.R. and Yeung, N. (2012). Memory and cognitive control in task switching. *Psychological Science* 23: 1256–1263. doi:10.1177/0956797612444613.

Rodríguez-Pujadas, A., Sanjuán, A., Fuentes, P. et al. (2014). Differential neural control in

early bilinguals and monolinguals during response inhibition. *Brain and Language* 132: 43–51. doi:10.1016/j.bandl.2014.03.003.

Sanders, A.E., Hall, C.B., Katz, M.J., and Lipton, R.B. (2012). Non-native language use and risk of incident dementia in the elderly. *Journal of Alzheimer's Disease* 29: 99–108. doi:10.3233/JAD-2011-111631.

Sandoval, T.C., Gollan, T.H., Ferreira, V.S., and Salmon, D.P. (2010). What causes the bilingual disadvantage in verbal fluency? The dual-task analogy. *Bilingualism: Language and Cognition* 13 (2): 231–252.

Scaltritti, M., Peressotti, F., and Miozzo, M. (2017). Bilingual advantage and language switch: What's the linkage? *Bilingualism: Language and Cognition* 20: 80–97. doi:10.1017/S1366728915000565.

Schwieter, J. and Ferreira, A. (2013). Language selection, control, and conceptual-lexical development in bilinguals and multilinguals. In: *Innovative Research and Practices in Second Language Acquisition and Bilingualism* (ed. J.W. Schwieter), 241–266. Amsterdam, The Netherlands: John Benjamins.

Schwieter, J. and Ferreira, A. (eds.) (2016). *Psycholinguistic and Cognitive Inquiries into Translation and Interpreting*. Amsterdam, The Netherlands: John Benjamins.

Shallice, T. (1994). Multiple levels of control processes. In: *Attention and Performance 15: Conscious and Nonconscious Information Processing* (ed. C. Umilta and M. Moscovitch), 395–420. Cambridge, MA: The MIT Press.

Shreve, G.M. and Diamond, B.J. (1997). Cognitive processes in translation and interpreting. Critical issues. In: *Cognitive Processes in Translation and Interpreting* (ed. J.H. Danks, G.M. Shreve, S.B. Fountain and M.K. McBeath), 233–251. Thousand Oaks, CA: Sage.

Spivey, M.J. and Marian, V. (1999). Cross talk between native and second languages: partial activation of an irrelevant lexicon. *Psychological Science* 10: 281–284.

Stocco, A. and Prat, C.S. (2014). Bilingualism trains specific brain circuits involved in flexible rule selection and application. *Brain and Language* 137: 50–61. doi:10.1016/j.bandl.2014.07.005.

Swainson, R., Cunnington, R., Jackson, G.M., and Rorden, C. (2003). Cognitive control mechanisms revealed by ERP and fMRI: evidence from repeated task-switching. *Journal of Cognitive Neuroscience* 15 (6): 785–799.

von Studnitz, R.E. and Green, D.W. (1997). Lexical decision and language switching. *International Journal of Bilingualism* 1: 3–24. doi:10.1177/136700699700100102.

Vygotsky, L.S. (1962). Thought and Language – Revised Edition. (E. Hanfmann & G. Vakar, Trans.). In: (ed. A. Kozulin). Cambridge, MA: MIT Press (Original work published 1934).

Weissberger, G.H., Gollan, T.H., Bondi, M.W. et al. (2015). Language and task switching in the bilingual brain: bilinguals are staying, not switching, experts. *Neuropsychologia* 66: 193–203. doi:10.1016/j.neuropsychologia.2014.10.037.

Wilson, R.S., Boyle, P.A., Yang, J. et al. (2015). Early life instruction in foreign language

and music and incidence of mild cognitive impairment. *Neuropsychology* 29: 292–302. doi:10.1037/neu0000129.

Wong, B., Yin, B., and O'Brien, B. (2016). Neurolinguistics: structure, function, and connectivity in the bilingual brain. *BioMed Research International* 2016: 1–22. doi:10.1155/2016/7069274.

Woumans, E., Ceuleers, E., Van der Linden, L. et al. (2015). Verbal and nonverbal cognitive control in bilinguals and interpreters. *Journal of Experimental Psychology: Learning, Memory, and Cognition* 41: 1579–1586. doi:10.1037/xlm0000107.

Zahodne, L.B., Schofield, P.W., Farrell, M.T. et al. (2014). Bilingualism does not alter cognitive decline or dementia risk among Spanish-speaking immigrants. *Neuropsychology* 28: 238–246. doi:10.1037/neu0000014.

Zhou, B. and Krott, A. (2016). Bilingualism enhances attentional control in non-verbal conflict tasks – evidence from ex-Gaussian analyses. *Bilingualism: Language and Cognition* 21 (1): 162–180. doi:10.1017/S1366728916000869.

25 Event-Related Potentials in Monolingual and Bilingual Non-literal Language Processing

ANNA SIYANOVA-CHANTURIA,
PAOLO CANAL, AND ROBERTO R. HEREDIA

1. Introduction

Non-literal language has figured prominently in linguistic and psycholinguistic research in the past few decades. Idioms and metaphors, in particular, have long been of interest to researchers working within the realm of online language processing, and the present chapter will largely focus on these two kinds of expressions. For instance, much of the research on idiom processing has focused on comprehension and production in young adults (e.g. Bobrow and Bell 1973; Cacciari and Tabossi 1988; Gibbs 1980; Konopka and Bock 2009; Swinney and Cutler 1979), children (e.g. Abkarian et al. 1992; Cacciari and Levorato 1989; Nippold and Rudzinski 1993), and speech and language impaired patients (e.g. Mondini et al. 2002; Van Lancker and Kempler 1987; Van Lancker-Sidtis et al. 2004). Most of this evidence, however, pertains to figurative language processing in a first language (L1). How idioms and other kinds of non-literal language are processed in second language (L2) speakers[1] is still an underresearched area. In addition, the bulk of current research with native speakers is based on the research that has employed a range of behavioural paradigms and methods. We still know relatively little about the electrophysiological markers involved in non-literal language processing. Even less is known about non-literal language processing in bilingual populations. Although recent years have seen a growing interest in the mechanisms associated with bilingual figurative language processing (e.g. Carrol et al. 2016; Carrol and Conklin 2014; Cieślicka 2006; Heredia and Cieślicka 2016; Matlock and Heredia 2002; Siyanova-Chanturia et al. 2011), few studies to date have employed event-related potentials (ERPs) to investigate the time-course and electrophysiological signature of such processing.

The lacuna left by this paucity motivated the present chapter, whose purpose is twofold. First, we outline the major findings in monolingual research on non-literal

The Handbook of the Neuroscience of Multilingualism, First Edition. Edited by John W. Schwieter.
© 2019 John Wiley & Sons Ltd. Published 2019 by John Wiley & Sons Ltd.

language processing that employed ERPs. Second, we review a handful of ERP studies that have looked at bilingual figurative language processing and highlight the need for further research. Some of the questions we address are: How do L1 and L2 users deal with the ambiguity of language? How does their processing differ for figurative speech compared with novel/literal phrases? Which ERP components are involved in figurative language processing in native and non-native speakers? Does language proficiency in L2 users play a role? How might the pattern of results differ depending on the type of non-literal language (idioms vs. metaphors)?

In the first part of the review, we discuss a number of theories put forward to account for non-literal language representation and access in an L1, as well as some of the pertinent studies with L2 speakers. We then centre on the ERP methodology and, specifically, the ERP components implicated in non-literal language processing. Finally, we review a selection of ERP studies on figurative language processing in monolingual participants, before turning to the studies on non-literal language processing in bilingual populations. We conclude with directions for future research.

2. Representation and Access of Non-literal Language: Theories and Evidence from Behavioural Studies

2.1. Non-literal Language Processing in an L1

Several theories have been put forward over the past decades to explain the representation and processing of figurative language. One characteristic, in particular, has received attention in the literature – the availability of two interpretations, figurative and literal, and how the former is accessed (i.e. idioms) or constructed (i.e. metaphors) in relation to the latter (e.g. Vega-Moreno 2001). Scholars have attempted to explain these processes by drawing either on one-step theories which hold that figurative meaning is directly available (e.g. Davidson 1978; Gibbs 1980), or two-steps theories, according to which figurative meanings are accessed only after the literal meaning has been found to be defective (e.g. Grice 1975; Searle 1979).

One fundamental distinction can be made between those expressions that have a conventional meaning stored in semantic memory, and those expressions that do not have such a meaning stored. On the one hand, in idioms, such as *tie the knot*, the figurative meaning does not directly result from the literal meaning of the words that make up the expression; the meaning is conventional (e.g. Nunberg et al. 1994). On the other hand, comprehension of metaphors, such as *my lawyer is a shark*, hinges on the interaction between the representation of the word *shark* and the larger context in which attributes of a *shark* are transferred to a *lawyer*. How this projection is achieved is a matter of debate. For example, the 'relevance theory' holds that metaphor requires conceptual adjustments (broadening or narrowing) of literal meanings (e.g. Sperber and Wilson 1985), whereas in other accounts, metaphors are understood directly as categorizations (a *lawyer* shares some properties of a *shark*) at a higher level of abstraction (e.g. Glucksberg 2001, 2003). It is noteworthy that this dimension – stored versus constructed – is a continuum, often labelled under the term 'familiarity'.[2]

Processing theories often emphasize the lexical/semantic nature of idioms: idioms are stored in special lists (e.g. idiom list hypothesis, Bobrow and Bell 1973) or represented in the mental lexicon akin to morphologically complex words (e.g. lexical representation hypothesis, Swinney and Cutler 1979), stored as configurations of words (e.g. the configuration hypothesis, Cacciari and Tabossi 1988) or as multiword lemmas – superlemmas (e.g. superlemma hypothesis, Sprenger et al. 2006). The matter of debate resides in how literal and figurative processing interact during ambiguous idiom comprehension. Concerning metaphor comprehension, the mental processes involved often deal with conceptual knowledge, pragmatic enrichment, and abstract thought. Still, the debate is always the same: How do literal and figurative meanings interact?

A range of theories of non-literal language processing has been put forth to account for how literal and figurative meanings are accessed and how they interact. We first briefly discuss the major theories specific to idiom processing, focusing, in particular, on the comprehension of ambiguous idioms (i.e. those that have both a figurative and literal meaning, e.g. *kick the bucket*; compared with *be on cloud nine*, which can only be used figuratively), before turning to those accounts that concern both idioms and metaphors.

The earliest idiom theory, known as the idiom list hypothesis (Bobrow and Bell 1973), proposes that literal meanings of ambiguous idioms are accessed, or attempted, before figurative ones. The literal interpretation is activated first and its plausibility within a given context is evaluated. If the literal interpretation fits the context, it is accepted and no further analysis takes place. If the literal interpretation is rejected, the figurative meaning is then activated and subsequently accepted. However, this serial order appears problematic in that the figurative meaning is almost always more frequent than the literal one. Thus, one would expect the more frequent meaning to be activated and accessed prior to the less frequent one (at least in the absence of a biasing context), akin to what has been found in the research on lexical ambiguity (e.g. Martin et al. 1999).

Another model of idiom comprehension is the lexical representation hypothesis (Swinney and Cutler 1979). In this account, figurative expressions are represented in the mental lexicon akin to morphologically complex words. The computation of the literal meaning and the retrieval of the figurative one are initiated simultaneously. However, because the computation of the literal interpretation is more time-consuming than the retrieval of the figurative one, the latter should be accessed first. With regard to this model and its view of idioms being akin to morphologically complex words, recent studies have shown that regular decompositional analyses are involved in the processing of idioms, at the level of semantics, syntax, and phonology (e.g. Konopka and Bock 2009; Sprenger et al. 2006).

Similar to the lexical representation hypothesis, the configuration hypothesis (e.g. Cacciari and Tabossi 1988) argues that, initially, both literal and figurative meanings of an idiom are accessed in parallel. Unique to this model, however, is the idea of a 'recognition point' – the point at which the conventional expression becomes uniquely recognizable as an idiom. According to this model, literal interpretations of an idiom's constituent words are activated up until the recognition point. As soon as the recognition point has been reached, the intended figurative meaning becomes activated, while the literal one is inhibited. However, the recognition point is not 'fixed' but depends on the context, and therefore, when frequent and conventional idioms are embedded in sentences that bias towards the figurative interpretation, the expression can be recognized as idiomatic before the reader reaches the recognition point.

Another prominent account of non-literal language processing – one that applies to both idioms and metaphors – is the direct access hypothesis (e.g. Gibbs 1980, 1986). According to this model, figurative meanings are accessed prior to, and processed faster than, literal ones. Figurative interpretations are thus thought to be accessed directly, rather than indirectly, that is, after the reader sees the literal meaning as defective (e.g. Grice 1975; Searle 1979), in particular, if supported by an appropriate context. Recent findings, however, do not offer support to this model. For example, in a reading experiment using the eye-movement technique, Siyanova-Chanturia et al. (2011) had native speakers of English read stories containing one of the following: an ambiguous idiom used figuratively, an ambiguous idiom used literally, or a control phrase. Analyses showed no significant differences in the reading of the literal and figurative meaning, suggesting that the two idiom interpretations were processed in a comparable way. Moreover, metaphor processing is often associated with processing costs, which are mitigated when context is supportive (e.g. Bambini et al. 2016), or when expressions are highly familiar (e.g. Lai et al. 2009).

Finally, the graded salience hypothesis (Giora 1997, 2003) puts forth yet another account of how non-literal language is processed. In line with this account, language processing is determined by the degree of salience of a given linguistic unit. That is, what matters is which of the two interpretations (figurative or literal) of an idiom or metaphor is more salient (i.e. familiar, frequent, prototypical, or conventional) as perceived by the language user. The meaning that is more prototypical and thus more salient will be processed first, irrespective of its status as literal or figurative, or the preceding context (e.g. Giora 1997, 2003). Correspondingly, the meaning that is less frequent and less familiar, and is thus less salient, will require more time to be activated and processed.

The models discussed thus far address the question of access of figurative versus literal meanings (items that are identical in form, but different in meaning). Researchers, however, have also been interested in the processing of figurative expressions versus matched novel (i.e. literal propositional) language. A notable example is an early study by Swinney and Cutler (1979) who found that idioms (*break the ice*) were processed more quickly than control phrases (*break the cup*). In another model, known as the idiom decomposition hypothesis, Gibbs et al. (1989) further explored the activation of the figurative meaning of a conventional phrase relative to a novel phrase. Gibbs et al. (1989) proposed that how an idiom is processed depends on whether it is decomposable or non-decomposable. That is, whether or not the literal meanings of individual constituents can be related to the overall figurative meaning of the idiom. Gibbs et al. (1989) proposed that decomposable items (*pop the question*) will be processed faster than controls (*ask the question*), because their components directly contribute to the figurative meaning. In contrast, non-decomposable idioms (*kick the bucket*) will be processed faster than control phrases (*fill the bucket*), because the idiom's constituents do not contribute to the figurative meaning. However, these predictions are not supported by some of the literature. For example, in Tabossi et al. (2009), participants were required to perform a semantic judgement task on decomposable and non-decomposable idioms, as well as their controls. Participants judged both decomposable and non-decomposable idioms faster than controls. Interestingly, clichés, also included in the study, showed a comparable advantage. Thus, the link between the meaning of the idiom's constituents and the overall figurative meaning, or lack thereof, did not affect the idiom processing.

2.2. *Non-literal Language Processing in an L2*

It is noteworthy that behavioural processing research with L2 speakers has primarily looked at idioms. Because idioms are ubiquitous in language, and some occur with high frequencies, there is clearly a need for L2 learners to acquire a rich repertoire of such phrases. The ability of L2 learners to use metaphors, on the contrary, has often not been seen as important (Littlemore and Low 2006). The review below thus centres on idiom processing in L2 speakers.

In one of the earliest such studies employing a cross-modal priming paradigm, Cieślicka (2006) had late second language learners listen to sentences that contained familiar idioms (*Peter was planning to tie the knot later that month*). L2 speakers then performed a lexical decision task on a word associated with the idiom's figurative meaning (*marry*), or its control (*limit*); a word associated with the idiom's literal meaning (*rope*), or its control (*ripe*). The results showed faster response times to the words associated with the idiom's literal meaning than to those linked to the idiom's figurative meaning. A similar finding was observed in Siyanova-Chanturia et al. (2011), who investigated ambiguous idiom processing in a biasing story context by native speakers of English and late L2 learners. They looked at idioms used figuratively (*at the end of the day* – 'eventually'), same sequences used literally (*at the end of the day* – 'in the evening'), and matched novel phrases (i.e., newly constructed phrases, matched in length and frequency with the individual components of the idioms, for example, *at the end of the war*). While native speakers read idioms more quickly than matched novel phrases, their reading of the idiom and the same sequence used literally did not differ. A different pattern of results was observed for L2 speakers, who did not read familiar idioms more quickly than novel language. Crucially, they needed more time to retrieve figurative senses than literal ones. Thus, figurative meanings required more rereading and reanalysis, despite the presence of a biasing context. Interestingly, in a more recent study employing a priming paradigm, Beck and Weber (2016) showed facilitation for both literal and figurative targets (relative to controls) in L2 learners of English. Additionally, the pattern of results observed for L2 speakers was similar to what was found for L1 speakers.

Based on these findings, there are two important conclusions we can arrive at. First, in late L2 learners, literal meanings may be activated and processed prior to their figurative counterparts (but see Beck and Weber 2016), and second, despite their frequency and conventionality, familiar idioms may not enjoy a processing advantage over novel propositional language. Slower reading and response times for idiom figurative uses observed in Cieślicka (2006) and Siyanova-Chanturia et al. (2011) imply that the link between the idiom and its meaning is not as strong as the link between the form and the meaning of the individual lexical items. This is, perhaps, unsurprising since L2 learners are likely to encounter and acquire idioms' constituent words and their literal senses before learning the idioms' figurative meaning. This may especially be the case with lower frequency idioms, such as *bury the hatchet* and *leave a bad taste in your mouth*, used in Cieślicka (2006) and Siyanova-Chanturia et al. (2011), respectively. (Of note, idioms, unlike other instances of formulaic language, such as collocations, lexical bundles, and binomials, are generally of lower frequency and are thus less likely to be encountered and acquired by L2 learners, in particular, where English has been learnt in an English as a Foreign Language context).

Finally, recent behavioural studies have also focused on the issue of L1 influence during idiom processing in an L2 (e.g. Carrol et al. 2016; Carrol and Conklin 2014). Using the eye-tracking paradigm, Carrol et al. (2016) investigated how L1 idiom knowledge was utilized in L2 idiom comprehension. Proficient L2 learners of English (L1 Swedish) read the following items in English: English-only idioms (i.e. those that exist only in English), Swedish-only idioms (i.e. those that exist only in Swedish) translated into English, and congruent idioms with similar L1/L2 form and meaning. Each idiom was paired with a matched control condition. Carrol et al. found a processing advantage not only for English idioms but also for L1 idioms over controls. Carrol et al. took their results to support the view according to which bilingual participants demonstrate 'ballistic activation' when processing language in their L2 (Phillips et al. 2004), wherein the L1 equivalent is automatically activated.

3.   ERPs and Non-literal Language Processing

The electroencephalogram (EEG) is the electrical activity produced by the synchronous firing of large populations of neurons in the cortex recorded from the scalp. ERPs represent the EEG activity time-locked to a particular stimulus and averaged over a large number of trials (e.g. Luck 2014; Rugg and Coles 1995). The greatest advantage of ERPs is their temporal precision, as based on zero-latency electrical transmission between the scalp and the electrodes. This electrophysiological research capitalizes on the neural activity (i.e. ERP components) generated in a brain module and reflecting the activity of a given computational operation (e.g. Kappenman and Luck 2012; Luck 2014). The observed ERP waveform consists of a series of peaks and valleys which derive from the summation of a set of underlying components. ERP components have typical polarity, latency, and scalp distribution. Critically, they have a functional interpretation. These components inform us about the nature of the cognitive processes involved in a linguistic task, such as lexical/semantic, syntactic, or pragmatic processing difficulty.

A number of ERP components have been found to be sensitive to linguistic manipulations. In sections 3.1–3.4, we briefly introduce those most relevant in the context of figurative language processing.

3.1.   N400

The N400 is a negative-going deflection typically occurring between 300 and 500 ms following stimulus onset, most prominent in the centroparietal scalp locations (e.g. Kutas and Federmeier 2011). The N400 has been shown to be sensitive to a variety of linguistic variables. The N400 component was first described by Kutas and Hillyard (1980) who observed that ERPs evoked by semantically incongruent sentence completions elicited larger negativity over posterior scalp locations than congruent sentence completions. After more than 30 years of research into the N400 component (e.g. Kutas and Federmeier 2011), we know that, amongst other factors, it is affected by word frequency (e.g. Van Petten and Kutas 1990), contextual predictability (e.g. Federmeier and Kutas 1999), and world knowledge (e.g. Hagoort and Van Berkum 2007). The N400 effect reflects facilitated access to lexical-conceptual representations (e.g. Lau et al. 2008).

3.2.   P300

The P300 is a positive-going deflection occurring between 250 and 400 ms (e.g. Sutton et al. 1965). The P300 is not a single component; rather, it represents a family of components, for example, the more anterior P3a and the more posterior P3b. Of interest to us is the P3b, which we will refer to as the P300. The P300 is often associated with cognitive mechanisms of context update (e.g. Donchin and Coles 1988) or context closure (e.g. Verleger 1988). Researchers have linked this component to 'template matching' mechanisms. The closer the match between the upcoming information and the mental template, the larger the P300 effects (Kok 2001). Kok (2001) has further linked the early positivity to participants' 'awareness that a stimulus belongs or does not belong to the category of a certain memorised target event' (p. 573). In Roehm et al. (2007, Experiment 1) uniquely constraining contexts (*The opposite of black is white*) resulted in larger P300 amplitudes on the final, highly predictable word (*white*), compared to the related word (*yellow*) and the unrelated word (*nice*). These authors concluded that the anticipated antonymous adjectives elicited larger P300 amplitudes because 'the correct identification of the predicted word does not require a lexical search (there is a unique prediction that may either be fulfilled or not)' (p. 1272).

3.3.   Later Positivities: Late Positive Component (LPC) and P600

3.3.1.   Late Positive Component (LPC)   Another ERP component associated with figurative language processing is the LPC, first reported by Pynte et al. (1996) for metaphor processing. The LPC is a positive deflection of the ERPs that occurs in a relatively late time interval (between 600 and 1000 ms) that can be found over parietal but also frontal scalp locations. The first studies that reported the LPC investigated memory and learning mechanisms (e.g. Neville et al. 1986), and the amplitude of this component was found to be predictive of subsequent memory recall. As described below in some detail, a number of studies on figurative language processing report late positive effects. However, positive effects are often labelled with different names. The studies on irony (e.g. Regel et al. 2011; Spotorno et al. 2013) or jokes (e.g. Coulson and Kutas 2001) discuss these positivities as P600 effects (the former) or simply late positivities (the latter). Compared to what we know about the N400 component, describing the LPC in terms of functional meaning for language processing is almost impossible. One reason for this is that rather few studies report the LPC. Further, there is no general rule that would allow a researcher to decide whether a late positive effect affects the LPC or other components occurring after the N400, such as the P600 component (e.g. Friederici 2011), or the post-N400 positivity (e.g. Van Petten and Luka 2012), because all these effects may occur during the same time window and may have similar topography.

3.3.2. P600 The P600 component is a slow positive shift emerging in a time window around 500–900 ms after stimulus onset (e.g. Osterhout and Holcomb 1992, 1995) that is usually recorded over posterior electrodes (e.g. Molinaro et al. 2011) but can also show a more anterior distribution (e.g. Kaan and Swaab 2003). Traditionally, the P600 component was interpreted as an index of syntactic structure reanalysis or revision processes (e.g. Friederici 2002), and was associated with the violation of syntactic information. More recently, this component has been linked to violations due to semantic information (e.g. Bornkessel-Schlesewsky and Schlesewsky 2008), as well as irony processing and pragmatic interpretation processes (e.g. Regel et al. 2011, 2014).

Whether or not the positive shifts observed in these studies reflect distinct or similar cognitive processes is beyond the scope of this chapter. However, it is worth noting that according to Brouwer and Hoeks's (2013) retrieval-integration hypothesis, language comprehension proceeds in N400-P600 cycles. The N400 reflects retrieval processes from semantic memory, while the P600 reflects the integration of this information with the unfolding representation of the discourse. If we could extend this hypothesis to include other types of positive shifts, we could accommodate the biphasic effects (the N400 followed by the LPC effect) that have been reported in the literature on figurative language.

3.4. ERP Studies on Monolingual Non-literal Language Processing

In this section, we review what is currently known about the processing of non-literal language – familiar and novel – in monolingual populations.

3.4.1. The Processing of Familiar Figurative Language Some of the research has linked conventional non-literal language processing to the modulations of the N400 (e.g. Canal et al. 2017; Laurent et al. 2006; Rommers et al. 2013; Strandburg et al. 1993; Vespignani et al. 2010; see also Liu et al. 2010; Zhang et al. 2013; Zhou et al. 2004) and, to a lesser extent, the P300 component (e.g. Molinaro and Carreiras 2010; Vespignani et al. 2010). One of the first ERP studies to investigate the neural correlates involved in the processing of figurative expressions was Strandburg et al. (1993). Patients with autism and a healthy control group performed a recognition task on conventional idioms, literal control phrases, and nonsensical phrases. Reduced N400s were elicited by the final word of conventional idioms compared with the other two conditions, with an ordered increase in the amplitudes from idiomatic to control to nonsensical phrases in both participant groups, suggesting progressive increases in the depth and difficulty of processing. In a similar study, Laurent et al. (2006) tested Giora's (1997, 2003) graded salience hypothesis that more salient meanings would exhibit a processing advantage compared with less salient ones. Healthy adult participants completed a semantic relatedness task on French idioms that were either strongly or weakly salient. Saliency was defined through conventionality, frequency, familiarity, and prototypicality. Strongly salient idioms were those that 'enjoy a high degree of entrenchment or fixedness' (p. 153), while weakly salient were novel metaphorical expressions. Drawing on the graded salience hypothesis, Laurent et al. (2006) proposed that N400 amplitudes should mirror the degree to which an idiom's meaning is 'foremost on our mind' (p. 151). N400 amplitudes were significantly affected by the degree of salience, with the final word of the strongly salient idioms eliciting reduced negativity compared to the final word of the weakly salient phrases. The authors took these findings to support the graded salience hypothesis and the idea that a more salient meaning will be processed more easily than a less salient one.

In another study, Vespignani et al. (2010) investigated electrophysiological correlates involved in the processing of highly predictable idioms in Italian. Three conditions were looked at: familiar idioms, substitution control condition, and violation control condition, presented in a sentence context. The authors hypothesized that the expectations driven by the activation of a prefabricated chunk (idiom) should differ from those driven by general discourse-based constraints. ERP waveforms were compared on and after the recognition point, defined in line with Cacciari and Tabossi's configuration hypothesis (1988). Vespignani and colleagues observed smaller N400 amplitudes on the word that represented the recognition point in idioms than in the other conditions, interpreted as a processing advantage and easier semantic integration for familiar phrases. Following the recognition point, the idiomatic sentence completions resulted in larger P300 amplitudes than the other conditions. It was proposed that the P300 effect was the result of categorical template matching that 'specifically operates for multiword expressions … when the compositional analysis must be integrated with the retrieval of prefabricated meaning from semantic memory' (p. 1696). A comparable effect was reported in Molinaro and Carreiras (2010) who investigated the comprehension of literal and figurative collocations and observed larger P300s on both types of collocations relative to novel strings of language. In addition, smaller N400 and larger P300 amplitudes were also observed in a recent ERP study looking at the processing of English binomial expressions, such as *bride and groom* (Siyanova-Chanturia et al. 2017). Although the target items in this study were literal and compositional, they were, nonetheless, conventional, akin to idioms used in Vespignani et al. (2010). It thus appears that familiar routinized language, irrespective of its figurative or literal status, may elicit a comparable EEG response, at least in L1 speakers.

Further evidence that idiom processing does not imply a greater lexico-semantic effort reflected in the behaviour of the N400 component comes from Rommers et al. (2013), and Canal et al. (2017). Rommers et al. (2013) showed that the N400 behaviour changes within and outside idiomatic expressions: in literal sentences the N400 is sensitive to subtle differences in semantic relatedness, whereas in idiom processing, expectations are directed towards the idiomatic completion only, suggesting that, to some extent, semantic integration may be switched off. In a more recent study, Canal et al. (2017) compared the processing of unpredictable and ambiguous idioms, such as *break the ice*, embedded in sentences that biased the interpretation of the string as either figurative or literal. Crucially, the cloze probability of the different idiomatic constituents was kept similarly highly constraining. The authors found that the difference associated with the reading of ambiguous expressions following idiomatic versus literal contexts did not modulate the N400 but rather a frontal positivity, interpreted as due to pragmatic processes of meaning enrichment taking place in idiom contexts only.

3.4.2. The Processing of Novel Figurative Language While the above and other similar studies have looked at the processing of highly familiar prefabricated non-literal strings of language, such as idioms and figurative collocations, other ERP studies have investigated the mechanisms involved in the processing of metaphor, irony and jokes. Metaphors, in particular, have received a lot of attention in the ERP research. In a series of experiments, Pynte et al. (1996) compared the processing of familiar (e.g. *those fighters are lions*) and unfamiliar (e.g. *those apprentices are lions*)[3] metaphors with literal sentences (e.g. *those animals are lions*), preceded by a relevant or irrelevant context. Pynte et al. (1996) reported larger N400 amplitudes for metaphorical endings compared with literal endings when metaphors were presented with no preceding context. The differences between novel and familiar metaphors were not reliable when presented in isolation, but emerged when the relevance of the preceding context was manipulated. Metaphors, either familiar or novel, elicited smaller N400 effects and larger LPC effects when preceded by relevant compared to non-relevant contexts. The research that has followed suggested a gradient increase in N400 amplitudes from literal phrases to familiar metaphors, to novel metaphors and to unrelated phrases (e.g. Arzouan et al. 2007; Lai et al. 2009), suggesting cognitively taxing processing for metaphors versus literal language, and for familiar versus unfamiliar metaphorical meaning.

The findings of Pynte et al. (1996) point to an important role of context during metaphor comprehension. It is noteworthy that much of the research has focused on metaphor processing in a minimal context. However, as pointed out by Bambini et al. (2016), in conversations, metaphors are not used in isolation; rather, they are embedded in linguistic and extra-linguistic contexts (also see Yang et al. 2013). Bambini et al. (2016) tested the role of context in the comprehension of literal phrases and metaphors. When the target stimuli were embedded in a minimal context (*Do you know what that fish is? A shark.* versus *Do you know what that lawyer is? A shark*), a biphasic N400-P600 pattern was observed. However, when embedded in a larger supportive context (*That fish is really aggressive. It is a shark.* versus *That lawyer is really aggressive. He is a shark.*), only a P600 effect emerged. Larger N400s in the minimal context condition were linked to the difficulty integrating the unexpected information (*shark*) given the preceding context (*lawyer*), whereas larger P600s were taken to index the cost of a pragmatic process of establishing the intended meaning of the metaphor. It was concluded that supportive linguistic context 'reduces the effort in retrieving lexical aspects of metaphors' (p. 12).

The most cited work on metaphor processing was carried out by Coulson and Van Petten (2002). These authors compared literal sentences (*He knows that whiskey is a strong intoxicant*) with literal mapping sentences (*He has used cough syrup as an intoxicant*) and metaphors (*He knows that power is a strong intoxicant*). According to the conceptual blending theory (Fauconnier and Turner 1998), literal mapping sentences do not require the construction of a metaphorical interpretation, which would be based on particularly abstract aspects of the concept, but still require the recognition of similarities and differences between two distant mental representations of the same concept (i.e. syrup as a medication and syrup as an intoxicant). The target words elicited a graded N400 effect, with literal sentences eliciting the smallest N400, metaphors associated with the largest N400 effect, and literal mapping sentences being in between. Further, it was found that literal mappings elicited a larger LPC across frontal sites, whereas metaphors elicited larger posterior LPC effects. The larger N400 in both literal mappings and metaphor conditions compared to control sentences was interpreted as being due to 'the fact that they both include an invitation to discover the similarity between two entities' (p. 965), whereas the parietal positivity was taken to reflect 'recovery and integration of additional material from semantic memory' (p. 966). The N400-LPC pattern has since been confirmed in several other studies (e.g. Coulson and Van Petten 2007; De Grauwe et al. 2010; Weiland et al. 2014).

Finally, irony and jokes have also been studied in the literature (e.g. Coulson and Kutas 2001; Regel et al. 2011, 2014). Coulson and Kutas (2001) recorded ERPs while participants were reading jokes and non-joke controls. Larger left anterior negative effects followed by late posterior positivity were observed on jokes when compared with literal sentences. In a more recent study, Regel et al. (2011) investigated the comprehension of sentences that contained irony versus control literal sentences (*You should take a break* used ironically or literally). Ironic completions elicited a P600 effect when compared with literal sentences. Interestingly, no differences between the two conditions were observed in the N400 window, suggesting absence of semantic integration difficulty. Regel et al. (2011) concluded that larger P600s, reflecting late inferential processes, might be a marker of the processing and integration of pragmatic information. This finding was further confirmed in Regel et al. (2014) and Spotorno et al. (2013), where ironic sentences were associated with a larger P600 effect compared to literal sentences.

Based on the above review, we can conclude that the processing differences between the various types of figurative language appear consistent in the ERP literature. On the one hand, language users benefit from the highly prefabricated nature of figurative expressions (e.g. conventional idioms vs. literal language), such that phrasal constituents become highly anticipated leading to reduced N400 amplitudes and larger P300s. On the other hand, metaphors – novel metaphors in particular – require more cognitive effort, which can affect lexical retrieval and semantic processing, resulting in larger N400s. Finally, when pragmatic inferences are needed to derive the final interpretation of the sentence, the LPC or P600 effects have been found, as in the case of ambiguous and unpredictable idioms, metaphors, and irony.

3.5.   *ERP Studies on Bilingual Non-literal Language Processing*

Language processing in bilinguals has firmly established itself as one of the key areas in psycholinguistic and neurolinguistic research. Yet, surprisingly few studies have looked at the processing of non-literal language in bilingual populations using ERPs.

In what is arguably the first ERP study looking at non-literal language processing in bilinguals, Moreno et al. (2002) investigated highly proficient English-Spanish bilingual speakers' comprehension of English idiomatic sentences (*Too many cooks can spoil the …*) ending either with a conventional English word (*broth*), its Spanish equivalent code switch (*caldo*), or an English lexical switch (*bouillon*). Expected completions (*broth*) elicited less negative responses in the N400 window than unexpected low probability completions (*bouillon*), suggesting that high probability completions were easier to integrate semantically. Interestingly, the bilinguals' responses to expected conditions in the N400 window were comparable to the amplitudes observed for the Spanish equivalent (*caldo*), suggesting that switching between the two languages did not render processing more effortful, and that it was less costly than processing unexpected within-language items (*bouillon*; for comparison, see behavioural evidence from Titone et al. 2015, who looked at the effect of code switching during idiom processing in English-French bilinguals). When more English-dominant and more Spanish-dominant bilinguals were looked at separately, the response in the N400 window was not found to be dependent on the English language proficiency. It was concluded that all participants, irrespective of language dominance, had equally strong expectations of the upcoming linguistic information. While no differences were found between the expected English completions and their Spanish translations in the N400 window, these conditions elicited distinct responses in a later 450–850 ms window. Spanish equivalents elicited an LPC, suggesting that these code switches were treated akin to unexpected, or improbable, events (Moreno et al. 2002). An alternative interpretation for this positive effect, in line with the studies reviewed in Section 3.4, is that code switches may require more pragmatic inferences to achieve comprehension (Moreno et al. 2002).

In another study, Paulmann et al. (2015) used ERPs to investigate the on-line processing of verb+preposition combinations used literally (*I heard that Mr Smith ran over the old bridge early this morning,* where *run over* = to walk over something) and phrasal verbs used figuratively (*I heard that Mr Smith ran over the old farmer early this morning,* where *run over* = to kill someone by driving). Paulmann et al. looked at the response elicited by disambiguating nouns (*farmer* vs. *bridge*) while monolingual English and proficient late Arabic-English bilinguals read target verbs embedded in neutral contexts. ERP analysis showed more negative amplitudes in the N400 window in response to literal interpretations than figurative ones. No group differences were observed. It was concluded that comparable mechanisms were involved in native and non-native speaker processing of sentences containing phrasal verbs with figurative meanings and verb+preposition combinations with literal meanings. The findings of this study suggest that, at least as far as comprehension is concerned, phrasal verbs are unlikely to cause difficulties for highly proficient L2 users (see Matlock and Heredia 2002, for comparable behavioural results). In cognitive terms, late L2 learners preferred the figurative interpretation over the literal one, just as the native speakers did (see, for example, Laurent et al. 2006; Strandburg et al. 1993; Vespignani et al. 2010). In addition, because no differences were found in the latency of the N400 peak amplitude between the two conditions, the results were interpreted as supporting theories of idiom processing that, in the absence of preceding disambiguating context, allow for parallel activation of figurative and literal meanings (e.g. Cacciari and Tabossi 1988). However, the unusual number of epochs per condition is of concern. The authors compared only 18 literal and non-literal sentences, while the norm in ERP research is to have at least 30 epochs per condition to achieve a satisfactory signal to noise ratio.

Electrophysiological correlates of metaphor processing have also been investigated in the context of bilingualism. Chen et al. (2013) looked at the processing of metaphors in late Chinese-English bilinguals. Participants saw Chinese literal (*Xiaobao is a worker*) and metaphorical (*Life is a music disc*) sentences, and English literal (*Jim is a teacher*) and metaphorical (*Zeal is fire*) sentences. The results showed that English metaphorical sentences elicited the most negative response in the N400 window, followed by English literal sentences, Chinese metaphorical sentences, and Chinese literal sentences, which evoked the smallest N400. Chen et al. took their results to support Giora's (1997) graded salience hypothesis, according to which the less salient stimuli will elicit larger N400s and require more processing effort than the more salient ones. Interestingly, while N400 amplitudes were found more negative for English metaphors than for English literal sentences, the difference in the N400 amplitude between Chinese metaphors and Chinese literal sentences was not significant. This finding may imply different processing mechanisms in an L1 and L2: while L2 literal sentences were easier to process than L2 metaphorical sentences, L1 literal and metaphorical sentences were characterized by comparable processing load. These findings appear to offer some support to Cieślicka's (2006) literal salience account of idiom processing in an L2. However, it is not clear why the authors chose to focus on the 350–600 ms window, rather than the typical N400 window (300–500 ms). Visual inspection of the grand averaged ERPs suggests more negative amplitudes for the Chinese metaphorical condition than the Chinese literal condition (akin to what was found for English sentences) – a difference that might have reached significance had a smaller N400 window been chosen. Further inspection of the included figures suggests that Chinese metaphors elicited the N400-LPC biphasic effect, with larger N400 amplitudes in the canonical time window (300–500 ms), followed by a larger LPC (500–800 ms). In contrast, English metaphors were associated with sustained N400 differences that occurred during the entire time-window (300–600 ms).

Additionally, Ibáñez et al. (2010), investigated the electrophysiological correlates of literal and metaphorical information processing, and how such processing might be modulated by gestures conveyed to participants with either high or low L2 proficiency (German). Native speakers of Spanish with varying L2 German proficiency watched video clips, in German, showing an actor uttering literal (*Those telephones are mobile phones/Those tools are hammers*) and metaphorical (*Those warriors are lions/Those virtues are diamonds*) sentences accompanied by either congruent (person using a phone [literal]/ doing 'a lion attacking' gesture [metaphorical]) or incongruent (person folding hands rather than imitating using a hammer [literal]/person holding a hand in front of the face [metaphorical]) gestures. No differences were observed in the (left anterior) N400 window for the lower proficiency group, whose processing of the four conditions was comparable. In the (left anterior) 500–700 (LPC) time window, the metaphorical incongruent condition evoked more negative waveforms than the other three conditions, which did not differ. The authors concluded that 'subtle differences of verbal expression were not processed in this group' (p. 48). For the higher proficiency speakers, in the N400 and LPC time windows, the metaphorical incongruent condition elicited the largest negativity followed by the literal incongruent condition. The two congruent conditions, metaphorical congruent and literal congruent, produced smallest negativities in these time windows and did not differ. Overall, the higher, but not lower, proficiency participants distinguished between congruent and incongruent gestural information, as well as between literal and metaphorical utterances. It is interesting to note that higher proficiency non-native speakers evoked neuronal responses in the LPC time window similar, in terms of waveform modulations and localization, to those reported for native speakers in another study by Ibáñez et al. (2011). This finding was taken to challenge the idea that there are fundamental differences between language processing in an L1 and L2. An alternative explanation, however, may point to the role of L2 proficiency.

Finally, in Jankowiak et al. (2017), proficient late Polish-English bilinguals performed a semantic decision task on novel (e.g. *to harvest courage*), conventional (e.g. *to gather courage*), literal (e.g. *to experience courage*), and anomalous (e.g. *to move courage*) metaphorical phrases, in L1 Polish and L2 English. In line with the literature on bilingual semantic processing (Moreno et al. 2008), between-language differences were observed in the early N400 window; L1 utterances evoked larger N400 amplitudes than L2 phrases. Larger N400 amplitudes in an L1 than L2 have been linked to greater interconnectivity for the native (dominant) language items (e.g. Midgley et al. 2009). Further, a 20 ms delay was found for L2 items relative to L1 items in the analysis of the N400 peak latency. This finding was interpreted as a delay in the activation of semantic representations in an L2, assumed to be due to lower frequency of occurrence of L2 items relative to L1 items (where participants are L1 dominant and late L2 learners). These between-language differences were found to be independent of utterance type. At the same time, a graded effect of utterance type – independent of language – was observed in the late N400 window. In line with the monolingual literature, smallest N400s were elicited by literal phrases, followed by conventional metaphors, novel metaphors, and anomalous phrases. The construction and lexico-semantic processing of novel metaphors was more taxing than meaning retrieval associated with the comprehension of familiar metaphors (in L1 and L2). Interestingly, between-language differences in metaphor processing did not surface until the LPC window. For L1 items, smaller (rather than larger, as the authors expected) LPC responses were elicited by novel metaphors than familiar metaphors and literal phrases; for L2 items, smaller LPC responses were found for both kinds of metaphors than literal phrases. Reduced LPC amplitudes were interpreted as sustained effort associated with access to the non-literal route during novel meaning computation in an L1 and L2.

4. Conclusion

A number of conclusions can be drawn with respect to the bilingual studies described in this chapter. First, the relevant ERP components have, for the most part, been the N400 and the LPC. Specifically, where the target stimuli were frequent and highly familiar word sequences, such as idioms (e.g. Moreno et al. 2002) and phrasal verbs (e.g. Paulmann et al. 2015), expected high probability figurative completions were associated with reduced N400s compared with unexpected, low probability literal endings, suggesting easier semantic integration for the former. This finding corroborates a body of research with monolingual populations (e.g. Laurent et al. 2006; Strandburg et al. 1993; Vespignani et al. 2010). When the target stimuli were metaphors, their processing was generally associated with larger N400s, smaller LPC responses (e.g. Jankowiak et al. 2017) and seemingly larger LPC responses (e.g. Chen et al. 2013) relative to literal phrases. (It is noteworthy that in the L1 literature, metaphor processing has been linked to both larger and smaller LPC amplitudes compared to literal phrases, depending on how supportive the context is). These findings have been taken to support the view that less salient metaphorical instances may require more processing effort than more salient literal ones. Interestingly, metaphor processing in an L2 has also been found comparable to that of literal phrases in the N400 and LPC windows (e.g. Ibáñez et al. 2010). However, Ibáñez et al. (2010) looked at multimodal integration of gestures and metaphors, which makes it difficult to directly link the observed ERP pattern to metaphor comprehension.

Second, current research with bilingual populations offers mixed support to the idea that distinct correlates may be involved in monolingual and bilingual language processing. Research into bilingual versus monolingual processing of semantic violations has shown a significant delay in the peak latency of the N400 for L2 speakers relative to L1 speakers (e.g. Moreno et al. 2008). In addition, N400 amplitudes have been found to be modulated by language proficiency, with less proficient language use associated with smaller amplitudes compared with more proficient language use (e.g. between-groups design: Hahne 2001; within-groups design: Kutas and Kluender 1994). Although it is believed that a late age of L2 exposure and a lower proficiency could be the factors contributing to this pattern of results (e.g. Moreno et al. 2008), an early age of L2 exposure does not necessarily imply a response akin to that in an L1 (e.g. Moreno and Kutas 2005). Although the general bilingual literature suggests a different time-course – at least in terms of the N400 peak latency – for semantic processing in monolinguals and bilinguals, Paulmann et al. (2015) found no differences between monolingual and bilingual participants in the analysis of N400 amplitudes or in the peak time analysis. Partial support for a different latency of the N400 effect can be found in the data presented in Chen et al. (2013), based on the visual inspection of the waveforms: when presented with English (but not Chinese) metaphors, late Chinese-English bilinguals exhibited a sustained N400 effect. More robust L1/L2 differences were found in a within-group design study by Jankowiak et al. (2017), who observed smaller N400 amplitudes on L2 than L1 utterances (irrespective of the type), and a small delay for L2 items in the analysis of the N400 peak latency. Between-language differences were also observed in metaphor processing in the LPC, but not N400, window.

Third, proficiency of the L2 speakers in question might be a determining factor in non-literal language processing. As noted by Hahne (2001, p. 252), 'proficiency level in L2 might be the most important variable'. As we have argued, higher proficiency L2 speakers in Ibáñez et al. (2010) elicited responses comparable to those reported for native speakers in the LPC window in Ibáñez et al. (2011). In comparison, lower proficiency L2 users differed both from their higher proficiency L2 speakers in the same study, as well as from monolinguals in Ibáñez et al. (2011).

Because ERP research in bilingual non-literal language processing is extremely limited, the conclusions we can arrive at are equally constraining. Clearly, research in bilingual figurative language processing is very much in its infancy, and there are a number of important questions that remain unanswered. Researchers working on bilingual figurative language processing employing ERPs can, however, draw on the monolingual literature on non-literal language processing, as well as on the bilingual literature more generally. For example, informed decisions need to be made with respect to whether a between-groups (e.g. Paulmann et al. 2015) or within-groups design (e.g. Chen et al. 2013; Jankowiak et al. 2017) is more appropriate or sensitive to accurately assess bilingual language processing. As noted by Moreno et al. (2008), ERP differences resulting from between-groups comparisons need to be interpreted with caution as ERPs can vary between groups in many different ways (p. 484). At the same time, within-subjects comparisons require a careful matching of L1 and L2 items, so that any observed effects are not merely reflecting possible differences in stimuli difficulty (Moreno et al. 2008, p. 484).

The processing of a wider range of non-literal language should also be considered in bilingual participants. As we have reviewed, the monolingual literature shows a variety of figurative expressions, such as two-word phrases (e.g. Strandburg et al. 1993), conventional idioms (e.g. Laurent et al. 2006; Vespignani et al. 2010), metaphors (e.g. Coulson and Van Petten 2002; Lai et al. 2009), irony (e.g. Regel et al. 2011, 2014; Spotorno et al. 2013), and jokes (e.g. Coulson and Kutas 2001). In comparison, bilingual studies have been limited to idiomatic expressions and metaphors. Future studies with bilingual populations might consider varying familiarity, predictability, and other factors known to affect idiom processing in L1 (e.g. Canal et al. 2017; Molinaro and Carreiras 2010; Vespignani et al. 2010). Because idiom comprehension largely depends on whether or not a language user knows the expression as prefabricated, or formulaic, one might expect to find differences in the N400 and, possibly, P300 windows between idioms and non-idioms in higher, but not lower, proficiency L2 speakers.[4] The modulation of the N400 and P300 may thus serve as an index of language proficiency.

Behavioural research into non-literal language comprehension in bilingual participants can also offer important insights to future ERP studies. For example, the issue of L1 influence during idiom processing in an L2 can further be fruitfully explored using ERPs. In Carrol et al. (2016), proficient L2 learners treated L1 (Swedish) idioms presented as translations in L2 (English) as conventional strings of language, even though these idioms do not exist in English. This finding implies that during L2 idiom processing, L1 knowledge is automatically activated. An interesting question is whether the electrophysiological markers associated with the comprehension of idioms in an L2 may differ for L1/L2 congruent versus incongruent idioms.

Finally, similar to the ERP studies with monolingual participants (e.g. Bambini et al. 2016; Pynte et al. 1996), future research with bilingual populations can tap into the role of context during non-literal language processing. Bambini et al. (2016) observed a biphasic N400-P600 pattern when metaphors were presented in a minimal context. In contrast, when embedded in a supportive context, a monophasic P600 was found, suggesting that the preceding linguistic context reduced the effort associated with retrieving lexical aspects of metaphors in monolingual participants. A question that lends itself to future interrogations is whether or not the supportive context might have the same facilitative effect in metaphor processing in an L2.

Through our inevitably selective review, we have covered some of the major studies and issues pertinent to L1 non-literal language processing, and hope to have set some ground for much needed research in bilingual non-literal language processing using ERPs. Despite the fact that ERPs have long been used in research on bilinguals, we still know remarkably little about the electrophysiological correlates involved in bilingual figurative language processing. Clearly, this line of research is at its very early stages. It can, however, fruitfully draw on the literature on the psychophysiology of monolingual processing of idioms, metaphors, irony, and jokes. We believe that by drawing on a variety of figurative language uses (that vary along the dimensions of frequency, predictability, salience, conventionality, familiarity, metaphoricity, and novelty), by looking at a range of L2 proficiency versus language dominance (e.g. Heredia and Cieślicka 2016) and background (high vs. low proficiency L2 users, early and late L2 learners), and by adopting a more rigorous approach to experimental design, data collection and analysis (akin to the norms in the L1 literature), as well as the careful selection of experimental tasks (e.g. implicit vs. explicit; Cieślicka et al. 2017; García et al. 2015), future studies will be able to address important unresolved issues and advance this emerging field of research.

NOTES

1   In this review, we use the terms second language speakers and bilinguals interchangeably. We thus adopt an inclusive approach to bilingualism, wherein both early and late learners of an additional language are deemed bilinguals. Where necessary we specify and discuss the role of proficiency and age of exposure.
2   As was noted by one of the reviewers, some idioms are naturally underpinned by metaphors. For example, although *tie the knot* is an idiom, it can be argued that there is also a metaphor of joining two things that motivates the idiom's overall meaning.
3   Here and throughout the chapter, we define familiar metaphors as conventional and 'readily interpretable' (Lai et al. 2009, p. 145) sequences, known to the speech community in question. In contrast, unfamiliar metaphors are novel, original, newly created strings of language that are 'harder to interpret' (Lai et al. 2009, p. 145).
4   The same argument applies to those formulaic sequences that are literal and compositional, such as lexical bundles (e.g. *to start with*), collocations (e.g. *fresh air*), and binomials (e.g. *knife and fork*). Higher, but not lower, proficiency L2 users may be sensitive to the differences – in terms of frequency and predictability – between conventional versus novel language in the N400 and P300 windows (see Siyanova-Chanturia et al. 2017 for a study with L1 speakers).

REFERENCES

Abkarian, G., Jones, A., and West, G. (1992). Young children's idiom comprehension: trying to get the picture. *Journal of Speech and Hearing Research* 35: 580–587.

Arzouan, Y., Goldstein, A., and Faust, M. (2007). Brainwaves are stethoscopes: ERP correlates of novel metaphor comprehension. *Brain Research* 1160: 69–81.

Bambini, V., Bertini, C., Schaeken, W. et al. (2016). Disentangling metaphor from context: an ERP study. *Frontiers in Psychology* 7: 559. https://doi.org/10.3389/fpsyg.2016.00559.

Beck, S. and Weber, A. (2016). Bilingual and monolingual idiom processing is cut from the same cloth: the role of the L1 in literal and figurative meaning activation. *Frontiers in Psychology* https://doi.org/10.3389/fpsyg.2016.01350.

Bobrow, S. and Bell, S. (1973). On catching on to idiomatic expressions. *Memory & Cognition* 1 (3): 343–346.

Bornkessel-Schlesewsky, I. and Schlesewsky, M. (2008). An alternative perspective on 'semantic P600' effects in language comprehension. *Brain Research Reviews* 59 (1): 55–73.

Brouwer, H. and Hoeks, J.C. (2013). A time and place for language comprehension: mapping the N400 and the P600 to a minimal cortical network. *Frontiers in Human Neuroscience* 7: 758. https://doi.org/10.3389/fnhum.2013.00758.

Cacciari, C. and Levorato, M. (1989). How children understand idioms in discourse. *Journal of Child Language* 16: 387–405.

Cacciari, C. and Tabossi, P. (1988). The comprehension of idioms. *Journal of Memory and Language* 27: 668–683.

Canal, P., Pesciarelli, F., Vespignani, F. et al. (2017). Basic composition and enriched integration in idiom processing: an EEG study. *Journal of Experimental Psychology: Learning, Memory, and Cognition* 43 (6): 928–943.

Carrol, G. and Conklin, K. (2014). Getting your wires crossed: evidence for fast processing of L1 idioms in an L2. *Bilingualism: Language and Cognition* 17 (4): 784–797.

Carrol, G., Conklin, K., and Gyllstad, H. (2016). Found in translation. The influence of the L1 on the reading of idioms in a L2. *Studies in Second Language Acquisition* 38:403–443.

Chen, H., Peng, X., and Zhao, Y. (2013). An ERP study on metaphor comprehension in the bilingual brain. *Chinese Journal of Applied Linguistics* 36 (4): 505–517.

Cieślicka, A.B. (2006). Literal salience in on-line processing of idiomatic expressions by second language learners. *Second Language Research* 22 (2): 115–144.

Cieślicka, A.B., García, T., and Heredia, R.R. (2017). Task effects in bilingual idiom comprehension. *Poznań Studies in Contemporary Linguistics* 53 (1): 95–117. https://doi.org/10.1515/psicl-2017-0005.

Coulson, S. and Kutas, M. (2001). Getting it: human event-related brain response to jokes in good and poor comprehenders. *Neuroscience Letters* 316 (2): 71–74.

Coulson, S. and Van Petten, C. (2002). Conceptual integration and metaphor: an event-related potential study. *Memory & Cognition* 30 (6): 958–968.

Coulson, S. and Van Petten, C. (2007). A special role for the right hemisphere in metaphor comprehension? ERP evidence from hemifield presentation. *Brain Research* 1146: 128–145.

Davidson, D. (1978). What metaphors mean. *Critical Inquiry* 5 (1): 31–47.

De Grauwe, S., Swain, A., Holcomb, P.J. et al. (2010). Electrophysiological insights into the processing of nominal metaphors. *Neuropsychologia* 48 (7): 1965–1984.

Donchin, E. and Coles, M. (1988). Is the P300 component a manifestation of context updating? *Behavioral and Brain Sciences* 11: 357–374.

Fauconnier, G. and Turner, M. (1998). Conceptual integration networks. *Cognitive Science* 22 (2): 133–187.

Federmeier, K. and Kutas, M. (1999). A rose by any other name: long term memory structure and sentence processing. *Journal of Memory and Language* 41: 469–495.

Friederici, A.D. (2002). Towards a neural basis of auditory sentence processing. *Trends in Cognitive Sciences* 6 (2): 78–84.

Friederici, A.D. (2011). The brain basis of language processing: from structure to function. *Physiological Reviews* 91 (4): 1357–1392.

García, O., Cieślicka, A.B., and Heredia, R.R. (2015). Nonliteral language processing and methodological considerations. In: *Bilingual Figurative Language Processing* (ed. R.R. Heredia and A.B. Cieślicka), 117–168. New York, NY: University of Cambridge Press.

Gibbs, R. (1980). Spilling the beans on understanding and memory for idioms in conversation. *Memory & Cognition* 8: 449–456.

Gibbs, R. (1986). Skating on thin ice: literal meaning and understanding of idioms in conversation. *Discourse Processes* 9: 17–30.

Gibbs, R., Nayak, N., and Cutting, C. (1989). How to kick the bucket and not decompose: analyzability and idiom processing. *Journal of Memory and Language* 28: 576–593.

Giora, R. (1997). Understanding figurative and literal language: the graded salience hypothesis. *Cognitive Linguistics* 7: 183–206.

Giora, R. (2003). *On our Mind: Salience, Context, and Figurative Language*. Oxford, UK: Oxford University Press.

Glucksberg, S. (2001). *Understanding Figurative Language: From Metaphor to Idioms*. Oxford, UK: Oxford University Press.

Glucksberg, S. (2003). The psycholinguistics of metaphor. *Trends in Cognitive Sciences* 7 (2): 92–96.

Grice, H.P. (1975). Logic and conversation. In: *Syntax and Semantics: Speech Acts*, vol. 3 (ed. P. Cole and J. Morgan), 41–58. New York, NY: Academic Press.

Hagoort, P. and Van Berkum, J. (2007). Beyond the sentence given. *Philosophical Transactions of the Royal Society, B: Biological Sciences* 362 (1481): 801–811.

Hahne, A. (2001). What's different in second-language processing? Evidence from event-related brain potentials. *Journal of Psycholinguistic Research* 30 (3): 251–266.

Heredia, R.R. and Cieślicka, A.B. (2016). Metaphoric reference: an eye movement analysis of Spanish–English and English–Spanish bilingual readers. *Frontiers in Psychology* 7: 439. doi:10.3389/fpsyg. 2016.00439.

Ibáñez, A., Manes, F., Escobar, J. et al. (2010). Gesture influences the processing of figurative language in non-native speakers: ERP evidence. *Neuroscience Letters* 471 (1): 48–52.

Ibáñez, A., Toro, P., Cornejo, C. et al. (2011). High contextual sensitivity of metaphorical expressions and gesture blending: a video event-related potential design. *Psychiatry Research: Neuroimaging* 191 (1): 68–75.

Jankowiak, K., Rataj, K., and Naskręcki, R. (2017). To electrify bilingualism: electrophysiological insights into bilingual metaphor comprehension. *PLoS One* 12 (4): e0175578. doi:10.1371/journal.pone.0175578.

Kaan, E. and Swaab, T. (2003). Repair, revision, and complexity in syntactic analysis: an electrophysiological differentiation. *Journal of Cognitive Neuroscience* 15 (1): 98–110.

Kappenman, E.S. and Luck, S.J. (2012). ERP components: the ups and downs of brainwave recordings. In: *The Oxford Handbook of Event-Related Potential Components* (ed. E. Kappenman and S. Luck), 3–30. Oxford, UK: Oxford University Press.

Kok, A. (2001). On the utility of P300 amplitude as a measure of processing capacity. *Psychophysiology* 38: 557–577.

Konopka, A. and Bock, K. (2009). Lexical or syntactic control of sentence formulation? Structural generalizations from idiom production. *Cognitive Psychology* 58 (1): 68–101.

Kutas, M. and Federmeier, K.D. (2011). Thirty years and counting: finding meaning in the N400 component of the event related brain potential (ERP). *Annual Review of Psychology* 62: 621–647.

Kutas, M. and Hillyard, S.A. (1980). Reading senseless sentences: brain potentials reflect semantic incongruity. *Science* 207 (4427): 203–205.

Kutas, M. and Kluender, R. (1994). What is who violating? A reconsideration of linguistic violations in light of event-related brain potentials. In: *Cognitive Electrophysiology* (ed. H.-J. Heinze, T.F. Munte and G.R. Mangun), 183–210. Boston, MA: Birkhauser.

Lai, V.T., Curran, T., and Menn, L. (2009). Comprehending conventional and novel metaphors: an ERP study. *Brain Research* 1284: 145–155.

Lau, E.F., Phillips, C., and Poeppel, D. (2008). A cortical network for semantics: (de) constructing the N400. *Nature Reviews Neuroscience* 9 (12): 920–933.

Laurent, J., Denhières, G., Passerieux, C. et al. (2006). On understanding idiomatic language. *Brain Research* 1068: 151–160.

Littlemore, J. and Low, G. (2006). Metaphoric competence, second language learning, and communicative language ability. *Applied Linguistics* 27 (2): 268–294.

Liu, Y., Li, P., Shu, H. et al. (2010). Structure and meaning in Chinese: an ERP study of idioms. *Journal of Neurolinguistics* 23 (6): 615–630.

Luck, S.J. (2014). *An Introduction to the Event-Related Potential Technique*. Cambridge, MA: MIT Press.

Martin, C., Vu, H., Kellas, G., and Metcalf, K. (1999). Strength of discourse context as a determinant of the subordinate bias effect. *The Quarterly Journal of Experimental Psychology* 52A (4): 813–839.

Matlock, T. and Heredia, R. (2002). Understanding phrasal verbs in monolinguals and bilinguals. In: *Bilingual Sentence Processing* (ed. R. Heredia and J. Altarriba), 251–274. Holland, The Netherlands: Elsevier Press.

Midgley, K.J., Holcomb, P.J., and Grainger, J. (2009). Language effects in second language learners and proficient bilinguals investigated with event-related potentials. *Journal of Neurolinguistics* 22 (3): 281–300.

Molinaro, N., Barber, H.A., and Carreiras, M. (2011). Grammatical agreement processing in reading: ERP findings and future directions. *Cortex* 47 (8): 908–930.

Molinaro, N. and Carreiras, M. (2010). Electrophysiological evidence of interaction between contextual expectation and semantic integration during the processing of collocations. *Biological Psychology* 83 (3): 176–190.

Mondini, S., Jarema, G., Luzzatti, C. et al. (2002). Why is 'red cross' different from 'yellow cross'?: a neurophysiological study of non-adjective agreement within Italian compounds. *Brain and Language* 81: 621–634.

Moreno, E., Federmeier, K., and Kutas, M. (2002). Switching languages, switching *palabras* (words): an electrophysiological study of code switching. *Brain and Language* 80: 188–207.

Moreno, E.M. and Kutas, M. (2005). Processing semantic anomalies in two languages: an electrophysiological exploration in both languages of Spanish-English bilinguals. *Brain Research. Cognitive Brain Research* 22 (2): 205–220.

Moreno, E.M., Rodrigues-Fornells, A., and Laine, M. (2008). Event-related potentials (ERPs) in the study if bilingual language processing. *Journal of Neurolinguistics* 21: 477–508.

Neville, H.J., Kutas, M., Chesney, G., and Schmidt, A.L. (1986). Event-related brain potentials during initial encoding and recognition memory of congruous and incongruous words. *Journal of Memory and Language* 25 (1): 75–92.

Nippold, M. and Rudzinski, M. (1993). Familiarity and transparency in idiom explanation: a developmental study of children and adolescents. *Journal of Speech and Hearing Research* 36: 728–737.

Nunberg, G., Sag, I.A., and Wasow, T. (1994). Idioms. *Language* 70 (3): 491–538.

Osterhout, L. and Holcomb, P.J. (1992). Event-related brain potentials elicited by syntactic anomaly. *Journal of Memory and Language* 31 (6): 785–806.

Osterhout, L. and Holcomb, P.J. (1995). Event-related potentials and language comprehension. In: *Electrophysiology of Mind: Event-Related Brain Potentials and Cognition* (ed. M.D. Rugg and M.G.H. Coles), 171–215. Oxford, UK: Oxford University Press.

Paulmann, S., Ghareeb-Ali, Z., and Felser, C. (2015). Neurophysiological markers of phrasal verb processing: evidence from L1 and L2 speakers. In: *Bilingual Figurative Language Processing* (ed. R.R. Heredia and A.B. Cieślicka), 245–267. New York, NY: Cambridge University Press.

Phillips, N.A., Segalowitz, N., O'Brien, I., and Yamasaki, N. (2004). Semantic priming in a first and second language: evidence from reaction time variability and event-related brain potentials. *Journal of Neurolinguistics* 17: 237–262.

Pynte, J., Besson, M., Robichon, F.-H., and Poli, J. (1996). The time-course of metaphor comprehension: an event-related potential study. *Brain and Language* 55 (3): 293–316.

Regel, S., Gunter, T.C., and Friederici, A.D. (2011). Isn't it ironic? An electrophysiological exploration of figurative language processing. *Journal of Cognitive Neuroscience* 23 (2): 277–293.

Regel, S., Meyer, L., & Gunter, T. C. (2014). Distinguishing neurocognitive processes reflected by P600 effects: Evidence from ERPs and neural oscillations. Retrieved from http://dx.plos.org/10.1371/journal.pone.0096840

Roehm, D., Bornkessel-Schlesewsky, I., Rösler, F., and Schlesewsky, M. (2007). To predict or not to predict: influences of task and strategy on the processing of semantic relations. *Journal of Cognitive Neuroscience* 19: 1259–1274.

Rommers, J., Dijkstra, T., and Bastiaansen, M. (2013). Context-dependent semantic processing in the human brain: evidence from idiom comprehension. *Journal of Cognitive Neuroscience* 25 (5): 762–776.

Rugg, M.D. and Coles, M.G. (1995). *Electrophysiology of Mind: Event-Related Brain Potentials and Cognition*. Oxford, UK: Oxford University Press.

Searle, J.R. (1979). Intentionality and the use of language. In: *Meaning and Use* (ed. A. Margalit), 181–197. New York, NY: Springer.

Siyanova-Chanturia, A., Conklin, K., Caffarra, S. et al. (2017). Representation and processing of multi-word expressions in the brain. *Brain and Language* 175: 111–122.

Siyanova-Chanturia, A., Conklin, K., and Schmitt, N. (2011). Adding more fuel to the fire: an eye-tracking study of idiom processing by native and nonnative speakers. *Second Language Research* 27: 251–272.

Sperber, D. and Wilson, D. (1985). Loose talk. In: *Proceedings of the Aristotelian Society,* vol. 86, 153–171. Oxford, UK: Oxford University Press on behalf of The Aristotelian Society.

Spotorno, N., Cheylus, A., Van Der Henst, J.B., and Noveck, I.A. (2013). What's behind a P600? Integration operations during irony processing. *PLoS One* 8 (6): e66839.

Sprenger, S., Levelt, W., and Kempen, G. (2006). Lexical access during the production of idiomatic phrases. *Journal of Memory and Language* 54: 161–184.

Strandburg, R., Marsh, J., Brown, W. et al. (1993). Event-related potentials in high-functioning adult autistics. *Neuropsychologia* 31: 413–434.

Swinney, D. and Cutler, A. (1979). The access and processing of idiomatic expressions. *Journal of Verbal Learning and Verbal Behaviour* 18: 523–534.

Tabossi, P., Fanari, R., and Wolf, K. (2009). Why are idioms recognized fast? *Memory & Cognition* 37 (4): 529–540.

Titone, D., Columbus, G., Whitford, V. et al. (2015). Contrasting bilingual and monolingual idiom processing. In: *Bilingual Figurative Language* (ed. R.R. Heredia and A.B. Cieślicka), 71–207. Cambridge, UK: Cambridge University Press.

Van Lancker, D. and Kempler, D. (1987). Comprehension of familiar phrases by left- but not by right-hemisphere damaged patients. *Brain and Language* 32: 265–277.

Van Lancker-Sidtis, D., Postman, W., and Glosser, G. (2004). Feast or famine: fixed expressions in the spontaneous speech of left hemisphere- and right hemisphere-damaged participants. *Brain and Language* 91: 47–48.

Van Petten, C. and Kutas, M. (1990). Interactions between sentence context and word frequency in event-related brain potentials. *Memory & Cognition* 18: 380–393.

Van Petten, C. and Luka, B.J. (2012). Prediction during language comprehension: benefits, costs, and ERP components. *International Journal of Psychophysiology* 83 (2): 176–190.

Vega-Moreno, R.E. (2001). Representing and processing idioms. *UCL Working Papers in Linguistics* 13: 73–109.

Verleger, R. (1988). Event-related potentials and cognition: a critique of the context-updating hypothesis and an alternative interpretation of the P300. *Behavioral and Brain Sciences* 11: 343–427.

Vespignani, F., Canal, P., Molinaro, N. et al. (2010). Predictive mechanisms in idiom comprehension. *Journal of Cognitive Neuroscience* 22 (8): 1682–1700.

Weiland, H., Bambini, V., and Schumacher, P.B. (2014). The role of literal meaning in figurative language comprehension: evidence from masked priming ERP. *Frontiers in Human Neuroscience* 8: 583.

Yang, F.-P.G., Bradeley, K., Huq, M. et al. (2013). Contextual effects on conceptual blending in metaphors: an event-related potential study. *Journal of Neurolinguistics* 26: 312–326.

Zhang, H., Yang, Y., Gu, J., and Ji, F. (2013). ERP correlates of compositionality in Chinese idiom comprehension. *Journal of Neurolinguistics* 26 (1): 89–112.

Zhou, S., Zhou, W., and Chen, X. (2004). Spatiotemporal analysis of ERP during Chinese idiom comprehension. *Brain Topography* 17 (1): 27–37.

Part IV Impairments and Disorders

26 Aphasia in the Multilingual Population

ELISA CARGNELUTTI, BARBARA TOMASINO, AND FRANCO FABBRO

1. Introduction

Aphasia is a clinical condition affecting language as a consequence of a lesion to the sensory, motor, or cognitive brain networks that support language. The lesion can impair production and/or comprehension of spoken and/or written language. Clinical manifestations of aphasia in people mastering more than one language are not generally distinguished from those observed in the monolingual population. Nevertheless, as we are going to see, the clinical profile of multilingual patients displays some peculiar features specifically related to their multilingual status. Noteworthy, aphasia may manifest differently in the diverse languages known by a patient. This means the languages are not necessarily equally compromised and that symptoms and deficits can differ. Further, problems related to the proper use of each language may occur. This chapter is therefore aimed at illustrating the diverse clinical patterns of impairment, in an attempt to shed light on the factors contributing to these profiles.

Every possible consideration is obviously dependent on the initial diagnosis. This implies an exhaustive and thorough assessment of the patient's aphasic symptoms in each language, because a rough evaluation may bias the actual impairment. Given the importance of aphasia assessment, we begin our dissertation by discussing this fundamental issue.

2. Assessment of Multilingual Aphasia

As a bilingual is not the mere sum of two monolinguals (Grosjean 1989), applying the procedure to assess aphasia in monolinguals also in people knowing more than one language is likely to be inadequate. The first tricky point concerns the evaluation of the actual impairment in each language. To this end, it is fundamental to establish the premorbid status of each language, as an individual's performance in one language might have been very poor already premobidly. Related to this, is the issue of the relative

The Handbook of the Neuroscience of Multilingualism, First Edition. Edited by John W. Schwieter.
© 2019 John Wiley & Sons Ltd. Published 2019 by John Wiley & Sons Ltd.

impairment of one language with respect to the other, with the additional complication that the lesion may affect dominance relations between languages (i.e. which language is the strongest or dominant and which is instead the weakest). Understanding this relation is important as it can be predictive of the impairment and also guide the setup of rehabilitation programs (Goral et al. 2013).

As regards the first point, since a direct evaluation of premorbid language proficiency is not possible, indirect information can be obtained by a retrospective evaluation, generally consisting in self-assessments through which patients rate their abilities. In some cases, self-ratings are integrated with, or replaced by (when self-rating is not possible), evaluations by the patient's relatives. However, this is a simplistic approach, as individuals can make a rough evaluation of their language skills and/or underestimate or overestimate them.

This difficulty could be partially overcome by structured interviews or specific questionnaires such as the language use questionnaire (LUQ, by Muñoz et al. 1999; see Kiran et al. 2010). These measures investigate different aspects related to language history, including the mode (e.g. spontaneous vs. formal) and age of appropriation (AoA) of each language and their context and frequency of use. The most recent evidence suggests that the combination of the two measures can provide a quite reliable evaluation (self-ratings and interviews, see Gollan et al. 2012).

With regard to evaluation of deficits, use of batteries developed for monolinguals is a debated issue. Amongst them, the Aachen aphasia test (AAT, Huber et al. 1984), the Boston diagnostic aphasia examination (BDAE, Goodglass and Kaplan 1972), the psycholinguistic assessment of language processing in aphasia (PALPA, Kay et al. 1992), and the Western aphasia battery (WAB, Kertesz 1982) are valuable measures to investigate aphasic deficits, particularly in the languages for which they have been developed. Their adaptation to other languages is not easy, as items need to be of comparable difficulty and have similar sociocultural valence. One language may appear to be impaired not because it is so, but because it differs from another under diverse linguistic aspects. Cultural inappropriateness is equally important: some items may refer to objects and concepts that are uncommon or improper in a given language (see Ivanova and Hallowell 2013, for a discussion on appropriate testing).

An aphasia battery for multilingual individuals was specifically developed by Paradis (Paradis and Libben 1987). The bilingual aphasia test (BAT), which is available in more than 70 languages, aims to provide the most systematic and congruent possible evaluation of aphasia deficits in each of the languages spoken by an individual. Its core feature is that the BAT versions are not mere translations but real adaptations, taking into account the structural and even cultural characteristics of the various languages.

The BAT consists of three main sections. Part A focuses on language history, which we have just stated to be a crucial point. Part B investigates competences in each language at the word, sentence, and discourse levels, and through four modalities (i.e. hearing, speaking, reading, and writing). The last section, Part C, is innovative because it is dedicated to specific language pairs (e.g. English-French or Japanese-Portuguese) to explore residual abilities in the two languages known by a patient. It evaluates translation abilities and critical aspects such as reversible contrastive features. These are obligatory elements of one language that are unacceptable in the other and whose exact translation is therefore considered to be an error (e.g. obligatory use of the future tense in French vs. use of the present tense in English). This is particularly useful when investigating language dominance, given that patients may recognize as incorrect only sentences in the strongest language containing features of the weakest, but not vice versa.

The clinical assessment validity of the BAT was widely demonstrated. Compared to other tests (see Peristeri and Tsapkini 2011), it provides a more exhaustive examination and a more fine-grained characterization of symptoms and enables discrimination between similar but distinct clinical conditions (e.g. Alzheimer's disease vs. mild cognitive impairment, Gómez-Ruiz and Aguilar-Alonso 2011).

In this discussion, we implicitly assumed that the assessment should involve all the languages employed by the patient; however, this is not generally so. However, all the languages should be considered, for two reasons: first, addressing only one of them prevents a global view of the problem and, second, it is ethically unacceptable, given the differential relevance that each language can have in the patient's social, emotional, and professional life.

3.   Typical Symptoms of Multilingual Aphasia

Assessing aphasia OR Aphasia assesment entails an evaluation of the symptoms that are peculiar to the multilingual status. For example, some lesions can impair the ability to translate or properly regulate the use of languages. Patients can involuntarily mix languages or switch between them or, on the contrary, be unable to purposefully shift between languages. As we are going to see, these phenomena are more likely following lesions to specific brain areas.

3.1.   *Mixing and Switching*

Multilingual individuals must properly handle the known languages by constantly regulating their mutual use. They need to know which language to use with which people and in which context. This concurrent activation/inhibition capacity introduces to Green's (1986, 1998) concept of control. This flexible language use requires a constant cognitive effort. A related skill concerns the ability to shift between languages, which is typical in bilingual communities where both languages are used.

Two specific phenomena are possible: *mixing*, which indicates the use of words from different languages within the same utterance, and *switching*, which consists in shifting to another language between utterances or sentences (see Albert and Obler 1978; Fabbro 1999; Paradis 1977). Following aphasia, individuals may lose the capacity to properly regulate their languages, with pathological episodes of mixing or switching. Mixing and switching deserve a thorough evaluation especially in bilingual communities, in order to clarify whether their occurrences are normal or pathological (see Bhat and Chengappa 2005; Chengappa et al. 2004; Muñoz et al. 1999).

Patients are usually aware of their improper language use and their unease increases when they involuntarily use a language that is not known by their interlocutor.

This unintentional shift was observed in a wide range of language pairs, with a more frequent shift from a non-native language to the native language than vice versa (e.g. Fabbro et al. 2000; Kong et al. 2014). However, this trend is not to be taken as a rule. In addition, these phenomena seem to have an increased probability of occurrence when involving two structurally close languages (e.g. Diéguez-Vide et al. 2012; Kong et al. 2014): the presence of similar words, or cognates, between these languages – despite generally proven to induce facilitatory effects during naming (e.g. Lalor and Kirsner 2001; Roberts and Deslauriers 1999) – is more likely to cause interference and possible mixing/switching phenomena in some clinical conditions (e.g. Abutalebi et al. 2009; Kurland and Falcon 2011). Nevertheless, interference phenomena were observed independently of language closeness and even across different language modalities. For instance, Leischner (1943) reported the case of a patient who switched between signs of native sign language and spoken and written modalities of the non-native language.

Mixing and switching terms are often used interchangeably, but they do not necessarily occur together in aphasia. Specifically, mixing was classified for the first time by Perecman (1984), who observed different possibilities: (i) use of a word that is the correspondent translation of the correct word in another language; (ii) word root of one language and suffix of another; (iii) syllables from different languages within a single word; (iv) words in a given language produced with the typical intonation or phonological rules of another; and (v) words of one language arranged in a sentence by using the syntactic rules of another.

A recent account identified two main reasons for pathological mixing (Neumann et al. 2016). The patient described by the authors was slightly more impaired in his native language, Yiddish, than in his second language, English, learned since childhood and trained in previous speech therapy. The patient used to mix the two languages and this occurred almost twice when speaking Yiddish. In Yiddish, the phenomenon was interpreted as a strategy to compensate for difficulties in lexical access; on the other hand, the fewer occurrences in English were mostly attributed to sociolinguistic differences (i.e. inability to find an equivalently evocative word or expression).

Concerning more specifically switching, the literature reports numerous cases, some observed to occur even in absence of other aphasic symptoms. Fabbro et al. (2000), for instance, studied a patient who began to speak his first language even with people that could not understand it, and he was aware of this. The patient was diagnosed with a brain tumour and underwent neurosurgery, following which he manifested a marked tendency to switch between languages, although not presenting other aphasic deficits.

This patient's lesion was located in the left prefrontal and cingulate cortices, which are amongst the regions proposed as belonging to the language control network regulating and monitoring language use (see Abutalebi and Green 2007). Both pathological switching and mixing have been observed particularly when lesions involve this specific network, which is located prevalently (but not exclusively) in the dominant hemisphere and includes, beside the mentioned frontal lobe areas, other non-language-specific regions.

Amongst them, the inferior parietal lobe seems to be involved in a sort of 'tuning in' to a given language, as already noticed by Pötzl (1925): lesions at this level are likely to cause pathological fixation on one language, meaning the exclusive use of only one of them, more likely the one spoken the most in the period immediately preceding the event. Other regions involved in language control are subcortical structures, with the basal ganglia (bidirectionally connected with the prefrontal cortex) playing a relevant role, as supported by mixing/switching phenomena consequent to their lesion (e.g. Abutalebi et al. 2000; Ansaldo et al. 2010). A possible involvement of the thalamus was also proposed (e.g. Mariën et al. 2005). Finally, there is also evidence of pathological mixing and switching following lesions in the classical frontotemporal language areas (e.g. Leemann et al. 2007). These episodes may be a strategy to compensate for lexical access difficulties in a given language, as previously hinted.

The involvement of these regions was supported by neuroimaging studies (see Abutalebi and Green 2016, for a recent review) and additional evidence was provided by the direct electrical stimulation of these sites during neurosurgery (e.g. Lubrano et al. 2012; Sierpowska et al. 2013; Tomasino et al. 2014). This technique further revealed the importance of the white matter fascicles connecting control and language-specific areas (e.g. superior longitudinal fasciculus), whose stimulation was capable of inducing involuntary switching (e.g. Moritz-Gasser and Duffau 2009; see Bello et al. 2006, for the importance of stimulating also the subcortical tracts). This suggests that lesion assessment should not be circumscribed to grey-matter sites, but should also look at the integrity in brain connectivity in order to fully understand a given clinical picture.

3.2. *Translation*

Another distinctive symptom of multilingual aphasia is represented by problems at the level of translation. In some cases, deficits seem to affect the process of translation per se: despite almost spared naming skills in each language (e.g. Gastaldi 1951) or capacity to recognize translation equivalents (e.g. Green et al. 2011), some patients are incapable of actively translating words they seemingly know. Very frequently, difficulties in translation generally reflect the global language impairment profile: translation appears to be more compromised when performed from less- to more-impaired languages rather than vice versa (e.g. Adrover-Roig et al. 2011). As suggested for mixing, deficits in translation are likely attributed to difficulties in lexical access in a weaker language.

Nevertheless, unexpected translation episodes were also reported. Some patients appeared unable to speak a given language, but were paradoxically capable of translating from the available language to the impaired one and not vice versa (Fabbro and Paradis 1995). The phenomenon is termed 'paradoxical translation' and is frequently observed in cases of antagonistic recovery (e.g. Paradis et al. 1982, see afterwards).

Another odd possibility is represented by patients with a compulsive tendency to translate from one language to another (e.g. García-Caballero et al. 2007), and, unexpectedly, unable to perform translation upon explicit request or to understand the meaning of words or sentences they had just translated (e.g. Perecman 1984). These cases demonstrated that translation is somehow an automatic process, which can also take place without access to semantics.

Overall, the reported evidence indicates how complex the mechanisms of translation are. Paradis et al. (1982) supported the existence of two different processes, one for each direction of translation (from language A to language B and vice versa), and independent of both language production and comprehension. Consequently, lesions may selectively affect one of these components, while sparing the other. In some cases, a pattern opposite to that just described can take place: translation skills are preserved, whereas naming is impaired, as observed in Ansaldo et al. (2010), who reported a case of spared translation, used as a strategy to compensate for naming deficits and also prevent mixing instances (the patient was instructed to mentally translate into the target language the word he was going to produce in the unrequested language before uttering it).

4. Patterns of Language Impairment

Besides language deficits peculiar to multilingual patients, another somewhat fascinating topic concerns the patterns of language impairment, meaning the extent of impairment of each language in relation to the others. After the insult, and comparable to monolingual individuals, multilingual patients go through different successive phases (see Fabbro 1999; Paradis 2004).

The acute phase, lasting a few weeks after the insult, is often characterized by initial temporary mutism, followed by unstable improvements in one or more languages. In the subsequent lesion phase, some language functions are more stably regained and it is possible to define the extent and type of impairment of each language. The regain of language functions in this post-onset period is usually indicated as spontaneous recovery. In the last stage, named late phase, the pattern of deficits is in fact steady and there is almost no margin for spontaneous improvements. Nevertheless, further recovery is still possible. There have been reports of rehabilitation continuing several years post-onset, with focused and intensive rehabilitation programs successfully promoting considerable recovery (e.g. Altman et al. 2012; Kurland and Falcon 2011).

There are a number of possible patterns of impairment. The first structured categorization was provided by Paradis (1977), who published the results of an international study during which hundreds of patients with multilingual aphasia had been monitored. This author adopted the term *recovery* to refer to the different observed patterns; nevertheless, in the literature confusion is sometimes generated by the use of both 'recovery' and 'impairment' when describing the reported cases. For this reason, in order to reduce such confusion, in this chapter we opted to consistently use the more general term of *impairment*, to generally refer to the profile of deficits resulting from aphasia.

In Paradis's reports (1977, 2001), the most commonly observed pattern was that of a parallel impairment, in which all languages displayed a comparable degree of deficits. Another frequent pattern was that of differential impairment, characterized by more severe deficits in one language (see also Albert and Obler 1978).

Other rarer and not mutually exclusive patterns of impairment were observed: selective impairment, affecting only one language; antagonistic, in which the decrease of deficits in one language is followed by their increase in another; blended (or mixed) impairment, causing interferences between languages, with the occurrence of mixing/switching phenomena. Finally, in the successive condition, one language begins to improve only after full improvements in the other. In the following sections, we mention some of the main reports on language impairments to elucidate the factors accounting for these diverse clinical manifestations.

5.   Main Factors Influencing Impairment

In impairment, multiple factors converge. These include clinical parameters (e.g. extent and location of the lesion) and variables related to both premorbid (e.g. language history) and postmorbid (e.g. language spoken during hospitalization) conditions. Other factors, such as language features, have also been shown to have an impact. In this section, we discuss some of the most salient factors.

Lesion site is one of the main predictors of impairment with regard not only to the nature of deficits (e.g. aphasia subtype), but also to the language affected the most (see Ibrahim 2008, for a discussion of the importance of lesion location). Each language has its own brain representation, partially overlapping with that of the other language. This is well demonstrated by direct electrical stimulation studies during neurosurgery. Overall, these studies (e.g. Lucas et al. 2004; Roux and Trémoulet 2002) revealed that there are brain regions supporting both languages and others specifically subserving each language. Only in rare cases did stimulation reveal uniquely shared sites, meaning completely overlapping functional networks between languages. This finding is in agreement with neuroimaging evidence from healthy individuals. Meta-analytic findings (e.g. Indefrey 2006; Sebastian et al. 2011) demonstrated that task performance in different languages partially recruited the same macro-areas, but also determined the activation of specific clusters (in particular, additional activations were observed when performing tasks in the non-native or low-proficiency language).

The brain representation of each language – and therefore its possible impairment –is primarily determined by age of acquisition (AoA). The importance of AoA is such that many authors tried to identify the cut-off age after which learning a new language may become problematic and introduced the concept of critical period, meaning the age after which a newly learned language hardly ever reaches a native-like performance. Different cut-offs were proposed such as (pre-)adolescence years (e.g. Long 1990). Other authors identified as a reasonable cut-off the age of 6 (e.g. Johnson and Newport 1989), which was then used to distinguish between early (AoA < 6) and late (AoA > 6) bilinguals.

The latter is considered critical in terms of developmental changes in the memory systems supporting learning. According to Paradis (1994, 2004, 2009, see also Ullman 2001, 2005, 2006), language acquisition before this age is prompted by implicit or procedural memory, allowing for language skills to be informally acquired and then be automatized. On the other hand, late-learned languages are mainly supported by explicit or declarative memory processes, especially if learning takes place in a formal manner. This language knowledge, being based on metalinguistic skills, is therefore more conscious and less automatic. The different age and method of appropriation – and the consequent different brain representation – are expected to influence the susceptibility to damage of that language.

The memory model has to further take into account the diverse linguistic domains within each language. In detail, the critical period was proposed to be particularly salient for phonological and morphosyntactic abilities. This means that competences related to these domains are strongly influenced by AoA, with late learning expected to prevent optimal achievement or at least entail consistent cognitive effort. If, however, high proficiency is achieved, even lately learned phonological and morphosyntactic abilities may become partially automatized and hence supported by implicit memory (see Ullman 2001). On the other hand, lexico-semantic skills, intended as conscious word knowledge, were mainly associated with proficiency, which is in turn determined by frequency of use. Hence, word knowledge is hypothesized to be supported by explicit memory also in the native language.

It appears evident that, along with AoA, another salient parameter is proficiency. Some authors consider premorbid proficiency the most relevant factor (see Gray and Kiran 2013), useful also for the prediction of rehabilitation outcomes (e.g. Druks and Weekes 2013; Edmonds and Kiran 2006). Languages should consequently be 'ordered' not according to a chronological age of appropriation but in terms of relative dominance. This seems to be a general rule when AoA and proficiency are not congruent, that is when the firstly acquired language is not the one mastered the most. In some extreme cases, a non-native language may become in life the dominant language and be more resistant to brain damage (e.g. Tiwari and Krishnan 2015). In the Section 6 we will discuss two parameters which are closely related to proficiency, namely language use and exposure.

6.   Parallel Impairment

The most probable clinical condition was parallel (i.e. comparable) impairment between languages. In a study on 20 bilingual patients, Fabbro (2001) reported this pattern of impairment in 65% of the cases. Nonetheless, published reports of parallel recovery are less frequent than expected, probably because the authors tend to describe exceptional and unusual cases, thus neglecting the less intriguing instances of parallel impairment (Paradis 1977, 2004).

A plausible interpretation for parallel impairment comes from early AoA. It is reasonable to assume that, if the non-native language is acquired within the critical period, it can show an impairment similar to the native language. Support for this hypothesis is lent by the study of Kendall et al. (2015): the only bilingual patient displaying parallel impairment had acquired both languages at a very early age. A comparable impairment was observed when both languages had been all learned at a late age (e.g. Goral et al. 2006). This provides evidence that, when language appropriation takes place within the same period (early vs. late), two languages are more closely connected and more likely to be similarly affected.

Nevertheless, Green et al. (2010) observed a comparable impairment between the native language and the non-native language in spite of the fact that the latter had been learned late. However, the two patients had been living in the UK for many years and the considerable exposure to English (their second and non-dominant language), both premorbidly and even more during hospitalization, could have influenced the process. This suggests that, apart from AoA and dominance, extent of use and exposure to a given language may be particularly relevant factors (see Goral et al. 2006).

Green and colleagues interpreted the findings in terms of language control, too. When control functions are disrupted and both languages heavily rely on control, a comparable impairment can be observed. Living in a foreign country and speaking a non-native language entails a considerable cognitive effort to regulate language use, including the dominant language which has to be constantly inhibited. In this regard, although for opposite reasons, both languages are impacted when control functions are disrupted.

7. Differential Impairment

A more consistent bulk of literature focuses on case reports of differential impairment between languages. More than a century ago, Ribot (1881) proposed that the less impaired language was more likely to be the native language, whereas Pitres (1895) claimed that the most familiar language was best preserved. Nowadays, these two stances, known as Ribot's and Pitres's rules, respectively, are considered rather simplistic, as many different factors concur to the patterns of impairment. In the work by Fabbro (2001) cited in Section 6, amongst patients displaying a differential impairment, 20% showed a better preservation of the first language versus 15% showing a better preservation of the second language (see Paradis 2004, 2009). This suggests that the most probable pattern is that in which the native language is the least impaired, at least when it was also the dominant one. Nevertheless, patients are roughly homogeneously distributed between the two conditions, suggesting that both patterns have a comparably high incidence.

7.1. *Impairment of a Non-native Language*

There are many reports of patients with a greater impairment of a non-native language. Although seemingly intuitive, this outcome is to a certain extent surprising as many of these cases concerned patients who had mastered the non-native languages and/or were primarily exposed to them in the period immediately preceding the insult (e.g. Diéguez-Vide et al. 2012; Koumadini Knoph 2011). These findings seem to go in the opposite direction of Pitres's rule and further contradict the evidence discussed before on the role that proficiency and exposure can have in preventing impairment. However, these patients were mostly late bilinguals, having possibly learned their non-native language only a few years before (as in Diéguez-Vide et al. 2012) or even in adult age (as in Koumadini Knoph 2011). Therefore, when non-native languages are learned after the critical period, language proficiency and use/exposure may be less relevant in preventing language impairment.

Another factor that can help explain a major impairment in a non-native language is the structural distance between the native and non-native language. Neuroimaging studies have provided evidence that distant (e.g. Indo-European vs. Asian) languages have a partially different neural representation (e.g. Bolger et al. 2005). In other words, the neural system developed for the native language could be inadequate when learning a distant language and additional brain areas should therefore be recruited (accommodation process). The above studies were focused on patients whose non-native languages differed to a certain extent from the native ones (e.g. Chinese-Spanish-Catalan in Diéguez-Vide et al. 2012; Farsi-Norwegian in Koumadini Knoph 2011). In these cases, the effect of language distance may be enhanced by late AoA, making the non-native language even more susceptible to damage.

In a study by Dai et al. (2012), the influence of AoA and language distance was controlled as the patient was an early bilingual speaker of two dialects of Chinese, namely Cantonese and Mandarin. At first, both dialects appeared to be equally impaired. However, more accurate testing revealed a slight impairment in naming actions – but not objects – only in Mandarin, the dialect that had been acquired later. This is a possible evidence of the fact that even in early and proficient bilinguals – also speaking two languages sharing several features – the second language is more vulnerable. However, this hypothesis needs further research.

7.2. *Impairment of the Native Language*

Almost a century ago, Minkowski (1927) described many patients manifesting a greater impairment in the native language versus the non-native language; he advanced several hypotheses for this, which are still considered to be useful in understanding how a non-native language can be spared by a brain insult.

Minkowski particularly stressed the importance of the degree of language use, which we have already discussed. This commonly refers to the extent a language has been used premorbidly. Nevertheless, post-insult conditions are important as well. The language spoken in the environment (i.e. hospital) is particularly relevant, especially during long hospitalizations, when patients are exposed to a language that is not their native language. This showed an impact on the rehabilitation outcome as well: when rehabilitation focused on the native language, which was not the language spoken in the environment, the effects were rather limited, as the potential improvements could not be applied in the natural environment (e.g. Goral et al. 2012).

The mechanisms of appropriation of a given language play a role, too. In some cases, formal appropriation could favour language preservation, because language functions can be restored through metalinguistic knowledge. In many cases, non-native languages are more consciously learned, whereas this occurs less frequently with the native language, which is often represented by mostly informally acquired languages or even dialects.

This is particularly true when individuals master their non-native language very well, such as the patient described by Samar and Akbari (2012) who manifested a better preservation of her second language, which she had learned at school, studied at university, and taught at school for 18 years. The particularly deep knowledge of this language may have effectively made it less susceptible to damage.

7.3. *Additional Factors Prompting Differential Impairment*

Beyond the factors discussed so far, other factors play a role in differential impairment. Irrespective of language distance, the features of each language per se need be taken into account. Because of their structure, some languages can pose greater cognitive demands, and related deficits may therefore reflect language complexity. This was demonstrated in different language domains (e.g. different performance in processing compounds between French and English, see Jarema et al. 2010) and especially in relation to orthography. For instance, reading in some languages such as Chinese or Japanese Kanji is particularly demanding. These writing systems are based on logographic characters, with no one-to-one morpheme–phoneme correspondence. Of note are the clinical studies on Japanese-Portuguese bilingual patients, documenting a relation between the observed deficits and cognitive demands posed by each language (e.g. Caramelli et al. 1994; Senaha and Parente 2012). Reading is demanding also in other languages, for instance in Hebrew, lacking vowels. In contrast to alphabetic phonological languages, reading in these languages cannot be performed automatically, but requires an obligatory access to semantics. Nevertheless, this kind of reading, despite being more demanding, might also promote recovery when conscious knowledge is preserved (e.g. Halpern 1941).

A last factor that deserves mentioning is the impact of the affective relevance of a given language and the consequent wish to recover it. Its relevance is demonstrated by the fact that facts and episodes of our lives are stored in our memory in a precise language (e.g. Marian and Neisser 2000). Recalling events in a given language has also been used as a therapeutic strategy in patients with aphasia (e.g. Altman et al. 2012). When it is feasible and makes sense, patients are given the opportunity to choose the language in which they wish to be trained and positive outcomes were seen when rehabilitation focused on a poorly mastered but emotionally relevant language (e.g. Miertsch et al. 2009). The affective significance of a language is also supported by cases of patients with neuropsychiatric disorders such as schizophrenia (see Paradis 2008). During a psychotic episode, many of these patients show a tendency to switch to a non-native language (e.g. Southwood et al. 2009). This can be explained by the fact that the non-native language, being perceived as more distant from their inner life, might help patients get emotionally detached.

8. Selective Impairment

We have so far discussed cases of overall language impairment affecting all languages to a greater or lesser extent. A debated question concerns selective damage, in which only one language is affected while the other is completely spared. This would be reasonable if we assumed that each language had completely distinct brain networks, as postulated by localizationist theories (e.g. Scoresby-Jackson 1867). We illustrated findings from neuroimaging and direct stimulation studies emphasizing the existence of language-specific brain sites; these differential sites were however shown to be located at a very close (millimetres) distance, whereas lesions are rarely so circumscribed. This suggests that the accounted reports of selective aphasia probably have to be attributed to some other (i.e. non-anatomical) reasons.

A common condition observed to cause selective language impairment is epilepsy. In the postictal period (i.e. after acute seizure), a temporary loss of one language, most frequently a non-native language, is often reported, at least when it has been learned late (e.g. Aladdin et al. 2008). This could happen because epileptic foci are frequently localized at the level of the temporal lobe, a brain site involved in explicit learning (see Paradis 2004, 2009). The reverse pattern (i.e. selective impairment of the native language) has also been reported but was likely to occur in the presence of right-sided lesions (e.g. Paradis and Goldblum 1989; Titiz et al. 2016). These inconclusive findings are further complicated by age of seizure onset: early onset may determine a reorganization of language functions in the right hemisphere, resulting in a more bilateral language representation (e.g. Woermann et al. 2003), which makes the prediction of language impairment more difficult.

In conclusion, a neurofunctional versus a neuroanatomical interpretation seems to account for selective deficits: some pathological conditions may temporarily inhibit one language by altering its activation threshold. When the condition resolves, inhibition is removed and the language recovers.

9.   Antagonistic Phenomena

In less frequent cases, there is no definite pattern of language impairment. Instead, distinct phases are observed, each characterized by the prevalent use of one language and the almost complete neglect of the other. Scholars define this condition as antagonistic, probably due to a dysregulation in control processes, with one language apparently inhibiting the other, in a sort of competition.

This phenomenon was accurately investigated for the first time by Paradis et al. (1982), who described two patients, both having acquired the two languages during childhood and having extensively used them in the years preceding the insult. The authors kept a diary in which they recorded the patients' daily linguistic profile. Surprisingly, the patients' performance in one language could be close to normal one day and severely impaired the day after, in a sort of alternating trend. Generally, these patients have good comprehension in both languages, but efficient production in only one of them. This phenomenon usually takes place in the initial post-onset weeks, after which it tends to normalize to a more stable profile (see also Nilipour and Ashayeri 1989).

10.   Subcortical Multilingual Aphasia

A specific subtype of aphasia is caused by lesions affecting the subcortical structures. Cases of subcortical aphasia in multilinguals are particularly interesting in that they help unravel the role of these structures by inspecting their differential involvement in each language. There is increasing evidence of the fundamental role of the basal ganglia in diverse language functions (see Arsalidou et al. 2013), spanning from articulation initiation and output control to morphosyntax and aspects related to semantics and phonology (see Fabbro and Paradis 1995). Lesion studies emphasized their involvement also in the automatic processes of language, such as the production of series or formulas (such as counting or playing prayers, e.g. Adrover-Roig et al. 2011; Speedie et al. 1993). Lesions at this level were also observed to cause an incapacity to prevent uncontrollable phenomena, resulting in echolalia, tachylalia, and compulsive repetition of words or utterances (e.g. Adrover-Roig et al. 2011). Finally, with specific reference to the multilingual population, we have already discussed the role of the basal ganglia in the regulation of the reciprocal use of languages.

The importance of these structures is related to their involvement in language acquisition through procedural processes (see Paradis 2009). Deficits were observed to disrupt especially the morphosyntactic competences across languages. This was seen also in late-learned languages, indicating, as already stated, that high proficiency and extensive use can result in at least partial automatization of the related grammatical aspects (e.g. Venkatesh et al. 2012). These studies showed that the lexicon (mainly supported by explicit memory in all languages) was instead generally preserved. Nevertheless, findings may differ according to which circuit is affected. Ullman (2006) supports the existence of two different frontostriatal circuits: one connecting the basal ganglia to Brodmann area (BA) 44 (involved in morphosyntax) and the other projecting to BA 45/47 (dedicated to lexico-semantics).

Concerning the greater involvement of the basal ganglia in implicit processes, it is also reasonable to assume that a lesion mainly affects the languages acquired early. Diverse clinical reports do support this. Moretti et al. (2001), for instance, illustrated the case of a patient manifesting a severe impairment in her native language following a lesion to the left caudate; when the lesion spread to frontotemporal areas, deficits surfaced also in the second, late-learned language. This provides evidence that early-acquired languages are mainly represented subcortically, whereas those learned at a late stage have a prevalent cortical representation (but see Jahangiri et al. 2011, for opposite findings).

Understanding the main role of the basal ganglia in first language performance can help explain cases of paradoxical recovery. Aglioti and Fabbro (Aglioti et al. 1996; Aglioti and Fabbro 1993) and García-Caballero et al. (2007) reported the cases of two patients having learned the second language at school and barely used it. Interestingly, following a lesion to the basal ganglia, these patients paradoxically began to express themselves in their barely mastered second language while completely neglecting their native language.

A condition that impairs the basal ganglia circuitry such as Parkinson's disease caused, in bilingual patients, a severe impairment of the native language (while the non-native language was almost spared) and particularly of morphosyntactic competences (e.g. Johari et al. 2013; Zanini et al. 2004, 2010). In this sense, the pattern is complementary to that of Alzheimer's disease and dementias in general, which are typically characterized by an atrophy in the structures subserving explicit memory (e.g. hippocampus) and are hence more likely to affect the late-learned non-native languages (e.g. McMurtray et al. 2009; Mendez et al. 2004; but see, for instance, Manchon et al. 2015, for a parallel impairment).

Other subcortical structures, such as the thalamus and cerebellum, were demonstrated as playing a central role in language. Clinical accounts come primarily from monolinguals (see Crosson 2013; De Smet et al. 2013), whereas reports on multilinguals are lacking, especially with regard to the cerebellum. A few more findings on thalamic aphasia were reported (e.g. Fabbro et al. 1997; Jahangiri et al. 2011), despite a full understanding of the deficits specifically attributed to this lesion has not yet been achieved. Nevertheless, a lesion to the thalamus is likely to primarily affect the lexico-semantics components of language (e.g. Jahangiri et al. 2011), as demonstrated for monolinguals (see Crosson 2013).

11.   Conclusion

This chapter aimed to provide an overview of the language impairments associated with multilingual aphasia. We illustrated some peculiar language deficits, the main patterns of impairment, and the factors that play a role in determining these clinical profiles. All these reports demonstrate how complex this phenomenon is. Lesion, age of appropriation of each language, and proficiency appear to be amongst the most relevant factors. Language features, manner of appropriation, degree of use and exposure, and even emotional and motivational variables play a role, too. Nevertheless, the complex interplay of all of these factors makes it difficult to predict a priori the actual impairment in each language. A better understanding of these mechanisms could be achieved by a proper deficit assessment, which should be performed in the diverse languages known by a patient and by means of multiple and adequate measures. We therefore stress the importance of a reliable assessment, as it constitutes a landmark for the development of rehabilitation programmes and the probability of their success.

REFERENCES

Abutalebi, J., Della Rosa, P.A., Tettamanti, M. et al. (2009). Bilingual aphasia and language control: a follow-up fMRI and intrinsic connectivity study. *Brain and Language* 109: 141–156. doi:10.1016/j.bandl.2009.03.003.

Abutalebi, J. and Green, D.W. (2007). Bilingual language production: the neurocognition of language representation and control. *Journal of Neurolinguistics* 20: 242–275. doi:10.1016/j.jneuroling.2006.10.003.

Abutalebi, J. and Green, D.W. (2016). Neuroimaging of language control in bilinguals: neural adaptation and reserve. *Bilingualism: Language and Cognition* 19: 689–698. doi:10.1017/S1366728916000225.

Abutalebi, J., Miozzo, A., and Cappa, S.F. (2000). Do subcortical structures control 'language selection' in polyglots? Evidence from pathological language mixing. *Neurocase* 6: 51–56. doi:10.1080/13554790008402757.

Adrover-Roig, D., Galparsoro-Izagirre, N., Marcotte, K. et al. (2011). Impaired L1 and executive control after left basal ganglia damage in a bilingual Basque–Spanish person with aphasia. *Clinical Linguistics & Phonetics* 25: 480–498. doi:10.3109/02699206.2011.563338.

Aglioti, S., Beltramello, A., Girardi, F., and Fabbro, F. (1996). Neurolinguistic and follow-up study of an unusual pattern of recovery from bilingual subcortical aphasia. *Brain* 119: 1551–1564. doi:10.1093/brain/119.5.1551.

Aglioti, S. and Fabbro, F. (1993). Paradoxical selective recovery in a bilingual aphasic following subcortical lesions. *NeuroReport* 4: 1359–1362.

Aladdin, Y., Snyder, T.J., and Ahmed, S.N. (2008). Pearls & Oy-sters: selective postictal aphasia: cerebral language organisation in bilingual patients. *Neurology* 71: e14–e17. doi:10.1212/01.wnl.0000325017.42998.d1.

Albert, M.L. and Obler, L.K. (1978). *The Bilingual Brain*. New York, NY: Academic Press.

Altman, C., Gil, M., and Walters, J. (2012). Language choice in bilingual aphasia: memory and emotions. In: *Aspects of Multilingual Aphasia* (ed. M.R. Gitterman, M. Goral and L.K. Obler), 51–68. Bristol, UK: Multilingual Matters.

Altman, C., Goral, M., and Levy, E.S. (2012). Integrated narrative analysis in multilingual aphasia: the relationship among narrative structure, grammaticality, and fluency. *Aphasiology* 26: 1029–1052. doi:10.1080/02687038.2012.686103.

Ansaldo, A.I., Saidi, L.G., and Ruiz, A. (2010). Model-driven intervention in bilingual aphasia: evidence from a case of pathological language mixing. *Aphasiology* 24: 309–324. doi:10.1080/02687030902958423.

Arsalidou, M., Duerden, E.G., and Taylor, M.J. (2013). The centre of the brain: topographical model of motor, cognitive, affective, and somatosensory functions of the basal ganglia. *Human Brain Mapping* 34: 3031–3054. doi:10.1002/hbm.22124.

Bello, L., Acerbi, F., Giussani, C. et al. (2006). Intraoperative language localization in multilingual patients with gliomas. *Neurosurgery* 59: 115–125. doi:10.1227/01. NEU.0000219241.92246.FB.

Bhat, S., & Chengappa, S. (2005). Code switching in normal and aphasic Kannada-English bilinguals. In J. Cohen, K. T. McAlister, K. Rolstad, & J. MacSwan (Eds.), Proceedings of the 4th International Symposium on Bilingualism (pp. 306–316). Somerville, MA: Cascadilla Press.

Bolger, D.J., Perfetti, C.A., and Schneider, W. (2005). Cross-cultural effect on the brain revisited: universal structures plus writing system variation. *Human Brain Mapping* 25: 92–104. doi:10.1002/hbm.20124.

Caramelli, P., Parente, M.A.M.P., Hosogi, M.L. et al. (1994). Unexpected reading dissociation in a Brazilian "nisei" with crossed aphasia. *Behavioural Neurology* 7: 165–170. doi:10.3233/BEN-1994-73-409.

Chengappa, S., Daniel, K.E., and Bhat, S. (2004). Language mixing and switching in Malayalam-English bilingual aphasics. *Asia Pacific Disability Rehabilitation Journal* 15: 68–76.

Crosson, B. (2013). Thalamic mechanisms in language: a reconsideration based on recent findings and concepts. *Brain and Language* 126: 73–88. doi:10.1016/j.bandl.2012.06.011.

Dai, E.Y.L., Kong, A.P.H., and Weekes, B.S. (2012). Recovery of naming and discourse production: a bilingual anomic case study. *Aphasiology* 26: 737–756. doi:10.1080/02687038.2011.645013.

De Smet, H.J., Paquier, P., Verhoeven, J., and Mariën, P. (2013). The cerebellum: its role in language and related cognitive and affective functions. *Brain and Language* 127: 334–342. doi:10.1016/j.bandl.2012.11.001.

Diéguez-Vide, F., Gich-Fullà, J., Puig-Alcántara, J. et al. (2012). Chinese–Spanish–Catalan trilingual aphasia: a case study. *Journal of Neurolinguistics* 25: 630–641. doi:10.1016/j.jneuroling.2012.01.002.

Druks, J. and Weekes, B.S. (2013). Parallel deterioration to language processing in a bilingual speaker. *Cognitive Neuropsychology* 30: 578–596. doi:10.1080/02643294. 2014.882814.

Edmonds, L. and Kiran, S. (2006). Effect of semantic naming treatment on crosslinguistic generalization in bilingual aphasia. *Journal of Speech Language and Hearing Research* 49: 729–749. doi:1092-4388/06/4904-0729.

Fabbro, F. (1999). Aphasia in multilinguals. In: *Concise Encyclopedia of Language Pathology* (ed. F. Fabbro), 335–340. Oxford, UK: Pergamon Press.

Fabbro, F. (2001). The bilingual brain: cerebral representation of languages.

Brain and Language 79: 211–222. doi:10.1006/brln.2001.2480.

Fabbro, F. and Paradis, M. (1995). Differential impairments in four multilingual patients with subcortical lesions. In: *Aspects of Multilingual Aphasia* (ed. M. Paradis), 139–176. Oxford, UK: Pergamon Press.

Fabbro, F., Peru, A., and Skrap, M. (1997). Language disorders in bilingual patients after thalamic lesions. *Journal of Neurolinguistics* 10: 347–367.

Fabbro, F., Skrap, M., and Aglioti, S. (2000). Pathological switching between languages after frontal lesions in a bilingual patient. *Journal of Neurology, Neurosurgery and Psychiatry* 68: 650–652. doi:10.1136/jnnp.68.5.650.

García-Caballero, A., García-Lado, I., González-Hermida, J. et al. (2007). Paradoxical recovery in a bilingual patient with aphasia after right capsuloputaminal infarction. *Journal of Neurology, Neurosurgery and Psychiatry* 78: 89–91. doi:10.1136/jnnp.2006.095406.

Gastaldi, G. (1951). Observations on a bilingual aphasia. *Sistema Nervoso* 3: 175.

Gollan, T.H., Weissberger, G.H., Runnqvist, E. et al. (2012). Self-ratings of spoken language dominance: a multi-lingual naming test (MINT) and preliminary norms for young and aging Spanish-English bilinguals. *Bilingualism: Language and Cognition* 15: 594–615. doi:10.1017/S1366728911000332.

Gómez-Ruiz, I. and Aguilar-Alonso, Á. (2011). Capacity of the Catalan and Spanish versions of the bilingual aphasia test to distinguish between healthy aging, mild cognitive impairment and Alzheimer's disease. *Clinical Linguistics & Phonetics* 25: 444–463. doi:10.3109/02699206.2011.560989.

Goodglass, H. and Kaplan, E. (1972). *Boston Diagnostic Aphasia Examination (BDAE)*. San Antonio, TX: Psychological Corporation.

Goral, M., Levy, E.S., Obler, L.K., and Cohen, E. (2006). Cross-language lexical connections in the mental lexicon: evidence from a case of trilingual aphasia. *Brain and Language* 98: 235–247. doi:10.1016/j.bandl.2006.05.004.

Goral, M., Naghibolhosseini, M., and Conner, P. (2013). Asymmetric inhibitory treatment effects in multilingual aphasia. *Cognitive Neuropsychology* 30: 564–577. doi:10.1080/02643294.2013.878692.

Goral, M., Rosas, J., Conner, P.S. et al. (2012). Effects of language proficiency and language of the environment on aphasia therapy in a multilingual. *Journal of Neurolinguistics* 25: 538–551. doi:10.1016/j.jneuroling.2011.06.001.

Gray, T. and Kiran, S. (2013). A theoretical account of lexical and semantic naming deficits in bilingual aphasia. *Journal of Speech Language and Hearing Research* 56: 1314–1327. doi:10.1044/1092-4388 (2012/12-0091).

Green, D.W. (1986). Control, activation and resource: a framework and a model for the control of speech in bilinguals. *Brain and Language* 27: 210–223. doi:10.1016/0093-934X(86)90016-7.

Green, D.W. (1998). Mental control of the bilingual lexico-semantic system. *Bilingualism: Language and Cognition* 1: 67–82. doi:10.1017/S1366728998000133.

Green, D.W., Grogan, A., Crinion, J. et al. (2010). Language control and parallel recovery in individuals with aphasia. *Aphasiology* 24: 188–209. doi:10.1080/02687030902958316.

Green, D.W., Ruffle, L., Grogan, A. et al. (2011). Parallel recovery in a trilingual speaker: the use of the bilingual aphasia test as a diagnostic complement to the comprehensive aphasia test. *Clinical Linguistics & Phonetics* 25: 449–512. doi:10.3109/02699206.2011.560990.

Grosjean, F. (1989). Neurolinguists, beware! The bilingual is not two monolinguals in one person. *Brain and Language* 36: 1–15.

Halpern, L. (1941). Beitrag zur Restitution der Aphasie bei polyglotten im Hinblick auf da Hebräische. *Schweitzer Archiv für Neurologie und Psychiatrie* 47: I50–I154.

Huber, W., Poeck, K., and Willmes, K. (1984). The Aachen aphasia test. *Advances in Neurology* 42: 291–303.

Ibrahim, R. (2008). Performance in L1 and L2 observed in Arabic-Hebrew bilingual aphasic following brain tumor: a case constitutes double dissociation. *Psychology Research and Behaviour Management* 1: 11–19.

Indefrey, P. (2006). A meta-analysis of hemodynamic studies on first and second language processing: Which suggested differences can we trust and what do they mean? *Language Learning* 56: 279–304. doi:10.1111/j.1467-9922.2006.00365.x.

Ivanova, M.V. and Hallowell, B. (2013). A tutorial on aphasia test development in any language: key substantive and psychometric considerations. *Aphasiology* 27: 891–920. doi:10.1080/02687038.2013.805728.

Jahangiri, N., Azarpazhooh, M.R., Ghaleh, M., and Seifhashemi, F. (2011). Thalamic and striatocapsular bilingual aphasia. *Asia Pacific Journal of Speech, Language and Hearing* 14: 187–196. doi:10.1179/jslh.2011.14.4.187.

Jarema, G., Perlak, D., and Semenza, S. (2010). The processing of compounds in bilingual aphasia: a multiple-case study. *Aphasiology* 24: 126–140. doi:10.1080/02687030902958225.

Johari, K., Ashrafi, F., Zali, A. et al. (2013). Grammatical deficits in bilingual Azari–Farsi patients with Parkinson's disease. *Journal of Neurolinguistics* 26: 22–30. doi:10.1016/j.jneuroling.2012.02.004.

Johnson, J.S. and Newport, E.L. (1989). Critical period effects in second language learning: the influence of maturational state on the acquisition of English as a second language. *Cognitive Psychology* 21: 60–99. doi:10.1016/0010-0285(89)90003-0.

Kay, J., Lesser, R., and Coltheart, M. (1992). *The Psycholinguistic Assessment of Language Processing Aphasia (PALPA)*. Hove, UK: Erlbaum.

Kendall, D., Edmonds, L., Van Zyl, A. et al. (2015). What can speech production errors tell us about cross-linguistic processing in bilingual aphasia? Evidence from four English/Afrikaans bilingual individuals with aphasia. *The South African Journal of Communication Disorders* 62: 1–10. doi:10.4102/sajcd.v62i1.111.

Kertesz, A. (1982). *The Western Aphasia Battery*. Philadelphia, PA: Grune & Stratton.

Kiran, S., Peña, E., Bedore, L., and Sheng, L. (2010). *Evaluating the relationship between category generation and language use and proficiency. In Proceedings of the Donostia Workshop on Neurobilingualism*. Spain: San Sebastian.

Kong, A.P.-H., Abutalebi, J., Lam, K.S.-Y., and Weekes, B. (2014). Executive and language control in the multilingual brain. *Behavioural Neurology* doi:10.1155/2014/527951.

Koumadini Knoph, M.I. (2011). Language assessment of a Farsi–Norwegian bilingual speaker with aphasia. *Clinical Linguistics & Phonetics* 25: 530–539. doi:10.3109/02699206.2011.563900.

Kurland, J. and Falcon, M. (2011). Effects of cognate status and language of therapy during intensive semantic naming treatment in a case of severe nonfluent bilingual aphasia. *Clinical Linguistics & Phonetics* 25: 584–600. doi:10.3109/02699206.2011.565398.

Lalor, E. and Kirsner, K. (2001). The role of cognates in bilingual aphasia: implications for assessment and treatment. *Aphasiology* 15: 1047–1056. doi:10.1080/02687040143000384.

Leemann, B., Laganaro, M., Schwitter, V., and Schnider, A. (2007). Paradoxical switching to a barely-mastered second language by an aphasic patient. *Neurocase* 13: 209–213. doi:10.1080/13554790701502667.

Leischner, A. (1943). Die Aphasie die Taubstummen. Beitrag zur Lehre von der Asymbolie. *Archiv für Psychiatrie* 115: 469–548.

Long, M.H. (1990). Maturational constraints on language development. *Studies in Second Language Acquisition* 12: 251–285.

Lubrano, V., Prod'hommed, K., Démonet, J.-F., and Köpke, B. (2012). Language monitoring in multilingual patients undergoing awake craniotomy: a case study of a German–English–French trilingual patient with a WHO grade II glioma. *Journal of Neurolinguistics* 25: 567–578. doi:10.1016/j.jneuroling.2011.08.002.

Lucas, T.H., McKhann, G.M., and Ojemann, G. (2004). Functional separation of languages in the bilingual brain: a comparison of electrical stimulation language mapping in 25 bilingual patients and 117 monolingual control patients. *Journal of Neurosurgery* 101: 449–457.

Manchon, M., Buetler, K., Colombo, F. et al. (2015). Impairment of both languages in late bilinguals with dementia of the Alzheimer type. *Bilingualism: Language and Cognition* 18: 90–100. doi:10.1017/S1366728914000194.

Marian, V. and Neisser, U. (2000). Language-dependent recall of autobiographical memories. *Journal of Experimental Psychology* 129: 361–368. doi:10.1037/0096-3445.129.3.361.

Mariën, P., Abutalebi, J., Engelborghs, S., and De Deyn, P.P. (2005). Pathophysiology of language switching and mixing in an early bilingual child with subcortical aphasia. *Neurocase* 11: 385–398. doi:10.1080/13554790500212880.

McMurtray, A., Saito, E., and Nakamoto, B. (2009). Language preference and development of dementia among bilingual individuals. *Hawaii Medical Journal* 68: 223–226.

Mendez, M.F., Saghafi, S., and Clark, D.G. (2004). Semantic dementia in multilingual patients. *Journal of Neuropsychiatry and Clinical Neurosciences* 16: 381.

Miertsch, B., Meisel, J.M., and Isel, F. (2009). Non-treated languages in aphasia therapy of polyglots benefit from improvement in the treated language. *Journal of Neurolinguistics* 22: 135–150. doi:10.1016/j.jneuroling. 2008.07.003.

Minkowski, M. (1927). Klinischer Beitrag zur Aphasie bei polyglotten, speziell im Hinblick aufs Schweizerdeutsche. *Schweizer Archiv für Neurologie und Psychiatrie* 21: 43–72.

Moretti, R., Bava, A., Torre, P. et al. (2001). Bilingual aphasia and subcortical-cortical lesions. *Perceptual and Motor Skills* 92: 803–814. doi:10.1080/02687038.2016.1184222.

Moritz-Gasser, S. and Duffau, H. (2009). Cognitive processes and neural basis of language switching: proposal of a new model. *NeuroReport* 20: 1577–1580. doi:10.1097/WNR.0b013e328333907e.

Muñoz, M.L., Marquardt, T.P., and Copeland, G.A. (1999). Comparison of the code switching patterns of aphasic and neurologically normal bilingual speakers of English and Spanish. *Brain and Language* 66: 249–274. doi:10.1006/brln.1998.2021.

Neumann, Y., Walters, J., and Altman, C. (2016). Codeswitching and discourse markers in the narratives of a bilingual speaker with aphasia. *Aphasiology* 31: 221–240. doi:10.1080/02687038.2016.1184222.

Nilipour, R. and Ashayeri, H. (1989). Alternating antagonism between two languages with successive recovery of a third in a trilingual aphasic patient. *Brain and Language* 36: 23–48.

Paradis, M. (1977). Bilingualism and aphasia. In: *Studies in Neurolinguistics*, vol. 3 (ed. H. Whitaker and H.A. Whitaker), 65–121. New York, NY: Academic Press.

Paradis, M. (1987). Neurolinguistic perspectives on bilingualism. In: *The Assessment of Bilingual Aphasia* (ed. M. Paradis and G. Libben), 1–17. Hillsdale, NJ: Erlbaum.

Paradis, M. (1994). Neurolinguistic aspects of implicit and explicit memory: implications for bilingualism. In: *Implicit and Explicit Learning of Second Languages* (ed. N. Ellis), 393–419. London, UK: Academic Press.

Paradis, M. (2001). Bilingual and polyglot aphasia. In: *Handbook of Neuropsychology*, 2nde, vol. 3 (ed. R.S. Berndt), 69–91. Oxford, UK: Elsevier Science.

Paradis, M. (2004). *A Neurolinguistic Theory of Bilingualism*. Amsterdam, The Netherlands: John Benjamins.

Paradis, M. (2008). Bilingualism and neuropsychiatric disorders. *Journal of Neurolinguistics* 21: 199–230. doi:10.1016/j. jneuroling.2007.09.002.

Paradis, M. (2009). *Declarative and Procedural Determinants of Second Languages*. Amsterdam: John Benjamins.

Paradis, M. and Goldblum, M.-C. (1989). Selective crossed aphasia in one of a trilingual's languages followed by antagonistic recovery. *Brain and Language* 36: 62–75.

Paradis, M., Goldblum, M.-C., and Abidi, R. (1982). Alternate antagonism with paradoxical transla-tion behavior in two bilingual aphasic patients. *Brain and Language* 15: 55–69.

Paradis, M. and Libben, G. (1987). *The Assessment of Bilingual Aphasia*. Hillsdale, NJ: Erlbaum.

Perecman, E. (1984). Spontaneous translation and language mixing in a polyglot aphasic. *Brain and Language* 23: 43–53. doi:10.1016/0093-934X(84)90005-1.

Peristeri, E. and Tsapkini, K. (2011). A comparison of the BAT and BDAE-SF batteries in determining the linguistic ability in Greek-speaking patients with Broca's aphasia. *Clinical Linguistics & Phonetics* 25 (6–7): 464–479.

Pitres, A. (1895). Etude sur l'aphasie chez les polyglottes. *Revue de Médecine* 15: 873–899.

Pötzl, O. (1925). Über die parietal bedingte Aphasie und ihren Einfluss auf das sprechen mehrerer sprachen. *Zeitschrift für die Gesamte Neurologie und Psychiatrie* 96: I00–I124.

Ribot, T. (1881). *Les maladies de la mémoire*. Paris, France: G. Baillère.

Roberts, P. and Deslauriers, L. (1999). Picture naming of cognate and non-cognate nouns in bilingual aphasia. *Journal of Communication Disorders* 32: 1–23. doi:10.1016/S0021-9924(98)00026-4.

Roux, F.-E. and Trémoulet, M. (2002). Organization of language areas in bilingual patients: a cortical stimulation study. *Journal of Neurosurgery* 97: 857–864.

Samar, R.G. and Akbari, M. (2012). A language teacher in the haze of bilingual aphasia: a Kurdish-Persian case. *Procedia – Social and Behavioral Sciences* 32: 252–257.

Scoresby-Jackson, R.E. (1867). Case of aphasia with right hemiplegia. *Edinburgh Medical Journal* 12: 696–706.

Sebastian, R., Laird, A.R., and Kiran, S. (2011). Meta-analysis of the neural representation of first language and second language. *Applied PsychoLinguistics* 1–21. doi:10.1017/S0142716411000075.

Senaha, M.L.H. and Parente, M.A.M.P. (2012). Acquired dyslexia in three writing systems: study of a Portuguese-Japanese bilingual aphasic patient. *Behavioural Neurology* 25: 255–272. doi:10.3233/BEN-2012-119001.

Sierpowska, J., Gabarrós, A., Ripollés, P. et al. (2013). Intraoperative electrical stimulation of language switching in two bilingual patients. *Neuropsychologia* 51: 2882–2892. doi:10.1016/j.neuropsychologia.2013.09.003.

Southwood, F., Schoemann, R., and Emsley, R. (2009). Bilingualism and psychosis: a linguistic analysis of a patient with differential symptom severity across languages. *Southern African Linguistics and Applied Language Studies* 27: 163–171.

Speedie, L.J., Wertman, E., Ta'ir, J., and Heilman, K.M. (1993). Disruption of automatic speech following a right basal ganglia lesion. *Neurology* 43: 1768. doi:10.1212/WNL.43.9.1768.

Titiz, A.P., Tezer, I., and Saygi, S. (2016). Speaking foreign language with expressive aphasia of native language during postictal period. *Journal of Neurological Sciences* 33: 147–154.

Tiwari, S. and Krishnan, G. (2015). Selective L2 cognate retrieval deficit in a bilingual person with aphasia: a case report. *Journal of Speech, Language and Hearing Research* doi:10.1179/2050572815Y.0000000008.

Tomasino, B., Marin, D., Canderan, C. et al. (2014). Involuntary switching into the native language induced by electrocortical stimulation of the superior temporal gyrus: a multimodal mapping study. *Neuropsychologia* 62: 87–100. doi:10.1016/j.neuropsychologia.2014.07.011.

Ullman, M.T. (2001). The declarative/procedural model of lexicon and grammar. *Journal of Psycholinguistic Research* 30: 37–69.

Ullman, M.T. (2005). A cognitive neuroscience perspective on second language acquisition: the declarative/procedural model. In: *Mind and Context in Adult Second Language Acquisition: Methods, Theory, and Practice* (ed. C. Sanz), 141–178. Washington, DC: Georgetown University Press.

Ullman, M.T. (2006). The declarative/ procedural model and the shallow structure hypothesis. *Applied PsychoLinguistics* 27: 97–105. doi:10.1017/S014271640606019X.

Venkatesh, M., Edwards, S., and Saddy, J.D. (2012). Production and comprehension of English and Hindi in multilingual transcortical aphasia. *Journal of Neurolinguistics* 25: 615–629. doi:10.1016/j. jneuroling.2011.10.003.

Woermann, F.G., Jokeit, H., Luerding, R. et al. (2003). Language lateralization by Wada test and fMRI in 100 patients with epilepsy. *Neurology* 61: 699–701.

Zanini, S., Tavano, A., and Fabbro, F. (2010). Spontaneous language production in bilingual Parkinson's disease patients: evidence of greater phonological, morphological and syntactic impairments in native language. *Brain and Language* 113: 84–89. doi:10.1016/j.bandl. 2010.01.005.

Zanini, S., Tavano, A., Vorano, L. et al. (2004). Greater syntactic impairments in native language in bilingual Parkinsonian patients. *Journal of Neurology, Neurosurgery, and Psychiatry* 75: 1678–1681. doi:10.1136/jnnp. 2003.018507.

27 Recovery and Rehabilitation Patterns in Bilingual and Multilingual Aphasia

CLAUDIA PEÑALOZA AND SWATHI KIRAN

1. Introduction

Bilingualism (hereafter also used to refer to multilingualism and the use of two or more languages) is, nowadays, an increasing defining trend of different societies due to globalization, immigration, and cross-cultural experience. As the bilingual population increases worldwide, the incidence of bilingual aphasia following stroke and other neurological conditions is also expected to increase especially in elderly individuals. Bilingual aphasia can be defined as the impairment of one or both languages in bilingual speakers that is not always followed by equal degrees of recovery across languages. Bilingual aphasia has motivated growing research interest in the last few decades due to an increasing demand of assessment and treatment options that are sensitive to the unique characteristics and needs of bilinguals. Nonetheless, several complexities regarding bilingualism and the functional organization of languages in the bilingual brain need to be considered to better understand language impairment and recovery in bilingual speakers affected by brain injury. In this chapter, we examine the recovery patterns and rehabilitation outcomes in individuals with bilingual aphasia. Section 2 of this chapter aims to provide an overview of language and cognitive control impairment in bilingual aphasia with specific focus on the premorbid language-related factors and lesion factors that influence the degree of impairment. Section 3 summarizes the patterns of language recovery and possible neural correlates in bilingual aphasia. In the fourth section, we discuss the existing evidence regarding treatment efficacy and outcomes involving the treated and untreated language. The section offers insights into the factors that modulate treatment outcomes including the type of rehabilitation provided and premorbid language proficiency. Section 5 is focused on the emerging neuroimaging evidence of language representation and treatment-induced recovery in bilinguals with aphasia. In the final section, we provide conclusions of our understanding of impairment and recovery in bilingual aphasia and suggestions for future research.

The Handbook of the Neuroscience of Multilingualism, First Edition. Edited by John W. Schwieter.

2.   Impairment in Bilingual Aphasia

2.1.   *Language Impairment and Control Impairment in Bilingual Aphasia*

An accurate characterization of the deficits that affect each language after brain damage is crucial to further our understanding of bilingual aphasia and to plan for optimal therapeutic interventions while considering factors that are inherently related to bilingualism. Initial approaches to describe language dysfunction in bilinguals with aphasia focused on the overall impairment of one language relative to the other. Following this approach, it has been suggested that languages can be affected according to the following patterns: (i) *parallel impairment* in which the first language (L1) and second language (L2) are equally affected, (ii) *differential impairment* in which one language is more impaired than the other relative to premorbid levels, and (iii) *selective impairment* in which one language is selectively impaired with no measurable deficits affecting the other (see Akbari 2014 for a review).

In an attempt to specify how brain damage affects the bilingual language system, early studies of bilingual aphasia have described overall equal levels of impairment across L1 and L2 (Watamori and Sasanuma 1976, 1978) but also differential impairments across languages with either greater impairment in speech production in L1 relative to L2 (Aglioti and Fabbro 1993; Silverberg and Gordon 1979) or greater impairment in L2 relative to L1 (Fabbro 2001). Also, differential impairments in morphology and syntax in L2 relative to L1 have been reported (Fabbro et al. 1997) albeit overall greater morphosyntactic than lexical-semantic impairment has been observed in aphasic bilinguals regardless of the pattern of bilingual impairment (Fabbro 2001). These early contributions provided relevant descriptions about the language history of the participants reported. Nonetheless, they also evidenced that as the field progressed, in-detail quantified examinations of language proficiency would be required to improve the interpretation of the relative impairment in each language with regards to its premorbid condition.

Other studies have provided a more refined description of the deficits observed in specific aspects of language processing in one language relative to the other in *premorbidly balanced bilinguals* (i.e. speakers with similar skills in both languages), thus using an initial approach to control for differences in premorbid proficiency across languages. It has been shown that lexical retrieval as measured by picture naming can remain comparable in both languages after brain damage in 30 Catalan-Spanish speakers (Junqué et al. 1989), 50 Spanish-Catalan bilinguals (Junqué et al. 1995), and 16 French-English bilinguals (Roberts and Dorze 1998). This last study also revealed similar impairment in semantic verbal fluency across languages.

Interestingly, other studies of bilingual aphasia have evidenced differences in naming performance according to specific word categories. It has been shown that picture-naming can be better for cognate than for non-cognate words across languages in a group of 15 French-English bilinguals (Roberts and Deslauriers 1999) although selective naming deficits for cognate words in L2 relative to L1 have been reported in a Kannada-Malayalam aphasic bilingual (Tiwari and Krishnan 2015). Two additional studies have also found selective deficits in picture-naming for verbs relative to nouns in a Spanish-Catalan bilingual (Hernàndez et al. 2008) and in 12 Greek-English aphasic bilinguals (Kambanaros and van Steenbrugge 2006) despite better comprehension for verbs and nouns in both languages (Kambanaros and van Steenbrugge 2006). The evidence reported here indicates that in bilinguals with aphasia with relatively balanced premorbid L1 and L2 proficiency, lexical retrieval can be impaired to similar degrees across languages. While cognateness seems to facilitate word retrieval across languages potentially due to shared phonological structure, deficits in lexical access can differentially impact grammatical categories (nouns vs. verbs) and input and output processes (production vs. comprehension).

Importantly, language impairment in bilingual aphasia could also reflect damage to the cognitive control system that regulates the selection of the target language and inhibition of interference of the non-target language in bilingual speech production. Most models of bilingual language processing agree in that the conceptual representations of bilinguals are associated with different lexical representations in L1 and L2 respectively (De Groot 1995; Kroll and Stewart 1994). Also, language coactivation is a particular phenomenon in bilinguals by which such lexical and phonological representations become activated from their common conceptual system in both the intended and the unintended language (Costa et al. 1999, 2000) and compete for selection in word production (Abutalebi and Green 2007). This particular characteristic of bilingualism calls for a cognitive mechanism that resolves competition across languages and ensures that the correct representations are selected and produced in the language intended for use. Cognitive control would enable bilingual speakers to filter irrelevant information and to inhibit inappropriate responses through interference suppression and response inhibition (Abutalebi and Green 2007; Rodríguez-Fornells et al. 2006). Thus, in bilingual aphasia, brain damage can also impact language capacity by impairing the cognitive control system, affecting the ability (i) to select between L1 and L2 language representations for use according to the appropriate linguistic context, or (ii) to resolve competition and control the activation of lexical representations in the non-targeted language (Abutalebi and Green 2007; Abutalebi et al. 2000).

It has been proposed that damage to cognitive control mechanisms in bilingual aphasia could explain selective impairment in one language, and interference between languages namely, pathological mixing (mixing L1 and L2 within the same utterance) and pathological mixing (mixing L1 and L2 within the same utterance) and pathological switching (alternating L1 and L2 in speech production across different utterances) (Abutalebi and Green 2007; Green et al. 2010). The few existing studies that have examined cognitive control in bilinguals with aphasia have shown that they are generally outperformed by healthy bilinguals in cognitive control tasks that involve response conflict and require the suppression of competing responses (Faroqui-Shah et al. 2016; Gray and Kiran 2016; Green et al. 2010; Verreyt et al. 2013). Moreover, initial evidence showing that congruency effects (i.e. a measure of cognitive control computed as the differences in accuracy and/or reaction times between conflict and non-conflict conditions) are not equally observed in linguistic versus non-linguistic control tasks (Dash and Kar 2014; Gray and Kiran 2016) points to a dissociation between language and domain-general cognitive control in bilingual aphasic speakers (Gray and Kiran 2016). However, recent research also suggests that cognitive control (as measured by the

Stroop paradigm) might not be associated with word retrieval in bilinguals with aphasia (Faroqui-Shah et al. 2016). Although the evidence of impaired cognitive control and reduced inhibitory mechanisms in bilinguals with aphasia with damage to the cognitive control network (described in Section 2.3) is consistent across studies, research focused on the association between cognitive control and language impairment in bilingual aphasia is still limited and preliminary. Studies with healthy bilinguals suggest an association between lexical retrieval and cognitive control (i.e. task switching and stop-signal tasks) in terms of behavioural performance (Shao et al. 2012) and overlap in neural activation (Braver 2012). Nonetheless, opposite findings have been reported by Bialystok et al. (2008) when using other measures of cognitive control (i.e. Simon task and Stroop task). The translation of these findings to bilingual aphasia is not that clear, hence, more research is needed to determine whether the relationship between bilingual language processing and cognitive control is consistent across experimental tasks, and under increased task difficulty increased task difficulty that taxes cognitive control mechanisms. Also, it is important to determine whether this association is consistent throughout the adult lifespan and if it is modulated by the severity of impairment such that associations between lexical access and control impairment could just reflect larger overall severity due to extensive regions with common neural damage.

In summary, the studies reviewed in this section suggest that: (i) parallel impairment is the most common condition in balanced bilinguals with aphasia, (ii) differential impairment in early reported cases of bilingual aphasia could be at least partially attributed to an underspecified assessment of premorbid language proficiency, and (iii) selective impairment in one language as well as pathological mixing and switching result from deficits in language control mechanisms.

2.2.   *Premorbid Language Factors that Influence Impairment: Age of Acquisition, Language Use and Proficiency*

Research with healthy bilinguals suggests that high L2 proficiency requires less effort for word retrieval in L2 relative to low L2 proficiency. Indeed, word retrieval in L2 might be more susceptible to cross-language interference and might require more inhibitory resources to suppress predominant L1 representations (Abutalebi and Green 2007; Kroll and Sholl 1992; Kroll and Stewart 1994). The degree of L2 proficiency might also modulate whether language processing requires the engagement of top-down control processes or more automatic processes as in highly proficient individuals (Abutalebi and Green 2007). Similarly, the age of acquisition of L2 can facilitate or constrain its degree of mastery (Birdsong 2006). Age of acquisition can especially influence grammatical processing (Johnson and Newport 1989) since L2 grammar may be more effortful to learn later in life through explicit declarative memory processes (Ullman 2004) as opposed to automatic implicit memory mechanisms supporting L1 acquisition (Paradis 1994; Paradis 2004; see Section 3 for a more detail discussion on the role of memory systems in L1 and L2 acquisition). Age of acquisition can also modulate lexical semantic processing, albeit to a lower extent than language proficiency (Hernandez and Li 2007). Besides, speech comprehension and production in L2 are influenced by L2 use and experience (Green 1998). Because age of acquisition and language proficiency and use can modulate differences in L1 and L2 processing in healthy bilinguals, it seems crucial that these factors are considered to characterize language impairment and to make appropriate inferences about the neural organization of language in bilinguals with aphasia. Two implications for language assessment in bilinguals with aphasia stem from this assumption. First, testing should be conducted in each language to accurately determine the spared/impaired language processing abilities in L1 and L2 (Paradis 2004). In addition, premorbid proficiency may directly influence performance on standardized tests. Therefore, testing should address the history of language acquisition, and premorbid use and proficiency through self-reports and questionnaires as to determine the degree of impairment in each language relative to premorbid skills and to plan treatment accordingly (Kiran and Roberts 2012).

Research on bilingual aphasia has evidenced the important role of premorbid language history in the characterization of language impairment. Muñoz and Marquardt (2003) demonstrated that different patterns of naming impairment could be determined for Spanish-English bilinguals with aphasia when considering premorbid language skills including proficiency and language use patterns. Likewise, Kiran and Iakupova (2011) examined a Russian-English bilingual with aphasia whose lower language performance in English compared with Russian could have been misinterpreted as an apparent differential impairment between the two languages. Yet, a further inspection of his premorbid proficiency (i.e. stronger for Russian compared to English before stroke) revealed an actual parallel impairment showing that the relative difference between the two languages continued after stroke.

More recent studies with Spanish-English bilinguals with aphasia have shown that self-rating measures of premorbid language proficiency can strongly predict postmorbid language deficits in comprehension and semantic processing (Gray and Kiran 2013) and in lexical retrieval as measured by picture-naming and word generation (Kiran et al. 2014). In line with these findings, Grasemann et al. (2011) developed a computational model that simulated naming impairment in 18 Spanish-English bilinguals with aphasia while accounting for premorbid language background. In this study, several individual models were first trained to simulate the premorbid language status of the participants including age of acquisition, relative exposure, and naming performance in both languages. Taking into account these premorbid language parameters was crucial to simulate post-stroke naming impairment and led the individual models to match the patients' actual post-stroke naming performance accurately in most cases. These findings suggest that considering language impairment in the light of these premorbid language factors is crucial in both clinical and research contexts.

2.3. Lesion Factors that Influence Language Impairment

Historically, lesion-deficit approaches have built the foundations of cognitive neuropsychology, informing models of brain organization and function about the relationships between brain and behaviour, and contributing to our understanding of impaired language and cognition following brain damage. Modern structural neuroimaging studies of monolingual aphasia have shown an overall reliable relationship between lesion location and language impairment according to aphasia subtypes (Henseler et al. 2014), and specific language abilities including speech production (Borovsky et al. 2007), comprehension (Dronkers et al. 2004), naming (Baldo et al. 2013), and repetition (Fridriksson et al. 2010). Moreover, lesion information and particularly lesion size can also help predicting the severity of post-stroke language and cognitive impairment (Forkel et al. 2014; Hope et al. 2013) suggesting that the less spared tissue is available, less cognitive resources can be recruited to cope successfully with a given linguistic or cognitive demand.

Importantly, both monolinguals and bilinguals with aphasia are sensitive to damage in the same brain regions, although bilinguals seem more sensitive to the functional disruption resulting from brain damage possibly depending on premorbid language proficiency (Hope et al. 2015). However, portraying the relationship between lesion and language dysfunction in bilingual aphasia is a more multifaceted effort when considering all the complexities that bilingualism adds to the representation and functional organization of two or more languages in the brain. Neuroimaging studies of healthy bilingual speakers suggest that, overall, the representation of L2 is predominantly overlapping with that of L1 in typical areas of the language network (see Abutalebi 2008; Abutalebi and Green 2007; Indefrey 2006, for a review). This is particularly true for bilinguals with early L2 acquisition (Perani et al. 2003) and high L2 proficiency (Sebastian et al. 2011) who seem to rely in a more automatic, native-like L2 processing (Abutalebi 2008). However, brain activity associated with L2 processing in bilinguals with low proficiency and/or late acquisition is more largely distributed, as it extends into adjacent regions to those recruited for L1 processing (Abutalebi 2008; Perani and Abutalebi 2005) and additional regions in the right hemisphere (Sebastian et al. 2011). This indicates not only a less efficient neural network for L2 processing that requires more cognitive effort and the recruitment of more extensive regions for low-L2 proficiency compensation (Sebastian et al. 2011; Stowe and Sabourin 2005) but also a higher reliance on controlled processing for L2 (Abutalebi 2008). In fact, bilingual language processing also involves other brain regions beyond the classical language areas. The cognitive control system including the prefrontal cortex, the inferior parietal cortex, anterior cingulate cortex/pre-supplementary motor area, and the basal ganglia would be key in the selection of the correct lexical representations in the intended language, the control and monitoring of the language in use and the resolution of competition and the inhibition of the non-target language (Abutalebi and Green 2007; Crinion et al. 2006). In this way, the engagement of this cognitive control network would facilitate the overall processing of a weaker L2 by controlling, inhibiting, and suppressing any competing representations of a predominant L1 in bilinguals (Abutalebi 2008; Sebastian et al. 2011).

In summary, based on the neuroimaging findings of healthy bilinguals and lesion evidence in bilingual aphasia, we suggest that the language impairment observed in bilinguals with brain damage is modulated by lesion location as follows. Bilingual aphasia may result from lesions affecting anatomical brain regions that involve the mostly overlapping or partially segregated representations of L1 and L2 (i.e. word form and meaning). This is supported by evidence of similar language impairment in L1 and L2 processing after brain damage within the left perisylvian language network (Fabbro 2001; Tschirren et al. 2011). Bilingual aphasia can also result from lesions affecting brain regions that are crucial for cognitive control. Lesions in the cognitive control system can account for selective impairment, and also cross-language interference involving pathological mixing and/or switching between L1 and L2 after damage to left prefrontal regions (Fabbro et al. 2000; Nardone et al. 2011; Sierpowska et al. 2013) and the basal ganglia (Abutalebi et al. 2000; Ansaldo et al. 2010; Keane and Kiran 2015; Mariën et al. 2005). Finally, as discussed in Section 5, functional connectivity studies suggest that bilingual aphasia deficits may also arise when the lesion affects the functional connections between language representation and control regions (Abutalebi et al. 2009; Radman et al. 2016).

3. Language Recovery in Bilingual Aphasia

As reviewed in the Section 2.2, the profile of language impairment that manifests as a direct and immediate consequence of brain injury in bilinguals with aphasia can be highly influenced by premorbid language factors and lesion location. However, language deficits tend to naturally improve during the following weeks to months post injury through spontaneous and therapy-induced processes, evolving into diverse profiles of language recovery. The behavioural patterns of language recovery in bilinguals with aphasia have been well-characterized in terms of the relative impairment and premorbid ability of each language and their progress over time (Paradis 2004). These patterns of language recovery are summarized in Table 1.

Despite the large variability of recovery patterns in bilingual aphasia, it is most frequently expected that the recovery of L1 and L2 parallels premorbid levels of proficiency in the absence of language control impairment (Green and Abutalebi 2008) as revealed by large patient sample studies (Fabbro 2001; Paradis 2001).

Table 1 Patterns of language recovery in bilingual aphasia.

Pattern of recovery	Profile of language processing abilities
Parallel recovery	Both languages show a similar extent of recovery that parallels premorbid relative ability.
Differential recovery	One language recovers better than the other relative to premorbid ability.
Selective recovery	Only one language shows clear improvement with no observable residual deficits while the other language remains impaired.
Antagonistic recovery	One language is initially recovered but it is lost with the recovery of the other.
Alternate antagonistic recovery	One language is available while the other is affected during alternating cycles of days or months.
Successive recovery	One language recovers before the other.
Blended recovery	Pathological involuntary switching between the two languages despite the voluntary effort of speaking only one language.

Source: Adapted from Paradis (2004).

Of interest, models of declarative and procedural memory systems involved in bilingual acquisition and processing (Paradis 1994, 2004; Ullman 2004) have suggested important considerations for language recovery in bilinguals. According to these models, L1 is predominantly acquired implicitly through the procedural memory system while L2 is more dependent on the declarative memory system. This is especially the case of late bilinguals because L2 is generally acquired through formal instruction (albeit higher reliance on the procedural system is expected with higher L2 proficiency, Green 2008). Thus, bilinguals may have a metalinguistic declarative knowledge about their L2 that they do not have for their L1 which is acquired and processed in an automatic and implicit manner. This suggests that the metalinguistic explicit knowledge of L2 may help compensate for L2 impairment and support its recovery (Paradis 2004).

Although important considerations have been proposed for the study of recovery patterns in bilingual aphasia through neuropsychological and neuroimaging methods (Green and Price 2001), the neural dynamics underlying spontaneous language recovery in bilingual aphasia have not been specifically examined. Nonetheless, structural neuroimaging evidence suggests similar sensitivity to damage in the same brain regions for bilinguals relative to monolinguals (Hope et al. 2015) and the description of the so-called acute lesion and late phase of recovery described in bilinguals with aphasia (Fabbro 2001) resembles the well-known stages of recovery in monolingual aphasia. Thus, it seems likely that the neural processes that support language recovery in bilinguals are similar to those reported in monolinguals. If this is the case, models of language recovery in monolingual aphasia (see Saur et al. 2006; Saur and Hartwigsen 2012, for a review) can be employed as a starting point for the study of the neural reorganization of the bilingual adult brain during spontaneous recovery while considering the neural mechanisms of lexical-semantic bilingual processing and crucially and those that govern language control.

4. Treatment-Induced Recovery of Bilingual Aphasia: Efficacy and Generalization Effects

Although several studies have provided in-detail descriptions about the patterns of impairment and recovery in bilingual aphasia, therapy studies with this population consist mostly of single-case or multiple-case studies and are largely variable in terms of the targeted language and treatment approach and duration, let alone the individual characteristics of the participants regarding language combinations, bilingual background, and language impairment. To date, several key issues remain unsolved in bilingual aphasia rehabilitation, including which language should be targeted in treatment, what type of treatment elicits the most optimal outcomes, and whether treatment gains can be generalized within and across languages. As a result, rehabilitation of bilingual aphasia continues to lack guidelines and recommendations on optimal treatment plans (Roberts and Kiran 2007). Nonetheless, a growing number of studies have addressed this gap by examining the efficacy and generalization effects of speech and language interventions for people with bilingual aphasia.

Studies of bilingual aphasia rehabilitation have generally shown that treatment targeting either L1 or L2 can lead to positive outcomes in the treated language, on both receptive and expressive skills, in the acute and the chronic phase. Specifically, the efficacy of such interventions has been evidenced for treatments targeting auditory comprehension (Abutalebi et al. 2009; Gil and Goral 2004; Khamis et al. 1996), word retrieval (Abutalebi et al. 2009; Edmonds and Kiran 2006; Gil and Goral 2004; Khamis et al. 1996; Kiran and Iakupova 2011; Kiran and Roberts 2010; Laganaro et al. 2003; Marangolo et al. 2009; Meinzer et al. 2007; Miertsch et al. 2009), morphosyntactic (Faroqui and Chengappa 1996), and syntactic deficits (Goral et al. 2010; see Faroqi-Shah et al. 2010 for a review).

Another measure of positive therapy outcome is the generalization of treatment gains to untreated items. Some treatment studies in bilingual aphasia have reported benefits that include within-language generalization effects across semantically related items (Edmonds and Kiran 2006; Kiran and Roberts 2010) and across language modalities (Galvez and Hinckley 2003). The generalization of treatment effects in bilinguals with aphasia can also involve the facilitation of language recovery in the untreated language (i.e. from L1 to L2 or vice versa). Although addressed less frequently, there is evidence that supports cross-language generalization in bilingual aphasia. For instance, significant improvements in the untreated language have been reported for treatments targeting receptive language skills in L2 (Faroqui and Chengappa 1996; Gil and Goral 2004; Khamis et al. 1996) and in L1 (Gil and Goral 2004; Junqué et al. 1989). Cross-language transfer effects have been also observed in studies addressing expressive language abilities in L2 (Faroqui and Chengappa 1996; Khamis et al. 1996; Knoph et al. 2017; Marangolo et al. 2009; Miertsch et al. 2009) and in L1 (Ansaldo et al. 2010; Croft et al. 2011; Edmonds and Kiran 2006; Gil and Goral 2004; Junqué et al. 1989; see Ansaldo and Saidi 2014; Faroqi-Shah et al. 2010; Kohnert 2009, for a review). Importantly, most bilinguals with aphasia showing cross-language effects had high premorbid proficiency in both L1 and L2 despite differences in their L2 age of acquisition. Nevertheless, other studies have not found transfer effects to the untreated language, and thus support existing evidence for only language-specific improvement (Galvez and Hinckley 2003; Hinckley 2003; Meinzer et al. 2007; Miller Amberber 2012; Radman et al. 2016). Moreover, other studies have shown opposite effects including cross-language interference and decreased language performance in the untargeted language (Abutalebi et al. 2009; Goral et al. 2013; Keane and Kiran 2015; Miertsch et al. 2009) possibly due to damage to regions involved in language control (Abutalebi et al. 2009). Overall, current available evidence for cross-language generalization is mixed, and more research is needed to determine the factors that facilitate cross-language transfer effects in bilinguals with aphasia.

Some studies suggest the possibility that cross-language generalization is modulated by the type of treatment and the type of items targeted in therapy. There is evidence that cross-language effects are likely to follow semantic treatment (Croft et al. 2011; Edmonds and Kiran 2006; Kiran and Iakupova 2011; Kiran and Roberts 2010; Kiran et al. 2013a) but not phonological treatment approaches (Abutalebi et al. 2009; Croft et al. 2011). Also, cross-language generalization is more likely to arise for items that are structurally and semantically similar (Kohnert 2009). For instance, generalization effects have been reported for cognate words but not for non-cognates (Kohnert 2004), for semantically related items across languages (Edmonds and Kiran 2006) and for languages with similar structure relative to the treated language (Miertsch et al. 2009, although see Kiran and Iakupova 2011, for evidence of cross-language transfer across distant languages). The exact mechanism underlying post-treatment generalization in bilingual aphasia remains to be determined, but a possible account for semantic treatment generalization effects can be suggested. Spreading activation is a generalized mechanism of increased activation of word representations in the mental lexicon involved in word production (see Schwartz 2014, for a review). In models of bilingual language processing with a unitary semantic store but separate lexical representations for each language (Kroll and Stewart 1994) the activation flows from the semantic to the phonological system for L1 and L2 in a target language-independent manner (Costa et al. 2006). Thus, treatments that strengthen semantic features may facilitate lexical access by inducing increased spreading activation from the semantic system to the target word forms and neighbours in the treated and the untreated language (Kiran et al. 2013a).

Language-related factors can also impact treatment outcomes and cross-language generalization in bilingual aphasia. Based on the computational model that simulated language impairment in bilingual aphasia commented above (Grasemann et al. 2011), Kiran et al. (2013b) compared the treatment outcomes of 17 Spanish-English bilingual speakers with aphasia with the treatment outcomes that were individually simulated for these participants through computational modelling. This study showed that, when taking into account premorbid language proficiency, age of acquisition, and language impairment, the computational model could accurately match the therapy gains in the trained language for most bilingual participants and the cross-language transfer effects when they occurred. In addition, therapy outcomes may be determined by the specific patterns of premorbid language proficiency across languages. In bilinguals with aphasia with premorbid balanced proficiency across languages, treatment can have equal benefits for both languages (Galvez and Hinckley 2003) and may be followed by cross-language transfer effects (Edmonds and Kiran 2006; Kiran and Roberts 2010). However, if bilinguals with aphasia show unbalanced premorbid proficiency across languages, treatment effects may be different depending on the language treated. For instance, treatment in the premorbid predominant language can lead to within-language but not to cross-language generalization (Edmonds and Kiran 2006) possibly due to stronger connections between the semantic system and the predominant language but weaker connections from the predominant to the less predominant language (Kroll and Stewart 1994). Conversely, treatment in the less proficient language can show the reverse pattern, with only cross-language but not within-language generalization (Edmonds and Kiran 2006), likely because of the weaker connections between the semantic system and the less predominant language but stronger connections from the less to the more predominant language (Kroll and Stewart 1994). Additionally, cross-language generalization has been reported after therapy provided in the language with highest postmorbid proficiency regardless of premorbid proficiency (see Ansaldo and Saidi, for a review). These results support the idea that true patterns of treatment outcomes can only be determined when considering language proficiency (Roberts and Kiran 2007) and suggest that examining the role of premorbid and postmorbid proficiency in more detail may offer a potential answer to the unsolved question of which language to treat in bilinguals with aphasia.

While more research is clearly needed, the overall findings commented here suggest that treating the weaker and less-proficient language, targeting cognates in language therapy, and using a semantic feature analysis approach are valid considerations for clinical practice to enhance therapy effects in bilinguals with aphasia (Ansaldo and Saidi 2014; Faroqi-Shah et al. 2010). The timing of treatment and language therapy regimen (intensity, dosage and duration) for bilinguals with aphasia has not been studied in detail. There is evidence that significant language improvement in the treated and untreated language can take place in both the subacute and chronic stages of bilingual aphasia (Faroqi-Shah et al. 2010; Kohnert 2009). Nonetheless, it remains to be determined whether bilinguals with aphasia also benefit most from language therapy delivered at high intensity, at high dose, and over long periods as shown in monolinguals with aphasia (Brady et al. 2016).

5. Neuroimaging Evidence of Treatment-Induced Recovery in Bilingual Aphasia

Only a few functional neuroimaging studies have been conducted with bilinguals with aphasia. Nonetheless, they have addressed important questions regarding the neural representation of bilingual language processing after brain damage and the functional changes that take place in treatment-induced language recovery (see Peñaloza and Kiran 2017, for a review). For instance, Sebastian et al. (2012) conducted an fMRI study on the neural representation of semantic processing of L1 and L2 in three Spanish (L1)-English (L2) bilinguals with aphasia who had stronger premorbid proficiency for L2 as compared to L1. Similar to the healthy bilingual controls, the three bilinguals with aphasia showed higher speed and accuracy on a semantic judgement task in the dominant L2 relative to their performance on the same task in the non-dominant L1. Additionally, fMRI findings revealed that, like the healthy controls, the bilinguals with aphasia presented an increased and more distributed bilateral activation in the frontal cortex and the cingulate gyrus when semantic processing took place in the non-dominant L1 relative to the dominant L2. As highlighted in Section 2.3, these findings from bilingual aphasia are in line with the neuroimaging evidence of healthy bilinguals that suggest that processing the non-proficient language involves the recruitment of more extensive brain regions of the language (Abutalebi 2008; Sebastian et al. 2011) and control network (Abutalebi and Green 2007) possibly to compensate for lower language proficiency to achieve effective language processing.

Single-case fMRI studies have also addressed the functional changes that take place in the language network following treatment in bilingual aphasia. The fMRI study conducted by Meinzer et al. (2007) examined an early bilingual with aphasia who was equally proficient in German and French prior to stroke and received language therapy and further intensive language training in German. The fMRI results revealed that naming improvement after therapy in German was associated with increased contralesional activation in right temporal regions as compared to naming in French. After further language training, improvement in picture-naming in German was associated with increased activation in perilesional and contralesional frontotemporal areas relative to picture-naming in the untrained language. Another fMRI study conducted by Marini et al. (2016) examined the recovery of a bilingual with aphasia who was equally proficient in Romanian (L1) and Italian (L2) prior to a severe traumatic brain injury and underwent speech therapy in L2 addressing communicative and language skills. The fMRI during a covert verb generation task in L1 and L2 at the chronic phase showed activation in the right middle temporal gyrus in the context of an extensive frontotemporo-parietal lesion in the left hemisphere. These studies show that language improvement following therapy in bilinguals with aphasia involves the recruitment of perilesional language regions and contralesional homologue regions as observed in spontaneous and therapy-induced recovery in monolinguals (see Crinion and Leff 2007; Crosson et al. 2007; Saur and Hartwigsen 2012, for a review).

Two additional fMRI studies have provided further evidence that changes in brain activation patterns following treatment can occur not only in the language network but also in the cognitive control network. Building upon their fMRI findings, these two studies also employed dynamic causal modelling (DCM) to determine changes in the connectivity of brain regions where changes in activation were detected and associated with language recovery. In the first study, Abutalebi et al. (2009) examined a bilingual speaker with equal premorbid proficiency for L1 (Spanish) and L2 (Italian) who received naming treatment in L2. His post-treatment fMRI findings showed a pattern of bilateral activation that involved the frontal, parietal, and occipital cortices, the right temporal cortex and the prefrontal and the anterior cingulate cortex in the control network which was more largely distributed in L2 as compared to naming in L1. These findings were attributed to the reactivation of the brain areas subserving language function only in the treated language. DCM analyses further revealed increased connection strength in the left hemisphere both within the naming network and between the naming and the control network for improved L2 naming, while worse L1 naming was associated with global decreased connection strength. In the second study, Radman et al. (2016) examined five bilinguals with aphasia, three of them were highly proficient in both French (L1) and English (L2) while the other two were highly proficient in Italian (L1) and French (L2) prior to stroke. At four months post-stroke and regardless of the type of treatment received, DCM analyses showed increased connectivity between language processing and control regions during naming performance in the recovered language. Moreover, for three bilinguals with aphasia showing parallel recovery, naming performance in L1 and L2 was associated with similar degrees of connectivity strength between language processing and control regions. Thus, these two studies additionally suggest that the recovery of language following treatment also relies on the functional interplay between the language and cognitive control systems. More research is needed to examine treatment-induced language recovery in bilinguals with aphasia.

6.   Conclusions

The last decades of research in bilingual aphasia have greatly contributed to our current knowledge of the deficits that characterize language impairment and behavioural recovery in bilingual aphasia. Yet, more recent evidence suggests that a better understanding of bilingual language impairment depends on an accurate and objective description of lesion-related factors including lesion size and location, profile of spared-impaired abilities in L1 and L2, and linguistic factors related to L2 age of acquisition and language use and proficiency before and after brain injury. In addition, cognitive control can be impaired in bilingual aphasia and it may influence language impairment, although the evidence on this relationship remains limited and deserves to be examined further. Overall, it is important that all these factors are extensively addressed and taken into account when evaluating treatment options and possible outcomes in bilingual aphasia. Indeed, there is a large degree of individual variability in the recovery of adults with bilingual aphasia because the effects of rehabilitation are multifactorial. Thus, outcomes in both the treated and the untreated language must be carefully interpreted in the context of the above mentioned factors. With regards to the rehabilitation of bilingual aphasia, treatment effects are generally positive in the targeted language with evidence of improvement for treated items and generalization to untreated items. However, the findings about cross-language generalization are mixed and remain inconclusive with some studies indicating that the effects of generalization are language specific, whereas others have shown that generalization to the non-treated language can take place in bilingual aphasia, especially when treating the less proficient language. Given that access to bilingual speech-language pathologists that can provide therapy in all the languages spoken by a person with aphasia is frequently not possible, determining the factors that promote and constrain cross-language generalization effects for close and distant languages is an urgent open question for future research. Neuroimaging studies suggest that a comprehensive view of language spontaneous and treatment-induced recovery in bilingual aphasia should consider the complex interactions between canonical language brain regions and those involved in cognitive control processes, while also considering the variability of stroke topography and language organization in the bilingual brain. Evidence from single-case studies already shows that the recovery of language following treatment is associated with the recruitment of preserved areas in the left language network and their homologues in the right hemisphere, and the functional coupling between regions within the language network but also between these regions and the cognitive control network. Nonetheless, further research in this field demands more group studies to more accurately represent and address the large variability of clinical profiles that can be found across bilingual adults with aphasia that stems from the complexity of bilingualism and language impairment. Simulations through computational modelling may facilitate the study of these multiple aspects in bilingual aphasia research.

REFERENCES

Abutalebi, J. (2008). Neural aspects of second language representation and language control. *Acta Psychologica* 128 (3): 466–478. doi:10.1016/j.actpsy.2008.03.014.

Abutalebi, J., Della Rosa, P.A., Tettamanti, M. et al. (2009). Bilingual aphasia and language control: a follow-up fMRI and intrinsic connectivity study. *Brain and Language* 109 (2): 141–156. doi:10.1016/j.bandl.2009.03.003.

Abutalebi, J. and Green, D. (2007). Bilingual language production: the neurocognition of language representation and control. *Journal of Neurolinguistics* 20 (3): 242–275. doi: 10.1016/j.jneuroling.2006.10.003.

Abutalebi, J., Miozzo, A., and Cappa, S.F. (2000). Do subcortical structures control 'language selection' in poliglots? Evidence from pathological language mixing. *Neurocase* 6 (1): 51–56. doi:10.1080/ 13554790008402757.

Aglioti, S. and Fabbro, F. (1993). Paradoxical selective recovery in a bilingual aphasic following subcortical lesions. *NeuroReport* 4 (12): 1359–1362. doi:10.1097/ 00001756-199309150-00019.

Akbari, M. (2014). A multidimensional review of bilingual aphasia as a language disorder. *Advances in Language and Literacy Studies* 5 (2): 73–86.

Ansaldo, A.I. and Saidi, L.G. (2014). Aphasia therapy in the age of globalization: cross-linguistic therapy effects in bilingual aphasia. *Behavioral Neurology* doi:10. 1155/2014/603085.

Ansaldo, A.I., Saidi, L.G., and Ruiz, A. (2010). Model-driven intervention in bilingual aphasia: evidence from a case of pathological language mixing. *Aphasiology* 24 (2): 309–324. doi:10.1080/ 02687030902958423.

Baldo, J.V., Arévalo, A., Patterson, J.P., and Dronkers, N.F. (2013). Grey and white matter correlates of picture naming: evidence from a voxel-based lesion analysis of the Boston naming test. *Cortex* 49 (3): 658–667. doi:10.1016/j.cortex.2012.03.001.

Bialystok, E., Craik, F., and Luk, G. (2008). Cognitive control and lexical access in younger and older bilinguals. *Journal of Experimental Psychology: Learning, Memory, and Cognition* 34 (4): 859–873. doi:10.1037/0278-7393.34.4.859.

Birdsong, D. (2006). Age and second language acquisition and processing: a selective overview. *Language Learning* 56: 949. doi:10.1111/j.1467-9922.2006.00353.x.

Borovsky, A., Saygin, A.P., Bates, E., and Dronkers, N. (2007). Lesion correlates of

conversational speech production deficits. *Neuropsychologia* 45 (11): 2525–2533. doi:10.1016/j.neuropsychologia.2007.03.023.

Brady, M.C., Kelly, H., Godwin, J. et al. (2016). Speech and language therapy for aphasia following stroke. *Cochrane Database of Systematic Reviews* 6: doi:10.1002/14651858. CD000425.pub4.

Braver, T.S. (2012). The variable nature of cognitive control: a dual mechanisms framework. *Trends in Cognitive Sciences* 16 (2): 106–113. doi:10.1016/j.tics.2011.12.010.

Costa, A., Caramazza, A., and Sebastian-Galles, N. (2000). The cognate facilitation effect: implications for models of lexical access. *Journal of Experimental Psychology: Learning, Memory, and Cognition* 26 (5): 1283–1296. doi:10.1037/0278-7393.26.5.1283.

Costa, A., La Heij, W., and Navarrete, E. (2006). The dynamics of bilingual lexical access. *Bilingualism: Language and Cognition* 9 (2): 137–151. doi:10.1017/S1366672890600249.

Costa, A., Miozzo, M., and Caramazza, A. (1999). Lexical selection in bilinguals: do words in the bilingual's two lexicons compete for selection? *Journal of Memory and Language* 41 (3): 365–397. doi:10.1006/ jmla.1999.2651.

Crinion, J.T. and Leff, A.P. (2007). Recovery and treatment of aphasia after stroke: functional imaging studies. *Current Opinion in Neurology* 20 (6): 667–673. doi:10.1097/ WCO.0b013e3282f1c6fa.

Crinion, J., Turner, R., Grogan, A. et al. (2006). Language control in the bilingual brain. *Science* 312 (5779): 1537–1540. doi:10.1126/ science.1127761.

Croft, S., Marshall, J., Pring, T., and Hardwick, M. (2011). Therapy for naming difficulties in bilingual aphasia: which language benefits? *International Journal of Language & Communication Disorders* 1–15. doi:10.3109/ 13682822.2010.484845.

Crosson, B., McGregor, K., Gopinath, K.S. et al. (2007). Functional MRI of language in aphasia: a review of the literature and the methodological challenges. *Neuropsychology Review* 17 (2): 157–177. doi:10.1007/s11065-007-9024-z.

Dash, T. and Kar, B.R. (2014). Bilingual language control and general purpose cognitive control among individuals with bilingual aphasia: evidence based on negative priming and flanker tasks. *Behavioral Neurology* doi:10.1155/2014/679706.

De Groot, A.M.B. (1995). Determinants of bilingual lexicosemantic organization. *Computer Assisted Language Learning* 8: 151–180. doi:10.1080/0958822940080204.

Dronkers, N.F., Wilkins, D.P., Van Valin, R.D. et al. (2004). Lesion analysis of the brain areas involved in language comprehension. *Cognition* 92 (1): 145–177. doi:10.1016/j.cognition.2003.11.002.

Edmonds, L.A. and Kiran, S. (2006). Effect of semantic naming treatment on crosslinguistic generalization in bilingual aphasia. *Journal of Speech, Language, and Hearing Research* 49 (4): 729–748. doi:10.1044/1092-4388(2006/053).

Fabbro, F. (2001). The bilingual brain: bilingual aphasia. *Brain and Language* 79 (2): 201–210. doi:10.1006/brln.2001.2480.

Fabbro, F., Peru, A., and Skrap, M. (1997). Language disorders in bilingual patients after thalamic lesions. *Journal of Neurolinguistics* 10 (4): 347–367. doi:10.1016/S0911-6044(97)00017-1.

Fabbro, F., Skrap, M., and Aglioti, S. (2000). Pathological switching between languages after frontal lesions in a bilingual patient. *Journal of Neurology, Neurosurgery & Psychiatry* 68 (5): 650–652. doi:10.1136/jnnp.68.5.650.

Faroqi-Shah, Y., Frymark, T., Mullen, R., and Wang, B. (2010). Effect of treatment for bilingual individuals with aphasia: a systematic review of the evidence. *Journal of Neurolinguistics* 23 (4): 319–341. doi:10.1016/j.jneuroling.2010.01.002.

Faroqui, Y. and Chengappa, S. (1996). Trace deletion hypothesis and its implications for intervention with a multilingual agrammatic aphasic patient. *Osmania Papers in Linguistics* 22–23: 79–106.

Faroqui-Shah, Y., Sampson, M., Pranger, M., and Baughman, S. (2016). Cognitive control, word retrieval and bilingual aphasia: is there a relationship? *Journal of Neurolinguistics* 1–15. doi:10.1016/j.jneuroling.2016.07.001.

Forkel, S.J., Thiebaut de Schotten, M., Dell'Acqua, F. et al. (2014). Anatomical predictors of aphasia recovery: a tractography study of bilateral perisylvian language networks. *Brain* 137 (7): 2027–2039. doi:10.1093/brain/awu113.

Fridriksson, J., Kjartansson, O., Morgan, P.S. et al. (2010). Impaired speech repetition and left parietal lobe damage. *The Journal of Neuroscience* 30 (33): 11057–11061. doi:10.1523/JNEUROSCI.1120-10.2010.

Galvez, A. and Hinckley, J.J. (2003). Transfer patterns of naming treatment in a case of bilingual aphasia. *Brain and Language* 87 (1): 173–174.

Gil, M. and Goral, M. (2004). Nonparallel recovery in bilingual aphasia: effects of language choice, language proficiency, and treatment. *International Journal of Bilingualism* 8 (2): 191–219. doi:10.1177/13670069040080020501.

Goral, M., Levy, E.S., and Kastl, R. (2010). Cross-language treatment generalization: a case of trilingual aphasia. *Aphasiology* 24 (2): 170–187. doi:10.1080/02687030902958308.

Goral, M., Naghibolhosseini, M., and Conner, P.S. (2013). Asymmetric inhibitory treatment effects in multilingual aphasia. *Cognitive Neuropsychology* 30 (7–8): 564–577. doi:10.1080/02643294.2013.878692.

Grasemann, U., Sandberg, C., Kiran, S., & Miikkulainen, R. (2011). *Impairment and rehabilitation in bilingual aphasia: A SOM-based model*. Presented at the 8th Workshop on Self-Organizing Maps (WSOM 2011), Espoo, Finland.

Gray, T. and Kiran, S. (2013). A theoretical account of lexical and semantic naming deficits in bilingual aphasia. *Journal of Speech, Language, and Hearing Research* 56 (4): 1314–1327. doi:10.1044/1092-4388(2012/12-0091).

Gray, T. and Kiran, S. (2016). The relationship between language control and cognitive control in bilingual aphasia.

Bilingualism: Language and Cognition 19 (3):
433–452. doi:10.1017/S1366728915000061.

Green, D.W. (1998). Mental control of the
bilingual lexico-semantic system.
Bilingualism 1 (2): 67–81. doi:10.1017/
S1366728998000133.

Green, D.W. (2008). Bilingual aphasia: adapted
language networks and their control. *Annual
Review of Applied Linguistics* 28: 25–48.
doi:10.1017/S0267190508080057.

Green, W.D. and Abutalebi, J. (2008).
Understanding the link between bilingual
aphasia and language control. *Journal of
Neurolinguistics* 21 (6): 558–576. doi:
10.1016/j.jneuroling.2008.01.002.

Green, D.W., Grogan, A., Crinion, J. et al.
(2010). Language control and parallel
recovery in individuals with aphasia.
Aphasiology 24 (2): 188–209.
doi:10.1080/02687030902958316.

Green, D.W. and Price, C.J. (2001). Functional
imaging in the study of recovery patterns in
bilingual aphasia. *Bilingualism: Language and
Cognition* 4 (2): 191–201. doi:10.1017/
S1366728901000281.

Henseler, I., Regenbrecht, F., and Obrig, H.
(2014). Lesion correlates of patholinguistic
profiles in chronic aphasia: comparison of
syndrome-, modality-, and symptom-level
assessment. *Brain* 137 (3): 918–930.
doi:10.1093/brain/awt374.

Hernàndez, M., Caño, A., Costa, A. et al.
(2008). Grammatical category-specific
deficits in bilingual aphasia. *Brain and
Language* 107 (1): 68–80. doi:10.1016/j.
bandl.2008.01.006.

Hernandez, A.E. and Li, P. (2007). Age of
acquisition: its neural and computational
mechanisms. *Psychological Bulletin* 133 (4):
638–650. doi:10.1037/0033-2909.133.4.638.

Hinckley, J.J. (2003). Picture naming treatment
in aphasia yields greater improvement in
L1. *Brain and Language* 87 (1): 171–172.

Hope, T.M.H., Parker Jones, '.ō., Grogan, A.
et al. (2015). Comparing language outcomes
in monolingual and bilingual stroke
patients. *Brain* 138 (4): 1070–1083.
doi:10.1093/brain/awv020.

Hope, T.M.H., Seghier, M.L., Leff, A.P., and
Price, C.J. (2013). Predicting outcome and
recovery after stroke with lesions extracted
from MRI images. *Neuroimage: Clinical* 2:
424–433. doi:10.1016/j.nicl.2013.03.005.

Indefrey, P. (2006). A meta-analysis of
hemodynamic studies on first and second
language processing: which suggested
differences can we trust and what do they
mean? *Language Learning* 56: 279–304.
doi:10.1111/j.1467-9922.2006.00365.x.

Johnson, J.S. and Newport, E.L. (1989). Critical
period effects in second language learning: the
influence of maturational state on the
acquisition of English as a second language.
Cognitive Psychology 21 (1): 60–99. doi:10.1016/
0010-0285(89)90003-0.

Junqué, C., Vendrell, P., and Vendrell, J. (1995).
Differential impairments and specific
phenomena in 50 Catalan–Spanish bilingual
aphasic patients. In: *Aspects of Bilingual
Aphasia* (ed. M. Paradis), 177–209. New
York, NY: Pergamon Press.

Junqué, C., Vendrell, P., Vendrell-Brucet, J.M.,
and Tobeña, A. (1989). Differential recovery
in naming in bilingual aphasics. *Brain and
Language* 36 (1): 16–22. doi:10.1016/
0093-934X(89)90049-7.

Kambanaros, M. and van Steenbrugge, W.
(2006). Noun and verb processing in Greek-
English bilingual individuals with anomic
aphasia and the effect of instrumentality
and verb-noun name relation. *Brain and
Language* 97 (2): 162–177. doi:10.1016/j.
bandl.2005.10.001.

Keane, C. and Kiran, S. (2015). The nature of
facilitation and interference in the
multilingual language system: insights from
treatment in a case of trilingual aphasia.
Cognitive Neuropsychology 32 (3–4): 169–194.
doi:10.1080/02643294.2015.1061982.

Khamis, R., Venkert-Olenik, D., and Gil, M.
(1996). Bilingualism in aphasia: the effect of
L2 treatment on language performance in
L1. *Journal of Speech, Language, and Hearing
Research* 19: 73–82.

Kiran, S., Balachandran, I., and Lucas, J.
(2014). The nature of lexical-semantic access

in bilingual aphasia. *Behavioral Neurology* doi:10.1155/2014/389565.

Kiran, S., Grasemann, U., Sandberg, C., and Miikkulainen, R. (2013b). A computational account of bilingual aphasia rehabilitation. *Bilingualism: Language and Cognition* 16 (2): 325–342. doi:10.1017/S1366728912000533.

Kiran, S. and Iakupova, R. (2011). Understanding the relationship between language proficiency, language impairment and rehabilitation: evidence from a case study. *Clinical Linguistics & Phonetics* 25 (6–7): 565–583. doi:10.3109/02699206. 2011.566664.

Kiran, S. and Roberts, P.M. (2010). Semantic feature analysis treatment in Spanish–English and French–English bilingual aphasia. *Aphasiology* 24 (2): 231–261. doi:10.1080/02687030902958365.

Kiran, S. and Roberts, P.M. (2012). What do we know about assessing language impairment in bilingual aphasia? In: *Aspects of Multilingual Aphasia* (ed. M.R. Gitterman, M. Goral and L.K. Obler), 35–51. Clevedon, UK: Multilingual Matters.

Kiran, S., Sandberg, C., Gray, T. et al. (2013a). Rehabilitation in bilingual aphasia: evidence for within- and between-language generalization. *American Journal of Speech-Language Pathology* 22 (2): 298–309. doi:10. 1044/1058-0360(2013/12-0085).

Knoph, M.I.N., Simonsen, H.G., and Lind, M. (2017). Cross-linguistic transfer effects of verb-production therapy in two cases of multilingual aphasia. *Aphasiology* 1–28. doi:10.1080/02687038.2017.1358447.

Kohnert, K. (2004). Cognitive and cognate-based treatments for bilingual aphasia: a case study. *Brain and Language* 91 (3): 294–302. doi:10.1016/j.bandl.2004.04.001.

Kohnert, K. (2009). Cross-language generalization following treatment in bilingual speakers with aphasia: a review. *Seminars in Speech and Language* 30 (3): 174–186. doi:10.1055/s-0029-1225954.

Kroll, J.F. and Sholl, A. (1992). Lexical and conceptual memory in fluent and nonfluent bilinguals. *Cognitive Processing in Bilinguals*

83: 191–204. doi:10.1016/S0166-4115(08)61495-8.

Kroll, J.F. and Stewart, E. (1994). Category interference in translation and picture naming: evidence for asymmetric connections between bilingual memory representations. *Journal of Memory and Language* 33 (2): 149–174. doi:10.1006/jmla.1994.1008.

Laganaro, M., Di Pietro, M., and Schnider, A. (2003). Computerized treatment of anomia in chronic and acute aphasia: an exploratory study. *Aphasiology* 17 (8): 709–721. doi:10.1080/02687030344000193.

Marangolo, P., Rizzi, C., Peran, P. et al. (2009). Parallel recovery in a bilingual aphasic: a neurolinguistic and fMRI study. *Neuropsychology* 23 (3): 405–409. doi:10.1037/a0014824.

Mariën, P., Abutalebi, J., Engelborghs, S., and De Deyn, P.P. (2005). Pathophysiology of language switching and mixing in an early bilingual child with subcortical aphasia. *Neurocase* 11 (6): 385–398. doi:10.1080/13554790500212880.

Marini, A., Galetto, V., Tatu, K. et al. (2016). Recovering two languages with the right hemisphere. *Brain and Language* 159: 35–44. doi:10.1016/j.bandl.2016.05.014.

Meinzer, M., Obleser, J., Flaisch, T. et al. (2007). Recovery from aphasia as a function of language therapy in an early bilingual patient demonstrated by fMRI. *Neuropsychologia* 45 (6): 1247–1256. doi:10.1016/j.neuropsychologia. 2006.1 0.003.

Miertsch, B., Meisel, J.M., and Isel, F. (2009). Non-treated languages in aphasia therapy of polyglots benefit from improvement in the treated language. *Journal of Neurolinguistics* 22 (2): 135–150. doi:10.1016/j.jneuroling.2008.07.003.

Miller Amberber, A. (2012). Language intervention in French–English bilingual aphasia: evidence of limited therapy transfer. *Journal of Neurolinguistics* 25 (6): 588–614. doi:10.1016/j.jneuroling. 2011.10.002.

Muñoz, M. and Marquardt, T. (2003). Picture naming and identification in bilingual speakers of Spanish and English with and without aphasia. *Aphasiology* 17 (12): 1115–1132. doi:10.1080/02687030344000427.

Nardone, R., De Blasi, P., Bergmann, J. et al. (2011). Theta burst stimulation of dorsolateral prefrontal cortex modulates pathological language switching: a case report. *Neuroscience Letters* 487 (3): 378–382. doi:10.1016/j.neulet.2010.10.060.

Paradis, M. (1994). Neurolinguistic aspects of implicit and explicit memory: implications for bilingualism and SLA. In: *Implicit and Explicit Language Learning* (ed. N. Ellis), 393–419. London, UK: Academic Press.

Paradis, M. (2001). Bilingual and polyglot aphasia. In: *Handbook of Neuropsychology*, 2nde (ed. R.S. Berndt), 69–91. Amsterdam, The Netherlands: Elsevier Science.

Paradis, M. (2004). *A Neurolinguistic Theory of Bilingualism*. Amsterdam, The Netherlands/ Philadelphia, PA: John Benjamins.

Peñaloza, C. and Kiran, S. (2017). Neuroimaging evidence in the treatment of bilingual/multilingual adults with aphasia. *Perspectives of the ASHA Special Interest Groups* 2 (SIG 2): 126–131.

Perani, D. and Abutalebi, J. (2005). The neural basis of first and second language processing. *Current Opinion in Neurobiology* 15 (2): 202–206. doi:10.1016/j.conb. 2005.03.007.

Perani, D., Abutalebi, J., Paulesu, E. et al. (2003). The role of age of acquisition and language usage in early, high-proficient bilinguals: an fMRI study during verbal fluency. *Human Brain Mapping* 19 (3): 170–182. doi:10.1002/hbm.10110.

Radman, N., Mouthon, M., Di Pietro, M. et al. (2016). The role of the cognitive control system in recovery from bilingual aphasia: a multiple single-case fMRI study. *Neural Plasticity* https://doi.org/10.1155/2016/8797086.

Radman, N., Spierer, L., Laganaro, M. et al. (2016). Language specificity of lexical-phonological therapy in bilingual aphasia: a clinical and electrophysiological study.

Neuropsychological Rehabilitation 26 (4): 532–557. doi:10.1080/09602011.2015.1047383.

Roberts, P.M. and Deslauriers, L. (1999). Picture naming of cognate and non-cognate nouns in bilingual aphasia. *Journal of Communication Disorders* 32 (1): 1–23. doi:10.1016/S0021-9924(98)00026-4.

Roberts, P.M. and Le Dorze, G. (1998). Bilingual aphasia: semantic organization, strategy use, and productivity in semantic verbal fluency. *Brain and Language* 65 (2): 287–312. doi:10.1006/brln.1998.1992.

Roberts, P.M. and Kiran, S. (2007). Assessment and treatment of bilingual aphasia and bilingual anomia. In: *Speech and Language Disorders in Bilinguals* (ed. A.A.E. Ramos), 109–131. New York, NY: Nova Science.

Rodríguez-Fornells, A., De Diego-Balaguer, R., and Münte, T.F. (2006). Executive control in bilingual language processing. *Language Learning* 56: 133–190. doi:10.1111/j.1467-9922.2006.00359.x.

Saur, D. and Hartwigsen, G. (2012). Neurobiology of language recovery after stroke: lessons from neuroimaging studies. *Rehabilitation of Neurological Language Disorders* 93 (1): 15–25. doi:10.1016/j. apmr.2011.03.036.

Saur, D., Lange, R., Baumgaertner, A. et al. (2006). Dynamics of language reorganization after stroke. *Brain* 129 (6): 1371–1384. doi:10.1093/brain/awl090.

Schwartz, M.F. (2014). Theoretical analysis of word production deficits in adult aphasia. *Philosophical Transactions of the Royal Society, B: Biological Sciences* 369 (1634): doi:10.1098/ rstb.2012.0390.

Sebastian, R., Kiran, S., and Sandberg, C. (2012). Semantic processing in Spanish–English bilinguals with aphasia. *Journal of Neurolinguistics* 25 (4): 240–262. doi:10.1016/j.jneuroling.2012.01.003.

Sebastian, R., Laird, A.R., and Kiran, S. (2011). Meta-analysis of the neural representation of first language and second language. *Applied PsychoLinguistics* 32 (4): 799–819. doi:10.1017/S0142716411000075.

Shao, Z., Roelofs, A., and Meyer, A.S. (2012). Sources of individual differences in the speed of naming objects and actions: the contribution of executive control. *The Quarterly Journal of Experimental Psychology* 65 (10): 1927–1944. doi:10.1080/17470218. 2012.670252.

Sierpowska, J., Gabarrós, A., Ripollés, P. et al. (2013). Intraoperative electrical stimulation of language switching in two bilingual patients. *Neuropsychologia* 51 (13): 2882–2892. doi:10.1016/j. neuropsychologia.2013.09.003.

Silverberg, R. and Gordon, H.W. (1979). Differential aphasia in two bilingual individuals. *Neurology* 29 (1): 51–51. doi:10.1212/WNL.29.1.51.

Stowe, L.A. and Sabourin, L. (2005). Imaging the processing of a second language: effects of maturation and proficiency on the neural processes involved. *International Review of Applied Linguistics in Language Teaching* 43 (4): 329–354. doi:10.1515/iral.2005.43.4.329.

Tiwari, S. and Krishnan, G. (2015). Selective L2 cognate retrieval deficit in a bilingual person with aphasia: a case report. *Speech,*

Language and Hearing 18 (4): 243–248. doi:10. 1179/2050572815Y.0000000008.

Tschirren, M., Laganaro, M., Michel, P. et al. (2011). Language and syntactic impairment following stroke in late bilingual aphasics. *Brain and Language* 119 (3): 238–242. doi:10.1016/j.bandl.2011.05.008.

Ullman, M.T. (2004). Contributions of memory circuits to language: the declarative/ procedural model. *Cognition* 92 (1–2): 231–270. doi:10.1016/j.cognition.2003.10.008.

Verreyt, N., De Letter, M., Hemelsoet, D. et al. (2013). Cognate effects and executive control in a patient with differential bilingual aphasia. *Applied Neuropsychology: Adult* 20 (3): 221–230. doi:10.1080/09084282.2012.753074.

Watamori, T.S. and Sasanuma, S. (1976). The recovery process of a bilingual aphasic. *Journal of Communication Disorders* 9 (2): 157–166.

Watamori, T.S. and Sasanuma, S. (1978). The recovery processes of two English-Japanese bilingual aphasics. *Brain and Language* 6 (2): 127–140.

28 Primary Progressive Aphasia in Bilinguals and Multilinguals

TARYN MALCOLM, AVIVA LERMAN,
MARTA KORYTKOWSKA, JET M. J. VONK,
AND LORAINE K. OBLER

1. Introduction

Primary progressive aphasia (PPA) is the result of neurodegeneration affecting language abilities that continue to decline as the disease progresses. There are three main variants of PPA: non-fluent, semantic, and logopenic. Deficits may occur in different areas of language, such as lexical retrieval, auditory comprehension, syntactic structure, processing morphological components, and repetition abilities. However, the impact on language is not comparable across all individuals with PPA; rather it differs for each of the different variants based on the underlying pattern of neural change.

In bilinguals or multilinguals with PPA, the language decline has an added layer of complexity. Decline may occur across the different languages in parallel, or differentially, and a number of factors may affect the pattern of decline. Recognizing the factors that most affect language decline in bilinguals and multilinguals with PPA, along with identifying the neural changes occurring in the brain, can increase our understanding of language organization in the bilingual or multilingual brain. It should be noted that language decline is not the only decline associated with PPA, as changes in cognition and behaviour have also been observed, particularly in the later stages (e.g. Rosen et al. 2006). However, language is the most salient decline in PPA so we focus on language in this chapter.

We analysed 13 case-studies of bilinguals and multilinguals with PPA published to date, which included all three variants of PPA, and found that language decline across languages within an individual can be differential and/or parallel. We discuss that in the cases of differential language decline, the factor that appears to most strongly affect the pattern of decline is the order of acquisition, in that the first-acquired language was better spared than any later-acquired languages. Other factors, such as proficiency,

The Handbook of the Neuroscience of Multilingualism, First Edition. Edited by John W. Schwieter.
© 2019 John Wiley & Sons Ltd. Published 2019 by John Wiley & Sons Ltd.

recency of use, manner of acquisition, age of acquisition, and language typology (which includes aspects like language distance) did not appear to have a strong effect on either differential or parallel decline. In most cases, aspects of parallel and differential decline were observed across different language domains. However, even in those domains where differential decline was observed, there was a shift towards parallel decline as the PPA progressed.

We will discuss language decline in bilinguals and multilinguals with PPA in relation to language decline in bilinguals with another degenerative disease (Alzheimer's disease) as well as in relation to sudden-onset aphasia in bilinguals as a result of a cerebrovascular accident (CVA). Due to the degenerative nature of PPA, carefully analysing language decline in bilinguals and multilinguals with PPA can add to our knowledge of bilingual and multilingual language organization in the brain and the effect of neural impairment on language.

For ease of reading, *bilinguals with PPA* will refer to either bilinguals or multilinguals for the remainder of this chapter, unless specifically stated otherwise. We begin the next section with a detailed explanation of PPA and its three main variants, following which we discuss different hypotheses of language organization in the bilingual brain, at the neural level. This will then lead us to an in-depth discussion about bilinguals with PPA, patterns of language decline, important factors affecting this decline and how all these support or conflict with exisiting models of language organization in the bilingual brain.

1.1.   Primary Progressive Aphasia

PPA is a subtype of dementia with progressive decline in language abilities over time relative to cognitive abilities that decline late in the disease. In contrast to sudden-onset aphasia, in PPA there is no defined lesion, nor is there diffuse cortical atrophy. Rather there is progressive atrophy initially to a somewhat confined region of the brain (Gorno-Tempini et al. 2008) as indicated, for example, by atrophy on magnetic resonance imaging (MRI) scans (Gorno-Tempini et al. 2004) or hypoperfusion on positron emission tomography (PET) scans (Sinnatamby et al. 1996). Even within these sites of cortical atrophy in patients with PPA, neuronal destruction is never fully complete, and the remaining neurons continue to participate in language function, but with altered patterns of neural network connectivity (Mesulam et al. 2014).

Different subtypes of PPA have been associated with volume loss in specific cortical regions. Despite differences in regional volume loss amongst the PPA subtypes, cortical atrophy is mostly confined to the left hemisphere in the non-fluent and logopenic variants (e.g. Gorno-Tempini et al. 2011; Mesulam 2007). In the semantic variant, by contrast, atrophy is usually seen in both hemispheres, yet in most cases, atrophy is more pronounced in the left hemisphere than the right hemisphere (Mion et al. 2010; Rogalski et al. 2011). Besides left-dominant atrophy, the semantic variant can also present with right-dominant atrophy (Gorno-Tempini et al. 2004). In such cases, early semantic decline is often more pronounced in the non-verbal than verbal domain. The subtle language impairment in the early stages of the right-dominant variant grows stronger with progression of the disease along with increasing atrophy in the left hemisphere

(Binney et al. 2016; Vonk et al. in preparation). In this chapter, however, we focus on the classic, more common left-dominant variant.

Language decline in PPA occurs as a result of these neuroanatomical changes of progressive cortical atrophy. Each of the three subtypes of PPA (non-fluent, semantic, and logopenic variants) presents with differential patterns of atrophy that result in different clinical symptoms and patterns of language decline.

In the non-fluent variant, cortical atrophy and hypometabolism are found in the left inferior frontoinsular area (Gorno-Tempini et al. 2011), although hypoperfusion has also been documented in the left superior and middle temporal areas secondary to the inferior frontal area (Grossman 2010). Damage to these areas results in impaired speech output, characterized by simple sentences, poor syntactic structure, and speech sound errors. Such speech is described as telegraphic since it omits essential morphological components (Gorno-Tempini et al. 2004). However, people with this variant of PPA have relatively preserved auditory comprehension for the majority of the duration of this decline (Hodges and Patterson 1996; Thompson et al. 1997).

In the semantic variant, atrophy is focused around the anterior and inferolateral temporal areas. As mentioned earlier in this section, atrophy in this variant is generally bilateral (Mion et al. 2010). However, it tends to be greater on the left than on the right, especially in the early stages of the disease (Rogalski et al. 2011). This pattern of atrophy results in severe deficits in confrontation naming (Hodges and Patterson 1996) due to deficits in semantic memory. Speech output appears fluent and is well-articulated but the content is empty, and errors include semantic paraphasias, circumlocutions, and non-specific names (e.g. Blair et al. 2007). Given that the deficit is found in semantic memory, language impairments are observed both in verbal expression as well as in comprehension and recognition of single words and objects (Mesulam 2003).

Logopenic PPA shows atrophy in the left posterior temporoparietal region or hypoperfusion in the same region early in the disease and later in the anterior temporal area (Gorno-Tempini et al. 2011). Symptoms include word-finding deficits, leading to frequent hesitations and pauses in speech. These hesitations make speech sound dysfluent, with increasing dysfluencies when content requires precision (Mesulam 2007; Wilson et al. 2010). Errors are characterized by phonemic paraphasias, decreased naming ability, and reduced repetition ability. Gorno-Tempini et al. (2011) further specified that in logopenic PPA there is an absence of frank agrammatism, differentiating it from the non-fluent variant.

This influence of brain atrophy on language impairment in the three variants is relatively consistent amongst monolinguals with PPA. Language impairment in bilinguals with PPA is more complex but can provide valuable information about how two or more languages are represented in the brain. We will now discuss a number of issues of bilingual brain organization which may help us better understand the patterns of language impairment in bilingual PPA. In Section 1.2, we will focus on bilingualism, rather than multilingualism, in the brain because that is the focus of the focus of the literature to date literature to date. Currently, differences between bilingualism and multilingualism at the neurological level are still unclear both generally and specifically in PPA.

1.2. Bilingualism in the Brain

With the development of neuroimaging techniques in the last three decades, knowledge of bilingual neural organization in healthy children and adults has increased, as well as in clinical populations such as bilinguals with sudden-onset aphasia and dementia. Together, behavioural and neuroimaging studies have provided much evidence that at least some language systems are shared by the first language (L1) and second language (L2; e.g. Kroll and Tokowicz 2005; Perea et al. 2008). However, there is also neuroimaging evidence of structural or functional differences in brain regions for L1 and L2. For example, studies of healthy adult bilinguals have found shared processing regions in high proficiency bilinguals, but limited overlap of processing regions in low proficiency bilinguals (e.g. Dehaene et al. 1997; Perani et al. 1998). Interestingly, the regions additionally activated for low-proficiency bilinguals were all in the right hemisphere: right middle temporal gyrus for L1, and right hippocampus, and superior parietal lobule for L2. Similarly, Kim et al. (1997) also showed differential activation for L1 and L2 when comparing early versus late age of acquisition, finding less overlap of regions in the left inferior frontal lobe during covert naming when L2 was acquired late.

Studies examining white matter pathways have also found differential effects in late bilinguals. Kuhl et al. (2016) examined late bilinguals immersed in the environment of the L2 compared with monolinguals. The study found white matter activation and diffusion to be bilaterally activated in bilinguals; in monolinguals activation is less bilateral. The bilingual group showed a correlation of duration and activation, such that those with longer immersion in the environment of the L2 exhibited less diffusion in white matter tracts (as measured by fractional anisotropy) in specific language pathways than those with shorter immersion in the environment of the L2.

Together, these studies suggest that factors such as level of proficiency, age of acquisition, and recency of use may alter the organization of language in the brain in healthy bilinguals. Nonetheless, the lack of consensus as to the neural representation of bilinguals' languages has resulted in the development of different models for language organization in the bilingual brain, based on factors related to individual profiles of bilinguals. Two of these well-supported but opposing models have dominated this field: the convergence hypothesis and the declarative-procedural model.

The convergence hypothesis (Green 2003) states that neurocognitive mechanisms of second language learning can improve with increased practice, thereby converging on L1 neural networks. Changes in proficiency are associated with shifts from more controlled to more automatic language processing (Abutalebi and Green 2007). In fact, rapid convergence of neural patterns has been shown both by functional magnetic resonance imaging (fMRI; Consonni et al. 2013; Golestani et al. 2006; Van de Putte et al. 2017) and event-related potential (ERP) data (Osterhout et al. 2006). However, this convergence may depend on linguistic variables other than (or as well as) proficiency, such as linguistic distance (Chen et al. 2007).

While current neuroimaging research is consistent with the position that the languages of bilinguals are at least partially represented in shared processing regions (e.g. Abutalebi et al. 2001), the literature has not yet fully accounted for evidence of differential organization – such as when languages are affected differently by brain damage. However, most agree that conceptual representations in different languages share a common substrate when considering lexical-semantic processing (e.g. Crinion et al. 2006; Stilwell et al. 2016) and there is also evidence of common regions mediating syntax (Golestani et al. 2006; Ullman 2015).

An alternative way to explain these differential findings is the declarative-procedural model which characterizes variability in language impairment following neural damage (Paradis 2003; Ullman and Pierpont 2005). In addition to proficiency, this model uses age of acquisition (early vs. late) and manner of acquisition (i.e. context of L2 acquisition) to explain why a second language may be represented differently in the brain. The model hypothesizes that a second language acquired early may be neurally represented differently from a late-acquired second language and that an early-acquired L2 will be more similarly represented in the brain to L1 than a late-acquired L2 under certain learning contexts, independent of proficiency (Ullman 2015). Additionally, L2 acquired in the home will be acquired more with procedural memory, i.e. implicitly, whereas acquiring an L2 at school will be accomplished more explicitly, therefore incorporating more declarative memory.

The declarative-procedural model proposes that both L1 and L2 use declarative memory to store idiosyncratic lexical knowledge in different linguistic domains, including simple words and their meanings, irregular morphology, and syntactic complements (Ullman 2015). At the same time, syntactic and morphological processes in L1 are mediated by the procedural system typically responsible for other cognitive and motor skills (Paradis 2008; Ullman 2015). L2 acquisition of syntactic and morphological processes can rely on the procedural system when acquired early, but the declarative system plays a crucial role in the representation of grammar if the L2 is acquired late. The use of declarative and procedural memory may result in differential effects of brain damage in L1 and L2, depending on age of acquisition and manner of acquisition. In bilinguals, when L2 is acquired late, the declarative system will play an important role in the production of morphological and syntactic forms that rely on the procedural system in L1. As L2 proficiency increases, the use of the procedural system to process it will likely increase, especially if it is acquired implicitly (e.g. via immersion; Ullman 2015). When the system is damaged, early bilinguals with high proficiency in both languages may have comparable performance in L1 and L2 in morphological and syntactic tasks.

These two models – the convergence hypothesis and the declarative-procedural model – follow a clear pattern, in that differential effects may be seen in brain damage based on individual factors of bilinguals. However, each model attributes differences in bilingual language organization to different factors: while the convergence hypothesis emphasizes proficiency and use of each language, the declarative-procedural model emphasizes manner and age of acquisition. To test which model best fits the patterns of language decline in bilinguals with PPA to date, we ask which factors are important for language decline in bilinguals with PPA and how these relate to language loss in other similar populations – i.e. sudden-onset aphasia and dementia in bilinguals.

2. Bilingual and Multilingual PPA

While the characterization of PPA began 30 years ago, much of the literature has examined monolingual individuals with PPA, establishing the three distinct variants mentioned previously. Cases of bilinguals or multilinguals with PPA began to be examined around the same time the current PPA classification was developed (in the early 2000s). To date, we have identified 12 published studies (one an abstract) on bilingual or multilingual PPA. All of these publications examined either single cases or two individuals with similar variants of the disorder. Two papers examined two individuals, one looking at two bilingual participants with the semantic variant (Mendez et al. 2004) and the other examining one multilingual participant and one bilingual participant, also both characterized as having the semantic variant (Liu et al. 2012). However, we removed the second case in the Liu study from consideration in this chapter, as his behavioural data indicated more widespread cognitive deficits than PPA usually allows for, throwing doubt to his PPA diagnosis.

After eliminating this one participant, we were left with 12 published studies which included 13 different case studies of bilinguals and multilinguals with PPA. Five have the non-fluent variant, four have the semantic variant, and four have the logopenic variant. Diagnoses and variant classifications were determined with both behavioural data from a variety of language and cognitive tasks, as well as neuroimaging data from MRI, PET, single-photon emission computerized tomography (SPECT), and/or computerized tomography (CT) scans. These case studies were analysed for the following factors: PPA variant, site of cortical atrophy, languages acquired, age of acquisition, dominance and/or proficiency, language(s) of the environment, and patterns of language abilities and decline in each language. See Table 1 for details of demographic information for each case study.

The most striking factor that can be observed when looking across all cases is that regardless of variant, in no case was L2 better preserved than L1. In all cases, either L1 was better preserved than L2, or both languages declined in parallel. Cases that found L1 better preserved than L2 assessed language decline via a variety of subtests; these varied across studies. For non-fluent PPA, all five studies showed that L2 was never better preserved than L1 for object and action naming (Druks and Weekes 2013; Hernàndez et al. 2008; Larner 2012; Machado et al. 2010; Zanini et al. 2011), a finding also present in one case with the logopenic variant (Lind et al. 2017). Similarly, two cases of multilinguals with the semantic variant showed greater decline in L2 than L1, with L3 being almost completely lost, in word comprehension and naming (Mendez et al. 2004). There was also a noted difference between tasks of grammatical processing in one case, with L2 declining more rapidly than L1 (Zanini et al. 2011).

Those areas of language showing parallel decline included lexical-semantic knowledge and access, phonological knowledge, comprehension of complex commands, and reading and writing abilities (Devaughn et al. 2016; Druks and Weekes 2013; Filley et al. 2006; Hernàndez et al. 2008; Liu et al. 2012; Zanini et al. 2011). Grammatical knowledge was also found to decline in parallel for one case (Druks and Weekes 2013). In the six cases tested at multiple time points, all deficits eventually declined in parallel as the disease progressed to the later stages. For example, Druks and

Table 1 Demographic information for 13 published case studies on bilinguals or multilinguals with PPA.

	PPA variant	Cortical atrophy	Languages	Age of L2 Acquisition	Dominant language / proficiency	Language of environment	Manner of acquisition of L2 (and/or L3)	Most preserved language overall
Mendez et al. (2004) – P1	Semantic	Left anterior temporal	L1-English L2-Spanish L3-German	N/A	Proficient in L1 and L2 L3[a]	L1	N/A	L1
Mendez et al. (2004) – P2	Semantic	Left anterior temporal	L1-Spanish L2-English L3-Polish	N/A	Proficient in L1 and L2	N/A	N/A	L1
Filley et al. (2006)	Logopenic	Left temporal and parietal	L1-Chinese L2-English	8 years	L2 dominant	L2	Formal, school context	L1 = L2
Hernández et al. (2008)	Non-fluent	Perisylvian cortex and hippocampus; right prefrontal region	L1-Spanish L2-Catalan	Before 4 years	Balanced, proficient	L1 and L2	Formal, school context	L1
Machado et al. (2010)	Non-fluent	Left temporal, anterior cingulate, and dorsolateral frontal	L1-Portuguese L2-French	4 years, then again as an adult	Balanced	L1	Acquired in the home	L1
Zanini et al. (2011)	Non-fluent	Left frontal, parietal and temporal	L1-Friulian L2-Italian	6 years	Balanced	L1 and L2	Acquired in the home	L1
Druks and Weekes (2013)	Non-fluent	Left perisylvian atrophy; intact medial temporal and posterior structures	L1-Hungarian L2-English	14 years	L2 dominant	L2	Formal, school context	L1 = L2
Kambanaros and Grohmann (2012)	Logopenic	Left temporal parietal	L1-Cypriot L2-Greek L3-English L4-Czech	L2 & L3 –Early exposure L4 – Late exposure	Highly proficient L1, L2, L3, L4	Mainly L1	Acquired in the home; and formal, school context	L1 (informally evaluated)

					Proficient in			
Liu et al. (2012)	Semantic	Left inferior temporal gyrus	L1-Taiwanese L2-Japanese L3-Mandarin Chinese	L2 – 7 years L3 – 11 years	L1, L2, L3	L1 and L3	Formal, school context	L1 = L2
Larner (2012)	Non-fluent	Left insular and anterior left temporal lobe	L1-Welsh L2-English	6 years[a]	N/A	L2	Formal, school context	L1
Meyer et al. (2015)	Logopenic	Left temporo-parietal	L1-Norwegian L2-English	7 years	L2 dominant	L2	Immersion in environment	L1 = L2
DeVaughn et al. (2016)	Semantic	N/A	L1-English L2-German	N/A	Balanced	L1	N/A	L1 = L2
Lind et al. (2017)	Logopenic[a]	Bilateral, large areas of the brain; not specified	L1-English L2-Norwegian	31 years	L1 dominant	L1 at home; L1 and L2 at work	Immersion in environment	L1

[a] indicates that the information has been inferred from the article, rather than explicitly stated by the authors.

N/A – information not available, even from inference.

Weekes (2013) found that most language tasks declined in parallel. However, in the two linguistic tasks where L1 was better spared than L2 at the first testing point two years post-onset (namely object and action naming), when retested one year later, L1 and L2 showed parallel decline in these two tasks along with the other language tasks. Similarly, Machado et al. (2010) found that L2 declined more drastically than L1 in their participant when tested two years post-onset, but within a year the L2 and L1 were similarly impaired. From these cases, we can see that language decline appears to become parallel over time in PPA, but how this decline progresses and under what circumstances the decline is parallel from the time of diagnosis, or whether the decline is differential from the time of diagnosis before changing to parallel at a later stage, remains unclear.

2.1. Factors Impacting Language Decline

While the literature on bilinguals with PPA seems to show that variant type has little effect on whether there is parallel decline or better L1 preservation, it is important to look at other factors that may impact how the two languages are organized in bilinguals, potentially resulting in differential decline. Here we ask whether age of acquisition, manner of acquisition, proficiency level, or recency of use (related to language of environment) impact better preservation of one language or if the languages decline in parallel. Due to the limited literature, it would be reasonable to compare the PPA literature with two better-studied fields in this regard: Alzheimer's disease (AD) and sudden-onset aphasia.

In bilinguals with AD, many researchers have documented better-preserved language abilities in L1 than in L2 (e.g. Ardila et al. 2008; Meguro et al. 2003; Mendez et al. 1999; Stilwell et al. 2016), although others have observed parallel deterioration between L1 and L2, especially as the disease progresses (e.g. Costa et al. 2012; Gómez-Ruiz et al. 2012; Manchon et al. 2015). In addition, language dominance rather than order of acquisition has been suggested to affect language performance in AD in some cases (see Stilwell et al. 2016, for a review), but closer analysis of the literature shows that the two studies they cite to support this hypothesis are not strong support at all. In one study by Gómez-Ruiz et al. (2012), the participants were balanced, early bilinguals of Catalan (L1) and Spanish (L2), and showed parallel deterioration overall. The only place the authors found a significant difference between L2 and L1 was in the one subtest related to reading and writing – namely verbal letter fluency (i.e. naming as many items as possible beginning with a given letter). In this population of bilinguals, the L2 (Spanish) was the language of schooling and the first (or in a few specific cases the only) language acquired for reading and/or writing. Clearly this single subtest is not good support for suggesting that language dominance may affect language performance more than order of acquisition in AD, since for literacy, Spanish was actually the first-acquired language.

In the second study by Gollan et al. (2011), two groups of participants were tested – L1 dominant and L2 dominant (premorbid dominance). Overall, the L2 dominant participants had relatively mild dementia compared to the L1 dominant group, where the dementia was more severe. The results showed that for the L1 dominant group, L2 was better spared than L1, but the results did not even approach significance. Also, the testing measure used (the Boston naming test; Kaplan et al. 1983), was noted by Gollan et al. to be problematic when comparing across English and Spanish, since the test was developed for English speakers residing in the US. The use of this test together with the more severe dementia, as well as the lack of significance, we would argue, is not strong evidence that L2 is sometimes spared more than L1 in AD. Therefore, we conclude, the two main patterns of language decline in bilinguals with AD are similar to those in bilinguals with PPA.

In sudden-onset aphasia, by contrast, several different parallel and non-parallel patterns have emerged to characterize language of bilinguals (Paradis 2001). Factors such as age of acquisition, proficiency, language dominance, and recency of use have all been found to contribute to language impairment (and recovery) post-stroke (e.g. Faroqi-Shah et al. 2010; Goral et al. 2012; Lorenzen and Murray 2008). The 13 PPA cases reviewed here have shown no distinct pattern as to individual factors. The only certainty is that at no point is L2 better preserved than L1, seemingly regardless of age of acquisition, manner of acquisition, proficiency level, or recency of use. For example, amongst the 13 cases, there was a range of ages of acquisition. In three cases, L2 was acquired very early in childhood (Hernàndez et al. 2008; Kambanaros and Grohmann 2012; Machado et al. 2010). A further five cases were characterized as having acquired L2 from age six up to puberty (Filley et al. 2006; Larner 2012; Liu et al. 2012; Meyer et al. 2015; Zanini et al. 2011). Only two cases discussed L2 acquisition post-puberty: Druks and Weekes' (2013) participant was age 14 and Lind et al.'s (2017) participant was age 31. The cases of DeVaughn et al. (2016) and Mendez et al. (2004) did not provide information about age of acquisition. For multilinguals, Liu et al. (2012) described a case where L3 was acquired later than L2, but still acquired pre-puberty, and Kambanaros and Grohmann (2012) described a case where L3 was acquired in early childhood and L4 acquired in adulthood. The range of ages of acquisition amongst these studies clearly demonstrates that, thus far, age of acquisition for a second language or later learned language is not a major factor for language decline in PPA.

As discussed in Section 1.2, the declarative-procedural model also pertains to how the manner of acquisition can impact language retention, with use of declarative or procedural memory to acquire different linguistic domains for L1 and L2. This use of different memory systems is hypothesized to explain differences found in language recovery from sudden-onset aphasia. Yet across all bilingual PPA cases examined, there was a range of manner of acquisition amongst participants, with some learning languages at home from a young age (Machado et al. 2010; Zanini et al. 2011), some learning in a formal, school context (Druks and Weekes 2013; Filley et al. 2006; Hernàndez et al. 2008; Larner 2012; Liu et al. 2012), some through immersion in the environment of the L2 (Lind et al. 2017; Meyer et al. 2015), and one multilingual case whose languages were acquired both at home from a young age and in a formal school context (Kambanaros and Grohmann 2012). As with age of acquisition, manner of acquisition was not observed to impact the overall outcomes of language decline in bilinguals and multilinguals with PPA.

Both proficiency level and recency of use have also been shown to be important factors for brain organization in healthy bilinguals, and as discussed in Section 1.2, the convergence hypothesis emphasizes them both. For proficiency, neuroimaging studies have shown that level of L2 proficiency can change the neural representation of a second language in the brain in healthy bilingual adults (Dehaene et al. 1997; Kuhl et al. 2016; Perani et al. 1998) resulting in relatively differential neural representations for low proficiency L2 users and relatively converged neural representations for high proficiency L2 users.

However, no studies to date in the bilingual PPA literature show that proficiency has a strong effect on the pattern of language decline. Of the 13 cases of bilingual and multilingual PPA, all 13 were found to be proficient in L2, with eight being described as balanced bilinguals or highly proficient in both languages (Devaughn et al. 2016; Hernàndez et al. 2008; Kambanaros and Grohmann 2012; Liu et al. 2012; Machado et al. 2010; both participants studied by Mendez et al. 2004; Zanini et al. 2011), three with L2 dominance (Druks and Weekes 2013; Filley et al. 2006; Meyer et al. 2015), and one with L1 dominance (Lind et al. 2017). Even when conditions seem most likely that L1 and L2 will be neurally similar, in the cases where early bilinguals were balanced in proficiency and used both languages daily, decline was not necessarily parallel as the bilingual aphasia literature would lead one to expect. For example, Hernàndez et al. (2008) and Zanini et al. (2011) described early, balanced bilinguals who used both languages daily, yet for both cases L1 was better preserved than L2, either in noun and verb naming (Hernàndez et al. 2008) or a variety of language tasks (Zanini et al. 2011).

The only hint that proficiency may affect language decline in PPA arises when we contrast the non-L1 languages in two cases of multilinguals. Mendez et al. (2004) describe one case of a multilingual whose L1 and L2 had been highly proficient, but L3 was less proficient. In this case, L3 appeared to be completely lost when he was tested, whereas L1 and L2 declined – but L1 was better spared relative to L2. Compare this with the study by Kambanaros and Grohmann (2012) of a multilingual who was highly proficient in all four of his languages, was tested in all but the L1, and showed language processing in non-L1 languages declining in parallel across all language domains: morphology, phonology, lexical semantics, comprehension, and repetition (Kambanaros and Grohmann 2012). It is important to note that even in this case, the authors described the L1 as being better preserved than the other three languages; however that conclusion was determined only informally since their testing methodology – THE BILINGUAL APHASIA TEST (Paradis 1987) – was not available in the participant's native language, Cypriot Greek (Kambanaros and Grohmann 2012). Based on these two cases, proficiency may be a factor in language decline in multilinguals with PPA, but order of acquisition still seems to be the strongest factor, such that L1 is better preserved even when other languages are as proficient as the L1.

Recency of use is a term used in the literature in relation to recovery from sudden-onset aphasia in bilinguals, where the most recent language is that being used at the time of the CVA (e.g. Faroqi-Shah et al. 2010; Goral et al. 2012). However, in the 13 cases of PPA in bilinguals and multilinguals that we reviewed, we did not find recency of use to be a critical factor affecting patterns of language decline. In fact, in all 13 cases, the L2 was used daily at least until the onset of PPA. In two cases, the participants were dominant in their L2 and rarely used their L1 (Druks and Weekes 2013; Filley et al. 2006). Even so, despite recency of use and immersion in L2, Filley et al. (2006) described L1 and L2 declining equally in naming after diagnosis of PPA, with more phonemic paraphasias noted in connected speech in the L2 – the most recently used language. Similarly, Druks and Weekes (2013) showed parallel decline in most language tasks, except for object and action naming, which declined more in the L2 – the most recently used language.

However, in both Filley et al. (2006) and Druks and Weekes (2013), it is difficult to tease apart the effects of premorbid proficiency from the effects of recency of use. The one case study that does differentiate between these factors is that of Larner (2012) who examined a case of a Welsh-English bilingual. Though Welsh was the participant's native language, she was highly proficient in English and primarily spoke English in the home at the time of her PPA diagnosis, at age 78. Again, despite being proficient in both L1 and L2, the most recently used language – English (her L2) – declined more than the less recently used L1.

Therefore, proficiency level and recency of use were not found to be major factors influencing language decline patterns between L1 and L2 in bilinguals and multilinguals with PPA. Filley et al. (2006) argued that their findings may have been due to the language distance of the specific language pair in the bilingual (Chinese and English), and this may have resulted in less overlap in the neural organization of the two languages than in two more similar languages due to a mismatch in the tasks administered. However, in the studies we reviewed, several different language combinations were examined: Hungarian-English (Druks and Weekes 2013), English-German (Devaughn et al. 2016), Spanish-Catalan (Hernàndez et al. 2008), Portuguese-French (Machado et al. 2010), Friulian-Italian (Zanini et al. 2011), Norwegian and English (Lind et al. 2017; Meyer et al. 2015), Cypriot-Greek-English-Czech (Kambanaros and Grohmann 2012), Taiwanese-Japanese-Mandarin (Liu et al. 2012), Welsh-English (Larner 2012), English-Spanish-German, and Spanish-English-Polish (Mendez et al. 2004). Again, regardless of the linguistic distance in any given language combination, the L2 was never better preserved than the L1, and most languages declined in parallel for most language tasks. The difficulty with characterizing PPA is that it does not follow the typical patterns, and does not appear to be influenced by the same factors, as sudden-onset aphasia in bilinguals; early age of acquisition, proficiency, and recency of use have been shown to have little effect on PPA decline. Therefore, the focus should be more on the degenerative nature of the PPA, since the patterns of language decline are more consistent with those seen in AD.

2.2. Neurological Basis of Language Decline in PPA

The bilingual PPA literature partially supports the theory of a shared neural substrate for two or more languages, in that atrophy to certain cerebral regions in the brain results in decline in both languages, albeit not necessarily in parallel. Furthermore, the patterns of decline are consistent, despite individual bilingual factors and different language typologies. What remains unknown is why brain atrophy in PPA affects language differently from sudden-onset aphasia that occurs after a CVA (stroke), when they occur in the same brain regions.

In stroke, lesions of brain damage are localized around major arteries, and as such, certain areas of the cortex are typically spared from damage, in particular, the temporal pole.

PPA, by contrast, is caused by protein abnormalities within a neuron. In healthy neurons, proteins, such as tau proteins, stabilize the shape of the cell. In neurodegenerative diseases, the pathway for these and other proteins become tangled, resulting in the inability to maintain the structure of the cell, and thus individual neurons start to degenerate (Iqbal et al. 2010). Neurodegeneration of cells in PPA has been linked to tauopathy, TDP-43 proteinopathy (for the non-fluent and semantic variants) and Alzheimer's pathology (for the logopenic variant) and these proteins are unable to sustain the vitality of neurons in a certain region (Grossman 2010; Santos-Santos et al. 2018). Due to the death of individual cells in PPA, damage is not limited to areas surrounding major cerebral arteries. Instead, each variant has a typical epicentre for atrophy where it starts and remains – but as the disease progresses, atrophy spreads to other regions, resulting in extensive degeneration.

The other crucial difference between sudden-onset aphasia and PPA is the type of neural damage. In a stroke, grey and contiguous white matter is suddenly destroyed. Contrastingly, neurodegenerative diseases – such as those resulting in PPA – can target specific layers and regions of the cerebral cortex (Mesulam et al. 2014). Despite localized regions of cortical atrophy in PPA, neuronal death in any given region is not complete. In the early stages of the disease, only some neurons have degenerated, and the remaining neurons continue to function for language tasks. Due to the gradual nature of neuronal loss, the existing neurons can reorganize, at least to an extent, and retain some language function until the end-stage of the disease process.

In a stroke, however, neural injury results in more abrupt damage, with sudden and sometimes complete loss of language function. As a result of this sudden loss, the brain cannot gradually reorganize to retain certain language processes, but instead may rely on alternative pathways to regain some function. These differences between gradual decline and sudden loss lead to subtle (or not-so-subtle) differences in language function between the two languages of a bilingual, depending on the aetiology of language impairment.

Another difference between the neural atrophy of PPA and the cerebrovascular lesions of stroke is the differential impairment of white matter pathways. While white matter can be impaired in PPA, typically this impairment is not as severe as that in patients after a stroke. An example of this is seen in logopenic PPA which, as mentioned, is characterized primarily by deterioration of cells in temporoparietal cortical regions. While a vascular lesion in the same neural regions should indicate Wernicke's aphasia, with poor comprehension and fluent, but empty speech, temporoparietal atrophy in logopenic PPA does not result in impaired comprehension. (For a more complete description of Wernicke's aphasia, see Kemmerer 2014). Mesulam et al. (2015) hypothesized that severe word comprehension deficits might only occur in PPA if white matter pathways are damaged, disconnecting posterior temporal regions from the anterior temporal lobe. The difference between atrophy and cerebrovascular lesions in similar areas demonstrates that the neural substrates of word and sentence comprehension are dissociable, and patients who have both word- and sentence-comprehension deficits typically have damage extending to subcortical white matter in addition to a temporoparietal lesion (Mesulam et al. 2015).

Furthermore, Calandri et al. (2014) have shown that bilinguals with PPA have greater microstructural integrity than monolinguals with PPA in the right uncinate fasciculus (UF). The UF has been proposed to play a role in lexical retrieval, semantic association, and aspects of naming that require connections from temporal to frontal areas which have been shown to undergo selective damage in the semantic variant of PPA. Calandri et al. (2014) suggest that the management of bilingual semantic knowledge could strengthen white matter pathways against degeneration, but suggest that further research is needed as this has just begun to be explored.

To summarize, PPA can provide crucial information about language organization over and above what we know from sudden-onset aphasia. Both the factors discussed above – gradual versus sudden loss, and different sites of neural damage – may provide a basis for differences in language impairment resulting from the two sources, such as language *loss* versus impaired language *access*. When language is suddenly impaired following a CVA, access to language is often due to disruption rather than loss. Therefore, full or partial recovery has the potential to occur, either spontaneously or with language treatment. In PPA, neural mechanisms can reorganize to at least partially compensate for language impairment. However, functions slowly degenerate, and the eventual decline will surpass compensation and result in the loss of language abilities, as seen in later stages of PPA. This language decline in PPA resulting from regional atrophy is less able to be recovered than language impairment resulting from a cerebrovascular lesion, and therefore intervention for PPA focuses on maintenance rather than restoration. It is important to mention that only one of the bilingual PPA studies investigated treatment effects on language (Meyer et al. 2015). The researchers found that the treatment did not restore function, but the treatment did slow decline, certainly for the treated language and possibly in the untreated language. Thus by studying language loss as a result of a degenerative disease, we can add to our knowledge of bilingual language organization on top of what we already know from studies of sudden-onset aphasia in bilinguals.

3.   Support for Language Models

Based on the bilingual and multilingual PPA cases reviewed in Section 2, the patterns of language decline are consistent across the three variants of PPA. Notably, language decline occurs in all languages of bilinguals and multilinguals with PPA, relative to the specific atrophy of the variant of PPA, and performance on some tasks declines in parallel across languages even in the beginning stages. This provides some support for Green's (2003) convergence hypothesis, with processing for L2 and L1 converging on shared brain regions for both languages (Abutalebi 2008; Abutalebi and Green 2007; Green 2003). However, the convergence hypothesis is not fully supported, since in many cases, at least some language tasks decline differentially in the early and middle stages of the disease. Furthermore, proficiency and recency of use do not appear to have a substantial effect on language decline between the L1 and L2 in bilinguals and multilinguals with PPA, contrary to the convergence hypothesis. Recall that the only support for the convergence hypothesis came from contrasting two cases of multilinguals with PPA

(Kambanaros and Grohmann 2012; Mendez et al. 2004, participant 2). This will be an interesting direction of research in the future when more cases of multilinguals with PPA are investigated.

Regarding Ullman's (2015) declarative-procedural model, little support is found from the bilingual and multilingual cases of PPA that we have reviewed. Although differential decline is observed in some cases and some language tasks, with L1 better preserved than L2, the patterns of differential decline do not follow the hypotheses of the declarative-procedural model. A lower age of L2 acquisition did not consistently result in parallel decline, and differences between implicit and explicit learning contexts did not result in parallel vs. differential decline respectively. Furthermore, specific language tasks that are related more to declarative (explicit) learning in both the first language and second languages (e.g. lexical knowledge) relative to other tasks that are considered more procedural in the first language and more declarative in the second (e.g. syntactic knowledge) did not show parallel decline relative to differential decline as might be expected from the declarative-procedural model. To summarize, neither model is fully supported by the bilingual and multilingual PPA literature.

What is also notable about the PPA literature are the striking similarities between bilinguals with AD and those with PPA. When language declines in AD, L1 has been found to be better preserved than L2 with both languages declining in parallel at the end-stage of the disease. Language decline in PPA parallels this pattern, which is hypothesized to be due to the process of neural atrophy and its effect on language loss. The bilingual PPA literature, we would argue, can be particularly useful in understanding how language is organized in the brain, as AD patients typically have concomitant cognitive deficits at the late stages of the disease, which is when language decline is most noticeable. These cognitive deficits in AD may confound the picture of language decline, but in PPA – especially in the earlier stages of the decline – the picture may be clearer when the focus is specifically on language.

4.   Conclusion

Studies on bilinguals with PPA can provide valuable information regarding language organization in the bilingual brain. Even with only 13 case studies covering a range of variants, languages, proficiency levels, ages of acquisition, manners of acquisition, and patterns of use, it is clear that the patterns of language decline fall into two main categories: parallel decline or L1 better spared than L2. Furthermore, as the PPA progresses, there is a trend towards parallel decline overall. Whether these two patterns will remain exclusive as more cases of bilinguals with PPA are studied and published, or whether there will be some cases of L2 being better spared than L1, remains to be seen.

For now, based on the published literature to date, we conclude that patterns of language decline in bilinguals with PPA are similar to those observed in bilinguals with AD; they do not support Ullman's (2015) hypothesis and only partially support Green's (2003) convergence hypothesis. More detailed cases of bilinguals with PPA are necessary to revise this, or other, models of bilingual language organization to fit better with the

PPA data. The degenerative nature of PPA, likely resulting in compensation for declining language abilities over the progressive decline, at least in the early stages, may explain why the two patterns of language decline converge to parallel decline over time. While the main factor driving the patterns of language decline is currently suggested to be order of acquisition, further research involving more cases of bilinguals with PPA, providing more details about language background and premorbid and postmorbid language abilities is essential. It is still unclear how other factors such as proficiency and/or dominance, age of acquisition, manner of acquisition, and patterns of use (such as recency of use) may interact with order of acquisition to determine the course of decline in any given bilingual with PPA.

In conclusion, longitudinal studies following the progression of the decline in both languages over time, including both behavioural and neuroimaging data, will be essential to understanding the progress of the degeneration, what compensation may occur, and how the deterioration affects languages in bilinguals with PPA. Further investigation of PPA in bilinguals should aid in our theoretical knowledge of language organization in the bilingual brain, particularly in areas that are still poorly understood, and should suggest avenues of approach for treatment to buffer against decline, enhance compensation, and maintain communication in order to uphold quality of life. The case studies that make up the current literature provide a first step towards understanding the complexity of language decline in bilinguals with PPA.

Acknowledgements

We would like to thank M. M. Mesulam for his helpful suggestions finding literature relating to the underlying neural degeneration in PPA. We also thank Ingeborg Sophie Ribu and an anonymous reviewer for thoughtful suggestions on an earlier draft.

REFERENCES

Abutalebi, J. (2008). Neural aspects of second language representation and language control. *Acta Psychologica* 128 (3): 466–478. doi:10.1016/j.actpsy.2008.03.014.

Abutalebi, J., Cappa, S.F., and Perani, D. (2001). The bilingual brain as revealed by functional neuroimaging. *Bilingualism: Language and Cognition* 4 (2): 179–190. doi:10.1017/S136672890100027X.

Abutalebi, J. and Green, D. (2007). Bilingual language production: the neurocognition of language representation and control. *Journal of Neurolinguistics* 20 (3): 242–275. doi:10.1016/j.jneuroling.2006.10.003.

Ardila, A., Ramos, E., Ardila, A., and Ramos, E. (2008). Normal and abnormal aging in bilinguals. *Dementia & Neuropsychologia* 2 (4): 242–247. doi:10.1590/S1980-57642009DN20400002.

Binney, R.J., Henry, M.L., Babiak, M. et al. (2016). Reading words and other people: a comparison of exception word, familiar face and affect processing in the left and right temporal variants of primary progressive aphasia. *Cortex* 82: 147–163.

Blair, M., Marczinski, C.A., Davis-Faroque, N., and Kertesz, A. (2007). A longitudinal study of language decline in Alzheimer's disease and frontotemporal dementia. *Journal of the International Neuropsychological Society* 13 (2): 237–245. doi:10.1017/S1355617707070269.

Calandri, I., Amengual, A., Chaves, H. et al. (2014). Bilingualism and language networks in the semantic variant of primary progressive aphasia. *Neurology* 82 (10 Supplement): P6.234.

Chen, L., Shu, H., Liu, Y. et al. (2007). ERP signatures of subject–verb agreement in L2 learning. *Bilingualism: Language and Cognition* 10 (2): 161–174. doi:10.1017/S136672890700291X.

Consonni, M., Cafiero, R., Marin, D. et al. (2013). Neural convergence for language comprehension and grammatical class production in highly proficient bilinguals is independent of age of acquisition. *Cortex* 49 (5): 1252–1258. doi:10.1016/j.cortex.2012.04.009.

Costa, A., Calabria, M., Marne, P. et al. (2012). On the parallel deterioration of lexico-semantic processes in the bilinguals' two languages: evidence from Alzheimer's disease. *Neuropsychologia* 50 (5): 740–753. doi:10.1016/j.neuropsychologia.2012.01.008.

Crinion, J., Turner, R., Grogan, A. et al. (2006). Language control in the bilingual brain. *Science* 312 (5779): 1537–1540. doi:10.1126/science.1127761.

Dehaene, S., Dupoux, E., Mehler, J. et al. (1997). Anatomical variability in the cortical representation of first and second language. *NeuroReport* 8 (17): 3809.

Devaughn, S., Chen, W., Burciaga, J., and Peery, S. (2016). A case of semantic variant of primary progressive aphasia in a balanced bilingual. *Archives of Clinical Neuropsychology* 31 (6): 588. doi:10.1093/arclin/acw043.14.

Druks, J. and Weekes, B.S. (2013). Parallel deterioration to language processing in a bilingual speaker. *Cognitive Neuropsychology* 30 (7–8): 578–596. doi:10.1080/02643294.2014.882814.

Faroqi-Shah, Y., Frymark, T., Mullen, R., and Wang, B. (2010). Effect of treatment for bilingual individuals with aphasia: a systematic review of the evidence. *Journal of*

Neurolinguistics 23 (4): 319–341. doi:10.1016/j.jneuroling.2010.01.002.

Filley, C.M., Ramsberger, G., Menn, L. et al. (2006). Primary progressive aphasia in a bilingual woman. *Neurocase* 12 (5): 296–299. doi:10.1080/13554790601126047.

Golestani, N., Alario, F.-X., Meriaux, S. et al. (2006). Syntax production in bilinguals. *Neuropsychologia* 44 (7): 1029–1040. doi:10.1016/j.neuropsychologia.2005.11.009.

Gollan, T.H., Salmon, D.P., Montoya, R.I., and Galasko, D.R. (2011). Degree of bilingualism predicts age of diagnosis of Alzheimer's disease in low-education but not in highly educated Hispanics. *Neuropsychologia* 49 (14): 3826–3830. doi:10.1016/j.neuropsychologia.2011.09.041.

Gómez-Ruiz, I., Aguilar-Alonso, Á., and Espasa, M.A. (2012). Language impairment in Catalan-Spanish bilinguals with Alzheimer's disease. *Journal of Neurolinguistics* 25 (6): 552–566. doi:10.1016/j.jneuroling.2011.06.003.

Goral, M., Rosas, J., Conner, P.S. et al. (2012). Effects of language proficiency and language of the environment on aphasia therapy in a multilingual. *Journal of Neurolinguistics* 25 (6): 538–551. doi:10.1016/j.jneuroling.2011.06.001.

Gorno-Tempini, M.L., Brambati, S.M., Ginex, V. et al. (2008). The logopenic/phonological variant of primary progressive aphasia. *Neurology* 71 (16): 1227. doi:10.1212/01.wnl.0000320506.79811.da.

Gorno-Tempini, M.L., Dronkers, N.F., Rankin, K.P. et al. (2004). Cognition and anatomy in three variants of primary progressive aphasia. *Annals of Neurology* 55 (3): 335–346. doi:10.1002/ana.10825.

Gorno-Tempini, M.L., Hillis, A.E., Weintraub, S. et al. (2011). Classification of primary progressive aphasia and its variants. *Neurology* 76 (11): 1006–1014. doi:10.1212/WNL.0b013e31821103e6.

Gorno-Tempini, M.L., Rankin, K.P., Woolley, J.D. et al. (2004). Cognitive and behavioral profile in a case of right anterior temporal lobe neurodegeneration. *Cortex* 40 (4): 631–644.

Green, D.W. (2003). Neural basis of lexicon and grammar in L2 acquisition. In: *The Lexicon Syntax Interface in Second Language Acquisition* (ed. R. van Hout, A. Hulk, F. Kuiken and R.J. Towel), 197–218. Amsterdam, The Netherlands: John Benjamins.

Grossman, M. (2010). Primary progressive aphasia: clinicopathological correlations. *Nature Reviews Neurology* 6 (2): doi:10.1038/nrneurol.2009.216.

Hernàndez, M., Caño, A., Costa, A. et al. (2008). Grammatical category-specific deficits in bilingual aphasia. *Brain and Language* 107 (1): 68–80. doi:10.1016/j.bandl.2008.01.006.

Hodges, J. and Patterson, K. (1996). Nonfluent progressive aphasia and semantic dementia: a comparative neuropsychological study. *Journal of the International Neuropsychological Society: JINS* 2: 511–524. doi:10.1017/S1355617700001685.

Iqbal, K., Liu, F., Gong, C.-X., and Grundke-Iqbal, I. (2010). Tau in Alzheimer disease and related tauopathies. *Current Alzheimer Research* 7 (8): 656–664. doi:10.2174/156720510793611592.

Kambanaros, M. and Grohmann, K.K. (2012). BATting multilingual primary progressive aphasia for Greek, English, and Czech. *Journal of Neurolinguistics* 25 (6): 520–537. doi:10.1016/j.jneuroling.2011.01.006.

Kaplan, E.F., Goodglass, H., and Weintraub, S. (1983). *The Boston Naming Test*, 2nd. Philadelphia: Lea & Febiger.

Kemmerer, D. (2014). *Cognitive Neuroscience of Language*, 80–84. New York, NY: Psychology Press.

Kim, K.H.S., Relkin, N.R., Lee, K.-M., and Hirsch, J. (1997). Distinct cortical areas associated with native and second languages. *Nature* 388 (6638): 40623. doi:10.1038/40623.

Kroll, J.F. and Tokowicz, N. (2005). Models of bilingual representation and processing: looking back and to the future. In: *Handbook of Bilingualism: Psycholinguistic Approaches* (ed. J.F. Kroll and A.M.B. De Groot). New York, NY: Oxford University Press.

Kuhl, P.K., Stevenson, J., Corrigan, N.M. et al. (2016). Neuroimaging of the bilingual brain: structural brain correlates of listening and speaking in a second language. *Brain and Language* 162 (Supplement C): 1–9. doi:10.1016/j.bandl.2016.07.004.

Larner, A.J. (2012). Progressive non-fluent aphasia in a bilingual subject: relative preservation of 'mother tongue'. *The Journal of Neuropsychiatry and Clinical Neurosciences* 24 (1): E9–E10. doi:10.1176/appi.neuropsych.11010019.

Lind, M., Simonsen, H.G., Ribu, I.S.B. et al. (2017). Lexical access in a bilingual speaker with dementia: changes over time. *Clinical Linguistics & Phonetics* 32 (4): 353–377. doi:10.1080/02699206.2017.1381168.

Liu, Y.C., Yip, P.K., Fan, Y.M., and Meguro, K. (2012). A potential protective effect in multilingual patients with semantic dementia: two case reports of patients speaking Taiwanese and Japanese. *Acta Neurologica Taiwanica* 21 (1): 25–30.

Lorenzen, B. and Murray, L.L. (2008). Bilingual aphasia: a theoretical and clinical review. *American Journal of Speech-Language Pathology* 17 (3): 299–317. doi:10.1044/1058-0360(2008/026).

Machado, Á., Rodrigues, M., Simões, S. et al. (2010). The Portuguese who could no longer speak French: primary progressive aphasia in a bilingual man. *The Journal of Neuropsychiatry and Clinical Neurosciences* 22 (1): 123.e31–123.e32. doi:10.1176/jnp.2010.22.1.123.e31.

Manchon, M., Buetler, K., Colombo, F. et al. (2015). Impairment of both languages in late bilinguals with dementia of the Alzheimer type. *Bilingualism: Language and Cognition* 18 (1): 90–100. doi:10.1017/S1366728914000194.

Meguro, K., Senaha, M.L., Caramelli, P. et al. (2003). Language deterioration in four Japanese–Portuguese bilingual patients with Alzheimer's disease: a trans-cultural study of Japanese elderly immigrants in Brazil. *Psychogeriatrics* 3 (2): 63–68. doi:10.1046/j.1479-8301.2003.00011.x.

Mendez, M.F., Perryman, K.M., Pontón, M.O., and Cummings, J.L. (1999). Bilingualism and dementia. *The Journal of Neuropsychiatry and Clinical Neurosciences* 11 (3): 411–412. doi:10.1176/jnp.11.3.411.

Mendez, M.F., Saghafi, S., and Clark, D.G. (2004). Semantic dementia in multilingual patients. *The Journal of Neuropsychiatry and Clinical Neurosciences* 16 (3): 381–381. doi:10.1176/jnp.16.3.381.

Mesulam, M.-M. (2003). Primary progressive aphasia – a language-based dementia. *New England Journal of Medicine* 349 (16): 1535–1542. doi:10.1056/NEJMra022435.

Mesulam, M.-M. (2007). Primary progressive aphasia: a 25-year retrospective. *Alzheimer Disease & Associated Disorders* 21 (4): S8. doi:10.1097/WAD.0b013e31815bf7e1.

Mesulam, M.-M., Rogalski, E.J., Wieneke, C. et al. (2014). Primary progressive aphasia and the evolving neurology of the language network. *Nature Reviews Neurology* 10 (10): 159. doi:10.1038/nrneurol.2014.159.

Mesulam, M.-M., Thompson, C.K., Weintraub, S., and Rogalski, E.J. (2015). The Wernicke conundrum and the anatomy of language comprehension in primary progressive aphasia. *Brain* 138 (8): 2423–2437. doi:10.1093/brain/awv154.

Meyer, A.M., Snider, S.F., Eckmann, C.B., and Friedman, R.B. (2015). Prophylactic treatments for anomia in the logopenic variant of primary progressive aphasia: cross-language transfer. *Aphasiology* 29 (9): 1062–1081. doi:10.1080/02687038.2015.1028327.

Mion, M., Patterson, K., Acosta-Cabronero, J. et al. (2010). What the left and right anterior fusiform gyri tell us about semantic memory. *Brain* 133 (11): 3256–3268. doi:10.1093/brain/awq272.

Osterhout, L., McLaughlin, J., Pitkänen, I. et al. (2006). Novice learners, longitudinal designs, and event-related potentials: a means for exploring the neurocognition of second language processing. *Language Learning* 56: 199–230. doi:10.1111/j.1467-9922.2006.00361.x.

Paradis, M. (1987). *Bilingual Aphasia Test*. Hillsdale, NJ: Lawrence Erlbaum Associates.

Paradis, M. (2001). The need for awareness of aphasia symptoms in different languages. *Journal of Neurolinguistics* 14 (2): 85–91. doi:10.1016/S0911-6044(01)00009-4.

Paradis, M. (2003). Differential use of cerebral mechanisms in bilinguals. In: *Mind, Brain, and Language* (ed. M.T. Banich and M. Mack), 351–370. Mahwah, NJ: Erlbaum.

Paradis, J. (2008). Are simultaneous and early sequential bilingual acquisition fundamentally different? Paper presented at the International Conference on Models of Interaction in Bilinguals, University of Wales, Bangor, UK.

Perani, D., Paulesu, E., Galles, N.S. et al. (1998). The bilingual brain. Proficiency and age of acquisition of the second language. *Brain* 121 (10): 1841–1852. doi:10.1093/brain/121.10.1841.

Perea, M., Duñabeitia, J.A., and Carreiras, M. (2008). Masked associative/semantic priming effects across languages with highly proficient bilinguals. *Journal of Memory and Language* 58 (4): 916–930. doi:10.1016/j.jml.2008.01.003.

Rogalski, E., Cobia, D., Harrison, T.M. et al. (2011). Progression of language decline and cortical atrophy in subtypes of primary progressive aphasia. *Neurology* 76 (21): 1804. doi:10.1212/WNL.0b013e31821ccd3c.

Rosen, H.J., Allison, S.C., Ogar, J.M. et al. (2006). Behavioral features in semantic dementia vs. other forms of progressive aphasias. *Neurology* 67 (10): 1752–1756.

Santos-Santos, M.A., Rabinovici, G.D., Iaccarino, L. et al. (2018). Rates of amyloid imaging positivity in patients with primary progressive aphasia. *JAMA Neurology* 75 (3): 342–352.

Sinnatamby, R., Antoun, N.A., Freer, C.E.L. et al. (1996). Neuroradiological findings in primary progressive aphasia: CT, MRI and cerebral perfusion SPECT. *Neuroradiology* 38 (3): 232–238. doi:10.1007/BF00596535.

Stilwell, B.L., Dow, R.M., Lamers, C., and Woods, R.T. (2016). Language changes in bilingual individuals with Alzheimer's disease. *International Journal of Language & Communication Disorders* 51 (2): 113–127. doi:10.1111/1460-6984.12190.

Thompson, C.K., Ballard, K.J., Tait, M.E. et al. (1997). Patterns of language decline in non-fluent primary progressive aphasia. *Aphasiology* 11 (4–5): 297–321. doi:10.1080/02687039708248473.

Ullman, M.T. (2015). The declarative/procedural model. In: *Theories in Second Language Acquisition: An Introduction* (ed. B. VanPatten and J. Williams), 135–158. New York: Routledge.

Ullman, M.T. and Pierpont, E.I. (2005). Specific language impairment is not specific to language: the procedural deficit hypothesis. *Cortex* 41 (3): 399–433. doi:10.1016/S0010-9452(08)70276-4.

Van de Putte, E., De Baene, W., Brass, M., and Duyck, W. (2017). Neural overlap of L1 and L2 semantic representations in speech: a decoding approach. *NeuroImage* 162 (Supplement C): 106–116. doi:10.1016/j.neuroimage.2017.08.082.

Vonk, J. M. J., Borghesani, V., Battistella, G., Younes, K., Welch, A., Miller, Z., Miller, B. L., & Gorno-Tempini, M. L. (in preparation). From side to side: Nine-year evolution of an early case of right anterior temporal degeneration.

Wilson, S.M., Henry, M.L., Besbris, M. et al. (2010). Connected speech production in three variants of primary progressive aphasia. *Brain* 133 (7): 2069–2088. doi:10.1093/brain/awq129.

Zanini, S., Angeli, V., and Tavano, A. (2011). Primary progressive aphasia in a bilingual speaker: a single-case study. *Clinical Linguistics & Phonetics* 25 (6–7): 553–564. doi: 10.3109/02699206.2011.566464.

29 Acquired Reading Disorders in Bilingualism

MIRA GORAL

1. Introductions

Not all languages have writing systems; those that do vary in the way their orthography maps visual forms (graphemes) onto language. Variation is found in the direction in which words are read (e.g. right to left, left to right), in the size of the sound unit that corresponds to a grapheme (e.g. phonemes, syllables), and in the degree of transparency and regularity of the correspondence between the written form and the spoken form (e.g. each grapheme corresponds to a unique phoneme vs. each grapheme corresponds to more than one phoneme and each phoneme is represented by more than one grapheme). For example, Finnish and Spanish have transparent orthographies, in which most graphemes consistently correspond to one phoneme, whereas English and French have more opaque orthographies, with graphemes that correspond to more than one phoneme and phonemes that can be written in a variety of graphemes or grapheme combinations. Finnish, Spanish, English, and French all use alphabetic orthographies, mapping graphemes onto phonemes; Chinese uses an orthography that maps graphemes to syllables or words.

Whereas spoken language is acquired by virtually all people, literacy skills have to be learned and not everyone learns to read. Reading aloud (or *word naming*) involves processes of visual perception and visual analysis, and of mapping print units into speech. Research studies have demonstrated that the process of reading utilizes neuronal networks specialized for reading. Evidence from lesion studies and from neuroimaging studies has converged on the finding that the analysis of visual word and letter form corresponds to the left occipito-temporal sulcus, along the fusiform gyrus, an area that has been termed the visual word form area (VWFA). Activation of the VWFA has been found regardless of language and orthography (Bolger et al. 2005; Dehaene et al. 2002). A meta-analysis of 25 studies summarized in Bolger et al. (2005) has confirmed that the left mid-fusiform gyrus is a part of a network involving the left ventral stream and temporal and frontal regions, which is associated with word reading across languages.

The Handbook of the Neuroscience of Multilingualism, First Edition. Edited by John W. Schwieter.
© 2019 John Wiley & Sons Ltd. Published 2019 by John Wiley & Sons Ltd.

The process of reading involves more than visual word form recognition and word naming. Beyond the decoding processes that are involved in word naming, processes of reading comprehension involve mapping print units onto units of meaning, which depend on additional language processes, including semantics and syntax. Neuroimaging studies have converged on findings associating several networks and regions with the various subprocesses of reading, including the activation of left occipital-temporal networks during visual orthographic form recognition, left parietal regions during the integration of orthographic, phonological, and semantic information, left superior and middle temporal regions during phonological and semantic processing, and left frontal regions during phonological, semantic, and syntactic processing (Bolger et al. 2005; Perfetti et al. 2017; Price and Mechelli 2005).

Learning to read can be a prolonged process, but once mastered, reading often becomes highly automatic and, in skilled readers, decoding written words can happen extremely fast (within milliseconds). Learning to read has been associated with increased activation in some of these networks mentioned above, and increased reading proficiency has been associated with decreased activation (e.g. in left temporal-occipital regions), suggesting that as reading processes become more efficient, they require decreased brain activation (Cao 2016). Bilingual individuals need to learn to read in each of their languages, especially when the languages employ different orthographies, although some knowledge may transfer when learning to read in a second language (L2) after reading has already been learned in the first language (L1; e.g. Geva 2014). Two mechanisms may be at play when learning to read in a second language: the neuronal networks which are associated with reading the first language become responsible for processing the second (known as the assimilation hypothesis); alternatively, additional networks are recruited to process reading in an L2 (known as the accommodation hypothesis; see van Heuven and Coderre 2015; Perfetti et al. 2017). These mechanisms depend, in part, on the degree of differences between the two orthographies – that of the L1 and that of the L2. Specifically, learning an L2 orthography that is more opaque than the L1 orthography may require the engagement of additional neuronal networks during L2 reading than learning a more transparent L2 orthography after a more opaque L1 (Liu and Cao 2016; Tan et al. 2003). Whereas the brain regions that are activated during reading in a second language have been found to be similar to those activated during reading in L1, some activation differences have been demonstrated, including for skilled biscriptal readers (see Section 3).

2. Models of Reading

The dominant model of word reading has been the dual-route model (e.g. Coltheart 2005). Within this framework, the lexical (direct) route allows the meaning of a written word to be accessed directly via its lexical entry (its representation in the mental lexicon); in the sublexical (indirect) route, a written word is processed via grapheme–phoneme conversion (GPC) and its meaning is retrieved via the spoken word lexical entry. Based on experimental findings and data from acquired reading impairments, a three-route model has been put forward, extending the two-route one. The extended model differentiates whether the semantic store is accessed during word reading. The three routes include a semantic lexical route, in which visual analysis leads to the orthographic lexicon, which is in turn linked to the semantic system, and from there the phonological output lexicon is accessed; a non-semantic lexical route, which links visual analysis to the orthographic lexicon, which in turn connects to the phonological output lexicon; and a non-lexical route, which links visual analysis via spelling–sound correspondence to the phonological output lexicon. A computational version of the dual-route model has been put forward, suggesting that reading can proceed in the two routes simultaneously (Coltheart 2005).

These models have been developed primarily based on English, but attempts to validate them in other languages have been made. To date, it is unclear whether all routes are useful in extremely transparent (one-to-one GPC) or extremely opaque (one-to-many, many-to-one GPC) orthographies, as will be discussed in Section 3.1. Connectionist models of reading have also been proposed, offering an alternative to the assumption that systematic aspects of language, such as the correspondence between phoneme and graphemes, are best represented with a set of rules (plus rules to account for exceptions to the rules). Instead, the parallel distributed processing model is based on statistical aspects of the relations between grapheme and phonemes in context (e.g. Plaut 1999). In this framework, the mental representation of specific words is not assumed; rather, based on repeated exposure and experience, readers are hypothesized to map the visual forms onto spoken forms.

3.   Acquired Reading Disorders in Bilingual and Biscriptal Adults

Acquired brain lesions to regions that are involved in the process of reading result in alexia, that is, impairment of reading. Impaired reading abilities may be due to an impairment in one or more of the processes that are involved, including visual, phonological, lexical, and semantic, leading to different types of alexia. Reading impairment can occur concomitantly with aphasia (central alexia) or as the main impairment, with or without comparable impairment of writing (peripheral alexia). Several types of alexia have been defined based on the main characteristics of the impairment (see, for example, Coslett 2000). Within the two- or three-route model of reading, phonological alexia, for example, results from an impairment to the non-lexical reading route and is characterized by greatly reduced nonword reading; deep alexia is defined as difficulty with the lexical reading route and a partially impaired sublexical conversion, and is characterized by semantic errors during reading. Surface alexia is defined as impaired lexical processing that, in turn, increases the reliance on the non-lexical reading route, and is characterized by difficulty reading irregular words compared to regular words. As in many classification systems in acquired brain lesions, not all individuals who acquire reading impairments can be neatly classified into the types of alexia identified.

The literature on acquired alexia in bilingual individuals (the term bilinguals is used in this chapter to denote individuals who use more than one language) comprises mostly single case studies, with a focus on the manifestation of the types of alexia across different orthographies. A review of the studies of acquired alexia in bilinguals has revealed two main controversies, as outlined in Sections 3.1 and 3.2. The first controversy concerns the degree to which orthography determines the nature of the reading impairment; the second addresses the implications of orthography differences for the underlying networks associated with reading. Most published studies provide information and findings that contribute to resolving the first controversy; few studies address directly the question that is at the focus of the second.

3.1. Orthography Effects on Reading Disorders

Controversy #1: Does orthography determine the process of reading and, consequently, the manifestation of acquired reading impairment across languages?

It has been hypothesized that languages with transparent orthographies, with a straightforward and regular correspondence between graphemes and phonemes, are likely to facilitate reliance on GPC, whereas languages with opaque orthographies, with complex and less-predicted correspondences between graphemes and phonemes, rely more on a direct (lexical or semantic lexical) route from the visual form to the word meaning than on the GPC (e.g. Katz and Frost 1992). This division is not categorical and evidence suggests that reading languages with transparent as well as opaque orthographies activates regions associated with phonological processing (Perfetti et al. 2017). Moreover, even in transparent orthographies, skilled readers use the lexical route, which is presumed to be more efficient (Coltheart 2005). Nevertheless, if one or another of the hypothesized reading routes bear less importance to opaque or to transparent orthographies, respectively, then the different types of alexia, observed initially in English, may be less likely in a given language. For example, deep alexia is less likely to be found in individuals who read a language with a transparent orthography in which the lexical route is less robust and there are few irregular words, and, similarly, surface alexia may be less likely in languages that rely less on GPC, a route that will result in numerous errors.

Whereas cross-language (cross-sectional) comparisons can be employed to test these predictions, an ideal way to support or refute the assumption that orthography type determines the manifestation of the impairment is to examine acquired reading impairment in bilingual and biscriptal individuals (Obler 1984; Weekes 2005). One source of evidence comes from the finding of dissociations in the reading impairment of bilingual readers of a language with opaque orthography (e.g. English, French), and a language of transparent orthography (e.g. Hindi, Spanish; see Table 1).

Ohno et al. (2002) described a Japanese-English bilingual man diagnosed with pure alexia (alexia without agraphia), resorting to letter-by-letter reading, following a left posterior cerebral artery (PCA) cerebral-vascular accident (CVA) that resulted in damage to the fusiform gyrus and the corpus callosum. His pure alexia, occurring without concomitant writing impairment or other language difficulties, was evident in the assessment conducted 30 days post-stroke: the participant's language abilities were intact, but he could not read in Japanese – in either kana (the syllabic orthography) or kanji (the logographic orthography that uses Chinese characters). Nevertheless, his

Table 1 Studies of acquired alexia in bilingual individuals.

Study	Languages	Aetiology	Impairment	
			Profile	Orthography Effect
Beaton and Davies 2007	Welsh, English	Left CVA	Three participants with deep alexia; comparable proportions of semantic errors in both languages; 2 of the 3 demonstrated better reading in English, their dominant language, than in Welsh	No, differences may be related to proficiency
Beland and Mimouni 2001	Arabic, French	Left CVA perisylvian region	Deep dyslexia in both languages with semantic errors in both; more reading errors in L1 Arabic than in L2 (French, from age 4) and translation errors from Arabic to French	Yes
Ibrahim 2009	Arabic, Hebrew	Left temporal lobe haemorrhage and right frontal subdural haemorrhage	Letter-by-letter reading; greater reading difficulties in L2 Hebrew (learned around age 9) than in L1 Arabic	Yes
Karanth 1981	Telugu, Kannada, Tamil, English	Not specified	Telugu L1; literate in Kannada and English (not Telugu); letter-by-letter reading in both Kannada and English; Kannada appeared more impaired than English	Yes
Karanth 2002	Hindi, English, Tamil, Bengali, Kannada	Head injury, left temporo-parietal fracture and haemorrhage	Greater difficulty reading in Hindi L1 than in English	Yes
Laganaro and Overton Venet 2001	Spanish, English	Head injury (gunshot) to left temporo-parietal-occipital	One participant (English learned in adulthood); comparable impairment in both languages. Cross-language generalization of some but not all therapy gains	No

Study	Languages	Lesion	Findings	Differential impairment
Lyman et al. 1938	Chinese, English	Brain tumour in left occipito-parietal region	Reading Chinese less impaired than reading English (L2 learned in childhood)	Yes
Ohno et al. 2002	Japanese, English	Left PCA CVA; fusiform, corpus callosum	Kana more impaired than kanji; English (learned in late childhood) only mildly impaired	Yes
Ratnavalli et al. 2000	Kannada, English; Telugu, Kannada, English, Hindi	Left occipital infarct, corpus callosum; Left parietal CVA	Pure alexia in both languages P1, alexia and agraphia in both languages in P2; comparable impairment in both languages; errors resulting in nonwords in Kannada and real words in English	Yes and no
Senaha and Parente 2012	Portuguese, Japanese	Traumatic brain injury to the left frontotemporal area	Greater impairment in Kanji and irregular Portuguese words than Kana, regular, and nonwords in Portuguese	Yes
Weekes et al. 2007	Mongolian, Chinese	Variable: left and right CVAs	In 3 of the 8 participants, greater reading impairment in Chinese L2 than Mongolian L1, at least in some tasks	Yes, but differences could be related to proficiency

Note: CVA = cerebral-vascular accident; P = participant; PCA = posterior cerebral artery; L1 = first acquired language; L2 = second language.

reading in kana was more impaired than his reading in kanji, which was in turn more impaired than his reading in English (which was only mildly impaired). Orthographic differences between English and Japanese may account for the differential impairment. We note that the most transparent orthography – kana – appeared to be most impaired. In addition, the difference in age of acquisition – the participant learned to read English in late childhood, after middle school – can account for the dissociation.

The authors also point to an early study, Lyman et al. (1938), in which reading Chinese was less impaired than reading English in a bilingual with acquired reading impairment. Furthermore, a dissociation (in the opposite direction) between the impairment in kanji and kana, the logographic and the syllabic orthographic systems in Japanese, was reported in Hashimoto and Uno (2016). Following a left temporal-parietal-occipital infarct, a Japanese speaker experienced mild anomia and difficulty reading. A thorough examination revealed that visual perception was intact, although written lexical decision was impaired in both scripts as well as reading high-frequency real words and reading nonwords. Also of note is that writing, which was impaired in this individual, was more affected in kanji than in kana.

Consistently, Senaha and Parente (2012) demonstrated that reading irregular words in Portuguese and reading kanji words in Japanese were more impaired than reading regular words in Portuguese and reading Japanese kana in a bilingual (triscriptal) Portuguese-Japanese speaker following a traumatic brain injury in the left frontotemporal region. His performance was consistent with surface alexia in Portuguese, evident in overreliance on the non-lexical reading route, leading the authors to interpret their findings as a selective impairment in the lexical route of reading. A very similar pattern was described in Meguro et al. (2003) for four Japanese-Portuguese individuals who developed dementia and had increasing difficulty reading. All four individuals demonstrated greater difficulty reading kanji and irregular Portuguese words compared to kana and regular words.

The findings reported in Senaha and Parente and in Meguro et al. are consistent with the notion that impaired reading performance following acquired brain lesions is the result of comparable impairment in all languages that is manifested differently, depending on the orthographic-specific characteristic of each writing system. The study of a single individual who has two languages and three writing systems offers a unique opportunity to dissociate orthography effects from language effects. That is, whereas differences between the reading impairments in two languages of a bilingual could be attributed to either differences in proficiency, age and acquisition, and other factors *or* to orthographic differences, differences in impairments in two orthographic systems of the same language could only be attributed to the orthographically unique characteristics of each script.

In another study with a bilingual with two languages of very different orthographies, Karanth (2002) reported on a case of a Hindi-English bilingual with acquired alexia due to a head injury resulting in left temporo-parietal fracture and haemorrhage. His alexia was central, that is, reading impairment concomitant with aphasia. He was a highly proficient reader in L1 Hindi, which has a syllabic orthography that is very transparent with few irregular words, as well as in his L2 English, which has opaque orthography. Following the stroke, the participant experienced greater difficulty reading in Hindi and preferred to receive therapy in English. In English, he made semantic errors, could not read via the letter-by-letter method, and showed no difference between reading regular and irregular words, all consistent with deep alexia. In Hindi, he made no semantic errors and his reading pattern appeared more consistent with pure alexia. These results were similar to those Karanth reported earlier for another case (Karanth 1981). The author suggested that reading in Hindi, a language with a transparent orthography, likely relies heavily on the sublexical (GPC) route and is less likely to rely on the lexical route, whereas English is assumed to rely on both routes. Therefore, the reading impairment manifested differently in each of the two languages. This interpretation is precisely what had been predicted for the manifestation of alexia in two different orthographies.

Although Beland and Mimouni (2001) diagnosed deep alexia in both languages of an Arabic-French bilingual man, they noted differences in the reading behaviour in the two languages. Their participant was a Lebanese man with Arabic as his L1 and French, spoken from age four, as his L2, who was educated in both languages. Arabic is written from right to left, the letters of a word are connected, and many letters have several different forms, depending on where in the word they appear (word initial, middle, final). Arabic may be written with or without diacritics – symbols that represent short vowels, amongst others. Arabic written without the diacritics (more common) makes for a more opaque orthography than when it is written with the diacritics (less common, mostly included for beginner readers and in some literary forms), and includes large numbers of homographs. French uses an alphabetic script but the GPC is not one-to-one and its orthography is considered opaque. Following a left CVA in the perisylvian region, the participant experienced aphasia and apraxia, as well as alexia characterized by semantic errors in both languages. However, the participant had committed more errors while reading in L1 than in L2. A series of reading aloud tasks at the letter, syllable, and word levels revealed impairment in both Arabic and French in both sublexical and lexical levels and better closed-class words than open-class words. His semantic error frequency was comparable in the two Arabic orthographies. Semantic errors were noted not only in reading but also in naming and repetition tasks. The authors administered lexical decision tasks with cross-language phonological priming, which in the case of Arabic and French is not orthographic nor visual, and found a difference between the two languages. Specifically, there was no priming effect in the Arabic nonword-prime/French word-target priming condition, whereas there was a significant priming effect in the French nonword-prime/Arabic word-target condition. The patient also made translation errors, seeing an Arabic word and saying the French translation (with fewer such instances in the opposite direction).

A similar dissociation has been reported in Ibrahim (2009) for a native speaker of Arabic who learned Hebrew formally at age nine and achieved high spoken and written proficiency in both languages. Arabic and Hebrew are similar in that both use orthography that, when written without the diacritics, is quite opaque, with multiple homographs and multiple shapes for each grapheme, although the Arabic orthography is considered more complex than the Hebrew one (e.g. more letters have multiple forms). Following a cerebral haemorrhage, the patient exhibited greater difficulty in Hebrew than in Arabic in various domains, including in his reading abilities. Whereas his greater impairment can be attributed to the fact that Hebrew was his L2, language-specific characteristics also appeared to determine his impairment. Specifically, due to his alexia, he resorted to letter-by-letter reading, which was less viable in Hebrew than in Arabic, according to the author.

Dissociations in the numbers of errors produced during reading in the two languages of bilinguals have been reported in several other studies, for a variety of language pairs of greater or lesser orthographic similarities, for example Spanish and English (Masterson et al. 1985), Turkish and English (Raman and Weekes 2005), and Chinese and Mongolian (Weekes et al. 2007). In Weekes et al. (2007), for example, three of the eight Mongolian (L1)-Chinese (early-learned L2) bilingual speakers with acquired alexia showed differential performance on one or more tasks related to reading. In some cases, the participants' L2, Chinese, appeared more impaired. This could be related to the fact that the second, less dominant language was less proficient before the acquired lesion and more impaired following it, as suggested by the authors. Specifically, the authors referred to Green's model of language inhibition (e.g. Green 2005), suggesting that L2 can be more inhibited following a stroke than L1 and therefore show greater impairment. However, the differential impairment in these bilingual individuals may also be related to the orthographic difference between Mongolian, an alphabetic script, and Chinese, a pictographic one.

In contrast to the dissociations reported above, several case studies of bilinguals have been reported for whom the acquired reading impairment was comparable in two languages, despite orthographic differences, or whose differential patterns do not align with the above predictions.

For example, Ratnavalli et al. (2000) studied two participants who were highly proficient in Kannada and English. Each participant demonstrated a different type of alexia, but both participants showed comparable reading impairment in both Kannada and English. The first participant had a left occipital infarct, extending into the corpus callosum. Following the stroke, he experienced, in addition to his alexia, anomia as well as colour anomia and word recognition impairment, while other language skills were not impaired. He demonstrated comparable reading performance in both languages, characterized by alexia without agraphia and severely impaired, letter-by-letter reading in both languages. The second case was a multilingual. He spoke and read, in addition to Kannada and English, Telugu (as his L1), and Hindi. Reading single words was slow but mostly accurate in both Kannada and English, although his errors included syllable substitution in Kannada. However, both participants made reading errors that resulted in nonwords in Kannada and real words in English. That is, despite overall similar impairments in two different languages, orthography-specific characteristics results in differing errors.

Two additional studies reported the absence of orthographic effects on the manifestation of alexia in two languages of different orthographic types: Beaton and Davies (2007) reported on Welsh, which has highly transparent orthography, and English, which has opaque orthography; and Laganaro and Overton Venet (2001) reported on Spanish, which has transparent orthography, and English.

Beaton and Davies (2007) examined three highly proficient Welsh-English bilingual individuals post left CVA, which resulted in central alexia with aphasia. All three were diagnosed with deep alexia. Based on the predictions outlined above, acquired deep alexia would result in more semantic errors in reading English than in reading Welsh. In contrast to this prediction, all three participants made comparable proportions of semantic errors in the two languages. Moreover, two of the three participants demonstrated better reading abilities in English, their dominant language, than in Welsh. However, whereas better performance in the more dominant language may be expected, greater difficulty with opaque than transparent orthography may have been predicted in deep alexia. Thus, the findings of this study do not lend support to a prevailing effect of orthography type on the manifestation of acquired reading.

Similarly, Laganaro and Overton Venet (2001) studied a Spanish-English bilingual man eight months after a traumatic brain injury (a gunshot to left temporo-partieal-occipital). Following surgery, the participant demonstrated central alexia, concomitant with right hemianopia, aphasia, and acalculia. His language comprehension was relatively intact and his expressive language skills were consistent with conduction aphasia. His overall language skills later improved but a phonological impairment remained. A detailed reading assessment in both languages (single word and nonword reading, visual lexical decision, narrative reading) revealed comparable performance in both languages. Nonword reading was more impaired than real word reading, with no effect of word length, consistent with phonological alexia. Reading aloud was slow and laborious in both languages, i.e. Spanish (the L1) and English (his L2, which was learned late).

In conclusion, the studies reviewed here suggest that there is evidence for the influence of orthography type on the manifestation of acquired reading impairment, although in some cases, orthography differences are confounded with language proficiency differences. Overall, there is no unequivocal evidence for a clear relationship between orthography type and alexia type. Perhaps, as suggested by Beland and Mimouni (2001), the two- or three-route models, suggested on the basis of dissociations and patterns amongst English-speaking individuals with acquired reading impairments, are less universal than was originally thought and do not capture the complex process of reading and the subtypes of alexia. As well, if, as is likely the case, all readers have access to all reading routes, an acquired impairment would alter the likelihood of reliance on one route or the other instead of completely impairing the process of reading.

3.2. Orthography Effects on Neuronal Organization

Controversy #2: Does selective manifestation of acquired alexia in bilingual individuals reflect differential underlying representation?

As evident in the studies reported in Section 3.1, in at least some instances, orthography-specific characteristics result in differential manifestation of impaired reading abilities in two languages following a single brain lesion. These reports, combined with the substantial orthographic differences seen across different languages, have given rise to the hypothesis that differing neuronal networks underlie different orthographic types. For example, although readers in all orthographies may make use of both lexical and sublexical reading routes, if in one language the GPC is more useful (e.g. Portuguese, Spanish) than in another (e.g. Mandarin), it is possible that reading in these different orthographies is mediated via different processes associated with different neuronal networks.

Before turning to the evidence that speaks to this hypothesis, it should be noted that the question of whether the (spoken) languages of bilingual individuals are processed via overlapping neuronal networks has been a matter of extensive discussion in the literature (e.g. Abutalebi et al. 2001; see also Chapter 9 in this volume), resulting in two main approaches. One view suggests that the two languages of a bilingual individual, especially if the languages have not been acquired simultaneously, may be represented and processed by distinct, or at least partially separate, neuronal networks. This assumption appeared necessary to account for differential degrees of impairment and recovery that have been reported for numerous bilinguals with stroke-induced aphasia (e.g. Paradis 2009).

In contrast, it has been hypothesized that any observed differential impairment of the two languages in bilingual individuals with aphasia is, in fact, differential degrees of activation and inhibition of the languages and that it is an impaired control mechanism, rather than a greater degree of language impairment, that results in the apparent differential impairment in the two languages (Abutalebi and Green 2008). Whereas the latter appears to be the more accepted view in the field today, it may be the case that while the underlying system for spoken language processing is shared for the two languages of a bilingual, written abilities, potentially learned more formally and processed via different cognitive processes, can have unique networks that have evolved to best match the orthography-specific demands of each language. It is possible that these differences would be found for beginning readers but not for skilled readers. It is also possible that regardless of whether the underlying networks have been assimilated and are shared for all reading processes in bilinguals, control mechanisms are needed to allow efficient and relevant processing during word reading. Similar issues are addressed in the literature of language selective versus non-selective processing in bilinguals, especially in studies of bilingual visual word recognition; a review of the extensive psycholinguistic research on this is beyond the scope of this chapter (but see Dijkstra and Van Heuven 2002; van Heuven and Coderre 2015).

Only a handful of studies of acquired reading disorders have addressed this question of differential neuronal representation directly. Most studies that report on bilingual individuals who acquire alexia have found that, even in the presence of a differential degree or nature of impairment, reading is typically impaired in both languages. None of the studies reviewed have found reading to be impaired in one language and completely intact in another. Nevertheless, several researchers have interpreted their findings as evidence for differential underlying representation of the two writing systems. Ohno et al. (2002) hypothesized that the differential degree of impairment in their participant's L1 Japanese and L2 English (described in Section 3.1) may be attributed to a differential underlying between- or within-hemispheric representation. Specifically, they proposed that the participant's learning to read English in late childhood, after middle school, may have been a factor in the dissociation they observed. The authors hypothesized that the participant's English was more right-localized than his Japanese, or that there were within-hemisphere differences in the representation of the two languages. Similarly, Ibrahim (2009) interpreted his find-ings for an Arabic-Hebrew biscriptal reader (described in Section 3.1) as support for the presence of at least partially distinct representations of L1 and L2 reading processes that result in differential vulnerability to impairment following brain damage.

Yet, several other studies with bilinguals with good reading proficiency in very different orthographies who acquired alexia provide evidence for shared neuronal rep-resentation, regardless of orthography, and a strong association between spoken and written language processing in the brain. For example, Weekes et al. (2007) found an orthographic effect on reading performance in only some of the tasks they administered and in only three of their eight Mongolian-Chinese bilingual participants. For instance, three of the participants demonstrated comparable difficulties on a variety of reading tasks in both languages; one participant had greater difficulty in Chinese in a written word comprehension test but comparable difficulty in the two languages on other reading tasks, and another showed greater difficulty in Chinese in oral reading but not in other tasks. Weekes and his colleagues argue that the patterns they observed can be explained with current models of reading and with respect to orthography-specific characteristics, and do not require the assumption of differential neuronal networks for the different orthographic systems.

Preliminary evidence from acquired reading disturbances in progressive neuro-logical diseases in bilinguals (e.g. Druks et al. 2012) are consistent with the findings of comparable reading impairments reported in aphasia, showing reading deteriora-tion in both orthographies. The participant demonstrated better reading in his L1, Hungarian, than his L2, English. The authors point to the role of language status in the degree of impairment but find no justification for assuming separate neuronal representation for the two languages. Indeed, differences in age of acquisition and/ or in levels of proficiency could potentially explain differences in reading impair-ment of the two languages of bilinguals reported in several of the studies reported above. For example, two of the three individuals reported in Beaton and Davies (2007) demonstrated better reading abilities in their more dominant language (English) than in their other language (Welsh), the patient reported in Ibrahim (2009) had greater difficulty in his L2 (Hebrew), and the three participants reported in Weekes et al. (2007) had greater reading impairment in one language experienced greater difficulty in their L2 (Chinese).

It may be concluded that, despite the prediction outlined above, in written language, as in spoken language, there is little evidence to suggest that separate neuronal mechanisms are associated with reading in different languages and across different orthographies. This conclusion is consistent with that drawn from recent neuroimaging studies with healthy biscriptal readers. Evidence from event-related potential (ERP) investigations and neuro-imaging studies with healthy skilled readers suggests that reading involves similar processes and overlapping underlying neuronal networks across languages, even those with opaque orthographies (van Heuven and Coderre 2015; Perfetti et al. 2017). Meta-analyses and reviews of neuroimaging findings from reading in different languages confirm that there is largely overlapping but also some variation in the brain networks that are associated with different writing systems (Nakada et al. 2001; Paulesu et al. 2000; Perfetti et al. 2017).

A meta-analysis by Liu and Cao (2016) showed coactivation in the left fusiform gyrus during reading in L1 and L2 in early (but not late) bilinguals, suggesting that differential activation could be related to neuronal accommodation. Furthermore, Roux et al. (2004) reported data from interoperative cortical stimulation with 19 bilingual patients, with a variety of languages, which point to comparable representation of reading in their two languages. The authors did report, however, several stimulation sites that led to interference in reading in only one language, consistent with previous findings for naming during cortical stimulation in bilinguals (e.g. Ojemann and Whitaker 1978).

Such dissociations can be related to orthography, as there is evidence for activation difference for the two routes of reading. For example, left temporal-occipital networks have been associated with sublexical reading whereas left fusiform gyrus and left frontal regions have been associated with lexical reading (Paulesu et al. 2000), as was greater activation of the temporal-occipital network in readers of transparent orthographies compared with greater activation of the temporal-frontal network in readers of opaque orthographies (e.g. Kumar 2014; Perfetti et al. 2017). Consistently, reading Chinese has been associated with greater left middle frontal gyrus than languages that use alphabetic writing systems (Perfetti et al. 2017; Tan et al. 2003) and with bilateral compared to left fusiform gyri (Bolger et al. 2005).

Thus, similar to evidence available for spoken language, data from bilingual readers point to largely shared underlying networks for reading across different orthographies but there is also evidence for differential neuronal networks involved with sublexical and lexical reading. It appears that, in part, conclusions regarding the underlying representation of two or more orthographic systems in the biscriptal brain are a matter of interpretation.

4.   Conclusion

Evidence from bilingual and biscriptal individuals who acquire alexia suggests that whereas most researchers report possible orthographic effects in the manifestation of reading impairment they found, the majority of bilinguals who experience reading impairment as a result of an acquired brain lesion demonstrate relatively comparable impairments in their two languages. Orthography-specific characteristics may affect the errors that individuals who acquire alexia produce during reading, and therefore may lead to differential diagnosis of alexia type in each language. Yet, the majority of cases reported in the literature demonstrate fewer differences than similarities in the reading impairment observed in the two languages and are thus consistent with the assumption of a shared representation of different languages and their reading systems in the brain. Furthermore, findings from acquired alexia in bilinguals can be taken as evidence that the traditional models of reading may not be adequate to account for reading processes and impairments in a variety of languages and orthographies (e.g. Beland and Mimouni 2001). Connectionism models of reading have been put forward (e.g. Plaut et al. 1996), but few studies of acquired alexia in bilinguals have set out to support or refute them.

Overall, despite the appealing possibility that variation across orthographies would lead to differential representation and/or differential processing associated with reading, current research evidence from bilinguals with acquired reading impairment and from healthy readers points to uniform underlying systems associated with the process of reading across different scripts.

Clinical implications from the above findings include the need to consider language-specific characteristics when assessing individuals who acquire alexia and to carefully analyse the errors produced in the context of the process of reading that is likely to dominate the specific language in question (e.g. greater reliance on GPC in transparent orthographies than in opaque ones). Assessment of reading may yield different results when reading is examined at the single word level versus the sentence level, during reading aloud versus reading for comprehension, and when reading frequent words versus rare words and nonwords. Furthermore, when intervention to ameliorate reading impairment is planned for bilingual (and biscriptal) individuals, the processes of reading that are impaired and thus targeted could be considered in terms of the subprocesses that are likely to be shared by the two languages in question in order to maximize cross-language generalization. As well, intervention studies could explore the role of orthographic similarities in cross-language effects. Little evidence exists to date regarding cross-language treatment generalization in bilinguals with acquired alexia, an area fertile for future research.

In addition, future studies of alexia in bilingual individuals could systematically examine errors in the respective languages to offer a subtler answer to the question of comparable vs. differential impairments. Another area that warrants further study is reading errors that illustrate cross-linguistic influences, orthographic effects, or translation errors, which have received little attention in the literature on bilingual alexia. One recent study that examined errors while reading aloud found that bilingual individuals with mild traumatic brain injury made more intrusion errors and more accent errors than healthy bilinguals (Ratiu and Azuma 2017). Future neuroimaging studies of bilingual individuals with alexia could shed light on the underlying neuronal networks that support processes of reading across orthographies. As in studies with bilingual individuals with aphasia, the dissociation between differential neuronal representation and differential activation associated with language control mechanism is challenging and will no doubt be addressed in future studies. The study of change in neuronal activity associated with improved reading skills following intervention could provide additional insight.

REFERENCES

Abutalebi, J., Cappa, S.F., and Perani, D. (2001). The bilingual brain as revealed by functional neuroimaging. *Bilingualism: Language and Cognition* 4: 179–190.

Abutalebi, J. and Green, D.W. (2008). Control mechanisms in bilingual language production: neural evidence from language switching studies. *Language and Cognitive Processes* 23 (4): 557–582.

Beaton, A.A. and Davies, N.W. (2007). Semantic errors in deep dyslexia: does orthographic depth matter? *Cognitive Neuropsychology* 24 (3): 312–323.

Beland, R. and Mimouni, Z. (2001). Deep dyslexia in the two languages of an Arabic/French bilingual patient. *Cognition* 82: 77–126.

Bolger, D.J., Perfetti, C.A., and Schneider, W. (2005). Cross-cultural effect on the brain revisited: universal structures plus writing system variation. *Human Brain Mapping* 25: 92–104.

Cao, F. (2016). Neuroimaging studies of reading in bilinguals. *Bilingualism: Language and Cognition* 19: 683–688.

Coltheart, M. (2005). Modeling reading: the dual route approach. In: *The Science of Reading: A Handbook* (ed. M.J. Snowling and C. Hulme), 6–23. Oxford, UK: Blackwell.

Coslett, H.B. (2000). Acquired dyslexia. *Seminars in Neurology* 20: 419–426.

Dehaene, S., Le Clec'H, G., Poline, J.B. et al. (2002). The visual word form area: a prelexical representation of visual words in the fusiform gyrus. *NeuroReport* 13: 321–325.

Dijkstra, A. and Van Heuven, W.J.B. (2002). The architecture of the bilingual word recognition system: from identification to decision. *Bilingualism: Language and Cognition* 5: 175–197.

Druks, J., Aydelott, J., Genethliou, M. et al. (2012). Progressive dyslexia: evidence from Hungarian and English. *Behavioural Neurology* 25: 185–191.

Geva, E. (2014). Introduction: the cross-language transfer journey – a guide to the perplexed. *Written Language and Literacy* 17 (1): 1–15.

Green, D.W. (2005). The neurocognition of recovery patterns in bilingual aphasics. In: *Handbook of Bilingualism: Psycholinguistic Approaches* (ed. J.F. Kroll and A.M.B. de Groot), 516–530. Oxford, UK: Oxford University Press.

Hashimoto, K. and Uno, A. (2016). Cognitive neuropsychological analysis of differential reading and spelling disorder mechanisms in a patient with aphasia. *Neurocase* 22 (3): 294–299.

van Heuven, W.J.B. and Coderre, E.L. (2015). Orthographic processing in bilinguals. In: *The Cambridge Handbook of Bilingual Processing* (ed. J.W. Schwieter), 308–326. Cambridge, UK: Cambridge University Press.

Ibrahim, R. (2009). Selective deficit of second language: a case study of a brain damaged Arabic-Hebrew bilingual patient. *Behavioral and Brain Functions* 5: 17.

Karanth, P. (1981). Pure alexia in a Kannada-English bilingual. *Cortex* 17: 187–198.

Karanth, P. (2002). The search for deep dyslexia in syllabic writing systems. *Journal of Neurolinguistics* 15: 143–155.

Katz, L., & Frost, R. (1992). The reading process is different for different orthographies: The orthographic depth hypothesis. Haskins Laboratories Status Report on Speech Research, SR-111/112, 147–160.

Kumar, U. (2014). Effect of orthography over neural regions in bilinguals: a view from neuroimaging. *Neuroscience Letters* 580: 94–99.

Laganaro, M. and Overton Venet, M. (2001). Acquired alexia in multilingual aphasia and computer-assisted treatment in both languages: issues of generalisation and transfer. *Folia Phoniatrica and Logopedica* 53: 135–144.

Liu, H. and Cao, F. (2016). L1 and L2 processing in the bilingual brain: a meta-analysis of neuroimaging studies. *Brain and Language* 159: 60–73.

Lyman, R.S., Kwan, S.T., and Chao, W.H. (1938). Left occipito-parietal brain tumor with observations on alexia and agraphia in Chinese and English. *Chinese Medical Journal* 54: 491–516.

Masterson, J., Coltheart, M., and Meara, P. (1985). Surface dyslexia in a language without irregularly spelled words. In: *Surface Dyslexia: Neuropsychological and Cognitive Studies of Phonological Reading* (ed. K. Patterson, J.C. Marshall and M. Coltheart), 215–223. London, UK: Lawrence Erlbaum.

Meguro, K., Constans, J.M., Shimada, M. et al. (2003). Corpus callosum atrophy, white matter lesions, and frontal executive dysfunction in normal aging and Alzheimer's disease. A community-based study: the Tajiri project. *International Psychogeriatrics* 15: 9–25.

Nakada, T., Fujii, Y., and Kwee, I.L. (2001). Brain strategies for reading in the second language are determined by the first language. *Neuroscience Research* 40: 351–358.

Obler, L.K. (1984). Dyslexia in bilinguals. In: *Dyslexia: A Global Issue* (ed. R. Malatesha and H.A. Whitaker). The Hague, The Netherlands: Martinus Nijho.

Ohno, K., Takeda, S., Kato, S., and Hirai, S. (2002). Pure alexia in a Japanese-English bilingual: dissociation between the two languages. *Journal of Neurology* 249: 105–107.

Ojemann, G. and Whitaker, H.A. (1978). The bilingual brain. *Archives of Neurology* 35: 409–412.

Paradis, M. (2009). *Declarative and Procedural Determinants of Second Languages*. Amsterdam, The Netherlands: John Benjamins.

Paulesu, E., McCrory, E., Fazio, F. et al. (2000). A cultural effect on brain function. *Nature Neuroscience* 3: 91–96.

Perfetti, C.A., Liu, Y., Fiez, J. et al. (2017). Reading in two writing systems: accommodation and assimilation of the brain's reading network. *Bilingualism: Language and Cognition* 10 (2): 131–146.

Plaut, D. (1999). A connectionist approach to word reading and acquired dyslexia: extension to sequential processing. *Cognitive Science* 23: 543–568.

Plaut, D., McClelland, J.L., Seidenberg, M.S., and Patterson, K. (1996). Understanding normal and impaired word reading: computational principles in quasi-regular domains. *Psychological Review* 103: 56–115.

Price, C.J. and Mechelli, A. (2005). Reading and reading disturbance. *Current Opinion in Neurobiology* 15: 231–238.

Raman, I. and Weekes, B.S. (2005). Acquired dyslexia in a Turkish–English speaker. *Annals of Dyslexia* 55: 71–96.

Ratiu, I. and Azuma, T. (2017). Language control in bilingual adults with and without history of mild traumatic brain injury. *Brain and Language* 166: 29–39.

Ratnavalli, E., Murthy, G.G., Nagaraja, D. et al. (2000). Alexia in Indian bilinguals. *Journal of Neurolinguistics* 13 (1): 37–46.

Roux, F.E., Lubrano, V., Lauwers-Cances, V. et al. (2004). Intra-operative mapping of cortical areas involved in reading in mono- and bilingual patients. *Brain* 127: 1796–1810.

Senaha, M.L.H. and Parente, M.A.M.P. (2012). Acquired dyslexia in three writing systems: study of a Portuguese-Japanese bilingual aphasic patient. *Behavioural Neurology* 25: 255–272.

Tan, L.H., Spinks, J.A., Feng, C.M. et al. (2003). Neural systems of second language reading are shaped by native language. *Human Brain Mapping* 18: 158–166.

Weekes, B.S. (2005). Acquired disorders of reading and writing: cross-script comparisons. *Behavioural Neurology* 16: 51–57.

Weekes, B.S., Su, I.F., Yin, W.G., and Zhang, X.H. (2007). Oral reading in bilingual aphasia: evidence from Mongolian and Chinese. *Bilingualism: Language and Memory* 10: 201–210.

30   Dementia and Multilingualism

MARIANA VEGA-MENDOZA, SUVARNA ALLADI, AND THOMAS H. BAK

1.   Introduction

The aim of this chapter is to provide an overview of studies examining the relationship between dementia and multilingualism. First, we will discuss the influence of dementia on multilingualism, i.e. the way in which different languages of a multilingual can be affected differentially by a dementing illness. We then move to the opposite, currently hotly debated question, whether multilingualism can influence dementia, in particular its age of onset and progression. We examine the evidence on whether bilingualism can delay the onset of dementia and, if yes, whether such an effect could depend on the type of bilingualism as well as the type of dementia. We discuss different studies arguing in favour as well as against this 'bilingualism effect' and possible factors, which could explain diverging results. Throughout this chapter we will use the terms 'bilingualism' and 'multilingualism' almost interchangeably. Strictly speaking, bilingualism is a special case of multilingualism, in which the individuals in question speak exactly two languages (as opposed to three, four, or more). However, many authors use the term 'bilingualism', as opposed to 'monolingualism', to refer to someone who speaks 'two or more' languages, and if this is the case, we will be following the original terms used in the sources we present.

2.   The Influence of Dementia on Multilingualism

Until a decade ago, the study of bilingualism and dementia had focused mainly on the question of how different languages spoken by a bi/multilingual individual are influenced by dementing illnesses. Much of this research has been influenced by older and more extensive literature on bilingual aphasia (see Paradis 1977, for an authoritative review). In most cases of bilingual aphasia, both languages of an aphasic are impaired (parallel impairment). In contrast, in case of a differential impairment

The Handbook of the Neuroscience of Multilingualism, First Edition. Edited by John W. Schwieter.
© 2019 John Wiley & Sons Ltd. Published 2019 by John Wiley & Sons Ltd.

(or a parallel initial impairment with a subsequent differential recovery) one language is more affected than other. The most often described pattern of differential impairment/recovery is Ribot's law: the first, native language of a patient is better preserved than those subsequently learned (Pearce 2005; Ribot 1882). However, other patterns have also been described, such as the best preservation of the language that the patient used most often prior to the onset of aphasia (Pitre's law; Pearce 2005).

Based on the analogy with aphasia, we could expect a frequent parallel impairment of all languages in dementia patients, with occasional cases of a differential impairment, corresponding to Ribot's and Pitre's law. But has this expectation been confirmed in the literature? One of the earliest systematic studies was that of Hyltenstam and Stroud (1993) who assessed the linguistic patterns of six female patients diagnosed with Alzheimer's disease (AD). The patients were Finnish native speakers who had acquired Swedish as a second language (L2) in late adulthood. The authors focused on the assessment of patterns of language choice when the L2 was required. Amongst the patients, two used their L2 appropriately (i.e. when required as target), three patients predominantly used their firstly acquired language (L1), even in situations in which L2 would have been appropriate, and one patient mixed the two languages. Because the authors found no conclusive pattern of association between severity of dementia and difficulties in language choice, they proposed that the observed pattern might reflect different patterns of premorbid L2 attainment. In this vein, in his review of 'bilingualism and neuropsychiatric disorders' (including psychoses and dementia), Paradis (2008) suggests that the aspects of language that are prone to deteriorate in early stages of dementia are those that depend on declarative memory such as semantic difficulties (e.g. observed for example in word generation tasks such as category/semantic fluency). Paradis points out that in contrast, aspects such as morphosyntax and phonology are not impaired until later stages of the disease (see Melvold et al. 1994) and, importantly, difficulties in appropriate language selection seem to decline more as the disease progresses to more advanced stages (see also De Santi et al. 1990).

Besides the age of acquisition, language proficiency has also been examined as a factor influencing language loss in bilingual AD. Gollan et al. (2010) assessed whether patients with AD would regress to using their most dominant language rather than the non-dominant language (i.e. the dominant language being that with more proficiency attained, whilst non-dominant language being that with less proficiency). Two groups of Spanish-English bilinguals, one with probable AD the other one a matched control group named pictures in both their dominant and non-dominant language. One of the main findings was that when using the dominant language, the control group outperformed the patients. However, this difference was smaller when using their non-dominant language. It was thus suggested that the dominant language is more prone to be affected in AD.

While much of the variation in the pattern of language loss in bilingual dementia patients might be due to individual differences in language acquisition, proficiency, and use, different types of dementia could also play a role. Like aphasia, dementia is very heterogeneous, with different aetiologies, pathologies, and clinical presentations. So the relationship between dementia and loss of language could differ from one type of dementia to the other. For example, in AD, remote memories tend to be more intact than recent ones, while in semantic dementia (SD) recent memories are better preserved (Hodges and Graham 1998). If similar differences apply to the relative loss and preservation of languages, we could expect that the first learned language will be better preserved in AD. In contrast, SD patients would show a better preservation of the language they used most frequently before the onset of the disease.

Such assumptions will need to be tested systematically in future studies. If confirmed, differential patterns of memory loss could have important practical implications for healthcare: with AD being the most common form of dementia – constituting between 60 and 70% of cases worldwide, according to the World Health Organization (2017) – the loss of later-acquired languages would have particularly damaging effects in immigrant communities. In many countries immigrants are encouraged to speak only the language of their new country at home and hence not to pass their original language to further generations (Bak and Mehmedbegovic 2017; Mehmedbegovic and Bak 2017). This might result in younger members of the families not being able to communicate with their parents, grandparents, and further relatives when they develop dementia.[1] Secondly, if dementia patients need to be admitted to a nursing home, it is unlikely that they will find staff able to communicate with them in their best-preserved language. This lack of verbal communication with family as well as with professional carers could deepen the social isolation associated with dementia. Thus, long-term planning for dementia care needs to take into account all languages spoken by future patients and potential shifts in language dominance which can be associated with dementia.

3.   Turning the Tables: Does Bilingualism Influence Dementia?

The seminal paper by Bialystok et al. (2007) opened an entirely new avenue in the research on dementia and bilingualism. The question asked by Bialystok et al. was not whether dementia influences bilingualism but whether bilingualism can influence the manifestation of dementia. They studied patients with dementia drawn from a memory clinic in Toronto. Bilingualism was classified as such by a group of 11 expert raters under the criteria that the patients must have spent most of their lives using at least two languages on a regular basis. Roughly half of the patients (51%) were classed as bilingual, the remaining group as monolinguals. The authors compared age of onset of symptoms of dementia as reported by the patients and the patient's family member or carer, age at first appointment, as well as performance on cognitive tasks measured by the Mini-mental State Examination (MMSE) administered at first appointment. Amongst the main findings, Bialystok and colleagues reported that bilingual patients showed onset of symptoms of dementia 4.1 years later than monolinguals and were diagnosed on average 3.2 years later than monolingual patients. An analysis including only patients with possible Alzheimer disease (as opposed to other types of dementia), showed an even greater delay in *onset of dementia symptoms*: 4.3 years later for AD bilinguals compared with their monolingual counterparts, and 3.5 years for other types of dementia.

However, as noted by the authors, the two groups differed not only in respect to bilingualism but also to other variables. The monolingual group had a higher level of education than the bilingual group, whereas the bilingual group was composed of more immigrants than the monolingual one. The authors attempted to address this issue by conducting an additional analysis of the immigrant sample within each group, although the monolingual immigrant group was quite small (monolingual immigrant group $n = 13/91$, compared to the bilingual immigrant group $n = 81/93$). These findings were followed up by another study from the same team but focusing only on patients with diagnosis of AD (Craik et al. 2010). The results were similar to those of Bialystok et al. (2007): bilinguals developed symptoms of dementia on average 5.1 years later than monolinguals, and were diagnosed 4.3 years later, despite the monolingual group having higher levels of education than the bilinguals. The authors reported that controlling for immigration status in their analysis showed the same pattern of results.

In a further study by the same research group, Bialystok et al. (2014) evaluated the relationship between bilingualism and age of onset of mild cognitive impairment (MCI) and AD. Their aims were threefold. The first aim was to improve the matching of monolingual and bilingual groups. The second was to employ a detailed executive functioning profile for the groups (thought to be the underlying component associated with the bilingual experience) controlling for variables such as diet, alcohol consumption, and physical activity, amongst others. The third was to carry out a longitudinal assessment composed of three evaluations at intervals of approximately six months to assess progression of decline in both conditions across the groups. Participants in the study were 149 patients from the Sam and Ida Ross Memory Clinic in Baycrest in Toronto. All participants were proficient in English fluently, but bilinguals spoke additionally a variety of languages (with bilingual and multilingual participants grouped together). Thirty-eight monolingual and 36 bilingual patients were diagnosed with MCI, and 35 monolingual and 40 bilingual with probable AD (of this latter group, 35 participants had been part of the Craik et al. 2010 study). Most monolingual (73%), but only less than half of the bilingual patients (31%) were born in Canada. Overall, immigrant patients had less formal education than non-immigrants. Bilingual patients reported later onset of symptoms than monolinguals in both the MCI (4.7 years later) and the AD (7.3 years later) groups, and likewise a later age of first appointment at the clinic (3.5 years for the MCI group, 7.2 years for the AD group). Patients with AD were older than MCI patients at both age of first symptoms and age of visit to the memory clinic. There was also an overall effect of language group, with bilinguals being older than monolinguals in both onset of symptoms and age of first appointment. Results of the executive functioning evaluations did not show differences between bilinguals and multilinguals in the initial evaluation (except a reported bilingual advantage on the Stroop effect and slower bilingual completion times in the number-letter switching task in the MCI group) nor in slope rate of cognitive decline on these functions indicating similar rate of cognitive decline over time post-diagnosis irrespective of bilingualism even though bilinguals had been diagnosed at a later age than monolinguals. The authors argued that later onset of dementia does not necessarily lead to a faster cognitive decline.

Chertkow et al. (2010) also used patients' records (in this case from a memory clinic in Montreal), but focused on the age of diagnosis – information on age of symptom onset was also obtained but only from a subsample of patients – and tried to reduce the influence of immigration status. The authors found a delay in diagnosis of dementia only for those who spoke more than two languages and the same pattern of results was observed in the subsample of participants whose age of symptom onset was obtained. In an attempt to reduce the potential confounds of immigration, they also compared the three languages groups in individuals who were classified as non-immigrant only (further divided into English native and French native speakers), and compared the three language groups in immigrant individuals (immigrant status was operational- ized as those individuals whose first language was neither English nor French, thus languages non-native to Canada). For the immigrant group, the protective effect was observed for those who spoke two or more languages (in line with Bialystok et al. 2007), whilst for their non-immigrant sample, a trend towards protective effect was observed in individuals whose first language was French, but not in those whose first language was English. Chertkow et al. pointed out the importance of considering factors such as genetics and environmental influences to explain differences between the groups.

The potential impact of external factors, in particular education, was investigated in more detail in a study by Gollan et al. (2011). In this study, the authors studied the age of diagnosis of probable AD in a group of Hispanic, Spanish-English bilinguals in California, and its relationship to degree of bilingualism, measured as a continuum. They focused on age of diagnosis and found that a higher degree of bilingualism was associated with a later age of diagnosis (they also mentioned that this result was the same for age of onset of symptoms of dementia), but importantly this effect was modulated by years of education, such that the effect was observed in low- but not high-education individuals.

The study by Alladi et al. (2013) compared the onset of dementia in monolingual and bilingual patients in a completely different social, cultural, and linguistic environment, in the city of Hyderabad in India. The majority of the population of Hyderabad has been bilingual for hundreds of years; accordingly, bilingualism in Hyderabad is not associ- ated with immigration, allowing the authors to examine an entirely non-immigrant sample. Moreover, since many bilinguals in India learn languages informally rather than in school, it was possible to compare monolingual and bilingual illiterates. In addition, the study examined four distinct subtypes of dementia: AD, frontotemporal dementia (FTD), vascular dementia (VaD), dementia with Lewy bodies (DLB), and mixed dementia (MD). The authors studied medical records in a large sample of 648 patients diagnosed with dementia from the memory clinic in Hyderabad: 391 bilinguals, 257 monolinguals. The age of onset of symptoms of dementia was 4.5 years later in bilinguals than in monolinguals, very similar to the two previous Toronto studies. The strongest effect was observed in FTD (6 years), followed by VaD (3.7 years), and AD (3.2 years). For the remaining two subtypes of dementia, although the difference was also in favour of bilinguals, it did not reach statistical significance: DLB (2.3 years) and MD (1.4 years; these two groups were, however, also the smallest). Interestingly, the bilingual delay in onset of symptoms of dementia in illiterate individuals was 6 years, even larger than that observed in the full sample. However, the authors did not find a difference depending on the number of languages spoken, i.e. knowing three or more languages did not seem to be an advantage over knowing two.

Given that the strongest effect of bilingualism in this study was found in FTD patients, a further paper by Alladi et al. (2017) explored a cohort of 193 FTD patients (121 bilingual, 72 monolingual) in more detail, specifically comparing the behavioural and language variant FTD (the behavioural variant is characterized above all by changes in personality, behaviour, social cognition, and executive functions, the language/aphasic variant, further divided into semantic dementia and non-fluent progressive aphasia, by prominent changes in language functions; see the current diagnostic criteria in Gorno-Tempini et al. 2011; Rascovsky et al. 2011). For bilinguals, the age of onset of predominantly behavioural FTD was 62.6 years old, for monolinguals 56.5, a significant difference of 6.1 years. In contrast, in the predominantly aphasic FTD, age of onset for monolinguals and bilinguals was 60.9 versus 60.6 years, almost identical. Taken together, the two bilingualism and dementia studies from Hyderabad suggest that the effect of bilingualism on the onset of dementia might be specifically related to the behavioural symptoms, in line with theories stressing that bilingualism has a particularly strong impact on executive functions (e.g. Bialystok et al. 2012). In contrast, progressive aphasic syndromes do not seem to be influenced by bilingualism. Similar observations were reported also for post-stroke cognitive syndromes: whereas vascular dementia and vascular MCI are significantly more common in monolinguals than bilinguals after stroke, there is no difference in the frequency of aphasia (Alladi et al. 2016), although the severity of post-stroke aphasia is more pronounced in monolinguals (Paplikar et al. 2018).

In a Belgian study using a similar design examining the age of onset of dementia, Woumans et al. (2015) assessed 69 monolingual and 65 bilingual patients with probable AD and retrospectively compared both the age of onset of symptoms *and* age of diagnosis on each group. The participants were a homogenous non-immigrant sample, matched for gender, education, occupation, and scores on MMSE at the age of diagnosis. Most bilinguals were speakers of Dutch and French and reported not to use language mixing. The delay in the manifestation of symptoms of AD was 4.6 years for bilinguals (4.1 years when controlling for the effect of age of acquisition of the second language by adding this variable into the regression model). A similar pattern was observed for the age of diagnosis, with bilingualism delaying the age of diagnosis by 4.8 years (4.6 years when age of acquisition of the second language was added to the model). There was no effect of the controlling variables, namely occupation, gender, education, MMSE, or L1. These results thus replicated earlier positive findings in a non-immigrant sample and in an L1 environment. As pointed out by the authors, this distinction might be relevant, since an L2 environment, requiring frequent use of the later-acquired and/or non-dominant language, may pose higher cognitive demands and thus inflate potential positive effects of language use on cognitive reserve.

Freedman et al. (2014) attempted to explain the contrasting findings of previous studies analysing in detail the methodology applied to measure contextual factors and language history. Whilst Bialystok et al.'s (2007) and Alladi et al.'s (2013) studies relied on age of the first manifestation of symptoms, Chertkow et al.'s (2010) focused on age of diagnosis. Freedman et al. also point out that differences in operationalization of immigration status might have played a role in the discrepancies (for a discussion of immigration in bilingualism research see also Bak and Alladi 2015; Bak 2016a).

4.   Possible Mechanisms

4.1.   *Ageing Studies*

Studies assessing the effects of bilingualism on dementia have largely based their hypotheses on healthy ageing studies suggesting a better cognitive performance in bilingual elderly populations. Bialystok et al. (2004) explored whether bilingualism would positively impact cognition in middle-aged and older adults, in a similar fashion to their previous observations in children. The authors used a stimulus-congruency executive control task (Simon task) that has been shown to capture declined processing speed associated with age (Van der Lubbe and Verleger 2002). Bialystok and colleagues reported that bilinguals' reaction times were faster than those of monolinguals and they also exhibited a reduced Simon effect, a finding that was consistent across the two age groups. These results led the authors to conclude that bilingualism offsets the age-related decline associated to these executive control processes.

Another study examining the relationship between multilingualism and ageing was conducted by Kavé et al. in 2008. The authors studied, in a longitudinal design consisting of three assessments, a sample of 814 older adults in Israel, who were 83 years old on average and according to self-reports bilingual, trilingual, and multilingual (in this generation, it would not have been possible to include a monolingual Israeli group). The cognitive assessment consisted of the Katzman et al. (1983) cognitive screening test (administered at the three evaluation points) and the Mini-Mental State Examination (administered on the second wave only). The number of languages predicted cognitive performance: older multilinguals who spoke four or more languages exhibited better cognitive performance than bilinguals and trilinguals. In addition, better cognitive performance was reported in people who were more fluent in a language other than their native tongue.

A further study providing support for a positive impact of bilingualism on cognitive decline was that of Perquin et al. (2013). Participants in Luxembourg were recruited from the general population as part of a cohort study on memory and dementia (MemoVie). A total of 232 volunteers, aged 65 years or over, who did not have dementia were recruited and assessed on cognitive and health tests and questionnaires including background variables such as socioeconomic status and language background abilities. The authors operationalized degree of multilingualism on the basis of ability to speak different languages fluently throughout their lives, also taking into account language practice patterns and age of acquisition. Furthermore, participants were classed as either presenting 'cognitive impairment no dementia (CIND)' or 'free of cognitive impairment (CIND-free)'. Since, as in the Israeli study, no monolinguals were included, the comparison group in this study was thus the bilingual group. Out of the 232 participants, 44 were diagnosed with CIND and the remaining 188 as CIND-free. Furthermore, individuals who actively practiced multilingualism were less likely to exhibit CIND, thus supporting the hypothesis that active multilingualism slows down the rate of cognitive decline in older age.

A Scottish study by Bak et al. (2014) introduced a novel approach by comparing baseline cognitive measures from childhood with cognitive performance by monolinguals and bilinguals in later life. It was based on a large sample of 853 participants, all English-native speakers, non-immigrants, who had been cognitively assessed as part of the Lothian Birth Cohort, a Scottish study which measured intelligence at age of 11 years in the year 1947. The cohort was followed up with a subsequent cognitive testing between 2008 and 2010. Because the study provided information on baseline cognitive measures of intelligence and it is well established that childhood intelligence is an important predictor of cognitive performance in later life, it was possible to evaluate cognitive performance associated with bilingualism (versus monolingualism) whilst accounting for baseline intelligence. Those participants who reported knowledge of more than one language (bilinguals) performed better than could have been predicted by their baseline intelligence from childhood. Importantly, further analysis showed that this effect was not dependent on whether the individuals were performing at a low (5th percentile), medium (50th percentile), or high (95th percentile) level when 11 years old: all three groups have benefited cognitively from the acquisition of another language.

4.2. *The Notion of Cognitive Reserve (CR)*

One of the most influential concepts in the explanation of bilingualism effects in older age is the notion of cognitive reserve (CR), defined as the 'cognitive processes or neural networks underlying task performance [which] allow some people to cope better than others with brain damage' (Stern 2009, p. 2016).[2] CR is thus believed to make the brain more resilient and adaptable in the presence of brain insults or disease, leading to better cognitive outcomes.

A range of factors has been proposed as potential contributors to cognitive reserve, such as education and occupation (Stern et al. 1994), physical activity (Colcombe and Kramer 2003), or musical experience (Hanna-Pladdy and MacKay 2011). The notion of CR applied in dementia research was studied by Valenzuela and Sachdev (2006) in a meta-analysis of longitudinal dementia studies. From the 22 final sample of studies assessed, the authors reported that factors contributing most to brain reserve were: education, such that individuals with higher education had 47% decreased risk of dementia, followed by occupation (44% decreased risk of dementia for high occupational status) and premorbid IQ (approximately 42% decreased risk of dementia).

4.3. *Comparison with Other Pathologies: Stroke*

As we have already seen in Section 3, the study by Alladi et al. (2013) from Hyderabad reported VaD as one of the four diagnostic categories of dementia. A detailed examination of the effects of bilingualism on stroke outcome has been subsequently presented in Alladi et al. (2016). Records of 608 stroke patients from the Hyderabad stroke registry were analysed and classified into VaD, vascular mild cognitive impairment (VaMCI), aphasia and history of stroke with normal cognition. There was no difference in the age of stroke, suggesting, that bilingualism was not associated with general health benefits (e.g. healthier diet or lifestyle, better access to medical services leading to identification and treatment of potential risk factors, etc.). However, twice as many bilinguals (143/353) as monolinguals (50/255) had normal cognition post-stroke. Conversely, a higher proportion of the monolingual group (175/255) showed post-stroke cognitive impairment including VaD and VaMCI compared with bilinguals (173/353). No differences were found in the proportion of aphasia outcome post-stroke between monolinguals (30/255) and bilinguals (37/353).

Based on the observation that bilinguals and monolinguals are equally likely to develop aphasia post-stroke (Alladi et al. 2016), Paplikar et al. (2018) explored further whether bilingualism might have an influence on its severity, in a study of 65 patients (38 bilingual, 27 monolingual) from Hyderabad with post-stroke aphasia. The severity of aphasia as assessed by the language subscale of the Addenbrooke's Cognitive Examination-Revised (ACE-R) was higher in monolinguals compared with bilinguals, suggesting that whilst bilingualism does not provide a protective effect against post-stroke aphasia per se, the severity of the condition is likely to be less pronounced in bilinguals than in monolinguals.

4.4. Neuroimaging

Another strand of investigation trying to explain differences in dementia onset between monolinguals and bilinguals is the exploration of a potential neural basis of these phenomena through neuroimaging techniques. Schweizer et al. (2012), part of the research group conducting seminal studies of the relationship between bilingualism and dementia (e.g. Bialystok et al. 2007), obtained computed tomography (CT) scans of 40 patients (with an equal number of monolinguals and bilinguals) with probable AD from a memory disorders clinic in Toronto to measure brain atrophy in brain areas commonly associated with AD. The groups did not differ in gender, age at CT scan, age at diagnosis, performance on cognitive tests, or functional status. The only difference between the two groups was that monolinguals had higher occupational status. There were no differences in levels of atrophy in frontal brain regions associated with AD (bicaudate ratio, Huckman's number, Evans ratio, and suprasellar cistern ratio). However, bilinguals showed greater brain atrophy than monolinguals in temporal areas associated to AD pathology: temporal horn ratio, third ventricle ratio, and radial width of the temporal horn. So the bilingual group, in spite of having more atrophy than monolinguals in brain regions linked to AD pathology, exhibited similar cognitive performance, thus suggesting that bilingualism could aid in building cognitive reserve and possibly better compensatory mechanisms against the disease.

Perani et al. (2017) provided further brain metabolic evidence in support of CR in bilingualism in AD in 40 monolingual and 45 bilingual patients with probable AD with a matched disease duration. Although the bilingual group had lower education than monolinguals and showed cerebral hypometabolism in additional brain structures compared with monolinguals, bilingual AD patients showed increased connectivity in areas related to executive control compared with the monolingual AD patients. At the behavioural level, bilingual patients with AD outperformed their monolingual counterparts on cognitive test measuring memory but no difference was found on language tasks between the groups. In addition, the bilingual patients in this study were on average five years older than their monolingual counterparts, suggesting a protective effect of bilingualism.

4.5. *Neurobiology*

A very recent line of research to address the impact of bilingualism on cognitive function in both healthy ageing and in dementia focuses on the use of biomarkers to explain the possible mechanisms underlying the idea of bilingualism as an aid to build cognitive reserve. Estanga et al. (2017) measured cognitive performance on a comprehensive neuropsychological test battery as well as the levels of AD biomarkers (t-tau, p-tau protein, amyloid-beta $A\beta_{1-42}$) in the cerebrospinal fluid (CSF) in healthy elderly monolinguals and early and late bilinguals. Compared with monolinguals, early bilinguals obtained better scores on the backward digit span (from the Wechsler Adult Intelligence Scale (WAIS)-III, an IQ test), and Judgement of Line Orientation (JLO), a standardised test of visuospatial skills. Late bilinguals scored better than monolinguals on Trail-Making Test B (a test of executive function and, more specifically, of task switching performance) and JLO. Results of the AD biomarkers in CSF (also adjusting for relevant variables such as age) showed that early bilingualism was associated with lower t-tau levels than monolingualism, thus showing not only behavioural evidence of a protective effect of bilingualism against AD, but also neurobiological evidence. Bak and Robertson (2017) offer a possible explanation for these findings hypothesizing through a sustained activation of noradrenergic pathways associated with the cognitive challenges of language learning and active bilingualism.

5. Papers Questioning Bilingualism Effects

The evidence suggesting a delaying effect of bilingualism on the onset of dementia has recently been questioned by a series of studies showing no significant differences in dementia onset between the groups.[3] Zahodne et al. (2014) studied a cohort of 1067 Spanish-English, Hispanic participants in New York who were part of a longitudinal prospective community ageing study (Washington/Hamilton Heights Inwood Columbia Ageing Project; WHICAP); all of them were immigrants. Bilingualism was measured through self-reports and assessed language proficiency through scores on a reading test (in English only), yielding a total of 430 bilinguals and 637 monolinguals. The bilingual group had significantly higher levels of education. The age of the initial assessment was significantly different by approximately a year with 75.66 years old on average for the monolingual group (range: 64–95) and 74.78 for the bilingual group (range: 64–94). The longitudinal assessment of cognitive functions included memory, language, executive function, and speed processing. The results of cognitive tests showed that bilinguals performed better than monolinguals at the initial assessment, in particular on memory and executive functions. However, within the group of 282 individuals who developed dementia, bilingualism did not reduce significantly the likelihood of developing it.

Lawton et al. (2015) compared the age of diagnosis of AD and VaD in monolingual and bilingual groups of Hispanic Americans, either immigrants or born in the US. Monolingualism and bilingualism were determined based on whether the participants reported speaking either English or Spanish (answering *'not at all'* or *'not very often'* to either question was classed as monolingual, whilst *'very often'* or *'almost always'* was classed as bilingual). In this prospective study, patients were drawn from a longitudinal community ageing study amongst Sacramento-dwelling individuals (Sacramento Area Latino Study on Ageing; SALSA). Out of the sample of 1789, secondary analyses of 81 patients who developed dementia were performed. Of these cases, 55 were AD and 26 VaD, without significant differences in proportions of cases of each type of dementia between monolinguals and bilinguals and the authors reported that this (null) effect was not modulated by immigration status. Amongst the background measures, bilinguals had significantly higher education than monolinguals, an effect moderated by immigration status. The authors reported no differences in age of diagnosis between monolinguals (mean age onset of diagnosis = 81.10 years old) and bilinguals (mean age onset of diagnosis = 79.31). Similarly, mean age of onset of dementia diagnosis did not differ overall between the US-born (79.0) and the immigrants (81.41). The authors therefore pointed out that the results of their prospective study in this population did not support those of previous retrospective studies (cf. Alladi et al. 2013; Bialystok et al. 2007; Craik et al. 2010) but are in line with three other community-sample studies that did not find a beneficial effect of bilingualism in delaying dementia (e.g. Zahodne et al. 2014, described above; Crane et al. 2009; Sanders et al. 2012).

Another prospective study failing to find a protective effect of bilingualism against dementia was that of Crane et al. (2009), who studied second-generation Japanese-American males in Hawaii who were part of the longitudinal Honolulu Asia Ageing Study. Participants ($n = 3139$) were divided according to self-reports of their knowledge (or lack thereof) of Japanese as follows: did not speak or read Japanese ($n = 561$), spoke but did not read Japanese ($n = 1847$), both spoke and read Japanese ($n = 731$). One of the main findings of this study was that the magnitude of the reduced risk for developing AD in the group that both spoke and read Japanese was comparable to the value obtained for the group that neither spoke nor read Japanese. This led the authors to conclude that there was no protective effect against dementia for those acquiring a second language.

Sanders et al. (2012) investigated whether speaking English as a non-native language would reduce incidence of dementia, taking into account also the impact of education, and similarly found no evidence of protective effects of bilingualism against dementia. Participants were part of a longitudinal community-based study on ageing and dementia, the Einstein Ageing Study in Bronx, New York, aged 70 years or more. The 1779 participants were divided into native English speakers ($n = 1389$) and non-native English Speakers ($n = 390$); 126 were diagnosed with dementia, out of whom 101 with probable AD. The authors used nested Cox proportional hazard regression models to analyse the association of non-native English speaking and incidence of dementia and AD. They report a non-significant association between being a non-native English speaking and incidence of dementia (for all dementia cases as well as for the AD analysis). They also pointed out a non-significant trend whereby non-native English speakers compared with native English speakers had a small increase in risk of dementia incidence, in contrast to previous positive findings. However, further analyses suggest that their results could have been modulated by education. The authors divided the participants by education level into three categories (low: 0–11 years; intermediate: 12–15 years, and high: equal to or over 16 years) and calculated the absolute dementia incidence in each education group, separately in native English and non-native English speakers. Results showed a decrease in absolute incidence rates with increasing education in native English speakers alone. In contrast, in the non-native English-speaking group, the absolute incidence rates were high for low and high education and lower in the intermediate group. Compared with native-English speakers, non-native English speakers from the low and intermediate education levels had a non-significant trend towards a smaller absolute incidence rates. In contrast, in the high education group, the incidence rate in non-native English speakers was higher than those of native English speakers. However, bilingualism here was operationalized only on the basis of being a non-native English speaker, and as pointed out by Zahodne et al. (2014), potential bilingualism was not assessed in native English speakers in Sanders et al. (2012).

The study of Yeung et al. (2014) explored the relationship between bilingualism and dementia in Manitoba, Canada. The cohort of participants in this study was part of a community-based prospective longitudinal study on ageing and cognition (Manitoba Study of Health and Ageing MSHA), 65 years old or older. There were two time-point evaluations and two types of analyses: a cross-sectional one including all participants of first assessment ($n = 1616$) and a prospective analysis including those individuals who completed the subsequent evaluation ($n = 990$). The participants were split into three groups: English monolinguals ($n = 913$), English bilinguals ($n = 81$), and bilinguals with English as a second language ($n = 622$). Amongst the background measures, the English as a second language group had a lower educational level than English monolinguals and English bilinguals, and significantly lower scores on English writing and reading fluency. Based on cognitive evaluation, participants were classed as either being cognitively intact, having cognitive impairment without dementia, or being diagnosed with dementia (without distinguishing subtypes of dementia).

Results of the cross-sectional analysis (first assessment) did not show an association between dementia and language group (percentage of dementia diagnosis reported by group: English monolingual 3.1%, English bilingual 0%, English as a second language 4.7%). The English as a second language group was more likely to exhibit cognitive impairment without dementia. The prospective analyses were reported in line with the cross-sectional ones: bilingualism was not associated with being diagnosed with dementia at the second evaluation in those individuals who had no cognitive impairment in the first evaluation (percentage of dementia diagnosis reported by group: English monolingual 9.4%, English bilingual 11.1%, English as a second language 9.7%). However, a serious limitation in this study, as noted by the authors themselves, was that since the cognitive tests were administered in English, this could have led to the observed cognitive impairment without dementia observed in the latter group (which is precisely the group with lower fluency in English).

5.1. Prospective vs. Retrospective Studies

Mukadam et al. (2017) attempted a systematic review and meta-analysis of the studies of the relationship between bi/multilingualism and dementia. The authors identified a total of 1174 articles of which 1156 were screened. From these, a final 13 were included for evaluation. Out of the 13 studies included, 5 were identified as prospective and 8 as retrospective. The authors discarded the retrospective studies and performed a meta-analysis confined to prospective studies, revealing an odds ratio of 0.96 of bilinguals developing dementia over monolinguals. Based on these results, they concluded that there is no bilingual advantage in protection against the effects of dementia.

Unfortunately, rather than analysing the specific strengths and weaknesses of individual studies, the authors simply assumed that prospective studies trump the retrospective ones. Accordingly, they paid no attention to the substantial limitations of the prospective studies they evaluated. For example, in practically all prospective studies, the bilingual group was largely composed of immigrants living in the country of assessment (mostly US, in one study Canada). In addition, due to the nature of prospective longitudinal studies, the number of individuals developing dementia is reduced compared to those of retrospective studies. Moreover, as pointed out by Woumans et al. (2017), in some prospective studies, such as Zahodne et al. (2014) and Lawton et al. (2015), the monolingual group could in fact have included bilinguals given the operationalization of bilingualism (i.e. Spanish L1 speakers without knowledge of English but living in the L2 environment in Zahodne et al. 2014). Another important point raised by Woumans and colleagues is the fact that the review carried out did not include all relevant papers: Wilson et al. (2015) and Bak et al. (2014), two studies favouring protective effect of bilingualism on MCI/cognitive decline were left out of the meta-analysis. Similar points are raised by Grundy and Anderson (2017). The authors point out conceptual and methodological flaws of the Mukadam et al. study, e.g. putting together heterogeneous studies and overlooking that retrospective studies usually examine *age of onset* of dementia as opposed to *incidence rate* of dementia in prospective studies. Furthermore, Bak and Alladi (2015) and Alladi et al. (2017) draw attention to a difference in the age of the cohorts included in different studies, with many prospective studies limited to older participants (e.g. aged over 65 years). Given that the biggest reported bilingualism effects have been described in frontotemporal dementia (Alladi et al. 2017), which can manifest well below the age of 65 years, this approach is likely to underestimate any potential effects of bilingualism. Finally, Bak (2016a) highlights the importance of taking into account environmental differences when comparing different sets of studies (for an extensive discussion on environmental confounding factors see also Bak 2016b).

6.   Relationship Between Bi/Multilingualism and Dementia: Complex and Multifactorial

As we have seen, there is a wide range of evidence for, as well as against, the hypothesis that bi/multilingualism leads to cognitive reserve and therefore might delay the curve of cognitive decline, delaying the onset of dementia. The relationship between bilingualism and dementia is a complex one and is affected by a number of factors that we have discussed throughout this chapter.

Arguably, the two confounding variables discussed most frequently in the research on bilingualism and cognition are immigration and education, and both have been mentioned throughout this chapter (for a more detailed discussion see Bak 2016a). Of the two, immigration is much easier to control. It is a major factor in countries in which bilingualism tends to be associated with recent immigration (US, Canada), but does not play a major role in places with a long tradition of bilingualism in situ (e.g. India, Belgium).

Education is more complex and one could argue that it exists in different forms in every human society. Even in illiterate populations, knowledge is being passed through from generation to generation, although it is much more difficult to quantify than the years of formal education used as a variable in most studies. In addition, different variables can be associated with education in different societies. In the UK and USA, low education is often associated with social deprivation (criminality, unemployment, drug and alcohol abuse, unhealthy diet and lifestyle, homelessness, etc.). However, this is not the case across the whole world; in India, for instance, one can find illiterate people functioning relatively well within the society, employed and living in stable families. Interestingly, it is exactly in the illiterate population that Alladi et al. (2013) found the largest effect of bilingualism on the onset of dementia. This issue has been further explored by Ramakrishnan et al. (2017), who assessed rates of cognitive decline in a sample of 115 MCI patients evaluated in Hyderabad. Comparisons between monolingual and bilingual participants, adjusting for high and low levels of education as potential confounding variables, showed that bilingual MCI patients had a delay in onset of MCI cognitive complains of 7.4 years later than monolinguals, with years of education not being associated with a significant delay onset. Interestingly, not all prospective studies conducted in the US found an effect of education (Bak and Alladi 2015). Given the complex interaction between education and bilingualism, we would suggest that rather than classifying education as a confounding variable in bilingualism studies, we should treat both as 'interacting variables'. Both are important and future research might be more productive if we examine their interaction rather than try to separate them.

Another important consideration for further studies is to focus on the potential influence of different types of dementia. As pointed out by Alladi et al. (2013), different subtypes of dementia may lead to different symptoms. Executive dysfunction can be encountered in most types of dementia, but to a different degree, and this difference might be crucial for the potential 'bilingualism effects' – the stronger the executive component, the more pronounced the influence of bilingualism (Alladi et al. 2017).

Finally, if bilingualism exerts a positive effect on dementia, language learning and practice could be used as prophylaxis and/or treatment of dementia, as suggested by Antoniou et al. (2013) and Bak (2016c). Effects of different forms of cognitive training on cognitive reserve have already been documented (e.g. Kivipelto et al. 2013; Valenzuela and Sachdev 2006); further research is necessary to determine whether similar effects can be found in language-based interventions.

NOTES

1   For an illustrative example, see https://www.pri.org/stories/2015-10-09/my-grandmothers-disease-has-stolen-her-memories-and-our-common-language
2   For a discussion on the notions of brain reserve and cognitive reserve, see Stern (2009, 2013).

3   Please note that in this chapter we review studies focusing on the relationship between bi/
multilingualism and dementia. For a recent meta-analysis challenging positive effects of
bilingualism in non-clinical populations please see for example Lehtonen et al. (2018).

REFERENCES

Alladi, S., Bak, T.H., Duggirala, V. et al. (2013). Bilingualism delays age at onset of dementia, independent of education and immigration status. *Neurology* 81 (22): 1938–1944.

Alladi, S., Bak, T.H., Mekala, S. et al. (2016). Impact of bilingualism on cognitive outcome after stroke. *Stroke* 47 (1): 258–261.

Alladi, S., Bak, T.H., Shailaja, M. et al. (2017). Bilingualism delays the onset of behavioral but not aphasic forms of frontotemporal dementia. *Neuropsychologia* 99: 207–212.

Antoniou, M., Gunasekera, G.M., and Wong, P.C. (2013). Foreign language training as cognitive therapy for age-related cognitive decline: a hypothesis for future research. *Neuroscience and Biobehavioral Reviews* 37 (10): 2689–2698.

Bak, T.H. (2016a). The impact of bilingualism on cognitive ageing and dementia: finding a path through a forest of confounding variables. *Linguistic Approaches to Bilingualism* 6 (1): 205–226.

Bak, T.H. (2016b). Cooking pasta in La Paz. *Linguistic Approaches to Bilingualism* 6 (5): 699–717.

Bak, T. (2016c). Language lessons to help protect against dementia. *BMJ* 354: i5039.

Bak, T.H. and Alladi, S. (2015). Bilingualism, dementia and the tale of many variables: why we need to move beyond the western world. Commentary on Lawton et al. (2015) and fuller-Thomson (2015). *Cortex* 74: 315–317.

Bak, T.H. and Mehmedbegovic, D. (2017). Healthy linguistic diet: the value of linguistic diversity and language learning. *Journal of Languages, Society and Policy* doi:10.17863/CAM.9854.

Bak, T.H., Nissan, J.J., Allerhand, M.M., and Deary, I.J. (2014). Does bilingualism influence cognitive aging? *Annals of Neurology* 75 (6): 959–963.

Bak, T.H. and Robertson, I. (2017). Biology enters the scene – a new perspective on bilingualism, cognition, and dementia. *Neurobiology of Aging* 50: iii–iv.

Bialystok, E., Craik, F.I.M., Binns, M.A. et al. (2014). Effects of bilingualism on the age of onset and progression of MCI and AD: evidence from executive function tests. *Neuropsychology* 28 (2): 290–304.

Bialystok, E., Craik, F.I.M., and Freedman, M. (2007). Bilingualism as a protection against the onset of symptoms of dementia. *Neuropsychologia* 45 (2): 459–464.

Bialystok, E., Craik, F.I., Klein, R., and Viswanathan, M. (2004). Bilingualism, aging, and cognitive control: evidence from the Simon task. *Psychology and Aging* 19 (2): 290.

Bialystok, E., Craik, F.I., and Luk, G. (2012). Bilingualism: consequences for mind and brain. *Trends in Cognitive Sciences* 16 (4): 240–250.

Chertkow, H., Whitehead, V., Phillips, N. et al. (2010). Multilingualism (but not always bilingualism) delays the onset of Alzheimer disease: evidence from a bilingual community. *Alzheimer Disease & Associated Disorders* 24 (2): 118–125.

Colcombe, S. and Kramer, A.F. (2003). Fitness effects on the cognitive function of older adults: a meta-analytic study. *Psychological Science* 14 (2): 125–130.

Craik, F.I., Bialystok, E., and Freedman, M. (2010). Delaying the onset of Alzheimer disease bilingualism as a form of cognitive reserve. *Neurology* 75 (19): 1726–1729.

Crane, P.K., Gibbons, L.E., Arani, K. et al. (2009). Midlife use of written Japanese and protection from late life dementia. *Epidemiology (Cambridge, Mass.)* 20 (5): 766.

De Santi, S., Obler, L., Sabo-Abramson, H. et al. (1990). *Discourse Ability and Brain Damage: Theoretical and Empirical Perspectives*. New York, NY: Springer.

Estanga, A., Ecay-Torres, M., Ibañez, A. et al. (2017). Beneficial effect of bilingualism on Alzheimer's disease CSF biomarkers and cognition. *Neurobiology of Aging* 50: 144–151.

Freedman, M., Alladi, S., Chertkow, H. et al. (2014). Delaying onset of dementia: are two languages enough? *Behavioural Neurology* 2014: 808137.

Gollan, T.H., Salmon, D.P., Montoya, R.I., and da Pena, E. (2010). Accessibility of the nondominant language in picture naming: a counterintuitive effect of dementia on bilingual language production. *Neuropsychologia* 48 (5): 1356–1366.

Gollan, T.H., Salmon, D.P., Montoya, R.I., and Galasko, D.R. (2011). Degree of bilingualism predicts age of diagnosis of Alzheimer's disease in low-education but not in highly educated Hispanics. *Neuropsychologia* 49 (14): 3826–3830.

Gorno-Tempini, M.L., Hillis, A.E., Weintraub, S. et al. (2011). Classification of primary progressive aphasia and its variants. *Neurology* 76 (11): 1006–1014.

Grundy, J.G. and Anderson, J.A. (2017). Commentary: the relationship of bilingualism compared to monolingualism to the risk of cognitive decline or dementia: a systematic review and meta-analysis. *Frontiers in Aging Neuroscience* 9: 344.

Hanna-Pladdy, B. and MacKay, A. (2011). The relation between instrumental musical activity and cognitive aging. *Neuropsychology* 25 (3): 378.

Hodges, J.R. and Graham, K.S. (1998). A reversal of the temporal gradient for famous person knowledge in semantic dementia: implications for the neural organisation of long-term memory. *Neuropsychologia* 36 (8): 803–825.

Hyltenstam, K. and Stroud, C. (1993). Second language regression in Alzheimer's dementia. In: *Progression and Regression in Language* (ed. K. Hyltenstam and A. Viberg), 222–242. Cambridge: Cambridge University Press.

Katzman, R., Brown, T., Fuld, P. et al. (1983). Validation of a short orientation-memory-concentration test of cognitive impairment. *American Journal of Psychiatry* 140: 734–739.

Kavé, G., Eyal, N., Shorek, A., and Cohen-Mansfield, J. (2008). Multilingualism and cognitive state in the oldest old. *Psychology and Aging* 23 (1): 70.

Kivipelto, M., Solomon, A., Ahtiluoto, S. et al. (2013). The Finnish geriatric intervention study to prevent cognitive impairment and disability (FINGER): study design and progress. *Alzheimer's & Dementia: The Journal of the Alzheimer's Association* 9 (6): 657–665.

Lawton, D.M., Gasquoine, P.G., and Weimer, A.A. (2015). Age of dementia diagnosis in community dwelling bilingual and monolingual Hispanic Americans. *Cortex* 66: 141–145.

Lehtonen, M., Soveri, A., Laine, A. et al. (2018). Is bilingualism associated with enhanced executive functioning in adults? A meta-analytic review. *Psychological Bulletin* 144 (4): 394–425.

Mehmedbegovic, D. and Bak, T.H. (2017). Towards an interdisciplinary lifetime approach to multilingualism: from implicit assumptions to current evidence. *European Journal of Language Policy* 9 (2): 149–167.

Melvold, J.L., Au, R., Obler, L.K., and Albert, M.L. (1994). Language during aging and dementia. *Clinical neurology of aging* 2: 329–246.

Mukadam, N., Sommerlad, A., and Livingston, G. (2017). The relationship of bilingualism compared to monolingualism to the risk of cognitive decline or dementia: a systematic review and meta-analysis. *Journal of Alzheimer's Disease* 58 (1): 45–54.

Paplikar, A., Mekala, S., Bak, T.H. et al. (2018). Bilingualism and the severity of poststroke aphasia. *Aphasiology* 1–15. doi:10.1080/02687038.2017.1423272.

Paradis, M. (1977). Bilingualism and aphasia. In: *Studies in Neurolinguistics*, vol. 3 (ed. H. Whitaker and H.A. Whitaker), 65–121. New York, NY: Academic Press.

Paradis, M. (2008). Bilingualism and neuropsychiatric disorders. *Journal of Neurolinguistics* 21 (3): 199–230.

Pearce, J.M. (2005). A note on aphasia in bilingual patients: Pitres' and Ribot's laws. *European Neurology* 54 (3): 127–131.

Perani, D., Farsad, M., Ballarini, T. et al. (2017). The impact of bilingualism on brain reserve and metabolic connectivity in Alzheimer's dementia. *Proceedings of the National Academy of Sciences* 114 (7): 1690–1695.

Perquin, M., Vaillant, M., Schuller, A.M. et al. (2013). Lifelong exposure to multilingualism: new evidence to support cognitive reserve hypothesis. *PLoS One* 8 (4): e62030.

Ramakrishnan, S., Mekala, S., Mamidipudi, A. et al. (2017). Comparative effects of education and bilingualism on the onset of mild cognitive impairment. *Dementia and Geriatric Cognitive Disorders* 44 (3–4): 222–231.

Rascovsky, K., Hodges, J.R., Knopman, D. et al. (2011). Sensitivity of revised diagnostic criteria for the behavioural variant of frontotemporal dementia. *Brain* 134 (9): 2456–2477.

Ribot, T. (1882). *Diseases of Memory: An Essay in the Positive Psychology*, vol. 43. New York, NY: Appleton.

Sanders, A.E., Hall, C.B., Katz, M.J., and Lipton, R.B. (2012). Non-native language use and risk of incident dementia in the elderly. *Journal of Alzheimer's Disease* 29 (1): 99–108.

Schweizer, T.A., Ware, J., Fischer, C.E. et al. (2012). Bilingualism as a contributor to cognitive reserve: evidence from brain atrophy in Alzheimer's disease. *Cortex* 48 (8): 991–996.

Stern, Y. (2009). Cognitive reserve. *Neuropsychologia* 47 (10): 2015–2028.

Stern, Y. (2013). Cognitive reserve: implications for assessment and intervention. *Folia Phoniatrica et Logopaedica* 65 (2): 49–54.

Stern, Y., Gurland, B., Tatemichi, T.K. et al. (1994). Influence of education and occupation on the incidence of Alzheimer's disease. *JAMA* 271 (13): 1004–1010.

Valenzuela, M.J. and Sachdev, P. (2006). Brain reserve and dementia: a systematic review. *Psychological Medicine* 36 (4): 441–454.

Van der Lubbe, R.H. and Verleger, R. (2002). Aging and the Simon task. *Psychophysiology* 39 (1): 100–110.

Wilson, R.S., Boyle, P.A., Yang, J. et al. (2015). Early life instruction in foreign language and music and incidence of mild cognitive impairment. *Neuropsychology* 29 (2): 292.

World Health Organization. (2017, December 12). Dementia. Retrieved from http://www.who.int/news-room/fact-sheets/detail/dementia

Woumans, E., Santens, P., Sieben, A. et al. (2015). Bilingualism delays clinical manifestation of Alzheimer's disease. *Bilingualism: Language and Cognition* 18 (3): 568–574.

Woumans, E., Versijpt, J., Sieben, A. et al. (2017). Bilingualism and cognitive decline: a story of pride and prejudice. *Journal of Alzheimer's Disease* doi:10.3233/JAD-170759.

Yeung, C.M., St. John, P.D., Menec, V., and Tyas, S.L. (2014). Is bilingualism associated with a lower risk of dementia in community-living older adults? Cross-sectional and prospective analyses. *Alzheimer Disease & Associated Disorders* 28 (4): 326–332.

Zahodne, L.B., Schofield, P.W., Farrell, M.T. et al. (2014). Bilingualism does not alter cognitive decline or dementia risk among Spanish-speaking immigrants. *Neuropsychology* 28 (2): 238–246.

31 Schizophrenia and Bilingualism

DARIA SMIRNOVA, SVETA FICHMAN, AND JOEL WALTERS

1. Introduction

Schizophrenia (SZ) is a complex mental disorder characterized by a variety of clinical phenotypes and extensive genetic heterogeneity, whose aetiology and biological underpinnings are still poorly understood despite more than a century of research (Jablensky 2006). The median lifetime prevalence of SZ is 0.4% and the lifetime morbidity risk is 0.7% in the general population (McGrath et al. 2008). Even though prevalence is stable across decades and does not significantly differ across gender or urban/rural residence, it differs for geographical sites and shows higher rates amongst migrants (migrant-to-native-born ratio median is 1.8), mostly due to interethnic differences and/or diagnostic inaccuracy related to the language of assessment and cross-cultural issues (McGrath et al. 2008). SZ patients display a variety of symptoms with different prognoses and outcomes which may change radically during the course of disorder. Thirty-nine percent of patients suffer from continuous disabling illness with significant functional deterioration and 62% develop partial remission or full recovery (Jablensky et al. 2000; Morgan et al. 2014). Despite the relatively high remission rate, a majority of SZ patients (76%) are unemployed and have serious difficulties in daily living, interpersonal relationships and social functioning, in particular due to persistent language and communication disturbances (Jablensky et al. 2000; Morgan et al. 2014). Language dysfunction thus represents a key feature in SZ, observed not only in patients diagnosed with SZ, but also in people at high risk for developing psychosis (Bedi et al. 2015). Language impairment is sometimes observed in clinically unaffected relatives as well (Levy et al. 2010), which suggests that it aggregates in families and may have a hereditary basis.

The diagnosis of SZ is based on a list of clinical criteria (DSM-5 2013; ICD-10 1993). The illness is considered to be more cognitive than affective, although both cognitive and emotional symptoms are present (Kahn and Keefe 2013). Unlike most clinical conditions, there are no pathognomonic biological markers to diagnose SZ, and different biological underpinnings may lead to similar psychotic manifestations (Clementz et al. 2016).

The Handbook of the Neuroscience of Multilingualism, First Edition. Edited by John W. Schwieter.
© 2019 John Wiley & Sons Ltd. Published 2019 by John Wiley & Sons Ltd.

The core positive symptoms (i.e. symptoms which are added to premorbid functioning or emerge as a result of illness) of SZ include auditory verbal hallucinations, formal thought disorder, and delusions (Hinzen and Rosselló 2015). Even though hallucinations and delusions are foremost amongst the diagnostic criteria in both the American Psychiatric Association (DSM-5 2013) and the World Health Organization (ICD-10 1993) diagnostic systems, two of the five diagnostic criteria in the DSM-5 (2013) and four of eight in the ICD-10 (1993) depend on language. Thus, social and communication behaviour, which is also language-dependent, is relevant in the diagnosis. As a result, cognitive and linguistic criteria overlap, which hampers diagnostic evaluation and treatment. In this vein, according to the DSM-5 (2013) and ICD-10 (1993), thought disorder, derailment, and incoherence are dysfunctions in both cognition and language. Brown and Kuperberg (2015) noted that 'language dysfunction is one of the core cognitive sequelae of schizophrenia, with verbal abilities often compromised relative to other cognitive domains' (p. 2). Performance on linguistic tasks serves as a marker of cognitive impairment, since it is used both as an assessment tool and a medium for therapeutic intervention.

SZ has been studied from a complex of neurobiological, cognitive, and linguistic perspectives. Bilingualism has also been approached from the same perspectives although, by definition, it is a linguistic phenomenon. Linguistic impairments in SZ cover the range of domains from phonology (e.g. clanging, echolalia) to pragmatics (e.g. tangentiality, misunderstanding of figurative language) and discourse (e.g. topic shifting, derailment) and across all domains of psychotic symptoms (positive, negative [i.e. features which are reduced or subtracted from premorbid functioning as a result of illness] and cognitive; Kuperberg and Caplan 2003). Healthy bilinguals can also experience a variety of linguistic challenges. Research has addressed bilinguals' difficulties related to lexical retrieval and performance on semantic tasks (Bialystok 2009; Sandoval et al. 2010). Studies on cross-language interference and code switching aim to offer insight into bilinguals' cognitive processes, in this way using linguistic tasks to gain insight into cognitive mechanisms (e.g. Hohenstein et al. 2006).

The remainder of the chapter is organized as follows: We first review studies on neurobiological underpinnings of SZ and bilingualism (BL) in order to provide a neurological basis for the comparison. In an attempt to isolate language phenomena which characterize individuals with SZ on the one hand and bilingual individuals on the other, we then provide a detailed description of linguistic characteristics of SZ and BL. Next, we examine the limited data suggesting potential effects of bilingualism on SZ. Since certain cognitive-based features are directly related to language (e.g. executive functions) in SZ and BL, we then offer an approach which attempts to integrate linguistic and cognitive aspects of 'bilingual schizophrenia'.

2.   Neurobiological Features Underlying SZ and BL

SZ is characterized by deviations in structure, volume, connectivity, activity, and lateralization across particular brain areas (e.g. frontal cortex, anterior cingulate cortex, inferior parietal lobules). These neurobiological and pathophysiological brain features correlate with positive, negative, and cognitive symptoms in SZ patients (e.g. auditory verbal hallucinations, formal thought disorder, reduced verbal fluency; see Table 1).

Table 1 Neurobiological and pathophysiological features associated with schizophrenia as a morbid process and located in brain areas typically involved in bilingual processing.

Frontal cortex areas

SZ grey matter volume loss in frontal lobes
- observed in SZ patients and those in transition to psychosis (Pantelis et al. 2007)
- in conjunction with progressive lateral ventricle volume increase; correlates with severity of negative symptoms in SZ (Hulshoff Pol and Kahn 2008)
- grey matter volume loss in frontal lobes is associated with poor cognitive functioning (attention and working memory deficits) in SZ (Antonova et al. 2004)

Dorsolateral prefrontal cortex (DLPFC)

SZ dysfunction
- deficient activity and associated cognitive control deficit observed from early disease stages and in medication-naive SZ patients (van Veelen et al. 2010)
- dysfunctional recruitment observed during proactive control tasks and associated with disorganization symptoms in SZ (Lesh et al. 2013)

BL recruitment
- involved in response selection for interfering contexts in BL; implicated in cognitive control (Collette et al. 2005)

Left prefrontal cortex (LPC)

SZ white matter disconnectivity
- intra- and inter-regional functional disconnectivity in SZ (Fornito et al. 2012)
- attributed to neurodevelopmental deficits in neuronal migration and synaptic plasticity associated with a decrease in reeling gene expression in SZ (Habl et al. 2012)

BL recruitment
- observed not only during language-switching tasks but also during word production and verbal fluency performance in bilinguals (Abutalebi and Green 2007)
- mostly engaged when using the weaker language (Parker Jones et al. 2012)
- responsible for response selection (Aron et al. 2014) and suppression, but not conflict monitoring (Green and Abutalebi 2013)

Right prefrontal cortex (RPC)

SZ blood perfusion deficit
- reduction in cerebral blood flow and perfusion in SZ (Walther et al. 2011)

BL recruitment
- related to response inhibition and activation (in particular, the right middle frontal gyrus) during processing of the dominant language (Videsott et al. 2010).

Left inferior frontal gyrus (LIFG)

SZ white matter disconnectivity
- disrupted white matter connectivity correlates with category fluency deficits in first-episode SZ (Ou et al. 2016)

(Continued)

Table 1   (Continued)

BL recruitment
- part of the language control network; monitors interference of irrelevant information from the dominant language (Abutalebi and Green 2016)
- involved in language-switching mechanisms (Branzi et al. 2016)

SZ reduced functional lateralization in Brodmann's areas 44–45
- reduced functional lateralization in language related frontal cortex in SZ (Li et al. 2007)

Inferior Parietal Lobules (IPL)
SZ grey matter volume loss in IPL
- bilateral grey volume loss correlates with clinical symptoms of violence and verbal working memory dysfunction (Puri et al. 2010) and with duration of SZ (Palaniyappan and Liddle 2012)
- right IPL cortical thinning in untreated SZ patients with Schneiderian first rank symptoms (Venkatasubramanian et al. 2011)

SZ volume changes in IPL
- correlates with severity of key psychotic symptoms (delusions, hallucinations) related to disruption in sensory integration, disturbances of body image and self-concept as well as with semantic and executive function deficits (Torrey 2007, for a review; Liu et al. 2016)

BL grey matter density increase in left IPL
- correlates with increased L2 vocabulary and proficiency (Abutalebi et al. 2015; Mechelli et al. 2004)

Supramarginal gyrus
SZ dysfunction
- hyperactivation in SZ during decision-making tasks, indicating dysregulated interaction between prefrontal and parietal cortex (Paulus et al. 2002)

SZ supramarginal and angular gyri decreased blood flow
- associated with psychomotor retardation syndrome (e.g. slow speech and decreased affect; Liddle et al. 1992)

SZ subregions dysfunctional connectivity
- abnormal connectivity between IPL subregions and visual and sensorimotor areas, increased connectivity with lingual, inferior occipital, mid-cingulate gyri (Liu et al. 2016).

BL intraparietal sulcus recruitment
- engaged in attention tasks in verbal and visual short-term memory processing in bilinguals (Majerus et al. 2010)

Temporal lobes connections with frontal and parietal areas
SZ grey matter volume loss in the left medium temporal gyrus (LMTG)
- observed in drug-naive, first-episode SZ patients and their unaffected relatives (Hu et al. 2013)

Table 1 (Continued)

SZ temporal areas dysfunctional connectivity

- reduced connectivity between LMTG and LIFG associated with auditory verbal hallucinations in SZ and between LMTG and left IPL in SZ (Zhang et al. 2017)
- decline in functional connectivity in the superior temporal gyrus (STG) and parietal areas associated with lower performance in speech recognition in speech-to-speech masking conditions (Li et al. 2017).

SZ right STG volume loss as a marker of reduced brain lateralization

- correlates with severity of language-related positive symptoms of thought disorder and hallucinations in SZ (Matsumoto et al. 2001)

Anterior Cingulate Cortex (ACC)

SZ decreased synaptic plasticity

- decreased synaptic density (both excitatory and inhibitory axospinous synapses) and the density of mitochondria (all axon terminals) correlate with deviant executive functioning in SZ (Roberts et al. 2015)

SZ dysfunction

- hypofunction (Harrison et al. 2007; Reid et al. 2010) observed during cognitive tasks in SZ (Blasi et al. 2010; Mathalon et al. 2002)
- hyperactivation in response to negative images in violent SZ male patients and associated with control of negative emotions and violent behaviour in SZ (Tikàsz et al. 2016)
- associated with deficits in attentional orienting, error monitoring, conflict monitoring, response inhibition (Barch et al. 2001; Braver et al. 2001) and disruption of error detection processing in SZ (Alain et al. 2002)

BL grey matter density increase

- observed in the dorsal ACC; presents in adult bilinguals compared to age-matched monolinguals (Abutalebi et al. 2012)

BL increased functional activity

- associated with bilingual performance (Abutalebi et al. 2012)
- dorsal ACC activity associated with language switching into the less-exposed language and language selection tasks; involvement when initiating speech in switching from one language to another (Abutalebi et al. 2007, 2012; Branzi et al. 2016; Luk et al. 2012).

Subcortical structures (basal ganglia, thalamus)

Basal ganglia

SZ volume increase

- associated with heightened dopaminergic tone in the striatum, thalamic hyperstimulation in SZ (Ellison-Wright and Bullmore 2009) and genetic vulnerability in SZ (Oertel-Knöchel et al. 2012)
- increased volumes in left and right caudate nuclei, putamen, and right globus pallidus correlated with changes in shape and positively with attention; but nucleus accumbens volume negatively correlated with positive symptoms (delusions; Mamah et al. 2007)

(Continued)

Table 1   (Continued)

SZ dysfunction
- associated with the goal-directed action and motor control impairments in SZ (Menon et al. 2001; Walther et al. 2011)

BL recruitment
- associated with motor, emotional and cognitive (inhibitory) control in bilinguals (Abutalebi et al. 2007, 2015)

BL Left caudate nucleus recruitment
- involved in translation (Lehtonen et al. 2005), language selection (Branzi et al. 2016) and language switching (Stocco et al. 2014) in production and comprehension in bilinguals (Abutalebi et al. 2007, 2015)

BL Left putamen recruitment
- associated with the control of articulatory processes in bilingual speaking (Abutalebi et al. 2013).

Thalamus
SZ blood perfusion deficit
- associated with SZ (Walther et al. 2011)

BL recruitment
- activated in lexical and semantic representations and in language production in bilinguals through connection with frontal regions, i.e. LIFG (Ford et al. 2013)

SZ Subcortical areas dysfunctional connectivity
- structural alterations in the pulvinar in the thalamus and N-Methyl-D-Aspartate hypofunction affect input signals in the higher order nuclei of thalamus; dysregulation of the cortico-thalamo-cortical connection in the frontal and parietal lobes and disturbance in sensorimotor integration (Dorph-Petersen and Lewis 2017; Vukadinovic 2014)

Cerebellum
SZ dysfunction
- altered functional topography in response to emotion and working memory tasks observed within cerebello-thalamo-cortical dysfunction in SZ (Bernard and Mittal 2015)
- disturbed prefronto-thalamo-cerebellar circuit in SZ mediates deficits in attention, working memory, verbal learning, and sensory discrimination (Yeganeh-Doost et al. 2011)

BL grey matter volume increase
- correlates with proficiency in L2 morphosyntax (Pliatsikas et al. 2014); but morphosyntactic features reported intact when cerebellum not activated in bilinguals (Mariën et al. 2014)

Most of these same brain regions are involved in bilingual processing and are engaged in language control mechanisms (e.g. language switching) in healthy bilingual adults. In the course of maturation and increasing second language proficiency, specific neurobiological changes have been reported, such as increased grey matter volume, increased neuronal connectivity, and increased brain activation. Table 1 summarizes studies of neurobiological underpinnings reported for SZ and BL in an attempt to specify which areas are common to the two populations.

A recent meta-analysis by Luk et al. (2012) showed eight main brain areas involved in bilingual cognitive control. Those areas, particularly for cognitive in language-switching mechanisms and for bilingual functioning in general, have been found to be impaired in SZ and associated with a variety of SZ clinical symptoms (Table 1), demonstrating common biological underpinnings of SZ as a morbid process (brain and language disorder) and BL as a natural brain and language phenomenon.

In an attempt to understand the interface of BL and SZ, we have focused on those brain areas reported to show (i) a decrease in functioning (e.g. worse connectivity, grey volume loss) for SZ and (ii) more active involvement or an increase in functioning (e.g. better connectivity, grey volume increase) for parallel areas in healthy bilinguals.

Since very few biological and linguistic studies have analysed data from bilinguals with SZ, it is premature to address beneficial versus harmful influences of BL on SZ or vice versa. Such analysis is crucial for an accurate clinical picture, diagnosis, and treatment of bilinguals with SZ. In lieu of appropriately designed biological studies of bilinguals with SZ, based on data from linguistic studies of bilinguals with SZ and theoretical assumptions from biological research on BL or SZ, we describe in Section 3 a pretheoretical approach to analyse interrelationships between SZ as a mental and language disorder and BL as a linguistic phenomenon influencing the brain.

3. Language Characteristics of SZ, BL and Their Interface

3.1. *Schizophrenia*

Language deviations figure amongst the most prominent impairments in patients with schizophrenia (Covington et al. 2005; Kim et al. 2015). However, not all patients show the same language abnormalities (Kuperberg 2010), and symptoms may vary in the course of the illness. In terms of particular language symptoms, some SZ patients show severe, profound and even constant disruption in language use, while others demonstrate fluctuating deviations with relatively preserved language functioning for different linguistic domains, especially during formal communication (Matulis 1977; Walder et al. 2006). Language impairment has been documented for SZ in structure, function, and content at micro- and macro-levels of linguistic organization (Brown and Kuperberg 2015; DeLisi 2001).

Clinically, linguistic impairments are assessed as reflecting formal thought disorder, which refers to form/organization rather than content of thought. It is often found in association with delusions (Goldberg and Weinberger 2000) and has been assessed via speech acts. For example, tangentiality of speech, a frequent symptom of SZ, is considered a thought disorder; it presents as impaired speech and communication.

Historically, the validity of equating speech disorder and thought disorder has been questioned (Bleuler 1911; Chaika 1974; Faber and Reichstein 1981; Kleist 1960; Kraepelin 1906, 1920; McKenna and Oh 2005). It has been argued that deviant patterns of psychotic speech reflect difficulties in ordering basic linguistic elements into meaningful language structures, and as such, should be analysed from a linguistic perspective. Formal thought disorder has also been discussed in terms of executive dysfunction and semantic deficits (Barrera et al. 2005). The present chapter does not resolve the conflation of thought and language in the SZ literature; it takes a more modest approach focusing on language and language-related executive functions in attempt to contribute to the relationship between language and cognition in SZ and BL.

Various classifications of language impairments in SZ have been proposed (Andreasen 1979, 1986; Chaika 1974; Chen et al. 1996; DeLisi 2001). Andreasen (1979, 1986) was amongst the first, characterizing 21 phenomena related to thought, language, and communication disorders. Liddle et al. (2002), whose classification targets mainly thought disorder, distinguished amongst impoverished thought and language, disorganized thought and language, and non-specific dysregulation of thought. Marini et al. (2008) compared linguistic features at the micro-level – within-sentence linguistic performance (phonology, lexis, syntax) – and at the macro-level – between-sentence language use (pragmatics and discourse); they concluded that, while microlinguistic processing was mildly impaired, macrolinguistic processing was significantly weaker in patients with SZ.

Table 2 lists most of the language, thought, and cognitive impairments found in the SZ literature, classified by linguistic domain. Cognitive domain/function is included at the bottom of the table. Many of the features here can be classified as belonging in more than one linguistic category, e.g. tangentiality, classified here as pragmatic, also has a discourse dimension and may also impinge on semantic aspects of referentiality. The classification has attempted to be loyal to its original meaning in the source cited.

The proposed classification and supporting research suggest that the domains of linguistic ability most vulnerable in SZ are semantics, pragmatics, and discourse, which tap mainly into macro-level organization and cognitive processes. Insight into how these macro-level skills are affected in SZ might serve as a bridge between speech/language and thought disorder in SZ. From amongst more than 50 linguistic characteristics of SZ reviewed in Table 2, more than half relate to semantics, pragmatics, and discourse domains and impinge on global-level cognitive processes in language use. Moreover, most of these symptoms have been observed during communicative or functional aspects of language use. Amongst impaired functional aspects of language are: semantic errors (Rodriguez-Ferrera et al. 2001), impaired semantic fluency (Fusar-Poli et al. 2012), disproportionate semantic deficit within action verbs but not mental state verbs (Smirnova et al. 2017), abnormal semantic activation (hyper- and hypo-priming; Pomarol-Clotet et al. 2008), excessive semantic activation during the initial stages of word processing (Kreher et al. 2009), difficulty identifying semantic violations (Kuperberg et al. 2006), and poverty of content (Andreasen 1979).

Disturbances of fluency are present in a wide range of linguistic symptoms, including perseveration, logorrhea, and echolalia at one end of a continuum and speech pressure, blocking, word finding, and lexical access problems at the other end. These markers of SZ are not always signs of impairment and may be compensatory resources in bilinguals with SZ, as has been shown for discourse markers and code switching (Smirnova et al. 2015). One view holds that lexical information is preserved

Table 2   Summary of language and cognitive impairments in schizophrenia literature.

Category	Disorder Impairment	Sources
Sound-based	Flattened intonation (aprosody)	Andreasen (1986), Cutting (1985)
	Phonetic paraphasias	Andreasen (1986)
	Echolalia	Andreasen (1986), Chaika (1974)
	Clanging	Andreasen (1979, 1986), Badcock et al. (2011), Kleist (1960), Kraepelin (1906, 1920), McKenna (1994), McKenna and Oh (2005)
	Inappropriate phonology	Chaika (1974)
Lexis	Blocking	Andreasen (1986), Andreasen and Grove (1986), Bersudsky et al. (2005), Miller et al. (1993), Smirnova et al. (2015), Sumiyoshi et al. (2005)
	Word finding/selection difficulties; impaired lexical access and retrieval	Allen et al. (1993), Marvel et al. (2004), McKay et al. (1996)
	Word approximations; paraphasias (metonyms)	Andreasen (1986), McKenna (1994), Silverberg-Shalev et al. (1981)
	Neologisms	Andreasen (1986), McKenna (1994)
	Lexical repetition/ perseveration, verbigerations	Andreasen (1986), Chaika (1974), Crider (1997), Lee (2004), Smirnova et al. (2015)
	Verbal fluency deficit	Allen et al. (1993), Marvel et al. (2004)
	Action verbs deficit	Badcock et al. (2011), Kambanaros et al. (2010), Marvel et al. (2004), Smirnova et al. (2017)
Semantics	Unclear reference	Bersudsky et al. (2005), Chaika (1974), Marini et al. (2008), Smirnova et al. (2015)
	Semantic paraphasias	Andreasen (1986), Marini et al. (2008), Oh et al. (2002)
	Lemma-level deficits	Kambanaros et al. (2010), Marini et al. (2008)
	Alogia, poverty of content, laconic speech	Andreasen (1986), Joyce et al. (1996), Miller et al. (1993)
	Semantic fluency deficit	DeLisi (2001), Marvel et al. (2004), Vogel et al. (2009)
Syntax	Incomplete, confused, odd syntax	Bersudsky et al. (2005), Chaika (1974), Kraepelin (1896, 1906), Marini et al. (2008), Morice and Mcnicol (1986), Smirnova et al. (2015)
	Reduced syntactic complexity	Radanovic et al. (2013), Thomas et al. (1990)
	Agrammatism	Semkovska (2010)

(Continued)

Table 2   (Continued)

Category	Disorder Impairment	Sources
Discourse	Topic shifting	Andreasen (1986), Harrow et al. (1983)
	Derailment/loose associations	Andreasen (1986)
	Incoherence, disorganized discourse	Allen et al. (1993), Andreasen (1986), Andreasen and Grove (1986), Chaika (1974), Docherty (2005)
	Circumstantiality	Andreasen (1979)
	Illogicality	Andreasen (1986), Andreasen and Grove (1986)
	Loss/weakening of goal	Andreasen (1979, 1986)
	Ordering/sequencing deficits	Docherty et al. (2000), Docherty et al. (2006)
	Word salad; unintelligible speech	Andreasen (1986), Chaika (1974)
	Logorrhea, perseveration	Andreasen (1986), Chaika (1974), Crider (1997), Lee (2004, Smirnova et al. (2015)
	Speech pressure	Andreasen (1986), Andreasen and Grove (1986), Chen et al. (1996)
Pragmatics	Literal meaning; failure to understand figurative language (idioms, metaphors, irony)	Cutting and Murphy (1990), Hoffman et al. (1985), Kuperberg (2010), Marini et al. (2008), Rodriguez-Ferrera et al. (2001)
	Concretism/lack of abstraction	Spitzer (1993)
	Exophoric-reference; overuse of self-reference	Bersudsky et al. (2005), Smirnova et al. (2015)
	Distractible speech	Andreasen (1979, 1986), Docherty et al. (2006), Langdon et al. (2002), Liddle et al. (2002)
	Tangentiality	Andreasen (1986), Docherty (2005), Smirnova et al. (2015)
	Manneristic/stilted speech	Andreasen (1986), Andreasen and Grove (1986)
	Planning	Docherty et al. (2006), Crider (1997)
	Abnormal use of context	Crider (1997), Vogel et al. (2009)
Cognitive domain	Impaired executive functions	Frommann et al. (2010), Fusar-Poli et al. (2012), Hardy-Baylé et al. (2003), Heinrichs and Zakzanis (1998), Kuperberg and Caplan (2003), Langdon et al. (2002), Pousa et al. (2008), Reichenberg and Harvey (2007)
	Attentional failure/selective attention	Caprile et al. (2015), Fusar-Poli et al. (2012), Hardy-Baylé et al. (2003), Kenny et al. (1997), Langdon et al. (2002), Pousa et al. (2008)

Table 2 (Continued)

Category	Disorder Impairment	Sources
	Working memory	Frommann et al. (2010), Fusar-Poli et al. (2012), Kenny et al. (1997), Kuperberg and Caplan (2003), Silver et al. (2003)
	Semantic memory access	Heinrichs and Zakzanis (1998), Henry and Crawford (2004), McKay et al. (1996), Kuperberg and Caplan (2003)
	Inhibitory control	Reichenberg and Harvey (2007), Wang et al. (2015)

in SZ, but the organization of the lexicon and access to words are impaired (Goldberg and Weinberger 2000). This view situates impairment at the level of discourse organization and implicates cognitive processing.

SZ speech, described as barely informative, empty of content, and containing unclear references embedded in vague and ambiguous discourse, can also be attributed to an inability to use pragmatic rules (Marini et al. 2008). These deficits at the discourse-pragmatic level stand out prominently because they affect communication. Indeed, SZ patients perform worse than healthy people in theory of mind and pragmatic conversation tasks (Mazza et al. 2008; Pickup and Frith 2001). However, these problems do not necessarily indicate cognitive decline or executive dysfunction in SZ. Rather, they are associated with impaired explicit/controlled processing, while implicit/automatic processing remains intact (Frith 2004). Frith (2004) maintains that SZ is characterized by deviations in meta-memory rather than general memory function and is a disorder of conscious reflection, which affects interpersonal communication and daily social functioning.

Of the 50+ manifestations of language dysfunction in SZ, most would appear to make learning a second language difficult, if not impossible. By way of example, second language learners who speak with flat intonation, unusual voice quality, and unintelligible utterances would be hard put to get their messages across. In terms of comprehension, impaired features such as selective attention deficit, distractibility, and failure to understand would make learning a new language challenging, whether in a classroom or in informal contexts. Yet, the limited research on second language learners with SZ shows otherwise (e.g. Bersudsky et al. 2005; Matulis 1977).

3.2. Bilingualism

Developing (and even proficient) bilingualism has been associated with weaknesses in lexis and morphosyntax, but strengths in non-verbal cognitive functioning. Weakness of bilinguals has been reported for verbal fluency tasks in both their original language (L1) and their second language (L2; Gollan et al. 2002; Rosselli et al. 2000). Relative to monolinguals, bilinguals have smaller vocabularies in both languages (Bialystok and Luk 2012; Mahon and Crutchley 2006) and problems with lexical retrieval (Bialystok 2009). They are slow in picture-naming (Gollan et al. 2005), show increased frequency of tip-of-the-tongue states (Gollan and Acenas 2004; Gollan and Silverberg 2001), experience more interference in lexical decision tasks (Ransdell and Fischler 1987), and display reduced verbal fluency (Portocarrero et al. 2007). Bilingual advantages have been reported for inhibition (Bialystok et al. 2006; Bialystok and Viswanathan 2009; Costa et al. 2008; Martin-Rhee and Bialystok 2008) as well as for storage and updating of information in working memory (Bialystok et al. 2004; Miyake et al. 2000).

The strengths associated with bilingualism have been shown for the inhibition of irrelevant information during executive function tasks, including non-linguistic executive functions (Bialystok 1999; Bialystok and Majumder 1998; Bialystok and Martin 2004; Bialystok and Viswanathan 2009; Bialystok et al. 2004, 2006, 2008; Carlson and Meltzoff 2008; Costa et al. 2008; Soveri et al. 2010). Bilingual advantages have also been noted for the processing of experimental trials that require inhibition of conflicting information (Bialystok and Viswanathan 2009; Bialystok et al. 2006; Costa et al. 2008; Martin-Rhee and Bialystok 2008) and for storing and updating information in working memory (Bialystok et al. 2004; Miyake et al. 2000). The causes of enhanced executive functioning have been linked to superior abilities in controlling inhibition, mental set shifting, and attention selection processes due to life-long experience managing two linguistic systems (Festman et al. 2010; Soveri et al. 2010; Stocco et al. 2014). Executive functioning has been related to Theory of Mind (the ability to take the perspective of the other, to step into the other person's shoes) and to attention and control (Carlson et al. 2004; Rubio-Fernández and Glucksberg 2012). Research has demonstrated a bilingual advantage for theory of mind tasks (for children, Bialystok and Senman 2004; Goetz 2003; for adults, Rubio-Fernández and Glucksberg 2012).

3.3.   *Interface of Schizophrenia and Bilingualism*

Several group studies (Bersudsky et al. 2005; Del Castillo 1970; Hemphill 1971; Smirnova et al. 2015; Smit et al. 2011), case reports (De Zulueta et al. 2001; Southwood et al. 2010; Theron et al. 2011), and four recent reviews (Dugan 2014; Marini et al. 2012; Paradis 2008; Seeman 2016) raise most of the critical issues related to the interface of SZ and BL. These issues differ in focusing on either BL or SZ as the predictor variable: (i) the extent to which BL affects (ameliorates/exacerbates) SZ symptoms; (ii) the extent to which SZ affects (impedes/assists) second language learning and BL performance. Our reading of the literature is that, by and large (with caveats regarding effective medication and severity level), SZ patients are able to learn a second language (Bersudsky et al. 2005; Matulis 1977). In the other direction, there is no evidence for a bilingual advantage in SZ, since no study has directly assessed bilingual advantage or disadvantage of SZ patients. These questions, while of interest to researchers in BL or SZ independently, do not get at the heart of the interaction of the illness with BL. Methodologically, examination of effects (of BL on SZ and SZ on BL) as well as the interaction between them would require multiple group comparisons of monolinguals and bilinguals with SZ patients and healthy adults (between-group) as well as within-group comparisons (L1 vs. L2) of bilinguals with SZ.

In an attempt to approach the question of disentangling language impairment in SZ from typical language use in L2, we first review one between-group study comparing bilinguals with SZ to healthy bilinguals and then several within-subject studies of bilinguals with SZ and the extent to which they show similar or different manifestations of SZ in L1 and L2.

Smit et al. (2011) recorded conversations of Afrikaans-English bilingual patients with SZ who were late bilinguals (they had acquired their L2 after puberty) and diagnosed after they acquired both their languages; the study included non-psychotic controls. Thirty minutes of conversation/spontaneous speech in L1/Afrikaans was immediately followed by 30 minutes in L2/English. Analyses compared frequencies and types of errors. Phonological, morphological, syntactic and lexical errors in bilinguals with SZ and bilingual controls were similar to typical L2 errors. Semantic errors differed quantitatively and qualitatively for the two groups. These group differences isolated semantics in L2/English as a source of impairment in SZ. Unfortunately, the authors did not analyse the conversation data from L1/Afrikaans, which would have allowed a within-subject analysis to see if SZ presented with the same manifestations in both languages.

Two studies which conducted within-group, cross-language comparisons focused on L1-L2 differences in linguistic and clinical markers of bilinguals with SZ (Smirnova et al. 2015; Southwood et al. 2010). Smirnova et al. (2015) examined a range of clinical, linguistic, and bilingual markers of SZ and BL in L1/Russian and L2/Hebrew in immigrants to Israel who acquired Hebrew following diagnosis. Impairment in SZ showed evidence for both similar and different manifestations in the two languages: clinical markers of SZ (blocking, topic shifting) were similar in L1 and L2, but four linguistic markers of SZ (incomplete syntax, lexical repetition, exophoric reference, and unclear reference) showed more frequent presentation in L2/Hebrew than in L1/Russian. Based on the clinical and linguistic markers, the authors concluded that despite the fact that the patients were relatively successful at learning a second language, SZ is nevertheless reflected in that second language. This fact is not surprising as these speakers have relatively greater difficulty in using L2 in the context of the cognitive and social difficulties underlying the SZ.

In addition, patients were able to manipulate two language features which show social awareness of interlocutors as well as the need to maintain fluency: discourse markers and code switching. The dissociation here between syntax/semantics and pragmatic aspects of language raises a number of issues. First, it is notable that people with SZ, for whom one indicator of impairment is social/occupational dysfunction, were able to manipulate two pragmatic aspects of language and do so differentially in their two languages. Since not all people with SZ are alike, and SZ is currently seen as a spectrum of symptoms within different endophenotypes, e.g. cognitively deficient and cognitively spared subtypes (Clementz et al. 2016; Jablensky 2006), it is possible that patients in this study were not impaired in certain pragmatic aspects of language, which allowed them to acquire L2, albeit with syntactic and semantic gaps. Another issue is related to the dissociation between clinical and linguistic markers of SZ. One possible conclusion from this study (which the authors did not draw) is that L2 does not adversely affect SZ, since the clinical markers were not more frequent, and in some cases less abundant than those found in another cohort from the same pool of patients (Bersudsky et al. 2005).

Southwood et al. (2010) report on a case study of a first psychotic episode of an Afrikaans-English bilingual patient. The patient was assessed with the MATRICS Consensus Cognitive Battery (Nuechterlein and Green 2006) in L2/English and interviewed with SCI-PANNS in L1 and L2 by a bilingual clinician. He was also assessed on verbal fluency and vocabulary in both languages. Proficiency was found to be better in L1 although the patient expressed a clear preference for L2/English, even switching to L2 in the initial evaluation. Psychotic symptoms were not confined to one language, but were more severe in L1 than in L2. During further assessment, L1 speech presented with many more psychotic features than L2, including: thought-disorder, delusions, tangentiality, derailment, and blunted affect, hearing Afrikaans-speaking voices. However, pragmatic features, such as topic selection and maintenance, pauses between utterances while avoiding eye contact, quantity of speech (too little or too much information) were appropriate in L1 but not in L2. In the semantic/lexical domain, specificity and accuracy of lexical selection and nonsensical statements were also impaired in L2 but not in L1.

The authors also point out that the patient spoke nonstandard varieties of both Afrikaans and English. For L1/Afrikaans, errors could be ascribed to dialectal differences, but for L2/Cape Flats English morphosyntactic errors (prepositions, inflexions) could not all be attributed to dialect differences, implying that they were a reflection of impairment. The patient also showed evidence of code interference in L2/English (adverb placement: *Went again the next morning out* instead of *Went out again the next morning*). The example of code interference here is not a dialect feature of Cape Flats English; thus it is more likely due to impaired syntax. This paper clearly distinguished L1 from L2, with more language pathology and/or less proficiency in L2 than in L1, despite greater preference for L2. Data also showed that errors in L1/Afrikaans but not in L2/English could be attributed to dialect differences. Finally, the study also isolated pragmatic/semantic impairment as more prominent in SZ than impairments in other linguistic domains.

In summary, the two studies reviewed here show different manifestations in the two languages of bilinguals with SZ.

3.4.   *Disentangling SZ and BL*

In an effort to synthesize the literature described in this section, we see that weaknesses or impairments in semantics and discourse/pragmatics emerge for both SZ and typical BL. No strengths have been reported for SZ (but the illness can present with relatively little or no impairment in some microstructure features of language, e.g. morphosyntax). Finally, the tasks that best discriminate SZ from BL pertain to executive functions, in particular, those involving inhibition and shifting.

One clearly productive way to begin to disentangle SZ and BL would be to examine bilinguals with SZ on a range of the executive function tasks to see if the discriminatory power of these tasks emerges in bilinguals with SZ. A more daring approach would be to examine the interaction of pragmatics and executive functions in bilinguals with SZ.

It has been proposed that theory of mind and pragmatics share a common foundation in executive functioning (Abdel-Hamid et al. 2009; Langdon et al. 2002). Inhibitory control mechanisms have been shown to be necessary (and possibly sufficient) to inhibit literal meaning in order to understand and produce figurative language. Inhibitory suppression mediated by frontal lobe regions and connections is deficient in SZ and may underlie impairment in working memory (Eich et al. 2014), in particular, verbal memory and language processing (Kuperberg and Caplan 2003; Silver et al. 2003), as reported for chronic schizophrenic patients (Frommann et al. 2010) and their first-degree relatives (Conklin et al. 2000).

Inhibitory mechanisms have also been proposed to account for semantic and selective attention deficits. For semantics, these mechanisms have been interpreted as underlying disorganized access to semantic memory and as related to formal thought disorder in SZ (Leeson et al. 2005). It has been theorized that inappropriate semantic forms are selected by patients with SZ as a result of impaired inhibition of less relevant items (Goldberg and Weinberger 2000). Selective attention deficits have been shown to be related to positive SZ symptoms (Caprile et al. 2015), and also to disruption of voluntary behavioural responses, e.g. negative symptoms of avolition (Reilly et al. 2008).

With more linguistically motivated tasks and analyses of pragmatic aspects of speech data, this line of research would go a long way towards dissociating cognitive and linguistic aspects of SZ. Healthy bilinguals should perform well on pragmatic tasks tapping into theory of mind abilities but less well on pragmatic tasks which involve idioms, metaphor, irony, and other aspects of figurative language which are learned via cross-cultural experience. This dissociation, however, would not take advantage of either the distinctive aspects of BL (e.g. code interference, code switching) or a within-subjects design. The distinctive aspects of BL include coping with cognitive demands associated with language control as a result of prolonged bilingual experience (Stocco et al. 2014), cognitive reserve (Bialystok 2009), neural reserve of bilingualism (Abutalebi and Green 2016),or use of various language features as compensatory resources (Bersudsky et al. 2005; Smirnova et al. 2015). It can thus be predicted that bilingual resources may positively affect brain functioning, clinical symptoms, and social outcomes in SZ patients. The advantages associated with intact executive functions (inhibition, shifting) in bilinguals are expected to create a positive impact in some of the most challenging domains in SZ: pragmatics and semantics. Yet the limited findings and heterogeneous population amongst even healthy bilinguals produce inconsistent results. For example, some executive functions (e.g. updating as part of working memory and response suppression) have not been shown as advantageous in bilinguals (Bialystok and Viswanathan 2009; Bialystok et al. 2008). These results indicate a multifaceted nature of executive functions, where only some processes related to inhibition show bilingual advantage. Moreover, the benefits of executive functions can be different at various stages of the lifespan (Bialystok and Viswanathan 2009). This alone calls for wide-scoped study including bilinguals with and without SZ at different stages of development. Interpretation of results is yet another challenge faced by research on bilingual functioning. Even those skills which show clear bilingual advantage can be interpreted differently in terms of the particular mechanisms underlying performance (Colzato et al. 2008).

We would suggest that superior language control mechanisms in bilinguals may trigger concomitant recruitment of bilingual resources and associated neurobiological changes (e.g. increase of grey matter volume, synaptic plasticity, connectivity, and activation) in the brain areas reviewed above (i.e. left prefrontal cortex, anterior cingulate cortex, pre-supplementary motor area, inferior parietal lobules bilaterally, left caudate) and might improve cognitive control, executive functions, verbal fluency and reduce related clinical symptoms of SZ.

In bilingual patients with SZ we should first look for enhanced performance on executive functions (since SZ patients are known to be weak in executive functions). Greater executive control is expected to decrease the severity of language disorders in the domains of semantics, pragmatics, and possibly discourse. Semantic deficits should be attenuated due to stronger inhibition abilities amongst bilinguals. And pragmatics and discourse abilities might benefit from availability of linguistic items in another language and possible transfer of global discourse skills.

If patients with SZ can learn and use L2 like healthy bilinguals, they should show lower symptom severity in L2 than in L1 (e.g. less blocking, derailment, topic shifting). Some linguistic markers of SZ may, however, be confused with features of typical L2 acquisition (e.g. syntactic and lexical difficulties). Language characteristics of L2 learners may also be taken for symptoms of a psychotic state. This raises the possibility of misdiagnosis, and makes it essential to examine data in both languages, as several studies reviewed above have done (De Zulueta et al. 2001; Smirnova et al. 2015; Southwood et al. 2010).

4.   Towards an Integrative Approach to the Study of the SZ–BL Interface

Three independent approaches to the study of SZ and BL and their interface can be identified in the literature reviewed in Section 3. One line of research, based on neuroimaging techniques, has isolated regions and connections responsible for SZ and BL. A second approach focuses on linguistic features that distinguish SZ and BL from the general population, but do not necessarily relate to the intersection of the two. A third, more conceptual perspective, involves psycholinguistic/neurolinguistic modelling of SZ impairment and BL. After delineating these approaches, this section concludes with recommendations for a more integrated effort to directly address the interface of SZ and BL.

4.1.   *Different Neural Mechanisms*

Beyond lateralization, which has been reported to be distinctive amongst SZ patients (Kircher et al. 2002; Oertel-Knöchel and Linden 2011), the review in Section 3 above showed evidence for deviations in structure, volume, connectivity, and activity in a wide range of brain regions, most prominent amongst them the frontal cortex, the anterior cingulate cortex, and inferior parietal lobules. These brain malfunctions were shown to correlate with reduced verbal fluency, formal thought disorder, and auditory verbal hallucinations. These same brain regions have been implicated in bilingual processing, in particular in language control processes (language switching) in healthy bilinguals, resulting in specific neurobiological changes (e.g. increased grey matter volume, increased neuronal connectivity, increased brain activation) as a function of age and second language proficiency.

4.2. Linguistic Markers Approach

A very broad range of linguistic and cognitive features have been linked to various clinical categories in SZ. By and large, the link between linguistic feature and clinical category represents simple correlations between SZ impairment (e.g. blocking) and linguistic features (e.g. word-finding or lexical access problems). Sometimes the clinical and linguistic terminology is overlapping, (e.g. topic shifting is both a clinical category; Fine 2006) and a linguistic descriptor. Research on bilingual adults has also generated a set of features such as incomplete acquisition, L1 attrition, code interference, and code switching. The review in Section 3 showed that semantic and pragmatic/discourse features of language (e.g. lexical difficulties, topic shifting) and executive function abilities (e.g. inhibition, shifting) are most relevant to the interface of SZ and BL.

4.3. Modelling of Impairment in Bilinguals with SZ

The approach we would propose is based on modularity and involves dissociation of both linguistic domains and languages (cf. differential diagnosis in clinical psychopathology).

Paradis (2004, 2008) proposed that different subsystems are responsible for L1 and L2 and are sustained by mechanisms of declarative and procedural memory. Drawing from Ullman (2001), L1 processing is more grammar-based and assumed to be grounded in procedural memory mechanisms for which frontal lobe and basal ganglia areas of the left hemisphere are the neurobiological substrates. L2 use is considered to more lexically based and to rely on declarative memory processes for which the left temporal lobe is responsible. Paradis makes use of these constructs for several reasons, the most relevant here, being to explain cases of selective impairment of L1 and L2 and '"reversibility" of symptoms, pointing to the inhibition and disinhibition of subsystems rather than their physical destruction' (Paradis 2008, p. 224).

Along these lines, procedural mechanisms would underlie sequencing difficulties in SZ reported by Docherty (2005) and should also be related to impaired syntactic abilities (e.g. Smirnova et al. 2015). Declarative mechanisms would be a source of lexical impairment including word-finding difficulties, lexical repetition, and blocking. Pragmatic impairment in SZ includes inability to use pragmatic rules and to make use of context (Bazin et al. 2000; Marini et al. 2012; Paradis 2004, 2008), but see Smirnova et al. (2015) who show BL SZ's abilities to manipulate one pragmatic feature of language (discourse markers).

In an effort to expand the profile of bilinguals with SZ in either or both languages, we suggest that in addition to pinpointing the domain of impairment and dissociations between subsystems, the interaction between and amongst them needs to be specified. Some of the linguistic–cognitive interactions have been proposed and reported on above. For example, blocking, word finding, and lexical access problems seem to be related to impaired inhibition, while topic shifting and derailment seem to be more related to impaired shifting abilities. Missing from this puzzle is an account for the distinctly bilingual aspects of the picture, viz. code interference and code switching. Green and Wei (2014) have provided this direction for control processes in code switching. In addition to including a wide range of motivations (both socio-pragmatic and psycholinguistic) and contexts (stable, enclaved, immigrant, second generation) for code switching, their model also accounts for speech planning and utterance production, specifying levels of connectivity between concept and lexeme in monolingual and bilingual speech modes (Green and Wei 2014; Grosjean 1999). This same kind of cognitive-linguistic specification can be applied to code interference as well. In the context of this wider framework, studies reporting on selective impairment, unsystematic code switching behaviour, and impaired fluency are useful pieces in the puzzle.

The interaction of cognitive mechanisms and linguistic features is not straightforward. In part this is due to the fact that cognitive mechanisms are not dedicated to a single linguistic domain, and a particular linguistic marker probably involves more than a single cognitive mechanism. We consider pragmatics, reported to be vulnerable in both SZ and BL, as a key to interaction, both between various linguistic domains as well as between linguistic domains and cognitive mechanisms.

Pragmatics is language use in context. In the heyday of syntax (1960s), it was called the garbage heap of linguistics, the place to deposit all those problems in syntax and semantics which had no solution (Leech and Thomas 1990). Today it is a 'domain' of linguistics in its own right, but really it cuts across, and actually entails all other linguistic domains. Words and sentences need context to be formulated into utterances. Sentences need to be sequenced in order to become coherent speech. Context involves many levels of processing: the words which precede or follow a word or phrase, the sentences which precede or follow an utterance. Context also involves social relationships, between speaker and listener and others in earshot of the conversation. A look at the long list of linguistic markers of SZ shows that all of them are pragmatic. Blunted affect, dull intonation, and overuse of self-reference (exophora) impact on the speaker's relationship to the listener in the act of communication.

In order to get at the lexical–pragmatic interaction, one needs a theory of speech processing, from planning to formulation. The linguistics of utterance planning begins with an idea or intention, translates this into lexical content, inserts words into syntactic slots, and then sends all this information to a phonological processor which allows emission of the utterance (e.g. Levelt 1989).

In terms of bilingual lexical processing of spoken language, the speaker begins with an intention (e.g. a response to a question in a clinical interview). Intentions are pragmatic (cf. illocutionary force, Searle 1969) and are not language-specific. The intention serves as the input to conceptual and semantic encoding (Levelt 1989). Concepts are not considered to be language-specific, but semantic processing is grounded in the bilingual mental lexicon with complex interactions between words in the two languages (researched extensively by Dijkstra and van Heuven 2002; Kroll et al. 2010). Research on bilingual lexical processing does not usually take into account pragmatic factors. But lexical choice involves a great deal of pragmatics. Context, both linguistic (e.g. the previous utterance) and social (e.g. recognition/ accommodation to the listener's language preferences and proficiency, age, gender, status) are amongst the pragmatic factors affecting lexical choice. Similar (but less influential) pragmatic choices are made at the stage of syntactic formulation. Green and Wei's (2014) comprehensive model of control processes in bilingual code switching bring this kind of analysis of speech planning and production to their cognitive bases, allowing examination of the language-cognitive interface.

Beyond speech itself, a wide range of factors in SZ as well as BL is worthy of systematic study. For SZ and BL these would include: biological age, age of onset (of SZ and of BL), individual factors (e.g. severity in SZ and aptitude in BL). For SZ, these include medication effects, data collection before, during, or after psychotic episode, and whether the diagnosis was before or after the second language was acquired. For BL, relevant factors include age of initial L2 exposure, length of exposure, manner of acquisition (informal/ classroom), frequency of use, proficiency/dominance, and preference. All these pose challenges for research examining the interaction of BL and SZ. One challenge is related to bidirectional influence: effects of BL on SZ and effects of SZ on BL. Each direction addresses different questions: the former is interested in how symptoms of SZ are manifested in bilinguals' first and second languages; the latter examines exposure to the second language *before* or *after* onset of psychotic symptoms and investigates second language acquisition amongst affected patients. A second challenge is related to measuring language proficiency in both languages of bilinguals, which is a difficult task even in healthy bilinguals (e.g. due to lack of norms for impaired populations) and should be more demanding in bilinguals with SZ.

On this background the following methodological guidelines are offered:

- Examine both languages in order to determine whether there is selective or non-selective impairment (which will assist in determining the language[s] for intervention).
- Probe a range of both linguistic and cognitive features in order to examine dissociations and interactions of domains and languages, e.g. for semantics: lexical accuracy, neologisms, lexical repetition; for pragmatics/discourse: topic shifting, coherence, discourse markers; pauses for planning; for executive functions: inhibition, attention control, and working memory.
- Look both under the SZ lamp post (pragmatic, semantic/lexical deficits, e.g. incoherence, unclear reference) and under the BL lamp post (word finding abilities, morphosyntax, e.g. prepositions, gender marking).
- Look also both at distinctive features of SZ (the language of hallucination and delusions, i.e. blocking, topic shifting, fluency markers) and BL (e.g. code switching, code interference).
- Examine structures which are typologically similar and different across languages and try to distinguish errors typical of BL/L2 use from errors uniquely attributable to SZ pathology.

REFERENCES

Abdel-Hamid, M., Lehmkämper, C., Sonntag, C. et al. (2009). Theory of mind in schizophrenia: the role of clinical symptomatology and neurocognition in understanding other people's thoughts and intentions. *Psychiatry Research* 165 (1): 19–26. doi:10.1016/j.psychres.2007.10.021.

Abutalebi, J., Brambati, S.M., Annoni, J.M. et al. (2007). The neural cost of the auditory perception of language switches: an event-related functional magnetic resonance imaging study in bilinguals. *Journal of Neuroscience* 27: 13762–13769. doi:10.1523/JNEUROSCI.3294-07.2007.

Abutalebi, J., Canini, M., Della Rosa, P. et al. (2015). The neuroprotective effects of bilingualism upon the inferior parietal lobule: a structural neuroimaging study in aging Chinese bilinguals. *Journal of Neurolinguistics* 33: 3–13. doi:10.1016/j.jneuroling.2014.09.008.

Abutalebi, J., Della Rosa, P., Ding, G. et al. (2013). Language proficiency modulates the engagement of cognitive control areas in multilinguals. *Cortex* 49 (3): 905–911. doi:10.1016/j.cortex.2012.08.018.

Abutalebi, J., Della Rosa, P.A., Green, D.W. et al. (2012). Bilingualism tunes the anterior cingulate cortex for conflict monitoring. *Cerebral Cortex* 22: 2076–2086. doi:10.1093/cercor/bhr287.

Abutalebi, J. and Green, D. (2007). Bilingual language production: the neurocognition of language representation and control. *Journal of Neurolinguistics* 20 (3): 242–275. doi:10.1016/j.jneuroling.2006.10.003.

Abutalebi, J. and Green, D.W. (2016). Neuroimaging of language control in bilinguals: neural adaptation and reserve. *Bilingualism: Language and Cognition* 19 (4): 689–698. doi:10.1017/S1366728916000225.

Alain, C., McNeely, H.E., He, Y. et al. (2002). Neurophysiological evidence of error-monitoring deficits in patients with schizophrenia. *Cerebral Cortex* 12 (8): 840–846. doi:10.1093/cercor/12.8.840.

Allen, H.A., Liddle, P.F., and Frith, C.D. (1993). Negative features, retrieval processes and verbal fluency in schizophrenia. *The British Journal of Psychiatry* 163 (6): 769–775. doi:10.1192/bjp.163.6.769.

Andreasen, N.C. (1979). Thought, language, and communication disorders. I: Clinical assessment, definition of terms, and evaluation of their reliability. *Archives of General Psychiatry* 36 (12): 1315–1321. doi:10.1001/archpsyc.1979.01780120045006.

Andreasen, N.C. (1986). Scale for the assessment of thought, language, and communication (TLC). *Schizophrenia Bulletin* 12 (3): 473. doi:10.1093/schbul/12.3.473.

Andreasen, N.C. and Grove, W.M. (1986). Thought, language, and communication in schizophrenia: diagnosis and prognosis. *Schizophrenia Bulletin* 12 (3): 348. doi:10.1093/schbul/12.3.348.

Antonova, E., Sharma, T., Morris, R., and Kumari, V. (2004). The relationship between brain structure and neurocognition in schizophrenia: a selective review. *Schizophrenia Research* 70 (2): 117–145. doi:10.1016/j.schres.2003.12.002.

Aron, A.R., Robbins, T.W., and Poldrack, R.A. (2014). Inhibition and the right inferior frontal cortex: one decade on. *Trends in Cognitive Sciences* 18 (4): 177–185. doi:10.1016/j.tics.2013.12.003.

Badcock, J.C., Dragović, M., Garrett, C., and Jablensky, A. (2011). Action (verb) fluency in schizophrenia: getting a grip on odd speech. *Schizophrenia Research* 126: 138–143. doi:10.1016/j.schres.2010.11.004.

Barch, D.M., Braver, T.S., Akbudak, E. et al. (2001). Anterior cingulate cortex and response conflict: effects of response modality and processing domain. *Cerebral Cortex* 11 (9): 837–848. doi:10.1093/cercor/11.9.837.

Barrera, A., McKenna, P., and Berrios, G. (2005). Formal thought disorder in schizophrenia: an executive or a semantic deficit? *Psychological Medicine* 35 (1): 121–132. doi:10.1017/S003329170400279X.

Bazin, N., Perruchet, P., Hardy-Bayle, M.C., and Feline, A. (2000). Context-dependent information processing in patients with schizophrenia. *Schizophrenia Research* 45 (1): 93–101. doi:10.1016/S0920-9964(99)00167-X.

Bedi, G., Carrillo, F., Cecchi, G.A. et al. (2015). Automated analysis of free speech predicts psychosis onset in high-risk youths. *NPJ Schizophrenia* 1: 15030. doi:10.1038/npjschz.2015.30.

Bernard, J. and Mittal, V. (2015). Dysfunctional activation of the cerebellum in schizophrenia. *Clinical Psychological Science* 3 (4): 545–566. doi:10.1177/2167702614542463.

Bersudsky, Y., Fine, J., Gorjaltsan, I. et al. (2005). Schizophrenia and second language acquisition. *Progress in Neuro-Psychopharmacology and Biological Psychiatry* 29 (4): 535–542. doi:10.1016/j.pnpbp.2005.01.004.

Bialystok, E. (1999). Cognitive complexity and attentional control in the bilingual mind. *Child Development* 70 (3): 636–644. doi:10.1111/1467-8624.00046.

Bialystok, E. (2009). Bilingualism: the good, the bad, and the indifferent. *Bilingualism: Language and Cognition* 12 (1): 3–11. doi:10.1017/S1366728908003477.

Bialystok, E., Craik, F., Klein, R., and Viswanathan, M. (2004). Bilingualism, aging, and cognitive control: evidence from the Simon task. *Psychology and Aging* 19 (2): 290–303. doi:10.1037/0882-7974.19.2.290.

Bialystok, E., Craik, F., and Luk, G. (2008). Cognitive control and lexical access in younger and older bilinguals. *Journal of Experimental Psychology: Learning, Memory, and Cognition* 34 (4): 859. doi:10.1037/0278-7393.34.4.859.

Bialystok, E., Craik, F.I., and Ryan, J. (2006). Executive control in a modified antisaccade task: effects of aging and bilingualism. *Journal of Experimental Psychology: Learning, Memory, and Cognition* 32 (6): 1341–1354. doi:10.1037/0278-7393.32.6.1341.

Bialystok, E. and Luk, G. (2012). Receptive vocabulary differences in monolingual and bilingual adults. *Bilingualism: Language and Cognition* 15 (2): 397–401. doi:10.1017/S136672891100040X.

Bialystok, E. and Majumder, S. (1998). The relationship between bilingualism and the development of cognitive processes in problem solving. *Applied PsychoLinguistics* 19 (1): 69–85. doi:10.1017/S0142716400010584.

Bialystok, E. and Martin, M.M. (2004). Attention and inhibition in bilingual children: evidence from the dimensional change card sort task. *Developmental Science* 7 (3): 325–339. doi:10.1111/j.1467-7687.2004.00351.x.

Bialystok, E. and Senman, L. (2004). Executive processes in appearance–reality tasks: the role of inhibition of attention and symbolic representation. *Child Development* 75 (2): 562–579.

Bialystok, E. and Viswanathan, M. (2009). Components of executive control with advantages for bilingual children in two cultures. *Cognition* 112 (3): 494–500. doi:10.1016/j.cognition.2009.06.014.

Blasi, G., Taurisano, P., Papazacharias, A. et al. (2010). Nonlinear response of the anterior cingulate and prefrontal cortex in schizophrenia as a function of variable attentional control. *Cerebral Cortex* 20 (4): 837–845. doi:10.1093/cercor/bhp146.

Bleuler, E. (1911). *Dementia Praecox, or the Group of Schizophrenias*. New York, NY: International Universities Press.

Branzi, F.M., Calabria, M., Boscarino, M.L., and Costa, A. (2016). On the overlap between bilingual language control and domain-general executive control. *Acta Psychologica* 166: 21–30. doi:10.1093/cercor/bhv052.

Braver, T.S., Barch, D.M., Gray, J.R. et al. (2001). Anterior cingulate cortex and response conflict: Effects of frequency, inhibition and errors. *Cerebral Cortex* 11 (9): 825–836. doi:10.1093/cercor/11.9.825.

Brown, M. and Kuperberg, G.R. (2015). A hierarchical generative framework of language processing: linking language perception, interpretation, and production abnormalities in schizophrenia. *Frontiers in Human Neuroscience* 9: 643. doi:10.3389/fnhum.2015.00643.

Caprile, C., Cuevas-Esteban, J., Ochoa, S. et al. (2015). Mixing apples with oranges: visual attention deficits in schizophrenia. *Journal of Behavior Therapy and Experimental Psychiatry* 48: 27–32. doi:10.1016/j.jbtep.2015.01.006.

Carlson, S.M., Mandell, D.J., and Williams, L. (2004). Executive function and theory of mind: Stability and prediction from ages 2 to 3. *Developmental Psychology* 40 (6): 1105–1122.

Carlson, S.M. and Meltzoff, A.N. (2008). Bilingual experience and executive functioning in young children. *Developmental Science* 11 (2): 282–298. doi:10.1111/j.1467-7687.2008.00675.x.

Chaika, E. (1974). A linguist looks at 'schizophrenic' language. *Brain and Language* 1: 257–276. doi:10.1016/0093-934X(74)90040-6.

Chen, E.Y., Lam, L.C., Kan, C.S. et al. (1996). Language disorganisation in schizophrenia: validation and assessment with a new clinical rating instrument. *Hong Kong Journal of Psychiatry* 6 (1): 4–13.

Clementz, B.A., Sweeney, J.A., Hamm, J.P. et al. (2016). Identification of distinct psychosis biotypes using brain-based biomarkers. *American Journal of Psychiatry* 173 (4): 373–384. doi: 10.1176/appi.ajp.2015.14091200.

Collette, F., Olivier, L., Van Der Linden, M. et al. (2005). Involvement of both prefrontal and inferior parietal cortex in dual-task performance. *Cognitive Brain Research* 24 (2): 237–251. doi:10.1016/j.cogbrainres.2005.01.023.

Colzato, L.S., Bajo, M.T., van den Wildenberg, W. et al. (2008). How does bilingualism improve executive control? A comparison of active and reactive inhibition mechanisms. *Journal of Experimental Psychology: Learning, Memory, and Cognition* 34 (2): 302. doi:10.1037/0278-7393.34.2.302.

Conklin, H., Curtis, C., Katsanis, J., and Iacono, W. (2000). Verbal working memory impairment in schizophrenia patients and their first-degree relatives: evidence from the digit span task. *The American Journal of Psychiatry* 157 (2): 275–277. doi:10.1176/appi.ajp.157.2.275.

Costa, A., Hernández, M., and Sebastián-Gallés, N. (2008). Bilingualism aids conflict resolution: evidence from the ANT task. *Cognition* 106: 59–86. 10.1016/j.cognition.2006.12.013.

Covington, M.A., He, C., Brown, C. et al. (2005). Schizophrenia and the structure of language: the linguist's view. *Schizophrenia Research* 77: 85–98. doi:10.1016/j.schres.2005.01.016.

Crider, A. (1997). Perseveration in schizophrenia. *Schizophrenia Bulletin* 23 (1): 63–74. doi:10.1093/schbul/23.1.63.

Cutting, J. (1985). *The Psychology of Schizophrenia*. Edinburgh, Scotland: Churchill Livingstone.

Cutting, J. and Murphy, D. (1990). Preference for denotative as opposed to connotative meanings in schizophrenics. *Brain and Language* 39 (3): 459–468. doi:10.1016/0093-934X(90)90151-6.

De Zulueta, F.I.S., Gene-Cos, N., and Grachev, S. (2001). Differential psychotic symptomatology in polyglot patients: case reports and their implications. *Psychology and Psychotherapy: Theory, Research and Practice* 74 (3): 277–292. doi:10.1348/000711201160966.

Del Castillo, J.C. (1970). Influence of language upon symptomatology in foreign-born patients. *American Journal of Psychiatry* 127: 160–162. doi:10.1178/ajp.127.2.242.

DeLisi, L.E. (2001). Speech disorder in schizophrenia: review of the literature and exploration of its relation to the uniquely human capacity for language. *Schizophrenia Bulletin* 27: 481–496. doi:10.1093/oxfordjournals.schbul.a006889.

Dijkstra, T. and van Heuven, W.J.B. (2002). The architecture of the bilingual word recognition system: from identification to decision. *Bilingualism: Language and Cognition* 5: 175–197. doi:10.1017/S1366728902003012.

Docherty, N.M. (2005). Cognitive impairments and disordered speech in schizophrenia: thought disorder, disorganization, and communication failure perspectives. *Journal of Abnormal Psychology* 114 (2): 269. doi:10.1037/0021-843X.114.2.269.

Docherty, N.M., Hall, M.J., Gordinier, S.W., and Cutting, L.P. (2000). Conceptual sequencing and disordered speech in schizophrenia. *Schizophrenia Bulletin* 26 (3): 723–735. doi:10.1093/oxfordjournals.schbul.a033489.

Docherty, N.M., Strauss, M.E., Dinzeo, T.J., and St-Hilaire, A. (2006). The cognitive origins of specific types of schizophrenic speech disturbances. *American Journal of Psychiatry* 163: 2111–2118. doi:10.1176/ajp.2006.163.12.2111.

Dorph-Petersen, K. and Lewis, D. (2017). Postmortem structural studies of the thalamus in schizophrenia. *Schizophrenia Research* 180: 28–35. doi:10.1016/j.schres.2016.08.007.

DSM-5 (2013). *Diagnostic and Statistical Manual of Mental Disorders*, 5the. Washington, DC: American Psychiatric Press.

Dugan, J.E. (2014). Second language acquisition and schizophrenia. *Second Language Research* 30 (3): 307–321. doi:10.1177/0267658314525776.

Eich, T., Nee, D., Insel, C. et al. (2014). Neural correlates of impaired cognitive control over working memory in schizophrenia. *Biological Psychiatry* 76 (2): 146–153. doi:10.1016/j.biopsych.2013.09.032.

Ellison-Wright, I. and Bullmore, E. (2009). Meta-analysis of diffusion tensor imaging studies in schizophrenia. *Schizophrenia Research* 108 (1): 3–10.

Faber, R. and Reichstein, M.B. (1981). Language dysfunction in schizophrenia. *The British Journal of Psychiatry* 139 (6): 519–522. doi:10.1192/bjp.139.6.519.

Festman, J., Rodriguez-Fornells, A., and Münte, T.F. (2010). Individual differences in control of language interference in late bilinguals are mainly related to general executive abilities. *Behavioral and Brain Functions* 6 (1): 5. https://doi.org/10.1186/1744-9081-6-5.

Fine, J. (2006). *Language in Psychiatry: A Handbook of Clinical Practice*. London, UK: Equinox.

Ford, A., Triplett, W., Sudhyadhom, A. et al. (2013). Broca's area and its striatal and thalamic connections: a diffusion-MRI tractography study. *Frontiers in Neuroanatomy* 7 (8): doi:10.3389/fnana.2013.00008.

Fornito, A., Zalesky, A., Pantelis, C., and Bullmore, E.T. (2012). Schizophrenia, neuroimaging and connectomics. *NeuroImage* 62 (4): 2296–2314. doi:10.1016/j.neuroimage.2011.12.090.

Frith, C.D. (2004). Schizophrenia and theory of mind. *Psychological Medicine* 34 (3): 385–389. doi:10.1017/S0033291703001326.

Frommann, I., Pukrop, R., Brinkmeyer, J. et al. (2010). Neuropsychological profiles in different at-risk states of psychosis: executive control impairment in the early— and additional memory dysfunction in the late—prodromal state. *Schizophrenia Bulletin* 37 (4): 861–873. doi:10.1093/schbul/sbp155.

Fusar-Poli, P., Deste, G., Smieskova, R. et al. (2012). Cognitive functioning in prodromal psychosis: a meta-analysis. *Archives of General Psychiatry* 69 (6): 562–571. doi:10.1001/archgenpsychiatry.2011.1592.

Goetz, P.J. (2003). The effects of bilingualism on theory of mind development. *Bilingualism: Language and Cognition* 6 (1): 1–15.

Goldberg, T.E. and Weinberger, D.R. (2000). Thought disorder in schizophrenia: a reappraisal of older formulations and an overview of some recent studies. *Cognitive Neuropsychiatry* 5 (1): 1–19. doi:10.1080/135468000395790.

Gollan, T.H. and Acenas, L.A.R. (2004). What is a TOT? Cognate and translation effects on tip-of-the-tongue states in Spanish-English and tagalog-English bilinguals. *Journal of Experimental Psychology: Learning, Memory, and Cognition* 30 (1): 246. doi:10.1037/0278-7393.30.1.246.

Gollan, T.H., Montoya, R.I., Fennema-Notestine, C., and Morris, S.K. (2005). Bilingualism affects picture naming but not picture classification. *Memory & Cognition* 33 (7): 1220–1234. doi:10.3758/BF03193224.

Gollan, T.H., Montoya, R.I., and Werner, G.A. (2002). Semantic and letter fluency in Spanish-English bilinguals. *Neuropsychology* 16 (4): 562. doi:10.1037/0894-4105.16.4.562.

Gollan, T.H. and Silverberg, N.B. (2001). Tip-of-the-tongue states in Hebrew–English bilinguals. *Bilingualism: Language and Cognition* 4: 63–83.

Green, D.W. and Abutalebi, J. (2013). Language control in bilinguals: the adaptive control hypothesis. *Journal of Cognitive Psychology* 25 (5): 515–530. doi:10.1080/20445911.2013.796377.

Green, D.W. and Wei, L. (2014). A control process model of code-switching. *Language, Cognition and Neuroscience* 29 (4): 499–511. doi:10.1080/23273798.2014.882515.

Grosjean, F. (1999). Bilingualism: individual. In: *Concise Encyclopaedia of Educational Linguistics* (ed. B. Spolsky), 284–290. Oxford: Elsevier Science.

Habl, G., Schmitt, A., Zink, M. et al. (2012). Decreased reelin expression in the left prefrontal cortex (BA9) in chronic schizophrenia patients. *Neuropsychobiology* 66 (1): 57–62. doi:10.1159/000337129.

Hardy-Baylé, M.C., Sarfati, Y., and Passerieux, C. (2003). The cognitive basis of disorganization symptomatology in schizophrenia and its clinical correlates: toward a pathogenetic approach to disorganization. *Schizophrenia Bulletin* 29 (3): 459–471. doi:10.1093/oxfordjournals. schbul.a007019.

Harrison, B.J., Yücel, M., Fornito, A. et al. (2007). Characterizing anterior cingulate activation in chronic schizophrenia: a group and single-subject fMRI study. *Acta Psychiatrica Scandinavica* 116: 271–279. doi:10.1111/j.1600-0447.2007.01002.x.

Harrow, M., Lanin-Kettering, I., Prosen, M., and Miller, J.G. (1983). Disordered thinking in schizophrenia: intermingling and loss of set. *Schizophrenia Bulletin* 9 (3): 354–367. doi:10.1093/schbul/9.3.354.

Heinrichs, R.W. and Zakzanis, K.K. (1998). Neurocognitive deficit in schizophrenia: a quantitative review of the evidence. *Neuropsychology* 12 (3): 426–445.

Hemphill, R.E. (1971). Auditory hallucinations in polyglots. *South African Medical Journal* 45: 1391–1394.

Henry, J.D. and Crawford, J.R. (2004). A meta-analytic review of verbal fluency performance following focal cortical lesions. *Neuropsychology* 18 (2): 284–295. doi:10.1037/0894-4105.18.2.284.

Hinzen, W. and Rosselló, J. (2015). The linguistics of schizophrenia: thought disturbance as language pathology across positive symptoms. *Frontiers in Psychology* 6: 971. doi:10.3389/fpsyg.2015.00971.

Hoffman, R.E., Hogben, G.L., Smith, H., and Calhoun, W.F. (1985). Message disruptions during syntactic processing in schizophrenia. *Journal of Communication Disorders* 18 (3): 183–202. doi:10.1016/0021-9924(85)90020-6.

Hohenstein, J., Eisenberg, A., and Naigles, L. (2006). Is he floating across or crossing afloat? Cross-influence of L1 and L2 in Spanish–English bilingual adults. *Bilingualism: Language and Cognition* 9 (3): 249–261.

Hu, M., Li, J., Eyler, L. et al. (2013). Decreased left middle temporal gyrus volume in antipsychotic drug-naive, first-episode schizophrenia patients and their healthy unaffected siblings. *Schizophrenia Research* 144 (1–3): 37–42. doi:10.1016/j.schres.2012.12.018.

Hulshoff Pol, H.E. and Kahn, R.S. (2008). What happens after the first episode? A review of progressive brain changes in chronically ill patients with schizophrenia. *Schizophrenia Bulletin* 34 (2): 354–366. doi:10.1093/schbul/sbm168.

Jablensky, A. (2006). Subtyping schizophrenia: implications for genetic research. *Molecular Psychiatry* 11 (9): 815. doi:10.1038/sj.mp.4001857.

Jablensky, A., McGrath, J., Herrman, H. et al. (2000). Psychotic disorders in urban areas: an overview of the study on low prevalence disorders. *Australian and New Zealand Journal of Psychiatry* 34 (2): 221–236. doi:10.1080/j.1440-1614.2000.00728.x.

Joyce, E.M., Collinson, S.L., and Crichton, P. (1996). Verbal fluency in schizophrenia: relationship with executive function, semantic memory and clinical alogia.

Psychological Medicine 26 (1): 39–49. doi:10.1017/S0033291700033705.

Kahn, R.S. and Keefe, R.S. (2013). Schizophrenia is a cognitive illness: time for a change in focus. *JAMA Psychiatry* 70 (10): 1107–1112. doi:10.1001/jamapsychiatry.2013.155.

Kambanaros, M., Messinis, L., Georgiou, V., and Papathanassopoulos, P. (2010). Action and object naming in schizophrenia. *Journal of Clinical and Experimental Neuropsychology* 32 (10): 1083–1094. doi:10.1080/13803391003733578.

Kenny, J.T., Friedman, L., Findling, R.L. et al. (1997). Cognitive impairment in adolescents with schizophrenia. *American Journal of Psychiatry* 154 (11): 1613–1615. doi: 10.1176/ajp.154.11.1613.

Kim, S.J., Shim, J.C., Kong, B.G. et al. (2015). The relationship between language ability and cognitive function in patients with schizophrenia. *Clinical Psychopharmacology and Neuroscience* 13 (3): 288.

Kircher, T., Liddle, P., Brammer, M. et al. (2002). Reversed lateralization of temporal activation during speech production in thought disordered patients with schizophrenia. *Psychological Medicine* 32 (3): 439–449. doi:10.1017/S0033291702005287.

Kleist, K. (1960). Schizophrenic symptoms and cerebral pathology. *Journal of Mental Science* 106: 246–255.

Kraepelin, E. (1896/1919). *Dementia Praecox and Paraphrenia*. Chicago, IL: Chicago Medical Book Company.

Kraepelin, E. (1906). *Über Sprachstörungen im Traume*. Leipzig, Germany: Verlag von Wilhelm Engelmann.

Kraepelin, E. (1920). Die Erscheinungsformen des Irreseins. *Zeitschrift für die gesamte Neurologie und Psychiatrie* 62 (1): 1–29.

Kreher, D., Goff, D., and Kuperberg, G. (2009). Why all the confusion? Experimental task explains discrepant semantic priming effects in schizophrenia under 'automatic' conditions: evidence from event-related potentials. *Schizophrenia Research* 111 (1): 174–181. doi:10.1016/j.schres.2009.03.013.

Kroll, J.F., van Hell, J.G., Tokowicz, N., and Green, D.W. (2010). The revised hierarchical model: a critical review and assessment. *Bilingualism: Language and Cognition* 13: 373–381. doi:10.1017/S136672891000009X.

Kuperberg, G.R. (2010). Language in schizophrenia part 1: an introduction. *Language and Linguistics Compass* 4 (8): 576–589. doi:10.1111/j.1749-818X.2010.00216.x.

Kuperberg, G.R. and Caplan, D. (2003). Language dysfunction in schizophrenia. In: *Neuropsychiatry*, 2nde (ed. R.B. Schiffer, S.M. Rao and B.S. Fogel), 444–466. Philadelphia, PA: Lippincott Williams & Wilkins.

Kuperberg, G.R., Sitnikova, T., Goff, D., and Holcomb, P.J. (2006). Making sense of sentences in schizophrenia: electrophysiological evidence for abnormal interactions between semantic and syntactic processing. *Journal of Abnormal Psychology* 115 (2): 251. doi:10.1037/0021-843X.115.2.251.

Langdon, R., Davies, M., and Coltheart, M. (2002). Understanding minds and understanding communicated meanings in schizophrenia. *Mind & Language* 17 (1–2): 68–104. doi:10.1111/1468-0017.00189.

Lee, J.W. (2004). Chronic 'speech catatonia' with constant logorrhea, verbigeration and echolalia successfully treated with lorazepam: a case report. *Psychiatry and Clinical Neurosciences* 58 (6): 666–668. doi:10.1111/j.1440-1819.2004.01318.x.

Leech, G. and Thomas, J. (1990). Language, meaning and context: pragmatics. In: *An Encyclopaedia of Language* (ed. N.E. Collinge), 173–206. London, UK: Routledge.

Leeson, V., Simpson, A., Mckenna, P., and Laws, K. (2005). Executive inhibition and semantic association in schizophrenia. *Schizophrenia Research* 74 (1): 61–67. doi:10.1016/j.schres.2004.07.011.

Lehtonen, H., Laine, A., Niemi, A. et al. (2005). Brain correlates of sentence translation in Finnish–Norwegian bilinguals. *NeuroReport* 16 (6): 607–610. doi:10.1097/00001756-200504250-00018.

Lesh, T.A., Westphal, A.J., Niendam, T.A. et al. (2013). Proactive and reactive cognitive control and dorsolateral prefrontal cortex dysfunction in first episode schizophrenia. *NeuroImage: Clinical* 2: 590–599. doi:10.1016/j.nicl.2013.04.010.

Levelt, W.E.M. (1989). *Speaking: From Intention to Articulation*. Cambridge, MA: MIT Press.

Levy, D., Coleman, M., Sung, H. et al. (2010). The genetic basis of thought disorder and language and communication disturbances in schizophrenia. *Journal of Neurolinguistics* 23 (3): 176–192. doi:10.1016/j.jneuroling.2009.08.003.

Li, X., Branch, C.A., Ardekani, B.A. et al. (2007). fMRI study of language activation in schizophrenia, schizoaffective disorder and in individuals genetically at high risk. *Schizophrenia Research* 96 (1): 14–24. doi:10.1016/j.schres.2007.07.013.

Li, J., Wu, C., Zheng, Y. et al. (2017). Schizophrenia affects speech-induced functional connectivity of the superior temporal gyrus under cocktail-party listening conditions. *Neuroscience* 359: 248–257. doi:10.1016/j.neuroscience.2017.06.043.

Liddle, P.F., Friston, K.J., Frith, C.D. et al. (1992). Patterns of cerebral blood flow in schizophrenia. *The British Journal of Psychiatry* 160 (2): 179–186. doi:10.1192/bjp.160.2.179.

Liddle, P.F., Ngan, E.T., Caissie, S.L. et al. (2002). Thought and language index: an instrument for assessing thought and language in schizophrenia. *The British Journal of Psychiatry* 181 (4): 326–330. doi:10.1192/bjp.181.4.326.

Liu, X., Zhuo, C., Qin, W. et al. (2016). Selective functional connectivity abnormality of the transition zone of the inferior parietal lobule in schizophrenia. *NeuroImage: Clinical* 11: 789–795. doi:10.1016/j.nicl.2016.05.021.

Luk, G., Green, D.W., Abutalebi, J., and Grady, C. (2012). Cognitive control for language switching in bilinguals: a quantitative meta-analysis on functional neuroimaging studies. *Language & Cognitive Processes* 27: 1479–1488. doi:10.1080/01690965.2011.613209.

Mahon, M. and Crutchley, A. (2006). Performance of typically-developing school-age children with English as an additional language on the British Picture Vocabulary Scales II. *Child Language Teaching and Therapy* 22 (3): 333–351. doi:10.1191/0265659006ct311xx.

Majerus, S., D'Argembeau, A., Martinez Perez, T. et al. (2010). The commonality of neural networks for verbal and visual short-term memory. *Journal of Cognitive Neuroscience* 22 (11): 2570–2593. doi:10.1162/jocn.2009.21378.

Mamah, D., Wang, L., Barch, D. et al. (2007). Structural analysis of the basal ganglia in schizophrenia. *Schizophrenia Research* 89 (1): 59–71. doi:10.1016/j.schres.2006.08.031.

Mariën, P., Ackermann, H., Adamaszek, M. et al. (2014). Consensus paper: language and the cerebellum: an ongoing enigma. *The Cerebellum* 13 (3): 386–410. doi:10.1007/s12311-013-0540-5.

Marini, A., Spoletini, I., Rubino, I.A. et al. (2008). The language of schizophrenia: an analysis of micro and macro-linguistic abilities and their neuropsychological correlates. *Schizophrenia Research* 105: 144–155. doi:10.1016/j.schres.2008.07.011.

Marini, A., Urgesi, C., and Fabbro, F. (2012). Clinical neurolinguistics of bilingualism. *The Handbook of the Neuropsychology of Language* 1 (2): 738–759.

Martin-Rhee, M.M. and Bialystok, E. (2008). The development of two types of inhibitory control in monolingual and bilingual children. *Bilingualism: Language and Cognition* 11: 81–93. doi:10.1017/s1366728907003227.

Marvel, C.L., Schwartz, B.L., and Isaacs, K.L. (2004). Word production deficits in schizophrenia. *Brain and Language* 89: 182–191. doi:10.1016/S0093-934X(03)00366-3.

Mathalon, D.H., Fedor, M., Faustman, W.O. et al. (2002). Response-monitoring dysfunction in schizophrenia: an event-related brain potential study. *Journal of Abnormal Psychology* 111 (1): 22–41. doi:10.1037/0021-843X.111.1.22.

Matsumoto, H., Simmons, A., Williams, S., and Hadjulis, M. (2001). Superior temporal gyrus abnormalities in early-onset schizophrenia: similarities and differences with adult-onset schizophrenia. *The American Journal of Psychiatry* 158 (8): 1299–1304. doi:10.1176/appi.ajp.158.8.1299.

Matulis, A.C. (1977). Schizophrenia: experiment in teaching a new foreign language to inpatients as an analeptic ego aid. *Dynamische Psychiatrie* 10: 459–472.

Mazza, M., Di Michele, V., Pollice, R. et al. (2008). Pragmatic language and theory of mind deficits in people with schizophrenia and their relatives. *Psychopathology* 41 (4): 254–263. doi:10.1159/000128324.

McGrath, J., Saha, S., Chant, D., and Welham, J. (2008). Schizophrenia: a concise overview of incidence, prevalence, and mortality. *Epidemiologic Reviews* 30 (1): 67–76. doi:10.1093/epirev/mxn001.

McKay, A.P., McKenna, P.J., Bentham, P. et al. (1996). Semantic memory is impaired in schizophrenia. *Biological Psychiatry* 39 (11): 929–937. doi:10.1016/0006-3223(95)00250-2.

McKenna, P.J. (1994). *Schizophrenia and Related Syndromes*. Oxford, UK: Oxford University Press.

McKenna, P.J. and Oh, T.M. (2005). *Schizophrenic speech: Making Sense of Bathroots and Ponds that Fall in Doorways*. Cambridge, UK: Cambridge University Press.

Mechelli, A., Crinion, J., Noppeney, U. et al. (2004). Neurolinguistics: structural plasticity in the bilingual brain. *Nature* 431 (7010): 757. doi:10.1038/431757a.

Menon, V., Anagnoson, R., Glover, G., and Pfefferbaum, A. (2001). Functional magnetic resonance imaging evidence for disrupted basal ganglia function in schizophrenia. *The American Journal of Psychiatry* 158 (4): 646–649. doi:10.1176/appi.ajp.158.4.646.

Miller, D.D., Arndt, S., and Andreasen, N.C. (1993). Alogia, attentional impairment, and inappropriate affect: their status in the dimensions of schizophrenia. *Comprehensive Psychiatry* 34 (4): 221–226. doi:10.1016/0010-440X(93)90002-L.

Miyake, A., Friedman, N.P., Emerson, M.J. et al. (2000). The unity and diversity of executive functions and their contributions to complex "frontal lobe" tasks: a latent variable analysis. *Cognitive Psychology* 41 (1): 49–100. doi:10.1006/cogp.1999.0734.

Morgan, V.A., McGrath, J.J., Jablensky, A. et al. (2014). Psychosis prevalence and physical, metabolic and cognitive co-morbidity: data from the second Australian national survey of psychosis. *Psychological Medicine* 44 (10): 2163–2176. doi:10.1017/S0033291713002973.

Morice, R. and Mcnicol, D. (1986). Language changes in schizophrenia: a limited replication. *Schizophrenia Bulletin* 12 (2): 239–251. doi:10.1093/schbul/12.2.239.

Nuechterlein, K.H. and Green, M.F. (2006). *MATRICS Consensus Cognitive Battery Manual*. Los Angeles, CA: MATRICS Assessment.

Oertel-Knöchel, V., Knöchel, C., Matura, S. et al. (2012). Cortical–basal ganglia imbalance in schizophrenia patients and unaffected first-degree relatives. *Schizophrenia Research* 138 (2–3): 121–127. doi:10.1016/j.schres.2012.02.029.

Oertel-Knöchel, V. and Linden, D. (2011). Cerebral asymmetry in schizophrenia. *The Neuroscientist* 17 (5): 456–467. doi:10.1177/1073858410386493.

Oh, T.M., McCarthy, R.A., and McKenna, P.J. (2002). Is there a schizophasia? A study applying the single case approach to formal thought disorder in schizophrenia. *Neurocase* 8 (2): 233–244.

Ou, J., Lyu, H., Hu, M. et al. (2016). Decreased white matter FA values in the left inferior frontal gyrus is a possible intermediate phenotype of schizophrenia: evidences from a novel group strategy. *European Archives of Psychiatry and Clinical Neuroscience* 1–10. doi:10.1007/s00406-016-0752-z.

Palaniyappan, L. and Liddle, P.F. (2012). Does the salience network play a cardinal role in psychosis? An emerging hypothesis of insular dysfunction. *Journal of Psychiatry & Neuroscience* 37 (1): 17–27. doi:10.1007/s00406-012-0314-y.

Pantelis, C., Velakoulis, D., Wood, S. et al. (2007). Neuroimaging and emerging psychotic disorders: the Melbourne ultra-high risk studies. *International Review of Psychiatry* 19 (4): 371–379. doi:10.1080/09540260701512079.

Paradis, M. (2004). *A Neurolinguistic Theory of Bilingualism*. Amsterdam, The Netherlands: John Benjamins.

Paradis, M. (2008). Bilingualism and neuropsychiatric disorders. *Journal of Neurolinguistics* 21 (3): 199–230. doi:10.1016/j.jneuroling.2007.09.002.

Parker Jones, '.Ō, Green, D.W., Grogan, A. et al. (2012). Where, when and why brain activation differs for bilinguals and monolinguals during picture naming and reading aloud. *Cerebral Cortex* 22: 892–902. doi:10.1093/cercor/bhr161.

Paulus, M.P., Hozack, N.E., Zauscher, B.E. et al. (2002). Parietal dysfunction is associated with increased outcome-related decision-making in schizophrenia patients. *Biological Psychiatry* 51 (12): 995–1004. doi:10.1016/S0006-3223(01)01358-0.

Pickup, G.J. and Frith, C.D. (2001). Theory of mind impairments in schizophrenia: symptomatology, severity and specificity. *Psychological Medicine* 31: 207–220. doi:10.1017/S0033291701003385.

Pliatsikas, C., Johnstone, T., and Marinis, T. (2014). Grey matter volume in the cerebellum is related to the processing of grammatical rules in a second language: a structural voxel-based morphometry study. *The Cerebellum* 13 (1): 55–63.

Pomarol-Clotet, E., Oh, T., Laws, K., and Mckenna, P. (2008). Semantic priming in schizophrenia: systematic review and meta-analysis. *The British Journal of Psychiatry* 192 (2): 92–97. doi:10.1192/bjp.bp.106.032102.

Portocarrero, J.S., Burright, R.G., and Donovick, P.J. (2007). Vocabulary and verbal fluency of bilingual and monolingual college students. *Archives of Clinical Neuropsychology* 22 (3): 415–422. doi:10.1016/j.acn.2007.01.015.

Pousa, E., Duñó, R., Brébion, G. et al. (2008). Theory of mind deficits in chronic schizophrenia: evidence for state dependence. *Psychiatry Research* 158 (1): 1–10. doi:10.1016/j.psychres.2006.05.018.

Puri, B., Counsell, S., Saeed, N. et al. (2010). Regional grey matter volumetric changes in forensic schizophrenia patients: a magnetic resonance imaging study comparing the brain structure of patients who have seriously and violently offended with those of patients who have not. *Annals of General Psychiatry* 9 (1): S154. doi:10.1186/1744-859X-9-S1-S154.

Radanovic, M., Sousa, R.T.D., Valiengo, L. et al. (2013). Formal thought disorder and language impairment in schizophrenia. *Arquivos de Neuro-Psiquiatria* 71 (1): 55–60. doi: 10.1590/S004-282x2012005000015.

Ransdell, S.E. and Fischler, I. (1987). Memory in a monolingual mode: when are bilinguals at a disadvantage? *Journal of Memory and Language* 26 (4): 392–405. doi:10.1016/0749-596X(87)90098-2.

Reichenberg, A. and Harvey, P.D. (2007). Neuropsychological impairments in schizophrenia: integration of performance-based and brain imaging findings. *Psychological Bulletin* 133 (5): 833. doi: 10.1037/0033-2909.133.5.833.

Reid, M., Stoeckel, L., White, D. et al. (2010). Assessments of function and biochemistry of the anterior cingulate cortex in schizophrenia. *Biological Psychiatry* 68 (7): 625–633. doi:10.1016/j.biopsych.2010.04.013.

Reilly, J., Harris, M., Khine, T. et al. (2008). Reduced attentional engagement contributes to deficits in prefrontal inhibitory control in schizophrenia. *Biological Psychiatry* 63 (8): 776–783. doi:10.1016/j.biopsych.2007.11.009.

Roberts, R., Barksdale, K., Roche, J., and Lahti, A. (2015). Decreased synaptic and mitochondrial density in the postmortem anterior cingulate cortex in schizophrenia. *Schizophrenia Research* 168 (1–2): 543–553. doi:10.1016/j.schres.2015.07.016.

Rodriguez-Ferrera, S., McCarthy, R.A., and McKenna, P.J. (2001). Language in schizophrenia and its relationship to formal thought disorder. *Psychological Medicine* 31 (2): 197–205.

Rosselli, M., Ardila, A., Araujo, K. et al. (2000). Verbal fluency and repetition skills in healthy older Spanish-English bilinguals. *Applied Neuropsychology* 7 (1): 17–24.

Rubio-Fernández, P. and Glucksberg, S. (2012). Reasoning about other people's beliefs: Bilinguals have an advantage. *Journal of Experimental Psychology: Learning, Memory, and Cognition* 38 (1): 211–217.

Sandoval, T.C., Gollan, T.H., Ferreira, V.S., and Salmon, D.P. (2010). What causes the bilingual disadvantage in verbal fluency? The dual-task analogy. *Bilingualism: Language and Cognition* 13 (2): 231–252.

Searle, J. (1969). *Speech Acts: An Essay in the Philosophy of Language*. New York, NY: Cambridge University Press.

Seeman, M.V. (2016). Bilingualism and schizophrenia. *World Journal of Psychiatry* 6 (2): 192–198. doi:10.5498/wjp.v6.i2.192.

Semkovska, M. (2010). Agrammatism in a case of formal thought disorder: beyond intellectual decline and working memory deficit. *Neurocase* 16 (1): 37–49. doi: 10.1080/13554790903193208.

Silver, H., Feldman, P., Bilker, W., and Gur, R.C. (2003). Working memory deficit as a core neuropsychological dysfunction in schizophrenia. *American Journal of Psychiatry* 160 (10): 1809–1816. doi:10.1176/appi.ajp. 160.10.1809.

Silverberg-Shalev, R., Gordon, H.W., Bentin, S., and Aranson, A. (1981). Selective language deterioration in chronic schizophrenia. *Journal of Neurology, Neurosurgery & Psychiatry* 44 (6): 547–551.

Smirnova, D., Clark, M., Jablensky, A., and Badcock, J. (2017). Action (verb) fluency deficits in schizophrenia spectrum disorders: linking language, cognition and interpersonal functioning. *Psychiatry Research* 257: 203–211. doi:10.1016/j. psychres.2017.07.044.

Smirnova, D., Walters, J., Fine, J. et al. (2015). Second language as a compensatory resource for maintaining verbal fluency in bilingual immigrants with schizophrenia. *Neuropsychologia* 75: 597–606. doi:10.1016/j. neuropsychologia.2015.06.037.

Smit, M., Conradie, S., and Schoeman, R. (2011). A grammatical analysis of the spontaneous L2 English use of schizophrenic bilinguals compared to typical bilinguals. *Southern African Linguistics and Applied Language Studies* 29 (4): 505–513. doi:10.2989/16073614.2011. 651946.

Southwood, F., Schoeman, R., and Emsley, R. (2010). Bilingualism and psychosis: a linguistic analysis of a patient with differential symptom severity across languages. *Southern African Linguistics and Applied Language Studies* 27: 163–171.

Soveri, A., Laine, M., Hämäläinen, H., and Hugdahl, K. (2010). Bilingual advantage in attentional control: evidence from the forced-attention dichotic listening paradigm. *Bilingualism: Language and Cognition* 14: 371–378. doi:10.1017/ s1366728910000118.

Spitzer, M. (1993). The psychopathology, neuropsychology, and neurobiology of associative and working memory in schizophrenia. *European Archives of Psychiatry and Clinical Neuroscience* 243 (2): 57–70.

Stocco, A., Yamasaki, B., Natalenko, R., and Prat, C. (2014). Bilingual brain training: a neurobiological framework of how bilingual experience improves executive function. *International Journal of Bilingualism* 18 (1): 67–92. doi:10.1177/1367006912456617.

Sumiyoshi, C., Sumiyoshi, T., Nohara, S. et al. (2005). Disorganization of semantic memory underlies alogia in schizophrenia: an analysis of verbal fluency performance in Japanese subjects. *Schizophrenia Research* 74 (1): 91–100. doi:10.1016/j.schres.2004.05.011.

Theron, J., Conradie, S., and Schoeman, R. (2011). Pragmatic assessment of schizophrenic bilinguals' L1 and L2 use.

Southern African Linguistics and Applied Languages Studies 29: 515–531. doi:10.2989/16073614.2011.651948.

Thomas, P., King, K., Fraser, W.I., and Kendell, R.E. (1990). Linguistic performance in schizophrenia: a comparison of acute and chronic patients. *The British Journal of Psychiatry* 156 (2): 204–210. doi:10.1192/bjp.156.2.204.

Tikàsz, A., Potvin, S., Lungu, O. et al. (2016). Anterior cingulate hyperactivations during negative emotion processing among men with schizophrenia and a history of violent behavior. *Neuropsychiatric Disease and Treatment* 12: 1397–1410. doi:10.2147/NDT.S107545.

Torrey, E.F. (2007). Schizophrenia and the inferior parietal lobule. *Schizophrenia Research* 97 (1): 215–225. doi:10.1016/j.schres.2007.08.023.

Ullman, M.T. (2001). The neural basis of lexicon and grammar in first and second language: the declarative/procedural model. *Bilingualism: Language and Cognition* 4 (2): 105–122. doi:10.1017/S1366728901000220.

van Veelen, N.M., Vink, M., Ramsey, N.F., and Kahn, R.S. (2010). Left dorsolateral prefrontal cortex dysfunction in medication-naive schizophrenia. *Schizophrenia Research* 123 (1): 22–29. doi:10.1016/j.schres.2010.07.004.

Venkatasubramanian, G., Jayakumar, P.N., Keshavan, M.S., and Gangadhar, B.N. (2011). Schneiderian first rank symptoms and inferior parietal lobule cortical thickness in antipsychotic-naive schizophrenia. *Progress in Neuro-Psychopharmacology and Biological Psychiatry* 35 (1): 40–46. doi:10.1016/j.pnpbp.2010.07.023.

Videsott, G., Herrnberger, B., Hoenig, K. et al. (2010). Speaking in multiple languages: neural correlates of language proficiency in multilingual word production. *Brain and Language* 113 (3): 103–112. doi: 10.1016/j.bandl.2010.01.006.

Vogel, A.P., Chenery, H.J., Dart, C.M. et al. (2009). Verbal fluency, semantics, context and symptom complexes in schizophrenia. *Journal of Psycholinguistic Research* 38 (5): 459–473.

Vukadinovic, Z. (2014). NMDA receptor hypofunction and the thalamus in schizophrenia. *Physiology & Behavior* 131: 156–159.

Walder, D.J., Seidman, L.J., Cullen, N. et al. (2006). Sex differences in language dysfunction in schizophrenia. *The American Journal of Psychiatry* 163 (3): 470–477.

Walther, S., Federspiel, A., Horn, H. et al. (2011). Resting state cerebral blood flow and objective motor activity reveal basal ganglia dysfunction in schizophrenia. *Psychiatry Research: Neuroimaging* 192 (2): 117–124.

Wang, Y.G., Shi, J.F., Roberts, D.L. et al. (2015). Theory-of-mind use in remitted schizophrenia patients: the role of inhibition and perspective-switching. *Psychiatry Research* 229 (1): 332–339.

World Health Organization (1993). *The ICD-10 Classification of Mental and Behavioural Disorders. Diagnostic Criteria for Research*. Geneva, Switzerland: World Health Organization.

Yeganeh-Doost, P., Gruber, O., Falkai, P., and Schmitt, A. (2011). The role of the cerebellum in schizophrenia: from cognition to molecular pathways. *Clinics* 66 (1): 71–77.

Zhang, L., Li, B., Wang, H. et al. (2017). Decreased middle temporal gyrus connectivity in the language network in schizophrenia patients with auditory verbal hallucinations. *Neuroscience Letters* 653: 177–182.

Part V Cognitive and Neurocognitive Consequences

32 Neurocognitive Effects of Multilingualism Throughout the Lifespan

A Developmental Perspective

HANNAH L. CLAUSSENIUS-KALMAN
AND ARTURO E. HERNANDEZ

1. Introduction

Plasticity and cognitive flexibility are paramount to the acquisition of multiple languages (Krizman and Marian 2015; Prior and Gollan 2011). Plasticity is the capacity of the cortex to reorganize its connections in response to perceptual, cognitive, and/or motor skill learning (Buonomano and Merzenich 1998). Early in development, high plasticity (especially of subcortical structures) may make the brain more reliably receptive to learning language (Fernandez-Coello et al. 2017; Hernandez and Li 2007). Research shows that multilinguals with an early age of acquisition (AoA) for their second language (L2) have more homogeneous brain activation in each of their three languages compared with those who acquired their L2 later in life (Bloch et al. 2009; Fernandez-Coello et al. 2017). Those who acquired their L2 later have more individual variability in processing of second and third languages, suggesting that individual differences play a larger role in late multilinguals. Therefore, the neurocognitive effects of multilingualism are best understood by examining individual differences.

One of the most widely discussed topics regarding the effects of multilingualism is its connection to increased executive function (Bialystok 2009; Dong and Li 2015; Green and Abutalebi 2013). However, multilingualism is a diverse variable that can take many shapes and does not necessarily lead to one set of effects. Instead, the effects are constrained by multiple factors that ultimately depend on cognitive flexibility (Green and Abutalebi 2013; Prior and Gollan 2011; Yim and Bialystok 2012; Yudes et al. 2011) and plasticity (Golestani and Pallier 2007; Sheppard et al. 2012; Ventura-Campos et al. 2013; Xiang et al. 2012).

The Handbook of the Neuroscience of Multilingualism, First Edition. Edited by John W. Schwieter.
© 2019 John Wiley & Sons Ltd. Published 2019 by John Wiley & Sons Ltd.

Some argue that practice with switching between languages leads to increased cognitive flexibility (Abutalebi and Green 2007), which is defined as the ability to switch between and adapt to changed circumstances (Diamond 2013). Although many have found an association between these two variables, it is not clear which comes first. It is possible that people who turn out to be bilingual may do so *because* they have higher cognitive control and cognitive flexibility, not as an effect of it (Li and Grant 2016). Genetic background may explain differences in language-use habits that relate to cognitive flexibility, such as code switching (Cools and D'Esposito 2011; Green and Abutalebi 2013; Hernandez et al. 2015; Stelzel et al. 2010; Vaughn et al. 2016). This suggests that people who are naturally better at switching might have an easier time dealing with the demands of a bilingual environment (Festman et al. 2010).

Additionally, while experiential factors (e.g. AoA, native language proficiency, and musical training) are known to affect L2 proficiency (Johnson and Newport 1989), evidence from studies of foreign language learning in adult monolinguals suggests that differences in neuroplasticity can predict language learning success (Archila-Suerte et al. 2015; Chai et al. 2016; Golestani et al. 2007; Mårtensson et al. 2012; Stein et al. 2014). This is especially true of plasticity in the auditory system (Krizman and Marian 2015). Because research on the neural bases of proficiency in bilinguals and multilinguals has mostly been correlational, this research leads us to consider the possibility that pre-existing neural differences can play a role in determining multilingual outcomes.

An understanding of individual differences in plasticity and cognitive flexibility is necessary in order to grasp the neurocognitive effects of multilingualism. Therefore, this chapter will begin by discussing the reason that AoA (which is deeply connected to plasticity) matters for multilingualism. It will then discuss the role of individual differences in determining multilingual outcomes within two foci: a genetic basis for cognitive flexibility and code switching; and how plasticity affects bilingual proficiency and adult foreign language learning success. Next, AoA and individual differences will be discussed in regards to hyperpolyglots. Finally, effects of multilingualism will be discussed within the constraints of individual differences, focusing on executive control, neuroprotective effects seen in older adults, and disadvantages and challenges.

2.   Age of Acquisition Matters for Multilingualism

Given that cortical representations are modified by experience (Buonomano and Merzenich 1998) it follows that neuroplasticity is necessary for the successful acquisition of any skill. When an L2 is acquired early, high neuroplasticity, especially of subcortical structures, may make the brain more reliably receptive to learning multiple languages (Fernandez-Coello et al. 2017; Hernandez and Li 2007). AoA is a strong predictor of bilingual proficiency, where early AoA is related to higher L2 proficiency (Flege et al. 1999; Granena and Long 2013; Johnson and Newport 1989; Piske et al. 2001; Trofimovich and Baker 2006). Because of this, some have argued for a critical period for language (e.g. Scovel 1988). However, this idea is debated because it implies a concrete cut-off point after which a skill cannot be learned (Knudsen 2004). With this said, many researchers would agree that there is at least a sensitive period during which the brain seems to be more receptive to language learning the earlier that exposure begins (Abrahamsson and Hyltenstam 2009; Granena and Long 2013). Furthermore, some domains (e.g. auditory perception, pronunciation, and grammar) have emerged as more sensitive to AoA than others (vocabulary; Scovel 1988; Weber-Fox and Neville 1999). The increased plasticity seen in early development is essential to learning multiple languages to a highly proficient level.

Because AoA is strongly associated with degree of foreign accent (Abrahamsson and Hyltenstam 2009; Flege and MacKay 2004; Granena and Long 2013; Piske et al. 2001), the earlier the AoA, the better the chance of mastering both languages with native-like accent (Flege et al. 1999). One driving factor in the association between AoA and L2 performance is that phonological abilities are most sensitive in infancy, but decline with age (Petitto et al. 2012; Piske et al. 2001). Research shows that infants are able to perceive differences between speech sounds from any foreign language that would not normally be perceivable by adults and that early bilingualism may allow this sensitive period to stay open longer, thereby serving as a perceptual wedge that allows for learning of additional languages (Petitto et al. 2012). The ability to produce native-like accent – a reflection of phonological perception – is better for those who acquired their L2 between 3 and 6 compared with those who acquired it between 7 and 15. For those who acquired their L2 after age 16, native-like accent production flattens out rather than continuing to decline (Granena and Long 2013). This is one reason that mastering a foreign accent is difficult for many adult foreign language learners: They must learn to produce sounds that they never dealt with as infants or children (Zhang et al. 2000).

Other language domains are affected differently by AoA (Neville et al. 1992). Syntactic processing (along with phonological perception and production) has an earlier sensitive period than semantic processing (Johnson and Newport 1989; Tokowicz and Macwhinney 2005; Weber-Fox and Neville 1999). Syntactic processing has not been found to be significantly better or worse as long as the AoA is earlier than age three (Weber-Fox and Neville 1999), but after this point implicit knowledge of syntax tends to rely on the first language (L1; Tokowicz and Macwhinney 2005). Meanwhile, differences in semantic processing performance only appear when the AoA is later than age 11 (Weber-Fox and Neville 1999). This is in line with the fact that even though children learn vocabulary at an accelerated rate, many adults continue augmenting their vocabulary throughout their entire lifetime (Nagy and Scott 2000).

It is possible that introducing more than one language during infancy extends the sensitive period for language (Petitto et al. 2012). Young infants up to the age of nine months old are able to discern between phonetic contrasts from any language, whether they have been exposed to that language before or not. Interesting enough, this is not the case for adults, who have difficulty distinguishing between speech sounds outside of their native language (Zhang et al. 2000). Petitto et al. (2012) used functional near-infrared spectroscopy (fNIRS), a neuroimaging technique that works by measuring blood oxygen levels, to test 34 bilingual and 27 monolingual babies between 2 and 16 months in an event-related design as they processed phonetic stimuli. The stimuli included native sounds, non-native sounds (taken from Hindi), and non-linguistic tones. They found that all infants had activation in the left superior temporal gyrus (STG) when listening to both native and non-native sounds and that this activation was greater for linguistic stimuli than musical tones. In addition, both the younger bilingual and younger monolingual infants showed similar left inferior frontal cortex (IFC) activation in response to linguistic stimuli. However, this was not the case for the older monolingual infants. While older (12-month-old) bilingual infants showed the same left IFC activation in response to native and non-native sounds, older monolingual infants showed greater left IFC activation only in response to speech sounds from their native language. In other words, at the age at which monolingual infants began to specialize to the needs of their own language, bilingual infants were still receptive to sounds from any language.

Based on these results, Petitto et al. (2012) suggested the perceptual wedge hypothesis. This hypothesis posits that while monolingual input results in sensitivity to that language, bilingual input may act as a "perceptual wedge" that allows for a lengthened period of plasticity in which the infant retains the ability to distinguish between sounds from any language. When the monolingual infant brain begins to prune away less-useful neural connections in favour of the more salient ones, the bilingual infant brain seems to maintain some of its neuroplasticity to deal with the demands of more diverse phonological input.

Although this sensitive period begins to diminish within the first year of life, there is evidence that this process is reversible for monolingual infants. Kuhl et al. (2003) took a group of nine-month olds who had been raised in a monolingual English environment and exposed them to Mandarin Chinese. At the end of 12 sessions, the infants were given a phonetic perception test. The infants who had interacted with a live Mandarin speaker performed as well as native Mandarin-speaking infants and did better than a control group that had been exposed to English instead of Mandarin for the 12 sessions. However, infants who were exposed to Mandarin via audio-visual input or solely auditory input demonstrated no phonetic learning. Thus, with sufficient personal interaction in a non-native language, it is possible for infants to regain phonetic perception at a level comparable to infants raised in that language from birth. The development of language skills begins at a time when the brain demonstrates plasticity to new sounds. This effect can rarely be replicated later in development or adulthood (Zhang et al. 2000). Thus, the type of input to which we are exposed in infancy may lay the groundwork for how we approach and integrate language-related information throughout the lifespan (Klein et al. 2014).

Indeed, research shows that the age at which a previous language was learned affects how new languages are represented in the brain (Bloch et al. 2009; Bradley et al. 2013; Dehaene et al. 1997; Fernandez-Coello et al. 2017). Bloch et al. (2009) compared the brain activation of multilinguals speaking in each of their three languages in order to test how age of L2 acquisition affects the cerebral representation of a third language (L3). They divided their participant group into simultaneous bilinguals (who had been exposed to their L2 since birth and acquired the L3 after age nine), sequential bilinguals (who had an L2 AoA between one and five years and acquired the L3 after age nine), and late bilinguals (with a L2 and L3 AoA later than age nine). They found that as AoA increased, so did individual variation of cerebral activation. Simultaneous bilinguals showed the lowest amount of individual variability in activation. Brain activation in all three of their languages was associated with regions traditionally linked to language production and comprehension: left Broca's and bilateral Wernicke's areas. Sequential bilinguals showed more variability in degree of activation in these areas, with late bilinguals showing the highest amount of variability. Late bilinguals had less homogeneous activation in their L2 and L3, with stronger activation in the basal ganglia and bilateral Broca's and Wernicke's areas. One interpretation of this result is that early exposure to two languages leads to the implementation of a language network that is able not only to maintain those two languages, but to facilitate the use of a third language. For the late bilinguals, more widespread activation may indicate an increased workload, which would require recruitment of areas outside of the language network. The particular areas they recruit are more subject to individual variability (Bloch et al. 2009).

Similarly, experimental evidence shows that experience with multiple languages may lead to more efficient learning of new languages (Bradley et al. 2013). Adult bilinguals and monolinguals, none of whom had experience with German, were asked to learn 100 German nouns and then make semantic judgments about the words in an MRI scanner. Not only did the bilinguals have faster reaction times than the monolinguals, but they showed differential brain activation. The monolinguals showed more activity in areas associated with higher-level cognition (right dorsolateral prefrontal cortex [DLPFC], left caudate, and right supplementary motor area [SMA]) and language control (left anterior cingulate cortex [ACC]). The bilinguals showed higher activation in the right putamen, which is associated with phonological and articulatory processes (Abutalebi et al. 2013). The authors interpreted this to mean that the bilinguals' previous experience managing multiple languages prepared them to rely on motor-based control, instead of higher-level cognitive processes, in order to more efficiently process the new vocabulary.

In sum, language experience gained early in life appears to affect future language processing and performance. When two languages are introduced early in life, the neural substrates related to phonological processing, phonological production, and syntactic processing are in a more malleable state (Chechik et al. 1998) that allows them to accommodate both languages. Language development proceeds in tandem with the development of the cerebral cortex (Sakai 2005), which is one reason that better L2 performance is associated with earlier AoA. The cerebral representation of later-acquired (L3 or beyond) languages, therefore, is affected by the age at which the L2 was acquired. Late bilinguals tend to show less homogeneous brain activation when speaking than early and simultaneous bilinguals, suggesting that adding an L2 later in life leads to more recruitment of areas outside of the language network in order to process additional languages. The high plasticity seen in early development is crucial to the language development process, and as AoA increases, individual differences become more important in determining language outcomes.

3. The Role of Individual Differences in Multilingual Outcomes

Language-use habits and proficiency levels have been associated with differences in cognitive flexibility and plasticity (Festman et al. 2010; Wong et al. 2007). These factors may be neurally and genetically influenced (Mosing et al. 2014; Vaughn et al. 2016;

Wong et al. 2012). Therefore, this section will discuss how differences in plasticity may affect proficiency and adult foreign language learning success, which will be followed by a discussion of a genetic basis for cognitive flexibility and code-switching preferences.

3.1.   *Plasticity*

Cortical representations are modified by experience (Buonomano and Merzenich 1998), and early development sees a period of heightened neuroplasticity compared to late development (Chechik et al. 1998). This is one reason that early AoA is associated with higher proficiency and more homogeneous brain activation across languages (e.g. Flege et al. 1999), but another means through which high plasticity can be achieved is that of individual differences. This section will discuss the neural correlates of bilingual proficiency, as well as evidence indicating that high plasticity, especially in the auditory system, is conducive to foreign language learning success in those who did not learn a foreign language early.

3.1.1.   The Link Between Proficiency and Plasticity   Experience-dependent factors, such as AoA (Flege et al. 1999), socioeconomic status, immigration timing (Mutchler and Brallier 1999), native language proficiency (Sparks et al. 2006), and musical training (Jäncke 2012) are all thought to affect language proficiency, but it may be the case that some people are better predisposed to language learning than others (Rueda et al. 2005; Vaughn et al. 2016; Wong et al. 2007). Even in environments that require use of both languages, some bilinguals still tend to favour one language more than the other (Grosjean and Li 2012). This suggests that environment may not fully account for proficiency.

Multilingualism is often assumed to be a product of environment in which multilingual input results in a multilingual child, but proficiency can vary significantly between individuals. One reason for this variation is that language proficiency can have more than one definition. For instance, an individual could have high cognitive/academic language proficiency (CALP, which refers to language relevant to the academic setting and is associated with academic achievement) but have lower basic interpersonal communication skills (BICS, which are the conversational skills that native speakers generally develop in childhood and are independent of academic achievement; Cummins 1979). By these metrics, even monolinguals vary in proficiency in their own language (Austin 2007). This is important because what is considered proficient by some standards may not always constitute high academic achievement (Cummins 1979).

Introducing multilingualism into the picture adds the topic of balance between languages. Whereas some multilinguals demonstrate high proficiency in two languages (balanced bilinguals), others favour one language over the other (unbalanced bilinguals; De Groot 2011). For multilinguals who may speak anywhere between three and 60 (or more) languages, balance may range considerably. Those who speak a high number of languages may have high proficiency in a few core languages and basic conversational skills in other languages (Erard 2012).

Language processing may differ between balanced and unbalanced bilinguals. Archila-Suerte et al. (2016) suggest that unbalanced bilingual children recruit brain regions more closely associated with attention, working memory, and error monitoring when processing L2 speech sounds, whereas balanced bilingual children simply rely on sensory areas. In a study by Archila-Suerte et al. (2013), unbalanced bilingual children taking part in a passive listening task showed increased activation in the left inferior frontal gyrus (IFG), bilateral middle frontal gyrus (MFG), bilateral anterior cingulate gyrus, and bilateral SMA. Balanced bilingual children showed increased activity in the right middle temporal gyrus, a lexico-semantic processing area. Unbalanced bilinguals seemed to rely on higher-order executive function frontal areas in order to make sense of the L2 speech sounds.

Previous experience handling multiple languages is associated with differing processing of novel sounds. Specifically, early bilinguals, late bilinguals, and monolinguals process sounds differently in the brain (Klein et al. 2014; Mechelli et al. 2004). For example, the perception of novel phonemes derived from English sounds was more strongly associated with activation of the bilateral STG in participants who were exposed to just one language during childhood (monolinguals and late bilinguals) than participants who had two languages in childhood (early bilinguals; Archila-Suerte et al. 2015). Additionally, late bilinguals relative to early bilinguals and monolinguals showed more activity in the bilateral rolandic operculum, which is a pre-motor area that allows for sub-vocal rehearsal (Li et al. 2012) and auditory processing (Koelsch et al. 2006). This suggests that late bilinguals may make use of subvocal rehearsal within the phonological loop in order to track speech sounds. Early bilinguals, on the other hand, showed more activation in the right middle frontal gyrus (MFG), which includes the right DLPFC and has been implicated in working memory, task-switching, and cognitive control. Therefore, the authors suggested that early bilinguals were able to use a more efficient top-down processing system to make sense of the sounds, while late bilinguals relied on L1 areas.

Multilingualism has been consistently connected to structural changes within the auditory system. One example is the inferior parietal cortex, which encompasses the supramarginal gyrus (SMG) and angular gyrus and is thought to be involved in phonological storage, lexical acquisition, and integrating auditory perception with motor production, possibly due to its connections with the primary auditory cortex (Jonides et al. 1998). For instance, Mechelli et al. (2004) found that bilinguals had higher grey matter density in the left inferior parietal cortex (IPC) than monolinguals, that this effect was stronger in early bilinguals than late bilinguals, and that increased IPC density was related to higher L2 proficiency. Activation of this area has also been associated with passive listening in bilingual compared to monolingual children (Archila-Suerte et al. 2013) and verbal fluency tasks (Perani et al. 2003). It has been suggested that increases in this region reflect increases in vocabulary size, an idea which is supported by research showing that multilinguals have higher grey matter density in the right posterior SMG than bilinguals (Grogan et al. 2012). Based on these studies, it is possible that either high proficiency results in changes to the left IPC, or people with greater grey matter density in this area are more easily able to achieve high proficiency.

3.1.2. Plasticity and Foreign Language Learning Success One problem with investigating the relationship between proficiency and brain activity in bilinguals is that it is difficult to discern which came first; does balanced use of two or more languages cause neural changes, or do individual differences cause better language learning? One way to determine causality here is by examining experiments of language learning that track how the brain changes throughout the process of foreign language acquisition. These studies show that plasticity in certain neural structures can be used to predict language learning success (Chai et al. 2016; Veroude et al. 2010).

Because learning to speak first requires listening, accurate phonological perception is one of the most important aspects of language learning. This poses a special problem for adult foreign language learners who tend to lack the highly plastic auditory processing system they once had as infants (Abrahamsson and Hyltenstam 2009; Granena and Long 2013; Johnson and Newport 1989; Kuhl et al. 2003; Petitto et al. 2012; Piske et al. 2001). Learning speech sounds is a different process for children than it is for adults (Saffran et al. 1996). While adult foreign language learning has been associated with changes to the STG and IFG (Mårtensson et al. 2012), children may be able to make use of virtually the entire auditory system, which is still in the process of development. In fact, the process of phonological attenuation to a native language may begin even before birth (Mampe et al. 2009). The cries of three- to five-day-old infants are distinguishable based on the language that was spoken around them while they were still in the womb (Mampe et al. 2009). fNIRS studies have shown that the left STG can respond to phonetic change in five-day-old infants (Imada et al. 2006). As the child develops, the language processing system will form a network that includes the STG (containing the primary auditory cortex and Wernicke's area), Broca's area (consisting of the pars triangularis and pars opercularis in the IFG), arcuate fasciculus connecting Broca's area to Wernicke's area, primary motor cortex, SMG, angular gyrus, and the rolandic operculum (Bear et al. 2007).

Even so, plenty of adults are capable of attaining foreign language fluency. The child brain is *more* plastic, but it is not the case that the adult phonological system cannot adapt at all. Longitudinal research shows that changes to the auditory system in the left STG and IFG are important for adult monolinguals to have success learning a foreign language (Mårtensson et al. 2012). This suggests that these areas maintain a certain amount of plasticity throughout adulthood and that changes to these areas are necessary for successful foreign language acquisition.

Individual differences in the auditory system may facilitate language learning (Golestani and Pallier 2007). As part of the primary auditory cortex, Heschl's gyrus plays a key role in accurate auditory perception of foreign sounds (Liegeois-Chauvel et al. 1991). Faster learning of non-native speech sounds is associated with higher white matter density in left Heschl's gyrus (Golestani et al. 2007) and higher activation in right Heschl's gyrus is associated with Japanese speakers' ability to discriminate between the English phonemes /ra/ and /la/ (Raizada et al. 2010). Additionally, accurate reproduction of foreign sounds has been associated with higher white matter density in the bilateral IPC, left insula, and left prefrontal cortex (PFC), which have been implicated in articulation and phonological working memory (Golestani and Pallier 2007). Finally, successful learners of pitch patterns that occur in tonal languages show increased activation in the left posterior superior temporal region post-training, whereas less-successful learners show higher activation in the right superior temporal region, right IFG, and frontal areas (Wong et al. 2007). Together, these results imply that changes to the auditory system are conducive for adult foreign language acquisition.

The notion that pre-existing individual differences affect learning outcomes is evidenced by research showing that resting state functional connectivity (rs-FC) between areas predominantly associated with articulation and phonological rehearsal predicts post-training results (Chai et al. 2016; Ventura-Campos et al. 2013; Veroude et al. 2010). Chai et al. (2016) asked a group of monolingual adults to participate in a 12-week French immersion course. fMRI scans showed that L2 lexical retrieval (i.e. responding to a prompt orally in the recently learned foreign language for two minutes) was linked to connectivity between the left posterior STG and the left anterior insula/frontal operculum (AI/FO), which is thought to allow for articulatory planning (Price 2010). Additionally, those with greater rs-FC between the left AI/FO and left STG, as well as between the left AI/FO and the dorsal ACC, had better performance on post-learning assessments overall. Furthermore, Ventura-Campos et al. (2013) found that the ability to correctly distinguish nonnative (i.e. Hindi) sounds post-training was associated with greater rs-FC between the AI/FO and left superior parietal lobule (SPL), as well as an increase in activation in the left SMG. The authors suggested that the left AI/FO and left SPL form a left frontoparietal network that facilitates top-down processing.

Another study showed that Dutch participants who demonstrated greater perceptual sensitivity to a weather report in Chinese (as measured by being able to correctly categorize the Chinese words in a word recognition task) had stronger functional connectivity between areas associated with phonological rehearsal: the left SMA, pre-central gyrus, insula, and rolandic operculum (Veroude et al. 2010). The left SPL has been implicated in auditory selective attention (Koenigs et al. 2009). It is possible that learners and non-learners differed in recruitment of the speech motor system during perception, which was taken to mean that stronger functional connectivity between the above mentioned areas may be favourable to processing foreign sounds (Veroude et al. 2010).

Learning a foreign language in adulthood requires a certain set of changes to take place (see Stein et al. 2014, for review). Longitudinal studies show that neural activation changes throughout the duration of the language learning process. Grant et al. (2015) tracked a group of classroom Spanish L2 learners over two semesters. fMRI scans were conducted in the first semester (Time 1) and second semester (Time 2), during which participants were asked to take part in a lexical decision task. The researchers found that, at Time 1, participants had stronger connections between control areas (between the IFG and MFG) and between conflict monitoring areas (the feedback loop between the MFG, medial surface of the frontal gyrus, and ACC). However, at Time 2, participants showed stronger connections between areas that process semantics/meaning (MTG to IFG). Thus, in monolinguals, learning appears to require more control networks initially, and as learning continues, this progresses to semantic-based processing.

Additionally, measurements of whole-cortex brain connectivity have found that increased global efficiency in phonological and articulatory areas is associated with more successful language learning (Sheppard et al. 2012). Global and local efficiency are measures of functional organization, which is thought to be essential for higher-level cognition and must meet the opposing demands of cognitive function: distributed processing (global efficiency) and segregated processing (local efficiency). Sheppard et al. (2012) recorded participants' fMRI responses during an auditory pitch discrimination task. They were also asked to learn spoken words of an artificial language.

The most successful language learners were the participants who demonstrated increased global efficiency and reduced local efficiency during the auditory pitch discrimination task. Less-successful learners had more PFC activation during the pitch discrimination task, while more-successful learners had more global efficiency in the bilateral DLPFC and the entire left IFG. The latter group also showed increased global efficiency in areas associated with the dorsal auditory stream and regional decreases in areas associated with verbal working memory. These results fit with the findings by Bloch et al. (2009) that language representation in those with early AoA tends to be associated with traditional language areas such as the left IFG, while language representation in late AoA individuals may be represented by more diverse areas of the brain. It seems to be the case that plasticity of the phonological and articulatory system facilitates language learning.

A large group of studies on language learning in adults has focused on phonological sensitivity, but this is not the only aspect of language learning. Syntactic learning and vocabulary acquisition may also depend on neural differences. For instance, connections from the left IFG (which encompasses the left AI/FO) to the posterior temporal lobe may reflect syntactic learning ability, while connections from the left IFG to the parietal lobe may reflect vocabulary learning (Xiang et al. 2012). As research on foreign language learning success continues, it may be possible one day to use neuroimaging to predict future language learning success and thus fine-tune pedagogy methods to the individual.

3.1.3.   Unanswered Questions   While language learning can be studied through experiments in adults, it is more difficult to retroactively pull apart the relationship between bilingual proficiency and neural activation. Therefore, future experiments should investigate brain responses to language learning in groups with differing levels of language experience, including monolingual, bilingual, and multilingual participants, as well as those with differing AoA.

3.2.   Cognitive Flexibility

Although it is not completely clear what causes differences in plasticity, one factor that may influence language learning is genetic background. One example is that genes related to dopamine have been associated with cognitive flexibility (Vaughn et al. 2016), a domain which some researchers believe may be related to bilingual language experience with switching between languages (Abutalebi and Green 2007). Although many studies document an association between bilingualism and increased cognitive flexibility, this association gives rise to one question in particular: Does bilingualism facilitate cognitive flexibility, or are more cognitively flexible people better able to acquire two languages? While it has often been assumed that the former is the best explanation, it may be the case that while language habits are largely shaped by environmental factors, they are also constrained by genetic effects (Green and Abutalebi 2013).

3.2.1.   The Link Between Bilingualism and Cognitive Flexibility   Multilingualism requires the ability to switch between languages that each have their own sets of grammar, vocabulary, intonations, and acceptable expressions; this ability may relate to cognitive flexibility.

In a general sense, cognitive flexibility means being able to change thinking paradigms and adapt to new situations. It is often measured as the ability to maintain and switch between multiple mental concepts and rules (Diamond 2013). Evidence for a more cognitively flexible system in bilinguals appears as early as infancy. For instance, one study found that infants raised in a bilingual environment learned to redirect their gaze in response to changes in auditory or visual cues more readily than monolingual infants (Kovács and Mehler 2009). The authors posited that the bilinguals were better able to suppress their trained response in favour of an updated prediction because processing and dealing with the multiple representations of two languages strengthened a domain general executive control mechanism. This suggests that a bilingual environment may affect executive function even before babies learn to speak. This effect is thought to continue throughout the lifetime: bilinguals often outperform monolinguals on rule-switching tasks aimed at measuring cognitive flexibility (Prior and Macwhinney 2010; Yudes et al. 2011), although the notion that bilinguals have an advantage in such tasks is not undisputed (see Paap and Greenberg 2013 for review).

Abutalebi and Green (2007) propose that non-linguistic cognitive control facilitates bilingual language switching through a network that includes the PFC, IPC, ACC, and inhibitory and excitatory connections of the basal ganglia. For example, task switching (a category under which language switching falls) requires the ability to inhibit a response to the current task and initiate an updated response to the new task (Abutalebi and Green 2007). It has been suggested that the ACC detects this response conflict and alerts the PFC that greater control will be needed to handle the situation. Then the PFC, which represents and maintains the task demands, implements the basal ganglia (Cools and D'Esposito 2011; MacDonald et al. 2000). Within the basal ganglia, the putamen employs dopamine to control higher-order movement (Hall et al. 2013). The putamen may play an important role in language switching in particular, as direct electrical stimulation to this region can lead to slurred speech and difficulty articulating words (Robles et al. 2005). Additionally, the caudate nucleus and ACC together seem to play an important role in both language switching and perceiving languages switches by another speaker (Abutalebi et al. 2007). Whereas the ACC is implicated in detection of response conflict (Abutalebi et al. 2008), the caudate nucleus is involved in speech articulation, cognitive control, control of word interference (Ali et al. 2010), response selection, and control (Duffau et al. 2014; Robles et al. 2005) and sequence planning (Graybiel 2000). Overlap in the regions that underlie both task switching (MacDonald et al. 2000) and language switching (Wang et al. 2007) provides evidence for the possibility that extended experience with switching between languages may enhance cognitive control.

3.2.2. Code Switching: Experiential Considerations   While most bilinguals are required to switch between languages at some point, how often they switch is partially subject to individual differences. Code switching is when, either intentionally or unintentionally, the bilingual speaker mixes words of one language into the other language (Moreno et al. 2002). Certain experiences have been correlated with code-switching frequency, such as social demands (Green and Abutalebi 2013) and historical context of the two languages (Bentahila and Davies 1995). Linguistic factors that influence this tendency include grammatical constraints and feeling that a word in the non-target language better conveys the message (Rodriguez-Fornells et al. 2012). Aside from social and linguistic contexts, AoA and proficiency are also associated with code switching, where simultaneous bilinguals self-report less daily code switching than sequential bilinguals (Rodriguez-Fornells et al. 2012). Additionally, in late bilinguals, there seems to be a tendency to make switches from the L2 into the L1, as opposed to switching from the L1 into the L2. This has been found in Spanish-Catalan bilinguals regardless of which language was learned first (Rodriguez-Fornells et al. 2012).

Bilinguals who switch between languages more often have been suggested to have better performance on non-linguistic switching tasks than those who switch less often (although this view is not unchallenged; see Paap and Greenberg 2013). For example, Spanish-English bilinguals (who reported more daily switching between languages) had faster reaction times on a shape-colour task than Mandarin-English bilinguals (who switched between languages less frequently throughout the day; Prior and Gollan 2011). In another study, Yudes et al. (2011) tested monolinguals, bilinguals, and simultaneous interpreters in a Wisconsin card sorting task and found that simultaneous interpreters required fewer attempts and made fewer errors compared with both bilinguals and monolinguals. This is interesting because interpreting is considered an extreme form of bilingualism that requires receiving information and producing translations simulta-neously and these results imply that this tight coordination between languages may require superior executive function (Yudes et al. 2011). Therefore, an increase in cognitive flexibility may be one way of adapting to an environment that requires the ability to switch between languages and inhibit unwanted intrusions.

In Green and Abutalebi's (2013) adaptive control hypothesis, the authors suggest that bilingual language-use habits are largely shaped by individual differences in environ-mental context (and that these differences may also be constrained by genetic effects). This framework predicts that different neural adaptations occur according to the control demands of three possible environments that bilinguals may experience: in a single lan-guage context, the non-native language is only spoken in certain situations (for example, English at work and Chinese at home); in a dual language context, both languages may be used in one context (e.g. at work), but each language is used with different speakers; and in a dense code-switching context speakers frequently interweave both languages within one utterance and may adapt words to fit the needs of both languages. Because each interactional context has particular demands, experience with different environ-ments may lead some bilinguals to code switch more often than others (see Section 5.1.1 for evidence regarding distinct neural bases that may facilitate language production in each context).

3.2.3. Individual Differences in Switching   Genetic background may influence how the brain responds to tasks that require cognitive flexibility (Stelzel et al. 2010; Vaughn et al. 2016). Switching in bilinguals may be influenced by genes affecting striatal dopamine availability (Vaughn et al. 2016). Dopamine is a neurotransmitter that is highly involved in conditioning, reward-based learning, motor control/stabilization, and cognitive con-trol (Graybiel et al. 1994). Dopamine levels affect behavioural outcomes, where too much is thought to be associated with attention-deficit hyperactivity disorder and schizophrenia, and too little can be detrimental to motor function (e.g. Parkinson's disease, Huntington's disease; Beaulieu and Gainetdinov 2011). One genetic variant associated with dopamine is the ANKK1 Taq1A polymorphism located within the dopamine receptor D2 (DRD2) gene, which has been shown to affect dopamine receptor density in the striatum and thereby influence dopamine availability. Stelzel et al. (2010) showed that a group of non-carriers of the A1 allele of the ANKK1 Taq1A polymorphism had increased task-switching costs compared with carriers. Furthermore, non-carrier status of this polymorphism was associated with increased prefrontal activity while switching tasks, especially in the inferior frontal junction, as well as increased functional connectivity in the dorsal frontostriatal circuits. This is in line with experimental research showing that administration of a DRD2 agonist called bromocriptine results in increased activity in the inferior frontal junction during task switching (Stelzel et al. 2013). These results suggest that dopamine availability is one factor that affects the processing of task switching.

To determine the role that genetic variation within the DRD2 gene might play in bilingual language control, Vaughn et al. (2016) asked 49 Spanish-English bilinguals to participate in tests of cognitive control (including a picture-naming task to test language production, a Simon task to test non-verbal inhibition, and a shape-colour task to test non-verbal switching) while in an fMRI scanner. They found that both genetic and language background variables predicted neural activity during the picture-naming task, but that only genetic background predicted activity during the shape-colour switching task. Specifically, during the picture-naming task, A1 carrier status and age of English acquisition were related to greater left IFG activity, and only A1 carrier status was related to greater right IFG activity. The authors posited that A1 carriers depended more on frontal regions when naming pictures in the L2 due to lesser striatal dopamine availability; however, ample dopamine availability in the basal ganglia may have permitted non-carriers of the allele to better automatize L2 picture naming. During the shape-colour switching task, A1 carriers showed a smaller difference in bilateral ACC activity between switch and non-switch tasks, which could be interpreted as more efficient switching. Together, these results suggest that neurogenetic factors may influence the cognition underlying tasks related to managing two languages, such as picture-naming and switching.

One example of how genetic variations may provide some explanation for bilingualism comes from a study that found that A1 carrier status was significantly more prevalent in a group of Hispanics compared with Caucasians. Hernandez et al. (2015) found that two-thirds of Hispanics carried the A1 allele and only one-third of the Caucasians were carriers. Because these participants were university students, it is possible that A1 carrier status allowed the Hispanic participants to more successfully transition to English due to increased cognitive flexibility, and therefore enter college and participate in such a study. Findings such as these are important to consider when examining previous associations between bilingualism and cognitive flexibility because some groups that are traditionally bilingual may be more likely to have a certain genetic profile than their monolingual counterparts.

Therefore, pre-existing differences may be one factor affecting language switching (Festman et al. 2010; Rueda et al. 2005). Individuals who have higher linguistic flexibility may prefer to code switch in conversation more than those who are not (Yim and

Bialystok 2012). In one study, Cantonese-English bilinguals were asked to generate as many items as possible that fit into a semantic category (e.g. sports or clothing) in a one-minute period. They then repeated this task in a new category, this time switching between languages every other word. Controlling for proficiency, a negative relationship was found between code-switching and verbal-switching cost. In other words, bilinguals who code switched more often were able to perform the verbal switching task more quickly and efficiently (Yim and Bialystok 2012).

The results discussed thus far lead to two possible conclusions. First, bilingualism may train the brain to have greater cognitive flexibility. Second, genetically influenced cognitive flexibility may influence language switching ability, making individuals with particular genetic backgrounds more likely to become bilingual. Findings that bilingualism is associated with cognitive flexibility, which are often interpreted to mean that bilingualism trains the brain's executive function abilities, may be confounded by genetic influences on cognitive flexibility. That is, individuals who naturally have greater cognitive flexibility may have an easier time coping with the demands of a bilingual environment, making them more likely to become bilingual. Attending to and maintaining more than one language is not merely a linguistic skill, but a cognitive one that is in part managed through neural substrates associated with switching. These neural substrates are influenced by both environmental influences and genetic background. Therefore, the role of genetics should not be ignored in the investigation of multilingualism.

3.2.4.   Unanswered Questions   More research is needed to determine the degree to which genetics, cognitive flexibility, and code switching are connected. While the above research discusses the association between genetics and cognitive flexibility in bilinguals, more needs to be done to understand how genetics affect code switching specifically. Additionally, it is possible that other genes implicated in cognitive control and attention (e.g. catechol-O-methyltransferase; Cools and D'Esposito 2011) or language disorders (Wong et al. 2012) affect language outcomes.

4.   Hyperpolyglotism: Genetic Jackpot or a Love for Language?

Although individual differences play a larger role in late L2 acquisition (Bloch et al. 2009; Dehaene et al. 1997), they should not be ignored in those with early L2 exposure. A hyperpolyglot (sometimes described as a linguistic genius) is someone who has attained high proficiency in a high number of languages post-puberty, with some defining it as fluency in six or more languages (Hyltenstam 2014) and others defining it as fluency in 11 or more languages (Erard 2012). Compared to the plethora of research on bilingualism, neuroimaging research on hyperpolyglots is relatively sparse. Based on available research, hyperpolyglotism is thought to occur through a combination of neural and environmental factors (Amunts et al. 2004; Erard 2012).

Although the circumstances that facilitate hyperpolyglotism are not completely understood, one possibility is that it has a genetic basis that is triggered by the environment, which results in hypertrophies to certain brain areas (Amunts et al. 2004).

One example is Emil Krebs (1867–1930), who fluently spoke more than 60 languages. He was known to attain languages rapidly, sometimes mastering a single language in less than nine weeks (Amunts et al. 2004). An analysis of his preserved brain showed that the cytoarchitecture of the cell bodies in the bilateral Brodmann area 44 and right Brodmann area 45 were significantly different from the same areas in 11 control brains. It is possible that he was born with these structural differences, but it is more likely that slight hypertrophies in these structures led to his affinity for languages, and his time spent training led to further structural changes in these areas (Amunts et al. 2004).

Another example is Daniel Tammet, a savant with Asperger's syndrome who speaks 10 languages. He also has exceptional mathematical abilities (he quickly multiplies six-digit numbers together), a strong memory (he once recited Pi to 22 514 decimal places), and experiences a form of synesthesia in which numbers are associated with shapes, colours, and textures (Baron-Cohen et al. 2007). fMRI scans showed hyperactivity in the lateral PFC when encoding digits, although the authors discussed this in terms of Asperger's syndrome and synesthesia rather than his linguistic ability. It is clear that Tammet processes information differently from most people, but an exact neural mechanism for his linguistic abilities is not clear.

Erard (2012) notes that hyperpolyglots are generally self-taught, highly self-motivated, and make use of reading materials and dictionaries instead of depending on classroom learning. Others emphasize efficient executive systems that permit switching between languages and avoiding interference (Biedroń and Pawlak 2016). They also tend to have enhanced long-term memory, working memory, and phonological perception, as well as a special interest in decoding and analysing grammar (Ioup et al. 1994; Novoa et al. 1988; Schneiderman and Desmarais 1988). Good speech imitating skills also point to the likelihood that they have exceptional perceptual abilities (Biedroń and Pawlak 2016). This final point is interesting to consider in light of the auditory plasticity differences noted in bilinguals. Since auditory processing is a keystone in language learning success, it could be the case that hyperpolyglots are able to learn so many languages due to enhanced phonological sensitivity that allows them to accurately imitate foreign sounds.

An affinity for language could result in a domino effect. The more languages a hyperpolyglot learns, the more the brain changes to support learning new languages, and the easier it is to pick up new languages. This is in line with studies that show that early multilinguals tend to use the same language areas to represent all three languages (Bloch et al. 2009). While it is not clear whether hyperpolyglotism necessitates an early AoA, previous experience learning foreign languages may allow for more efficient learning of new languages. In fact, behavioural research shows that people who speak more than one language have faster reaction times when making judgements of newly learned foreign words (Bradley et al. 2013).

In sum, while certain cognitive advantages may facilitate hyperpolyglotism, it is also clear that a passion for language learning is one of the driving factors in hyperpolyglotism. Furthermore, the individual differences that predict L2 learning success seem to apply to hyperpolyglots as well (e.g. enhanced phonological perception and mimicking abilities). With this said, it is still possible that hyperpolyglotism is best explained by some yet-to-be-explored neural difference.

4.1.   Unanswered Questions

Due to a smaller population, relatively few neuroimaging studies have been done on hyperpolyglots. More research will be needed in order to determine whether hyperpolyglotism is an extension of multilingualism that is achievable by anyone with the motivation and will, or if it is an effect of environmental and/or neurogenetic factors.

5.   Other Effects of Multilingualism

5.1.   Executive Control

Learning to perceive and control multiple languages may alter neural structures that also underlie executive attention and cognitive control (Bialystok 2017). Some have argued that bilingual language production always requires inhibiting one language or the other due to both languages constantly being active. This idea is called joint activation (Bialystok and Kroll 2013; Sunderman and Kroll 2006). The relationship between enhanced executive control and bilingualism is thought to stem from this experience managing two competing languages.

An example of evidence for joint activation is an electroencephalography (EEG) study that showed that Chinese-English bilinguals had reduced N400 components when reading English words that, when translated to Chinese, contained a character repetition (compared with English words that did not have this type of translation). When bilinguals and monolinguals were later asked to read the translated versions of these words in Chinese, the same reduction in the N400 component was found for the words containing the character repetition. This was interpreted to mean that, even if it was unconscious, bilingual students were activating some representation of the words in Chinese as they read in English (Thierry and Wu 2007). This could mean that speaking one language always requires inhibiting the other to avoid intrusions (see Costa et al. 2016, for an alternative account that coactivation can be explained by native language influence on non-native language organization).

It is therefore possible that bilingual experience results in a domain-general inhibitory skillset (Kroll et al. 2008). Behavioural studies have shown a bilingual advantage on the Stroop task even for children as young as two years old (Poulin-Dubois et al. 2011). Bilinguals outperform monolinguals on inhibition tasks such as flanker (Costa et al. 2009; Poarch and Bialystok 2015), Stroop (Heidlmayr et al. 2014; Yang and Yang 2017), and Simon tasks (see Dong and Li 2015, for review), although some studies fail to replicate this effect (see Paap et al. 2015, for review). Additionally, there is some experimental evidence showing that a short period of language switching leads to increased non-verbal cognitive control in bilinguals (Zhang et al. 2015) and that this is reflected in a reduction in activity post-training in cognitive control regions such as the ACC and caudate nucleus (Kang et al. 2017).

Some have made the argument that the key to language control lies in how language and control regions are connected, not necessarily whether or not they are activated. Studies examining anatomical connectivity patterns have found two underlying networks in early bilinguals that may explain the ability to control multiple languages

(García-Pentón et al. 2014). In a group of early Basque-Spanish bilinguals, greater anatomical connectivity relative to monolinguals was found in a left hemisphere network containing the insula, STG, pars triangularis, pars opercularis, SMG, and medial superior frontal gyrus. This network may be involved in controlling phonological, syntactic, and semantic interference between languages. A second network was identified that included the left superior occipital and parietal gyri, superior temporal pole, angular gyrus, and right superior frontal gyrus. This network may be associated with word recognition, reading, and semantic processing. In both networks, connections to frontal structures may allow for control and switching between languages (García-Pentón et al. 2014; although differences in sample selection and neuroimaging method may lead to different results between studies; see García-Pentón et al. 2016, for review). Based on these results, experience with more than one language could lead to neural connections that allow for more efficient processing of language demands.

5.1.1. Executive Control: Experiential Considerations Different interactional contexts may foster the development of different control processes. The adaptive control hypothesis (Green and Abutalebi 2013) proposes that because bilingual speakers face increased cognitive demands to deal with language selection, experience with these skills affects eight different control processes in differing degrees (goal maintenance, conflict monitoring, interference suppression, salient cue detection, selective response inhibition, task disengagement, task engagement, and opportunistic planning), depending on interactional context. As mentioned in Section 3.2.2, three possible contexts of bilingualism include single language, dual language, and dense code switching.

Different contexts would, then, lead to individual differences in neural adaptations that best accommodate the environmental demands specific to that person (Green and Abutalebi 2013). For example, the main objective of speakers with extensive experience in a single language context is to maintain the target language and avoid cross-language intrusions; the authors speculate that this may result in changes to the dorsal left frontal cortex and parietal cortex, which have previously been associated with sustained inhibition (Guo et al. 2011). Speakers in a dual language context would aim to have both languages ready for recall rather than completely suppressing one language, and therefore would recruit thalamic and basal ganglia regions (this would allow them to attend to salient cues and select the correct language at the proper moment). They would also recruit frontal and parietal regions in order to deal with conflict monitoring, interference suppression, and task changes. Finally, speakers in a dense code-switching context would find it beneficial to jointly activate both languages, which the authors associate with adaptive change to the left inferior frontal and right cerebellar circuit to mediate language switching and integrate appropriate morphosyntax. From this perspective, neural processes associated with language control depend somewhat on interactional context.

5.2. Neuroprotective Effects Seen in Older Populations

Multilingualism has important clinical implications for older adults. Not long ago, it was suggested that bilingualism could have detrimental effects on normal ageing, such that cross-language interference would create special problems and exacerbate dementia symptoms (Mendez et al. 1999). However, more recent research suggests the opposite: a lifetime of speaking multiple languages may have neuroprotective effects against the onset of cognitive decline as well as dementia symptoms (Alladi et al. 2013; Bialystok et al. 2007; Chertkow et al. 2010; although not all findings are consistent; see Lawton et al. 2015). Multilingualism may create a larger 'cognitive reserve' that acts as a buffer against age-related cognitive decline.

Several studies point to an association between bilingualism and slowed cognitive decline in older adults, and this is reflected in brain structure. Using diffusion tensor imaging (DTI), a neuroimaging technique that detects the diffusion of water molecules to measure white matter, Luk et al. (2011) showed that a group of older lifelong bilinguals had enhanced white matter connectivity in the corpus callosum and its projections to the bilateral superior longitudinal fasciculi, right inferior frontal-occipital fasciculus, and uncinate fasciculus. This is important to older populations in particular given that white matter integrity is known to decrease with age. Other structural differences in older bilinguals include increased grey matter volume in the bilateral inferior parietal lobule (IPL; Abutalebi et al. 2015a) and ACC (Abutalebi et al. 2015b). Differences in these areas could reflect possible neural correlates of a cognitive reserve (Luk et al. 2011).

In addition, Gold et al. (2013) found both behavioural advantages and processing differences in bilingual compared to monolingual older adults. In a perceptual task-switching paradigm, bilinguals had faster task switching, and this effect was not explained by education level, socioeconomic status, or IQ. During the task, fMRI scans showed that the group of older bilinguals had less activation in the left DLPFC, left ventrolateral PFC, and ACC, which are thought to be involved in a network involved in task switching (Kehagia et al. 2010). The authors posited that because the PFC is involved in slower, more effortful processing (Rypma et al. 2002), lifelong bilingualism may improve the neural efficiency of these areas.

If the above-mentioned areas are involved in executive function networks, they may allow for a bigger cognitive reserve that can compensate for cognitive decline, making it less severe (Luk et al. 2011). However, this idea is contended. A meta-analysis by Mukadam et al. (2017) found that bilingualism did not significantly predict delayed cognitive decline or dementia when only prospective studies (studies that randomly sampled from community-dwelling participants), rather than retrospective studies (studies that sampled from clinics specializing in memory assessment), were included. They suggested that retrospective studies on dementia and bilingualism are often confounded with factors like education and cultural differences. Therefore, this issue should be further investigated to understand whether bilingualism can buffer against cognitive decline, or the controlling factors actually have more to do with socioeconomic status, education, or experience living in other countries.

5.3.   *Cognitive Disadvantages, Costs, and Challenges*

Although the current paradigm is one that focuses on the advantages of bilingualism, many used to fear that exposure to multiple languages during development would contaminate and delay the child's 'normal' development (see Baker and Sienkewicz 2000). Not only is this not true, but bilingualism today is frequently associated with cognitive advantages (Bialystok 2009). With this said, a few disadvantages of bilingualism have been identified. Specifically, bilinguals experience more frequent occurrences of anomia (Gollan and Acenas 2004), smaller vocabulary size in each language[1] (Perani et al. 2003; Portocarrero et al. 2007), and slower picture naming (Gollan et al. 2005; Kaushanskaya and Marian 2007).

Although tip-of-the-tongue (TOT) states are a normal part of life for any language speaker (even users of sign language experience tip-of-the-fingers states; Thompson et al. 2005), bilinguals report this state more often than monolinguals. One possible reason for more frequent anomia is that bilinguals have more words available to them (i.e. two words for everything), so it takes them longer to find the correct word. Gollan and Acenas (2004) induced TOT states in Spanish-English bilinguals, Tagalog-English bilinguals, and monolinguals by asking them to partake in a picture-naming task where half of the pictures were cognates (words that have similar-sounding translations such as *vampire* and *vampiro*) and half were non-cognates. Bilinguals had more TOT states than monolinguals, a result which was obtained even when accounting for proficiency level and therefore did not have to do with lacking familiarity with the target words.

However, when the English target words had cognate translations, bilinguals actually had fewer TOT states. Because the majority of bilinguals reported English as their dominant language, the authors inferred that the non-dominant language affects processing in the dominant language (Gollan and Acenas 2004). In the right circumstances, having two languages available can allow for each language to support the other. This implies that one benefit of speaking two languages of the same origin (e.g. two Romance languages) is an increased amount of carry-over between them.

Bilinguals and monolinguals also differ in how long it takes them to name words. Monolinguals outperform bilinguals in picture-naming tasks, whether the bilinguals are in their dominant or non-dominant language (Gollan et al. 2011; Ivanova and Costa 2008). While it is possible that this is due to competition between the two languages, some have argued that less time spent in each language results in weaker connections between words and concepts (Gollan et al. 2008).

Finally, bilinguals have a smaller vocabulary in each language (Bialystok et al. 2010; Mahon and Crutchley 2006; Oller et al. 2007). In an analysis of 1738 children ranging from 3 to 10 years old, monolinguals had higher vocabulary than bilinguals in every age group. Each group had a normal distribution, but the monolinguals were always approximately nine points above the bilinguals (Bialystok et al. 2010). This may simply be an effect of spending less time in each language. These results should be considered along with the fact that while vocabulary in one language may be smaller, bilinguals hold a larger total vocabulary than that of monolinguals. The authors of this study emphasized that these results do not characterize a developmental delay, but instead aim to describe the norm for bilingual children in school.

Overall, while monolinguals and bilinguals differ in lexical access abilities, this is not thought to cause significant disruption in daily life (Dong and Li 2015). Further, the ability to communicate in multiple languages, as well as the advantages associated with it, is generally thought to outweigh the aforementioned costs. Examining these differences in cognition at face value, rather than categorizing them as good or bad, can inform our understanding of the natural development of bilingualism.

6.   Conclusion

To summarize, plasticity and cognitive flexibility are crucial factors in language learning at any point in life. Early development sees a period of heightened plasticity, especially in auditory and motor pathways, which is one reason for findings that early AoA is correlated with higher L2 proficiency. Later AoA, however, is correlated with more variation in cortical representation of languages (Bloch et al. 2009), suggesting that individual differences take on a larger role as development continues. Foreign languages can still be acquired at later points in development, but it might be easier for people who have higher plasticity in sensory areas related to language. Additionally, cognitive flexibility, which is often considered to be an effect of multilingualism, may actually be an individual difference that makes it easier for some people to switch between languages. Genetic evidence shows that this is one potential explanation for variation in code-switching preferences in bilinguals. Although individual differences play a larger role in late L2 acquisition than they do in early L2 acquisition, they are still present for those with early L2 exposure, which may help explain hyperpolyglotism. However, the interaction between L2 AoA and individual differences should be further explored in order to best understand multilingualism.

Finally, an important distinction between child and adult learning is that while children have the chance to learn organically, adult classroom learning generally focuses on rote memorization of vocabulary and grammar rules. The latter method may suffice for some individuals, but with less than 1% of people in the US having learned a foreign language to a proficient level in school (Snyder and Dillow 2015), it is clear that this method has room for improvement. As neuroimaging research in this area continues, it is likely that we will one day be able to pinpoint the best methods for language learning and tune them to individual needs.

NOTE

1   Note that this may be affected by language origin. Evidence from Gollan and Acenas (2004) shows that speaking languages of the same origin may actually facilitate vocabulary knowledge between languages.

REFERENCES

Abrahamsson, N. and Hyltenstam, K. (2009). Age of onset and nativelikeness in a second language: listener perception versus linguistic scrutiny. *Language Learning* 59 (2): 249–306. doi:10.1111/j.1467-9922.2009.00507.x.

Abutalebi, J., Annoni, J.M., Zimine, I. et al. (2008). Language control and lexical competition in bilinguals: an event-related FMRI study. *Cerebral Cortex* 18 (7): 1496–1505. doi:10.1093/cercor/bhm182.

Abutalebi, J., Brambati, S.M., Annoni, J.M. et al. (2007). The neural cost of the auditory perception of language switches: an event-related functional magnetic resonance imaging study in bilinguals. *The Journal of Neuroscience* 27 (50): 13762–13769. doi:10.1523/JNEUROSCI.3294-07.2007.

Abutalebi, J., Canini, M., Della Rosa, P.A. et al. (2015a). The neuroprotective effects of bilingualism upon the inferior parietal lobule: a structural neuroimaging study in aging Chinese bilinguals. *Journal of Neurolinguistics* 33: 3–13. doi:10.1016/j.jneuroling.2014.09.008.

Abutalebi, J., Della Rosa, P.A., Gonzaga, A.K. et al. (2013). The role of the left putamen in multilingual language production. *Brain and Language* 125 (3): 307–315. doi:10.1016/j.bandl.2012.03.009.

Abutalebi, J. and Green, D. (2007). Bilingual language production: the neurocognition of language representation and control. *Journal of Neurolinguistics* 20 (3): 242–275. doi:10.1016/j.jneuroling.2006.10.003.

Abutalebi, J., Guidi, L., Borsa, V. et al. (2015b). Bilingualism provides a neural reserve for aging populations. *Neuropsychologia* 69: 201–210. doi:10.1016/j.neuropsychologia.2015.01.040.

Ali, N., Green, D.W., Kherif, F. et al. (2010). The role of the left head of caudate in suppressing irrelevant words. *Journal of Cognitive Neuroscience* 22 (10): 2369–2386. doi:10.1162/jocn.2009.21352.

Alladi, S., Back, T.H., Duggirala, V. et al. (2013). Bilingualism delays age at onset of dementia, independent of education and immigration status. *Neurology* 81: 1938–1944.

Amunts, K., Schleicher, A., and Zilles, K. (2004). Outstanding language competence and cytoarchitecture in Broca's speech region. *Brain and Language* 89 (2): 346–353. doi:10.1016/s0093-934x(03)00360-2.

Archila-Suerte, P., Munson, B.A., and Hernandez, A.E. (2016). The role of executive function in the perception of L2 speech sounds in young balanced and unbalanced dual language learners. In: *Cognitive Control and Consequences of*

Multilingualism: Bilingual Processing and Acquisition (ed. J.W. Schwieter), 71–96. doi:10.1075/bpa.2.04arc.

Archila-Suerte, P., Zevin, J., and Hernandez, A.E. (2015). The effect of age of acquisition, socioeducational status, and proficiency on the neural processing of second language speech sounds. *Brain and Language* 141: 35–49. doi:10.1016/j.bandl.2014.11.005.

Archila-Suerte, P., Zevin, J., Ramos, A.I., and Hernandez, A.E. (2013). The neural basis of non-native speech perception in bilingual children. *NeuroImage* 67: 51–63. doi:10.1016/j.neuroimage.2012.10.023.

Austin, D. L. B. (2007). The impact of age of acquisiiton of English, extent of language use, and first language proficiency on the bilingual language skills of Spanish-English bilinguals. (PhD dissertation), University of Houston.

Baker, C. and Sienkewicz, A. (2000). *The Care and Education of Young Bilinguals: An Introduction for Professionals (ch. 4)*. Clevedon, UK: Multilingual Matters.

Baron-Cohen, S., Bor, D., Billington, J. et al. (2007). Savant memory in a man with colour form-number synaesthesia and Asperger syndrome. *Journal of Consciousness Studies* 14 (9–10): 237–251.

Bear, M.F., Connors, B.W., and Paradiso, M.A. (2007). *Neuroscience – Exploring the Brain*, 2e. Baltimore, MD: Lippincott, Williams & Wilkins.

Beaulieu, J.M. and Gainetdinov, R.R. (2011). The physiology, signaling, and pharmacology of dopamine receptors. *Pharmacological Reviews* 63 (1): 182–217. doi:10.1124/pr.110.002642.

Bentahila, A. and Davies, E.E. (1995). Patterns of code-switching and patterns of language contact. *Lingua* 96: 75–93.

Bialystok, E. (2009). Bilingualism: the good, the bad, and the indifferent. *Bilingualism: Language and Cognition* 12 (01): 3. doi:10.1017/s1366728908003477.

Bialystok, E. (2017). The bilingual adaptation: how minds accommodate experience. *Psychological Bulletin* 143 (3): 233–262. doi:10.1037/bul0000099.

Bialystok, E., Craik, F.I., and Freedman, M. (2007). Bilingualism as a protection against the onset of symptoms of dementia. *Neuropsychologia* 45 (2): 459–464. doi:10.1016/j.neuropsychologia.2006.10.009.

Bialystok, E. and Kroll, J.F. (2013). Understanding the consequences of bilingualism for language processing and cognition. *Journal of Cognitive Psychology* 25 (5): 1–22. doi:10.1080/20445911.2013.799170.

Bialystok, E., Luk, G., Peets, K.F., and Yang, S. (2010). Receptive vocabulary differences in monolingual and bilingual children. *Bilingualism: Language and Cognition* 13 (4): 525–531. doi:10.1017/S1366728909990423.

Biedroń, A. and Pawlak, M. (2016). New conceptualizations of linguistic giftedness. *Language Teaching* 49 (2): 151–185. doi:10.1017/s0261444815000439.

Bloch, C., Kaiser, A., Kuenzli, E. et al. (2009). The age of second language acquisition determines the variability in activation elicited by narration in three languages in Broca's and Wernicke's area. *Neuropsychologia* 47 (3): 625–633. doi:10.1016/j.neuropsychologia.2008.11.009.

Bradley, K.A., King, K.E., and Hernandez, A.E. (2013). Language experience differentiates prefrontal and subcortical activation of the cognitive control network in novel word learning. *NeuroImage* 67: 101–110. doi:10.1016/j.neuroimage.2012.11.018.

Buonomano, D.V. and Merzenich, M.M. (1998). Cortical plasticity: from synapses to maps. *Annual Review of Neuroscience* 21: 149–186.

Chai, X.J., Berken, J.A., Barbeau, E.B. et al. (2016). Intrinsic functional connectivity in the adult brain and success in second-language learning. *The Journal of Neuroscience* 36 (3): 755–761. doi:10.1523/JNEUROSCI.2234-15.2016.

Chechik, G., Meilijson, I., and Ruppin, E. (1998). Synaptic pruning in development: a computational account. *Neural Computation* 10 (7): 1759–1777.

Chertkow, H., Whitehead, V., Phillips, N. et al. (2010). Multilingualism (but not always bilingualism) delays the onset of Alzheimer disease: evidence from a bilingual community. *Alzheimer Disease & Associated Disorders* 24 (2): 113–125. doi:10.1097/WAD.0b013e3181ca1221.

Cools, R. and D'Esposito, M. (2011). Inverted-U-shaped dopamine actions on human working memory and cognitive control. *Biological Psychiatry* 69 (12): e113–e125. doi:10.1016/j.biopsych.2011.03.028.

Costa, A., Hernandez, M., Costa-Faidella, J., and Sebastian-Galles, N. (2009). On the bilingual advantage in conflict processing: now you see it, now you don't. *Cognition* 113 (2): 135–149. doi:10.1016/j.cognition.2009.08.001.

Costa, A., Pannunzi, M., Deco, G., and Pickering, M.J. (2016). Do bilinguals automatically activate their native language when they are not using it? *Cognitive Science* 41 (6): 1629–1644. doi:10.1111/cogs.12434.

Cummins, J. (1979). Cognitive/academic language proficiency, linguistic interdependence, the optimum age question and some other matters. *Working Papers on Bilingualism* 19: 121–129.

De Groot, A.M.B. (2011). *Language and Cognition in Bilinguals and Multilinguals*. New York, NY: Psychology Press.

Dehaene, S., Dupoux, E., Mehler, J. et al. (1997). Anatomical variability in the cortical representation of first and second language. *NeuroReport* 8: 3809–3815.

Diamond, A. (2013). Executive functions. *Annual Review of Psychology* 64: 135–168. doi:10.1146/annurev-psych-113011-143750.

Dong, Y. and Li, P. (2015). The cognitive science of bilingualism. *Language and Linguistics Compass* 9 (1): 1–13. doi:10.1111/lnc3.12099.

Duffau, H., Moritz-Gasser, S., and Mandonnet, E. (2014). A re-examination of neural basis of language processing: proposal of a dynamic hodotopical model from data provided by brain stimulation mapping during picture naming. *Brain and Language* 131: 1–10. doi:10.1016/j.bandl.2013.05.011.

Erard, M. (2012). *Babel No More: The Search for the World's Most Extraordinary Language Learners*. New York, NY: Free Press.

Fernandez-Coello, A., Havas, V., Juncadella, M. et al. (2017). Age of language acquisition and cortical language organization in multilingual patients undergoing awake brain mapping. *Journal of Neurosurgery* 126 (6): 1912–1923. doi:10.3171/2016.5. JNS152791.

Festman, J., Rodriguez-Fornells, A., and Münte, T.F. (2010). Individual differences in control of language interference in late bilinguals are mainly related to general executive abilities. *Behavioral and Brain Functions* 6: 5. doi:10.1186/1744-9081-6-5.

Flege, J.E. and MacKay, I.R.A. (2004). Perceiving vowels in a second language. *Studies in Second Language Acquisition* 26 (1): 1–34. doi:10.1017/s0272263104026117.

Flege, J.E., Yeni-Komshian, G.H., and Liu, S. (1999). Age constraints on second-language acquisition. *Journal of Memory and Language* 41: 78–104.

García-Pentón, L., Fernández, A.P., Iturria-Medina, Y. et al. (2014). Anatomical connectivity changes in the bilingual brain. *NeuroImage* 84: 495–504. doi:10.1016/j. neuroimage.2013.08.064.

García-Pentón, L., García, Y.F., Costello, B. et al. (2016). The neuroanatomy of bilingualism: how to turn a hazy view into a full picture. *Language, Cognition and Neuroscience* 31 (3): 303–327. doi:10.1080/232 73798.2015.1068944.

Gold, B.T., Kim, C., Johnson, N.F. et al. (2013). Lifelong bilingualism maintains neural efficiency for cognitive control in aging. *The Journal of Neuroscience* 33 (2): 387–396. doi:10.1523/JNEUROSCI.3837-12.2013.

Golestani, N., Molko, N., Dehaene, S. et al. (2007). Brain structure predicts the learning of foreign speech sounds. *Cerebral Cortex* 17 (3): 575–582. doi:10.1093/cercor/bhk001.

Golestani, N. and Pallier, C. (2007). Anatomical correlates of foreign speech sound production. *Cerebral Cortex* 17 (4): 929–934. doi:10.1093/cercor/bhl003.

Gollan, T.H. and Acenas, L.-A.R. (2004). What is a TOT? Cognate and translation effects on tip-of-the-tongue states in Spanish-English and Tagalog-English bilinguals. *Journal of Experimental Psychology: Learning, Memory, and Cognition* 30 (1): 246–269. doi:10.1037/0278-7393.30.1.246.

Gollan, T.H., Montoya, R.I., Cera, C., and Sandoval, T.C. (2008). More use almost always means a smaller frequency effect: aging, bilingualism, and the weaker links hypothesis. *Journal of Memory and Language* 58 (3): 787–814. doi:10.1016/j. jml.2007.07.001.

Gollan, T.H., Montoya, R.I., Fennema-Notestine, C., and Morris, S.K. (2005). Bilingualism affects picture naming but not picture classification. *Memory & Cognition* 33 (7): 1220–1234. doi:10.3758/BF03193224.

Gollan, T.H., Slattery, T.J., Goldenberg, D. et al. (2011). Frequency drives lexical access in reading but not in speaking: the frequency-lag hypothesis. *Journal of Experimental Psychology: General* 140 (2): 186–209. doi:10.1037/a0022256.

Granena, G. and Long, M.H. (2013). Age of onset, length of residence, language aptitude, and ultimate L2 attainment in three linguistic domains. *Second Language Research* 29 (3): 311–343. doi:10.1177/0267658312461497.

Grant, A.M., Fang, S.Y., and Li, P. (2015). Second language lexical development and cognitive control: a longitudinal fMRI study. *Brain and Language* 144: 35–47. doi:10.1016/j. bandl.2015.03.010.

Graybiel, A.M. (2000). The basal ganglia. *Current Biology* 10 (14): R509–R511. doi:10.1016/S0960-9822(00)00593-5.

Graybiel, A.M., Aosaki, T., Flaherty, A.W., and Kimura, M. (1994). The basal ganglia and adaptive motor control. *Science* 265 (5180): 1826–1831. doi:10.1126/science.8091209.

Green, D.W. and Abutalebi, J. (2013). Language control in bilinguals: the adaptive control hypothesis. *Journal of Cognitive Psychology (Hove, England)* 25 (5): 515–530. doi:10.1080/20445911.2013.796377.

Grogan, A., Parker Jones, O., Ali, N. et al. (2012). Structural correlates for lexical efficiency and number of languages in non-native speakers of English. *Neuropsychologia* 50: 1347–1352. doi:10.1016/j.neuropsychologia.2012.02.019.

Grosjean, F. and Li, P. (2012). *The Psycholinguistics of Bilingualism*. New York, NY: Wiley.

Guo, T., Liu, H., Misra, M., and Kroll, J.F. (2011). Local and global inhibition in bilingual word production: fMRI evidence from Chinese-English bilinguals. *NeuroImage* 56 (4): 2300–2309. doi:10.1016/j.neuroimage.2011.03.049.

Hall, J.J., Batterson, J.R., and Snow, J.H. (2013). Tic disorders. In: *The Neuropsychology of Psychopathology* (ed. C.A. Noggle and R.S. Dean), 187–199. New York, NY: Springer.

Heidlmayr, K., Moutier, S., Hemforth, B. et al. (2014). Successive bilingualism and executive functions: the effect of second language use on inhibitory control in a behavioural Stroop colour word task. *Bilingualism: Language and Cognition* 17 (3): 630–645. doi:10.1017/S1366728913000539.

Hernandez, A.E., Greene, M.R., Vaughn, K.A. et al. (2015). Beyond the bilingual advantage: the potential role of genes and environment on the development of cognitive control. *Journal of Neurolinguistics* 35: 109–119. doi:10.1016/j.jneuroling.2015.04.002.

Hernandez, A.E. and Li, P. (2007). Age of acquisition: its neural and computational mechanisms. *Psychological Bulletin* 133 (4): 638–650. doi:10.1037/0033-2909.133.4.638.

Hyltenstam, K. (2014). Language awareness in polyglots. Paper presented at the 12th International Conferences Association for Language Awareness, Hamar, Norway.

Imada, T., Zhang, Y., Cheour, M. et al. (2006). Infant speech perception activates Broca's area: a developmental magnetoencephalography study. *NeuroReport* 17: 957–962.

Ioup, G., Boustagui, M., El Tigi, M., and Moselle, M. (1994). Reexamining the critical period hypothesis: a case study of successful adult SLA in a naturalistic environment. *Studies in Second Language Acquisition* 16 (1): 73–98.

Ivanova, I. and Costa, A. (2008). Does bilingualism hamper lexical access in speech production? *Acta Psychologica* 127 (2): 277–288. doi:10.1016/j.actpsy.2007.06.003.

Jäncke, L. (2012). The relationship between music and language. *Frontiers in Psychology* 3: 123–124. doi:10.3389/fpsyg.2012.00123.

Johnson, J.S. and Newport, E.L. (1989). Critical period effects in 2nd language-learning – the influence of maturational state on the acquisition of English as a second language. *Cognitive Psychology* 21 (1): 60–99. doi:10.1016/0010-0285(89)90003-0.

Jonides, J., Schumacher, E.H., Smith, E.E. et al. (1998). The role of parietal cortex in verbal working memory. *Journal of Neuroscience* 18 (13): 5026–5034.

Kang, C., Fu, Y., Wu, J. et al. (2017). Short-term language switching training tunes the neural correlates of cognitive control in bilingual language production. *Human Brain Mapping* 38 (12): 5859–5870. doi:10.1002/hbm.23765.

Kaushanskaya, M. and Marian, V. (2007). Bilingual language processing and interference in bilinguals: evidence from eye tracking and picture naming. *Language Learning* 57 (1): 119–163. doi:10.1111/j.1467-9922.2007.00401.x.

Kehagia, A.A., Murray, G.K., and Robbins, T.W. (2010). Learning and cognitive flexibility: frontostriatal function and monoaminergic modulation. *Current Opinion in Neurobiology* 20 (2): 199–204. doi:10.1016/j.conb.2010.01.007.

Klein, D., Mok, K., Chen, J.K., and Watkins, K.E. (2014). Age of language learning shapes brain structure: a cortical thickness study of bilingual and monolingual individuals. *Brain & Language* 131: 20–24. doi:10.1016/j.bandl.2013.05.014.

Knudsen, E. (2004). Sensitive periods in the development of the brain and behavior. *Journal of Cognitive Neuroscience* 16 (6): 1412–1425. doi:10.1162/0898929042304796.

Koelsch, S., Fritz, T., Cramon, D.Y. et al. (2006). Investigating emotion with music: an fMRI study. *Human Brain Mapping* 27 (3): 239–250. doi:10.1002/hbm.20180.

Koenigs, M., Barbey, A., Postle, B., and Grafman, J. (2009). Superior parietal cortex is critical for the manipulation of information in working memory. *The Journal of Neuroscience* 29 (47): 14980–14986. doi:10.1523/JNEUROSCI.3706-09.2009.

Kovács, A.M. and Mehler, J. (2009). Cognitive gains in 7-month-old bilingual infants. *Proceedings of the National Academy of Sciences* 106 (16): 6556–6560. doi:10.1073 pnas.0811323106.

Krizman, J. and Marian, V. (2015). Neural consequences of bilingualism for cortical and subcortical function. In: *The Cambridge Handbook of Bilingual Processing* (ed. J.W. Schwieter), 614–630. Cambridge, England: Cambridge University Press.

Kroll, J.F., Bobb, S.C., Misra, M., and Guo, T. (2008). Language selection in bilingual speech: evidence for inhibitory processes. *Acta Psychologica* 128 (3): 416–430. doi:10.1016/j.actpsy.2008.02.001.

Kuhl, P.K., Tsao, F.-M., and Liu, H.-M. (2003). Foreign-language experience in infancy: effects of short-term exposure and social interaction on phonetic learning. *Proceedings of the National Academy of Sciences* 100 (15): 9096–9101. doi:10.1073/pnas.1532872100.

Lawton, D.M., Gasquoine, P.G., and Weimer, A.A. (2015). Age of dementia diagnosis in community dwelling bilingual and monolingual Hispanic Americans. *Cortex* 66: 141–145. doi:10.1016/j.cortex.2014.11.017.

Li, P. and Grant, A. (2016). Second language learning success revealed by brain networks. *Bilingualism: Language and Cognition* 19 (04): 657–664. doi:10.1017/s1366728915000280.

Li, R., Qin, W., Zhang, Y. et al. (2012). The neuronal correlates of digits backward are revealed by voxel-based morphometry and resting-state functional connectivity analyses. *PLoS One* 7 (2): e31877. doi: 10.1371/journal.pone.0031877.

Liegeois-Chauvel, C., Musolino, A., and Chauvel, P. (1991). Localization of the primary auditory area in man. *Brain* 114: 139–151.

Luk, G., Bialystok, E., Craik, F.I., and Grady, C.L. (2011). Lifelong bilingualism maintains white matter integrity in older adults. *The Journal of Neuroscience* 31 (46): 16808–16813. doi:10.1523/JNEUROSCI.4563-11.2011.

MacDonald, A.W., Cohen, J.D., Stenger, V.A., and Carter, C.S. (2000). Dissociating the role of dorsolateral prefrontal cortex and anterior cingulate cortex in cognitive control. *Science* 288: 1835–1838.

Mahon, M. and Crutchley, A. (2006). Performance of typically-developing school-age children with English as an additional language on the British Picture Vocabulary Scales II. *Child Language Teaching and Therapy* 22 (3): 333–351. doi:10.1191/026 5659006ct311xx.

Mampe, B., Friederici, A.D., Christophe, A., and Wermke, K. (2009). Newborns' cry melody is shaped by their native language. *Current Biology* 19 (23): 1994–1997. doi:10.1016/j.cub.2009.09.064.

Mårtensson, J., Eriksson, J., Bodammer, N.C. et al. (2012). Growth of language-related brain areas after foreign language learning. *NeuroImage* 63 (1): 240–244. doi:10.1016/j.neuroimage.2012.06.043.

Mechelli, A., Crinion, J.T., Noppeney, U. et al. (2004). Structural plasticity in the bilingual brain: proficiency in a second langauge and age at acquisition affect grey-matter density. *Nature* 431 (7010): doi:10.1038/431757a.

Mendez, M.F., Perryman, K.M., Ponton, M.O., and Cummings, J.L. (1999). Bilingualism and dementia. *Journal of Neuropsychiatry and Clinical Neurosciences* 11 (3): 411–412. doi:10.1176/jnp.11.3.411.

Moreno, E.M., Federmeier, K.D., and Kutas, M. (2002). Switching languages, switching palabras (words): an electrophysiological study of code switching. *Brain and Language* 80 (2): 188–207. doi:10.1006/brln.2001.2588.

Mosing, M.A., Madison, G., Pedersen, N.L. et al. (2014). Practice does not make perfect: no causal effect of music practice on music ability. *Psychological Science* 25 (9): 1795–1803. doi:10.1177/0956797614541990.

Mukadam, N., Sommerlad, A., and Livingston, G. (2017). The relationship of bilingualism compared to monolingualism to the risk of cognitive decline or dementia: a systematic review and meta-analysis. *Journal of Alzheimer's Disease* 58 (1): 45–54. doi:10.3233/JAD-170131.

Mutchler, J.E. and Brallier, S. (1999). English language proficiency among older Hispanics in the United States. *Gerontologist* 39 (3): 310–319.

Nagy, W.E. and Scott, J.A. (2000). Vocabulary processes. In: *Handbook of Reading Research*, vol. 3 (ed. M.L. Kamil, P. Mosenthal, P.D. Pearson and R. Barr), 269–284. Mahwah, NJ: Erlbaum.

Neville, H.J., Mills, D.L., and Lawson, D.S. (1992). Fractionating language – different neural subsystems with different sensitive periods. *Cerebral Cortex* 2 (3): 244–258. doi:10.1093/cercor/2.3.244.

Novoa, L., Fein, D., and Obler, L. (1988). Talent in foreign language: a case study. In: *The Exceptional Brain: Neuropsychology of Talent and Special Abilities* (ed. L.K. Obler and D. Fein), 294–302. New York, NY: Guilford.

Oller, D.K., Pearson, B.Z., and Cobo-Lewis, A.B. (2007). Profile effects in early bilingual language and literacy. *Applied PsychoLinguistics* 28 (2): 191–230. doi:10.1017/S0142716407070117.

Paap, K.R. and Greenberg, Z.I. (2013). There is no coherent evidence for a bilingual advantage in executive processing. *Cognitive Psychology* 66: 232–258. doi:10.1016/j.cogpsych.2012.12.002.

Paap, K.R., Johnson, H.A., and Sawi, O. (2015). Bilingual advantages in executive functioning either do not exist or are restricted to very specific and undetermined circumstances. *Cortex* 69: 265–278. doi:10.1016/j.cortex.2015.04.014.

Perani, D., Abutalebi, J., Paulesu, E. et al. (2003). The role of age of acquisition and language usage in early, high-proficient bilinguals: an fMRI study during verbal fluency. *Human Brain Mapping* 19 (3): 170–182. doi:10.1002/hbm.10110.

Petitto, L.A., Berens, M.S., Kovelman, I. et al. (2012). The 'perceptual wedge hypothesis' as the basis for bilingual babies' phonetic processing advantage: new insights from fNIRS brain imaging. *Brain and Language* 121 (2): 130–143. doi:10.1016/j.bandl.2011.05.003.

Piske, T., MacKay, I.R.A., and Flege, J.E. (2001). Factors affecting degree of foreign accent in an L2: a review. *Journal of Phonetics* 29: 191–215. doi:10.006/jpho.2001.0134.

Poarch, G.J. and Bialystok, E. (2015). Bilingualism as a model for multitasking. *Developmental Review* 35: 113–124. doi:10.1016/j.dr.2014.12.003.

Portocarrero, J.S., Burright, R.G., and Donovick, P.J. (2007). Vocabulary and verbal fluency of bilingual and monolingual college students. *Archives of Clinical Neuropsychology* 22 (3): 415–422. doi:10.1016/j.acn.2007.01.015.

Poulin-Dubois, D., Blaye, A., Coutya, J., and Bialystok, E. (2011). The effects of bilingualism on toddlers' executive functioning. *Journal of Experimental Child Psychology* 108 (3): 567–579. doi:10.1016/j.jecp.2010.10.009.

Price, C.J. (2010). The anatomy of language: a review of 100 fMRI studies published in 2009. *Annals of the New York Academy of Sciences* 1191: 62–88. doi:10.1111/j.1749-6632.2010.05444.

Prior, A. and Gollan, T.H. (2011). Good language-switchers are good task-switchers: evidence from Spanish-English and Mandarin-English bilinguals. *Journal of the International Neuropsychological Society* 17 (4): 682–691. doi:10.1017/S1355617711000580.

Prior, A. and Macwhinney, B. (2010). A bilingual advantage in task switching. *Bilingualism: Language and Cognition* 13 (02): 253. doi:10.1017/s1366728909990526.

Raizada, R.D., Tsao, F.M., Liu, H.M., and Kuhl, P.K. (2010). Quantifying the adequacy of neural representations for a cross-language phonetic discrimination task: prediction of individual differences. *Cerebral Cortex* 20 (1): 1–12. doi:10.1093/cercor/bhp076.

Robles, S.G., Gastignol, P., Capelle, L. et al. (2005). The role of dominant striatum in language: a study using intraoperative electrical stimulations. *Journal of Neurology, Neurosurgery, and Psychiatry* 76: 940–946.

Rodriguez-Fornells, A., Krämer, U.M., Lorenzo-Seva, U. et al. (2012). Self-assessment of individual differences in language switching. *Frontiers in Psychology* 2: 388. doi:10.3389/fpsyg.2011.00388.

Rueda, M.R., Rothbart, M.K., McCandliss, B.D. et al. (2005). Training, maturation, and genetic influences on the development of executive attention. *Proceedings of the National Academy of Sciences* 102 (41): 14931–14936. doi:10.1073/pnas.0506897102.

Rypma, B., Berger, J.S., and D'Esposito, M. (2002). The influence of working- memory demand and subject performance on prefrontal cortical activity. *Journal of Cognitive Neuroscience* 14: 721–731.

Saffran, J.R., Aslin, R.N., and Newport, E.L. (1996). Statistical learning by 8-month-old infants. *Science* 274: 1926–1928.

Sakai, K.L. (2005). Language acquisition and brain development. *Science* 310 (5749): 815–819. doi:10.1126/science.1113530.

Schneiderman, E. and Desmarais, C. (1988). The talented language learner: some preliminary findings. *Second Language Research* 4 (2): 91–109.

Scovel, T. (1988). *A Time to Speak: A Psycholinguistic Inquiry into the Critical Period for Human Speech*. Cambridge, MA: Newbury House.

Sheppard, J.P., Wang, J.P., and Wong, P.C. (2012). Large-scale cortical network properties predict future sound-to-word learning success. *Journal of Cognitive Neuroscience* 24 (5): 1087–1103. doi:10.1162/jocn_a_00210.

Snyder, T.D. and Dillow, S.A. (2015). *Digest of Education Statistics 2013 (NCES 2015–011)*. Washington, DC: U.S. Department of Education.

Sparks, R.L., Patton, J., Ganschow, L. et al. (2006). Native language predictors of foreign language proficiency and foreign language aptitude. *Annals of Dyslexia* 56 (1): 129–160.

Stein, M., Winkler, C., Kaiser, A., and Dierks, T. (2014). Structural brain changes related to bilingualism: does immersion make a difference? *Frontiers in Psychology* 5: 1116. doi:10.3389/fpsyg.2014.01116.

Stelzel, C., Basten, U., Montag, C. et al. (2010). Frontostriatal involvement in task switching depends on genetic differences in d2 receptor density. *Journal of Neuroscience* 30 (42): 14205–14212. doi:10.1523/JNEUROSCI.1062-10.2010.

Stelzel, C., Fiebach, C.J., Cools, R. et al. (2013). Dissociable fronto-striatal effects of dopamine D2 receptor stimulation on cognitive versus motor flexibility. *Cortex* 49 (10): 2799–2811. doi:10.1016/j.cortex.2013.04.002.

Sunderman, G. and Kroll, J.F. (2006). First language activation during second language lexical processing: an investigation of lexical form, meaning, and grammatical class. *Studies in Second Language Acquisition* 28: 387–422.

Thierry, G. and Wu, Y.J. (2007). Brain potentials reveal unconscious translation during foreign-language comprehension. *Proceedings of the National Academy of Sciences* 104: 12530–12535. doi:10.1073/pnas.0609927104.

Thompson, R., Emmorey, K., and Gollan, T.H. (2005). 'Tip of the fingers' experiences by deaf signers. *Psychological Science* 16 (11): 856–860. doi:10.1111/j.1467-9280.2005.01626.x.

Tokowicz, N. and Macwhinney, B. (2005). Implicit and explicit measures of sensitivity to violations in second language grammar – an event-related potential investigation. *Studies in Second Language Acquisition* 27 (2): 173–204. doi:10.1017/S0272263105050102.

Trofimovich, P. and Baker, W. (2006). Learning second language suprasegmentals: effect of L2 experience on prosody and fluency characteristics of L2 speech. *Studies in Second Language Acquisition* 28 (1): 1–30. doi:10.1017/S0272263106060013.

Vaughn, K.A., Ramos Nuñez, A.I., Greene, M.R. et al. (2016). Individual differences in the bilingual brain: the role of language background and DRD2 genotype in verbal and non-verbal cognitive control. *Journal of Neurolinguistics* 40: 112–127. doi:10.1016/j.jneuroling.2016.06.008.

Ventura-Campos, N., Sanjuan, A., Gonzalez, J. et al. (2013). Spontaneous brain activity predicts learning ability of foreign sounds. *Journal of Neuroscience* 33 (22): 9295–9305. doi:10.1523/JNEUROSCI.4655-12.2013.

Veroude, K., Norris, D.G., Shumskaya, E. et al. (2010). Functional connectivity between brain regions involved in learning words of a new language. *Brain and Language* 113 (1): 21–27. doi:10.1016/j.bandl.2009.12.005.

Wang, Y., Xue, G., Chen, C. et al. (2007). Neural bases of asymmetric language switching in second-language learners: an ER-fMRI study. *NeuroImage* 35 (2): 862–870. doi:10.1016/j.neuroimage.2006.09.054.

Weber-Fox, C.M. and Neville, H.J. (1999). Functional neural subsystems are differentially affected by delays in second language immersion: ERP and behavioral evidence in bilinguals. In: *Second Language Acquisition and the Critical Period Hypothesis* (ed. D. Birdsong), 23–38. Mahwah, NJ: Erlbaum.

Wong, P.C., Morgan-Short, K., Ettlinger, M., and Zheng, J. (2012). Linking neurogenetics and individual differences in language learning: the dopamine hypothesis. *Cortex* 48 (9): 1091–1102. doi:10.1016/j.cortex.2012.03.017.

Wong, P.C., Perrachione, T.K., and Parrish, T.B. (2007). Neural characteristics of successful and less successful speech and word learning in adults. *Human Brain Mapping* 28 (10): 995–1006. doi:10.1002/hbm.20330.

Xiang, H., Dediu, D., Roberts, L. et al. (2012). The structural connectivity underpinning language aptitude, working memory, and IQ in the perisylvian language network. *Language Learning* 62 (2): 110–130.

Yang, H. and Yang, S. (2017). Are all interferences bad? Bilingual advantages in working memory are modulated by varying demands for controlled processing. *Bilingualism: Language and Cognition* 20 (1): 184–196. doi:10.1017/S1366728915000632.

Yim, O. and Bialystok, E. (2012). Degree of conversational code-switching enhances verbal task switching in Cantonese-English bilinguals. *Bilingualism: Language and Cognition* 15 (4): 873–883. doi:10.1017/S1366728912000478.

Yudes, C., Macizo, P., and Bajo, M. (2011). The influence of expertise in simultaneous interpreting on non-verbal executive processes. *Frontiers in Psychology* 2 (1–9): 309.

Zhang, H., Kang, C., Wu, Y. et al. (2015). Improving proactive control with training on language switching in bilinguals. *NeuroReport* 15 (26): 354–359. doi:10.1097/WNR.0000000000000353.

Zhang, Y., Kuhl, P. K., Imada, T., Iverson, P., Pruitt, J., Kotani, M., & Stevens, E. (2000). Neural plasticity revealed in perceptual training of a Japanese adult listener to learn American /l-r/ contrast: a whole-head magnetoencephalography study. Paper presented at the Sixth International Conference on Spoken Language Processing, Beijing, China.

33 The Intense Bilingual Experience of Interpreting and Its Neurocognitive Consequences

YANPING DONG AND FEI ZHONG

1. Introduction

Interpreting experience is an intense bilingual experience. In consecutive interpreting (CI), interpreters have to listen to and remember (and sometimes take notes of) a stretch of speech and produce the message in another language as efficiently as possible. In simultaneous interpreting (SI), interpreters have to listen to and remember a certain segment of speech while almost at the same time producing the previous segment of speech they have received. In either mode of interpreting, the interpreter is working under great time pressure. Classical questions in bilingual processing such as bilingual word access and language control are pertinent and critical questions in interpreting, and research on these questions in interpreting may reveal insights into the mechanisms of general bilingual processing.

A hotly debated issue concerning the mechanisms of general bilingual processing is whether or why learning or using two languages enhances one's executive functioning (e.g. Green 1998; Bialystok et al. 2004; Paap and Greenberg 2013; Paap et al. 2015; Bialystok 2017). The main debate centres on the existence or non-existence of a 'bilingual advantage', based on the presence or absence of performance advantages by bilinguals compared with monolinguals in non-linguistic tasks that are typically assumed to test one's executive functioning (EF). A related topic in interpreting is 'interpreter advantage', i.e. whether or how interpreting experience enhances performances in EF tasks. There seems to be no controversy on whether interpreting experience enhances EF because every study (Yudes et al. 2011; Dong and Xie 2014; Morales et al. 2015; Woumans et al. 2015; Becker et al. 2016; Dong and Liu 2016; Babcock and Vallesi 2017; Dong and Zhong 2017) has found an interpreter advantage in one aspect or another. What is controversial is the presence of an interpreter advantage in a specific executive function such as

The Handbook of the Neuroscience of Multilingualism, First Edition. Edited by John W. Schwieter.
© 2019 John Wiley & Sons Ltd. Published 2019 by John Wiley & Sons Ltd.

cognitive flexibility or inhibitory control. A further question would be: Why does a certain executive function exhibit an interpreter advantage in one study but not in another? Research on this question will probably help answer the parallel question in bilingual research.

Similar paradigms have been used in the investigation of bilingual advantage and interpreter advantage. Most empirical studies on bilingual advantage have followed the tripartite model by Miyake and Friedman (2012), i.e. a model illustrating the unity and diversity of mainly three executive functions: inhibition, switching, and updating. There are corresponding tasks typically employed to test these functions (although no task is pure in this correspondence). Inhibitory control is generally tested in the tasks of flanker (e.g. de Abreu et al. 2012; Dong and Zhong 2017), Stroop (e.g. Bialystok et al. 2008; Xie and Dong 2017), Simon (e.g. Bialystok et al. 2004; Woumans et al. 2015), and the more complex attentional network task (ANT; e.g. Costa et al. 2008; Marzecová et al. 2013). The switching function is often tested in colour-shape tasks (e.g. Prior and Macwhinney 2010; Babcock and Vallesi 2017) and the Wisconsin card sorting test (WCST; e.g. Yudes et al. 2011; Dong and Xie 2014), and updating is tested in the n-back task (e.g. Morales et al. 2015; Dong and Liu 2016). Research on interpreter advantage also covers the executive function of working memory (WM), the most basic component in the construct of executive functions as illustrated by Diamond (2013).

According to Diamond (2013), there are three sets of basic executive functions: WM, inhibitory control, and cognitive flexibility, with WM supporting the latter two, and with inhibitory control supporting cognitive flexibility. Higher-order functions like problem-solving depend on these basic functions. Although overlapping with the tripartite model by Miyake and Friedman (2012), Diamond's model is more comprehensive, and thus more appropriate for the current review. In fact, memory, especially WM, is often considered vital to success in interpreting. Interpreters need to temporarily store and process the incoming utterances and update their representations in their WM; they need to focus their attention on the relevant information or language, and to inhibit distractions, so that they can switch efficiently between listening in one language and speaking in another language. This indicates the involvement of all the sets of basic executive functions in interpreting, which raises the question of how interpreting experience affects the executive functions of WM, inhibitory control and cognitive flexibility. Although this question is of value itself, it is especially of value to the issue of bilingual advantage or the broader issues of bilingualism and brain plasticity.

2.   Interpreting Experience and Its Consequences on WM

2.1.   *Working Memory in Interpreting*

The task of interpreting places a heavy demand on memory, which is recognized in theoretical models such as the effort models proposed by Gile (1997/2002) and the process models proposed by Cowan (1988) and Mizuno (2005). The effort models, as functional models, illustrated what efforts an interpreter has to make to be successful in his or her renditions. In the effort model for SI (simultaneous interpreting) – *SI = L (listening) + P (production)* + M *(memory)* + C *(coordination)* – the M component makes possible language comprehension and production and is essential to coordination, which refers to the orchestration of the different components. The efforts for CI (consecutive interpreting) are described separately in two phases. In the input phase *–CI (listening)* = L *(listening)* + M *(memory)* + N *(note-taking)* + C *(coordination)* – the M component sustains the L and C efforts, as in the SI model, and also supports the efforts related to note-taking. In the output phase – *CI (reformulation)* = *Rem (remembering)* + *Read (note-reading)* + P *(production)* – the Rem component refers to retrieving the to-be-conveyed meaning from memory and from the notes. Note-taking and note-reading, features distinguishing CI from SI, are aids for the function of memory when segments of speech are too long.

Although the M component in the effort models mainly refers to a functional view of short-term memory (STM), WM plays an important role in all the M, P, and L efforts, as illustrated in Gile (2009). What the models emphasize is that for an interpretation to be successful, the total processing capacity available should exceed or at least be equal to the processing capacity required. The notion that the various efforts involved in interpreting need support from an interpreter's limited cognitive resources is consistent with the key feature of the function of WM, which is frequently defined as a cognitive system with a limited capacity that is responsible for temporarily holding information and for manipulating it. STM, simply defined as holding information in mind, is also considered important, and frequently tested together with WM in research in interpreting (e.g. Padilla et al. 1995; Köpke and Nespoulous 2006).

The process model proposed by Darò and Fabbro (1994) mainly explicates how WM and long-term memory work together to support SI. Compared with the classical multicomponent model of WM proposed by Baddeley and colleague (e.g. Baddeley 2000), this SI process model highlights the importance of the phonological loop in interpreting which consists of a phonological store and subvocal rehearsal.

Based on the embedded-processes model of memory (Cowan 1988, 2005), Mizuno (2005) proposed the other influential process model for interpreting. According to Cowan (1988, 2005), human memory is a single storage system composed of elements at various levels of activation. Those elements that are above the threshold of activation are considered to be in STM, and those that fall into the focus of attention (FOA) are in a hyperactivated state and are maintained or manipulated with conscious effort, and thus considered to be in WM. Mizuno's model is an integration of Cowan's model with the comprehension and production processes in interpreting.

It is therefore widely recognized (both in interpreting training and in theoretical research) that good WM is essential to success in interpreting. Previous research in the literature has tested different aspects of WM in interpreting, such as the phonological loop (e.g. Padilla et al. 1995; Köpke and Nespoulous 2006), WM spans (almost all the studies on this topic), WM updating (e.g. Morales et al. 2015; Dong and Liu 2016) and coordination (e.g. Strobach et al. 2015).

2.2. Interpreter Advantage in WM

Since the task of interpreting places an intense and unique demand on the function of WM, the question of how interpreting experience affects WM arises. If this influence is an additional benefit compared with similar experiences such as general L2 experience, it is considered to be an interpreter advantage in WM. A dozen studies have been published on this topic of interpreter advantage in WM, with most of them supporting the existence of this advantage in one way or another. We will describe most of them in this section, and leave a few to the next section in which we will try to explain why some of the findings are a little mixed and what could be done in the future.

WM and STM are frequently tested together in studies concerned with interpreter advantage, and are sometimes not distinguished or hardly distinguishable from each other in some manipulations of tasks. We try to distinguish them in the present chapter, but we are aware that other people may have different views. Apart from classical WM tasks such as complex verbal spans (e.g. reading, listening and speaking spans in either first language [L1] or second language [L2]) and STM tasks such as digit and word spans, a typical task frequently used in memory research in interpreting is the task of free recall with or without articulatory suppression, a task making use of the phonological loop (e.g. Padilla et al. 1995; Köpke and Nespoulous 2006). In the non-articulatory suppression condition, participants read and remember several lists of words visually presented, and at the end of each list, report verbally as many words as possible. In the articulatory suppression condition, however, participants have to repeat the same syllable such as 'bla' while reading the words presented. Simple free recall is a typical task for STM, while free recall with articulatory suppression can be considered a task of WM. Interpreting experience may enhance this special feature of WM because it is closely connected with the feature of the interpreting task (SI) in which interpreters have to listen, remember, and speak almost at the same time. Another WM task that is probably related to remembering and processing features in interpreting is the category probe task, in which participants listen to lists of words. At the end of each list, participants see a phonological or semantic probe word, and are asked to judge whether the probe word rhymes with or belongs to one of the words in the list. All these tasks are mainly intended as tests of WM spans, although no task is pure.

As regards interpreters' WM, what is more important than a large WM span is probably a more efficient functioning of the WM component of 'central executive' in Baddeley's (2000) model. As skills in central executive, updating, and coordination are frequently measured in empirical studies by n-back tasks and dual tasking. Updating, which is also considered central to the tripartite model by Miyake and Friedman (2012) and frequently reported together with other executive functions such as inhibitory control and cognitive flexibility (e.g. Morales et al. 2015; Dong and Liu 2016), can be tested in different versions of the n-back task. In the visuo-spatial version of the 2-back task, for example, participants are asked (at unpredictable intervals) to match the location of the current square with the location of the square before the previous one on the computer screen. As far as we know, coordination is best tested in dual tasking, in which participants are asked to respond to a main task and a following secondary task, with probably different SOAs (stimulus-onset asynchrony) between the two tasks. A typical main task, for example, is an auditory task, asking participants to listen to a tone and judge whether it is high, medium, or low, and a typical secondary task is a visual task, asking participants to judge whether a triangle is large, medium, or small.

Studies on WM span advantages for interpreters have found mixed results. Padilla et al. (1995) was probably the first study reporting interpreter advantages in the WM tasks of reading span and free recall with articulatory suppression, and in the STM tasks of digit span and simple free recall. Four groups of participants were compared: 10 interpreters, 10 non-interpreter controls, 10 student interpreters with some SI training, and 10 without. The key result was that the group of interpreters outperformed the other groups in the two tasks of digit and reading spans, and free recall with articulatory suppression (but not free recall without articulatory suppression). This pattern was replicated in a later study (Padilla et al. 2005).

Christoffels et al. (2006) conducted a well-controlled study and found evidence for interpreter advantages in the WM tasks of speaking and reading spans (with no restriction on recall order) and in the STM task of word span (recall order as presented), all administered in both L1 and L2. In this study, 13 professional Dutch-English interpreters were compared with 15 Dutch-English teachers matched in age (48.5 vs. 43.5 years old), educational background, and professional experience, and 39 unbalanced Dutch-English bilingual students with a mean age of 21.1 years. The professional interpreters outperformed the students and the teachers in almost all the WM and STM tasks except in L1 reading.

Köpke and Nespoulous (2006) found interpreter advantages in the WM tasks of listening span, free recall with articulatory suppression, and category probe, but not in the STM tasks of digit and word spans, but these WM advantages were mainly brought about by novice interpreters rather than expert interpreters. To explain this unexpected result, Köpke and Signorelli (2012) suggested that novice interpreters may have better memory skills because they frequently encounter cognitive overload, whereas interpreting experts may have developed specific strategies or schemas that are less reliant on WM. We believe that the factor of age may have also played a role, which was verified in Signorelli et al. (2012).

Signorelli et al. (2012) compared four groups of participants in the tasks of L2 reading span, nonword repetition, order- and category- cued recall: 12 interpreters with a mean age of 34.5, 11 non-interpreters with a mean age of 31.8, 13 interpreters with a mean age of 56.2, and 11 non-interpreters with a mean age of 63.6. The result is that interpreters outperformed non-interpreters in reading span and nonword repetition, but not in cued recall, suggesting that interpreters are better at WM and storing sublexical phonological representations, but not at short-term retention of words. However, younger interpreters were marginally better than the other groups in nonword repetition and cued recall, suggesting the important role of age.

There were also studies failing to find evidence for an interpreter advantage in WM. Chincotta and Underwood (1998), for example, found no interpreter advantage in WM and STM in the task of digit span administered in L1 and L2 with or without articulatory suppression. Twelve interpreting students with about 100 hours of interpreting practice were compared with 12 bilingual students majoring in English. The result was that no group effect was found for digit span in any conditions. In the study by Liu et al. (2004), three groups of participants were compared in the listening span task: 11 professional interpreters, 11 advanced student interpreters, and 11 beginning student interpreters. The result was that the three participant groups differed significantly in SI performance but not in WM capacity.

Apart from the above studies testing mostly different aspects of STM and WM spans, three more recent studies tested how interpreting experience influenced WM updating ability and found evidence supporting such an interpreter advantage in WM updating. Timarová et al. (2014) found positive correlations between interpreting performance and updating ability, with professional interpreters of higher accuracy in a letter 2-back task performing better in the interpretation of numbers (but not other indexes of interpreting performance). Morales et al. (2015) reported higher updating skills from simultaneous interpreters (SIs) when compared to general bilinguals. To overcome potential weaknesses in cross-sectional studies, Dong and Liu (2016) tested three comparable groups of participants twice with one semester in between during which one group received interpreting training, and the other two received written translation or general L2 training. The most relevant result is that interpreting training significantly enhanced updating ability, while the two control groups of written translation or general L2 training made only marginal or no progress, indicating an interpreter advantage in WM updating.

One recent study, Strobach et al. (2015), investigated the issue of interpreter advantage in dual tasking, which consisted of a primary auditory task and a secondary visual task with three SOAs of 50, 100, and 400 ms manipulated in the mixed blocks. The main results showed that interpreters outperformed the controls in the primary task in the single-task blocks, and the group difference was enlarged when responding to the primary task in the mixed block. These results suggest better task coordination skills in SIs, with an optimized activation of relevant task information (as indexed by enlarged group difference in the primary task in the mixed blocks), but not better regulation of bottleneck access (as indexed by no further boost of group difference in the secondary task in the mixed blocks). Becker et al. (2016) conducted a similar study using the fMRI technique, and the most relevant result is that the SIs exhibited an advantage in dual tasking when compared with professional multilingual controls.

To sum up, most relevant research in the literature indicates an interpreter advantage in WM, although specific findings are not necessarily consistent in all the studies. To date, the three studies investigating an updating advantage (Timarová et al. 2014; Morales et al. 2015; Dong and Liu 2016) and the two studies investigating a coordination advantage (Strobach et al. 2015; Becker et al. 2016) have found evidence supporting an interpreter advantage in WM central executive. The role of 'coordination' is depicted in Gile (1997/2002), while the advantage in updating is probably due to the fact that successful interpreting requires frequent storage of information and highly efficient replacement of obsolete information with information that is new and relevant for the current task. As for WM or STM spans, the findings are mixed.

2.3. Limitations in Current Research and Directions in Future Research

A few confounding factors may have contributed to the mixed findings about interpreter advantage in WM. The first one is age, which was not matched amongst participant groups in some of the studies. Professional interpreters are generally older than novice or student interpreters, and research on individual differences in WM shows that WM capacity declines as a function of age (e.g. Park et al. 2003). It is therefore possible that age may have counteracted or neutralized a potential WM advantage in older professional interpreters when compared with younger novice interpreters. This age factor may explain the results in Köpke and Nespoulous (2006) and Liu et al. (2004; see Section 2.2 for details). The second factor is L2 proficiency, which has been found to play a role in WM capacity (e.g. Service et al. 2002) but was seldom matched amongst participant groups. As found in Tzou et al. (2012), participants with higher L2 proficiency showed larger WM capacity than those with lower L2 proficiency. The third factor is the small sample size in some of the studies (e.g. 9 in Tzou et al. 2012; 10 in Padilla et al. 1995; 11 in Liu et al. 2004; 12 in Chincotta and Underwood 1998; less than 13 in Signorelli et al. 2012). Studies with small sample sizes can be problematic, as discussed in Button et al. (2013). Briefly speaking, a small sample size is associated with low statistical power, which means that the possibility of observed results being true is low. Even if the effect size is large, it could be inflated, and it may be hard to reproduce the same result if replicated.

To investigate how interpreting experience affects WM, it is probably more fruitful to conduct more longitudinal research in the future. Macnamara and Conway (2014) tested a group of 21 bimodal bilinguals twice with two years in between in which participants received SI training between American Sign Language and English, and found that interpreting training enhanced the WM processes of coordination and transformation (as tested by backward digit span and letter–number sequencing), but not storage and processing (as tested by reading span and operation span). To better investigate the issue of interpreter advantage, Dong et al. (2018) tested two groups of participants twice with four months in between. One group (48 university students) received interpreting training and the comparable control group (43 university students) received general L2 training. Liu et al. found that interpreting training made a unique contribution to WM updating efficiency (as tested in n-back), but not to spans (as tested in L2 listening span and running letter span), suggesting an interpreter advantage in updating efficiency.

In short, future studies testing an interpreter advantage in WM may need to pay more attention to research design, in particular as regards participants' age, language proficiency (and language learning history), the number of participants in each group, and the use of a control group in longitudinal studies. There are also other factors such as the use of different WM tasks, and different manipulations of the same task. Many studies selected tasks or manipulated tasks in a way that corresponds to the features of interpreting, regardless of typical manipulations in the literature. For example, some studies testing interpreters' WM did not require order in the recall of items (e.g. Christoffels et al. 2006; Signorelli et al. 2012), although others did follow the typical requirement of order in recall (e.g. Köpke and Nespoulous 2006). Will this specific difference lead to different results? More research is thus needed, especially longitudinal studies with more rigorous research designs.

3. Interpreting Experience and Its Consequences on Inhibitory Control

As illustrated in Sections 1 and 2.1, interpreting is a cognitively complex and demanding task, and interpreters have to manage at almost the same time different components such as listening, speaking, note-taking, reading, etc. under time pressure. They must concentrate on their job, not be disturbed by the many surrounding distractions (the other language, different people speaking, etc.), and must restrain themselves from saying or doing things which are incompatible with their role as interpreters. The question thus arises whether interpreting experience enhances inhibitory control, or as preferred in the present review, whether interpreting experience adds more benefits to inhibitory control when compared with general L2 experience, i.e. the issue of interpreter advantage in inhibitory control.

According to Diamond (2013), inhibitory control helps regulate one's attention, thoughts, emotions, and behaviour to ensure daily life management. It consists of response inhibition, and interference control which in turn consists of cognitive inhibition and selective/focused attention. Cognitive inhibition, the resistance to prepotent mental representations, is seldom connected with interpreting advantage in the literature, while selective attention and response inhibition have been investigated in a few studies and are therefore what we will review in this section. Selective attention is inhibition at the attentional level, focusing attention on the present task or goal while resisting irrelevant information. Response inhibition is inhibition at the behavioural level, suppressing prepotent responses.

So far, five paradigms have been employed to explore how interpreting experience affects inhibitory control: tasks of flanker, ANT, Simon, Stroop, and antisaccade. What they share is that they are all composed of three types of stimulus conditions: congruent, incongruent, and neutral. In the tasks of flanker and ANT (attentional network task, a combination of the flanker task with attentional cues), the incongruent condition is created by the mismatch between the direction of the central arrow and that of its flankers. In the Simon task, it is created by the mismatch between the response elicited by the colour of the stimuli (pressing a button on the left or right side) and the response tendency elicited by the position of the stimuli (in the left or right side of the screen). In the Stroop task, it is created by the mismatch between the reference of a colour word and the print colour of the word. The smaller the reaction time (RT) difference between the incongruent and the congruent conditions, the better the inhibitory ability. Besides, shorter global RT in these tasks is considered an index of better monitoring ability, i.e. participants were better at monitoring situations containing conflicts. The antisaccade task is different to a certain extent. Apart from solving the conflict between the direction of the arrow and its position in the left or right side of the screen, participants also have to inhibit the distraction of the preceding cue that is positioned in the opposite direction of the screen.

The description of the tasks above seems to indicate some correspondences between these tasks and the different types of inhibitory control. The flanker task (together with the ANT) seems to be a typical task testing how participants could focus on the goal (central arrow) and ignore distractions (flankers), while the Simon, Stroop, and antisaccade tasks tend to test how participants can inhibit prepotent responses (the position, the reference of the word, etc.). However, we certainly do not think there is a clear-cut line between these two types of inhibitory control, because inhibiting prepotent responses also requires participants to focus their attention on the more 'mute' feature of a stimulus (e.g. the colour of the print of a colour word such as 'red'). In other words, no task is 'pure' (Valian 2015), and focusing attention is essential to good performance in any task containing conflicts and/or distractions. The current chapter, therefore, does not try to differentiate between the two types of inhibitory control unless there is a special need, and we will use the general term 'inhibitory control' to refer to both, for the sake of convenience.

Since success in interpreting requires intense language control (partly as coordination described in Gile's effort model, 1997), it seems reasonable to hypothesize that constant practice of interpreting may enhance inhibitory control. However, empirical data collected with behavioural methods have not yet found strong support for this hypothesis. Three of the studies (Yudes et al. 2011; Morales et al. 2015; Babcock and Vallesi 2017) compared the performance of a group of professional interpreters and a comparable group of general bilinguals (with no interpreting experience), respectively in the task of Simon, ANT, and Stroop (together with ANT), and found that professional SIs and general bilinguals did not differ in their performance. With both professional SIs and student SIs compared with bilingual and monolingual controls, Köpke and Nespoulous (2006) again did not find interpreter advantage in the Stroop task. Neither did Dong and Xie (2014) with CI students compared with general bilinguals in the flanker task. Woumans et al. (2015) tested the inhibitory control performance of student interpreters, balanced bilinguals, unbalanced bilinguals, and monolinguals in the ANT and Simon tasks. The results showed that student interpreters exhibited superior performance on accuracy rates over the unbalanced bilinguals but not the balanced bilinguals, indicating that L2 proficiency rather than interpreting training was the main source of this advantage. In their longitudinal study, Dong and Liu (2016) failed to find any evidence supporting an interpreter advantage in inhibitory control tested in the Stroop task, although they did find an advantage in updating.

Timarová et al. (2014) was probably the first behavioural study that has found some evidence supporting an interpreter advantage in inhibitory control. They employed 28 professional SIs in a series of tasks of executive functioning including the flanker and the antisaccade tasks and analysed correlations between the EF indexes and participants' background data (e.g. length of interpreting experience, age) together with various interpreting performance indexes. The results showed that the performance of the flanker task significantly correlated with interpreting experience (calculated in years or days), although the performance of the antisaccade task did not.

All the above studies examining the inhibitory control advantage were conducted with behavioural methods, and the results could be a coordination of several processes (Luck 2005). To dissociate the inhibitory processes and to examine the processing of the inhibitory task in earlier stages, Dong and Zhong (2017) employed student CIs with different amount of interpreting training and compared their performance in the task of flanker using the event-related potential (ERP) technique. They analysed the N1, N2, and P3 components, with N1 reflecting early attentional processing and N2 and P3 indexing inhibition processes. Larger N2 and smaller P3 amplitudes in the incongruent condition with no group differences in the congruent condition were regarded as an advantage of interference suppression while larger N2 and smaller P3 amplitudes in both conditions were regarded as an advantage of conflict monitoring. The results indicated that interpreting experience enhanced early attentional processing, conflict monitoring, and interference suppression (i.e. selective or focused attention in Diamond 2013) along the time course of processing. To be more specific, Experiment 1 suggested advantages of early attentional processing in the N1 time window (30–130 ms), of conflict monitoring in the N2 (240–380 ms) and the first half of P3 time window (320–440 ms), and of interference suppression in the second half (440–520 ms) and in the RT. These results were successfully replicated in Experiment 2 in which a new group with less interpreting (training) experience was recruited. However, the advantage of selective attention in Experiment 2 appeared earlier, in the first half of P3 time window, and it decreased earlier, leading to only a marginal interpreter advantage indexed in RT. A comparison of the two experiments suggests that the reason why no inhibitory control advantage has been found by behavioural methods in the literature is probably that the advantage may have appeared and decreased before participants respond by pressing a certain button.

To sum up, except for one study (Timarová et al. 2014), all the behavioural studies failed to find any evidence supporting an interpreter advantage in inhibitory control (Köpke and Nespoulous 2006; Yudes et al. 2011; Dong and Xie 2014; Babcock and Vallesi 2017; Morales et al. 2015; Woumans et al. 2015; Dong and Liu 2016). And yet, the two flanker experiments conducted with the ERP technique in Dong and Zhong (2017) found robust advantages and illustrated how an inhibitory control advantage (specifically selective attention advantage) emerged along the time course, and how it may disappear gradually when the conflicts were solved and the disadvantageous group caught up in RT.

The 'temporal' and 'distributed' nature of selective attention as illustrated in Dong and Zhong (2017) merits further research. Selective attention seems distributed along the time course of processing, with the supposedly advantageous group being better at early attentional processing around 100 ms, at monitoring ability during some time interval after about 200 ms and at interference suppression during some time interval after about 300 ms. Each manifestation of the selective attention advantage along the time course of processing seems temporal and temporary, and the supposedly disadvantageous group may then catch up. More replications are needed to reach firm conclusions. In addition, it may be worthwhile to test the difference between selective attention and response inhibition with the ERP technique.

Future research needs to further investigate the issue of interpreter advantage along the time course of processing, with participants of various contrasts. For example, if the two groups of participants in Dong and Zhong (2017) differed more in the amount of interpreting training (such as professional interpreters and comparable bilinguals), the inhibitory control advantage in the ERP experiments may have appeared earlier and disappeared earlier, leaving no more advantage in RT. If this hypothesis is correct, it will be instructive to investigate the developmental trajectory of interpreter advantage in each executive function, including inhibitory control.

4.   Interpreting Experience and Its Consequences on Cognitive Flexibility

As illustrated in Section 2, interpreters have to switch efficiently between listening to one language and speaking in another language. Even when they are listening to one language, their mind is probably switching back and forth between the two languages because they may have been searching for equivalents of words, phrases, clauses in the other language even before an input sentence is finished (e.g. Macizo and Bajo 2006; Dong and Lin 2013). Will this intense language-switching experience help enhance the non-linguistic executive function of cognitive flexibility?

Cognitive flexibility is more or less the same as switching in Miyake and Friedman's (2012) tripartite model, and a synonym for 'mental set shifting'. As one of the three sets of basic executive functions in Diamond (2013), cognitive flexibility is the ability to switch perspectives or switch between tasks or courses, or to adapt to changed environments. In addition, cognitive flexibility needs to be supported by the other two sets of executive functions, i.e. WM and inhibitory control (Diamond 2013). For example, when switching from one task to the other, participants need to inhibit the previous task rule and load the new rule into WM.

The typical tools used to explore how interpreting experience influences cognitive flexibility are the colour-shape task and the Wisconsin card sorting task (WCST), although again no task is process pure. The colour-shape task consists of (i) single-task blocks in which participants are asked to judge on only one dimension of the stimulus throughout (e.g. 'green or red' vs. 'square or triangle' for a coloured shape), and (ii) mixed-task blocks in which participants are asked to judge the colour or the shape of each stimulus according to cues given. Three indexes are generally calculated as indicators of cognitive flexibility, or how well the task is performed: switch cost, mixing cost, and global RT. Switch cost is the difference between switch and non-switch trials in the mixed-task blocks; mixing cost is the difference between non-switch trials in the mixed-task blocks and trials in the single-task blocks, and global RT is the average RT in the mixed-task blocks. An adapted version of the bivalent colour-shape task just described is the univalent colour-shape task, in which each stimulus can be defined by only one dimension (e.g. a colourless shape). The main difference between the two versions of the task is that inhibitory control is more involved in the bivalent version because when making judgements about one dimension of a stimulus (e.g. the colour of a coloured shape), participants have to inhibit the other dimension of the same stimulus (e.g. shape).

With regard to the WCST, participants are asked to match a response card with one of the four stimulus cards. There are three dimensions for a response card: colour, shape, and number (e.g. a response card with three green squares), and each response card matches one of the four stimulus cards by one of the three dimensions. Participants have to guess the current rule of sorting (e.g. match the response card with a stimulus card by their shared colour or shape or number), and adjust their rule in their next trial according to the 'correct' or 'wrong' feedback they receive. The number of completed categories and various error rates are the main indicators of WCST performance. When compared with the colour-shape task (bivalent or univalent), the WCST seems therefore more dependent on WM, because participants have to remember and calculate many things (the three dimensions, the previous dimension they selected and its feedback), and to efficiently change their mental set if the feedback is 'wrong'.

Two studies with the WCST task (Yudes et al. 2011; Dong and Xie 2014) have found evidence supporting an interpreter advantage in cognitive flexibility. In Yudes et al.'s (2011) WCST experiment, professional SIs outperformed their bilingual counterparts in three aspects. They needed fewer attempts to find out the correct rules, and made fewer overall errors and fewer previous category errors (i.e. errors made as a repetition of a previous trial even if told in the feedback that it was wrong, Hartman et al. 2001). Dong and Xie (2014) conducted a similar experiment with student CIs and comparable control groups, and found that only interpreting experience, but not L2 proficiency, L2 exposure, or L2 use, significantly predicted WCST performance.

Two studies with the (bivalent) colour-shape task (Becker et al. 2016; Babcock and Vallesi 2017) also found evidence supporting an interpreter advantage but not necessarily in cognitive flexibility. Babcock and Vallesi's (2017) study with professional SIs showed that the interpreters exhibited shorter overall RT and a smaller mixing cost, but no group difference was found in switch cost. A smaller mixing cost is regarded as an advantage in sustained control, and can be taken as a reflection of a monitoring advantage of interpreters. As for the smaller overall RT, the authors ascribed it to the interpreters' faster information processing ability, for the reason that the faster responses were exhibited not only in the mixed-task block, but also in single-task block, where no group differences were expected.

Becker et al. (2016) used the fMRI technique to examine the same issue with professional SIs. The behavioural results were similar to the results in Babcock and Vallesi (2017), revealing an interpreter advantage in overall RT and mixing cost but not in switch cost. The fMRI data indicated that with regard to brain structure, interpreters showed more grey matter (GM) volume in the left frontal pole (BA 10) when compared with controls. Besides, the volume in this region predicted variances in mixing cost with marginal significance, but only with interpreters, and there was a negative partial correlation between the left frontal pole cluster and mixing cost. The resting-state functional brain data revealed that, in the voxel-based morphometry (VBM) frontal pole cluster, the interpreters enjoyed greater global efficiency and node degree (the amount of edges connected to a particular node), compared to controls. Moreover, interpreters also exhibited stronger functional connectivity between the frontal pole cluster and the left MFG/left IFG. Furthermore, SIs' superior performance in mixing cost may be due to their better developed (left) frontopolar cortex (FPC), as it is related to task switching and attention shifting, and its connectivity with IFG is stronger in SIs. Therefore, it can be concluded that SI experience helps enhance EF (but not necessarily cognitive flexibility) and has structural and functional neurocognitive consequences.

Cross-sectional studies were not able to draw conclusions with regard to causal effects. To overcome such shortcomings, Dong and Liu (2016), as reported in Section 2.2, tested three comparable groups of bilingual students twice with one semester in between when the three groups respectively took a course in interpreting, translation, or general L2. The results of the univalent colour-shape task showed that the interpreting experience significantly reduced the switch cost (but not mixing cost or global RT), indicating an interpreter advantage in cognitive flexibility when compared with the control groups. This pattern of an interpreter advantage was replicated in the post-test WCST as reported in the supplementary material of the paper (because the WCST was not conducted in the pre-test).

To sum up, empirical studies exploring how interpreting experience influences cognitive flexibility have found evidence for an interpreter advantage, but not necessarily in cognitive flexibility. The three studies conducted with either professional SIs or student CIs in the WCST task (Yudes et al. 2011; Dong and Xie 2014; Dong and Liu 2016) did find an interpreter advantage in cognitive flexibility, evidenced by fewer errors and/or more completed categories. Nevertheless, the two studies conducted with professional SIs in the bivalent colour-shape task (Becker et al. 2016; Babcock and Vallesi 2017) showed only an interpreter advantage in monitoring (smaller mixing cost) and faster information process (smaller global RT including the single task), but not in the typical index of cognitive flexibility (switch cost). Only one study (Dong and Liu 2016) found an advantage in cognitive flexibility with the univalent colour-shape task.

We believe that this pattern of empirical findings can be explained by the different features of the tasks. The WCST task has found evidence for an interpreter advantage in cognitive flexibility, probably because this task is more dependent on WM than the colour-shape task. The colour-shape task in Becker et al. (2016) and Babcock and Vallesi (2017) failed to find such an advantage, probably because the bivalent version was more dependent on inhibitory control. As reviewed in Section 3, it seems easier to find an interpreter advantage in WM than in inhibitory control. Indeed, when the colour-shape task was conducted in its univalent version as in Dong and Liu (2016), the advantage in switch cost appeared, probably because the dependence on inhibitory control was lessened. More research is needed to verify this explanation, which will help explicate the relationship between the different components in either the tripartite model by Miyake and Friedman (2012) or the EF model by Diamond (2013).

5. Conclusion

Interpreting experience is a cognitively demanding task, which raises the question of how interpreting experience affects EF, or more specifically, how interpreting experience affects the executive functions of WM, inhibitory control, and cognitive flexibility. A comprehensive review reveals three major findings. First, those executive functions that are most exercised in interpreting tend to produce an interpreter advantage, such as WM updating and coordination, selective attention, and cognitive flexibility. Second, behavioural methods may not be so appropriate to test the temporal and distributed nature of selective attention. Third, the mixed results of cognitive flexibility are probably related to how much the switching task involves WM and inhibitory control.

Interpreting experience is an intense bilingual experience, and research on its neurocognitive consequences helps solve corresponding questions in bilingual research. There are a few implications. First, if the bilingual experience is intense enough, it will probably produce certain EF benefits. Dong and Liu (2016) suggest that high processing demand in training is probably a vital factor in the absence or presence of cognitive benefits, since it was oral interpreting rather than written translation that exhibited a cognitive flexibility advantage, although both modes involve similar language-switch practice.

Second, only those executive functions that are intensively exercised in bilingualism may get enhanced. Previous research on the topic of bilingual advantage mainly focuses on inhibitory control and cognitive flexibility, because it is assumed that compared with a monolingual, a bilingual has to inhibit the other language not needed at the moment, and a bilingual may have to switch between languages. Since the findings are so mixed (e.g. Paap et al. 2015), we may have to come back to the issue of what bilingualism exactly means. Since the bilingual spectrum is very broad, it may be too difficult to generalize features that are relevant and true, and it may be necessary to split it into special groups, such as the bilingual group of interpreters. The final result may dispel the concept of 'bilingual advantage', but it will certainly help reveal the nature of bilingualism.

Third, with all the mixed results and conflicting conclusions in the literature of bilingual advantage, we may have to pay more attention to the methods used in collecting data. As analysed in this chapter, some studies may contain flaws such as an insufficient sample size and the incomparability of participant groups. The correspondence between a task and the function the task is assumed to test is also a problem. In addition, it may be useful to compare behavioural results with neurological results.

All in all, the research on the neurocognitive consequences of interpreting experience has provided not only tentative answers to the question itself but also some insights into bilingual research, as we have illustrated. But more research is certainly needed.

REFERENCES

Babcock, L. and Vallesi, A. (2017). Are simultaneous interpreters expert bilinguals, unique bilinguals, or both? *Bilingualism: Language and Cognition* 20 (2): 403–417.

Baddeley, A.D. (2000). The episodic buffer: a new component of working memory? *Trends in Cognitive Sciences* 4 (11): 417–423.

Becker, M., Schubert, T., Strobach, T. et al. (2016). Simultaneous interpreters vs. professional multilingual controls: group differences in cognitive control as well as brain structure and function. *NeuroImage* 134: 250–260.

Bialystok, E. (2017). The bilingual adaptation: how minds accommodate experience. *Psychological Bulletin* 143 (3): 233.

Bialystok, E., Craik, F.I.M., Klein, R., and Viswanathan, M. (2004). Bilingualism, aging, and cognitive control: evidence from the Simon task. *Psychology and Aging* 19 (2): 290–303.

Bialystok, E., Craik, F.I.M., and Luk, G. (2008). Cognitive control and lexical access in younger and older bilinguals. *Journal of Experimental Psychology: Learning, Memory, and Cognition* 34 (4): 859–873.

Button, K.S., Ioannidis, J.P.A., Mokrysz, C. et al. (2013). Power failure: why small sample size undermines the reliability of neuroscience. *Nature Reviews Neuroscience* 14 (5): 365–376.

Chincotta, D. and Underwood, G. (1998). Non temporal determinants of bilingual memory capacity: the role of long-term representations and fluency. *Bilingualism: Language and Cognition* 1 (2): 117–130.

Christoffels, I.K., De Groot, A.M., and Kroll, J.F. (2006). Memory and language skills in simultaneous interpreters: the role of expertise and language proficiency. *Journal of Memory and Language* 54 (3): 324–345.

Costa, A., Hernandez, M., and Sebastian-Galles, N. (2008). Bilingualism aids conflict resolution: evidence from the ANT task. *Cognition* 106 (1): 59–86.

Cowan, N. (1988). Evolving conceptions of memory storage, selective attention, and their mutual constraints within the human information processing system. *Psychological Bulletin* 104 (2): 163–191.

Cowan, N. (2005). *Working Memory Capacity.* New York, NY/Hove, UK: Psychology Press.

de Abreu, P.M.E., Cruz-Santos, A., Tourinho, C.J. et al. (2012). Bilingualism enriches the poor enhanced cognitive control in low-income minority children. *Psychological Science* 23 (11): 1364–1371.

Darò, V. and Fabbro, F. (1994). Verbal memory during simultaneous interpretation: effects of phonological interference. *Applied Linguistics* 15 (4): 365–381.

Diamond, A. (2013). Executive functions. *Annual Review of Psychology* 64: 135–168.

Dong, Y. and Lin, J. (2013). Parallel processing of the target language during source language comprehension in interpreting. *Bilingualism: Language and Cognition* 16 (3): 682–692.

Dong, Y. and Liu, Y. (2016). Classes in translating and interpreting produce differential gains in switching and updating. *Frontiers in Psychology* 7: 1297.

Dong, Y., Liu, Y., and Cai, R. (2018). How does consecutive interpreting training influence working memory: a longitudinal study of potential links between the two. *Frontiers in Psychology* 9: 875.

Dong, Y. and Xie, Z. (2014). Contributions of second language proficiency and interpreting experience to cognitive control differences among young adult bilinguals. *Journal of Cognitive Psychology* 26: 506–519.

Dong, Y. and Zhong, F. (2017). Interpreting experience enhances early attentional processing, conflict monitoring and interference suppression along the time course of processing. *Neuropsychologia* 95 (2017): 193–203.

Gile, D. (1997/2002). Conference interpreting as a cognitive management problem. In: *The Interpreting Studies Reader* (ed. F. Pöchhacker and M. Shlesinger), 162–176. London, UK: Routledge.

Gile, D. (2009). *Basic Concepts and Models for Interpreter and Translator Training* (Rev. ed.). Amsterdam, The Netherlands/Philadelphia, PA: John Benjamins.

Green, D.W. (1998). Mental control of the bilingual lexico-semantic system.

Bilingualism: Language and Cognition 1 (2): 67–81.

Hartman, M., Bolton, E., and Fehnel, S.E. (2001). Accounting for age differences on the Wisconsin card sorting test: decreased working memory, not inflexibility. *Psychology and Aging* 16 (3): 385.

Köpke, B. and Nespoulous, J.L. (2006). Working memory performance in expert and novice interpreters. *Interpreting* 8 (1): 1–23.

Köpke, B. and Signorelli, T.M. (2012). Methodological aspects of working memory assessment in simultaneous interpreters. *International Journal of Bilingualism* 16 (2): 183–197.

Liu, M., Schallert, D.L., and Carroll, P.J. (2004). Working memory and expertise in simultaneous interpreting. *Interpreting* 6 (1): 19–42.

Luck, S.J. (2005). *An Introduction to the Event-Related Potential Technique.* Cambridge, MA: The MIT Press.

Macizo, P. and Bajo, M.T. (2006). Reading for repetition and reading for translation: do they involve the same processes? *Cognition* 99: 1–34.

Macnamara, B.N. and Conway, A.R. (2014). Novel evidence in support of the bilingual advantage: influences of task demands and experience on cognitive control and working memory. *Psychonomic Bulletin & Review* 21 (2): 520–525.

Marzecová, A., Asanowicz, D., Kriva, L.U., and Wodniecka, Z. (2013). The effects of bilingualism on efficiency and lateralization of attentional networks. *Bilingualism: Language and Cognition* 16 (3): 608–623.

Miyake, A. and Friedman, N.P. (2012). The nature and organization of individual differences in executive functions: four general conclusions. *Current Directions in Psychological Science* 21: 8–14.

Mizuno, A. (2005). Process model for simultaneous interpreting and working memory. *Meta: Journal des traducteurs* 50 (2): 739–752.

Morales, J., Padilla, F., Gomez-Ariza, C.J., and Bajo, M.T. (2015). Simultaneous interpretation selectively influences working memory and attentional networks. *Acta Psychologica* 155: 82–91.

Paap, K.R. and Greenberg, Z.I. (2013). There is no coherent evidence for a bilingual advantage in executive processing. *Cognitive Psychology* 66 (2): 232–258.

Paap, K.R., Johnson, H.A., and Sawi, O. (2015). Bilingual advantages in executive functioning either do not exist or are restricted to very specific and undetermined circumstances. *Cortex* 69: 265–278.

Padilla, P., Bajo, M.T., Canas, J.J., and Padilla, F. (1995). Cognitive processes of memory in simultaneous interpretation. In: *Topics in Interpreting Research* (ed. J. Tommola), 61–72. Turku, Finland: University of Turku.

Padilla, F., Bajo, M.T., and Macizo, P. (2005). Articulatory suppression in language interpretation: working memory capacity, dual tasking and word knowledge. *Bilingualism: Language and Cognition* 8 (03): 207–219.

Park, D.C., Welsh, R.C., Marshuetz, C. et al. (2003). Working memory for complex scenes: age differences in frontal and hippocampal activations. *Journal of Cognitive Neuroscience* 15 (8): 1122–1134.

Prior, A. and Macwhinney, B. (2010). A bilingual advantage in task switching. *Bilingualism: Language and Cognition* 13 (2): 253–262.

Service, E., Simola, M., Metsaenheimo, O., and Maury, S. (2002). Bilingual working memory span is affected by language skill. *European Journal of Cognitive Psychology* 14 (3): 383–407.

Signorelli, T.M., Haarmann, H.J., and Obler, L.K. (2012). Working memory in simultaneous interpreters: effects of task and age. *International Journal of Bilingualism* 16 (2): 198–212.

Strobach, T., Becker, M., Schubert, T., and Kühn, S. (2015). Better dual-task processing in simultaneous interpreters. *Frontiers in Psychology* 6.

Timarová, Š., Čeňková, I., Meylaerts, R. et al. (2014). Simultaneous interpreting and working memory executive control. *Interpreting* 16: 139–168.

Tzou, Y.-Z., Eslami, Z.R., Chen, H.C., and Vaid, J. (2012). Effect of language proficiency and degree of formal training in simultaneous interpreting on working memory and interpreting performance: evidence from mandarin–English speakers. *International Journal of Bilingualism* 16 (2): 213–227.

Valian, V. (2015). Bilingualism and cognition. *Bilingualism: Language and Cognition* 18 (1): 3–24.

Woumans, E., Ceuleers, E., Van der Linden, L. et al. (2015). Verbal and nonverbal cognitive control in bilinguals and interpreters. *Journal of Experimental Psychology: Learning, Memory, and Cognition* 41 (5): 1579–1586.

Xie, Z. and Dong, Y. (2017). Contributions of bilingualism and public speaking training to cognitive control differencs among young adults. *Bilingualism: Language and Cognition* 20 (1): 55–68.

Yudes, C., Macizo, P., and Bajo, T. (2011). The influence of expertise in simultaneous interpreting on non-verbal executive processes. *Frontiers in Psychology* 2: 309.

34   The Bilingual Advantage Debate
Quantity and Quality of the Evidence

KENNETH PAAP

1.   Introduction

More than 100 published articles have tested the hypothesis that bilingualism causes an enhancement in general executive functioning (EF). The hypothesis is predicated on the assumption that coordinating two languages requires extensive use of general-purpose EFs. Although many of these articles report statistically better performance for bilinguals compared with monolinguals, recent reviews have drawn attention to alternative explanations for many of these positive results and have suggested that the bilingual advantages may be trivial in magnitude or restricted to very special cases (Hilchey et al. 2015; Paap et al. 2014, 2015, 2016). The bilingual advantage hypothesis is difficult to test for many reasons and one is the complexity of the EF construct (see Paap and Sawi 2014 and Valian 2015, for extended discussions). Both the conceptualization of EF and its operational definition in empirical studies may be contributing to the inconsistencies in the findings.

EFs consist of a set of general-purpose control processes that are central to the self-regulation of thoughts and behaviours and that are instrumental to accomplishing goals. Research on EF has often focused on the three components initially identified by Miyake et al. (2000) using latent variable analyses: updating, switching,[1] and inhibitory control. Inhibitory control was inferred from performance measures in three different tasks that all involve competition and therefore require some type of conflict resolution such as the inhibition of a prepotent response. Likewise, a general switching ability was inferred from performance on three different tasks that frequently required participants to switch from one task (e.g. judgements about colour) to another (e.g. judgements about shape). The third latent variable – updating of working memory representations – requires monitoring and coding incoming information for task relevance and then appropriately revising the information held in working memory. In Miyake et al. (2000) each of three observed measures significantly loaded on the expected latent variable, establishing that these three EFs can be considered as separate abilities. Furthermore, at the higher level of the analysis, the three latent variables also correlated

The Handbook of the Neuroscience of Multilingualism, First Edition. Edited by John W. Schwieter.
© 2019 John Wiley & Sons Ltd. Published 2019 by John Wiley & Sons Ltd.

with one another and this is consistent with the assumption that the latent variables are components of a common EF ability.

Miyake and Friedman (2012) now favour a variation on the simple hierarchical model described above. They compared the fit of the simple hierarchical model to a more complex second-order ('nested') model where the nine observed measures are allowed to load on common EF and the three latent variables compete in accounting for the remaining variance. The best solution for the second-order model resulted in all nine measures loading on the common EF and with only two of the nested components (updating and switching) still making unique contributions. Putting this together, the model supports a theory of a general EF ability with separate updating and switching components and an inhibition component that is not separable, but moderately linked to general EF ability. This analysis led Miyake and Friedman (2012) to conclude that EF has both unity (a common EF) and diversity (additional specific abilities associated with switching and updating).

There are other frameworks, also based on latent variable analyses, that are somewhat different. Using similar latent variable methods Engelhardt et al. (2015) used data from 505 third- to eighth-graders and 12 different tasks to test five different models, but the second-order unity–diversity model favoured by Miyake and Friedman was not amongst those evaluated. The best-fitting model included the inhibitory control and switching components, but also separates working memory capacity (WMC) from updating.

Drawing WMC into the web of EF adds further complications as WMC is known to correlate with general fluid (gF) intelligence at about 0.45 at the level of individual tests and at around 0.72 at the latent variable level (Kane et al. 2005).

In turn, Unsworth et al. (2014) showed that this strong relationship between WMC and gF is completely mediated by latent factors for capacity, secondary memory, and attention control. Capacity refers to the ability to apprehend and maintain distinct items in a highly active state. Secondary memory refers to the ability to successfully encode information into secondary memory and, most important, to bring task relevant information back into primary memory when needed. Attention control refers to the ability to select and actively maintain items in the presence of internal and external distraction, especially when goal-relevant information must be maintained in a highly active state in the presence of distraction.

One reason why the bilingual advantage debate continues is because studies target a variety of different executive functions and types of bilinguals. On the other hand, if the components of EF are highly related to one another, then one might expect that bilinguals who actively use two languages (regardless of other differences) would show fairly consistent advantages across an array of different tests of EF.

2.   Quantity of Evidence

To address the quantity of evidence supporting the bilingual advantage hypothesis, one needs to carve up the vast literature in a way that minimizes, at least to some extent, combining apples with oranges. The newest wave of meta-anlayses on the bilingual advantage has minimized the apples and oranges problem (Ioannidis 2016) by separately analysing results targeting inhibition, updating of working memory, and switching. That said, meta-analyses focusing on a single component of EF are still challenged by differences in tasks and types of bilingual experience that cause heterogeneity across studies.

2.1. Inhibition

The results of a meta-analysis we first summarized at a meeting of the Psychonomic Society (Paap et al. 2017) is presented in detail here. The analysis was restricted to measures of interference control derived from non-verbal interference tasks. Verbal tests were not included because bilinguals often show small, but significant disadvantages on verbal tasks. The non-verbal tasks all included both incongruent trials, where conflict resolution is required, and congruent trials, where there is no competition between task relevant and irrelevant information. Five databases (PsycARTICLES, PsycINFO, PsycEXTRA, Academic Search Complete, and Education Research Complete) were searched for documents satisfying this Boolean expression: bilingual AND ([Stroop OR Simon OR flanker OR ANT] OR [congruent AND incongruent]). The databases included dissertations, but unpublished experiments were not solicited because authors often do not respond to requests for additional information and this may add another layer of bias to the selection process (see de Bruin et al. (2015) for a specific example of requesting information about unpublished conference abstracts). The full text of the 586 studies was then examined and a study was eliminated if it did not report new empirical results, if only verbal tasks were used (e.g. a standard Stroop colour-word task), if reaction times (RTs) were not reported and analysed, or if there was no monolingual comparison group. These steps resulted in the selection of 109 studies that reported RT statistics for 193 language-group comparisons.[2] In a final step, comparisons involving participants with mean ages less than six years old were removed. The final sample consisted of 99 studies that reported RT statistics for 177 language-group comparisons.

Comparisons using preschool children were removed because differences between preschoolers are more likely to occur in accuracy rather than latency. Latency measures obtained from preschoolers are usually treated as flotsam and jetsam and including these in the meta-analysis may qualify as the practice of 'mega-silliness' or 'garbage in-garbage out' as Eysenck (1978) warned.

For the meta-analysis of non-verbal interference scores the primary dependent variable is the interference score (mean correct RT on incongruent trials minus mean correct RT on congruent trials) that measures the difference in processing time when competition and conflict resolution occurs relative to when it does not. Note that the term interference score is agnostic with respect to whether conflict resolution may involve upregulation of task-relevant information, inhibition of task-irrelevant information, selection by spatial attention, or any other mechanism.

Of the 177 comparisons in the final database, 174 reported a statistical test comparing the interference effects of the two language groups. There were 26 (14.7%) statistically significant bilingual advantages at the standard alpha of 0.05 and only 4 (2.3%) monolingual advantages. The vast majority of the tests yielded null results (144, 81.4%). These percentages are very close to the results we have published before that were based on a much smaller number of studies (Paap et al. 2014, 2015).

Of the 177 comparisons in the final database, 152 reported either the mean interference score for each group and/or the magnitude of the bilingual advantage (mean interference score for monolinguals minus mean interference score for bilinguals). Most of the studies that did not report means simply reported that the differences between the groups were not significant. Consequently, it is important to keep in mind that there is a reporting bias within the studies identified that is above and beyond the file drawer and publication biases. That is, studies that did not report specific effect sizes are very likely to be studies with small and nonsignificant group differences.

The boxplot of the 152 effect sizes shown on the left side of Figure 1 reveals outliers as far as nine standard deviations above the mean of 21.7 ms. The six most extreme effect sizes are the six effects reported by Bialystok et al. (2004). One of the coauthors, Ray Klein, later noted that the largest bilingual advantages were driven by Simon effects for the monolingual groups that were 'strikingly anomalous' and in the range of 500–1800 ms for the monolingual groups (Hilchey and Klein 2011; Klein 2015). Simon effects for young adults are usually about 30 ms (Lu and Proctor 1995) and the effect in older adults seems to peak at around 70 ms (Van der Lubbe and Verleger 2002). As discussed in Paap (2018) these extreme outcomes may have been caused by the confluence of small samples sizes (10–32 with a mean of 15.4), inadequate matching (bilinguals living in India or Hong Kong compared with monolinguals living in Canada), and an unusually small number of trials per condition (as few as 14 in Study 1). Given these issues, the effect sizes from the Bialystok et al. (2004) study were eliminated from subsequent analyses.

The boxplot for the remaining 146 bilingual advantages is shown in the right panel of Figure 1. As shown in Table 1 the mean bilingual advantage across all 146 comparisons is +4.4 ms. If the 146 effect sizes are treated as a single sample the Bayes Factor (using the JZS prior and Rouder's calculator) favouring the alternative is 2.87, an odds ratio that according to Jeffrey's (1961) guidelines is 'barely worth mentioning'. This very small but statistically significant advantage would likely drift to zero if publication and reporting bias could be taken into account.

The meta-analysis of bilingual advantages in interference control reported above has the virtue of focusing only on non-verbal interference tasks, but did not eliminate any studies because of: (i) missing standard errors, (ii) missing inferential statistical tests, or (iii) multiple comparisons obtained from the same participants. The benefits of maintaining a larger pool of studies are not cost free as the effect sizes reported were not standardized and multiple comparisons (e.g. Simon and flanker effects) from the same participants were not statistically independent as required by typical procedures for combining studies in a meta-analysis. Fortunately, the outcome of our meta-analysis converges with a new formal meta-analysis reported by Lehtonen et al. (2018). This meta-analysis used a wider definition of inhibitory control and identified a more heterogeneous set of 212 effect sizes compared with ours, but only included datasets that were both independent and allowed standardized effect sizes. Also, the Lehtonen et al. meta-analysis was restricted to studies using participants 18 years and older, whereas the Paap meta-analysis includes participants 6 years and older. The mean effect size for

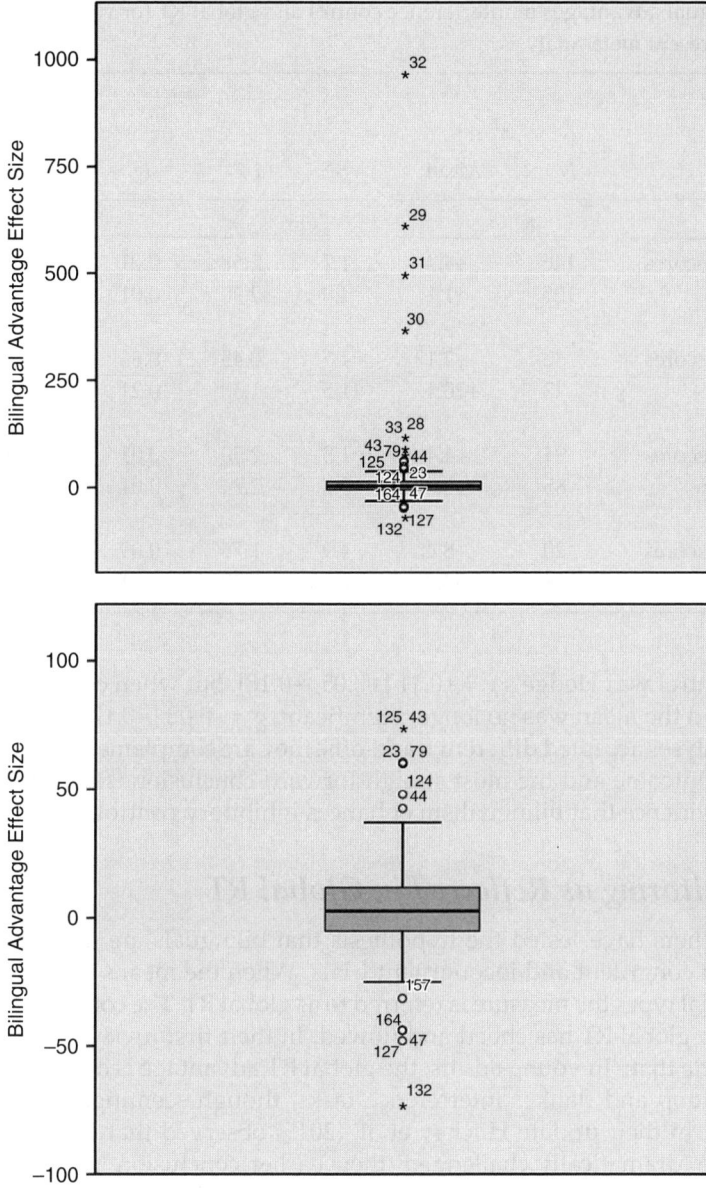

Figure 1   Boxplots of the mean effect size (bilingual advantage in interference scores) when the six extreme outliers from Bialystok et al. (2004) are included (left side) compared to when they are deleted (right side).

Table 1   Bilingual advantages in interference control and global RT for various age groups based on the present meta-analysis.

Measure	N	Mean	SE	t	sig.	95% CI lower	95% CI upper
All Ages							
Interference scores	146	+4.4	1.7	2.68	0.01	+0.97	+7.97
Global RT	125	+11.1	4.0	2.70	0.01	+3.41	+19.26
Ages 6 to 15							
Interference scores	32	+2.1	4.5	0.45	0.66	−7.48	+11.69
Global RT	22	+20.1	11.5	1.30	0.21	−9.50	+52.98
Ages 19 to 51							
Interference scores	94	+4.4	1.8	2.50	0.01	+0.90	+7.89
Global RT	85	+10.0	3.7	2.74	0.01	+27.05	+40.64
Ages 60 to 81							
Interference scores	20	+8.4	4.9	1.76	0.09	−0.80	+19.0
Global RT	18	+4.8	12.8	0.37	0.71	−20.58	+26.30

inhibitory control was Hedge's $g = +0.11$ [+0.05, +0.18], but when corrected by the PET-PEESE method the mean was no longer significant, $g = −0.02$ [−0.12, +0.08]. Because the two meta-analyses accepted different trade-offs, they are complementary. They converge on the same outcome and the most straightforward conclusion is that they provide no compelling evidence that bilingualism enhances inhibitory control.

2.2.   *Monitoring as Reflected in Global RT*

Many researchers have tested the hypothesis that bilinguals are faster than monolinguals on both congruent and incongruent trials. When the means are simply averaged across both trial types the measure is referred to as global RT. The consistency of bilingual advantages in global RT has ebbed and flowed. In their first review, Hilchey and Klein (2011) conclude that: 'In young adults, the global RT advantage is detected ubiquitously on spatial Stroop and flanker interference tasks, though seemingly not in the Simon task' (p. 645). In their update Hilchey et al. (2015) observed that the last two years of research have 'dramatically challenged' their earlier conclusion because the bilingual advantages in global RT with school children, young adults, and the elderly all vanished in the flood of null results reported in newer, often larger, and often better-controlled studies. However, the Hilchey et al. review included only 30 tests for bilingual advantages in global RT whereas our database includes 132 inferential statistical tests and 125 specific effect sizes.

Considering all studies that reported statistical tests of global RT 81.1% reported null effects, 16.7% reported significant bilingual advantages, and 2.3% reported significant monolingual advantages. As shown in Table 1 the bilingual advantage in global RT shows that bilinguals were, on average, 11.1 ms faster than monolinguals. The Bayes Factor favouring the alternative for these 125 effect sizes is 3.18 and edges into the interval that is worth mentioning. However, the reporting bias is also likely to be substantial as only 125 of the 177 potential comparisons in the final database reported effect sizes for global RT.

Lehtonen et al.'s (2018) meta-analysis of the monitoring component included 184 effect sizes that were primarily derived from global RT (82 comparisons), congruent trial RT (65), and mixing costs (26). Their mean effect size of $g = +0.06$ [0.00, +0.13] was not significantly different from zero and when corrected by PET-PEESE for bias crossed-over to a negative $g = -0.07$ [−0.17, +0.04].

Given the propensity of authors to interpret bilingual advantages in global RT as a bilingual advantage in EF a theoretical discussion of the global RT measure is warranted.

Consider the subset of outcomes (15 in our database) that find comparable bilingual advantages on both congruent and incongruent trials and, consequently, no group differences in interference control. This pattern can only occur if there is a processing advantage that applies equally to both types of trials. One class of 'explanation' assumes that bilinguals are better at managing trial-to-trial variation with respect to presence or absence of conflict under the rubric of 'monitoring' (Costa et al. 2009), 'coordination' (Bialystok 2011), or 'mental flexibility' (Kroll and Bialystok 2013). How monitoring, coordination, or mental flexibility actually leads to a bilingual advantage in these non-verbal interference tasks is not always clear. What needs to be monitored? The same simple task schema (e.g. press the right key when the target is an arrow pointing right) is always in play across both types of trials in the experimental block and because the Stimulus-Response (S-R) rule remains constant and never needs reconfiguration (as it would in a switching task) it is unclear what needs to be coordinated or how flexibility enters the equation. Note that if bilinguals were better at monitoring for and preparing for conflict this should lead to greater advantages on incongruent trials and not equal benefits for both types of trials.

A hypothesis put forth by Hilchey and Klein (2011) describes a mechanism that could provide equivalent advantages for both trial types. Relying on the general conflict-monitoring literature (e.g. Botvinick et al. 2001) and the specific neuroscientific findings of Luk et al. (2010), Hilchey and Klein hypothesise that coordinating two languages leads to the ability to rapidly reroute processing depending on the presence or absence of conflict. Thus, in bilinguals one route is optimized for processing nonconflicting (congruent) trials and the other for conflict resolution (incongruent trials). The division of labour between functionally distinct processing streams and the consequent freeing up of processing resources leads to the global RT advantage. The Hilchey and Klein hypothesis does provide a specific mechanism for generating the global RT advantage, but it could be a 'just so story'. Why does having two dedicated processing stream lead to *equivalent* benefits in behavioural RT compared with having one stream, especially when one task is more difficult than the other? If the answer is that it just happens to work out that way in some samples, then this raises the rejoinder that most (81.1%) comparisons show no global RT advantages at all and, by implication, the division of labour usually provides no processing advantage.

Mining a different vein, it seems that a ubiquitous condition of everyday life is to monitor for conflict between task relevant and irrelevant information and to selectively attend to the relevant. Is it reasonable to suggest that the additional demands of coordinating two languages are the just-sufficient-difference that triggers a two-stream reorganization of cortical networks in bilinguals that is absent in monolinguals? Hilchey and Klein's interesting hypothesis leads to the prediction that the correlation between congruent and incongruent trial RTs should be higher in monolinguals (a single processing stream for both) than in bilinguals (two functionally distinct processing streams). To explore this hypothesis, the composite database described in Paap et al. (2014) was used. For the Simon task, there were 171 bilinguals and 207 monolinguals. The correlation between congruent and incongruent RTs was +0.92 for bilinguals and +0.94 for monolinguals which do not differ (p = 0.18). For the flanker task there were 100 bilinguals and 111 monolinguals. The correlations between trial types were +0.89 and +0.94, respectively. For the flanker task the monolingual correlation is significantly larger (p = 0.011). Thus, there is some indirect evidence from the flanker task that bilinguals, but not monolinguals, employ functionally different networks on congruent and incongruent trials. However, given the constraints imposed by the test–retest reliability of the flanker task (Paap and Sawi 2016), the fact that all of the correlations are in the neighbourhood of +0.90 is striking. It appears that any individual differences in abilities that are unique to incongruent trials are quite modest as about 81% of the variance in incongruent trial RTs can be predicted from congruent trial RTs. To summarize, only 16.7% of the tests yielded a bilingual advantage in global RT, the effect size of the bilingual advantage was 11.1 ms, and explanations for why bilingualism should equally enhance both congruent and incongruent trials are murky.

2.3. *Working Memory*

Bialystok (2017) asserts that working memory (WM) capacity, conceptualized not as storage space, but as the extent to which resources are available to control attention (Engle and Kane 2004) 'is compatible with the evidence found across the lifespan for bilingualism-dependent plasticity' (p. 249). A recent meta-analysis by von Bastian et al. (2017) evaluated this conceptualization of EF for bilingual advantages. A set of 88 studies with 108 independent comparisons was included. The average effect size was $g = +0.11$ [+0.03, +0.19]. Considering the Bayes Factor associated with each effect size, there was a high degree of heterogeneity, mostly null effects, and little evidence for the alternative hypothesis. Neither age (children, younger adults, older adults) nor task mode (verbal versus non-verbal) moderated the variability in effect sizes. Lehtonen et al. (2018) also examined the WM domain and their meta-analysis of 243 effect sizes yielded a mean effect size of $g = +0.07$ [0.00, +0.13] that shifted to a disadvantage when corrected for bias, $g = -0.07$ [−0.17, +0.03]. The Lehtonen et al. meta-analysis reinforces the conclusion of von Bastian et al. that the findings challenge executive-attention accounts of bilingual advantages.

2.4. Switching

Another popular paradigm for testing the bilingual advantage in EF hypothesis involves switching between two non-verbal tasks such as colour (e.g. Is the target red or green?) or shape (e.g. Is the target a circle or triangle?). In the most common instantiation a pre-cue precedes the target and signals whether the upcoming decision should be based on colour or shape. Thus, each trial (after the first) can be classified as a repeat trial (e.g. two colour decisions in a row) or a switch trial (e.g. a colour decision preceded by a shape decision). A measure referred to as switch cost is defined as the mean correct RT on switch trials minus the mean correct RT on repeat trials. Most switching studies also include single-task blocks where every trial requires the same type of decision and obviously no task switching occurs. A measure referred to as mixing cost is defined as the mean correct RT on the repeat trials of the mixed block minus the mean correct RT in the single-task blocks. A third measure that is sometimes reported and analysed is the mean of all the mixed trials minus the mean on the single-task blocks. For clarity this measure will be referred to as global mixing costs. There seems to be a consensus view that these cued switching task require EF as participants must monitor for and encode the precue, update the cue in working memory, and on switch trials reconfigure the S-R rules of the task schema. It is often assumed that reconfiguration requires inhibition of the previous rule. A meta-analysis of switching cost and mixing cost now follows that, in the interest of avoiding apples and oranges comparisons, was restricted to studies using the colour-shape switching task and also to studies that included a group of monolinguals.

In a seminal study Prior and MacWhinney (2010) were the first to report a bilingual advantage in switching cost. The advantage in switching costs looked like one that should easily replicate given that the estimated effect size was $d = 0.52$ (with 44 participants in each group) and that the estimated power for a one-tailed test with an alpha equal to 0.05 was 0.78. However, as shown in Table 2 the bilingual-advantage with young adult participants obtained by Prior and MacWhinney has replicated twice, but yielded null results 25 times.

The mini meta-analysis for the colour-word switching task shown in Table 2 generalizes to Lehtonen et al.'s meta-analysis of 77 effect sizes of which 45 were derived from a colour-shape switching task. A small significant bilingual advantage was present in the uncorrected analysis, $g = +0.15$ [+0.06, +0.24], but this advantage was not sustained when corrected for bias, $g = +0.02$ [−0.09, +0.14]. Again, despite many differences in selection criteria and methods the two meta-analyses converge on the outcome that there is very little evidence for a bilingual advantage in switching ability.

Table 2 also lists studies that have used the cued colour-shape switching task and reported mixing costs. Nineteen (90%) of the tests yielded null results and there was one significant bilingual advantage balanced by one significant monolingual advantage. Mixing costs are often used as a measure of monitoring and that is how they were treated in the Lehtonen et al. meta-analysis.

The main purpose of Table 2 was to show that the colour-shape switching task yields overwhelmingly null results between groups of bilinguals and monolinguals for both

Table 2   Results of tests for bilingual advantages in colour-shape switching tasks.

Study	n Per Group	Age	Switch Cost	Mixing Cost	Global Cost
Prior and MacWhinney (2010)					
various bilinguals	44	19.5	B+	ns	
Prior and Gollan (2011)					
Spanish-English bilinguals	41	20.0	B+	ns	
Mandarin-English bilinguals	43	19.4	ns	ns	
Tare and Linck (2011)					
various bilinguals	35	27.7	ns	ns	
Barac and Bialystok (2012)					
Chinese-English bilinguals	30	6.0			B+
French-English bilinguals	28	6.2			B+
Spanish-English bilinguals	20	6.2			B+
Gold et al. (2013)					
Exp. 1: various bilinguals	15	63.3			B+
Exp. 2: various older bilinguals	20	older			ns
Exp. 2: various young bilinguals	20	younger			ns
Prior and Gollan (2013)					
Spanish-English bilinguals	30	20.3	ns	ns	
Hebrew-English bilinguals	6	25.0	ns	ns	
Mandarin-English bilinguals	16	20.0	ns	ns	
Paap and Greenberg (2013)					
Study 1: various bilinguals	34	US	ns	ns	
Study 2: various bilinguals	36	US	ns	ns	
Study 3: various bilinguals	52	US	ns	ns	
Hernández et al. (2013)					
Experiment 1: Spanish-Catalan bilinguals	87	20.6	ns		
Experiment 2: Spanish-Catalan bilinguals	20	20.4	ns		
Experiment 3: Spanish-Catalan bilinguals	38	19.9	ns		
Rodriguez-Pujada et al. (2013)					
Catalan-Spanish bilinguals	18	23.1	ns		
Paap and Sawi (2014)					
Day 1: various bilinguals	58	US	ns	ns	
Day 2: various bilinguals	39	US	ns	ns	
Mor et al. (2014)					
Hebrew-English bilinguals	20	24.8	ns	ns	
Moradzadeh et al. (2014)					
Non-musicians: various bilinguals	36	21.5	ns	ns	
Musicians: various bilinguals	36	22.5	ns	ns	

Table 2   (Continued)

Study	n Per Group	Age	Switch Cost	Mixing Cost	Global Cost
Wiseheart et al. (2016)					
various bilinguals	31	19.2	ns	B+	
Houtzager et al. (2017)					
middle-aged: Dutch-Frisian bilinguals	25	46.0	ns	ns	
elderly: Dutch-Frisian	25	73.2	B+	ns	
de Bruin et al. (2015)					
older active Gaelic-English bilinguals	28	71.9	ns	ns	
older inactive Gaelic-English bilinguals	24	70.5	ns	ns	
Shulley and Shake (2016)					
various bilinguals	58	21.3	ns		
Branzi et al. (2016)					
Exp. 2: Spanish-Catalan bilinguals	91	US	ns		
Paap et al. (2017)					
various bilinguals	110/95	22	ns	M+	
Ratiu et al. (2017)					
Exp. 2: various bilinguals	19	19	ns		

Note: B+ = significant bilingual advantage at $p < 0.05$; US = university students; ns = non-significant.

switching costs and mixing costs. However, there are studies using other cued-switching tasks or which do not include a monolingual group that appear to support the hypothesis that bilinguals are advantaged in switching ability. Christoffels et al. (2015) obtained a switch-cost advantage for 17-year-old Dutch-English bilinguals who were enrolled in bilingual education versus bilinguals who were enrolled in a monolingual education program. The baseline group was not monolingual as their L2 proficiency was within 85% of the bilingual education group on both subjective ratings of proficiency and an objective measure of vocabulary.

If one opens the doors to comparisons that do not include 'pure' monolinguals, then one must also permit entry to von Bastian et al. (2015) who used a k-means clustering procedure to consider three continuous dimensions: age of second language (L2) acquisition, non-first language (L1) usage, and the L1/L2 proficiency ratio. These three dimensions of bilingual experience have been hypothesized to play important roles in fostering bilingual advantages in EF. There were no advantages in switching costs for colour shape, animacy size, or parity magnitude tasks for any measure of bilingualism. In contrast to the von Bastian et al. results, Marzecová et al. (2013) found a bilingual advantage in switch costs when switching to a gender decision about pictures of faces, but no differences when switching to an age decision. This finding for one dimension (gender) of one task (gender/age) pales in comparison to the consistently null results across three tasks reported by von Bastian et al. (2015).

Hartanto and Yang (2016) obtained an intriguing advantage of dual-language bilinguals (those who frequently switch languages within the same utterance or conversation) over single language bilinguals (those who tend to use a single language in any given situation). In a standard analysis, the dual-language bilinguals had significantly smaller switch costs, but there were no group differences in mixing costs. The data were also modelled using the diffusion model (Ratcliff 1978) and the dual-language advantage was manifest in the non-decision time parameter, not the drift rate, and this was interpreted as bilingualism enhancing task-set reconfiguration rather than modulating the amount of proactive interference.

3. Methodological and Statistical Issues

In our target article (Paap et al. 2015) for the *Cortex* forum we evaluated the studies that did report significant bilingual advantages and found a variety of concerns. An abbreviated version of those arguments are presented in this section.

3.1. *Confounds and ANCOVA*

Testing for bilingual advantages in EF usually involves a comparison between two naturally occurring groups that may systematically differ on other attributes that affect EF and, consequently, create confounded tests. Because participants cannot be randomly assigned to be bilingual or monolingual, large sample sizes do not guarantee that the groups will be approximately matched on all factors other than bilingualism. From a dynamical-systems perspective Paap et al. (2016) argue that confounds with multilingualism are inevitable and may actually differ in direction across locations. For example, bilinguals are more likely to be better educated in Hyderabad, but less educated in Houston. When a simple between-group design is used, the best first step is to measure the usual suspects: age, culture, immigrant status, education, general fluid intelligence (gF), parents' education, childhood family income, videogame play, music performance, etc. The second step is to determine which of these factors affected the dependent measures of interest. If a factor, say age, does not correlate with performance (perhaps because the range in the sample is small), then it can be ignored. If a factor, say gF, does correlate with performance then it critically matters whether the means are balanced or confounded across the language groups. When the factor is confounded a significant main effect of group has two plausible explanations. The most common tactic is to use ANCOVA to 'statistically control' for the confounding. However, the confound violates the assumption that the covariate and the grouping variable be independent. In their landmark article Miller and Chapman (2001) assert that 'controlling' or 'removing' non-trivial group differences is an inappropriate use of ANCOVA and that when the independence assumption is violated the regression adjustments may either obscure part of the grouping effect or produce spurious effects.[3] A better approach, assuming an adequate sample size, is to precisely match a subset of the participants and redo the test.

When the independence assumption is not violated, but the covariate predicts the outcome variable, then ANCOVA is an excellent tool for increasing the power of the analysis because variance accounted for by the covariate is no longer treated as unaccounted for error.

3.2.   Potential Confounds Measured Continuously

Many factors that may independently affect or moderate the influence of bilingualism on measures of EF are usually measured continuously. GF is highly correlated with measures of EF. In a large sample study (Paap 2018), 201 participants completed four non-verbal interference tasks and the interference scores were standardized and averaged to form a composite measure of interference control. In a stepwise regression with 11 potential predictors of the interference scores Raven's scores had the highest zero-order correlation ($r = -0.37$) and the largest standardized regression coefficient ($\beta = -0.35$).[4]

In the Paap et al. study several factors that sometimes showed significant relationships with various measures of EF in earlier work did not predict the composite interference scores: videogame play (e.g. Hutchinson et al. 2016), music performance (e.g. Moradzadeh et al. 2014), music training (e.g. Moreno et al. 2011), meditation (Colzato et al. 2015), and socioeconomic status (SES; e.g. Calvo and Bialystok 2014; Hartanto et al. 2018). Two points serve our discussion for how these factors entangle the tests of the bilingual advantage hypothesis. First, the existence or potency of these effects are sometimes just as controversial as the debate on the bilingual advantage. For example, Unsworth et al. (2015) showed that videogame play is unrelated to a wide range of cognitive abilities and point out methodological problems in studies that do report differences. Second, as Valian (2015) discussed at length, reverse causality is highly plausible in many of these domains because, for example, although music performance may enhance EF it is also likely that general EF contributes to mastery, excellence, the motivation to play more often, and opportunities for more advanced training.

The effects of SES on EF may be closely tied to the age of the participants. In several of our large-sample studies using university participants (Paap and Greenberg 2013; Paap and Sawi 2014; Paap et al. 2018) the correlations between parents' educational levels and a variety of measures of EF were always non-significant and often near zero. In contrast Calvo and Bialystok (2014) tested six-year-olds and reported main effects for both bilingualism and SES on both the flanker and Stroop effects. Hartanto et al. analysed dimensional change card sort data from five- to seven-year-olds and found positive effects of bilingualism for the low SES groups, but not the high SES groups. We have conjectured that the lower SES students in our college student population either had enriching early experience despite their parent's education and income or have otherwise managed to compensate for disadvantages in early childhood. Early advantages of bilingualism in low SES groups may not persist.

A factor that isn't often measured in studies testing the bilingual advantage in EF hypothesis is experience or ability in sports. Paap and Greenberg (2013) introduced this item: 'Team sports often involve dividing your attention between a ball, a goal, your opponents, and your teammates. Do you excel at these sports?' In separate regression analyses, this self-rating significantly predicted flanker effects and switching costs, but not Simon effects. In Paap et al. (2018) team-sports ability predicted the composite interference scores that included both flanker and Simon tasks.

Another study using more objective measures showed a strong relationship between team-sports and EF. Vestberg et al. (2012) tested soccer players with different levels of advanced skills using the D-KEFS battery of executive functions (Homacka et al. 2005). The design fluency component requires participants to remember previous responses by updating working memory and inhibition skills in order to not repeat previous responses. Also included was a colour-word Stroop test and the trail making test. Players from the Swedish highest national soccer leagues outperformed players from the lower division on all of these measures of EF who, in turn were well above the published norms. Furthermore, the EF test scores obtained in the autumn of 2007 were used to predict a performance measure that combines goals and assists over a 17-month interval in 2008 and 2009. The correlation (+0.54, p = 0.006) was statistically significant and noteworthy in magnitude. These results are consistent with the interpretation that high EF facilitates team-sports performance and also the possibility that playing sports at increasingly competitive levels enhances EF. At a more practical level team-sports ability is yet another factor that may confound comparisons between bilinguals and monolinguals and a potent one at that.

3.3. *Potential Confounds that Are Nominal Categories*

Bilinguals and monolinguals are recruited from other naturally occurring groups distinguished by sex, race, culture, immigrant status, and so forth. In many English-speaking countries, bilinguals are more likely than monolinguals to be immigrants. The existence of a healthy immigrant effect is widely cited in disciplines ranging from epidemiology to psychology. Kennedy et al. (2015) characterize the evidence in support of the hypothesis as strong and further suggest that selectivity plays an important role in the observed better health of migrants. Furthermore, immigrants are, to various extents, more highly educated than native-born speakers in Canada, the United States, the United Kingdom, Australia, and New Zealand. Assuming that the healthy immigrant effect extends to better EF, advantages observed with bilingual samples dominated by immigrants may have little or nothing to do with bilingualism (see also Fuller-Thomson and Kuh 2014). There is circumstantial but quite consistent evidence that bilingual advantages reported for specific ages and tasks tend to vanish when immigrant status is controlled (e.g. Guido Mendes 2015; Kousaie and Phillips 2012; Kirk et al. 2014; Morton and Harper 2007).

When immigrant status is confounded it is also likely that there are differences in culture across the language groups. Even when studies match the groups with respect to measured SES and immigrant status there may be cultural differences that can confound tests of bilingual advantages. A study by Carlson and Choi (2009) provides a dramatic demonstration of the entanglement between culture and bilingualism. Using six different measures of EF, they found significant bilingual advantages comparing a group of Korean-English bilinguals (n = 67) living in the United States to a matched sample of American monolinguals ($n =53$). However, the performance of the Korean-American bilinguals was indistinguishable from a third group of matched Korean monolinguals ($n =69$). This challenges the interpretation that the obtained group differences were due to bilingualism and strongly supports the view that cultural differences play an influential role in the development of EF.

Gender is another important potential confound because male advantages in interference control have been reported. The Paap et al. (2018) study that used four different non-verbal interference tasks reported a four-way ANOVA treating *language group* and *sex* as between-subject factors and *task* and *congruency* as within-subject factors. There was no main effect of language group nor did language group interact with any other factor. However, the sex x congruency interaction was significant with males showing smaller interference effects than females. Although sex was confounded with the Raven's measure of gF, when the 52 males were each matched to a female with an identical Raven's score the magnitude of the male advantage remained the same (37.9 ms versus 36.6 ms). Similar male advantages have been reported in studies using the spatial Stroop task (Evans and Hampson 2015; Stoet 2017).

3.4. Interpreting Interactions

Paap et al. (2015) and Hilchey et al. (2015) discuss several examples where significant language group x congruency interactions were interpreted as evidence for a bilingual advantage in inhibitory control when the interpretation was not warranted. The language group x congruency interaction shown in Paap et al.'s (2015) Figure 3 occurs because the groups differ on the congruent trials (where they are expected to be the same, but the monolinguals are faster), but do not differ on the incongruent trials (where they should differ if bilinguals are better at interference control). Six of the 22 bilingual advantages in interference control in our final database are associated with non-trivial monolingual advantages on the congruent trials that drive the interaction (Bialystok et al. 2008; Rubio-Fernandez and Glucksberg 2012; Salvatierra and Rosselli 2011, both older groups; Schroeder and Marian 2012; Woumans et al. 2015). The presence of a significant group by congruency interaction does not automatically signal a bilingual advantage in inhibitory control.

4. Counterarguments

4.1. Young Adults and Null Results

Proponents of the bilingual advantage in EF hypothesis frequently brush aside the multitude of null results by suggesting that they stem exclusively from studies using young adults and that young adults are immune to the positive effects of bilingualism: 'One simple possibility is that it is difficult for high functioning young adults to respond much faster than they already do – across most of these studies the mean RT for young adults is about 500 ms and it is difficult to see how an experiential difference could move an entire group to a significantly faster time' (Bialystok 2016, p. 5).

In a direct test of the 'ceiling' hypothesis Paap et al. (2014) reported that for a group of eight young adults, the mean RTs on both congruent and incongruent trials of a flanker task decreased substantially by about 100 ms over the course of 20 daily sessions. The magnitude of the flanker effect itself also decreased by about 30 ms. The results demonstrate that the 'experience' of practising the same task can 'move an entire group to a significantly faster time'. These young adults were not at a performance ceiling. Thus, if bilinguals experience ubiquitous practice of general EF during their everyday language control they should show better interference control in a first session because neither group is at a performance ceiling. Given that young adults are not at a performance ceiling, then it is not surprising that extensive music training produced an advantage compared with non-musicians (Moradzadeh et al. 2014) and reprises the question as to why the same study showed no bilingual advantage.

Bialystok (2016) appeals to Fisher's (1935) famous assertion that 'failure to reject the null is not grounds for accepting the null' and indicts Paap and Greenberg (2013) for taking their null results as evidence that bilingualism has no effect on cognition. Both Paap and colleagues and the Basque Center on Cognition, Brain and Language (BCBL) group have consistently used Bayes Factor analyses in addition to null hypothesis testing. A Bayes Factor is a ratio of the probability of the null hypothesis being true given the data over the probability of the alternative being true given the data.[5] Jeffrey's (1961) guidelines suggest that Bayes Factors in the range of 0–3 are not very meaningful, but provide substantial evidence that the null is true as they grow in the range of 3–10. Paap et al. (2014) computed Bayes Factors for 12 different measures of EF comparing bilinguals to monolinguals and 9 of the 12 produced 'substantial' Bayes Factors in the range of 5–9. The only measure in the not-very-meaningful range was the Simon effect that surprisingly showed a monolingual advantage! Across the BCBL studies, Bayes Factor analyses showed substantial support for the null hypothesis in the flanker task (5.6), colour-word Stroop (5.6), and numerical Stroop (3.6).

4.2.   *Older Adults, School-Age Children, and Null Results*

A complementary part of the narrative that young adults do not show bilingual advantages is that advantages are consistently observed with children and older adults. Bialystok et al. (2014) go so far as to say that studies failing to find bilingual advantages '… have ALL been conducted with ONLY young adults' (emphasis added; p. 697). Likewise, Ye et al. (2017) state that: 'in most research that has found no bilingual advantage, the participants were young adults' (p. 2). In fact, only 5 of the 20 studies in our final database that tested older adults obtained bilingual advantages using non-verbal interference tasks and as shown in Table 1 the mean effect size of all 20 studies was only +8.4 ms and nonsignificant.

With respect to preschoolers through adolescents, the claim that null results only occur with young adults is, well, equally false. Very large-scale studies with highly proficient bilingual children living in language communities where language switching occurs all the time have shown no bilingual advantages in non-verbal interference tasks (Antón et al. 2014; Duñabeitia et al. 2014; Gathercole et al. 2014). Bialystok (2017) dismisses these results because they 'examine an unusually large age range without convincing control over the role of age in performance' (p. 238) but all of these studies analyse the results in separate and narrow age bands with no hint that age or years of bilingual experience matters.

Related to the claim that young adults are at ceiling in the standard versions of the flanker or Simon, it has been hypothesized that bilingual advantages may occur if the difficulty of these tasks is sufficiently boosted. The expectancy of an incongruent trial has become a standard trope since Costa et al. (2009) showed that global RT advantages in a flanker task are likely to occur when congruent and incongruent trials are equally likely, but did not occur when the ratio was 80:20 or 20:80. Although the proportion effect is probably robust, it becomes a fig leaf to cover the fact that the bilingual advantages in flanker effects reported by Costa et al. when congruent and incongruent trials are equally likely (the 'difficult' condition) are rarely replicated (e.g. Antón et al. 2014; Paap et al. 2015).[6] In summary, bilingual advantages in flanker effects are not consistently observed when 'difficulty' is enhanced by increasing uncertainty.

Another touted example (e.g. Friesen et al. 2014) of the critical importance of preventing young adults from performing at ceiling is to extend the two-colour Simon task to a more demanding task where there are four colours, two assigned to each response. The argument first gathered strength in the seminal, but flawed study by Bialystok et al. (2004) that observed a bilingual advantage for their middle-aged participants in the four-colour task, but not the two-colour version. However, Salvatierra (2007) and Salvatierra and Rosselli (2011) reported no language-group differences for young adults in either a two- or four-colour Simon task. Likewise, Billig and Scholl (2011) found no bilingual advantages in global RTs (they do not report Simon interference effects) in a four-colour Simon task for either their younger or older groups. Guido Mendes (2015) found no language-group differences in either global RT or Simon effects for both the two-colour and four-colour Simon task. In summary, bilingual advantages in the Simon task are not consistently observed in the four-colour version despite the increased demands on working memory.

5.   Reformulations

The key starting point for predictions of bilingual advantages in EF is the plenitude of evidence consistent with the hypothesis that both languages are coactivated even when the language context supports only one of them and that some general-purpose aspect of EF is recruited to facilitate the selection of the target language and avoid intrusions from the non-target language. Both Dijkstra and van Heuven's (1998) bilingual interactive activation model and Green's (1998) inhibitory control model were highly influential in establishing inhibition as a likely control candidate that resolved the competition between the lexicons and, consequently, grew stronger through ubiquitous practice in coordinating two languages.

5.1.   Selective Attention, Not Inhibition

Bialystok (2015) and others no longer believe that there is a bilingual advantage in inhibitory control: 'rather it is the failure of bilinguals to inhibit attention to the nontarget language that leads to the involvement of executive function and the eventual consequences for its development ... executive function is recruited to maintain attention to the target language' (p. 4).

Friesen, Latman, Calvo and Bialystok (2014) tested the bilingual advantage in selective attention (SA) hypothesis by using visual search tasks that involved either feature or conjunctive searches (Treisman and Gelade 1980). Feature searches are easy because the distinctive target pops-out and exogenously attracts attention. Conjunctive searches require the integration of two features, are endogenously controlled, and take increasingly longer as the number of distractors in the display increases. Bilinguals were faster than monolinguals, $F(1,107) = 4.19, p = 0.04$, but only in the most difficult condition that combined low discriminability and conjunctive search. The results are consistent with the hypothesis that bilinguals enjoy better selective attention. The degree to which conjunctive search is free of interference control and isolates attentional control from other aspects of EF is arguable. If, for example, the target is defined as a blue triangle then encountering a distractor that is a blue diamond could cause competition because the colour is consistent with a 'yes' decision while the mismatching shape must override and support a 'no' decision. In fact, a different way of describing the difference between feature and conjunctive searches is that distractors in the latter having competing dimensions.

Friesen et al. reasonably mention that future research should use eye-tracking to investigate the time course of engaging and disengaging attention when scanning the display. Ratiu et al. (2017) report a series of three elegant experiments that use eye movements to separate search time from decision time during conjunctive searches. The study is data rich and if bilingualism confers attentional, EF, or WM advantages a consistent difference should have been observed across the three experiments. The only reliable group difference was observed in Experiment 3 and that was a bilingual disadvantage in decision times. Ratiu et al. conclude that their results show no apparent bilingual advantage in attentional guidance, response initiation, or overall search performance. In understatement, it appears that conjunctive search does not consistently yield bilingual advantages.

5.2.   *Disengagement of Attention*

Another interesting facet of the reformulated bilingual advantage hypothesis is that bilinguals are better at disengaging attention. Grundy et al. (2017) review evidence that bilinguals disengage from previous distracting information more rapidly than monolinguals. That review starts with the claim 'bilinguals show smaller switch costs than monolinguals' (p. 44), but as reviewed in Section 2.4 significant advantages in switch costs occur in a very small minority of studies. They also cite Mishra et al. (2012), finding that high-proficiency bilinguals display inhibition-of-return effects at earlier stimulus onset asynchronies (SOAs) than low-proficiency bilinguals. The study did not include monolinguals. In a study that actually did compare bilinguals ($n = 24$) to monolinguals ($n = 28$) there were no group differences in the time course of IOR (Hernández et al. 2010). Furthermore, in a replication and extension of their earlier work, Saint-Aubin et al. (2018) tested a large sample of English-French bilinguals living in Canada, but neither subjective nor objective measures of proficiency affected the time course or

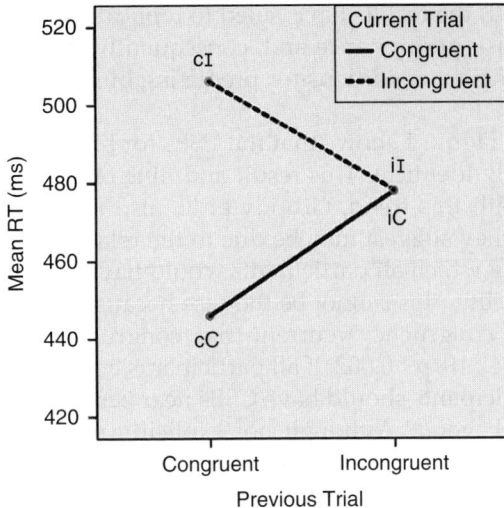

Figure 2   The CSE derived from the Simon task reported in Paap and Greenberg (2013), Experiment 3.

magnitude of the IOR. The authors conclude that there is no reliable evidence that mastering a second language leads to faster or more potent disengagement of endogenous attention.

Grundy et al. (2017) further pursued the hypothesis that bilinguals are better than monolinguals at disengaging attention by comparing the magnitude of congruency sequence effects (CSEs). CSEs are robust context effects observed in many choice RT tasks that include both congruent and incongruent trials.[7] Figure 2 shows the CSE derived from a Simon task in Study 3 of Paap and Greenberg (2013). Following a common convention, the congruency of a previous trial will be designated with lowercase and the congruency of a current trial with uppercase. For this dataset, the congruency effect (cI – cC) following a congruent trial is 60.3 ms compared to only 0.3 ms (iI – iC) following an incongruent trial. Thus, the magnitude of the CSE is 60.0 ms for this dataset and more generally is: CSE = (cI – cC) – (iI – iC). For the experiment shown in Figure 2, there was an equal number of congruent and incongruent trials and under these conditions, it is often the case that CSE consists of two relatively symmetrical effects: (i) a speed-up when incongruent trials repeat (see the broken line in Figure 2) and (ii) a slow-down when a congruent trial follows an incongruent one (see the solid line).

In their first two experiments using a flanker task, Grundy et al. observed no language group differences in the magnitude of the simple flanker effect, but bilinguals did have significantly smaller CSEs in comparison to monolinguals. The smaller CSE is interpreted as reflecting 'more rapid disengagement of attention and greater ability to refocus on the current trial' (p. 45). The findings are asserted to 'provide insight into why some studies show bilingual advantages on executive control tasks and some do not' (p. 52). The CSE results are most interesting, but two somewhat orthogonal issues deserve examination: (i) the results have failed to replicate and (ii) CSE magnitudes are unrelated to overall task performance and, consequently, do not provide insights into the necessary and sufficient conditions for predicting bilingual advantages that matter in everyday life.

Paap et al.'s (2016), Figure 1 shows that the CSEs for bilinguals and monolinguals in a Simon task are nearly identical. This result and nine other null results are shown in Table 3. Consistent with this trend, Grundy et al. also reported a null result in their Experiment 3, which they suggest may be due to the relatively long response stimulus intervals (RSIs) 'during which all participants would have had sufficient time to disengage attention' (p. 51), but, this cannot be the case because the CSE was robust and the critical previous-trial congruency × current-trial congruency interaction was highly significant, $F(1, 109) = 42.10$, $p < 0.002$. If all participants had sufficient time to disengage attention, then all participants should have CSEs near zero.

Why is a small CSE good? Although not explicitly noted by Grundy et al., their conclusion seems to require a very specific variant of the attention-shifting account of CSEs (see Weissman et al. 2014, for various accounts), namely, that the attentional shift is not a preparation for the next trial, but an unintended carryover effect from the control exercised on trial n-1. If CSEs are simply lingering effects of the control applied to the previous trial, then consider the limiting case of complete disengagement, there would be no CSE. However, a CSE of zero is not informative within this attention-shifting account because it provides no index as to whether the *within-trial* control on an incongruent trial was effective (e.g. resolved the conflict with little or no latency cost) or ineffective. In fact, it would seem that the overall congruency effect, not the CSE, would be the better index of the effectiveness of an individual's *within-trial* control. This brings us full circle because in the Grundy et al. data there were no group differences in the overall congruency effect.

Instead of appealing to disengagement of attentional control exercised on the previous trial Grundy and Bialystok could adopt Botvinick et al.'s conflict monitoring model with the additional assumption that the activation of the control plan for trial n (triggered by the amount of conflict on trial n-1) decays as the response–stimulus interval (RSI) lengthens. This subtly different account should not be characterized as attentional 'disengagement' because it is not the attentional control exercised on trial n-1 that matters, but rather the control planned for the upcoming trial n on the basis of the amount of conflict detected on trial n-1. Logically, a smaller CSE could be attributed to problems in any step in the process: a failure to detect the conflict on trial n-1, an underestimation of the amount of conflict, under regulation relative to the magnitude of conflict detected, or faster decay of the control plan. None of these provides a rationale for why a smaller CSE should be considered 'better' or indicative of an 'advantage'. In fact, each can be viewed as a 'defect' in the ideal control process.

We have previously argued that the question of bilingual advantages is inherently a hypothesis about advantages in performance (Paap and Liu 2014; Paap et al. 2014). From this perspective, one wants to know if bilinguals can accomplish a task faster and/or more accurately than monolinguals. If true, this could be because: (i) the same functions are superior in bilinguals because of ubiquitous practice in controlling two languages or (ii) because the neural reorganization that is caused by managing two languages enables

Table 3   Congruency sequence effects for monolinguals and bilinguals.

	Trial Type		c Effect	Trial Type		i Effect	CSE	Effect	Global
							c Ef.-I Ef.		
	cC	cI	cI-cC	iC	iI	iI-iC	I Ef.	I-C	RT
Paap and Greenberg (2013)									
Simon									
Monolingual	450	503	53	480	477	−2	**55**	25	477
Bilingual	442	510	68	476	479	3	**65**	36	477
Flanker									
Monolingual	526	631	105	542	623	81	**24**	93	580
Bilingual	533	648	114	550	630	80	**34**	97	590
Paap and Sawi (2014, Session 1)									
Simon									
Monolingual	435	491	56	464	458	−5	**61**	25	462
Bilingual	439	502	64	475	481	6	**58**	35	474
Flanker									
Monolingual	488	580	93	499	578	80	**13**	86	536
Bilingual	500	583	83	513	576	63	**20**	73	543
Paap and Sawi (2014, Session 2)									
Simon									
Monolingual	423	475	52	447	453	6	**46**	29	462
Bilingual	423	481	57	452	462	10	**48**	34	474
Flanker									
Monolingual	474	554	80	476	549	73	**7**	77	513
Bilingual	469	540	72	474	539	66	**6**	69	505
Guido Mendes (2015)									
Simon									
Monolingual	444	490	46	477	468	−9	**55**	19	470
Bilingual	440	491	51	478	471	−7	**58**	22	470
Flanker									
Monolingual	464	571	107	479	570	91	**16**	99	521
Bilingual	485	592	107	498	581	83	**24**	95	539
Antón and Duñabeitia (personal communication, unpublished)									
Simon									
Monolingual	465	515	50	493	475	−18	**68**	16	487
Bilingual	406	480	74	466	445	−21	**95**	27	449
Flanker									
Monolingual	399	437	38	399	443	44	**−6**	41	420
Bilingual	384	433	49	387	423	36	**13**	43	407

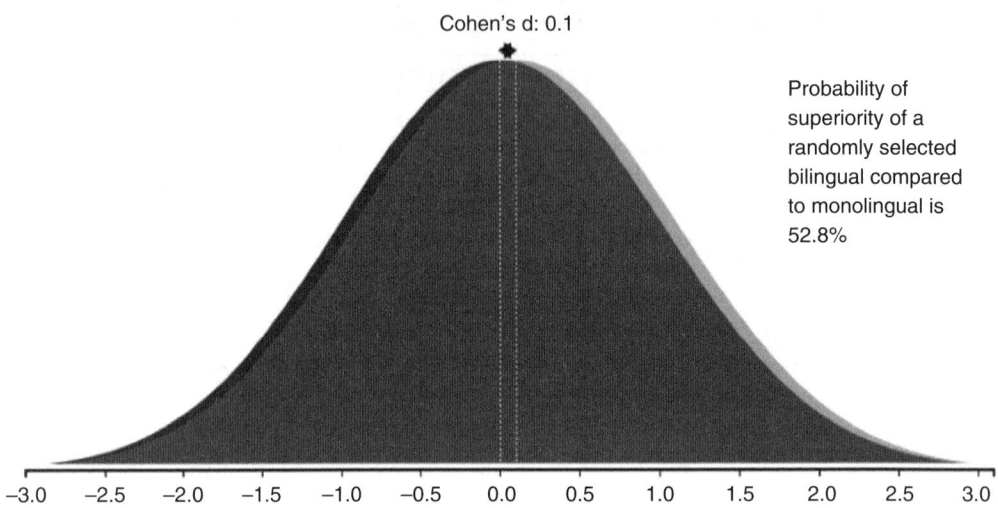

For an effect size of Cohen's d = .1, 96% of the 2 Distributions Overlap

Cohen's d: 0.1

Probability of superiority of a randomly selected bilingual compared to monolingual is 52.8%

Figure 3   96% of the population distributions with mean differences of d = 0.1 overlap.

bilinguals to use different neural pathways to resolve conflict compared with monolinguals and those alternative or additional pathways yield better performance. From either perspective, it is useful to examine individual components of the system and ask if they are controlled in ways that tend to optimize overall system performance.[8] With respect to CSEs, the surprising answer is that they are not typically controlled in ways that optimize (or even improve) performance. Rather, the control is more homeostatic, that is, regulated to maintain stable and consistent conditions. As shown back in Figure 2, the gain in speed when an incongruent trial is followed by another tends to be matched by the loss in speed when it is followed by an equiprobable congruent trial. At least on average, it does not appear to be the case that control can be exercised in a manner that produces a more favourable cost–benefit ratio. From this perspective the smaller CSEs observed by Grundy et al. should not be considered as a bilingual advantage because they are not contributing to either a global RT advantage or to a decrease in the overall congruency effect.

6.   Conclusion and Frequently-Asked-Questions

Statistically significant bilingual advantages are in a clear minority: about 15% for interference scores, 17% for global RT, and 10% for switching. The incidence of significant bilingual advantages would be even smaller if the record could be corrected for the file-drawer problem and publication biases that favour positive results. An anonymous reviewer of an earlier version of this chapter shared a thought that many may harbour and that goes something like this: Surely hundreds of scientists around the world have not manufactured the positive results they report. Are you really suggesting that all available studies, across several continents, many dozens of labs and across many accomplished scholars suffer from bad statistics and methodological issues?

Before answering the question, it is interesting to note that hundreds of scientists have not published positive results. The meta-analysis of non-verbal interference tasks found a total of 109 studies, the Lehtonen et al. meta-analysis of six domains of EF found 152 studies, and the von Bastian et al. meta-analysis of WM capacity found 88 studies. Furthermore, there is overlap between the Lehtonen et al. meta-analysis and each of the other two. These meta-analyses yield a relatively small proportion of positive results and report very small mean effect sizes even before any corrections for bias. The accumulated effect of a steady drip of positive findings can be easily overestimated compared with the flow of null results when viewed through the lens of confirmation bias, primacy effects, and belief persistence (Bacon and Fowler 1889; Paap 2014).

Proponents of the bilingual advantage hypothesis who believe that the selection criteria for this new wave of meta-analyses are biased should publish analyses with different and justified selection rules. For example, this chapter does not cover the research literature on infants, toddlers, and preschoolers where measures of EF are derived from many different age-appropriate tasks. A similarly-inspired meta-analysis of infants to five-year-olds would be well worthwhile. Bialystok's (2017) qualitative review of this literature suggests that in these age ranges, bilinguals outperform monolinguals in a variety of tasks that appear to be related to selective attention or cognitive flexibility. Whether these should always be considered bilingual advantages in EF is arguable and it will be a difficult challenge to assess their convergent validity using latent variable analyses similar to the models tested by Engelhardt et al. (2015) for third- and eighth-grade children. A meta-analysis on toddlers and preschoolers may show more consistent evidence for bilingual advantages and lead to a developmental account of some of the inconsistencies in the literature.

It has not been my intent to imply that researchers reporting null findings are superb methodologists and those reporting positive results are not. One purpose of this chapter and of our *Cortex* forum article (Paap et al. 2015) was to show that a fair number of the positive results (which we have seen is not that many in populations age six and older) may be caused by other factors: inappropriate use of ANCOVA, questionable interpretations of interactions, a plethora of confounding factors, and small sample sizes compounded by failures to report all experiments or all analyses. The designs and analyses of studies reporting null effects are equally challenged by potential confounds and an outcome showing no differences in, say, a flanker task could be due to a bilingual advantage in inhibitory control being cancelled out by a monolingual advantage in SES. As pointed out in Section 3, there are cases where bilingual advantages fail to reproduce in conceptual replications that explicitly remove a confound through matching. Furthermore, as we have documented multiple times in the past (Paap et al. 2014, 2015), null results are associated with larger sample sizes and positive results with riskier small sample sizes. The null results often yield Bayes Factors strongly supporting the null, but Bayes Factors are rarely reported for positive findings.

Another frequently asked question, echoed by the anonymous reviewer, is why not interpret the mix of null and positive results as suggesting a need to understand the dynamic process better instead of abnegating any possible effect at all? Such a question would misrepresent the conclusions offered here and captured in the titles of our articles: 'Bilingual advantages in executive functioning either do not exist or are restricted to very specific and undetermined circumstances' (Paap et al. 2015). This conclusion seems to be completely consistent with the new wave of meta-analyses described in this chapter as significant effects are infrequent and mean effect sizes are small.

Rather than abnegating the phenomenon and walking away we have helped lead the way by exploring both empirically and by systematic review answers to the question: 'Are bilingual advantages dependent upon specific tasks or specific bilingual experiences?' (Paap et al. 2014). In this study, both subgroup ANOVAs and regression analyses were used to test for possible effects of the L2/L1 proficiency ratio, age-of-acquisition, and number of languages spoken. In other work we have explored effects of script similarity (Paap et al. 2014), frequency of language switching (Paap et al. 2017), and the mean number of languages spoken per interactional context or the frequency of code switching within single utterances (Paap et al. 2018). In each case no significant relationships were observed between the specific aspect of bilingual experience and multiple measures of different components of EF. The earlier discussion of Hartanto and Yang's study on the consequences of different types of language switching confirms our interest in EF effects within bilinguals and our belief that there may be sufficient conditions for producing a bilingual advantage.

What is not likely to change is that a vast majority of individuals who consider themselves bilingual, will not show EF advantages across the lifespan compared with those who consider themselves monolingual. As illustrated in Figure 3, even if there is a small, but real bilingual advantage (say Cohen's d = 0.1) only 4% of the bilingual distribution lies to the right of that for monolinguals and the probability of a randomly selected bilingual having superior EF is barely above chance, namely p = 0.528.

A final frequently asked question, especially appropriate for a handbook of the neuroscience of multilingualism, runs along these lines: Isn't there overwhelming evidence that the brain adapts both structurally and functionally to the bilingual experience? Surely there has to be some adaptation? Absolutely. I have always agreed that bilingual brains are different from monolingual brains, but that it is very difficult to interpret functional or anatomical differences. The most extended discussion is presented in Paap et al. (2014) and is concisely recapitulated here. As documented in other chapters in this volume, cortical areas shown to be involved in managing two languages overlap with those shown to be involved with EF. It is also clear from the neuroimaging results that the neural processing of bilinguals and monolinguals differs during the performance of EF tasks. This is consistent with the view that coordinating two languages leads to a reorganization of neural networks in cortical areas involved in language control and EF. However, reorganization to accommodate bilingualism does not logically need to result in more efficient performance. Alternatively, it can lead to comparable performance or even to a compromise that results in inferior performance. Thus, it is imperative that the observed neural differences be aligned with the behavioural differences so that bilingual advantages in actual performance can be confirmed. The assumption that the existence of a behavioural phenomenon can only be adjudicated at the behavioural level, an argument first advanced by Hilchey and Klein (2011), is sound. Paap et al. (2014) described many studies where the neuroscience results fail to align with the behavioural results. Furthermore, they show that neuroscience measures that fail to align with behavioural differences often suffer from a valence ambiguity because increasing neural scores are interpreted as advantages by some researchers and as disadvantages by others. In summary, the fact that the brain shows plasticity and that bilingualism induces cortical reorganization is interesting in its own right, but cannot override the behavioural facts regarding the relative performance of bilinguals and monolinguals on tasks reflecting EF. If you want to select the best candidate for an air-traffic controller, you should do so by comparing behavioural performance on tasks relevant to air-traffic control and not on the basis of concurrent brain imaging.

NOTES

1   Miyake et al. use the term 'shifting', but we will use 'switching' in deference to the vast literature on task switching.
2   Ideally accuracy and composite measures of speed and accuracy such as the efficiency score would also be included. However, a large number of studies do not report the mean proportion correct and/or merely report that for the accuracy measure there was no main effects or interaction involving language group. In the age ranges analysed it is rare (but see Blumenfeld and Marian 2014, for an exception) for bilingual advantages to occur in proportion correct or efficiency scores, but not in the interference score derived from RTs.
3   See Paap et al. (2014) for a more detailed treatment of the ANCOVA problem and specific examples of using covariates in an attempt to statistically control for confounds in gF and parent's education.
4   The close relationship between EF and gF presents a conundrum. On the one hand, it seems necessary to match the language groups on gF. On the other hand, if that close relationship occurs because both the EF and gF tasks rely on a common general ability, then matching may reduce or eliminate the group difference under investigation.
5   The Bayes Factor ratio is often inverted and readers must attend to whether odds greater than 1 support the null (as in this paragraph) or the alternative hypothesis.
6   It is fair to note that it is other research groups, not Costa's, that tend to cite Costa's null effects at extreme congruency proportions as demonstrating the importance of using more difficult tasks.
7   Alternative names include the Gratton Effect (Gratton et al. 1992), sequential congruency effects (SCEs), and conflict adaptation effects. We will use the term CSE descriptively to describe a specific outcome, namely, that the congruency effect is significantly smaller following incongruent trials than following congruent trials.
8   This sense of optimizing overall task performance is clearly different from the sense used, for example, by Shenhav et al. (2013) when they describe the decision to adjust the current control specification on the basis of the expected rewards and costs on the next trial by choosing the 'optimal' control candidate. When these best bets are accumulated across trials they need not lead to optimal, or even improved performance as seen in the typical CSE.

REFERENCES

#A study included in the meta-analysis of non-verbal interference task described in Section 2.1.

*A study cited in the text and also included in the meta-analysis.

#Abutalebi, J., Della Rosa, P.A., Green, D.W. et al. (2012). Bilingualism tunes the anterior cortex for conflict monitoring. *Cerebral Cortex* 22 (9): 2076–2086.

#Abutalebi, J., Guidi, L., Borsa, V. et al. (2015). Bilingualism provides a neural reserve for aging populations. *Neuropsychologia* 69: 201–210.

#Ansaldo, A.I., Ghazi-Saidi, L., and Adrover-Roig, D. (2015). Interference control in elderly bilinguals: appearances can be misleading. *Journal of Clinical and Experimental Neuropsychology* 1–16.

#Antón, E., Carreiras, M., & Duñabeitia, J. A. (2017). On the Effects of Bilingualism on Executive Functions and Working Memory in Young Adults. Manuscript submitted for publication.

*#Antón, E., Duñabeitia, J.A., Estévez, A. et al. (2014). Is there a bilingual advantage in the ANT task? Evidence from children. *Frontiers in Psychology: Language Sciences* 5 (398): 1–12.

#Antón, E., Fernández Garcia, Y., Carreiras, M., and Duñabeitia, J.A. (2016). Does bilingualism shape inhibitory control in the elderly? *Journal of Memory and Language* 90: 147–160.

#Antón, E., Garcia, Y.F., Carreiras, M., and Duñabeitia, J.A. (2016). Does bilingualism shape inhibitory control in the elderly? *Journal of Memory and Language* 90: 147–160.

#Antoniou, K., Grohmann, K.K., Kambanaros, M., and Katsos, N. (2016). The effect of childhood bilectalism and multilingualism on executive control. *Cognition* 149: 18–30.

#Arredondo, M.M., Xiao-Su, H., Satterfield, T., and Kovelman, I. (2017). Bilingualism alters children's frontal lobe functioning for attentional control. *Developmental Science* 20 (3): 1–25.

Bacon, F. and Fowler, T. (1889). *Novum Organum*. Oxford, UK: Clarendon Press.

Barac, R. and Bialystok, E. (2012). Bilingual effects on cognitive and linguistic development: role of language, cultural backgound, and education. *Child Development* 83 (2): 413–422.

#Barrac, R., Moreno, S., and Bialystok, E. (2016). Behavioral and electrophysiological differences in executive control between monolingual and bilingual children. *Child Development* 87 (4): 1277–1290.

#Berroir, P., Ghazi-Saidi, L., Dash, T. et al. (2017). Interference control at the response level: functional networks reveal higher efficiency in the bilingual brain. *Journal of Neurolinguistics* 43: 4–16.

#Bialystok, E. (2006). Effect of bilingualism and computer video game experience on the Simon task. *Canadian Journal of Experimental Psychology* 60 (1): 68–79.

#Bialystok, E. (2010). Global-local and trail-making tasks by monolingual and bilingual children: beyond inhibition. *Developmental Psychology* 46 (1): 93–105.

Bialystok, E. (2011). Coordination of executive functions in monolingual and bilingual children. *Journal of Experimental Child Psychology* 110: 461–468.

Bialystok, E. (2015). Bilingualism and the development of executive function: the role of attention. *Child Development Perspectives* 9 (2): 117–121.

Bialystok, E. (2016). The signal and the noise: finding the pattern in human behavior. *Linguistic Approaches to Bilingualism* 1–18.

Bialystok, E. (2017). The bilingual adaptation: how minds accommodate experience. *Psychological Bulletin* 143 (3): 233–262.

#Bialystok, E., Barac, R., Blaye, A., and Poulin-Dubois, D. (2010). Word mapping and executive functioning in young monolingual and bilingual children. *Journal of Cognition and Development* 11 (4): 485–508.

#Bialystok, E., Craik, F.I.M., Grady, C. et al. (2005). Effect of bilingualism on cognitive control in the Simon task: evidence from MEG. *NeuroImage* 24: 40–49.

*#Bialystok, E., Craik, F.I.M., Klein, R., and Viswanathan, M. (2004). Bilingualism, aging, and cognitive control: evidence from the Simon task. *Psychology and Aging* 19 (2): 290–303.

Bialystok, E., Craik, F., and Luk, G. (2008). Cognitive control and lexical access in younger and older bilinguals. *Journal of Experimental Psychology: Learning, Memory, and Cognition* 34 (4): 859–873.

#Bialystok, E., Craik, F.I.M., and Ryan, J. (2006). Executive control in a modified antisaccade task: effects of aging and bilingualism. *Journal of Experimental Psychology: Learning, Memory, and Cognition* 32 (6): 1341–1354.

#Bialystok, E. and DePape, A.-M. (2009). Musical expertise, bilingualism, and executive functioning. *Journal of Experimental Psychology: Human Perception and Performance* 35 (2): 565–574.

#Bialystok, E., Hawrylewicz, K., Wiseheart, M., and Toplak, M. (2017). Interaction of bilingualism and attention-deficit/hyperactivity disorder in young adults. *Bilingualism: Language and Cognition* 20 (3): 588–601.

#Bialystok, E., Martin, M.M., and Viswanathan, M. (2005). Bilingualism across the lifespan: the rise and fall of inhibitory control. *International Journal of Bilingualism* 9 (1): 966–971.

Bialystok, E., Poarch, G., Luo, L., and Craik, F.I.M. (2014). Effects of bilingualism and aging on executive function and working memory. *Psychology and Aging* 29 (3): 696–705.

#Bice, K. and Kroll, J.F. (2015). Native language change during early stages of second language learning. *Neuroreport* 26 (16): 966–971.

*#Billig, J.D. and Scholl, A.P. (2011). The impact of bilingualism and aging on inhibitory control and working memory. *Organon* 51: 39–52.

#Blackburn, A. M. (2013). A study of the relationship between code switching and the bilingual advantage: Evidence that language use modulates neural indices of language processing and cognitive control (Doctoral dissertation, University of Texas at San Antonio).

#Blom, E., Boerma, T., Bosma, E. et al. (2017). Cognitive advantages of bilingual children in different sociolinguistic contexts. *Frontiers in Psychology* 8: 552.

#Blumenfeld, H.K. and Marian, V. (2011). Bilingualism influences inhibitory control in auditory comprehension. *Cognition* 118: 245–257.

*#Blumenfeld, H.K. and Marian, V. (2014). Cognitive control in bilinguals: advantages in stimulus-stimulus inhibition. *Bilingualism: Language and Cognition* 17 (3): 610–629.

#Bogulski, C.A., Rakoczy, M., Goodman, M., and Bialystok, E. (2015). Executive control in fluent and lapsed bilinguals. *Bilingualism: Language and Cognition* 18 (3): 561–567.

Botvinick, M.M., Braver, T.S., Barch, D.M. et al. (2001). Conflict monitoring and cognitive control. *Psychological Review* 108: 624–652.

Branzi, F.M., Calabria, M., Gade, M. et al. (2016). On the bilingualism effect in task switching. *Bilingualism: Language and Cognition* 1–14. doi: 10.1017/S136672891600119X.

#Cachia, A., Del Maschio, N., Borst, G. et al. (2017). Anterior cingulate cortex sulcation and its differential effects on conflict monitoring in bilinguals and monolinguals. *Brain and Language* 175: 57–63.

*#Calvo, A. and Bialystok, E. (2014). Independent effects of bilingualism and socioeconomic status on language ability and executive functioning. *Cognition* 130: 278–288.

Carlson, S. M., & Choi, H. P. (2009, April). Bilingual and bicultural: Executive function in Korean and American children. Paper presented at the 2009 biennial meeting of the society for research in child development, Denver, Colorado.

#Chabal, S., Schroeder, S.R., and Marian, V. (2015). Audio-visual object search is changed by bilingual experience. *Attention, Perception, & Psychophysics* 77 (8): 2684–2693.

Christoffels, I.K., de Haan, A.M., Steenbergen, L. et al. (2015). Two is better than one: bilingual education promotes the flexible mind. *Psychological Research* 79: 371–379.

#Coderre, E.L. and van Heuven, W.J.B. (2014). The effect of script similarity on executive control in bilinguals. *Frontiers in Psychology* 5 (1070).

#Coderre, E.L., Smith, J.F., van Heuven, W.J.B., and Horwitz, B. (2016). The functional overlap of executive control and language processing in bilinguals. *Bilingualism: Language and Cognition* 19 (3): 471–488.

Colzato, L.S., Sellaro, R., Samara, I., and Hommel, B. (2015). Meditation-induced cognitive-control states regulate response-conflict adaptation: evidence from trial-to-trial adjustments in the Simon task. *Consciousness and Cognition* 35: 110–114.

*#Costa, A., Hernández, M., Costa-Faidella, J., and Sebastián-Gallés, N. (2009). On the bilingual advantage in conflict processing: now you see it, now you don't. *Cognition* 113: 135–149.

#Costa, A., Hernández, M., and Sebastián-Gallés, N. (2008). Bilingualism aids conflict resolution: evidence from the ANT task. *Cognition* 106: 59–86.

#Cox, S.R., Bak, T.H., Allerhand, M. et al. (2016). Bilingualism, social cognition and executive functions: a tale of chicken and eggs. *Neuropsychologia* 91: 299–306.

*#de Bruin, A., Bak, T.H., and Della Sala, S. (2015). Examining the effects of active versus inactive bilingualism on executive control in a carefully matched non-immigrant sample. *Journal of Memory and Language* 85: 15–26.

de Bruin, A., Treccani, B., and Della Sala, S. (2015). The connection is in the data: we should consider them all. *Psychological Science* 26 (6): 947–949.

#De Cat, C., Gusnanto, A., and Serratrice, L. (2017). Identifying a threshold for the executive function advantage in bilingual children. *Studies in Second Language Acquisition* 1–33.

#de Leeuw, E. and Bogulski, C.A. (2016). Frequent L2 language use enhances executive control in bilinguals. *Bilingualism: Language and Cognition* 19 (5): 907–913.

Del Maschio, N., Guidi, L., Weekes, B. S., & Abutalebi, J. (2017). Bilingual experience maintains cognitive control performance in seniors. Manuscript submitted for publication.

Dijkstra, T. and van Heuven, W. (1998). The BIA-model and bilingual word recognition. In: *Localist Connectionist Approaches to Human Cognition* (ed. J. Grainger and A. Jacobs), 189–225. Hillsdale, NJ: Erlbaum.

Dijkstra, T. and van Heuven, W.J.B. (2002). The architecture of the bilingual word recognition system: from identification to decision. *Bilingualism: Language and Cognition* 5: 175–197.

*#Duñabeitia, J.A., Hernández, J.A., Antón, E. et al. (2014). The inhibitory advantage in bilingual children revisited: myth or reality? *Experimental Psychology* 61: 234–251.

#Duncan, H.D., Segalowitz, N., and Phillips, N.A. (2016). Differences in L1 linguistic attention control between monolinguals and bilinguals. *Bilingualism: Language and Cognition* 19 (1): 106–121.

Engelhardt, L.E., Briley, D.A., Mann, F.D. et al. (2015). Genes unite executive functions in childhood. *Psychological Science* 26 (8): 1151–1163.

Engle, R.W. and Kane, M.J. (2004). Executive attention, working memory capacity, and a two-factor theory of cognitive control. In: *The Psychology of Learning and Motivation*, vol. 44 (ed. B. Ross), 145–199. New York, NY: Elsevier.

#Emmorey, K., Luk, G., Pyers, J.E., and Bialystok, E. (2008). Cognitive control in bilinguals: evidence from bimodal bilinguals. *Psychological Science* 19 (12): 1201–1206.

#Engel de Abreu, P.M.J., Cruz-Santos, A., and Puglisi, M.L. (2014). Specific language impairment in language-minority children from low-income families. *International Journal of Language and Communication Disorders* 49 (6): 736–747.

#Engel de Abreu, P.M.J., Cruz-Santos, A., Tourinho, C.J. et al. (2012). Bilingualism enriches the poor: enhanced cognitive control in low-income minority children. *Psychological Science* 23: 1364–1371.

Evans, K.L. and Hampson, E. (2015). Sex-dependent effects on tasks assessing reinforcement learning and interference inhibition. *Frontiers in Psychology* 6: 1044.

Eysenck, H.J. (1978). An exercise in mega-silliness. *American Psychologist* 33 (5): 517.

Eysenck, H.J. (1981). *Intelligence: The Battle for the Mind*. London, UK: Pan.

Fisher, R.A. (1935). *The Design of Experiments*. London, UK: Macmillan.

#Freeman, M.R., Blumenfeld, H.K., and Marian, V. (2017). Cross-linguistic phonotactic competition control in bilinguals. *Journal of Cognitive Psychology* 29 (7): 783–794.

Friesen, D.C., Latman, V., Calvo, A., and Bialystok, E. (2014). Attention during visual search: the benefit of bilingualism. *International Journal of Bilingualism* 19: 693–702.

Fuller-Thomson, E. and Kuh, D. (2014). The healthy migrant effect may confound the link between bilingualism and delayed onset of Alzheimer's disease. *Cortex* 52: 128–130.

*#Gathercole, V.C.M., Thomas, E.M., Kennedy, I. et al. (2014). Does language dominance affect cognitive performance in bilinguals? Lifespan evidence from preschoolers through older adults on card sorting, Simon, and metalinguistic tasks. *Frontiers in Psychology* 5: 11.

Gold, B.T., Kim, C., Johnson, N.F. et al. (2013). Lifelong bilingualism maintains neural efficiency for cognitive control in aging. *The Journal of Neuroscience* 33 (2): 387–339.

#Grady, C.L., Luk, G., Craik, F.I.M., and Bialystok, E. (2015). Brain network activity in monolingual and bilingual older adults. *Neuropsychologia* 66: 170–181.

#Grant, A. and Dennis, N. (2017). Increased processing speed in young adult bilinguals: evidence from source memory judgments. *Bilingualism: Language and Cognition* 20 (2): 327–336.

Gratton, G., Coles, M.G., and Donchin, E. (1992). Optimizing the use of information: strategic control of activation of responses. *Journal of Experimental Psychology: General* 121: 480–506.

Green, D.W. (1998). Mental control of the bilingual lexico-semantic system. *Bilingualism: Language and Cognition* 1: 67–81.

*#Grundy, J.G., Chung-Fat-Yim, A., Friesen, D.C. et al. (2017). Sequential congruency effects reveal differences in disengagement of attention for monolingual and bilingual young adults. *Cognition* 163: 42–55.

*#Guido Mendes, C. (2015). The impact of bilingualism on conflict control. (Doctoral dissertation, University of Otago, Dunedin, New Zealand).

#Gutierrez, M. (2015). Strengthening cognitive development in minority populations: A study of the beneficial effects of bilingualism (Doctoral dissertation, University of Texas at El Paso).

Hartanto, A., Toh, W.X., and Yang, H. (2018). Bilingualism narrows socioeconomic disparities in executive functions and self-regulatory behaviors during early childhood: evidence from the early childhood longitudinal study. *Child Development* 1–21.

Hartanto, A. and Yang, H. (2016). Disparate bilingual experiences modulate task-switching advantages: a diffusion model analysis of the effects of interactional context on switch costs. *Cognition* 150: 10–19.

*#Hernández, M., Costa, A., Fuentes, L.J. et al. (2010). The impact of bilingualism on the executive control and orienting networks of attention. *Bilingualism: Language and Cognition* 13 (3): 315–325.

*#Hernández, M., Martin, C.D., Barceló, F., and Costa, A. (2013). Where is the bilingual advantage in task-switching? *Journal of Memory and Language* 69: 257–276.

Hilchey, M.D. and Klein, R.M. (2011). Are there bilingual advantages on non-linguistic interference tasks? Implications for plasticity of executive control processes. *Psychonomic Bulletin and Review* 18: 625–658.

Hilchey, M.D., Saint-Aubin, J., and Klein, R.M. (2015). Does bilingual exercise enhance cognitive fitness in non-linguistic executive processing tasks. In: *Cambridge Handbook of Bilingual Processing* (ed. J.W. Schwieter), 586–613. Cambridge, UK: Cambridge University Press.

Homacka, S., Lee, D., and Ricco, C.A. (2005). Test review: Delis-Kaplan executive function system. *Journal of Clinical and Experimental Neuropsychology* 27 (5): 559–609.

Houtzager, N., Lowie, W., Sprenger, S., and de Bot, K. (2017). Age-related differences between German monolinguals and Dutch-Frisian bilinguals. *Bilingualism: Language and Cognition* 20 (1): 69–79.

#Humphrey, A. D., & Valian, V. V. (2012, November). Multilingualism and cognitive control: Simon and flanker task performance in monolingual and multilingual young adults. Presentation at the 53rd annual meeting of the Psychonomic Society, Minneapolis, MN.

#Hutchison, L. A. (2012). Relations between executive functioning, second language fluency, and externalizing behavior problems in early childhood (Doctoral dissertation, George Mason University).

Hutchinson, C.V., Barrett, D.J., Nitka, A., and Raynes, K. (2016). Action video game training reduces the Simon effect. *Psychonomic Bulletin and Review* 23 (2): 587–592.

Ioannidis, J.P.A. (2016). The mass production of redundant, misleading, and conflicted systematic reviews and meta-analyses. *The Milbank Quarterly* 94 (3): 485–514.

Jeffreys, H. (1961). *Theory of Probability*, 3e. Oxford, UK: Oxford University Press, Clarendon Press.

#Jiao, L., Liu, C., Wang, R., and Chen, B. (2017). Working memory demand of a task modulates bilingual advantage in executive functions. *International Journal of Bilingualism* 1–16. doi: 10.1177/1367006917709097.

Kane, M.J., Hambrick, D.Z., and Conway, A.R.A. (2005). Working memory capacity and fluid intelligence are strongly related constructs: comment on Ackerman, Beier,

Boyle (2005). *Psychological Bulletin* 131 (1): 66–71.

#Kapa, L.L. and Colombo, J. (2013). Attentional control in early and later bilingual children. *Cognitive Development* 28: 233–246.

#Keijzer, M.C.J. and Schmid, M. (2016). Individual differences in cognitive control advantages of elderly Dutch-English bilinguals. *Linguistic Approaches to Bilingualism* 6 (1/2): 64–85.

Kennedy, S., Kidd, M.P., McDonald, J.T., and Biddle, N. (2015). The healthy immigrant effect: patterns and evidence from four countries. *Journal of International Migration and Integration* 16 (2): 317–332.

*#Kirk, N.W., Fiala, L., Scott-Brown, K., and Kempe, V. (2014). No evidence for reduced Simon cost in elderly bilinguals and bidialectals. *Journal of Cognitive Psychology* 26: 1–9.

Klein, R.M. (2015). On the belief that the cognitive exercise associated with the acquisition of a second language enhances extra-linguistic cognitive functions: is "Type-1 incompetence" at work here? *Cortex* 73: 340–341.

*#Kousaie, S. and Phillips, N.A. (2012). Aging and bilingualism: absence of a 'bilingual advantage' in Stroop interference in a nonimmigrant sample. *The Quarterly Journal of Experimental Psychology* 65: 356–369.

#Kousaie, S. and Phillips, N.A. (2017). A behavioural and electrophysiological investigation of the effect of bilingualism on aging and cognitive control. *Neuropsychologia* 94: 23–35.

#Kousaie, S., Sheppard, C., Lemieux, M. et al. (2014). Executive function and bilingualism in young and older adults. *Frontiers in Behavioral Neuroscience* 8 (250): 1–12.

Kroll, J.F. and Bialystok, E. (2013). Understanding the consequences of bilingualism for language processing and cognition. *Journal of Cognitive Psychology* 25: 497–514.

#Ladas, A.I., Carroll, D.J., and Vivas, A.B. (2015). Attentional processes in low-socioeconomic status bilingual children: are they modulated by the amount of bilingual experience? *Child Development* 86 (2): 557–578.

Lehtonen, M., Soveri, A., Laine, A. et al. (2018). Is bilingualism associated with enhanced executive functioning in adults? *Psychological Bulletin* 144 (4): 394–425.

#Linck, J.A., Hoshino, N., and Kroll, J.F. (2008). Cross-language lexical processes and inhibitory control. *The Mental Lexicon* 3 (3): 349–374.

Lu, C.-H. and Proctor, R.W. (1995). The influence of irrelevant location information on performance: a review of the Simon and spatial Stroop effects. *Psychonomic Bulletin & Review* 2 (2): 174–207.

*#Luk, G., Anderson, J.A.E., Craik, F.I.M. et al. (2010). Distinct neural correlates for two types of inhibition in bilinguals: response inhibition versus interference suppression. *Brain and Cognition* 74: 347–357.

#Luk, G., De Sa, E., and Bialystok, E. (2011). Is there a relation between onset age of bilingualism and enhancement of cognitive control? *Bilingualism: Language and Cognition* 14: 588–595.

#Marian, V., Chabal, S., Bartolotti, J. et al. (2014). Differential recruitment of executive control regions during phonological competition in monolinguals and bilinguals. *Brain and Language* 139: 108–117.

#Martin-Rhee, M.M. and Bialystok, E. (2008). The development of two types of inhibitory control in monolingual and bilingual. *Bilinguaism: Language and Cognition* 11 (1): 81–93.

#Marzecová, A., Asanowicz, D., Krivá, L., and Wodniecka, Z. (2013). The effects of bilingualism on efficiency and lateralization of attentional networks. *Bilingualism: Language and Cognition* 16 (3): 608–623.

*#Marzecová, A., Bukowski, M., Correa, A. et al. (2014). Tracing the bilingual advantage in cognitive control: the role of flexibility in temporal preparation and category switching. *Journal of Cognitive Psychology* 25 (5): 586–604.

Miller, G.A. and Chapman, J.P. (2001). Misunderstanding analysis of covariance. *Journal of Abnormal Psychology* 110 (1): 40–48.

Mishra, R.K., Hilchey, M.D., Singh, N., and Klein, R.M. (2012). On the time course of exogenous cueing effects in bilinguals: high proficiency in a second language is associated with more rapid endogenous disengagement. *The Quarterly Journal of Experimental Psychology* 65 (8): 1502–1510.

Miyake, A. and Friedman, N.P. (2012). The nature and organization of individual differences in executive functions: four general conclusions. *Current Directions in Psychology* 21 (1): 8–14.

Miyake, A., Friedman, N.P., Emerson, M.J. et al. (2000). The unity and diversity of executive functions and their contributions to complex 'frontal lobe' tasks: a latent variable analysis. *Cognitive Psychology* 41: 49–100.

#Mohades, S.G., Struys, E., Van Schuerbeek, P. et al. (2014). Age of second language acquisition affects nonverbal conflict processing in children: An fMRI study. *Brain and Behavior* 4 (5): 626–642.

*#Mor, B., Yitzhaki-Amsalem, S., and Prior, A. (2014). The joint effect of bilingualism and ADHD on executive functions. *Journal of Attention Disorders* 19 (6): 527–541.

Moradzadeh, L., Blumenthal, G., and Wiseheart, M. (2014). Musical training, bilingualism, and executive function: A closer look at task switching and dual-task performance. *Cognitive Science* 39: 1–29.

#Morales, J., Calvo, A., and Bialystok, E. (2013). Working memory development in monolingual and bilingual children. *Journal of Experimental Child Psychology* 114: 187–202.

Moreno, S., Bialystok, E., Barac, R. et al. (2011). Short-term music training enhances verbal intelligence and executive function. *Psychological Science* 22 (11): 1425–1433.

*#Morton, J.B. and Harper, S.N. (2007). What did Simon say? Revisiting the bilingual advantage. *Developmental Science* 10: 719–726.

#Nair, V.K., Biedermann, B., and Nickels, L. (2017). Effect of socio-economic status on cognitive control in non-literate bilingual speakers. *Bilingualism: Language and Cognition* 20 (5): 999–1009.

#Namazi, M. and Thordardottir, E. (2010). A working memory, not bilingual advantage, in controlled attention. *International Journal of Bilingual Education and Bilingualism* 13 (5): 597–616.

#Nicolay, A.C. and Poncelet, M. (2013). Cognitive advantage in children enrolled in a second-language immersion elementary school program for three years. *Bilingualism: Language and Cognition* 16 (3): 597–607.

Paap, K.R. (2014). The role of componential analysis, categorical hypothesizing, replicability and confirmation bias in testing for bilingual advantages in executive functioning. *Journal of Cognitive Psychology* 26 (3): 242–255.

Paap, K.R. (2018). Bilingualism and executive functioning. In: *An Introduction to Bilingualism: Principles and Processes*, 2nde (ed. J. Altarriba and R. Heredia), 191–224. New York, NY: Routledge.

Paap, K. R., Anders, R., Mikulinsky, R., Mason, & Alvarado (2017, November). Congruency effects in nonverbal interference tasks are predicted by fluid intelligence and biological sex, but not by bilingualism, self control, or impulsivity. Paper presented at the meeting of the Psychonomics Society, Vancouver, Canada.

*#Paap, K.R., Anders-Jefferson, Mikulinsky, R. et al. (2018). Is there a general domain-free inhibitory control ability that is moderated by bilingualism? *Journal of Memory and Language* under review.

Paap, K.R., Darrow, J., Dalibar, C., and Johnson, H.A. (2014). Effects of script similarity on bilingual advantages in executive control are likely to be negligible or null. *Frontiers in Psychology* 5: 1539.

*#Paap, K.R. and Greenberg, Z.I. (2013). There is no coherent evidence for a bilingual advantage in executive processing. *Cognitive Psychology* 66: 232–258.

Paap, K.R., Johnson, H.A., and Sawi, O. (2014). Are bilingual advantages dependent upon specific tasks or specific bilingual experiences? *Journal of Cognitive Psychology* 26 (6): 615–639.

Paap, K.R., Johnson, H.A., and Sawi, O. (2015). Bilingual advantages in executive functioning either do not exist or are restricted to very specific and undetermined circumstances. *Cortex* 69: 265–278.

Paap, K.R., Johnson, H.A., and Sawi, O. (2016). Should the search for bilingual advantages in executive functioning continue? *Cortex* 74 (4): 305–314.

Paap, K.R. and Liu, Y. (2014). Conflict resolution in sentence processing is the same for bilinguals and monolinguals: the role of confirmation bias in testing for bilingual advantages. *Journal of Neurolinguistics* 27 (1): 50–74.

Paap, K.R., Myuz, H.A., Anders, R.T. et al. (2017). No compelling evidence for a bilingual advantage in switching or that frequent language switching reduces switch costs. *Journal of Cognitive Psychology* 29 (2): 89–112.

*#Paap, K.R. and Sawi, O. (2014). Bilingual advantages in executive functioning: problems in convergent validity, divergent validity, and the identification of the theoretical constructs. *Frontiers in Psychology* 5 (962): 1–15.

Paap, K.R. and Sawi, O. (2016). The role of test-retest reliability in measuring individual and group differences in executive functioning. *Journal of Neuroscience Methods* 274: 81–93.

Paap, K.R., Sawi, O.M., Dalibar, C. et al. (2014). Brain mechanisms underlying the cognitive benefits of bilingualism may be extraordinarily difficult to discover. *AIMS Neuroscience* 1 (3): 245–256.

Paap, K., Wagner, S., Johnson. H., Bockelman, M., Cushing, D., & Sawi, O. (2014, May). 20,000 flanker task trials: Are the effect stable reliable, robust, and stable? Poster presented at the Association for Psychological Science meeting, San Francisco, CA.

#Pelham, S. D. (2015). Monolinguals and bilinguals' attentional control in the presence of cognitive and emotional distraction (Doctoral dissertation, University of Florida).

#Pelham, S.D. and Abrams, L. (2014). Cognitive advantages and disadvantages in early and late bilinguals. *Journal of*

Experimental Psychology: Learning, Memory and Cognition 40 (2): 313–325.

#Poarch, G.J. and Bialystok, E. (2015). Bilingualism as a model for multitasking. *Developmental Research* 1 (35): 113–124.

#Poarch, G.J. and van Hell, J.G. (2012). Executive functions and inhibitory control in multilingual children: evidence from second-language learners, bilinguals, and trilinguals. *Journal of Experimental Child Psychology* 113: 535–551.

Prior, A. and Gollan, T.H. (2011). Good language-switchers are good task-switchers: Evidence from Spanish–English and Mandarin–English bilinguals. *Journal of the International Neuropsychological Society* 17: 682–691.

Prior, A. and Gollan, T.H. (2013). The elusive link between language control and executive control: a case of limited transfer. *Journal of Cognitive Psychology* 25 (5): 622–645.

*#Prior, A. and MacWhinney, B. (2010). A bilingual advantage in task switching. *Bilingualism: Language and Cognition* 13: 253–262.

#Rainey, V.R., Davidson, D., and Li-Grining, C. (2016). Executive functions as predictors of syntactic awareness in English monolingual and English-Spanish bilingual language brokers and nonbrokers. *Applied PsychoLinguistics* 37: 963–995.

Ratcliff, R. (1978). A theory of memory retrieval. *Psychological Review* 85: 59–108.

Ratiu, I., Hout, M.C., Walenchok, S.C. et al. (2017). Comparing visual search and eyemovements in bilinguals and monolinguals. *Attention, Perception, & Psychophysics* 79 (6): 1695–1725.

#Rodrigues, L.R. and Zimmer, M.C. (2016). Inhibitory and attentional control: the interaction between "professional activity" and bilingualism. *Psicologia: Reflexão e Crítica* 29 (36): 1–10.

Rodriguez-Pujada, A., Sanjuan, A., Ventura-Campos, N. et al. (2013). Bilinguals use language-control brain areas more than monolinguals to perform non-linguistic switching tasks. *PLoS One* 8 (9): e73028.

#Roselli, M., Ardila, A., Lalwani, L.N., and Vélez-Uribe, I. (2016). The effect of language proficiency on executive functions in balanced and unbalanced Spanish-English bilinguals. *Bilingualism: Language and Cognition* 19 (3): 489–503.

#Ross, J. and Melinger, A. (2016). Bilingual advantage, bidialectal advantage or neither? Comparing performance across three tests of executive function in middle childhood. *Developmental Science* 20 (4): 1–21.

*#Rubio-Fernandez, P. and Glucksberg, S. (2012). Reasoning about other people's beliefs: bilinguals have an advantage. *Journal of Experimental Psychology: Learning, Memory, and Cognition* 38 (1): 211–217.

#Ryskin, R.A., Brown-Schmidt, S., Canseco-Gonzalez, E. et al. (2014). Visuospatial perspective-taking in conversation and the role of bilingual experience. *Journal of Memory and Language* 74: 46–76.

Saint-Aubin, J., Hilchey, M.D., Mishra, R. et al. (2018). Does the relation between the control of attention and second language proficiency generalize from India to Canada? *Canadian Journal of Experimental Psychology* 72 (3): 208–218.

*#Salvatierra, J. L (2007). The effect of bilingualism and aging on inhibitory control. (Dissertation, Florida Atlantic University. Boca Raton, Florida).

*#Salvatierra, J.L. and Rosselli, M. (2011). The effect of bilingualism and age on inhibitory control. *International Journal of Bilingualism* 15 (1): 26–37.

#Sampson, M. (2016) An investigation of inhibitory control in bilingual aphasia. (Dissertation, University of Maryland, College Park, Maryland).

#Scaltritti, M., Peressotti, F., and Miozzo, M. (2017). Bilingual advantage and language switch: What's the linkage? *Bilingualism: Language and Cognition* 20 (1): 80–97.

*#Schroeder, S.R. and Marian, V. (2012). A bilingual advantage for episodic memory in older adults. *Journal of Cognitive Psychology* 24 (5): 591–601.

#Schroeder, S.R., Marian, V., Shook, A., and Bartolotti, J. (2016). Bilingualism and musicianship enhance cognitive control. *Neural Plasticity* 2016: 1–11.

Shenhav, A., Botvinick, M.M., and Cohen, J.D. (2013). The expected value of control: an integrative theory of anterior cingulate cortex function. *Neuron* 79: 217–240.

Shulley, L.J. and Shake, M.C. (2016). Investigating the relationship between bilingualism, cognitive control, and mind wandering. *Journal of Cognitive Psychology* 28 (3): 257–274.

#Slevic, L.R., Davey, N.S., Buschkuehl, M., and Jaeggi, S.M. (2016). Tuning the mind: Exploring the connections between musical ability and executive functions. *Cognition* 152: 199–211.

#Sorge, G.B., Toplak, M.E., and Bialystok, E. (2017). Interactions between levels of attention ability and levels of bilingualism in children's executive functioning. *Developmental Science* 20 (e12408): 1–16.

Stoet, G. (2017). Sex differences in the Simon task help to interpret sex differences in selective attention. *Psychological Research* 81: 571–581.

#Tao, L., Marzecova, A., Taft, M. et al. (2011). The efficiency of attentional networks in early and late bilinguals: The role of age of acquisition. *Frontiers in Psychology* 2: 123.

Tare, M., & Linck, J. (2011, November). *Exploring bilingual cognitive advantages when controlling for background variables*. Poster presented at the 52nd Annual Meeting of the Psychonomic Society, Seattle, WA.

#Tran, C.D., Arredondo, M.M., and Yoshida, H. (2015). Differential effects of bilingualism and culture on early attention: a longitudinal study in the U.S., Argentina, and Vietnam. *Frontiers in Psychology* 6 (795): 1–15.

Treisman, A. and Gelade, G. (1980). A feature-integration theory of attention. *Cognitive Psychology* 12: 97.136.

Unsworth, N., Fukuda, K., Awh, E., and Vogel, E.K. (2014). Working memory and fluid intelligence: capacity, attention control, and secondary memory retrieval. *Cognitive Psychology* 71: 1–26.

Unsworth, N., Redick, T.S., McMillan, B.D. et al. (2015). Is playing video games related to cognitive abilities? *Psychological Science* 26 (6): 759–774.

Valian, V. (2015). Bilingualism and cognition. *Bilingualism: Language and Cognition* 18 (1): 3–24.

Van der Lubbe, R.H. and Verleger, R. (2002). Aging and the Simon task. *Psychophysiology* 39 (1): 100–110.

#Vaughn, K.A., Nunez, A.I.R., Greene, M.R. et al. (2016). Individual differences in the bilingual brain: the role of language background and DRD2 genotype in verbal and non-verbal cognitive control. *Journal of Neurolinguistics* 40: 112–127.

Vestberg, T., Gustafson, R., Maurex, L. et al. (2012). Executive functions predict the success of top-soccer players. *PLoS One* 7 (4): e34731.

von Bastian, C., de Simoni, C., Kane, M., Carruth, N., & Miyake, A. (2017, November). Does being bilingual entail advantages in working memory? A meta-analysis. Paper presented at the meeting of the Psychonomic Society, Vancouver.

von Bastian, C.C., Sousa, A.S., and Gade, M. (2015). No evidence for bilingual cognitive advantages: a test of four hypotheses. *Journal of Experimental Psychology: General* 216 (2): 246–258.

Weissman, D.H., Jiang, J., and Egner, T. (2014). Determinants of congruency sequence effects without learning and memory confounds. *Journal of Experimental Psychology: Human Perception and Performance* 40 (5): 2022–2037.

Wiseheart, M., Viswanathan, M., and Bialystok, E. (2016). Flexibility in task switching by monolinguals and bilinguals. *Bilingualism: Language and Cognition* 19 (1): 141–146.

*#Woumans, E., Ceuleers, E., Van der Linden, L. et al. (2015). Verbal and nonverbal cognitive control in bilinguals and interpreters. *Journal of Experimental Psychology: Learning, Memory, and Cognition* 41 (5): 1579–1586.

#Woumans, E., Surmont, J., Struys, E., and Duyck, W. (2017). The longitudinal effect of bilingual immersion schooling on cognitive control and intelligence. *Language Learning* 66 (52): 76–91.

#Xie, Z. and Dong, Y. (2017). Contributions of bilingualism and public speaking training to cognitive control differences. *Bilingualism: Language and Cognition* 20 (1): 55–68.

#Yang, E. (2016). Cognitive effects of bilingualism: Executive functions and language practice (Doctoral dissertation University at Buffalo, State University of New York).

#Yang, S. and Yang, H. (2016). Bilingual effects on deployment of the attention system in linguistically and culturally homogeneous children and adults. *Journal of Experimental Child Psychology* 146: 121–136.

Ye, Y., Mo, L., and Wu, Q. (2017). Mixed cultural context brings out bilingual advantage on executive function. *Bilingualism: Language and Cognition* 20 (4): 844–852.

#Yudes, C., Macizo, P., and Bajo, T. (2011). The influences of expertise in simultaneous interpreting on non-verbal executive processes. *Frontiers in Psychology* 2: 1–9.

35 The Bilingual Advantage Debate

Publication Biases and the Decline Effect

ANGELA DE BRUIN AND SERGIO
DELLA SALA

1. Introduction

The question whether bilinguals have a cognitive advantage compared with mono-linguals has been the topic of fierce debates over the past few years. Several studies have suggested that bilinguals show enhanced inhibitory control (e.g. Bialystok et al. 2004), better conflict monitoring (e.g. Costa et al. 2009), and superior task-switching performance (e.g. Prior and MacWhinney 2010) compared with monolinguals. A wide range of tasks has been used to study these effects of bilingualism. For instance, in the frequently used Simon task, participants need to respond with a right or left button press to a stimulus that appears on the left or right side of the screen. On some trials, the required button press and presentation side will mismatch, requiring par-ticipants to suppress task-irrelevant information (i.e. the side of the screen) in order to make the correct response. Bilinguals have been found to respond faster to these incongruent trials in particular but also to respond faster overall on this type of conflict tasks as compared to control tasks without conflict. Other studies have used different types of task-switching paradigms, such as the colour-shape switching task requiring participants to indicate the colour or shape of an object while switching between these two tasks.

Effects of bilingualism on these and other tasks have been reported for all age groups, including children (e.g. Bialystok and Martin 2004), younger adults (e.g. Costa et al. 2008), and older adults (e.g. Bialystok et al. 2004). Additionally, different types of bilin-guals have been studied to examine whether effects may be more likely to occur in some types of bilinguals, for instance those with an earlier age of acquisition (Luk et al. 2011) or those who switch more often between their languages in daily life (e.g. Prior and Gollan 2011).

The Handbook of the Neuroscience of Multilingualism, First Edition. Edited by John W. Schwieter.
© 2019 John Wiley & Sons Ltd. Published 2019 by John Wiley & Sons Ltd.

Because of its large societal impact, this so-called bilingual advantage has received a great amount of media attention and has often been presented as an undisputed fact. More recent years, however, have seen an upsurge of studies challenging these findings with comparisons between large samples of bilinguals and monolinguals not showing any differences on various executive control tasks (e.g. Duñabeitia et al. 2014; Paap and Greenberg 2013). Estimations furthermore suggest that over 80% of tasks presented in recent studies do not observe a positive effect of bilingualism on executive control (cf. Paap et al. 2015). Along these lines, Paap (Chapter 34, Table 2 of this volume) presents an overview of studies examining bilingual–monolingual differences on colour-shape switching tasks, showing that only two studies have replicated the bilingual effects on switching costs reported by Prior and MacWhinney (2010). In contrast, 25 studies yielded null results on these tasks. Recent meta-analyses, furthermore, do not show consistent effects of bilingualism on executive control tasks (Lehtonen et al. 2018; Donnelly 2016).

In addition to increased attention to failed replications, the quality of studies on this topic is often criticized. This includes the degree to which participant groups are matched on background variables such as immigrant status or socioeconomic status, over-interpretation of the data, and the incorrect use of statistical analyses (cf. Paap et al. 2015). Thus, the debate whether or not bilingualism affects executive control is still ongoing (see, for example, the various papers that form part of Cortex Bilingualism Forum in response to Paap et al. 2015).

In this chapter, we discuss another variable that influences this debate: publication bias. Both quantitative and qualitative reviews are often based on published data only. However, positive results may be more likely to be published than null or negative findings, a phenomenon known as 'publication bias'. In this chapter, we will discuss evidence suggesting that a publication bias is at play in the literature on bilingualism and executive control. This bias as such does not inform us about the existence or size of a bilingual effect but being aware of biases does improve the interpretation of the literature. We will furthermore evaluate whether this bias has changed over time. In addition, the positive effects of bilingualism appear to have diminished over time (also generally referred to as the 'decline effect'). We will discuss how (publication) biases may relate to this decline effect in the field of bilingualism and executive control.

2.   Publication Bias

Publication biases have been studied and observed in many different research fields (see Ioannidis et al. 2014, for an overview of publication biases in cognitive science). Taking advantage of preregistration (cf. Chambers 2013), biases have been studied particularly often in relation to clinical research studying e.g. the effects of medication (e.g. Easterbrook et al. 1991; Dickersin et al. 1992; Ioannidis and Trikalinos 2007; Scherer et al. 2007). Easterbrook et al. (1991) examined the publication fate of 487 clinical research projects that had been approved by an ethics committee. A direct comparison of publications per result type showed that 34% of studies with null results had been published in a journal as compared to 60% of studies with significant findings. A further examination of the type of journal in which the study had been published showed that articles with positive findings on average appeared in journals with a higher impact factor.

This gap between positive and null results can occur in different stages of the publication process. Firstly, authors can decide not to publish null or negative results that do not fit their hypotheses or are incompatible with the current zeitgeist. Some studies have suggested that biases indeed occur at the level of the authors. For instance, Easterbrook's survey showed that null results were given as the main reason for not submitting or writing up a paper with null results. Dickersin et al. (1992), too, suggested that the existence of a publication bias in clinical studies was mainly driven by the researchers themselves.

Secondly, reviewers may respond more negatively to studies with null effects and editors may be more likely to reject papers that do not show positive effects that are easily sellable to a wider audience. Mahoney (1977) stated that biases are at least partly driven by the review process. Reviewers were given studies with positive, negative, mixed, or null results that reported the exact same methodological procedure. Nevertheless, positive studies were reported to be methodologically sounder than papers with negative, null, or mixed results. Furthermore, papers with positive results typically received acceptance with moderate revisions while other result types received major revisions or rejections. More recently, similar findings were observed by Emerson et al. (2010) who showed that papers with positive results were more likely to be recommended for publication by reviewers. Their method section, furthermore, received a better evaluation compared with the manuscript version with null effects.

While publication biases have been studied relatively elaborately in clinical sciences, publication biases and failures to replicate positive effects have been observed and discussed extensively in the field of psychology too (e.g. Bakker et al. 2012; Ferguson and Heene 2012; Francis 2012; Francis 2014; Nosek et al. 2015). Through a survey asking researchers about several questionable practices, it was estimated that approximately two-thirds of researchers selectively only submit for publication studies that show the desired findings (John et al. 2012). Others have argued that the amount of positive findings in psychology publications exceeds the expected number. Sample sizes in published papers are often too small to detect small to medium effect sizes. Considering this, more studies with null effects are expected but are not found in the published literature (e.g. Bakker et al. 2012; Francis 2014).

3.   Publication Bias in Bilingualism and Executive Control

Considering the existence of a publication bias in other research fields and the suggestion that positive studies are overrepresented in psychology, biases are expected to occur in the literature on the 'bilingual advantage' too. An overview of publication outcomes of studies presented at conferences suggested that this is indeed the case (De Bruin et al. 2015a). A search through 169 conferences organized between 1999 and 2012 yielded 104 conference abstracts on the topic of bilingualism and executive control. These were classified into four categories: studies supporting a bilingual advantage (38%), studies with mixed results mainly supporting an advantage (13%), studies with mixed results mainly challenging an advantage (32%), and studies with null or negative effects of bilingualism (16%). Half of the studies presented in the conference abstracts were published in a scientific journal before or in February 2014. Examining the publication rates per result type showed that studies with positive results were more likely to be published (68%) than studies with null or negative findings (29%). Studies with mixed results fell in between these two (50% of mixed-supporting studies were published and 39% of mixed-challenging studies). Crucially, the studies that did and did not show positive effects of bilingualism did not differ in terms of average sample size and average year of conference. They used similar tasks and had a similar power to detect the various effect sizes observed in the literature. However, studies showing positive effects of bilingualism on average reported fewer tasks than studies (mainly) reporting null or negative effects.

While the sample sizes did not differ between abstracts supporting or challenging a bilingual effect, it is interesting to note that differences in sample size have been observed in the published literature. For instance, Paap (see Chapter 34 in this volume) observed smaller bilingual–monolingual differences in studies with larger sample sizes. It is possible that researchers collect more data after conference presentations and that this is done in particular for null results, leading to relatively larger sample sizes in the literature. In addition, not all conference abstracts (23%) reported sample sizes and they should therefore be treated with caution.

The original analysis (De Bruin et al. 2015a) included both tasks with non-verbal and tasks with verbal materials. However, as bilinguals may have a disadvantage on pure lexical tasks (cf. Bialystok 2009), the analysis was repeated with non-verbal tasks only (De Bruin et al. 2015b). The difference in publication outcome remained present for positive (70% published) studies compared to null effects (23% published).

The analysis presented in de Bruin et al. (2015a) furthermore included a wide range of bilinguals varying in age of acquisition, proficiency, language use, and languages spoken. It has frequently been suggested that cognitive effects may be observed only for certain types of bilinguals. However, as conference abstracts often do not include detailed information about the participants' language profiles, it could not be examined whether certain findings may have been easier to publish for certain types of bilingualism.

In an attempt to examine why null effects in the bilingualism and executive control field had been published less often, a survey was sent out to the researchers of unpublished conference abstracts. Unfortunately, the majority of contacted authors did not reply or refused to complete the survey. The few replies that were received suggest that the majority of authors from a null-result study had not submitted their work to a journal (De Bruin et al. 2015b). However, the low number of replies, particularly from productive research groups on this topic, hinders the understanding of the mechanisms behind a publication bias in this field.

Furthermore, while tracking the publication record of conference abstracts may inform us about publication biases existing at the level of publishing in journals, a bias may already exist at the level of conference submission. Researchers may not only decide not to submit null results to journals, but they can choose not to present these data at conferences either. If this is the case, the data reported by de Bruin et al. (2015a) revealing a publication bias may underestimate the problem.

It should be emphasized, as described, that the literature on this particular topic is not the only one suffering from biases. While it is extremely difficult to compare bias analyses across studies due to differences in methodology, results on the topic of bilingualism and executive control appear similar to those on clinical studies such as medical trials. Firstly, half of the studies reported in conference abstracts on bilingualism and executive control were subsequently published in a scientific journal. Easterbrook et al. (1991) also report that 52% of their clinical trials had been published. Dickersin et al. (1992) too studied clinical research and suggested that approximately 30–60% of registered studies are eventually published. Moreover, the percentages of published papers per result type in de Bruin et al. (2015a) are in line with those reported by Easterbrook et al. (1991): respectively 68% and 60% of positive studies were published compared with 29% and 34% of null effects.

4.   The Decline Effect

The existence of a publication bias does not mean that an effect does not exist. However, it does suggest that the published literature presents a distorted impression of the actual effect size. Furthermore, being aware of biases can help to understand the shifting patterns in the literature on bilingualism and executive control. Recent years have seen an increase in the number of studies with null effects as compared with early years predominantly reporting positive effects. Examining published papers addressing cognitive effects of bilingualism across a wide range of tasks, de Bruin and Della Sala (2015) showed an increase in the number of studies not showing a bilingual advantage. Furthermore, keeping in mind the overall increase of the number of published papers on this topic, there was a relative decrease of studies showing a positive effect of bilingualism. A recent overview (Sanchez-Azanza et al. 2017) also showed a shift in publication trends with an increase of studies with null effects from 2014 onwards.

While de Bruin and Della Sala (2015) and Sanchez-Azanza et al. (2017) show an increase in studies with null results in recent years, they also show that approximately half of recent studies support a positive effect of bilingualism. These reviews are based on a holistic approach, classifying the results and conclusions of a paper as a whole. In contrast, when individual statistical tests are examined (e.g. Paap et al. 2015), the vast majority show null results. The discrepancy between these two review methods may be related to several large sample studies being weighted differently. For instance, Paap and Greenberg (2013) reported multiple tasks each yielding multiple measurements of executive control. While this study was only included once as a whole in e.g. de Bruin and Della Sala (2015), ten individual tests were included in Paap et al. (2015).

The recent increase of null results is also noticeable when comparing Hilchey and Klein's (2011) review on bilingualism and executive control with their review in 2015 (Hilchey et al. 2015). While they observed a strong and consistent effect of bilingualism on overall response times in interference tasks in 2011, in their 2015 review they conclude that the evidence for this effect has evaporated in recent years.

Apart from assessing the publication trends in terms of the types of results being published, others have assessed the actual effect sizes reported. One of the first and seminal studies on this topic (Bialystok et al. 2004) observed effect sizes up to $d = 3$. This effect size is much larger than those typically observed in psychology and even goes beyond the effect size labelled as 'huge' ($d = 2$; Sawilowsky 2009). Since then, many other studies have been published showing positive effects of bilingualism but with far more modest effect sizes. For instance, Klein (2015) showed that larger differences between bilinguals and monolinguals on the Simon and flanker task were predominantly observed in early studies while later studies show smaller or no differences. Similarly, de Bot (2017) examined effect sizes on Simon tasks across time and observed a decrease across the years.

A decrease in the size of bilingual–monolingual differences across the years in combination with an increase of published null results suggests that a decline effect is present. This refers to the observation that there is a relative decrease in positive evidence after a strong initial finding. A decline effect, similar to publication biases, is not specific to this particular line of research but has been found for several clinical research studies (Ioannidis 2006) as well as experimental psychology (Francis 2012). There may be several reasons underlying a decline effect (see De Bruin and Della Sala 2015; Lehrer 2010; Schooler 2011). Firstly, regression to the mean is often presented as a mechanism behind decreasing effect sizes. While the first reports may show an inflated effect size due to errors, subsequent studies will show effect sizes closer to the average due to statistical self-correction. Publication biases and selectively reporting experiments that work may be another prominent mechanism behind this effect. Initial studies may only be deemed interesting when a strong, positive effect is found. This effect may be observed on the first experiment that is run and may be published immediately without self-replication. Alternatively, several experiments may be needed to find an effect, but only the 'successful' one gets published. Initial replications failing to observe an effect may be less likely to be published or even submitted because they are inconsistent with the expected positive effects. It is possible that, with time, and when theories get more established, an increased interest in null effects may arise. However, Ferguson and Heene (2012) warn against so-called 'undead theories', suggesting that theories can stay around for a long time despite failures to replicate.

In the case of bilingualism in particular, there has been increased interest in assessing which types of bilinguals (e.g. only those with a high proficiency level) and which types of tasks (e.g. only those with a high conflict level) are most likely to elicit an effect. In this attempt to establish the boundaries of a potential effect, null results are expected to occur in certain conditions but not others and may add to the relative increase of null results.

5.   Reassessing a Publication Bias in Recent Years

Publication biases may (at least partly) explain why initial publications showed large, positive effect sizes of bilingualism on executive control tasks that have later been challenged. In overviews assessing publication trends on this topic (e.g. De Bruin and Della Sala 2015; Sanchez-Azanza et al. 2017), the year 2014 is deemed to be the turning point regarding the publication of null results. In general, these recent years have seen an increase in interest for failed replications and biases (e.g. Francis 2012; Nosek et al. 2015). Within the field of bilingualism in particular, the shift in 2014 may be related to Paap and Greenberg's study that was published in 2013 (cf. Sanchez-Azanza et al. 2017). Paap and Greenberg assessed possible bilingual–monolingual differences across multiple executive control tasks using large sample sizes. No positive effects of bilingualism were observed on any of the tasks. This publication of null results may have paved the path for other researchers to submit and for editors to accept studies with null effects.

The overview of publication bias presented in de Bruin et al. (2015a) was based on conference abstracts until 2012 and publications until February 2014. The increase of null results in studies published from 2014 onwards suggests that publication biases may be diminishing. We therefore examined publication outcomes of conference abstracts presented in more recent years (2013–2015). The same conferences were searched through as in de Bruin et al. (see Table 1 in 2015a). In addition, we included relevant abstracts from the *International Workshop on Bilingualism and Cognitive Control* (Krakow, Poland, 2013) and the *Bilingualism and Executive Function: An interdisciplinary approach* workshop (New York, US, 2015). Abstracts examining effects of bilingualism on executive control components in a wide range of tasks and all age groups were included. Similar to the previous analysis, we included tasks using both verbal and non-verbal materials. In recent years, an increased interest exists to study bilingual–monolingual differences in terms of brain activation or structure. However, considering that these studies do not inform us about a behavioural *advantage* as such (cf. Treccani and Mulatti 2015), abstracts discussing only brain differences without behavioural data and not drawing conclusions about a bilingual advantage were not included in the current overview. For instance, abstracts discussing only grey matter differences between bilinguals and monolinguals were not included. A large number of abstracts had to be excluded because they studied characteristics of bilingualism (e.g. the amount of language switching in a group of highly proficient bilinguals) in relation to executive control. In the absence of a (monolingual) control group, these abstracts could not be classified. We furthermore excluded abstracts reporting effects of short-term language training in adults (e.g. comparing monolinguals who took part in a language learning course with a control group who did not attend such a course), abstracts reporting already published studies, abstracts reporting a meta-analysis, as well as all abstracts that did not report results or did not draw any conclusions about a possible advantage. Studies presented multiple times at different conferences were included only once.

In total, 75 abstracts met the criteria and were included in the analysis. These abstracts were then classified following the criteria described in de Bruin et al. (2015a) as fully supporting a bilingual advantage ('yes'; 19 studies, 25%); predominantly supporting ('mixed-yes'; 9 studies, 12%); predominantly challenging ('mixed-no'; 25 studies, 33%); or fully challenging ('no'; 22 studies, 29%, see Figure 1, Table 1). Thus, whereas 52% of the abstracts presented until 2012 were mainly or fully supporting a bilingual advantage, this was the case for only 37% of the abstracts between 2013 and 2015. Furthermore, there was an increase in the number of bilingual disadvantages reported. In the analysis until 2012, 4% of abstracts reported a bilingual disadvantage. In the current analysis, 13% of the abstracts reported a bilingual disadvantage in some (but not necessarily all) tasks or participant groups. We then checked whether the reported studies had been

Table 1 Overview of the abstracts included in the analysis between 2013 and 2015. The classification 'yes' refers to studies fully supporting a bilingual advantage. 'Mixed-yes' and 'Mixed-no' respectively refer to those mainly supporting and mainly challenging a bilingual advantage. 'No' refers to studies fully challenging a positive effect of bilingualism on executive control.

Study	Classification	Published?
Bovee et al. (2013)	Yes	No
Hutchison et al. (2015)	Yes	No
Kakvan et al. (2015)	Yes	No
Pakulak et al. (2013)	Yes	No
Suarez et al. (2014)	Yes	No
Teubner-Rhodes et al. (2013)	Yes	No
Yoon et al. (2013)	Yes	No
Zhou et al. (2015)	Yes	No
Birke Hansen et al. (2015)	Yes	Yes
Blom et al. (2013)	Yes	Yes
De Leeuw et al. (2013)	Yes	Yes
Grant & Dennis (2015)	Yes	Yes
Grundy et al. (2015)	Yes	Yes
Heidlmayr et al. (2013)	Yes	Yes
Incera & McLennan (2014)	Yes	Yes
Poncelet & Nicolay (2013)	Yes	Yes
Sullivan et al. (2014)	Yes	Yes
Van der Hoeven-Houtzager et al. (2013)	Yes	Yes
Vega-Mendoza et al. (2014)	Yes	Yes
Dosi et al. (2015)	Mixed-yes	No
Morales et al. (2015)	Mixed-yes	No
Soto-Añari et al. (2015)	Mixed-yes	No
Bosma et al. (2015)	Mixed-yes	Yes
Friend et al. (2015)	Mixed-yes	Yes
Laloi et al. (2014)	Mixed-yes	Yes
Morales et al. (2014)	Mixed-yes	Yes
Verhagen et al. (2014)	Mixed-yes	Yes
Woumans et al. (2013)	Mixed-yes	Yes
Babcock et al. (2013)	Mixed-no	No
Balilah & Archibald (2015)	Mixed-no	No
Cannon & Yoshida (2015)	Mixed-no	No
Chrysochoou et al. (2015)	Mixed-no	No
Fernandez & Chrysikou (2013)	Mixed-no	No
Finger et al. (2013)	Mixed-no	No
Gonzalez-Barrero & Nadig (2015)	Mixed-no	No
Guerrero et al. (2015)	Mixed-no	No

(Continued)

Table 1 (Continued)

Study	Classification	Published?
Joret et al. (2015)	Mixed-no	No
Marton et al. (2013)	Mixed-no	No
Melecio-Vaquez et al. (2015)	Mixed-no	No
Mills et al. (2015)	Mixed-no	No
Moore et al. (2014)	Mixed-no	No
Oberhofer et al. (2015)	Mixed-no	No
Ravid et al. (2013)	Mixed-no	No
Stevenson et al. (2015)	Mixed-no	No
Timmer et al. (2015)	Mixed-no	No
Vinerte & Sabourin (2014)	Mixed-no	No
Antoniou et al. (2013)	Mixed-no	Yes
De Cat et al. (2015)	Mixed-no	Yes
Ghazi Saidi et al. (2013)	Mixed-no	Yes
Grundy & Bialystok (2015)	Mixed-no	Yes
Heidlmayr et al. (2014)	Mixed-no	Yes
Keijzer & Schmid (2015)	Mixed-no	Yes
Xie & Dong (2015)	Mixed-no	Yes
De Simoni & Gade (2013)	No	No
Drozdzowicz et al. (2013)	No	No
Eriksen & Foursha-Stevenson (2015)	No	No
Gjorgieva et al. (2015)	No	No
Hayward et al. (2014)	No	No
Kolak et al. (2015)	No	No
Levari & Snedeker (2015)	No	No
Lopez et al. (2015)	No	No
Moore et al. (2015)	No	No
Robbins & Higgins (2015)	No	No
Sawi et al. (2015)	No	No
Senderecka et al. (2013)	No	No
Schonfeld et al. (2014)	No	No
Tran et al. (2015)	No	No
Darrow et al. (2015)	No	Yes
De Bruin et al. (2014)	No	Yes
Kirk et al. (2013)	No	Yes
Loher et al. (2015)	No	Yes
Mielicki et al. (2013)	No	Yes
Paap et al. (2015)	No	Yes
Prior et al. (2013)	No	Yes
Sawi et al. (2013)	No	Yes

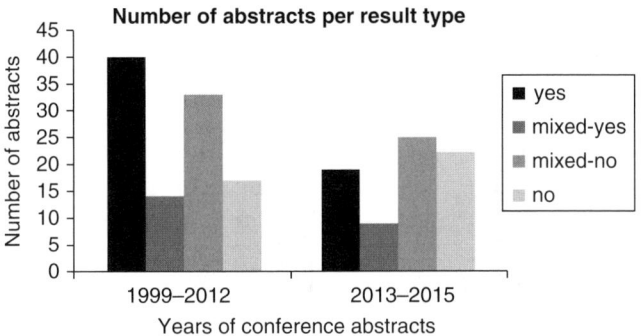

Figure 1   Number of conference abstracts reporting positive effects of bilingualism ('yes'), mixed effects predominantly supporting a bilingual advantage ('mixed-yes'), mixed effects predominantly challenging a bilingual advantage ('mixed-no'), and abstracts showing no or negative effects of bilingualism ('no'). The left side reports abstracts presented until 2012, the right side reports abstracts between 2013 and 2015.

published in a scientific journal before July 2017 (either as an in-press or published article). Fifty-eight percent of fully supporting and 67% of mainly supporting abstracts had been published. Combining these two classifications, 61% of abstracts fully or mainly supporting a bilingual advantage had been published. In comparison, 36% of the fully challenging abstracts had been published and 28% of the mainly challenging abstracts. This leads to a publication rate of 32% for predominantly challenging abstracts. Comparing studies fully or mainly supporting versus fully or mainly challenging a bilingual advantage shows that there still is a difference of 29% in publication rates. This percentage difference is similar to the gap reported for abstracts until 2012. However, focusing on the publication rates of the fully challenging and fully supporting abstracts shows some shifts (see Figure 2). Firstly, a decrease is observed for publication of abstracts fully supporting a bilingual advantage (68% of abstracts until 2012 were published compared with 58% of abstracts from 2013 onwards). In contrast, abstracts fully challenging a bilingual advantage were slightly more likely to be published in recent years (29% until 2012 as compared with 36% after 2013). When comparing the fully supporting versus fully challenging studies only, the publication gap has diminished from 39% until 2012 to 22% in 2015. However, neither the increase in publication rate for null effects nor the decrease for positive effects was significant.

5.1.   *The Number of Tasks Reported*

These data suggest there is still a difference in publication outcome, especially when comparing the more general classification of fully or mainly supporting versus fully or mainly challenging result types. However, numerically, null results were published more often in more recent years. At the same time, there seems to be a decrease in publication rates for studies fully supporting a bilingual advantage. This may be related to a crucial difference in the number of reported tasks. On average, and when these data

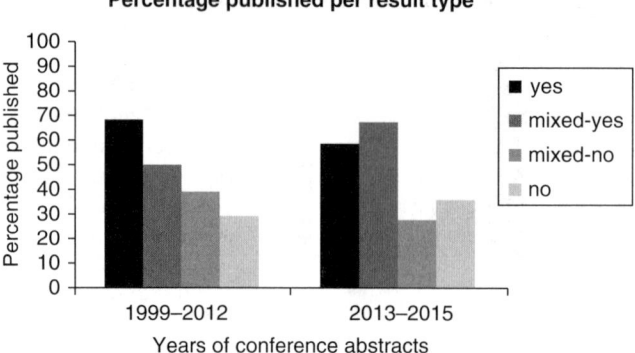

Figure 2   Percentage of published studies for conference abstracts with positive effects of bilingualism ('yes'), mixed effects predominantly supporting a bilingual advantage ('mixed-yes'), mixed effects predominantly challenging a bilingual advantage ('mixed-no'), and abstracts showing no or negative effects of bilingualism ('no'). The left side shows abstracts presented until 2012, the right side shows abstracts between 2013 and 2015.

were reported, studies showing a bilingual advantage typically only reported one task ($M = 1.31$, $SD = 0.70$). In contrast, all other result types reported on average between 2.2 and 2.4 tasks. In terms of the number of participants, no differences were observed between abstracts fully supporting (average of 36 participants per group) and abstracts fully challenging (average of 39 participants per group). Studies with mixed results reported slightly, but not significantly, more participants per group (76 for mixed-yes and 54 for mixed-no).

Failed replications are increasingly receiving more attention. For instance, Nosek et al. (2015) attempted to replicate 100 studies and observed significant results for only 36% of these studies, often with much smaller effect sizes. This study received great attention (shown, for instance, by the more than 1000 citations gathered) and as such may make it more difficult to submit papers reporting only one task without any self-replications in a relatively small sample size. Indeed, regardless of the type of results, in our overview, only 28% of studies reporting one task were published. In contrast, 51% of abstracts with two or more tasks resulted in a publication. While this very rarely concerned replications as such, the inclusion of more than one task (e.g. using inhibition and task-switching paradigms) appears related to an increased likelihood of publication.

The analysis of abstracts until 2012 also observed a difference in terms of the number of tasks reported. Positive studies on average reported fewer tasks than abstracts with other result types, similar to the pattern observed in the more recent analysis. Interestingly though, in the 2012 analysis, abstracts reporting more than one task were *less* likely to be published than those reporting only one task. Thus, it appears that only in recent years, studies with only one task are less likely to be published. This could explain the relative publication decrease for studies with positive effects largely reporting only one task.

Additionally, within the field of bilingualism and executive control in particular, there is increased interest in examining the types of bilingualism and the types of tasks that may or may not elicit a positive effect. For instance, Von Bastian et al. (2016) assessed effects of three dimensions of bilingualism (proficiency, age of acquisition, and use) on nine cognitive abilities, each assessed by three different tasks. As such, studies assessing performance on only one (type of) task may not be sufficiently compatible with the current trends in this research area to be submitted for publication and/or accepted by a journal.

In summary, a comparison of publication outcomes of abstracts presented until or after 2012 shows various interesting findings. First of all, the publication difference between studies fully or mainly supporting versus challenging remains present and suggests that studies with positive findings are still more likely to be published than studies with null or negative findings. At the same time, when only comparing the studies fully supporting or fully challenging a positive bilingual effect (leaving out the mixed results), the publication difference has become smaller. This is a combination of an increase of publication chances of null results as well as a decrease for positive findings. In this respect, the number of tasks reported may explain the relative decrease in the publication of positive results in studies reporting one task only.

5.2. *An Increase in the Number of Null Results*

Apart from a difference in the publication trends, the relative increase in the total number of conference abstracts found is also noteworthy (104 abstracts presented in the 13 years between 1999 and 2012 as compared to 75 within only three years between 2013 and 2015). While we searched through the same conferences in both analyses and used the same classification criteria, the latest analysis also included two workshops specifically organized on the topic of bilingualism and executive control and as such yielded a large number of abstracts. However, the general increase of conference abstracts is in line with the increase of papers on this topic. Sanchez-Azanza et al. (2017) observed an increase in the number of papers published between 2014 and 2016 challenging a bilingual advantage. A similar increase can be observed in terms of conference abstracts (see Figure 1). While studies fully challenging a positive bilingual effect only encompassed 16% of all abstracts until 2012, they form 29% of the total between 2013 and 2015. Together, the fully and mainly challenging abstracts now form over 60% of the abstracts. These data are compatible with a decline effect as they reflect an increase in null effects in combination with a relative decrease of positive studies. In addition, the relatively large number of abstracts with null effects in recent years suggests that the earlier analyses until 2012 may indeed have already been biased at the level of conference submission, which may have diminished over the past few years.

6. A Delay Effect?

Apart from publication biases, there may also be a delay regarding *when* the different result types are published. We therefore examined how much time passed between the presentation of the conference abstract and the publication of papers for the abstracts presented until 2012 (De Bruin et al. 2015a). We also evaluated whether those abstracts that were unpublished in 2014 had been published since. Of the 52 previously unpublished abstracts, 16 had been published between 2014 and 2017. This includes 38% of yes studies, 17% of no studies, and 57% and 25% of mixed-yes and mixed-no studies respectively. Thus, even when more time is given for papers to be published, a publication bias remains present for abstracts presented until 2012. Furthermore, the publication delay was very similar for all result types, ranging from 2.44 (mixed-no studies) to 2.64 (mixed-yes studies) years. This suggests that all result types are published at an equal rate. Thus, the difference in publication rates appears to be related to certain result types not being published at all rather than with a delay.

7.   Why Does a Publication Bias Matter?

Neither publication biases nor decline effects mean that an effect of bilingualism does not exist. In addition, a single null effect does not cancel out the positive effects that have been observed. While there may have been an increase in null results, there are still many recent studies reporting positive effects of bilingualism (e.g. Houtzager et al. 2017; Verreyt et al. 2016; Woumans et al. 2016).

However, biases do affect our understanding of potential effects of bilingualism. Firstly, meta-analyses are inevitably biased when based on a biased literature. While they attempt to provide a reflection of the cognitive effects of bilingualism, their outcomes are unreliable when not corrected for publication bias. For example, Lehtonen et al. (2018) observed a small positive effect of bilingualism in some cognitive domains when not correcting for publication bias. However, after taking these biases into account, these positive effects did not survive.

Secondly, having access to all result types is not only important when forming a coherent and unbiased interpretation of the existing data, but is also crucial for the formulation and testing of theoretical frameworks. The literature on bilingualism and executive control has been criticized for lacking a theoretical framework (e.g. Jared 2015). Considering the multifaceted nature of both bilingualism as well as executive control, we are unlikely to reach a yes/no answer to a question such as 'does bilingualism enhance executive control?' (e.g. Luk and Bialystok 2013). As such, any theoretical framework on this topic should take into account the multiple components of bilingualism (e.g. proficiency, language use) and the different types of executive control components that exist (e.g. switching, conflict monitoring), as well as the likelihood that multiple different relations exist between these different components. Indeed, there is an increasing interest in studying the types of bilingual groups and types of tasks that may or may not elicit an effect. An attempt to establish such a framework, and specifically taking into account the role that language switching and use could play, was formulated in the adaptive control hypothesis (Green and Abutalebi 2013). Within this framework, multiple possible relations between types of bilinguals and types of executive control are established. For instance, only bilinguals who have to follow stricter patterns of language switching in a dual-language context experience high language control in daily life and may show advantages on interference suppression and conflict monitoring. In contrast, those bilinguals who can freely switch without any constraints recruit lower levels of language control in daily life and may not show such advantages.

Relatedly, some studies (e.g. Costa et al. 2009) have suggested that effects of bilingualism may occur only in tasks with a high amount of conflict. Thus, whether or not a bilingual advantage occurs may largely depend on the type of bilinguals tested and the type of executive control tasks used. While frameworks such as the adaptive control hypothesis may be used to explain why positive effects are found for some type of bilinguals but not others, they cannot be evaluated properly unless we have access to all outcomes, both positive and negative. If we want to explore the factors modulating a possible effect of bilingualism on executive control, it is crucial that we have access to all data. After all, establishing the boundaries of an effect entails that the effect will not be observed in all tasks, conditions, or participant groups. In this sense, not only null effects but mixed results comparing different tasks and participants may be particularly informative.

Lastly, it should be emphasized that biases exist in many (if not all) research fields. However, due to the societal interest in the topic of a possible bilingual advantage, biases may also lead to an exaggerated claim in the society. Various media outlets have published claims such as 'Why it's smart to be bilingual' (Schwartz 2011, Newsweek) or 'Bilingual brains are more healthy' (Fox 2011, The Guardian). While it is undoubtedly good to emphasize the positive aspects of bilingualism (e.g. in terms of increased communication possibilities), public claims will be exaggerated when based on a biased literature. In this sense, it is not only publishing null or negative results that matters but also the way publications are presented to the media. As exaggerations in press releases have been found to be closely related to exaggerations in the media (e.g. Sumner et al. 2014), it is important that researchers do not just submit for publication all data regardless of the outcome but also present these data in an appropriate manner to the general audience.

8.   Possible Solutions

Many researchers are moving away from the term 'bilingual advantage' and are instead talking about differences between different types of bilinguals and monolinguals. This focus on multifaceted differences rather than considering bilingual advantages as a static concept is a positive change and will hopefully allow for a more open debate.

In general, initiatives are arising at various levels to increase openness and diminish selective reporting (cf. Nosek et al. 2016, for a description of transparency and openness promotion [TOP] guidelines). Several journals are now requesting research disclosure statements upon submission, confirming, amongst others, that all variables (both showing positive or null effects) have been reported. Other journals offer registered reports as a way to preregister the task and analysis details (cf. Chambers 2013). In this type of report, papers are evaluated based on their introduction and methods prior to data collection. This firstly gives the researchers an opportunity to improve the design based on the reviewers' comments. Furthermore, acceptance of the registered report's introduction and method section guarantees acceptance of the final version, regardless of the actual results. This may increase the researcher's motivation to actually publish null effects as a large part of the writing has already been completed. Lastly, preregistration does not only encourage researchers to submit null effects but can also be used as a way to examine whether all results have been included. As all tasks need to be preregistered, it can easily be checked whether any unsuccessful tasks have been omitted from the final manuscript.

Preregistration may be particularly important for replication studies. In line with this, more exact replications may be needed in order to further examine the effects of bilingualism found in previous studies. Conceptual replications are needed to assess whether different types of bilinguals and different tasks can elicit different patterns of results. However, exact replications are needed too to evaluate the replicability of the initial findings (cf. Pashler and Harris 2012). While these exact replications may be difficult to publish, especially when they don't replicate the original findings, this would be avoided through registered reports.

With several platforms available for data sharing and journals encouraging preregistration of planned studies, the possibilities for more transparent research and data sharing are expanding. However, the main necessity concerns a change in attitude. Authors are free to preregister their studies and can easily decide not to do so. Additionally, it is not just the inclusion of data but also the data-interpretation that may be biased. When examining the actual results of individual tasks, Paap and colleagues found that over 80% did not show a positive effect of bilingualism. When basing the classification on the results and conclusions as a whole, the data from recent conference abstracts suggest that challenging studies take up approximately 60% of the total. Thus, there appears to be something of a discrepancy between the two types of analyses. This can be for various reasons. For instance, a wider range of tasks has been included in the analyses of conference abstracts than in Paap et al. (2015). Furthermore, analyses based on overall results may differ from those based on individual comparisons as studies including multiple tasks and measurements with multiple null results are compressed to one data point (e.g. in the case of Paap and Greenberg 2013). Moreover, the results of individual tasks do not always correspond to the actual conclusions. Paap and colleagues provide the example of Calvo and Bialystok (2014), who conclude that bilinguals outperformed monolinguals on the executive control tasks included in their study. However, when examining the actual data, little evidence can be found for this claim and no bilingual–monolingual differences are observed in terms of response times, the measurement typically included in meta-analyses. Opposite effects (e.g. increased or decreased white matter) have also been taken to support the same conclusion regarding positive effects of bilingualism (cf. Treccani and Mulatti 2015). Thus, the conclusions drawn may show an over-interpretation of the actual data observed.

9. Conclusions

The current chapter examined the existence of a publication bias in the literature on bilingualism and executive control, suggesting that positive studies are more likely to be published than studies with null or negative effects. This bias could be one of the explanations for the decline effect that is also observed in this literature. While initial studies predominantly reported positive results with large effect sizes, there has been an increase of null results in recent years. At the same time, while positive results are still published frequently, the effect sizes are becoming smaller. Consistently, an analysis of publication outcomes of abstracts presented at recent conferences showed a small increase of the percentage of null effects being published in combination with a decrease of positive results being published. However, the latter finding may be more related to the reportage of single tasks. Furthermore, the publication gap between studies supporting versus challenging remains present. In addition, an analysis of possible delay biases (i.e. the time between conference reports and publications) suggests that studies with null effects do not get published later than positive effects. Rather, it implies that many do not get published at all.

This evaluation shows that biases may be decreasing and that more null effects have been published in recent years. However, a publication gap remains present and the bias existing in earlier years does not appear to diminish through delayed publication. This publication bias is problematic at multiple levels. Firstly, in order to examine the existence and nature of an effect, it is crucial to have access to all data. The interpretation of meta-analyses is hindered when based on a biased literature. In the case of possible bilingual cognitive effects, null results too are needed to establish the boundaries of such an effect. Subjective data presentation is not only problematic for the examination of existing data, but also for the development and evaluation of theoretical frameworks. It is therefore crucial for researchers to present all data regardless of the outcome and for reviewers and editors to evaluate manuscripts regardless of the results reported.

REFERENCES

Bakker, M., van Dijk, A., and Wicherts, J.M. (2012). The rules of the game called psychological science. *Perspectives on Psychological Science* 7 (6): 543–554.

Bialystok, E. (2009). Bilingualism: the good, the bad, and the indifferent. *Bilingualism: Language and Cognition* 12 (01): 3–11.

Bialystok, E., Craik, F.I., Klein, R., and Viswanathan, M. (2004). Bilingualism, aging, and cognitive control: evidence from the Simon task. *Psychology and Aging* 19 (2): 290–303.

Bialystok, E. and Martin, M.M. (2004). Attention and inhibition in bilingual children: evidence from the dimensional change card sort task. *Developmental Science* 7 (3): 325–339.

Calvo, A. and Bialystok, E. (2014). Independent effects of bilingualism and socioeconomic status on language ability and executive functioning. *Cognition* 130 (3): 278–288.

Chambers, C.D. (2013). Registered reports: a new publishing initiative at cortex. *Cortex* 49 (3): 609–610.

Costa, A., Hernández, M., Costa-Faidella, J., and Sebastián-Gallés, N. (2009). On the bilingual advantage in conflict processing: now you see it, now you don't. *Cognition* 113 (2): 135–149.

Costa, A., Hernández, M., and Sebastián-Gallés, N. (2008). Bilingualism aids conflict resolution: evidence from the ANT task. *Cognition* 106 (1): 59–86.

De Bot, K. (2017). The bilingual advantage and the life cycle of theories. Internal publication, University of Pannonia.

De Bruin, A. and Della Sala, S. (2015). The decline effect: how initially strong results tend to decrease over time. *Cortex* 73: 357–377.

De Bruin, A., Treccani, B., and Della Sala, S. (2015a). Cognitive advantage in bilingualism: an example of publication bias? *Psychological Science* 26 (1): 99–107.

De Bruin, A., Treccani, B., and Della Sala, S. (2015b). The connection is in the data: we should consider them all. *Psychological Science* 26 (6): 947–949.

Dickersin, K., Min, Y.I., and Meinert, C.L. (1992). Factors influencing publication of research results: follow-up of applications submitted to two institutional review boards. *JAMA* 267 (3): 374–378.

Donnelly, S. (2016). Reexamining the bilingual advantage on interference-control and task-switching tasks: A meta-analysis. (Doctoral dissertation submitted to the Graduate Center, CUNY, CUNY Academic Works).

Duñabeitia, J.A., Hernández, J.A., Antón, E. et al. (2014). The inhibitory advantage in bilingual children revisited. *Experimental Psychology* 61 (3): 234–251.

Easterbrook, P.J., Gopalan, R., Berlin, J.A., and Matthews, D.R. (1991). Publication bias in clinical research. *The Lancet* 337 (8746): 867–872.

Emerson, G.B., Warme, W.J., Wolf, F.M. et al. (2010). Testing for the presence of positive-outcome bias in peer review: a randomized controlled trial. *Archives of Internal Medicine* 170 (21): 1934–1939.

Fox, K. (2011, 12 June). Bilingual brains are more healthy. The Guardian. Retrieved from https://www.theguardian.com/technology/2011/jun/12/ellen-bialystok-bilingual-brains-more-healthy

Ferguson, C.J. and Heene, M. (2012). A vast graveyard of undead theories: publication bias and psychological science's aversion to the null. *Perspectives on Psychological Science* 7 (6): 555–561.

Francis, G. (2012). Too good to be true: publication bias in two prominent studies from experimental psychology. *Psychonomic Bulletin & Review* 19 (2): 151–156.

Francis, G. (2014). The frequency of excess success for articles in psychological science. *Psychonomic Bulletin & Review* 21 (5): 1180–1187.

Green, D.W. and Abutalebi, J. (2013). Language control in bilinguals: the adaptive control hypothesis. *Journal of Cognitive Psychology* 25 (5): 515–530.

Hilchey, M.D. and Klein, R.M. (2011). Are there bilingual advantages on nonlinguistic interference tasks? Implications for the plasticity of executive control processes. *Psychonomic Bulletin & Review* 18 (4): 625–658.

Hilchey, M.D., Saint-Aubin, J., and Klein, R.M. (2015). Does bilingual exercise enhance cognitive fitness in traditional non-linguistic executive processing tasks? In: *The Cambridge Handbook of Bilingual Processing* (ed. J.W. Schwieter). Cambridge, UK: Cambridge University Press.

Houtzager, N., Lowie, W., Sprenger, S., and De Bot, K. (2017). A bilingual advantage in task switching? Age-related differences between German monolinguals and Dutch-Frisian bilinguals. *Bilingualism: Language and Cognition* 20 (1): 69–79.

Ioannidis, J.P. (2006). Evolution and translation of research findings: from bench to where? *PLoS Clinical Trials* 1 (7): e36.

Ioannidis, J.P., Munafo, M.R., Fusar-Poli, P. et al. (2014). Publication and other reporting biases in cognitive sciences: detection, prevalence, and prevention. *Trends in Cognitive Sciences* 18 (5): 235–241.

Ioannidis, J.P. and Trikalinos, T.A. (2007). An exploratory test for an excess of significant findings. *Clinical Trials* 4 (3): 245–253.

Luk, G. and Bialystok, E. (2013). Bilingualism is not a categorical variable: interaction between language proficiency and usage. *Journal of Cognitive Psychology* 25 (5): 605–621.

Jared, D. (2015). What is the theory? *Cortex* 73: 361–363.

John, L.K., Loewenstein, G., and Prelec, D. (2012). Measuring the prevalence of questionable research practices with incentives for truth telling. *Psychological Science* 23 (5): 524–532.

Klein, R.M. (2015). Is there a benefit of bilingualism for executive functioning? *Bilingualism: Language and Cognition* 18 (01): 29–31.

Lehrer, J. (2010, December 13). The truth wears off. *The New Yorker*. Retrieved from http://www.newyorker.com/reporting/2010/12/13/101213fa_fact_lehrer?currentPage=all.

Lehtonen, M., Soveri, A., Laine, A. et al. (2018). Is bilingualism associated with enhanced executive functioning in adults? A meta-analytic review. *Psychological Bulletin* 144 (4): 394–425.

Luk, G., De Sa, E.R.I.C., and Bialystok, E. (2011). Is there a relation between onset age of bilingualism and enhancement of cognitive control? *Bilingualism: Language and Cognition* 14 (4): 588–595.

Mahoney, M.J. (1977). Publication prejudices: an experimental study of confirmatory bias in the peer review system. *Cognitive Therapy and Research* 1 (2): 161–175.

Nosek, B.A., Alter, G., Banks, G.C. et al. (2015). Promoting an open research culture. *Science* 348 (6242): 1422–1425.

Nosek, B. A., Alter, G., Banks, G., Borsboom, D., Bowman, S., Breckler, S., … Christensen, G. (2016). Transparency and Openness Promotion (TOP) Guidelines.

Paap, K.R. and Greenberg, Z.I. (2013). There is no coherent evidence for a bilingual advantage in executive processing. *Cognitive Psychology* 66 (2): 232–258.

Paap, K.R., Johnson, H.A., and Sawi, O. (2015). Bilingual advantages in executive functioning either do not exist or are restricted to very specific and undetermined circumstances. *Cortex* 69: 265–278.

Pashler, H. and Harris, C.R. (2012). Is the replicability crisis overblown? Three arguments examined. *Perspectives on Psychological Science* 7 (6): 531–536.

Prior, A. and Gollan, T.H. (2011). Good language-switchers are good task-switchers: evidence from Spanish–English and mandarin–English

bilinguals. *Journal of the International Neuropsychological Society* 17 (4): 682–691.

Prior, A. and MacWhinney, B. (2010). A bilingual advantage in task switching. *Bilingualism: Language and Cognition* 13 (02): 253–262.

Sanchez-Azanza, V.A., López-Penadés, R., Buil-Legaz, L. et al. (2017). Is bilingualism losing its advantage? A bibliometric approach. *PLoS One* 12 (4): e0176151.

Sawilowsky, S.S. (2009). New effect size rules of thumb. *Journal of Modern Applied Statistical Methods* 8 (2): 597–599.

Scherer, R.W., Langenberg, P., and Von Elm, E. (2007). Full publication of results initially presented in abstracts. *Cochrane Database of Systematic Reviews* 2 (2): MR000005.

Schooler, J. (2011). Unpublished results hide the decline effect. *Nature* 470: 437.

Schwartz, C. (2011, 8 July). Why it's smart to be bilingual. Newsweek. Retrieved from https://www.newsweek.com/why-its-smart-be-bilingual-67163

Sumner, P., Vivian-Griffiths, S., Boivin, J. et al. (2014). The association between exaggeration in health-related science news and academic press releases: retrospective observational study. *British Medical Journal* 349: g7015.

Treccani, B. and Mulatti, C. (2015). No matter who, no matter how… and no matter whether the white matter matters. Why theories of bilingual advantage in executive functioning are so difficult to falsify. *Cortex* 73: 349–351.

Verreyt, N., Woumans, E., Vandelanotte, D. et al. (2016). The influence of language-switching experience on the bilingual executive control advantage. *Bilingualism: Language and Cognition* 19 (1): 181–190.

Von Bastian, C.C., Souza, A.S., and Gade, M. (2016). No evidence for bilingual cognitive advantages: a test of four hypotheses. *Journal of Experimental Psychology: General* 145 (2): 246–258.

Woumans, E., Surmont, J., Struys, E., and Duyck, W. (2016). The longitudinal effect of bilingual immersion schooling on cognitive control and intelligence. *Language Learning* 66 (S2): 76–91.

36 Speech-Sign Bilingualism
A Unique Window into the Multilingual Brain

ROBIN L. THOMPSON AND EVA
GUTIERREZ-SIGUT

1. Introduction

Bilingualism provides a unique window into language processing and its underlying neurocognitive mechanisms. To date, the majority of bilingual research has been based on spoken-language bilinguals who know two or more spoken languages. This chapter focuses instead on bilinguals who know both a signed and spoken language (speech-sign bilinguals). Research on speech-sign bilinguals is a young, but quickly expanding area. This is due to its potential as a valuable and unique window into the nature of bilingualism and the bilingual brain. By exploring differences between spoken-language bilinguals and speech-sign bilinguals, we can gain insight into how the brain represents and processes two languages in different sensorimotor modalities. Additionally, we can better understand the relationship between language and more general cognitive processes. This chapter contributes to the ongoing discussion by compiling and interpreting the findings that relate to speech-sign bilingualism in the brain. Specifically, it provides an overview of the relevant research to date placed in a wider language context by extending the study of bilingualism to languages in two different sensorimotor modalities, but at the same time focusing on results that provide critical insight into multilingualism more broadly.

1.1. Thinking About Signed Languages

Sign languages are natural languages that develop when Deaf[1] individuals come together in a group. Wherever communities of deaf individuals exist, sign languages naturally arise, fulfilling the same linguistic, social, and cognitive functions as spoken languages. A common misconception held by people unfamiliar with signed languages is that they are a signed version of the surrounding spoken language. However, natural

The Handbook of the Neuroscience of Multilingualism, First Edition. Edited by John W. Schwieter.
© 2019 John Wiley & Sons Ltd. Published 2019 by John Wiley & Sons Ltd.

sign languages evolve with their own unique grammars and lexicons, independent of the majority-spoken language in the area in which they arise (for review see Petitto 1994; Emmorey 2002; Sandler and Lillo-Martin 2006).

Another common misconception about sign languages is that there is a single universal language used around the world. This belief may stem from a further misconception that sign languages are invented and transmitted to deaf individuals through formal instruction. The logical conclusion of this (incorrect) belief is that, of course, only one system would need to be invented. However, sign languages develop naturally in much the same way as spoken languages: when deaf individuals form a community of language users. Since Deaf communities tend to be smaller and traditionally more isolated from other Deaf communities, there can sometimes be more sign languages than spoken languages in a given geographical location. For example, in Northern Ireland, Irish Sign Language (ISL) is used by Catholic Deaf people and British Sign Language (BSL) is used by Protestant Deaf people. This language division arises because historically Catholic and Protestant children were educated separately (Sutton-Spence and Woll 1999). As this example highlights, while sign languages are passed down from one generation to the next, similarly to spoken language transmission, language development and transmission for sign languages has centred around schools for the Deaf where Deaf communities tend to form.

Importantly, when babies are exposed to a sign language from birth, it will be acquired naturally as a native language along the same general timeline as a spoken language. Sign language acquisition has been shown to parallel spoken language acquisition in onset, rate, and patterns of development (for reviews see Chamberlain et al. 2000; Morgan and Woll 2002).

There are no known examples of fully developed natural sign languages[2] arising in a community with only hearing people. Sign languages come about as a communication solution when members of the community are deaf. However, it is estimated that only 8% of the deaf population are born to Deaf signing parents (study of the deaf population in America only; Mitchell and Karchmer 2004), with the remaining 92% born to hearing parents who may prefer to use their own spoken language, exposing their deaf child to sign language only as a second choice. Interestingly, while a sign language does not arise in the absence of a Deaf community to use it, there may in fact be more native signers who are hearing (i.e. signers exposed to the language from birth as their first language). This is because Deaf parents, who are the most likely to sign with their babies from birth, are more likely to have hearing babies than deaf babies. Therefore, unusually, while the core of the sign language community consists of Deaf signers, language transmission from parent to child may most frequently be from Deaf parent(s) to a hearing child.

1.2. *Signers are Bilingual*

The vast majority of signers are bilingual, learning both a sign language and the spoken language of the surrounding community. In the UK, for example, Deaf children born to Deaf parents will acquire BSL as their native language, but they will also acquire English as a second language through the education system. Deaf children born into hearing families who are exposed to BSL will also be exposed to English through the education system. Hearing children exposed to BSL from their Deaf parents will acquire spoken English as a native language from the surrounding hearing community. Monolingual native signers are quite rare and occur only in communities that do not send deaf children to school to learn the surrounding spoken language. Such rare communities have been identified in Bali (Zeshan 2003). In Israel, there is a high incidence of deafness which means that Al-Sayyid Bedouin Sign Language is accessible to deaf children through the prevalence of signing in the wider community, even when they are born to hearing parents (Sandler et al. 2005).

1.3.   *Speech-sign Bilinguals*

'Speech-sign bilingual' is the broad term adopted here to refer to anyone who knows both a signed and spoken language. However, speech-sign bilinguals are not a homogenous group. As with all bilingual groups, it is not possible to neatly divide speech-sign bilinguals into cohesive uniform groups. However, the three most common groupings applied in the literature reflect the broadest natural divisions where differences can be found. These are: hearing status (whether a signer is deaf or hearing), age of acquisition (i.e. age of exposure to the sign language), and proficiency (how fluent bilinguals are in their languages).

Hearing status: While few differences have been found in terms of sign language processing for Deaf or hearing bilinguals, there are (sometimes profound) differences in processing in terms of the spoken language because Deaf individuals do not have the same easy and full access to a spoken language as they do to a signed language. Deafness also appears to drive language dominance for signers. Deaf people who know a signed and spoken language will likely be dominant (and by extension more proficient) in their signed language. This makes sense since it is the only language they can fully access. Alternatively, while some hearing signers may learn a sign language as their first and native language, for the most part, language dominance switches to their spoken language after they are exposed to it (Emmorey et al. 2016). Native hearing signers usually report a switch in dominance when they enter school (Pizer et al. 2013), presumably because this is a time when they begin to interact more often with people that use their spoken language than with those that use their signed language.

Age of acquisition: The age at which someone is exposed to a sign language has been shown to impact both speed and accuracy in processing as well as patterns of brain activation while performing language tasks over and above proficiency. While more recent statistical analyses can factor in the specific age of sign onset, traditionally age of sign onset is divided into native signers, early signers, and late signers. Native signers can be either deaf or hearing and are those signers who learn a sign language from their Deaf parent(s) or an older Deaf sibling. Early signers are those who learn to sign before a certain age. The cut-off age varies across studies from five to seven or even nine years of age, depending on the individual study, with the researchers basing their criteria on starting-school age or on the predicted end of the critical period for language, or clear patterns from the data itself. Early signers are deaf children who have hearing parents that either do not discover their child's deafness until sometime after birth, or who attempt to teach their child a spoken language and then later add a signed language (e.g. when deaf children start attending a deaf nursery or school where they can be exposed to a signed language for the first time). It is rare for a hearing person to begin signing at this age if they are not native. Late signers can be Deaf or hearing. Often deaf individuals will discover sign language when they enter school, or even as teens or adults after primarily using a spoken language up to that point. Non-native speech-sign bilinguals usually learn a signed language as adults through classes in high school or university or by coming into contact with Deaf signers.

Proficiency: This simply refers to the relative fluency of a given individual. For the most part, in bimodal bilingual studies the proficiency in the signed language is measured, while proficiency in the spoken language is less often assessed.

Two terms, tapping directly onto hearing status, have been widely used in the literature to refer to speech-sign bilinguals: bimodal bilinguals and sign-print bilinguals.

Bimodal bilinguals: 'Bimodal bilingual' is the term used to describe hearing bilinguals who know both a signed and spoken language. For spoken-language bilinguals it is physically impossible to produce, and extremely difficult to comprehend two spoken languages at the same time. However, for bimodal bilinguals who command both a signed and spoken language, distinct sensory-motor modalities allow for production and comprehension of two languages simultaneously (Emmorey et al. 2005; Emmorey et al. 2008a). This bimodality suggests the existence of unique action and perception systems for two languages that work together. Bimodal bilinguals, therefore, not only allow us to understand how modality affects bilingual language processing but also provide a unique window into understanding the consequences of dual-processing both when using language (e.g. during code blending), and more generally.

For both deaf signers and bimodal bilinguals signing and speaking simultaneously is common, but perhaps more so for hearing bimodal bilinguals both in comprehension (input to bimodal bilingual children is frequently from parents who sign and speak simultaneously; Petitto et al. 2001) and production (many social situations require simultaneous sign and speech, e.g. when interacting with a mixed group of deaf signers and hearing non-signers).

Sign-print bilinguals: Deaf signers are, for the most part, also fluent in the majority-spoken language. However, many Deaf bilinguals access spoken language through the visual modality only (i.e. through print or through the visual mouth patterns of speakers) and are therefore not *bimodal* bilinguals. Deaf speech-sign bilinguals are therefore sometimes referred to as sign-print bilinguals (Neuroth-Gimbrone and Logiodic 1992; Dufour 1997) or deaf unimodal sign-speech bilinguals (Woll and MacSweeney 2016) to highlight that they acquire a written second language (L2) in the same modality as sign. Here we adopt the term sign-print bilingual since it highlights the primary role of orthography in providing access to spoken language for deaf people. Importantly, however, Deaf signers can also be bimodal bilingual to some extent, fully accessing a sign language, and producing and comprehending some auditory form of spoken language. This is particularly true of Deaf signers who wear hearing aids or have a cochlear implant.

This section's overview of speech-sign bilinguals will provide the reader with a better picture of the heterogeneous mix of people who call themselves signers. Importantly, while differences based on individual experiences with first language (L1) and L2 learning have been an important area of interest for spoken-language bilingual research (see, e.g. Bialystok 1988, 2017), speech-sign bilingualism has, for the most part, not yet addressed the potential impact of hearing status, age of acquisition, and proficiency on brain function for processing a signed or spoken language. We will now discuss what studies there are in this area.

2.   Bilingual Language Activation

One important question in bilingual research is how a bilingual's two languages are represented and processed in the brain. There is mounting evidence that spoken-language bilinguals do not process language in a substantively different way from monolinguals. One meta-analysis of word production tasks (e.g. neuroimaging studies during picture-naming, word repetition, word completion) demonstrated overlapping activation in the expected left frontal and temporo-parietal brain areas, similar to those engaged when monolinguals perform the same tasks (Indefrey 2006). Furthermore, the results suggest that bilinugals' two languages share the same neural network. In general, this finding is replicated across linguistic domains in neuroimaging studies which have shown overlapping areas of activation in the same brain regions for both of a bilingual's languages (e.g. Klein et al. 1995; Illes et al. 1999; see Perani and Abutalebi 2005, for review).

Early research on sign languages in the brain concentrated on lateralization. Given that the majority of the population is left lateralized for language, but that the right hemisphere specializes in visual-spatial information, the central issue of this early research was how the brain would treat a language expressed in the visual-spatial modality. Studies investigating sign language processing have revealed large overlap between the brain areas recruited for signed and spoken language processing. Lesion data has shown that damage to the left hemisphere causes sign language aphasias in deaf signers, but damage to the right hemisphere does not (Poizner et al. 1987; Corina 1998). More recently, neuroimaging studies with brain-intact signers have found evidence for strong left lateralization of both sign comprehension and production (e.g. for comprehension: Neville et al. 1998; Petitto et al. 2000; MacSweeney et al. 2002, 2008a, b; Leonard et al. 2012; for production: Braun et al. 2001; Corina et al. 2003; Emmorey et al. 2007; Gutierrez-Sigut et al. 2015; Gutierrez-Sigut et al. 2016). This research has identified a similar, although not identical, neural network supporting both speech and sign processing.

2.1.   *Speech-Sign Bilingual Activation*

For speech-sign bilinguals, perhaps the clearest way to determine the similarity of brain systems that are engaged for both languages is by direct comparisons within a single bimodal bilingual participant. Using a within-participant design, early speech-sign lesion studies and neuroimaging research have demonstrated a common neural circuitry for sign and speech, similar to that of spoken-language bilinguals. During comprehension tasks, sign-print and bimodal bilinguals activated the superior temporal cortex bilaterally, both in speech-based and sign-based tasks. Indeed, despite the fact that sign languages are perceived visually, there is some evidence that sign language (along with other visual stimuli) activates the auditory cortex for Deaf people (e.g. Finney et al. 2001; Cardin et al. 2013). During production, both signing and speaking tasks have been found to activate a similar left-lateralized frontotemporal network in bimodal bilinguals (for reviews see Emmorey 2002; MacSweeney et al. 2008a; Corina et al. 2013).

When asking what aspects of language processing are supramodal, and which are modality dependent, most research to date suggests that, while linguistic aspects of processing appear largely similar, there are differences between sign and speech processing that appear to reflect modality-specific processing. Importantly, as the instruments and methodologies become more sensitive, more detailed information emerges.

2.2. *Activation During Comprehension*

In comprehension, research on bimodal bilinguals has investigated the extent to which modality plays a role in language processing. In two similar positron emission tomography (PET) studies (Söderfeldt et al. 1994, 1997), activation for Swedish Sign Language (SSL) and audiovisual spoken Swedish were contrasted in native bimodal bilinguals. In the first study, Söderfeldt et al. (1994) found no significant differences in brain activation for speech and sign. However, the later study (Söderfeldt et al. 1997), using a more sensitive imaging analysis and a more comprehensive experimental design, found differences in language perception areas as a function of language modality. While the overlap remained between SSL and Swedish in classic perisylvian language regions, perception of spoken language alone (sound track paired with a motionless face) selectively activated the auditory cortex in the superior temporal lobe bilaterally. Conversely, perception of sign language selectively activated visual integration areas.

In one early neuroimaging study of language comprehension, both Deaf and hearing native American Sign Language (ASL) signer showed activation in left hemisphere language regions for their native languages, with additional activation in homologous areas within the right hemisphere during ASL sentence comprehension (Neville et al. 1998). However, the comparison was to reading English sentences (shown one word at a time). Thus, the difference may be attributable to the different cognitive requirements of each type of task (reading for English vs. watching video stimuli of signers in motion) rather than to linguistic processing of signs. When brain activation elicited by sign language comprehension was instead compared with activation for a better-matched task such as comprehension of audiovisual speech (i.e. looking at a person who is talking), there was no evidence of greater right hemisphere recruitment for BSL (MacSweeney et al. 2002). As in previous studies, MacSweeney et al. (2002) reported similar left-dominant activation for both sign (BSL) and speech (English) processing. Furthermore, they observed bilateral activation within inferior prefrontal and superior temporal regions, which was similar for both languages and is likely to be due to domain-general visual-spatial processing (MacSweeney et al. 2002; see also Capek et al. 2004). Thus, when natural language inputs (sign and audio-visual speech) are compared directly, there is no indication of greater involvement of the right hemisphere for sign language. Similarly, in a magnetoencephalography (MEG) study Levänen et al. (2001) found that right hemisphere areas (inferior frontal gyrus and superior temporal sulcus) were activated when both deaf signers and hearing non-signers passively watched sign language, supporting the view that these right hemisphere areas subserve general action observation processes. The stronger activation found in this study for signers compared with non-signers in the right superior temporal sulcus was attributed to processing of emotional facial expressions and prosody by deaf signers.

Activation of right hemisphere regions during sign processing has also been linked to shallower and effortful processing in non-proficient signers. A recent study used MEG to investigate the spatial–temporal dynamics of lexical access in hearing beginning learners of ASL. Brain activation was measured during a semantic matching task (i.e. does a picture followed by a signed, spoken, or written word match?) for two different time windows: the first associated with word encoding and the second with lexico-semantic processing. Importantly, results showed that the three types of stimuli were processed in a similar left-dominant network that involved classical perisylvian language areas in both time windows. The extra activation found for signs in contrast to English in a network of right hemisphere regions was similar to that previously observed for spoken-language bilinguals. Activation of this right neural network is thought to reflect shallow and effortful processing of semantic content (Leonard et al. 2013). Further support for this view comes from a longitudinal study with deaf adults who had learned ASL after adolescence. A leftward shift in brain activity elicited by well-known and familiar signs was found after sustained ASL experience (see Ferjan Ramirez et al. 2014).

This is not the end of the story as some researchers suggest that right-hemisphere engagement found during sign language comprehension may also be important for sign-specific linguistic use of visual-spatial processing (e.g. Corina et al. 2013). Using event-related potentials (ERP), Capek et al. (2009) showed deaf native signers ASL sentences including verbs that encode information about the grammatical object. The grammatical object is marked spatially by moving a verb to a spatial location in which the object referent has been associated. In critical trials, 'incorrect' movement of the verb in space was to a new location not associated with the object. This new and unexpected visual-spatial information elicited a more bilaterally distributed anterior negativity than other types of syntactic violations in signers, perhaps reflecting visual-spatial processing unique to sign language comprehension.

2.3.   *Activation During Production*

In production, neuroimaging studies have consistently reported strong activation in the left inferior frontal regions for signed languages as well as left-hemisphere dominance in 'classical language areas' (e.g. Broca's and Wernicke's areas) and surrounding regions (McGuire et al. 1997; Petitto et al. 2000; Emmorey et al. 2003; Kassubek et al. 2004; San Jose-Robertson et al. 2004). In a recent study, Gutierrez-Sigut et al. (2015) measured the strength of lateralization during language production in bimodal bilinguals. Participants performed overt phonological and semantic fluency tasks in BSL and English, while undergoing functional transcranial Doppler sonography (fTCD). FTCD measures event-related changes in blood flow to both middle cerebral arteries simultaneously, thus allowing the calculation of a laterality index. While stronger left hemisphere lateralization was found during BSL sign production compared with English for bimodal bilinguals, a non-sign repetition task with hearing controls did not show the same pattern of stronger left hemisphere activation. Similarly, strong left lateralization for sign production was also found for deaf native signers for overt language generation tasks and also for covert tasks, which did not involve movement of the articulators (Gutierrez-Sigut et al. 2016). These findings were consistent with those from Corina et al. (2003), who asked participants to produce ASL signs with either their right or left hand and found left hemisphere activation regardless of the hand that was used to sign.

Taken together, these results show that this strong left lateralization for sign production is not driven by right-handed signing (i.e. because the left-hemisphere controls the right hand and most signers are right-handed). Rather than being due to the greater motoric demands of coordinating multiple time-locked articulators, strong left lateralization seems to be driven by specific linguistic requirements during sign encoding (e.g. differences between sign and speech in the nature of phonological encoding or the increased use of self-monitoring mechanisms for sign processing). In fact, both fMRI and PET speech-sign studies have identified the left parietal lobe (implicated in multimodal integration) as playing a greater role in sign than speech production (e.g. Braun et al. 2001; Emmorey et al. 2014a). In bimodal bilinguals, parietal, and left posterior middle temporal cortex activation was larger during signing than during speaking (Zou et al. 2012a).

In terms of modality differences in core language processing areas, Horwitz et al. (2003) investigated the potential for modality-specific processing in Broca's area. Probabilistic brain maps of bimodal bilinguals were used to determine the two cyto-architectonically defined regions that make up Broca's area: BA44 and BA45. Then, PET was used during the production of language narratives. The results show that BA45, but not BA44, is activated by both speech and signing (when contrasted to a baseline that subtracts the activations from generation of movements and sounds during language production). This suggests that BA45 is fundamental to the modality-independent aspect of language generation. Conversely, the extensive activation in BA44, but not in BA45, for the motor tasks compared with rest indicates that BA44 is engaged in the production of complex movements of both the oral and manual articulators.

Overall, using more sophisticated methods and a within-participant design possible with bimodal bilinguals, we can begin to uncover the degree to which language articulators (i.e. the hands vs. the vocal tract, the eyes vs. the ears) as well as modality-specific linguistic devices afforded (e.g. the grammatical use of space) have an impact on the neural substrate for language (for overview see Corina et al. 2013).

2.4. *Activation and the Role of Experience*

Bilingualism can create changes in the structural and functional organization of the brain (for a review, see Gullberg and Indefrey 2006). There is recent evidence to suggest that learning a sign language as an L2 may impact the functional brain network of the spoken L1 in bimodal bilinguals. Using fMRI, for Mandarin-Chinese Sign Language bilinguals, Zou et al. (2012b) compared bimodal bilinguals with monolinguals during picture-naming in their Chinese L1 and found five pairs of brain regions with increased connectivity in the bimodal bilinguals relative to the monolinguals. These findings indicate that sign language experience modulates the functional brain network of the first language in bimodal bilinguals in a way that is similar to how learning a second spoken language does.

The specific experience and environment of a bilingual can also play a role in how the brain develops. The age that a language is learned, and the level of fluency in that language are important aspects of the bilingual experience (Perani et al. 2003). As is found for spoken-language bilinguals, age of exposure to the second language can result in measurable differences in sign language processing (e.g. Mayberry and Fischer 1989; Mayberry and Eichen 1991; Emmorey et al. 1993, Emmorey et al. 1995; Corina and Hildebrandt 2002; Carreiras et al. 2008). For example, in a semantic-relatedness task comparing deaf bilinguals and late (less proficient) ASL-English bimodal bilinguals, both groups showed interference effects for semantically unrelated pairs when the underlying ASL sign translations were phonologically related (Morford et al. 2014). However, unlike the sign-print bilinguals, late bimodal bilinguals showed no facilitation effect when the pairs were semantically related (i.e. when the answer was 'yes' they are related). This pattern of results is similar to what is found with L2 processing for spoken-language bilinguals. Specifically, there may be weaker cross-language activation of the L2 during L1 comprehension when L2 proficiency is lower (see for example, Van Hell and Dijkstra 2002; Van Hell and Tanner 2012).

During a BSL phonological judgement task MacSweeney et al. (2008a) found a similar neural network supporting phonological similarity judgments made in a signed (BSL) and spoken (English) language. Hearing people making the same rhyming judgements in English also recruited the same network. However, greater activation was found in the left inferior frontal cortex in Deaf non-native signers (age of acquisition was not reported) compared with Deaf native signers. An increase of activation in this region has also been found as a function of proficiency during L2 processing in speech bilinguals (Klein et al. 2006). Importantly, differences were found not only during BSL judgements, in which both groups had different language experience, but also during English judgements, in which both groups had more similar experiences.

In a series of fMRI experiments, native and late hearing bimodal bilinguals showed differences in parietal activation in the right hemisphere when processing ASL sentences (Newman et al. 2002). Specifically, native, but not late acquisition of ASL was associated with recruitment of the right angular gyrus during sign language comprehension. Newman et al. (2002) argue that the activation of this region during sign language perception might be a neural signature of native sign language acquisition such that there is a critical period for recruitment of processing in this visual-spatial region (see also Atkinson et al. 2004).

However, in a meta-analysis of studies comparing monolinguals and spoken-language bilinguals, Hull and Vaid (2007) report more bilateral activation for comprehension tasks of early bilinguals compared with monolingual speakers. Their meta-analysis suggests that early bilinguals show greater bilateral involvement in language comprehension than late bilinguals. Therefore, it is possible that the greater right hemisphere involvement observed by Newman et al. (2002) for early ASL-English bilinguals is a consequence of the early acquisition of two languages rather than due to early acquisition of a signed language per se.

Deafness is another obvious potential influencing factor and we can ask the extent to which status (hearing or deaf) impacts the neural systems recruited for language processing. In general, comparison of native bimodal bilingual signers and deaf native signers on sign language comprehension tasks generally reveals little or no differences in neural activation for the two groups (Söderfeldt et al. 1994; Neville et al. 1998; MacSweeney et al. 2002). However, comprehending spoken language for Deaf individuals requires significantly more neural resources and sustained activation in auditory cortices compared with comprehending sign language (e.g. Finney et al. 2001; Cardin et al. 2013). In addition, MacSweeney et al. (2002) found that hearing native users of BSL exhibited less extensive activation along the left superior temporal gyrus (STG) compared with deaf native signers when comprehending BSL sentences. MacSweeney et al. (2002) suggest that auditory processing of speech has privileged access to more anterior regions of STG (adjacent to primary auditory cortex), such that hearing signers engage this region much less during sign language processing (see also Emmorey and McCullough 2009).

Overall, many aspects of the Deaf experience could drive differences in neural activation. A person who is immersed in a sign language culture and in a family with many generations of deaf individuals (occurring in families with genetically based deafness) will necessarily encounter different world experiences and undergo a different path to cognitive development than a signer who learned to sign only later in life. These differences could translate into changes in brain function. Importantly, Deaf late-learners of a signed language, who constitute the majority of deaf signers and whose language development tends to lag behind that of the early signer (Mayberry and Lock 2003), tend not to have a secure first language that is learned in infancy because of limited access to a spoken language (Campbell et al. 2008).

While still in its infancy, studies investigating effects of age of acquisition and experience in speech-sign bilinguals also find differences in the neural signature of sign language processing comparable to what has been reported for spoken-language bilinguals (Emmorey and McCullough 2009; Emmorey et al. 2014a; also see Emmorey et al. 2016 for a review). In the future, speech-sign bilingual studies may be helpful in teasing apart potential differences due to proficiency and age of exposure. This is because Deaf late-learners of a sign language are likely to become immersed in Deaf culture and life and develop a high level of proficiency. Alternatively, native hearing signers (bimodal bilinguals) are likely to become more proficient in their spoken L2, despite first exposure to a signed language.

One research question that has yet to be sufficiently addressed, but that could be vital in determining language policy for deaf children, is the potential for differences in how language is processed when access to an L1 is limited or delayed (as is often the case when deaf children are exposed only to a spoken language). Lack of exposure to a fully accessible language early in life may have implications for the neural systems supporting not only that language, but also for subsequently learned languages. Mayberry shows important consequences for late acquisition of a sign language for deaf individuals who she terms 'late L1 signers'. For these signers, the establishment of language in typical brain regions may not hold (Mayberry et al. 2002; Mayberry and Lock 2003). For a discussion of differences in acquisition for L1 and L2 signers see, Cormier et al. 2012).

3.   Speech-Sign Bilingual Language Processing

So far, we have discussed speech-sign bilinguals and what different patterns of activation tell us about the neural correlates of language processing in general. In this section, we discuss the ways in which a speech-sign bilingual's two languages interact. What is the evidence for shared, or independent storage, access and processing for their signed and spoken languages, and to what degree is this modulated by modality? What happens when a bilingual's two languages are distinct in terms of the motoric systems used to produce and comprehend them? An understanding of the processing differences that arise from different language modalities is critical for understanding the interaction of language processing with perception and action systems.

3.1.   *Phonology and the Speech-Sign Bilingual Difference*

Speech-sign bilinguals have no overlap between their spoken and signed phonology. Similarly to spoken languages, signed languages have a phonological system, or a sub-lexical level of representation from which words are formed. Signs are composed of four basic phonological parameters: handshape, location (place of articulation), movement, and palm orientation (for a discussion, see Brentari 1998; Sandler and Lillo-Martin 2006).

Evidence for these parameters comes from minimal pairs: signs that are identical except for one feature, such that if you substitute one feature for another, it changes the meaning of the sign. Minimal pairs in a sign language (see Figure 1 for BSL examples) 'rhyme' in a way similar to minimal pairs in English (e.g. 'bat' and 'pat' in English are minimal pairs). When making rhyming judgements in BSL and English, Deaf sign-print bilinguals exhibit frontoparietal activation that is left lateralized, similar to that found for phonological processing in a spoken language. This provides support that phonological processing is not driven by modality (MacSweeney et al. 2008a).

3.2.   *Speech-Sign Bilingual Comprehension*

For spoken languages, it is generally uncontroversial that information is processed almost immediately, as it comes in (e.g. Rayner and Clifton 2009). During such incremental moment-by-moment language processing listeners are faced with many possible alternatives that match the current acoustic-phonetic input. Empirical evidence suggests instead of waiting until temporary ambiguities are resolved, partial activation of possible words (i.e. lexical competitors) that match current phonological information proceeds, with potential words being eliminated as more information becomes available (e.g. McClelland and Elman 1986; Gaskell and Marslen-Wilson 1997).

For bilinguals who know two spoken languages, a large body of evidence has shown that their languages are not 'separable', with activation of both languages during

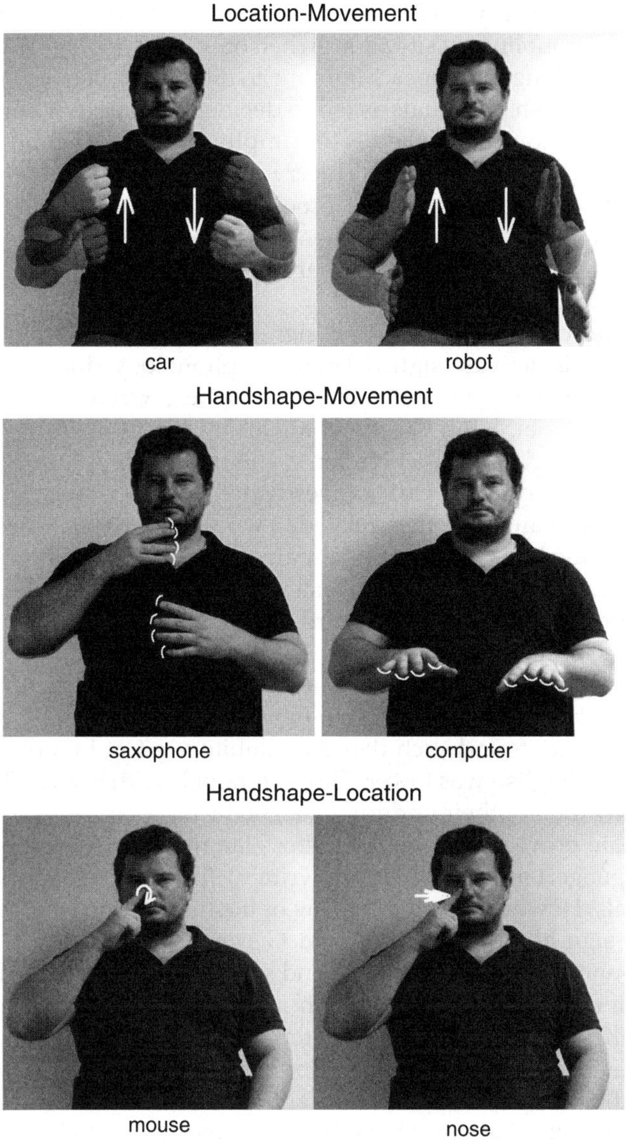

Location-Movement

car   robot

Handshape-Movement

saxophone   computer

Handshape-Location

mouse   nose

Figure 1   Examples of phonological minimal pairs in BSL. Top: *car* and *robot* share location and movement (up and down) parameters, but differ in handshape. Middle: *saxophone* and *computer* share handshape and movement (finger wiggle) features, but differ in location. Bottom: *mouse* and *nose* share handshape and location features, but differ in movement (*mouse*, with a twisting movement and *nose* with a tapping movement).

listening (Marian and Spivey 2003), speaking (Kroll et al. 2006), and reading (Dijkstra 2005) tasks, even in monolingual situations when only one language is in use. Activation for spoken-language bilinguals appears immune to differences between the two language systems: Chinese-English bilinguals asked to decide whether two English words were semantically related showed reduced N400 amplitudes when Chinese translations of the English words shared a character (Thierry and Wu 2007). Similarly to the competition model of monolingual language processing, for spoken-language bilinguals, cross-language activation during comprehension is generally assumed to be bottom-up and based on lexical competition from shared phonology (Dijkstra and Van Heuven 2002; Shook and Marian 2013).

Similarly, studies of both bimodal and sign-print bilinguals provide evidence that speech-sign bilinguals activate signed language phonology during spoken language tasks when the sign language is not actively in use (e.g. Ormel et al. 2012; Shook and Marian 2012; Kubuş et al. 2014; Giezen et al. 2015; Chiu et al. 2016; Villameriel et al. 2016). However, the origin of this activation is still unknown.

For example, Morford et al. (2011) investigated whether semantic judgements to printed English word pairs ('are they related?') would be primed when the underlying ASL translation equivalents were minimal pairs. Underlying phonological relatedness of the ASL translation equivalents led to faster 'yes' judgements and slower 'no' judgements in deaf bimodal bilinguals (Morford et al. 2011; see also Kubuş et al. 2014 for similar effects in German Sign Language and German: i.e. an interference effect for semantically unrelated pairs of German words when the German Sign Language translations were phonologically similar). In a follow-up study (Morford et al. 2014), proficiency effects were found such that the inhibitory effect in 'no' trials was greater when proficiency in English was lower. Thus, bilinguals with lower L2 proficiency may have stronger activation of their underlying signed L1.

Research to date provides evidence for cross-language activation between a signed and spoken language (either spoken, or written) for both sign-print bilinguals and bimodal bilinguals. However, in an overview of the findings on cross-language interactions for speech-sign bilinguals, Ormel and Giezen (2014) point out that despite the similar effects found for spoken-language and speech-sign bilinguals, it is possible that the underlying mechanisms of coactivation are different. For speech-sign bilinguals, behavioural studies do not allow us to determine whether cross-language activation stems from bottom-up lexical competition (outside of phonology), or instead, relies on top-down activation from semantic or conceptual levels (however, see Thompson and Langdon 2017, for a recent attempt to address this question with behavioural data).

In a recent behavioural study, Morford et al. (2017) found effects of coactivation when deaf ASL-English bilinguals made semantic judgements on pairs of English words that could be phonologically related or unrelated in ASL. Importantly, those effects were found at short intervals (300 ms) between the stimulus words, which argues in favour of implicit coactivation of ASL. Likewise, in an ERP study (Meade et al. 2017) provided insight on the time course of cross-language activation in Deaf ASL-English bilinguals during a semantic relatedness judgement task. Specifically, they found a reduced negativity in the N400 time window for English word pairs with underlying phonologically related ASL translations than for those with unrelated translations. The direction of the effect and timing of this N400 effect was consistent with previous research in spoken-language bilinguals. This suggests that the same lexico-semantic mechanism underlies implicit coactivation of a non-target language, irrespective of language modality. However, there were some discrepancies with results from spoken-language bilinguals in the distribution of the ERP effect (anterior right as opposed to central as is typically found in spoken-language bilinguals) and in the behavioural data (interference for word pairs with phonologically related translations) that suggest weaker suppression of the non-target language by bimodal than unimodal bilinguals.

3.3. Speech-Sign Bilingual Production

Tip-of-the-tongue states (TOTs) are the experience of knowing a given word and yet not being able to recall it. The existence and nature of TOTs in spoken languages suggests that independent processing stages provide access to word meanings and word forms (e.g. Garrett 1975; Levelt et al. 1999). Deaf signers also experience 'tip-of-the-fingers' (TOFs) parallel to TOTs suggesting that, as with spoken languages, semantic information can be retrieved independently of phonological information (e.g. signers may know all about a target sign but are unable to access its word form; Thompson et al. 2005).

For spoken-language bilinguals, there is a greater incidence of TOTs compared with matched monolinguals (Gollan and Silverberg 2001; Gollan and Acenas 2004). This result has been obtained with several groups of spoken-language bilinguals (Hebrew-English, Spanish-English, and Tagalog-English bilinguals), and in both laboratory and natural settings (Gollan et al. 2001), and even when bilinguals were tested exclusively in their dominant language (Gollan and Acenas 2004). Because the increased TOT rate was observed in the bilinguals' strongest language it appears that spoken-language bilingualism is associated with a processing cost.

For speech-sign bilinguals, a similar cost is found. Specifically, ASL-English bimodal bilinguals experienced similar numbers of TOTs in English as Spanish-English bilinguals, and significantly more TOTs than monolinguals (Pyers et al. 2009). The findings support a theory under which TOTs reflect a failure to activate lexical representations because of reduced frequency accessing them (Gollan et al. 2008). Specifically, all bilinguals must divide their language use between two languages, whether signed or spoken, and therefore experience increased TOT rates.

Most theories of language production assume that lexical access requires selection of the most highly activated lexical node from the set of activated nodes. Selection is required because, in addition to the target node, other semantically related lexical nodes are also activated (e.g. Dell 1986; Levelt 1989; Caramazza 1997; Green 1998). Thus, there is competition within a single language of multiple potential words at the semantic level during lexical selection. In spoken-language bilinguals between-language competition is also found. For example, spoken-language bilinguals are slower to name pictures compared with monolinguals both in their dominant and non-dominant language. This effect has been explained in terms of competition from the non-target language during production tasks (e.g. Costa et al. 1999; Costa et al. 2000).

Bimodal bilinguals are also slower than Deaf signers during picture-naming in their non-dominant language compared to their dominant language. However, when they name pictures in their dominant language (English) they show similar speed and accuracy to that of English monolinguals (Emmorey et al. 2013). Hence, lexical access to the dominant language does not seem to suffer from the presence of the non-dominant language when it is in a different modality. Such a finding may indicate that there is only unidirectional competition for bimodal bilinguals (i.e. from the spoken language to the signed language). However, further research is needed to investigate this hypothesis as there may be costs associated with language competition that are more subtle for bimodal bilinguals. For example, in a recent study ASL-English bilinguals retrieved fewer items than English monolinguals during an English letter fluency task, reflecting language interference (Giezen and Emmorey 2017).

4.   Articulating Two Languages Simultaneously

The visual-gestural modality available to signers offers a multichannel system in which linguistic information can be expressed simultaneously by not only the hands, but also the body, head, face, and mouth, all of which can have both lexical and grammatical functions. Some mouth patterns can express adjectival or adverbial information, while other specific mouth patterns (termed mouth gestures) are an integral part of a lexical sign and are time-locked to the production of a sign's manual component (i.e. hand movement; Boyes Braem and Sutton-Spence 2001). Mouth gestures use abstract vocal properties (e.g. inhalation and exhalation, mouth shape, articulation) to reflect properties of the manual signs themselves (Woll and Sieratzki 1998).

Another unique mouth pattern that is relevant for bilingual research is the forming of silent words corresponding to the spoken language. These mouth patterns are based directly on the pronunciation of words in a spoken language, and originate as borrowed forms from the surrounding spoken language. Spoken language mouth patterns that co-occur with signs can be used to distinguish between ambiguous sign forms. For example, the BSL signs for *eat* and *meal* have the same sign form, but can be distinguished by English-based mouthings. However, such mouthings also commonly occur with signs that are not ambiguous.

The occurrence of speech-based mouth patterns with signs has been documented in many sign languages (for a partial list, see Woll and MacSweeney 2016). Their simultaneous occurrence and synchronization with the hands during sign production suggests that they are the product of shared lexical representations, at least at the semantic level. However, the status of speech-based mouthings within a sign language has been controversial. Specifically, they have been described as part of the sign language lexicon, such that both the speech-based mouth pattern and the signing hands form a single lexical representation (e.g. Vogt-Svendsen 2001), or alternatively, as an independent representation that is accessed separately from the sign language (i.e. as is found in simultaneous bimodal bilingual production; e.g. Boyes Braem and Sutton-Spence 2001).

Vinson et al. (2010) provide experimental evidence for the latter claim. Specifically, using a semantically blocked picture-naming task in BSL, dissociations were found on the mouth and the hands when errors were produced (e.g. mouthing 'banana' and signing 'apple'). The results provide the first strong evidence that speech-based mouthings reflect the activation of representations based on a spoken language that occur simultaneously, but independently, from sign-based representations. That speech-based mouthings could be incidental to manual-form retrieval, rather than being integrated before phonological encoding reflects the unique fact that speech-sign bilinguals need not suppress one language while producing another, at least at the lexical level.

In support of the behavioural data, fMRI data show that speech-based mouthings and mouth gestures dissociate in a similar way to watching speech or watching BSL during comprehension (Capek et al. 2008). That is, a speech-based mouthing condition (silent video of someone speaking) generated greater activation in middle superior temporal regions while the sign-based mouth gestures generated more activation in posterior and inferior temporal regions. For bimodal bilinguals, the difference was not as marked (evidence was found only in the mouth gesture > speech-based mouthings contrast, but not in speech-based mouthings > mouth gesture contrast). The authors suggest that the difference in strength may be due to greater reliance on speech-reading for deaf compared to hearing signers. Importantly, the findings are consistent with the claim that signs and spoken-language mouthings are accessed independently.

The face also plays an important role in both sign production and comprehension for sign languages researched to date. Everyone (both signers and non-signers) uses their face to convey emotion, with expressions of happiness, sadness, and anger thought to be universal (Ekman 1992). Additionally, during sign production signers use facial expressions to convey a variety of linguistic contrasts (Liddell 1980). For example, in ASL, raised eyebrows mark conditionals, while furrowed eyebrows mark wh-questions (e.g. who, what, where).

Emotional facial expressions and linguistic facial expressions differ in their scope and timing and in the facial muscles that are used (for ASL, see Baker-Schenk 1983; Reilly et al. 1990). Facial expressions with a grammatical function have a clear onset and offset and are coordinated with specific parts of a signed sentence. Emotional expressions have more global and inconsistent onset and offset patterns, and their timing is not linked to specific signs or grammatical structures.

Pyers and Emmorey (2008) monitored eyebrow movements during a speaking task that elicited both conditionals and wh-clauses while ASL-English bimodal bilinguals were partnered with English-speaking monolinguals. Bimodal bilinguals produced significantly more ASL-appropriate facial expressions than non-signers and synchronized their expressions with the English clause onset (Pyers and Emmorey 2008). The simultaneous production of distinct morphosyntactic elements from two languages argues for a dual-language architecture in which grammatical information can be integrated and coordinated at all levels of processing (see e.g. Hartsuiker et al. 2004; Goldrick et al. 2016; Hartsuiker and Bernolet 2017).

4.1. *Code-blending*

As mentioned in Section 1.3, speech-sign bilinguals can perceive and produce their languages simultaneously. This means producing or perceiving semantically converging, but quite distinct phonological information in two modalities. In cognitive science, there is a known tendency for detection of a signal to be faster when stimuli are presented in two modalities simultaneously (i.e. a light and a sound that both signal go) compared with when either signal is presented alone (Todd 1912; Miller 1982). However, for spoken-language bilinguals, there is some evidence that simultaneous perception of translation equivalents across modalities can interfere with processing (e.g. Mitterer and McQueen 2009). Therefore we can ask: What are the processing costs or benefits of simultaneous production and comprehension of two languages?

Spoken-language bilinguals tend to 'code-switch', or switch between their languages. Such code-switching is an effortful process during language production, made possible by language inhibition (Green 1998; although see Finkbeiner et al. 2006; Bobb and Wodniecka 2013; Declerck and Philipp 2015, for a different view). In contrast, ASL-English bilinguals prefer to 'code-blend', or simultaneously produce both spoken and signed languages together (Emmorey et al. 2008a). Code-blends are characterized by temporally matched onsets of signs and English words that convey the semantically equivalent, or closely related content (Emmorey et al. 2008a). Thus, when articulatory constraints are removed, bilinguals may prefer to produce two languages simultaneously rather than suppress one language while using the other.

In a similar way, during comprehension ASL-English bimodal bilinguals demonstrated a processing advantage for dual input of semantically equivalent ASL and English in a semantic decision task (e.g. Is it edible?) compared with English words presented alone (Emmorey et al. 2012). Thus, dual-language input from multiple languages in distinct modalities may be beneficial for comprehension.

In support of this, using fMRI, Weisberg et al. (2015) found that simultaneous input of a sign and spoken word (again using a semantic relatedness judgement) elicited reduced activation in bilateral prefrontal and visual extrastriate cortices relative to signed ASL presented alone, and in auditory association cortex relative to spoken English alone. Further, comprehension of simultaneous English and ASL (i.e. code-blended) did not result in recruitment of cognitive control regions. Therefore, the findings, which are also consistent with the previously mentioned facilitation during semantic decisions (Emmorey et al. 2012), suggest that redundant signals of semantic content result in efficient neural processing in language and sensory regions during bimodal language integration. Importantly, although bimodal bilinguals can use their two languages simultaneously, language control is still demanding because the two languages differ in grammatical structure (Emmorey et al. 2005; Zou et al., 2012a). Therefore code-blends tend to be one or two words long.

In production, we might predict that code-blending would incur a processing cost because motor planning and retrieval for two lexical representations might be more effortful than retrieval of a single representation. However, initial evidence provides mixed results. Specifically, in a comparison of picture naming for ASL–English bilinguals (ASL only, or ASL–English code-blend), Emmorey et al. (2012) found that code-blending did not slow lexical retrieval and, further, found code-blending facilitated retrieval of low-frequency ASL signs (see also Kaufmann et al. 2018, for German and German Sign Language [DGS]). However, English-only picture naming was faster than producing ASL-English code-blends. Emmorey et al. (2012) conclude that facilitation is driven by translation priming (e.g. Costa et al. 1999), but that code-blending was slower than

English because bimodal bilinguals delayed the onset of speech in order to synchronize words and signs (i.e. delaying speech onset until the hand reaches the target location of the sign).

4.2. *Code Switching*

Although code-blending is more common for bimodal bilinguals, there are situations where code-switch between the two languages occurs (Emmorey et al. 2008a). Since signed and spoken languages do not share articulators, language selection is not obligatory. This coupled with greater practice code-blending, might lead to repercussions for the control mechanisms needed during code switching.

The language-switching paradigm has been extensively used in studies of unimodal bilinguals (e.g. Meuter and Allport 1999; Costa and Santesteban 2004). Typically, this paradigm involves the production of a word in response to sequentially displayed stimulus (e.g. naming a picture or colour), with the target language for each trial indicated by a cue (e.g. a specific shape or colour is associated with each language). Therefore, trials can be a switch trial, which requires a response in a different language from the immediately preceding one, or a repeat trial (that requires a response in the same language). For unimodal bilinguals there is a language switch cost, reflected in longer response times and higher error rates for switch than repeat trials that is often larger when participants are switching from their non-dominant to their dominant language (see e.g. Declerck and Philipp 2015, for review). It is thought that language switch costs are due to non-target language interference that results in language suppression. That is, in a switch trial the target language is still inhibited from the previous trial and the system must overcome this inhibition, thus taking longer to produce a response (see Koch et al. 2010, for review).

The few studies on language switching in bimodal bilinguals to date have found significant costs associated to switching between the two modalities. However, it is not clear yet whether the same language control mechanisms are used by bimodal and unimodal bilinguals. Emmorey et al. (2014b) found a switch cost for English (ASL to English) but not for ASL. Indeed, they found an advantage of switching into ASL that they interpreted in terms of an anticipatory preparation for manual response (allowed by the lack of competition between the articulators). However, in a recent study Dias et al. (2017) found language switch costs for both languages in proficient (including native and late signers) Spanish and Spanish Sign Language (LSE) bilinguals. Furthermore, consistent with previous findings in unimodal bilinguals, the language switch cost was larger when switching from the non-dominant to the dominant language (LSE to Spanish). Kaufmann et al. (2018) studied unimodal (spoken English to spoken German) and bimodal (spoken German to DGS) language switches within the same group of hearing late learners of German Sign Language. A smaller switch cost was found for bimodal compared to unimodal switches, which might indicate different, although still inhibitory, control mechanisms for language switches between modalities.

Kovelman et al. (2009) found brain activation patterns consistent with this view in a functional near infrared spectroscopy (fNIRS) study with proficient English-ASL bilinguals. This study compared unimodal contexts (either English or ASL utterances) and bimodal contexts, in which English and ASL were produced simultaneously (code-blends) or in rapid succession (code-switches). The data revealed a greater recruitment of left posterior temporal brain regions (within the language network) for both bilingual contexts compared to the monolingual context. However, there was no engagement of frontal areas linked to general control mechanisms (e.g. dorsolateral prefrontal cortex, anterior cingulated cortex), which suggest that bimodal bilinguals do not need to solve motor-articulatory competition as unimodal bilinguals do.

Emmorey et al. (2014b) further explored the mechanisms at use when switching into or out of a code-blend by contrasting switches from English to code-blending and switches from ASL to code-blending. They found no cost of switching into code-blends (similar response times compared to non-switch trials) but there was a cost of switching out of a code-blend into either English or ASL. These results were taken as an indication that for bimodal bilinguals there is not an additional processing cost associated with re-activating a previously inhibited language. However, there is a cost associated with inhibiting one of the languages. Similar results were found in a recent behavioural study that compared language switch costs when participants produced either a signed or verbal response alone or a code-blended response (Kaufmann and Philipp 2017). Although language switch costs were found for all three types of response, they were smaller for code-blending than for the sign only responses. Remarkably, it was more difficult to switch from a code-blending to a single (either signed or verbal) response than in the opposite direction. These results suggest again that inhibition alone might not be enough to explain language control mechanisms in bimodal bilinguals, rather persisting activation of the previous (blend) trial must be taken into account. As there are more possibilities for mixing their languages for bimodal bilinguals than there are for unimodal bilinguals, further research is needed to determine whether control mechanisms are the same for bimodal and unimodal bilinguals and, crucially, to fully understand the influence of the output modality, especially when both modalities use them simultaneously.

5.   Cognition and Speech-Sign Bilingualism

We are just beginning to understand how language is shaped by and interdependent with other aspects of cognition: non-linguistic cognitive processes such as executive control and working memory impact language processing (e.g. Hussey and Novick 2012) and language processing in return impacts these cognitive processes (e.g. Bialystok and Feng 2009; Bialystok et al. 2012). The unique need for spoken-language bilinguals to manage multiple languages while their executive control mechanisms are developing is claimed to result in long-term cognitive advantages on inhibitory control processes that generalize beyond the language domain (Bialystok et al. 2008; Costa et al. 2008; Martin-Rhee and Bialystok 2008; however, see de Bruin et al. 2015).

The cognitive demands on lexical processing may also be higher for speech-sign bilinguals compared with monolinguals as, similarly to spoken-language bilinguals, speech-sign bilinguals must represent two sets of lexical items (one for each language). In an fNIRS study, bimodal bilinguals demonstrated greater signal intensity within posterior temporal regions when using both languages either simultaneously or in rapid alternation compared with when they used only one language (Kovelman et al. 2014). However, because signed and spoken language processing engage different sensory and motor systems for perception and production, for speech-sign bilinguals there may not be high demands on executive control processes (e.g. conflict monitoring, inhibition) because the competing non-target language is in a different modality from the target language.

In line with this theory, a study with bimodal bilinguals shows that they are not better than monolingual speakers on cognitive control tasks (Emmorey et al. 2008b). Specifically, performance on a flanker task was compared for monolinguals, spoken-language bilinguals, and bimodal bilinguals. While spoken-language bilinguals showed enhanced cognitive control, performing more quickly on incongruent trials compared with monolinguals, bimodal bilinguals instead paralleled monolinguals in their performance (Emmorey et al. 2008b). Thus, while all participants performed similarly on the control condition, spoken-language bilinguals were faster compared with both monolinguals and bimodal bilinguals on the condition requiring executive control. The authors conclude that this difference is driven by the lower demands on language control for bimodal bilinguals who can both perceive and produce more than one language simultaneously and therefore do not need to monitor their languages as often to ensure that the correct language is being selected. They further suggest that, in contrast to spoken-language bilinguals, who need to attend to and perceptually discriminate between two spoken languages, perceptual cues of language identity are unambiguous and easy to distinguish for bimodal bilinguals.

5.1. Cognitive Benefits of Speech-Sign Bilingualism

Previous studies have reported that bimodal bilinguals show enhanced non-linguistic visuospatial abilities including motion processing, face perception, and mental imagery, all of which are directly tied to processing requirements for sign language (Emmorey et al. 1993; Emmorey and Kosslyn 1996; Emmorey and McCullough 2009). Exposure to sign language also influences patterns of functional brain activity, leading to a left lateralized network for perception of movements rather than the typically bilateral or right hemisphere dominance for both motion processing (Bavelier et al. 2001) and recognition of facial expressions (Emmorey and McCullough 2009).

For example, signers look at their conversational partner's face almost exclusively when perceiving visual linguistic input (Emmorey et al. 2008c). The signer's face is important for comprehension both as a central location to perceive unpredictable movement from their signs, and as the location of grammatical and prosodic information. Because deaf signers must attend to the face for both affective and linguistic input in order to interpret signed sentences, they may develop unique processing mechanisms that maximize their ability to gather information from expressive faces. Interestingly, there is evidence that ASL-English bilinguals are better at face discrimination tasks compared with English monolinguals (Bettger 1992; McCullough and Emmorey 1997).

ASL-English bilinguals do not outperform English monolinguals on tests of global face processing, or on face recognition from memory. However, they have shown enhanced face discrimination abilities that were likely linked to the local featural processing required for grammatical facial expressions (McCullough and Emmorey 1997). Such featural processing appears to be mediated by the left fusiform gyrus (Hillger and Koening 1991). However, neuroimaging evidence provides support for effects of sign language experience during processing of grammatical facial expressions in sign (McCullough et al. 2005; Emmorey and McCullough 2009). Using fMRI, McCullough et al. (2005) found that deaf ASL signers exhibit a strong left hemisphere asymmetry in the fusiform gyrus for processing linguistic facial expressions (i.e. static pictures depicting adverbial mouth gestures with ASL verb signs, compared to pictures of non-linguistic emotional facial expressions) when compared with English monolingual speakers, who exhibited a slight right hemisphere asymmetry. The authors interpret this difference as resulting from a signer's need to rapidly analyse local facial features during online sign language processing. The results suggest that experience with ASL may alter the laterality of the neural circuitry underlying face processing.

Importantly, specialization for linguistic facial expressions appears to be affected by deafness, such that the same linguistic stimuli did not elicit strong left lateralization in hearing signers. The difference between deaf and hearing signers may be due to the effect of neuroplasticity: as the temporal cortex is not specialized for auditory processing in deaf signers, it can be recruited for linguistic processing of a signed language (Emmorey and McCullough 2009).

Several studies have also suggested that the acquisition of a signed language during development affects certain non-linguistic visual-spatial abilities (see Emmorey 2002, for a review). Several studies have shown that hearing ASL-English bilinguals (and deaf native signers) exhibit left hemisphere dominance for motion processing in the visual periphery compared with monolingual English speakers who tend to exhibit a right hemisphere asymmetry (Neville and Lawson 1987; Bavelier et al. 2001; Bosworth and Dobkins 2001). Thus, early acquisition of a signed language can alter the neural areas responsible for certain aspects of non-linguistic motion perception.

Finally, long-term cognitive benefits in terms of grey matter volume have been attributed to bilinguals. Specifically, an increased grey matter volume in brain areas underpinning executive control has been identified as a beneficial neural change of bilingualism. It has been proposed that such a change may protect the brain from age-induced atrophy (Perani and Abutalebi 2015). For speech-sign bilinguals, Li et al. (2017) showed that all bilinguals, regardless of language modality, exhibited higher grey matter volume compared with monolinguals. This finding highlights the general beneficial neuroprotective effects provided by experience with handling two language systems, whether signed or spoken.

6.   Conclusion

There is a growing appreciation that learning and using more than one language is a natural and prevalent circumstance of cognition. Research on speech-sign bilinguals can help identify to what extent the segregation of languages into different sensory-motor systems alters the cognitive and linguistic demands of representing and controlling two languages within a single brain. Research on speech-sign bilingualism is therefore likely to have a sustained and compelling influence on how we understand the effects of bilingualism on cognitive control, on language processing, and on the neural systems that support these functions.

NOTES

1   By convention, uppercase Deaf indicates individuals who are deaf, but also use sign language and are members of the Deaf community, while lowercase deaf represents audiological status.
2   Although see Pfau (2012) for information on alternative manual communication systems that have been developed.

REFERENCES

Atkinson, J., Campbell, R., Marshall, J. et al. (2004). Understanding 'not': neuropsychological dissociations between hand and head markers of negation in BSL. *Neuropsychologia* 42 (2): 214–229.

Baker-Schenk, C. (1983). *A micro-analysis of the nonmanual components of questions in American Sign Language.* (Doctoral dissertation, University of California, Berkeley, CA).

Bavelier, D., Brozinsky, C., Tomann, A. et al. (2001). Impact of early deafness and early exposure to sign language on the cerebral organization for motion processing. *Journal of Neuroscience* 21 (22): 8931–8942.

Bettger, J. (1992). *The Effects of Experience on Spatial Cognition: Deafness and Knowledge of ASL.* Champagne- Urbana: University of Illinois.

Bialystok, E. (1988). Levels of bilingualism and levels of linguistic awareness. *Developmental Psychology* 24 (4): 560.

Bialystok, E. (2017). The bilingual adaptation: how minds accommodate experience. *Psychological Bulletin* 143 (3): 233.

Bialystok, E., Craik, F.I.M., and Luk, G. (2008). Cognitive control and lexical access in younger and older bilinguals. *Journal of Experimental Psychology: Learning, Memory, and Cognition,* 34: 859–873.

Bialystok, E., Craik, F.I.M., and Luk, G. (2012). Bilingualism: consequences for mind and brain. *Trends in Cognitive Science* 16 (4): 240–250.

Bialystok, E. and Feng, X. (2009). Language proficiency and executive control in proactive interference: evidence from monolingual and bilingual children and adults. *Brain and Language* 109 (2/3): 93–100.

Bobb, S.C. and Wodniecka, Z. (2013). Language switching in picture naming: what asymmetric switch costs (do not) tell us about inhibition in bilingual speech planning. *Journal of Cognitive Psychology* 25 (5): 568–585.

Bosworth, R.G. and Dobkins, K.R. (2001). Visual field asymmetries for motion processing in deaf and hearing signers. *Brain and Cognition* 49: 170–181.

Boyes Braem, P. and Sutton-Spence, R. (eds.) (2001). *The Hands are the Head of the Mouth.* Hamburg, Germany: Signum Press.

Braun, A.R., Guillemin, A., Hosey, L., and Varga, M. (2001). The neural organization of discourse: an H2 15O-PET study of narrative production in English and American Sign Language. *Brain* 124 (10): 2028–2044.

Brentari, D. (1998). *A Prosodic Model of Sign Language Phonology*. Cambridge, MA: The MIT Press.

Campbell, R., MacSweeney, M., and Waters, D. (2008). Sign language and the Brain: a review. *Journal of Deaf Studies and Deaf Education* 13 (1): 3–20.

Capek, C., Bavelier, D., Corina, D.P. et al. (2004). The cortical organization of audio-visual sentence comprehension: an fMRI study at 4 Tesla. *Cognitive Brain Research* 2: 111–119.

Capek, C.M., Grossi, G., Newman, A.J. et al. (2009). Brain systems mediating semantic and syntactic processing in deaf native signers: biological invariance and modality specificity. *Proceedings of the National Academy of Sciences* 106 (21): 8784–8789.

Capek, C.M., Waters, C., Woll, B., and MacSweeney, M. (2008). Hand and mouth: Cortical correlates of lexical processing in British Sign Language and speechreading English. *Journal of Cognitive Neuroscience*, 20 (7): 1220–1234.

Caramazza, A. (1997). How many levels of processing are there in lexical access? *Cognitive Neuropsychology* 14: 177–208.

Cardin, V., Orfanidou, E., Rönnberg, J. et al. (2013). Dissociating cognitive and sensory neural plasticity in human superior temporal cortex. *Nature Communications* 4: 1473.

Carreiras, M., Gutiérrez-Sigut, E., Baquero Castellanos, S., and Corina, D.P. (2008). Lexical processing in Spanish Sign Language (LSE). *Journal of Memory and Language* 58: 100–122.

Chiu, Y., Kuo, W., Lee, C., and Tzeng, O.J.L. (2016). The explicit and implicit phonological processing of Chinese characters and words in Taiwanese deaf signers. *Language and Linguistics* 17 (1): 63–87.

Chamberlain, C., Morford, J.P., and Mayberry, R.I. (eds.) (2000). *Language Acquisition by Eye*. Mahwah, NJ: Erlbaum.

Corina, D.P. (1998). The processing of sign language: evidence from aphasia. In: *Handbook of Neurology* (ed. H. Whitaker and B. Stemmer), 313–329. San Diego, CA: Academic Press.

Corina, D.P. and Hildebrandt, U. (2002). Psycholinguistic investigations of phonological structure in ASL. In: *Modality and Structure in Signed and Spoken Language* (ed. R.P. Meier, K. Cormier and D. Quinto–Pozos), 88–111. New York, NY: Cambridge University Press.

Corina, D.P., Lawyer, L.A., and Cates, D. (2013). Cross-linguistic differences in the neural representation of human language: evidence from users of signed languages. *Frontiers in Psychology* 3: 587.

Corina, D.P., San Jose-Robertson, L., Guillemin, A. et al. (2003). Language lateralization in a bimanual language. *Journal of Cognitive Neuroscience* 15: 718–730.

Cormier, K., Schembri, A., Vinson, D., and Orfanidou, E. (2012). First language acquisition differs from second language acquisition in prelingually deaf signers: evidence from sensitivity to grammaticality judgement in British Sign Language. *Cognition*, 124 (1): 50–65.

Costa, A., Albareda, B., and Santesteban, M. (2008). Assessing the presence of lexical competition across languages: evidence from the stroop task. *Bilingualism: Language and Cognition*, 11 (1): 121–131.

Costa, A., Caramazza, A., and Sebastian-Galles, N. (2000). The cognate facilitation effect: implications for models of lexical access. *Journal of Experimental Psychology: Learning, Memory and Cognition* 26 (5): 1283–1296.

Costa, A., Miozzo, M., and Caramazza, A. (1999). Lexical selection in bilinguals: do words in the bilingual's two lexicons compete for selection? *Journal of Memory and Language* 41: 491–511.

Costa, A. and Santesteban, M. (2004). Lexical access in bilingual speech production: evidence from language switching in highly proficient bilinguals and L2 learners. *Journal of Memory and Language* 50 (4): 491–511.

de Bruin, A., Treccani, B., and Della Sala, S. (2015). Cognitive advantage in bilingualism: an example of publication bias? *Psychological Science* 26: 99–107.

Declerck, M. and Philipp, A.M. (2015). A review of control processes and their locus in language switching. *Psychonomic Bulletin & Review* 22 (6): 1630–1645.

Dell, G.S. (1986). A spreading activation theory of retrieval in sentence production. *Psychological Review* 93: 283–321.

Dias, P., Villameriel, S., Giezen, M.R. et al. (2017). Language switching across modalities: evidence from bimodal bilinguals. *Journal of Experimental Psychology: Learning, Memory, and Cognition* 43 (11): 1828.

Dijkstra, T. (2005). Bilingual visual word recognition and lexical access. In: *Handbook of Bilingualism: Psycholinguistic Approaches* (ed. J.F. Kroll and A.M.B. de Groot), 179–201. New York, NY: Oxford University Press.

Dijkstra, T. and Van Heuven, W.J.B. (2002). The architecture of the bilingual word recognition system: From identification to decision. *Bilingualism: Language and Cognition* 5: 175–197.

Dufour, R. (1997). Sign language and bilingualism: modality implications for bilingual language representation. In: *Tutorials in Bilingualism: Psycholinguistic Perspectives* (ed. J.F. Kroll and A.M.B. de Groot), 301–330. Mahwah, NJ: Erlbaum.

Ekman, P. (1992). Facial expression of emotion: an old controversy and new findings. In: *Processing the Facial Image* (ed. V. Bruce), 63–69. Oxford, UK: Clarendon Press.

Emmorey, K. (2002). *Language, Cognition, and the Brain: Insights from Sign Language Research*. Mahwah, NJ: Lawrence Erlbaum & Associates.

Emmorey, K., Bellugi, U., Friederici, A., and Horn, P. (1995). Effects of age of acquisition on grammatical sensitivity: evidence from on-line and off-line tasks. *Applied Psycholinguistics* 16 (1): 1–23.

Emmorey, K., Borinstein, H. B., Thompson, R. L. (2005). Bimodal bilingualism: Code-blending between spoken English and American Sign Language. In K. McAlister, K. Rolstad, & J. MacSwan (Eds.), ISB4: Proceedings of the 4th International Symposium on Bilingualism (pp. 663–673). Somerville, MA: Cascadilla Press.

Emmorey, K., Borinstein, H.B., Thompson, R.L., and Gollan, T.H. (2008a). Bimodal bilingualism. *Bilingualism: Language and Cognition* 11 (1): 43–61.

Emmorey, K., Giezen, M.R., and Gollan, T.H. (2016). Psycholinguistic, cognitive, and neural implications of bimodal bilingualism. *Bilingualism: Language and Cognition,* 19 (2): 223–242.

Emmorey, K., Grabowski, T., McCullough, S. et al. (2003). Neural systems underlying lexical retrieval for sign language. *Neuropsychologia* 41: 85–95.

Emmorey, K. and Kosslyn, S. (1996). Enhanced image generation abilities in deaf signers: a right hemisphere effect. *Brain and Cognition* 32: 28–44.

Emmorey, K., Kosslyn, S.M., and Bellugi, U. (1993). Visual-imagery and visual spatial language: enhanced imagery abilities in deaf and hearing ASL signers. *Cognition* 46 (2): 139–181.

Emmorey, K., Luk, G., Pyers, J., and Bialystok, E. (2008b). The source of enhanced cognitive control in bilinguals: evidence from bimodal bilinguals. *Psychological Science* 19: 1201–1206.

Emmorey, K. and McCullough, S. (2009). The bimodal bilingual brain: effects of sign language experience. *Brain and Language* 109 (2–3): 124–132.

Emmorey, K., McCullough, S., Mehta, S., and Grabowski, T.J. (2014a). How sensory-motor systems impact the neural organization for language: direct contrasts between spoken and signed language. *Frontiers in Psychology* 5: 484.

Emmorey, K., Mehta, S., and Grabowski, T.J. (2007). The neural correlates of sign versus word production. *NeuroImage* 36 (1): 202–208.

Emmorey, K., Petrich, J.A.F., and Gollan, T.H. (2012). Bilingual processing of ASL–English code-blends: the consequences of accessing two lexical representations simultaneously. *Journal of Memory and Language* 67: 199–210.

Emmorey, K., Petrich, J.A.F., and Gollan, T.H. (2013). Bimodal bilingualism and the frequency-lag hypothesis. *Journal of Deaf Studies and Deaf Education* 18 (1): 1–11. https://doi.org/10.1093/deafed/ens034.

Emmorey, K., Petrich, J. A. F., & Gollan, T. H. (2014b). Evidence from bimodal bilinguals indicates 'turning a language ON' is not costly but 'turning a language OFF' is. Presented at the 55th Annual Meeting of the Psychonomic Society, Long Beach, CA.

Emmorey, K., Thompson, R.L., and Colvin, R. (2008c). Eye gaze during comprehension of American Sign Language by native and beginning signers. *Journal of Deaf Studies and Deaf Education* 14: 237–243.

Ferjan Ramirez, N., Leonard, M.K., Davenport, T.S. et al. (2014). Neural language processing in adolescent first-language learners: longitudinal case studies in American Sign Language. *Cerebral Cortex* 26 (3): 1015–1026.

Finkbeiner, M., Almeida, J., Janssen, N., and Caramazza, A. (2006). Lexical selection in bilingual speech production does not involve language suppression. *Journal of Experimental Psychology: Learning, Memory, and Cognition* 32 (5): 1075–1089.

Finney, E.M., Fine, I., and Dobkins, K.R. (2001). Visual stimuli activate auditory cortex in the deaf. *Nature Neuroscience* 4: 1171–1173.

Garrett, M.F. (1975). The analysis of sentence production. In: *The Psychology of Learning and Motivation*, vol. 9 (ed. G.H. Bower), 133–177. New York, NY: Academic Press.

Gaskell, M.G. and Marslen-Wilson, W.D. (1997). Integrating form and meaning: a distributed model of speech perception. *Language and Cognitive Processes* 12: 613–656.

Giezen, M.R., Blumenfeld, H.K., Shook, A. et al. (2015). Parallel language activation and inhibitory control in bimodal bilinguals. *Cognition* 141: 9–25.

Giezen, M.R. and Emmorey, K. (2017). Evidence for a bimodal bilingual disadvantage in letter fluency. *Bilingualism: Language and Cognition* 20 (1): 42–48.

Goldrick, M., Putnam, M., and Schwarz, L. (2016). Coactivation in bilingual grammars: a computational account of code mixing. *Bilingualism: Language and Cognition* 19 (5): 857–876.

Gollan, T.H. and Acenas, L.A. (2004). What is a TOT? Cognate and translation effects on tip-of-the-tongue states in Spanish-English and Tagalog-English bilinguals. *Journal of Experimental Psychology: Learning, Memory, & Cognition* 30: 246–269.

Gollan, T.H., Montoya, R.I., and Bonanni, M.P. (2001). Proper names get stuck on bilingual and monolingual speakers' tip of the tongue equally often. *Neuropsychology* 19 (3): 278.

Gollan, T.H. and Silverberg, N.B. (2001). Tip-of-the-tongue states in Hebrew–English bilinguals. *Bilingualism: Language and Cognition* 4: 63–83.

Gollan, T.H., Montoya, R.I., Cera, C., and Sandoval, T.C. (2008). More use almost always means a smaller frequency effect: aging, bilingualism, and the weaker links hypothesis. *Journal of Memory and Language* 58: 787–814.

Green, D.W. (1998). Mental control of the bilingual lexico-semantic system. *Bilingualism: Language and Cognition* 1: 67–81.

Gullberg, M. and Indefrey, P. (2006). *The Cognitive Neuroscience of Second Language Acquisition*. Malden, MA: Blackwell.

Gutierrez-Sigut, E., Daws, R., Payne, H. et al. (2015). Language lateralization of hearing native signers: a functional transcranial Doppler sonography (fTCD) study of speech and sign production. *Brain and Language* 151: 23–34.

Gutierrez-Sigut, E., Payne, H., and MacSweeney, M. (2016). Examining the contribution of motor movement and language dominance to increased left lateralization during sign generation in native signers. *Brain and Language* 159: 109–117. https://doi.org/10.1016/j.bandl.2016.06.004.

Hartsuiker, R.J. and Bernolet, S. (2017). The development of shared syntax in second language learning. *Bilingualism: Language and Cognition* 20 (2): 219–234.

Hartsuiker, R.J., Pickering, M.J., and Veltkamp, E. (2004). Is syntax separate or shared between languages? Cross-linguistic syntactic priming in Spanish-English bilinguals. *Psychological Science* 15 (6): 409–414.

Hillger, L.A. and Koening, O. (1991). Separable mechanisms in face processing: evidence from hemispheric specialization. *Journal of Cognitive Neuroscience* 3: 42–58.

Horwitz, B., Amunts, K., Bhattacharyya, R. et al. (2003). Activation of Broca's area during the production of spoken and signed language: a combined cytoarchitectonic mapping and PET analysis. *Neuropsychologia* 41: 1868–1876.

Hull, R. and Vaid, J. (2007). Bilingual language lateralization: a meta-analytic tale of two hemispheres. *Neuropsychologia* 45: 1987–2008.

Hussey, E.K. and Novick, J.M. (2012). The benefits of executive control training and the implications for language processing. *Frontiers in Psychology* 3: 158.

Illes, J., Francis, W.S., Desmond, J.E. et al. (1999). Convergent cortical representation of semantic processing in bilinguals. *Brain and Language* 70: 347–363.

Indefrey, P. (2006). A meta-analysis of hemodynamic studies on first and second language processing: which Ssggested differences can we trust and what do they mean? *Language Learning* 56: 279–304.

Kassubek, J., Hickok, G., and Erhard, P. (2004). Involvement of classical anterior and posterior language areas in sign language production, as investigated by 4T functional magnetic resonance imaging. *Neuroscience Letters* 364: 168–172.

Kaufmann, E., Mittelberg, I., Koch, I., and Philipp, A.M. (2018). Modality effects in language switching: evidence for a bimodal advantage. *Bilingualism: Language and Cognition* 21 (2): 243–250.

Kaufmann, E. and Philipp, A. (2017). Language-switch costs and dual response costs in bimodal bilingual language production. *Bilingualism: Language and Cognition* 20: 418–434.

Klein, D., Milner, B., Zatorre, R.J. et al. (1995). The neural substrates underlying word generation: a bilingual functional-imaging study. *Proceedings of the National Academy of Sciences* 92: 2899–2903.

Klein, D., Zatorre, R.J., Chen, J.K. et al. (2006). Bilingual brain organization: a functional magnetic resonance adaptation study. *NeuroImage* 31: 366–375.

Koch, I., Gade, M., Schuch, S., and Philipp, A.M. (2010). The role of inhibition in task switching – a review. *Psychonomic Bulletin & Review* 17: 1–14.

Kovelman, I., Shalinsky, M.H., Berens, M.S., and Petitto, L. (2014). Words in the bilingual Brain: an fNIRS brain imaging investigation of lexical processing in sign-speech bimodal bilinguals. *Frontiers in Human Neuroscience* 8: 606.

Kovelman, I., Shalinsky, M.H., White, K.S. et al. (2009). Dual language use in sign-speech bimodal bilinguals: fNIRS brain-imaging evidence. *Brain and Language* 109 (2–3): 112–123.

Kroll, J.F., Bobb, S.C., and Wodnieka, Z. (2006). Language selectivity is the exception, not the rule: arguments against a fixed locus of language selection in bilingual speech. *Bilingualism: Language and Cognition* 9: 119–135.

Kubuş, O., Villwock, A., Morford, J.P., and Rathmann, C. (2014). Word recognition in deaf readers: cross-language activation of German Sign Language and German. *Applied Psycholinguistics* 36 (4): 831–854.

Li, L., Abutalebi, J., Emmorey, K. et al. (2017). How bilingualism protects the brain from aging: insights from bimodal bilinguals. *Human Brain Mapping* 38: 4109–4124.

Levelt, W.J.M. (1989). *Speaking: From Intention to Articulation*. Cambridge, MA: MIT Press.

Levelt, W.J.M., Roelofs, A., and Meyer, A.S. (1999). A theory of lexical access in speech production. *Behavioral and Brain Sciences* 22: 1–75.

Liddell, S.K. (1980). *American Sign Language Syntax*, vol. 52. Berlin, Germany: Mouton De Gruyter.

Leonard, M.K., Ramirez, N.F., Torres, C. et al. (2012). Signed words in the congenitally deaf evoke typical late lexicosemantic responses with no early visual responses in left superior temporal cortex. *The Journal of Neuroscience* 32 (28): 9700–9705.

Leonard, M.K., Ferjan Ramirez, N., Torres, C. et al. (2013). Neural stages of spoken, written, and signed word processing in beginning second language learners. *Frontiers in Human Neuroscience* 7: 322.

Levänen, S., Uutela, K., Salenius, S., and Hari, R. (2001). Cortical representation of sign language: comparison of deaf signers and hearing non-signers. *Cerebral Cortex* 11 (6): 506–512.

MacSweeney, M., Woll, B., Campbell, R. et al. (2002). Neural systems underlying British Sign Language and audio-visual English processing in native users. *Brain* 125: 1583–1593.

MacSweeney, M., Capek, C.M., Campbell, R., and Woll, B. (2008a). The signing brain: the neurobiology of sign language. *Trends in Cognitive Science* 12: 432–440.

MacSweeney, M., Waters, D., Brammer, M.J. et al. (2008b). Phonological processing in deaf signers and the impact of age of first acquisition. *NeuroImage* 40: 1369–1379.

Marian, V. and Spivey, M.J. (2003). Competing activation in bilingual language processing: within-and between-language competition. *Bilingualism: Language and Cognition* 6: 97–115.

Martin-Rhee, M.M. and Bialystok, E. (2008). The development of two types of inhibitory control in monolingual and bilingual children. *Bilingualism: Language and Cognition* 11: 1–13.

McClelland, J. and Elman, J. (1986). The TRACE model of speech perception. *Cognitive Psychology,* 18: 1–86.

McGuire, P.K., Robertson, D., Thacker, A. et al. (1997). Neural correlates of thinking in sign language. *NeuroReport* 8: 695–699.

Mayberry, R.I. and Eichen, E.B. (1991). The long-lasting advantage of learning sign language in childhood: Another look at the critical period for language acquistion. *Journal of Memory and Language* 30 (1): 486.

Mayberry, R.I. and Fischer, S.D. (1989). Looking through phonological shape to lexical meaning: the bottleneck of nonnative sign language processing. *Memory and Cognition,* 17: 740–754.

Mayberry, R.I. and Lock, E. (2003). Age constraints on first versus second language acquisition: evidence for linguistic plasticity and epigenesis. *Brain and Language* 87: 369–384.

Mayberry, R.I., Lock, E., and Kazmi, H. (2002). Development: linguistic ability and early language exposure. *Nature* 417 (6884): 38.

McCullough, S. and Emmorey, K. (1997). Face processing by deaf ASL signers: evidence for expertise in distinguishing local features. *Journal of Deaf Studies and Deaf Education* 2 (4): 212–222.

McCullough, S., Emmorey, K., and Sereno, M. (2005). Neural organization for recognition of grammatical and emotional facial expressions in deaf ASL signers and hearing nonsigners. *Cognitive Brain Research* 22 (2): 193–203.

Meade, G., Midgley, K.J., Sevcikova Sehyr, Z. et al. (2017). Implicit co-activation of American Sign Language in deaf readers: an ERP study. *Brain and Language* 170: 50–61.

Meuter, R.F. and Allport, A. (1999). Bilingual language switching in naming: asymmetrical costs of language selection. *Journal of Memory and Language* 40 (1): 25–40.

Miller, J. (1982). Divided attention: evidence for coactivation with redundant signals. *Cognitive Psychology* 14 (2): 247.

Mitchell, R.E. and Karchmer, M.A. (2004). Chasing the mythical ten percent: parental hearing status of deaf and hard of hearing students in the United States. *Sign Language Studies* 4 (2): 138–163.

Mitterer, H. and McQueen, J.M. (2009). Foreign subtitles help but native-language subtitles harm foreign speech perception. *PLoS One* 4 (11): e7785.

Morford, J.P., Wilkinson, E., Villwock, A. et al. (2011). When deaf signers read English: do written words activate their sign translations? *Cognition* 118 (2): 286–292.

Morford, J.P., Kroll, J.F., Piñar, P., and Wilkinson, E. (2014). Bilingual word recognition in deaf and hearing signers: effects of proficiency and language dominance on cross-language activation. *Second Language Research* 30 (2): 251–271.

Morford, J.P., Occhino-Kehoe, C., Pinar, P. et al. (2017). The time course of cross-language activation in deaf ASL–English bilinguals. *Bilingualism: Language and Cognition* 20 (2): 337–350.

Morgan, G. and Woll, B. (eds.) (2002). *Directions in sign Language Acquisition.* Amsterdam, The Netherlands: John Benjamins.

Neuroth-Gimbrone, C. and Logiodic, C.M. (1992). A cooperative bilingual language program for deaf adolescents. *Language Studies* 74: 79–91.

Neville, H.J., Bavelier, D., Corina, D. et al. (1998). Cerebral organization for language in deaf and hearing subjects: biological constraints and effects of experience. *Proceeding of the National Acadamy of Science* 95: 922–929.

Neville, H.J. and Lawson, D. (1987). Attention to central and peripheral visual space in a movement detection task: an event-related potential and behavioral study. II. Congenitally deaf adults. *Brain Research* 405 (2): 268–283.

Newman, A.J., Bavelier, D., Corina, D. et al. (2002). A critical period for right hemisphere recruitment in American Sign Language processing. *Nature Neuroscience* 5 (1): 76–80.

Ormel, E. and Giezen, M. (2014). Bimodal bilingual cross-language interaction: pieces of the puzzle. In: *Bilingualism and Bilingual Deaf Education* (ed. M. Marschark, G. Tang and H. Knoors), 74–101. Oxford, UK: Oxford University Press.

Ormel, E., Hermans, D., Knoors, H., and Verhoeven, L. (2012). Cross-language effects in written word recognition: the case of bilingual deaf children. *Bilingualism: Language and Cognition* 15 (2): 288–303.

Pfau, R. (2012). Manual communication systems: evolution and variation. In: *Sign Language. An International Handbook* (ed. R. Pfau, M. Steinbach and B. Woll), 513–551. Berlin, Germany: Mouton de Gruyter.

Perani, D. and Abutalebi, J. (2005). Neural basis of first and second language processing. *Current Opinion of Neurobiology,* 15: 202–206.

Perani, D. and Abutalebi, J. (2015). Bilingualism, dementia, cognitive and neural reserve. *Current Opinion in Neurology* 28: 618–625.

Perani, D., Abutalebi, J., Paulesu, E. et al. (2003). The role of age of acquisition and language usage in early, high-proficient bilinguals: an fMRI study during verbal fluency. *Human Brain Mapping* 19 (3): 170–182.

Petitto, L.A. (1994). Are signed languages 'real' languages? Evidence from American Sign Language and Langue des Signes Québecoise. *Signpost (International Quarterly of Sign Linguistics Association)* 7 (3): 1–10.

Petitto, L.A., Zatorre, R.J., Gauna, K. et al. (2000). Speech-like cerebral activity in profoundly deaf people pro- cessing signed languages: implications for the neural basis of human language. *Proceedings of the National Academy of Science* 97: 13961–13966.

Petitto, L.A., Katerelos, M., Levy, B.G. et al. (2001). Bilingual signed and spoken language acquisition from birth: implications for the mechanisms underlying early bilingual language acquisition. *Journal of Child Language* 28: 453–496.

Pizer, G., Walters, K., and Meier, R.P. (2013). 'We communicated that way for a reason': language practices and language ideologies among hearing adults whose parents are deaf. *Journal of Deaf Studies and Deaf Education* 18: 75–92.

Poizner, H., Klima, E.S., and Bellugi, U. (1987). *What the Hands Reveal about the Brain. MIT press Series on Issues in the Biology of Language and Cognition.* Cambridge, MA: The MIT Press.

Pyers, J.E., Gollan, T.H., and Emmorey, K. (2009). Bimodal bilinguals reveal the source of tip-of-the-tongue states. *Cognition* 112: 323–329.

Pyers, J.E. and Emmorey, K. (2008). The face of bimodal bilingualism: grammatical markers in American Sign Language are produced when bilinguals speak to English monolinguals. *Psychological Science* 19: 531–535.

Rayner, K. and Clifton, C. (2009). Language processing in reading and speech perception is fast and incremental: implications for event-related potential research. *Biological Psychology* 80: 4–9.

Reilly, J.S., McIntire, M., and Bellugi, U. (1990). Faces: the relationship between language and affect. In: *From Gesture to Language in Hearing and Deaf Children* (ed. V. Volterra and C. Erting), 128–141. New York, NY: Springer-Verlag.

San Jose-Robertson, L., Corina, D.P., Ackerman, D. et al. (2004). Neural systems for sign language production: mechanisms supporting lexical selection, phonological encoding, and articulation. *Human Brain Mapping* 23 (3): 156–167.

Sandler, W. and Lillo-Martin, D. (2006). *Sign Language and Linguistic Universals.* Cambridge, UK: Cambridge University Press.

Sandler, W., Meir, I., Padden, C., and Aronoff, M. (2005). The emergence of grammar in a new sign language. *Proceedings of the National Academy of Sciences* 102 (7): 2661–2665.

Shook, A. and Marian, V. (2012). Bimodal bilinguals co-activate both languages during spoken comprehension. *Cognition* 124: 314–324.

Shook, A. and Marian, V. (2013). The bilingual language interaction network for comprehension of speech. *Bilingualism: Language and Cognition* 16: 304–324.

Söderfeldt, B., Ronnberg, J., and Risberg, J. (1994). Regional cerebral blood-flow in sign language users. *Brain and Language* 46: 59–68.

Söderfeldt, B., Ingvar, M., Rönnberg, J. et al. (1997). Signed and spoken language perception studied by positron emission tomography. *Neurology* 49: 82–87.

Sutton-Spence, R. and Woll, B. (1999). *The linguistics of British Sign Language: An introduction.* Cambridge, UK/New York, NY: Cambridge University Press.

Thierry, G. and Wu, Y.J. (2007). Brain potentials reveal unconscious translation during foreign language comprehension. *Proceedings of the National Academy of Sciences* 104 (30): 12530–12535.

Thompson, R.L., Emmorey, K., and Gollan, T. (2005). Tip-of-the-fingers experiences by ASL signers: insights into the organization of a sign-based lexicon. *Psychological Science* 16 (11): 856–860.

Thompson, R. L., & Langdon, C. (2017). Cross-modal bilingual activation in ASL signers: The role of language experience. Architectures and mechanisms of language processing (AMLaP, 2017), Lancaster University, England.

Todd, J.W. (1912). Reaction to multiple stimuli. In: *Archives of Psychology, 25.* New York, NY: Science Press.

Van Hell, J.G. and Dijkstra, T. (2002). Foreign language knowledge can influence native language performance in exclusively native contexts. *Psychonomic Bulletin & Review* 9: 780–789.

Van Hell, J.G. and Tanner, D. (2012). Second language proficiency and cross-language lexical activation. *Language Learning* 62: 148–171.

Villameriel, S., Dias, P., Costello, B., and Carreiras, M. (2016). Cross-language and cross-modal activation in hearing bimodal bilinguals. *Journal of Memory and Language* 87: 59–70.

Vinson, D.P., Thompson, R.L., Skinner, R. et al. (2010). The hands and mouth do not always slip together in British Sign Language: dissociating articulatory channels in the lexicon. *Psychological Science* 21: 1158–1167.

Vogt-Svendsen, M. (2001). A comparison of mouth gestures and mouthings in Norwegian Sign Language (NSL). In: *The Hands are the Head of the Mouth: The Mouth as Articulator in Sign Languages* (ed. P. Boyes-Braem and R.L. Sutton-Spence), 9–40. Hamburg, Germany: Signum Press.

Weisberg, J., McCullough, S., and Emmorey, K. (2015). Simultaneous perception of a spoken and a signed language: the brain basis of ASL-English code-blends. *Brain and Language* 147: 96–106.

Woll, B. and MacSweeney, M. (2016). Let's not forget the role of deafness in sign/speech bilingualism. *Bilingualism: Language and Cognition* 19 (2): 253–255.

Woll, B. and Sieratzki, J.S. (1998). Echo phonology: signs of a link between gesture and speech. *Behavioral & Brain Sciences* 21: 531–532.

Zeshan, U. (2003). Indo-Pakistani sign language grammar: a typological outline. *Sign Language Studies* 3 (2): 157–212.

Zou, L., Abutalebi, J., Zinszer, B. et al. (2012a). Second language experience modulates functional brain network for the native language production in bimodal bilinguals. *NeuroImage* 62 (3): 1367–1375.

Zou, L., Ding, G., Abutalebi, J. et al. (2012b). Structural plasticity of the left caudate in bimodal bilinguals. *Cortex* 48: 1197–1206.

Index

Page references to Figures are followed by the letter 'f' , while references to Tables are followed by the letter 't'. References to Notes are indicated by the page number followed by 'n' and the Note number.

Aachen aphasia test, 534

Abutalebi, J., xxxviii, 22, 40, 131, 134, 135, 137, 139, 140, 205, 219, 220, 224, 225, 234, 244, 258, 265–266, 365, 450–452, 455, 456, 667, 668

AC model *see* adaptive control (AC) model

ACC (anterior cingulate cortex) *see* anterior cingulate cortex (ACC)

accent, 137, 148
  age of acquisition (AoA), 659
  errors, 605
  in L2 speech, 201, 472, 473
    late learning, 201, 467
  native-like, 234, 238, 659
  rating of, 150t, 152t, 158, 166

Acenas, L.-A.R., 675, 676n1

acquisition of language, 23
  see also under adulthood; language; native language (L1); second language (L2)/ second language acquisition (SLA)
  and ability, 257–267
  age of acquisition (AoA) *see* age of acquisition (AoA)
  language dominance, 266
  proficiency, 259–261t, 263–266
  third language/LN, 395–396

activations
  "abstract" conceptual level, 42n5
  bilingual, 758–764
    during comprehension, 759–760
    during production, 760–761
    and role of experience, 761–764
    speech-sign activation, 758–759
  brain tissue, 8
  categories, 35
  cerebral, 345–346
  false positives, 37
  fMRI data analysis, 37–39
  inhibition-related, 134
  language coactivations, 75, 77
  language mode model, in multilingualism, 8
  mapping, 38
  and variation studies, 37–38

AD *see* Alzheimer's disease (AD)

Adamou, E., 477

adaptive control (AC) model
  contexts and processes, 62–63
  neural correlates of language control, 63–64

adaptive control hypothesis, 450, 452, 488, 748

Adesope, O.O., 364

adjectives, 88, 433, 496, 514

adoptees, language forgetting in, 148–149
  see also forgotten languages, memory traces
  adults, 148, 156–157, 164–165, 166
  behavioural tasks, 159–162
  children, 148, 157
  fMRI studies, 156–157
adulthood
  see also OAs (older adults), learning in; YAs
    (younger adults), learning in
  acquired reading disorders in bilingual/
    biscriptal adults, 594–604
  brain
    adaptations and neurological indices of
      processing in SLA, 170–196
    anatomical changes in healthy ageing,
      410–411
    plasticity, 180–181
    real-time measures, 106–110
    structure and regions of interest in SLA,
      181–183
  fMRI studies 156–157, 180–181
  language forgetting in adoptees, 156–157,
    164–165, 166
  older adults, school-age children and null
    results, 716–717
  second language acquisition, xl, 170–196,
    408–426
    adult adoptees, 148, 164–165, 166
    brain structure and regions of interest,
      181–183
    critical period hypothesis, evidence base,
      171–176
    designing L2 experiences to enhance
      older adults' L2 learning, 417–419
    real-time brain measures, 106–110
    savings paradigm, 164, 166
  younger adults and null results, bilingual
    advantage debate, 715–716
African-American English, 470
Afrikaans-English bilinguals, 637, 638
age and language development, 414–416
age of acquisition (AoA)
  see also acquisition of language
  accent, 659
  bilingualism 51, 57, 68, 501
  and cerebral cortex, 233
  cortical representation, 257–263, 266–267
  functional magnetic resonance imaging
    (fMRI), 359–361t, 378

impairment, 539
multilingualism, 657, 658–661
  multilingual processing, factors affecting,
    377–378
  neuroimaging studies, 127, 129, 138, 139
neurobiology, 417
and proficiency, 259–261t, 266–267
speech-sign bilingualism, 756–757
age of onset (AoO), 171, 620
age regression hypnosis, 147–148,
  154–156, 165
ageing
  acquisition of language *see* age of
    acquisition (AoA)
  bilingualism and ageing brain, 244–245
  and dementia, 614–615
  healthy, brain-based cognitive-linguistic
    changes in, 409–414
    anatomical, 410–411
    cognitive, 411–413
    linguistic, 413–414
  individual differences, cortical
    representation, 255–256
  normal, pedagogical approaches, 417–418
  protection against age-related cognitive
    decline, 139–140
Aglioti, S., 455, 545
Akbari, M., 542
Akimoto, Y., 346
Alain, C., 412
alexia, 594, 595, 596–597t, 599, 601
Alladi, S., xlii, 612, 613, 615, 616, 620, 621
Allport, A., 78, 491
Altarriba, J., xxxix, xl, 318, 319, 401–403
Altmann, G.T.M., 89, 90f
Alzheimer's disease (AD), xlii, 245, 268,
  413, 580
  executive control (EC), 499, 500
  multilingualism and dementia, 609,
    611, 616
American Sign Language (ASL), 28, 57, 691,
  759, 760
amygdala, 323, 346
Anderson, J.A.E., 245, 620
Anderson, S., *A-Morphous Morpholoy*, 299
Andreasen, N.C., 632
Andrews, E., xxxvii, 22, 23, 36, 37, 39, 43n14
angular gyrus, 131, 282
ANKK1 Taq1A polymorphism, 669

Ansaldo, A.I., 538
ANT (attentional network task), 686, 692, 693
antagonistic phenomena, aphasia, 544
anterior cingulate cortex (ACC)
  see also cerebral cortex
  bilingual models, 59, 61, 66
  brain structure and regions of interest, 182
  developmental perspective, in multilingualism, 661
  humour perception, 345
  language-switching networks, 129, 130f
  and plasticity, 233–234, 264, 667
anterior superior temporal lobe, 20
anterior temporal cortex (ATC), 344
anterior temporal lobe (ATL), 182, 234
anterior thalamic radiation (ATR), 185, 241, 242
antisaccade tasks, 692, 693
Antoniou, M., 409, 621
Aparicio, X., 59
aphasia
  see also neurodegenerative disease
  bilingual, xli–xlii, 456–458, 554–560
  and dementia, 609, 613
  language impairment in *see* impairment, language
  lesions, 533–539, 543–546, 565
    bilingual, 457, 557–559
    primary progressive aphasia (PPA), 573, 583, 584
  multilingual, xli, 533–552
  primary progressive aphasia (PPA), 572–591
  psychotic, 543
  and stroke, 616
  sudden-onset, 573, 576, 582, 584, 585
applied linguistics, 12
Arabic, 599, 600, 603
Archila-Suerte, P., 378, 662–663
arcuate fasciculus (AF), 240
Aronoff, M., 299
articulatory suppression, 688, 689
artificial grammar learning (AGL), 186
As, A., 154
Asperger's syndrome, 671
assessment
  see also measurement
  dynamic, 15

multilingualism, xxxvii
  aphasia, 533–535
  proficiency testing, 36
  publication bias, reassessing, 741–742, 743–744t, 745
  self-ratings, 14
associated use networks, 10
associative learning processes, 203
asymmetrical costs, 53, 60, 78, 111
asymmetrical mappings, bilingual memory, 394–395
ATL (anterior temporal lobe), 182, 234
ATR (anterior thalamic radiation), 185, 241, 242
Attardo, S., 340, 341
attention
  see also attentional states; language control
  versus awareness, 419
  changes in, 413
  disengagement of, 718–720, 721t, 722
  focus of, 129, 432, 435, 437, 438, 687
  selective, 717–718
  supervisory attentional system (SAS), 53, 61
attentional network task (ANT), 686, 692, 693
attentional states
  code switching, 432–435, 439, 440, 441n2
  dissociable, 440
  dynamics of in a speech act, 436–439
  internal orientation, 436
  and language control, xl, 427–446
  metastability, 437–440
  in monolingualism, 496
  neural signatures, topics with, 434–436
  review, 438–440
  signatures, 433–436
  types, 441n5
attrition, language, 5–6
Au, J., 158
Au, T.K., 158, 160, 162
autobiographical memory, 315
automaticity, 25
awareness, 419
axial diffusivity (AD), 239
axon bodies, 181
Ayçiçeği-Dinn, A., 325
Azim, E., 345

Babcock, L., 380, 696, 697
Baddeley, A., 412, 687, 688
Bahrick, H., 5, 163

Bak, T.H., xlii, 614–615, 617, 620, 621
Baldeweg, T., 255–256
Bambini, V., 517
Barenholtz, E., 399
Bartolo, A., 345
basal ganglia (BG)
  aphasia, 545
  bilingual language use affecting, 65
  conditional routing (CR) model, 64
  language-switching networks, 129, 130f
  neural basis of BLC and EC, 451
  and plasticity, 237, 238
  schizophrenia, bilinguals with, 641
  subthalamic nucleus (STN), 135, 136
basal language centres, 31
basic interpersonal communication skills
  (BICS), 662
Basque Center on Cognition, Brain and
  Language (BCBL), 716
Basque-Spanish bilinguals, 673
Bauer, L.M., 319
Baumeister, J.C., 320, 321
Baus, C., xl, 284–286, 289
Bayes Factor, 704, 707, 708, 716, 725n5
Beaton, A.A., 600–601, 603
Beatty-Martínez, A.L., xli, 112, 437, 478
Beck, S., 512
Becker, M., 243, 690, 696, 697
Becker, T.M., 66
behavioural methodologies/tasks
  emotion/emotion concepts, processing and
    use, 314–319
  forgotten languages, memory traces, 157–162
  memory and L2 studies, 398–399
Beland, R., 599, 601
Bell, N.D., 347–348
Benati, A., 305
Berken, J.A., 234, 238, 243
Berns, M., 14
BG *see* basal ganglia (BG)
BIA-d model *see under* bilingual interactive
  activation (BIA) models
BIA+ model *see under* bilingual interactive
  activation (BIA) models
Bialystok, E., 7, 174–175, 409, 610–614, 704,
  705f, 708, 716, 717, 720, 723, 750
bidirectional cognate facilitation effects, 77
bilaterality of language, 39–40
bilingual advantage debate, xliii, 701–753

colour-shape tasks, 736, 737
confounds
  and ANCOVA, 712–713, 725n3
  as nominal categories, 714–715
  potential, measured continuously, 713–714
evidence, 701–735
  ANOVAs, 715, 724
  Bayes Factor, 704, 707, 708, 716, 725n5
  boxplots, 705f
  'ceiling' hypothesis, 716
  conflict resolution, 707
  congruency sequence effects (CSEs),
    719–720, 721t
  counterarguments, 715–717
  databases, 703
  disengagement of attention, 718–720,
    721t, 722
  global RT, monitoring as reflected in,
    706–708
  latency measures, 703
  meta-analyses, 702–703, 708
  monitoring, 706–708
  null results, 715, 716
  PET-PEESE method, 706, 707
  quantity of, 702–712
  Raven's scores, 713, 715
  regression, 724
  switching, 709–712
  trials, 707
  working memory (WM), 708
executive functioning (EF), 701, 702, 713,
  724, 725n4
flanker task, 714, 716, 717, 719, 723, 741
  quantity of evidence, 703, 704, 706, 708
general fluid (gF) intelligence, 702, 712, 715,
  725n3, 725n4
inhibition, 703–704, 705f, 706
interactions, interpreting, 715
methodological/statistical issues, 712–715
publication bias, 736–753
questions, 722–725
reformulations
  disengagement of attention, 718–720,
    721t, 722
  questions, 722–725
  selective attention, 717–718
Stimulus-Response (S-R) rule, 707
Stroop task, 214, 703, 706, 713, 715, 716
switching, 709–712

bilingual aphasia, xli–xlii
  see also aphasia; multilingual aphasia;
        primary progressive aphasia (PPA)
  bilingual aphasia test (BAT), 534–535
  and executive control, 456–458
  generalization effects, 561–562
  impairment in
    language and control, 554–556
    lesion factors influencing, 457, 557–559
    premorbid language factors influencing,
        556–557
  language recovery in, 559–560
  neuroimaging studies, 558, 563–564
  premorbidly balanced bilinguals, 554, 555
  recovery and rehabilitation patterns
    efficacy and generalization effect,
        560–563
    language recovery, 559–560
    neuroimaging evidence of treatment-
        induced recovery, 563–564
    treatment-induced recovery, 560–564
  treatment-induced recovery
    efficacy and generalization effect,
        560–563
    neuroimaging studies, 563–564
bilingual interactive activation (BIA) models,
        48, 49, 50f
  BIA-d model, 51–52
    decreased excitatory form-level
        connections, 58–59
    increased inhibition between word
        forms, 59
    increased L2 proficiency strengthening
        connections to the semantic store, 59
  BIA+ model, 49–51, 60, 393
    inhibitory control model compared, 53
    key regions of interest, 55–56t
    lexical production, 76
    neural evidence for
      BIA-d model, 58–59
      inhibitory control (IC) model, 60–62
      integrated L1-L2 lexical networks, 54, 57
      non-selective lexical access, 57–58
    repetition enhancement effects, 57
    word recognition, 92n1
bilingual language control (BLC), 447, 448
  deficits, 454–460
    bilingual aphasia *see* bilingual aphasia
    neurodegenerative disease, 458–460

neural basis, 451–453
  overlap of mechanisms with EC, 460
bilingual models
  adaptive control (AC) model, 62–64
  bilingual interactive activation (BIA)
      models *see* bilingual interactive
      activation (BIA) models
  conditional routing (CR) model, 64–66
  N400 (ERP component), effects of, 58–60
  and neurocognition of multiple languages,
      xxxvii, 48–74
  nodes, 49–51, 53, 68–69
  revised hierarchical model (RHM), 51, 52
bilingual simple recurrent model (BSRN), 52
bilingual single network (BSN), 52
bilingual word production *see* word
      production, bilingual
bilingualism
  see also monolingualism; multilingualism;
      Russian-English bilinguals; second
      language (L2)/second language
      acquisition (SLA)
  acquired reading disorders in bilingual/
      biscriptal adults, 594–604
  advantages, 494–498
    cognition, 497–498
    component language structures,
        496–497
    linguistic attentional control, cognitive
        and L1, 496–497
    metalinguistics and grammaticality,
        495–496
  age of acquisition (AoA) 51, 57, 68, 501
  aphasia *see* bilingual aphasia
  basal ganglia, bilingual language use
      affecting, 65
  bilingual language control (BLC), 447, 448,
      451–460
  bilinguals compared with monolinguals,
      225, 450, 675, 708, 736, 762
    bilingual advantage debate, 741, 742
    and dementia, 615–617
  brain of bilinguals, 11
    in ageing, 244–245
    bilingual brain, translating and
        interpreting in, 485–507
    cortical connections, 65–66
    differences between monolinguals and
        bilinguals, 279–280

effects of bilingual language use on brain
structure, 67–68
effects on grey matter, 232–238
effects on white matter, 239–242
implications of bilingualism for
translating and interpreting, 490–493
networks underlying bilingual language
processing, 66–67
neural bases of cognitive control, 54–62
neural organization of language centres/
language-related areas, 34
primary progressive aphasia (PPA),
575–576
research limitations, 22
speech-sign bilingualism, 754
translating and interpreting in, 485–507
in children, 103, 239, 314, 495–497, 662–663,
675, 716
balanced or unbalanced, 663
cognates, 81
and cognition, 188, 326, 409, 620, 716
advantages of, 497–498
models, 69
speech-sign bilingualism, 772–774
cognitive control
bilingual aphasia, 555, 564
bilingual brain, translating and
interpreting in, 489
neural bases in bilingualism, 54–62
and cognitive flexibility, 666–667
compound, xl, 303, 389, 390, 391
considered the exception in the Western
world, 3
coordinate, xl, 389, 390, 391
cortical stimulation, in bilinguals, 604
and dementia, 610–613, 620–621
questioning effects of bilingualism on,
617–620
disadvantages, 222, 500
dual-coding theory, 392
effects on grey matter, 232–238
cerebellum, 238
cerebral cortex, 233–235
subcortical structures, 235–238
ERP studies on bilingual non-literal
language processing, 518–521
executive control, effect on, 66
immersive, 236, 237f, 239
individual differences in, 68–69

language organization *see* language
organization
language use, variability in and
implications for language processing,
475–478
late acquisition, 35, 126–127, 186, 258, 262,
576, 617, 659
learning and memory, 389–407
conceptual meaning versus lexical
representations, 389
distinguishing memory models, 399–403
L2 studies, methodological
considerations for, 396–399
learning of languages in bilingualism,
389–407
theories and models, 390–396
and multilingual aphasia, 533
neural bases of cognitive control in, 54–62
increased inhibition between word
forms, 59
increased L2 proficiency strengthening
connections to the semantic store, 59
integrated L1-L2 lexical networks, 54, 57
key regions of interest (BLA and IC
models), 55–56t
non-selective lexical access, 57–58
neurocognition of multiple languages,
bilingual models for *see* bilingual
models
neuroplasticity, 184–188, 486
neuroprotective effects, 498–499
neutrality, 500
null results, 715–717
picture-naming tasks, 636, 758
aphasia, 554, 555, 557, 563, 564
speech-sign bilingualism, 762, 767, 768,
770
word production, 216, 217, 219, 225
primary progressive aphasia (PPA), 577,
578–579t, 580
publication bias, 738–740
and schizophrenia *see* schizophrenia,
bilinguals with
selective versus non-selective access, 11
sentence processing, 467–484
simultaneous learning of two languages,
258, 262
simultaneous versus sequential
bilinguals, 236–237, 500

bilingualism (*cont'd*)
  specific groups of bilinguals
    Afrikaans-English, 637, 638
    Basque-Spanish, 673
    Cantonese-English, 149, 669
    Cantonese/Mandarin-Dutch, 161
    Catalan-Spanish, 498
    Chinese-English, 79, 302, 321, 322,
      376, 672
    Deaf ASL-English, 766, 768, 773–774
    Dutch-English, 79, 81, 400, 711
    English-French, 186, 718–719
    English-Spanish, 57, 58, 59, 320, 399
    Flemish-French, 216
    French-Chinese, 157
    French-Dutch, 458
    German-Dutch, 163
    German-English, 84, 86
    German-French, 219
    German-Spanish, 322
    Japanese-American English, 154–155
    Korean-Chinese, 381
    Korean-Dutch, 161
    Korean-English, 375–376
    Mandarin-English, 216
    Mongolian-Chinese, 603
    Russian-English, 59, 149, 155, 557
    Spanish-Catalan, xxxix, 216–217, 267,
      284–285, 292, 316
    Spanish-English, 57, 58, 59, 81, 88, 219,
      316, 320, 323, 557
    Spanish-German, 322
    Swedish-English, 154
    Swedish-Korean, 160, 161
    Welsh-English, 434
  speech networks, 121–123
  speech-sign *see* speech-sign bilingualism
  switching and interference, control of,
    487–490
  'tip-of-the tongue' (TOT) phenomenon, 675
  variable input, role in language processing,
    471–475
  word production *see* word production,
    bilingual
bimodal bilinguals, 757, 759, 766, 767–768,
  771–773
biomarkers, 617
biphasic effect, 180, 515, 520
Birdsong, D., 40

Blackburn, A.M., xxxvii–xxxix
Blanco-Elorrieta, E., 64
BLC (bilingual language control) *see* bilingual
  language control (BLC)
Bley-Vroman, R., 415
Bloch, C., 126–127, 378, 660, 666
blocked-language switching paradigms,
  78–79
blood-oxygen-level dependent (BOLD)
  response, 34, 42n8, 67, 87
Blumenfeld, H.K., 90–91
Bock, J.K., 83, 84, 85
Bögels, S., 430
BOLD signal *see* blood-oxygen-level
  dependent (BOLD) response
Bolger, D.J., 592
Boliek, C.A., 241
Bolinger, D., 23, 24, 42n6
Booj, G., *Construction Morphology*, 299
Boston diagnostic aphasia examination
  (BDAE), 534
Bowden, H.W., 109
Bowers, J., 158
Bowers, J.S., 316
brain
  see also basal ganglia; brain basis; Broca's
    area; neurobiology; Wernicke's area;
    *specific areas, such as inferior fronto-
    occipital fasciculus (IFOF)*
  adaptations in adulthood second language
    acquisition, 170–196
  adult
    adaptations and neurological indices of
      processing, 170–196
    anatomical changes in healthy ageing,
      410–411
    plasticity, 180–181
    real-time measures, 106–110
    structure and regions of interest in SLA,
      181–183
  anatomical changes, in healthy ageing,
    410–411
  of bilinguals, 11
    in ageing, 244–245
    cortical connections, 65–66
    differences between monolinguals and
      bilinguals, 279–280
    effects of bilingual language use on brain
      structure, 67–68

effects on grey matter, 232–238
effects on white matter, 239–242
networks underlying bilingual language processing, 66–67
neural bases of cognitive control, 54–62
neural organization of language centres/language-related areas, 34
primary progressive aphasia (PPA), 575–576
research limitations, 22
speech-sign bilingualism, 754
translating and interpreting, 485–507
cerebellum, 238
cerebral cortex, 233–235
differences between monolinguals and bilinguals, 279–280
and endogenous factors influencing learning, 280–291
frontal lobe, 19
grey matter *see* grey matter (GM)
imaging studies *see* neuroimaging studies
knowledge of, xliii
language as separate entities in, 11–13
and learning
    effect of language learning, 184–188
    endogenous factors influencing, 280–291
of monolinguals, compared with bilinguals, 279–280
of multilinguals, 9–11, 22
    effects on grey matter, 232–238
    effects on white matter, 239–242
    executive function/metacognition, 365
    neuroimaging studies *see* neuroimaging studies
    plasticity/neuroplasticity *see* plasticity/neuroplasticity
    real-time measures, 100–120
native-like activity, 109, 177–178, 238
networks underlying bilingual language processing, 66–67
neurocognitive consequences of interpreting, 685–700
neuronal organization, orthography effects *see* orthography effects
plasticity *see* plasticity/neuroplasticity
primary progressive aphasias, neurological basis, 583–585
real-time responses *see* real-time measures of brain, in multilingualism

remapping of language in, 19–22
schizophrenia and bilingualism, neurological features underlying, 626, 627–630t, 631
structural connectivity, 280
structure
    bilingual language use, effects on, 67–68
    and regions of interest in L2 acquisition, 181–183
    subcortical structures, 20, 235–238
    translation of humour in, 340–342, 347
    white matter *see* white matter (WM)
brain basis
    L2 grammar, 202–204
    L2 lexico-semantics, 204–206
    L2 phonology, 200–202
    language control, 206
brain stimulation studies, 452
Branigan, H.P., 85
Branzi, F.M., 63
Braver, T., 459
Briellmann, R.S., 127, 128f
Bright, P., xxxix–xl
British Sign Language (BSL), 755, 756, 765f
Broca's area
    BA44 and BA45, 761
    brain anatomical changes, 410
    cognitive neuroscience, 19, 20, 22, 28, 37, 41n1, 41n2
    developmental perspective, in multilingualism, 661
    language organization, 203
    speech-sign bilingualism, 761
Brodmann area, 545, 671
Broersma, M., 14
Brouwer, H., 515
Brown, M., 626
Bultena, S., 476
Burgaleta, M., xxxix, 221, 236, 238, 290
Button, K.S., 691

Cabeza, R., 411
Cacciari, C., 510, 516
Caffarra, S., 468
Cage, S., 158
Calabria, M., xl, 455
Calandri, I., 585
Caldwell-Harris, C.L., 321, 325

Calvin, W.H., 21, 41n1
Calvo, A., 750
Calvo, N., 409
Campbell, D.W., 346
Canal, P., xli, 516
Cantonese-English bilinguals, 149, 669
Cantonese-English-Mandarin trilinguals, 455
Cantonese-Mandarin-Dutch trilinguals, 161
Cao, F., 604
Capek, C.M., 760
Caplan, D., 375, 376
Caramazza, A., 24, 42n5
Cardoso, W., 381
Cargnelutti, E., xli
Carlson, S.M., 714
Carrasco-Ortiz, H., 109–110
Carreiras, M., 516
Carrillo, D.F., 327
Carrol, G., 513
Catalan-Spanish bilinguals, 498
category-switching, 60, 64, 113
Cattaneo, G., 459
caudate nucleus/left caudate nucleus (LCN), 236–238, 245, 497
CDST (complex dynamic systems theory), 9, 13, 15
CEFR *see* Common European Framework of Reference for Languages (CEFR)
central alexia, 594
cerebellum, 238
    left, 345
cerebral cortex, 233–235, 584, 661
cerebrospinal fluid (CSF), 617
cerebrovascular accident (CVA)/stroke
    and aphasia, 616
    and dementia, 615–616
    post-stroke cognitive impairment, 616
    and primary progressive aphasia (PPA), 573, 582–585
    and reading disorders, acquired, 595, 599, 600
Chai, X.J., 665
Chan, Y.-C., 346
Chapman, J.P., 712
Chee, M.W.L., 216
Chelsea (linguistic isolate), 173
Chen, S.H., 314, 323
Chertkow, H., 612, 613
Chiaro, D., 341, 348

children
    see also bilingualism; second language (L2)/
        second language acquisition (SLA)
    adoptees, language forgetting in, 157
    bilingual, 103, 239, 314, 495–497, 662–663, 675, 716–717
        balanced or unbalanced, 663
    linguistic isolates in, 173–174
    monolingual, 174
    multilingual, 106, 137, 263
    overhearing, 148, 157, 158–159, 165
    school-age, and bilingual advantage debate, 716–717
    second language learners, 163–164
Chincotta, D., 689
Chinese-English bilinguals, 79, 302, 321, 322, 376, 672
Choi, H.P., 714
Chomsky, N., *Syntactic Structures*, xxxix, 299
Christianson, K., 375, 376
Christoffels, I.K., 60, 223, 689, 711
Cieślicka, A.B., 512, 513, 520
circumlocutions, 31, 32f, 33f
Cisneros, S., 113
Clahsen, H., 380
Claussenius-Kalman, H.L., xlii
clinical settings, applied work in, 324–328
    interpreters, use of, 326–327
cluster-based inference, 37
code-blending, 769–771, 772
code switching, xli, xlii, 6, 12, 86, 188, 268, 325, 403
    see also language switching; switching
    articulating two languages simultaneously, 771–772
    bilingual models, 62, 63
    cognitive flexibility, xlii, 667–670
    density, 188, 268, 450
        bilingual models, 63, 64f
        developmental perspective, in multilingualism, 668, 673
        language control and attention, 433, 434, 437–440, 441n3
    existence of, questioning, 12
    individual differences, 668–670
    language control and attention, 432–435, 439, 440, 441n2
    learning and memory, 389, 391

Russian-English, 155
sentence processing, bilingual, 469, 475, 477, 478
Coderre, E., 453
Coggins, P.E., 239, 240
cognate words, 77, 78, 91, 223
cognition, xxxiv, xxxvi, 10, 83, 106, 135, 188, 199, 270, 324
  and bilingualism, 326, 409, 620, 716
    advantages of, 497–498
    models, 69
    speech-sign bilingualism, 772–774
  and brain damage, 557
  disembodied, 42n5
  domain general, 479
  embodied, 22, 24–26, 39, 42n3, 42n5
  higher-level, 364, 661, 665
  and language, 9, 31, 410, 626, 632
  longitudinal studies, 497, 619
  and multilingualism, 244, 246, 307, 357, 365
    neurocognitive effects, 669, 675
cognitive/academic language proficiency (CALP), 662
cognitive control
  see also neurocognition, multiple languages
  and articulation, 137–138
  bilingualism
    bilingual aphasia, 555, 564
    bilingual brain, translating and interpreting in, 489
    neural bases in, 54–62
  changes, in healthy ageing, 412–413
  network, 130f
  neural bases in bilingualism, 54–62
    increased inhibition between word forms, 59
    increased L2 proficiency strengthening connections to the semantic store, 59
    integrated L1-L2 lexical networks, 54, 57
    key regions of interest (BLA and IC models), 55–56t
    non-selective lexical access, 57–58
cognitive control, neural bases in bilingualism
  see also bilingual interactive activation (BIA) models; inhibitory control (IC) model
cognitive flexibility, 658, 666–670
  and bilingualism, 666–667
  code switching, xlii, 667–668

developmental perspective, in multilingualism, 657, 667–668
  genetic basis, xlii
  and interpreting, 694–697
  and plasticity, 658, 676
  unanswered questions, 670
cognitive impairment
  mild cognitive impairment (MCI), 611
  with no dementia (CIND), 614
  post-stroke, 616
  vascular mild cognitive impairment (VaMCI), 615
cognitive linguistics, 23
cognitive neuroscience, 19–47
  bilaterality of language, 39–40
  evaluation, 40–41
  experimental design, 25
  imaging in cognitive neurolinguistic research, 27–34
    second language acquisition (SLA), 23, 35, 36, 39
  intermediate time frame, 25
  limitations of classic model, 19–20
  localization/explanation fallacy, 20–21
  longitudinal studies, 36, 39, 41
  mindsharing, 25–26
  and multilingualism, 19–47
    multilingualism as the norm, 22
  names of regions, 22
  variation studies, 37–38, 40–41
cognitive overload, 689
cognitive reserve (CR), 413, 615, 617, 621, 674
cognitive slowing, 411
Colbeck, K.L., 316
Collins, L., 381
Colomé, A., 78
colour
  colour-coded functions, 30f
  colour naming, 316
  colour-shape tasks
    bilingual advantage debate, 736, 737
    bivalent, 697
    interpreting, 686, 695–697
    switching, 488, 709, 710t, 736, 737
    univalent, 696, 697
  colour-word tasks, 316, 692, 709
    Stroop, 455, 703, 714, 716
  hot colours, 240f
Coltheart, M., 300

Common European Framework of Reference for Languages (CEFR), 13, 36
communities of practice, 23–25, 41n3
competitive queuing (CQ), 429
complementarity principle, 8
complex dynamic systems theory (CDST), 9, 13, 15
compositional analysis, 516
compound bilingualism, xl, 303, 389, 390, 391
compound words, 202, 299, 301–302, 303
comprehension
  bilingual activation during, 759–760
  and emotion word processing, 317–319
  event-related potentials (ERPs), xxxvii
  idioms, 510
  lexical, 80–81
  metaphors, 510, 517
  priming in, 86–87
  sentences, 35
  and speech production, 20, 35
computerized tomography (CT), 577, 616
conditional routing (CR) model, 64–66
  bilingual language use affecting basal ganglia, 65
  cortical connections, effects of bilingualism on, 65–66
confederate-scripting technique, 85, 86
confidence, versus performance, xl
configuration hypothesis, 510, 516
confounds
  and ANCOVA, 712–713, 725n3
  as nominal categories, 714–715
  potential, measured continuously, 713–714
congruency sequence effects (CSEs), 719–720, 721t
conjunction analysis, 61–62
connectionist models
  bilingual/multilingual memory, 392–394
  reading, 594, 604
Conrad, M., 322
consciousness, defining, 25
consonants, 280
Consonni, M., 205
contact, language
  measuring, 7–8
  role in multilingualism, 6
contingent negative variation (CNV), 105
convergence hypothesis, in PPA, 575, 576, 585, 586

conversation, xxxiv, xl, 7, 8, 62, 174, 268, 336, 477, 501, 517, 712, 773
  contexts, 435, 439, 441n3
  developmental perspective, in multilingualism, 662, 669
  face-to-face, 428
  fluency, 430
  language control and attention, 416, 427–433, 435–440, 441n3
  learning and memory, 391, 399
  multilingualism
    psycholinguistic research methods, 83, 86
    real-time measures of brain, 113, 114
  natural, 113, 477
  recording, 637
  schizophrenia, bilinguals with, 635, 637, 642
  speech acts, 428
  turn-taking, 429–430, 432, 433
Conway, A.R., 691
Cook, V., 9
coordinate bilingualism, xl, 389, 390, 391
Cop, U., 400–401
Corina, D.P., 27–28, 29, 31, 32f, 254, 761
corpus callosum (CC), 183, 239, 240, 242, 595
cortical atrophy, in PPA, 573–574, 584
cortical representation
  exposure to language, 267–268
  factors affecting, 252–276
  individual differences
    age, 255–256
    gender, 255
    genetics, 256–257
    verbal intelligence, 254–255
  language acquisition
    age of acquisition (AoA), 257–263
    fMRI studies, 259–261t, 263
    interaction of AoA and proficiency, 259–261t, 266–267
    language dominance, 266
    proficiency, 263–266
  language-and task-specific attributes, 253
  language environment and use, 268
  language experience, 267–268
  language modularity, 254
  language similarity, 253–254
  number of languages and neuroprotection, 268–269

overlap in during speech production, xxxviii–xxxix, 126–129
cortical stimulation, 10
  in bilinguals, 604
  direct, 29, 123
  intraoperative, 604
  mapping *see* cortical stimulation mapping (CSM)
  metacognition measurement, 362
cortical stimulation mapping (CSM), 27–29, 31, 32–33f
  data produced, 29
  electrodes, implanting of grids in initial surgery, 29, 30f
  epilepsy, 28
  error types
    circumlocutions, 31, 32f, 33f
    naming errors, 31, 32f
    neologisms, 31, 32f, 33f
    no-response errors, 29, 31, 32f, 33f
    performance errors, 31, 32f
    phonological paraphasias, 31, 32f
    semantic paraphasias, 31, 32f
  implications for understanding language representations in the brain, 28
  limitations, 29
  localization, 28, 29
  multilingual language control, 140
  reliability issues, 29
  and single-neuron mappings, 28
  verbal intelligence, 254
cortical surface area (CSA), 232
cortical thickness (CT), 232, 494
Costa, A., xl, 77, 222, 717, 725n6
costs
  asymmetrical, 53, 60, 78
  switching, 477, 669, 737
    asymmetrical, 78, 111
    behavioural, 53
    bilingual advantage debate, 711, 714
    cortical representation, 265
    interpreting and bilingual brain, 485, 488, 491–493
    language switching, 61, 82
    neuroimaging studies, 134, 135
    symmetrical, 53
Costumero, V., 66
Coughlin, C., 375
Coulson, S., 344, 517, 518

counselling, applied work, 324–328
Cowan, N., 686, 687
Cox, J.G., 415, 418
Cox proportional hazard regression models, nested, 618
CR model *see* conditional routing (CR) model
Craik, F.I., 611
Crane, P.K., 618
Crinion, J., 452
critical periods, second language learning, xxxviii, 414
  animal models, 278
  critical period hypothesis, evidence base, 170, 171–176
  event-related brain potentials (ERPs), use in language processing research, 177–178
  terminology, 189n1
  traditional interpretation of, 469
cross-language task performance and neuroplasticity, 486, 493–494
cross-sectional studies
  inflexion, 204
  second language acquisition, in adulthood, 185–186
CSM *see* cortical stimulation mapping (CSM)
culture
  cultural issues and culture-specific treatment strategies, 327–328
  interaction with language, 23
Cummine, J., 241
Cummins, J., 495
Cunnings, I., 376
Curtiss, S., 173–174
Cutler, A., 510, 511

Dai, E.Y.L., 542
Darò, V., 687
Dash, T., 457
data analysis, functional magnetic resonance imaging (fMRI), 37–39
Davidson, D., 43n13
Davies, C., 341–342
Davies, N.W., 600–601, 603
De Baene, W., 453
de Bleser, R., 216
de Bot, K., xxxvii, 11, 22, 27, 35, 163, 166
de Bruin, A., xliii, 134, 135, 740, 742
De Grauwe, S., 186

de Groot, A.M.B., 11
De Zulueta, F., 325
Deaf ASL-English bilinguals, 766, 768,
    773–774
declarative memory, 459, 560, 576
declarative-procedural model, in PPA, 575,
    576, 586
Declercq, M., 85, 86
decline effect, publication bias, 740–741
default mode network (DMN), 37, 243
Degner, J., 319
DeKeyser, R.M., 415
Del Maschio, N., xxxviii
Della Sala, S., xliii, 740
DeLuca, V., xxxviii
dementia, 576, 608–624
    see also memory theories/models
    age of onset (AoO), 620
    ageing studies, 614–615
    Alzheimer's disease (AD), xlii, 245, 268,
        413, 499, 500, 580, 609, 611
    and aphasia, 609, 613
    and bilingualism, 610–613, 620–621
        questioning of effects on dementia,
            617–620
    cognitive impairment no dementia
        (CIND), 614
    and cognitive reserve (CR), 413, 615,
        617, 621
    comparison with other pathologies,
        615–616
    compensatory mechanisms in AD, 245
    free of cognitive impairment
        (CIND-free), 614
    frontotemporal, 612, 613
    Hyderabad, studies from, 612, 613
    incidence rate, 620
    with Lewy bodies, 612
    longitudinal studies, 617, 619, 620
    and mild cognitive impairment (MCI), 611
    mixed, 612
    and multilingualism, 608–610, 620–621
    neurobiology, 617
    neuroimaging, 616
    possible mechanisms, 614–617
    post-stroke cognitive impairment, 616
    prospective versus retrospective studies,
        619–620
    semantic, 610

vascular, 612, 615, 616
vascular mild cognitive impairment
    (VaMCI), 615, 616
dementia with Lewy bodies (DLB), 612
dendrites, 231
Deng, Z., 283
density
    axonal, 239
    code switching, 188, 268, 450
        bilingual models, 63, 64f
        developmental perspective, in
            multilingualism, 668, 673
        language control and attention, 433, 434,
            437–440, 441n3
    grey matter (GM), 138, 189, 282
        developmental perspective, in
            multilingualism, 663, 664
        and plasticity, 232–234, 238
        schizophrenia and bilingualism, 628t, 629
        word production, bilingual, 220, 221
    receptor, 257, 669
    synaptic, 629
dental-retroflex contrast, 280–282
Desikan-Killiany atlas, 68
Desmet, T., 85, 86
detachment effect, 325
DeVaughn, S., 581
developmental perspective, in
    multilingualism, xxxix, 657–684
    age and language development, 414–416
    age of acquisition and multilingualism,
        658–661
    cognitive flexibility, 657, 666–670
    cognitive neuroscience, 24
    conversation, 662, 669
    individual differences in multilingual
        outcomes, role of, 661–670
    and plasticity, 657
        and foreign language learning success,
            663–666
        link with proficiency, 662–663
        unanswered questions, 666
Di Sciullo, A.-M., 299
dialogic communication, 26
Diamond, B.J., 492, 500, 686, 692, 695
Dias, P., 771
Díaz, B., xxxix, 285–286, 287, 289
Dickersin, K., 738
diffusion tensor imaging (DTI), 68, 283, 674

diffusion-weighted MRI (DW-MRI)
  tractography techniques, 494
digit and word span tasks, 688, 689
Dijkstra, T., 49, 51, 59, 61, 80, 81, 717
direct access hypothesis, 511
DLPFC (dorsolateral prefrontal cortex) *see*
  dorsolateral prefrontal cortex (DLPFC)
Docherty, N.M., 641
Doedens, W.J., 86
Dolan, R.J., 345
Donald, M., 25–26, 42n3
Dong, Y., xliii, 691, 693, 694, 696, 697
dopamine, 256, 668, 669
dopamine receptor D2 (DRD2) gene, 669
dorsolateral prefrontal cortex (DLPFC), 113
  age of acquisition (AoA), 258
  bilingual models, 60, 61, 66
  brain structure and regions of interest, 182
  developmental perspective, 661
  humour perception, 345
  language-switching networks, 129, 130
  metacognitive processing, 361
  and plasticity, 233, 264
  word production, bilingual, 216, 218, 219
Doughty, C.J., 418, 419
Dowens, M.G., 109
Druks, J., 577, 580, 583
Drury, J.E., 479n1
DTI (diffusion tensor imaging), 68
dual-coding theory, bilingualism, 392
dual-language context, 432–433, 441n1,
  450, 452
dual mechanisms of control (DCM)
  model, 450
'dual stream' models of language processing,
  21f, 200, 283
Duffau, H., 31
Dussias, P.E., xli, 88, 112, 376, 437, 473,
  474, 478
Dutch-English bilinguals, 79, 81, 400, 711
Dutch-English-French trilinguals, 80
Dutch-English-German trilinguals, 61
dynamic assessment (DA), 15
dynamic causal modelling (DCM), 564
dyslexia, 292

early left anterior negativity (ELAN)
  see also left anterior negativity (LAN)
  interpretation, 108, 479n1

real-time measures of brain, in
  multilingualism, 108, 109
sentence processing, bilingual, 468
early posterior negativity (EPN), 322
Easterbrook, P.J., 737
Ebbinghaus, H., 162, 165
Ecke, P., 155
EEG *see* electroencephalography (EEG)
EF *see* executive functioning (EF)
Einstein Ageing Study, 618
Eklund, A., 37
ELAN (early left anterior negativity) *see* early
  left anterior negativity (ELAN)
electroencephalography (EEG), xxxvii, 22,
  322, 468, 513, 672
  humour, utilizing in, 343–344
  real-time measures of brain, in
    multilingualism, 100–104
electromyography (EMG), facial, 320
electrophysiological studies, xxxvii, xli, 19,
  290, 322, 361, 468, 520
Ellis, R., 415
Elmer, S., 233, 238, 241
embodied cognition, 24–26, 42n5
Emmorey, K., 769, 770, 771, 772
emotion/emotion concepts, processing and
  use, 313–334
  applied work in clinical and counselling
    settings, 324–328
  behavioural tasks, 314–319
  cultural issues and culture-specific
    treatment strategies, 327–328
  electrophysiological work, 322
  emotion-laden words, 319
  future research, 328–329
  interpreters, use in clinical settings, 326–327
  neuroimaging and related work, 323–324
  psychophysiological work, 320–322
  qualitative differences in L1 and L2
    emotion processing, 323
  rapid serial visual presentation (RSVP)
    paradigm, 82, 315, 316
  research findings and implications for
    practice, 324–326
  Stroop task, 314–316, 319, 322
  word acquisition, storage and retrieval,
    315–317
  word processing and comprehension,
    317–319

emotion, role in encoding, storage and
    retrieval of information, xxxix
emotional enhancement of memory
    (EEM), 317
emotive function, speech acts, 42n7
encephalography, xxxvii
    advantages, 103
    compared with other methods, 102–104
    real-time measures of brain, in
        multilingualism, 101–104
end-of-the-sentence grammaticality
    judgement tasks, 82
Engelhardt, L.E., 723
English-French bilinguals, 186, 718–719
English-Spanish bilinguals, 57, 58, 59,
    320, 399
epilepsy, 28, 543–544
epileptogenic zone, 29
episodic buffer, 412
episodic memory changes, in healthy ageing,
    411–412
Erard, M., 671
ERPs *see* event-related potentials (ERPs)
errors
    accent, 605
    circumlocutions, 31, 32f
    cortical stimulation mapping (CSM), 31, 32f
    determiner-noun agreement errors, 110
    naming, 31, 32f, 219
    neologisms, 31, 32f
    no-response, 29, 31, 32f, 33f
    performance, 31, 32f
    phonological paraphasias, 31, 32f
    in schizophrenia, 637
    semantic paraphasias, 31, 32f
    syntactic processing, measuring, 82
Ervin, S.M., 390, 391
Estanga, A., 617
event-related fields (ERFs), 104
event-related potentials (ERPs)
    bilingual models, 54, 57
    biphasic effect, 180, 515, 520
    cognitive neuroscience, 22, 36
    comprehension of language, xxxvii
    critical periods, 176, 177–178
    emotion processing, 322
    humour, utilizing in, 343–344
    language control and attention, 427, 430
    memory and L2 studies, 396–398

mismatch negativity (MMN), 105, 286–289
    in monolingual and bilingual non-literal
        language processing, 508–529
    N400 component *see* N400 (ERP
        component), effects of
    and non-literal language processing
        bilingual, 518–521
        figurative language, 515–518
        late positive component (LPC) and P600,
            514–515
        monolingual, 515–518
        N400, 513–514
        P300, 514, 518
    P300 component, 514, 518
    P600 component *see* P600 (ERP component),
        effects of
primary progressive aphasia (PPA), 575
psycholinguistic research methods,
    multilingualism, 78–79
reading disorders, acquired, 603
real-time measures of brain, in
    multilingualism, 102
    interpretation, 105–106
    language switching, 110, 114
speech-sign bilingualism, 760
time-averaged, 468
use in language processing research,
    176–180
waveforms, 177, 513, 516, 520, 521, 522
word production, bilingual, 222–223
evidence
    see also bilingual interactive activation
        (BIA) models; cognitive control;
        functional magnetic resonance
        imaging (fMRI); inhibitory control (IC)
        model; neurocognition, multiple
        languages; neuroimaging studies
    bilingual advantage debate, 701–735
        quantity of evidence, 702–712
    bilingualism-induced neuroplasticity,
        184–188
    critical period hypothesis, second language
        acquisition, 170, 171–176
    fMRI studies, 156–157
    neural
        bilingual interactive activation (BIA)
            models, 54–59
        increased inhibition between word
            forms, 59

increased L2 proficiency strengthening
connections to the semantic store, 59
inhibitory control (IC) model, 55–56t,
60–62
integrated L1-L2 lexical networks, 54, 57
non-selective lexical access, 57–58
neuroimaging studies, 140–141
executive control (EC)
see also language control
adaptive control hypothesis, 450, 452, 488
and bilingual aphasia, 456–458
bilingual language control (BLC), 447, 448,
451–460
deficits, 454–460
domain-general, 489
dual mechanisms of control (DCM)
model, 450
effect of bilingualism on, 66
experiential considerations, 673
generalized, versus language control, 61–62
and language/language switching, 447–466
multilingualism, 672–673
networks, 674
neural basis, 451–453
and neuroplasticity, 485–507
publication bias, 738–740, 748
theoretical perspectives, 448–451
executive functioning (EF), xliii, 183, 219
bilingual advantage debate, 701, 702, 713,
724, 725n4
in bilingual brain, 496, 497
in dementia, 611
and interpreting, 685, 693
and metacognitive regulation 358–362
in schizophrenia, 636, 638
experience
and bilingual activation, 761–764
cortical representation, 267–268
executive control (EC), 673
of language, 267–268
of second language (L2)/second language
acquisition (SLA), to enhance older
adults' L2 learning, 267–268
experimental design, 25
experimental design and intermediate time
frame, 25
experimental paradigms, 77, 82
external symbols, 25, 42n3
eye-tracking

bilingual advantage debate, 718
evaluation of, 91, 92
eye-movement research, 87–88, 400, 511
Eyelink device, 317
fixations, 88
independent components analysis
(ICA), 102
infrared-based, 399
measuring bilingual language processing
with, 87–91
reading studies, 87–88
saccades, 88
and visual world paradigm, 88–89

Fabbro, F., xli, 455, 536, 541, 545, 687
Fan, L., 322
Faroqui-Shah, Y., 457
Felser, C., 380
Felton, A., 240
Fernandez-Duque, D., 360
Ferré, P., 316
Fichman, S., xlii
figurative language, processing of, 512,
515–518
familiar, 515–517
novel, 517–518
Filippi, R., xxxix–xl, 238
Filley, C.M., 583
FIRST (Bayesian analytical approach), 236
first language (L1) *see* native language (L1)
flanker task, 773
bilingual advantage debate, 714, 716, 717,
719, 723, 741
quantity of evidence, 703, 704, 706, 708
interpreting, 692–694
speech-sign bilingualism, 773
Flavell, J., 358
Flemish-French bilinguals, 216
flexibility, cognitive *see* cognitive flexibility
fMRI *see* functional magnetic resonance
imaging (fMRI)
fNIRS (functional near infrared spectroscopy)
see functional near-infrared
spectroscopy (fNIRS)
focus of attention (FOA), 129, 435, 687
see also attention; attentional states
broad, 437, 438
narrow, 432, 437, 439
Folke, T., 363, 364f

Footnick, R., 155
forgotten languages
    adoptees, language forgetting in, 148–149
        adult adoptees, 148, 156–157, 164–165, 166
        child adoptees, 157
    attrition types, 5–6
    behavioural tasks in uncovering memory
        remnants, 157–162
        adoptees, 148, 159–162
        childhood overhearers, 148, 157,
            158–159, 165
    immediate forgetting in a learning
        situation, 5–6
    memory traces, uncovering, 5, 147–169
        age regression hypnosis, 147–148,
            154–156, 165
        behavioural tasks, 148, 157–162
        fMRI research, 148, 156–157
        retention of forgotten language, 5, 6
        savings paradigm, 162–165
        studies, 150–153t, 156–157
    repressed versus suppressed, 155–156
    savings paradigm, xxxviii, 162–165
        adult adoptees, 164–165
        adult L2 learners, 164
        child L2 learners, 163–164
    suppressed versus repressed, 155–156
    verbs versus nouns, 149
Foroni, F., 320
Forster, K., 300, 301
fractional anisotropy (FA), 181, 239, 283
Frazier, L., 86
Freedman, M., 613
French-Chinese bilinguals, 157
French-Dutch bilinguals, 458
Frenck-Mestre, C., 186
Fricke, M., 437
Friederici, A.D., 109, 242
Friedman, N.P., 366, 686, 688, 695, 702
Friesen, D.C., 718
Frith, C.D., 635
Fromm, E., 154–155
frontal lobe, Broca's area *see* Broca's area
frontopolar cortex (FPC), 696
frontotemporal dementia (FTD), 612, 613
functional magnetic resonance imaging
        (fMRI), xxxvii, xxxviii, 27, 31
    activations and variation, 37–39
    age of acquisition (AoA), 359–361t, 378

artifactual signal loss, 34
bilingual language use, effect on brain
        structure, 67, 68
BOLD signal, 34, 42n8, 67, 87
brain differences between monolinguals
        and bilinguals, 279
cognitive control, neural bases in
        bilingualism, 54
cognitive flexibility, 696
combining with other techniques, 36
conditional routing (CR) model, 66
controlled articulation and lexical selection
        in multilinguals, 136
cortical representation, factors affecting,
        259–261t, 263
criticism, 39–40
data analysis, 37–39
developmental perspective, 671
emotion processing, 323
humour, utilizing in studies of,
        344–346
inter-subject averaging, 155
language control, 63, 427
language organization, 199, 201
language switching and interference, 488
learning and brain, endogenous factors
        influencing, 282, 283
limitations, 128
memory
    memory remnants of forgotten
        languages, recovering, 148, 155,
        156–157, 166
    second language (L2)/second language
        acquisition (SLA) studies, 396–398
metacognitive processing, 361
parametric statistical methods, 37
primary progressive aphasia (PPA), 575
psycholinguistic research methods,
        multilingualism, 79
real-time measures of brain, in
        multilingualism, 103
scanner noise, 34
speech-sign bilingualism, 761–762,
        769, 770
studies of language, 34–39
subtractive methodology, 34
training studies, 281
treatment-induced recovery in bilingual
        aphasia, 563–564

variation studies, 37–38
word production, bilingual, 216, 217–218, 221
functional near-infrared spectroscopy (fNIRS), 104, 440, 659
speech-sign bilingualism, 771–772
functional transcranial Doppler sonography (fTCD), 760–761
funniness *see* humour
fusiform gyrus, 595

Gabriele, A., 178
Gabryś-Barker, D., 418
Third Age Learners of Foreign Language, 417
Gallese, V., 24, 42n5
Garbin, G., 452
García-Caballero, A., 545
García-Pentón, L., 68, 240
gender, 255, 345, 346, 711–712
general fluid (gF) intelligence, 702, 712, 715, 725n3, 725n4
genetic factors, xlii, 256–257
Genie (linguistic isolate), 173–174
German-Dutch bilinguals, 163
German-English bilinguals, 84, 86
German-French bilinguals, 219
German-Spanish bilinguals, 322
gestures, 768
Geyer, A., 58
Gibbs, R., 511
Gierhan, S.M.E., 242
Giezen, M., 766
Gile, D., 686, 687, 690, 693
Gilley, P.M., 470
Gindis, B., 149
Giora, R., 515, 520
Giraudo, H., 301–302
globus pallidus, 237, 457
goal maintenance, 63
Goel, V., 345
Gold, B.T., 245, 498, 674
Golestani, N., 281, 282, 283, 290
Gollan, T.H., 77, 222, 580–581, 609, 612, 675, 676n1
Gómez-Ruiz, I., 580
Goral, M., xlii
Gorno-Tempini, M.L., 574
Grabois, H., 149
graded silence hypothesis, 511

Grady, C.L., 245
Grainger, J., 51, 301–302
grammar
artificial grammar learning (AGL), 186
brain basis of L2 grammar, 202–204
end-of-the-sentence grammaticality judgement tasks, 82
grammatical knowledge, 7, 107, 414, 577
inflectional processes, 202
judging grammaticality, 495–496
second language (L2)/second language acquisition (SLA), 107, 202–204
Grant, A.M., xxxvii, 59, 665
grapheme–phoneme conversion (GPC), 593, 594
graphemes, xlii, 592
Grasemann, U., 557
Gratton Effect, 725n7
Gray, T., 457
Green, D.W., xl, 40, 224, 265–266, 365, 441n2, 449–452, 457, 535, 540, 585, 586, 642, 643, 667, 668, 717
Greenberg, Z.I., 716, 719, 740, 742
Grendel, M., 13
grey matter (GM), 231, 232f
see also white matter (WM)
brain imaging, 181, 182f
brain structure and regions of interest, 182
cortical, effects of cerebral cortex on, 235
density, 138, 189, 282
developmental perspective, in multilingualism, 663, 664
and plasticity, 232–234, 238
schizophrenia and bilingualism, 628t, 629
word production, bilingual, 220, 221
destruction in stroke, 584
effects of bi-/multilingualism on, 232–238
bilingual language use, 67, 68
bilingualism-induced neuroplasticity, 185
subcortical, effects of subcortical structures on, 236–238
views, 232f
volume, 138, 206, 234, 453, 497
cortical representation, 263, 265
increased, 279, 630, 639, 641, 674, 696, 774
schizophrenia, bilinguals with, 627t, 628t, 630, 641

Grogan, A., 233, 236
Grohmann, K.K., 581, 582
Grosjean, F., 8, 9, 54
Grundy, J.G., 620, 718, 719, 720, 722
Guijarro-Fuentes, P., 171
Guo, T., 60, 61, 79
Gusnard, D.A., 37
Gutierrez-Sigut, E., xliii, 760

Hagoort, P., 10, 20, 37
Hahne, A., 109, 522
Hakuta, K., 174–175
Halle, M., 299
Hämäläinen, S., 240
Hansen, L., 164, 167n4
Hartanto, A., 712, 713
Hartsuiker, R., 11, 85
Hashimoto, K., 598
Hebrew, 543, 599, 600, 603, 637
Hejazi, Z., xl
Hempelmann, C.F., 340
Heredia, R.R., xl, xli
Hernandez, A.E., xlii, 139, 216, 218–219,
    323, 669
Hernàndez, M., 582
Herschensohn, J., 472
Hervais-Adelman, A., 65, 234, 495
Heschl's gyrus (HG), 233, 282–284, 290, 664
Hickock, G., 19, 20, 37, 41n2
hierarchical models, bilingual/multilingual
    memory, 394–395
  revised hierarchical model (RHM), 51, 52,
    304, 394, 395
Hilchey, M.D., 706, 707, 708, 725, 740
Hillyard, S.A., 513–514
Hindi language, 158, 280
Hispanics, 669
Hoeks, J.C., 515
Hofmann, J., xxxix
Hofstetter, S., 241
Holland, A.C., 315
Hopp, H., 381
Hopper, P., 12
Horwitz, B., 761
Hosoda, C., 241
Hoversten, L.J., 58
Hsu, C.-T., 323
Huettel, S.A., 31, 34
Huibregste, I., 14

Hull, R., 762
humour, xxxix, 335–354
  3WD (model and test), 339, 340
  ambiguity, 340, 346
  and amusement, 337
  appreciation, 336, 346, 348–349
  cartoons, 338, 339, 344
  cognitive theories, 338
  compromise, 342
  cortical regions selective for perception
    of, 345
  defining, 336–337
  EEG and ERPs, studies utilizing, 343–344
  elaboration, 346
  equivalence, 341, 342
  fMRI studies, 344–346
  and gender, 345, 346
  general theory of verbal humour
    (GTVH), 340
  incongruity-resolution, 339, 340, 346
  invasive techniques, studies utilizing, 347
  jokes, 338, 339, 341–342, 346
  language learning, 347–348
  MEG, studies utilizing, 344–346
  neural processes, 342–347
  nonsense, 339, 340, 346
  PET, studies utilizing, 344–346
  processing and appreciation, 342–347
  production, 336, 348–349
  and resources, hierarchically
    structured, 347
  semantic theory, 340
  sense of, 349
  sexual, 339
  SPECT, studies utilizing, 344–346
  switchable jokes, 342
  in text, 340
  translation of, 340–342, 347
  verbal, theories of, 338–347
Hyderabad (India), dementia studies, 612, 613
Hyltenstam, K., 160, 161, 609
Hymes, D.H., 41n3
hyperpolyglotism, xlii, 670–672
  see also multilingualism
  neuroprotective effects in older
    populations, 673–675
  unanswered questions, 672
hyperscanning, 440
hypnosis, 147–148, 154–156, 165

Iakupova, R., 557
Ibáñez, A., 520, 521, 522
Ibrahim, R., 599, 603
IC model *see* inhibitory control (IC) model
ICA (independent components analysis), 102
idioms
 see also metaphors; non-literal language
  processing
 decomposable and non-decomposable,
  511, 512
 figurative meaning, 512
 idiom list hypothesis, 510
 idiom representation hypothesis, 510
 lower frequency, 513
 and metaphors, 508–511
IFG (inferior frontal gyrus) *see* inferior frontal
 gyrus (IFG)
IFOF (inferior fronto-occipital fasciculus) *see*
 inferior fronto-occipital fasciculus
 (IFOF)
immigration, 6, 149, 414, 553, 637, 662
 dementia and multilingualism, 612,
  620, 621
 immigration status, 611–613
impairment, language, xli–xlii
 see also aphasia
 access, 585
 in aphasia
  bilingual, 554–559
  multilingual, 538–544
  primary progressive aphasia (PPA), 574
 comparable versus differential, 605
 differential, 541–543
 factors affecting
  lesions, 539, 557–559
  main factors, 539–540
  premorbid language, 556–557
 loss, 585
 native language, 542–543
 neurological basis of language decline in
  PPAs, 583–585
 non-native language, 541–542
 parallel, 540–541, 554
 patterns of, 538–539
 in schizophrenia, 641–643
 selective, 543–544, 554
incidence studies, neuroprotective effects, 499
incongruity-resolution theory, 339, 340, 346
Indefrey, P., 38, 86, 87

independent components analysis (ICA),
 102, 490
individual differences
 bilingualism, 68–69
 code switching, 668–670
 constraints on, xliii
 cortical representation, 254–257
 L2 proficiency, 67
 multilingual outcomes, 661–670
 speech perception, 277–296
inferior frontal cortex, 126, 216, 660
inferior frontal gyrus (IFG), 182, 345
 bilateral, 186, 233, 238, 241, 243, 245
 bilingualism, 61, 67
  bilingualism-induced neuroplasticity, 186
 cortical representation, factors affecting,
  252, 253, 259t, 260t, 262–265, 267, 269
 IFG pars opercularis (IFGop), 233, 497
 IFG pars orbitalis (IFGorb), 234
 IFG pars triangularis (IFGtr), 233
 left inferior frontal gyrus (LIFG)
  cortical representation, 252, 253, 259t,
   260t, 262, 264, 265, 267, 269
  developmental perspective, in
   multilingualism, 666, 669
  executive control (EC), 453
  interpreting, 696
  language control, 489
  and plasticity, 233, 234, 240, 243
 multilingual language control, 127
 right inferior frontal gyrus (RIFG), 55t, 66,
  264, 345, 664, 669
  neuroimaging studies, 130, 132t, 134
  and plasticity, 234, 241, 243
 word production, bilingual, 218
inferior fronto-occipital fasciculus (IFOF), 31,
 183, 185, 239, 240
 bilateral, 186, 233, 238, 241, 243, 245
inferior longitudinal fasciculus (ILF), 31,
 185, 241
inferior parietal cortex (IPC), 663
inferior parietal lobe (IPL), 130f, 131, 182, 258,
 536–537
inflexion, 204
inhibition
 activation, inhibition-related, 134
 bilingual advantage debate, 703–704, 705f,
  706, 717–718
 increase in inhibitory activity, 31, 33

inhibition (*cont'd*)
  increased, between word forms, 59
  inhibition–activation cycle, 487
  multiple levels of, 61–62
  selective response inhibition, 63
inhibitory control (IC) model, 49, 52–53,
      78, 717
  executive control (EC), 449
  and interpreting, 691–694
  key regions of interest, 55–56t
  multilingual language control, 134, 138
  multiple levels of inhibition, 61–62
  neural evidence for, 55–56t, 60–62
  proficiency-modulated lemma activation,
      60–61
  schemas, 60
insula, 67, 218, 233
interference
  control of, 63, 487–490
  picture-picture interference task, 77
  suppression, 490
interpreting/interpretation, xliii, 205, 238,
      380, 474, 501, 509
  see also translation
  alternative, 375
  antisaccade tasks, 692, 693
  basal ganglia, bilingual language use
      affecting, 65
  bilingual advantage debate, 715, 723
  of data, 737, 748, 750
  difficulties, 329
  ELAN/LAN effects, 108, 479n1
  executive functioning (EF), 685, 693
  expert interpreters, 689
  figurative interpretation, 511, 516, 519
  flanker task, 692–694
  functional interpretation, 513
  idioms, 511
  impairment, 540, 554, 599
  implications of bilingualism for, 490–493
  'interpreter advantage,' 685, 690
  interpreters, use in clinical settings, 326–327
  language and executive control, 459
  and language switching, 485, 486, 487–490
  literal interpretation, 510, 516, 529
  long dialogue or complex text, 491
  meta-analyses, 751
  misinterpretation, 429
  neural correlates, language control, 63

  neuroanatomical, 544
  neurocognitive consequences, 685–700
      on cognitive flexibility, 694–697
      on inhibitory control, 691–694
  novice interpreters, 689, 691
  numerical, 690
  parallel impairment, 540
  pragmatic interpretation, 515
  proactive control, 460
  of real-time brain responses, 104–106
  research limitations, 690–691
  of results, 179, 289–290, 335, 468, 661, 714
  separate sentence interpretation hypothesis
      (SSIR), 375
  Simon task/effect, 692, 693
  simultaneous interpreting (SI), 492–493,
      686–687, 690, 693, 695–696, 697
  of speech, xxxii, 41n3
  Stroop task, 492, 493, 692, 693
  success of, 687
  traditional, of critical periods, 469
  use of interpreters in clinical settings,
      326–327
  of words and affect, 327
  and working memory (WM), 376, 686–687
      interpreter advantage, 687–690
intransitives, 85
IPL (inferior parietal lobe), 130f, 131, 182, 258
Irish Sign Language (ISL), 755
Isel, F., 54
isolates, linguistic, 173–174
Isurin, L., xxxviii, 148–149, 164, 166
item-by-item switching paradigms, 78, 79
Ivanova, A., 77, 222
Iwase, M., 344

Jackendoff, R., 299
Jackson, G., 111
Jakobson, R., 23, 26, 42n7, 43n15
Janowsky, J.S., 360
Japanese-American English bilinguals,
      154–155
Japanese language, 598
Javier, R.A., 326
Jeffrey, H., 704
Jeong, H., 204, 253
Jin, Y., 289
Joanisse, M.F., 240
Johari, K., 459

Johns, M.A., xli
Johnson, J.S., 414
Johnson, M., 23
jokes, 338, 339, 341–342, 346
    see also humour
    ambiguity, 346
    bridging-inference, 346
    exaggeration, 346
    switchable, 342
Jonczyk, R., 322
Judgement of Line Orientation (JLO)
    test, 617

Kaan, E., 479
Kaiser, A., 263
Kambanaros, M., 581, 582
Kamide, Y., 89, 90f
Kandel, E.R., 41n1
Kantola, L., 86
Kar, B.R., 457
Karanth, P., 598, 599
Katzman, R., 614
Kaufmann, E., 771
Kavé, G., 614
Kazanas, S.A., xxxix, 319
Kendall, D., 540
Kennedy, S., 714
Kensinger, E.A., 315
Kersten, K., 347
Keysar, B., 325
Kim, A.E., 470
Kim, J., xl, 375, 376
Kim, K.H.S., 575
Kiran, S., xli, 457, 557, 562
Klaus, J., xxxviii
Klein, D., 216, 234
Klein, R.M., 707, 708, 725, 740
knowledge, xliii, 165, 201, 257, 291, 315, 326,
        348, 358, 395, 410, 543, 564, 577
    of bilingualism or multilingualism, 66, 342,
        403, 573, 575, 585
        cognitive neuroscience, 35, 37
        defining and assessing multilingualism,
        6, 7
    conceptual, 307, 346, 429, 487, 510
    critical period hypothesis, evidence base,
        277, 278
    dementia and multilingualism, 618,
        620, 621

early, 468–469
explicit, 415, 560
forgotten or lost languages, 5, 147, 154, 155,
        158, 161, 163, 164, 166
general, xxxii, xxxiv
grammatical, 7, 107, 414, 577
and humour, 335, 340, 341, 347, 348
implicit, 158, 415, 659
integrated, 297, 302
of initial language/L1, 149, 523
lexical, 163, 299, 303, 576, 586
    lexical-semantic/lexico-semantic,
        203, 577
linguistic, xxxviii, 106, 174, 207, 230, 278,
        298, 335, 392, 471, 539
    forgotten languages, memory traces,
        157, 163
    language control, 454, 497
    metalinguistic, 174, 539, 542
metacognitive, 357, 360
metalinguistic, 174, 539, 542
of new/second languages, 4, 107, 199, 201,
        230, 390, 391, 560
    lack of or loss of, 147, 199
non-literal language processing, 513, 514
preserved, 150t, 157, 158
semantic, 204, 585
    lexical-semantic/lexico-semantic,
        203, 577
syntactic, 106, 586
theoretical, 357, 587
transfer of, 395, 593
vocabulary, 13, 14, 441n1
of words, 7, 298, 514, 540
Kohn, N., 345
Kok, A., 514
Kong, A.P.H., 455
Kootstra, G.J., xxxvii, 86, 437
Köpke, B., 689, 691, 693
Korean-Chinese bilinguals, 381
Korean-Dutch bilinguals, 161
Korean-English bilinguals, 375–376
Korean language, 159, 160
Korsakoff syndrome, 361
Korytkowska, M., xlii
Kousaie, S., 243
Kovelman, I., 771–772
Krass, K., xxxvii
Krebs, E., 671

Kuhl, P.K., 241, 575, 660
Kuperberg, G.R., 626
Kutas, M., 344, 513–514, 518

L1 *see* native language (L1)
L2 *see* second language (L2)/second language
    acquisition (SLA)
L3 *see* third language (L3)
La Heij, W., 11
Laganaro, M., 600, 601
Lakoff, G., 23, 24, 42n5
LAN (left anterior negativity) *see* left anterior
    negativity (LAN)
language, 268–269
  see also language experience and
      proficiency questionnaire (LEAP-Q);
      language history questionnaire (LHQ)
  acquisition *see* acquisition of language
  articulating two languages simultaneously,
      768–772
    code-blending, 769–771
    code switching, 771–772
  attrition, 5–6
  bilaterality of, 39–40
  brain networks underlying bilingual
      processing of, 66–67
  and cognition, 9, 31, 410, 626, 632
  contact, measuring, 7–8
  control of *see* language control
  cross-language task performance and
      neuroplasticity, 486, 493–494
  defining, 16, 41n3
  domains, 7, 10
  dominance, 266
  dual-language context, 432–433, 441n1, 450,
      452, 712
  environment and use, 268
  experience of, 267–268
  exposure to, 267–268
  familiar figurative, processing of, 515–517
  fMRI studies, 34–39
  forgotten languages *see* forgotten
      languages, memory traces
  forgotten, searching for memory traces *see*
      forgotten languages
  functional anatomy, dual-stream model, 21f
  heritage, 6
  and humour, 347–348
  impairment *see* impairment, language

interaction with culture, 23
language mode model, in multilingualism, 8
linguistic knowledge, 335, 392, 471, 539
  forgotten languages, memory traces,
      157, 163
  language control, 454, 497
  metalinguistic, 471, 539, 542
links between elements, 11–12
memory stores, 390–392
mixed-language context, word production
    in, 218–221
modularity, 254
national, 6
native *see* native language
non-native *see* non-native language
novel figurative, processing of, 517–518
organization of *see* language organization
premorbid factors influencing impairment,
    556–557
remapping in brain, 19–22
as separate entities in the brain, 11–13
as serial process, 21
similarity, 253–254
single-language context, 215–218, 432–433,
    450, 452
switching *see* code switching; switching,
    language
and task-specific attributes, 253
typology and status, 381–382
language control, 427–446
  see also executive control (EC); language;
      language organization; language
      representation; language switching
  and attentional states, xl, 431–434
    code switching, 432–435, 439, 440, 441n2
    dynamics of in a speech act, 436–438
    review, 438–440
    signatures, 433–436
    topics with neural signatures, 434–436
  bilingual language control (BLC), 447, 448,
      451–460
  conversation, 416, 427–433, 435–440, 441n3
  dissociation between language and non-
      linguistic control, 457
  functional magnetic resonance imaging
      (fMRI), 63, 427
  and generalized executive control, 61–62
  goal maintenance, 63
  impairment, in bilingual aphasia, 554–556

interference, 63
local versus global, 61
monitoring systems versus response
    selection systems, 63
multilingual, 129–140
    age-related cognitive decline, protection
        against, 139–140
    brain basis, 206
    controlled articulation and lexical
        selection in multilinguals, 136–139
    language-switching networks, 129–131
    language-switching studies, 131,
        132–133t, 134–136
    neural correlates of, 63–64
    neuroimaging studies, 129–140, 435
    selective, 434
language experience and proficiency
        questionnaire (LEAP-Q), 7, 14
Language Go Task (LGT), 58
language history questionnaire (LHQ), 7, 14
language organization
    see also language; language control;
        language representation; language
        switching
    age factors, 256
    in bilingual and multilingual brain, 199–213
    brain basis for second language acquisition
        grammar, 202–204
        language control, 206
        lexico-semantics, 204–206
        phonology, 200–202
    cross-sectional studies, 204
    'dual stream' models of language
        processing, 200
    functional magnetic resonance imaging
        (fMRI), 199, 201
    morphological parsing, 203–204
    morphological processing, dual-route
        models, 202–203
    and multilingualism, 199–213, 256
    neuroimaging studies, 199, 202, 205
    phonetic learning, 201–202
    picture-naming tasks, 202, 205
    syntactic distance effect, 204
    syntactic processing, 203
language representation
    cortical stimulation mapping (CSM), 28
    levels of, 400–401
    nature of, 401–403

language switching, xxxvii, xxxviii, 40, 279,
        319, 361, 410
    see also code switching; language; language
        control; language organization;
        language representation; switching
    aphasia, 535–537
    bilingual advantage debate, 709–712
    bilingual models, 53, 60, 61, 63–65
    blocked-language switching paradigms,
        78–79
    cognitive flexibility, 658
    complexity, 65
    continuous, 220
    cortical representation, 267, 268
    costs, 61, 82
    dominant language, into, 476
    dual mechanisms of control (DCM)
        model, 450
    and executive control, 448, 449, 450, 453,
        454–456, 458, 459
    hemodynamics, 219–220
    inhibitory control (IC) model, 53
    and interference, control of, 487–490
    and interpreting, 485, 486, 487–490
    item-by-item switching paradigms, 78, 79
    and language control, 206, 427
    in multilinguals
        networks, 129–131
        studies, 132–133t, 134–136
    networks, 129–131
    neuroimaging studies, 130, 136–139
    overt, 134
    pathological, 452, 454–456
    and plasticity, 235–239, 244–246
    production, 113
    proficiency-modulated lemma
        activation, 60
    psycholinguistic research methods, 78,
        79, 82
    real-time brain measures, 105, 106, 110–114
    studies, 131, 132–133t, 134–136
    weaker language, into, 142, 476
    word production, bilingual, 219, 220, 221,
        223, 225
language use questionnaire (LUQ), 534
Larner, A.J., 583
late positive component (LPC), 105
    and P600, 514–515
lateral prefrontal cortex, 361

lateralization, 758, 761
lateralized readiness potential (LRP), 105
Latter Day Saints, 5
Lau, H., 362
Laurent, J., 515, 516
Lawton, D.M., 617–618
LCN (left caudate nucleus), 236–238, 245
Le Berre, A.P., 361
LEAP-Q *see* language experience and
    proficiency questionnaire (LEAP-Q)
learning of languages
    see also second language (L2)/second
        language acquisition (SLA)
    in adulthood *see* adulthood
    child and adult learning compared, 676
        see also children
    dental-retroflex contrast, 280–282
    effect on brain, 184–188
    endogenous factors influencing learning
        and brain, 280–291
        natural language learning studies,
            284–290
        training studies, 280–284
    exogenous factors influencing, xxxix,
        278–279
    explicit, 415
    first language *see* native language (L1)
    frequency- and usage-based approaches
        to, 379
    giftedness, 291, 348
    and memory, in bilingualism, 389–407
        distinguishing memory models, 399–403
        L2 studies, methodological
            considerations for, 396–399
        theories and models of bilingual/
            multilingual memory, 390–396
    natural language learning studies, 284–290
        good perceivers (GPs) and poor
            perceivers (PPs), 286–290
    phonemic learning, 284
    plasticity and foreign language learning
        success, 662–663
    second language *see* second language (L2)/
        second language acquisition (SLA)
Leech, R., 435, 436, 438, 439–440
Leemann, B., 455
left anterior negativity (LAN)
    see also early left anterior negativity (ELAN)

real-time measures of brain, in
    multilingualism, 105, 108
sentence processing, bilingual, 468
left caudate nucleus (LCN), 236–238, 245
left inferior frontal gyrus (LIFG)
    see also inferior frontal gyrus (IFG); right
        inferior frontal gyrus (RIFG)
    cortical representation, 252, 253, 259t, 260t,
        262, 264, 265, 267, 269
    developmental perspective, in
        multilingualism, 666, 669
    executive control (EC), 453
    interpreting, 696
    language control, 489
    and plasticity, 233, 234, 240, 243
left putamen, 220
Legault, J., xxxvii
Lehtonen, M., 704, 707, 708, 709, 723
Leischner, A., 536
Lemhöfer, K., 14
lemma activation, proficiency-modulated,
    60–61
Lenneberg, E.H., 170, 171, 173, 175, 185, 414
Leonard, M.K., 57
Lerman, A., xl, xlii
lesions
    acquired, 594, 598, 600
    acute, 560
    aphasia, 533–539, 543–546, 565
        bilingual, 457, 557–559
        primary progressive aphasia (PPA), 573,
            583, 584
    cerebrovascular, 584, 585
    contralesional areas, 563
    delineation, 361
    frontal, 360
    location, 539, 557, 558, 559
    perilesional areas, 563, 564
    prefrontal, 361
    reading disorders, acquired, 601, 604
    size, 558, 565
    studies, 36, 544, 592, 758
    subcortical, 455, 544
    thalamic, 546
    vascular, 584
Levänen, S., 760
lexical processing
    bilingual, 642–643
    conceptual restructuring, 305

congruent lexicalization, 433
cross-language tasks, 486
lexical access, 57–58, 675
lexical attrition, 149
lexical comprehension, 80–81
lexical decision task (LDT), 80, 81, 322
lexical gender, 110
lexical networks, integrated L1 and L2, 54, 57
lexical nodes, 767
lexical priming, 398–399
lexical production, 76–79
lexical representation hypothesis, 510
lexical selection, 136–139, 643
lexicalism/lexicalist framework, 299
lexico-semantics, second language, 204–206
logogen model, 300
measurement, 76–81
morphemes, 299, 301, 302
multilingual connections, modelling, 304–307
notion of a mental lexicon, 298–301
    functional architecture, 304–307
    as a list, 300
    roots in generative linguistics, 299
    roots in psycholinguistics, 300–301
and reorganization, 297–312
revised hierarchical model (RHM), 51, 52, 304
in schizophrenia, 632, 635
structurally complex words as meeting ground, 301–304
LexTale (five-minute test for English vocabulary), 13–14
LHQ *see* language history questionnaire (LHQ)
Li, L., 243, 774
Li, P., xxxvii, 3, 54
Libben, G., xxxix, 297, 302, 303
Liddle, P.F., 632
Linck, J., 377
Lind, M.F., 581
Lindquist, K.A., 318
linguistics
    see also acquisition of language; language; learning of languages; native language (L1); psycholinguistic research methods; second language (L2)/ second language acquisition (SLA)

cognitive, 23
and humour, 340
linguistic changes, in older adults, 413–414
linguistic markers approach, schizophrenia in bilinguals, 641
linguistic theory
    foundational concepts, 23–26
    meaning and speech acts, understanding, 26
    sociolinguistics, 7, 23–24
    studies, 23–24
Litcofsky, K.A., 476
Littmann, S.K., 328
Liu, H., 53, 217, 381, 604
Liu, M., 689, 691
Liu, Y.C., 581, 697
Llama, R., 381
Llungberg, J.K., 497
localization/explanation fallacy, 20–21, 27
locus coeruleus (LC), 434
Loebell, H., 83, 84, 85
logogen model (Morton), 300
long-term memory (LTM), 687
longitudinal fasciculus *see* inferior longitudinal fasciculus (ILF); middle longitudinal fasciculus (MdLF); superior longitudinal fasciculus (SLF)
longitudinal studies, xxxvii, 65, 409, 597, 665, 760
    brain adaptation, 179, 184, 185, 188
    cognition/cognitive neuroscience, 36, 39, 41, 497, 619
    cognitive control, 489
    dementia, 617, 619, 620
    interpreting, 691, 693
    language forgetting, 148–149
    and plasticity, 234, 494
    primary progressive aphasia (PPA), 587
    real-time measures, 110, 114
    training studies, 184, 234
low-frequency fluctuations (ALFF), 283
LPC *see* late positive component (LPC)
Luk, G., 239, 243, 244, 245, 631, 707
Luo, H., 37
Lyman, R.S., 598

macaques, neuronal studies, 135
MacClelland, J.L., 49
McConnell-Ginet, S., 41n3

MacDonald, M.C., 430
MacDonald, M.J., 223
Machado, A., 580
Mackey, A., 416
McLaughlin, J., 179
McLean, J.S., xxxix
Macnamara, B.N., 691
MacSweeney, M., 759, 762, 763
MacWhinney, B., 109
magnetic resonance imaging (MRI)
    age of acquisition (AoA), 378
    cortical thickness (CT), 494
    diffusion-weighted MRI (DW-MRI)
        tractography techniques, 494
    event-related potentials (ERPs), 176
    functional magnetic resonance imaging
        (fMRI) *see* functional magnetic
        resonance imaging (fMRI)
    high-definition, 231
    learning and brain, endogenous factors
        influencing, 282
    in multilingualism
        controlled articulation and lexical
            selection in multilinguals, 137
        metacognitive processing, 361
        and plasticity, 230, 231
        real-time measures of brain, 103
    non-native perception, individual
        differences, 290
    primary progressive aphasia (PPA),
        573, 577
    second language (L2)/second language
        acquisition (SLA) in adulthood, 180–181
    structural, 361
magnetoencephalography (MEG), xxxvii, 36
    bilingual models, 57, 64
    event-related potentials (ERPs), 176
    humour, utilizing in studies of, 344–346
    language-switching networks, 130
    real-time measures of brain, in
        multilingualism, 100–104, 106, 111, 114
    sentence processing, bilingual, 470
    speech-sign bilingualism, 760
Maguire, E., 230
Mahon, B.Z., 24, 42n5
Mahoney, M.J., 738
Malcolm, T., xlii
Malott, K.M., 327
Mamiya, P.C., 185, 187, 241

MANCOVA (multivariate analysis of
    variance), 36, 39, 43n14
Mandarin-Chinese Sign Language, 761–762
Mandarin-English bilinguals, 216
Mandarin language, 660
Maniscalo, B., 362
Manitoba Study of Health and Ageing
    (MSHA), 619
Marcos, L.R., 325
Marian, V., 14, 89, 90–91
Marini, A., 564
Marinis, T., 379
Marinkovic, K., 345
Marquardt, T., 557
Mårtensson, J., 185, 187, 234
Martín, M.C., 81
Marzecová, A., 711
MATRICS Consensus Cognitive Battery, 638
Mattys, S., 158
Mayeux, R., 41n1
mean diffusivity (MD), 181, 239
measurement
    see also assessment
    lexical processing, 76–81
    metacognitive processing, 362–363
    proficiency, 13–14, 36
    syntactic processing, 82–83
    working memory capacity (WMC), 373–374
Mechelli, A., 233, 663
MEG *see* magnetoencephalography (MEG)
Meinzer, M., 563
memory
    see also learning of languages; working
        memory capacity (WMC); working
        memory (WM)
    autobiographical, 315
    in bilingualism, 389–407
        conceptual meaning versus lexical
            representations, 389
        distinguishing memory models, 399–403
        L2 studies, methodological
            considerations for, 396–399
        learning of languages in bilingualism,
            389–407
        theories and models of bilingual/
            multilingual memory, 390–403
    conversation, 391, 399
    declarative, 459, 560, 576
    embedded-processes model, 687

emotion word acquisition, storage and
retrieval, 315–317
emotional enhancement of memory
(EEM), 317
episodic, changes in, 411–412
fMRI research, 148, 155, 156–157
future research, 403–404
hierarchical models, 394–395
L2 studies, methodological considerations
for, 396–399
behavioural methodologies, 398–399
fMRI and ERP, 396–398
language memory stores, 390–392
long-term memory (LTM), 687
loss of *see* dementia
memory-task priming paradigm, 84
procedural, 560, 576
short-term memory (STM), 687, 688
storage and retrieval, 358
theories and models
connectionist models, 392–394
distinguishing between, 399–403
findings related to levels of language
representation, 400–401
findings related to the nature of language
representations, 401–403
model of L3/LN acquisition, 395–396
traces of a forgotten language, uncovering,
147–169
adult adoptees, 148, 156–157,
164–165, 166
age regression hypnosis, 147–148,
154–156, 165
behavioural tasks, 148, 157–162
child adoptees, 157
fMRI research, 148, 155, 156–157
language forgetting in adoptees, 148–149,
156–157, 164–165
savings paradigm, xxxviii, 162–165, 166
studies, 150–153t, 156–157
verbal, 31
Mendez, M.F., 581, 582
Menjot de Champfleur, N., 31
mesolimbic reward system, 345
metacognition/metacognitive processing,
xxxix–xl, 25
confidence judgements, 361
description and critique of methods used to
measure, 362–363

metacognitive regulation and executive
function
conceptual overlap, 358–359
neuroanatomical considerations, 360–362
and multilingualism, 357–371
metacognitive efficiency (MRatio), 362–363
metalingual function, speech acts, 42n7
metalinguistics, advantages of bilingualism
in, 495–496
metaphors, 328, 395
see also idioms; non-literal language
processing
Chinese, 520, 522
comprehension, 508–510, 517
dominant, 298
English, 520
familiar, 517, 521, 524n3
lexical processing, 300, 307
non-literal language, 508–512, 514, 516–518,
521, 523, 524n2
novel, 516, 517, 521
processing, 511, 514, 517–518, 520, 521–523
metastability, 437–440
see also attention; attentional states;
language control
degree of, 440
high and low, 438, 439
network of, 437–438, 439
Meuter, R.F., 78, 491
MFG (middle frontal gyrus), 59, 127, 182, 663
MHM (modified hierarchical model), 305, 307
middle frontal gyrus (MFG), 59, 127, 182, 663
middle longitudinal fasciculus (MdLF), 31
middle temporal gyrus (MTG), 20, 59, 186
left, 345
migration *see* immigration
mild cognitive impairment (MCI), 611
Miller, D., xxxviii
Miller, G.A., 712
Mimouni, Z., 599, 601
mindsharing, 25–26
Mini-mental State Examination (MMSE),
610, 613
Minkowski, M., 542
Miozzo, M., 78
Mishra, R., 718
mismatch negativity (MMN), 105, 286–289,
292, 412
Misra, M., 78

misunderstanding, 26
mixed dementia (MD), 612
mixing, in multilingual aphasia, 535–537
Miyake, A., 366, 686, 688, 695, 701, 702, 725n1
Mizuno, A., 686, 687
MMN (mismatch negativity), 105, 286–289, 292, 412
modified hierarchical model (MHM), 305, 307
Molinaro, N., 516
Mongolian-Chinese bilinguals, 603
monolingualism
    see also bilingualism; multilingualism; native language (L1)
    attention control, 496
    brain differences between monolinguals and bilinguals, 279–280
    conflict resolution abilities, 206
    critical period hypothesis, evidence base, 174
    as exception or the norm, 3, 22
    fMRI studies, 35
    language control and attention, 430
    links between elements, 12
    monolinguals compared with bilinguals, 225, 450, 675, 708, 736, 762
        bilingual advantage debate, 741, 742
        and dementia, 615–617
    monolinguals compared with multilinguals, 202, 206
    reading, 400
    syntactic processing, 203
    variable input, role in language processing, 469–471
Montreal Neurological Institute (MNI) atlas, 38
Montrul, S., 160
Moreno, E.M., xxxvii, 112, 518–519, 523
Morford, J.P., 766
morphemes, 109, 433, 543
    lexical processing, 299, 301, 302
morphology
    agreement, 375
    brain, 280, 282, 289
        cerebral cortical, 290
    impairment, 554
    inflectional, 204, 379, 380
    irregular, 576
    morphological parsing, 203–204
    morphological processing, dual-route models, 202–203

morphology-syntax interface, 396
    overgeneralization of rules, 396
    and psycholinguistic models, 301
    rules, 396
    theoretical, 299
    word, 391
morphosyntax, 63, 109, 204, 609, 673
    see also syntax
    aphasia, 544, 545
    forgotten languages, uncovering memory traces, 150t, 152t, 158
    morphosyntactic processing, 177–179, 377, 378
    morphosyntactic violations, 179
    schizophrenia, bilinguals with, 630t, 635
    second language (L2)/second language acquisition (SLA), 171, 174–175, 178–179
        in older adulthood, 414, 420
Morton, J., 300
mother-tongue *see* native language (L1)
mouth gestures, in signers, 768–769
moving window task, 82
MRI *see* magnetic resonance imaging (MRI)
MTG *see* middle temporal gyrus (MTG)
Mukadam, N., 619, 620, 674
multicompetence model, multilingualism, 9
multilingual aphasia, xli, 533–552
    see also aphasia; bilingual aphasia; primary progressive aphasia (PPA)
    antagonistic phenomena, 544
    assessment of, 533–535
    mixing and switching, 535–537
    subcortical, 544–546
    translation, 537–538
    typical symptoms, 535–538
multilingual processing, factors affecting, 372–388
    age of acquisition (AoA), 377–378
    exposure and language use, 379–380
    language typology and status, 381–382
    processing speed, 380–381
    proficiency, 376–377
    working memory capacity (WMC), 372–376
multilingualism, xxxvii, xxxviii
    see also bilingualism; brain; monolingualism; third language (L3)
    and age of acquisition, 658–661
    age of acquisition (AoA), 657, 658–661

multilingual processing, factors affecting, 377–378
neuroimaging studies, 127, 129, 138, 139
aphasia *see* multilingual aphasia
brain of multilinguals, 9–11, 22
    effects on grey matter, 232–238
    effects on white matter, 239–242
    executive function/metacognition, 365
    neuroimaging studies *see* neuroimaging studies
    and plasticity *see* plasticity/ neuroplasticity
    real-time measures, 100–120
in children, 106, 137, 263
and cognition, 246
cognitive disadvantages, costs and challenges, 674–675
and cognitive neuroscience, 19–47
competency during childhood, 263
conflict resolution abilities, 206
controlled articulation and lexical selection in multilinguals, 136–139
as daily use of two or more languages, 4
defining, xxxvii, 3–4
and dementia, 608–610, 620–621
developmental perspective *see* developmental perspective, in multilingualism
dynamic nature of, xxxvii
early acquisition, 35, 138, 203, 262–263
effects on grey matter, 232–238
    cerebellum, 238
    cerebral cortex, 233–235
    subcortical structures, 235–238
executive control (EC), 672–673
and executive function/metacognition, 365
factors affecting processing, 372–388
individual differences in multilingual outcomes, role of, 661–670
language control
    age-related cognitive decline, protection against, 139–140
    controlled articulation and lexical selection, 136–139
    language-switching networks, 129–131
    language-switching studies, 131, 132–133t, 134–136
language organization *see* language organization

language switching in multilinguals
    networks, 129–131
    studies, 132–133t, 134–136
late acquisition, 657
    cortical representation, 262–263, 269
    language organization, 200, 203, 204
    neuroimaging studies, 137, 138
    processing, 376, 378
lexical processing and reorganization, 297–312
magnetic resonance imaging (MRI) in
    controlled articulation and lexical selection in multilinguals, 137
    metacognitive processing, 361
    and plasticity, 230, 231
    real-time measures of brain, 103
memory theories/models, 390–396
and metacognition, 363–365
models, 8–9
multilinguals compared with monolinguals, 202, 206
neurocognitive effects, 658
neuroimaging studies, 35, 121–146
    and bilingual speech networks, 121–123
    cortical representation, 252
    magnetic resonance imaging (MRI), 103, 138, 230, 231
    and multilingual speech networks, 123–141
as the norm, 3, 22
picture-naming tasks, 669, 675
primary progressive aphasia (PPA), 577, 578–579t, 580
processing *see* multilingual processing, factors affecting
psycholinguistic research methods *see* psycholinguistic research methods, multilingualism
rationale for, 4–5
real-time measures *see* real-time measures, multilingualism
Simon task/effect, 669, 672
speech networks, 123–141
    language control, 129–140
    overlap in cortical representation during speech production, xxxviii, 126–129
    patient populations, evidence from, 140–141

multimodality, 24–26
multivariate analysis of variance
        (MANCOVA), 36, 39, 43n14
Munakata, Y., 449
Muñoz, M., 557
Musser-Granski, J., 327
myelin/myelination, 181, 239, 241

N400 (ERP component), effects of, 322, 377,
        397, 672
    see also event-related potentials (ERPs);
        P600 (ERP component), effects of
    amplitudes, 106, 107, 111, 473, 516–518,
        520–522, 766
    bilingual models, 58–60
    biphasic effect, 180
    and non-literal language processing,
        513–523, 524n4
    real-time measures of brain, in
        multilingualism, 101, 105–108, 110–114
    second language acquisition (SLA), 177f,
        178–180
    sentence processing, bilingual, 473, 476, 478
    speech-sign bilingualism, 766, 767
    subject-verb agreement violations, 179
names
    blocked, 217, 219, 220
        blocked-language switching paradigms,
        78–79
    colour naming, 316
    L1 and L2, 217, 219, 220
    naming errors, 31, 32f, 219
    naming of pictures *see* picture-naming tasks
    object and action naming, 583
    of regions, 22
    word naming studies, 92n2, 592
National Committee for Adoption, 167n2
National Institute on Ageing, US, 408
native language (L1), xxxviii
    see also monolingualism; second language
        (L2)/second language acquisition
        (SLA); third language (L3)
    accent, 473
    acquisition of, 23
    attrition, 6
    emotion processing, xxxix, 323
    grammatical processing, 82
    impairment, 542–543
    influence of L2 on, 473–474

integrated L1-L2 lexical networks, 54, 57
    knowledge of, 149, 523
    limited variation in, 277
    linguistic attentional control, 496–497
    migration, 6
    naming, 217, 219, 220
    neurobiology, 416–417
    non-literal language processing, 509–512
    processing, 203, 224, 376, 469, 558, 641
        and emotion, 320, 323
        sentence processing, bilingual, 472–473
    shared neural representations, 215
    similarities and differences with the
        learned language, 279
    word recognition studies, 472
native-like activity, 109, 177–178, 238
    see also native language (L1)
    accent, 234, 238, 659
natural language learning studies, 284–290
    good perceivers (GPs) and poor perceivers
        (PPs), 286–290
Nelson, T., 162–163
neologisms, 31, 32f, 33f
Nespoulous, J.L., 689, 691, 693
network-based statistic (NBS), 494
neuroanatomy, 544
    metacognition, 360–362
neurobiology
    and dementia, 617
    of first and second languages, 416–417
neurobiology, of first and second languages,
        416–417
neurocognition of multiple languages,
        bilingual models for, 48–74
    adaptive control (AC) model, 62–64
    bilingual interactive activation (BIA)
        models, 48, 49, 50f
        BIA-d model, 51–52, 58–59
        BIA+ model, 49–51, 60, 393
        neural evidence for, 54–59
    brain networks underlying bilingual
        language processing, 66–67
    conditional routing (CR) model, 64–66
    effects of bilingual language use on brain
        structure, 67–68
    individual differences in bilingualism,
        68–69
    inhibitory control (IC) model, 49, 52–53
        neural evidence for, 60–62

neural bases of cognitive control in
  bilingualism, 54–62
  increased inhibition between word
    forms, 59
  increased L2 proficiency strengthening
    connections to the semantic
    store, 59
  integrated L1-L2 lexical networks, 54, 57
  key regions of interest (BLA and IC
    models), 55–56t
  non-selective lexical access, 57–58
  new research directions, 66–69
neurodegenerative disease, xli, 451, 454, 461,
  501, 584
  see also specific diseases, such as aphasia
  bilingual and executive control, 458–460
  cerebral cortex, affecting, 584
  neuroprotective effects, 498–499
neuroimaging studies, xxxvii–xxxviii
  see also computerized tomography (CT);
    diffusion tensor imaging (DTI);
    diffusion-weighted MRI (DW-MRI)
    tractography techniques;
    electroencephalography (EEG);
    encephalography; functional magnetic
    resonance imaging (fMRI); functional
    transcranial Doppler sonography
    (fTCD); magnetic resonance imaging
    (MRI); magnetoencephalography
    (MEG); positron emission tomography
    (PET); single photon emission
    computed tomography (SPECT);
    transcranial magnetic stimulation
    (TMS)
  age of acquisition (AoA), 127, 129
  bilingualism
    bilingual aphasia, 558, 563–564
    bilingual speech networks, 121–123
    see also bilingualism
  brain basis, of L2 phonology, 202
  cognitive neurolinguistic research, 27–34
    cortical stimulation mapping (CSM),
      27–29, 30f, 31, 32–33f
    functional magnetic resonance imaging
      (fMRI) *see* functional magnetic
      resonance imaging (fMRI)
    hemodynamic technologies, xxxvii, 19
    see also cognitive neuroscience;
      neuroimaging studies

and dementia, 616
electrophysiological work, xxxvii, 322
emotion word processing and
  comprehension, 323–324
evidence from patient populations,
  140–141
functional magnetic resonance imaging
  (fMRI) *see* functional magnetic
  resonance imaging (fMRI)
hemodynamic technologies, xxxvii, 19
L2 syntax, 204
language control, 129–140, 435
language organization, 199, 202, 205
language switching, 130, 136–139
lexico-semantics, brain basis, 205
magnetic resonance imaging (MRI) *see*
  magnetic resonance imaging (MRI)
multilingualism, 121–146
  brain of multilinguals, 9–10
  cortical representation, 252
  fMRI studies, 35
  speech networks, 123–141
  see also multilingualism
neurons, 135–136
non-native speech sounds, word
  learning, 283
picture-naming tasks, 126, 127, 139, 323
primary progressive aphasia (PPA),
  575–576
Simon task/effect, 134, 135, 323
neurological embodiment, 42n6
neuronal organization
  orthography effects *see* orthography
    effects
neurons, 100, 101, 410
  and brain structure, 181, 231, 233
  changes in activity, 103
  cortical, 101, 265, 513
  death of, 584
  imaging studies, 31, 135–136, 176
  orthography effects on neuronal
    organization, 601–604
  parietal, 24
  primary progressive aphasia (PPA),
    573, 584
  real-time measures of brain, in
    multilingualism, 100–101
neurophysiology, 221–223, 415
neuroplasticity *see* plasticity/neuroplasticity

neuroprotection/neuroprotective effects
  bilingualism, 498–499
  incidence studies, 499
  in normal ageing and neurodegenerative
      disease, 498–499
  and number of languages, 268–269
neuroscience *see* cognitive neuroscience;
      neurocognition, multiple languages
Neville, H.J., 106, 107, 108
Newman, A.J., 763
Newport, E.L., 414
Ng, S., 57
Nichols, E.S., 240
Nicoladis, E., 149
no-response errors, 29, 31, 32f, 33f
nodes
  see also regions of interest (ROIs)
  activated, 49, 767
  bilingual models, 49–51, 53, 68–69
  conceptual, 393f
  generalized, 393f
  lexical, 767
non-literal language processing, 508–529
  direct access hypothesis, 511
  and ERP studies, 513–521
    bilingual non-literal language processing,
        518–521
    late positive component (LPC) and P600,
        514–515
    monolingual non-literal language
        processing, studies, 515–518
    N400, 513–514
    P300, 514, 518
  familiar figurative language, 515–517
  graded silence hypothesis, 511
  idioms *see* idioms
  in an L1, 509–512
  in an L2, 512–513
  metaphors *see* metaphors
  monolingual, ERP studies, 515–518
  N400 (ERP component), effects of,
      513–523, 524n4
  P600 (ERP component), effects of, 517,
      518, 523
    and late positive component (LPC),
        514–515
  recognition point, 510–511
  representation and access, 509–513
nonsense humour, 339, 340, 346

Norman, D.A., 359
Nosek, B.A., 746
nouns
  complex, 375–376
  concrete, 392, 496
  determiner-noun agreement errors, 110
  disambiguating, 519
  English, 218
  first and second, 88
  French, 54–55
  German, 54–55
  lexical gender, 110
  lexical selection, 139
  phrases, 375–376, 429
  proper, 412
  and relative clause, 88
  switched, 113, 433
  uncountable, 396
  and verbs, 112, 127, 149, 216, 555
nucleus accumbens, 345

OAs (older adults), learning in, 408–426
  see also adulthood; second language (L2)/
      second language acquisition (SLA)
  brain-based cognitive-linguistic changes in
      healthy ageing, 409–414
    anatomical changes, 410–411
    cognitive changes, 411–413
    linguistic changes, 413–414
  cognitive-linguistic aptitude and L2
      acquisition, 416
  cognitive slowing, 411
  language development and age, 414–416
  neurobiology of first and second languages,
      416–417
  neuroprotective effects of multilingualism,
      673–675
  normal ageing and pedagogical
      approaches, 417–418
  pedagogical approaches, 417–419
  second language acquisition (SLA),
      414–416
    designing experiences to enhance,
        417–419
    pedagogical approaches, 418–419
  'tip-of-the tongue' (TOT) phenomenon,
      414, 675
  and younger adults (YAs), 410–413, 415,
      416, 418, 419

object-verb-subject (OVS) sentences, 85
Obler, L.K., xl, xlii, 414
Oh, J., 159, 160, 162
Ohno, K., 595, 602
Ojemann, G.A., 21, 27, 28, 31, 41n1
Ojima, S., 109, 178
older adults, second language learning in *see*
　　OAs (older adults), learning in; second
　　language (L2)/second language
　　acquisition (SLA)
Olsen, R.K., 245
Olulade, O.A., 233
operation span task (OSpan task), 373, 374
opportunistic planning, 63
Ormel, E., 766
Ortega, L., 171
orthographies
　　in bilingualism, 49, 593
　　effects on neuronal organization,
　　　601–604
　　effects on reading disorders, 595, 596–597t,
　　　598–601
　　transparent, 592, 598
Ortiz, H.C., xxxvii
Osaka, N. and M., 344
Osgood, C.E., 390, 391
OSpan task, 373, 374
Osterhout, L., 110, 179, 234
Ouchikh, Y., xl
Ouzia, J., xxxix–xl
Overton Venet, M., 600, 601
OVS (object-verb-subject) sentences, 85

P300 (event-related component), 514, 518
P600 (ERP component), effects of, 179,
　　180, 496
　　see also event-related potentials (ERPs);
　　　N400 (ERP component), effects of
　　non-literal language processing, 517,
　　　518, 523
　　and late positive component (LPC),
　　　514–515
　　real-time measures of brain, in
　　　multilingualism, 101, 105, 107–110, 114
　　second language acquisition (SLA), 177f,
　　　178–180
　　sentence processing, bilingual, 468, 470
Paap, K.R., xliii, 708, 713, 715, 716, 719, 720,
　　724, 725n3, 739, 740, 742, 750

Padilla, P., 688
Pallier, C., 156, 157, 159–160
Palmer, S.D., 397
Pang, E.W., 223
Paone, T.R., 327
Paradis, M., 10, 11, 22, 38, 257–258, 415, 534,
　　537, 538, 544, 641
parahippocampal gyri, 346
Parente, M.A.M.P., 598
parietal cortex, 457
Parker-Jones, O., 202, 218
Parkinson's disease (PD), 454, 458–460, 545
pars triangularis, 218
Paulmann, S., 519, 522
Pavlenko, A., 305
PCA (principal components analysis), 102
PCC (posterior cingulate cortex), 127, 435, 440
PCG (precentral gyrus), 67, 233
PD *see* Parkinson's disease (PD)
pedagogical approaches
　　and normal ageing, 417–418
　　in second language acquisition, 418–419
Peeters, D., 61
Peñaloza, C., xli
Penfield, W., 170, 414
Perani, D., 216, 217, 225, 245, 258, 417, 616
perceptual wedge hypothesis, 660
Perecman, E., 536
performance errors, 31, 32f
peripheral alexia, 594
permastore, 163
Perquin, M., 614
Perrachione, T.K., 283–284
PET *see* positron emission tomography (PET)
Petersson, K.M., 187
Petitto, L.A., 659, 660
PFC *see* prefrontal cortex (PFC)
phatic function, speech acts, 42n7
phonemes, xlii, 80, 148, 160, 592
　　non-native speech perception, individual
　　　differences, 284, 289
phonetic learning, 201–202
phonological alexia, 601
phonological processing, 201, 235, 453, 595,
　　642, 661, 764
　　multilingual processing, factors affecting,
　　　377, 378
　　non-native speech perception, individual
　　　differences, 282, 284–286, 289, 292

phonological representation, 49, 137, 263, 555, 689
  non-native speech perception, individual differences, 285, 286
phonology, 31, 32f, 49, 50, 79, 106, 189n1, 205, 263, 766
  see also phonological alexia; phonological processing; phonological representation
  acoustic-phonological analysis, 201
  competitors, 90, 91
  forgotten languages, uncovering memory traces, 148, 150t, 155, 159, 160
  L2, brain basis, 200–202
  neuroimaging studies, multilingual speech, 131, 138, 139
  non-native speech perception, individual differences, 279, 285
  phonological advantage, 161, 162
  phonological minimal pairs, 764, 765f
  phonological paraphasias, 31, 32f
  and plasticity, 235, 243
  retrieval, 79, 138
  sharing, 77, 766
  and speech-sign bilingual difference, 754, 764, 765f
  word production, bilingual, 214, 215, 219, 222, 224
Piaget, J., 24
Pickering, M., 11
picture-naming tasks, 236, 254, 267, 323, 430, 457
  bilingualism, 636, 758
    aphasia, 554, 555, 557, 563, 564
    speech-sign bilingualism, 762, 767, 768, 770
    word production, 216, 217, 219, 225
  blocked, 217, 219
  covert, 217
  language organization, 202, 205
  lexical production, 76
  multilingualism, 669, 675
  neuroimaging studies, 126, 127, 139, 323
  overt, 125t, 202, 217, 218, 260t
  picture-naming paradigm, 61, 139
  psycholinguistic research methods, 76, 77
  tacit, 219
picture-picture interference task, 77
Piñar, P., 376

Pisano, T.S., xl
Pitres, A., 541
planum temporale, 218
plasticity/neuroplasticity, xxxviii, xli
  bilingualism, 184–188, 486
  cerebellum, 238
  and cognitive flexibility, 658, 676
  and cross-language task performance, 486, 493–494
  defining, 657
  developmental perspective, in multilingualism, 657
    and foreign language learning success, 663–666
    link with proficiency, 662–663
    unanswered questions, 666
  experience-dependent, 68
  and foreign language learning success, 663–666
  function, 242–244
  grey matter (GM), 231, 232f
    effects of bi-/multilingualism on, 232–238
  and language switching, 235–239, 244–246
  longitudinal studies, 234, 494
  and multilingualism, 230–251
  resting state functional connectivity, 243–244
  second language acquisition, in adulthood, 170
    bilingualism-induced neuroplasticity, structural and functional evidence for, 184–188
    cross-sectional studies, 185–186
    fMRI studies, 180–181
  subcortical structures, 235–238
  terminology, 189n2
  white matter, 231, 232f
    effects of bi-/multilingualism on, 239–242
  and working memory (WM), 240–242, 245
Pliatsikas, C., xxxviii, 185, 186, 204, 225, 236, 237, 237f, 239, 240f, 379
Poeppel, D., 19, 20, 37, 41n2
poetic function, speech acts, 42n7
Polish-English-German trilinguals, 80
Pomerantz, A., 347–348
positron emission tomography (PET), xxxvii, xxxviii, 34

humour, utilizing in studies of, 344–346
language organization, 199, 201
multilingual language control, 136, 140
speech-sign bilingualism, 759, 761
word production, bilingual, 215–216, 221
posterior cingulate cortex (PCC), 127, 435, 440
posterior superior temporal gyrus
 (pSTG), 378
postsynaptic potentials (PSPs), 100
PPAs *see* primary progressive aphasia (PPA)
pragmatics, 642
precentral gyrus (PCG), 67, 233, 323
prefrontal cortex (PFC)
 and cognition, 497
 dorsolateral *see* dorsolateral prefrontal
  cortex (DLPFC)
 language-switching networks, 129, 130f
 lateral, 361
 lexico-semantic processing, 205–206
 neural basis of BLC and EC, 451
 ventro-medial prefrontal cortex (VMPFC),
  243, 345, 361
Prehn, K., 186, 238
prelexical language, 35
prepositions, 433, 470, 496, 519, 638
Price, C.J., 35–36, 37
primary progressive aphasia (PPA), 572–591
 see also aphasia; bilingual aphasia;
  multilingual aphasia;
  neurodegenerative disease
 bilingual and multilingual, 573, 577,
  578–579t, 580
 case studies, 572–573
  demographic information, 577, 578–579t
 convergence hypothesis, 575, 576, 585, 586
 cortical atrophy, 573–574, 584
 declarative-procedural model, 575, 576, 586
 degenerative nature, 573, 587
 event-related potentials (ERPs), 575
 factors impacting language decline,
  580–583
 hypometabolism, 574
 language decline, 574, 583–585
 language impairment in, 574
 logopenic variant, 573, 574, 577, 584
 monolinguals with, 574
 neurodegeneration of cells in, 584
 neuroimaging studies, 575–576
 neurons, 573, 584

non-fluent variant, 573, 574, 577, 584
semantic variant, 573, 574, 577, 584, 585
subtypes, 573–574
support for language models, 585–586
telegraphic speech, 574
priming
 comprehension, 86–87
 lexical, 398–399
 memory-task priming paradigm, 84
 non-literal language processing, 512
 semantic, 319
 structural, 83–87
 subword, 303
principal components analysis (PCA), 102
procedural memory, 560, 576
processing instruction theory, 418
processing speed, 380–381
production
 bilingual activation during, 760–761
 of humour, 336, 348–349
 language production studies, 135
 language switching, 113
 lexical, 76–79
 native language (L1), xxxviii
 second language (L2)/second language
  acquisition (SLA), xxxviii
 of speech
  and comprehension, 20
  covert production, 137
  fMRI studies, 35
  overlap in cortical representation during,
   xxxviii, 126–129
 speech-sign bilingual, 767–768
 structural priming in language
  production, 84–86
 of words *see* word production, bilingual
proficiency
 assessment/measurement, 13–14, 36
 BIA+ model, 51
 controlled processing, 265
 differences in, 10
 experiential factors, 658
 increased L2 proficiency strengthening
  connections to the semantic store, 59
 interaction with AoA, 266–267
 L2, individual differences, 67
 language acquisition, 263–266
 lemma activation, proficiency-modulated,
  60–61

proficiency (*cont'd*)
  lexical and semantic retrieval tasks in lower
      proficiency languages, 264
  lower proficiency languages, 264–266
  multilingual processing, 376–377
  and plasticity, 662–663
  premorbid language, 534
  speech-sign bilingualism, 757
  word production, bilingual, 224–225
pseudowords, 35, 283
psycholinguistic research methods,
      multilingualism, xxxvii, 75–99
  compared to real-time measures, 103
  confederate-scripting technique, 85, 86
  event-related potentials (ERPs), 78–79
  experimental paradigms, 77, 82
  eye-tracking, measuring bilingual language
      processing with, 87–91
  language switching, 78, 79, 82
  lexical decision task, 80, 81
  lexical processing measurement, 76–81
  picture-naming tasks, 76, 77
  roots of mental lexicon in psycholinguistics,
      300–301
  self-paced reading-listening
      paradigms, 82–83
  structural priming, 83–87
  syntactic processing, measuring, 82–83
  traces of a forgotten language,
      uncovering, 147
  verbal fluency task, 79
  visual world paradigm, 88–89, 91
psychophysiological work, 320–322
publication bias, 736–753
  see also reformulations
  in bilingualism and executive control,
      738–740
  decline effect, 740–741
  delay effect, 747–748
  executive control (EC), 738–740, 748
  importance of, 748–749
  meta-analyses, 748, 751
  null results, increase in number, 747
  number of tasks reported, 745–747
  reassessing, 741–742, 743–744t, 745
  replication studies, 750
  solutions possible, 749–750
pupil dilation, 434
putamen, 220, 236–237, 457

Pyers, J.E., 769
Pylkkänen, I., 64
Pynte, J., 514, 517

quadrilinguals, 127

radial diffusivity (RD), 239
Radman, N., 456
Raichle, M.E., 31, 34, 37
Ramakrishnan, S., 621
Ramírez Gómez, D., 416, 419, 420
  Language Teaching and the Older Adult, 417
rapid instructed task learning (RITL)
      paradigm, 496
rapid serial visual presentation (RSVP)
      paradigm, 82, 315, 316
Raskin, V., 340
Ratiu, I., 718
Ratnavalli, E., 600
Raven's scores, 713, 715
reaction time (RT), 692, 696, 703
  behavioural, 707
  global, 706–708
reading
  acquired disorders *see* reading disorders,
      acquired
  learning to read, 593
  mind-wandering during, 434
  monolingualism versus bilingualism, 400
  process of, 593
  reading-listening paradigms, self-paced,
      82–83, 87, 375
  reading span task (RST), 373, 374, 376
  studies, eye-tracking, 87–88
reading disorders, acquired, xlii, 592–607
  alexia, 594, 595, 596–597t, 599, 601
  in bilingual and biscriptal adults, 594–604
  models of reading, 593–594
  orthography effects, 595, 596–597t, 598–601
  on neuronal organization, 601–604
real-time measures of brain, in
      multilingualism, 100–120
  adult second language learning, 106–110
  compared to psycholinguistic measures, 103
  electroencephalography (EEG), 100–104
  encephalography, 101–104
    advantages, 103
    compared with other methods, 102–104
  event-related potentials (ERPs), 102

interpretation, 105–106
language switching, 110, 114
N400 (ERP component), effects of, 101,
  105–108, 110–114
P600 (ERP component), effects of, 101,
  105, 107–110, 114
interpreting real-time brain responses,
  104–106
language switching, 110–114
magnetoencephalography (MEG), 100–104,
  106, 111, 114
scalp-recorded electromagnetic signals,
  101, 104
recognition point, 510–511
referential function, speech acts, 42n7
Regel, S., 518
regions of interest (ROIs)
  bilingual interactive activation (BIA)
    models, 55–56t
  fMRI data, analysis, 37
  second language acquisition in adults,
    181–183
regression, 88, 724
  age regression hypnosis, 147–148,
    154–156, 165
  Cox proportional hazard regression
    models, nested, 618
relative clauses (RCs), 375
relevance theory, 509
repressed versus suppressed language, 155
  see also forgotten languages
response–stimulus interval (RSI), 720
Ressel, V., 233
resting-state functional connectivity (rs-FC),
  243–244, 282, 283, 665
revised hierarchical model (RHM), 51, 52, 304,
  394, 395
RHC (right hippocampus), 182
Ribot, T., 541, 609
right cingulate, 60
right hippocampus (RHC), 182
right inferior frontal gyrus (RIFG), 55t, 66,
  264, 345, 664, 669
  see also inferior frontal gyrus (IFG); left
    inferior frontal gyrus (LIFG)
  neuroimaging studies, 130, 132t, 134
  and plasticity, 234, 241, 243
RITL (rapid instructed task learning)
  paradigm, 496

Roberts, L., 170, 376, 380, 414
Robertson, I., 617
Rodden, F.A., xxxix
Rodriguez-Fornells, A., 219, 416, 418, 452
Roebers, C.M., 364
Roehm, D., 514
ROIs *see* regions of interest (ROIs)
rolandic operculum, 67
Rommers, J., 516
Rosselli, M., 717
Rossi, E., xxxvii, 82, 239–240
Rossi, S., 109, 185
Rothman, J., xxxviii, 172
RST (reading span task), 373, 374, 376
RSVP (rapid serial visual presentation)
  paradigm, 82, 315, 316
Ruch, W., 339, 340
Rumelhart, D.E., 49
Russian-English bilinguals, 59, 149, 155, 557

saccades (eye movements), 88
  antisaccade tasks, 692, 693
Sachdev, P., 616
Sachs, R., 416
Sacramento Area Latino Study on Ageing
  (SALSA), 618
Sagarra, N., 88, 473
Saint-Aubin, J., 718–719
Salamoura, A., 86
salient cue detection, 63
Salis, C., 412
Salvatierra, J.L., 717
Samar, R.G., 542
Sanchez-Azanza, V.A., 740, 747
Sanders, A.E., 618
Sanz, C., 415, 418
SAS (supervisory attentional system), 53, 61
savings paradigm, memory traces of
  forgotten languages, xxxviii,
  162–165, 166
scalpel model, L3/LN acquisition, 395–396
Scheepers, C., 85
schemas, 24, 60, 487
schizophrenia, bilinguals with, xlii, 625–654
  conversation, 635, 637, 642
  delusions, 626
  diagnosis, 625–626
  hallucinations, 626
  impairment, modelling, 641–643

schizophrenia, bilinguals with (*cont'd*)
  integrative approach to study of SZ–BL
      interface, 640–643
    different neural mechanisms, 640–641
    linguistic markers approach, 641
    modelling of impairment, 641–643
  interface of schizophrenia and
      bilingualism, 636–638
    integrative approach to study of,
        640–643
  language characteristics
    bilingualism, 635–636
    disentangling schizophrenia and
        bilingualism, 638–640
    interface of schizophrenia and
        bilingualism, 636–638, 640–643
    schizophrenia (SZ), 631–632, 633–635t
  linguistic and clinical markers, 637
  neurological features underlying, 626,
      627–630t, 631
    different neural mechanisms, 640–641
  prevalence, 625
  psychosis, 632, 638, 643
  symptoms, 626
Schlegel, A.A., 240–241
Schmid, M., 6
Schoonbaert, S., 86
Schriefers, H., xxxviii
Schwartz, J.H., 41n1
Schweizer, T.A., 245, 616
Schwieter, J.W., xxxix, xl, 305
SCRs (skin conductance responses), 320, 321
Sebastian-Galles, N., xxxix, 284–286,
    289, 290
second language (L2)/second language
    acquisition (SLA), xxxviii, 67, 170, 643
  see also bilingualism; learning of languages;
    native language (L1); third
    language (L3)
  adulthood learning, xl, 170–196, 408–426
    adult adoptees, 148, 164–165, 166
    brain structure and regions of interest,
        181–183
    critical period hypothesis, evidence base,
        171–176
    designing L2 experiences to enhance
        older adults' L2 learning, 417–419
    older adults, 408–426
    real-time brain measures, 106–110

savings paradigm, 164, 166
younger adults, 410–413, 415, 416,
    418, 419
attrition, 6
bilingualism-induced neuroplasticity,
    structural and functional evidence for,
    184–188
brain basis/brain-based challenges,
    408–426
  age and language development,
      414–416
  anatomical, 410–411
  cognitive control, 412–413
  cognitive-linguistic aptitude, 416
  cognitive-linguistic changes in healthy
      ageing, 409–414
  designing L2 experiences to enhance
      older adults' L2 learning, 417–419
  episodic and working memory,
      411–412
  grammar, 202–204
  language control, 206
  lexico-semantics, 204–206
  linguistic changes, 413–414
  neurobiology of first and second
      languages, 416–417
  phonology, 200–202
in childhood, 163–164
cognitive-linguistic aptitude, 416
cognitive neuroscience/cognitive
    neurolinguistic imaging, 23, 35, 36, 39
cortical representation, 258, 262, 278
critical period *see* critical periods, second
    language learning
cross-sectional studies, 185–186
early acquisition, 35, 126, 186, 258, 262
emotion processing, 323
empirical research requirements, 408, 414,
    415, 417
endogenous factors influencing learning
    and brain, 280–291
  natural language learning studies,
      284–290
  training studies, 280–284
exogenous factors influencing learning,
    278–279
exposure to, degree of, 225
fMRI studies, 180–181

grammar/grammatical processing, 82, 107, 202–204
  inflexion, 204
  influence on the native language, 473–474
  integrated L1-L2 lexical networks, 54, 57
  language development and age, 414–416
  longitudinal studies, 409
  methodological considerations
    behavioural methodologies, 398–399
    fMRI and ERP, 396–398
  morphosyntax, 171, 174–175, 178–179, 414, 420
  naming, 217, 219, 220
  native-like way, whether L2 learners process language in, 177–178
  neurobiology, 416–417
  neuroimaging studies of L2 syntax, 204
  non-literal language processing, 512–513
  P600 (ERP component), effects of, 177f, 178–180
  pedagogical approaches, 418–419
  perception discrimination of sounds, 158
  proficiency, individual differences, 67
  second language learners (SLLs), 148, 163–164, 414, 512, 635
  shared neural representations, 215
  speech perception, individual differences, 277–296
Seidel, C., 164, 166
Seidenberg, M., 411–412
seizures *see* epilepsy
selective response inhibition, 63
self-paced reading-listening paradigms, 82, 87, 375
self-ratings, 14
Selfridge, O., 300
semantic dementia (SD), 610
Semantic Go Task (SGT), 58
semantic judgement relatedness task, 80
semantic opacity, 302
semantic paraphasias, 31, 32f
semantic priming, 319
semantic relatedness paradigm, 81
semantic store, increased L2 proficiency strengthening connections to, 59
semantic/syntactic ambiguity, 35
Semin, G.R., 320
Senaha, M.L.H., 598
sensory-motor alignment, 24

sensory-motor systems, 25
sentences
  comprehension, 35
  end-of-the-sentence grammaticality judgement tasks, 82
  object-verb-subject (OVS) sentences, 85
  probabilistic or exposure-based processing models, 379
  sentence processing, bilingual, xli, 467–484
    N400 (ERP component), effects of, 473, 476, 478
    P600 (ERP component), effects of, 468, 470
    separate sentence interpretation hypothesis (SSIR), 375
    variable input
      role in bilingual language processing, 471–475
      role in monolingual language processing, 469–471
separate sentence interpretation hypothesis (SSIR), 375
sequential congruency effects (SCEs), 725n7
Serafini, S., 28
SFG (superior frontal gyrus), 233
Shallice, T., 359
shallow structure hypothesis (SSH), 186
Sharp, D.J., 435, 436, 438, 439–440
Shekari, E., xl
Shen, X.R., 477
Shenhav, A., 725n8
Sheppard, J.P., 68, 665
Shibata, M., 346
short-term memory (STM), 687, 688–689
Shreve, G.M., xli
sign languages, 754–755
  see also speech-sign bilingualism
  American Sign Language (ASL), 28, 57, 691, 759, 760
  British Sign Language (BSL), 755, 756, 765f
  defining, 754
  Irish Sign Language (ISL), 755
  Mandarin-Chinese Sign Language, 761–762
  phonological minimal pairs, 764, 765f
  Spanish Sign Language (LSE), 771
  Swedish Sign Language (SSL), 759
sign-print bilinguals, 757, 759, 766
signal detection theory, 362
signification, 41–42n3

Signorelli, T.M., 689
Simon-switch task, 53
Simon task/effect, 53, 412, 556, 614
    bilingual advantage debate, 704, 706, 708,
        714, 716, 717, 719f, 720
    emotion, 317, 323
    interpreting, 692, 693
    multilingualism, 669, 672
    neuroimaging studies, 134, 135, 323
Singh, L., 161
Singh, N.C., 240
single-language context, 215–218, 432–433,
        450, 452
single photon emission computed
        tomography (SPECT), 139, 577
    humour, utilizing in studies of, 344–346
single resources (SR) model, 375
Siyanova-Chanturia, A., xli, 511, 512, 513
skin conductance responses (SCRs),
        320, 321
SLA (second language acquisition) *see under*
        second language (L2)/second
        language acquisition (SLA)
Slate, J., 149
SLLs (second language learners), 148,
        163–164, 414, 512, 635
SMA (supplementary motor area), 61,
        67, 219
SMG *see* supramarginal gyrus (SMG)
Smirnova, D., xlii, 637, 641
Smit, M., 637
socioeconomic status (SES), 713
sociolinguistics, 7, 23–24
Soltano, E.G., 402–403
Soto-Faraco, S., 285
sounds, perception discrimination of, 158
Southwood, F., 638
Spanish-Catalan bilinguals, xxxix, 267, 316
    non-native speech perception, individual
        differences, 284–285, 292
    word production, bilingual, 216–217
Spanish-English bilinguals, 219, 557
    bilingual models, 57–59
    emotion processing, 316, 320, 323
    psycholinguistic research methods, 81, 88
Spanish-German bilinguals, 322
Spanish Sign Language (LSE), 771
SPECT *see* single photon emission computed
        tomography (SPECT)

speech
    communities of practice, 23–25, 41n3
    comprehension, 20, 35
    fMRI studies, 35
    motor speech areas, for naming, 31
    networks *see* speech networks
    non-native perception, individual
        differences, 277–296
        brain differences between monolinguals
            and bilinguals, 279–280
        exogenous factors influencing language
            learning, xxxix, 278–279
    production of
        and comprehension, 20
        covert, 137
        fMRI studies, 35
        overlap in cortical representation during,
            xxxviii, 126–129
        speech-sign bilingual, 767–768
    speech acts, 26, 42n7, 436–438
    speech communities, 23, 24, 25
    speech-sign bilingualism *see* speech-sign
        bilingualism
speech acts
    attentional states, dynamics, 436–439
    conversation, 428
    functions, 42n7
    linguistic theory, 26
speech networks
    bilingual, 121–123
    multilingual, 123–141
        language control, 129–140
        overlap in cortical representation
            during speech production,
            126–129
        patient populations, evidence from,
            140–141
speech-sign bilingualism, xliii, 754–783
    see also sign languages
    age of acquisition (AoA), 756–757
    articulating two languages simultaneously,
        768–772
        code-blending, 769–771, 772
        code switching, 771–772
    bilingual language activation, 758–764
        during comprehension, 759–760
        during production, 760–761
        and role of experience, 761–764
        speech-sign, 758–759

bimodal bilinguals, 757, 759, 766, 767–768, 771–773
and cognition, 772–774
comprehension
  activation during, 759–760
  language processing, 764, 766–767
Deaf parents, 755
fMRI studies, 761–762, 769, 770
hearing status, 756
language processing, 764–768
  comprehension, 764, 766–767
  phonology and speech-sign bilingual difference, 764, 765f
  production, 767–768
mouth gestures, in signers, 768–769
N400 (ERP component), effects of, 766, 767
phonology and speech-sign bilingual difference, 764, 765f
proficiency, 757
sign languages, 754–755
sign-print bilinguals, 757, 759, 766
signers as bilingual, 755–756
speech-sign bilinguals, 756–758
'tip-of-the tongue' (TOT) phenomenon, 767
Spivey, M., 89
SPL (superior parietal lobule), 234
Spotorno, N., 518
Squires, L., 470
Steinhauer, K., 479n1
STG (superior temporal gyrus) *see* superior temporal gyrus (STG)
stimulus-onset asynchrony (SOAs), 688, 690, 718
STN *see* subthalamic nucleus (STN)
Stocco, A., 64
Stoessel, S., 163, 166
Stowe, L., 10, 38, 39–40, 41n2
Strandburg, R., 515
stratium, 263
Strijkers, K., 222, 223
Strobach, T., 690
stroke
and aphasia, 616
and dementia, 615–616
post-stroke cognitive impairment, 616
and primary progressive aphasia (PPA), 573, 582–585
and reading disorders, acquired, 595, 599, 600

Stroop task, 245
bilingual advantage debate, 214, 703, 706, 713, 715, 716
colour-word, 455, 703, 714, 716
emotional, 314–316, 319, 322
executive control and language, 455, 457
interpreting, 492, 493, 692, 693
numerical, 716
Stroud, C., 609
structural priming, 83–87
in language comprehension, 86–87
in language production, 84–86
subcortical structures, 20, 235–238
effects on subcortical grey matter, 236–238
and putamen, 236–237
subject-verb agreement, 381
violations of, 109, 179, 380
subset hypothesis (Paradis), 11
subthalamic nucleus (STN), 135, 136
subword priming, 303
Sue, S., 328
Suls, J.M., 338, 339
superior frontal gyrus (SFG), 233
superior longitudinal fasciculus (SLF), 130, 183, 239, 537, 674
superior parietal lobule (SPL), 234, 665
superior temporal cortex, 253
superior temporal gyrus (STG), 20, 127, 219, 263, 497, 659–660, 664
adult second language learning, 182, 186
left, 345
posterior superior temporal gyrus (pSTG), 378
supervisory attentional system (SAS), 53, 61
supplementary motor area (SMA), 61, 67, 219, 661
suppressed versus repressed language, 155–156
see also forgotten languages
supramarginal gyrus (SMG), 66, 131, 182, 218, 233, 282, 497, 663
surface alexia, 594
Sutton, T.M., 317, 401
Swedish-English bilinguals, 154
Swedish-Korean bilinguals, 160, 161
Swedish Sign Language (SSL), 759
Swinney, D., 510, 511

switching
  asymmetrical, 78, 111
  backward, 56t, 61
  behavioural, 53
  bilingual advantage debate, 709–712
  category-switching, 60, 64, 113
  code *see* code switching
  conscious and automatic, xxxiv
  costs, 477, 669, 737
    asymmetrical, 78
    behavioural, 53
    bilingual advantage debate, 711, 714
    cortical representation, 265
    interpreting and bilingual brain, 485, 488,
      491–493
    language switching, 61, 82
    neuroimaging studies, 134, 135
  delayed, 130
  forced, 55t, 56t, 62
  forward, 55t, 61
  language *see* language switching
  response delays, 265
  between schemas, 487
  tasks *see* task-switching
  trials, 129
  unintended, 140
syllables, xlii
symbols, 25, 42n3, 218, 403, 599
syntactic persistence/priming *see* structural
    priming
syntactic processing, 109, 186, 203, 242, 375,
    458, 496, 593
  developmental perspective, in
    multilingualism, 659, 661
  language organization, 203, 204
  measuring, 82–83
  sentence processing, bilingual, 468, 469
syntactic satiation, 471
syntax, 37, 83, 92, 173, 186, 189n1, 204, 224,
    278, 420, 593, 659
  see also morphosyntax; syntactic processing
  aphasia, 554, 576
  morphology-syntax interface, 202
  multilingual processing, factors affecting,
    392, 398, 400
  and pragmatics, 642
  schizophrenia, bilinguals with, 637,
    638, 642
  sentence processing, bilingual, 467, 472

SZ *see* schizophrenia, bilinguals with
Szubko-Sitarek, W., 80, 382

Tabossi, P., 510, 511, 516
Taft, M., 301
Talairach coordinates, 38
Tammet, D., 671
Tanenhaus, M., 89
Tanner, D., 178–179
task-switching, 268, 358, 359, 411, 451,
    452, 498
  see also language switching; switching
  bilingual models, 55t, 56t, 60–61, 65
tasks
  see also task-switching
  colour *see under* colour
  flanker *see* flanker task
  Simon *see* Simon task/effect
  Stroop *see* Stroop task
  task engagement/disengagement, 63
tauopathy, 584
TDP-43 proteinopathy, 584
temporal lobe, Wernicke's area *see* Wernicke's
    area
temporo-parietal junction, 345
thalamus
  anterior thalamic radiation (ATR), 185,
    241, 242
  aphasia, 545, 546
  lesions, 546
  and plasticity, 236–238
  subthalamic nucleus (STN), 135, 136
theory of mind (TOM), 365, 636
Thierry, G., 111
third agers *see* OAs (older adults), learning in
third language (L3), 35, 77
  see also multilingualism; trilingualism
  acquisition model, 395–396
Thompson, R.L., xliii
Timarová, S., 690, 693
time frames, 25
'tip-of-the-tongue' (TOT) phenomenon, 414,
    675, 767
TMHM (trilingual modified hierarchical
    model), 305–307
TMS (transcranial magnetic stimulation),
    36, 103
Tokowicz, N., 109
Tomasino, B., xli

TOT *see* 'tip-of-the tongue' (TOT)
    phenomenon
tract-based spatial statistics (TBSS), 239
Trail-Making Test B, 617
training studies, 67, 204, 235, 240, 280–284,
    281f, 290
    longitudinal, 184, 234
transcranial direct current stimulation
    (tDCS), 360
transcranial magnetic stimulation (TMS),
    36, 103
translation
    see also interpreting/interpretation
    aphasia, 537–538
    compromises, 341
    equivalence, 341
    of humour, 340–342, 347
    implications of bilingualism for, 490–493
    linguistic meaning and speech acts, 26
    multilingual aphasia, 537–538
    pragmatic, 341
    studies, 341
    translatability, 341
Treisman, A., 297
Tremblay, A., 375
trilingualism
    see also multilingualism; third language (L3)
    Cantonese-English-Mandarin
        trilinguals, 455
    Cantonese-Mandarin-Dutch trilinguals, 161
    cognates, 80–81
    Dutch-English-French trilinguals, 80
    Dutch-English-German trilinguals, 61
    French-English-Spanish trilinguals, 59
    Polish-English-German trilinguals, 80
    trilingual modified hierarchical model
        (TMHM), 305–307
    Uighur-Chinese-English trilinguals, 60
    word production, 217, 218
tuning hypothesis, 379
Tzou, Y.-Z., 691

Uighur-Chinese-English trilinguals, 60
Ullman, M.T., 203, 257–258, 377, 379, 380,
    545, 586
uncinate fasciculus (UF), 239, 585
Underwood, G., 689
Uno, A., 598
Unsworth, N., 373, 702

Vaid, J., 348, 762
Valdés Kroff, J.R., xli
Valenzuela, M.J., 616
Valian, V., 713
Vallesi, A., 696, 697
Van Assche, E., 79
van Gompel, R.P.G., 86
Van Hell, J.G., 80, 476
van Heuven, W.J., 49, 717
Van Petten, C., 517
VanPatten, B., 418
variation studies, 37–38, 40–41
vascular dementia (VaD), 612, 615, 616
vascular mild cognitive impairment (VaMCI),
    615, 616
Vasquez, C., 326
Vaughn, K.A., 669
VBM *see* voxel-based morphometry (VBM)
Vega-Mendoza, M., xlii
ventro-medial prefrontal cortex (VMPFC),
    243, 345, 361
Ventura-Campos, N., 282, 665
Ventureyra, V., 159–160
verbal fluency task, 79, 126
verbal humour, theories, 338–347
verbal intelligence, 254–255
verbs, 149, 216, 238, 555
    action, 632
    complex, 238
    covert generation, 264, 564
    finite, 83
    French, 433
    generating, 102, 127, 139, 258, 264, 564
    mental state, 632
    and nouns, 112, 127, 149, 216, 555
    object-verb-subject (OVS) sentences, 85, 493
    past tense, 381
    phrasal, 519, 521
    psycholinguistic research methods,
        multilingualism, 86, 87, 88, 90f
    regular and irregular, 139, 379
    rule-based formation, 139
    subject-verb agreement, 581
        violations of, 109, 179, 380
    verb-agreement errors, 110
    visually presented, 139
Veroude, K., 66, 186
Verreyt, N., 457–458
Verspoor, M., 12

Vespignani, F., 516
Videsott, G., 127, 217
Vingerhoets, G., 126, 217, 218
Vinson, D.P., 768–769
visual word form area (VWFA), 592
visual world paradigm, 88–89, 91
vocabulary
    associative learning processes, 203
    knowledge, 13, 14, 441n1
    LexTale (five-minute test for English
        vocabulary), 13–14
voice onset time (VOT), 160, 381
Von Bastian, C.C., 711, 747
Vonk, J.M.J., xlii
vowels, 284, 285, 287, 599
voxel-based morphometry (VBM), 289, 696
    and plasticity, 232, 233, 236, 239, 245
voxel-wise inference, 37
Vygotsky, L., 15, 495
    Thought and Speech, 24

Waldron, E.J., 139
Walters, J., xlii
Wang, Y., 60
Wartenburger, I., 417
Waters, G.S., 375, 376
Wattendorf, E., 137, 378
Weber, A., 512
Weber-Fox, C.M., 106, 107, 108
Weber, K., 86, 87
Wechsler Adult Intelligence Scale
        (WAIS)-III, 617
Weekes, B.S., 580, 583, 600, 603
Wei, L., 6, 642, 643
Wei, M., 234
Weinreich, U., *Languages in Contact*, 43n12
Weisberg, J., 770
Weiss-Croft, L. J., 255–256
Weissberger, W., 453
Wells, J.B., 470
Welsh-English bilinguals, 434
Wernicke's area
    aphasia, 584
    brain anatomical changes, 410
    cognitive neuroscience, 19, 20, 22, 28, 37,
        41n1, 41n2
    developmental perspective, in
        multilingualism, 661
Whitaker, H.A., 27

white matter (WM)
    see also grey matter (GM)
    bilingualism, effect, 67, 239–242
    brain imaging, 181, 182f
    brain structure and regions of interest,
        183, 184f
    destruction in stroke, 584
    fibre tracts, 31
    integrity, 283
    multilingualism, effect, 239–242
    pathways, 183, 284, 410, 575, 584, 585
    and plasticity, 231, 232f
    views, 232f
    volume, 410
Wicha, N.Y.Y., xxxvii, 57
Wickes, K., 149
Wilck, A.M., xl
Wild, B., 344–345
Williams, E., 299
Williams, J.N., 86, 419
Wilson, R.S., 620
Wisconsin card sort test (WCST), 686, 695–697
WM *see* white matter (WM); working
        memory (WM)
WMC *see* working memory capacity (WMC)
Wong, P.C., 283–284
Woods, D.L., 412
word production, bilingual, 92n1, 214–229
    common or distinct neural signatures,
        215–221
    event-related potentials (ERPs), 222–223
    factors moderating neural representations,
        224–225
    fMRI studies, 216, 217–218, 221
    in a mixed-language context, 218–221
    neurophysiology of timing aspects, 221–223
    PET studies, 215–216, 221
    proficiency, 224–225
    in a single-language context, 215–218
    spatial and temporal signatures, 223
words
    activation results, 35
    bilingual word production *see* word
        production, bilingual
    cognate, 77, 78, 91, 223
    covert generation, 128f
    emotion-laden, 319
    emotion word acquisition, storage and
        retrieval, 315–317

increased inhibition between word
  forms, 58, 59
knowledge of, 7, 298, 514, 540
non-cognate, 223
non-native speech sounds in word
  learning, 283
prefixed, 301
pseudowords, 35, 283
rating of, 318
recognition, 92n1
retrieval and articulation, 35
semantically opaque, 302
structurally complex, 301–304
subword priming, 303
unknown, 429
word naming studies, 92n2
word recognition, 92n1, 472
word-to-concept mapping, 305
working memory capacity (WMC)
  bilingual advantage debate, 702
  effects on language processing, 375–376
  language effects in multilinguals, 374
  large, 376
  measuring, 373–374
  multilingual processing, 372–376
  operation span task (OSpan task), 373, 374
  reading span task (RST), 373, 374, 376
working memory (WM), xl
  see also working memory capacity (WMC)
  bilingual advantage debate, 708
  central executive, 688
  changes, in healthy ageing, 411–412
  classical multicomponent model, 687
  classical tasks, 688, 689
  contrasted with episodic memory, 412
  and interpreting, 376, 686–687
    interpreter advantage, 687–690
  language aptitude, 416
  language switching, 488

meta-analyses, 723
and plasticity, 240–242, 245
storage, 374
World Health Organization (WHO), 610
Woumans, E., 613, 620
writing systems, 303, 543, 592, 598, 602–604
Wu, Y.J., 111, 434

Xiang, H., 67, 241
Xie, Z., 696
Xu, X., 11
Xu, Y., 136

Yang, H., 712
Yang, J., 69
YAs (younger adults), learning in, 410–413,
    415, 416, 418, 419
  see also adulthood; OAs (older adults),
    learning in
  bilingual advantage debate, 715–716
Ye, Y., 716
Yetkin, O., 126
Yiddish, 536
Young-Scholten, M., 472
younger adults, learning in *see* YAs (younger
    adults), learning in
Yudes, C., 668, 695–696

Zahodne, L.B., 499, 617, 619, 620
Zanini, S., 459, 582
Zatorre, R., 281, 282, 290
Zhang, T., 302, 303
Zhang, Y., 61
Zhao, X., xxxvii, 3
Zhong, F., xliii, 693, 694
Zhuravleva, A., 7
zone of proximal development (ZPD),
    Vygotsky, 15
Zou, L., 762